SCIENCE FICTION, FANTASY, AND WEIRD FICTION MAGAZINES

Recent Titles of
Historical Guides to the World's Periodicals and Newspapers

This series provides historically focused narrative and analytical profiles of periodicals and newspapers with accompanying bibliographical data.

Black Journals of the United States
Walter C. Daniel

Mystery, Detective, and Espionage Magazines
Michael L. Cook

American Indian and Alaska Native Newspapers and Periodicals, 1826-1924
Daniel F. Littlefield, Jr., and James W. Parins

British Literary Magazines: The Augustan Age and the Age of Johnson, 1698-1788
Alvin Sullivan, editor

British Literary Magazines: The Romantic Age, 1789-1836
Alvin Sullivan, editor

British Literary Magazines: The Victorian and Edwardian Age, 1837-1913
Alvin Sullivan, editor

Children's Periodicals of the United States
R. Gordon Kelly, editor

International Film, Radio, and Television Journals
Anthony Slide, editor

SCIENCE FICTION, FANTASY, AND WEIRD FICTION MAGAZINES

Edited by

Marshall B. Tymn

and

Mike Ashley

Historical Guides to the World's Periodicals and Newspapers

Greenwood Press
Westport, Connecticut • London, England

HOUSTON PUBLIC LIBRARY

Library of Congress Cataloging in Publication Data

Tymn, Marshall B., 1937-
  Science fiction, fantasy, and weird fiction magazines.

  (Historical guides to the world's periodicals and
newspapers, ISSN 0742-5538)
  Includes bibliographies and index.
  1. Science fiction—Periodicals—History. 2. Fantastic
fiction—Periodicals—History. I. Ashley, Michael.
II. Title. III. Series.
PN3433.T9 1985   809.3'876   84-11523
ISBN 0-313-21221-X (lib. bdg.)

Library of Congress Catalog Card Number: 84-11523
ISBN 0-313-21221-X
ISSN 0742-5538

First published in 1985

Greenwood Press
A division of Congressional Information Service, Inc.
88 Post Road West
Westport, Connecticut 06881

Printed in the United States of America

10 9 8 7 6 5 4 3 2 1

Contents

Preface

This volume was compiled to fill a gap in the library of reference works currently available in the field of fantastic literature. Although the contents of science fiction, fantasy and weird fiction magazines have been partially indexed by Donald B. Day for the 1926–1950 period, by Norm Metcalf for the 1951–1965 period, and by the New England Science Fiction Association from 1966 to the present, no guide as comprehensive in scope as this has ever been published. This volume gives full coverage of the pulp age of science fiction and fantasy, beginning with the general pulp magazines such as *Argosy*, which was first published in 1882 and regularly included science fiction and fantasy, through the decades of specialist pulp titles that began with the publication of *Weird Tales* in 1923, up to the contemporary pulps of the early 1980s. It was during the pulp era (roughly from 1926 until the early 1950s) that fantastic literature separated itself from the mainstream of publishing. A long line of specialist pulp titles appeared that were to remain virtually the only outlet for science fiction and fantasy writers during this period. A knowledge of that era is crucial to an understanding of the history of this literature. It was the pulp era that determined the directions in which the genre would develop and laid the groundwork for future writers. Thomas D. Clareson's introduction to this volume provides a balanced historical perspective on this important period in the history of science fiction and fantasy literature.

Our purpose in compiling this volume is to provide scholars, researchers and the general reader with a useful tool for evaluating the science fiction, fantasy and weird fiction magazines as a historical and literary phenomenon, and to furnish a bibliographic apparatus for documenting the appearance of these magazines in all their various phases. Except as it appears scattered througout general histories of this genre, and in capsule form in Peter Nicholls' *The Science Fiction Encyclopedia* (1979), commentary on these magazines has never been available in any sustained form. This volume provides that commentary for the historian and general reader, not only for titles for which information is partially available, but for those titles which have never before been researched.

The volume is divided into four sections: Section I: English-Language Magazines (279 titles), Section II: Associational English-Language Anthologies (15 titles), Section III: Academic Periodicals and Major Fanzines (72 titles), and Section IV: Non-English-Language Magazines, by Country (184 titles). In addition, it includes two appendixes: an index to major cover artists and a chronology.

Section I, which makes up the bulk of this volume, contains magazines published in the United States, Great Britain, Canada and Australia that are devoted wholly or in part to science fiction, fantasy and weird fiction in all of its forms and variations, beginning with the publication of *Argosy* in 1882 and ending with the early 1980s. It includes all of the important, as well as all of the less significant, magazines meeting these criteria. The cornerstone of the volume is the *Analog Science Fiction/Science Fact* entry, which presents the editorial policies of John W. Campbell in a new light.

Section I concentrates on fiction magazines in the broad spectrum of science fiction, fantasy and weird fiction and does not generally include nonfantasy and nonfiction magazines. A few general fiction or nonfiction titles are included, however, either because of their historical importance or for associational significance. Hence, although the first English-language all-fantasy magazine was *Weird Tales* in 1923 and the first all-science fiction magazine was *Amazing Stories* in 1926, several earlier magazines figure in the history and development of science fiction and fantasy magazines, the most obvious being the general fiction magazine *Argosy*. Because of its importance, an entry is given to *Argosy* and its companion, *All-Story*. The same reasoning applies to the inclusion of *The Thrill Book*, which is often erroneously cited as the first science fiction magazine but is more properly considered a precursor to the fantasy magazine *Weird Tales*. *Science and Invention*, Hugo Gernsback's nonfiction technical magazine, which published some science fiction, was another direct antecedent to the science fiction magazine, and it, too, is included. *The Black Cat* magazine is often cited as an early supernatural magazine, although it was no such thing, and we felt that an entry was necessary to clarify this situation, especially as another short-lived Canadian fantasy magazine of the same name claimed to revive the spirit of the original publication.

Like Gernsback's *Science and Invention*, two modern popular science magazines, *Omni* and *Ad Astra*, also include science fiction. Most of the magazines in Section I, however, are devoted primarily to fiction, although nearly all of the science fiction magazines have carried an occasional nonfiction article. *Omni* and *Ad Astra* are included for their science fiction and because of their relevance to the science fiction field. Magazines that concentrate on the cinema or other aspects of fantasy and the occult, with only a passing acknowledgment to fiction, including one or two stories an issue—and these frequently reprints—are excluded. Thus, you will find no entries for *Famous Monsters of Filmland*, *World of Horror*, *New Witchcraft*, and their ilk, although *Questar* is included because it was making a serious attempt to publish relevant science fiction before it suspended publication.

It was not our initial intention to deal with mystery, crime and thriller magazines, as these are included in another volume in Greenwood's Historical Guides to the World's Periodicals and Newspapers, Michael L. Cook's *Mystery, Detective, and Espionage Magazines*. However, it was inevitable that there would be some overlap if only because so many horror stories are also mysteries. Some of the overlaps were obvious, such as Gernsback's *Scientific Detective Monthly*, but once one accepted the inclusion of that title in this book, it left the way open to a number of other borderline magazines such as *Ace Mystery*. This in turn opened the door to the weird-menace or terror pulps. These pulps have been included when (a) their contents to some extent justify inclusion, (b) their titles might imply a fantasy connection, and confusion might arise through their exclusion, and (c) their contributors are of associational interest. We would make special reference to the entries on *Dime Mystery Magazine*, *Terror Tales*, *Horror Stories* and *Thrilling Mystery* for further clarification. Our emphasis is on the supernatural, weird or science fiction aspects of the magazines, as opposed to Cook's emphasis on the detective or mystery story.

This same dichotomy affected the hero pulps. Although it was a simple enough decision to include such titles as *Doc Savage* and *Dusty Ayres*, where there was a close enough affinity with the science fiction field, the definition became more hazy as we drifted toward such bizarre crime fighters as *The Scorpion* and *The Octopus*. Once into the realms of *The Shadow* and *The Avenger*, we decided that we had come too far. The dividing line, however, is vague and arbitrary, and the decision was made to exclude all those that usually offered a natural explanation for bizarre events, where that explanation was discovered by natural means. Here again, there is some overlap between our volume and Cook's, but the emphasis in our book is different from that in Cook's.

The entries in Section I, which are arranged alphabetically, follow a standard format. Each entry begins with a narrative section on the magazine's history and development. This section provides a view of the magazine's editorial policies and emphases as well as changes in those policies; an idea of the nature of the magazine's contents; the people who played a role in its founding and development; the magazines it influenced and those that influenced it; and an assessment of its significance within the field.

The narrative section is followed by two appended sections, outlining the basic details of the magazine's publication history and providing location sources and sources for further information. This information will be particularly useful to those wishing to do further research. Each section uses the following format:

Information Sources

BIBLIOGRAPHY: Lists reference sources specific to the magazine.
INDEX SOURCES: Lists sources where the magazine is indexed.

REPRINT SOURCES: Gives full details of other English-language reprint editions of the magazine, such as British or Canadian editions of an American magazine, and of later magazines that reprinted chiefly from a source magazine. This section also cross-references to foreign-language editions included in Section IV. In addition, it provides information on any derivative anthologies that either drew their contents entirely from the magazine or relied heavily on it as a source publication.

LOCATION SOURCES: Lists locations of partial and complete runs of the magazine in academic and public library collections.

Publication History

TITLE: Gives the original full title of the magazine, with references to subtitle where relevant, and all title changes and variations with relevant issue dates.

VOLUME DATA: Gives the full volume and issue sequence, using cover dates and qualifying all changes and errors. Also specifies magazine schedule (quarterly, bi-monthly, monthly, weekly, etc.) and all changes in schedule, together with the total number of issues published.

PUBLISHER: Lists the publisher(s) and place of publication. In some instances the publisher's location may be different from the editorial and executive offices, and such variations are noted.

EDITORS: Lists all editors directly responsible for the selection of stories and assembling of issues. When duties are divided, that is so indicated.

FORMAT: Gives the size and shape of the magazine as well as the number of pages in the magazine. The following general terms are used:

Pulp: Magazines printed on cheap, pulp stock usually measuring 7 by 10 inches, although dimensions vary by up to half an inch either way.

Large Pulp: Magazines printed on the same cheap paper as pulps but measuring 8½ by 11 inches, again with variations; sometimes referred to as ''bedsheet.''

Neo-pulp: Also magazines printed on pulp paper but of slightly better quality. Dimensions are usually slightly smaller than the pulps, about 6 by 9 inches, but with variations.

Digest: Magazines usually printed on pulp stock, 5 by 7½ inches.

Large Digest: In between neo-pulp and digest in size, measuring 5½ by 8½ inches. Used for a while by *Astounding* and *New Worlds*.

Slick: Glossy magazines printed on coated stock throughout, usually measuring 8 by 11 inches.

Large-size: Usually a pulp magazine masquerading as a slick, with glossy, coated covers and some coated interior sheets, but printed predominantly on pulp stock. Dimensions are usually 8 by 11 inches.

Pocketbook: Paperback format, usually measuring 4 by 7 inches. The number of pages is given after the format designations. All pages are counted exclusive of covers and regardless of the actual numbering within the magazine. Other variations are usually specified within the entry. Magazines can be either perfect bound, or glued with a spine on which the magazine's title and off-sale date are printed, or saddle-stapled in booklet form, with no spine.

PRICE: Gives the cover price at time of sale in the country of publication, together with any variations.

In addition to the alphabetical arrangement of the entries in this section, entries providing cross-references will aid the reader in locating the entries on magazines that underwent name changes or merged with other magazines. Moreover, whenever an entry refers to a magazine that has a separate entry in this volume, an asterisk (*) after the first mention of that magazine so indicates.

Greenwood's Historical Guides to the World's Periodicals and Newspapers are not designed to include books. Yet in the science fiction field, there is, at times, a close affinity between original paperback anthologies and magazines. The 1970s paperback series *Infinity*, for instance, was a direct descendant of the 1950s magazine *Infinity*. Omitting such anthologies altogether would create a gap in coverage. Thus, Section II was devised to include those paperback anthology series that have a close affiliation with magazines. It does not include showcase anthologies, such as *The Berkley Showcase*, *New Voices* or the *Clarion* volumes, or even all original anthologies or anthology series. Because of their importance to the field, *Orbit*, *New Dimensions* and *Universe* are included, along with *Infinity*, *Nova* and *New Writings in S.F. Chrysalis* was a borderline case, but we opted for inclusion. You will not find *Continuum*, *SF Emphasis*, *Pulsar*, or even *New Writings in Horror and the Supernatural* because these were planned solely as anthology series with no tug of the forelock to magazines.

Nor is the distinction between magazines and anthologies as obvious as one might expect. Donald A. Wollheim, editor of the *Avon Fantasy Reader*, always asserted, for instance, that the *Reader* was a series of paperback anthologies; yet, because it appeared on a fairly regular basis at a time when paperback anthologies were the exception rather than the rule, the persuasion of the fan field was to accept the *Reader* as magazines, and as such they are still indexed today. Thus, the *Avon Fantasy Reader* appears in Section I. James Baen, on the other hand, launched *Destinies* as a magazine in book form, and Forrest Ackerman treated the U.S. editions of *Perry Rhodan* in the same manner. These two series appear in Section II. A number of British wartime magazines, such as *Strange Tales*, *Strange Love Stories* and *Occult*, were issued in book form by way of convenience. Although one can argue either way regarding their placement, they appear in Section I. Whenever there could be some question as to whether an entry would be in Section I or II, there is a cross-reference referring the reader to the proper section.

In addition to the number of fantastic fiction magazines that has existed since the late 1920s, fanzines and, more recently, academic journals have provided a wealth of material about science fiction and fantasy. This volume would not be complete if it did not provide some information on these nonfiction magazines, for they contain much that is of interest to both the scholar and the fan. Section III includes brief entries on a selected list of nonfiction fanzines and scholarly journals. The list is limited to magazines that contain a strong, continuing body of worthwhile information, contain at least one solid, continuing feature of value to the reader, or are of historical significance.

Nor is fantastic fiction limited to the English-speaking world. It has developed as a well-defined genre in a number of countries around the world, and, as in the United States and Great Britain, that development has been nurtured by a variety of active magazines. Information on these magazines is limited in the English-speaking world, and the serious study of fantastic literature would be greatly enhanced by a comprehensive world bibliography of science fiction and fantasy magazines and series. We have provided a beginning in Section IV. That section includes an annotated listing of 178 titles, identifying the classic, as well as a few other, magazines from twenty-three countries.

Finally, both the general subject index and the appendixes help to provide access to the material in this volume. Since the cover artist played an important role in the success or failure of many magazines, Appendix I is an Index to Major Cover Artists. As such, it will help the reader to locate information on artists of particular interest. Appendix II, a chronology that lists the magazines by their founding dates, will help those interested in a particular time period to locate magazines of interest.

Acknowledgments

The essays in this volume are all the products of the individual contributors, and though reference will have been made to many of the books listed in the Bibliography, and where necessary cited within the essay, all essays are original. Specific reference, however, must be made to the following books, which were used for cross-checking to ensure that no titles had been omitted: Donald H. Tuck, *A Handbook of Science Fiction and Fantasy* (Hobart, Tasmania: Tuck, 1959), which includes entries on all the magazines published as of 1958 (the magazine section forms part of Volume 3 of Tuck's *The Encyclopedia of Science Fiction and Fantasy* [Chicago: Advent, 1982], which is current to 1968—this printing was not consulted in the preparation of the present volume); and Bradford M. Day, *The Complete Checklist of Science-Fiction Magazines* (New York: Day, 1961), which was complete up to 1960. Day's work was updated by William H. Desmond, in *The Science-Fiction Magazine Checklist, 1961–1972* (Cambridge, Mass.: Archival Press, 1972), but this guide was not consulted for the present volume. Rather, from 1960 onward the selection of items included was based on the collection of Mike Ashley, with further suggestions by Robert Weinberg for the hero pulps, Frank H. Parnell for some of the rare, short-lived fantasy magazines, Jon Harvey for some of the semi-professional publications, and Graham Stone for the Australian titles.

Apart from the contributors, who include the above four devotees, special thanks must go to Robert A.W. Lowndes for his research into the archives of Gernsback Publications for information on *Science and Invention*, and for reading and vetting the entries on the magazines he edited; to Donald A. Wollheim, for the help on the many magazines with which he has been associated, in particular *Uncanny Tales*, *Orbit* and *Saturn*; to Paul Allen, ex-publisher/editor of *Fantasy Newsletter*, for his spontaneous action which enabled entries to be made for *Chillers*, *Ares*, *S.F. Digest* and *Rod Serling's The Twilight Zone*; to Alistair Durie and Terry Hill, both of whom tirelessly delved through their collections of old pulps for snippets of information in editorials, letter columns or publishers' statements; to Forrest J Ackerman, for his help on obscure details of historical import; to Michael L. Cook for his help on some knotty problems with borderline mystery magazines; to Cele G. Lalli, Bea Mahaffey, Joseph Wrzos, Frederik Pohl, Robert Silverberg and Robert Hoskins for their help in providing background data on the publications with which they were associated; and to Howard DeVore, Paul Spencer, John Robert Colombo, Robert A. Madle and Robert Weinberg for being there and responding promptly to so many obscure queries.

Finally thanks to Malcolm J. Edwards for helping read manuscripts way back when this all started, and to Will Murray for his help and advice in reading the final copy.

Introduction

At times one becomes uncertain how to handle the general introduction to an encyclopedic volume such as *Science Fiction, Fantasy, and Weird Fiction Magazines*. Marshall B. Tymn, series editor for the Greenwood Press series on science fiction and fantasy, originally saw the need for a book providing extended discussions of the publishing histories and editorial policies of the many magazines—primarily American—that have shaped the field of science fiction from the 1920s onward. In this final form, he and Mike Ashley have expanded the scope of that dreamed-of volume. Nor should one forget either Joe Sanders, who undertook the task of describing the academic journals and fanzines, or Robert Weinberg, who has been particularly valuable in that he has provided accounts of many of the associational magazines, particularly *Weird Tales* and many of the ''hero pulps'' of the 1930s, which helped to prepare an audience for the specialist science fiction magazines.

The result is the most comprehensive appraisal yet published of magazines and original anthologies dealing with science fiction, fantasy, and horror fiction published in the twentieth century. It will remain the basic research tool for those studying the magazines for a long time. Together with the magazine runs which Greenwood Press has already published—and hopefully those additional series which it will publish in the future—this volume provides the basic raw data which are needed for a definitive history of the three categories of magazines.

What *Science Fiction, Fantasy, and Weird Fiction Magazines* has accomplished may be realized, in part at least, through a consideration of numbers. First, it includes 279 English-language magazines which have published relevant fiction in the United States and the British Commonwealth nations. Second, it gives the history of 15 original anthology series—and though one title appeared as early as the 1950s, one should not forget that during the 1970s especially the original anthologies were where the action was in terms of experimentation and expansion of the field. Third, primarily through the effort of Joe Sanders, it chronicles (in 78 titles) the response of the readers/enthusiasts and students (if such a distinction can or should be made) of the field of science fiction and fantasy, for not only did those journals and fanzines provide an outlet for many of the new talents which have shaped the field within the past several decades, but they also revealed the critical response to the field both in terms of literary criticism (as opposed to reviews) and intellectual history. Finally, it has shown that science fiction and fantasy can no longer be regarded as a specialized literary response primarily of the Anglo-American nations, for it gives the history of 178 magazines published in a language other than English. As already suggested, no other single volume has yet provided a more comprehensive coverage of the field in the twentieth century.

This coverage brings one full circle to the original problem regarding an introduction to *Science Fiction, Fantasy, and Weird Fiction Magazines*. First and foremost, such an introduction must not become a catalogue of titles, editors and authors. To do so would risk the danger of becoming perfunctorily repetitious. It would be pointless to attempt a highly detailed discussion of any one of the magazines, editors or writers dealt with in the volume, for individual entries afford a tremendous variety of information—ranging from the tenure of editors and publishers to the number of volumes, the regularity and place of publication, as well as the significant attitudes which shaped the contributors of each magazine and the memorable works published in them. If the reader/researcher wishes information about a particular title, he or she has only to go to the appropriate entry.

As a result, the task of the introduction should be to sketch, essentially, the literary context which gave rise to an increased emphasis upon science fiction resulting in the specialized periodicals appearing from the 1920s onward. Because *Science Fiction, Fantasy, and Weird Fiction Magazines* emphasizes SF, fantasy and horror, one may well ask why such an approach should be taken. No matter how detailed the specific account of any magazine is, certain questions and/or problems arise which only a consideration of the literary background can confront. These questions cover a wide spectrum. For example: (1) Why did the specialist magazines come into being at the time they did within the broad field of popular pulps, and why did they survive when the pulp field disappeared? (2) To what extent is a historical perspective imperative to an understanding of the evolution of modern science fiction and fantasy? (3) What are the basic and necessary assumptions needed to distinguish and define science fiction? and (4) most important of all, Is Science Fiction a distinct and separate genre, or is it merely another form of fantasy? (This same question may be asked of horror fiction, although to do so might well involve special problems involving psychology and literary realism.) In short, *Science Fiction, Fantasy, and Weird Fiction Magazines* may be an essential weapon in the debate over why the twentieth century (perhaps more to the point, recent criticism) has fragmented a single field into a number of forms which should not be separated.

Within recent years a number of events, as well as trends in publishing and film making, have brought this problem of distinctly separate identity into sharp focus. In the introduction to his *Science Fiction Writers* (1982), E. F. Bleiler suggested that the basic difficulty in definition lies in the fact that one person's science fiction may well be another's fantasy.[1] Despite such a view, however, he is now editing a companion volume which he has entitled *Supernatural Fiction Writers*. At the Modern Language Association meeting in New York City in December 1981, Barry Malzberg insisted that science fiction be confined to the specialist magazines of the last half century and that his academic audience agree that writers like Frank Stockton did *not* write science fiction. He further argued that SF is better able to give insight into the social, psychological and political quandaries of the twentieth century than any other literary form. Many writers and editors whose careers have been tied to the magazines—sometimes since the 1930s and 1940s—share his opinions.

On the other hand, many writers, editors and critics use a variety of criteria to differentiate between "hard" and "soft" science fiction. Patricia Warrick, current president of the Science Fiction Research Association (SFRA), said that at the Eaton Conference at the University of California–Riverside in the spring of 1983, participants seemed to have a difficult time agreeing exactly what "hard" science fiction is. At the same conference in the spring of 1982, when the topic focused upon SF and fantasy films, there was a similar disagreement in which some participants wanted to speak of some films as "horror" rather than either SF or fantasy. Nor should one ignore that within the past year or so several major publishing houses have sharply curtailed or dropped their science fiction lines in favor of fantasy. Del Rey Books, Bantam Books and Pocket Books carefully designate a given title as "fantasy" or "science fiction," although on occasion, as in the instance of the paperback edition of Piers Anthony's *Juxtaposition* (1982), Del Rey identifies novels as "science fiction/fantasy." Quantitatively, one suspects that during 1982 and 1983 more titles have been issued under the label of fantasy than science fiction. One may, of course, argue that such a trend simply indicates the current popular literary taste and represents no problem in definition. Yet if one examines the recent books closely, one finds a surprising mixture of science fiction "furniture" and fantasy within the same story, as in the works of Jean Lorrah, Sterling E. Länier and C. J. Cherryh. Should these examples be dismissed because they represent writers active only during the past decade, then one must point out that some of the highly regarded masters in the field have produced both science fiction and fantasy: Clifford D. Simak, Jack Williamson, L. Sprague de Camp, Ray Bradbury and H. P. Lovecraft among them. In this respect, perhaps the most bitterly amusing incident of the past several years involved Gene Wolfe's *The Shadow of the Torturer* (1980). It was nominated for but did not win the Nebula Award; it did not gain a nomination for the Hugo; but it won the World Fantasy Award and the British Science Fiction Society (BSFS) Award as the best novel of the year. In the *World Fantasy Convention 1983* booklet, an advertisement for *The Book of the New Sun*, the tetralogy of which *The Shadow of the Torturer* was the first volume, includes the assertion by Greg Benford, himself a winner of the Nebula Award, that Wolfe's series is among the "true classics of modern science fantasy."[2]

The Science Fiction Encyclopedia acknowledges that that term "has never been clearly defined," suggesting perhaps hopefully that it has been superseded in recent years by "sword and sorcery" or "heroic fantasy"; after alluding to a "well-known magazine" by that title (dealt with in this volume), the passage goes on to differentiate "science fantasy" from "weird fantasy" by declaring that the former emphasizes "the strange and bizarre," and the latter "the horrible and obviously SUPERNATURAL."[3] Other instances of such careful distinctions, including some from scholarly journals, could be cited. On one point, however, there can be no disagreement. Within the past few years fantasy, whether as fiction or film, has undergone a resurgence of interest. The International Association for the Fantastic in the Arts (IAFA), whose current president is Roger Schlobin, has grown out of the annual Conference on the Fantastic held by Florida Atlantic University at Boca Raton in March. In the Fall 1983 newsletter of World Science Fiction (WSF), president Brian Aldiss expressed the wish that there could be "close liaison" between the two organizations.

Perhaps not everyone, especially those younger persons new to the field, realizes that the term *science fiction* did not come into general usage until after the simplification of Hugo Gernsback's awkward, tongue-twisting *scientifiction*. For a time during the 1930s "space fiction" was considered as a possible label for the supposedly new field, while earlier the British critic Dorothy Scarborough had met no opposition when she proposed "scientific romance" to describe the work of Wells and his contemporaries. Aldiss has suggested that the first use of the term *science fiction* occurred in the middle of the nineteenth century. The novelist Gustavus W. Pope, for example, called his *Journey to Mars* (1894) a "scientific novel." In the 1960s and 1970s, attempting to maintain the acronym "SF," writer and critic Samuel R. Delany advanced the name "speculative fiction" in order to escape the restrictions set up by the practices of editors and writers during the 1930s and 1940s. Harlan Ellison, Robert Silverberg and Barry Malzberg are among those who have suggested abandoning the term *science fiction* altogether because it is no more than a convenient publishers' label used to assure a certain minimal sale of a given work.

In addition, the work of a number of individuals—Mike Ashley, Brian Aldiss, James Gunn, Sam Moskowitz, Thomas Clareson, H. Bruce Franklin, I. F. Clarke, Mark Hillegas, Jack Williamson and E. F. Bleiler, to name only those who come immediately to mind—has established the historical ties of "modern" SF to the literary tradition which goes back to the eighteenth century, at least, and to the utopian romance beginning with Sir Thomas More. Aldiss has argued persuasively that Mary Shelley's *Frankenstein* (1818) is the fountainhead of the genre as a distinct form of literature, and she certainly gave lasting expression to one of the basic myths of the field. Some have stressed the works of Edgar Allan Poe and Fitz-James O'Brien; others, Edward Everett Hale, Ambrose Bierce and Mark Twain. Sam Moskowitz, one of the few scholars to search extensively through the popular magazines of the nineteenth century, unhesitatingly stresses the importance of writers like Edward Page Mitchell (*The Crystal Man*, 1973) and Robert Duncan Milne (*Into the Sun and Other Stories*, 1980); indeed, his *Science Fiction in Old San Francisco: History of the Movement from 1854 to 1890* (1980), as the title indicates, establishes that city as a nerve-center of the new form at least as early as New York, London and Paris.

Such an emphasis upon American authors, as students of the literary history of the development of science fiction and fantasy know, distorts the picture. The work of I. F. Clarke provides a case in point. His earliest study involved a bibliography of *The Tale of the Future* (1961, 1972) in which the first entries dated from 1644, 1733 and 1763. He has also documented the growth of the so-called future war motif, which mushroomed after the publication of Sir George Tomkyns Chesney's "The Battle of Dorking" in *Blackwood's Magazine* in the spring of 1871. One has little difficulty tracing the evolution of that basic plot from those late Victorian jingoistic narratives—emulated both on the Continent and in America—through the narratives of the "space operas" of writers like "Doc" Smith and Edmond Hamilton to the contemporary treatments of the motif, ranging from Joe Haldeman's *The Forever War* (1974) to such films as *Star Wars* and *Return of the Jedi*. Indeed, one realizes the irony of how deeply a part of modern popular culture these forecasts of future struggles have become when the *Newsweek* cover referring to the outbreak of the Falkland Islands affair in the spring of 1982 was entitled "The Empire Strikes Back."

To understand the problem of definition, one must be acquainted with the variety within the literary tradition from which science fiction evolved in the late nineteenth and early twentieth centuries before the specialist magazines came into existence. Greenwood Press will soon publish an annotated bibliography primarily of American titles between 1870 and 1930, as well as a history of that period. At present both E. F. Bleiler's *The Checklist of Science Fiction and Supernatural Fiction* (1978)—originally published as *The Checklist of Fantastic Literature* (1948)—and R. Reginald's *Science Fiction and Fantasy Literature* (1979) are standard bibliographies of the field, but neither of them supplies annotations, so that frequently irrelevant titles have been included, especially in the pioneering first edition of Bleiler.

Science Fiction, Fantasy, and Weird Fiction Magazines is also a pioneering venture, for until now there has been no comprehensive, annotated description of the relevant twentieth-century magazines. Unfortunately, there is no similar volume to cover the late nineteenth century. Frank Luther Mott's five-volume *History of American Magazines* does not touch the "pulps" as they developed after the turn of the century. In his *Golden Multitudes: The Story of Best Sellers in the United States*, the chapter, "The Cheap 'Libraries' of 1875–1893" has importance for its discussion of Erastus F. Beadle, the originator of the so-called dime novel. He also makes passing reference to such publishers as John B. Alder, Norman L. Munro, and Street and Smith, but his brief references to Verne and Wells have little value. One of the most important sources is E. F. Bleiler's two-volume *Frank Reade, Jr.* anthology (1979); one wishes his introduction were more extended, but he does acknowledge the indebtedness of the Reade stories to Jules Verne and declares that such "newspaper" series, reprinted several times and obviously aimed at a juvenile audience, expressed the "utmost in science-fiction adventure" during the 1880s and 1890s; "Frank Reade embodied the science fiction of his day in America."[4] Yet young Reade was not alone. Only the format changed as Street and Smith issued in book form George Manville Fenn's *The Young Inventor* (1892). The way was open for Tom Swift and his cohorts.

Although Frank Munsey's *All-Story* and *Argosy*, under their various names, did more to emphasize the field and create a market for it than did any other pulp periodical during the first quarter of this century, what is overlooked is that some science fiction and fantasy was published in virtually every American magazine during the late nineteenth and early twentieth centuries. As early as 1889 *Colliers'* serialized Frank Stockton's *The Great War Syndicate*; in 1911 *Hampden's Magazine* issued Robert W. Chambers' *A Matter of Eugenics*, which saw book publication as *The Gay Rebellion*; during the autumn of 1914 the *Saturday Evening Post* published Arthur Train and Robert William Wood's *The Man Who Rocked the Earth*; and in 1915 *McClure's* ran Cleveland Moffet's *The Conquest of America*. This was not a new fad. As early as the 1870s *Scribner's* and *Lippincott's* serialized the fiction of Jules Verne, while at the turn of the century *Cosmopolitan* published the romances of H. G. Wells. Garrett P. Serviss' sequel to Wells' *The War of the Worlds*—*Edison's Conquest of Mars*—first appeared in the New York *Evening Standard* in 1898 and then was lost until Carcosa House issued it in book form in 1947.

As mentioned earlier, however, to emphasize only American magazines distorts the picture. One can gain a good idea of the complexity of the field and the problems of definition by considering the contents of such recent anthologies as *Science Fiction by the Rivals of H. G. Wells* (Castle Books, 1979). The competitors of Wells produced such stories as the following. In W. L. Allen's "The Purple Death" a German "scientific person" develops a strain of bacillus capable of decimating the population; he dies and it is buried with him, but the narrator fears that someday builders—urban developers—will break the bottle so that the plague scourges the Earth (how like contemporary concern for toxic wastes, to say nothing of germ warfare). Grant Allen's "The Thames Valley Catastrophe" focuses upon a series of volcanic eruptions which destroy the Thames Valley and, of course, London. L. J. Beeston's "A Star Fell" centers upon the theft and destruction of an advanced form of aircraft so that the inventor/ narrator wonders whether or not such research should be undertaken (an odd echo of the Frankenstein theme). A Darwinian fantasy, Frank T. Bullen's "The Last Stand of the Decopods," portrays a prehistoric struggle between whales and octopi for the supremacy of the deep ocean. Wardon Allan Curtis' "The Monster of Lake Lametre" allows the narrator to report the existence in a lake in Wyoming of a prehistoric saurian monster apparently capable of absorbing the human intellect of those it devours. In Rudolph de Cordova's "The Microbe of Death" a jealous lover kills the man who has married the woman they both loved only to find that she really loves the man he was, so that he still loses her. George Griffith's "The Raid of *Le Vengeur*" averts a threatened invasion of Britain, while his "Stories of Other Worlds" (rewritten and published as *A Honeymoon in Space*) simply lets its newlyweds tour the solar system and marvel at the varied wonders of Earth-like planets. The narrator of Cutcliffe Hyne's "The Lizard" encounters a prehistoric beast in a cave near the village of Kettlewell in Yorkshire. His "London's Danger" is one of several narratives in which the great city is threatened with destruction, this time a vast fire after cold water freezes the water mains. His classic novel, *The Lost Continent*, whose scene is ancient Atlantis, has also been reprinted in the anthology. E. Tickner-Edward's "The Man Who Meddled with Eternity" may provide a final example from the thirty works included in *The Rivals of H. G. Wells*. A former rival takes possession of the body of the husband of the woman they both loved; when he learns that she really loved him instead of her husband and wishes to be released so that she may go off with him, he commits suicide, for he cannot reverse the process which has given him her husband's form. Because the anthology is made up of photographic reproductions from the periodicals in which the stories originally appeared, one immediately learns that many of them came from *Pearson's Magazine*, although *The Strand*, *Cassell's* and *The Windsor Magazine* also are represented.

One might find the same variety in the magazines from which George Locke's *Worlds Apart* (1972) and David G. Hartwell and L. W. Currey's *The Battle of the Monsters* (1976, American stories) are drawn. Douglas Menville and R. Reginald's two anthologies, *Ancestral Voices* (1975) and *Dreamers of Dreams* (1978), dealing with early science fiction and fantasy, respectively, take their selections from early books for the most part, although many of their stories were first published in magazines.

There are several problems involving such a listing of specific examples. First, there are persons now who will not accept some of that early fiction as SF, for the simple reason that their definitions do not include such plotlines. Second, such catalogues can give only a sampling of the fiction from the period. Yet if one turns to the works of Sir Arthur Conan Doyle, Frank Stockton, Jack London, Edward Page Mitchell and Ralph Duncan Milne—to name only those early writers who have had single-author anthologies published within the last decade—one finds the same plotlines, the same concerns, granting the individual genius of those writers, as illustrated by Jack London's "The Red One" (1918), which has been republished a half dozen times since its first reprinting in *A Spectrum of Worlds* (1972). Their narratives reflect the imaginative interests of their period: new weapons, electricity, the survival of prehistoric animals, the threat of plagues, communication with other planets, the threat of ecological or man-made catastrophes—to cite some of the principal recurrent motifs, a number of which have evolved, perhaps, but remain popular in the 1970s and 1980s.

Such patterns repeated themselves in the Munsey magazines dealt with in this volume, although both *All-Story* and *Argosy* gave particular emphasis to the imaginary voyage and the lost race motif as exemplified in the works of such individuals as A. Merritt, Charles B. Stilson and Ralph Milne Farley. Other Munsey serials, like those of Garrett Smith, focused upon a technologically sophisticated Earth. When the tales did involve other worlds, as in the trilogy which J. U. Giesy introduced with *Palos of the Dog Star Pack*, not only does one find adaptations of the imaginary voyage and the lost race, but the protagonist dutifully returns to present-day Earth as often as possible, frequently to do no more than deliver another installment of his narrative. (If one looks for a common narrative convention, perhaps none was more prevalent than the discovery or presentation of a manuscript which supposedly gave feasibility to the wildest imaginings.)

Although Garrett Smith and, to a large extent, Ray Cummings anticipated some of the interest of the specialist magazines of the 1930s, one should re-member that none of the motifs mentioned has completely disappeared from the later scene. Indeed, two of the most popular magazines from 1939 until the early 1950s were *Famous Fantastic Mysteries* and *Fantastic Novels*, which first re-printed extensively from the Munsey magazines before expanding their scope to include first magazine publication of novels, both British and American, which had previously appeared only in book form. During World War II, though its frequency of appearance was cut back, *Famous Fantastic Mysteries*, devoted almost exclusively at the time to ''classics'' appearing in the Munsey magazines, survived the exigencies of the war, although John W. Campbell abruptly cut off *Unknown Worlds*, which was devoted to fantasy—or perhaps one should say to stories, like those of Sprague de Camp, relying less on ''hard'' science—in order to continue regular publication of *Astounding Science Fiction*.

Mike Ashley is essentially correct, therefore, when he asserts that before 1926 ''there were three types of science fiction: first, the scientific romance epitomized by Burroughs and Merritt that appeared in the Munsey magazines; second, the scientific extrapolation of Gernsback; and third, the weird and bizarre science fiction of *Weird Tales*.''[5] As the author of the four-volume *The History of the Science Fiction Magazine*, although each volume is in large part an anthology devoted to a single decade between 1926 and 1965, Ashley has done one of the most thorough historical surveys, especially of the British magazines in his various introductions. Even though he works in those volumes with the specialist magazines, he acknowledges the importance of the late nineteenth-century pe-riodicals in establishing an interest in and readiness to accept the new form by an enthusiastic audience. To some degree, in naming the three types of SF, he probably oversimplifies, especially—as illustrated by the future war motif em-phasized by I. F. Clarke—since one can undoubtedly show the evolution of each motif from its early inception to the present day (the 1970s and 1980s), allowing for certain changes that are dictated by the shifts of interest and innovations of the writers of each successive generation (the mystery and western fields may provide additional evidence of such changes).

From Robert Silverberg to Barry Malzberg, two of the most severe critics of the early specialist magazines, one hears variations of the assertion that once in the magazines, science fiction abandoned serious thematic concerns in favor of story and became "mere motion for motion's sake, hollow and pointless adventure fiction."[6] Much the same criticism has been leveled at Edgar Rice Burroughs, who certainly transformed the imaginary voyage and the lost race motif in his various series, although he has been dismissed as a "one plot" writer. Again, from James Gunn and Ted Dikty to various academic critics, one hears the cry that the magazines "ghettoized" SF and for at least twenty years removed it from the general reading public and thus deprived it of serious critical assessment. One must hasten to remind the reader, however, that if this was the case, it applied more to the American scene than to the British. One recalls Brian Aldiss and John Brunner, for example, speaking of the "Yank magazines" which they read in their youth and which became so influential in determining their own careers. As an examination of this volume should readily indicate, the specialist magazine has been primarily an American vehicle, for the British accepted and published SF directly in book form, as in the cases of Olaf Stapledon, Aldous Huxley and George Orwell, although such writers as John Wyndham and Arthur C. Clarke contributed to the American magazines from the beginnings of their careers.

One could also show that to dismiss the magazines as "pointless adventure fiction" not only loses sight of the importance of story as an element of fiction but also ignores the literary climate which first produced the dime novel, then the "boys' libraries," and finally the pulp magazines. In the introduction to *The Shudder Pulps* (1975), Robert Kenneth Jones reminds his readers that "originally, pulps were mass-produced as a cheap thrill for the working man (and schoolboy) eager for light reading of a sensational nature."[7] One recalls a similar remark about freight cars filled with dime novels shipped to the Union army during the Civil War in order to keep the youthful troops of the Army of the Potomac out of the usual difficulties besetting soldiers in camp. One need not rehearse here the history of popular publishing in America. Suffice it to say that not until 1896 did the first true pulp magazine appear when Frank Munsey transformed *The Argosy* into an all-fiction magazine. In 1905 he followed it with *The All-Story Magazine*. The specialized pulps followed: *Snappy Stories* (1912), *Detective Story Magazine* (1915), *Western Story Magazine* (1919), *Thrill Book* (1919)—the first attempt at a magazine devoted largely to science fiction—*Weird Tales* (1923) and, of course, *Amazing Stories* (1926).

More to the point is the problem of definition. *The Science Fiction Reference Book*, edited by Marshall Tymn, cites Isaac Asimov's definition of science fiction as "that branch of literature which deals with the human response to changes in science and technology."[8] He goes on to say that because the worlds created in SF differ from the present only because of the changes in science and technology, a reader can infer the "set of continuous changes" leading from the here-and-now to the world portrayed in the fiction. He also emphasizes the basic rationality ("sanity") of both the characters and the worlds in science fiction.

One should recall that Asimov began publishing in the late 1930s: variations of his definition echo through those advanced by other writers whose careers began about that time. His criteria very aptly describe one strain which has persisted from the earliest science fiction to the present day. It lies at the basis of the comparison often made between SF and the detective story in that it stresses that both forms are a kind of "puzzle story." It covers all of those works in which the protagonist is faced with a problem which must be solved before the narrative can end. Significantly, the basic optimism of this part of the field reveals itself in that whatever the problem is, it is successfully overcome. Murray Leinster's "First Contact" (1945) affords a perfect example. Somewhere near the Crab Nebula Earthmen aboard the *Llanvabon* encounter an alien ship; neither crew dares to return to its home world for fear that the other will follow and destroy its world. They exchange ships. That future security—that is, the ability of Earthmen and aliens to get along with one another—is couched in what some would regard as a sexist jest merely dates the narrative.

Ironically, Asimov's criteria do not apply to what is undoubtedly his most famous short story, "Nightfall" (1941); the astronomers have deduced that a total eclipse is responsible for the 2,000-year cycle which has governed the rise and fall of civilization on their planet, Lagash. Yet irrational fear seizes the characters in the story, as well as the unseen populace of Saro City, as each either encounters complete darkness or sees the "thirty thousand mighty suns" amid which their solar system exists. Nor is there any implication that those persons secreted in the "Hideout" will survive the ordeal and remain sane. The cycle thus will repeat itself once again. (Interestingly—not only for Asimov himself but for modern science fiction as a whole, Asimov has said that John W. Campbell inserted the reference contrasting the "thirty-six hundred" stars visible from Earth, perhaps to heighten the effect of thirty thousand suns. Asimov himself did not want any reference whatsoever to Earth.) In its own way, then, while containing the stuff of "hard" science fiction, "Nightfall" can also be called a horror story.

Nor does his definition apply to another early classic, Stanley G. Weinbaum's "A Martian Odyssey" (1934). That story is most notable for its sympathetic treatment of the ostrich-like Martian, Tweel. But no problem is solved. The Earthman, Jarvis, lost from his ship, is accompanied by Tweel as he trudges across the sand-swept planet; by convenient chance he and Tweel are rescued by a man from Jarvis' ship at a crucial moment, although Tweel runs away and is not found despite a search. Dominated by the Martian landscape as the narrative is, Earth cannot be forgotten; the last line implies that Jarvis has obtained the means of curing cancer. A few may regard that potential as an irrelevancy—a flaw—but such matters were a convention of the early period. Recall that before Hiroshima many thought that advanced science and technology would provide a panacea curing all of mankind's woes; it would produce, in short, a veritable earthly paradise.

One might include John W. Campbell's much acclaimed "Twilight" (1934) as a final example of an early work which falls outside of Asimov's definition. Within the narrative frame of an encounter between a present-day man and an individual from the future, the narrative is primarily concerned with Ares Sen Kenlin's account of his experience when he is projected 7 million years into the future to a time when the Earth and Sun are dying and, far worse, when mankind has become "little men—bewildered—dwarfed" who have lost their curiosity. Ares Sen Kenlin escapes from that future, returning to 1932 instead of his own time so that he may tell Jim Bendell his story. Before he left the distant future, however, he set a task for one of the machines he activated; he "ordered it to make a machine which would have what man had lost. A curious machine."[9] Then he fled from "the lingering, dying glow of man's twilight." He can only hope that the machine solved the problem he had set for it, but even such success would not reestablish man's glory. The story is thus a lament for the death of mankind, the death of the universe.

What is most important about the use of these four stories as examples is that they all come from *The Science Fiction Hall of Fame* (1970). Its selections were chosen by the vote of the members of the Science Fiction Writers of America (SFWA) as the finest short stories written before December 31, 1964, thereby making it impossible for them to be considered for the newly founded Nebula Award. In short, in the opinions of those men and women writing science fiction in 1965, these stories merited the Nebula Award had it existed at the time they were written. Yet only one of them fits within Asimov's excellent definition.

Perhaps the difficulty lies in that any single definition, whoever advances it—editor, writer, academic scholar—cannot encompass a field that exists as part of a literary tradition going back at least to the eighteenth century. What such definitions do is try to freeze science fiction as an unchanging form. That, of course, is ridiculous. For example, the earlier vision of an earthly paradise has certainly been replaced within the last generation, at least, by the vision of an earthly hell. To put it another way, the vision of utopia has been replaced by one of dystopia. Some individuals like to suggest that a pivotal change of vision occurred when Clifford D. Simak's series of "dog" stories published in *Astounding* during the period of World War II were gathered together and published as *City* (1951). John W. Campbell rejected the last of the stories, "Trouble with Ants" (1951), which saw magazine publication in *Amazing Stories*. Granted that Simak's extraordinary beast fable was not the first dystopian view of the future, it did totally condemn mankind as a species incapable of dealing with its individual and societal problems, and it was published in the popular, specialized magazines. A second revolution, so to speak, occurred during the 1960s when writers—primarily British, at least at first—gathered themselves around Michael Moorcock's *New Worlds*, undoubtedly the most important of the British magazines, and launched what was denounced as "the new wave." Harlan Ellison's *Dangerous Visions* (1967) provided another landmark, for never again could the field be the same. And with the 1970s came a mixture of science fiction "furniture" and the magic of fantasy which had not been seen before, even the so-called weird-menace magazines of the 1930s, which did blend together horror, science fiction, fantasy and sexuality to the point of sadism.

Perhaps one final example will suffice. As mentioned earlier, at the turn of the century and in the decades immediately following, the lost race motif, as given shape by Sir H. Rider Haggard and Edgar Rice Burroughs, became one of the most popular motifs in the field of science fiction and fantasy. From the nineteenth century onward, one can trace the focal points of exploration during any given period by reading the imaginary voyages and lost race novels. From the Arctic, where the quest for the Northwest Passage remained an obsession for Americans and Europeans alike even after the Franklin and Andree disasters, and the Antarctic, which excited the imagination with John C. Symmes' theory of the hollow Earth and Poe's *The Narrative of Arthur Gordon Pym* (1838), to the Africa of Haggard and Burroughs and their imitators and either South or Central America, the storyteller moved his setting until, by the time of the romances of ''Ganpat'' and James Hilton's *Lost Horizon* (1933), only the interior of Asia was left uncharted for the imagination of the fantasist to work with. The South Seas had been a favorite place to journey from the time of Captain Cook and Herman Melville's *Typee* (1846) to a hundred romances early in this century, to say nothing of Joseph Conrad and William Somerset Maugham. But during World War II millions of Americans and their allies fought their way through the islands of the South Pacific and Southeast Asia. They found that the Burma Road did not lead to Shangri-la. Since World War II, one notices the paucity of the traditional lost race novel; only Aldous Huxley's *Island* (1962) and Jacquetta Hawkes' *Providence Island: An Archaeological Tale* (1959) come readily to mind unless one returns to the polar regions with Ian Cameron.

The problem of definition remains unsettled. There will be innumerable definitions because any one will restrict the field too much; a person looks at the field and finds that it evolves dynamically in response to new writers, just as the novel itself has evolved and yet retained all of its older conventions. Perhaps the 1980s will see a new fusion of science fiction, fantasy and horror fiction. That fusion may already be under way. Yet that is an issue for the future to decide. Just as the vision of mid-century sent the imagination soaring to other worlds and galaxies in the starships—the generation ships, as Robert Heinlein called them—so, too, present and future writers will mold the materials to the needs and interests of their own visions. What is most important at the moment is that *Science Fiction, Fantasy, and Weird Fiction Magazines* provides the most comprehensive view of what the complex field has been like in the relevant magazines of the twentieth century. For that the enthusiast and the scholar must thank Marshall Tymn and Mike Ashley and their contributors. They have provided the insight to show their readers how various and how new the field has always been.

Notes

1. E. F. Bleiler, ed., ''Introduction,'' *Science Fiction Writers* (New York: Charles Scribner's Sons, 1982), pp, xi–xii.

2. *World Fantasy Convention 1983* (Oak Forest, Ill.: Weird Tales Ltd., 1983), p. 38.

3. Peter Nicholls, ed., *The Science Fiction Encyclopedia* (Garden City, N.Y.: Doubleday, 1975), p. 521.

4. E. F. Bleiler, ed., "Introduction," *The Frank Reade Library* (New York: Garland Publishing Co., 1979), I: xiii.

5. Michael Ashley, ed., *The History of the Science Fiction Magazine: 1926–1935* (Chicago: Henry Regnery Company, 1976), I: 21.

6. Robert Silverberg, ed., "Introduction," *The Mirror of Infinity* (New York: Harper & Row, 1970), p. viii.

7. Robert Kenneth Jones, "Introduction," *The Shudder Pulps* (West Linn, Ore.: Fax Collector's Editions, 1975), p. xi.

8. Thomas D. Clareson, "Toward a History of Science Fiction," in *The Science Fiction Reference Book*, ed. Marshall B. Tymn (Mercer Island, Wash.: Starmont House, 1981), p. 3.

9. John W. Campbell, Jr., "Twilight," in *The Science Fiction Hall of Fame*, ed. Robert Silverberg (Garden City, N.Y.: Doubleday, 1970), p. 41.

Thomas D. Clareson

Abbreviations

ASFI	Stone, *Australian Science Fiction Index*
Cockcroft, IWFM	Cockcroft, *Index to the Weird Fiction Magazines*
Day, IWFM	Day, *An Index on the Weird and Fantastica in Magazines*
FRG	Ashley, *Fantasy Reader's Guide*
IBSF	Australian Science Fiction Association, *Index to British Science Fiction Magazines: 1934–1935*
ISFM	Day, *Index to the Science-Fiction Magazines 1926–1950*
ISFM-II	Lewis, *Index to the Science Fiction Magazines 1966–1970*
ISFM-III	Boyajian and Johnson, *Index to the Science Fiction Magazines: 1983*
ISPF	Boyajian and Johnson, *Index to the Semi-Professional Fantasy Magazines: 1982*
ISPF-2	Boyajian and Johnson, *Index to the Semi-Professional Fantasy Magazines: 1983*
IWG	Cook, *Fred Cook's Index to the Wonder Group*
MIT	Strauss, *The MIT Science Fiction Society's Index to the S-F Magazines, 1951–1965*
MT	Parnell, *Monthly Terrors*
NESFA	New England Science Fiction Association, The N.E.S.F.A. Index. Science Fiction Magazines: 1971–1972
NESFA-II	———, *The N.E.S.F.A. Index. Science Fiction Magazines: 1973*

NESFA-III	————, *The N.E.S.F.A. Index. Science Fiction Magazines: 1974*
NESFA-IV	————, *The N.E.S.F.A. Index. Science Fiction Magazines: 1975*
NESFA-V	————, *The N.E.S.F.A. Index. Science Fiction Magazines: 1976*
NESFA-VI	————, *The N.E.S.F.A. Index. Science Fiction Magazines: 1977–1978*
NESFA-VII	————, *The N.E.S.F.A. Index. Science Fiction Magazines: 1979–1980*
NESFA-VIII	————, *The N.E.S.F.A. Index. Science Fiction Magazines: 1981*
NESFA-IX	————, *The N.E.S.F.A. Index. Science Fiction Magazines: 1982*
Nicholls, *Encyclopedia*	Nicholls. *The Science Fiction Encyclopedia*
SFM	Hall, *The Science Fiction Magazine*
Tuck	Tuck, *The Encyclopedia of Science Fiction and Fantasy Through 1968.* Vol. 3: Miscellaneous

Abbreviations

ASFI	Stone, *Australian Science Fiction Index*
Cockcroft, IWFM	Cockcroft, *Index to the Weird Fiction Magazines*
Day, IWFM	Day, *An Index on the Weird and Fantastica in Magazines*
FRG	Ashley, *Fantasy Reader's Guide*
IBSF	Australian Science Fiction Association, *Index to British Science Fiction Magazines: 1934–1935*
ISFM	Day, *Index to the Science-Fiction Magazines 1926–1950*
ISFM-II	Lewis, *Index to the Science Fiction Magazines 1966–1970*
ISFM-III	Boyajian and Johnson, *Index to the Science Fiction Magazines: 1983*
ISPF	Boyajian and Johnson, *Index to the Semi-Professional Fantasy Magazines: 1982*
ISPF-2	Boyajian and Johnson, *Index to the Semi-Professional Fantasy Magazines: 1983*
IWG	Cook, *Fred Cook's Index to the Wonder Group*
MIT	Strauss, *The MIT Science Fiction Society's Index to the S-F Magazines, 1951–1965*
MT	Parnell, *Monthly Terrors*
NESFA	New England Science Fiction Association, The N.E.S.F.A. Index. Science Fiction Magazines: 1971–1972
NESFA-II	———, *The N.E.S.F.A. Index. Science Fiction Magazines: 1973*

NESFA-III	——, *The N.E.S.F.A. Index. Science Fiction Magazines: 1974*
NESFA-IV	——, *The N.E.S.F.A. Index. Science Fiction Magazines: 1975*
NESFA-V	——, *The N.E.S.F.A. Index. Science Fiction Magazines: 1976*
NESFA-VI	——, *The N.E.S.F.A. Index. Science Fiction Magazines: 1977–1978*
NESFA-VII	——, *The N.E.S.F.A. Index. Science Fiction Magazines: 1979–1980*
NESFA-VIII	——, *The N.E.S.F.A. Index. Science Fiction Magazines: 1981*
NESFA-IX	——, *The N.E.S.F.A. Index. Science Fiction Magazines: 1982*
Nicholls, *Encyclopedia*	Nicholls. *The Science Fiction Encyclopedia*
SFM	Hall, *The Science Fiction Magazine*
Tuck	Tuck, *The Encyclopedia of Science Fiction and Fantasy Through 1968*. Vol. 3: Miscellaneous

Section I

ENGLISH-LANGUAGE MAGAZINES

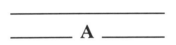

A. MERRITT'S FANTASY MAGAZINE

When the first issue of *A. Merritt's Fantasy Magazine* appeared, dated December 1949, it looked like a sure success. It was part of the Popular Publications chain, a well-established line that had kept *Famous Fantastic Mysteries** going since 1939 and that recently had reactivated *Super Science Stories** and *Fantastic Novels** with apparent success. In particular, both *Famous Fantastic Mysteries* and *Fantasic Novels* had demonstrated that all-reprint SF and fantasy magazines could thrive; *AMF*'s policy was virtually identical with *Fantastic Novels'*, since both reprinted their contents from earlier general fiction pulp magazines in the Munsey chain, such as *The Argosy.** In fact, since *AMF* began as a bi-monthly publication alternating with *Fantastic Novels*, the two could be said to form one monthly magazine. Based on time-tested policy and solid backing, the new magazine appeared to be a safe bet. In fact, however, it lasted less than a year. Its fifth issue, dated October 1950, was its last.

Since, in policy, content, format, even illustrators, *AMF* was of a piece with apparently successful magazines, perhaps the most distinctively interesting thing about it, thus, is its abrupt collapse. Several possible reasons have been suggested for that failure.

In *The Science Fiction Encyclopedia*, for one, Malcolm Edwards suggests that the attempt to build on Merritt's popularity made it unlikely that the magazine would last long, since Merritt had died in 1943.[1] That explanation seems unlikely. Merritt's novels and stories had appeared much earlier, but they were popular throughout the 1940s, and still are. Recent paperback reprints carry the banner: "Over 5,000,000 copies of A. Merritt's Books Sold in Avon Editions."[2] It thus appears that Merritt's name must have had considerable sales power.

In another suggestion for the magazine's failure, Sam Moskowitz offers an ingenious reversal of Edwards' notion: instead of overusing Merritt's popularity,

AMF underused it. Merritt was not a prolific writer, and much of his work had been recently reprinted in *Fantastic Novels*. To stretch out the available Merritt material, *AMF* ran only three pieces by Merritt in its five issues—one novel, "Creep, Shadow!," in the first issue, one short story, "Three Lines of Old French," in the second, and one novella, "The Face in the Abyss," in the fourth—all of which were available relatively easily in Avon paperback editions. There was, in addition, a portrait of Merritt by Virgil Finlay in the last issue. Moskowitz faults the magazine's editor for not selecting stories by other writers that more closely resembled Merritt's work, pointing out that stories from the same magazine, written in the same era, even dealing with the same theme, may be different in flavor. Thus, Moskowitz argues, *AMF* did not use intelligently the drawing power it had.[3]

In fact, Merritt's popularity may have created still another problem for the magazine, making it difficult to obtain reprint rights to Merritt's work. The editorial comments in *AMF* suggest as much. The editor began with the promise to print "the complete works of Abraham Merritt."[4] When readers began making specific suggestions, however, the editor hedged that the magazine "shall at some time or other print all the Merritt stories which we are able to reprint," adding that "if we can secure rights to any of his poetry or non-fiction articles, they will also be included."[5] The editor later remarked that "*A. Merritt's Fantasy* will publish as many stories as we have the rights to."[6] If Merritt's popularity was considerable, as indicated by the 1949 paperback collection of his short fiction, *The Fox Woman*, reprint rights to his work would have been worth protecting. And, in fact, Moskowitz reports that Popular Publications had given the rights back to Merritt earlier. He also reports seeing a letter written to Popular at this time by Merritt's widow protesting about the magazine reprints.[7]

Finally, in addition to these possible reasons for the failure of *A. Merritt's Fantasy*, the fact is that the Popular SF magazines were less robust than they appeared. *Fantastic Novels* and *Super Science Stories* ceased publication within a year of *AMF*, while *Famous Fantastic Mysteries* survived only a little longer.[8] Unable, for one reason or another, to establish a clear identity of its own, *AMF* may have been merely the first to sink.

Nevertheless, the magazine's contents are of some interest. The second issue, for instance, featured "The Smoking Land" by George Challis, one of the many pseudonyms of Frederick Faust. This printing represented the novel's only other magazine appearance outside the original serialization in *Argosy* in 1937, and only recently was it published in book form. The third issue carried one of Jack Mann's detective novels featuring Gees, "The Ninth Life," which is equally scarce. The last issue ran George Allan England's "The Elixir of Hate." There were also several worthy stories including "The Seal Maiden" by Victor Rousseau, "The Little Doll Died" by Theodore Roscoe and "Footsteps Invisible" by Robert Arthur. *AMF* also carried occasional articles, such as "The Science of Time Travel" by Ray Cummings, plus the traditional letter column. The first letter to be printed welcoming the arrival of the new magazine was by a fourteen-year-old Robert Silverberg.

Notes

1. Peter Nicholls, ed., *The Science Fiction Encyclopedia* (Garden City, N.Y.: Doubleday, 1979), p. 29.
2. A. Merritt, *The Ship of Ishtar* (New York: Avon, n.d.), n.p.
3. Sam Moskowitz, telephone conversation, July 15, 1980. Moskowitz also believes, based on prose style of editorial material and on the fact that one of the novels in *A. Merritt's Fantasy* had already been reprinted in *Famous Fantastic Mysteries*, that the anonymous editor of *A. Merritt's* was not Mary Gnaedinger (editor of *Famous Fantastic Mysteries* and *Fantastic Novels*) but some uninformed editorial hack.
4. "Calling All Fantasy Fans" [editorial], *A. Merritt's Fantasy Magazine* 1 (December 1949): 8.
5. Reply to letter in "Readers' Column," *A. Merritt's Fantasy Magazine* 1 (April 1950): 123.
6. Reply to letter in "Readers' Column," *A. Merritt's Fantasy Magazine* 1 (July 1950): 123.
7. Moskowitz, telephone conversation, July 15, 1980. A check of current editions of Merritt's novels confirms that even when original copyright is to the magazine publisher a later copyright is to the author. In the case of *The Ship of Ishtar*, for example, the novel is copyrighted 1924 by the Frank A. Munsey Company but then copyrighted 1926 by A. Merritt.
8. With the passing of *Fantastic Novels*, a tenuous extension of *A. Merritt's Fantasy* also ended. What turned out to be the last issue of the latter magazine had promised that the next issue would feature Merritt's "The Face in the Abyss." The January 1951 editorial for *Fantastic Novels* began with Mary Gnaedinger's announcement: "A. Merritt has returned to *Fantastic Novels*! The March issue will feature 'The Snake Mother,' with superb new illustrations and a beautiful new cover by Virgil Finlay! It has been decided to publish the remaining Merritt stories occasionally, in *Fantastic Novels* from now on" (p. 6). It is difficult to account for this if reprint rights actually were in dispute, unless the editor thought she could get around the problem by reprinting the *magazine* version of Merritt's work. In any event, that question proved to be moot. "The Snake Mother" did not appear in the next *Fantastic Novels*; the editorial in the June issue mentioned it vaguely as something that would "appear in a latter issue"—but that was *Fantastic Novels*' last issue.

Information Sources

BIBLIOGRAPHY:
Nicholls. *Encyclopedia.*
Tuck.
INDEX SOURCES: ISFM; MT; SFM; Tuck.
REPRINT SOURCES: Identical Canadian reprint edition by subsidiary of Popular. Back Cover advertisement changed, and magazine half-inch longer.
LOCATION SOURCES: M.I.T. Science Fiction Library; Toronto Public Library.

Publication History

TITLE: *A. Merritt's Fantasy Magazine*.
VOLUME DATA: Volume 1, Number 1, December 1949–Volume 2, Number 1, October
    1950. 4 issues per volume; bi-monthly to April 1950, then quarterly. Total run:
    5 issues.
PUBLISHER: Recreational Reading, Inc., an affiliate of Popular Publications, Kokomo,
    Indiana. Editorial Offices at East 42nd St., New York.
EDITOR: Not listed in magazine. Mary Gnaedinger was editor for Popular Publications'
    other fantasy magazines, but see Note 3 above.
FORMAT: Pulp, 132pp.
PRICE: 25¢.

Joe Sanders

ACE MYSTERY

Ace Mystery was a short-lived rival to the weird terror pulps dominated by
Dime Mystery Magazine,* *Horror Stories** and their like. It was published in
1936 by Aaron Wyn (1898–1967), who in later years established the Ace imprint
of paperbacks. Only three bi-monthly issues appeared, but they were of reasonably good quality, considering the state of the field, and featured a higher than
average quota of fantasy. It took the same format as the other terror pulps—a
lead "novel" supported by several short stories. The novels in the three issues
were the work of Frederick C. Davis, a prolific pulpster though not noted for
any contributions to the regular SF pulps. His themes would not have been out
of place in Gernsback's early magazines, especially *Scientific Detective Monthly*,*
although his treatment was poles apart from that magazine's. The first novel,
for instance, dealt with a directional loudspeaker that aims a high-pitched note
at the heroine to induce a homicidal frenzy. The second novel, "The Destroying
Angel," concerns a sculptor who shrinks corpses down to tiny miniatures. By
coincidence it appeared the same month that MGM released its film version of
A. Merritt's *Burn Witch Burn!*, retitled *The Devil Dolls*, with its own miniature
assassins.

Short stories were by such pulp regulars as Paul Ernst, Hugh B. Cave and
John Knox, but the one story worthy of singular credit is "Coyote Woman"
(July 1936) by the little-known Charles Marquis Warren. Pulp historian Robert
K. Jones goes so far as to call it " . . . among the most effective vampire stories
to appear in the pulps."

Ace Mystery, however, failed to make an impression on the terror pulp market
and soon folded.

Information Sources

BIBLIOGRAPHY:
Desmond, William H. *Science Fiction Times*, No. 4 (August 1979): 15.
Jones, Robert K. *The Shudder Pulps*. West Linn, Ore.: Fax Collector's Editions, 1975.

Weinberg, Robert. "The Horror Pulps: 1933–1940." In *Horror Literature*, ed. Marshall B. Tymn. New York: R. R. Bowker, 1981.
Tuck.
INDEX SOURCES: MT; Tuck.
REPRINT SOURCES: None known.
LOCATION SOURCES: University of California-Los Angeles Library (Vol. 1, No. 1, only).

Publication History

TITLE: *Ace Mystery*.
VOLUME DATA: Volume 1, Number 1, May-June 1936–Volume 1, Number 3, September-October 1936. Bi-monthly. Total run: 3 issues.
PUBLISHER: Periodical House, a subsidiary of Ace Magazines, New York.
EDITOR: Harry Widmer.
FORMAT: Pulp, 128 pp.
PRICE: 10¢.

Mike Ashley

AD ASTRA

At first glance *Ad Astra* could be considered a poor man's *Omni*,* although any direct comparison between the two magazines would be as unfair as comparing a Cunard liner with a rowboat. *AA* was a pop-science magazine with a modicum of science fiction and a budget that probably would not have paid for one page in *Omni*. Yet it managed to continue for sixteen issues, establishing a small corner for itself in the British market, but unfortunately one too small to survive.

AA started in a small way in 1978 and progressed steadily. The editor and power behind the magazine, James Manning, had conceived the idea of a combined science fact/fiction magazine one night in general conversation with friends. Unlike others, however, who drop such ideas in the cold light of day, Manning determined to follow it through.

The basic philosophy of the magazine is to cover science fact, astronomy and space exploration and uses of technology in simple terms so that people can understand not only what is going on, but its importance and implications to them. Secondly, to publish science fiction stories from not only known authors . . . but also from people who are just starting, as these offer alternative views of the future. Finally, there is a middle ground of future speculation/mysteries which embraces such subjects as UFOs, astrology, alternative energy, etc.[1]

Somehow, Manning managed to establish a satisfactory equilibrium of these strange bedfellows, although the letter column repeatedly carried pleas from those who wanted more of one particular category and less of another. The science and quasi-science articles placed special emphasis on astronomy and technology, interlaced with items on astrology and space mysteries. As issues passed Manning spread his coverage to general science and media news, film coverage becoming a regular feature.

Limiting our attentions, however, to *AA*'s position in the science fiction field, the magazine could only be considered minor, but not through editorial failings. It carried, on average, only two stories an issue, both very short, so that its sixteen issues printed only as much SF wordage as one might find in two issues of a standard SF magazine. On this basis the presence of four or five good stories was a reasonable batting average.

At the outset the fiction was amateurish, and its quality remained variable, but *AA* has attracted contributions from some of Britain's better new writers. Standards rose with the fourth issue in June 1979, which introduced *AA*'s readers to Ian Watson and David Langford. Watson's enigmatic "The False Braille Catalogue" was an especially effective story that attracted much comment and interest. Brian Stableford, Garry Kilworth, Robert Holdstock and John Brunner all appeared in its pages. The Brunner story, "He Who Fights," was of above-average length for *AA* and unfortunately had to be serialized in two parts, which lessened its impact considerably.

AA did not confine itself to British writers. As early as the third issue Manning reprinted Larry Niven's tongue-in-cheek look at Superman's love life, "Man of Steel, Woman of Kleenex." The sixth issue carried an article by Isaac Asimov entitled "Comets and Asteroids," while the seventh issue included an interview with Norman Spinrad, who was also present in the eighth issue with the story "The Perils of Pauline."

Certain issues placed special emphasis on some aspect of science or fiction. The ninth issue, for instance, had a resume and forecast, "The Soviet Achievement in Space," by Boris Belitzsky, plus an interview with the Strugatsky Brothers by Vladimir Gakov. The twelfth issue had George Hay looking back over the career of L. Ron Hubbard in "The Man Who Did" and also included a short story by Hubbard, "One Was Stubborn." Paul Collins gave the thirteenth issue an Australian flavor with "The View Down Under" plus his own short story "A Walk on the Wild Side."

At the start *AA* carried only black and white covers but progressed to color with the fourth issue. Distribution, always a problem with any specialist magazine, improved after the third issue, giving Manning the incentive to continue to experiment and help the magazine evolve. A plan to issue the magazine on a six-weekly schedule never eventuated, and though undated, the magazine continued to appear on an approximate bi-monthly program. Although the printing and presentation of the issues left much to be desired at times, each issue contained something of interest, even merit, in either the fact or fiction field.

After billing itself as ''Britain's Premier Sci-Fact Sci-Fi Magazine,'' and thereby threatening to alienate the core of SF fans, the magazine began to sport the innocuous subtitle ''Future Fact and Fiction.''

Manning is to be admired for his single-handed efforts in issuing such a formidable task as a dual-purpose SF/fact magazine, and within its financial limits *AA* proved itself an adventurous magazine always willing to challenge accepted scientific beliefs, and with no strict taboos on science fiction. It thus has some significance in the SF field. At length, however, *AA*'s circulation of 18,000 was too small to support the venture in Britain. Endeavors to secure European distribution seemed hopeful at one point but proved fruitless, and with that course closed Manning decided to suspend the magazine. It is unlikely to be revived.

Note

1. James Manning, private communication, March 1979.

Information Sources

INDEX SOURCES: SFM.
REPRINT SOURCES: None known.
LOCATION SOURCES: None known.

Publication History

TITLE: *Ad Astra*.
VOLUME DATA: Volume 1, Number 1, October-November 1978–Number 16 (undated: September/October 1981). Bi-monthly. Only first two issues dated, 6 issues per volume for first two volumes. Volume 3, first issue designated Number 13, followed by Number 2, followed by Number 15. Volume numbering discontinued from Number 16.
PUBLISHER: Rowlot Ltd., London.
EDITOR: James Manning.
FORMAT: Slick, 28 pp. first issue, thereafter 32 pp.
PRICE: 45p., Number 1–Number 7; thereafter 55p.

Mike Ashley

ADVENTURES IN HORROR

From a publisher that was more interested in sex books and magazines, *Adventures in Horror*, which began publication in 1970 and subsequently was retitled *Horror Stories*, was an attempt to cash in on the new liberated fiction. The stories, illustrated by photographs and film stills, placed a greater emphasis on sexual rather than supernatural adventures and were, on the whole, insignificant and uninspiring. Rather than feature ''fiction,'' the contents were disguised in the manner of the confession magazines with ''True Tales of the Unknown'' bearing such titles as ''The Blood-Drenched Corpse of the Priestess of Satan'' and "It Takes Two for Terror," and usually involving witchcraft, satanism or some other aspect of the occult. No authors of note appeared in the two issues sighted, and the names suggest pseudonymity. The magazine is decidedly a noncollector's item.

Information Sources

INDEX SOURCES: MT.
REPRINT SOURCES: None known.
LOCATION SOURCES: None known.

Publication History

TITLE: *Adventures in Horror*, October–December 1970. Retitled *Horror Stories*, February–October 1971.
VOLUME DATA: Volume 1, Number 1, October 1970–Volume 1, Number 7, October 1971. Bi-monthly. Total run: 7 issues.
PUBLISHER: Stanley Publications, Fifth Avenue, New York.
EDITOR: Theodore S. Hecht.
FORMAT: Slim Neo-pulp, 64pp.
PRICE: 60¢, first two issues; thereafter 50¢.

Mike Ashley/Frank Parnell

AIR WONDER STORIES

Founded by Hugo Gernsback as a companion to *Science Wonder Stories* (*Wonder Stories**), *Air Wonder Stories* was the first of the "specialist" SF magazines. Since the SF magazines were themselves still an infant breed and almost as specialist, the idea of publishing stories with such a narrow range may almost seem like painting oneself into a corner. In the event that is just what happened, but in 1929, when the first issue was published, it seemed like a good idea. Interest in air flight was at a peak in the United States. Although heavier-than-air flight had been possible for over a quarter of a century, it was only two years since Charles Lindbergh had made his epic nonstop transatlantic flight and focused the nation's attention on its real possibilities. The airship rather than the airplane still seemed the transport of the future, and this kind of controversy was what had inspired Gernsback. "*Air Wonder Stories* has been created to explore the path of aviation and see whither it is bound," Gernsback declared in one of his promotional advertisements. "Progress in any line of endeavour is impossible unless we can project ourselves into the future."

Moreover, a number of air-war pulp magazines like *War Birds* and *Aces High* were proving to be immensely popular, and many more would follow in their wake, including some SF titles, among them *Dusty Ayres and His Battle Birds** and *G-8 and His Battle Aces.** So, although from today's vantage point *AWS* seemed doomed to failure from the start, at the time such a pulp seemed inevitable.

In his first editorial, Gernsback announced that *AWS* would present "solely

flying stories of the future, strictly along scientific-mechanical-technical lines.''
Furthermore, to prevent ''gross scientific-aviation misinformation'' from reaching his readers, Gernsback created a panel of experts to authenticate the stories—
three professors and one Air Corps Reserve major.

Gernsback also said that *AWS* would not contain stories about air bandits, yet
he chose as his lead serial for the first issue ''The Ark of the Covenant'' by
Victor MacClure. Originally published in hardcover by Harper's in New York
in 1924, this novel is entirely about air bandits, although it is revealed that they
are the Robin Hoods of the future, plundering banks for financial aid in the hope
of preventing another world war. Gernsback reprinted another novel in *AWS*,
''The Flying Legion'' by George Allan England (originally serialized in *All-
Story Weekly* [*Argosy**] during 1919), which showed the opposite bias to
MacClure's work. In England's novel a band of ex-officers, bored with peace-
time, help themselves to a new airliner and set off in search of adventure.

Gernsback also sought out some specialist articles on aviation. From his own
pen came ''The Airplane of the Future'' (September 1929), while from the
German rocket pioneer Max Valier came ''Berlin to New York in One Hour''
(February 1930). The prolific German writer Hans Dominik was present with
''Airports for World Traffic'' (January 1930). It is surprising that Gernsback
failed to publish one of the more important works of air-SF from Germany in
the shape of Kurt Siodmak's *FP1 Does Not Reply*, which appeared in Germany
in 1930 but which would have been available in manuscript earlier. Siodmak
had already been published in Gernsback's *Amazing Stories*,* and here was an
opportunity missed. *AWS* did not last long enough to reprint the novel, but in
fact Gernsback never picked it up for any of his magazines.

Instead, most of the stories were provided by the growing stable of new writers
that mushroomed with the appearance of *Amazing*. Edmond Hamilton provided
the first new serial, ''Cities in the Air'' (November–December 1929), which
may prove to be the single best story published in *AWS*. With the discovery of
anti-gravity, cities now hover in the atmosphere like Swift's Laputa and at length
become involved in a global war.

Raymond Z. Gallun sold his first story, ''The Crystal Ray,'' to *AWS* (November 1929), and here too appeared such SF regulars as David H. Keller, Ed
Earl Repp, Harl Vincent and Jack Williamson, whose ''The Second Shell''
(November 1929) suggested invisible electronic life existing in the upper atmosphere. A surprising number of writers made the major part of their SF sales
to *AWS* and scarcely appeared elsewhere. Lowell Howard Morrow, for instance,
sold four stories to *AWS* starting with ''Islands in the Air'' in the first issue, yet
all are forgotten. If he is remembered at all it is for his poignant ''Omega, the
Man,'' probably written at about the same time, which finally surfaced in *Amazing Stories* in 1933. Edward E. Chappelow was another flash in the pan, with
three stories in *AWS* including a short series about the Air Master.

One service *AWS* did perform was to inspire P. Schuyler Miller's first sale.
The February 1930 issue presented another of Gernsback's regular cover com-

petitions, asking readers to submit stories based on Paul's cover painting. Miller won, but his story, "The Red Plague," saw print in *Wonder Stories*. Another competition had asked readers to suggest a slogan that best typified the intent of *AWS* and could be used as a banner on the magazine. The winning entry was "Future Flying Fiction" and was sent in by John Beynon Harris (who twenty years later turned himself into John Wyndham), but the winner's name and the accompanying explanatory letter were printed in the September 1930 *Wonder Stories*, not in *AWS*.

After less than a year Gernsback realized that *AWS* was too limiting in scope. It did not attract as many readers as its companion; many were probably dissuaded from buying *AWS* because it promised less than the wondrous interplanetary and future adventures in *Science Wonder Stories*. In the eleven issues published, the writers had fully explored the subject of future aviation, and already repetition was becoming a problem. And so, following the May 1930 issue, *Air Wonder Stories* was combined with *Science Wonder Stories* to form the much more exciting *Wonder Stories*.

Information Sources

BIBLIOGRAPHY:
Arnold, Francis. "The High-Flier That Flopped," *Cosmos Science-Fantasy Review*, No. 3 (June/July 1969): 8–9.
Nicholls. *Encyclopedia*.
Tuck.
INDEX SOURCES: ISFM; IWG; Okada, Masaya, *Illustrated Index to Air Wonder Stories* (Vol. 1, No. 1–Vol. 1, No. 11, July 1929–May 1930), Nagoya, Japan: Masaya Okada, 1973; SFM; Tuck.
REPRINT SOURCES: None known.
LOCATION SOURCES: M.I.T. Science Fiction Library.

Publication History

TITLE: *Air Wonder Stories*.
VOLUME DATA: Volume 1, Number 1, July 1929–Volume 1, Number 11, May 1930. Monthly. Total Run: 11 issues.
PUBLISHER: Stellar Publishing Corp., New York.
EDITOR: David Lasser [Managing Editor].
FORMAT: Large Pulp, 96 pp.
PRICE: 25¢.

Mike Ashley/Robert J. Ewald

ALIEN WORLDS

Early in 1966 two Manchester fans, Harry Nadler and Charles Partington, terminated their fanzine *Alien*, which they had edited for sixteen issues since 1963, and invested their time, effort and money to produce a professional magazine. The resultant *Alien Worlds* was a commendable achievement, with multitone colored covers and interior artwork. A small, slim booklet with sixty-four varityped pages, it appeared in July 1966. The featured story was "Contact Man" by Harry Harrison, with supporting tales by Kenneth Bulmer and Ramsey Campbell. There were also film articles, including one on the impending *2001: A Space Odyssey*. As a first attempt it was good, but the cost was prohibitive. The prospects for a second issue decreased as the months passed, and in the end it was abandoned. The time was not opportune for a semi-professional magazine and, with limited bookstall distribution, *AW* had to appeal to the core of fandom who knew of the publication through specialist dealers. For this reason *AW* should have been priced as a specialty, perhaps ten shillings instead of half a crown, and should have contained more variety than the average fiction it featured. But it was a lesson learned, and one that would have its reward when David Sutton and Stephen Jones issued *Fantasy Tales** a decade later. Charles Partington became the publisher of *New Worlds** in 1977.

Information Sources

BIBLIOGRAPHY:
Nicholls. *Encyclopedia*.
Tuck.
INDEX SOURCES: Tuck.
REPRINT SOURCES: None known.
LOCATION SOURCES: M.I.T. Science Fiction Library.

Publication History

TITLE: *Alien Worlds*.
VOLUME DATA: Number 1, 1966 (July).
PUBLISHER: Privately published, Manchester, England.
EDITORS: Charles Partington and Harry Nadler.
FORMAT: Booklet, 64 pp.
PRICE: 2/6d.

Mike Ashley

THE ALL-STORY MAGAZINE/ALL-STORY WEEKLY

See THE ARGOSY.

AMAZING DETECTIVE TALES

See SCIENTIFIC DETECTIVE MONTHLY.

AMAZING SCIENCE FICTION [STORIES]

See AMAZING STORIES.

AMAZING SCIENCE STORIES

From March 1950 to June 1952 a publisher in Sydney, Australia, produced twenty-three issues of *Thrills, Incorporated*,* Australia's first real SF magazine. In 1951 the Manchester firm of Pemberton's reissued the second and third issues as a large-size pulp, *Amazing Science Stories*. Stories such as "Jet-Wheel Jockey" and "Rogue Robot" bore such unlikely by-lines as Wolf Herscholt and Belli Luigi. What must have puzzled English fans was to find appended to all this juvenilia two stories pirated from the April 1949 *Super Science Stories**: "Son of the Stars" by F. Orlin Tremaine in the first issue, and "The Earth Killers" by A.E. van Vogt in the second.

Both issues are unmemorable and for devoted collectors only.

Information Sources

BIBLIOGRAPHY:
Tuck.
INDEX SOURCES: IBSF; MIT; SFM; Tuck.
REPRINT SOURCES: None known.
LOCATION SOURCES: M.I.T. Science Fiction Library.

Publication History

TITLE: *Amazing Science Stories* (first issue entitled *Amazing Science Magazine* inside).
VOLUME DATA: Number 1 [March 1951]–Number 2 [April 1951]. Monthly. Total run:
    2 issues.
PUBLISHER: Pemberton's, Manchester, England.
EDITOR: Not named; possibly Stafford Pemberton.
FORMAT: Large Pulp, 64 pp.
PRICE: 1/-.

Mike Ashley

AMAZING STORIES

Amazing Stories [hereinafter designated *AS*] was the first English-language magazine devoted entirely to science fiction. Science fiction had formed a regular and, at times, major part of earlier magazines such as *Argosy*,* *All-Story*, *The Thrill Book** and Hugo Gernsback's *Science and Invention*.* There had even been foreign-language magazines with a heavy dose of SF and fantasy such as the Swedish *Hugin* and Germany's *Der Orchideengarten*. But it was *AS* that lit the beacon for science fiction as a distinct fictional genre and gave the public what it wanted. Its publisher, Hugo Gernsback, stated that the prime purpose of *AS* was to educate—to impart "knowledge, and even inspiration, without once making us aware that we are being taught."[1] Although *AS* ceased to be a trendsetter after 1929, it was always a significant magazine, and its pages frequently reflected the trends prevalent elsewhere in SF. For that reason this essay treats the magazine at greater length than most other periodicals in this work.

The first issue of *AS* was dated April 1926 and appeared on the newsstands on March 5, 1926[2]—a Friday, a good day for workers to buy a copy to read over the weekend. Gernsback relied on three people in particular to help prepare and edit the magazine: Dr. T. O'Conor Sloane, C.A. Brandt, and Wilbur C. Whitehead. The associate editor (identified as managing editor for the first issue only) was Dr. T. O'Conor Sloane, then seventy-four years old and more prone to look back on his past glories as a professor and inventor than forward to the glittering future. His duties, according to Sam Moskowitz, were "not to select stories, but to check on the accuracy of the science, handle the mechanics of expediting copy for text and illustrations and generally to co-ordinate the publication's functions."[3]

Gernsback himself acted as editor, with the final say on contents, but he had two first readers who sorted through the new manuscripts and recommended reprints. These were Brandt and Whitehead, both of whom were billed as literary editors. At the time of Whitehead's death in 1931, Sloane remarked that Whitehead had "influenced the conduct of the magazine by his advice. He had an extensive knowledge of scientific fiction which was his hobby."[4] Brandt, however, was the greater influence. German by birth, he later settled in the United States, where his knowledge and collection of SF was made known to Gernsback. It was Brandt who selected the reprints for *Amazing*, translating, where necessary, from the original German.

Finally, to illustrate the magazine, Gernsback employed Frank R. Paul, whom Gernsback had first used in 1914 in *The Electrical Experimenter*. Although Paul could not draw people effectively, his vivid imagination and past experience enabled him to capture precisely the technological visions that Gernsback desired. His bold use of yellows and reds made every one of his covers eye-catching and memorable.

AS immediately caught the public eye. It was not a standard pulp magazine but was larger, measuring 8 by 11 inches, and was printed on a heavier stock, made, so Gernsback claimed, especially for its requirements and dubbed "Amazing Stories Bulky Weave."[5] It made the magazine's hundred or so pages look twice as thick. With Paul's colorful cover, illustrating a scene from Jules Verne's "Off on a Comet," not even the high cover price of twenty-five cents daunted prospective purchasers. The original print run was probably 100,000 and sold out. Gernsback later reported that they were printing 150,000 copies and that sales were climbing month after month. These were respectable figures for a specialist magazine, and even today only *Analog Science Fiction** and *Isaac Asimov's Science Fiction Magazine** can claim to have exceeded the 100,000 figure. (This excludes *Omni,** which is primarily a popular science magazine and boasts a circulation of over 800,000.)

The first two issues of *AS* consisted entirely of reprinted material, mainly because it was less expensive to use reprints. Gernsback had made a block deal to reprint all of Jules Verne's work, Edgar Allan Poe was out of copyright, and Gernsback had probably acquired all serial rights to stories published in his own technical magazines. The serial rights to other stories, including those of H. G. Wells, were probably relatively cheap at that time. Moreover, the names Verne, Wells and Poe on the cover had considerable pulling power and, as their work exemplified Gernsback's own definition of scientifiction,[6] it was obvious that he would present them in the first issue.

The lineup for that inaugural issue was "Off on a Comet"[Part 1], Jules Verne; "The New Accelerator," H. G. Wells; "The Man from the Atom" [Part 1], G. Peyton Wertenbaker; "The Thing from—Outside," George Allan England; "The Man Who Saved the Earth," Austin Hall; and "The Facts in the Case of M. Valdemar," Edgar Allan Poe. It was a safe, well-balanced lineup, probably decided jointly by Gernsback and Brandt. The Verne novel, while not his most scientific, was one of his most imaginative in terms of pure fun and frolics in space. The Wells short was more in line with Gernsback's credo—a new invention coupled with scientific observation. Similarly, Poe's tale of a man's brain kept alive after death through hypnotism had elements of Gernsback's banner: "Extravagant Fiction Today—Cold Fact Tomorrow."

The contents were obviously selected to attract a maximum readership. Wells, Verne and Poe were respectable names to any reader. Both England and Hall were popular contributors to the Munsey pulps, *Argosy* and *All-Story*, and England's best novels had appeared in book form.[7] Only Wertenbaker was unknown, although regular readers of *Science and Invention* would have encountered the story in the special SF issue three years earlier.

The May issue was an even better bargain. Paul's stunning cover illustrated a scene from Wells' "The Crystal Egg,"[8] while the conclusion of Verne's serial heralded a new one, and one of Verne's best, "A Trip to the Center of the Earth." There was a sequel to Wertenbaker's earlier story, plus short tales by Poe and Charles C. Winn.

The response to Gernsback's new venture was overwhelming. He was deluged by letters from "scientifiction fans," as he called them, and when he asked readers' views as to whether *AS* should go semi-monthly or remain monthly, an astonishing 33,000 responded, with all except 498 asking that the frequency be doubled. *AS* was literally an overnight success, and the history of science fiction had entered a new phase.

The immediate results of this avalanche were twofold. First, Gernsback established a letter column, called "Discussions," which soon became a forum of opinion on all matters scientific and scientifictional. By publishing the correspondents' addresses, Gernsback encouraged fans to contact each other and thereby indirectly helped organize SF fandom, which ever since has remained a potent force within the genre. Second, Gernsback considered for some time the possibility of *AS* appearing twice a month and all but promised this in the January 1927 issue in response to a letter writer's request. He subsequently revised his plans and instead issued *Amazing Stories Annual*,* which in turn led to a regular *Amazing Stories Quarterly*.*

Another reason Gernsback relied heavily on reprints during the first year was that few good new stories were forthcoming. Two years later Gernsback would write that, "until very recently, there were not enough new scientifiction stories to go around, and . . . the few that were submitted, were not always good enough to publish."[9] C. A. Brandt shared his opinion.

This poses an interesting question. There were plenty of competent SF writers around—Murray Leinster, George Allan England, Ray Cummings, Abraham Merritt, Edgar Rice Burroughs, Philip M. Fisher, and even Edmond Hamilton, Otis Adelbert Kline and J. Schlossel. Cummings already sold regularly to Gernsback, but he had no original story in *Amazing* during Gernsback's tenure. Leinster was also reprinted regularly in *AS*, but offered no new stories. Hamilton made seven sales to *Weird Tales** before he eventually turned to *AS*. The first new story in *AS* was "The Coming of the Ice" by G. Peyton Wertenbaker in the June 1926 issue, though this may already have been on hand. Wertenbaker was then a precocious teenager who managed to charge his story with the emotional maturity of a man twice his age. Clearly, here was a writer of talent who would not remain within the restrictive confines of the pulps if he could afford it. Indeed, in a letter that Gernsback quoted in his editorial "Fiction versus Facts" in the July 1926 issue, Wertenbaker hinted that *AS* might not be the best vehicle for his future work: "The danger that may lie before *Amazing Stories* is that of becoming too scientific and not sufficiently literary." These were wise words. The sentiments were echoed two years later in a letter from Dr. Miles J. Breuer, one of Gernsback's most discerning contributors, who held that the stories lacked a modern literary quality. None of Gernsback's editors or advisors had any literary talent. All except Whitehead were scientists, and one had only to read Gernsback's fiction or Sloane's editorials to discover that both were blind to style. Moreover, English was not the first language of either Brandt or Gernsback.

AS remained, therefore, first and foremost a science magazine in fictional form and thereby attracted contributors who were predominantly scientists, not writers. The true scientific adventure writers were perfectly at home in *The Argosy* and other pulps, with no need to write for Gernsback. A secondary factor in the absence of major names was payment. The Munsey pulps paid well and often prior to publication; Gernsback paid poorly and frequently long after publication. This distinction would have a significant effect on *AS*'s formative years.

The minimum payment which a pulp magazine regularly gave at this time was one cent a word, often more for short stories and proportionately less for longer stories. It also varied according to the popularity of the author. Thus, the well-known Edgar Rice Burroughs' 93,000-word "The Chessmen of Mars" was purchased by *All-Story* in 1921 for $3,500, or 3.7¢ a word; Francis Stevens'

"Serapion" sold to *Argosy* for $600 in 1920, at the height of her fame, equal to 1.5¢ a word; while the neophyte Austin Hall received .7¢ a word for "Almost Immortal" in 1916. All these payments were made before publication.

Hugo Gernsback ignored the payment practice. In March 1926 he acquired second serial rights to Burroughs' "The Land That Time Forgot" for just $100, or a quarter of a cent a word, a tenth of what *Blue Book* had paid eight years earlier. In 1927, after much wrangling, Gernsback paid Burroughs $1,266 for his latest Martian novel, "Vad Varo of Barsoom." This was two cents a word, astonishingly high for Gernsback, but for the biggest name in the SF field, and for the surefire success of the *Annual*, it was a small price to pay. But as a result of Gernsback's poor treatment of Burroughs he would never again be given an opportunity to publish Burroughs in *AS*. This was not an isolated incident. His cheapness and long delays in paying also alienated H. P. Lovecraft, not just against Gernsback, but against all SF magazines in general. New writers received even worse treatment. E. E. Smith's now classic "The Skylark of Space" was purchased in 1927 and paid for in 1928 with $125. At 90,000 words that was less than one-seventh of a cent a word. The serial was the most popular *AS* ever published, and when Sloane bought the sequel "Skylark Three," he offered an "extravagant" three-quarters of a cent a word to Smith. By that time Gernsback had gone, however.

Not surprisingly, few people wanted to write for Gernsback. The only people who did write for him were scientists and new writers, few of whom had any literary qualities and certainly would not acquire them from Gernsback, Brandt and Sloane. Those writers who had any literary aspirations soon deserted Gernsback, as in the case of Wertenbaker. Others soon found better paying markets when the first upsurge in the SF field began in 1930. On a more positive note, one might point out that, at the time of the Depression, even Gernsback's poor late payments were better than no money at all. Moreover, as many of the writers held other jobs, the payments were not as important as one might think. *AS* was an outlet for their wonder-filled and bizarre imaginations where they were appreciated by other starry-eyed visionaries whom the outside world regarded as crackpots. *AS* therefore became a home not for writers but for dreamers, and it was in this way that the real "ghettoization" (as it has come to be known) of SF began.

Since *AS* was such a publishing success, it is evident that the readers were happy to forego literary appeal in favor of vision. With the Depression looming, the American public was glad to escape in dreams of alien worlds, lost lands or the future. Gernsback had gambled on the public's desire for a "sense of wonder" and had won.

The first new story which Brandt accepted for *AS* was "Beyond the Pole" by A. Hyatt Verrill (1871–1954). Because of its length, the story was serialized in the October and November 1926 issues. Most of Verrill's stories, including "Beyond the Pole," "Through the Crater's Rim" (December 1926) and "Into the Green Prism" (March–April 1929), were stories of lost civilizations in the tradition of Rider Haggard, Conan Doyle and, more recently, Abraham Merritt. Lost world stories proved extremely popular in *AS* and were featured extensively. Gernsback even reprinted Merritt's "The People of the Pit" (March 1927) and "The Moon Pool" (May–July 1927), though it is hard to see how Gernsback could defend the inclusion of Merritt's fantastic stories on the grounds of scientific instruction.

Verrill, however, was not averse to writing purely scientific stories, and in "The Astounding Discoveries of Doctor Mentiroso" (November 1927) he wrote one containing a deliberate mistake. Several more "find-the-flaw" stories appeared in *AS*, including "Ten Million Miles Sunward" (March 1928) by Geoffrey Hewelcke, and always brought a great response in the letter column.

Verrill was the first regular contributor of new stories to *AS* and fell into the category of eminent scientist writing fiction for his own amusement. Much the same could be said of the next initiate, Miles J. Breuer, a Nebraskan doctor for whom SF was a serious hobby. His first story, "The Man with the Strange Head" (January 1927), revolved around the idea of an automaton body created to house a man's withered frame. "The Riot at Sanderac" (December 1927) was one of the earliest tales about a machine that artificially controls emotions. Breuer also delved into other dimensions. "The Appendix and the Spectacles" (December 1928) concerns hyperdimensional surgery and inspired two sequels, "The Captured Cross-Section" (February 1929) and "The Book of Worlds" (July 1929). The original story was written as a professional rebuttal to Bob Olsen's "Four Dimensional Surgery" (February 1928). Olsen, another popular contributor, had more or less cornered the field of the fourth dimension with his first sale, "The Four Dimensional Roller Press" (June 1927), and wrote his own sequel to "Four Dimensional Surgery" in "Four Dimensional Robberies" (May 1928), where the amazing hyperforceps are used to rob a safe deposit vault.

Breuer should also be remembered for his help and encouragement of a young, fledgling writer, Jack Williamson, who debuted in the December 1928 *AS* with his Merrittesque "The Metal Man." Later, Williamson and Breuer collaborated on a novel and a short story. Breuer also collaborated with another writer, Clare Winger Harris, one of the few women contributors to the early SF pulps. Mrs. Harris had been lured to *AS* by the $500 Cover Competition announced in the December 1926 issue. Paul had painted an enticingly puzzling cover around which Gernsback asked readers to build a story. Harris came in third with "The Fate of the Poseidonia," which was published in the June 1927 *AS*.

While Harris had only five other stories published in *AS*, her name is closely associated with the early days of the magazine, probably because she apparently wrote no more SF after 1930. Her most popular contribution was almost certainly "The Miracle of the Lily" (April 1928), one of the earliest surprise-ending stories, where the alien "insects" invading another planet turn out to be humans.

Harris had earlier sold "A Runaway World" to *Weird Tales* (July 1926). Another *Weird Tales* regular who became a mainstay at *AS* was Edmond Hamilton. He first appeared in the January 1928 issue with "The Comet Doom," the kind of story that would soon earn him the nickname of "World-Saver" Hamilton. Over the next few years Hamilton subjected the Earth to invasions from space, other dimensions or inside the Earth, but "our hero" always saved the day at the end. It was a tune that Hamilton played with limited variations, yet it remained popular.

Hamilton was one of the pioneers of the superscience extravaganza, and he had already been plotting his stories on a cosmic scale in *Weird Tales*. During its early days *AS* had remained fettered to the solar system until E. E. Smith came along. Readers of the *Quarterly* would have had a cosmic hors d'oeuvre in the Spring 1928 issue with J. Schlossel's "The Second Swarm," but those who had missed that issue were about to be overwhelmed by the galaxy-shattering adventures of Richard Seaton and the villainous Blackie DuQuesne in "The Skylark of Space" (August–October 1928). It was not as if Smith was doing anything new. Recent research has revealed that Robert W. Cole had set the stage for cosmic space opera as early as 1900 in his novel *The Struggle for Empire* (London: E. Stock, 1900), though it was probably read at most by only a few thousand. Homer Eon Flint had staggered readers of *All-Story Weekly* in 1918 with his short novel "The Planeteer" (complete in the March 9 issue), wherein the Earth is shifted in its orbit around the sun to the outer limits of Jupiter's domain. But popular though that story was, it was read by a general readership, not specifically by SF fans. And even though Edmond Hamilton had been moving planets in *Weird Tales*, that magazine's circulation was only a fraction of *Amazing*'s.

For the first time, therefore, the true superscience epic, as epitomized by "The Skylark of Space," was delivered undiluted to the eager masses of *Amazing*'s readership, and the story rocketed to immortality. Despite the stilted prose, the overriding Victorian delivery of plot and the laughable dialogue, the novel contained an identifiable hero, heroine and villain against a stupendous and breathtaking backcloth that left the reader intoxicated by his own stimulated imagination. As Sam Moskowitz states, because of the impact of "Skylark" on the readers of *AS*, "science fiction would never again be the same."[10]

If "The Skylark of Space" was the most popular, and arguably the most important, story published in *AS* between 1926 and 1929, then the single most popular and certainly the most prolific contributor was David H. Keller. Unlike many of his contemporaries who lost track of individual human beings in the relentless cold front of scientific advance, Keller brought his professional knowledge as a practicing physician and psychiatrist to bear on studying the effects of technology on society. Unlike most of Gernsback's writers, he had a social conscience, and although his writing was crude and his characterization and plotting poor, his ideas were effective and therefore memorable. His first story in *AS* was "The Revolt of the Pedestrians" (February 1928), which told of a future where the elite automobilists had lost the use of their lower limbs because of their reliance on transport, while the pedestrians had been relegated to second-class citizenship. "A Biological Experiment" (June 1928) reveals a future where people are sterilized and babies are produced parthenogenetically, but natural maternal and paternal instincts eventually win the day. "The Psychophonic Nurse" (November 1928) explores the problem from another angle with robots employed to rear children in a future of emancipated women. Possibly Keller's best story along these lines, appearing in the Fall 1928 *Quarterly*, is "Stenographer's Hands," which looks at the results of breeding a deliberate class of beings solely for dictating purposes. While other writers were lighting the torch of scientific freedom, Keller was building a multivarious fireguard to caution people that the ends do not always justify the means.

By 1929 Gernsback had built up his own stable of regular writers. Apart from the more important writers cited above, there were Charles Cloukey, a youthful genius whose "Sub-Satellite" (March 1928) was the first story to consider the consequences of firing a bullet from a gun on the moon; Francis Flagg, whose "The Machine-Man of Ardathia" (November 1927) set the pattern for so many "far-future evolution" tales; Philip Francis Nowlan, who in "Armageddon—2419 A.D." (August 1928) created the immortal character of Anthony (Buck) Rogers; Alexander M. Phillips, who originated the idea (in the pulps) that the Earth had been visited by intelligent aliens in prehistoric times in "The Death of the Moon" (February 1929); and other popular writers such as Harl Vincent, Stanton Coblentz, Fletcher Pratt and Wallace West.

In addition to its regular contributors, *Amazing*'s early issues were full of solo appearances by unknown writers who were probably subscribers to *Science and Invention* and dabbled with an idea that appealed to them out of pure self-indulgence. Others, inspired by a first sale, made one or two others but have now been long forgotten. One such writer was W. Alexander, who introduced the idea of organ transplants in "New Stomachs for Old" (February 1927) and then stayed in the same rut for his five other stories, so that by the time we encounter his "One Leg Too Many" (October 1929) his plot can be anticipated. "The Singing Weapon" (May 1927) marked Ben Prout's only appearance, but introduced the idea of supersonic weapons as a means of defense. Thomas R. Jones' only contribution, "Reprisal" (October 1928), was an early example of a scientist using his knowledge to hold the world to ransom, a plot that would be worked to death throughout the 1930s. In this case he threatens to plunge the British Isles back into the Ice Age by the simple expedient of diverting the Gulf Stream. The pseudonymous Marius (Steve Benedict)[11] took the idea one stage further in "The Sixth Glacier" (January–February 1929), where he plunges the whole world back into the Ice Age.

In the thirty-seven issues of *Amazing* under his control, Gernsback opened up new horizons to his readers and gave substance to that sense of wonder. Unknowingly, however, he had set an unstoppable ball in motion, the entire history of which has yet to be completed. That *AS* was a success and that his readers clamored for more are undeniable; that Gernsback had also unleashed on the world an animal that even he did not understand is also a certainty. Just as Baron Frankenstein had let loose his monster on the world for failing to understand it for what it really was, so, in 1929, when Gernsback lost control of *AS*, science fiction was left to fend for itself in a world of commercial publishing that had no real idea of what it was all about.

The full story of how Gernsback and *AS* parted in 1929 has been discussed in some depth in more recent issues of *AS*.[12] Suffice it to say that through his own financial mismanagement (mostly in connection with his radio station, but symptomatic of his habit of not paying debts until he had to) Gernsback's Experimenter Publishing Company was declared insolvent in the spring of 1929. Gernsback promptly established a new company and within months had launched three new SF magazines: *Science Wonder Stories (Wonder Stories*)*, *Air Wonder Stories** and *Science Wonder Quarterly (Wonder Stories Quarterly*)*. After three years *AS* was no longer the only SF magazine and never would be again. But its first three years were significant not just for the stories it published and the new authors it discovered, but also for the future authors it inspired. Fritz Leiber would not enter the SF field for another ten years, but he had been a convert from the very first issue of *AS*. So had John W. Campbell, Jr., while A. E. vanVogt became hooked when he saw the November 1926 issue. Likewise, Robert A. Heinlein, Clifford D. Simak, Robert Bloch and Arthur C. Clarke all encountered the magazine during these first years, and it influenced them beyond all record.

Writers and readers were not the only avid followers of *AS*. Rival publishers and editors, always with an eye to success, were aware of the potential. Harry Bates, one of the editors at Clayton Publishing, charged with establishing a new magazine, considered the possibilities offered by *AS* and came up with *Astounding Stories of Super Science (Analog Science Fiction*)*.[13] *Amazing*, therefore, was the seed from which grew not only the first two generations of leading SF writers, but also the first independent rival magazine, which in turn became the premier SF publication. There are solid grounds, therefore, to say that the period 1926–1929 was probably the most significant in the whole of SF history and historically (not literarily) more important than *Astounding*'s Golden Age.

During the months immediately following Gernsback's departure and while the Experimenter Publishing Company's finances were being evaluated, a temporary business manager was installed along with a new editor, Arthur Lynch. Lynch had past experience with radio magazines, but probably had little knowledge of SF. Hence, while he was nominally editor of the magzine, T. O'Conor Sloane continued to serve as acting editor. When the company was officially wound up and *Amazing* was sold to Bergan MacKinnon, Sloane assumed the role of editor in title as well as in name.

Without Hugo Gernsback the nearly eighty-year-old Sloane lacked verve and sparkle. The magazine rapidly grew dull and uninspiring. Gone were the vision and wonder inspired by Gernsback. Gernsback was a disciple of the future; Sloane was a shadow of the past. Gernsback's editorials, seldom more than a page long, were vibrant and stimulating; Sloane's editorials grew increasingly longer and more tedious, and could hardly have been less inspiring. No sooner had he moved into the editorial chair than Sloane was proclaiming, "Interplanetary travel . . . appears an impossible achievement."[14] And he did not just say it once but repeatedly, his grounds being that "pressure will be so enormous that, in order to reach a planet, or even to reach the moon in any reasonable time, it would probably be sufficient to kill the person."[15] SF fans were used to the uninitiated scorn of space travel, but for the editor of the premier magazine to declare it was tantamount to sacrilege. Not content with avowing that man will never leave the Earth's surface alive, Sloane compounded his sin by stating that "it is somewhat doubtful if Mount Everest will ever be ascended."[16]

Sloane remained at the helm for another eight years, assisted in the basic duties by Miriam Bourne. C. A. Brandt remained associated with the magazine, although for a brief period he crossed sides to work with Gernsback at *Wonder Stories*.

Not surprisingly, *AS* lost most of its readers to the competition, especially Gernsback's new magazine, *Wonder Stories*, established in the summer of 1929, and *Astounding*, which entered the fray at Christmas 1929. Over the years the readership dwindled, driven away by the dullness of Sloane's editorials and attracted by the exciting revolution that was revitalizing SF in the pages of *Wonder Stories* and *Astounding*. Although *AS* retained most of its readership until 1932, by 1934 circulation had sunk to as low as 23,000.[17] Thus, while the survey of *Amazing*'s first three years is an analysis of a success story, coverage of the next eight years becomes a postmortem. Yet, despite Sloane, *AS* did publish several worthy stories, as we shall shortly discuss, and even experimented dramatically with presentation.

After Frank R. Paul followed Gernsback to *Wonder Stories*, Sloane and MacKinnon chose Hans Wessolowski as the new regular artist; he painted the covers only briefly before becoming the mainstay at *Astounding*. His place was taken by the Peruvian Leo Morey, who illustrated most of the covers and interiors until 1938. Morey was a capable artist, more adept at drawing people than Paul had been, but with less imagination when it came to machines and dramatic scenes. His covers lack the immediate impact of Paul's, and his use of softer colors added to the generally solemn tone of the Sloane *AS*. For a few months in 1933 the publisher experimented with some symbolic covers painted by an artist called Sigmund. Visually, these were less attractive than either Paul's or Morey's, although they may have been aesthetically more satisfying. Certainly they did not reflect the pulp image, and they were not generally appreciated by the majority of readers. After six issues, Morey returned.

Perhaps MacKinnon should have persisted with the Sigmund covers for a while longer, because by 1933 a major division had developed between scientific respectability and juvenile sensationalism. Paul's dramatic covers had undoubtedly attracted the right readers, but they had also given the magazine an indelible image with the general public. When an attempt was made to disguise the magazine in order to attract the more discriminating reader, sales did not pick up. On one hand, one could therefore conclude that the pulp image was not the proper one for science fiction and that it should never have been compartmentalized. On the other hand, sales proved that by popularity alone the pulps were the right place. It is a dichotomy that SF has never successfully resolved and that still plagues it today.

For his fiction, Sloane initially relied on *Amazing*'s newfound regulars, in particular Edmond Hamilton and David H. Keller, both of whom were so prolific that they appeared frequently in both Gernsback's new magazines and *AS*. Some of Hamilton's best early work appeared at this time, as he revealed that he could produce more than the cosmic disaster story. In "The Man Who Saw the Future" (October 1930) he produced a simple tale about a fifteenth-century apothecary who is condemned to death as a sorcerer after trying to explain the wonders he has seen after a temporary transfer to the twentieth century. Hamilton also explored the variant possibilities in the themes of evolution and mortality. Although his masterwork on the theme, "The Man Who Evolved," appeared in *Wonder Stories* (April 1931), he worked a neat twist into "Devolution" (December 1936), wherein the survivor of a group of explorers in northern Canada discovers that man has not evolved but devolved from a supraintelligent protoplasmic alien team that visited the Earth millennia ago. The poignant "Intelligence Undying" (April 1936) follows the alpha and omega of the lives of a scientist who is able to transfer his memory and his accumulated knowledge to a newborn baby, and so on down through each successive generation. All of these stories are little more than synopses of what could have been novel-length works but, typical of the stories of the period, they exist purely as vehicles for an idea, with no character or plot development.

Keller had twenty stories in *AS* during this period, including three serials, of which the most memorable was "Life Everlasting" (July–August 1934), about a serum that cures all and perpetuates life but that mankind eventually rejects in favor of the pleasures of growing old. Though not as good a writer as Hamilton, Keller, through his medical background, was able to focus on human and social aspects. "Unto Us a Child Is Born" (July 1933) portrays an episode in a regimentalized, controlled future and lets it speak for itself. "No More Tomorrows"(December 1932) is an especially clever story about a scientist who perfects a serum that eradicates man's ability to comprehend the existence of the future. "The Ambidexter" (April 1931) deals with brain and limb transplants and details the relationship between the world's two greatest surgeons. One of these surgeons, Wing Loo, reappears in "The Cerebral Library" (May 1931), one of a number of stories by Keller to feature the detective Taine of San Francisco.

Other already established writers continued to contribute to *AS*, including Verrill, Olsen and Williamson. But a more important reflection of Sloane's standing as an editor is the number of new writers he apparently encouraged or even discovered. The question of encouragement can soon be discounted. Both Jack Williamson[18] and Frederik Pohl[19] denigrated his talents in that area. And yet, technically, Sloane "discovered" Pohl, buying his poem "Elegy to a Dead

Planet: Luna'' and using it as a filler in the October 1937 issue. With regard to discoveries of new talent, Sloane can be credited with discovering Clifford D. Simak. He accepted Simak's first story, "The Cubes of Ganymede," in early 1931, but for reasons known only to him, he never published it and eventually returned it to Simak in 1935.[20] By then Simak had debuted in *Wonder Stories*.

Sloane almost blundered a second time with John W. Campbell, Jr. He had accepted Campbell's story "Invaders from the Infinite" early in 1929 but subsequently lost it,[21] possibly following Gernsback's departure. Sloane, however, had also acquired Campbell's second story, "When the Atoms Failed," which he ran in the January 1930 issue, heralding, perhaps, the most important of Sloane's discoveries. Campbell became a regular contributor thereafter, and *AS* published the first of his popular series about the team of superscientists Wade, Arcott and Morey, "Piracy Preferred" (June 1930). The series continued in the *Quarterly*, where Campbell's best work appeared and where he established himself as a powerful rival to E. E. Smith as a writer of superscience extravaganzas. The year 1930 represents a plateau for the superscience epic in *AS*. Edmond Hamilton's serial, "The Universe Wreckers" (May–July 1930), was followed to rapturous approval by Doc Smith's "Skylark Three" (August–October 1930), which was running while Campbell's "The Black Star Passes" appeared complete in the Fall 1930 *Quarterly*.

Although Campbell later established a new identity for himself as Don A. Stuart with his controlled Wellsian "mood" stories in *Astounding*, the first indication of this change came in *AS* with "The Last Evolution" (August 1932).

P. Schuyler Miller technically was another Sloane discovery, although once again Sloane delayed publication with the result that "Through the Vibrations" came out in May 1931 after Miller had debuted in *Wonder Stories*. "Cleon of Yzdral" (July 1931), "The Arrhenius Horror" (September 1931), "The Pool of Life" (October 1934) and "The People of the Arrow" (July 1935) were Miller's other worthy contributions to *AS*.

The October 1932 issue saw the first appearance of the by-line Eando Binder with "The First Martian." At this time the by-line accurately named the two writers Earl and Otto Binder, who collaborated on their stories until Earl retired in the mid-1930s. John Russell Fearn debuted with a short novel, "The Intelligence Gigantic" (June–July 1933). Here too, in August 1936, was the first solo appearance of Henry Hasse,[22] with a story since considered a classic, "He Who Shrank." Overlooked at the time, but of greater significance now, is the October 1932 issue, which included "Wrath of the Purple" by Howard M. Fast, who would go on to international fame as the author of *Spartacus*. "As a kid a long, long time ago, I was utterly enthralled by the original *Amazing Stories*," Fast later wrote. "It became a very unique part of my life. I never missed an issue, and to me it was absolutely the most wonderful manifestation of the late 1920s and the 1930s."[23]

Sloane's record of discovery, while impressive, was more a result of good fortune than of design. In the same way Sloane acquired a few memorable stories by writers who appeared more frequently elsewhere. S. P. Meek, for instance, appeared most regularly in *Astounding*, yet all the stories for which he is remembered appeared in *AS*: the novel "Drums of Tapajos" (November 1930–January 1931), the novelette "Submicroscopic" (August 1931) and its sequel "Awlo of Ulm" (September 1931). These left an indelible impression on the eleven-year-old Isaac Asimov, and the cover for "Awlo of Ulm" attracted the eye of twenty-year-old C. L. Moore, who "from that moment on . . . was a convert."[24]

John Beynon Harris, still twenty years away from his John Wyndham persona, was a regular contributor to *Wonder Stories* and appeared only once in *AS*, and yet that story, "The Lost Machine" (April 1932), is probably the best of his early work and is significant in its portrayal of an alien robot. Charles R. Tanner, while a Gernsback discovery, is remembered today for two stories, "Tumithak of the Corridors" (January 1932) and "Tumithak in Shawm" (June 1933), both from *AS*.

If any stories most typify the Sloane *AS*, however, they are the Professor Jameson series by Neil R. Jones. "The Jameson Satellite" (July 1931) had introduced the Professor who, after his death, was buried in space in Earth orbit. Millennia later, passing aliens—the Zoromes—discover the tomb. The Zoromes are brains encased in robot bodies, and they revive the Professor's own brain and house it in a spare Zorome body. Thereafter the Professor accompanies the Zoromes on their travels in story after story. Twelve in all appeared in *AS* alone up to "The Music Monsters" (April 1938) and were among the most popular stories Sloane ever published.

Sloane's best years at *AS* were 1930 and 1931, when *AS* was still regarded as the aristocrat among SF magazines. Within a couple of years all that had changed. Since 1926 *AS* had retained its large format; in October 1933 it converted to the standard pulp size. *Wonder* had temporarily toyed with this format in 1931, and it now changed for good from the November 1933 issue. Coincidentally, in October 1933 *Astounding* was revived by Street and Smith, also in the pulp format. *Amazing*'s readers responded to the change with howls of anguish; the large format had kept an aura of dignity that had set *AS* apart from the common adventure pulps. Now all were equal in appearance. *Astounding* had the edge on cover price, costing twenty cents rather than the twenty-five cents charged for *AS* and *Wonder*. This was important during the Depression years, when seventy cents for three magazines each month was a large sum. Consequently, contents and covers played a big part over the next year. Both *Astounding* and *Wonder* experimented with challenging new stories, shaking off old themes. Because *Astounding* paid reliably on acceptance, it attracted the writers' first submissions. *Wonder* and *Amazing* usually paid on publication, or long after, and writers became loathe to rely on them. *Wonder* later reduced its cover price to fifteen cents, leaving *Amazing* out in the cold. Furthermore, *Wonder* could boast the bold reds and yellows of Frank R. Paul's covers, while some of *Astounding*'s best covers were by Howard V. Brown. Leo Morey's covers were pallid in comparison.

By 1935, therefore, *Astounding* and *Wonder* represented all that was exciting in the SF field, while *Amazing* gathered dust. Sloane even went through a period when he reprinted such works as Jules Verne's "Measuring a Meridian" (May–August 1934), of only minimal SF import; Edward Everett Hale's "The Good Natured Pendulum" (May 1933), of no SF relevance at all; Edgar Allan Poe's "The Gold Bug" (April 1934), a good tale of cryptograms and treasure hunting, but not SF; and Fitz-James O'Brien's dated and cumbersome "The Diamond Lens" (October 1933). Clearly, Sloane had lost all contact with SF and merely assembled issues as he saw fit from whatever happened to appeal to his whim for that month. Few writers of any lasting merit, except those who stood little chance of selling elsewhere, continued to contribute to the magazine. Names like Isaac R. Nathanson, Joe W. Skidmore, Henry J. Kostkos, Abner J. Gelula (whose "Automaton" in the November 1931 issue was the first SF pulp story to be filmed) and William K. Sonneman were all mummies in *Amazing*'s tomb. The last issue of any import under Sloane was that for April 1934, with the final installment of Doc Smith's "Triplanetary." By then *Astounding* was in full swing, *Wonder* was about to launch Stanley G. Weinbaum on an unsuspecting world, and *AS* held nothing in reserve.

It was inadvertently revealed in 1935 that the magazine's circulation had plummeted to the low 20,000s, and from the October 1935 issue the magazine went bi-monthly. Circulation continued to fall, reaching rock bottom at 15,000. The publishers called it a day, and the magazine was sold to the Chicago firm of Ziff-Davis. At the recommendation of Ralph Milne Farley, the young and enthusiastic fan Raymond A. Palmer was installed as editor. Sloane had edited his last issue at the age of eighty-six; Palmer edited his first at twenty-seven. That difference became evident in editorial strategy from the start.

Palmer's first issue was dated April 1938. Ziff-Davis had officially taken over with the previous issue, which had been prepared by Sloane and published by Teck on behalf of Ziff-Davis. Sloane may not have known about his impending replacement. (His comments in the letter column refer to plans for future issues.) To the very end, he denied the possibility of space travel.[25] By contrast, fans were going to discover over the next few years that there was little that new editor Raymond A. Palmer did not believe in.

Palmer turned *AS* upside down. Harry Warner reports that he rejected all but one of over a hundred manuscripts accepted by Sloane.[26] He hastily circulated a bulletin to many of the leading SF writers telling of the changing circumstances at *AS* and outlining the type of stories now being sought. It also announced that the word rate for stories was to be doubled. At the same time the cover price dropped to twenty cents.

Palmer had only two weeks in which to assemble his first issue and could not wait for a full response from the circular. The contents came from two sources: local contacts and the agent Julius Schwartz, a close fan-colleague of Palmer.

The area around Chicago and Milwaukee was a spawning-ground for writers, and Robert Moore Williams, Ross Rocklynne, Charles R. Tanner and Ralph Milne Farley were all able to contribute new stories. From Schwartz, Palmer obtained two stories by English writer John Russell Fearn, of which "A Summons from Mars" proved to be the most popular in the first issue. He instigated a chatty editorial, "The Observatory," full of news, comment and behind-the-scenes gossip, which was to become Palmer's trademark. Sloane's stuffiness was replaced by Palmer's exuberance. The tedious "Science Questionnaire," which asked questions about scientific principles mentioned in the stories, was replaced by a more informative "Science Quiz" and "Questions and Answers," plus an illustrated "Amazing Facts of Science." The new AS was profusely illustrated, but no longer by Morey. From Ziff-Davis' own art department came Jay Jackson and Harold McCauley to do the basic interior illustrations. A new addition was an illustrated back cover. McCauley drew "This Amazing Universe" showing the family of planets plus the nearest star and plotting how long it would take the world's fastest airplane to reach them. The back cover was further described in an inside feature.

For the front cover Palmer and his art editor Herman Bollin utilized the resources of *Amazing*'s elder companion magazine, *Popular Photography*, to produce a photographic cover. Although it was a science fiction first, it was not an overwhelming success, as it produced stilted, lifeless results. Palmer, however, soon acquired the services of Robert Fuqua (the "brush name" of Joe Tillotson) who, along with McCauley and Julian S. Krupa, soon became one of the predominant cover artists. Unlike the previous situations, however, no one artist dominated the cover. The work of Palmer and Bollin should be justly acknowledged in making *Amazing* and its later companion, *Fantastic Adventures*,* the most attractive and eye-catching magazines on the stalls during the 1940s.

Reaction to the new AS was generally favorable, though many fans had reservations. There was relief that the stale AS of Sloane had gone, but there was some fear that Palmer would sell the fans short in his desire to pander to younger readers. To all intents AS rapidly became a teenage adventure magazine capably illustrated by a bevy of artists of which the best were J. Allen St. John, Harold McCauley and the much overlooked Rod Ruth. Palmer took one further step with his new magazine. One criticism of early SF had been that the action was slowed down by the hero lecturing at length on scientific theory at relevant moments. Palmer removed these passages from the text and inserted them as explanatory footnotes, to be read if desired.

As far as most readers were concerned, Palmer was right in his judgments. Circulation rose impressively and was soon back at the 100,000 level, and still rising. By October 1938, the monthly schedule had been restored.

As soon as AS reverted to a monthly schedule Palmer brought back serials, although they never remained a regular feature, the bumper complete lead novel being the new selling point. The first serial, however, was "Revolution of 1950"

(October–November 1938), a short novel left unfinished by Stanley G. Weinbaum and completed by Ralph Milne Farley. Palmer also convinced Ziff-Davis to publish a hardcover edition of Weinbaum's early superman novel, *The New Adam* (Chicago: Ziff-Davis, 1939), and a slightly abridged version was later serialized in *AS* (February–March 1943).

Palmer soon began to establish a stable of local, regular writers. Some had only recently started to contribute to the genre, and others were old hands, though the largest category was new writers whom Palmer introduced. The first category included writers like Robert Moore Williams and Robert Bloch. Bloch had hitherto contributed predominantly to *Weird Tales*, but "Secret of the Observatory" (August 1938) was his first venture into SF. Thereafter, Bloch appeared frequently, although he was more at home in *Fantastic Adventures*. His best contribution to *AS* at this time was "The Strange Flight of Richard Clayton" (March 1939), an early example of the psychological aspects of space travel. Robert Moore Williams had just started to sell stories to *Astounding* when Palmer contacted him for material. Palmer is reputed to have rejected Williams' now classic story "Robot's Return" (*Astounding*, September 1938) in favor of rip-roaring adventure yarns, and by 1939 Williams was writing in the groove. A few of the longer works, such as "Survivors from 9000 BC" (July 1941), are still readable, but on the whole Williams' contributions were unmemorable. Twelve years later, Palmer's successor bought Williams' spiritual successor to "Robot's Return," "The Metal Martyr" (July 1950), the best story Williams ever had in *AS*.

The typical story in Palmer's *AS* appealed to the adventurous spirit of adolescents rather than to the cerebral wonder of more mature minds. For this reason few stories of any lasting quality appeared during his editorship. Fortunately, there are some exceptions.

One such writer, and another relative newcomer, was Nelson S. Bond. He provided several of *Amazing*'s series, of which the best, set fifteen centuries in the future when society has returned to primitivism, concerns Meg the Priestess, who leads her clan back on the road to civilization. The first in the series, "The Priestess Who Rebelled" (October 1939), appeared in *AS*, the second, "The Judging of the Priestess," in *Fantastic Adventures* (April 1940); but it is some measure of its merit that Palmer lost the third and final story, "Magic City," to *Astounding* (February 1941). On the lighter side, Bond wrote the Horsesense Hank stories for *AS*, starting with "The Scientific Pioneer" (March 1940), while his ubiquitous spaceman Lancelot Biggs, who started out in *Fantastic Adventures* in 1939 and moved to *Weird Tales* in 1941, ended up in *AS* in 1942. Bond was a skillful writer whose talent showed through the often mischievous plots, and even his adventure stories were a cut above the average for *AS*. His two serials, "Sons of the Deluge" (January–February 1940) and "Gods of the Jungle" (June–July 1942), stand up well today.

Among the more established writers of 1938, Palmer attracted Eando Binder, John Russell Fearn and Ed Earl Repp. An accomplished writer with an eye for plot development, Binder produced one of the best stories of 1939 in "I, Robot" (January 1939), where the robot, Adam Link, is given the full Frankenstein's monster treatment and receives the full sympathy of the readership. It remains an important story in the development of the robot theme. Palmer also published much work by British writers, although most of the stories by Benson Herbert, Festus Pragnell and, of course, Fearn were formulaic. The unswerving William F. Temple, however, wrote one of his best stories for Palmer, and certainly the best that *Amazing* presented in 1939, "The Four-Sided Triangle" (November 1939), a tale of matter duplication and a fateful *ménage à quatre*! John Wyndham, writing as John Beynon at this time, appeared twice. "Judson's Annihilator"[27] (October 1939) was a routine future war story, but "Phoney Meteor" (March 1941) was a clever tale that set the trend for visiting aliens being destroyed by insecticide.

Palmer also pandered to the fan's natural nostalgia by bringing back to *Amazing* some of the great names and series from SF's early days. Ralph Milne Farley briefly revived Myles Cabot in "The Radio Man Returns" (June 1939) in the same issue that saw the return of Frank R. Paul to *AS*, illustrating not only the interior, but also the back cover with his idea of the "Future Space Suit." From July 1940, and for nearly two years thereafter, the back cover became the resident Paul spot as he illustrated scenes and cities on other worlds. The typically vivid colors and imaginative creativity made these some of Paul's best work. Another short-lived revival was Hawk Carse, one of the most popular space heroes of the Clayton *Astounding*. "The Return of Hawk Carse" by Anthony Gilmore (Harry Bates, July 1942) did not prove as popular the second time around, however.

Palmer's greatest service to SF fans in his early editorial days was to bring Edgar Rice Burroughs into the pages of *Amazing* and have J. Allen St. John illustrate the stories. Palmer had already presented two Burroughs stories of dubious origin. "The Scientists Revolt" in the July 1939 *Fantastic Adventures* had been an early nonfantasy rewritten by Palmer, while "John Carter and the Giant of Mars" (January 1941), which led off the Burroughs revival in *AS*, was predominantly the work of Burroughs' son, John Coleman. The remaining stories, however, were all genuine E.R.B. and had been written at a furious pace during 1940. He had written twelve novelettes, four for each of his three SF series concerning Carson Napier, John Carter and Alan Innes. The Napier stories ran in *Fantastic Adventures*, while "The City of Mummies" heralded the John Carter series in the March 1941 *Amazing*, running through to "Invisible Men of Mars" (October 1941), all with St. John covers. The Pellucidar series began with "The Return to Pellucidar" in February 1942, followed in the next two issues by the remaining stories. For some reason Burroughs delayed completion of the final story, "Savage Pellucidar," and though it was finally finished in 1944, Palmer never published it. It finally found its way into the November 1963 issue of *AS* and was even nominated for a Hugo Award. If Burroughs could still have that impact in 1963, it is easy to see what a wave of triumph

Palmer and *AS* were riding twenty years earlier. Burroughs did write one further John Carter story for Palmer, "Skeleton Men of Jupiter" (February 1943).

Palmer encouraged a host of new writers, some of whom hinted at more talent than *AS* required. Some, like Mark Reinsberg and W. Lawrence Hamling, were local fans. Some were aspiring writers whom chance brought Palmer's way. Such a one was Isaac Asimov, whose desire it was to sell to Campbell's *Astounding*. But in September 1938 he had submitted "Marooned off Vesta" to *Amazing*, and six weeks later it was accepted. It appeared in the March 1939 issue and marked Asimov's first professional appearance.

The majority of contributors to *AS* became a stable of staff writers who produced masses of hack material under numerous pseudonyms. One of the earliest was Don Wilcox, who was a competent adventure writer, but after regular writing of formula stories, he had degenerated into another hack writer. Another was William P. McGivern. Although he became one of America's foremost thriller writers, McGivern debuted in *AS* in the May 1940 issue with "John Brown's Body," written in collaboration with his friend David Wright O'Brien. O'Brien was one of the most prolific and promising writers for *AS*. A nephew of *Weird Tales* editor Farnsworth Wright, O'Brien first appeared in the February 1940 *AS* with "Truth Is a Plague" and over the next four years sold over a hundred stories to *AS* and *FA*, many under such pseudonyms as John York Cabot, Duncan Farnsworth, and Clee Garson. Unfortunately, O'Brien was shot down over Berlin in 1944 before his full talent was allowed to develop. Chester S. Geier was another of the team of writers. He entered the Palmer domain with "The Sphere of Sleep" in the December 1942 *AS*, and he appeared regularly thereafter.

Along with only slightly less prolific writers such as David Vern, Leroy Yerxa and Berkeley Livingston, these were the predominant contributors to *AS* during the first half of Palmer's editorship, 1938–1944. *AS* prospered, and Ziff-Davis was sufficiently encouraged to increase the number of pages at a time when, due to wartime restrictions, most other magazines had reduced theirs. For the fifteenth anniversary issue in May 1941, readers were treated to a 240-page issue, and a year later this rose to 272 pages. It settled at 240 again for several months before dropping to 208 in 1943. Despite the paper restrictions, Ziff-Davis preferred to keep *AS* bulky, so by November 1943 its schedule slipped to bi-monthly and then quarterly from May 1944. Palmer and Davis clearly preferred quantity to quality. *AS* still sported some of the gaudiest covers of all the pulps, which earned it the nickname of the "comic-book of science fiction." Malcolm Smith and Robert Gibson Jones were two new regular artists, as well as James B. Settles, who replaced Paul on the back covers.

As the war neared its end, however, certain events occurred that would split *AS* down the middle. It started in a small way in the January 1944 issue when Palmer published a letter from a Pennsylvanian welder, Richard S. Shaver, that purported to give the key to an ancient alphabet which he claimed was the mother tongue of all languages—Mantong, the lost language of Lemuria. Almost immediately readers responded, and, sufficiently encouraged, Shaver submitted a manuscript entitled "Warning to Future Man." Atrociously typed, and in the form of a letter, the manuscript nevertheless held strong appeal. Palmer immediately set about recasting the letter into a story format, retitling it "I Remember Lemuria!" In his first statement about the story, Palmer claimed to have conducted rigorous research; in an account given sixteen years later, however, he claimed he simply rewrote Shaver's letter-manuscript without any intensive investigation.

The Shaver Mystery as set out in "I Remember Lemuria!" (March 1945) and many stories that followed related Shaver's experiences in caverns deep under the Earth where live the races of the evil "deros" (detrimental robots) and the good "teros" (integrative robots). These people, Shaver contended, were descendants of the "abandondero," the humans left on Earth millennia ago when two immortal races of giants, the Titans and the Atlans, abandoned the planet when they realized that the sun's cosmic rays were causing them to age and die. Initially to escape the rays, they had built vast subterranean cities, but even here they were not safe. It was here, however, among the mighty machines that they only half understood, that the deros found themselves, and over the centuries they have used such machines as the "telaug" (telepathic augmentor) and the disintegrating rays to torment the surface inhabitants. The deros are responsible for all the wrecks, crashes and accidents on Earth, and were themselves the basis of such legends as demons, ghosts and gremlins.

By chance, the issue in which "I Remember Lemuria!" appeared had had an extra 50,000 copies run off, and all 185,000 copies sold out, with reorders. *Amazing*'s offices were deluged with letters from readers who averred their belief in the story and cited instances of their own experiences in support. Palmer knew when he was on to a good thing and rushed into print "Thought Records of Lemuria" (June 1945), which was followed by another flood of mail.

Enough has been written on the Shaver phenomenon elsewhere[28] to warrant no detailed analysis here, but it was an important moment in the history of magazine SF. It caused a major rift between Palmer and the core of active SF fans. They were already opposed to Palmer for filling *AS* with too many juvenile, formula-written stories, some lifted from the pages of W. Lawrence Hamling's semi-professional magazine *Stardust*, but now they were up in arms at Palmer's pandering to the "lunatic fringe." They were afraid that the SF world, already viewed as being a "bunch of nuts" by non-SF critics, would now all be grouped in with the crackpot Shaver followers and that it would prove harmful to the future of SF. Palmer was accused of sensationalism and of prostituting science fiction. Had not the atom bomb been detonated at this time, which momentarily made SF respectable, SF as a whole would likely have suffered considerably from the Shaver Mystery. As it was, the mass media took only passing note of it as yet another fad and then forgot it.

The Shaver stories increased *Amazing*'s circulation, enabled it to resume monthly publication, and led to Palmer's elevation to editor-in-chief. *AS* became totally saturated with Shaver fever, culminating in the special Shaver issue in June 1947. Overcome with the response to the stories, Palmer found himself becoming increasingly enmeshed with the world of strange happenings, which led him eventually to UFOs and flying saucers. By 1948 he was moonlighting from *AS*, having established his own publishing company, and he issued a new magazine devoted to true stories of the strange and unusual, *Fate*. Eventually he would leave *AS*, and though he retained an interest in SF through his magazine *Other Worlds Science Stories*,* he channeled his energies predominantly into *Fate*, and later *Mystic Magazine*.* No editor and publisher would abandon a lucrative editorial post to follow a dream unless he felt it had some substance, and it is clear in hindsight that Palmer was genuine in his presentation of the Shaver stories, despite his contradictions over the years.

Because of the inevitable emphasis on the Shaver stories, it is easy to overlook the good stories Palmer acquired for *AS* in the last half of his editorship: 1944–1949. Before the Shaver phenomenon really took hold, Palmer published a few stories by Ray Bradbury: "I, Rocket" (May 1944), "Final Victim" (February 1946, with Henry Hasse) and "Chrysalis" (July 1946). The December 1945 issue introduced readers to Rog Phillips, the best-known pseudonym of Roger Phillips Graham who, like Shaver, was a welder, working in the shipyards during the war. Phillips' talent as a writer was often stifled under Palmer, but he helped keep a sense of balance during the Shaver period by producing some of the more readable stories. He started out with a series of nuclear-future stories, the inevitable aftermath of the atom bomb. These included "Atom War" (May 1946), "The Mutants" (July 1946), "Battle of the Gods" (September 1946) and "So Shall Ye Reap!" (August 1947). On a more cosmic scale, Phillips showed he could produce agreeable space opera in "Starship from Sirius" (August 1948). Few of these stories have stood the test of time, but in the late 1940s they were a welcome relief from the excesses of Shaverism.

Perhaps the greatest surprise in any issue of *AS* during the 1940s was the work of Henry S. Whitehead. Whitehead had been a popular contributor to *Weird Tales* before his death in 1932. Somehow Palmer had acquired two of his few surviving unpublished stories: "Scar Tissue" and "Bothon," which he presented in the July and August 1946 issues. "Scar Tissue," a tale of inherited memory of the days of Atlantis, fitted in well with the Shaver vogue, but was nontheless welcome. Theodore Sturgeon also made a surprise appearance with "Blabbermouth" (February 1947), although even this had overtones of psychic phenomena as its theme.

The German writer and traveler Heinrich Hauser, temporarily resident in Chicago, provided *AS* with one of its most popular novels, indirectly inspired by the Shaver Mystery. "Agharti" (June 1946) tells of the vast underground city in Central Asia ruled by "the King of the World," an immortal who plans to emerge and establish a new world civilization when mankind is ready.

Perhaps the most popular novel published in *AS* at this time, however, was "The Star Kings" by Edmond Hamilton, published complete in the September

1947 issue. Space opera deluxe, it told the story of John Gordon, an Earthman, who exchanges bodies with Zarth Arn, a scientist from 2,000 centuries in the future, and also son of the greatest ruler in the Galaxy.

Palmer finally left Ziff-Davis' employ in 1949; he had been responsible for 117 issues of *AS*, more than any other single editor before or since. (Sloane had had direct responsibility for only 92.) While Palmer was a shrewd and capable editor, he seemed to respond directly to Ziff-Davis' natural desire for *AS* to be a commercial success rather than a specialist magazine, and in doing so he lost respect in the SF field.

From 1947 to 1949 Palmer remained nominal editor of *AS*, while establishing his own company with *Fate* and *Other Worlds*. Most of his duties were carried out by W. Lawrence Hamling. When Palmer departed, Howard Browne, who had served as associate editor until 1947 and was on a leave of absence to write three mystery novels, was recalled to assume full editorship, with Hamling still handling the basic duties. After Hamling left he was succeeded by Lila Shaffer, who had originally replaced Browne as associate editor in 1947. Browne recalled Shaffer as "a very bright young woman and an excellent editor," and the team of Browne and Shaffer produced some highly respectable issues of *AS*.

On the face of it Browne was an odd choice as editor. He openly admitted that he disliked science fiction. In addition, his forté was the mystery, and he had first been employed by Ziff-Davis as editor of *Mammoth Detective*. Ziff-Davis felt that *AS* now needed Browne's level-headedness to restore some respectability to *AS*, and Browne gave it a good try. He wrote off over 300,000 words worth of Shaver material in the inventory and declared plans to make *AS* a mass-market deluxe slick magazine, paying top word rates. His plans fell through when America entered the Korean War, and all such experiments were shelved.

Plans had been well advanced, however, and Browne had been acquiring material in readiness. These stories now found their way into the old pulp *AS*, which suddenly began to sprout leading SF names among its regular hacks. Fritz Leiber was one of the first with his novel "Let Freedom Ring" (April 1950). William F. Temple returned for the first time in over ten years with "For Each Man Kills" (March 1950). Fredric Brown had "From These Ashes" (August 1950) and "Gateway to Glory" (October 1950), while Clifford D. Simak brought down the curtain on Browne's first year with "Seven Came Back" (October 1950) and "Bathe Your Bearings in Blood" (December 1950; also known as "Skirmish").

Several new writers were also welcomed. Mack Reynolds first appeared in *Amazing* with "United We Stand" (May 1950), having debuted in *Fantastic Adventures* one month earlier. Similarly, John Jakes was ushered into the SF world first in *Fantastic Adventures*, followed the next month in *AS* with "Your Number Is Up!" (December 1950). Paul W. Fairman, who was soon to have a major effect on *AS*, first appeared under his own name in the February 1950 issue with "No Teeth for the Tiger." Milton Lesser, better known today as historical writer Stephen Marlowe, debuted in the November 1950 *AS* with "All Heroes Are Hated" and became a regular contributor for the next six years. Meanwhile, the January 1951 *AS* brought two new names to SF that would soar to great heights during the ensuing decade: Charles Beaumont with " 'The Devil, You Say?' " and Walter M. Miller, Jr., with the retitled "Secret of the Death Dome." For a first year's record of new writers, this was an impressive list.

In 1951 some of the more prestigious stories planned for the now aborted deluxe *AS* found their way into the pulp pages, including "Operation R.S.V.P.," by H. Beam Piper (January 1951) and "Satisfaction Guaranteed" by Isaac Asimov (April 1951). Both stories were sophisticated SF by pulp standards and more in line with the quality Horace Gold was establishing at *Galaxy Science* *.* With the budgeted money now spent and no more forthcoming, Browne could no longer plan the future he wanted, and his natural disdain for SF returned. Thus, by 1952 *AS* had once again become a routine space adventure magazine. The high spot came with the Michael Flanagan trilogy written in the style of Edgar Rice Burroughs by Stuart J. Byrne under the alias John Bloodstone. "Land beyond the Lens" (March 1952) was followed by the "Golden Gods" (April 1952) and subsequently, by popular demand, by "The Return of Michael Flanagan" (August 1952).

Opportunity presented itself again during 1952 when Ziff-Davis decided to experiment with a digest-format fantasy magazine, *Fantastic*.* Its success resulted in the merger of *Fantastic Adventures* with *Fantastic* and the conversion of *Amazing* from a pulp to a digest. As a further tidbit, Browne was given a new mystery magazine, *Conflict*, which suprisingly lasted only one issue. Browne now had a second chance to obtain high-quality stories and pay top rates. For the first digest *AS*, dated April/May 1953, he presented a formidable lineup. Robert Heinlein, with his nuclear thriller "Project Nightmare," Theodore Sturgeon and "The Way Home," Richard Matheson with his powerfully telling "The Last Day," Murray Leinster and "The Invaders," and the only reprint— because his promised new story did not come through in time—"Here There Be Tygers" by Ray Bradbury. Browne's one lapse of judgment was in his mock exposé about the seamy side of Mars in "Mars—Confidential" by Jack Lait and Lee Mortimer. Internal illustrations, mostly the work of art editor Leo Ramon Summers, were in two-tone, with an element of overconfident slickness that gave an up-market appeal but that must have reacted against contact with the usual pulp magazine readership.

Although the general trend was toward digest magazines, they were not universally liked. The pulp readers, especially those used to the bumper pulps of *Amazing*'s past decade containing up to 150,000 words, were now presented with an emaciated *AS* of little over 60,000 words. In one sweep gone were all the departments which for twenty-five years had given *AS* something of a family atmosphere. The absence of a letter column was perhaps the gravest sin, and Browne soon realized it would have to come back. When he did revive it, he dropped the long familiar "Discussions" title because Browne would have no affiliation with the readers; instead, he called it " . . . Or So You Say." The new *AS* had no atmosphere at all; it was almost clinical. The magazine was aimed at a readership poles apart from that of only a few years earlier, and no magazine can change its approach so radically without some dramatic results. *Galaxy* and *The Magazine of Fantasy and Science Fiction** had set out already aiming at that market, and *Amazing* was now trying to compete with these two titles with a background that was utterly incongruous. The one asset *AS* had had over the other magazines had been personality, and that was the one thing Browne killed.

The magazine's circulation dropped in equal proportion to its wordage, and while other overheads had been cut in the change to digest, the increased word rates and production costs had not been totally covered by the rise in cover price. Ziff-Davis immediately felt the pinch and began to tighten the purse strings again. Word rates were once again cut, production suffered, and, before Browne knew it, his promising new venture was suffocating. The quality material Browne had acquired was rationed over the ensuing year, but the issues steadily deteriorated. Only such stories as Arthur C. Clarke's "Encounter in the Dawn" (June/July 1953), Philip K. Dick's "The Commuter" (August/September 1953), Henry Kuttner's "Or Else" (August/September 1953) and Walter M. Miller's "Death of a Spaceman" (February/March 1954) were deservedly memorable.

Browne once again lost interest in the magazine, and so he increasingly left the main editorial duties to his managing editor, Paul W. Fairman. Fairman wrote prolifically for the magazine under various pseudonyms and in 1954 left to write full-time. Ziff-Davis' budget precluded taking on a replacement. Browne, with no further respect for SF, with a limited budget and a desire to write, not edit, took the easy way out. He took on contract a group of free-lance writers who could churn out a fixed wordage a month to be published under a fleet of house names. This way Browne did not have to read too many manuscripts, and, providing he fed each writer with the correct balance of stories required, editing became a formality.

Browne's strongest point was that he recognized good writing talent. The main group who mass-produced stories by the yard were Robert Silverberg, Harlan Ellison, Henry Slesar and Milton Lesser. In addition, Paul Fairman stayed with the market, and on some occasions Robert Moore Williams, Randall Garrett and Rog Phillips chipped in. These writers produced almost the entire contents of *AS* (and *Fantastic*) between June/July 1955 and December 1957. Their own names appeared alongside such alter egos as O. H. Leslie (Slesar), C. H. Thames (Lesser), Ralph Burke (Silverberg), Adam Chase (Lesser and Fairman), Ellis Hart (Ellison), Darius John Granger (Lesser) and E. K. Jarvis (Williams).

Only one issue of *AS* did not follow this format during the mid-1950s, and that was the thirtieth anniversary issue in April 1956. This issue, compiled by Paul Fairman with the help of Sam Moskowitz, contained 256 pages of mostly reprinted stories. These came predominantly from the magazine's early years with nothing more recent than 1942. In addition, there was a retrospect on

Amazing's early stories in "What Man Can Imagine" by Sam Moskowitz, plus a compendium of "Predictions: 2001 A.D." from a variety of eminent personalities including Sid Caesar, Philip Wylie, Salvador Dali, Dr. Robert Lindner and a dozen more. Robert Heinlein contributed a longer "As I See Tomorrow."

With the return of Paul Fairman in 1956 and *Amazing*'s monthly schedule restored in the November 1955 issue, Howard Browne left *AS* for Hollywood. The change in editorship was not apparent. Fairman continued Browne's production line techniques, and the contract authors still sent in their required wordage. *AS* had become one of the least inspiring and most monotonous magazines on the bookstalls, equal almost to the final issues under Sloane, twenty years earlier. One complaint that could never have been levied against Raymond Palmer was that of tedium, but in 1957, under Fairman, *AS* was nothing short of boring.

Fairman, like Browne, was more interested in writing than in editing and progressively handed over his duties to his assistant, Cele Goldsmith. It was the most fortuitous action of his editorship, for *AS* was about to enter, belatedly, upon its golden age.

With the departure of Bernard Davis, who had been the driving force behind the fiction magazines at Ziff-Davis, Paul Fairman and the young Cele Goldsmith were left to their own devices. Early in 1957 Goldsmith had risen from assistant to managing editor, and the more operating responsibilities she took on, the happier Paul Fairman was. He contented himself with writing many of the magazines' contents under a squad of pseudonyms. Finally, in 1958, he left to write full-time, and Goldsmith was left to go it alone.

With Fairman's departure, Norman Lobsenz was installed as editorial director. He signed his name to the editorials, and as it was more prominent than Cele Goldsmith's on the masthead, it gave the impression that he controlled the magazine's contents. This was far from the case.

Cele Goldsmith was not the first woman editor of a fantasy magazine, but she was by far the best. Under her seven-year editorship, *AS* and *Fantastic* blossomed as never before. During her tenure *AS* came its closest to greatness. She had a combination of talents that past editors had possessed only in some measure. She was not only enthusiastic and respectful, but was also willing to encourage new and old writers, to instill fresh ideas into SF, and to bring back the vivacity that had been missing in the field since the end of World War II. As Goldsmith herself has observed, aspiring writers began to see the change in *AS* and *Fantastic*, submitted stories, and received swift replies; these prompt personal responses engendered a loyalty that helped cement firm relations among the magazine, its editor and its contributors. The additional ingredient of prompt, if low, payment and acceptance resulted in one of the most astonishing tranformations the SF magazine world has ever seen.

Goldsmith's early and surprisingly short period of transition ended with the March 1959 issue. The cover boasted two big names: Isaac Asimov and E. E. Smith. For Asimov, March 1959 marked his twentieth anniversary as a writer, and *AS* had commissioned him to write a sequel to his first sale. "Anniversary" appeared alongside a reprint of "Marooned off Vesta," together with two letters by Asimov written twenty years apart. For "Doc" Smith, it was his first appearance since 1934 in the magazine that had started his career thirty years earlier, and it was with a new novel, "The Galaxy Primes," serialized in three parts and enticingly illustrated by Virgil Finlay.

Letters of appreciation flooded in, indicating that the editors were on the right road. With the next issue they showed how far they could break with the past by publishing "Golden the Ship was . . . O! O! O!" by the enigmatic Cordwainer Smith, and also introduced new writer Keith Laumer with "Greylorn." Laumer was the first of an impressive number of new writers who would owe their early sales to Cele Goldsmith.

The May 1959 issue led with "Initiative" by Boris and Arkady Strugatski, the first Soviet SF story to be translated for an American SF magazine. The next few months introduced readers to the works of Ron Goulart, Poul Anderson, Lloyd Biggle, Arthur Porges, Jack Sharkey and David R. Bunch, none of whom had previously appeared in *AS*. Bunch's story, "The Flesh-Man from Far Wide" (November 1959), was the first of his many stories of Moderan which readers either hated or loved but which always provoked response. Perhaps the most controversial story for 1959, however, was Harlan Ellison's "Sound of the Scythe" (October).

It was not long before another story set the letter column buzzing. "Transient" by Ward Moore (February 1960) was controversial because of its casual references to sex and because it was arguably more fantasy than science fiction. But if a story could provoke such a response, then *AS* was clearly back in the top league, for SF should not merely entertain, it should provoke.

Goldsmith had clearly restored *AS*. For the first time it was nominated for the Hugo Award as Best Magazine in 1960, and in 1962 Goldsmith received a Special Committee Award for her handling of the magazines. During these years *AS* published the first stories by Albert Teichner ("Man Made," January 1960), Neal Barrett, Jr. ("Made in Archerius," August 1960), Roger Zelazny ("Passion de Play," August 1962) and Sonya Dorman ("The Putnam Tradition," January 1963). Soon authors such as Piers Anthony, Thomas M. Disch, Ursula K. LeGuin, Robert Rohrer and Larry Eisenberg took their places in *AS* alongside such regular contributors as Poul Anderson, Fritz Leiber, Robert Sheckley, Brian W. Aldiss, J. G. Ballard, Philip José Farmer, James H. Schmitz, Gordon R. Dickson, Leigh Brackett, Ben Bova, Raymond F. Jones and Edmond Hamilton. For Hamilton, the new *AS* marked a resurgence in his fiction, as he now produced some of the best and most powerful stories of his career: "Requiem" (April 1962), "The Stars, My Brothers" (May 1962) and "Sunfire!" (September 1962), plus two new Star Kings stories, "The Kingdom of the Stars" (September 1964) and "The Shores of Infinity" (April 1965).

At last *AS* had regained a feeling of excitement, but without the juvenile sensationalism that had marred the 1940s and the scientific suffocation that had spoiled the 1930s. The stories speak for themselves: "The Trouble with Tycho" by Clifford D. Simak (October 1960); "Before Eden" by Arthur C. Clarke (June 1961); "The Towers of Titan" by Ben Bova (January 1962); "Quinquepedalian" by Piers Anthony (November 1963), in the same issue as the rediscovered "Savage Pellucidar" by Edgar Rice Burroughs; "The Days of Perky Pat" by Philip K. Dick (December 1963), which formed the basis of his novel *The Three Stigmata of Palmer Eldritch* (New York: Doubleday, 1965); "The Dowry of Angyar" by Ursula K. LeGuin (September 1964); "He Who Shapes" by Roger Zelazny (January–February 1965), co-winner of the 1965 Nebula for Best Novella, and so many more.

Nor was *AS* deaf to nonfiction. Sam Moskowitz began his series of SF personality profiles in the September 1960 issue with a study of Hugo Gernsback. Most of the articles that compose his volume *Seekers of Tomorrow* (Cleveland: World, 1966) first appeared here. Moskowitz also selected and introduced a series of "Classic Reprints" of stories from *AS*'s past (mostly the period 1928–1936). Lester del Rey began a series of science articles with "Homesteads on Venus" (October 1960). His role was subsequently taken over by Frank Tinsley, who looked at the early and projected space program, and he in turn was supplanted by Ben Bova, who was approached to contribute a series of articles on the possibilities of life in space. There were also the occasional one-off articles such as Arthur C. Clarke's "A New Look at Space" (July 1960) and Alexander Kazantsev's "A Soviet View of American SF" (May 1963).

Goldsmith also endeavored to make *AS* one of the most attractive SF magazines. With the help of interior illustrations by Ed Emsh and Virgil Finlay, and covers by Alex Schomburg, Lloyd Birmingham, Robert Adragna and again Ed Emsh, she succeeded admirably.

And then it all came to an end. Much respected though *AS* was, it was an anomaly for the publisher. Ziff-Davis had long since dropped all its other fiction titles and now concentrated on its glossy money-spinners *Popular Photography*, *Popular Electronics*, *Car and Driver* and *Modern Bride*. *AS* and *Fantastic* were its least lucrative titles and did not fit into its new drive for slick, special interest magazines with enormous advertising potential. The titles went up for sale after twenty-seven years with the same publisher, and were bought by Sol Cohen, who had left *Galaxy* and, with Arthur Bernhard, had formed the Ultimate Publishing Company. Goldsmith opted to stay at the well-established Ziff-Davis firm and took on an editorial post with *Modern Bride* where, in 1982, she became overall editor.

In the meantime, Sol Cohen found a managing editor in Joseph Wrzos, an English teacher who had had a long involvement with SF, as far back as the Gnome Press days of the early 1950s. Wrzos anglicized his name to Joseph Ross and began work.

The first few issues of the Ultimate *AS*, leading up to the fortieth anniversary issue in April 1966, were well received and circulation increased dramatically. The August 1965 issue boasted thirty-two extra pages and carried only two reprints. The three remaining stories and one article, by Keith Laumer, Robert F. Young, Arthur Porges and Robert Silverberg, respectively, were all new and legacies from Cele Goldsmith.

With the old inventory soon used up, Ross carefully rationed his budget for new fiction. Despite this handicap, he acquired two new novels by Murray Leinster—"Killer Ship" (October–December 1965) and "Stopover in Space" (June–August 1966)—and such stories as "On the Sand Planet" by Cordwainer Smith (December 1965), "Your Appointment Will Be Yesterday" by Philip K. Dick (August 1966) and "Ensign Flandry" by Poul Anderson (October 1966). He also purchased new novels by John Brunner ("Born under Mars," December 1966–February 1967) and Frank Herbert ("The Heaven Makers," April–June 1967, and "Santaroga Barrier," October 1967–February 1968). For the rest, however, he had to fill up with reprints.

Cohen soon found himself in a head-on collision with the newly formed Science Fiction Writers of America (SFWA) under its president, Damon Knight. When Cohen refused to make additional payments to authors whose stories were reprinted on the grounds that Gernsback, Teck and Ziff-Davis had acquired all serial rights to the stories, SF writers declared a boycott of *AS*. Later came the endorsement that sales to the magazines by a new writer did not constitute an immediate right of membership to the organization. The argument over the use of reprints dogged *AS* for the next few years. It resulted in a bitter period when once again *AS* reached a low ebb. After two years Ross felt he had exhausted both himself and the best of *Amazing*'s archives, especially since the archives were also being extensively mined by the new companion reprint magazines (see *Science Fiction Classics*,* *Great Science Fiction** and *Thrilling Science Fiction**). With Cohen unwilling to purchase more new material and to phase out the reprints, Ross resigned.

His replacement was Harry Harrison. Harrison knew Cohen from the early 1950s, and he stepped in to make peace between Cohen and the SFWA. After Harrison set up an amicable interim arrangement, Cohen asked him to edit the two magazines. Harrison agreed on the basis that all reprints would be phased out within a year, to which Cohen acceded.

Harrison reinstated *AS*'s variety of departments, reinstigated the letter column, commissioned a new science series, "The Science of Man," started a series of "London Letters," and obtained the services of Fritz Leiber, Robert Silverberg, James Blish and others in the book review column. For new fiction he secured an extract from Samuel Delany's forthcoming novel, *Nova*, published as "House-A-Fire" (July 1968), plus stories from Mack Reynolds, Ben Bova, Brian Aldiss, and R. A. Lafferty, among others.

Harrison also strove to restore a personality to the magazine, but, after five months, during which time Cohen still seemed adamant about keeping the reprints, Harrison resigned. He recommended Barry Malzberg as his replacement. The situation did not change, however, because Malzberg also wanted to phase out the reprints and Cohen was just as stubborn that they should remain.

Malzberg lasted only six and a half months. During this time he secured a new novel by Richard C. Meredith ("We All Died at Breakaway Station," January–March 1969), as well as new stories from Dean R. Koontz and Ray Russell. But Malzberg grew rapidly frustrated with Cohen's attitudes. It was evident in the only editorial he wrote: " . . . the reprint policy of these magazines will continue for the foreseeable future; publisher prerogative being as significant here as it is in any other branch of publishing."[29]

All this time *Amazing* lacked any sparkle. Poor printing, poor layout and cheap covers reprinted from European sources gave the magazine a cheap and uninteresting look. In an effort to improve the magazine's appearance, Malzberg commissioned a cover painting which Cohen then refused either to use or even to pay for. Cohen fired Malzberg, having already acquired a new editor, Ted White, behind Malzberg's back. Within only a few months White succeeded in reducing the reprints to one per issue and finally dropped them altogether after the January 1972 issue. This was accomplished by the simple expedient of shifting the reprints into a number of new all-reprint magazines and yearbooks. In the period 1969 to 1971, Cohen flooded the market with such titles as *Space Adventures,** *Strange Fantasy** and *Weird Mystery.** It was, apparently, a necessary sacrifice in order to have an all-new *Amazing*.

Ted White had Palmer's editorial approach, without Palmer's extremism. He promptly restored the chatty editorials and fan-related departments, and reinstigated "The Club House," which had been dropped twenty years earlier when *AS* converted to digest form. He also brought back the letter column (which Malzberg had dropped), designed as a forum for discussion and comment. The book review column was handed over to a variety of contributors such as Richard Delap, Richard Lupoff, Alexei Panshin and Hank Stine. As a result of Stine's perceptive review of Thomas M. Disch's novelization of *The Prisoner* and David McDaniel's *Number Two*,[30] Stine was commissioned to write the third Prisoner novel, *A Day in the Life* (New York: Ace, 1970). Finally, when Leon Stover's science series ended, White commissioned Gregory Benford (initially assisted by David Book) to write his own regular column, "The Science in Science Fiction."

Hitherto, Cohen had always managed the layout and production of the magazines himself. Now, White became increasingly more involved, and he soon had the satisfaction of replacing the reprint covers with the works of Jeff Jones, Mike Hinge, Dan Adkins and John Pederson. A similar transformation took place in the magazine's interior, so that by the end of White's first year, both *AS* and *Fantastic* were attractive and presentable.

White's record for new fiction was also commendable. The serials for the first few years included "Orn" by Piers Anthony (July–September 1970), "One Million Tomorrows" by Bob Shaw (November 1970–January 1971), "The Lathe of Heaven" by Ursula K. LeGuin (March–May 1971), "The Second Trip" by Robert Silverberg (July–September 1971), "The Wrong End of Time" by John Brunner (November 1971–January 1972) and Bob Shaw's "slow glass" novel,

"Other Day's, Other Eyes" (May–July 1972). White also encouraged new writers, including Gordon Eklund, Grant Carrington, Gerard Conway and Thomas F. Monteleone.

Once again *AS* found itself a contender for the Best Magazine Hugo, and later Ted White received a nomination for the award as Best Editor. Neither magazine nor editor won an award, and, curiously, only one short story ever reached the final ballot form, Grant Carrington's powerful and poignant tale of the last living actors, "His Hour upon the Stage" (March 1976).

For the fiftieth anniversary issue, published in April 1976 but with a cover date of June, White assembled several good stories. Apart from a novelty item by Isaac Asimov, "Birth of a Notion," there were "Natural Advantage" by Lester del Rey, "Strange Wine" by Harlan Ellison and "The Death of Princes" by Fritz Leiber.

Part of *AS*'s strength under White lay in its serials. In the last half of White's editorship he acquired John Brunner's "The Stone That Never Came Down" (October–December 1973) and "Total Eclipse" (April–June 1974), as well as Jack Vance's "Trullion: Alastor 2262" (March–June 1973), "The Domains of Koryphon" (August–October 1974), and "Marune: Alastor 933" (July–September 1975). But when the magazine's schedule dropped from bi-monthly to quarterly, it was no longer practical to run serials, and *AS* was consequently much the weaker.

Another area of *AS*'s strength, and its most lasting, was its artwork, especially the fine work of Stephen Fabian, who illustrated both covers and interiors.

Finally, Ted White's own comments in the editorials and letter columns were often controversial and always stimulating. These comments sometimes antagonized readers more than attracted them, and this also became true of the fiction, from the shapeless quips of Barry Malzberg, who was the most frequent contributor, to such excesses as Rich Brown's "Two of a Kind" (March 1977), which went out of its way to be provocative.

Whereas White still encouraged new writers, a disincentive was introduced by way of a twenty-five cent "handling charge" which had to accompany the submission of manuscripts from untried and untested writers.[31] The money was used to pay assistant editors who helped White sift through the slush pile of unsolicited manuscripts. In other words, *AS* contributors, instead of the publisher, were reimbursing the assistant editors for their time and judgment. Although this practice was widely opposed, it nevertheless went into effect and remained in force for eighteen months before it was dropped.

AS was a far cry from the mighty pulp of the mid-1940s when it had carried over three times the wordage and had been edited by a team of salaried editors, illustrated by a squad of artists under contract, and filled with fiction by a cluster of staff writers and when, seemingly, money was no object. Now, by 1978, *Amazing* was edited from home by just one man, Ted White, aided by two or three unsalaried assistants at their own homes, and with White also acting as the art director, responsible for the full layout of the magazines. Cohen had progressively relinquished more and more of his duties to White, and although the end product was artistically and egotistically satisfying to White, the work it entailed and the time it absorbed when he needed to supplement his income by other writing became frustrating. White finally resigned in October 1978 after Cohen sold his stock in Ultimate Publishing to his partner, Arthur Bernhard, who became sole proprietor.

White returned all the manuscripts accepted for publication but not paid for. Thus, after the February 1979 issue Ultimate had nothing in its inventory. Once more *AS* entered a transitional period under a new eidtor, Elinor Mavor. She assumed the male alias of Omar Gohagen because both she and her employer felt that a woman's name as editor would not go down well in the SF field— despite *AS*'s glorious past under Cele Goldsmith.

Ted White's ten years of hard work were instantly obliterated. *AS* resorted to an all-reprint policy and was assembled in a patchy, untidy fashion. Gradually, Mavor contacted new writers and artists. Once again it took about a year for the new editor to become acquainted with the field, and en route she encountered help from Thomas Easton and Darrell Schweitzer, as well as new writer Wayne Wightman and artist Gary Freeman. With the May 1980 issue reprints were dropped and some of the more established writers began to return. Subsequent issues featured Greg Benford, Barry Malzberg, David R. Bunch and Harlan Ellison. With the November 1980 issue *AS* absorbed *Fantastic* and increased slightly in size. The combined magazine allowed the publisher to cut his losses and focus on producing one good-quality magazine instead of two average publications. Thereafter *AS* included a measure of fantasy in its contents.

Amazing's circulation showed a slight increase in its second year under Mavor, and there was a marked increase in the quality of its contents and presentation. Each issue still contained one reprinted story, but its significance was enhanced by a new introduction provided by the author on the origin and importance of the story. A new variety of departments was added, including author interviews, science news, book reviews and a fan column. There were new stories by Roger Zelazny, Manly Wade Wellman and Somtow Sucharitkul, as well as superior artwork by Stephen Fabian, Gary Freeman and Alicia Austin. *AS* had redeemed itself.

In 1982 Arthur Bernhard decided to sell the magazine and, for a while, its future was in doubt. In March the title was acquired by TSR Hobbies through a subsidiary company Dragon Publishing. For the first time since 1938 *AS* was in the hands of a publisher with sufficient capital and enthusiasm to give it the backing and promotion needed. Moreover, George Scithers, the former editor of *Isaac Asimov's Science Fiction Magazine* and recently appointed vice-president of the parent company, became editor.

The July and September 1982 issues were transitional, with Mavor still serving as editor, Scithers assuming full control from November. The magazine increased its size to 160 pages but, perhaps surprisingly, retained the digest format. The trend in recent years had been toward more slick magazines with greater market appeal. Instead Scithers, virtually overnight, tranformed *AS* to a near twin of his former magazine. Authors who had been regular contributors to *Asimov's*— such as Somtow Sucharitkul, Avram Davidson, Darrell Schweitzer and John M. Ford—now became *AS* regulars. Likewise, artists George Barr, Karl Kofoed, Jack Gaughan and others transferred to the new market. There is such a striking similarity between the cover of the May 1983 *AS* and that of the Winter 1977 *Asimov's*—both by Kelly Freas—as to resolve any question that Scithers was out to capture the same audience he had acquired so rapidly with *Asimov's*. But it did not happen. Most likely the absence of the not inconsiderable attraction of Asimov's name on the bookstalls was the most prominent factor, but after two years under new management *AS*'s circulation had dropped from around 17,500 to a little over 11,300, scarcely enough to make it a profitable venture. Although it has published some good stories it now needs to concentrate on reestablishing its circulation or the magazine is seriously in danger of seeing its final issue.

In a life that spans six decades *AS* has had a checkered history. It has published both the best and the worst of science fiction, it has discovered many of the leading writers in the field, and it has published some of the most damaging fiction in the shape of the Shaver stories. It has been edited by a man who had no liking for SF; it was started by a man who wanted it to act as a forum for disseminating scientific knowledge through the medium of fiction; it was even edited by a man who did not believe man would conquer Everest; and it is now in the hands of a publisher who was able to buy the title from the proceeds of marketing SF and fantasy games. Its history has reflected the rise and fall and struggles of the SF field, and with good fortune will continue to do so. In its various forms since 1926 *AS* has, in effect, been eight different magazines; nevertheless, it has remained one of the pillars of the SF magazine scene, and it would be hard to imagine the field without it.

Notes

I must thank Joseph Wrzos, Cele Lalli, Robert Silverberg, Harry Harrison and Barry Malzberg for their memories of their part in this story, plus special thanks to Alistair Durie and Terry Hill for devotedly ploughing through their long runs of early *Amazings* for bibliographical and editorial information.

1. Hugo Gernsback, "A New Sort of Magazine" [editorial], *Amazing Stories*, April 1926; reprinted in issue for April 1966.

2. In his essay on Hugo Gernsback, Sam Moskowitz states that the first issue appeared on April 5. However, the magazine's indicia clearly state that the magazine is published on the fifth day of the preceding month (*Explorers of the Infinite* [Cleveland: World, 1963], p. 225).

3. Ibid., p. 227.

4. [T. O'Conor Sloane], Obituary of Wilbur C. Whitehead, *Amazing Stories*, September 1931, p. 484.

5. Hugo Gernsback, "Idle Thoughts of a Busy Editor" [editorial], *Amazing Stories*, March 1927.

6. Gernsback's definition was given in his first editorial, "A New Sort of Magazine." It ran: "By 'scientifiction' I mean the Jules Verne, H. G. Wells, and Edgar Allan Poe type of story—a charming romance intermingled with scientific fact and prophetic vision."

7. Four of England's SF novels had seen book publication by 1926, among them *Darkness and Dawn* (Boston: Small Maynard, 1914), originally serialized in *The Cavalier* during 1912, and *Cursed* (Small Maynard, 1919). Of special interest, however, is *The Golden Blight*, published in New York in 1916 by H. K. Fly, the same H. K. Fly who in 1930 would become co-publisher, with B. A. McKinnon, of *Amazing Stories*.

8. This cover was reprinted in David Kyle's *A Pictorial History of Science Fiction* (Feltham: Hamlyn, 1976), p. 58.

9. Hugo Gernsback, "The Rise of Scientifiction" [editorial], *Amazing Stories Quarterly*, Spring 1928.

10. Sam Moskowitz, *Seekers of Tomorrow* (Cleveland: World, 1966), p. 10.

11. "Marius" is identified as Steve Benedict by Norm Metcalf in his *Index of Science Fiction Magazines 1951–1965*, where it is listed that Benedict also had a single story in *Astounding SF* for January 1953.

12. See "Mythology Deluxe" by Thomas Perry, *Amazing Stories*, July 1977, pp. 4ff., followed by Sam Moskowitz's letter printed in " . . . Or So You Say," *Amazing Stories*, October 1977, pp. 4ff., followed by Tom Perry's "Experiment in Bankruptcy," *Amazing Stories*, May 1978, pp. 101ff.

13. See Harry Bates, "To Begin" [editorial], *A Requiem for Astounding* (Chicago: Advent, 1964).

14. T. O'Conor Sloane, "Editorial," *Amazing Stories*, May 1929.

15. Sloane, "Editorial," *Amazing Stories*, November 1929.

16. Sloane, "Editorial," *Amazing Stories*, May 1930.

17. See *Amazing Stories*, June 1935, p. 5.

18. Jack Williamson, *The Early Williamson* (Garden City, N.Y.: Doubleday, 1975), p. 34.

19. Frederik Pohl, *The Way the Future Was* (New York: Ballantine Books, 1978), p. 43.

20. See Moskowitz, *Seekers of Tomorrow*, p. 270.

21. Ibid., p. 32.

22. Hasse had had two earlier stories published, collaborations with A. Fedor starting with "The End of Tyme," a fannish spoof in the November 1933 *Wonder Stories*.

23. Howard Fast, in R. Reginald's *Science Fiction and Fantasy Literature*, Vol. 2 (Detroit: Gale Research, 1979), p. 896.

24. See Moskowitz, *Seekers of Tomorrow*, p. 306. Note also Isaac Asimov's comments on the story in *The Early Asimov* (Garden City, N.Y.: Doubleday, 1972).

25. See *Amazing Stories*, April 1938, p. 141.

26. See Harry Warner, *All Our Yesterdays* (Chicago: Advent, 1969), p. 76. That one story may have been "Space Pirate," a genuine collaboration between Earl and Otto Binder. Earl had ceased being one of the team a few years earlier, and Sloane's habit of hanging on to manuscripts for a long time may support that surmise.

27. Earlier published as "Beyond the Screen," *Fantasy*, No.1, 1938.

28. Apart from the editorials and letter columns of *AS* from December 1944 onwards to September 1947, the more relevant items are *The Hidden World*, Spring 1961, subtitled "The True Story of the Shaver Mystery," with an editorial and essay, "Invitation to Adventure" by Palmer, and ten items by Richard S. Shaver on every aspect of the

Mystery, plus " 'I Remember Lemuria!' " complete; "The Shaver Mystery" by Shaver, serialized in *Mystic*, starting in October 1955 issue; *Fantastic*, July 1958, a special Shaver issue containing articles by Shaver, Palmer and others; *Amazing Stories*, June 1947, the all-Shaver issue; Palmer, "Flying Saucers and the Stymie Factor," *Science Fiction Review*, No. 25 (May 1978): 60ff. Reference might also be made to L. Sprague de Camp, *Science Fiction Handbook* (New York: Hermitage, 1953), pp. 92f., and Michael Ashley, *The History of the Science Fiction Magazine, Part 3* (London: New English Library, 1976), pp. 19–24.

 29. Barry Malzberg, "Editorial," *Amazing Stories*, January 1969, p. 138.

 30. The review was published in *Fantastic*, April 1970, pp. 112–113f., and notice of Stine's commission in *Fantastic*, December 1970, p. 140.

 31. See Ted White's editorial in *Amazing SF*, October 1974, pp. 4ff.

Information Sources

BIBLIOGRAPHY:

Gernsback, Hugo. "Science Fiction That Endures." *Amazing Stories*, April 1961; repr. December 1967. (Discusses the origins of *AS*.)

Herwald, Michelle Hope. "Amazing Artifact: Cultural Analysis of *Amazing Stories* 1926–1938." Ph.D. dissertation, University of Michigan, 1977.

Lowndes, Robert A.W. "Yesterday's World of Tomorrow." *Future SF*, Summer 1957–August 1959. (Series of editorials discussing the contents of *AS* month by month for 1927–1929.)

Nicholls. *Encyclopedia*.

Panshin, Alexei. "The Nature of Creative Fantasy." *Fantastic*, February 1971; repr. in *SF in Dimension*. Chicago: Advent, 1976.

————. "The Short History of Science Fiction." *Fantastic*, April 1971; repr. in *SF in Dimension*. Chicago: Advent, 1976.

Schweitzer, Darrell. "Interview with Ted White." *SF Voices*. Baltimore: T-K Graphics, 1976. (Gives background of White's involvement with *AS*.)

Tuck.

White, Ted. "Editorial." *Amazing Stories*, May 1971. (A potted history. See also White's other editorials and columns in *SF Review*, *Algol* and *Thrust*.)

INDEX SOURCES: ISBF; ISFM; ISFM-II; ISFM-III; MIT; NESFA; NESFA-II; NESFA-III; NESFA-IV; NESFA-V; NESFA-VI; NESFA-VII; NESFA-VIII; NESFA-IX; SFM; Tuck.

REPRINT SOURCES:

 Rebound Editions: Unsold issues of *AS* were rebound, three to a volume with a new cover and reissued as *Amazing Stories Quarterly*. Volume 1, Number 1, Winter 1940 [rebinding of issues April, May, June 1940]–Volume 4, Number 1, Winter 1943; 13 issues, 35¢. Second series, unnumbered, Winter 1947–Winter 1951, 15 issues, 50¢.

 Reprint Magazines: See entries for *Astounding Stories Yearbook*, *Great Science Fiction*, *Thrilling Science Fiction* and *Science Fiction Classics Annual*.

 Reprint Editions:

  British: Three series. First series, 1 issue, undated, released November 1946 by Ziff-Davis, London. Pulp, 64 pp., 2/-. Reprints four stories from issues Feb 39, May 40, Jul 46. [Note: Brad Day cites a second issue, but none is listed in Stone or Tuck.]

Second series, 24 issues, undated, released June 1950–November 1953, by Thorpe & Porter, Leicester. Pulp, 160pp.–96pp., 2/-. Abridged U.S. versions correspond as follows: 1, Apr 50; 2, Mar 50; 3, May 50; 4, Sep 50; 5, Oct 50; 6, Aug 50; 7, Feb 51; 8, Nov 51; 9, Feb 50; 10, Dec 50; 11, Apr 52; 12, Mar 51; 13, Apr 51; 14, May 51; 15, Aug 51; 16, Jun 51; 17, Sep 51; 18, Oct 51; 19, Nov 52; 20, May 52; 21, Jul 50; 22, Feb 53; 23, Jan 53; 24, Dec 51.

Third series, 8 issues, undated, released December 1953–January 1955 by Thorpe & Porter, Leicester. Digest, 128pp., 1/-. Corresponds to U.S. editions August/September 1953–October/November 1954.

Japanese: 7 issues, April–October 1950. Pulp, 256pp., 100 yen. Selected chiefly from *AS* 1948–1950, but also from early years and from *Fantastic Adventures*.

Derivative Anthologies: Joseph Ross, ed., *The Best of Amazing* (New York: Doubleday, 1967), 9 stories from 1926–1962; Ted White, ed., *The Best from Amazing* (New York: Manor Books, 1973), 8 stories from 1953–1964.

Microform: Greenwood Press Periodical Series.

LOCATION SOURCES: Brigham Young University Library; Dallas Public Library; Florida International University Library; Harvard University Library; Lilly Library of Indiana University; Michigan State University Library; M.I.T. Science Fiction Library; New York Public Library; Northern Illinois University Library; Pennsylvania State University Library; Red Wing, Minnesota, Public Library; San Francisco Public Library; Sarah Lawrence College Library; State University of New York-Albany Library; Syracuse University Library; Texas A&M University Library; Tulane University Library; University of Arizona Library; University of California Library; University of California-Riverside Library; University of Maryland Baltimore County Library; University of Montana Library; University of New Brunswick Library; University of New Mexico Library; University of Texas-Austin Library; University of Winnipeg Library; University of Wisconsin-Milwaukee Library.

Publication History

TITLE: *Amazing Stories*, April 1926–February 1958; *Amazing Science Fiction*, March–April 1958; *Amazing Science Fiction Stories*, May 1958–September 1960; *Amazing Stories* [subtitled "Fact and Science Fiction"], October 1960–June 1965; *Amazing Stories*, August 1965–July 1970; *Amazing Science Fiction Stories* [on cover and masthead only; spine and indicia retained *Amazing Stories*], September 1970–May 1972 [spine converted to *Amazing Science Fiction* in May 1972]; *Amazing Science Fiction* [on cover and spine, but not masthead], July 1972–February 1979; *Amazing Stories*, May 1979–August 1980; *Amazing Science Fiction Stories* [combined with *Fantastic*], November 1980– [spine reads *Amazing/Fantastic* and indicia read simply *Amazing*].

VOLUME DATA: Unnecessarily complicated by *AS*'s recent conversion to *Fantastic*'s volume sequence; the full data are as follows: Volume 1, Number 1, April 1926–Volume 8, Number 12, April 1934, 12 issues per volume, monthly (August/September 1933 issues combined); Volume 9, 11 issues (May 1934–March 1935, monthly); Volume 10, 13 issues (April 1935–December 1936; monthly to August 1935, then bi-monthly); Volume 11, 6 issues, bi-monthly (February–December

1937); Volume 12, 7 issues (February–December 1938; bi-monthly to October 1938, then monthly); Volume 13, Number 1, January 1939–Volume 16, Number 12, December 1942, 12 issues per volume, monthly; Volume 17, 10 issues (January–November 1943; monthly to September, then bi-monthly); Volume 18, 5 issues (January–December 1944; bi-monthly to May, then quarterly); Volume 19, 4 issues, March–December 1945, quarterly; Volume 20, 9 issues (February–December 1946; quarterly to May, then monthly); Volume 21, Number 1, January 1947–Volume 26, Number 12, December 1952, 12 issues per volume, monthly; Volume 27, 8 issues (January 1953–December 1953/January 1954; monthly to March, then bi-monthly); Volume 28, 5 issues, March–November 1954, bi-monthly; Volume 29, 7 issues (January–December 1955; bi-monthly to November, then monthly); Volume 30, Number 1, January 1956–Volume 38, Number 12, December 1965, 12 issues per volume, monthly; Volume 39, 6 issues, January–June 1965, monthly; Volume 40, 10 issues, August 1965–February 1967, bi-monthly; Volume 41, Number 1, April 1967–Volume 49, Number 5, March 1976, 6 issues per volume, bi-monthly (April 1968 issue dated June on cover, and followed by July 1968 issue; March 1973 followed by June 1973; December 1974 followed by March 1975); Volume 50, 5 issues, June 1976–July 1977, quarterly; Volumes 51 and 52, 4 issues per volume, October 1977–August 1979, quarterly. After Volume 52, Number 4, *AS* adopted concurrent numbering with *Fantastic*: Volume 27, Number 5, November 1979–Number 12, May 1981, quarterly to November 1980, then bi-monthly. Volume 28, July 1981–January 1983, 9 issues, bi-monthly. Volume numbering then corrected to Volume 56, Number 5, March 1983. Volume 57 began May 1983, 6 issues per volume, bi-monthly.

PUBLISHER: Experimenter Publishing Co., 230 Fifth Ave., New York, April 1926–April 1929; Experimenter Publishing Co., in receivership, 381 Fourth Ave., New York, May 1929–October 1930; Radio-Science Publications, Inc., Jamaica, New York, November 1930–September 1931; Teck Publishing Corp., New York, October 1931–February 1938; Ziff-Davis, Chicago, April 1938–February 1951; Ziff-Davis, New York, March 1951–June 1965; Ultimate Publishing Co., Flushing, New York, August 1965–February 1979; Ultimate Publishing Co., Scottsdale, Arizona, May 1979–June 1982; Dragon Publishing, Lake Geneva, WI, September 1982–.

EDITORS:

Editors-in-Chief: Hugo Gernsback, April 1926–April 1929; Arthur H. Lynch, May–October 1929; T. O'Conor Sloane, November 1929–April 1938; Bernard G. Davis, June 1938–February 1947; Raymond A. Palmer, March 1947–December 1949; Howard Browne, January 1950–August 1956; Paul W. Fairman, September 1956–November 1958; Norman Lobsenz, December 1958–June 1965; Sol Cohen, August 1965–November 1969; Ted White, January 1970–February 1979; Elinor Mavor, May 1979–September 1982; George Scithers, November 1982–.

Managing Editors: T. O'Conor Sloane [Associate], April 1926–October 1929; Miriam Bourne, November 1929–November 1932; T. O'Conor Sloane, December 1932–April 1938; Raymond A. Palmer, June 1938–February 1947; William Lawrence Hamling, March 1947 [Associate], then January 1948 [Managing]–February 1951; Lila E. Shaffer, March 1951–March 1953; Paul W. Fairman, April/May 1953–November 1954; Howard Browne, January 1955–May 1956; Paul W. Fairman, June 1956–February 1957; Cele Goldsmith, March 1957–November 1958, [Editor]

December 1958–June 1965; Joseph Ross, August 1965–October 1967; Harry Harrison, December 1967–September 1968; Barry N. Malzberg, November 1968–March 1969; Ted White, May 1969–February 1979; Elinor Mavor, May 1979–September 1982 (under alias Omar Gohagen until August 1980 issue); George Scithers, November 1982–.

FORMAT: [Note: Some of the early issues of *AS* carried extra pages of advertising, some of special coated stock. With the fluctuating number only serving to confuse, they have been ignored in the following, which concentrates on the pulp pages.]

Large Pulp, 96pp., April 1926–August/September 1933; Pulp, 144pp., October 1933–April 1941; 240pp., May 1941–March 1942; 272pp., April–July 1942; 240pp., August 1942–May 1943; 208pp., June 1943–June 1945; 176pp., September 1945–June 1948; 162pp., July 1948; 160pp., August 1948; 152pp., September 1948–May 1949; 144pp., June–August 1949; 160pp., September 1949–February 1950; 192pp., March–August 1950; 176pp., September 1950; 160pp., October 1950–March 1953; Digest, 160pp., April/May–August/September 1953; 144pp., October/November 1953; 128pp., December 1953/January 1954–February 1958 [except April 1956, 256pp.]; 144pp., March 1958–July 1962 [except April 1961, 192pp.]; 128pp., August 1962–June1965; 160pp., August 1965–October 1967 [except April 1966, 192pp.]; 144pp., December 1967–November 1970; 128pp., January 1971–August 1980; Large Digest, 128pp., November 1980–November 1981; Digest, 128pp., January–September 1982; Digest, 160pp., November 1982–.

PRICE: 25¢, April 1926–April 1938; 20¢, June 1938–April 1941; 25¢, May 1941–March 1953; 35¢, April/May 1953–April 1963; 50¢, May 1963–September 1969; 60¢, November 1969–June 1974; 75¢, August 1974–September 1975; $1.00, November 1975–January 1978; $1.25, May 1978–February 1979; $1.50, May 1979–November 1983; $1.75, January 1984–.

Mike Ashley

AMAZING STORIES ANNUAL

Hugo Gernsback's phenomenal success with *Amazing Stories** led him to consider first a twice monthly publication, and then an annual of the year's best stories. It was probably his initial intention to make the *Annual* all-reprint, but correspondence with Edgar Rice Burroughs in April 1927 gave Gernsback the opportunity to publish an entirely new Martian novel, at that stage entitled *Vad Varo of Barsoom*. Burroughs' asking price was rather more than Gernsback would have liked to have paid, so he made the sale conditional on the success of the *Annual*, Surprisingly, Burroughs accepted this "tales-I-win-heads-you-lose" deal. It was probably at this point that Gernsback decided to issue such a bumper-sized annual, running to 128 bedsheet-size pages, but at the same time he increased the price to fifty cents.

The *Annual* was released in July 1927, and its 100,000-print run sold out. Gernsback had settled on the title "The Master Mind of Mars," which has remained with subsequent book publications. Frank R. Paul painted one of his usual colorfully arresting covers portraying the brilliant Martian surgeon Ras Thavas in his House of the Dead. While Burroughs was having trouble finding editors willing to accept his new stories, he had no such worries about his public acceptance. He was arguably the most popular adventure writer of his day.

It is indicative of the public's reception of the story to listen to Frederik Pohl reminisce (in 1975) about his encounter of Burroughs' story in the *Annual*.

> Burroughs used Mars to comment on Earth, just as Swift used Lilliput and Laputa. In *The Master Mind of Mars* he ridiculed religion, an act not without courage. In all the books he jabbed at prudery (the Barsoomians ornamented their bodies instead of concealing them). The stately "formal dances" of the Barsoomian nobles no doubt reflect his displeasure with the Charleston and the Bunny Hug. And so on; I will not labour the point, but if the man was writing adventure it was not *just* adventure.
>
> It was even scientifically accurate. That, I admit, is a claim for Burroughs not often heard, but I think it is defensible. True, Burroughs' Barsoom is not much like the Mars of the Mariner photographs. But it is very like the Mars of Percival Lowell, and that was all that science knew of Mars at the time.[1]

Gernsback knew exactly what his readers wanted; he knew the Fred Pohls were out there in mass, waiting to be instructed—even mesmerized. It is interesting to compare the above statement by Pohl with Gernsback's own introduction to the story.

> E.R.B. has written many interesting stories, but we believe, for downright originality, and exciting interest, "The Master Mind of Mars" is hard to equal. There is hardly a page that does not hold your interest. Once the story gets under way, hair-raising episodes seem to tumble over each other—they come so quickly.
>
> Besides this the science is excellent and no matter how strangely the tale reads, it always, somehow or other, seems to have an element of truth in it.[2]

Gernsback used the statement "besides the science is excellent" so often when introducing stories that it became a shibboleth, almost a *sine qua non* of the SF genre. Yet, in many ways Gernsback saw himself as something of a missionary, bringing science to the people.

The remaining stories in the *Annual*, bar one, were those that had brought the most popular response from readers of *Amazing*, where the stories had been printed during the past year. They were "The Feline Light and Power Company Is Organized" by Jacque Morgan, "The People of the Pit" by A. Merritt, "Under the Knife" by H. G. Wells, "The Man Who Saved the Earth" by Austin Hall and "The Man Who Could Vanish" by A. Hyatt Verrill. The one exception was the novella "The Face in the Abyss," also by Merritt, and also a reprint, but one that had not yet had an airing in the Gernsback magazines.

As was his custom, Gernsback asked readers of the *Annual* whether they wanted more stories in this vein and, if so, how frequently. The response was overwhelming and, in return, the following January Gernsback launched *Amazing Stories Quarterly.** The *Quarterly* was a continuation, indeed a substitute, for the *Annual*, and as a consequence no further *Annuals* appeared.

Notes

1. Frederik Pohl, "Ragged Claws," in *Hell's Cartographers*, ed. Brian W. Aldiss and Harry Harrison (New York: Harper & Row, 1975), pp. 148–49.
2. Hugo Gernsback, "Editorial," *Amazing Stories Annual*, p. 3.

Information Sources

BIBLIOGRAPHY:
Nicholls. *Encyclopedia*.
Tuck.
INDEX SOURCES: ISFM; SFM; Tuck.
REPRINT SOURCES:
  No reprint editions or derivative anthologies appeared, but *The Master Mind of Mars* was first published in hardcover by A. C. McClurg, Chicago, in 1928, and is currently available in a paperback edition from Ballantine Books, New York.
  Microform: Greenwood Press Periodical Series.
LOCATION SOURCES: M.I.T. Science Fiction Library; Pennsylvania State University Library.

Publication History

TITLE: *Amazing Stories Annual*.
VOLUME DATA: Volume 1, Number 1, 1927 (July). Only issue.
PUBLISHER: Experimenter Publishing Co., New York.
EDITOR: Hugo Gernsback.
FORMAT: Large Pulp, 128pp.
PRICE: 50¢.

Milton Wolf

AMAZING STORIES QUARTERLY

Following the successes of *Amazing Stories** in 1926 and *Amazing Stories Annual** in 1927, Gernsback was satisfied that there was a sufficiently large market to launch a companion magazine. Although readers had voted almost unanimously for a fortnightly *Amazing*, Gernsback decided to issue the companion on a quarterly basis. He also followed in the footsteps of *Annual* by making the *Quarterly* the home of full-length novels which otherwise could only be serialized in the monthly magazines. *Amazing Stories Quarterly*, therefore, was a bumper publication, in large pulp format and running to 144 pages. The cover price was twice that of the monthly—fifty cents—but on a quarterly basis this was not so expensive.

Hitherto Gernsback had only serialized reprinted novels in *Amazing Stories*. A. Hyatt Verrill's "Beyond the Pole" (October–November 1926) had been only of novella length, and the first original novel serialized in *Amazing* would not materialize until E. E. Smith's *The Skylark of Space* appeared in the issues for August, September and October 1928. The *Quarterly* was, therefore, the only place where the SF devotee would find new novel-length stories. Although in the first issue Gernsback did reprint H. G. Wells' *When the Sleeper Wakes*, it was the only time he did feature nonoriginal material, except for his own novel *Ralph 124C 41 +*.

The first issue, dated Winter 1928 and released in January, led with a short novel, "The Moon of Doom" by Earl L. Bell, an early example of the grand tradition of disaster stories in which the moon swings in closer to the Earth, with all the resultant catastrophes. Earl Leaston Bell is not noted for his contributions to SF. He had only one other story in *Amazing Stories* and two in *Weird Tales*,* but as the first bat in *ASQ* he will be remembered in the annals of SF. By today's standards "The Moon of Doom" is an unexceptional, almost naive story, but in 1928 it was noted for its abundance of ideas and action.

The complete-novel policy was an immediate success with the readers, and Gernsback realized that he had another winner on his hands. Always garnering reader response, Gernsback instigated another letter column, "Your Viewpoint," and, from the third issue, inaugurated a competition for the best editorial letters submitted by readers on scientifictional themes. The first $50 prize went to the now famous SF writer but then unknown fan, Jack Williamson. What he said, in part, was:

> The chief function of scientifiction is the creation of real pictures of new things, new ideas, and new machines. Scientifiction is the product of the human imagination, guided by the suggestion of science. It takes the basis of science, considers all the clues that science has to offer, and then adds a thing alien to science—imagination. It goes ahead and lights the way. And when science sees the things made real in the author's mind, it makes them real indeed. It deals only with that which it can see, weigh, or measure; only with logical hypothesis, experiment and influence and calculation. Scientifiction begins with the ending of science.[1]

Evidence seems to indicate that Gernsback used the *Quarterly* as a place to experiment. Certainly, a higher quota of new authors debuted in its pages than in the monthly, and by allowing readers their own voice in the editorial Gernsback was encouraging a rapid development of the genre. Miles J. Breuer made a very valid point in his own prize-winning editorial:

Scientific fiction as a fine art is truly new. Rarely does any fine art spring fully developed from the brow of its goddess. Years, decades of painful evolution will yet be necessary before Scientifiction can take its seat at the banquet, fully recognized by her sisters, Drama, Historical Romance, the Novel, etc. Scientifiction of today is not yet perfect; and those of us who write it recognize that fact better than does anyone else. When we attempt to wed two such dissimilar personalities as Science and Literary Art, it is but natural that there should be a period of adjustment before conjugal life is perfect. But the point I make is, that progress is being made, *right now*.

Amazing Stories is a pioneer. Our magazine is ineradicably down in history as the leader with the far-flung vision. A hundred or a thousand years in the future, men will point back to it as the originator of a new type of literary art.[2]

Breuer was perhaps even more prophetic in his nonfiction than in his fiction, for who else in 1928 would imagine that in years to come we would be looking back at the significance of *Amazing*'s pioneering years? Such was the faith of the early devotees in their newfound genre.

The question of prophetic fiction was in fact brought to focus in another of the prize-winning editorials, this time by Alexander M. Phillips.

At one time the advance of human knowledge depended upon more or less isolated individuals . . . working alone. Today science, like everything else, is being commercialized; invention is becoming a systematized industry. Rich and powerful corporations, Westinghouse, for example, maintain vast laboratories for no other purpose than research work. . . .

Few consider what is, after all, the vital question, namely, the consequences and effects, of these oncoming inventions and discoveries. Will they result in the betterment or detriment of civilization? The answer is, of course, that it depends on their application. That application, however, should not be left to chance, as is the tendency, for commercialized science is interested only indirectly in the welfare of the state; its primary objective is dividends. . . .

We do not need more scientists, but more men to direct the sane and beneficent application of inventions and discoveries. Unfortunately, political and social sciences are far behind the natural and technical ones, and are contstantly receiving severe jolts in consequence. Our attempts at world peace are a belated recognition of the fact that science has made war at best suicidal.[3]

In an age of almost constant recall of faulty products, cars, airplanes, even nuclear reactors, it is instructive to return to the prophetic extrapolations that emanated from a genre of literature that was being born in *Amazing Stories* and its companion *Quarterly*. Over and over again, SF has decried mankind's failure to develop his facility for imagination, the "what if" that just might save him from self-extermination. Isaac Asimov puts it this way:

> What is important about science fiction, even crucial, is the very thing that gave it birth—the perception of change through technology. It is not that science fiction predicts this particular change or that that makes it important; it is that it predicts *change*.
>
> Since the Industrial Revolution first made the perception of change through technology clear, the rate has continued to increase, until now the wind of change has risen from a zephyr to a hurricane. It is change, continuing change, inevitable change, that is the dominant factor in society today. No sensible decision can be made any longer without taking into account not only the world as it is, but the world as it will be—and naturally this means that there must be an accurate perception of the world as it will be. This, in turn, means that our statesmen, our businessmen, our everyman must take on a science fictional way of thinking, whether he likes it or not, or even whether he knows it or not. Only so can the deadly problems of today be solved.[4]

Not that all the fiction in *ASQ* borē this dictum in mind. Most of the fiction was written for entertainment and, in Gernsback's hope, to educate, but at the same time that element of prescience was always there.

Superscience fiction may not have been born in *ASQ*, but it was certainly the most encouraging nursery. "The Second Swarm" by the little-known J. Schlossel in the second issue (Spring 1928) had ushered in the era with a mighty invasion from Sirius, and other authors followed. Edmond Hamilton presented "Locked Worlds" in the Spring 1929 issue, and by 1930 John W. Campbell had the bit between his teeth with his stories "The Voice in the Void" (Summer 1930), "The Black Star Passes" (Fall 1930), "Islands of Space" (Spring 1931) and "Invaders of the Infinite" (Spring-Summer 1932).

The third issue of *ASQ*, dated Summer 1928, began to show the encouragement of new writers coming to fruition. Stanton A. Coblentz led the issue with his novel "The Sunken World," while R. F. Starzl debuted with "Out of the Sub-Universe." The issue, however, has greater significance for its contribution by David H. Keller, four connected stories under the general title "The Menace." Here Keller, a Philadelphia psychiatrist, handled the racial theme of blacks versus whites with a chilling foresight of ghetto riots, Black Panthers, and economic repression and retaliations. In his book *Strange Horizons*, Sam Moskowitz says:

> In "The Menace," a plot is uncovered by private detective Taine of San Francisco, in which Negroes have discovered how to make gold and are systematically buying up Harlem and other areas of New York City. They have also discovered a chemical which can turn their skin white. In the

course of the narrative Dr. Keller is brutally frank in his treatment of the race question. The other three stories deal with a series of other efforts by Negro scientists and leaders to destroy the United States for its behavior towards the Negro, almost succeeding before being foiled by Taine of San Francisco.[5]

Little wonder, then, that Gernsback could say with great self-satisfaction that America would "become known as the hotbed of scientifiction."[6]

Keller had seven stories in the *Quarterly*, and if "The Menace" was the most controversial, "Stenographer's Hands" (Fall 1928) was arguably the most significant, dealing with the specialist breeding of humans.

Gernsback reprinted his own prophetic "novel," "Ralph 124C 41 + ," in the Winter 1929 issue, which may have been the first time many readers had seen it. However, of possible greater import in that same issue was "The Murgatroyd Experiment," a story of humans injected with superchlorophyll so that they can draw their sustenance directly from the sun, but which also turns them into plant-men. It marked the debut of S. P. Meek. Also in that issue was "The Evolutionary Monstrosity" by Clare Winger Harris, one of the earliest stories to have a human artificially evolved into a monster.

The Spring 1929 *ASQ* was the last under Gernsback's control. It carried as its lead novel "After 12,000 Years" by Stanton A. Coblentz, which, though not on a par with Wells' *When the Sleeper Wakes*, which closed the first issue, has much in common in basic theme.

For the next couple of years T. O'Conor Sloane edited the *Quarterly* with remarkable selectivity, as some of the best SF of the early years appeared here. "Paradox" by Charles Cloukey (Summer 1929) was one of the earliest stories to consider the consequences of time travel rather than use it purely as a means to an end. "The Bridge of Light" (Fall 1929) is considered by many to be one of A. Hyatt Verrill's best novels, following his time-honored theme of a lost civilization in South America. "The Birth of a New Republic" (Winter 1930) by Miles J. Breuer and Jack Williamson parallels the independence of the Moon to the American War of Independence in much the same way that Robert A. Heinlein would thirty-five years later in *The Moon Is a Harsh Mistress* (see *If**). "Paradise and Iron" (Summer 1930) by Miles J. Breuer, possibly his best work, is still a highly regarded story of machines taking over society. "White Lily" (Winter 1930) was one of two novels by John Taine run in *ASQ*. This one dealt with a strange form of crystalline life, while "Seeds of Life" (Fall 1931) looks at man mutated into superman.

While it is true even after 1931 that the stories published in *ASQ* continued to carry bold and ingenious ideas, it is also true that, with the exception of John Campbell's novels and possibly "The Ant with the Human Soul" by Bob Olsen, the stories grew less inspiring and less entertaining. This was almost certainly attributable to aging editor Sloane. His editorials were much less inspiring and messianic than Gernsback's. His style tended toward the pedantic and his choice of subjects toward those involving mechanical engineering, like the problems in raising a crippled submarine or the mechanics behind rotary force. By 1933 the *Quarterly* had become irregular and, with the Winter 1933 issue, turned totally to reprinting earlier works. By then the Depression was helping to weed out all but the heartiest publications, and money for the expensive *Quarterly* did not come easily. With *Amazing*'s own circulation plummeting, there is no doubt that the *Quarterly* was already on the borders of poverty, but the publishers themselves showed no signs of dropping the magazine. If anything, its end was due to Sloane's apathy. In answer to a reader's enquiry in 1935, almost a year after the last *ASQ* had appeared, Sloane said, "The *Quarterly* will be somewhat irregular in dates of publication. We have sometimes felt like discontinuing it definitely."[7] With such a lack of interest it is perhaps not surprising that no further issues appeared.

ASQ has perhaps been unjustly overshadowed by its senior monthly partner, but in retrospect it is clear that *ASQ* contributed as much, if not more, to the development of science fiction by allowing writers to expand and explore their concepts at greater length, and also allowed Gernsback to experiment further with the possibilities of his new publishing offspring.

[Note: The issues of *ASQ* released between 1940 and 1943 and again in 1949–1951 were rebound issues of *Amazing Stories*, and not a separate magazine in its own right.]

Notes

1. Jack Williamson, "Scientifiction, Searchlight of Science" [editorial], *Amazing Stories Quarterly*, Fall 1928, p. 435.

2. Miles J. Breuer, "The Future of Scientifiction" [editorial], *Amazing Stories Quarterly*, Summer 1929, p. 291.

3. Alexander M. Phillips, "Do We Need More Scientists?" [editorial], *Amazing Stories Quarterly*, Winter 1930, p. 3.

4. Isaac Asimov, Foreword to *Encyclopedia of Science Fiction* (London: Octopus Books, 1978), p. 7.

5. Sam Moskowitz, *Strange Horizons* (New York: Charles Scribner's Sons, 1976), p. 61.

6. Hugo Gernsback, "Editorial," *Amazing Stories Quarterly*, Spring 1928, p. 147.

7. T. O'Conor Sloane, editorial comment in letter column, *Amazing Stories*, May 1935, p. 140.

Information Sources

BIBLIOGRAPHY:
Nicholls. *Encyclopedia*.
Tuck.
INDEX SOURCES: ISFM; SFM; Tuck.
REPRINT SOURCES: No magazine or anthology derives its contents entirely from the pages of *ASQ*, but *Science Fiction Classics* No. 3, Winter 1967, draws five of its seven stories from *ASQ*. Most of the lead novels mentioned above were also reprinted in hardcover and sometimes paperback during the 1950s and 1960s.

Microform: Greenwood Press Periodical Series.
LOCATION SOURCES: Florida International University Library; Lilly Library of Indiana University; M.I.T. Science Fiction Library; Pennsylvania State University Library; University of Montana Library; University of Winnipeg Library; University of Wisconsin–Milwaukee Library.

Publication History

TITLE: *Amazing Stories Quarterly*.
VOLUME DATA: Volume 1, Number 1, Winter 1928–Volume 7, Number 2, Fall 1934. First 4 volumes, 4 issues per volume, quarterly. Volume 4, Number 1, dated Winter 1930, is actually Winter 1931. Volume 5, 3 issues only (Spring-Summer 1932 and Fall-Winter 1932 issues combined). Volume 5, Number 3 followed erroneously by Volume 6, Number 4, Spring-Summer 1933. Volume 7, 2 issues only (Winter 1933 and Fall 1934). Total run: 22 issues.
PUBLISHER: Experimenter Publishing Co., Fifth Avenue, New York (Winter 1928–Spring 1929); Irving Trust Company as trustee in bankruptcy of Experimenter Publishing Co., 233 Broadway, New York (Summer 1929); Experimenter Publishing Co., Fourth Avenue, New York (Fall 1929–Summer 1930); Radio-Science Publications, Fourth Avenue, New York (Fall 1930–Summer 1931); Teck Publising Corp., Washington and Dunellen (Fall 1931–Fall 1934).
EDITORS: Hugo Gernsback, Winter 1928–Spring 1929; T. O'Conor Sloane, Summer 1929–Fall 1934.
FORMAT: Large Pulp, 144pp.; last two issues, 128pp.
PRICE: 50¢.

Milton Wolf/Mike Ashley

AMAZING STORIES SCIENCE FICTION NOVEL

When first mentioned in March 1957 (with the title *Amazing Science Fiction Novels*), this magazine was intended to contain novels only and was projected as a quarterly publication "if Ziff-Davis [could] get the right novels for it."[1] On the same date, Ziff-Davis SF editor Paul Fairman announced that *Amazing Stories** and *Fantastic** would run no more serials.[2] Thus, the new magazine may have been intended eventually to serve as a repository for longer stories of the heavy-action, light-thought variety that Z-D generally preferred. The initial issues, however, were to have a very specific audience: monster movie fans. The first report described plans to publish an adaption of the Columbia movie (then near release) "2,000,000 [*sic*] Miles to Earth," illustrated with stills from the film.[3] At that time, no writer had been chosen for the project.

Later, the plans were amended slightly. Reproduction of the movie stills proved unsatisfactory, so the novel ultimately was illustrated by line drawings based on the film. These and the cover painting were done by Novick and Edward Valigursky respectively, both regulars in the Z-D SF magazines.[4]

When it actually appeared on the stands, in June 1957, the magazine's title had been changed to *Amazing Stories Science Fiction Novel* (note noun change to singular). The *Amazing Stories* logo from that magazine was simply reproduced in a box at the upper left-hand corner; the rest of the title was run in small type to the right. The larger title ''20 Million Miles to Earth'' dominated the cover, just above Valigursky's picture of a grimacing monster standing with a girl in one hand and a torn-off lamppost in the other. No editor, publishing schedule or subscription rate was mentioned; in fact, the magazine had the look of a one-shot. Henry Slesar (a frequent contributor to Z-D) did the novelization; it has the distinction of being his longest piece of SF. Lacking the charm of Ray Harryhausen's special effects in the film, though, the novelization was thoroughly routine. The text ran from page 8 to page 120, biographies of the performers filling the last pages of the magazine. A later summary of Ziff-Davis news included the following:

> No plans are underway for a second issue of *Amazing Stories Science Fiction Novel*, until the complete returns of the first issue come in. Normally, a Distributing Company will give spot returns shortly after a new mag comes out, but, in this case, *Amazing Novel* was distributed by American News, which is no longer in that branch of business and thus Z-D will not know how the mag made out until all returns are in. The mag is still listed as a quarterly.[5]

So *Amazing Science Fiction Novel* may have been killed by the marketing uncertainty that followed American News' decision to get out of magazine distribution. However, the changes in title and lack of schedule information in the published magazine suggest that the decision had already been made, that Z-D had realized it could produce juvenile SF on its own without the complication of working with a movie studio. The ''Amazing Stories Science Fiction Novel'' name was used for a special section of *Amazing* itself, when the magazine added sixteen pages and began running a ''Complete Book-Length Novel'' each issue.[6] That began with the March 1958 issue, when *Amazing* began running E. E. Smith's ''The Galaxy Primes'' as a serial, and following that any short novels were simply incorporated into the regular contents. Under Cele Goldsmith, the Ziff-Davis SF magazines were moving away from monster-movie novelizations.

Notes

1. ''Another New S-F Publication Coming from Ziff-Davis: 'AMAZING S-F NOVELS,' '' *Fantasy-Times* [fanzine], No. 266 (first March 1957 issue): 1. The story is dated February 21.

2. ''No More Serials for Amazing or Fantastic,'' *Fantasy-Times* [fanzine], No. 266 (first March 1957 issue): 3.

3. ''Another New S-F Publication,'' p. 4.

4. ''AMAZING S-F NOVELS, Due out in June, 1957, Dream World Delayed Again,'' *Fantasy-Times* [fanzine], No. 267 (second March 1957 issue): 1.

5. "B. G. Davis Resigns As President of Z-D," *Science Fiction Times* [fanzine], No. 275 (second July 1957 issue): 2.

6. "Amazing Stories SF Novel 'Combines with' Amazing Stories," *Science-Fiction Times* [fanzine], No. 286 (first January 1958 issue]: 3.

Information Sources

BIBLIOGRAPHY:

Nicholls. *Encyclopedia.*

Prieto, Frank R. Jr. "The Science Fiction Record," *Science-Fiction Times* [fanzine], No. 275 (second July 1957 issue): 5.

Tuck.

INDEX SOURCES: MIT; Tuck.

REPRINT SOURCES: None known.

LOCATION SOURCES: M.I.T. Science Fiction Library.

Publication History

TITLE: *Amazing Stories Science Fiction Novel.*

VOLUME DATA: No volume or date printed in issue. Copyright is 1957, and the only issue appeared on the newsstands in June. Planned schedule was quarterly. Total run: 1 issue.

PUBLISHER: Ziff-Davis Publishing Co., New York.

EDITOR: Paul W. Fairman (not credited in magazine).

FORMAT: Digest, 128pp.

PRICE: 35¢.

Joe Sanders

AMERICAN FICTION

A British pocketbook series (1944–1946) that was as much anthologies as magazines. A few associated items could be regarded as magazines and are given separate entries here. See STRANGE LOVE STORIES, STRANGE TALES and THRILLING STORIES.

AMERICAN SCIENCE FICTION [MAGAZINE]

This series, published in Australia from 1952 to 1955, was a curious anomaly and qualifies more as a monthly anthology series than a magazine. A thirty-two page digest-sized booklet, it usually contained two or three short stories, but the cover only announced the first. The series title appeared only in small print on the cover, and even though after the first twenty-four issues it added "Magazine" to the title, there was never a date, number, contents page or any other usual feature of a magazine. Yet, the series did appear on a regular monthly schedule, and the back cover announcement of the forthcoming title often added "Next

Month." The publishers acquired book, not serial, rights for Australian printing, and as they purchased stories that had already been selected from the original American magazines for subsequent book publication this helped keep the quality high. The package was enhanced by the covers, mostly the work of Stanley Pitt.

Stories selected included "The Man Who Sold the Moon" by Robert A. Heinlein (July 1952), "The Thing from Another World" (the film retitle of "Who Goes There?") by John W. Campbell (September 1952), "The Monster" by Nelson S. Bond (January 1953), "There Shall Be Darkness" by C. L. Moore (April 1954) and "Common Time" by James Blish (March 1955).

ASF had a later companion, *Selected Science Fiction*,* but shortly after its appearance both publications ended abruptly, probably through their failure to compete with the British imported magazines.

Information Sources

BIBLIOGRAPHY:
Nicholls. *Encyclopedia*.
Tuck.
INDEX SOURCES: ASFI; Tuck.
REPRINT SOURCES: None known.
LOCATION SOURCES: Futurian Society of Sydney Library; M.I.T. Science Fiction
    Library.

Publication History

TITLE: *American Science Fiction*, May 1952–April 1954. Retitled *American Science
    Fiction Magazine*, May 1954–September 1955.
VOLUME DATA: Unnumbered and undated. Monthly from May 1952 to September
    1955. Total run: 41 issues.
PUBLISHER: Malian Press, Sydney.
EDITOR: Not identified.
FORMAT: Digest (saddle-stapled), 32pp.
PRICE: First three issues, 8d.; thereafter 9d.

Graham Stone/Mike Ashley

ANALOG SCIENCE FICTION/SCIENCE FACT

Known for much of its life as *Astounding* (or *ASF*), *Analog* was the leading science fiction magazine for nearly thirty years and today remains one of the genre's quality publications. Speculative science and the literary values of popular entertainment fiction have regularly found a congenial home in its pages. Its longest tenured editor, John W. Campbell, Jr., was SF's single most influential force throughout his career. His views of the relationship between science and technology and society and the larger universe provide important insights into the American response to the technologically pervaded modern world. *ASF*'s prominence in the field and its success have continued through four separate publishers but only five editors since the first issue appeared in 1930. It is nearly sixty years old, and it still makes a profit by selling fiction to an audience rather than by selling an audience to advertisers.

ASF's history well illustrates the role of economics in the publishing business and also the rare example of art and commerce working together to produce both a quality product and a profit.[1] The resources of publishing chains and their access to mass distribution channels enabled *ASF* to survive both the Depression and the transformation of the publishing industry after World War II, but the commercial imperatives of those publishers also played a role in raising literary standards in the field. Their ability to pay top-scale rates swiftly and *regularly* helped the editors get the kind of submissions they wanted. Their administrative services allowed Campbell in particular to give the authors and stories the devoted personal attention which kept the magazine a leader for so long.[2]

I. The Clayton Years

ASF was founded in 1929 by Clayton Publishing Company; its first issue was dated January 1930. Clayton paid above-scale rates, offsetting higher editorial labor costs by ruthlessly minimizing production costs. The first editor, Harry Bates, was not a science fiction enthusiast, and had no experience in the field. As an adventure professional, he sought to set ordinary adventure stories against an alien background, an editorial strategy that did not earn *ASF* much respect from the fledgling fan community. However, the magazine did find an audience among other readers, and also managed to begin attracting readers from the Hugo Gernsback magazines (*Amazing Stories*,* and later, *Science Wonder Stories* [*Wonder Stories**]). Bates himself apparently warmed to the genre, and he began to write some of *ASF*'s stories himself, as well as in collaboration with his assistant editor, Desmond Hall. The best known of these stories were a series of thrillers featuring Hawk Carse, a stereotypical interplanetary sheriff pursuing an equally stereotyped oriental villain drawn after Sax Rohmer's Fu Manchu.[3] Later, on his own, Bates wrote "Farewell to the Master" (October 1940), which was transformed into the Michael Rennie film, *The Day the Earth Stood Still*.

ASF's first cover would become a genre stereotype on its own, a malevolent monster fighting a hero defending a frightened young woman. The inaugural story titles say a lot about the tenor of Bates' early efforts: the cover story, "The Beetle Horde," "The Cave of Horror," and "Phantoms of Reality." Despite the generally unrespected nature of the stories in the Clayton *ASF*, they included works by Murray Leinster, Ray Cummings, Arthur J. Burks, Donald Wandrei, and Jack Williamson.

What Bates published in the Clayton *ASF* was in the long run crucial to SF's development. Pulp adventures were not literary masterpieces, but they did have their standards—basic literacy, good plotting, and action interrupted as little as possible by long soliloquies on science or philosophy—and it was these standards that Bates brought to science fiction through *ASF*.

Clayton paid two cents per word on acceptance, premium pay as well as fast and regular—as long as he stayed in business. During the Depression, that proved to be impossible. Unwilling to lower labor costs by reducing rates, Clayton reverted to the standard practice of payment on publication, but it was too late. The Clayton *ASF* ceased in March 1933. As in the case of the Gernsback bankruptcy, publishing economics, not the content of the magazine, were most responsible for the failure.[4]

II. The Tremaine Years

ASF was acquired by Street and Smith Publications in mid-1933, and published its first issue under the new ownership in October. One of the largest and oldest of the pulp magazine publishers, and a pioneer in the production of specialized genre magazines, Street and Smith was among the premier mythmakers in American popular culture, publishers of Ned Buntline's Buffalo Bill Cody stories.[5] The firm offered all of the chain publishing advantages Clayton had, but on a far larger scale. As at Clayton, *ASF* was given to editors whose training and priorities were rooted in popular fiction rather than in science fiction enthusiasm.

The early years of the Street and Smith *ASF* were crucial to its later success under John Campbell, and as early as 1934-1935 it was beginning to be recognized as the most exciting of the science fiction magazines.[6] *ASF*'s indexer, Mike Ashley, attributes much of the credit to Desmond Hall. Hall worked under the direction of F. Orlin Tremaine, Street and Smith's chief editor and the man to whom *ASF*'s success in these years is usually credited. Hall certainly had a greater influence than is generally recognized.

One of the key elements in *ASF*'s escalating reputation was its publication of E. E. Smith's "The Skylark of Valeron" (beginning August 1934); in Smith *ASF* had acquired the leading science fiction writer of the period, and it was Hall who approached the author about the series.[7] Ashley also points to Jack Williamson's recollection of working primarily with Hall, along with a most provocative interview with H. L. Gold, who sold his first stories to *ASF* and whose recollection is that in the best years of the pre-Campbell magazine Hall was its real editor.[8]

While the editorial policies in the early Street and Smith years were built on a foundation of traditional adventure, they were soon adorned with a key innovation, the "thought-variant" story. This was a story propelled primarily by the interest generated by a novel speculative concept (as opposed to a technological device, as in a Gernsbackian story), extrapolated from existing scientific knowledge or theory. The first thought-variant, Nat Schachner's "Ancestral Voices" (December 1933), was essentially a political commentary. Schachner took an old paradox—the time traveler who kills an ancestor in the past and makes his own existence impossible—and turned it into social satire. When the traveler kills a barbarian sacking Rome, the traveler disappears, along with thousands of other twentieth-century people, including a deliberately drawn caricature of Adolf Hitler.

The author was able to use a commercial magazine in a period of intense racism to point out that "racial characteristics" are palpably absurd, given the degree to which genetic lines have been mixed through history. But it is also worth mentioning that most of the responses to the story commented on the merits of Schachner's logic—if the traveler never exists, how can he go back and kill his ancestor?—than with his political point. As late as 1979, Lester del Rey was taking the same critical tack.[9] As prepared as were some writers and editors for such social and political speculation, the SF community revealed a distinct preference for the intellectual games of extrapolation rather than for real issues and real lives.

These factors account for the popularity and memorability of such later thought-variants as "Colossus" (January 1934), by Donald Wandrei, with its concept of whole universes as atomic components of infinitely larger ones; "Born of the Sun" (March 1934), by Jack Williamson; "Sidewise in Time" (June 1934), by Murray Leinster; and "Old Faithful" (December, 1934), by Raymond Z. Gallun.

The Street and Smith *ASF* even made some progress in characterization and depiction of personality. In pulp fiction, the line between a strong, independent woman and a more stereotyped headstrong woman is quite fuzzy, but the women in "Born of the Sun" and in Stanley Weinbaum's "The Parasite Planet" (February 1935) are clearly on the strong, independent side. Leinster's "Sidewise in Time" is only superficially concerned with its speculative phenomenon (the interpenetration of parallel time tracks) and is really about the personality changes that an obscure mathematics professor goes through when he realizes that he can use the phenomenon to find a time track in which his lot is better than that he enjoys at home. Perhaps equally important was the degree to which the depiction of alien life was becoming more realistic and sympathetic, as in Gallun's Martian astronomer Number 774 in "Old Faithful."

In their first year, Tremaine and Hall had brought a whole new approach to science fiction, a sympathy for alien characters, and a new respect for atmosphere and mood over scientific exuberance and adventurous space heroics.[10] Veterans like Harl Vincent, Wandrei, Leinster, and Williamson participated in these developments, but Gallun and the spectacular Weinbaum led in them, along with John Campbell, under his own name and the pseudonym, Don A. Stuart. The fact that Campbell and Stuart were respectively regarded as *ASF*'s two best writers from 1935 on is itself evidence of the magazine's eclecticism. Campbell's ability to continue and expand this diversity would make the *ASF* he would later edit so memorable.

Campbell was known as an adventure writer, and his first appearance in *ASF* was supposed to be "The Mightiest Machine" (December 1934), a fit companion for Williamson's "Legion of Space" (April 1934) and E. E. Smith's "Skylark of Valeron." But *ASF* also published "Sidewise in Time" and "Old Faithful" that year, along with C. L. Moore's "Bright Illusion" (October 1934) with its unusual love story between a man and an indescribably alien female.[11] Moore's other stories of the time, which appeared in *Weird Tales*,* highlight the eclecticism, along with the *ASF* appearances of the quintessential *Weird Tales* author,

H. P. Lovecraft ("At the Mountains of Madness," February 1936; "The Shadow out of Time," June 1936). Campbell's first appearance in the magazine was not an adventure, but "Twilight" (November 1934), a piece that depended entirely on mood and that had previously been rejected by every other science fiction magazine.[12] The final element of the "Golden Age" *ASF* was soon in place too—similarly eclectic nonfiction articles from authors as diverse as German refugee rocket researcher Willy Ley and the iconoclastic (and less respectable) Charles Fort. Campbell contributed here too, with "A Study of the Solar System," eighteen articles that appeared after June 1936, and additional articles under the pseudonyms Arthur McCann and Karl Van Campen.

These were the components of the leading science fiction magazine in the field, even before Campbell began his fabled tenure. Its success was built on several factors: the highest wordage rates (an advantage Campbell would not always have); a large, solvent publisher with good access to distribution outlets and display space; an editorial team that seemed to combine general pulp experience with science fiction experience; and an editorial strategy that encompassed both adventures and more speculative stories, that provided room both for the adventurous celebration of the power of the new science and technology and for a substantially lower-key consideration of the more complex implications of scientific development. In addition, as in any good business, the transfer of power to a new generation of managers was accomplished when Campbell was brought on board, first as assistant editor replacing Hall, and later as overall editor.

III. The Campbell Years

In many ways Campbell's career embodied both the contradictory requirements of good science fiction and their resolution. He was an enthusiast for scientific and technological progress in the Gernsback mode, and he had the scientific education to back it up. His promotional zeal made Gernsback's seem pale, but he began writing for money and his earnings from science fiction saw him through the Depression. His writing became popular for its adventurous qualities, yet, under the psedonym Don A. Stuart, he would later become known for some of the best thought-variants, while still developing what passed for realism in pulp fiction.

Campbell's editorial methods were as synthetic and synergistic as they were innovative in the field. *ASF* was already SF's leading magazine before he took it over, and he himself was at least partially shaped by the magazine before he began shaping it. Having earned a reputation for adventure, he was able to develop more speculative concepts in *ASF* which did violence neither to realistic science nor to his plausible, if jaundiced, view of human nature. *ASF* also provided him with an early outlet for his argument that progress in the physical sciences would lead to developments in nonphysical sciences and ultimately to parapsychological human powers.

Campbell was hired as an assistant editor for *ASF* at Street and Smith in 1937, and he took full charge in May 1938. To the leading science fiction magazine he brought his own insatiable appetite for plausible but unorthodox speculation, his passion for technological development and lengthy, speculative editorial bull sessions, and, above all, his sense of a good science fiction story. His Gerns-backian concern for science was subordinated to his taste for a good story, a point he made explicit in an introduction to a 1951 collection of the Stuart stories: "A weak idea can be carried by a strong story." But he would also point out that a strong idea was a tempting crutch on which to carry a weak story.[13] Perhaps that realization, and the judgment that enabled Campbell to know when an idea's limits to carry a story had been reached, were the secrets of his success as an editor. Certainly the *ASF* issues that appeared between 1938 and 1945 demonstrate his eclecticism and the quality of his taste in popular fiction, while many, but far from all, of the later issues show what could happen when he allowed his speculative interests to override them.

Campbell's takeover at *ASF* coincided with new competition within the SF genre. Shortly afterwards, twelve new SF magazines joined *Amazing Stories* and *Thrilling Wonder Stories* in competition with *ASF* for the limited entertainment dimes of the pulp readership. *ASF* benefited from Street and Smith's distribution, and that distribution paid for the top-of-scale rates the writers received promptly on acceptance (although the two other top magazines could match the rates). To these competitive advantages, Campbell added his own involvement. He read all the manuscripts himself and the rejects were returned as promptly as were the checks that were Campbell's only notification of acceptance. It was worth a hard-working writer's best efforts to try to sell to him because he paid well and quickly, and was generous and helpful (if often lengthy) in both written and oral suggestions for suitable revisions.

The conflict between popular art and commerce was resolved into a successful marriage in which Campbell's taste and judgement, his technological enthusiasm, and his up-to-date education supported Street and Smith's profits while Street and Smith, having helped train Campbell as an editor, supported his policies with their profits. He would later describe his relationship with his publishers in terms of an admirable *laissez-faire*: it was his magazine as long as it made money.[14]

Campbell knew what he wanted: according to Lester del Rey, "a very human story, told from the view of a man involved in the events, and detailing his emotions and reactions, rather than being a story of a gadget." "I want reactions," the editor warned would-be contributors in the 1938 *Writers' Yearbook*, "not mere actions. Even if your character is a robot, human readers need human reactions from him."[15] In May 1941, offering Robert Heinlein's "Future History" stories and the outline of an imaginary future world in which they took place as models, Campbell noted that the realistic background gave Heinlein's stories a "lived-in" world in which conflicts inherent in the times produced the situations (and in which the author had the chance to make good use of knowledge denied the protagonists) ("History to Come," May 1941).

ASF, however, retained a considerable commitment to Gernsbackian premises; the scientific content of stories was supposed to be a reasonable extrapolation from what was then known (and Campbell had both the fertile imagination and the scientific background to help many writers do that better than they would have on their own). He insisted that "Science Fiction is written by technically-minded people, about technically-minded people, for the satisfaction of technically-minded people." When he invited new writers to submit their manuscripts to *ASF* in 1946, he expected them to come from the ranks of technicians released from war work. Although he claimed always to be open to new angles and approaches, he warned that generally only readers of science fiction could meet his standards and that technical people stood the best chances of hitting the top ("Our Monthly Contest," December 1946). He still wanted heroes in *ASF* too, "remarkable men to do remarkable things."[16]

Campbell sought balance. *ASF* would still contain wonders, but only in stories that were well plotted, motivated, characterized, and developed. Campbell's missionary temperament and the missionary impulses in Gernsbackian science fiction reinforced each other. Del Rey is quite right to point out that *ASF* was in fact attempting to cross-breed what C. P. Snow would later call "the two cultures" of science and the humanities, however limited those attempts might now seem to contemporary critics.[17]

Within the SF category, this represented the final integration of the various aspects of its split personality. This integration was later pursued by editors who were at once Campbell's competitors and former *ASF* writers, but it was first accomplished by Campbell. Like his predecessors, Campbell built on a foundation laid by others, but also like them he began to discover or develop an entirely new group of writers whose abilities he was able to organize and present in the magazine's pages. It takes nothing from his reputation to note that he was able to utilize both a generation of experienced professionals and a generation of people who had read a lot of science fiction and were just then moving to the writing of it.[18] As often as not, writers from both groups cited Campbell's policies at *ASF* for their enthusiasm and the quality of much of what they wrote.

Particularly for those readers who came to *ASF* in the years when Campbell made it more of a rigid and doctrinaire collection of favored ideas and ideological hobbyhorses, the eclecticism of the "Golden Age" magazine is striking. Heinlein's grimmest tales of technology and society could appear along with the off-the-wall and often equally mordant humor of Lewis Padgett's drunken inventor Galloway Gallegher, or alongside the violent adventures of E. E. Smith's Galactic Patrol. A prototypical fan-aspiring-to-professionalism like Isaac Asimov appeared in the same pages as the veteran confession and radio soap opera writer A. E. van Vogt; and both shared space with a newcomer like Theodore Sturgeon, a midwestern journalist like Clifford Simak, and free-lance science and history popularizers like Schachner, L. Sprague de Camp, Fletcher Pratt, and, of course,

Willy Ley. Nor should one forget L. Ron Hubbard, a veteran of the adventure pulps who established a good reputation as an *ASF* writer before founding Dianetics and its offshoot, Scientology.

The degree to which Campbell influenced the writers in his "stable" varied with each individual. Few were as unformed as Asimov, a writer to whom Campbell represented a teacher as well as a figure on the road out of the confines of his father's candy store; but many did similarly benefit from Campbell's speculations and his detailed critiques of unsuitable or marginal work. Many of the more established writers and those who lived farther away from the offices than Asimov did had more conventional writer-editor relationships, even as they recognized him as the best editor controlling the most desirable market.

The most influential of these "Campbell writers" was Robert Heinlein. Campbell did not create Heinlein, but Heinlein's writing was exactly what Campbell had in mind. He was prolific and he appeared very frequently in *ASF* and its fantasy companion, *Unknown.** His distinctive diction and narrative style marked his early maturity as a popular writer, and he was a hit with the readers too. His rise to prominence was remarkably rapid. But even the powerful influence of the Campbell-Heinlein combination did not destroy *ASF*'s variety during the "Golden Age." That was what made it a Golden Age.

Within that diversity, however, strong themes of historic and social forces ran through a great many of *ASF*'s stories. Van Vogt's "Black Destroyer" (July 1939) borrowed heavily from the bug-eyed monster tradition, although it told the story largely from the monster's point of view; but it turned not on a test of strength or of technology, but rather on a correct understanding of an historical and astronomical situation. Echoes of *Elmer Gantry* and of pulp mobs sound through Asimov's "Trends" (July 1939); the only monsters are human. Yet it too turns on a correct understanding of history and sociology. Most of what Heinlein wrote was explicitly set within a framework of "future history" heavily dependent on an elitist view of people and on the development of chemically and biologically based psychological sciences. Finally, one ought not to forget that Smith's "Lensman" or "Galactic Patrol" novels, the largest space opera of them all, were also cast in the form of a crude historical epic.

This emphasis on historical and social forces necessarily changed the nature of *ASF*'s science fiction. In Smith's early fiction, for example, a "sense of wonder" at a newfound human ability to travel throughout the cosmos is at the heart of all matters, along with a similarly awestruck celebration of the growth of human powers. The alienness of the setting or of the future was emphasized in early science fiction, even when that setting was nominally contemporary, as it was in the "Skylark" stories. A Campbell-Heinlein "lived-in" future implied the essential familiarity of even the most alien or futuristic setting; Campbell's the essential familiarity of even the most futuristic setting; Campbell's intent in pointing up Heinlein's achievement in his future history was to emphasize the degree to which people would have to cope with change in their daily lives as new and wondrous scientific discoveries were made. But a familiar base was required. Critics have noted the limitations this placed on science fiction; language, personal interaction, and elements of social and economic structure did not change as a result of technological development in science fiction as they do in reality. However, at the price of a loss in the traditional sense of wonder, *ASF* had made possible a link between technological development and the history which its readers and writers would make in their lifetimes. Nevertheless, this should not be overestimated. The end product of *ASF*'s development prior to the explosion of the atomic bomb was a popular category fiction, no more. While the genre's potential had been expanded, most of it was still unrealized.

The specific theories of history that appeared were most often variations on technological determinism limited primarily by human irrationality. Science and its fruits were the principal motive forces in human history except when overridden or defeated by emotionalism, which was defined as irrational. Human beings reached their full potential only while attempting to use reason and science to master their environment. In this intellectual environment, nuclear energy played a dual role, as the most powerful of technologies and as a symbol of the great power people could control—a power great enough to overwhelm the constraints and requirements of all social, political, and economic systems. At best, *ASF* writers wrote, the development of technology would, if permitted, usher in a rich material utopia in which science and reason would triumph over emotion and maintain a dominant (or at least significant) role in the making of social decisions. At the same time, stories paid at least lip service to conventional American political and social virtues such as simple patriotism, civil equality, free enterprise entrepreneurship, freedom of speech, press, and inquiry, and the separation of church and state.

The problem was complex; these were often contradictory values to hold. The first decade of Campbell's tenure at *ASF* saw the development of several extraordinary technologies which would challenge the staying power of the traditional virtues. SF art was anticipating life, but SF writers had only the vaguest foreknowledge of how right they were. When that became apparent, their uncritical acceptance of traditional social values left them largely stripped of intellectual tools to cope with the changes they had anticipated. The violence of at least one science fiction writer's reaction to this social transformation demonstrated just how ambivalent American reaction to the future could be. "Machines," says L. Ron Hubbard's hero in "Final Blackout" (April–June 1940), "only make unemployment and, ultimately, politicians out of otherwise sensible men. . . . When each man does his best with his materials at hand, he is proud of his work and is happy with his life. Hatred only rises when some agency destroys those things of which we are most proud—our crafts, our traditions, our faith in man." It was an astonishing passage to appear in *ASF*, a critique of virtually every assumption common to science fiction.

Throughout the Golden Age, *ASF* showed a marked distaste for the large and complex institutions and politics that had developed along with high technology. Increasingly, these institutions were seen as obsolete holdovers from a society rendered irrelevant by modern science. Two of Heinlein's most important stories, "Blowups Happen" (September 1940) and "Solution Unsatisfactory" (May 1941), make the point most explicitly. In both, corporate and political institutions are incompetent to manage world-threatening crises brought on by the development of nuclear power. Both comprise an engineer's critique of the public office and corporate boardroom, and point toward a world in which scientists and technicians make social decisions. Nuclear energy, the most significant of science fiction's new technologies, provided most of the opportunities for both this critique and the suggested alternatives. In addition to the Heinlein stories, Clifford Simak's "Lobby" (April 1944) specifically advanced the proposition that the development of cheap commercial nuclear power would create conditions under which a real world government could grow, run by scientists educated for rule, as doctors and engineers are trained for their technical specialties.

Enough of this was directed at the corporations to seem liberal in the political context of the day; the economic concerns of business generally were treated as simply one special case in the series of parochial, emotional, and irrational obstacles people could be expected to place in the way of progress—with executives' concern for profits seen as either cupidity or senseless conservatism. Economics was considered to be as irrational as religious fanaticism. But as much of the same critique was directed at the institutions of political democracy in ways that seem quite authoritarian, despite their sources in the stories of writers whose expressed politics ran across the usual American spectrum.

ASF published some depressing examples of the genre's distrust of democratic politics during the Golden Age. Heinlein pays lip service to American traditions, but throughout his early "future history" stories runs the thread of human irrationality interfering with technological progress and otherwise mucking up life for the rational minority. Isaac Asimov, unlike Heinlein in age, social background, education, and political direction, made the theme of irrational popular religious opposition to scientific research and intellectual freedom the central focus of "Trends," his first *ASF* story. In the "Foundation" stories, he developed the proposition that from the ashes of a Galactic Empire would emerge a democratic-capitalist state ostensibly at the core of a second Empire but in truth secretly dominated by a "Second Foundation" which guides and protects it in a highly paternalistic fashion ("... And Now You Don't," November 1949–January 1950). Not only must psychological sciences be brought to the aid of the physical sciences in governing the universe, but the universe's people must also be secretly and decisively "aided" in living happier and more prosperous lives.

The relationship which this last convention bears to the general imagery of science and scientists is curious. Despite the greater awareness of the industrial context of twentieth-century science which *ASF* displayed under Campbell, and of the virtues of organized research and development over solitary thinking noted by Brian Aldiss, most of *ASF*'s scientists during the World War II years were either individuals or members of extremely small groups held together by interpersonal loyalty.[19] Oddly enough, E. E. Smith drew one of the few pictures of an organized conference of scientists to appear while the Manhattan Project was operating, in an episode of "Gray Lensman" (October 1939–February 1940). The picture is neither complimentary nor democratic, though. The scientists are so brilliant as to be unstable, and they are unable to work together toward a common goal without the tactful leadership of soldiers. Willy Ley's articles on German research did nothing to erase such impressions; Ley's experiences with the German Rocket Society gave him more than sufficient cause to distrust the bureaucratization of science ("The End of the Rocket Society," August 1943; "V-2: Rocket Cargo Ship," May 1945; "Pseudoscience in Naziland," May 1947).

If organized science had acquired negative connotations, positive connotations still applied to individual scientists, who were often portrayed as eccentric individualists. Their eccentricities ranged from the crusty cynicism of Heinlein's older heroes and Asimov's Ebling Mis in "The Mule" (November 1945) to the disarming naivete of younger, more casually and intuitively inventive men such as Heinlein's Andrew Jackson Libby ("Misfit," November 1939; "Methuselah's Children," July-September 1941), the drunken inventor Gallegher in Padgett's "The Proud Robot" (October 1943), or Anthony Boucher's clear-headed robot mechanic Doug Quimby in "Q.U.R." (March 1943). Their scientific accomplishments are also more the results of some inherent special talents than of any education or intellectual discipline: Libby is a lightning calculator, Quimby can "see things straight," and Gallegher is only a brilliant inventor when his subconscious is released while he is drunk. Lester del Rey introduced a corollary: the scientist either partially trained, or trained in a seemingly irrelevant discipline who can draw on intuition, unorthodox approaches or eccentric personal experience to solve a problem (in "Nerves," September 1942). While not forgetting that these scientists appear in good stories, one notes that the imagery makes of scientists a separate, gifted elite apart from the rest of humanity, a separation that cannot be bridged by education or other traditional American tools of social mobility.

This perceived separation between scientists and humanity at large had appeared in *ASF* for some time, but it became extraordinarily explicit in the shadow of Hiroshima and Nagasaki. At its gloomiest, the situation might lead to the violent persecution of scientists and intellectuals, as it does in Pendleton Banks' "Turning Point" (March 1947), where fugitive technicians are burned to death by an ignorant mob straight out of the most clichéd monster movies. The theme was carried to a world-wearily cynical political conclusion by L. Ron Hubbard in "The End Is Not Yet" (August–October 1947). In that story, apparently democratic scientists oppose an established order controlled by villainous international businessmen from a secret community hidden in North Africa's Atlas Mountains, much as Los Alamos had been hidden in New Mexico. They defeat their enemies only to realize that their rule can be little different from that of their corrupt and tyrannical predecessors. Their technological devices will only make it more efficient. Realizing this, the most idealistic of the survivors leave civilization entirely, heading for China, where bitter revolution was then actually in progress, "to sing songs of Kubla Khan"!

Thus, the convention of the solitary scientist led to the seemingly contradictory convention of the paternalistic technocratic elite, an anachronistic individualism to acceptance of the most authoritarian of political systems, and forced those holding to both the rationalism of science and to broadly defined democratic values to hope for nothing more than escape to frontier perceived as unpopulated or undeveloped—where the drama would most likely simply recur. Thus was history not only cyclical, moving in response to a conflict between scientific reason and popular irrationality, but the concept of a rational elite also bred a sense of vulnerability. History was also increasingly the working out of a conspiracy, either one of the elite's or one of their enemies'.

This imagery of science and its accompanying political ideology developed in an *ASF* increasingly preoccupied with real and quite immediate struggles: the integration of nuclear power into the structure of American society and the emerging Cold War with the Soviet Union. The questions were not new: the ample treatment science fiction writers had given atomic energy before it really existed contributed to the brief spell of semi-respectability SF achieved following the news from Hiroshima and Nagasaki (and nearly all the serious consideration of nuclear matters had been in *ASF*); but the actual development of nuclear power gave *AFS*'s treatment of the subject some urgency.

Nuclear power had appeared in nearly all of *ASF*'s elements, stories, articles, editorials, and letters-to-the-editor. Campbell's factual articles for the magazine had continued after he became editor and by the postwar period had become a regular feature from many contributors: Campbell, Ley, de Camp, and, in the 1950s, Isaac Asimov. The editor had also appropriated the pages previously reserved for promotional blurbs and transformed them into his own platform for commentary on technology and the world at large. Nuclear power was among the first issues he addressed. He took over in May 1938. The following month he was able to note that "the discoverer of the secret of atomic power is alive on Earth today. His papers and researches are appearing regularly; his name is known. But the exact handling of the principles he's discovered—not even he knows now" ("The Editor's Page," June 1938).

In succeeding editorials, Campbell discussed prospective uses for nuclear energy in industry, in radiation medicine, and in the generation of electricity. He was not as sanguine about technology's ability to transform the world as Simak would be later in "Lobby," however. The month following his acknowledgment of Otto Hahn and Enrico Fermi, Campbell noted that many great inventions were never fully developed because they were too complicated, or because they involved hidden costs that made the older technologies more economical. Rarely, he suggested, had practical inventions actually been suppressed by special interests. Later still, he would caution that even atomic energy would have to be "worked into the scheme of things gradually," as it was developed; and he pointed out that nuclear energy could not substitute for coal in some uses involving the chemical composition of the mineral, a need for easy handling, and/or low cost ("Atomic Power vs. Coal," August 1941). In November 1942, he even wrote that there was a need to develop direct applications of solar energy to generate electricity, suggesting that, due largely to cost factors, there was really no need for atomic power plants on Earth. These commentaries may surprise the magazine's more recent readers, for Campbell's attitude later changed drastically.

All these uses for atomic energy were civilian and peaceful. Military uses elicited rather different reactions, largely because Campbell and at least one of his writers, Heinlein, recognized that the enormously greater power released by nuclear weapons would change warfare in kind as well as in degree. Under the pseudonym Anson MacDonald, Heinlein wrote "Solution Unsatisfactory" (May 1941), in which the development of nuclear weapons (in this view, radioactive dust which contaminates all it touches when dropped) creates a situation in which every advanced industrial nation can attack every other, while no adequate defense can be developed. The only conceivable result is immediate, constant warfare and mass destruction until the industrial capacity of all nations has been reduced below the level that can support weapons manufacture. The only alternative is an International Peace Patrol armed with the dust and under the jurisdiction of a worldwide American military dictatorship which keeps all countries (including the United States) in line. The social structures within which nuclear weapons are developed are made obsolete by its power.

This last was another aspect of science fiction's view of nuclear energy; it was a literary metaphor for the enormous power at the command of human intelligence and the scientific method.[20] Throughout the early 1940s, perhaps most explicitly in Isaac Asimov's early "Foundation" stories, "Bridle and Saddle" (June 1942) and "The Big and the Little" (August 1944), possession of atomic power is presented as the touchstone of modernity and technological progress. Along with space flight, nuclear energy was considered a milestone in human evolution. But such evolutionary steps put both individuals and the species at risk. In "Atomic Age" (November 1945), his first post-Hiroshima editorial, Campbell proclaimed that the atomic bomb meant "the death of an era, and the death of a cultural pattern based on a balance of military power controlled exclusively by big and wealthy nations. Atomic war is as suicidal as a duel between two men armed with flame throwers in a vestibule. Neither party can have the slightest hope of surviving."

The entire situation might have been the concept for a thought-variant story: what would happen if nuclear weapons were unexpectedly developed in an international society that was unprepared to cope with their power? Of course, one of the things that happened was that science fiction writers wrote "atomic doom" stories depicting the consequences of nuclear war. These dominated other SF magazines more than they did *ASF*. Campbell did publish some, most notably "Tomorrow's Children" (March 1947), by F. N. Waldrop and Poul Anderson. Brian Aldiss is able to comment on the blackness of *ASF*'s outlook in these years, and the pain with which writers and fans digested the implications of a real atomic bomb and its relationship to all the pre-Hiroshima power fantasies.[21] However, most of the nuclear war stories in *ASF* dealt with ways in which technology might evade a nuclear war, since the roots of conflict were assumed to be part of human nature and as such an irrational obstacle to the progress which rational technology ought to bring. Some of these stories dealt with alternative technologies obviating for neutralizing atomic bombs: George O. Smith's "The Answer" (February 1947) and Poul Anderson's "The Perfect Weapon" (February 1950), for example. Others were concerned with how the United Nations or some other world organization, often disturbingly authoritarian, could use a technology of its own to limit the military ambitions of nuclear-armed nations, as in Arthur Leo Zagat's "Slaves of the Lamp" (August 1946).

Science fiction responses to the bomb took other directions as well. In the 1940s, *ASF* reflected the fad that had grown up around Count Alfred Korzybski and his book *Science and Sanity* in the fan community. Among the most interested in the Count's ideas was A. E. van Vogt, who wrote his interest in Semantics and Korzybski's concept of "non-Aristotelian logic" into "The World of Null-A" (August–October 1945). The story was written and scheduled for publication before the explosion of the atomic bomb, but after *ASF*'s three-month lead-time, it appeared in the August 1945 issue, which went out to subscribers two weeks before the news from Hiroshima.

Prophetic and timely in a way he could not entirely have anticipated, Campbell's introduction to the story, in his editorial "Science to Come," argued the necessity of research into "mental science," on grounds that must have been chilling in the contemporary context:

> I'm fairly well convinced that the race is fairly indestructible, and will survive any next war. But our present culture is finished.
>
> Either it will learn something about how men live and think and react, so it can be discarded in favor of a cultural system that can prevent warfare, or the next gross failure on its part will produce a war in which the ancient cry of "Wolf! Wolf!" will not be a false alarm—they really will have the weapon that can't be stopped.

Its coincidental appearance alongside the headlines gave van Vogt's story additional impact. Within it, lessons learned through the use of Semantics and null-A logic give individuals enormous personal powers and permit them to group together in communities sufficiently rational and self-disciplined to dispense with conventional social organizations and relationships. One fan actually suggested to Campbell that a series by van Vogt on Semantics was the only alternative to nuclear war or worldwide psychoanalysis.[22]

The concept permitted *ASF* writers to construct scenarios in which the power of nuclear physics forced the creation of new psychological disciplines, which in turn made possible anarchic societies poles removed from the centralized authoritarianism in Zagat or Asimov. Significantly, this happy state would later be seen, as by Heinlein in *Time Enough for Love* (New York: G. P. Putnam's, 1973), as attainable only by a small, hereditary, and/or specially trained elite. In his own way, Hubbard would advance a similar utopian vision as one consequence of the widespread adoption of Dianetics.[23]

ASF also published stories set in a more immediate future which routinely dealt with nuclear weapons in contemporary fashion. Chandler Davis, for example, wrote cautionary tales of the difficulties of civil defense and crisis management under the shadow of nuclear war like "The Nightmare" (May 1946). Theodore Sturgeon, at first enthusiastic about the status the bomb brought to the field, wrote into "Memorial" (April 1946; the first bomb story to appear after Hiroshima) a caustic assessment of the way he and his colleagues had handled nuclear matters:

> All . . . were quite aware of the terrible potentialities of nuclear energy. Practically all . . . were scared silly of the whole idea. They were afraid for humanity, but they themselves were not really afraid, except in a delicious drawing room sort of way, because they couldn't conceive of this Buck Rogers event happening to anything but posterity.

And then Sturgeon wrote his most important story: "Thunder and Roses" (November 1947).

Singular in his denunciation of nuclear retaliation as immoral, Sturgeon pointed out that while one nuclear strike might destroy a country, or even a hemisphere, retaliatory strikes could exterminate all life on Earth. Chandler Davis wrote of this notably influential story's impact on him, and of his continuing commitment to its moral premises, in 1976:

> When I look back on the formation of my ideas on nuclear deterrence, from SOLUTION UNSATISFACTORY to ON THERMONUCLEAR WAR, a story which stands out is THUNDER AND ROSES. . . . it remains the sharpest statement of the thesis that policy ought never to be founded on threats of nuclear retaliation because that retaliation would always be wrong. A whole generation of "strategy theorists" would be making an advance in their theory if they would throw out their treatises on mutual deterrence and read THUNDER AND ROSES.[24]

As a piece of literary craftsmanship, the story also represents a crucial transition in science fiction writing. Its style and structure are pulp stock, as are its characters, but its use of stereotype is useful. Like the thought-variants, the concept is important. Real characters would get in the way. Here stereotyping helps universalize the situation. Of course the situation is in a way trite—a sergeant's infatuation with a television sex symbol—but it exists in a very urgent context. The emotions, so often seen as irrational obstacles to human progress in science fiction, are here shown as providing a superior vision of reality. At the very least the sentimental variety of emotion and love had found a legitimate place in *ASF*, although it was seldom followed up.

The explosion of the atomic bomb had a peculiar effect on science fiction. On the one hand, it established science fiction in the public eye as something more realistic than Buffalo Bill fantasies in technological dress, and it contributed to a postwar category publishing boom that lasted until the middle 1950s. On the other hand, many writers and fans became convinced that their perceptions of human irrationality and hostility to reason had been far too accurate.

ASF's editorials now began speculating about contemporary development, more often than not complaining about the directions that development was taking. A few years later, those editorials became the magazine's most distinctive feature. It is all too easy to underestimate the literary quality of *ASF* from 1950 to 1965, but it is not possible to fully understand the magazine in those years without understanding its editorials and the ways in which the audience responded to them as well as the stories.

Many of the points Campbell raised in his editorials from the early atomic age are now common property; many of the dilemmas he first saw are now the stuff of congressional debate and international negotiation. Most prescient of these was the futility of widespread security systems in preserving the American nuclear monopoly: "Nature is a blabbermouth," he would remind anyone who would listen. He knew too that security would neither keep the USSR from developing its own arsenal nor prevent nuclear proliferation to myriad smaller countries.

But *ASF* and Campbell were not pioneers of the anti-nuclear movement. Quite the contrary. In fact, when Campbell reported on the 1948 opening of the Brookhaven National Laboratories, he celebrated this first large civilian nuclear research facility, his relief at the complexity and obvious expense involved readily apparent ("Brookhaven Sketches," July 1949). Economics might provide temporary safety where science and technology and police could not, and the Bomb might remain in what he considered the relatively responsible hands of the United States.

In some ways, Campbell was anticipating Dwight Eisenhower's "Atoms for Peace" proposals for civilian nuclear industrial development. But, for all his fear of nuclear proliferation, he missed the link of the nuclear fuel cycle which ties military and civilian uses to each other permanently, and like most nuclear enthusiasts of his generation never paid much attention to the problem of waste disposal. Generally, he remained an uncritical celebrant of nuclear reactors.

The shock of the military and governmental involvement in science revealed by the Manhattan Project was one cause of *ASF*'s transition away from the characteristics of the Golden Age. The magazine now published a plethora of overtly didactic stories dealing with nuclear weapons and the aftermath of their use. The writers' preferences for the rational control of technology were taking a beating right after the war, with the Truman administration sponsoring a projected Atomic Energy Act which would give the military virtually full control of all nuclear matters. Unauthorized disclosure of information which had been part of ordinary scientific discourse would carry the death penalty. The proposed legislation set off a storm of protest in *ASF*'s editorial and letter columns.

In the end, Congress established a civilian Atomic Energy Commission, but Campbell assaulted it, as he had attacked the original proposal, for its stringent security provisions, which he believed would strangle research ("Secrecy and Death," June 1946; "Spanish Atoms," September 1946; "The Lead Curtain," October 1946).

ASF's concern was more for the nature of American control mechanisms than for the issues of international war and control. The perceived irrationality of the congressional response to the issue of nuclear energy had reinforced well-entrenched attitudes about popular politics which were inextricably bound up with a dislike of bureaucratic scientific establishments. Military security and the free exchange of scientific ideas were the specific issues, but the obviousness and the pervasiveness of security bureaucracies provided a focus of the *ASF* readership's deeply held distrust of bureaucratic structures in general.

Campbell suggested that excessive security could diminish military preparedness if bureaucratization created less than optimum working conditions for scientists. Not even the intensification of the Cold War could change Campbell's mind, or the minds of writers and readers who ordinarily disagreed with him on other political and social issues. Paradoxically, the development of science fiction's most cherished fantasies (nuclear weapons and large rockets) had reinforced the development of the detested structures which regulated, guarded, financed, and, worst of all, organized science and technology, and *ASF*'s writers made clear their resentment of that.[25]

One must remember that this reaction against bureaucracy was appearing in a magazine whose readership was increasingly employed in such structures. Readership surveys published by Campbell in 1949 and 1958 indicate that a relatively large number of readers were employed in scientific or technological fields and that an even higher proportion of readers had scientific education. Their earnings were already higher than the American average and their incomes would rise through the 1950s and 1960s at a faster rate than the American average.[26] Nevertheless, *ASF*'s editorial pages and stories continuously assaulted the concept of big bureaucracy in every field throughout the remainder of Campbell's life.

This paradox was particularly mirrored in Campbell's editorials. His distaste for bureaucracy did not keep him from referring repeatedly to his friendships with the employees of the Bell Labs located near his New Jersey home or from pointing with pride to their portentous work in semi-conductors and their development of the transistor and other solid state electronic components. Earlier,

Heinlein had been able to see that some of the same forces influenced the conduct of both business and government bureaucracies. But even he considered government and academic bureaucracies more rigid and less far-sighted than business, even while he suggested that the inspired entrepreneur was apt to be the most far-sighted of all.

Of course, Heinlein's elitism is reflected in the number of his heroes who are conspirators, even within nominally democratic politics, as in "Double Star" (February–March 1956). The engineers' critique of the boardroom increasingly became a critique of the government agency and popular democracy, an assault on the academic department, and the links of grant mechanisms between agencies, departments, and the public support for research. In Campbell's editorials, this critique became increasingly shrill and alienated, and an intellectual highway to the political authoritarianism which marked his last writing, despite his fundamentally anti-authoritarian temperament and inclinations.

Campbell wanted *ASF* to be considered what today would be called a futurological magazine, but he was never able to sell that idea to his advertisers. Even when his efforts were perfectly orthodox, like changing the magazine's size, it didn't work out. Many of the science articles in *ASF* during the 1950s were soundly written by Isaac Asimov, but Campbell's hobbyhorses are remembered and the kudos for publishing Asimov's early science popularizations lost. Perhaps it was because Campbell integrated the unorthodox articles with the magazine's fiction far more thoroughly than he did the more respectable ideas.

For example, G. Harry Stine, an engineer, contributed both stories and articles that supported or illustrated Campbell's theses—under his own name or the pseudonym Lee Correy. Although one of his early stories, "Galactic Gadgeteers" (May 1951), possibly alienated at least one reader from *ASF* (Brian Aldiss refers to its glib superficiality), he did produce a series of contemporary stories showing human situations in which very real rocket experimenters might find themselves ("Pioneer," August 1953; "Design Flaw," February 1955; and "Test Stand," March 1955).[27] In 1960, he wrote an article on amateur rocketry, pointing to the honorable heritage it shared with the early rocket societies and providing tips on making it safe and respectable in the community ("Demon in a Bottle," April 1960). But then, a year later, he wrote a series of articles in conjunction with Campbell's promotion of the so-called Dean Drive (on which he would eventually work as a development engineer) whose titles reflect some of Campbell's 1950s themes: "Time for Tom Swift" (January 1961), "Progress Report: Super V-2 Program" (a critical look at the development of the Saturn V rocket for the Apollo program, February 1961), and (most provocatively) "Science Fiction Is Too Conservative" (May 1961).

This last title is the tip-off. Campbell hankered for establishment respectability without losing his role as SF's goad into the future. That objective eluded him, despite the elimination of the breathless old pulp title, *Astounding*, in October 1960. *ASF*'s science articles were not cited in any more than informal discussions. The failed attempt did give the magazine some attributes of an underground forum without status or respectability. But this underground network of *ASF* readers was thoroughly middle-class and tied into the existing order of things for their manifest economic advantages. If Campbell's interpretation of their role as "decision-influencing executives" was even partially correct, they were helping to build the establishments *ASF* disliked so much, those structures, depersonalized and substituting advanced technology for people, that "made the modern world modern."[28]

The demography of the *ASF* readership has been well established since the end of World War II, and the bulk of it falls into a curious new social class: managerial in job function and identification, upper-middle in terms of income and social status, thoroughly proletarian in economic dependence on wages.[29] Recent research in the social history of industrial technology documents the ways in which scientific, technical, and research people eventually found their social status transformed from independent professional to bureaucratic employee in a fashion not altogether different from that which had transformed the world of the mechanic.[30] If *ASF*'s pages are any guide, they didn't like it, regarded it as destructive, and sought to understand and explain it in terms they could understand. It could sometimes be a very political magazine: a right-wing magazine.

As previously, the perceived conflict between the forces of reason and those of emotion constituted history's prime mover, inhibiting technology's ability to develop and move the human race forward. Identifying this inhibition with government, bureaucracy, and scientific establishmentarianism, Campbell gradually moved into an intellectual thicket which he, and many of the writers who wrote to his hobbyhorses, attempted without success to domesticate. If the development of established orthodoxy in science had permanently limited the creative possibilities of technology, how could unorthodox technologies be developed free of those limitations, and how could a legitimate but unorthodox science be differentiated from either magic or simple charlatanry? Many of the enthusiasms which Campbell made notorious in the last twenty years of his tenure were related to this problem and were thoroughly enmeshed in its tangles. Generally, the solutions proposed propelled both Campbell and *ASF*'s fiction further and faster toward an anti-democratic elitism.

The problem developed progressively. With standards of professionalism tied so thoroughly to their place in organizations, legitimate though unorthodox scientists were becoming harder to identify and intellectual standards by which to gauge the value of their work less objective. Eventually, even in *ASF*, the ability of humans to solve the problem without the intervention of some *deus ex machina* came increasingly into question. In the process, the scientific method of hypothesis and experiment itself almost disappeared from view.

For example, in May 1947, T. L. Sherred's "E for Effort" describes the invention of a time viewer by a technician with impeccable, if limited, conventional credentials who utilizes a principle ignored by more established scientists for whom he has previously worked as a technician. Stine's "Galactic Gadgeteers" is about an obsolete starship with an undisciplined crew which is actually a secret research facility. None of the men know it, but in throwing highly intelligent and unorthodox people against a powerful enemy in an inadequate vessel, the high command expects them to come up with new and unpredictable weapons which can then be deployed throughout the fleet. The system works *because* the men are unorthodox and work in an unstructured research environment under conditions that make success a very immediate and personal necessity. But Aldiss' assessment of the story is accurate; it is glib. Inspiration and accident play a larger part in the new developments than does organized research or even tinkering. Stine struck a further blow against orthodox specialization in "Amateur" (February 1954), which presents a gifted amateur as explicitly more useful in the long run than a specialized professional.

Perhaps the most explicit statement of *ASF*'s perspective on the unorthodox scientist was "The Great Gray Plague" (February 1962), by Raymond F. Jones. Here, unorthodox science is portrayed in several modes successively: a creative physicist who simply lacks a Ph.D., an untutored farmer who has apparently invented an operating telepathic communications device, and, finally, a government bureaucrat who, having seen the light, rewrites the establishment's criteria for research grants. But there was an extra twist at the end: almost imperceptibly over the years, *ASF*'s portrayal of appropriate unorthodox science had changed from one of an organized, labored investigation to one of appreciation of an intuitive vision. And the results of such visions are not replicable, nor do they respect equal opportunity.

Campbell and *ASF* writers never explicitly rejected the experimental method; in fact, it was continuously offered as a method preferred to theorization. Campbell defended each of his notorious enthusiasms with its own record of accomplishment in defiance of academic, established theory. However, Isaac Asimov has a very revealing anecdote in his autobiography showing how Campbell was capable of fudging experimental results that did not fit his preconceived notions.[31] Campbell's defense of his outspoken belief in parapsychological powers offered the example of dowsing rods used as mine detectors in Viet Nam; but the experiments are remembered less fondly by combat veterans.[32]

These enthusiasms were never quite as absurd as their detractors remember; certainly speculation on such matters is more than legitimate in science fiction. The trouble was, as Brian Aldiss sees it, that "Campbell, convinced of the profound worth of science fiction, tried to live some of it."[33]

To most readers, this process first became apparent in 1950, when *ASF* printed L. Ron Hubbard's long article on Dianetics (May 1950). Campbell had been talking privately about Hubbard's "dabblings in amateur psychiatry" for some time.[34] Hubbard, an adventure pulpster who had moved into science fiction at the beginning of Campbell's editorship, claimed to have been doing his research while writing, before and after the war. But *ASF* had published some hoax articles, notably Asimov's "The Endochronic Properties of Resublimated Thiotimoline" (March 1948), and at first many readers took the Dianetics article for another. Not as far as Campbell was concerned!

Barry Malzberg believes that Campbell was "at least . . . co-creator" of Dianetics, but he also suggests that the editor was "unable to cut loose of his position, his prerogatives, and his science fictional cachet."[35] Campbell promoted Dianetics, editorialized about it, lectured on its behalf, and eventually broke with Hubbard, although he was never as soft a touch for a story pandering to it as he was reputed to be. In *ASF* editorials, he approached Dianetics as an example of the way in which a scientific orthodoxy in alliance with a bureaucratic establishment could smother a potentially revolutionary idea. He also placed Hubbard's ideas squarely in the tradition of adapting psychological science and technology to solve the problems created by physical science and technology. Once the "engrams" or scars of trauma in people's "reactive mind" were erased by Dianetic therapy, fully rational "clears" might make a gigantic "evolutionary breakthrough." Hubbard himself spoke of exploring the stars.[36]

Dianetics was but one of Campbell's hobbyhorses. His beliefs in parapsychology, or in a machine like the Dean Drive, would dominate the editor's thinking and *ASF*'s pages for some time, and on each occasion Campbell would tout its revolutionary potential. Then would come the awareness of the real world as demonstrated by the existence of a complicated and expensive development phase for even the most probable of these ideas. The intensity of Campbell's enthusiasms has diverted attention from this pattern, which was repeated with each of them. The editor's enthusiasm for more orthodox technologies like nuclear power and space exploration followed much the same pattern. Each episode convinced him more thoroughly than the last that American society was unprepared to consider new ideas, and that the failure was of extraordinary import to its future.

There was at the time an emerging consensus that the literary leadership in the field had passed to *Galaxy Science Fiction** and *The Magazine of Fantasy and Science Fiction.** While that is true, it would be a mistake to underestimate the merits of *ASF* fiction during the last twenty years of Campbell's life. His personal reputation within science fiction might be higher if his tenure had ended in 1950, as Malzberg suggests it should have; but despite the noticeable influx of stories that catered to Campbell's preoccupations, the accepted view of *ASF* during the fifties and sixties does an injustice to a lot of writers and to Campbell too.[37]

To be sure, there was a retreat to the more didactic side of Gernsbackian science fiction that marked the stories more closely identified with Campbell's hobbyhorses (Randall Garrett, "Gentlemen, Please Note," October 1957, and "Damned If You Don't," May 1960; Hank Dempsey, "A Matter of Timing," January 1965; Charles Harness, "The Alchemist," May 1966 [on scientific orthodoxy]; David Gordon, " . . . Or Your Money Back," September 1959 [on the Hieronymous Machine and parapsychology]; and "By Proxy," September 1960 [on the Dean Drive]). But not all of these were sterile works; Laurence

Janifer's ''Hex'' (May 1959) manages to include paternalistic welfare bureau-cracies along with parapsychology in a little chiller of a horror story.

And there were the ''hard'' science fiction writers in *ASF*, who were integrating science and literature far more effectively than ever before, with considerably less compromise of the science and with considerably more sensitivity to char-acter and even a new ear for dialogue. Harry Stubbs (writing as Hal Clement) was among the earliest of these, with ''Needle'' (May 1949) and ''Mission of Gravity'' (April–July 1953), and Poul Anderson eventually published more in *ASF* than any writer in the fifties. Frank Herbert's *Dune* was probably the best-selling science fiction novel of the sixties and early seventies and was first published in *ASF* during some of its least well regarded years (as ''Dune World,'' beginning December 1963, and ''Prophet of Dune'' [not to be confused with *Dune Messiah*, originally serialized in *Galaxy*], beginning January 1965).

This emerging mode of ''ecological science fiction,'' tied far more rigorously to contemporary scientific knowledge than anything Gernsback had published, went together with stories continuing Campbell's favored integration of the technological and adventurous concerns of a Jules Verne with the sociological and historical concerns of an H. G. Wells. Poul Anderson's ''The Man Who Counts,'' the adventures of the interplanetary entrepreneur Nicholas Van Rijn, was serialized beginning in February 1958; Gordon Dickson's ''Dorsai!'' in May 1959. Harry Harrison's ''Deathworld,'' with its exploration of the ways in which violence feeds upon itself, began in January 1960. Despite Campbell's reputation for accepting stories slanted toward his point of view, and despite the political conservatism he was increasingly expressing in his editorials, at least some of these stories were developing quite different positions. Mack Reynolds, a one-time lecturer for the Socialist Labor party, was able to publish ''Black Man's Burden'' beginning in December 1961, which was based on Reynolds' concern for the Third World and acceptance of racial equality, despite Campbell's genteel racism and America-first attitudes. Harry Harrison's attack on the CIA, and his equation of it with the Soviet KGB in ''In Our Hands, the Stars'' (December 1969–February 1970), probably appealed to Campbell for its depiction of an independent individual Israeli scientist despite the editor's thoroughly conven-tional patriotism.

Despite a residual diversity in ideas, approach, craftsmanship, and overall tone, *ASF* exhibited a considerably different tenor during the latter half of Camp-bell's editorial career. He was willing to print stilted, poorly developed, sim-plistic, and occasionally boring stories that fit his ideas. Even some of his friends recounted stories of his obsessive behavior and the way it influenced his editorial judgment. Harry Harrison, for example, has said, ''When John Campbell was talking, a lot of solemn nodding went on all round!''[38] On another occasion, with Campbell present (Harrison was giving a very favorable introduction to a Campbell speech), he would note, ''John never fights [with an author], he just wins.''[39] But Mike Ashley's research indicates that, contrary to the conventional picture of Campbell imposing his enthusiasms on the writers, there were cases where enthusiasms grew from new ideas in some of the stories.[40] The "symbiotic relationship" between Campbell and his writers, noted by Randall Garrett, was still functioning.[41]

Probably the import of the new tenor in *ASF* is best seen in the better stories which did not relate directly to the enthusiasms. For example, *ASF* stories had usually assumed that exploration of the space frontier was essential to the development of human history and that failure to travel through space was symptomatic of the decline of social life on Earth. However, the number of stories in the post-World War II *ASF* which featured that idea against a mood of sadness and failure reminiscent of Campbell's "Twilight" is quite striking: Jack Williamson's "The Equalizer" (March 1947) and Lester del Rey's "The Years Draw Nigh" (October 1951) are only two. James Blish's "Okie" or "Cities in Flight" stories (which appeared between 1953 and 1958) were set against the backdrop of economic depression and police state rule on Earth. This sort of thing is not the blackness of which Aldiss writes in reference to the post-atomic war stories, but rather a series of sad farewells to many of the genre's fondest hopes and exuberant expectations.

Aldiss notes that the field and *ASF* in particular had never been blindly celebratory of advanced technology; if technological advance had created no conflict, there would be little good science fiction at all. However, a good stiff dose of even more technology had been prescribed as a remedy.[42] Despite Campbell's enthusiasms, that prescription was missing from *ASF*'s fiction in the fifties to a surprising degree. Gone completely was a sense of control. In its place stood a new awareness of social context which, while it contributed to the emerging "hard" science fiction, also drew heavily on the anti-democratic and elitist elements that had been present in *ASF* fiction for some time.

Perhaps the story most representative of all these developments is Tom Godwin's "The Cold Equations" (August 1954). Godwin's point in this story is that people on Earth can have a great deal of unhindered, uncaring freedom, since an established society and a friendly environment shelter them from the worst consequences of their actions in a universe that is fundamentally indifferent to the concerns of human beings. On a frontier, that shelter does not exist; there is no margin for error or ignorance.

As James Gunn points out, "The Cold Equations" is a touchstone story for Campbell's science fiction.[43] The people *must* accept the conditions imposed by the laws of nature or die. No alternatives exist. It is not a matter of heroism, or chivalry, or cruelty. That is just the way things are. The rules cannot be changed, nor can any last-minute inspiration or invention prevent the only possible outcome. Two years after it was published, Campbell used it as an example of good science fiction in "Science Fiction and the Opinion of the Universe" (*Saturday Review*, May 12, 1956), an answer to "The Myth of Science Fiction," which had appeared in the same magazine in August 1955.

Campbell described the hapless pilot of the emergency craft in the story as an example of the "Universe-Directed" individual whose thinking was dominated not by tradition, inner drives, or the opinions of others, but by "the facts of the universe." Such a man is not cold-blooded or authoritarian, but the universe is, he maintained. However, students asked to comment on "The Cold Equations" almost invariably pick up the implicit condescension toward ordinary people and the impression that Godwin is quite judgmental, and simultaneously rather sexist in his use of a "dumb blonde" stereotype. They get from the text the unspoken assessment that aside from the crewman on the space frontier, people get no more than they deserve. A similarly jaundiced view of humanity appears in Mark Clifton's "What Have I Done?" (May 1952). Clifton took a hackneyed convention, the invasion of Earth by aliens who can assume human form, and turned it into an extraordinarily bitter commentary on humans' inhumanity to their own species.

ASF had been an elitist magazine ever since Campbell had begun editing it. As the years went by, however, the life of that elite was increasingly presented as dominated by sadness, alienation, condescension, and hostility: for example Campbell's editorials "The Group and the Individual" (April 1956), "The One-eyed Guide" (March 1960), "Utopian Voters" (February 1962), and many others. That syndrome accounts for a good deal of the libertarian science fiction that *ASF* published during the early fifties, at a time when few were attacking the likes of Joe McCarthy and Richard Nixon (even obliquely) except for "a few senators, Edward R. Murrow, and just about every science fiction writer in the world."[44]

Perhaps the fate of such libertarian elitism in *ASF* after McCarthy's fall from grace is indicative of what lay in store for similar contemporary liberal political thought. It is worth noting that Henry Kuttner and Algis Budrys both published on the theme of the relationship between the ordinary run of humanity and mutants with superior powers: Kuttner the "Baldy" stories of the middle forties, Budrys "Nobody Bothers Gus" (November 1955). But the Kuttner series is firmly set within communities, while Budrys has each of his individual *homos superior* isolated and reduced to social impotence. In Poul Anderson's fiercely libertarian "Sam Hall" (August 1953), an organized resistance to a computerized tyranny exists, and eventually triumphs, but only through the independent efforts of an alienated senior technician who subverts a national surveillance network and disrupts the repressive political system for essentially personal reasons. When the resistance wins, their pledges of reforms ring just true enough to create the suspicion that they will need their own resistance before too long. The cycle of Hubbard's "The End Is Not Yet" is repeated, at a higher level of literary sophistication. Once more, and even more strongly than earlier, *ASF* writers adopted the engineer's critique of economic and political society, merged it with elitist preconceptions, and denigrated the ability of ordinary people to act effectively and progressively in the making of history.

These ideas and attitudes were *ASF*'s distinguishing charcteristics as it faced new and stiff competition. Campbell was true enough to his conservative creed to respond very well to competition; the *ASF* Golden Age had coincided with a general expansion of the category magazines at the end of the thirties, and *ASF*'s original dominance had been established in competition with many other pulps. In 1949 and 1950, two new science fiction magazines of quality appeared, *The Magazine of Fantasy and Science Fiction* and *Galaxy*, which seized the literary leadership from *ASF*. *Galaxy*'s first issue was described by Isaac Asimov as "just about the best issue of any science-fiction magazine I had ever seen."[45] In the years to come, Campbell was able to see *The Magazine of Fantasy and Science Fiction* as too literary for the pulp science fiction market, but he did recognize *Galaxy* as a serious commercial challenger. It reflected different editorial tastes and priorities, but it was well-financed, and it was the first pulp in the category to pay writers three cents a word. For the first time, *ASF* had to scramble to catch up with the rates paid by another magazine, and for the first time, *ASF*'s lead in circulation was threatened. On top of this new competition in a traditional mode, *ASF* had to survive the drastic changes in the publishing industry forced by the advent of television and the forced closing of the largest magazine distributor in the country, the American News Company.[46] Eventually, it also had to survive the demise of Street and Smith.

Of course, *ASF* did survive the demise of Street and Smith. And it survived television, and American News, and the defection of the droves of fans who were supposed to have been alienated by Campbell's increasingly cranky editorials. The most important assets underwriting this record of survival continued to be the stories, and that means the writers and Campbell's editorial tastes, no matter how diminished by his interests beyond fiction or his prejudices. The writers included Anderson, Asimov, Blish, Bova, Budrys, Clement, del Rey, Dickson, Godwin, Harrison, Heinlein, on through Anne McCaffrey, H. Beam Piper, Norman Spinrad, and Kate Wilhelm, as well as two regular nonfiction contributors, J. R. Pierce (a noted information scientist with Bell Labs, who wrote as "J. J. Coupling"), and, most regular of all, P. Schuyler Miller, the monthly book reviewer.

The fan who wanted "hard" science fiction, stories dealing directly with new technology and the men who worked with it, would find its cradle in *ASF* during the last ten years of Campbell's life. The nuts-and-bolts tendencies which literary-oriented critics assailed may have appeared as a positive advantage to segments of the readership to which the literary experimentation and political alienation of the sixties were anathema. This fiction was still published and distributed by a large corporation with a substantial base outside the contracting pulp market. If this would later pose coordination problems for the publishing management of Condé Nast, it was a useful cushion for *ASF* during the difficult latter half of the Campbell years.

Campbell's last Hugo Award for editing, in 1965, coincided with the publication of the second half of *Dune* and marks an important point in *ASF*'s history. Although it continued as a fiction magazine and would publish some good fiction right up to the end of Campbell's life, by the middle sixties it had become a quasi-political magazine and not notably more biased or shrill than others publishing at the same time. The editorials concentrated on the issues of the day, such as race relations, the War on Poverty, and the War in Viet Nam. However, there was a considerable continuity of theme from earlier pieces informing these: the distrust of the democratic political process and the detestation of theory, whether in the physical or social sciences.

Campbell was most vocal in his criticism of the sociological political thinking that so influenced the liberal political initiatives of the sixties, a criticism that originated with his segregationist assaults on the Supreme Court's 1954 school desegregation decision and that then spread throughout Campbell's writing as it spread through the right-wing generally. This put him in somewhat of an ideological bind, since, without a true "science of society," the alternatives were limited to "amateurs," elected public officials who could lead people. But that necessitated a political process which Campbell distrusted to begin with and which he insisted had been debased by too great an emphasis on the doctrines of equality, which he held to be invalid. "A government can work," he wrote, "and work well, which denies the vote to 80% of its people—provided that 80% is simply strong, determined, courageous, numerous, but stupid" ("Utopian Voters," February 1962; "Constitution for Utopia," March 1961; "Pie in the Sky," August 1961). But without any criteria by which to select an elite electorate, and without a science of sociology, which his approach to unorthodox science had rendered impossible, Campbell was truly adrift politically. He increasingly detested the direction in which the country was going and was increasingly vocal about it, but, increasingly, he had no alternative to offer save violence. Ironically, he revealed this in endorsing George Wallace for the Presidency in 1968. Certainly the most brutal and violent of the candidates, Wallace was perhaps the most thoroughgoing of the twentieth century's right-wing populists and hardly a supporter of the kinds of elites Campbell liked to talk about.

All in all, Campbell and the writers who were playing with his ideas were approaching an intellectual dead end, even in their alternative methods of scientific investigation. While he had been criticizing the scientific establishment, which he saw as linked with the political establishment, Campbell had been writing out his own ideas for more productive methods of research. He was quick to dismiss investigations which were not carried out according to his ideas of experimentation, dismissing Dr. Joseph Rhine's study of ESP at Duke as too statistical.[47]

And his ideas were running up against the realities of the American social and economic structure. As early as September 1952, he had elaborated on "The Laws of Speculation," which summarized the way he thought new ideas and technologies ought to be developed. In 1958, in the wake of the disastrous public failure of the Vanguard rocket's attempt to follow the Soviet launching of the first artificial Earth satellite, he picked up on a suggestion by Dr. Edward Teller that science needed a band of strong "rooters" who would support it. Campbell noted that true fans were loyal to a game, rather than to any specific team, and that as hecklers they could, on occasion, force changes on a team. Science fans, he argued, ought to be participating junior members in the scientific game. He thought that, although practicing scientists did not want laity breaking up their game, they were wrong in sniffing at the largest group of science's fans and supporters. The 200,000 science fiction fans could provide a useful and informed check on the scientists' work, even if few could follow specialized details ("Concerning Science Fans," June 1958).

Of course, that kind of professional-amateur interaction had been part of science fiction fandom for years and it had been productive for the genre, but the singular interchange that goes on at a science fiction convention is the diametrical opposite of the compartmentalized and bureaucratic industrial, military, and research establishments of modern science. It is likely that Campbell never understood what an old beehive he was unsuccessfully trying to stir up. As CalTech historian Daniel Kevles points out, the hydra-headed scientific establishment had grown over a period of nearly one hundred years as the result of long struggles over the financing of increasingly expensive research, and it was thoroughly grounded in a "best science" ideology which deliberately favored the largest, best-known, and best-connected institutions and personnel, on the grounds that they were the most productive for the public money being spent.[48] It was *intended* to be a screening device eliminating just the sort of unorthodox research efforts and amateur tinkerers Campbell liked. Neither he nor his readers seemed to realize just how subversive they were. Nor, despite their injunctions to follow evidence instead of theory, were they able to recognize when reality had beaten them.

One of Campbell's enthusiasms actually made it off an inventor's drawing board and into the test-bed stage: the so-called Dean Drive. Dean, a Washington, D.C., civil servant—a bureaucrat!—claimed to have built a machine that could convert the angular momentum of two contra-rotating masses into straight-line motion without producing or requiring an equal reaction in the opposite direction. If it worked as claimed, it could propel a spaceship without rockets and fuel; it would be a "true space drive." But if it worked, Newton's Third Law of Motion no longer did.

Dean's failure to convince the military to put Newton aside long enough to examine his machine and test results, and his inability to patent the machine without making its mechanism public, angered Campbell. He rose, not necessarily, he claimed, to defend Dean, but to attack the methods through which his efforts had been stymied and to defend the concept he so cherished: that *anyone* might make a true breakthrough, regardless of credentials, if the insight were there. But for once his agitation had some effect, and the Huyck Corporation of Connecticut decided to undertake a small development program. They even appointed engineers of whom Campbell approved, Stine and William Parsons, an Air Force Colonel with a Ph.D. in physics and a record as a practically minded manager of early rocket test flights. But Dean and Huyck could not come to terms, and the machines Parsons and Stine built to replicate his results without infringing on his patent did not display the results Dean had claimed. Huyck shelved the project as unprofitable.[49]

Campbell's last writing on the Dean Drive was a report of the beginning of Huyck's research, a parting shot at the official unwillingness to test fairly unorthodox propositions. But even in sympathetic hands, the project was not exempt from the economic limits of the existing research system. It would have been an insight of importance had Campbell realized it; regardless of the merits of the Dean Drive, the lesson that significant technological development might be held up by a near-sighted concentration on short-term profits has not been completely learned as of this writing. Campbell knew that there was a problem, but he was entirely unable to fashion an argument about it in economic terms.

If there was a time in *ASF*'s history when it could be perceived as a dogmatic collection of Campbell's prejudices, that time would begin after the Dean Drive affair, although Campbell was wont to dwell more on parapsychology than on that machine. *ASF*'s eclecticism was considerably diminishing, and many writers and observers, who now had many competing outlets available, blamed Campbell, who, by this time, was seemingly a safe target. But if its quality was sinking, it had clearly not passed the Plimsoll line. It was continuing to showcase, if it no longer developed, new writers. Campbell published "Birth of a Salesman" (March 1968), the first appearance of "James Tiptree, Jr." (biochemist Dr. Alice Sheldon), who would become one of the field's pre-eminent new talents in the seventies. *ASF* also published "Weyr Search" (October 1967) and "Dragonrider" (December 1967–January 1968), the first volume of Anne McCaffrey's series of novels on the adventures of telepathic teleporting dragons, who with their riders protect the planet of Pern.

In overview, by the late sixties *ASF* was moribund, dominated by Campbell's astonishing, often illogical, and surprisingly authoritarian and brutal conservatism. Yet it was still publishing good fiction along with a lot of junk. It appears that Campbell never entirely lost his instinct for a good story or his judgment to determine when a slippery idea might be carried by a good story. He just exercised it less regularly than he once had. Then too, some of the new good stories were in accordance with, or at least did not do violence to, Campbell's ideas. Near the end Campbell claimed that *ASF* enjoyed a circulation nearly as large as that of the three nearest competitors, and he himself was well regarded enough to earn Hugo awards for editing in 1953, 1955, 1957, 1961, 1964, and 1965.[50] If his cranky views of science and society became simply obtuse and brutal at the end, that was because he had worked himself into an intellectual corner with his increasing rejection of the role of established, organized science and scientific theory. In the scientific world, this reduced him to a crank, futilely protesting against a system from which he and those like him were excluded.

An advocate of a revolution in the organization of science who never realized that he *was* a revolutionary, Campbell fell back into reaction, retreating to what seemed to be the certainties of the American middle-class life in which he had grown up, and willing to justify the killing of people who refused to accept many, if not most, of the premises and policies of that culture. Thus, the transformation of middle-class life brought about by the organization of Campbell's beloved technology in the giant corporation, university, and government bureaucracies, combined with the conservative views traditional in that social group, led to a fearfully rigid authoritarianism, support of George Wallace, and excuses for the killing of anti-war demonstrators at Kent and Jackson State universities in 1970.

Campbell died on July 11, 1971; his principal legacy was *ASF* and what it had done in the science fiction field. The magazine was not at the peak of its reputation when he died, but it was in sound financial condition, with a larger circulation than any contemporary competitor and none of the shaky future that afflicted others at the same time. The editor had fulfilled his half of the bargain with the publisher to the end: it was his magazine and it made money. Its pages of fiction were by then out of fashion, but they had continued to feature more substantial stories than many of their critics usually remember, and they fulfilled a useful function as an incubator for "hard" science fiction which has proven more durable than some of the fiction fashionable in 1971.

ASF was not built by Campbell, nor did it die with him, but his tenure made it the focal point of developments within the genre for all the years between the winter of 1937-1938 and the summer of 1971. The magazine had always prospered when its editors and publishers were most interested in integrating disparate stories and articles, in merging the utopian hopes and fears for technology of Gernsback with the more mundane concerns of popular fiction. Campbell allowed that integration to slip considerably at the end, but it never disappeared entirely. Even in its poor years after 1965, *ASF* was able to provide a harbor for nuts-and-bolts fiction which after 1971 could be enriched by literary tools developed by "New Wave" writers whom Campbell would not have published and by the new astronomical and biological discoveries of the seventies.[51] That is to say, that as Campbell had received the magazine from the hands of capable predecessors who made his own inestimable contributions to the genre possible, he preserved it in a manner fit for the new contributions of new editors (and, eventually, publishers), who would take it in their directions as Campbell had taken it in his.

IV. The Post-Campbell Years

The death of John Campbell was a shock. He was only sixty-one and might otherwise have edited *ASF* for another fifteen or twenty years, or at least have retired gracefully. Eric Frank Russell, who was Campbell's own favorite author, though his work had been woefully absent from the magazine for the last decade, sent an appreciation to the publishers. "John Campbell's virtues far outshone whatever human faults he may have had. The latter were given some publicity by the petty-minded and the envious. The former remained well concealed; for John was essentially a modest man. People who did not know him personally could be misled by his liking for ruthless argument and his sly needling of opponents, all of which arose from his love of discussion and his pixieish sense of humor."[52] Elsewhere in that appreciation Russell wrote, "He [Campbell] towered like a giant above the ordinary mass of us and it was largely under his aegis that we were brought—or, in some cases dragged—from the comparatively primitive days of the 1930s and into today's far larger science-fiction world."

While that may be Campbell's epitaph, it is also an anti-climax, for although Campbell continued to help and nurture new talent his major contribution to science fiction was the overnight transformation of the pulp genre between 1938 and 1942. Although Campbell continued to publish much of the best science fiction of the forties and, to a lesser extent, the fifties and sixties, it was no longer his domain. But, unlike the case of Hugo Gernsback, who had created a genre that finally turned on him, Campbell attracted true science fiction apostles.

The paramount question after his death was who could replace him. When he had taken up the editorial reins, many of the writers he helped establish had been only children or had not yet been born. At length the lot fell to Ben Bova. Bova, then aged thirty-eight, was not unknown in the science fiction field. He had first appeared in 1959 with a novel in the respected Winston Juvenile SF series The Star Conquerors. Some short stories had appeared in the SF magazines, including a few in *ASF*, but he was probably best known at this time for his scientific articles, which had started with a series called Life in Space published in *Amazing* during the early sixties.

Bova and Campbell shared many qualities. Both were technophiles, and Bova was actively involved in exploiting futurological ideas in his capacity as marketing manager.[53] Moreover, Bova expressed much the same sentiments as Campbell in his first editorial:

> For more than thirty years, this magazine has been a place where you could go window shopping for the future; where you could look at possible tomorrows, judge their shape, their color, their texture, and prepare yourself mentally for what comes next.
>
> That's the kind of magazine Analog will continue to be.
>
> No, I don't mean "relevant" stories about how terrible it all is, and how a poor pitiful human being hasn't got a chance in this great big scary world. Hell, this world was made by human beings, its problems and its joys are the work of men and women. Men and women can solve those problems and appreciate those joys.[54]

There was the passion for resolving the future and establishing a human/machine harmony. Bova emphasized that the stories in *ASF* would continue to be *science* fiction and that the problems would generally arise from the interplay between technology and human emotions. He also emphasized that the characters in the stories would be human beings, "who lose more than they win, who were alive before the first page of the story and will continue to live in your mind after the story is over."[55]

Bova advised that *ASF* would change, because life is change, and indeed no one expected *ASF* to carry on as before. Nevertheless, the publishers were not advocating a radical departure from the Campbell formula, and so the transition from Campbell to Bova was surprisingly smooth. Campbell had left a large inventory of stories. He had purchased sufficient material and assembled issues as far ahead as December. Bova's duties officially began with the January 1972 issue, but at this stage it was still not possible to be sure which stories had been acquired by which editor. This led to a number of blunders by a small cadre of *ASF* readers who were staunch followers of Campbell and clearly expected Bova to watch his step. Their immediate complaint centered upon the excessive use of sex, or "genital recreation," as one correspondent put it. The first story to cause a stir was, curiously, Jack Wodhams' spoof "Foundlings Father" (December 1971) with its inexcusable illustration by Kelly Freas. Bova happily pointed out that Campbell had purchased both story and illustration.

Two other stories proved even more distressing to many readers: "The Gold at the Starbow's End" by Frederik Pohl (March 1972) and "Hero" by Joe W. Haldeman (June 1972). Letters arrived from readers expressing disgust with the overt use of sex and threatening to cancel their subscriptions. Such remonstrations were clearly in the minority, however, for *ASF*'s subscription sales rose steadily during the seventies. Of more immediate gratification, both stories were nominated for the Hugo Award (Pohl's story also received a Nebula nomination), and Bova received the Hugo Award in 1973 as Best Professional Editor.

The more rational reaction to the changeover was one of relief. While Bova did not have Campbell's charisma, or the inclination to reply at great length on near-successful submissions, neither did he have a penchant for wild schemes which, as we have seen, first secluded and then almost alienated Campbell from much of the SF field during the sixties. Moreover, Bova was not afflicted by Campbell's limiting prejudices, and as 1972 progressed it became very evident that the windows were once again opening at *ASF*. Nevertheless, such comments must be made with reserve, because there is absolutely no way of knowing whether Campbell would have bought either Pohl's or Haldeman's stories. There is a strong suspicion that he would have, though it is also more than likely that he would have taken issue with both authors over their science, especially the black hole physics that Haldeman expostulated. This would have provided ample material for one or more editorials and doubtless Campbell would have generated responses from other writers. To some extent this is just what happened with Bova, because within months appeared "He Fell into a Dark Hole" by Jerry Pournelle (March 1973), and "The Hole Man" by Larry Niven (January 1974), which went on to win the Hugo Award.

For a short period, *ASF* experienced something of the excitement of the 1940s. Not only did many of the regulars (Poul Anderson, Gordon R. Dickson, Christopher Anvil) continue to appear, but Bova also began to attract some exciting new talent from the ranks of either the unestablished or the well known in the field who had never previously been published by Campbell. In this last category were such names as Gene Wolfe, Barry Malzberg, Ron Goulart, Roger Zelazny, and even Harlan Ellison. Now these writers appeared with some traditional, but more often radically un-Campbellian stories reflecting the breadth of Bova's editorial policy. This was perhaps most ironic in the case of Malzberg, who in many ways represented every opposite of Campbell. Yet Malzberg received the first John W. Campbell Memorial Award for the Best SF Novel of the Year in 1973, for *Beyond Apollo* (New York: Random House, 1972). Poul Anderson instantly went on record protesting the misuse of Campbell's name for an award to a novel which, according to Anderson, was "gloomy, involuted, and technophobic, perhaps the three qualities which John most strongly opposed."[56] This was the start of a clash between Anderson and Harry Harrison (one of the award judges) and other readers in the letter column, all of which highlighted the fact that science fiction was going to continue to progress and not stagnate just because Campbell had passed away. Hardly had this debate settled than Bova published a short story by Barry Malzberg in the March 1974 issue, "Closing the Deal."

The appearance of Roger Zelazny in *ASF* was an occasion for celebration. Zelazny, one of the hottest SF properties of the sixties, had never succeeded in selling to Campbell simply because he never wrote in the Campbell mode. His work of the seventies was even further from it, but the stories in question were received rapturously. In all there were two stories and a novel. All three were nominated for the Hugo and Nebula awards with "Home Is the Hangman" (November 1975) taking both of them.

Perhaps of more significance was the space Bova was giving to new or relatively new writers. Almost certainly the most successful was George R. R. Martin who, although he debuted in *Galaxy*, rapidly established himself as an *ASF* author. His stories were frequently nominated for the major awards and almost as frequently won them. Curiously, his first appearance in *ASF* was with an article, "The Computer Was a Fish" (August 1972), which gave no measure of the writer as a fictioneer. His story debut, therefore, "The Second Kind of Loneliness" (December 1972), showed that here was a writer sensitive to mood and atmosphere as well as one with a talent for creating believable people, aliens, and situations. Martin's talent was rapidly recognized. "With Morning Comes Mistfall" (May 1973) received a Nebula nomination, while "A Song for Lya" (June 1974), also nominated for the Nebula, won the Hugo Award. Martin is a good example of a Bova/Campbell hybrid author. His stories have all the mood of the early Campbell "Stuart" stories, but some, like "A Song for Lya," carry rather more explicit sex than Campbell would have liked. It had never been the fashion to flaunt sex in SF during the bulk of Campbell's period as editor, but when it could be accomplished with reason Campbell usually accepted it. He did, after all, publish Anne McCaffrey's "A Womanly Talent" (February 1969), which carried just as much sex as some of the stories that came after Campbell, and indeed created something of a stir in *ASF*'s letter column, but it tends to be overlooked when evaluating Campbell's acceptance of sex in SF.

Once Bova had established himself at *ASF*, distinct changes began to occur.

Some of the changes were of Bova's own making. Fiction aside, the long-established Analytical Laboratory was dropped after 1976. But there were other changes. Kay Tarrant, the assistant editor, retired in 1972 and was succeeded by Diana King. King was in turn succeeded, after three years, by Victoria Schochet. P. Schuyler Miller, *ASF*'s much respected book reviewer, who had reviewed books intermittently from April 1945 and then regularly each month from October 1950 (initiating the standard "Reference Library" a year later), died in 1974. His successor was a man equally revered, Lester del Rey. Later, however, del Rey's connections with Ballantine Books and their own subsequent imprint Del Rey Books brought some criticism from various parties, not least Barry Malzberg, over del Rey's vested interests which, unfortunately, brought a rather sour flavor to *ASF*'s letter column for a while.

Perhaps more noticeable was the increasing absence of Kelly Freas. Freas was synonymous with *ASF*, and there was scarcely an issue—sometimes scarcely a story—that he did not illustrate. But during the seventies his work was less in evidence. On the other hand Jack Gaughan, who had found that he just could not work for Campbell, appeared as soon as Bova was settled, and some of his best work appeared on the cover as well as inside the Bova issues. Bova also used the artistic talents of Vincent diFate to good effect, although he had debuted in Campbell's day. Perhaps the most effective artist developed during the seventies was Rick Sternbach, whose work was ideally suited to *ASF*. This was almost certainly reflected in Sternbach's winning the Hugo Award for Best Professional Artist in both 1977 and 1978.

Finally, long-term readers would have noticed that, although Bova continued with the tradition established by Campbell of providing long, and at times controversial, editorials, these were far less radical than Campbell's, and not as frequent, because Bova regularly handed over his editorial space to guest writers.

One tradition of Campbell's that Bova did continue was to read and comment on all the manuscripts himself. With a similar eye for good or potential talent, Bova continued to cultivate writers who had perhaps just sold one or two stories previously to Campbell or other markets, and discovered a few himself. As already mentioned, George R. R. Martin was perhaps the most successful. In a similar mold was P. J. Plauger, the president of a computer software company, who debuted in *ASF* with "Epicycle" (November 1973) but who established himself with "Child of All Ages" (March 1975), a poignant tale of a girl whose aging process was arrested before puberty and who must periodically disappear from public notice so that her secret is never discovered. At the other extreme is Spider Robinson, whose contributions, since his first appearance with "The Guy with the Eyes" (February 1973), fall into a series of tall yarns told in Callahan's Bar in the tradition of Lord Dunsany's Jorkens tales or Arthur Clarke's *Tales from the White Hart*. Robinson's stories cannot pretend to be "hard" science in the *ASF* tradition, but then neither could many of those contributed in the fifties by Eric Frank Russell or Randall Garrett, and there is much in the way of their humor in Robinson's work. Robinson could, however, change the mood completely as he did when teamed with his wife on the much praised "Stardance" (March 1977) and its novel-length sequel.

"Stardance" was indicative of a trend that was especially noticeable in *ASF* during the seventies but that surprisingly started in the late Campbell days: science fiction stories in the mood and style of fantasies. This had been evident in some of the stories by Poul Anderson and Randall Garrett, especially when depicting feudal societies, but Anne McCaffrey probably achieved more than anybody in establishing the approach with her stories about the Dragonriders of Pern. Many of the stories by George R. R. Martin fall into this framework, especially his collaboration with Lisa Tuttle on "The Storms of Windhaven" (May 1975), which features many of the Pern hallmarks without any deliberate imitation. Frank Herbert's Dune series also possessed this fantastic quality. While Campbell had helped develop the Dune premise and had published the first two serials that constituted *Dune*, *ASF* had not acquired the original sequel, *Dune Messiah*. It did, however, capture the third novel of the sequence, *The Children of Dune*, which was serialized from January to April 1976.

One new writer who brought the flavor of the fantastic to his SF was Orson Scott Card, possibly one of Bova's major discoveries. His very first sale, "Ender's Game" (August 1977), had been a Hugo nominee, and thereafter he notched up sales with startling rapidity. Solidly in the fantasy mold was "Mikal's Songbird" (May 1978—another Hugo and Nebula nominee) and its sequel "Songhouse" (September 1979), two stories Campbell would probably never have purchased, though *ASF* would have been the poorer without them.

Surprisingly, the one author of the seventies for whom Bova apparently had a blind spot was John Varley, who exploded on the scene with stories in *Galaxy* and *The Magazine of Fantasy and Science Fiction*, most of which had been submitted first to Bova. At length Bova did acquire serial rights to Varley's most ambitious work at that stage, *Titan*, although it was serialized in the issues after Bova's departure.

Bova promoted the work of female SF writers. Some have argued that Campbell was anti-feminist; others, however, point to the many women writers he published in *ASF*, especially Katherine MacLean, Anne McCaffrey, C. L. Moore, and the pseudonymous James Tiptree, Jr. (Alice Sheldon). Two female writers who firmly established themselves during the seventies in the pages of *ASF* were Vonda McIntyre and Joan D. Vinge. McIntyre's work held some of the fantasy soupçon, especially her Snake sequence, which began with the award-winning "Of Mist, and Grass, and Sand" (October 1973).

With a number of good stories by female writers on hand, Bova compiled a special women's issue of *ASF* in June 1977. While there were a few who objected to Bova segregating women in such a manner rather than integrating them, the issue was not only well received, but it also provided two award winners. To Joan Vinge went the Hugo for "Eyes of Amber" and to Raccoona Sheldon (a less disguised alias of Alice Sheldon's) went the Nebula for "The Screwfly Solution."

Bova put out two other special issues; these were divided by theme rather than sex. One, issued in October 1974, was devoted to discussing the works of Immanuel Velikovsky; the second, two issues later, was a special Mars issue. These were the exception rather than the rule, however.

Bova succeeded in making *ASF* a voice for every type of writer and was not averse to experimentation, even when Greg Benford, normally a "hard" science writer, deliberately wrote a non-Campbellian piece in "Doing Lennon" (April 1975). This story was nominated for both the Hugo and Nebula Awards. While under Bova *ASF* retained its individuality, its personality underwent a slight transformation. Under Bova *ASF* took on renewed life, retaining much of the feel of Campbell's days but removing the shackles of tradition that had built up through 34 years and 409 issues by one editor. In recognition of his success as an editor, Bova won the Hugo Award for every year he edited *ASF*.

He also experimented beyond *ASF*, initiating the series of Analog Books, which included *Analog Annual* and the subsequent *Analog Yearbook* which were, in effect, a thirteenth annual issue of *ASF*.

When Bova achieved all that he wanted with the magazine he quit, recommending Stanley Schmidt as his successor. Bova had intended to return to full-time writing, but with his departure he was recontacted by Frank Kendig and Bob Guccione, who were in the final stages of launching a new popular science magazine, then called *Nova* (*Omni**). Guccione had previously contacted Bova while he was still editor of *ASF*, but Bova had had no intention of leaving then. However, within a week of leaving *ASF*, he became *Omni*'s fiction editor.

Bova had served *ASF* well; only a rare editor could have achieved more than he had. Probably his most important achievement was destroying some of the unnecessary myths surrounding Campbell. He had showed that while the man was unique, he was not irreplaceable and that *ASF* could prosper adequately without him.

Stanley Schmidt, like Bova and Campbell, was a technophile. A lecturer in physics, he had contributed regularly to *ASF* and was a Campbell discovery, having debuted with "A Flash of Darkness" in September 1968. His most ambitious project had been the Lifeboat Earth series which had run during Bova's editorship and consisted of a novel and five novelettes. It tells of the discovery that the sun will become a nova and of the attempts and consequences of moving the Earth away from its orbit out and beyond the solar system.

Schmidt was a less dominant person than Bova and certainly than Campbell, and his early presence in *ASF*'s pages was low-key. While under Campbell readers had always expected good reading, it was often tinged with elements of surprise and sometimes of the outrageous. Bova ensured that he provided solidly good SF, and he made *ASF* a forum to present startling new ideas. Schmidt, on the other hand, still endeavored to obtain good material, but stepped out of the limelight in trying to present the ideas. These he left to either guest writers for the editorial, or columnists Harry Stine and Jerry Pournelle. As a result, during Schmidt's editorship *ASF* has ceased to be as preeminent a magazine as it had always been hitherto, and has begun to lose its individuality. This is a result not so much of the magazine's contents as events that are beyond Schmidt's control. That *ASF* is still capable of producing award-winning stories is evidenced by Edward Bryant's "giANTS" (August 1979), Clifford D. Simak's "Grotto of the Dancing Deer" (April 1980), Gordon R. Dickson's "The Cloak and the Staff" (August 1980), and Poul Anderson's "The Saturn Game" (February 2, 1981). But there is now far less of a sense of occasion about *ASF*.

Part of the cause lies with changing trends in SF readers' habits during the seventies, which are not limited to *ASF*. Circulation statistics of the magazine reveal that subscription sales have increased while newsstand sales have dropped. In 1967, for instance, *ASF* sold 63 percent of its total print run, and only a third of those sales were by subscription, with the bulk selling over the counter. The percentage of sales to print run remained more or less constant during the seventies, but by 1979 the subscription accounted for 50 percent of sales, and for 58 percent by 1981. A similar pattern can be found in the other SF magazines. By and large the distributors had lost interest in the few remaining digest magazines, and readers who wanted to ensure that they received copies found it more reliable to subscribe. Where issues were displayed on sale, they usually sold, but more often they just languished in the distributors' or wholesalers' warehouses. This was suicidally expensive for the publisher.

Condé Nast, *ASF*'s publisher since 1961, was no longer geared to publish a magazine such as *ASF*. Its other publications, such as *Vogue, Mademoiselle*, and *House and Garden*, were all slick magazines aimed up-market. All the while newsstand sales remained healthy, Condé Nast's distribution outlet could handle *ASF*, even though it was something of an anachronism for them. But once the counter sales dropped to only 40 percent, *ASF* became little more than a burden.

There was no trouble in finding a new publisher. Joel Davis had sought to acquire the magazine for some time. As publisher of *Ellery Queen's Mystery Magazine*,[57] and more recently SF's latest success story, *Isaac Asimov's Science Fiction Magazine*,* Davis was one of the few remaining major publishers of digest magazines and had the means to handle extensive subscription lists. *ASF* changed hands with the September 1980 issue, less than two years after Schmidt had become editor. Within months Joel Davis increased the magazine's publication schedule from monthly to four-weekly, thus squeezing in a genuine thirteenth issue per year. Aside from marginally enlarging the market from the writer's viewpoint, it was a shrewd move because it placed *ASF* on the newsstands at times of the month when magazine releases were slack and thus increased the potential display space. It is still too early to evaluate the experiment, but first signs indicate that *ASF*'s newsstand sales have continued to diminish. Even more alarming is the fact that so too have the subscription sales, although this may be temporary. If *ASF*'s circulation continues to decrease, it can only be the result of first, the loss of its individuality and second, the rivalry from without.

This competition comes from three sources: *Omni, Asimov's*, and *Destinies*. The friendly rivalry with its own stable mate should not be of major consequence.

Certainly *Asimov's* rise to fame has been meteoric and coincides with *ASF*'s fall from grace, but that is almost certainly accidental. It also coincides with the passing of *Galaxy*, and *Asimov's* was more likely to capture its readers from that magazine than from *ASF*, which remains predominantly the scientists' magazine.

As the most science-oriented of the SF magazines, *ASF* has championed scientific progress since the 1930s, much as Gernsback had previously. By the 1970s, however, much of the SF appearing was technophobic in nature, the thrill of adventure having been syphoned away from SF to fantasy. From 1978, however, *ASF* has had to contend with *Omni*, which glorifies science in a way that *ASF* can not possibly match. Moreover, with Bova initially as fiction editor, *Omni* attracted much the same type of fiction that had previously appeared in *ASF*, and there can be no doubt that *Omni* satisfies a quota of the science-oriented readership who gradually forsook *ASF*. The original feeling that *ASF* would benefit from *Omni*'s presence does not seem to be the case, for although *Omni* is no substitute so far as its SF is concerned, it does serve for those who purchased *ASF* predominantly for its nonfiction. *Omni*'s success, of course, generated imitations, and the conversion of *Science Digest* to the same format only siphoned off *ASF*'s dwindling readership. Any interest in SF generated by *Omni* was served more by books than by magazines. By 1980 SF was on the crest of a wave of popularity. Among the many books available was Jim Baen's *Destinies*, which was another technophilic publication carrying much of the flavor of the Campbell/Bova *ASF*, as well as many of the regular authors. Thus, *ASF*'s strength in content and authors was being plundered, and its once unvanquishable prestige was being eroded.

With *ASF* having been the top SF magazine since 1934, it is still hard to imagine that it can be anything but the most prestigious, and its name still holds much respect. Despite Stanley Schmidt's laudable efforts, however, *ASF* is no longer the unquestioned leader in the field. Although reliability and readability are important, that sense of excitement and of unpredictability that powered the early Campbell, and even early Bova issues, cannot be dismissed. That sense is now woefully absent. It is present in *Omni* and is there in greater measure in *Asimov's*, *The Magazine of Fantasy and Science Fiction* and even *Amazing*. As of 1984, *ASF* had much work to do to regain its standing in SF.

Notes

1. Lester del Rey, *The World of Science Fiction: The History of a Subculture* (New York: Del Rey/Ballantine Books, 1979), pp. 52–53, gives an example of how this worked at *ASF* under Clayton Publishing.

2. John W. Campbell, Jr., address at Illinois Institute of Technology, Chicago, Illinois, April 27, 1971.

3. Del Rey, *World of SF*, pp. 55–56. See also Alva Rogers, *A Requiem for Astounding* (Chicago: Advent Publishers, 1964), including its introductory recollections of the first three editors of *ASF*, Bates, F. Orlin Tremaine and John W. Campbell.

4. Del Rey, *World of SF*, pp. 57–58.

5. For a profound and scholarly review of Street and Smith's historic mythmaking influence, see Henry Nash Smith, *Virgin Land: The American West as Symbol and Myth* (New York: Vintage Books, 1950), pp. 115ff.

6. Del Rey, *World of SF*, p. 87; Isaac Asimov, *Before the Golden Age: A Science Fiction Anthology of the 1930s* (Garden City, N.Y: Doubleday & Co., 1974), p. 442; Mike Ashley, letter to Albert I. Berger, April 20, 1982.

7. Sam Moskowitz, *Seekers of Tomorrow: Masters of Modern Science Fiction* (New York: Ballantine Books, 1967), pp. 25–26, describes the influence of the Smith story while mentioning only editor Tremaine. Ashley to Berger, April 20, 1982, for role of Desmond Hall.

8. Ashley to Berger, April 20, 1982.

9. Paul A. Carter, *The Creation of Tomorrow: Fifty Years of Magazine Science Fiction* (New York: Columbia University Press, 1977), p. 118; del Rey, *World of SF*, p. 60.

10. Brian Aldiss, *Billion Year Spree: The True History of Science Fiction* (New York: Schocken Books, 1973), pp. 232–34; del Rey, *World of SF*, p. 80.

11. Carter, *Creation of Tomorrow*, chap. 7; del Rey, *World of SF*, pp. 68, 80.

12. John W. Campbell, Jr., interview with Albert I. Berger in the *ASF* offices, New York City, January 28, 1971.

13. John W. Campbell, Jr., Introduction to *Who Goes There?* (N.p: Shasta, 1971).

14. Campbell, interview, January 28, 1971; Campbell, IIT address, April 27, 1971.

15. This paraphrase of Campbell's requirements is found in del Rey, *Worlds of SF*, pp. 153–54.

16. John W. Campbell, Jr., "Science Fiction We Can Buy," *The Writer*, September 1968.

17. Del Rey, *World of SF*, p. 155.

18. Asimov, *Golden Age*, p. 495; Aldiss, *Spree*, p. 232; Donald Wollheim, *The Universe Makers: Science Fiction Today* (New York: Harper & Row, 1972), chap. 18; del Rey, *World of SF*, pp. 91–102.

19. Aldiss, *Spree*, pp. 229–30; Albert I. Berger, "The Triumph of Prophecy: Science Fiction and Nuclear Power in the Post-Hiroshima Period," *Science-Fiction Studies* No. 9, Vol. 3(2) (July 1976); Albert I. Berger, "Nuclear Energy: Science Fiction's Metaphor of Power," *Science-Fiction Studies* No. 18, Vol. 6(2) (July 1979).

20. Ibid.

21. Aldiss, *Spree*, pp. 246–47.

22. Albert Manly, "Brass Tacks" (letter to the editor), *Astounding Science Fiction*, September 1948, p. 160.

23. L. Ron Hubbard, *Dianetics: The Modern Science of Mental Health* (New York: Paperback Library, 1968).

24. Chandler Davis letter to R. Dale Mullen, January 12, 1976; quoted with the kind permission of Mr. Davis.

25. Albert I. Berger, "Science Fiction Critiques of the American Space Program, 1945–1958," *Science-Fiction Studies* No. 15, Vol. 5(2) (July 1978).

26. Albert I. Berger, "Science Fiction Fans in Socio-economic Perspective: Factors in the Social Consciousness of a Genre," *Science-Fiction Studies* No. 13, Vol. 4(3) (November 1977). See also two published readership surveys of *ASF*: "The Analytical Laboratory," July 1949, and "A Portrait of You," March 1958; and S. E. Finer, "A Profile of Science Fiction," *Sociological Review*, 2 (new series), 1954, pp. 239–55.

27. Aldiss, *Spree*, p. 233.

28. Harold L. Berger, "Anti-utopian Science Fiction of Mid-Twentieth Century," Ph.D. dissertation, University of Tennessee, 1970, cited by Martin Harry Greenberg and Joseph Olander in the introduction to their anthology *Science Fiction of the Fifties* (New York: Avon Books, 1979), pp. xx–xxi.

29. See Berger and others cited in Note 26 above.

30. See David F. Noble, *America by Design: Science, Technology, and the Rise of Corporate Capitalism* (New York: Oxford University Press, 1977).

31. Isaac Asimov, *In Joy Still Felt* (New York: Avon Books, 1980), p. 53. Campbell turned Asimov's polite evasion of direct questions on the performance of the parapsychological Hieronymous Machine into data.

32. These comments were gleaned in informal conversations between Albert I. Berger and United States Marine Corps combat veterans of Viet Nam on the island of Okinawa from January to March 1980.

33. Aldiss, *Spree*, p. 241.

34. Isaac Asimov, *In Memory Yet Green* (New York: Avon Books, 1979), p. 570.

35. Barry Malzberg, "Afterword to 'Sam Hall,' " in *The End of Summer: Science Fiction of the Fifties*, ed. Barry Malzberg and Bill Pronzini (New York: Ace Books, 1979), p. 117.

36. Hubbard, *Dianetics*, p. 400.

37. Malzberg, *Summer*, p. 117.

38. Cited in Aldiss, *Spree*, p. 241.

39. Harry Harrison, Introduction to Campbell, IIT address.

40. Mike Ashley, letter to Albert I. Berger, n.d.

41. Asimov, *In Memory*, p. 630.

42. Aldiss, *Spree*, pp. 230–31.

43. James Gunn, *The Road to Science Fiction #3: From Heinlein to Here* (New York: New American Library, 1979), pp. 244–46.

44. Frederik Pohl, in conversation with Mike Hodel on "Hour 25," KPFK-FM, Los Angeles, Fall 1978.

45. Asimov, *In Memory*, p. 602.

46. Del Rey, *World of SF*, pp. 191–96.

47. Campbell, IIT address.

48. See Daniel Kevles, *The Physicists: The History of a Scientific Community in Modern America* (New York: Vintage Books, 1979).

49. G. Harry Stine, "Detesters, Phasers and Dean Drives," *Analog*, June 1976.

50. Leon E. Stover, "Campbell, John W(ood), Jr.," in *Twentieth Century Science Fiction Writers*, ed. Curtis C. Smith (New York: St. Martin's Press, 1981), p. 97.

51. Poul Anderson's remarks on this new synthesis to a University of Arizona seminar in February 1975 are reported in Carter, *Creation of Tomorrow*, p. 285.

52. Eric Frank Russell, "An Appreciation," *Analog*, November 1971, pp. 169ff.

53. See "Galaxy Stars," *Galaxy*, January 1971, p. 113.

54. Ben Bova, "The Popular Wisdom," *Analog*, February 1972, p. 178.

55. Ibid.

56. Poul Anderson, *Analog*, October 1973, pp. 167ff.

57. Prior to its ownership by Joel Davis, *Ellery Queen's Mystery Magazine* had been owned by Mercury Press, which publishes *The Magazine of Fantasy and Science Fiction*. Indirectly, therefore, *Ellery Queen's Mystery Magazine* stands as a stepsister between *The Magazine of Fantasy and Science Fiction* and *ASF*.

Information Sources

BIBLIOGRAPHY:

Aldiss, Brian. *Billion Year Spree: The True History of Science Fiction*. Garden City, N.Y.: Doubleday & Co., 1973.

Asimov, Isaac. *Before the Golden Age: A Science Fiction Anthology of the 1930s*. Garden City, N.Y.: Doubleday & Co., 1974.

————. *The Early Asimov or, Eleven Years of Trying*. Garden City, N.Y.: Doubleday & Co., 1972.

————. *In Joy Still Felt: The Autobiography of Isaac Asimov, 1954–1978*. Garden City, N.Y.: Doubleday & Co., 1980.

————. *In Memory Yet Green: The Autobiography of Isaac Asimov, 1920–1954*. Garden City, N.Y.: Doubleday & Co., 1979.

Berger, Albert I. "Love, Death, and the Atomic Bomb: Sexuality and Community in Science Fiction, 1935–1955." *Science-Fiction Studies*, Vol. 8, 1981. Pp. 280–96.

————. "The Magic That Works: John W. Campbell and the American Response to Technology." *Journal of Popular Culture*, Vol. 5(4), Spring 1972. Pp. 867–942.

————. "Nuclear Energy: Science Fiction's Metaphor of Power." *Science-Fiction Studies* No. 18, Vol. 6(2), July 1979. Pp. 121–28.

————. "Science Fiction Critiques of the American Space Program, 1945–1958." *Science-Fiction Studies*, Vol. 5, 1978. Pp. 99–109.

————. "Science Fiction Fans in Social and Economic Perspective: Factors in the Social Consciousness of a Genre." *Science-Fiction Studies*, Vol. 4, 1977. Pp. 232–46.

————. "The Triumph of Prophecy: Science Fiction and Nuclear Power in the Post-Hiroshima Period." *Science-Fiction Studies*, Vol. 3, 1976. Pp. 143–50.

Carter, Paul A. *The Creation of Tomorrow: Fifty Years of Magazine Science Fiction*. New York: Columbia University Press, 1977.

Del Rey, Lester. *The World of Science Fiction: The History of a Subculture*. New York: Del Rey/Ballantine Books, 1979.

Franklin, H. Bruce. *Robert A. Heinlein: America as Science Fiction*. New York: Oxford University Press, 1980.

Greenberg, Martin Harry, and Joseph Olander, eds. *Science Fiction of the Fifties*. New York: Avon Books, 1979.

Gunn, James. *Alternate Worlds: The Illustrated History of Science Fiction*. Englewood Cliffs, N.J.: Prentice Hall, 1975.

————, ed. *The Road to Science Fiction: From Wells to Heinlein*. New York: New American Library Mentor Books, 1978.

————, ed. *The Road to Science Fiction: From Heinlein to Here*. New York: New American Library Mentor Books, 1979.

Hubbard, L. Ron. *Dianetics: The Modern Science of Mental Health*. New York: Paperback Library, 1968.

Kevles, Daniel. *The Physicists: The History of a Scientific Community in Modern America*. New York: Vintage Books, 1979.

Malzberg, Barry, and Bill Pronzini, eds. *The End of Summer: Science Fiction of the Fifties*. New York: Ace Books, 1979.

Moskowitz, Sam. *Seekers of Tomorrow: Masters of Modern Science Fiction*. Cleveland, Ohio: World, 1966, rpt. Westport, CT:1 Hyperion Press, 1974.

Noble, David F. *America by Design: Science, Technology, and the Rise of Corporate Capitalism.* New York: Oxford University Press, 1977.

Rogers, Alva. *A Requiem for Astounding.* Chicago: Advent Publishers, 1964.

Smith, Curtis C., ed. *Twentieth-Century Science-Fiction Writers.* New York: St. Martin's Press, 1981.

Smith, Henry Nash. *Virgin Land: The American West as Symbol and Myth.* New York: Vintage Books, 1950.

Tuck.

Wollheim, Donald A. *The Universe Makers: Science Fiction Today.* New York: Harper & Row, 1971.

INDEX SOURCES: Ashley, Mike, *The Complete Index to Astounding/Analog*, Oak Forest, Ill.: Robert Weinberg Publications, 1981; ISFM; ISFM-II; ISFM-III; IWSF; MIT; NESFA; NESFA-II; NESFA-III; NESFA-IV; NESFA-V; NESFA-VI; NESFA-VII; NESFA-VIII; NESFA-IX; SFM; Tuck.

REPRINT SOURCES:

British Edition: One continuous series from Atlas Publishing, London, though in three incarnations. 222 issues. Pulp (with slight variations), August 1939–October 1953; Digest (with slight variations), November 1953–August 1963. Abridged versions of U.S. editions, usually corresponding to U.S. issues but with one or two stories selected from earlier or later issues to balance the page count. Initially 96pp., dropping to 80pp. in March 1940, then to 64pp. in December 1940. Rose to 128pp. with digest size in November 1953. Price, 9d. until October 1953, 1/6d. until February 1961, then 2/6d. The only SF magazine published in Britain throughout the war. Began as a direct continuation of U.S. series bearing the same volume numbering and published concurrently. Monthly, August 1939–January 1942, but no issues in May or October 1941. U.K. December 1941 = U.S. October 1941, but all other issues correspond. Thereafter irregular. U.K. issues correspond approximately to U.S. issues as follows (U.K. dates first): Mar 42 = Feb 42; May 42; Aug 42 = Jun 42; Oct 42 = Sep 42; Jan 43 = Oct 42; Feb 43 = Dec 42; Apr 43 = Mar 43; Jun 43; Jul 43; Dec 43 = Sep 43; Feb 44 = Oct 43; Apr 44 = Nov 43; Jun 44 = Feb 44; Aug 44 = May 44; Oct 44 = Jun 44; Dec 44 = Sep 44; Feb 45 = Oct 44; May 45 = Nov 44; Jul 45 = Feb 45; Sep 45 = Jun 45; Nov 45 = May 45; Jan 46 = Apr 45; Mar 46 = Oct 45; May 46 = Dec 45; Jul 46 = Feb 46; Sep 46 = May 46; Dec 46 = Jun 46; Jan 47 = Sep 46; Apr 47 = Jul 46; Jun 47 = Nov 46; Aug 47 = Mar 47; Oct 47 = Apr 47; Dec 47 = Jun 47; Feb 48 = Jul 47; Apr 48 = Dec 47; Jun 48 = Feb 48; Aug 48 = Sep 47; Oct 48 = Oct 47; Dec 48 = Apr/Aug 48; Feb 49 = Sep 48; Apr 49 = May 48; Jun 49 = Dec 48; Sep 49 = Apr 49; Oct 49 = Jun 49; Jan 50 = Mar 49; Feb 50 = Sep 49; May 50 = Dec 49; Jun 50 = Jan 49; Aug 50 = Jan 50; Oct 50 = Mar 50; Dec 50 = Jul 50; Feb 51 = Aug 50; Apr 51 = Sep 50; Jun 51 = May 50; Aug 51 = Feb 51; Oct 51 = Apr 51; Dec 51 = Jun 51; Feb 52 = Aug 51; Mar 52 = Sep 51; Apr 52 = May 51; May 52 = Jan 52; Jun 52 = Feb 52; Jul 52 = Mar 51. From the August 1952 issue successive issues corresponded in sequence with the U.S. issue cover dated five months earlier, Aug 52 = Mar 52 and so on, monthly. Exceptions as follows: Jan 57 = Aug 56, but Feb 57 = Oct 56, and thereafter a four-month gap until Apr 58 = Dec 57, then May 58 = Feb 58. No U.K. issues for Sep or Oct 59, so Nov 59 = Jun 59; Dec 59 = Jul 59; Jan 60 = Aug 59; Feb 60 = Nov 59; Mar 60 = Dec

59; Apr 60 = Jan 60; May 60 = Oct 59; Jun 60 = Feb 60; and thereafter continues in sequence with a four-month gap until Aug 63 = Apr 63. Began with U.S. volume numbering Volume 23, Number 6, August 1939–Volume 31, Number 1, April 1943. Unnumbered, June 1943–December 1944. Then volume numbering continued treating August 1939 issue as Volume 1, Number 1, thus Volume 4, Number 9, February 1945–Volume 19, Number 8, August 1963. For index of issues up to December 1953 see Graham Stone, *Index to British Science Fiction Magazines* (Sydney: Australian SF Assoc., 1977), and for November 1953–August 1963 Jim and Shirl Diviney, *Index to British Edition of Astounding/Analog Nov 53-Aug 63* (Huntingdon, U.K.: p.p., n.d.).

Foreign Editions: See entries in Section IV under Denmark—*Planetmagazinet*, Italy—*Scienza Fantastica*.

Derivative Anthologies:

Showcase Anthologies: John W. Campbell, ed., *The Astounding Science Fiction Anthology* (New York: Simon & Schuster, 1952), 22 stories, 1 article selected between 1940 and 1951; *Prologue to Analog* (Garden City, N.Y.: Doubleday, 1962), 10 stories between 1953 and 1960; *Analog 1* (Doubleday, 1963), 8 stories from Sep 60–Dec 61; *Analog 2* (Doubleday, 1964), 8 stories from Apr 62–Jan 63; *Analog 3* (Doubleday, 1965; paperbacked as *A World by the Tale*), 8 stories from 1963; *Analog 4* (Doubleday, 1966; paperbacked as *The Permanent Implosion*), 7 stories from 1964; *Analog 5* (Doubleday 1967; paperbacked as *Countercommandment!*), 9 stories from 1965; *Analog 6* (Doubleday, 1968), 13 stories, 1 article from 1966; *Analog 7* (Doubleday, 1970), 9 stories from 1967; *Analog 8* (Doubleday, 1971), 9 stories from Jul 68–Dec 69. Ben Bova, ed., *Analog 9* (Doubleday, 1973), 6 stories from Nov 70–Jun 72; *The Best of Analog* (New York: Baronet, 1978), 15 stories from 1972–1977.

Retrospective Anthologies: Harry Harrison and Brian W. Aldiss, eds., *The Astounding-Analog Reader* (Doubleday, 2 vols., 1972/3), Vol. 1, 15 stories between 1937 and 1946, Vol. 2, 21 stories between 1947 and 1965; Tony Lewis, ed., *The Best of Astounding* (New York: Baronet, 1978), 7 stories between 1944 and 1949; Stanley Schmidt, ed., *The Analog Anthology #1: 50 Years of the Best* (New York: Davis, 1980; casebound as *Analog's Golden Anniversary Anthology*, Dial, 1981), 18 stories plus articles and editorials from 1934–1979; *The Analog Anthology #2: Readers' Choice* (Davis, 1982), 10 stories selected from readers' lists of top tens; *The Analog Anthology #3: Children of the Future* (New York: Davis, 1982; casebound Dial, 1982); *The Analog Anthology #4: Analog's Lighter Side* (New York: Davis, 1982; casebound Dial, 1983); *The Analog Anthology #5: Writer's Choice* (New York: Davis, 1983; casebound Dial, 1983) 11 stories selected by Analog's contributors; *The Analog Anthology #6: Analog's War and Peace* (New York: Davis, 1983; casebound, Dial, 1983); *The Analog Anthology #7: Aliens From Analog* (New York: Davis, 1983; casebound, Dial, 1983); *The Analog Anthology #8: Writer's Choice #2* (New York: Davis, 1984); *The Analog Anthology #9: From Mind to Mind* (New York: Davis, 1984); Martin Harry Greenberg, *Astounding* (Carbondale: Southern Illinois University Press, 1981), facsimile of July 1939 issue plus commentaries by three contributors.

Associational Anthologies: Brian W. Aldiss and Harry Harrison, eds., *Decade the 1940s* (London: Macmillan, 1975), 8 stories all from 1940s *ASF*; Terry Carr, ed.,

Classic Science Fiction: The First Golden Age (New York: Harper & Row, 1978), 12 stories, 8 from *ASF* between 1940 and 1942; Groff Conklin, ed., *Best of Science Fiction* (New York: Crown, 1946), 40 stories plus an introduction by John W. Campbell, 25 stories from *ASF* during 1930–1945; *A Treasury of Science Fiction* (Crown, 1948), 30 stories, 25 from *ASF* between 1938 and 1947; Martin Greenberg, ed., *Journey to Infinity* (New York: Gnome Press, 1951), 12 stories, 10 from *ASF* during 1940s; *Men against the Stars* (Gnome, 1950), 12 stories, 11 from *ASF* between 1938 and 1946; *The Robot and the Man* (Gnome, 1953), 10 stories, 9 from *ASF* between 1938 and 1948; Raymond J. Healy and J. Francis McComas, eds., *Adventures in Time and Space* (New York: Random House, 1946), 33 stories, 2 articles, 31 from *ASF* during 1934–1945; Damon Knight, ed., *Science Fiction of the Thirties* (Bobbs-Merrill, 1975), 18 stories, 13 from *ASF* between 1931 and 1939.

Non-Fictional Anthologies: Martin Greenberg, ed., *Coming Attractions* (New York: Gnome Press, 1957), 11 articles, 7 from *ASF* between 1938 and 1955. Harry Harrison, ed., *Collected Editorials from Analog* (Garden City, N.Y.: Doubleday, 1966).

Original Anthologies: Harry Harrison, ed., *Astounding: John W. Campbell Memorial Anthology* (New York: Random House, 1973), 13 stories continuing series that owe much to Campbell, plus foreword by Isaac Asimov. Ben Bova, ed., *Analog Annual* (New York: Pyramid, 1976), 3 stories, 1 article and 1 novel; *Analog Yearbook* (New York: Baronet, 1978), 6 stories, 4 articles, plus editorial by Greg Benford. Stanley Schmidt, ed., *Analog Yearbook II* (New York: Ace Books, 1981), 11 stories.

LOCATION SOURCES: Runs of *ASF*, not all complete, are held in the following university libraries and in various private collections: California State University–Fullerton Library; Eastern New Mexico University–Portales Library; Michigan State University Library; M.I.T. Science Fiction Library; Northern Illinois University Library; Ohio State University Library; Texas A&M University Library; Tulane University Library; University of Arizona Library; University of California–Los Angeles Library; University of Kentucky Library; University of Maryland (Baltimore County) Library; University of New Mexico–Alberquerque Library; University of Wisconsin–Milwaukee Library.

Publication History

TITLE: *Astounding Stories of Super-Science*, January 1930–January 1931, and January–March 1933; *Astounding Stories*, February 1931–November 1932, and October 1933–February 1938; *Astounding Science-Fiction*, March 1938–January 1960 (hyphen dropped from November 1946); *Astounding/Analog Science Fact & Fiction*, February 1960–September 1960; *Analog Science Fact-Fiction*, October 1960–November 1961; *Analog Science Fact-Science Fiction*, December 1961–March 1965; *Analog Science Fiction-Science Fact*, April 1965–.

VOLUME DATA: Volume 1, Number 1, January 1930–Volume 102 [Number 1 dated January 4, 1982]. Three issues per volume, monthly, until Volume 10, Number 3, June 1932. Volume 11, three issues, bi-monthly, September 1932–January 1933. Volume 12, six issues, March 1933, then monthly from October 1933. Thereafter, six issues per volume, monthly, until Volume 93, Number 6, August 1974. Volume 94, five issues, monthly, September 1974–January 1975. Volume

95 begins with Number 2, February 1975–Number 12, December 1975. Thereafter volume sequence corresponds to year, twelve issues per volume, monthly, until Volume 100, Number 12, December 1980. Volume 101, thirteen issues, January 5, 1981–December 7, 1981, four-weekly. Volume 102, thirteen issues, January 4, 1982–. [Full cover date printed until March 29, followed by May issue, and month only designation.]

PUBLISHER: Clayton Magazines, Inc., New York, January 1930–March 1933 [initially under the imprint Publisher's Fiscal Corp., followed by Readers Guild, Inc.]; Street & Smith Publications, October 1933–January 1961; Condé Nast Publications, February 1961–August 1980; Davis Publications, September 1980–.

EDITORS: Harry Bates, January 1930–March 1933; F. Orlin Tremaine, October 1933–November 1937; John W. Campbell, Jr., December 1937–December 1971; Ben Bova, January 1972–November 1978; Stanley Schmidt, December 1978–.

FORMAT: Pulp, 144pp., January 1930–February 1934; 160pp., March 1934–December 1941; Large Pulp, 132pp., January 1942–April 1943; Pulp, 160pp., May–October 1943; Digest, 176pp., November 1943–February 1947; 160pp., March 1947–December 1959, and February 1960 [an eight-page photographic supplement was included as extra between August 1951 and July 1953, except May 1953]; 176pp., January 1960–February 1963 [except February 1960]; Large-size, 96pp., March 1963–March 1965; Digest, 160pp., April 1965–July 1966; 176pp., August 1966–December 1984; 192pp., mid-December 1984–.

PRICE: 20¢, January 1930–December 1941; 25¢, January 1942–July 1951; 35¢, August 1951–October 1959; 50¢, November 1959–July 1966; 60¢, August 1966–June 1974; 75¢, July 1974–February 1975; $1.00, March 1975–March 1977; $1.25, April 1977–March 1980; $1.50, April 1980–November 1982; $1.75, December 1982–December 1984; $2.00, mid-December 1984–.

Albert I. Berger (sections I–III)
Mike Ashley (section IV)

THE ARGOSY and ALL-STORY

Neither *The Argosy* nor *All-Story* was a science fiction or fantasy magazine, and yet they probably influenced the course of science fiction more than any other magazine either within or outside of the field with the exceptions of *Astounding Science-Fiction* (*Analog Science Fiction**) and *Amazing Stories.** Moreover, their names are held in such nostalgic esteem that, despite the fact that most of the fiction they carried was nonfantastic, the two magazines might just as well have been devoted entirely to fantasy, since, were it not for the SF and fantasy genre, the history of either title would doubtless long have been forgotten.

Argosy and *All-Story* were companion pulp fiction magazines from the great publishing empire of Frank A. Munsey. Indeed, it was *Argosy* that had started it all when it became the first all-fiction pulp magazine in 1896. It had existed long before that, originating as a children's weekly called *The Golden Argosy* on December 9, 1882. The "Golden" was dropped in 1888, and it changed from a weekly to a monthly in 1894. During this period, when it carried both stories and articles, it offered little in the way of SF, although Andre Laurie's "The Conquest of the Moon," first published in France in 1888, was serialized in *The Argosy* at the end of 1889.

When Munsey took the bold step of converting *Argosy* to an all-fiction men's magazine and soon thereafter reduced the stock to coarse pulp paper, the whole package selling for just ten cents, everything changed. The first pulp number, dated December 1896, carried one SF story, "Citizen 504" by C. H. Palmer. An anti-utopia set in a future of arranged marriages, the story was reprinted by Sam Moskowitz in his *Science Fiction by Gaslight* (Cleveland: World, 1968).

Although probably not a deliberate policy, such pseudo-scientific tales became regular items in *Argosy's* makeup, with at least one such piece an issue, either a short story or the installment of a serial. There were a few bleak periods, and in the early years few of the names were of much consequence, although Tudor Jenks and Frank Aubrey were known for their general adventure fiction, and latterly, thanks to the delvings of historians like Sam Moskowitz, Wardon Allan Curtis has taken on a belated, albeit minor, significance.

It was not until the early 1900s that greater names began to make their mark. James Branch Cabell, for instance, made his debut in the February 1902 issue with "An Amateur Ghost." July 1903 saw the first episode of "A Round Trip to the Year 2000" by William Wallace Cook, the first of many SF stories and serials that this talented dime novelist would contribute to the pulps. At this time, though, the bulk of what passed as science fiction was served up in the form of madcap inventions, mostly from the pens of writers Edgar Franklin and Howard R. Garis. W. W. Cook aside, the most original contributor for the period was Frank Lillie Pollock, whose excellent end-of-the-world story, "Finis," appeared in the June 1906 issue and has frequently been reprinted.

Munsey had launched a number of other magazines, but the first genuine all-fiction companion was *The All-Story Magazine*, with the premier issue dated January 1905. It was the first real sign that the pulp magazine war was on, with other companies bringing out rival publications. Street and Smith had released *The Popular Magazine* in November 1903, while in May 1905 the Story-Press Corporation issued *The Monthly Story Magazine*. Two years later this became *The Blue Book Magazine*, one of the most prestigious of all pulps, perhaps second only to *Adventure*. There were many, many more such magazines, and all to a greater or lesser extent published at least some fantasy: indeed, *Blue Book* discovered George Allan England. But the real future of SF in the pulps was governed predominantly by *All-Story* and, to a lesser degree, by *Argosy*.

Science fiction was evident in *All-Story* from the first issue with the serial "When Time Slipped a Cog" by W. Bert Foster, about a man who loses a year of his life, and "The Great Sleep Tanks," a short story by Margaret P. Montague that looks at the idea of sleep as being a tangible essence which can be extracted from the atmosphere and stored in great tanks, leaving the population sleepless.

Other contributors in the early years included Don Mark Lemon, Edgar Franklin and even M. R. James, but by 1909 the SF in *All-Story* was beginning to feature major contributors. The first big names were Garrett P. Serviss and George Allan England. Serviss had already established himself in the SF field with "Edison's Conquest of Mars" in 1898, and his novel from 1900, "The Moon Metal," was reprinted in the May 1905 issue. The year 1909 saw a new Serviss serial, possibly his best: "A Columbus of Space," serialized between January and June. England, in the meanwhile, had contributed such stories as "The House of Green Flame," "The Time Annihilator" and the serial "Beyond White Seas."

If these two authors were all set to establish themselves as *All-Story*'s cornerstone fantasists, that opportunity was wrenched from their grasp in 1912 with the appearance of Edgar Rice Burroughs. The publication of "Under the Moons of Mars" as a six-part serial starting in the February 1912 issue of *All-Story* and the inclusion of "Tarzan of the Apes" complete in the October 1912 issue must go down as the two most important events in the early history of magazine SF.

Burrough's Martian and jungle novels became so popular that they did more than spawn imitators: they helped *All-Story* go weekly in March 1914. *Argosy* would follow as a weekly in 1917. During the war years fantasies spilled from the pens of Perley Poore Sheehan, George Allan England, John U. Giesy, Achmed Abdullah, H. Bedford-Jones, Victor Rousseau and Charles B. Stilson. Stilson offered one of the best imitations of the Burroughs novels in his Polaris trilogy, set in a lost land in Antarctica. Starting with "Polaris of the Snows" (*All-Story Weekly [ASW]*, 1915), the series continued with "Minos of Sardanes" (*ASW*, 1916) and "Polaris and the Goddess Glorian" (*ASW*, 1917). In the same vein, though set on a planet orbiting Sirius, was the Jason Croft trilogy by J. U. Giesy: "Palos of the Dog Star Pack" (*ASW*, 1918), "The Mouthpiece of Zitu" (*ASW*, 1919) and "Jason, Son of Jason" (*Argosy*, 1921).

By this time many of the new generation of major fantasy writers were emerging. Gertrude Bennett, better known as Francis Stevens, had sold her first story to *ASW* in 1916 and became a regular contributor of fantasy stories and serials, mostly to *Argosy* from 1917 onward. Perhaps her best-known work from its pages was "The Citadel of Fear" (*Argosy*, 1918), and she would later appear in *The Thrill Book** and *Weird Tales.**

Austin Hall made an auspicious debut in *ASW* for October 7, 1916, with "Almost Immortal" and went on to write many such immortal stories including the classic novel "The Blind Spot" (*Argosy*, 1921), written in collaboration with Homer Eon Flint, who had started to establish himself as a powerful fantasy author in his own right with such stories as "Lord of Death" (*ASW*, May 10, 1919) and "The Queen of Life" (*ASW*, August 16, 1919). Then there were Philip M. Fisher, Tod Robbins and even Max Brand, whose early stories "Devil Ritter," "John Ovington Returns" and "That Receding Brow" (all in *ASW* during 1918–1919) were pure fantasies and would surprise devotees of his later westerns or the Dr. Kildare stories.

But during 1918 and 1919 three major names emerged who would lead SF on into the next stage of its evolution: Abraham Merritt, Murray Leinster and

Ray Cummings. Merritt, certainly to be numbered among the greatest of all fantasy writers, was the harbinger. His adventure in other dimensions, "Through the Dragon Glass," marked his debut in the November 24, 1917 *ASW*. It was followed by the immortal "The Moon Pool" (*ASW*, June 22, 1918), which led to the novel-length sequel "The Conquest of the Moon Pool" (*ASW*, 1919). Merritt went on to be, possibly, the most popular writer for the magazine. Certainly when *Argosy* conducted a poll in 1938 to find what was the most popular story it had published in its long history, Merritt's "The Ship of Ishtar," from 1924, came out on top. Merritt's work influenced many writers, among them Jack Williamson and Hannes Bok, and his work still sells steadily today, forty years after his death.

Ray Cummings debuted in *All-Story* while Merritt's "Conquest of the Moon Pool" was still running, making the March 15, 1919 issue something of a bonanza. So popular was Cummings' "The Girl in the Golden Atom" that the author continued to rewrite the same plot for years to come. Cummings was an author who appeared at the right time, with the right story. Although much revered among old-timers, he failed to make the most of his talent and by the 1930s had become a prolific, albeit competent, hack for the terror and weird mystery magazines. Although his name continued to appear in the SF magazines right through to the 1950s and although he was among the most prodigious of the early writers, he never again achieved the popularity of his first sale, although his stories in the early Clayton issues of *Astounding Stories* could rival that claim.

Murray Leinster was the most accomplished writer to emerge from this period as far as *science* fiction was concerned, although his early stories, such as "Oh, Aladdin" (*ASW*, January 11, 1919) and the oft-reprinted "The Runaway Sky-scraper" (*Argosy*, February 22, 1919), flaunted their misuse of science. Leinster had already been selling nonfantasies to Munsey since 1918 and was equally at home writing westerns, jungle adventures and SF, but it was in the latter genre that he was most revered. His first real claim to greatness came with the pub-lication of "The Mad Planet" (*Argosy*, June 12, 1920), an imaginative tour de force set 30,000 years in the future.

In July 1920 *All-Story* and *Argosy* combined, but the magazine stayed weekly until 1941. During the 1920s and 1930s it continued to feature SF regularly, and it was a mark of prestige among SF writers not to sell to the regular SF magazines, but to appear in *Argosy*. Apart from those already mentioned, Ralph Milne Farley, R. F. Starzl, Otis Adelbert Kline, Harl Vincent, Donald Wandrei, Robert E. Howard, Jack Williamson, Arthur Leo Zagat, Paul Ernst, Nelson S. Bond and Henry Kuttner all made its pages, and there was, in addition, SF from the pens of Erle Stanley Gardner, Theodore Roscoe, George F. Worts, Garrett Smith, J. Allan Dunn and many other pulp regulars. SF was gradually phased out of the magazine in the 1940s, however, when it was acquired by Popular Publications, which already published several SF and fantasy magazines of its own, and it was converted to a general men's magazine, later still publishing less and less fiction of any kind. The last SF of note listed in most bibliographies was C. L. Moore and Henry Kuttner's serial "Earth's Last Citadel," which ran from April to July 1943.

While *Argosy* was still a major market during these last twenty years and served as an incentive to writers, it was not as powerful an influence on SF as it had been for the previous twenty years. By allowing writers a free rein with their imaginative concepts and, indeed, by openly encouraging such endeavors, *All-Story* in particular, under its much-loved editor Robert H. Davis, did more to advance SF than any other magazine before *Amazing Stories*. Although it made a few mistakes—Davis rejected E. E. Smith's *The Skylark of Space*, for instance—these were minimal. Instead, the effect of the magazine upon the mind and imagination of such fledgling writers as Edmond Hamilton—who found the inspiration to become a writer in the stories of *Argosy*—and no doubt many others, was to repay the fiction field multifold. When Jacob Henneberger started *Weird Tales* in 1923 it attracted many writers from *Argosy*. When Gernsback launched *Amazing* in 1926 he reprinted many stories from *Argosy* and *All-Story*, predominantly those of Leinster, Burroughs and Merritt. When the SF field entered a boom period in the late 1930s, the Munsey Corporation issued its own entrant, *Famous Fantastic Mysteries*,* and drew its contents almost entirely from the pages of *Argosy* and *All-Story* (and another Munsey magazine, *Cavalier*). This time the stories were illustrated by Virgil Finlay and, later, Lawrence Stevens, and the combination of beautiful artwork and nostalgia was irresistible to the fans.

In the days before SF took itself too seriously, *Argosy* and *All-Story* offered stories that were powerful in their innocence, powerful in their originality, and powerful in their durability. That so many of these stories can still be read and enjoyed today, even when many of the concepts are long outmoded, is a testament to their strength. With no pretentions to grandeur, but with an intense enjoyment and satisfaction in what they wrote, men like Charles B. Stilson, Abraham Merritt, Murray Leinster, Ray Cummings and Austin Hall laid a solid platform on the foundations already established by Jules Verne and H. G. Wells whereupon the tower of science fiction would be built. Although it was Hugo Gernsback who laid the first few courses of that tower, it was not from his tradition that the SF in *Amazing Stories* owed its origins, even though he brought writers from *Science and Invention** into *Amazing*. In the end it was the *Argosy* adventure tradition that prevailed, and it is more than justifiable to regard *Argosy*, Frank Munsey and Bob Davis, rather than Hugo Gernsback, as the magazine antecedents of science fiction.

Information Sources

BIBLIOGRAPHY:
Dewart, William T. "The Story of Argosy." *Argosy Weekly*, December 10, 1932.
Moskowitz, Sam. "A History of Science Fiction in the Popular Magazines, 1891–1911."

Introduction to *Science Fiction by Gaslight*. Cleveland, Ohio: World, 1968. (Also includes three stories from *The Argosy*.)
————. "A History of the 'Scientific Romance' in the Munsey Magazines, 1912–1920." Afterword in *Under the Moons of Mars*. New York: Holt, Rinehart and Winston, 1970. (Also includes eight stories and episodes from the two magazines.)
Porges, Irwin. *Edgar Rice Burroughs: The Man Who Created Tarzan*, 2 vols. Provo, Utah: Brigham Young University Press, 1975.
INDEX SOURCES: Hasse, Henry, *Index to Fantasy and Science Fiction in Munsey Publications*, Alhambra, Calif.: Munsey Publications, 1976); IWFM; Tuck.
REPRINT SOURCES: See entries for *Famous Fantastic Mysteries, Fantastic Novels* and *A. Merritt's Fantasy Magazine*. See also Moskowitz items in bibliography.
LOCATION SOURCES: Pennsylvania State University Library; U.C.L.A. Special Collections.

Publication History (Abbreviated)

TITLE: *The All-Story Magazine*, January 1905–March 1914; *All-Story Weekly*, March 7, 1914–May 9, 1914; *All-Story Cavalier Weekly* [magazine merged with *The Cavalier*], May 16, 1914–May 8, 1915; *All-Story Weekly*, May 15, 1915–July 17, 1920. Thereafter merged with *Argosy*. Total run: 444 issues.
The Golden Argosy, December 9, 1882–November 24, 1888; *The Argosy*, December 1, 1888–September 1917; *Argosy Weekly*, October 6, 1917–July 17, 1920; *Argosy All-Story Weekly*, July 24, 1920–September 28, 1929; *Argosy Weekly*, October 5, 1929–October 4, 1941; *The Argosy*, November 1, 1941 and thereafter.
VOLUME DATA: Weekly, December 9, 1882–March 31, 1894 (591 issues); monthly, April 1894–September 1917 (282 issues); weekly, October 6, 1917–October 4, 1941 (1,253 issues); bi-monthly, November 1, 1941–May 1942 (4 issues); thereafter monthly, from July 1942. The issue for July 1943 is generally regarded as the last SF issue. Counting from the first all-fiction issue in October, 1896, that gives a total relative run of 1,522 issues (*Argosy* only).
PUBLISHER: E. G. Rideout, December 9, 1882–September 1, 1883; Frank A. Munsey, September 8, 1883–December 26, 1925; William T. Dewart, January 2, 1926–May 1942; Popular Publications, July 1942 and thereafter.
EDITORS:
All-Story: Robert H. Davis.
Argosy: Frank A. Munsey, December 9, 1882–November 27, 1886; Matthew White, Jr., 1886–June 2, 1928. Subsequent editors include A. H. Bittner (1928–1930), Don Moore (1930–1931), Albert J. Gibner (1931–1936); Chandler H. Whipple (1937–1939); George W. Post (1940–1942); Henry Steeger (1942–1948).
FORMAT: The number of pages varied considerably for both magazines, especially in the later years, but it was predominantly Pulp, 192 pp., for most of the relevant issues.
PRICE: Varied, 10¢ for most issues.

Mike Ashley

ARGOSY SPECIAL

Argosy Special was a one-shot reprint magazine issued by the publishers of *Argosy** in 1977 as Number 8 of a series of special issues devoted to a variety of topics. Nine stories were drawn from *Super Science Stories*,* which the publishers had issued nearly thirty years earlier. The stories were not of any special value, although included was Chad Oliver's first sale, ''The Land of Lost Content.'' Of greater value were the accompanying illustrations, also reproduced from the original magazine and including some examples of Virgil Finlay's work. For completist collectors only.

Information Sources

BIBLIOGRAPHY:
Mandler, Peter. Letter to *Locus* 202 (July 1977): 7. (See also *Locus* 203, p. 10 [letter by George Flynn], and *Locus* 208, pp. 6 and 8 [Magazine Survey].)
INDEX SOURCES: Boyajian, Jerry, and Kenneth R. Johnson, *Index to the Science Fiction Magazines: 1977*, Cambridge, MA: Twaci Press, 1982; SFM.
REPRINT SOURCES: None known.
LOCATION SOURCES: M.I.T. Science Fiction Library.

Publication History

TITLE: *Argosy Special—Science Fiction.*
VOLUME DATA: Number 8 in a series, undated [Summer 1977].
PUBLISHER: Popular Publications, New York.
EDITOR: Lon Sahadi.
FORMAT: Digest, 64 pp.
PRICE: 75¢.

Mike Ashley

ARIEL, THE BOOK OF FANTASY

Ariel started life in the fall of 1976 as a large, semi-professional art-orientated fanzine. The first issue featured Frank Frazetta with two short articles and the first half of a two-part interview, abundantly illustrated by selections of Frazetta's artwork. The issue also contained articles on Hogarth and Tarzan, the changing face of Batman, and pulp magazine covers; and ''Conan the Existential'' was reprinted from *Amra* and illustrated by Marvel Comics' version of Conan to give some connection to the comics scene. Some poems by Robert E. Howard and two stories were also included, and the issue was completed by an excerpt from the Richard Corben/John Jakes graphic novel *Bloodstar* and a reprint of Corben's *Den* from the underground comic *Grim Wit 2*. This last item carried the only color artwork to be featured within the issue. No credits were given to the reprints. The overall impression was of a very attractive package, though on closer inspection it is seen to be lightweight, employing many comic-strip reprints and Frazetta paintings to fill the large spaces that would otherwise surround the text.

The second issue was a great improvement. The Frazetta interview was completed and a further episode of *Den* appeared, as did a good selection of fiction by some top authors, an interesting comic strip by Bruce Jones, plus articles and fillers. Some material was again reprint, but this time it was credited.

Nevertheless, there was once again an ersatz quality about the production: it was characterized by artwork that was not always first class and by inflated fillers which would better have been forgotten. Fortunately these could be ignored in the presence of Frazetta, Corben, and Jeff and Bruce Jones.

Issues 3 and 4 were distributed by Ballantine Books, which should have boosted sales and brought the magazine professional material of good quality. Instead, the opposite was true. Issue 2 was the best of the run, issues 3 and 4 being failures in comparison. While some of the artwork in these issues was first rate, much was brightly colored trivia, and sometimes hazy, sepia photographs were used. The quality of the fiction was disappointing; not even names like Roger Zelazny, Harlan Ellison and Larry Niven salvaged *Ariel*. The appearance of an early, previously unpublished Elric story by Michael Moorcock, "The Last Enchantment," enhanced only the collectability of the issue, not the quality. The remainder of the text consisted of insipid fillers overblown by artwork.

The impression that *Ariel* left was one of stunning but superficial quality which failed to deliver the goods that the appearance promised. Whether this was the direct result of *Ariel*'s demise or whether, as has been suggested, it was Ballantine Books' fault due to its poor distribution of the last two volumes, with consequent poor sales, is not clear. A publication such as *Ariel* is not a viable newsstand commodity. Its large format, full color, extensive artwork and heavy gloss stock take it beyond the league of *Time* and *Playboy*. As a specialist publication, it did not sell in the local stores because it looked and *was* expensive. Not only was Ballantine Books at fault; so were its publisher and editor. Nevertheless, the failure of *Ariel* was unfortunate. Despite its faults, it was one of a kind.

Information Sources

BIBLIOGRAPHY:
Nicholls. *Encyclopedia*.
INDEX SOURCES: MT.
REPRINT SOURCES: None known.
LOCATION SOURCES: M.I.T. Science Fiction Library.

Publication History

TITLE: *Ariel, the Book of Fantasy*.
VOLUME DATA: Volume 1, Autumn 1976–Volume 4, October 1978. No separate issue
    numbers. Publication irregular. Issue 2 dated 1977, issue 3, April 1978.
PUBLISHER: Ariel Books (Armand Eisen).
EDITOR: Thomas Durwood.
FORMAT: Large-size (12"x 9"); first two issues 80 pp., last two 96 pp.
PRICE: Number 1, $5.95; Numbers 2 and 3, $6.95; Number 4, $7.95.

Jon Harvey

THE ARKHAM COLLECTOR

By the mid-1960s the administration of Arkham House was increasingly taxing the time and limited finances of its co-founder and editor-manager August Derleth. He chose to curtail his frequent stock-lists and announcements and to embody them in a new magazine for sale to interested customers. The little journal would also answer many of the typical questions that Derleth frequently received by post and thus help reduce his correspondence. (Derleth answered almost all his many letters within forty-eight hours.)

The first issue of *The Arkham Collector* appeared in the summer of 1967 and established the format all subsequent issues followed. It was neatly typeset, small (5'' by 7½''), coverless and with sequentially paged numbers through successive issues within the volume. Even more modest than its predecessor, *The Arkham Sampler*,* the magazine would have the same professional and literary tone that stamped nearly all of Derleth's publications.

Besides the Arkham book announcements, the first issue featured extracts from an essay by H. P. Lovecraft on science fiction, news from the field including notice of other periodicals and books of related interest, plus several poems. The first fiction did not appear until the third issue: "The Cyprus Shell" by Brian Lumley. Thereafter issues would carry usually two, sometimes three stories. It allowed Derleth to showcase new writers, such as Lumley, who had four stories in all, as well as Alan Dean Foster, Gary Myers and James Wade. Lumley and Myers both had subsequent volumes of fiction published by Arkham House.

Some of the tales published in *TAC* were by early writers. Lovecraft was present with two minor pieces. Also featured were Robert H. Barlow, Carl Jacobi, Howard Wandrei and Donald A. Wollheim. "The Waiting Room" (Spring 1971) was an example of Robert Aickman's understated but unnerving stories. Lin Carter, at that time still establishing himself as a writer and editor, was represented by two stories, and George Wetzel, pioneer Lovecraft bibliographer, had a vignette, "The Shadow Game," in the last issue.

Few of the stories are of major significance. There were twenty-six fictional items in *TAC*'s ten issues. Of greater import was the poetry, on which Derleth placed considerable emphasis. He published nearly eighty items in all, ranging from short squibs to relatively long narratives. They also ranged from early work by such elder poets as Thomas Bailey Aldrich, Clark Ashton Smith, H. P. Lovecraft and William Hope Hodgson, to work by such relative newcomers as Donald Sidney-Fryer—whose poetry volume would be the last Arkham House book in Derleth's lifetime—and Richard L. Tierney. Others included were Joseph Payne Brennan, Donald Wandrei, Edna Meudt, the acrostic poet Walter Shedlofsky, Wade Wellman, James Wade, Lin Carter and L. Sprague de Camp, whose verse Arkham House would also assemble into a small volume.

Occasional photographs and prose pieces, including obituaries of fantasy authors, filled out the issues. The journal was taken for granted as a rather marginal publication, but its abrupt cessation at Derleth's death had great effect. Two readers are known to have driven all the way to Arkham House in Wisconsin, offering to continue the *Collector*, but their offer was declined. Soon other, more lavish publications arose, some admittedly trying to fill the void. If *TAC* had any direct successor it was *Whispers*,* but *TAC* was an inspiration to many key periodicals of the 1970s small press movement. This may, in the final analysis, be the magazine's major importance, especially when considering the influence of the emerging small press poets of the 1970s.

Information Sources

BIBLIOGRAPHY:
Eng, Steve. "August Derleth, Friend of Fantasy Poetry." In Richard Fawcett's forth-coming volume of critical essays on Derleth.
Jaffery, Sheldon. *Horrors and Unpleasantries: A Bibliographic History and Collector's Price Guide to Arkham House*. Bowling Green, Ohio: Bowling Green University Popular Press, 1982.
INDEX SOURCES: Retrospective index to Volume 1 in final issue; MT.
REPRINT SOURCES:
Volume 1 was rebound in hardback in two differing states by Arkham House in 1971.
LOCATION SOURCES: Duke University Library; East New Mexico University Library; Steve Eng collection; Florida State University Library; Free Library of Philadelphia; Library of Congress; Memphis State University Library; M.I.T. Science Fiction Library; University of California-Riverside Library.

Publication History

TITLE: *The Arkham Collector*.
VOLUME DATA: Number 1, Summer 1967–Number 10, Summer 1971, treated as Volume 1. Bi-annual. Total run: 10 issues.
PUBLISHER: Arkham House, Sauk City, Wisconsin.
EDITOR: August Derleth.
FORMAT: Booklet. Pages varied as follows: Number 1, 24 pp.; Number 2, 28 pp.; Numbers 3 and 4, 36 pp.; Numbers 5–7, 32 pp.; Number 8, 36 pp.; Number 9, 44 pp.; Number 10, 48 pp. (Total, 348 pp.)
PRICE: 50¢.

Steve Eng

THE ARKHAM SAMPLER

The Arkham Sampler was an offshoot of August Derleth's Arkham House book publishing program. It was a short-lived quarterly, running for eight issues. Like *The Arkham Collector** two decades later, it served both as a showcase for the type of material Derleth wanted to publish and as a vehicle for printing some of the surplus material that might otherwise wait too long to appear in book form.

Derleth had originally founded Arkham House in 1939 with Donald Wandrei to publish H. P. Lovecraft's works, but they soon developed a small but regular market for other books of fantasy fiction and, subsequently, poetry. During the postwar science fiction boom it began to look as though all fantasy—even supernatural and weird fiction—might flourish. Optimistically, Derleth increased his publishing program. He had high hopes that a fantasy literary quarterly might prove self-supporting. At that time few fanzines had high literary quality (*The Acolyte* being an exception), and their design and printing were almost always amateur. The first issue of *TAS*, dated Winter 1948, was distinguished from its fanzine counterparts by its detached literary tone, attractive design, professional printing and layout, and quality book paper. The serious format well suited the fiction, poetry, articles and knowledgeable book reviews.

While not of major importance as a fiction magazine, *TAS* published many noted authors. Of special significance was H. Russell Wakefield, neglected in his native England, who found a saving mentor in Derleth. Wakefield's "Messrs. Turkes and Talbot" led the first issue, and he was also present in the final issue with his terse conversational chiller "The Triumph of Death." Robert Bloch contributed one story, "Change of Heart" (Autumn 1948), plus frequent reviews and articles. Ray Bradbury was represented by a number of short science fiction pieces, while the noted poet and colorful fiction stylist Clark Ashton Smith had one tale, "The Root of Ampoi" (Spring 1949), and many poems. Bookman Malcolm Ferguson departed pleasantly from Coleridge's "Kubla Khan" in "A Damsel with a Dulcimer" (Spring 1948); Lord Dunsany offered one of his Jorkens tall tales, "The Sign" (Autumn 1948), and there were other contributions by Leah Bodine Drake, Fritz Leiber and Derleth himself under his "Stephen Grendon" alias.

Needless to say, Lovecraft formed a prominent part of the magazine. The first issue presented not only a short essay by Lovecraft on the "History and Chronology of the Necronomicon" but also the first part of a four-part serialization of "The Dream-Quest of Unknown Kadath," which had earlier appeared in Arkham's Lovecraft omnibus *Beyond the Wall of Sleep* (1943). The second issue continued the serial and presented a group of letters by Lovecraft, plus some random notes on the Cthulhu Mythos by George T. Wetzel and on "The Lurker at the Threshold" by Derleth. These items, in the form of reminiscences, analyses or memorabilia, ran throughout *TAS*'s existence.

The Winter 1949 issue was a special science fiction number and featured stories by Ray Bradbury, A. E. van Vogt and John Beynon Harris; an article on "The Case for Science Fiction" by Sam Moskowitz; and a symposium on "A Basic Science Fiction Library" with contributions by Forrest Ackerman, Everett Bleiler, David H. Keller, Sam Merwin, Jr., P. Schuyler Miller, Sam Moskowitz, "Lewis Padgett," Paul L. Payne, A. Langley Searles, Theodore Sturgeon, A. E. van Vogt and Donald Wandrei.

To cut costs Derleth began to rely more on reprints. Much of the Spring 1949 issue was taken up by J. A. Mitchell's 1889 short novel "The Last American." The Summer 1949 issue carried Jules Verne's "In the Year 2889," plus the first part of a new serial, "Journey to the World Underground," the 1741 classic by Lewis (*sic*) Holberg.

By 1949, however, it was clear that Derleth's literary and somewhat self-indulgent, if time-consuming, experiment had failed to pay for itself, and with regret he stopped the magazine, trying to sell back copies at cover price for several years. Today, single issues may fetch up to twenty times their original cost. Although *TAS* carried a number of competent new stories, that had not been its prime purpose. Derleth's quarterly had tried to elevate the fields of weird and horror fantasy, and to some degree science fiction, with distinguished critical writing and reviewing. In this respect *TAS*, however unprofitable, was decades before its time.

Note

The author would like to thank Gary Crawford, Richard Minter, Richard Wald and Betsy Fisher for information and loaning of materials.

Editor's Note

The name *The Arkham Sampler* was revived in 1983 by the small press publisher R. Alain Everts as the title of a small (7'' by 5'') quarterly chapbook. It was rather more in the mold of *The Arkham Collector* as it served in one capacity as the catalogue of Evert's The Strange Company, but its main purpose was as a supplement to the magazine *Etchings & Odysseys** which Everts had also revived. The new *TAS* was only 32 pages long and each issue, while featuring a variety of poetry, has varied in purpose. Issue 3 (December 1983), for example, was a portfolio of twenty-eight previously unpublished photographs of H. P. Lovecraft. Issue 4 (March 1984) was a special poetry issue in memorial to Jim Spencer (1944-1983). Issue 5 (June 1984) was a "horror and phantasy art special," while issues 6 and 7 (September and December 1984) have concentrated on short horror fiction. *TAS* can be ordered from The Strange Company, P.O. Box 864, Madison, Wisconsin 53701 at $2.50 each issue, and it is indexed fully in MT.

Information Sources

BIBLIOGRAPHY:
Jaffery, Sheldon. *Horrors and Unpleasantries: A Bibliographic History and Collector's Price Guide to Arkham House*. Bowling Green, Ohio: Bowling Green University Popular Press, 1982.
Nicholls. *Encyclopedia*.
Tuck.
INDEX SOURCES: Retrospective index in the final issue, Autumn 1949; Derleth, August, *Arkham House: The First Twenty Years: 1939–1959*, Sauk City, Wis.: Arkham House, 1959 (enlarged ed., *Thirty Years of Arkham House 1939–1969* [1969]); MT; Tuck.
REPRINT SOURCES: None known.
LOCATION SOURCES: Library of Congress, Washington D.C.; M.I.T. Science Fiction Library; University of California–Berkeley Library; Pennsylvania State University Library.

Publication History

TITLE: *The Arkham Sampler*.
VOLUME DATA: Volume 1, Number 1, Winter 1948–Volume 2, Number 4, Autumn
    1949. Four issues per volume; quarterly. Total run: 8 issues.
PUBLISHER: Arkham House, Sauk City, Wisconsin.
EDITOR: August Derleth.
FORMAT: Intermediate (9''x 6''), 100 pp.; last two issues, 128 pp.
PRICE: $1.00.

Steve Eng

ASIMOV'S SCIENCE FICTION MAGAZINE

See ISAAC ASIMOV'S SCIENCE FICTION MAGAZINE.

ASIMOV'S SF ADVENTURE MAGAZINE

This magazine was started as a deliberate attempt to recapture an older mode of science fiction.[1] In the first issue, dated Fall 1978, Isaac Asimov traced the development of adventure-oriented magazines, finding their demise in the mid-1950s to be a result of a gradual shift in the science fiction readership of earlier times. Thus, by historical accident " 'adventure' has come to mean 'pulp' and both have come to mean 'bad writing.' "[2] This equation was rejected by Asimov, and quality adventure stories in a science fictional setting were promised that would be enjoyable by all ages.

By the third issue the adventure concept had been expanded to include occasional "stories in the tradition of Robert E. Howard and his Conan the Barbarian; of Fritz Leiber and his Fafhrd and the Gray Mouser; of J.R.R. Tolkien and his tales of Middle Earth."[3] Asimov went on to characterize these as being set in a prescientific universe and thus not science fiction, but still adventure.

Stories by Asimov appeared in some issues, among them "Fair Exchange?" in the first. Here a protagonist saves the lost Gilbert and Sullivan operetta "Thespis," but the alterations in subsequent history lead to his wife's death. The third issue had a much lighter piece, a satire on the biblical and scientific versions of creation.

The cover story of the first issue was a rewritten version of Poul Anderson's 1951 "Captive of the Centaurianess," which originally ran in *Planet Stories*.* The changes were mainly to allow for some advances in astronomical knowledge.

The magazine was a receptive host to series stories, although serials were felt to be inappropriate in a quarterly. The first issue had a Stainless Steel Rat story by Harry Harrison, although it might be noted that the protagonist's personality had long since shifted so much from the early works in the series that the appellation is hardly justified. Feghoots (short short puns by Reginald Bretnor) appeared. The "Starschool" series by the Haldeman brothers began in this magazine, later to be published as their first novel in collaboration.

The announced bias in favor of adventure stories and the later inclusion of fantasy permitted "Ghosts" by Keith Minnion to appear in the third issue. This story combines a trite science fictional rescue in orbit around Uranus with ghosts who are crucial to performing the rescue. The significance of this story is that it seems to be the first published science fiction to mention the rings of that planet, which were discovered in March 1977. Another entry under the expanded theme was Samuel R. Delany's "The Tale of Gorgik," which could be regarded as a Conan-type adventure. Roger Zelazny placed several of King Arthur's acquaintances in our world with "The Last Defender of Camelot." Both were later incorporated into longer works.

Alan Dean Foster's "Bystander" in the first issue suggested, as is usual with this author, acceptance of numerous scientific errors. This was, however, a frequent concomitant of the vanished adventure-oriented pulps Asimov hoped to revive.

Nonfictional materials included a centerfold poster of the cover art, without lettering; an editorial by Asimov; letters; and, starting in the second issue, a column of activities related to science fiction in Hollywood.

The magazine ceased publication with its fourth issue. Sales had been poor despite the lengthy newsstand exposure of a quarterly. This may have been due partially to its large size, which kept it separate from the other science fiction displayed, and the audience may have changed too much to appreciate the kind of fiction Asimov remembered nostalgically and tried to repopularize.

Notes

1. "Adventure!," editorial by Isaac Asimov, *Asimov's SF Adventure Magazine*, Fall 1978, pp. 6ff.

2. Ibid., p. 8.

3. "The Pre-Scientific Universe," editorial by Isaac Asimov, *Asimov's SF Adventure Magazine*, Summer 1979, p. 7.

Information Sources

INDEX SOURCES: NESFA-VI; SFM.
REPRINT SOURCES: None known.
LOCATION SOURCES: M.I.T. Science Fiction Library.

Publication History

TITLE: *Asimov's SF Adventure Magazine*.
VOLUME DATA: Volume 1, Number 1, Fall 1978–Volume 1, Number 4, Fall 1979.
    Quarterly, but no Winter 1979 issue. Total run: 4 issues.
PUBLISHER: Davis Publications, Inc., New York.

EDITOR: George Scithers.
FORMAT: Large Pulp (saddle-stapled), 116 pp., but last issue 112 pp.
PRICE: $1.75, but last issue $1.95.

Thomas W. Hamilton

ASTONISHING STORIES

The 1940s began as a bull market for science fiction magazines. The desperate years of the Depression were receding fast. Frederik Pohl, a brash young science fiction fan from New York, still in his teens, had developed the habit of visiting that city's editorial offices on the lookout for job possibilities. Wednesday, October 15, 1939, proved a most fateful day. He visited the offices of Robert O. Erisman, the editor of *Marvel Science Stories** and *Dynamic Science Stories** plus a string of less than respectable terror pulps. As Pohl recalls:

I remember deciding that I knew as much about science fiction as he did and so I asked him if he would like to hire me as his assistant. He politely declined the offer, but instead of throwing me out of his office he sent me across town to see Rogers Terrill, managing editor of Popular Publications. Popular had just started a cut-rate half-cent-a-word line of magazines and seemed to be in the market for additional titles; Terrill offered me a job, and at the nineteen I found myself editor of two science fiction magazines. One was *Astonishing Stories*. It sold for a dime, ran to 112 pulp-sized pages, used about 45,000 words of material an issue, and had a budget of $405. That was not just for stories; that was for stories *and* black-and-white art *and* an oil painting to be used for a cover.[1]

The other magazine was *Super Science Stories*,* which concentrated on longer stories, the two titles appearing in alternate months. The small budget severely hampered Pohl's chances of obtaining quality material, although by the end of 1940 it was increased to allow payment of a bonus for the better stories. Yet, despite this restriction, Pohl had two valuable resources on which to draw: a keen critical perspective and his membership in the Futurians.

The Futurians started as a group of precocious young New Yorkers brought together by an interest in science fiction. They read it and discussed it avidly, but they also wanted to write it, and write it they did, with what proved to be conspicuous success. Since Isaac Asimov was already selling to John Campbell's *Astounding* (*Analog Science Fiction**), Pohl had to be content with his rejects, but there were other talented Futurians. As one of their number, Damon Knight, recalled in later years:

During their first year of existence, Pohl's two bi-monthly magazines . . .
published thirteen stories by active Futurians (and two more by James
Blish, who became active later). Four were by Isaac Asimov, two by Pohl,
two by Wollheim (one under Lowndes's name), one by Wilson; the rest
were collaborations involving Pohl, Kornbluth, Wilson and Dockweiler in
various combinations.[2]

They were young writers whose best work lay in the future, but some of SF's
better writers and editors matured from the group. It also helped Pohl's own
writing interests, for often when he did not have enough copy to fill an issue,
he would insert material that he had written under various pseudonyms. Usually
his alias was "James MacCreigh," but he also borrowed the name "Dirk Wylie"
from another Futurian, Harry Dockweiler, and when he was collaborating with
Cyril Kornbluth they usually became "S. D. Gottesman." No other genre seems
to have science fiction's propensity for author collaborations. Damon Knight
recalls one case in point:

> At one point, Pohl . . . found himself ten thousand words short of the
> wordage he needed to fill an issue of *Astonishing*, and there was something
> like $35 left in his budget. Cyril Kornbluth and Dick Wilson volunteered
> to fill the gap. They wrote a story in alternate sections, taking turns at the
> typewriter; it was called "Stepsons of Mars"—a Foreign Legion epic
> transferred to the Martian sands. "Cyril would write a few sections,"
> Wilson told me, "and then I would take it and go on from there, and
> eventually we got it finished. It was a rather disjointed piece, as you may
> imagine; and Dirk Wylie [Dockweiler] then took this manuscript and re-
> wrote it. Then it was submitted to Fred, and he edited it further before it
> was published. And the pen name on it was 'Ivar Towers.' "[3]

Pohl's own efforts included "Earth, Farewell!," written under the MacCreigh
alias and published in the February 1943 issue. It is a tightly plotted, thought-
provoking tale in which the author handles the unsympathetic point of view of
his dehumanized narrator with a skill that anticipates his masterful use of the
device in later novels.

Jack Williamson has said of *Astonishing*: "If the magazine itself was not very
distinguished, it was at least a fine training ground for newcomers to the field."[4]
This judgment may be unduly harsh, for while it is true of such stories as "The
Last Drop" by L. Sprague de Camp and L. Ron Hubbard (November 1941),
which was below standard for both writers, and of the contributions by Leigh
Brackett and Ray Cummings, which were scarcely a notch above mediocre, there
was much that was memorable in *Astonishing*, both by way of immediate appeal
and of more lasting quality.

In the first category, for instance, came the continuing adventures of Professor
Jameson, a human whose brain had been transferred to a robot body and who

joined his rescuers in a series of adventures throughout the universe. The series, written by Neil R. Jones, had started in the pages of *Amazing Stories** in 1931 and was conventional space opera written in a very flat style; yet, although the episodes repeated the same basic pattern with minor variations, the fans still enjoyed them.

More understandable was the enthusiastic response to Henry Kuttner's "Soldiers of Space" (February 1943). This tale of a handful of veteran pilots holding off a treacherous attack until the fleet arrived appealed to the mood of the country in the midst of a hard-fought war, though it seems sentimental and dated to modern eyes. The same issue contained Robert Bloch's "It Happened Tomorrow." This realistic account of the extermination of mankind by machines is weak in both characterization and plot development, but its powerful sense of a civilization running amok struck as responsive a chord in readers as did the tales of heroism.

Pohl had been an astute observer of SF magazines and knew that any publication which catered to its readership, as Hugo Gernsback had done originally with *Amazing*, would stand a fair chance of success. In the first issue Pohl had declared that *Astonishing*'s motto would be "What you wish—that you shall have," and Pohl, more than most editors, kept his word. Two of the most memorable performances in *Astonishing* were Alfred Bester's "The Pet Nebula" (February 1941), which treats the old idea of the irresponsible scientist letting loose a menace upon the world with just the right touch of humor; and Ross Rocklynne's series on energy beings, "Into the Darkness" (June 1940), "Daughter of Darkness" (November 1941) and "Abyss of Darkness" (December 1942). In these the author succeeds not only in creating aliens who are both believable and unhuman, but also in exploring important themes, like the self-destruction that results from abandoning responsibility to others to pursue personal pleasure. The series eventually made its way into book form as *The Sun Destroyers* (New York: Ace Books, 1973).

Pohl also pandered to the SF devotee in other forms. He included a section on fanzines, giving pertinent data on the various magazines around the country, including names and addresses, and a lively letter column, "Viewpoints." Perhaps most significant were the review sections. As Paul Carter has pointed out, "In *Astonishing Stories* and *Super Science Stories*, book reviewing for the first time began to merit the term 'literary criticism,' and it was in those magazines that the custom began of paying attention to science fiction on the stage and screen."[5] Donald A. Wollheim handled most of the book and film reviews, but there were contributions by Forrest J Ackerman, Dick Wilson and John Michel, who even did a review of the theme music to the classic SF film, *Things to Come*. Wollheim's section of reviews was later expanded into the well-received section on fantasy material called "Fantasy Circle."

On the whole the artwork was poor, which, considering the budget, is not surprising. Pohl had to rely heavily on the work of fan artists, and some of their work was mediocre, but, just as with some of the writers, a few were excellent and went on to establish themselves in the field of SF art. One of the fan artists who went on to become something of a celebrity was Hannes Bok. Bok's works were distinctly different from those of many of his contemporaries; his interior illustrations had a wood-block aura about them (as did the works of two other imitative *Astonishing* artists, Gabriel Mayorga and Marconette), but Bok gave the unusual impression of freezing space and time. His detractors often found his work static, yet his style, once seen, is never forgotten. Ray Bradbury praised Bok's work in the August 1940 letter column. Later, in April 1943, when Bradbury had a story printed in *Astonishing*, it was Bok who did the illustrations.

Some of the other artists whose work appeared in the magazine were Jack Binder (the brother of writers Earl and Otto Binder), Matt Fox, Gerald Thorp, Leslie Perri (the pseudonym of Doris Baumgardt, whom Pohl married in 1940), John Giunta, Angus Dunn, Bob Sherry, Dave Kyle (another Futurian), J. B. Musacchia, Milton Luros, Dorothy Les Tina (who became Pohl's second wife in 1945) and Boris Dolgov.

As the magazine matured, the professional calibre of the art increased. Frank R. Paul, Leo Morey and Hans Wesso supplied interior and cover art. Starting with the June 1942 issue *Astonishing* gave full credit to the artists on the contents page, and that same issue featured a cover by the very popular Virgil Finlay. Finlay was probably more noted for his black and white interiors, particularly his voluptuous and sensuous women and his horrific aliens. His style is often characterized by painstaking detail in a stippled effect. Lawrence Stevens, noted for his macabre imagination, signed his alias Stephen Lawrence to several il- lustrations, although recent research by Robert Weinberg has revealed that at least some of these were the work of Stevens' son Peter. A. Leydenfrost could also bring forth the horrific and macabre; it has been said that "his style might be described as a blending of Finlay and Bok."[6]

Astonishing featured a fine blend of new and old talent, artists and writers alike. Alongside the hopefuls were such established names as Clifford S. Simak, Harl Vincent, E. E. Smith, Nelson S. Bond, Frank Belknap Long and L. Ron Hubbard. This mixture reflected the changing tone of SF during the early 1940s. The space opera with epic adventure and bug-eyed monsters still held sway, but the optimistic future, which had for so long been a mainstay of SF, was beginning to wane. The newer writers were starting to suspect that everything was not necessarily for the best—that technology had a Janus-face.

But World War II ended all that: most of the SF writers and artists were being drafted. The shortages created by the war, particularly of paper, brought to an end the SF boom, and for *Astonishing* the death knell was sounded when Pohl donned Uncle Sam's uniform. The April 1943 issue was the last published. Except from early summer 1941 to the beginning of 1942, when he had a disagreement with Popular Publications, Pohl, under the direction of Alden H. Norton, did most of the editorial work. When he departed for the war, Ejler Jakobsson was brought in to put together the final issue.

At a time when *Astounding* dominated the SF scene, it would be idle to pretend that *Astonishing* was other than average, or at times slightly above, but it is worth remembering for two reasons. First, along with its companion, it initiated a meaningful book review column, and second, it served as a valuable training ground, not only for some talented young writers, but also for its young editor. Looking back on those days, Pohl writes, "With what I know now I could have made those magazines sing, but as it was they just lay there."[7]

In many respects Pohl's contribution to the history of SF magazines has never been fully appreciated; he was really an SF *wunderkind*. There were other editors who, for their time, were greater than Pohl, but few who could have achieved so much, starting with so little. Pohl was, and is, a survivor—a more modern, more sensitive Gernsback. Knowing just how little money he had on which to operate, his direction of the contents and format shows considerable acumen, which would later come to full fruition in his editorial work on *Star Science Fiction** and *Galaxy Science Fiction.** Even if *Astonishing* did not sing loud and clear, it at least strove to find its voice with more determination and success than most of its rivals.

Notes

1. Frederik Pohl, "Ragged Claws," in *Hell's Cartographers*, ed. Brian W. Aldiss and Harry Harrison (New York: Harper & Row, 1975), p. 155. See also Pohl, *The Way the Future Was: A Memoir* (New York: Ballantine, 1979), p. 95; and Pohl, *The Early Pohl* (Garden City, N.Y.: Doubleday, 1976), pp. 23–24.

2. Damon Knight, *The Futurians* (New York: John Day, 1977), pp. 46–47.

3. Ibid., p. 46.

4. Jack Williamson, "The Years of Wonder," in *Voices for the Future*, Vol. 1, ed. Thomas Clareson (Bowling Green, Ohio: Bowling Green University Popular Press, 1976), pp. 10–11.

5. Paul Carter, *The Creation of Tomorrow* (New York: Columbia University Press, 1977), p. 296.

6. [Jon Gustafson], "Science Fiction Art," in Brian Ash, *The Visual Encyclopedia of Science Fiction* (New York: Harmony Books, 1977), p. 288.

7. Pohl, *Way the Future Was*, p. 108.

Information Sources

BIBLIOGRAPHY:
Nicholls. *Encyclopedia*.
Tuck.
INDEX SOURCES: ISFM; SFM; Tuck.
REPRINT SOURCES:
   Reprint Magazine: See separate entry for Canadian edition.
   Microform: Greenwood Press Periodical Series.
LOCATION SOURCES: M.I.T. Science Fiction Library; Pennsylvania State University
      Library.

Publication History

TITLE: *Astonishing Stories.*
VOLUME DATA: Volume 1, Number 1, February 1940–Volume 4, Number 4, April
    1943. Four issues per volume. Volumes 1 and 2, bi-monthly. Volume 3, irregular,
    September and November 1941, March and June 1942; Volume 4, bi-monthly
    from October 1942. Total run: 16 issues.
PUBLISHER: Fictioneers, Inc., a subsidiary of Popular Publications, Chicago and New
    York.
EDITORS: Frederik Pohl, February 1940–September 1941; Alden H. Norton, November
    1941–April 1943.
FORMAT: Pulp, 112 pp.
PRICE: 10¢.

Milton Wolf/Raymond H. Thompson

ASTONISHING STORIES (Canadian)

The Canadian edition of *Astonishing Stories* was instigated by Popular Publications when wartime import/export restrictions were levied. The three issues
were fairly straightforward reprint numbers, but with a slight twist. The first,
dated January 1942, was a reprint of stories and departments from American
*Astonishing Stories** of November 1941. The second, dated March 1942, was,
however, a reprint of the November 1941 *Super Science Stories** with the exclusion of "Pendulum" by Ray Bradbury and Henry Hasse, and the artwork.
The third and final issue, dated May 1942, reprinted the textual contents of the
March 1942 *Astonishing.*

The only difference in the three Canadian issues was the artwork. Each featured
an original, unsigned color cover and three unsigned pieces of interior art which
did not come from the U.S. edition and were very attractive.

It is interesting to note that the last issue was followed three months later by
the first issue of the Canadian *Super Science Stories,** which continued to reprint
alternate issues of the U.S. original titles and is thus to a great extent a continuation of this magazine under a new title. The reason for the name change is
not known.

Information Sources

BIBLIOGRAPHY:
Tuck.
INDEX SOURCES: Tuck.
REPRINT SOURCES: None known.
LOCATION SOURCES: M.I.T. Science Fiction Library.

Publication History

TITLE: *Astonishing Stories.*
VOLUME DATA: Volume 1, Number 1, January 1942–Volume 1, Number 3, May
    1942. Bi-monthly. Total run: 3 issues.

PUBLISHER: Popular Publications, Inc., Toronto, Canada.
EDITOR: Not identified.
FORMAT: Pulp, 96 pp. (dimensions slightly larger than U.S.).
PRICE: 10¢.

Grant Thiessen

ASTOUNDING SCIENCE-FICTION (1938–1960)

See ANALOG SCIENCE FICTION/SCIENCE FACT.

ASTOUNDING S[cience] F[iction] (1970)

See ASTOUNDING STORIES YEARBOOK.

ASTOUNDING STORIES

See ANALOG SCIENCE FICTION/SCIENCE FACT.

ASTOUNDING STORIES OF SUPER SCIENCE

See ANALOG SCIENCE FICTION/SCIENCE FACT.

ASTOUNDING STORIES YEARBOOK

One of the many digest magazines to be issued by Sol Cohen's Ultimate Publishing Company in the period 1966–1971, *Astounding Stories Yearbook* reprinted stories from early issues of *Amazing Stories.** Only two numbers of this magazine appeared. The first, released in the summer of 1970, was treated as a yearbook, while a second, dated Fall 1970, was retitled *Astounding SF*.

The title should not be confused with the original *Astounding*, the forerunner of today's *Analog Science Fiction,** although one look at the magazines would clear up any confusion. Nevertheless, the use of the hallowed name raised eyebrows in the SF community, where many were anxious to protect the memory of the original *Astounding*. In response to one such letter from respected fan Roy Tackett in the September 1970 *Analog*, John W. Campbell said: "Legally, when we changed our title to *Analog* we abandoned the *Astounding* title, putting it into the public domain. Thus anyone who wants to could appropriate it. Someone did." Perhaps Cohen realized that he was treading on dangerous ground, or perhaps the sales did not warrant the continuation of the title, for no further issues appeared.

The stories selected came mostly from the Sloane and Palmer *Amazing*s, and none was worthy of resurrection.

Information Sources

BIBLIOGRAPHY:
Nicholls. *Encyclopedia.*
INDEX SOURCES: ISFM-II; SFM.
REPRINT SOURCES: None known.
LOCATION SOURCES: M.I.T. Science Fiction Library.

Publication History

TITLE: *Astounding Stories Yearbook* (first issue, 1970). Retitled *Astounding SF*, Number 2, Fall 1970.
VOLUME DATA: *Yearbook*, unnumbered, 1970; Number 2, Fall 1970.
PUBLISHER: Ultimate Publishing Co., Flushing, New York.
EDITOR: Sol Cohen (not identified within issues).
FORMAT: Digest, 128 pp.
PRICE: *Yearbook*, 60¢; Number 2, 50¢.

Mike Ashley

AUTHENTIC SCIENCE FICTION

Authentic was the third point of the triangle of leading British SF magazines of the mid-1950s, with *New Worlds** and *Nebula Science Fiction** as companions. Yet it was originally conceived not as a magazine, but as a book series. The publishers, Hamilton and Company, had already experimented unsuccessfully with SF (including the magazines *Strange Adventures** and *Futuristic Stories**), but in 1949 they called in Gordon Landsborough to reorganize their lists. The decision was made to issue a science fiction novel twice a month, with the first—*Mushroom Men from Mars* by the pseudonymous Lee Stanton—released on January 1, 1951. As a paperback it took the standard pocketbook format with an identifying banner on the cover declaring the "Authentic Science Fiction Series."

The second novel, released on January 15, was *Reconnoitre Krellig II* by Jon J. Deegan, the first of what became a very popular series about the escapades of the crew of the spaceship "Old Growler." Deegan was at the time suspected to be the pseudonym of Herbert J. Campbell, who had joined Landsborough as technical editor and subsequently succeeded him as full editor. (Robert Reginald has since identified the Deegan books as the work of R. C. Sharp.)

Over the next few months changes came thick and fast as Landsborough and Campbell experimented with the publication's format and content. They hid behind the persona of "L. G. Holmes," who supplied an editorial to the third and subsequent issues, and they also started a letter column, ''Projectiles''; so from the third issue, now bearing the banner ''Science Fiction Fortnightly,'' the series began to assume the shape of a magazine. More editorial features, including book reviews, were added as issues passed and as the compilation of each issue took longer; by issue 9 in May 1951, it became *Science Fiction Monthly*, with the identifying *Authentic* added with issue 13 in September.

All this time the fiction consisted of simply one novel, but the editorial for issue 25 asked the relevant question ''Short—or Long?'' Plans were in hand to convert *Authentic* to a formal magazine, and a further step in this direction came with the introduction of a serial, ''Frontier Legion'' by Sydney J. Bounds, in issue 26. The full-length novels were now transferred to Hamilton's new SF line, Panther Books, and Landsborough, satisfied at the success of having made *Authentic* Hamilton's biggest steady seller, went to pastures new, leaving H. J. Campbell in full control.

The first real magazine issue was Number 29, published in January 1953. It still relied on a strong lead novel—''Immortal's Playthings'' by William F. Temple—and apart from another episode in Bounds' serial, the only other story was ''Welcome, Brothers!,'' a reprint of Ray Bradbury's ''Mars Is Heaven.'' As issues passed, however, the percentage of short stories increased, although initially the majority were reprints from U.S. magazines.

Campbell's main claim to fame at this time was the first publication of Charles L. Harness' short novel ''The Rose,'' now regarded as a notable contribution to the superman theme, but at that time rejected by all the leading American markets. *Authentic* was also the first magazine to publish a piece by Brian W. Aldiss—though not a story, indeed not an intended submission, but a long and serious letter supporting the need for a reliable British SF magazine. Given the title ''Now Consolidate,'' it was published complete in the November 1953 issue.

From the August 1953 issue *Authentic* phased out reprints and printed only new stories (although reprints reappeared in June 1956). The lead novels were considerably reduced in length, and while still labeled as such they were seldom more than 25,000 words.

Campbell, as a qualified scientist, placed an emphasis on non-fiction with short articles on a variety of topics. Starting with issue 35 (July 1953) art editor John Richards (under the alias ''Davis'') began a series of covers depicting the conquest of space which ran for fourteen issues and was then followed by another series on the solar system. These covers and their supporting notes were among the most pleasing on any British SF magazine, and in comparison covers on later issues were drab and lifeless.

Authentic featured a number of short stories by writers who seldom contributed to magazines and were known more for their novels—writers like Bryan Berry, Charles Eric Maine and Edmund Cooper. A few authors owe their first sales to H. J. Campbell, including Arthur Sellings (''The Haunting,'' October 1953), Clifford C. Reed (''Jean—Gene—Jeanne,'' November 1954) and Robert Presslie

("Trespassers Will Be Prosecuted," June 1955). As a rule, however, the magazine's contents varied between minor works by writers unknown outside of fandom, and average stories by writers like Kenneth Bulmer, Jonathan Burke and E. C. Tubb, one of whom appeared in almost every issue. Tubb in particular was at his most prolific in the mid-1950s, and he frequently had two or more stories per issue under pseudonyms. This increased in 1955 when H. J. Campbell tired of editing and, wishing to get back to his first love as a research chemist, handed the editorship of *Authentic* over to Tubb, whose first issue appeared in February 1956. Tubb found a shortage of good manuscripts, and in order to deliver copy on deadline he fleshed out issues himself or resorted to American reprints.

Under Tubb's editorship the nonfiction content was phased out except for a few regular departments mostly written by Tubb. Interior illustrations were also decreased and, from March 1957, *Authentic* enlarged from pocketbook to digest format. Tubb felt that *Authentic* was being overlooked on the stands because of the proliferation of paperbacks and that a conversion to digest size would increase sales—circulation had been dwindling over the last few years. It did not work. The publishers were convinced that the future lay in paperbacks and eventually axed *Authentic* in favor of boosting the Panther line.

Authentic was always readable, but, with the exception of Harness' "The Rose," published little fiction of any lasting quality. It was nevertheless a valuable market for aspiring writers, and its folding was the first major casualty on the British SF scene and a foretaste of the blight that would run riot over the next six years.

Information Sources

BIBLIOGRAPHY:
Nicholls. *Encyclopedia.*
Tuck.
INDEX SOURCES: IBSF; MIT; SFM; Tuck.
REPRINT SOURCES: None known.
LOCATION SOURCES: M.I.T. Science Fiction Library; Pennsylvania State University
     Library.

Publication History

TITLE: *Authentic Science Fiction Series*, Number 1, January 1, 1951–Number 2, January
     15, 1951; *Science Fiction Fortnightly*, Number 3, February 1, 1951–Number 8,
     April 15, 1951; *Science Fiction Monthly*, Number 9, May 15, 1951–Number 12,
     August 15, 1951; *Authentic Science Fiction*, Number 13, September 15, 1951–
     Number 28, December 15, 1952 and Number 69, May 15, 1956–Number 77,
     February 1957. Intervening issues Numbers 29–68 and 78–85 were *Authentic*
     Science Fiction Monthly.
VOLUME DATA: No volume numbering; issues numbered sequentially. First two issues
     unnumbered and undated (January 1 and 15, 1951); Number 1–Number 8 (April

15, 1951), fortnightly; Number 9, May 1951–Number 85, October 1957, monthly. Total run: 85 issues.

PUBLISHER: Hamilton & Co., London.

EDITORS: "L. G. Holmes" (Gordon Landsborough), Number 1 (January 1, 1951)–Number 27 (November 15, 1952); H. J. Campbell, Number 28 (December 15, 1952)–Number 65 (January 15, 1956); E. C. Tubb, Number 66 (February 15, 1956)–Number 85, October 1957.

FORMAT: Pocketbook, 128 pp., Number 1–Number 6; 112 pp., Number 7–Number 25; 128 pp., Number 26–Number 28; 144 pp., Number 29–Number 40; 160 pp., Number 41–Number 46; 144 pp., Number 47–Number 56; 128 pp., Number 57–Number 59; 160 pp., Number 60–Number 77; Digest, 128 pp., Number 78–Number 85.

PRICE: 1/6d., Number 1–Number 59 (July 1955); thereafter 2/-.

Mike Ashley

AVON FANTASY READER

Between 1947 and 1952 Donald A. Wollheim edited a total of eighteen issues of *Avon Fantasy Reader*. Although the cover of the first issue was numbered but undated, its title page indicates that it was released in February 1947, and the announcement was made that it would be "published every other month." That plan never materialized. Thereafter, the issues were numbered consecutively, the year of publication was given, but there were no monthly or quarterly designations. A total of five were published in 1947, three in 1948, three in 1949, three in 1950, three in 1951, and only one in 1952.

This seemingly irregular publication schedule is deceptive; although *AFR* appeared in the format of the digest-size periodical magazines, Wollheim himself has asserted that both he and the publisher, Joseph Meyers, thought of the *Reader* as a series of books, never as a magazine. (It should be remembered that by 1947 Meyers sponsored *Avon Modern Short Story Monthly* and a "New Avon Library" made up of novels and short story collections by single authors ranging from Somerset Maugham, John Steinbeck and Erskine Caldwell to Agatha Christie, Leslie Charteris and John O'Hara.) In short, from the beginning the two men regarded the venture as a deliberate experiment; Wollheim said as much in the introduction to the first issue: "In establishing AVON FANTASY READER we seek to set up a periodic anthology at a price available to all wherein may be found, volume after volume, the outstanding creations of fantastic imagination by the leading fantasy writers. No type of imaginative romancing will be neglected."

Technically, then, *AFR* should not have been included in the indexes to science fiction magazines of the period. That the *Reader* should be regarded as a series of distinctly separate anthologies gains credence by its listing in L. W. Currey's *Science Fiction and Fantasy Authors* (1979) and Robert Reginald's *Science Fiction and Fantasy Literature* (1980) among the books which Wollheim edited.

At the time, however, paperback anthologies, let alone regular series, were rarities, and by reader reaction the series came to be regarded as a magazine.

This concept of each number of the *Reader* as an anthology complete within itself had at least one direct effect upon Wollheim's editorial policy. It automatically excluded serials. A typical issue printed between eight and twelve stories. Almost without exception they were reprints, drawing mostly upon works published during the 1920s and 1930s, although some earlier titles were included, a few going back to John Kendrick Bangs, M. R. James, and Ambrose Bierce (significantly, no Poe, no Verne, and only two of Wells' stories were included in the entire run of *Avon Fantasy Reader*). Increasingly, Wollheim featured a few selections from the 1940s, perhaps most notably six stories by Ray Bradbury, five by Wollheim himself, two by Cyril Kornbluth and one by Anthony Boucher—"The Pink Caterpillar," reprinted from *Adventure*. While the Boucher title may seem something of a maverick, it underscores one of the unjust evaluations made of the *Reader*; namely, that it relied almost exclusively on reprints from *Weird Tales*.*

The key to Wollheim's editorial policy lay in his assertion that "no type of imaginative romancing will be neglected." An examination of the table of contents of the first number of *Avon Fantasy Reader* reveals the pattern of what he attempted to achieve throughout the series by drawing from both magazines and books:

Murray Leinster, "The Power Planet," *Amazing Stories*,[*] June 1931.

August Derleth, "The Shuttered House," *Weird Tales*, April 1937.

William Hope Hodgson, "The Voice in the Night," from *Men of Deep Waters* (London, 1914).

A. Merritt, "The Woman of the Wood," *Weird Tales*, August 1926; January 1934.

H. G. Wells, "The Truth About Pyecraft," from *Twelve Stories and a Dream* (London, 1903).

Clark Ashton Smith, "The Vaults of Yoh Vombis," *Weird Tales*, May 1932; from *Out of Time and Space* (Salt Lake City: Arkham House, 1942).

H. Russell Wakefield, "The Central Figure," from *Imagine a Man in a Box* (New York: Appleton, 1931).

Lord Dunsany, "The Three Infernal Jokes," from *The Last Book of Wonder* (Boston, 1916).

Certainly Wollheim relied upon *Weird Tales*; no one questions that *per se*, but one might argue that at the time—the late 1940s—he had to do so in order to obtain every "type of imaginative romancing" for the *Reader*. What has been overlooked is how extensively he drew upon a wide variety of authors. This is no place for a catalogue of writers and titles; yet when one checks closely the reprints he selected, one finds that at least forty contributors to *Weird Tales* are represented in *AFR* by a single tale. In short, most frequently Wollheim chose the story rather than the author. One other factor should be noted: many of these stories had been newly copyrighted by Arkham House for inclusion in one of its books. Wollheim thus secured permission to reprint from Arkham House.

In addition, of course, he drew from other magazines: *All-Story* (*Argosy**), *Thrill Book*,* *Astounding* (*Analog Science Fiction**) and *Amazing*. Perhaps even more important, as often as he reprinted from the older magazines, he contracted with the author for the rights to stories which had seen—or were to see—publication only in hardcover form. Thus, for example, he preserved—or brought to the attention of the mass market at a time when fantasy was not in great favor in America—titles by such authors as Maurice Baring, Algernon Blackwood, Thomas Burke, G. K. Chesterton, John Collier and Edward Lucas White. He reprinted White's "Amina" (*Lukundoo, and Other Stories*, 1927), passing over two which had been published much earlier by *Weird Tales*.

His close relationship with Arkham House paid off. He secured the rights to "The Man Who Never Grew Young" and "The Dreams of Albert Moreland" by Fritz Leiber, Jr., before their publication in *Night's Black Agents* (1947) and to "Original Sin" by S. Fowler Wright before its first American appearance in *The Throne of Saturn* (1949). But his greatest service undoubtedly came through his devotion to William Hope Hodgson and Lord Dunsany; he reprinted five stories by Hodgson and six by Dunsany at a time when their short fiction was not widely available in America. Unfortunately, subsequent bibliographers have unintentionally created a problem. In all instances when Wollheim included a story taken from some book, the indexes to the science fiction magazines make a dutiful entry to *Avon Fantasy Reader*, but they do not mention the story's previous appearance in hardcover because none of the indexes was prepared to make such references. This inadequacy unwittingly commits a double disservice. First, it does not acknowledge the breadth of the field outside the specialist magazines; second, it does not recognize the lengths to which Wollheim went to find the best possible stories for the *Reader*.

In 1947, in the introduction to the first issue, after quoting from Clark Ashton Smith's poem, "The Hashish Eater," Wollheim enunciated a basic principle governing his selection of stories: "Our empire of dreams is fed from the ever-flowing currents of literature, and our crown is the crown of fantasy, the countless volumes, and the innumerable magazines, extant and extinct, wherein may lie some vivid vision or spine-tingling tale worth the retelling." In the second issue, concluding a statement about the power of the imagination to bind together the past, present and future, he advanced what some may consider a controversial definition of fantasy, one which echoes what he himself, Jack Williamson, and Lester del Rey were later to say of science fiction: "Fantasy is the implement that permits progress, that permits invention, that raises man above all other creatures. We alone can imagine change." Several editorials later he explicitly named science fiction as a part of the broader field of fantasy when he wrote:

"Whether they be science-fiction, as some are, or pure fantasy, or ghostly tales, all are selected for their memorable qualities both in literary value and imaginative impact."

One cannot underestimate the importance of Wollheim's views, for both in his theory and in his practice, he strengthens the view that fantasy—and therefore science fiction—has remained a significant part of the tradition of modern fiction, reaching one of its high points during the so-called Gothic period and then splitting into a number of parallel streams as various influences, ranging from science to folklore, appealed to individual writers. His views remain important not only because of their date, but because he has remained one of the most influential editors in the contemporary field.

As noted, he most frequently chose the story rather than the author. Thus, for example, despite reader demand, he used only three stories by C. L. Moore, although by the third issue he readily acknowledged that "most of you readers included requests [for her work]." There were, of course, exceptions to whom he turned time and again: Mary Elizabeth Counselman (4); Robert E. Howard (7); Frank Belknap Long (6); H. P. Lovecraft (7); A. Merritt (5); Clark Ashton Smith (8); Donald Wandrei (3). With the recent publication of a collection of Mary Elizabeth Counselman's works, all of these writers have been published extensively, if not exclusively, by Arkham House, which also issued a number of titles by William Hope Hodgson, whom Wollheim reprinted more frequently than any other individual who had appeared only in hardback.

His practice of drawing from books as frequently as from magazines has led to further bibliographical confusion when the failure to cite a book implies that Wollheim was publishing original material in the *Reader*. The difficulty arose when Avon Book Company purchased a renewal of copyright (or second serial rights) from an individual author, as had occurred with S. Fowler Wright's "Automata" in the second issue; Avon bought the rights from him so that the entry is dated 1947—"Reprinted by permission of the author." If one checks the entry, the word "reprinted" destroys the suggestion of first publication; however, Donald Day's *Index to the Science-Fiction Magazines 1926–1950* contains the entry "AFR #2 97," nothing more. Only by going to Thomas G. L. Cockcroft's *Index to the Weird Fiction Magazines* or to Bradford Day's *An Index on the Weird & Fantastica in Magazines* does one find that "Automata" was originally published in *Weird Tales* for September 1929.

Wollheim did purchase a number of original items for the *Reader*, and a listing of those titles seems important, if only to emphasize that *AFR* was not just a reprint magazine.

No. 3 (1947), August Derleth, writing as Stephen Grendon, "Bishop's Gambit," published in *Mr. George and Other Odd Persons* (Arkham House, 1963).

No. 4 (1947), A. E. van Vogt, "Defense," published in *Destination Universe* (Farrar, Straus, 1952).

No. 5 (1947), Carl Jacobi, "The Random Quantity" (no indication of subsequent publication).

No. 6 (1948), Joseph E. Kelleam, "From the Dark Waters" (no indication of subsequent publication).

No. 7 (1948), A. Merritt, "When Old Gods Wake," published in *The Fox Woman* (Avon, 1949).

No. 9 (1949), Robert Bloch, "The Unspeakable Betrothal," published in *Living Demons* (Belmont, 1967).

No. 14 (1950), Ray Bradbury, "Ylla," published in *The Martian Chronicles* (Doubleday, 1950).

No. 14 (1950), Clive G. B. Jackson, "The Still Small Voice" (no indication of subsequent publication).

No. 16 (1951), Louise Leipiar, writing as L. Major Reynolds, "The River," published in *Science Fiction Digest** (1954) and *Nebula Science Fiction** (1957).

No. 17 (1951), Frank Owen, "One-Man God," reprinted in *Avon Science Fiction and Fantasy Reader** in 1953.

No. 18 (1952), Robert E. Howard, "The Witch from Hell's Kitchen," published in Donald A. Wollheim and George Ernsberger, eds., *The Avon Fantasy Reader* (Avon, 1968).

As publisher, Joseph Meyers influenced the *Reader* in at least three obvious ways. In an effort to make a bigger profit with a cheaper design, beginning with Number 5 (the last issue in 1947) he reduced the gloss cover from 80 to 60 pounds, and while the quality of the paper itself remained the same, there was an additional change from perfect to saddle binding. In addition, although at least two of the first four covers had been taken from grotesque drawings by earlier European artists which Meyers had collected, beginning with Number 5 a scantily clad girl in a precarious situation dominated each of the remaining covers. One infers that Meyers believed this, too, would help sales. He also attempted to attract readers by substituting suggestive titles. Number 15 (1951), for example, featured Stanley A. Weinbaum's "A Man, a Maid, and Saturn's Temptation," which was called—ambiguously—a "hitherto unobtainable story," although the table of contents indicates that it had been entitled "Flight on Titan" when it appeared in *Astounding Stories* in 1935.

Despite the pressures of the marketplace, Wollheim successfully edited a "chain of book anthologies," as he himself recently referred to the *Reader,* at a time when fantasy was not widely popular on the American mass market. It is to his credit that he brought its readers a wide variety of fiction. At the very least *Avon Fantasy Reader* deserves historical attention both as an experiment in publishing and as an illustration of how complex modern fantasy has become, ranging as it does from "hard" science fiction to sword and sorcery heroics, all flourishing simultaneously.

Information Sources

BIBLIOGRAPHY:
Nicholls. *Encyclopedia.*
Tuck.
INDEX SOURCES: ISFM; MIT; MT; SFM; Tuck.
REPRINT SOURCES:
   Derivative Anthologies: The Avon Fantasy Reader (New York: Avon Books, 1968) and *The Second Avon Fantasy Reader* (New York: Avon Books, 1969), both edited by Donald A. Wollheim and George Ernsberger; 7 stories and 9 stories, respectively.
LOCATION SOURCES: M.I.T. Science Fiction Library; Pennsylvania State University Library.

Publication History

TITLE: *Avon Fantasy Reader.*
VOLUME DATA: No volume numbering; all issues sequentially numbered. Number 1 [February 1947]–Number 18 [1952]. Originally quarterly, but schedule thereafter irregular.
PUBLISHER: Avon Book Company, 1947–1948; Avon Publishing Co., Inc., 1948–1949; Avon Novels, Inc., 1949–1952, New York City.
EDITOR: Donald A. Wollheim.
FORMAT: Digest, 128 pp. Formal binding changed to saddle-stapled from Number 5.
PRICE: 35¢.

Thomas D. Clareson

AVON SCIENCE FICTION AND FANTASY READER

In January 1953 Joseph Meyer and a new editor, Sol Cohen, revived the former *Avon Fantasy Reader** and *Avon Science Fiction Reader** under the title *Avon Science Fiction and Fantasy Reader.* Donald Wollheim's concept of a serial anthology was abandoned, for the new magazine had been transformed into a quarterly which featured "ALL NEW STORIES." For the first time each story was illustrated, the principal artists being Everett Raymond Kinstler, John Giunta and Gerald McCann. By and large their work had an erotic flavor, although the cover artist, Leo Manso, abandoned the damsel in distress who had become a trademark of the earlier *Readers* in favor of abstractions tied to no specific narrative. The final innovation was "The Space Ark," a book review column by Noah Gordon, the assistant editor. In short, *Avon Science Fiction and Fantasy Reader* lost any distinctive characteristics it had developed during the editorship of Wollheim and became, simply, another commercial magazine.

With one exception, Frank Owen's "One-Man God," which had appeared as recently as *Avon Fantasy Reader #17* (1951), all of the fiction was first-run. Alfred Coppel provided the lead story, "For Humans Only," an exploration of the theme of racial prejudice focusing upon a robot's attempt to escape human persecution by fleeing to Mars. Other science fiction selections included Arthur C. Clarke's "The Forgotten Enemy," concerned with the coming of a new glacial age, and Theodore R. Cogswell's "The Short Count," an off-trail sketch of a writer and his wife reminiscing at the moment of an atomic attack. John Christopher's "Mr. Kowtshook" and Glen Malin's "Agratha" represented traditional fantasy, while E. Everett Evans' "The Shed" and Charles L. Harness' "The Call of the Black Lagoon" both presented encounters with alien creatures evoking a combination of fantasy and horror rather than depicting a scientific meeting with civilized creatures. All in all, the twelve stories making up the first issue—none longer than seventeen pages, most as short as six or eight pages—had a distinctively dystopian tone when they did not rely upon the emotion of terror.

The second issue, dated April 1953, featured Jack Vance's "DP!"—a tale of the emergence from the depths of the earth and the destruction of a long-isolated segment of the human race; only Vance's narrative technique—a reliance upon newspaper articles and other official reports—gives freshness to this account of "displaced persons." No less than five authors who had had stories in the first issue repeated in the second. Most notable of these were Arthur C. Clarke, with "The Parasite," and John Christopher, with "Breaking Point." Dr. R. S. Richardson contributed an article, "A Night on Mars Hill," giving an account of his personal trip with friends to Flagstaff to observe the planet Mars and, it was hoped, to see its canals.

Essentially, the second issue maintained the dystopian tone of the first. Significantly, one cannot find record of the stories being widely reprinted. Nor is the *Avon Science Fiction and Fantasy Reader* mentioned thus far in any of the histories of the field. The attempt to convert it to a regular quarterly magazine survived for two issues. Undistinguished and without sufficient individuality, it was lost in the deluge of SF magazines then on the bookstalls.

Information Sources

BIBLIOGRAPHY:
Nicholls. *Encyclopedia.*
Tuck.
INDEX SOURCES: MIT; MT; Perry, Brian, "Index to Avon Fantasy and Science Fiction Readers," *Xenophile*, No. 9 (1974) and No. 10 (1975); SFM; Tuck.
REPRINT SOURCES: None known.
LOCATION SOURCES: M.I.T. Science Fiction Library; Pennsylvania State University Library.

Publication History

TITLE: *Avon Science Fiction and Fantasy Reader*.
VOLUME DATA: Volume 1, Number 1, January 1953–Volume 1, Number 2, April
1953. Quarterly. Total run: 2 issues.
PUBLISHER: First issue: Avon Novels, Inc., New York. Second issue: Stratford Novels,
Inc., New York.
EDITOR: Sol Cohen.
FORMAT: Digest, 128 pp.
PRICE: 35¢.

Thomas D. Clareson

AVON SCIENCE FICTION READER

In 1951–1952, with Donald A. Wollheim as editor, Avon Novels, Inc. brought
out *Avon Science Fiction Reader* as a companion "pocket-priced anthology" to
the successful *Avon Fantasy Reader*.* It survived for only three issues: two in
1951 and one in 1952.

The main reason for *ASFR*'s short life was the departure of Donald Wollheim
who left to help establish Ace books. Nevertheless *ASFR* has never had the
honors bestowed on its companion despite the similarity of content. Perhaps its
lack of success lay in that, even more than *Avon Fantasy Reader*, it relied upon
reprints—at a time when both *Galaxy Science Fiction** and *The Magazine of
Fantasy and Science Fiction** emerged to strengthen and broaden the field.
Moreover, unlike its companion, it did not include stories which had seen previous publication only in hardback editions. The two exceptions were Lord
Dunsany's "The Rebuff" from *The Fourth Book of Jorkens*, first published by
Jarrolds in 1947 and then by Arkham House in 1948, and S. Fowler Wright's
"PN 40," published in *The Throne of Saturn* by Arkham House in 1949. The
remainder of its selections came from the science fiction and fantasy magazines
of the 1920s and 1930s. Only six other stories, including Wollheim's "Blind
Flight" and Thorp McClusky's "The Ultimate Paradox" from *Weird Tales*,*
had publication dates in the 1940s, and none had dates after 1945. In short,
Wollheim did not show the same astuteness in his selection that he had shown
in *Avon Fantasy Reader*, although perhaps the fault lay in the publisher rather
than in his own preferences.

The first issue featured Edmond Hamilton's "The War of the Sexes," first
published in *Weird Tales* in 1933. In an editorial which promoted Hamilton's
tale of the struggle of the sexes to destroy each other, Wollheim called it "fantasy
at its strangest—this is the new thrill of science-fiction which defies the commonplace to tear aside the veil of the future and bare the wonders to come!"
He promised that *ASFR* would include "the most astonishing classics of the
imagination, stories whispered of by devotees but hard to locate, stories of
unusual themes taken from the hidden files of out-of-print volumes and the

crumbling pages of treasured magazines.'' Unfortunately, the selection never truly lived up to that promise.

The lead story of the second issue was Sewell Peaslee Wright's ''Priestess of the Flame'' from *Astounding Stories* (*Analog Science Fiction**) in 1932; that of the third and last number is Frank Belknap Long's ''The Robot Empire,'' originally published in *Astounding* in 1934 as ''The Vapor Death.'' In short, an analysis of the content of *ASFR* reveals, not surprisingly, that the majority of the stories were written by authors who had appeared in *Avon Fantasy Reader*: Frank Belknap Long, A. Merritt, Clark Ashton Smith, Donald Wandrei, Mary Elizabeth Counselman, among others. Murray Leinster, Jack Williamson and Miles J. Breuer were also represented.

Information Sources

BIBLIOGRAPHY:
Nicholls. *Encyclopedia.*
Tuck.
INDEX SOURCES: MIT; MT; SFM; Tuck.
REPRINT SOURCES: None known.
LOCATION SOURCES: M.I.T. Science Fiction Library; Pennsylvania State University
    Library.

Publication History

TITLE: *Avon Science Fiction Reader.*
VOLUME DATA: No volume numbering; issues numbered sequentially. Number 1
    (1951)–Number 3 (1952). Schedule irregular. Total run: 3 issues.
PUBLISHER: Avon Novels, Inc., New York.
EDITOR: Donald A. Wollheim.
FORMAT: Digest (saddle-stapled), 128 pp.
PRICE: 35¢.

Thomas D. Clareson

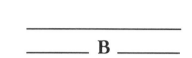

B

THE BEST OF OMNI SCIENCE FICTION

Derivative anthology in magazine format which includes some new fiction. See OMNI, Reprint Sources.

THE BEST SCIENCE FICTION FROM WORLDS OF IF

Derivative anthology. See IF.

THE BEST SCIENCE FICTION FROM WORLDS OF TOMORROW

Derivative anthology. See WORLDS OF TOMORROW.

BEYOND FANTASY FICTION

Beyond was a short-lived but high-quality digest magazine devoted to fantasy which ran for ten bi-monthly issues from July 1953 until January 1955. It was launched by Horace L. Gold as a companion to his SF magazine *Galaxy Science Fiction,** much as John W. Campbell had issued *Unknown** as a stablemate for *Astounding* (*Analog Science Fiction**). Thus, *Beyond* continued the tradition of fantasy originally identified with *Unknown* a decade earlier, and its importance lies partly in its role as the successor to that influential magazine, introducing a new generation of readers to a type of fantasy that was rational and sophisticated, certainly by pulp standards. Also, *Beyond* encouraged those writers who were working along the open borderland between SF and fantasy to experiment and expand the genre.

The parallels between *Beyond* and *Unknown* suggest that Gold saw himself in the role of a latter-day Campbell. Certainly his expectations for *Beyond* were such that he thought to exert an influence on the genre in the fifties similar to that of *Unknown* a decade or more earlier. "If *Beyond* had come first," Gold would later write, "I think it would have had the same effect and same misty memories as *Unknown*."[1] Earlier, Gold had been something of a Campbell protégé, contributing two stories to *Astounding* (1938–1939) and four more, plus a novel, *None but Lucifer* (a collaborative effort with L. Sprague de Camp) to *Unknown* (1939–1940) prior to becoming an editor himself, just as Campbell had done before him. The Gold/Campbell parallel gains further emphasis in the first and only editorial Gold would write for his new magazine. He wrote that "*Beyond* will have the same impact on fantasy that *Galaxy* has had on science fiction,"[2] thus echoing almost verbatim Campbell's earlier claim about the relation between *Astounding* and *Unknown*. Even their taste in fantasy was similar. Each magazine published stories written predominantly by SF writers who had been regular contributors to the flagship SF magazines. Each preferred a mixture of myth, magic and social comedy to the action/adventure, heroic or traditional Gothic fantasy. The parallels extended beyond the style and tone of the two magazines to their eventual fates—*Beyond* did not survive its second winter. *Unknown* was a casualty of the World War II paper shortage, and *Beyond* perished in the great pulp shakeout of the mid-fifties, following the glutting of the market earlier in the decade. *Beyond*'s untimely demise, however, cannot be blamed entirely on market forces; it may have fallen victim also to Horace L. Gold's preference for irony over wonder.

It was the rational fantasy of *Unknown* on which Gold doted, and he sought the story that would give him that effect. There were many readers who agreed with Gold and who remember *Beyond* with nearly as much fondness as the greater *Unknown*, despite the fact that *Beyond* seems to have produced fewer memorable stories. It is difficult to interpret such selective reader recall. One theory is that it is the nostalgic recollection of the bright promise with which *Beyond* was begun, reviving the expectations of *Unknown*'s surviving readership. But Gold was unable to recover that former contingent of subscribers and add enough new names to give his magazine the subscription base it needed. Even though *Beyond* offered the obvious market for rational and stylish fantasy in a wasteland of immaturity, Gold may have made a costly misjudgment of his readership by assuming that his taste in fantasy was theirs also. It may have been what was omitted, those heroic and naive forms of fantasy, that limited the appeal of the magazine and insulated it from a more vitalizing tradition.

Gold's one editorial (an ill omen in itself) established the basis for the type of fantasy *Beyond* was to champion—popular rather than literary in tradition and ironic rather than sentimental in tone. It would treat myth in a curious, demythologized spirit, one that would both reflect and instruct the mind of its readers. The criteria against which the fantastic was to be evaluated would come out of SF and a spirit of popular psychological realism. Emphasis would be placed on mythic themes and psychological effects since both were associated in Gold's mind with two privileged sciences: psychology and anthropology. Gold's bias toward SF is revealed in several other important ways which served to shape the content of the magazine and helped determine its character. Sensational pulp stories were clearly out, as they were with *Galaxy*, and so were chillers in the Poe/Lovecraft vein. Equally unwelcome were the sword and sorcery melodramas in the tradition of Burroughs, Howard and Kline. Perhaps more serious was the exclusion of literary fantasy in the English tradition of Morris, Dunsany, Chesterton, Williams, Lewis and Tolkien. Gold's definition of fantasy as "the unconscious interpretation of reality,"[3] while scarcely illuminating the nature of the genre, does offer an important clue to the editorial preferences of the magazine. In developing his idea of an unconscious interpretation of the real world, Gold contrasts fantasy with the occult, arguing that myth is a kind of unsystematic psychology devised by the ancients rather than an aspect of fantasy. Gold presses the reader to accept the notion that the mythic often proves historically or factually true (or at least may be taken as the expression of universal human experience). Gold seems to have been unsympathetic to stories of fantasy with strong religious or archetypal elements, and was unprepared to take seriously either dragons or dwarfs. Where we find myth or the traditional machinery of fantasy in a story we can be sure that they will be treated with humor or irony.

The unconscious euhemerism of the lead editorial was the closest Gold ever got to taking fantasy seriously as literature. His was essentially the embarrassment of the rationalist at finding himself attracted to a form of literature which is not only critical of modern rationalism, empiricism and materialism but also seems to imply the acceptance of transcendent realities. Neither Campbell nor Gold was prepared to hazard his credentials as a scientific man even for imagined instances of supernaturalism. Nor was either about to identify his magazine, however distantly, with the sensational fantasy action pulps which had given the word "fantasy" such a bad reputation among American adult readers.

Beyond departed from the successful Campbell format for *Unknown* in forsaking novel-length works, which were precluded to some extent, perhaps, by the digest format, whereas the bi-monthly printing schedule made serialization awkward. Gold settled instead for using one long story or novella as the keystone, committing *Beyond* to reliance upon short fiction in order to build its reputation.

Given these self-imposed limitations, *Beyond* successfully followed in the footsteps of its predecessor, however briefly. The first issue was built around Damon Knight's "Babel II," a story that could well have appeared in *Galaxy* because the basic premise—that New York City becomes a modern Babel, cursed by the collapse of intelligible communications among people—could have had a supernatural cause just as readily as an extraterrestrial one.

The second issue is built around the only story from *Beyond* to have become a consensus classic: "The Wall around the World" by Theodore R. Cogswell. Flawlessly simple, the story portrays an attempt by a youngster to escape the confinement of a society totally enclosed by a wall. It is a symbolic story that can be read on several levels and at the same time an entertaining escape fantasy. This story would have been perfectly at home in *Unknown*.

L. Sprague de Camp and Fletcher Pratt published a Harold Shea novella, "The Green Magician," in the penultimate issue of *Beyond*. It is not vintage Harold Shea, perhaps, but it was certainly worth the price of a copy and would have attracted the notice of fantasy readers. If the problem did not lie with production and distribution, we must look elsewhere for the reason that *Beyond* failed to attract enough subscription and newsstand readers to survive.

Whereas Campbell's *Unknown* established a stable of writers as regular contributors (as indeed Gold's *Galaxy* also did), *Beyond* never successfully achieved that kind of identification or continuity. Perhaps, given time, such a relationship would have evolved. Of the fifty-six or so authors who appeared in *Beyond*, only eighteen appeared a second time, and only four of that number a third time—Jerome Bixby, Evelyn E. Smith, Roy Hutchins and Theodore Cogswell. Cogswell is the closest thing there was to a *Beyond* author, contributing four stories. "Wolfie" (January 1954), Cogswell's second contribution, is a clever story about an attempt to commit the perfect murder and how it backfires. "Lover Boy" (March 1954) reworks the same theme using a similar device but arrives at a startlingly different conclusion. Both stories rely on the familiar theme of man dabbling in the unknown with fatal results, a theme mined to near exhaustion in successive issues of the magazine. Earlier, Jerome Bixby's "Can Such Beauty Be?" (September 1953) gave this theme a special twist by showing that even the Devil himself does not always come out the winner in the end.

Gold published a formidable array of leading writers in the pages of *Beyond*, but he was not notably successful in getting their best work. Ray Bradbury contributed a story that is now a period piece, "The Watchful Poker Chip" (March 1954). Theodore Sturgeon had two stories, the underrated novella " . . . And My Fear Is Great" (July 1953), a forceful study of an old woman with the power to control others, and the overrated "Talent" (September 1953), a macabre tale of a child with the ability to transform others. Frederik Pohl's "The Ghost Maker" (January 1954) makes use of an amulet that conjures up the whole ghost of a being from any portion of its remains. Philip José Farmer's "The God Business" (March 1954) deserves to be better known. It blends a mixture of warped mythologies and switched time-streams. James E. Gunn's entertaining novella, "Sine of the Magus," is a detective story variant of the Harold Shea formula and stands out as one of the best of *Beyond*. It served later as the basis for Gunn's often reprinted novel, *The Magicians* (New York: Scribner's, 1976).

Also in *Beyond* are stories by T. L. Sherred, Richard Matheson, Philip K. Dick, Algis Budrys, Randall Garrett, Fredric Brown, Robert Bloch and Isaac Asimov. However, their contributions do not represent their best work. Ted

Reynolds made his first story sale with "Just Imagine" (November 1953) as a teenager, but it would be more than twenty years before he would return to the field. Some lesser-known authors contributed good stories, such as Roy Hutchins, whose "Stream of Consciousness" in the last issue is a delightful, sentimental chronicle of a New England river with both a personality and a temperament.

Despite the auspicious beginnings and the continued offering of good-quality, if somewhat specialized, fantasy, *Beyond* failed to attract a sufficiently broad base of subscriber support. Market conditions were not favorable, but other magazines survived the crisis. Perhaps *Beyond* became too specialized for mass appeal or Gold's editorial policy too restrictive to attract stories good enough to insure survival. Also, Gold's well-known waspishness was a potential factor in *Beyond*'s failure to establish a stable of regular authors of top rank. Possibly Gold was simply unfortunate in his timing and, given the limitations within which he worked, failure was inevitable.

If Gold is to be blamed for the fate of his magazine, possibly an unfairly severe judgment, then he must be given the credit he deserves for reestablishing a market for well-written fantasy. On the whole, *Beyond* appears to be a magazine that deserved a better fate and deserves to be better remembered. If the magazine produced few classic stories, it consistently published interesting, entertaining and often very good stories, many of which deserve a new reading.

Notes

1. Horace L. Gold, "Looking Aft," *Galaxy*, October 1975, p. 29.
2. Horace L. Gold, "Beyond" [editorial], *Beyond Fantasy Fiction*, July 1953, p. 2.
3. Ibid.

Information Sources

BIBLIOGRAPHY:
Nicholls. *Encyclopedia.*
Tuck.
INDEX SOURCES: MIT; MT; SFM; Tuck.
REPRINT SOURCES:
   Reprint Editions: A British edition saw four issues from Strato Publications, Leicester, published bi-monthly from January to July 1954, corresponding to the first four U.S. issues slightly abridged.
   Derivative Anthologies: [Thomas A. Dardis], *Beyond* (New York: Berkley, 1963) contains nine stories.
LOCATION SOURCES: East Carolina University Library; M.I.T. Science Fiction Library; Pennsylvania State University Library; State University of New York–Albany.

Publication History

TITLE: *Beyond Fantasy Fiction*, July 1953–September 1954; *Beyond Fiction*, last two issues, undated [December 1954–March 1955].

VOLUME DATA: Volume 1, Number 1, July 1953–Volume 2, Number 4, [March 1955].
    Bi-monthly until September 1954. Last two issues identified by whole numbers
    9 and 10. Six issues per volume. Total run: 10 issues.
PUBLISHER: Galaxy Publishing Corporation, New York.
EDITOR: Horace L. Gold.
FORMAT: Digest, 160 pp., July 1953–July 1954; 128 pp., September 1954–March 1955.
PRICE: 35¢.

Donald L. Lawler

BEYOND INFINITY

Only one issue of this magazine appeared, in 1967, and it passed by all but
unnoticed. The idea behind it was to publish a variety of "what if?" stories of
the fantastic, but the editorial promise was not fulfilled by the stories. This might
seem surprising considering that the lineup included Ben Bova, John Brunner,
Christopher Anvil and John Christopher, but these stories must have been bottom-
drawer rejects. "Whirligig" by Brunner, for instance, is related to a short series
of jazz stories that the author had published in *Science Fantasy** eleven years
earlier.[1] The other stories had little to offer, and titles such as "Mommy, Mommy,
You're a Robot" by Dexter Carnes and "Revenge at the TV Corral!" by J. de
Jarnette Wilkes were not likely to arouse much enthusiasm.

The editor, Doug Stapleton, was not unknown to science fiction. He had
appeared in *Thrilling Wonder Stories* (*Wonder Stories**) in 1942 and again in
1954. What is strange, however, is that even though the magazine was edited
in Hollywood, only a few blocks away from Forrest Ackerman's mansion,
Stapleton did not enlist the help of Ackerman's agency. Ackerman recalls that
he knew nothing about the magazine, and when he discovered it on his doorstep,
he promptly sent some material to the editor, but heard no more. There is no
trace today of a Doug Stapleton in the Hollywood telephone directory. No further
issues of *BI* appeared. It may be that the bad printing and appalling illustrations,
combined with the poor quality of the fiction, turned readers away. Or it may
simply be that the editor decided that the publication was not worth the bother.
The photographs of Stapleton that adorn the inside of the front and back covers
show a tired, rather bewildered old man, and with all the time and hopes that
were probably invested in *BI*, the end result would be enough to dishearten even
the boldest SF devotee.

Note

1. The series concerned Tommy Caxton and his Solid Six, and he featured in "The
Man Who Played the Blues," *Science Fantasy* 17 (February 1956) and "When Gabriel,"
Science Fantasy 19 (August 1956).

Information Sources

BIBLIOGRAPHY:
Nicholls. *Encyclopedia*.
Tuck.
INDEX SOURCES: ISFM-II; MT; SFM; Tuck.
REPRINT SOURCES: None known.
LOCATION SOURCES: M.I.T. Science Fiction Library; Pennsylvania State University
    Library.

Publication History

TITLE: *Beyond Infinity*, subtitled "Strange Tales from Other Dimensions."
VOLUME DATA: Volume 1, Number 1, November/December 1967. Listed as bi-monthly,
    but no further issues appeared.
PUBLISHER: I. D. Publications, Hollywood.
EDITOR: Doug Stapleton.
FORMAT: Digest, 160 pp.
PRICE: 50¢.

Mike Ashley

BEYOND THE FIELDS WE KNOW

Original title for magazine combined with *Dragonbane* to form *Dragonfields*.
See DRAGONFIELDS.

BIZARRE

Walter Marconette was a well-known SF fan of the 1930s who, starting in
January 1938, issued a typical hectographed fan magazine on a bi-monthly
schedule called *Scienti-Snaps*. With the sixth issue (February 1939) he switched
to mimeograph form. With the fifteenth issue (January 1941), he changed the
title to *Bizarre* and produced a semi-professional magazine.

Marconette was probably influenced by William Hamling's magazine *Stardust*,* another semi-professional venture issued in 1940. Marconette had acquired
as co-editor Jack Chapman Miske of Cleveland, and together they contacted
Hamling, freely acknowledging his help with preparation and printing. They
probably intended to go professional in time, but their early sales were aimed
at the core of fandom, and they consequently retained those features commonly
found in fan magazines. The result is thus something of a hybrid.

Bizarre's main features were its illustrations and its fiction. The front cover,
printed in red and black, was by Hannes Bok, and was of excellent quality.
Interior illustrations were by Bok and Marconette; they were printed on book
paper and were superior to most magazine illustrations on standard pulp paper.

The magazine presented two pieces of fiction. One, "The Thing in the Moon-light," was one of a handful of fragments found after H. P. Lovecraft's death, and this was its first appearance in print. August Derleth would later include it in *Marginalia* (Sauk City, Wis.: Arkham, 1944) and again in *Dagon and Other Macabre Tales* (Arkham, 1965). Later still, Brian Lumley was given the op-portunity to complete the story. His version was published in the Winter 1969 *Arkham Collector** and most recently in the Winter 1979 *Fantasy Tales*.*

The other story, the original ending by A. Merritt to his classic novel *Dwellers in the Mirage*, is perhaps of greater significance. When the novel was sold to *The Argosy** (where it was serialized in 1932), the editors asked Merritt to provide a happy ending. This he did, and that ending has remained in all hard-cover editions of the novel. His original ending, however, was placed with Farnsworth Wright for publication in *Weird Tales*,* but when Wright left the magazine, the new proprietor returned the story. Its appearance in *Bizarre* thus marked its first publication, and this ending was used in all paperback editions of the novel.

Of special interest was the magazine's quota of nonfiction. John W. Campbell wrote on how a writer's personality influences his writing style and took as an example L. Ron Hubbard's *Final Blackout*. He discussed how L. Sprague de Camp and Lester del Rey would have presented the same basic story. Edward Elmer Smith contributed a piece on keeping an open mind, striking back at fan Milton Kaletsky, who had started a controversy. Doc Smith was well known for his discussions in the fan columns and was never known to back away from an argument.

Elsewhere, Hannes Bok contributed a short autobiography where he revealed his poverty-stricken youth. Unfortunately, he would spend the rest of his life in similar circumstances. Earl Singleton, a brilliant fan of the period, presented a sonnet, "On H. P. Lovecraft's 'The Festival.' " Some months later, Singleton, overwhelmed with school and fan obligations, hoaxed fandom by faking his suicide and quietly disappeared from the fan scene.

The magazine presents a few other minor items of historic interest, such as the advertisements where one finds Harry Warner, Jr., selling his fanzine *Space-ways* for a dime; Bob Tucker offering his humorous *Le Zombie* for a nickel, or free to persons in the British Army; and even August Derleth, still offering copies of H. P. Lovecraft's *The Outsider* for five dollars, two years after its publication.

The editorial mentions the vast amount of work involved in preparing and presenting the issue, and promises improvements for the future. Partial contents were specified for future issues, with the next issue, March 1941, scheduled for January publication. It never appeared. Presumably, lack of finances and time made it impossible to continue. Probably both editors were drafted during World War II, and in time they simply vanished in the limbo that swallows so many SF fans. Miske briefly resurfaced in 1950 when he spent an evening with Howard DeVore and Wilson Tucker, and that was probably his last public appearance.

Information Sources

INDEX SOURCES: MT.
REPRINT SOURCES: None known.
LOCATION SOURCES: None known.

Publication History

TITLE: *Bizarre* (previously entitled *Scienti-Snaps* in fanzine format).
VOLUME DATA: Volume 4, Number 1, January 1941; only one issue as a semi-professional magazine. Earlier issues as *Scienti-Snaps* ran Volume 1, Number 1, January 1938–Volume 3, Number 3, Summer 1940; fourteen issues.
PUBLISHER: Privately published by the editors in Cleveland, Ohio. Printed by W. L. Hamling.
EDITORS: Jack Chapman Miske and Walter E. Marconette.
FORMAT: Digest, 22 pp.
PRICE: 20¢.

Howard DeVore

BIZARRE FANTASY TALES

Bizarre Fantasy Tales was one of several small magazines issued by Health Knowledge Inc. as companions to the *Magazine of Horror** in an attempt to overcome the problem of distribution. There was little to distinguish its contents from that of the other magazines, although Robert A. W. Lowndes determined to run long lead novellas in each issue. In the first issue, which appeared in the fall of 1970, he performed a great service by resurrecting Henry S. Whitehead's rare science fantasy, "The Great Circle," from the June 1932 *Strange Tales*.* The second issue featured Algernon Blackwood's John Silence adventure, "The Nemesis of Fire." Clark Ashton Smith was present in the second issue with "The Holiness of Azederac," and both issues contained new stories by Eddy C. Bertin.

BFT had a more liberal policy than its companions, including *Magazine of Horror*, and it was the most promising of the new magazines. The third issue would have carried "Daughter of Darkness" by Ross Rocklynne from *Astonishing Stories*, but unfortunately that issue never appeared. *BFT* and its companions were axed in 1971 by Countrywide Publications, which had taken over the parent company, Acme News, late in 1970.

Information Sources

BIBLIOGRAPHY:
Lowndes, Robert A. W., "The Health Knowledge Years." *Outworlds*, No. 28/29 (October 1976). (See also letter by Lowndes in *Science-Fiction Collector*, No. 8 [October 1979]: 45–47.)

INDEX SOURCES: ISFM-II; Marshall, Gene, and Carl F. Waedt, "An Index to the
    Health Knowledge Magazines," *Science-Fiction Collector*, No. 3 (1977): 3–42;
    MT; NESFA; SFM.
REPRINT SOURCES: None known.
LOCATION SOURCES: M.I.T. Science Fiction Library.

Publication History

TITLE: *Bizarre Fantasy Tales*.
VOLUME DATA: Volume 1, Number 1, Fall 1970–Volume 1, Number 2, March 1971.
    Intended schedule quarterly, then bi-monthly. Total run: 2 issues.
PUBLISHER: Health Knowledge Inc., New York.
EDITOR: Robert A. W. Lowndes.
FORMAT: Digest (saddle-stapled), 128 pp.
PRICE: 60¢, first issue; 75¢, second issue.

Mike Ashley

BIZARRE! MYSTERY MAGAZINE

A borderline suspense/horror fiction magazine, *Bizarre*! featured some science
fiction, notably a fifty-page condensation of Pierre Boulle's *Planet of the Apes*
(New York: Vanguard, 1963) in the second issue. *BMM* was a digest-sized
magazine of 144 pages selling for fifty cents. It was launched in October 1965
on a monthly schedule. The editors promised to provide "carefully selected
doses of far-out fiction—the supernatural, the weird, the wild, the fantastic."
Stories were both new and reprint, and the first issue presented a varied blend.
The lead story was Cornell Woolrich's "One Drop of Blood," a straightforward
mystery with a macabre payoff. It had originally appeared in the April 1962
Ellery Queen's Mystery Magazine. Also included were H. P. Lovecraft's "The
Horror at Red Hook" and new stories by Arthur Porges, Avram Davidson and
Thomas M. Disch. The second issue, apart from the Boulle novel, included one
of those increasingly rare events of the 1960s, a new short story by Arthur C.
Clarke, a vignette called "The Last Command."

The third issue was a month late but was able to boast only one reprint (a
Mickey Spillane story) and sixteen new stories written especially for *BMM*,
including "Walpurgisnacht" by August Derleth, "Too Nice a Day" by Cornell
Woolrich, "The Way to a Man's Heart" by Tom Disch and John Sladek, and
"Faddist" by James H. Schmitz.

None of the stories was above average. Further issues were promised, but
none appeared. *BMM* had a companion magazine of spy and suspense stories
called *Intrigue*.

Information Sources

BIBLIOGRAPHY:
Nicholls. *Encyclopedia*.
Tuck.

INDEX SOURCES: Cook, Michael L., *Monthly Murders*, Westport, Conn.: Greenwood Press, 1982; ISFM-II; MT; SFM; Tuck.
REPRINT SOURCES: None known.
LOCATION SOURCES: M.I.T. Science Fiction Library; Pennsylvania State University Library.

Publication History

TITLE: *Bizarre! Mystery Magazine.*
VOLUME DATA: Volume 1, Number 1, October 1965–Volume 1, Number 3, January 1966. First two issues monthly, third bi-monthly. Total run: 3 issues.
PUBLISHER: Pamar Enterprises Inc., Concord, New Hampshire. (Editorial offices were at East 42nd Street, New York.)
EDITOR: John Poe (Publisher: Gerald Levine).
FORMAT: Digest, 144 pp.
PRICE: 50¢.

Mike Ashley

THE BLACK CAT (1895–1923)

This entry is by way of clarification and to lay to rest the ghost of a myth. Almost without exception, histories of weird and fantasy fiction relating to the magazines refer to *The Black Cat*, published from 1895 to 1923, as an early repository of such tales. It is accorded an entry in Bradford Day's *The Complete Checklist of Science-Fiction Magazines* (New York: Day, 1961) and, more significant, in Peter Nicholls' *The Encyclopedia of Science Fiction* (New York: Doubleday, 1979). Yet the truth is that *The Black Cat* almost certainly published less science fiction and fantasy than the average nongenre fiction magazine of its day.

The myth may well have originated because of the supernatural connotations of the publication's title, but the feline that beamed out from the magazine's cover was more at home in a pantomime than in a witch's coven. Because copies of the magazine were rare, dealers no doubt inflated its collectability and referred to what few off-trail stories the magazine did publish as if they were the norm. Among them were Jack London's first sale, "A Thousand Deaths" (May 1899), the highly popular "The Mysterious Card" by Cleveland Moffett (February 1896) and its sequel "The Mysterious Card Unveiled" (August 1896), "My Invisible Friend" by Katherine Kip (February 1897), "In re State vs Forbes" by Warren Earle (July 1906), "The Mansion of Forgetfulness" by Don Mark Lemon (April 1907) and "John Jones's Dollar" by Harry Stephen Keeler (August 1915). The latter story, about teaching by television, was picked up by Hugo Gernsback and reprinted in the April 1927 *Amazing Stories.**

These few stories in their own right, however, are insufficient to account for the legend that *The Black Cat* was a fantasy magazine. Certainly Seabury Quinn was under the impression that it was. Writing a birthday retrospective for the twenty-fifth anniversary issue of *Weird Tales*,* Quinn said, in part:

> Until the advent of *Weird Tales* the longest-lived magazine dedicated to the supernatural story was the *Black Cat* which first saw the light of print October, 1895 and perished in September, 1906, after eleven years of superservice to discerning readers on both sides of the Atlantic.

Quinn had his facts wrong on every account. Where he obtained his information is not known, and in fact Quinn was actively writing at the time *The Black Cat* was in its final incarnation and could even have contributed to it. He may have been misled by Clark Ashton Smith, who had contributed poetry to the magazine. In any event, Quinn's notice in *Weird Tales* must have sent the collectors scurrying and thus perpetuated a myth. Moreover, once a fan has acquired issues of a magazine at enormous cost, only to be disappointed, he is not likely to deflate the price of the magazine by announcing that it has nothing of interest for the fantasy fan.

The Black Cat went in for unusual stories, but there was nothing unusual in its treatment of any theme. It is a fascinating and rewarding magazine for the bibliophile to collect but it is not a specialty for the fantasy fan. Enough has been written in the bibliographic sources listed below to give the complete picture of the magazine insofar as it is of interest to the fantasy fan.

Information Sources

BIBLIOGRAPHY:
Haining, Peter. *The Fantastic Pulps*. London: V. Gollancz, 1975, pp. 25–27.
Jones, Bob. "The Best Ten Cents' Worth on Earth." *WSFA Journal*, Oct/Nov 1969, pp. 5–8.
Moskowitz, Sam. *Science Fiction by Gaslight*. Cleveland: World Pub. Co., 1968, pp. 31–33. Rpt. Westport, CT:1 Hyperion Press, 1974.
Nicholls. *Encyclopedia*.
Quinn, Seabury. "Weird Tales, A Retrospective." *Weird Tales*, March 1948, pp. 3, 37.
Tuck.
Umbstaetter, H. D. "The Story of the Black Cat." *The Black Cat*, No. 58 (July 1900): v–vi.
INDEX SOURCES: Tuck.
REPRINT SOURCES:
    Reprint Editions: A British edition ran February 1898–February 1900, monthly, 25 issues; it included new stories as well as reprints, but hardly any fantasy.
    Derivative Anthologies: *The Red-Hot Dollar and Other Stories from "The Black Cat,"* ed. Herman D. Umbstaetter (Boston: L. C. Page, 1911), contains little of fantasy interest.
LOCATION SOURCES: Boston Public Library; Pennsylvania State University Library.

Publication History

TITLE: *The Black Cat*, October 1895–September 1919. Retitled *The Thriller*, October 1919–April 1923(?).

VOLUME DATA: Volume 1, Number 1, October 1895–Volume 27, Number 4, April 1923. Details as per Brad Day's *The Complete Checklist of Science Fiction Magazines* are Volume 1, 15 issues (Oct. 1895–Dec. 1896), Vols. 2 and 3, 12 issues each for 1897–98. Volume numbering dropped after Vol. 3. Whole issue numbering had followed since Number 1 and continued to Number 72 (Sept. 1901). Followed by Vol. 7, No. 1 (Oct. 1901) and continued 12 issues per volume (sequential numbering discontinued) to Vol. 24, No. 12 (Sept. 1919). All issues monthly. Retitled *The Thriller* with Vol. 25, No. 1 (Oct. 1919), skipped one month, and ceased publication with Vol. 25, No. 12 (Oct. 1920). Revived January 1922 (not listed in Day), Vol. 26, No. 1, and ran monthly until April 1923, Vol. 27, No. 4. Total run: 316 issues.

PUBLISHER: Shortstory Publishing Co., Boston, Massachusetts, 1895–1912; Shortstory Pub. Co., Salem, Massachusetts, 1913–1919; Black Cat Pub. Co., New York, 1919–1920 (reincorporated as Black Cat Magazine Inc., February–October 1920); William Kane, Highland Falls, New York., 1922–1923.

EDITORS: Herman D. Umbstaetter, 1895–1912; Theresa E. Dyer, 1913; T. H. Kelly, 1914; Harold E. Bessom, 1915–1920; William R. Kane, 1922–1923.

FORMAT: Intermediate (9''x 6''), 46 + xviii pp. (variations in the amount of additional pages for advertisements), October 1895–March 1913; Pulp (but on coated stock initially), 128 pp., April 1913–October 1920; 36 pp., 1922–1923.

PRICE: 5¢, 1895–1907; 10¢, 1908–1917; 15¢, 1918; 20¢, 1920.

Mike Ashley

THE BLACK CAT (1970)

Not to be confused with the turn-of-the-century magazine of the same name, this 1970 publication was a slim neo-pulp magazine printed on better quality stock and with stiff card covers. The front cover, in black and white, looks like the work of Virgil Finlay, though it is not credited. The back cover is by Finlay, as are a number of the interior illustrations.

The entire magazine was reprint. The contents page bore the same visage of the friendly cat that was besported on the original *Black Cat* (1895–1923), and publisher George Henderson regarded the new venture as the reincarnation of the old magazine, but devoted to fantasy and science fiction. It can thus be considered as a spiritual successor to a misunderstood myth.

The magazine contained twelve stories, most of them familiar to the fantasy collector. They included "The Cask of Amontillado" and "The Murders in the Rue Morgue" by Edgar Allan Poe; "Frankenstein's Monster," an extract from Mary Shelley's novel; "The Silent Prison" by Charles Dickens; "The Man with the Brain of Gold" by Alphonse Daudet; and "How It Feels to Die" from Leo Tolstoy's "The Death of Ivan Ilyitch."

Such a readable and balanced selection might lead one to expect the magazine to be a big success. But shortly after it was printed and handed over to the distributor, the distributor went bankrupt. Henderson was forced to drop what had been, for him, a pet project.

Note

The authors wish to thank John Robert Colombo of Toronto for his help in the research for this essay.

Information Sources

INDEX SOURCES: MT.
REPRINT SOURCES: None known.
LOCATION SOURCES: None known.

Publication History

TITLE: *The Black Cat.*
VOLUME DATA: Number 1, Winter 1970/71. Only issue.
PUBLISHER: Memory Lane Publications [George Henderson], Toronto, Canada.
EDITOR: George Henderson.
FORMAT: Neo-pulp, 64 pp.
PRICE: 50¢.

Mike Ashley/Frank H. Parnell

THE BOOK OF TERROR

A rare Canadian publication, *The Book of Terror*, which appeared in 1949, has hitherto been overlooked in histories of the field. A large-size, slim magazine on pulp paper, it bore an imitation Hannes Bok cover by an artist who signed himself Lorenstein. There was a similar Bok-like frontispiece in place of a table of contents. This page declared "STRANGE TERRORS OF WEIRD FANTASIES."

Although most of the contributors are unknown, two names do stand out: E. Hoffman Price with "Dark Depths of Human Madness" and Robert Leslie Bellem with "Nameless Dread of the Savage Sirens"; these help provide a clue to the origin of the stories. Although individual stories have not been identified, the contents appear to be reprinted from 1930s issues of *Spicy Mystery*, to which Price, Bellem and Carl Moore (present here with "A Nightmare of Spawned Mysticism") were regular contributors. The stories may have been retitled. They were accompanied by new illustrations or, in certain cases, photographs, some of which appear to have been lifted from a naturist magazine.

Beyond its rarity the magazine has little merit.

Information Sources

BIBLIOGRAPHY:
Tuck.
INDEX SOURCES: MT; Tuck.
REPRINT SOURCES: None known.
LOCATION SOURCES: None known.

Publication History

TITLE: *The Book of Terror.*
VOLUME DATA: Unnumbered, December 1949.
PUBLISHER: Metropolitan Publishing Co., Toronto, Canada.
EDITOR: Credited as "The Black Prince"; identity unknown.
FORMAT: Large pulp, 32 pp.
PRICE: 25¢.

Mike Ashley/Frank H. Parnell

A BOOK OF WEIRD TALES

This single-issue magazine appeared in 1960 as an experiment by Veevers and Hensman, a firm of printers in North England, to venture into publishing. Had the magazine succeeded, a string of companion titles would have followed, covering mystery, westerns, romance and suspense. The founding editor of the magazine was Cliff Lawton, who had acted as art editor on the earlier British magazine *Phantom.** A glance at the contents, however, will show that the real man behind *BoWT* was Forrest J Ackerman who, because of his considerable help, was credited as associate editor.

The magazine contained six stories, plus an article about Bela Lugosi, "The Terror from Transylvania," written by Ackerman under one of his spoof pen names, Dr. Acula, and reprinted from Ackerman's *Famous Monsters of Filmland.* Of the six authors present, four were represented by Ackerman's Literary Agency and the remaining two would certainly have been handled by Ackerman. Furthermore, for the most part the stories came from sources not readily available in England, but readily accessible to Ackerman.

Three of the stories—"The Curse of Amen-Ra" by Victor Rousseau, "The Dead Walk Softly" by Sewell Peasless Wright and "The Hunters from Beyond" by Clark Ashton Smith—came from the October 1932 *Strange Tales.** "Chained to a Bed of Roses," by Jack Bechdolt, first appeared in the July 1926 *Ghost Stories.** Both these sources were acknowledged in the magazine, but so too were *Malcolm's Magazine*—an obscure mystery digest of the 1950s—and *Unknown Worlds* (*Unknown**). No story from *Unknown* was present, and it is possible that it had to be omitted at the last minute because of length. The story from *Malcolm's* (January 1954 issue) was "Second Chance" by L. Major Reynolds, another of Ackerman's clients.

Today, however, what makes *BoWT* a collector's item is the appearance of a rare short story by Marion Zimmer Bradley, "The Wild One," the tale of a strange woman in the Catskill Mountains.

The magazine was of readable quality and is of interest to specialist collectors, but it was not suited to the general reading public in Britain in 1960. It sank without a trace, and no more issues were published. It was a bold and brave gamble, but was also misguided and mistimed.

Information Sources

BIBLIOGRAPHY:
Tuck.
INDEX SOURCES: MIT; MT; SFM; Tuck.
REPRINT SOURCES: None known.
LOCATION SOURCES: M.I.T. Science Fiction Library.

Publication History

TITLE: *A Book of Weird Tales*.
VOLUME DATA: Volume 1, Number 1 (undated, but released 1960).
PUBLISHER: Veevers & Hensman, Burnley, Lancashire.
EDITOR: Cliff Lawton. (Associate Editor [U.S.], Forrest J Ackerman.)
FORMAT: Digest, 128 pp.
PRICE: 2/6d.

Mike Ashley

BRIEF FANTASTIC TALES

Virtually unknown today, this abortive experiment by a Canadian publisher lasted only one issue. Although that issue was undated, one of its three companion magazines, *Dimebook Detective*, was dated August 1952, so it is possible the issue also appeared that year.

A small, vestpocket-sized magazine, it contained only four stories. Although not credited, research shows that at least three of them originated in the earlier Canadian magazine *Uncanny Tales* (1941–1943)*, and it is possible that the fourth may be a retitled story or from a companion magazine. This implies either that the magazine pirated its contents or that it may have been put out by the publisher of *Uncanny Tales* under a new company name.

Brief Fantastic Tales is an extremely rare item; for the record, the contents are "Strong Fingers of Death" by D. H. Fairley (*Uncanny Tales*, November 1941), "The Man Who Remembered" by Thomas S. Gardner (*Uncanny Tales*, February 1942), "The Thing Creeps" by Geoffrey Myers (*Uncanny Tales*, May 1941) and "Nightmare Murder" by Lyle Cranston (origin untraced). As the titles suggest, the stories fitted mainly within the framework of supernatural terror stories. Although *BFT* is of interest because of its scarcity, the fiction is not of notable quality.

Information Sources

INDEX SOURCES: MT.
REPRINT SOURCES: None known.
LOCATION SOURCES: None known.

Publication History

TITLE: *Brief Fantastic Tales*.
VOLUME DATA: Undated, unnumbered, probably 1952.
PUBLISHER: Studio Publications, Toronto, Canada.
EDITOR: Not identified.
FORMAT: Small Pocketbook (5¾" x 3¾") (saddle-stapled), 64 pp.
PRICE: 10¢.

Grant Thiessen/Mike Ashley

THE BRITISH SCIENCE FICTION MAGAZINE

See VARGO STATTEN SCIENCE FICTION MAGAZINE.

THE BRITISH SPACE FICTION MAGAZINE

See VARGO STATTEN SCIENCE FICTION MAGAZINE.

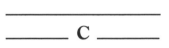

C

CAPTAIN FUTURE

Captain Future, first published in 1940, was the only hero pulp magazine to come totally within the SF genre. The story of its origin, as perpetuated by Sam Moskowitz, is that, while attending the first World SF Convention in New York in July 1939, Leo Margulies was so overcome by the sincerity of the fans that he and his editor, Mort Weisinger, "went into a huddle" and "discussed plans . . . for a new idea in fantasy magazines."[1]

Although there is no doubt that Margulies did announce his plans at the convention, the seeds for *Captain Future* had already been sown. Moreover, if *CF* did reflect Margulies' impression of the SF fans, then it cannot have been very high, for *CF* was a juvenile adventure magazine of pure space opera, with no sophistication or pretensions of grandeur.

Weisinger and Margulies had already been considering a magazine along the lines of *CF* for over a year. In 1938 Edmond Hamilton had submitted a novel for Standard Magazines' new publication, *Startling Stories.** Called "The Three Planeteers," it eventually saw print in the January 1940 issue of *Startling*, carefully planned to coincide with the launching of *Captain Future*. The novel told of the intrepid adventures of an Earthman, a Venusian and a Mercurian as they swept across the solar system. At the request of Margulies, Hamilton planned a new adventure novel around the idea of "Mr. Future, Wizard of Science," but following a meeting in New York, where Hamilton put forward further ideas, the full character of Captain Future was born.[2]

Captain Future was Curt Newton, a tall, cheerful, red-headed superscientist who lived in laboratories on the Moon with three sidekicks: Grag, a seven-foot robot of immense strength, Otho, a rubbery android of incredible agility and speed, and the disembodied brain of Curt's mentor, Simon Wright. The romantic interest was maintained by Curt's girl friend, Joan Randall. In issue after issue, the intrepid trio helped Curt and Joan save the solar system. Another colleague was Ezra Gurney, an Interplanetary Police Agent. Villains were numerous, although the most villainous was the Magician of Mars, son of the man who had killed Curt's father, Roger, and a half-breed Martian. He appeared in three of the novels: "The Seven Space Stones" (Winter 1941), "The Magician of Mars" (Summer 1941), and "The Solar Invasion" (Fall 1946), where stand-in author Manly Wade Wellman killed him off.

The Captain Future novels were unabashed space opera written with considerable knowledge by Edmond Hamilton. Hamilton also wrote a number of features within the magazine where he gave further background data on the future history he had created, and the background of the Futuremen. Initially they were confined to the solar system, but with the ninth issue, "The Quest beyond the Stars" (Winter 1942), Hamilton broke all barriers and discovered "the birthplace of matter," and in so doing Captain Future saves the entire universe.

There were seventeen issues of *CF* magazine, and Hamilton wrote all but two of the lead novels. The others were the work of Joseph Samachson, better known in the SF field as William Morrison. The novel by Manly Wade Wellman, which finished off the Captain Future series, appeared later in *Startling Stories*. Hamilton would have continued to write the novels, but in 1942, suspecting that he was about to be called up into the army, he told Leo Margulies to be prepared and have other authors stand by. In the event, Hamilton was not inducted, but by then Samachson had already been commissioned and Margulies had concocted the name "Brett Sterling" as a new house name to mask the identity of new writers. Three of Hamilton's novels also appeared under the Sterling name.

CF was popular, possibly because of Hamilton's presence. But it did not rely solely on the lead novels and Future-departments. As Standard Magazines had acquired the right to *Wonder Stories** from Hugo Gernsback, some of the stories were reprinted in much abridged form as serials. David H. Keller's "The Human Termites," originally serialized in *Science Wonder Stories* in 1929, appeared in the first four issues, followed by a truncated version of Laurence Manning's "The Man Who Awoke," originally published in 1933. *CF* also included a few short stories, and it is perhaps surprising that it was in its pages that SF readers first saw the work of Fredric Brown, whose brief "Not Yet the End" appeared in the Winter 1941 issue.

Although *CF* was not a magazine of quality, on the level for which it was conceived it was a success, and it is fondly remembered by old-time readers. The magazine, however, was right for a period, and it is unlikely that had wartime paper shortages not killed it, it would have lasted much longer. Three further Future novels appeared in *Startling Stories* after *CF* folded, but when an attempt was made to revive the series in *Startling* in 1950, it proved less successful. Such superheroes did not belong in the atomic age of the new "mature" SF reader. Their place was in the comic books.

Notes

1. Sam Moskowitz, *The Immortal Storm* (Westport, Conn.: Hyperion Press, 1974), p. 219, and *Seekers of Tomorrow* (Cleveland: World Publishing, 1966), p. 112.
2. Edmond Hamilton, "Fifty Years of Heroes," in *Weird Heroes*, Vol. 6, ed. Byron Preiss (New York: Pyramid, 1977), pp. 118–22.

Information Sources

BIBLIOGRAPHY:
Goulart, Ron. *An Informal History of the Pulp Magazine*. New York: Ace Books, 1973. Pp. 168–69.
Hamilton, Edmond. "Fifty Years of Heroes." In *Weird Heroes*, Vol. 6, ed. Byron Preiss. New York: Pyramid, 1977. Pp. 118–22.
Nicholls. *Encyclopedia*.
Tuck.
Weinberg, Robert, and Lohr McKinstry. *The Hero Pulp Index*. Evergreen, Colo.: Opar Press, 1971.
INDEX SOURCES: IWG; ISFM; SFM; Tuck; Weinberg, Robert, *The Hero Pulp Index*. Evergreen, Colo.: Opar Press, 1971 (lists lead novels only).
REPRINT SOURCES:
Foreign Editions: See entry on Sweden—*Jules Verne Magasinet* in Section IV.
Novels: Thirteen novels were reprinted in pocketbook form by Popular Library, New York, during 1968/69. Titles with original publication dates as follows: *Danger Planet* ("Red Sun of Danger," *Startling Stories*, Spring 1945), *The Solar Invasion* (*Startling Stories*, Fall 1946), *Outlaw World* (*Startling Stories*, Winter 1946), *Quest beyond the Stars* (Winter 1942), *Outlaws of the Moon* (Spring 1942), *The Comet Kings* (Summer 1942), *Planets in Peril* (Fall 1942), *Calling Captain Future* (Spring 1940), *Captain Future's Challenge* (Summer 1940), *Galaxy Mission* ("The Triumph of Captain Future," Fall 1940), *The Magician of Mars* (Summer 1941), *The Tenth Planet* ("Days of Creation," Spring 1944) and *Captain Future and the Space Emperor* (Winter 1940).
LOCATION SOURCES: M.I.T. Science Fiction Library; Pennsylvania State University Library.
Publication History

Publication History

TITLE: *Captain Future*.
VOLUME DATA: Volume 1, Number 1, Winter 1940–Volume 6, Number 2, Spring 1944. Three issues per volume. Quarterly, but no Fall 1943 issue. Total run: 17 issues.
PUBLISHER: Better Publications, Inc., Chicago and New York.
EDITORS: Leo Margulies, Editorial Director. Mort Weisinger, Winter 1940–Summer 1941; Oscar J. Friend, Fall 1941–Spring 1944.
FORMAT: Pulp, 128 pp.
PRICE: 15¢.

Mike Ashley/Robert Ewald

CAPTAIN HAZZARD

Published by Ace Magazines in 1938 as an attempt to copy the *Doc Savage** formula for success, *Captain Hazzard* lasted but one issue. Science fiction played a large role in the fairly routine lead novel featuring the title hero and written by the pseudonymous Chester Hawks. Captain Hazzard was a genius with telepathic powers who used them to fight supercriminals. The villain of the novel, titled "Python-Men of the Lost City," planned on using the energy of a harnessed volcano in a mad plan of world conquest.

Following the usual pattern of Ace Magazines, the Captain Hazzard novel was fairly short, leaving room for a number of short stories. Unfortunately, all were by lesser pulp authors and none had much science fiction or fantasy material.

Information Sources

BIBLIOGRAPHY:
Tuck.
Weinberg, Robert, and Lohr McKinstry. *The Hero Pulp Index*. Evergreen, Colo.: Opar Press, 1971.
INDEX SOURCES: Tuck; Weinberg, Robert, and Lohr McKinstry. *The Hero Pulp Index*. Evergreen, Colo.: Opar Press, 1971.
REPRINT SOURCES: The lead novel, *Python-Men of the Lost City* by Chester Hawks, was reprinted without the accompanying stories by Robert Weinberg as *Pulp Classics 2* (Oak Lawn, Ill.: Weinberg, 1974).
LOCATION SOURCES: San Francisco Academy of Comic Art.

Publication History

TITLE: *Captain Hazzard*.
VOLUME DATA: Volume 1, Number 1, May 1938. Only issue.
PUBLISHER: Ace Magazines, New York.
EDITOR: Rose Wynn.
FORMAT: Pulp, 96 pp.
PRICE: 10¢.

Robert Weinberg

CAPTAIN ZERO

In an attempt to combine the single-character pulp hero concept with the more realistic style of hardboiled detective fiction so popular in hardcover and paperback after World War II, Popular Publications launched *Captain Zero*, the last of the hero pulps, in 1949. The stories were written by veteran pulp fictioneer G. T. Fleming-Roberts and were primarily mystery stories with a science fiction background. Lee Allyn, not up to the physical standards needed to join the armed forces, volunteered as a human guinea pig for the Lockridge Research Foundation, testing radiation and drugs in the treatment of leukemia. The huge jolts of radiation had a bizarre effect on Allyn. At midnight his body turned completely transparent and stayed invisible till dawn. Deciding to use his strange power in the cause of justice, Allyn became a crime fighter, dubbed "Captain Zero" by the newspapers. Zero's powers were not known by either the papers or the police, but they did know he got results through unexplainable methods.

Except for the unusual power of Lee Allyn, the Zero novels were nothing more than straight mystery novels with a sleuth who could discover secrets because of his invisibility. The science fiction angle of the series was not played up, and the novels were all quite pedestrian. The magazine folded after three bi-monthly issues, the potential of the ideas never developed.

Long novels dominated the three issues of this pulp, leaving little room for departments or short stories. The token editorial feature was titled "The Zero Hour" and mainly related supposedly true stories of "nameless" crime fighters. Short stories in the three issues were by Don James, Everett Ortner, John Bender, James Booth, Alan R. Anderson and Walt Sheldon. None had any trace of SF or fantasy. All read as if they had been taken from other Popular Publications mystery pulps and used to fill up the extra pages in *Captain Zero*.

Information Sources

BIBLIOGRAPHY:
Tuck.
Weinberg, Robert, and Lohr McKinstry. *The Hero Pulp Index*. Evergreen, Colo.: Opar Press, 1971.
INDEX SOURCES: Tuck; Weinberg, Robert, and Lohr McKinstry. *The Hero Pulp Index*. Evergreen, Colo.: Opar Press, 1971 (lead novels only).
REPRINT SOURCES:
 Reprint Editions: Identical Canadian edition, of slightly larger format and variant back cover advertisements.
LOCATION SOURCES: M.I.T. Science Fiction Library; University of California–Los Angeles Library (Vol. 1, No. 1 only).

Publication History

TITLE: *Captain Zero*.
VOLUME DATA: Volume 1, Number 1, November 1949–Volume 1, Number 3, March 1950. Bi-monthly. Total run: 3 issues.
PUBLISHER: Recreational Reading, Inc., Kokomo, Indiana, an affiliate of Popular Publications, New York. (Editorial offices in New York.)
EDITORS: Mary Gnaedinger, originating editor. Alden H. Norton, all issues.
FORMAT: Pulp, 128 pp.
PRICE: 25¢.

Robert Weinberg

CHACAL

The mid-1970s were particularly fertile years for a new breed of fanzine within the fantasy and science fiction fields, the result of a much greater awareness of the values of quality production. The rise of the semi-professional magazine leaned heavily toward the sword and sorcery brand of heroic fantasy exemplified in such magazines as *REH: Lone Star Fictioneer, REH: Two-Gun Raconteur, Cross Plains, The Howard Collector, Fantasy Crossroads, Phantasy Digest** and others. *Chacal* was born out of *REH: Lone Star Fictioneer* with editors Byron Roark and Arnie Fenner honorably trying to extend the boundaries of the semi-prozine. "*Chacal* is an experiment of sorts," wrote Fenner in his editorial. "The title is the French term for 'jackal,' a creature whose nourishment is gained from feeding off any and everything." Such avowed eclecticism began to emerge in the first issue, dated Winter 1976, although the bias was still heavily slanted toward heroic fantasy with a lengthy, previously unpublished tale by Robert E. Howard, entitled "The Road of Azrael." There were more sword and sorcery adventures from Karl Edward Wagner with "Sing a Last Song of Valdese" and the first part of David C. Smith's "The End of All Days." The issue's high points, and a good indication of the direction in which the editors were heading, were Tom Reamy's "Mistress of Windraven" and Howard Waldrop's "Der Untergang Des Abenlandesmenchen," which was runner-up for the British Fantasy Society's award for Best Short Story 1976. News, reviews and articles plus some fine artwork completed the package, a debut that caused quite a stir and led to the magazine receiving a nomination for a World Fantasy Award in the Special Non-Professional Category, 1976.

The second issue saw a major shift in management, with Byron Roark leaving and Pat Cadigan being appointed associate editor. The swords and sorcery imbalance leveled out with another Kane story by Wagner, "Raven's Eyrie" and the conclusion of David C. Smith's "The End of All Days." Additional fiction included a Jack the Ripper tale, "The Adventures of the Grinder's Whistle" by Sir Simon Malone, edited by Howard Waldrop; and a William Hope Hodgson satire, "The Next to Last Voyage of the Cuttle Sark" by M. M. Moamrath, edited by Bill Wallace and Joe Pumilia. Perhaps the best pieces in the issue were Steve Utley's "To 1966" and the new associate editor's own "Last Chance for Angina Pectoris at Miss Sadie's Saloon," which was nominated for the BFS Best Short Story Award 1977.

Thereafter the editors, wishing to rid *Chacal* of the Robert E. Howard image, buried the old *Chacal* and started again with *Shayol.**

Information Sources

INDEX SOURCES: MT.
REPRINT SOURCES: None known.
LOCATION SOURCES: M.I.T. Science Fiction Library.

Publication History

TITLE: *Chacal*.
VOLUME DATA: Volume 1, Number 1, Winter 1976–Volume 1, Number 2, Spring
    1977. Quarterly. Total run: 2 issues.
PUBLISHER: Arnie Fenner.

EDITORS: First issue, Byron Roark. Second issue, Arnie Fenner and Pat Cadigan.
FORMAT: Slick; 57 pp., first issue; 72 pp., second issue.
PRICE: $3.50.

Gordon Larkin

CHILLERS

Chillers is a more recent example of a new magazine turned failure in the field. Perhaps we can see from this magazine an example of yet another publisher who will never learn. There will be those who will readily blame the failure of the magazine on its editor, Roger Elwood, if only because Elwood so swamped the field with anthologies in the early 1970s as to temporarily blight the anthology market. But SF anthologies continue to appear unabated, and others have compiled more volumes than Elwood with no dire consequences, so perhaps the blame should be placed elsewhere.

A magazine is first and foremost the responsibility of the publisher. The editor is but one of the cogs in his wheel, no less but no more important than, say, the art director. A good editor is worth his weight in rare manuscripts, but even a good editor can do little working under a publisher with no market sense when it comes to the SF and weird fiction fields.

Chillers was put out by Charlton Publications, which has a history of disasters in the field, among them *Fantastic Science Fiction* (1952)* and *Tales of Terror from the Beyond.** The idea behind the magazine was to cash in on the popularity of chiller movies, as an anonymous announcement calls them—the kind of film that *The Exorcist*, *The Omen* and *Carrie* had generated. *Chillers* was therefore predominantly a film magazine, not unlike *Famous Monsters*, but one that would also feature fiction.

Chillers was not alone as a film magazine; there are literally hundreds, and not a few specialize in SF and fantasy films. They are slick, glossy affairs, produced with much panache and requiring substantial finances to launch and establish them.

Chillers had none of these. It was a drab, lifeless-looking magazine with no interior color, printed on very poor pulp stock. It was illustrated mostly with film stills, but also by some of the worst artwork seen in any magazine. A magazine's success can also be measured by the number of prestigious advertisements included, but *Chillers* carried only the usual syndicated ads that appear in hundreds of cheap newspapers and periodicals and have done so throughout pulp history: "Be an Instant Battery Genius," "Gain Up to 5, 10, 15 Pounds," "Automatic Mind Command," and so on. The amount that these ads contribute to the finances of the magazine is negligible compared to the number of potential readers they turn away.

The magazine concentrated on film previews and interviews with film producers, directors and, inevitably, Stephen King. The fiction was limited to two or three stories per issue that tended to take a back seat. One story, for instance, was scattered through the length of the magazine, filling in spaces at the end of featured articles. On the whole the fiction was adequate. The first issue carried George Zebrowski's "Fire of Spring," a brief horror fantasy strong on atmosphere but weak on plot. Howard Goldsmith's "Homecoming" was a standard haunted house story, while Gail Kimberly's "Requiem" was a powerful story that probably found its way into the magazine because it involved sharks, and thus would appeal to the *Jaws* market.

George Zebrowski was present with another plot outline in the second issue, "Earth around His Bones." In addition was a reprint of a Victorian tale, "The Witch of the Marsh," written by H. B. Marriott-Watson; for some reason it was credited to Ethel Marriott-Watson. (Curiously the story had earlier been reprinted in the January 1965 *Magazine of Horror* under the original title "The Devil of the Marsh" but that time credited to E. B. Marriott-Watson.)

By the third issue the magazine was resorting to such cheap tricks as proclaiming stories as "too terrifying to illustrate," but at least no illustrations were better than the atrocities readers had otherwise to suffer. The issue contained another out-of-copyright reprint, "The Demon Cat" by Lady Wilde, another sign that the magazine had a very low production and editorial budget. By the third issue it must also have been evident that sales of the first issue had been poor. Indeed, *Chillers*' distribution was extremely limited, and many potential readers never knew it existed.

While *Chillers* provided only a limited market for weird fiction, it was nevertheless an outlet. To the publisher, however, the weird fiction was only an aside to the main idea of latching onto a trend with only the meagerest of publications, and the result was inevitable.

Information Sources

INDEX SOURCES: MT; SFM.
REPRINT SOURCES: None known.
LOCATION SOURCES: None known.

Publication History

TITLE: *Chillers*.
VOLUME DATA: Volume 1, Number 1, July 1981–Volume 1, Number 3, November
        1981. Bi-monthly. Total run: 3 issues.
PUBLISHER: Charlton Publications Inc., Derby, Connecticut.
EDITOR: Roger Elwood.
FORMAT: Pulp (saddle-stapled), 64 pp.
PRICE: $1.50.

Mike Ashley

COMET

Of the many magazines that appeared at the beginning of World War II, few offered such promise as *Comet*, for it marked the return of F. Orlin Tremaine to editing. Tremaine had steered *Astounding* (*Analog Science Fiction**) to a position of unrivaled dominance in the field of science fiction from 1933 to 1937, before handing over the task to the redoubtable John W. Campbell in order to assume broader responsibilities as assistant editorial director for Street and Smith's various magazines. Tremaine left Street and Smith the following year, however, and his return marked the first, and what was to prove the only, venture of H-K Publications into the then proliferating field of science fiction magazines.

The readers' expectations of so successful an editor were reflected in their letters to him, and in his opening editorial in the first issue, which appeared in December 1940, Tremaine wrote: "Tell your friends that I'm back aboard and urge them to try just one trip with us. . . . I'll gather the finest writers in the field together for you, and the best artists, and between us we'll make *our* 'COMET' so worthwhile that it will reach out to new fields and a new audience." In each bi-monthly issue Tremaine returned to the theme of steady improvement, using the metaphor of the comet blazing a trail for others to follow. In the second issue he spoke of the magazine's "gathering momentum," and by the fifth he could write with some satisfaction, "At last our wings are tapered to new speeds," though he promised continued progress.

Ironically, however, this fifth issue was to prove the last, for *Comet* was one of the earliest casualties of the magazine recession that was just starting. The problem was money. Unlike many of its competitors, *Comet* paid a full penny a word for material, but H-K Publications lacked the resources of the larger publishing companies. To succeed, the magazine needed to capture a sizable share of the market, and this awareness lay behind Tremaine's repeated requests to readers to introduce their friends to *Comet*. In his opening editorial he proclaimed, "We need a bigger audience every month to support the program of the COMET." To win readers Tremaine promised to be receptive to their views, and it was in response to appeals from fans like Sam Moskowitz for stories by new writers that he introduced the "Short, Short Story Corner" for newcomers, though he also encouraged more established writers to submit tales ordinarily too brief to be published.[1] Though it yielded no literary gems, this experiment proved popular with the fans, and among the authors published were Robert W. Lowndes and Donald A. Wollheim (under the pseudonym "Millard V. Gordon"). Less happy was a feature by Warner Van Lorne called "The Spacean," an imaginary newssheet from the year 2008. Readers expressed initial interest in the concept, but soon found that it grew tiresome and, as one put it, "childish."

The harsh economic pressures probably accounted for Tremaine's well-known outrage at Wollheim, the editor of *Cosmic Stories** and *Stirring Science Stories,** who was gathering stories for nothing but the promise of payment should the magazines succeed. Tremaine had already complained in the first issue of *Comet* that the field was "cluttered with titles"; he later told the young Isaac Asimov that "any author who donated stories to Wollheim, and thus contributed to the destruction of competing magazines who paid, should be blacklisted in the field."[2] Given such an uncompromising attitude, it was no surprise that when the publisher's failure to pay authors and competition winners prompted growing complaints, Tremaine resigned. He never returned to science fiction editing.

This was a genuine loss, for Tremaine had been true to his word when he promised steady improvement. As the brash young Asimov remarked in a letter to the editor, the first issue was good only as first issues go. Most of the authors were established writers, but they seem to have submitted manuscripts rejected elsewhere. Perhaps the liveliest and certainly the best appreciated was Eando Binder's "Momus' Moon": this story of two astronauts who nearly die laughing served to many as an ironic counterpoint to the bloody struggle in Europe. In response to appeals from aspiring writers among the fans, more material from newcomers appeared in the second issue, including Sam Moskowitz's first story, "The Way Back," and Robert W. Lowndes' second, "A Green Cloud Came." Both tales were marred by youthful sentimentality and immaturity, however, though the latter did create an interesting situation.

Yet, if this issue was little better than the first, the third did indeed substantiate Tremaine's claim that *Comet* was gathering impetus. The editor's extravagant assurance that Ross Rocklynne's "The Immortal" would prove a classic was rightly rejected by the fans, though they did appreciate the haunting atmosphere evoked in the story. They preferred Robert Moore Williams' "Dark Reality," one of the author's better stories. They also enjoyed Jack Williamson's "The Star of Dreams," an intriguing and well-paced adventure which succeeds in involving the reader despite the implausibly optimistic ending (a feature fans of the era readily accepted) and the obviousness of the answer to the mystery that baffles the hero. By contrast, most disliked Stanton Coblentz's "Headhunters of Nuamerica," a timely satirical farce about young men being sacrificed to preserve the lives of influential people. After this the fourth issue was something of a disappointment, apart from P. Schuyler Miller's "The Facts of Life," which makes skillful use of atmosphere to create suspense. However, the last issue marked another major improvement in quality.

The feature story was "Vortex Blaster," the first of what was to be a series by E. E. Smith.[3] The hero, "Storm" Cloud, combines absolute fearlessness, the split-second reactions of a natural athlete, and the ability to perform complex calculations with the lightning speed of a mathematical genius in order to disintegrate highly destructive atomic vortices (the Red Adair of the future!). It was a well-told adventure story that managed to generate both suspense and excitement. Leigh Brackett and Frank Belknap Long contributed two above-average adventure yarns, while Manly Wade Wellman created a challenging setting on "The Devil's Asteroid," where evolution operated in accelerated reverse. Unfortunately, characterization and plot failed to rise above stereotype, so that the intriguing possibilities for character study and suspense were largely wasted. These action stories were balanced by two in a more thoughtful vein: Robert Arthur's carefully ironic "The Indulgence of Negu Mah," and perhaps the best story to appear in *Comet*, "The Street That Wasn't There" by Clifford D. Simak and Carl Jacobi. The latter account of reality dissolving as aliens seize control of the very form of the world combines effective characterization with a perceptive comment upon both the subjective nature of reality and the folly of failing to appreciate life and the world around us.

It also served as an ironically appropriate symbol of the magazine itself, for after this issue both *Comet* and Tremaine disappeared from the science fiction world. The artwork of the magazine had never been good: few readers cared for the interior illustrations, and while Frank Paul's two covers were competent, the three by Leo Morey were poor. Yet, the stories had improved in quality, and this development augured well. While *Comet* deserved to survive, circumstances dictated otherwise. Tremaine voiced no distinctive policy, nor did he assemble a stable of writers who would submit their best work to him, so that his magazine held no special appeal to any group of readers. Improvement was not fast enough to challenge established magazines and to capture enough readers in an already saturated market. An editor of Tremaine's style needed more time to build the magazine's impetus. Unfortunately, the publishers did not provide the necessary resources, and in July 1941 time ran out.

Notes

1. The idea was later adopted by Campbell in *Astounding*, where the department was called "Probability Zero."

2. Isaac Asimov, *In Memory Yet Green* (Garden City, N.Y.: Doubleday, 1979), pp. 283–84. Since Asimov had already contributed a story to Wollheim he was considerably embarrassed.

3. Two more stories in this series were published in *Astonishing Stories.** They were subsequently collected and published as part of the Lensman series.

Information Sources

BIBLIOGRAPHY:
Nicholls. *Encyclopedia.*
Tuck.
INDEX SOURCES: ISFM; SFM; Tuck.
REPRINT SOURCES:
Microform: Greenwood Press Periodical Series.
LOCATION SOURCES: M.I.T. Science Fiction Library; Pennsylvania State University Library.

Publication History

TITLE: *Comet* (subtitled "Stories of Time and Space" on the cover of the first four issues only).

VOLUME DATA: Volume 1, Number 1, December 1940–Volume 1, Number 5, July
    1941. First issue monthly, thereafter bi-monthly. Total run: 5 issues.
PUBLISHER: H-K Publications, New York.
EDITOR: F. Orlin Tremaine.
FORMAT: Pulp, 128 pp.
PRICE: 20¢.

Raymond H. Thompson

COPPER TOADSTOOL

Copper Toadstool was one of a number of magazines—the others are *Dark
Fantasy,* Borealis, Stardock* and *Dragonfields**—produced by a small group
of Canadian fans. Each editor assembles his own magazine and contributes to
and relies on contributions from the others. This arrangement is not as incestuous
as it sounds, for while each can boast contributions from the others and each
draws from a small stable of writers and artists, that stable is very competent
and allows each magazine to retain its individuality. Each title also attracts its
own set of contributors.

The first tentative issue of *CT*, a thin digest production, was dated Winter
1977. The contents consisted mostly of the work of its two editors, the brothers
Dale and Tim Hammell. It exhibited no signs of originality, but was merely a
collection of amateurish stories and poems accompanied by equally poor illustrations. A second issue followed in July, merely a larger version of the first.
By now, Dale Hammell had emerged as the editor/publisher while Tim was
satisfied with the position of editorial assistant and resident artist.

It was with the third issue that *CT*'s personality surfaced—dually created by
Dale's editorship and by the group of contributors that had been attracted to the
magazine. These included Charles R. Saunders, the creator of Imaro, Galad
Elflandsson and Albert Manachino, whose stories of "St. George" are little
gems. There are also artists like Gene Day and *CT*'s major discovery, Larry
Dickison. The magazine's layout was still a trifle disorganized, but the contents
were good throughout. The fourth issue appeared only a few months later and
was a rerun of the previous issue in both material and layout. The only difference
was the cover illustration. Until then, the Hammells had experimented with
hand-painted covers. With Number 4, and thereafter, color photographic prints
were pasted onto the card covers. As an experiment it worked remarkably well,
especially on the fifth issue, where the print blended in with the rest of the black
and white wraparound.

The magazine advanced considerably with the fifth issue. Quality was the key
word in layout, printing and paper stock, all of which enhanced the excellent
material presented. Deserving special mention is the centerpiece of the magazine:
Galad Elflandsson's novella "The Basilisk," superbly illustrated by Larry Dick-

ison and given a marvellous presentation on parchment stock. It is an example of what even the professional publishers should strive to produce.

The sixth and seventh issues were combined under the title *The Storyteller* and printed in trade paperback format. It had been Dale Hammell's dream to publish a book, and this was it. *CT* was also destined to continue in this format, or so Dale stated. The issue featured Galad Elflandsson, Al Manachino and Larry Dickison at their best, and these plus Charles Saunders, Wendy Pini and others were promised for the eighth issue. Such was not to be. Dale married his new co-editor Sharon Sinner in October 1979 and *CT* was lost in the process.

Within the space of three years *CT* had developed from a run-of-the-mill fanzine into one that still takes some beating. It may yet return, and Dale Hammell has stated that he may one day publish a collection of Albert Manachino's "St. George" stories. We await that day with interest.

Information Sources

INDEX SOURCES: MT.
REPRINT SOURCES: None known.
LOCATION SOURCES: None known.

Publication History

TITLE: *Copper Toadstool* (issues 6/7 combined under the general title *The Storyteller*).
VOLUME DATA: No volume numbering. Issue 1, Winter 1977–Issue 6/7, July 1979.
  Schedule irregular. Number 2, July 1977; Number 3, January 1978; Number 4,
  May 1978; Number 5, June 1979. Total run: 6 issues.
PUBLISHER: Soda Publications [Dale Hammell], Vancouver, Canada.
EDITORS: Dale Hammell. First issue co-editor Tim Hammell. Issue 6/7 co-editor Sharon
  Sinner.
FORMAT: Digest, first five issues; Large Digest, final issue. Page counts as follows: 1,
  40 pp.; 2, 84 pp.; 3, 104 pp.; 4, 98 pp.; 5, 94 pp.; 6/7, 148 pp.
PRICE: $1.50, Numbers 1–4; $2.00, Number 5; $3.00, Number 6/7.

Jon Harvey

COSMIC SCIENCE FICTION (1941)

See COSMIC STORIES.

COSMIC SCIENCE FICTION (1950)

See COSMIC SCIENCE STORIES.

COSMIC SCIENCE STORIES

In the early 1950s the United Kingdom saw a spate of reprint editions of American magazines. The majority retained the same title and contents as the originals, apart from some abridgment. A few, however, were retitled to give the appearance of completely new magazines. One such magazine in the SF field was *Cosmic Science Stories*, its single sixty-four-page pulp edition being a reprint of five stories from the September 1949 *Super Science Stories.**

Information Sources

BIBLIOGRAPHY:
Tuck.
INDEX SOURCES: IBSF; SFM; Tuck.
REPRINT SOURCES: None known.
LOCATION SOURCES: M.I.T. Science Fiction Library.

Publication History

TITLE: *Cosmic Science Stories* (*Cosmic Science Fiction* on contents page).
VOLUME DATA: Unnumbered and undated; one issue, June 1950.
PUBLISHER: Popular Press, London.
EDITOR: Not identified (possibly Tom V. Boardman).
FORMAT: Pulp, 64 pp.
PRICE: Unpriced, probably retailed at 1/-.

Mike Ashley

COSMIC STORIES

Cosmic Stories, like its companion *Stirring Science Stories*,* was the brain-child of Donald A. Wollheim who, late in 1940, persuaded Albing Publications to launch the two magazines.[1] Unfortunately, the company was a marginal operation, a father and son with a line of credit from a news distributor, and although they offered to provide a little money for artwork, they were willing to pay both writers and the editor himself only in the event that the magazines succeeded financially. Anxious to gain experience, Wollheim agreed and set about rounding up stories.

This attempt to gather material without payment aroused the wrath of F. Orlin Tremaine, editor of another new science fiction magazine, *Comet.** Tremaine feared that Wollheim's venture would "'siphon readership from those magazines that paid,'" and he told a young Isaac Asimov, "'any author who donated stories to Wollheim, and thus contributed to the destruction of competing magazines who paid, should be blacklisted in the field.'"[2] Asimov was appalled because he had himself contributed a tale to *Cosmic Stories*. He confessed his action, plead-ing ignorance, but insisted that he had been paid for the story, which seemed to mollify Tremaine, though it led to a dispute with Wollheim.[3]

Yet if this episode left Asimov understandably reluctant to contribute unpaid stories to Wollheim, other members of the Futurians, the talented New York fan society to which both belonged, remained eager to get into print and to help a friend, and their contributions made up the bulk of both magazines. Although many went on to become major figures in the field of science fiction, their early efforts exposed their inexperience. This weakness was compounded by the fact that Wollheim seems to have included the better material in *Stirring Science Stories*. Many of the stories reveal potential, particularly in their development of irony, humor and fast-paced adventure; but the irony and humor are often pointless, while the adventures ramble on with little sense of direction. Thus, Asimov's "The Secret Sense" teaches a bitterly ironic lesson about the perils of self-indulgence but fails to develop character sufficiently to give it force; Cyril Kornbluth, writing as Cecil Corwin, produced a typically bizarre parody of stories about the soldier of fortune in "The Reversible Revolutions" and a sequel entitled "The City in the Sofa," but the humor soon starts to pall, and the confusion grows tiresome rather than clever. However, he managed to attain tighter control over his material in "What Sorghum Says," an amusing tale of time travel by a hillbilly bootlegger, which exploits a limited point of view to considerable effect.[4] Under a variety of pseudonyms, Kornbluth was the major contributor of fiction to *Cosmic Stories*; as Martin Pearson he even wrote an article entitled "So You Want to Be a Space-Flier?" in which he humorously deflates romantic illusions about space travel by graphically describing the inconvenience of life in confined quarters without gravity and companionship. John Michel (as Hugh Raymond) and James Blish also contributed regularly: "The Last Viking" by the former deploys point of view to thoughtful effect, while "The Real Thrill" by the latter uses the sentimentality that mars so many stories of this era to make a poignant comment upon the plight of those left behind by progress.

Yet, despite some modest achievements, the stories generally gave the impression of being too hastily written. In the first issue Wollheim expressed his support for the policy of encouraging "new names—new ideas," but went on to admit that the veterans' "second-rate material is often better written (if less original) than a newcomer's first-rate original stuff" (p. 126). Without funds to attract more carefully written stories, however, the editor was unable to find worthy material to fill one magazine, let alone two. Although the name on the cover of the second and third issues was changed to *Cosmic Science-Fiction* (it remained *Cosmic Stories* on the title page), the magazine only lasted for three issues, which appeared in March, May and July 1941. The magazine was certainly not without merit. Despite the absence of full-color covers, the art was above average, particularly the illustrations by Hannes Bok; moreover, the magazine served both as an outlet for the embryonic talents of some fine writers and as a valuable training ground for Wollheim, who developed into one of the great editors in the field of science fiction. If the readers of *Cosmic Stories* were given little to enthuse over, later generations have been amply rewarded by the achievements of those who learned part of their craft in its pages.

Notes

1. See Damon Knight, *The Futurians* (New York: John Day, 1977), p. 87.

2. Isaac Asimov, *In Memory Yet Green* (New York: Doubleday, 1979), pp. 283–84.

3. Learning that some of his fellow Futurians would be publishing under pseudonyms, Asimov had asked either that his story appear under a pseudonym too, or else that he receive a token payment of $5, for "it suddenly occurred to me that even though the story might be worth nothing, my name was worth something" (*In Memory Yet Green*, p. 284). Wollheim paid the $5, but the check was accompanied by what the author recalls as "a remarkably ungracious" letter. In *The Early Asimov* (Garden City, N.Y.: Doubleday, 1972), which reprints "The Secret Sense" with a biographical introduction, Asimov remembers the event differently in that he states that he made his request to Wollheim after, not before, his interview with Tremaine.

4. This story seems to parody L. Sprague de Camp's *Lest Darkness Fall*, just as "The City in the Sofa" parodies Ray Cummings' many stories in microscopic worlds. The stories written under the Cecil Corwin pseudonym were later collected and edited by James Blish in *Thirteen O'Clock and Other Zero Hours* (New York: Dell, 1970).

Information Sources

BIBLIOGRAPHY:
Asimov, Isaac. *In Memory Yet Green*. Garden City, N.Y.: Doubleday, 1979.
Knight, Damon. *The Futurians*. New York: John Day, 1977.
Nicholls. *Encyclopedia*.
Tuck.
Wollheim, Donald A. *The Universe Makers*. New York: Harper & Row, 1971.
INDEX SOURCES: IBSF; ISFM; SFM; Tuck.
REPRINT SOURCES:
   Microform: Greenwood Press Periodical Series.
LOCATION SOURCES: M.I.T. Science Fiction Library; Pennsylvania State University
   Library.

Publication History

TITLE: *Cosmic Stories*. Retitled *Cosmic Science-Fiction* on cover only, May–July 1941.
VOLUME DATA: Volume 1, Number 1, May 1941–Volume 1, Number 3, July 1941.
   Bi-monthly. Total run: 3 issues.
PUBLISHER: Albing Publications, New York.
EDITOR: Donald A. Wollheim.
FORMAT: Pulp, 130 pp.; last issue, 116 pp.
PRICE: 15¢.

Raymond H. Thompson

COSMOS SCIENCE FICTION AND FANTASY
MAGAZINE (1953–1954)

"Why one more?" was the pointed question asked in the back cover editorial in the first issue of *Cosmos*. *Cosmos Science Fiction and Fantasy Magazine* was launched at the very height of the SF magazine boom in 1953, and the editors and publishers knew they had to do something special to stand a chance of surviving amid so much competition. The answer, if the editorial was to be believed, was in placing an emphasis on story and entertainment rather than on gadgetry and gimmick. And by way of proof the magazine boasted some of the major names in SF, including Arthur C. Clarke, Poul Anderson and Ross Rocklynne. Surely names such as these would not contribute to a get-rich-quick publisher, and yet *Cosmos* showed signs of being a magazine designed to cash in on the field's current popularity. Neither the publisher nor the editor—J. A. Kramer and L. B. Cole—was known in the SF field, so how serious was their intent?

The truth was that *Cosmos* had something of a split personality: a young and very inexperienced editor who was a tremendous fan of SF, and a publisher who was chiefly in it for the money. And the editor was not L. B. Cole, as the masthead declared, although he did exist, but Larry M. Harris, better known today by his ancestral name, Laurence M. Janifer. Janifer explains how it all came about:

> At the time I was working for Scott Meredith, the literary agency which seems to have employed almost every sf writer in or near New York at one time or another. Scott began to make arrangements for the packaging of magazines of various sorts. For one mystery magazine, which paid very high rates . . . and published the very top names, I was (under still another name) Managing Editor. I worked on a scattering of others, and the scattering included *Cosmos*, which did not pay high rates. The policy was set by mutual agreement between Scott and the publishers, but it wasn't much of a policy. We were to pay low rates (about a cent a word), not get *too* damned experimental, and draw our material either from stories written for *Cosmos* by clients of the agency, including me, or from the backlog of sf stories which we had at the agency and hadn't sold to higher-pay markets. . . . no writers except agency clients could be considered.

As Janifer said, Scott Meredith represented most of the major SF names at that time, which was why so many top writers appeared in *Cosmos* during its short run. It also explains why the quality of the fiction varied from good—the stories by major writers—to poor—the unsold stories.

Janifer did all the work on the magazine, including acting as art director, blurb-writer and so on. His inexperience may have resulted in Evan Hunter's name appearing as a contributor on the cover of the first issue, though there was no story by him inside. In his editorial for that issue, however, Janifer stated that the final lineup for the first issue had been several thousand words overweight and that the contents had been selected from 600,000 words of copy! The Hunter story appeared in the second issue.

The first issue was also, possibly, the best. The lead story was Poul Anderson's "The Troublemakers," one of the threads in his Future History tapestry and a keen study of two strong but opposing characters in space. "The Fiends in the Bedroom" was a science fiction horror story by John Jakes on the effects of interdimensional worlds impinging. "The Great C," an early story by Philip K. Dick, portrays a post-nuclear world and how a formidable computer continues to survive. "The Curse" was a brief but nonetheless memorable story by Arthur C. Clarke blending the memorable lines of Shakespeare's epitaph with another post-nuclear doom. Other stories were by A. Bertram Chandler, Charles E. Fritch and Ross Rocklynne, and Robert S. Richardson contributed an article on asteroids.

The second issue had a few worthwhile contents, including one of the rare SF appearances of one of literature's major mystery men, B. Traven, and contributions by Carl Jacobi, Jack Vance and Alfred Coppel, as well as Janifer's first story, "Expatriate."

The initial bi-monthly schedule then began to waver, and the final two issues dropped considerably in quality. Vance had a story, "When the Five Moons Rise," in the third issue, and the fourth had stories by Anderson, Gordon R. Dickson and Algys Budrys, but it was clear that many of the poorer stories were now being used. Circulation figures were now in to show that *Cosmos'* sales were poor and that the magazine was losing money, and it was promptly cancelled.

Cosmos might have made a name for itself at the right moment, but it was just another face in the crowd in 1953. Its history is remarkable only for the great lengths to which the publishers went to keep secret the actual identity of the magazine's editor. Janifer recalls that they even hired an empty office and a spare phone line booked in the names of the relevant aliases. If this much legerdemain had been invested in marketing *Cosmos* the magazine may well have had a longer life.

Note

The author wishes to thank Laurence M. Janifer for his help in the research on this entry.

Information Sources

BIBLIOGRAPHY:
Nicholls. *Encyclopedia.*
Tuck.
INDEX SOURCES: MIT; SFM; Tuck.
REPRINT SOURCES: None known.
LOCATION SOURCES: M.I.T. Science Fiction Library; Pennsylvania State University
    Library.

Publication History

TITLE: *Cosmos Science Fiction and Fantasy Magazine.*
VOLUME DATA: Volume 1, Number 1, September 1953–Number 4, July 1954. Volume
    numbering dropped with issue 3. Bi-monthly for first two issues, then irregular.
    Issue 3, March 1954. Total run: 4 issues.
PUBLISHER: Star Publications, New York.

EDITOR: Laurence M. Janifer (not identified in issues, where credit is given to L. B. Cole).
FORMAT: Digest, 128 pp.
PRICE: 35¢.

Mike Ashley

COSMOS SCIENCE FICTION AND FANTASY MAGAZINE (1977)

Cosmos was one of a number of new magazines that appeared like a whirlwind in the mid-1970s and soon blew themselves out. The SF magazine field could rightly be said to have been in turmoil at this time. *Galaxy Science Fiction,** one of the most respected titles in the field, was on the rocks, while small press publications like *Galileo** and *Unearth,** scarcely out of diapers, were apparently flourishing. There were new magazines in all forms, among them *Isaac Asimov's Science Fiction Magazine,** a traditional digest, and *Cosmos*, a larger quasi-slick. At the time of its birth in 1977 everyone seemed sure that *Cosmos* was quality and would survive. Its sudden death after four issues had nothing to do with quality; it was a question of finances.

Cosmos originated because of publisher Norman Goldfind's special liking for the SF and fantasy field. He wanted to start a new magazine but "a major obstacle was [his] own lack of knowledge about the field."[1] He secured the services of David G. Hartwell, who knew the field as well as anyone. As Goldfind and Hartwell planned their first issue, they consulted with other editors, "and they all agreed that we are in an immensely fertile and creative explosion in sf in the 1970s, with everyone who edits in the sf and fantasy field receiving more good material on submission than they can publish or that their editorial policy can incorporate."[2]

Goldfind was sure that here was an area for development: "We felt we could do a superior magazine that in some ways stretched beyond what had been available at the time in other magazines. We also felt we were on the crest of an expanding wave of interest in the field."[3] Its goals were broad and far-reaching: get the best writers and the best illustrators, use some color printing for interior artwork, and include special features on current SF trends. These goals were largely attained.

By employing the slick as opposed to digest size, the scope and quality of the artwork were greatly improved. Jack Gaughan accepted the post of art editor and brought in some of the top SF artists. Together with the editor and publisher, Gaughan arranged for a color spread by some of the best artists to be displayed on a two-page layout in the centerfold. The four artists represented were Paul Lehr, Will Eisner, Ron Miller and Eddie Jones. Their work became the focus of "The Center Section," a "magazine within a magazine" as Hartwell called it, which contained the regular features of book reviews by Robert Silverberg,

"The Media Scene" by Charles N. Brown, "A Fan's Notes" by Ginjer Buchanan, and art by fans. Buchanan spoke of her experiences with fans and commented on fans, fannish gatherings and conventions. A letter column was added with later issues, as were occasional science articles.

Cosmos started with a bang and continued that way. The lead cover story for the first issue, "The House of Compassionate Sharers" by Michael Bishop, was selected by three different anthologists for inclusion in their annual volumes of the year's best SF.[4] George R. R. Martin's "Bitterblooms" from the final issue also made its way into a year's best selection, while "Camera Obscura" by Thomas Monteleone, from the second issue, was a Nebula nominee. The magazine was studded with top names—Fritz Leiber, Larry Niven, Gordon R. Dickson, Norman Spinrad, Joe Haldeman, Brian W. Aldiss, Harlan Ellison—and looked attractive and promising. It carried only one brief serial during its run, "Rime Isle" by Fritz Leiber, perhaps the most complex story in his long-running but extremely popular series about Fafhrd and the Gray Mouser. It seems likely that, given the right distribution, *Cosmos* would have been a sales-winner.

But a magazine needs time to build a readership, and *Cosmos* did not have that time. Sales of each issue hovered around 40,000. When the same publisher's movie magazine *Bijou* suddenly failed, the entire company was left dependent on *Cosmos*, whose circulation was too small to bear the burden. Norman Goldfind felt that *Cosmos* failed for two reasons: "under-capitalization and insufficient exposure on the newsstand."[5]

It was a bitter blow, because, had *Cosmos* succeeded, there is little doubt that it would have helped reshape SF into the 1980s. Instead, other publishers viewed the experiment with caution and kept to the tried and tested paths.

Notes

1. Norman Goldfind, "From the Publisher," *Cosmos*, May 1977, p. 38.
2. David G. Hartwell, "Editorial," *Cosmos*, May 1977, p. 40.
3. Norman Goldfind, letter to George Laskowski (quoted with permission).
4. Terry Carr, *The Best Science Fiction of the Year #7* (New York: Holt, Rinehart and Winston, 1978); Gardner Dozois, *Best Science Fiction Stories of the Year: Seventh Annual Collection* (New York: Dutton, 1978); Donald A. Wollheim, *The 1978 Annual World's Best SF* (New York: DAW Books, 1978).
5. Norman Goldfind, letter to George Laskowski (quoted with permission). See also news item, "Cosmos Suspends Publication," *Locus* 205 (October 1977): 1.

Information Sources

BIBLIOGRAPHY:
Nicholls. *Encyclopedia*.
INDEX SOURCES: NESFA-VI; SFM.
REPRINT SOURCES: None known.
LOCATION SOURCES: M.I.T. Science Fiction Library.

Publication History

TITLE: *Cosmos Science Fiction and Fantasy Magazine* on masthead of first two issues; cover and masthead (of last two issues) dropped "Magazine." Indicia designated title solely as *Cosmos.*

VOLUME DATA: Volume 1, Number 1, May 1977–Volume 1, Number 4, November 1977. Bi-monthly. Total run: 4 issues.

PUBLISHER: Baronet Publishing Company, New York.

EDITOR: David G. Hartwell.

FORMAT: Slick (pulp-paper), 72 pp.

PRICE: $1.00, first two issues; $1.25, last two issues.

George J. Laskowski/Thomas W. Hamilton

COVEN 13

Once in a while a new magazine appears that *tries*. The fantasy field is so used to publishers producing magazines in the hope of making a quick buck at what seems an opportune time when in reality their heart is not in the magazine's contents, that it is a relief to welcome those rare publications that show that both publisher and editor really care for the genre. This is relatively common in the semi-professional field, almost by definition, but in the professional world of commercialism it is rare. Almost inevitably such publications are a financial failure but, paradoxically, an artistic and literary success.

Coven 13, which debuted in September 1969, was the brainchild of Arthur H. Landis, who worked for a small Los Angeles publisher editing a trade journal in the motorcycle field, *Dealer's Voice*. Landis, in his early fifties, had a passionate love for the traditional, realistic supernatural story, not the sensationalistic blood-and-gore horror that has so often masqueraded as the occult in recent years. He convinced his publisher that there was a gap that should be filled, and the result was a neat digest magazine attractively illustrated by William Stout, *Coven 13*.

From the start, Landis set out to make *C13* a magazine of principle. In his first editorial he emphasized that "ours will be a sophisticated quality magazine directed to the truly mature and to the still existing adult audience." He was perhaps more forceful in his second editorial:

No. No, and NO! *Coven 13* will present no ridiculous, freaked-out monster mummy to gurgle tana leaves, and to drag itself along at ⅛ of a mile per hour, through the fuzz-patroled, well-lighted suburbs of an American city: and no fruity King Kong will grace our pages to threaten the peace and quiet of our populace and thereby distract them from their *real* problems. We would suggest that the only King Kongs amongst us today are those not evidenced by their size but rather by their neanderthal thinking.

Such were the editor's principles; but did he practice what he preached? The first issue had ample evidence to support him. There was the first part of what became a four-part serial, ''Let There Be Magick,'' written by Landis himself under the alias James R. Keaveny. It was subsequently published in paperback as *A World Called Camelot* (New York: DAW Books, 1976). It was a fantasy in the tradition of *Unknown Worlds* (*Unknown**), with a galactic agent being sent to the world of Camelot to try to find out about an impending war on a planet where magic works, and has much in common with Christopher Stasheff's popular novel *The Warlock in Spite of Himself* (New York: Ace, 1969). The feature novelette was ''Odile,'' a mature and sensible treatment of witchcraft by Alan Caillou, and there was a handful of short stories which looked at traditional themes with a common sense approach.

The second issue maintained this level of quality with ''Rock God'' by Harlan Ellison, ''Pia'' by Dale Donaldson, and another *Unknown*-style novelette, ''The Transmogrification of Ridgely P. Winters'' by Joseph Harris. All was well, the editorial implied, and distribution and sales were sufficiently encouraging to indicate that *C13* was here to stay. But with the third issue, Landis was admitting in his editorial that the magazine's distribution was causing big problems. When *C13* made the newsstands, sales were good, but a large percentage of the magazine's print run of 80,000 was not being displayed. This was nothing new. It had been the plague of specialist fiction magazines throughout the twentieth century. The distributor has caused the death of more SF and fantasy magazines than any other single factor. It did not matter that the majority of the stories were among the best fantasy around if the magazine did not reach its potential market. Two more issues appeared, both with more than enough good fantasy to make many other magazines envious. By then, however, it became evident that the wall was too high to scale: the financial burden of publishing a national magazine was too heavy for a small, local publisher with no influence in the major outlets. After just four issues, one of the most promising markets for new fantasy to appear for sixteen years (in fact, since *Beyond Fantasy Fiction** and *Fantasy Magazine**) had to be sold off so that the publisher could keep his trade journal, *Dealer's Voice*, solvent.

Coven 13's subscription list and inventory were taken over by William Crawford, no stranger to publishing little magazines (among them *Marvel Tales*,* *Fantasy Book** and *Spaceway**). *Spaceway* had, in fact, been struggling, and Crawford was looking for partners in the hope of expanding his publishing enterprises. He teamed up with longtime devotee Gerald Page and artist Jerry Burge, Page becoming the new editor of the magazine and Burge the art director.

Crawford had made a new deal with a national distributor, but again the distributor dictated the terms. Plans to continue the magazine in the same format and title had to be changed. The name became *Witchcraft & Sorcery* and the magazine went large-size. Since the fifth issue had already been prepared in the old format, this led to delays and production problems and a natural loss of momentum.

When *W&S* did appear it was a handsome publication, although printed on cheap pulp stock with tiny print. There had been a major change in approach. Whereas *C13* had concentrated on light fantasy, *W&S* emphasized sword and sorcery and bolder dark tales.

The result was a magazine heading in a totally different direction than *C13*. The fiction was equally entertaining, though lacking in polish. The artwork was good and grew better with new work by Jeff Jones, Tim Kirk and Stephen Fabian in addition to that of Jerry Burge. There was a regular column of reminiscences by E. Hoffman Price, "Jade Pagoda," which for nostalgia buffs was the high spot of the magazine. The first few issues presented stories from old and new alike: Brian Lumley, Glen Cook, August Derleth, Emil Petaja and Ross Rock-lynne. It adopted the policy of featuring a long novelette each issue, and these included "Dragon's Daughter" by E. Hoffman Price; "Thirst" by Gerald W. Page; "The Castle at the World's Edge," again by Page under the alias Carleton Grindle; "Death God's Doom" by E. C. Tubb; and "Gola's Hell" by Emil Petaja; but on the whole the magazine lacked some of the force and sparkle that had made *C13* so promising.

Crawford was left high and dry when, after two issues, the distributor withdrew his support. At that stage sales had been promising. Now Crawford had to rely on specialist outputs, and *W&S* soon became little more than a semi-professional magazine. Somehow it struggled on through four more issues, but once again costs mounted and sales decreased. The final issue to appear was Number 10, after which Crawford left his option open to continue but temporarily rested the magazine. The last issue featured one of those occasional experiments, the round-robin story, never a literary success but an interesting novelty. Here the Love-craftian tale "Othuum" was started by Brian Lumley, continued by David Gerrold, Miriam Allen deFord and Emil Petaja, and completed by Ross Rocklynne. A deliberate spoof, it was not a sales-winner.

Although *W&S* lacked the polish and promise of *Coven 13*, it was a readable magazine that included a few worthwhile stories. With the right support it might have become a major publication, but the SF/fantasy world is full of might-have-beens.

Information Sources

BIBLIOGRAPHY:
Nicholls. *Encyclopedia.*
INDEX SOURCES: Cook, Michael L., *Monthly Murders*, Westport, Conn.: Greenwood Press, 1982; ISFM-II; MT; NESFA; NESFA-II; NESFA-III; SFM.
REPRINT SOURCES: None known.
LOCATION SOURCES: M.I.T. Science Fiction Library; Pennsylvania State University Library.

Publication History

TITLE: *Coven 13*, September 1969–March 1970. Retitled *Witchcraft & Sorcery*, January/February 1971–1974.

VOLUME DATA: Volume 1, Number 1, September 1969–Number 10, 1974. Volume numbering ceased after issue 6 (still Volume 1). *Coven 13*, bi-monthly; *W&S* intentionally bi-monthly but issues irregular: 5, Jan./Feb. 1971; 6, May 1971; 7, [Spring] 1972; 8, [Summer] 1972; 9, [Summer] 1973; 10, [Spring] 1974. Total run: 4 + 6, 10 issues.

PUBLISHER: *Coven 13*: Camelot Publishing Co., Los Angeles, California. *W&S*: Fantasy Publishing Co. Inc., Alhambra, California.

EDITOR: *Coven 13*: Arthur H. Landis. *W&S*: Gerald W. Page.

FORMAT: *Coven 13*: Digest, 144 pp. *W&S*: Large pulp (saddle-stapled); issues 6 and 7, 64 pp.; 7, 28 pp.; 8, 36 pp.; 9, 44 pp.; 10, 36 pp.

PRICE: *Coven 13*: 60¢. *W&S*: issues 5–8, 60¢; 9, 75¢; 10, $1.00.

Mike Ashley

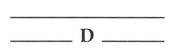

D

DARK FANTASY

Dark Fantasy appeared steadily for nearly a decade, a long time for a fanzine and an achievement that indicated the dedication of its publisher/editor, the artist Gene Day. At the outset *DF* was the typical little fanzine. The June 1973 debut issue, produced on a manual typewriter with a cloth ribbon and bound together with a wraparound card cover stapled from front to back, was no indication of what was to come. However, fortune smiled on *DF* when it received a very favorable review from Warren Publishing, the publishers of *Creepy*, *Eerie* and *Vampirella*. As a consequence *DF*'s sales increased, subscriptions rose and new manuscripts arrived. The third issue showed an improvement in the printing and binding, and with the fourth issue (July 1974) the quality of the fiction improved. It was that issue that contained the first episode of a two-part story by a new author called Charles R. Saunders. The story introduced a black sword and sorcery hero, Imaro, who has since proved inordinately popular. The prose was careless at times, revealing a still immature hand, but it also displayed promise. *DF* has, more than any other publication, championed the work of Charles Saunders and, in particular, the Imaro stories. In fact, Imaro appeared in seven issues of *DF*, and the eighteenth issue (December 1978) was an "all Imaro special." Two of the stories from *DF* have been included in Saunders' first book, *Imaro* (New York: DAW Books, 1981).

DF continued to develop, although in 1977 it almost folded. The twelfth issue was to have been "star-studded" with fiction by Tevis Clyde Smith and Al Manachino, with a cover by Steve Fabian. The completed issue 13 accompanied issue 12 to the printers. The printer accepted them, plus the prepaid printing costs, and disappeared. The loss of the material and the money was almost too much for a fan magazine. (Indeed, the same fate befell the rather more prosperous *Midnight Sun*.*) However, *DF* had by that time established a devoted following that pledged enough subscription money to save it. Much of the fiction scheduled for issues 12 and 13 appeared in later issues, but the artwork was irretrievably lost. It meant that issue 11 was followed by issue 14, but two years later Day brought out a retrospective twelfth issue, and he planned to produce a thirteenth in time.

As *DF* progressed, it attracted a number of professional and semi-professional writers: the late David Madison first appeared in issue 8, Tevis Clyde Smith in 14, Galad Elflandsson in 15, Ardath Mayhar in 20 and Charles de Lint in 21. Nevertheless, Day never forgot the fannish roots of *DF* and continued to present work by newcomers. The same applies to artwork. While names like Steve Fabian and Neal Adams have adorned some issues, and though Day himself became an established comic-book artist with work in several of the Marvel Comics titles, he still welcomed the work of newcomers.

Day worked too hard to fulfill all his endeavors. At the age of thirty-one, in October 1982, he died of a heart attack. *Dark Fantasy* remains as a tribute to his talent as an artist and an editor.

Information Sources

INDEX SOURCES: MT.
REPRINT SOURCES: None known.
LOCATION SOURCES: None known.

Publication History

TITLE: *Dark Fantasy*.
VOLUME DATA: Number 1, Summer 1973–Number 23, November 1980. Issues irregular, with from two to four per year.
PUBLISHER: Gene Day, Gananoque, Ontario, Canada.
EDITOR: Gene [Howard] Day.
FORMAT: Digest (saddle-stapled from issue 3). Issues 1 and 2, 68 pp.; 3–6, 32 pp.; 7, 28 pp.; 8–11, 44 pp. (9, 40 pp.); 14 and 15, 48 pp.; 16, 44 pp.; 17, 40 pp.; 18, 44 pp.; 19, 48 pp.; 12 retrospective, 20 and 21, 52 pp.; 22 and 23, 48 pp.
PRICE: $1.00, all issues except: 2, $1.25; 3, 50¢; 4–7, 75¢; 22 and 23, $1.50.

Jon Harvey

DIME MYSTERY MAGAZINE

Dime Mystery, which appeared in December 1932, was the pioneer terror fiction magazine and started what has been called the weird-menace trend of the 1930s. In general terror/weird-menace stories were neither fantasy nor SF, and were seldom supernatural, so in principle they have no place in this volume. However, *DM* and its later companions and imitators are included for two reasons. First, some of their titles imply that they might be supernatural story magazines, as in the cases of *Horror Stories** and *Uncanny Tales,** and second, there is some SF and fantasy scattered through the issues that is worth recording.

A third reason is that the terror pulps were extremely popular for a while, and their success had side effects on both the supernatural front—especially in *Weird Tales**—and on the SF scene, for example, in *Marvel Science Stories.**

The basic idea of the terror tale was that of a bizarre mystery where our hero, and more often our heroine, is menaced by some character with a warped sense of justice. As the field "developed," or perhaps degenerated, there was an increasing emphasis on sex and sadism, the menaces grew more macabre, the villains more grotesque. Often they were escaped lunatics, or dwarves, or beast-men. The denouement, however, no matter how bizarre the mystery, usually had a mundane explanation. Only rarely did SF or supernatural elements creep in. Usually they were discouraged. The weird-menace pulps, therefore, are basically mystery magazines with hyper-bizarre plots.

DM started out in life as a straightforward mystery magazine for its first ten issues (December 1932–September 1933), but the policy change to Gothic terrors was implemented by publisher Henry Steeger from the October 1933 issue and remained in effect for the rest of the 1930s. The magazine turned to the more traditional detective format with the October 1938 issue. Thus, only 60 out of a total run of 159 issues were in the weird-menace vein, and yet those 60 issues were of far greater influence than the remaining 99.

DM had a regular stable of writers who soon learned the ropes and became trendsetters. The leading contributor was Wyatt Blassingame with nearly forty stories in those sixty issues. Others were Paul Ernst, Arthur Leo Zagat, Wayne Rogers, John H. Knox and Hugh B. Cave. At least three of those names are equally well known in the SF and supernatural fiction fields, and yet, paradoxically, the few stories in that vein that appeared in *DM* were by nonfantasy authors.

John H. Knox, for instance, contributed at least two recognizable SF stories, "Man out of Hell" (March 1934), where the menacing creature turns out to be a remote-controlled robot, and "Frozen Energy" (December 1933), where a drug is administered to a man which slows down his awareness of time. When he is released three hours later he has aged by thirty years. A third story by Knox has elements of the Jekyll-Hyde theme. "Nightmare" (May 1934) concerns a psychiatrist who weakens his patient's will but unwittingly releases the sub-conscious "nightmare beast" that lurks in all of us, causing the patient to murder the psychiatrist.

Paul Ernst did contribute at least one quasi-fantasy, "Caia the Cruel" (July 1935), which involves the workings of a Persian talisman, and a more conventional fantasy in "The Devil's Doorstep" (October 1935), about a fireplace that is an entrance to hell. But probably the most important fantasy to appear in *DM* was, unconventionally, a series, about the curse of the Harcourts. Written by Chandler H. Whipple, the series began with "The Son of Darkness" (February 1935) and ran for six episodes, concluding with "The Last Harcourt" (October 1935). Each story followed the conflicts between the accursed heads of the

Harcourt family down successive generations and the respective reincarnations of the evil Signor Pirelli who first cursed the family.

Such bona fide supernatural elements were rare, however. Nevertheless, the increasing ingenuity with which authors plotted the methods of revenge in each story was as fantastic as some true fantasies. "The Pool Where Horror Dwelt" by Richard Race Wallace (December 1934), for instance, uses as its central device an old legend about a sea monster that used to terrorize a length of coast. As a means of driving the hero mad and taking over control of the estate, the trustee goes to the great lengths of constructing a sea-monster outfit that he can wear!

Preposterous though all this seems, *DM* was read by hundreds of thousands of men and women every month. It ceased publication in 1950.

Note

The author wishes to thank Robert K. Jones for his help in the compilation of this article.

Information Sources

BIBLIOGRAPHY:
Jones, Robert K. *The Shudder Pulps*. West Linn, Ore.: Fax Collector's Editions, 1975. Tuck.
Weinberg, Robert. "Horror Pulps." In *Horror Literature*, ed. Marshall B. Tymn. New York: Bowker, 1981.
INDEX SOURCES: Austin, William N., *Macabre Index*, Seattle, Wash.: FAPA 59, 1952 (features an incomplete issue index from December 1932 to May 1941); Jones, Robert, "Popular's Weird Menace Pulps," in *The Weird Menace*, ed. Camille Cazedessus, Jr., Evergreen, Colo.: Opar Press, 1972 (carries an author index for the issues October 1933–September 1938); Tuck.
REPRINT SOURCES:
Derivative Publication: John H. Knox's two stories, "Man out of Hell" and "Frozen Energy," were reprinted in The Weird Menace (Evergreen, Colo.: Opar Press, 1972).
LOCATION SOURCES: Pennsylvania State University Library; University of California–Los Angeles Library (Vol. 1, No. 1, Vol. 33, No. 4; Vol. 34, No. 3, only).

Publication History

TITLE: Entitled *Dime Mystery Magazine* for the duration of the weird-menace period. Its first few issues appeared as *Dime Mystery Book*, and in its final days it became *15 Mystery*.
VOLUME DATA: Volume 1, Number 1, December 1932–Volume 40, Number 3, October/November 1950. Four issues per volume. Monthly, December 1932–February 1941 (but no issue July 1940); bi-monthly, March/April 1941–July/August 1947; monthly, September 1947–January 1948; bi-monthly, February/March 1948–October/November 1950. Weird-menace issues ran from Volume 3, Number 3, October 1933 to Volume 18, Number 2, September 1938 (60 issues). Total run: 159 issues.

PUBLISHER: Popular Publications, New York.
EDITOR: Overall editor during the weird-menace period was Rogers Terrill.
FORMAT: Pulp, 128–144 pp.
PRICE: 10¢.

Mike Ashley

DOC SAVAGE

In 1933 Street and Smith began publishing a new character pulp, with hopes of duplicating the success of *The Shadow*.* Originally, the thought was to publish a magazine titled *The Phantom*, but this concept collapsed when Standard Publications issued *The Phantom Detective*. Instead, circulation manager Henry Ralston came up with the character Doc Savage. The notion was further developed by S&S editor John Nanovic. The job of actually writing the novels was given to Missouri-born Lester Dent. Dent, an imaginative writer, was a master of unusual plot ideas. Whereas the Shadow was primarily developed as a detective character, Doc Savage was an adventurer and righter-of-wrongs throughout the world.

Dr. Clark Savage, Jr., was a physical and mental superman. He was aided in his adventures by five companions, each a specialist in one field of endeavor and one of the great geniuses of the world. Every day, to remain in perfect physical shape, Doc Savage engaged in two hours of vigorous exercises that strongly resembled isometrics. These exercises generated so much interest from the readership of the magazine that the pulp actually published a series of articles detailing the exercises for practice by Doc Savage fans.

Doc Savage sold extremely well and rivaled *The Shadow* in popularity if not frequency. The magazine never changed to a twice-a-month schedule for complex business reasons, not for lack of circulation. *Doc Savage* began on a monthly basis and remained so until March 1947, when it switched to bi-monthly. In September 1948, like almost all of the Street and Smith pulps still being published, it became a quarterly, as S&S began phasing out its pulp publishing.

Lester Dent used a pulp magazine master fiction plot for nearly all of his Doc Savage novels, so the stories had very similar plots and maintained little mystery as to the identity of the true villain. However, Dent was extremely imaginative and inventive and used many science fiction devices and concepts in his stories to add novel twists to the formula adventures. Oftentimes what seemed like an event explainable only through the use of some fantastic machine turned out to be a masterpiece of misdirection, with the true answer being quite simple. Hoaxes mingled freely with superscience, and the reader was never sure what the true explanation was for any of Dent's bizarre happenings until the end of the novel.

As with all pulp adventurers, Doc Savage encountered lost races and forgotten people all over the world. In the first novel of the series, "The Man of Bronze," Doc found a lost valley in Central America. After saving the natives of a lost civilization from an evil plotter, Doc was rewarded with a steady supply of gold bullion whenever he needed it, so that he could wage a constant battle against the forces of evil throughout the world.

The second novel had another "lost world," this time in the Conan Doyle, King Kong tradition, as Doc and his men traveled to "The Land of Terror," a Pacific island inhabited by dinosaurs. In all, Doc Savage and his men found three such dinosaur havens in the course of their 181 adventures. There were also lost cities in the midst of the Arabian desert and the Sargasso Sea, and other lost races scattered throughout the unexplored regions of the world.

Doc Savage was a master scientist, and he and his men used many super-scientific devices throughout their many adventures. These were needed to battle some of the most outlandish inventions ever found in the character pulps, including a teleportation device, a machine that could cause earthquakes, rocket bombers, and all sorts of machines that could kill at a distance.

In one of the most unusual novels ever to appear in the pulps, "Resurrection Day" (November 1936), Doc Savage found the means to bring a man back from the dead. After much debate, the person chosen was King Solomon. Needless to say, after much adventure, another man—an evil king from the same period—was revived. While an excellent science fiction concept degenerated quickly into a routine adventure story, it was still an unusual idea for a science fiction magazine, much less a single-character pulp.

While *Doc Savage* was not a science fiction magazine in the truest sense, it did promote science fiction among pulp readers; and because the ads for *Astounding Science Fiction* (*Analog Science Fiction**) ran in the magazine, it probably did provide a small but steady stream of readers for the SF companion. *DS* also published numerous science fantasy novels, though in the single-character vein. If not major works of science fiction, they nevertheless compared favorably with much of the SF that was appearing in the genre magazines of the period and should be recognized as a legitimate part of the early SF field.

Most issues of *DS* also featured short stories, usually tales of adventure by lesser known pulp writers from the Street and Smith stable. However, even though *DS* did have strong elements of SF in its pages, its publisher regarded it as an adventure pulp, and the short stories were in turn adventure tales and not SF or fantasy. Regular contributors were Laurence Donovan, Steve Fisher and William Bogart. After the failure of *The Skipper* (an adventure-oriented single-character pulp which ran from December 1936 to December 1937 and featured a sea-going Doc Savage-type character) a novelette featuring this character, written under the house name "Wallace Brooker" (predominantly Norman Daniels), ran regularly for the next few years.

There was a Doc Savage club, which consisted primarily of a page giving the code of Doc Savage and how to obtain a club pin, and letters from members. For several years a feature on the Doc Savage fitness exercises also ran in the magazine.

Information Sources

BIBLIOGRAPHY:

Farmer, Philip José. *Doc Savage: His Apocalyptic Life*. Garden City, N.Y.: Doubleday, 1973.

Goulart, Ron. "Doc Savage and His Circle." Chapter 6 of *Cheap Thrills*. New Rochelle, N.Y.: Arlington House, 1972. Retitled *An Informal History of the Pulp Magazines*. New York: Ace Books, 1973.

Murray, Will. *Doc Savage Supreme Adventurer*. Greenwood, Mass.: Odyssey Press, 1980.

Sampson, Bob. "Dinosaur!" *Xenophile*, No. 11 (1975).

Tuck.

Weinberg, Robert. *Lester Dent, The Man Behind Doc Savage*. Oak Lawn, Ill.: Pulp Press, 1976.

Weinberg, Robert, and Lohr McKinstry. *The Hero Pulp Index*. Evergreen, Colo.: Opar Press, 1971.

INDEX SOURCES: Clark, William J., *An Author Index to the Doc Savage Magazine*, Los Angeles: M & B Publishers, 1971; Cook, Michael L., *Monthly Murders*, Westport, Conn.: Greenwood Press, 1982 (includes an issue index for the issues from January 1944 to September/October 1948); Murray, Will, "The Duende Doc Savage Index," *Duende*, No. 2 (1977): 28–32; Tuck.

REPRINT SOURCES:

Reprint Editions: Both short-run Canadian and British editions appeared during the 1940s textually identical to the U.S. edition.

Novels: The lead novels are being reprinted by Bantam Books, New York, with the intention that they all be restored to print. The reprinting began with *Man of Bronze* (1964) and continues.

LOCATION SOURCES: M.I.T. Science Fiction Library; Pennsylvania State University Library; San Francisco Academy of Comic Art; Street and Smith Collection, Syracuse University Library.

Publication History

TITLE: *Doc Savage* (subtitle "Science Detective" added from September/October 1947).

VOLUME DATA: Volume 1, Number 1, March 1933–Volume 31, Number 1, Summer 1949. Volumes 1–28, six issues per volume, monthly. Volume 29, six issues, bi-monthly. Volume 30, bi-monthly, March–September 1948, four issues; thereafter quarterly. Volume 31, one issue only. Total run: 181 issues.

PUBLISHER: Street and Smith, New York.

EDITORS: John Nanovic, March 1933–November 1943; Charles Moran, December 1943–May 1944; Babette Rosmond, June 1944–June 1948; William DeGrouchy, July 1948–September 1948; Daisy Bacon, Winter 1949–Summer 1949.

FORMAT: Pulp, 128 pp., March 1933–October 1939; 112 pp., November 1939–December 1943; Digest, January 1944–September/October 1948; Pulp, 128 pp., Winter 1949–Summer 1949.

PRICE: 10¢, March 1933–March 1943; 15¢, April 1943–February 1947; 25¢ thereafter.

Robert Weinberg

DOCTOR DEATH

The only single-character pulp ever to feature a title character with actual supernatural powers, *Doctor Death* evolved from Dell Magazine's *All Detective* in 1935. Starting in the August 1934 issue, *All Detective* featured a series of four novelettes by Edward Norris (a purported pen name) in which a diabolical criminal, Doctor Death, battled insurance investigator Nibs Holloway for the possession of a series of rare gems. In the January 1935 novelette, "Thirteen Pearls," Doctor Death was killed. However, that same issue announced that *All Detective* was changing its title with the next issue to *Doctor Death* magazine.

The new magazine featured an entirely different Doctor Death from the villain in *All Detective*. Dr. Rance Mandarin was a mad scientist who felt that the material benefits of civilization were destroying mankind. Mandarin was a master of supernatural powers and worked to destroy civilization and send mankind back into a new Stone Age. Doctor Death used black magic, zombies, fire elementals, Egyptian magic and more to battle the forces of law and order. His nemesis were James Holm, a criminologist with a good grasp of magic; John Ricks, Police Chief of New York, a typical pulp stereotype of the hard-boiled old-fashioned inspector; and Mandarin's assistant, Nina Fererra. The stories were listed as being written by "Zorro" but were the work of Harold Ward. At the end of each novel, an attempt was made to explain that any of Doctor Death's powers were actually science made to look like magic, but the explanations were feeble attempts to give the stories a veneer of plausibility. The novels were just too unbelievable. Death's powers were so vast that it seemed ludicrous that he should be opposed by only the New York Police Force. In fact, the President of the United States appeared in the first novel, threatened by Death's powers, but his presence added little to the credibility of the series.

In keeping with the supernatural theme of the lead novels, the short stories in *DD* were odd combinations of detective and horror stories. Most read as if they were hangovers from *All Detective*'s inventory. Arthur J. Burks had two stories to his credit and may well have written others under pen names, possibly being Damascus Blount, the author of "The Beast That Talked," about a scientist who turns himself into an ape.

Information Sources

BIBLIOGRAPHY:
Cervon, Bruce. "Reader's Guide to Doctor Death." *Collecting Paperbacks?* Vol. 3, No. 3 (July 1981): 30.
DeWitt, Jack. "The Return of Doctor Death." *Bronze Shadows*, No. 5 (July 1966): 8.
Johnson, Tom. "Jimmy Holm, Supernatural Detective vs. Dr. Death." *Doc Savage Club Reader*, No. 10 (1981): 8.
Tuck.
INDEX SOURCES: MT; SFM; Tuck; Weinberg, Robert, and Lohr McKinstry. *The Hero Pulp Index*. Evergreen, Colo.: Opar Press, 1971 (lead novels only).

REPRINT SOURCES:
  Novels: The three lead novels were reprinted in paperback in 1966 by Corinth Books, San Diego, under their original titles: *12 Must Die*, *The Gray Creatures* and *The Shriveling Murders*, credited to "Zorro."
  Derivative Anthology: Six of the stories from *DD* plus four others were reprinted as *Stories from Doctor Death and Other Terror Tales*, ed. Jon Hanlon (San Diego: Corinth, 1966).
LOCATION SOURCES: San Francisco Academy of Comic Art; University of California–Los Angeles Library (Vol. 1, No. 1 only).

Publication History

TITLE: *Doctor Death*.
VOLUME DATA: Volume 1, Number 1, February 1935–Volume 1, Number 3, April 1935. Monthly. Total run: 3 issues.
PUBLISHER: Dell Publishing Co., New York.
EDITOR: Carson Mowre.
FORMAT: Pulp, 128 pp.
PRICE: 15¢.

Robert Weinberg

DR. YEN SIN

Dr. Yen Sin, issued in 1936, was Popular Publications' second attempt to capitalize on the Fu Manchu readership as well as on the growing apprehension in the United States over the Japanese "Yellow Peril" (the first attempt being *The Mysterious Wu Fang**). The novels for the three issues were written by Donald Keyhoe, who was to win fame in later years for his book on flying saucers. The magazine owed more than a little to *Wu Fang*—for one thing, the first cover for *DYS* was a painting originally prepared for the eighth, unpublished issue of *Wu Fang*. Like Wu Fang, Yen Sin was a sinister oriental mastermind intent on conquest. He was the master of a huge network of spies and agents and was for this reason billed as "The Invisible Menace." Fighting the evil doctor was Michael Traile, the Man Who Never Sleeps. Traile had been the victim of an accident years earlier that had caused an unusual condition whereby he never slept. During his eternal wakefulness he studied everything he could so that he knew as much as several men. He was also a perfect physical specimen.

DYS offered little change from the pattern established by Sax Rohmer and copied so often in the pulps. The magazine was dropped after three issues when someone pointed out a possible sexual connotation to the villain's name.

All of the stories in *DYS* reflected the oriental flavor of the magazine. Included was early work by Frank Gruber, Arch Oboler (later to gain fame for his work on the radio show *Lights Out*), Arden Pangborn, Moran Tudury and Alden H. Norton (later to become associate publisher of the Popular chain). Two issues also featured a column, "Fei Lu Fei Ma," from the annals of the Chinatown Squad. The stories were little more than adventure or spy tales with oriental villains or tortures added to fit the magazine's format.

Information Sources

BIBLIOGRAPHY:

Carr, Nick. "Introducing the Yellow Peril." *Megavore*, No. 12 (December 1980): 39–41.

Goulart, Ron. *Cheap Thrills*. New Rochelle, N.Y.: Arlington House, 1972. Reprinted as *An Informal History of the Pulp Magazine*. New York: Ace Books, 1973.

Gruber, Frank. *The Pulp Jungle*. Los Angeles: Sherbourne Press, 1967.

Hardin, Nils. "An Interview with Henry Steeger." *Xenophile*, No. 33 (July 1977): 3–18.

————, and George Hocutt. "A Checklist of Popular Publications Titles 1930–1955." *Xenophile*, No. 33 (July 1977): 21–24.

Hickman, Lynn. "Checklist." *The Pulp Era*, No. 75 (Spring 1971): 11.

Tuck.

Weinberg, Robert, and Lohr McKinstry. *The Hero Pulp Index*. Evergreen, Colo.: Opar Press, 1971.

INDEX SOURCES: Lewandowski, Joseph, "An Index to Dr. Yen Sin," *Age of the Unicorn*, No. 4 (1979); Tuck; Weinberg, Robert, and Lohr McKinstry, *The Hero Pulp Index*, Evergreen, Colo.: Opar Press, 1971 (lead novels only).

REPRINT SOURCES:

Novels: The lead novel in the first issue, "The Mystery of the Dragon's Shadow," was reprinted by Robert Weinberg as *Pulp Classics 9* (Oak Lawn, Ill.: Pulp Press, 1976).

LOCATION SOURCES: San Francisco Academy of Comic Art; University of California–Los Angeles Library (Vol. 1, No. 1 only).

Publication History

TITLE: *Dr. Yen Sin*.

VOLUME DATA: Volume 1, Number 1, May/June 1936–Volume 1, Number 3, September/October 1936. Bi-monthly. Total run: 3 issues.

PUBLISHER: Popular Publications, New York.

EDITOR: Edythe Seims.

FORMAT: Pulp, 112 pp.

PRICE: 10¢.

Robert Weinberg

DRAGONBANE

See DRAGONFIELDS.

DRAGONFIELDS

In 1977 two aspiring Ottawa-based SF/fantasy writers, Charles Saunders and Charles de Lint, discussed the possibility of producing a new semi-professional magazine. Out of that discussion was born Triskell Press, and its first publication was *Dragonbane* 1, which made its debut in the spring of 1978.

In appearance *Dragonbane* was neat if uninspiring. On the cover stands a fierce-looking barbarian in suitable pose. Most interior illustrations also picture fierce-looking barbarians in suitable poses! However, this lackluster package brought with it some very good fiction, from Tanith Lee's gentle "Tiger Sleeping," through Galad Elflandsson's tale of necromancy, "How the Darkness Came to Carcosa" and on to David Madison's decadent sword and sorcery tale, "From under the Hills"; compared to these, Saunders' own Imaro tale and a story by de Lint seem pedestrian.

Nevertheless, as a first attempt *Dragonbane* was commendable. A second issue was well into production, with contributions from Michael Moorcock, Andrew Offutt and Karl Wagner, when Triskell Press decided to start a second magazine. If *Dragonbane* featured straightforward heroic fantasy, *Beyond the Fields We Know* offered a more gentle type of fantasy. However, *Beyond* took itself a little too seriously. There is a feeling of pseudo-intellectualism about the magazine that does not quite come off—an article on William Morris, an interview with Terry Brooks, stories based on folk legends and songs. Even with the presence of authors like Thomas Burnett Swann and Galad Elflandsson, the package is dry and, above all, disappointing.

Neither *Dragonbane* 2 nor *Beyond* 2 appeared. Instead, after a pause of nearly two years and the publication of a small portfolio and a booklet, Triskell Press issued another magazine. *Dragonfields*, in both name and content, is a combination of the two previous magazines. It also continued the numbering by designating itself the third issue. This time the editor and publisher achieved a balance. Gone is the immaturity that spoiled *Dragonbane* and the affected seriousness that pervaded *Beyond*. Here there was rich variety, from a tale in the Tiana cycle by Richard K. Lyon and Andrew Offutt, through the sparkling poetic prose of Caradoc Cador and Tanith Lee, to the wit of a Marcus and Diana tale by the late David Madison. The whole is packaged with some interesting articles, good poems and refreshing illustrations.

Lack of finances and the editors' increased preoccupation with their own writing activities delayed the appearance of *Dragonfields* 4 for three years. Not as striking in appearance as the third issue it was nevertheless a pleasing blend of fact and fiction with a special section devoted to Tanith Lee.

Information Sources

INDEX SOURCES: ISPF-2; MT.
REPRINT SOURCES: None known.
LOCATION SOURCES: M.I.T. Science Fiction Library.

Publication History

TITLE AND VOLUME DATA: *Dragonbane* 1, Spring 1978. *Beyond the Fields We Know* 1, Autumn 1978. *Dragonfields* 3, Summer 1980. *Dragonfields* 4, Winter 1983.

PUBLISHER: Triskell Press, Ottawa, Ontario, Canada.

EDITORS: Charles R. Saunders and Charles de Lint.

FORMAT: Variable. *Dragonbane*, 64 pp.; *Beyond . . .*, 92 pp.; *Dragonfields* 3, 120 pp.; *Dragonfields* 4, 76 pp.

PRICE: *Dragonbane*, $3.00; *Beyond . . .*, $4.50; *Dragonfields*, $5.00.

Jon Harvey

DREAM WORLD

Dream World, subtitled "Stories of Incredible Powers," was a digest-sized magazine scheduled for bi-monthly publication that ran for only three issues: February, May and August 1957. Published by Ziff-Davis, *DW* was edited by Paul W. Fairman, a regular contributor to the Ziff-Davis publications and editor of other Ziff-Davis magazines. The assistant editor of *DW* was Cele Goldsmith, who also worked in various editorial capacities for Ziff-Davis.

The fiction in *DW* is remarkably homogeneous, even formulaic. Written by male authors for a male audience, the stories concern unusual physical and mental powers and their consequences. Often a meek individual turns the tables on persons who exploit or harass him. Female characters, generally, are stereotypically shrewish, childlike or sexually enticing. While impossibly voluptuous women often reward the protagonist, the stories, to Fairman's credit, are good-humored, never sadistic or excessively violent.

In editorials in the last two issues, Fairman describes the kind of stories *DW* published. In "A New Kind of Fiction—" (May 1957), Fairman contrasts *DW*'s brand of fantasy with "grim, preachy, dreary" fiction. In the name of realism,

no coach and six for Cinderella. She must stay in her rags and learn forebearance [*sic*] because turning a pumpkin into a carriage is ridiculous. . . . Rather than publishing a new kind of fiction, we are actually going back to the original concept of what fiction was meant to be. We are giving the glass slipper back to Cinderella; we are taking Peter Pan off Pier 26 and putting him back into Never Never Land.

In "Of Men and Dreams—" (August 1957), Fairman equates *DW*'s stories with daydreaming:

I wish I could walk into that bank and come out with enough money to pay my bills. This is wishful thinking and such is the fabric from which all dreams are woven.

And what is a day dream other than the vicarious wielding of incredible powers?

Wish fulfillment, Fairman suggests, is the *raison d'être* of *DW*.

DW's covers and interior illustrations are crude and, more often than not, lascivious. Presumably illustrating Leonard G. Spencer's "The Man with the X-Ray Eyes," the February cover is by Edward Valigursky, formerly associate art director for Ziff-Davis. A man looks through a brick wall at a sensuous girl undressing. Depicting a scene from C. H. Thames' "The Man Who Made His Dreams Come True," the cover of the May issue is by John Parker. The "dream girl," Jeanette, breasts and hips accentuated, appears to Alex, in bed the night before his wedding. Valigursky illustrates the August cover with the torso of a living, nearly nude woman rising from a block of granite. Virgil Finlay's black and white rendering of the same scene from Adam Chase's "His Touch Turned Stone to Flesh" is one of the few interior illustrations with style or grace. All three issues, the first especially, contain cartoons, often depicting stupid or voluptuous women, whom men either ridicule or ogle.

Some of *DW*'s stories are published under house names or pseudonyms. As Darius John Granger, Milton Lesser contributed "Time Out" to the February issue and "He Fired His Boss" to the May issue. Lesser's "The Man Who Made His Dreams Come True," in the May issue, is attributed to C. H. Thames. The identity of writers using other Ziff-Davis house names cannot easily be ascertained. In all three issues are stories by Adam Chase, a house name used by both Lesser and Paul Fairman. Stories also appear under two other Ziff-Davis house pseudonyms: Leonard G. Spencer (used by Robert Silverberg and Randall Garrett, as well as by lesser-known writers) and Ivar Jorgenson (used by Paul Fairman, Harlan Ellison, Randall Garrett and Robert Silverberg).[1] Ellison, Garrett and Silverberg all contributed to the magazine under their own names. The names or pseudonyms of the other contributors are not traceable through science fiction's biographical sources.

The February issue of *DW*, the weakest both in art and fiction, is fleshed out with two reprints. Having little in common with *DW*'s other fiction, P. G. Wodehouse's "Ways to Get a Gal" is a lighthearted, witty tale about a butler who wins the affection of a girl with whom his employer is infatuated. Thorne Smith's "Sex, Love, and Mr. Owen," belatedly acknowledged in the May issue as a reprint of a chapter from the novel *Rain in the Doorway*, is a far less happy choice than the Wodehouse piece. Mr. Owen, who knows nothing of either books or sex, works in the pornography section of a department store. He and the brassy salesgirls converse tediously at cross purposes with various customers, twisting what they say into sexual innuendoes or nonsense.

Adam Chase's "Legs on Olympus" (February), Darius John Granger's "He

Fired His Boss'' (May) and G. L. Vandenburg's "The Man Who Couldn't Lose" (August) are representative examples of *DW*'s fiction. "Legs" is a slangy, irreverent treatment of a myth, a vehicle for much rhapsodizing about female sexual attributes. Abner Paris, a beauty contest judge, is staying at the Troy Hotel in Atlantic City. Because of the coincidence of names, he is transported magically to Mount Ida to decide whether Hera, Athena, or Aphrodite is the most beautiful. Granger's "He Fired His Boss" is one of several stories in which a meek individual gets revenge on his persecutors. Tom Anderson is fired by his tyrannical boss, Mr. Smedley, because he fails to secure an advertising contract from Penelope Standish, head of a perfume company. When a great-aunt dies, leaving Tom controlling interest in Smedley's company, he becomes chairman of the board, fires Smedley, and has his way with both Penelope and Smedley's daughter. Similarly, George Wellington, the mousey protagonist of "The Man Who Couldn't Lose," is bullied unmercifully by an unmarried sister. Following the instructions of the disembodied voice of Red Lundigan, a dead gangster, George becomes rich at the race track and succeeds in frightening the men who killed Lundigan into signing a confession. Under Lundigan's influence, George, for the first time, commands respect from other people.

As these plot summaries suggest, *DW*'s contributors are more concerned with the escapism that characterizes daydreams than with their psychological implications. One story, however, almost transcends the *DW* formula in its representation of a woman supernaturally divided into two warring personas. In C. H. Thames' "The Man Who Made His Dreams Come True," Alex Hammer, rather unenthusiastically, plans to marry Janey, who is remarkable only for a total lack of outstanding qualities, good or bad. The night before the wedding, Alex is visited by Jeanette, a gorgeous being who claims to be Janey's "dream girl," the person Janey dreams about being but keeps locked in a dream city, "Paris on the Euphrates." While Alex and Janey honeymoon in the real Paris, Jeanette continues her efforts to undermine Janey and finally spirits Alex away to her oriental city. Its sensuous pleasures turn nightmarish when Alex is pursued by a jealous sultan threatening to castrate him. Finally, Alex is granted three wishes; the last is that Janey and Jeanette be joined together in one person. While "The Man Who Made His Dreams Come True" is not an exceptional story, the scenes in "Paris on the Euphrates" are genuinely dreamlike, with persons from Alex's waking life appearing in surprising contexts. Furthermore, in a publication that presents relationships between men and women simplistically, the Jamesian idea that sexual repression should give rise to a ghost is startling.

Randall Garrett, Robert Silverberg and Harlan Ellison are the only *DW* contributors likely to be familiar to readers today. Garrett wrote "The Devil Never Waits" (February) and "You Too Can Win a Harem" (May). "The Devil" is an unremarkable story about a man impatient with waiting, cursed with the power to transport himself to places instantaneously. In "You Too," Edgar Farnsworth wins a "mystery prize" on a quiz show. (An opponent is unable to identify "thiotimoline," an in-joke alluding to "The Endochronic Properties of Resublimated Thiotimoline," Isaac Asimov's mock doctoral dissertation published in *Astounding [Analog Science Fiction*]*.)[2] The mystery prize is the Pearl Palace, owned by the Shah of oil-rich Khivat. Dependent on the country's oil, U.S. government officials coerce Edgar into living at the palace, where he is pampered by harem slaves and threatened by one of the Shah's political enemies. Garrett's two contributions are formula fiction, pleasant and unexceptional.

Because Robert Silverberg uses his protagonist's special powers not merely to provide his reader with vicarious gratification, but also to ridicule the stultifying conservatism of American colleges, his "Anything His Heart Desires" (August) is one of *DW*'s best stories. When Professor Howard Lockridge announces that he has modest psychic powers, he is fired from MacFlecknoe College and students and faculty are forbidden to associate with him. Under emotional stress, Lockridge's powers proliferate. At the request of the students, he speaks at a football game, and the college president sends campus police to stop him. Levitating above their heads, Lockridge finishes his address in triumph.

Unlike Silverberg, who uses a protagonist with special powers as an occasion to satirize resistance to new ideas, Harlan Ellison makes no pretense of redeeming social importance. As is characteristic of *DW*, the incredible powers of the protagonists of Ellison's "A Bucketful of Diamonds" (February) and "The Big Trance" (August) bring them fantastic wealth and the ability to manipulate others. In "A Bucketful," Davey Baer, a "second storey man," receives the ability to walk up walls and to make people turn their heads while he is robbing them. In "The Big Trance," Victor Mainwaring, an unassertive attendant at an orange juice stand, sends for a book on hypnotism advertised in a pulp magazine and succeeds in hypnotizing all of New York. After a week of kissing beautiful women and helping himself to luxuries in stores and restaurants, he gives New Yorkers the posthypnotic suggestion to send him money regularly and brings the city out of its trance. Ellison's magical book is a spoof on the exaggerated claims made for books and courses advertised in the pulps; but, even more significant, *The Power of Hypnosis* by Ramakalandra III (*"set in Tangibility Bold, set to read in any language the owner desires"*) is a delightful addition to the library of imaginary, forbidden books, initiated by H. P. Lovecraft with the *Necronomicon* and augmented by Robert Bloch, August Derleth, Clark Ashton Smith and others. Ellison's playfulness and exuberance of tone, the sly insincerity with which he manipulates the *DW* formula, make other contributors seem plodding by comparison. Even the leering sexism with which Ellison treats his female characters is so outrageous that the effect is ironic.

"You only live twice, or so it seems, / One life for yourself and one for your dreams." The title song from the James Bond film sums up Paul Fairman's conception of *Dream World*. Stories by Randall Garrett, Robert Silverberg, Harlan Ellison and lesser-known and pseudonymous writers are, for the most part, variations on a basic plot: a commonplace man is suddenly endowed with unusual powers, generally bringing him wealth or love. With a few exceptions, *DW*'s stories are pleasant formula constructs, without much psychological insight or social commentary.

Notes

1. See Susannah Bates, *The Pendex: An Index of Pen Names and House Names in Fantastic, Thriller and Series Literature* (New York: Garland, 1981); Barry McGhan, *Science Fiction and Fantasy Pseudonyms*, rev. ed. (Dearborn, Mich.: Misfit Press, 1979); and James A. Rock, *Who Goes There?* (Bloomington, Ind.: Rock, 1979).

2. *Astounding Science-Fiction*, March 1948, p. 120.

Information Sources

BIBLIOGRAPHY:
Nicholls. *Encyclopedia.*
Tuck.
INDEX SOURCES: MIT; MT; SFM; Tuck.
REPRINT SOURCES: None known.
LOCATION SOURCES: Eastern New Mexico University, Golden Library (not available through interlibrary loan); Massachusetts Institute of Technology, MIT Science Fiction Society (not available through ILL); Michigan State University, Special Collections; Northern Illinois University, University Library, Rare Books and Special Collections (no ILL or microfilm, but partial photocopying of some issues *may* be possible); Ohio State University Libraries, Division of Special Collections; Queen's University, Special Collections (Vol. 1, Nos. 2–3 only; no ILL or microfilm); San Francisco Academy of Comic Art, Science Fiction Room; Temple University, Paley Library, Paskow SF Collection (not available through ILL); Texas A&M University, Special Collections; University of Arizona, Special Collections; University of California–Los Angeles (a microfilm may be produced, the negative to remain at UCLA and the patron to pay for negative and print); University of Georgia Libraries, Periodicals Department; University of Kansas, Spencer Research Library (Vol. 1, Nos. 1–2 only).

Publication History

TITLE: *Dream World* (subtitled "Stories of Incredible Powers").
VOLUME DATA: Volume 1, Number 1, February 1957–Volume 1, Number 3, August 1957. Intended schedule bi-monthly, but published quarterly. Total run: 3 issues.
PUBLISHER: Ziff-Davis Publishing Co., New York.
EDITOR: Paul W. Fairman.
FORMAT: Digest, 128 pp.
PRICE: 35¢.

Wendy Bousfield

DUSTY AYRES AND HIS BATTLE BIRDS

In an attempt to pump new life into the ailing pulp *Battle Birds*, Popular Publications commissioned Robert Sidney Bowen, Jr., to convert the magazine into a single-character pulp. Bowen, who had been writing numerous air-war stories for the pulps, wanted to try his hand at a continuing monthly character with his own titled magazine. Henry Steeger, president of Popular, agreed, and the two men devised the concept of *Dusty Ayres*. Not wanting to be in direct competition with *G-8 and His Battle Aces*,* Popular's top-selling World War I air-war pulp, Steeger and Bowen decided to set *Dusty Ayres* in the near future. Asiatic hordes, under the leadership of the mysterious Fire-Eyes, had conquered the world, with only the United States remaining free. Dusty Ayres was America's top pilot and was usually given the job of stopping the latest plot devised by Fire-Eyes to conquer America.

As with most single-character pulp series, the novels in the Dusty Ayres canon soon settled into a predictable mold. Dusty would learn of a new device or plot by the Black Invaders, usually the work of their chief flyer, the Black Hawk. With the aid of his friend and spy among the Invaders, Jack Horner, Dusty would destroy the menace just in time to save the United States from invasion. Also aiding Dusty were two sidekicks, Curley Brooks and Biff Bolton.

After a number of issues, it became apparent that the series was not selling sufficiently well to continue the magazine. In an unusual break with tradition, Bowen penned "The Telsa Raiders," in which Fire-Eyes, the leader of the Black Invaders, is killed and the invasion threat ended, with the world set free. There was even an editorial in the same issue announcing the cancellation of the magazine.

Dusty Ayres was a science fiction magazine. All of the air menaces used to threaten the United States were science fiction in both concept and use. The setting of the novels, the immediate future with all the world conquered, was typical pulp but also typical SF.

Adding to the uniqueness of *Dusty Ayres* was the fact that the entire magazine was written by Bowen. Each issue featured several short stories, all dealing with the Black Invasion (on land, sea and air) and all the work of Bowen. These were usually just war stories with a touch of SF added, usually a new invention or secret device that has to be defeated by the resourceful hero (just like the lead novels). Even the editorial department, "Hanger Flying," was by Bowen. In it, the author wrote about the latest in aviation and answered readers' questions. About the only thing Bowen did not do for the magazine was illustrate it!

While the magazine had little if any influence on modern SF, it highlighted the close relationship between the interests in aviation and science fiction that had existed since the first attempt at manned flight and which had earlier materialized in the shape of Hugo Gernsback's *Air Wonder Stories*.*

Information Sources

BIBLIOGRAPHY:
Goulart, Ron. *Cheap Thrills*. New Rochelle, N.Y.: Arlington House, 1972. Retitled *An Informal History of the Pulp Magazine*. New York: Ace Books, 1973.
Weinberg, Robert. *The Hero Pulp Index*. Evergreen, Colo.: Opar Press, 1971.

INDEX SOURCES: Weinberg, Robert, and Lohr McKinstry, *The Hero Pulp Index*, Evergreen, Colo.: Opar Press, 1971 (lead novels only).

REPRINT SOURCES:

Novels: Five novels were reprinted in paperback by Corinth Books, San Diego, in 1966 under the titles *Black Lightning*, *Crimson Doom*, *Purple Tornado*, *The Telsa Raiders* and *Black Invaders vs the Battle Birds*.

LOCATION SOURCES: M.I.T. Science Fiction Library; San Francisco Academy of Comic Art.

Publication History

TITLE: *Dusty Ayres and His Battle Birds* (retitling of original magazine, *Battle Birds*).

VOLUME DATA: Continued the numbering of *Battle Birds*: Volume 5, Number 4, July 1934–Volume 8, Number 3, July/August 1935. Four issues per volume. Monthly. Total run: 12 issues.

PUBLISHER: Popular Publications, New York.

EDITOR: Rogers Terrill.

FORMAT: Pulp, 128 pp.

PRICE: 15¢.

Robert Weinberg

DYNAMIC SCIENCE FICTION

Dynamic Science Fiction, not to be confused with the earlier *Dynamic Science Stories*,* was the fourth SF pulp magazine to be published by Louis Silberkleit but was also his last new title. Satisfied with the sales of *Future Science Fiction* (*Future Fiction**), and with the SF boom at its height, Silberkleit issued the new magazine in late 1952, with the cover date December. Once again Robert W. Lowndes edited in his usual competent manner.

Although *DSF* saw only six issues, it published a number of memorable stories, surprising when one considers that it was the second stablemate to a magazine that had to rely heavily on material not aimed at the Big Three (*Astounding Science Fiction*,* *Galaxy Science Fiction*,* and the *Magazine of Fantasy and Science Fiction**) in the SF field. Nevertheless, at this time Silberkleit was paying good (though not top) rates, and on acceptance, which would have helped to attract writers, as would the knowledge that Lowndes would not meddle with their manuscripts.

The first issue led with Lester del Rey's hard-hitting SF thriller "I Am Tomorrow." The second issue featured Arthur C. Clarke's clever story about the origin of the lemmings, "The Possessed." The fourth issue was dominated by the novel "The Duplicated Man" by James Blish and Michael Sherman [Lowndes], an early work by the two writers and their first attempt at the novel length. It saw a hardcover edition from Avalon Books in 1959. Prophetically, the final issue carried Poul Anderson's "The Chapter Ends."

DSF, like the other Lowndes magazines, was strong in nonfiction. James E.

Gunn had two long essays that were serialized: "The Philosophy of Science Fiction" (March–June 1953) and "The Plot Forms of Science Fiction" (October 1953–January 1954), an analysis of the field that still stands up well today. Anthony K. van Riper provided a critical analysis of the work of E. E. Smith in "Skylark Smith: An Appreciation" (October 1953), while it was in the pages of *DSF* that Robert A. Madle's column of news and nostalgia, "Inside Science Fiction," began (June 1953–January 1954). It later spread to the three other Lowndes magazines.

DSF, however, had little to offer the majority readership at a time when there were scores of SF pulps and digests fighting for survival on the stalls. In recent correspondence Lowndes commented on *DSF*'s final days.

By the summer of 1953 returns showed that sales had fallen off. As Milton Luros once (not once—often!) remarked, Silberkleit played the magazines the way one plays the stock market—a fall-off in sales resulted in immediate cut-backs. I could not use so much higher-rate material, and payment was deferred to schedule, meaning when the issue containing the story was closed; still before actual publication.

In 1953 Silberkleit had experimented with a digest-sized *Science Fiction Stories*, which indicated that the pulps were clearly on the way out. Silberkleit converted *Future Science Fiction*, but rather than continue *DSF* he folded it in favor of reviving *Science Fiction*.

Information Sources

BIBLIOGRAPHY:
Nicholls. *Encyclopedia.*
Tuck.
INDEX SOURCES: MIT; SFM; Tuck.
REPRINT SOURCES:
    Reprint Editions: British edition published by Thorpe & Porter, Leicester. Three issues in January, June and November 1954; Pulp, 96 pp., 1/-. Related to U.S. issues as follows: 1, June 1953; 2, December 1952; 3, January 1954.
    Derivative Anthologies: Six of the seven stories in *Way Out*, ed. Ivan Howard (New York: Belmont Books, 1963), are from *DSF*, mostly the first issue. Four of the eight stories in *Novelets of SF*, ed. Ivan Howard (1963), are from various issues.
LOCATION SOURCES: M.I.T. Science Fiction Library; Pennsylvania State University Library.

Publication History

TITLE: *Dynamic Science Fiction.*
VOLUME DATA: Volume 1, Number 1, December 1952–Volume 1, Number 6, January 1954. First two issues, quarterly. Thereafter bi-monthly, though last issue on quarterly schedule. Total run: 6 issues.

PUBLISHER: Columbia Publications, Holyoke, Massachusetts. (Editorial offices in Church
    Street, New York.)
EDITOR: Robert W. Lowndes.
FORMAT: Pulp, 128 pp., first four issues; thereafter 96 pp.
PRICE: 25¢.

Mike Ashley

DYNAMIC SCIENCE STORIES

Lasting only two issues, *Dynamic Science Stories* was introduced by Western
Fiction Publishing as a companion pulp to *Marvel Science Stories*.*[1] Its two
numbers coincided with the February 1939 and April–May 1939 (Vol. 1, Nos.
3–4) issues of *Marvel*. Like that magazine, *Dynamic* was edited by Robert O.
Erisman,[2] used the art of Paul and of Norman Saunders on its covers, and featured
writers who were typical of the pulp style before it was transformed by John
Campbell at *Astounding*.

For its two cover stories, *Dynamic* used "The Lord of Tranerica" by Stanton
Coblentz and "Prison of Time" by Eando Binder (Earl and Otto Binder). Despite
differences in tone—the Coblentz piece aims for some satire on American habits
of labor and leisure, whereas Binder's offers a more desperately heroic reaction
to the international tensions of 1939—both stories are built around undaunted
American males who enter another time or dimension, where they triumph over
oppressive dictatorial powers.

The remaining stories in *Dynamic* offer a representative sample of the period's
pulp conventions. There is a lost world in the Amazon jungle and a secret
laboratory in the polar ice. There is an abundance of personal combat on (and
between) Jupiter, Mercury, Mars and Venus. There are clever gadgets and menacing ray-guns, aliens of a benign or a menacing cast, and scientists both brilliant
and mad. And there are the women—haughty or hapless, but always attracted
to the dashing American males who lead the action.

Amid all these conventions, a few of the stories do offer flashes of greater
skill. In "The Message from the Void" by Hubert Mavity (Nelson S. Bond),
this skill lies in the idea—a failure in first contact due to the differing modes of
human and alien abstraction. In L. Sprague de Camp's "Ananias," the skill lies
in sharp observation, which deftly skewers bureaucracies (particularly military
bureaucracies) for the blundering to which they are prone. Less incisive than
either of these, Manly Wade Wellman's "Insight" nonetheless displays a control
of tone and plot construction from which other stories in *Dynamic* (and *Marvel*)
would have benefited.

Such flashes do not come often enough, however, to enrich *Dynamic* with
any substantial distinction. Like most of its pulp competitors, it remains satisfied
with what is representative and routine for the genre.

Notes

1. In *The Science Fiction Encyclopedia* (p. 52), Malcolm J. Edwards notes that publishers could increase the shelf life of their magazines by putting out two titles on a bi-monthly schedule rather than one on a monthly basis.

2. As is the case with the pre-World War II numbers of *Marvel*, Erisman's name does not appear as editor in either issue of *Dynamic*. And the magazine's statement of ownership again cites Martin Goodman as publisher, editor and managing editor. Nonetheless, Ashley, Nicholls and Tuck all name Erisman as *Dynamic*'s editor.

Information Sources

BIBLIOGRAPHY:
Nicholls. *Encyclopedia.*
Tuck.
INDEX SOURCES: ASFI; ISFM; SFM; Tuck.
REPRINT SOURCES:
  Reprint Editions: A British edition identical to the first issue was released in 1939, undated.
  Microform: Greenwood Press Periodical Series.
LOCATION SOURCES: M.I.T. Science Fiction Library; Pattee Library, Pennsylvania State University.

Publication History

TITLE: *Dynamic Science Stories.*
VOLUME DATA: Volume 1, Number 1, February 1939–Volume 1, Number 2, April/May 1939. Bi-monthly. Total run: 2 issues.
PUBLISHER: Western Fiction Publishing Co., Chicago. (Editorial offices in Radio City, New York.)
EDITOR: Uncredited [Robert O. Erisman].
FORMAT: Pulp, 112 pp.
PRICE: 15¢.

Joseph J. Marchesani

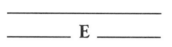

E

EERIE MYSTERIES

Despite the title, this was not a fantasy magazine but one of the weird-menace pulps that proliferated in the 1930s. First appearing in August/September 1938, it was the third and final attempt by Aaron Wyn to enter the field, following *Ace Mystery*,* which at least did contain some fantasy, and *Eerie Stories*,* which did not. The stories all appear to have been published under house names, and a number have been identified as reprints from Wyn's other magazine, *Ten Detective Aces*. *EM* is of little interest to the fantasy fan.

Information Sources

BIBLIOGRAPHY:

Jones, Robert K. *The Shudder Pulps*. West Linn, Ore.: Fax Collector's Editions, 1975. P. 131.

Jones, Robert K. "The Weird Menace Magazines." *Bronze Shadows*, No. 10 (June 1967): 3–8; No. 11 (August 1967): 7–13; No. 12 (October 1967): 7–10; No. 13 (January 1968): 7–12; No. 14 (March 1968): 13–17; No. 15 (November 1968): 4–8.

Tuck.

Weinberg, Robert. "The Horror Pulps." In *Horror Literature*, ed. Marshall Tymn. New York: Bowker, 1981. Pp. 381, 395.

INDEX SOURCES: Austin, William N., *Macabre Index*, Seattle, Wash.: FAPA 59, 1952 (lists first three issues only); MT; Tuck.

REPRINT SOURCES: None known.

LOCATION SOURCES: University of California–Los Angeles Library (Vol. 1, No. 1 only).

Publication History

TITLE: *Eerie Mysteries*.
VOLUME DATA: Volume 1, Number 1, August/September 1938–Volume 1, Number
    4, April/May 1939. Listed as bi-monthly, but appeared quarterly. Total run: 4
    issues.
PUBLISHER: Ace Magazines, New York.
EDITOR: Harry Widmer.
FORMAT: Pulp, 128 pp.
PRICE: 15¢.

Mike Ashley

EERIE STORIES

Like *Eerie Mysteries*,* which followed *Eerie Stories* a year later, *ES* was not
a supernatural magazine, as the title suggests, but one of a number of weird-
menace magazines, best typified by *Dime Mystery Magazine** and *Terror Tales*.*
It is included in this volume for clarification only, especially since a magazine
with a similar title, *Eerie Tales*,* *was* a fantasy magazine.

Only one issue of *ES* appeared, in August 1937, carrying twelve stories under
house pseudonyms. At least one, "Mate of the Beast" by Leon Dupont, was a
reprint from *Ace Mystery** with a pepped-up title change from "Wolf Vengeance." Except for the lead story, "Virgins of the Stone Death" by Gates
Alexander, which includes a drug that induces near instantaneous rigor mortis,
the stories contain no elements of SF or fantasy.

Information Sources

BIBLIOGRAPHY:
Jones, Robert K. *The Shudder Pulps*. West Linn, Ore.: Fax Collector's Editions, 1975.
    P. 130.
Jones, Robert K. "The Weird Menace Magazines." *Brgnze Shadows*, No. 10 (June
    1967): 3–8; No. 11 (August 1967): 7–13; No. 12 (October 1967): 7–10; No. 13
    (January 1968): 7–12; No. 14 (March 1968): 13–17; No. 15 (November 1968):
    4–8.
Tuck.
Weinberg, Robert. "The Horror Pulps." In *Horror Literature*, ed. Marshall Tymn. New
    York: Bowker, 1981. Pp. 381, 394.
INDEX SOURCES: Austin, William N., *Macabre Index*, Seattle, Wash.: FAPA 59,
    1952; MT; Tuck.
REPRINT SOURCES: None known.
LOCATION SOURCES: None known.

Publication History

TITLE: *Eerie Stories*.
VOLUME DATA: Volume 1, Number 1, August 1937. Designated bi-monthly, but no
    further issues appeared.

PUBLISHER: Ace Magazines, New York.
EDITOR: Harry Widmer.
FORMAT: Pulp, 112 pp.
PRICE: 10¢.

Mike Ashley

EERIE TALES

A short-lived rival publication to the Canadian *Uncanny Tales*,* *Eerie Tales* survived for one issue in 1941 and was all but indistinguishable in content and quality from the former magazine's early issues. Indeed, it is possible that *Eerie* was a companion magazine, despite the different publisher and publishing address, because of the odd circumstances under which *Uncanny* appeared. The list of contributors was almost identical, dominated, as were all Canadian fantasy publications at this time, by Thomas P. Kelley. Kelley had two genuine items in the issue and probably a third under the alias "Valentine Worth." One of the stories, "The Man Who Killed Mussolini," awkwardly written wish-fulfillment SF, was a companion piece to "The Man Who Killed Hitler" by the same author in the concurrent issue of *Uncanny Tales* (cover date June 1941). Kelley also contributed the first part of a serial, "The Weird Queen." This comprises the opening four chapters of Kelley's book, *The Face That Launched a Thousand Ships*, published in October 1941 by Adam Publishing Company of Toronto as its "Handy Library Book #1," probably the first original Canadian paperback SF novel. Adam Publishing was also the publisher of *Uncanny Tales*.

The remaining contents were poor, with only Leslie A. Croutch's "A Dictator Dies" justifying itself as SF. "The Phantom Trooper" by Scott Malcolm is a western with ghostly vengeance on the last page to convert it to a nominal fantasy; "Horror in the Dungeon" by George Grant presents us with the concept of a dank, moldy dungeon in the Sahara, while "Tales of Long Ago" by Ethel G. Preszcator is a nonfiction historical anecdote.

ET is collectable only for its rarity, not quality.

Information Sources

BIBLIOGRAPHY:
Tuck.
INDEX SOURCES: MT; Tuck.
REPRINT SOURCES: None known.
LOCATION SOURCES: None known.

Publication History

TITLE: *Eerie Tales*.
VOLUME DATA: Volume 1, Number 1, July 1941. Only issue.
PUBLISHER: C. K. Publishing Co., Toronto, Canada.

EDITOR: Not identified, but may be Melvin Colby, as per *Uncanny Tales*.
FORMAT: Pulp, 64 pp.
PRICE: 15¢.

Grant Thiessen

THE ELECTRICAL EXPERIMENTER

Technical magazine known better by its subsequent title, *Science and Invention*. See SCIENCE AND INVENTION.

EROTIC SCIENCE FICTION STORIES

Erotic Science Fiction Stories was a one-shot magazine from a publisher of pornography who was clearly looking for a new front to peddle his wares. The editor and publisher was David Sullivan, whose company changes names fairly frequently. At the time of *ESFS* it was Figcrest Publications, a company that ran from March 1977 to October 1978 and which brought out at least one erotic SF book called *The Orgasm Test*, a collection of short stories. The book may even have been a paperback edition of the magazine since there is a story called "The Test" in *ESFS* which could fit that title story. Neither the book nor the story is credited, but most of the stories in the magazine are attributable to Michael Ginley, and other by-lines may be pseudonyms.

In his editorial Sullivan proclaims that the "magazine is dedicated to stories that are 100% Science Fiction-Fantasy, and out of the unknown." He attempts to give the magazine a veneer of respectability when he adds, "Some of the stories are of a slightly erotic nature and for this reason we are restricting sales to Adults Only, but please do not confuse it with ordinary sex magazines as this is not the aim of this publication."

If that was not the aim, then the publication was clearly aimless. The stories are all science fiction; all are set in the future and deal with oppressive societies and, occasionally, other dimensions; but the SF element is merely an excuse for a new angle on sexploitation. The stories do not match the bona fide erotic SF stories of Philip José Farmer, Charles Platt or Hank Stine for either eroticism or originality of treatment.

Note

The author wishes to thank Norman Lazenby and Terry Hill for their help in the research for this essay.

Information Sources

BIBLIOGRAPHY:
Lester, Colin. *The International Science Fiction Yearbook*. London: Pierrot, 1978.
    P. 87.
INDEX SOURCES: None.
REPRINT SOURCES: None known.
LOCATION SOURCES: None known.

Publication History

TITLE: *Erotic Science Fiction Stories* on cover, but in editorial and subscription form it
    is referred to as *Science Fiction Stories* only.
VOLUME DATA: Number 1, undated (mid-1977).
PUBLISHER: Figcrest, Ltd., London.
EDITOR: David Sullivan (not identified in issue).
FORMAT: Slick, 68 pp.
PRICE: 80p.

Mike Ashley

ETCHINGS & ODYSSEYS

Etchings & Odysseys is a small-press magazine that has seen two existences. It was originally launched as the official publication of the ''MinnCon''—the name given to a small convention of fans of the works of H. P. Lovecraft held in Minneapolis in August 1971. Assembled by Eric A. Carlson and John J. Koblas it was duplicated in a small print run of 250 copies in an attractively spiral-bound quarto edition. Originally concentrating on the work of local writer Carl Jacobi, who is interviewed in the first issue, the magazine attracted so many contributions that in the end it ran the whole gamut of weird fiction, although H. P. Lovecraft and Robert E. Howard remained the main influences. There were contributions by Joseph Payne Brennan, Richard L. Tierney, Eddy C. Bertin, Darrell Schweitzer and many more, and the issue was sold out in advance orders before its Spring 1973 publication. Despite its success and the amount of material submitted for future issues, finances precluded continued publication and to all intents and purposes *E&O* folded.

Ten years later, however, R. Alain Everts, a much respected researcher and small-press publisher, helped Koblas and Carlson re-launch *E&O* in a highly professional format. The idea was to maintain a quarterly schedule, although other commitments have precluded this at present. Four issues have been published since the revival, undated, but appearing in May and October 1983 and May and December 1984. All have maintained a Lovecraftian flavor, especially issue 5 which was a special ''Cthulhu Mythos'' volume. Issue 4 was devoted to the memory of Henry Kuttner while issues 2 and 3 focused on memories of *Weird Tales** magazine. All issues contain a blend of fiction, articles, poetry, and interviews and are liberally illustrated. Of special interest in issue 2 is an interview with the leading *Weird Tales* cover artist of the thirties, Margaret Brundage, plus a previously unpublished short story by William Hope Hodgson, "The Room of Fear."

Everts also publishes a supplement to *E&O* in the form of a small chapbook, *The Arkham Sampler.**

Information Sources

BIBLIOGRAPHY:
Everts, R. Alain. "Introduction to The Arkham Sampler." *The Arkham Sampler*, Volume 1, Number 2, pp. 2–4.
INDEX SOURCES: ISPF-2.
REPRINT SOURCES: None known.
LOCATION SOURCES: M.I.T. Science Fiction Library.

Publication History

TITLE: *Etchings & Odysseys.*
VOLUME DATA: Number 1, Spring 1973; Number 2, May 1983; Number 3, October 1983; Number 4, May 1984; Number 5, December 1984. Current.
PUBLISHER: Number 1, MinnCon Publications, Duluth, Minnesota. Number 2–, The Strange Company, Madison, Wisconsin.
EDITORS: Eric Carlson and John J. Koblas, with R. Alain Everts from Number 2.
FORMAT: Large Quarto. First issue, spiral bound, thereafter perfect bound, page count varies.
PRICE: Number 1, $2.50; Numbers 2 and 3, $6.00; Number 4, $5.00; Number 5, $7.50.

Mike Ashley

ETERNITY SCIENCE FICTION

Eternity Science Fiction was one of the few science fiction fanzines of the 1970s to strive for semi-professionaldom. It was becoming increasingly common in the fantasy field, where the lack of any regular professional market caused the fans to create their own semi-professional magazines, but in the SF field, which had comparatively more regular professional SF magazines, there was little need for semi-prozines. *Space and Time** and *Eternity* were the two notable exceptions.

With the first issue of *Eternity*, dated July 1972 but published a little later, editor/publisher Stephen Gregg managed to obtain a limited newsstand distribution. However, the magazine was fanzine in format and design, prepared on a standard manual typewriter with fannish artwork scattered throughout. Gregg stated that two of his main aims were to exploit areas that the professional SF magazines avoided—SF poetry and graphic art. Poetry he certainly promoted. The first issue contained a short piece, "Morning with Music," by Roger Zelazny, and there were others by Susan Jane Clark, Bill Gard and assistant editor

Scott Edelstein. Later issues continued this emphasis with further poems by Zelazny, Edelstein, Peter Dillingham, David R. Bunch and others.

The graphics proved less successful. The first three issues contained some scattered comic strips, few of which were of any consequence, and some joke items that were immediately forgettable, including Jack Gaughan's supposedly humorous "Genii."

In its standard artwork, *Eternity* had much greater success. Stephen Fabian provided the covers to the first and third issues and some interior work, and Vincent DiFate, Tim Kirk, Ed Romero and Darrel Anderson all put in appearances.

The articles and features, as with many fanzines, were often the most interesting aspect of the magazine. The first issue contained a telling "Notes Made Late at Night by a Weary SF Writer" by Philip K. Dick, the third issue an article on "Science Fiction Poetry" by Peter Dillingham, and there were interviews with Thomas M. Disch, Kate Wilhelm and Damon Knight.

But the main purpose of any SF magazine is the science fiction, which was present in abundance. The first issue was able to boast such names as Andrew J. Offutt, Barry Malzberg, Edward Bryant, Robert E. Margroff and Joseph Green, whose "The Seventh Floor" was the most powerful and perhaps best item in the issue, and a vindication for the semi-professional market, because this was the sort of story that would not have appeared in most of the professional magazines of the time.

Arthur Byron Cover, David R. Bunch, Glen Cook, Kris Neville and Barry Malzberg, and Grant Carrington were among the contributors to the second issue. Glen Cook's story in particular, "Sunrise," gave evidence of the great promise he showed as a writer at this stage.

One of the highlights of the third issue was Roger Zelazny's Dilvish story, "A Knight for Merytha," beautifully illustrated by Steven Fabian. Although not credited, the story had originally appeared in the September 1967 issue of the fanzine *Kallikanzaros*, which had had very limited circulation and was thus almost unknown. Malzberg, Bunch, Offutt, Margroff and Cover again appeared, along with Janet Fox, Pg Wyal and Robert Wissner.

The fourth issue was the most professional in appearance, although the quality of fiction dropped slightly. Nevertheless, *Eternity* was gradually becoming accepted, and one might have expected issues to continue to appear. More were certainly planned, as Gregg announced in his editorial, but the months turned into years and nothing happened.

In his second issue, Gregg had stated that in order to help finance his magazine, which at that stage cost $700 per issue, he needed a regular schedule which would attract subscribers. In the event, *Eternity* was about the most irregularly published magazine around, and Gregg probably lost a lot of money on those four issues.

But in 1979 he came back with a vengeance. This time he converted the magazine into a more professional format, which must have cost far in excess of what all four of his earlier issues did, and he strove for a regular schedule.

The new issue reverted to Number 1, indicating that the original *Eternity* was now regarded as a forerunner to the new magazine and that there was no continuity. Gregg selected some of the better stories from the earlier issues for reprinting along with some new items, and he extensively advertised the renewed presence.

Unfortunately, despite this drive for attention, *Eternity* did not succeed the second time around. It showed tremendous promise, with the same emphasis on poetry and graphics, but failed to attract a sufficient readership.

Information Sources

BIBLIOGRAPHY:
Nicholls. *Encyclopedia*.
INDEX SOURCES: NESFA-IV, SFM.
REPRINT SOURCES: None known.
LOCATION SOURCES: M.I.T. Science Fiction Library.

Publication History

TITLE: *Eternity Science Fiction*.
VOLUME DATA: First series: Number 1, July 1972–Number 4, February 1975. Initial schedule quarterly, but issue 2, undated [1973], and issue 3, May 1974. Second series: Number 1, November 1979–Number 2, Spring 1980. Quarterly. Total run: 4 + 2, 6 issues.
PUBLISHER: First series, Stephen Gregg, Sandy Springs, South Carolina. Second series from Gregg at Clemson, South Carolina.
EDITOR: Stephen Gregg.
FORMAT: A4 Printed. Pages as follows: issue 1, 36 pp.; issues 2–4, 48 pp.
PRICE: First series, issues 1–3, $1.00; issue 4, $1.25; second series, $1.75.

Mike Ashley

EXTRO SCIENCE FICTION

Extro was the first and, to date, only science fiction magazine to emanate from Northern Ireland. This despite the fact that there has been a thriving SF community there for many years, most notably in the 1950s when Walt Willis, Bob Shaw, John Berry, and James White were a fan group unique unto themselves and where *Slant* (and later *Hyphen*) was required reading for all fannish fans.

Even before its first issue in early 1982, *Extro* had had a chequered career. It had originated as a fanzine under the name *Popular Music and Science Fiction Journal*, issued from Manchester by Irish fan Robert Allen. By profession a journalist, Allen had the drive and direction to convert the magazine from a fanzine to a professional magazine but lacked the finances. After three issues of *Popular Music* (dated April, July, and September 1979), which were an odd and rather unsatisfactory mixture of rock music news and SF bibliography plus an immature SF serial, Allen retitled the magazine *Extro* but kept the original numbering sequence. By now Allen had returned to Northern Ireland where he hoped to raise the capital to turn *Extro* professional. At the same time he planned a news magazine which eventually saw two broadsheet issues as *SF News*. During 1980 and 1981 issues of *Extro* were few and far between. At length a Northern Irish colleague, Paul Campbell, took matters into his own hands and succeeded in launching *Extro* on a professional basis. This led to some acrimony between Allen and Campbell, though Campbell was undeterred.

The first issue, dated February/March 1982, was printed large size on glossy stock paper but was cramped with four columns of print per page, small type face and little by way of artwork to alleviate the eye strain. It was a clear transition from fanzine to prozine. The issue was, however, able to boast an interview with Stephen Donaldson and fiction from Christopher Priest, Garry Kilworth and Ian Watson representing much that was typical of the new generation of British writers. For a first issue it sold moderately well.

The second and third issues showed more promise. A new cover logo and striking artwork by Gerard Quinn made the magazine instantly recognizable, and fiction by Bob Shaw, James White, Richard Cowper, Brian W. Aldiss and Steve Rasnic Tem made the magazine an interesting and worthwhile investment. A new type size and internal layout also made it more readable.

All this time, however, Campbell was struggling to achieve adequate distribution. Through his own efforts he was able to secure adequate circulation in Ireland but the English distributor failed to breach the walls of Britain's major bookseller W. H. Smith. Subscriptions were promising but insufficient to keep the magazine afloat and despite his determination and perseverance Campbell at last admitted defeat.

The loss of *Extro* was perhaps predictable but was no less sorry for that. It is interesting to compare the approach and fate of *Extro* with its contemporary *Interzone** which has managed to survive by not overreaching itself. In the final analysis although the failure to secure distribution was the major cause of *Extro*'s death it was Campbell's own exuberance that sealed its fate.

Information Sources

INDEX SOURCES: SFM.
REPRINT SOURCES: None known.
LOCATION SOURCES: M.I.T. Science Fiction Library.

Publication History

TITLE: *Extro Science Fiction.*
VOLUME DATA: Volume 1, Number 1, February/March 1982; Number 2, April/May 1982; Number 3, July/August 1982. Bi-monthly.
PUBLISHER: Specifi Publications, Belfast, Northern Ireland.
EDITOR: Paul Campbell.
FORMAT: Slick. Number 1, 38 pp., thereafter 46 pp.
PRICE: 75p.

Mike Ashley

___ F ___

FAMOUS FANTASTIC MYSTERIES

Although fantasy and science fiction had never been completely absent from the American magazines, before the appearance of *Weird Tales** and the magazines specializing in science fiction, such titles as *Cavalier*, *All-Story*, and *Argosy*,* published by the Frank A. Munsey Company, had provided the chief source of fantasy and SF for the twentieth-century popular audience. In his fine anthology, *Under the Moons of Mars* (1970), Sam Moskowitz has outlined the history of those mass-circulation periodicals, emphasizing that the high point of their influence in shaping American tastes in the field came between 1912 and 1920.[1] One might argue that the later specialist magazines could not have succeeded had not the Munsey chain created a receptive audience. Nor should one forget that *Argosy* continued to include such titles as Ralph Milne Farley's "The Golden City," Murray Leinster's "The War of the Purple Gas," and Arthur Leo Zagat's "Tomorrow" throughout the 1930s.

In the autumn of 1939, beginning with a combined September/October issue, Munsey began publication of *Famous Fantastic Mysteries*. The tables of contents of the first four numbers announced the editorial policy: "This magazine is the answer to thousands of requests we have received over a period of years, demanding a second look at famous fantasies which, since their original publication, have become accepted classics. Our choice has been dictated by *your* requests and our firm belief that these are the aces of imaginative fiction." Those first title pages also indicated that *FFM* was being handled by The Continental Publishers and Distributors, Ltd. in Great Britain and by Hachette & Cie in France.

A second number followed immediately in November "as a result of the spontaneous response and acceptance of the first issue." For six months *FFM* remained a monthly magazine before going bi-monthly after the creation in July 1940 of a companion title, *Fantastic Novels*.* Its success can perhaps be best measured by another factor. It survived the war, although from 1943 through 1945 it appeared on a quarterly basis; thereafter it maintained a bi-monthly schedule (the significance of this may be fully realized only when one recalls that John Campbell sacrificed the highly successful *Unknown** in order to assure having sufficient paper for *Astounding* (*Analog Science Fiction**) during the wartime shortages). From the outset Mary Gnaedinger edited *FFM*.

Initially, *FFM* reprinted only works which had been published in the Munsey magazines. The lead story of the first issue was A. Merritt's "The Moon Pool" (1918). Others included Todd Robbins' "The Whimpus" (1919), Ray Cummings' "The Girl in the Golden Atom" (1919)—the text that makes up the first eight chapters of the expanded novel—Donald Wandrei's "The Witch-Makers" (1936) and J. U. Giesy's "Blind Man's Buff" (1920). The November issue introduced early short stories by two authors who were to be among the most frequently reprinted authors in *FFM*: "The Man with the Glass Heart" (1911) by George Allan England and "Almost Immortal" (1916) by Austin Hall, as well as a short form of Garrett P. Serviss' "The Moon Metal," which had appeared in *All-Story* in 1905 (the full-length novel had been published by Harper in 1900).

The chief innovation of that issue resulted from what the "editors" called the readers' demand for "the long classics of science fiction in serial form." The first installment of A. Merritt's "The Conquest of the Moon Pool" (1919) led off seven selections. In December began the serialization, intentionally in three parts, of Ralph Milne Farley's "The Radio Man" (1924), which was rushed to completion in the February 1940 number by combining Parts 3 and 4. Apparently Gnaedinger misread the desire for serials. In the May/June 1940 issue, after only three of six promised episodes, Austin Hall and Homer Eon Flint's "The Blind Spot" (1921) was abruptly cut short; "The Editors' Page" explained that beginning in July the "complete long stories for which many readers have been asking" would be featured in the "brand new, 144 page" *Fantastic Novels*. The initial selection would be "The Blind Spot," which would be "discontinued as a serial" in *FFM*. "Everyone seems to have realized," the editorial statement continued, "that although [the] set-up of five to seven stories with two serials running, was highly satisfactory, that the long list of novels would have to be speeded up somehow."

The policy decreed that the companion magazines be offered in alternate months; moreover, both would offer a complete novel in each issue "because there is no doubt that the book-length classics are the best."

After its fifth issue in April 1941 *Fantastic Novels* ceased publication until 1948. It was combined with *FFM*, which again briefly resumed a monthly schedule in June 1942. Besides suggesting that Gnaedinger and Munsey were juggling titles to gain the widest reader appeal, *Fantastic Novels* influenced *FFM* in two lasting ways. First, instead of five to seven stories, the standard offering became the full-length novel augmented by a novelette or possibly by one or two short stories. On occasion, as in the instance of Francis Stevens' "The

Citadel of Fear'' (February 1942), the novel was so long that no other fiction was included. Second, with the exception of Austin Hall's ''Into the Infinite'' (October 1942–March 1943), *FFM* never again serialized a novel.

One other innovation came during this early period. The first five covers of *FFM* had merely listed the stories in the current issue. Beginning in March 1940, however, cover illustrations either by Virgil Finlay or (less often) by Paul became a trademark of the magazine. These two artists—Finlay especially—also did the interior art during these early years. Indeed, one may argue that Virgil Finlay attained his hold upon the devotees of fantasy primarily through his work with *FFM* and *Fantastic Novels*.[2]

Munsey retained control of *FFM* through the end of 1942. Throughout the period 1939–1942 it remained essentially a reprint magazine, drawing almost exclusively upon works originally published in the Munsey chain. So far as reprints from other sources were concerned, through twenty-six issues only three exceptions occurred: H. P. Lovecraft's ''The Colour out of Space'' (October 1941), Guy de Maupassant's ''The Horla,'' translated by George Allan England (September 1942), and Robert W. Chambers' ''The Demoiselle D'Ys'' (November 1942). The only original work to appear was a series of four short stories ''written especially for'' *FFM* during the brief period when *Fantastic Novels* was published. Those stories included Eando Binder's ''Son of the Stars'' (February 1940); Harry Walton's ''Bomb from Beranga'' (March 1940); Stanton A. Coblentz's ''Fire Gas'' (April 1940); and Henry Kuttner's ''Pegasus'' (May/June 1940). Finlay's artwork was original, of course, as was ''The Reader's Viewpoint,'' the letters to the editor department.

Gnaedinger featured a relatively small number of writers repeatedly. She turned to A. Merritt most frequently. His fiction appeared in the first eight issues of *FFM*: ''The Moon Pool'' (September/October 1939), ''The Conquest of the Moon Pool'' (November 1939–April 1940) and ''Three Lines of Old French'' (May/June 1940). Four other novels by him also appeared: ''The Face in the Abyss'' (October 1940), ''The Metal Monster'' (August 1941), ''Burn, Witch, Burn!'' (June 1942) and ''Creep Shadow!'' (August 1942). This tabulation ignores his titles in *Fantastic Novels*, and one should note that most of his works were reprinted in the late 1940s and early 1950s. As in the case of Virgil Finlay, one may make the case that A. Merritt's reputation owes a great deal to Mary Gnaedinger.[3]

Other favorite contributors included Austin Hall, George Allan England and Ralph Milne Farley. Hall was second only to Merritt: ''Almost Immortal'' (November 1939), ''The Man Who Saved the Earth'' (February 1940), ''The Rebel Soul'' (August 1940) and ''Into the Infinite'' (October 1942–March 1943), as well as the previously mentioned ''The Blind Spot'' appeared. After several of England's short stories, *FFM* issued the three parts of his ''Darkness and Dawn'' trilogy and followed that with ''The Elixir of Hate'' (October 1942). Ralph Milne Farley had three novels included—''The Radio Man'' (December 1939–February 1940), ''Radio Planet and the Ant Men'' (April 1942) and ''The Golden

City'' (December 1942). Francis Stevens was the only other author to have three major titles: "Claimed" (April 1941), "The Citadel of Fear" (February 1942) and "Serapion" (July 1942). Other high points during the Munsey period included Charles B. Stilson's "Polaris of the Snows" (July 1942) and J. U. Giesy's "Palos of the Dog Star Pack" (October 1941) and "The Mouthpiece of Zitu" (November 1942).

No cursory analysis of this body of fiction could be adequate. Yet several observations do seem valid. For the most part, the featured stories look backward to the themes—like the catastrophe motif and the lost city/civilization—that had developed before World War I. One notices, too, how many of the longer works center on a love story which surely owes something of its tone to Rider Haggard (a sharp contrast to the new magazines specializing in science fiction, where during this early period few writers other than Stanley G. Weinbaum dared write a love story, as in *The Black Flame*). Finally, perhaps one should call this body of fiction science fantasy, for, as in A. Merritt's works, one finds that the occult and the scientific are thoroughly intermixed. These characteristics gave *FFM* a special historical significance because it preserved (and introduced a new generation to) the older traditions from which modern science fiction emerged.

At the end of 1942 Munsey sold *Famous Fantastic Mysteries* to Popular Publications. One cannot be certain how suddenly this decision was made. "The Editors' Page" for December 1942, signed by Mary Gnaedinger, scheduled forthcoming Munsey stories and spoke of a February issue. Although she remained editor (and Finlay remained artist), when the next issue did appear in March 1943, the editorial policy had changed radically. The new publishers explained that out of "deference" to the many readers following Hall's "Into the Infinite" they were publishing the concluding (fourth) installment of that serial. "In the future FAMOUS FANTASTIC MYSTERIES will feature either new stories or stories which have appeared only in book form." For that March number Popular Publications had purchased the "first magazine rights" to John Hawkins' *Ark of Fire*. *FFM* appeared only twice more during 1943. In September John Taine's "The Iron Star" was augmented by Robert W. Chambers' "The Yellow Sign" and C. L. Moore's new story, "Doorway into Time." The December issue featured J. Leslie Mitchell's 1932 novel, "Three Go Back"; introduced William Hope Hodgson through his short story, "The Derelict"; included Robert W. Chambers' "The Mask"; and published another original story, Ray Bradbury's "King of the Gray Spaces."[4] The covers of the last two issues for 1943 informed the potential reader that all of the stories were either new or had never appeared in any magazine. As though to emphasize the new look, the December cover was by Lawrence.[5]

During 1944 and 1945 *FFM* remained a quarterly, but in 1946 it resumed a bi-monthly schedule, failing to meet it only in 1950, when no December number was issued. (Sax Rohmer's "Brood of the Witch-Queen" had been announced; it appeared in the January 1951 issue, the delay caused perhaps by a brief three-issue change of format.) Although the source of its fiction had changed, *FFM* remained essentially a reprint magazine. In March 1944 G. K. Chesterton's "The Man Who Was Thursday" was the featured novel; successive issues introduced Algernon Blackwood, Lord Dunsany and Arthur Machen. In December 1945 it published an H. Rider Haggard novel for the first time: "The Ancient Allan"; in October 1946, H. G. Wells' "The Island of Dr. Moreau" appeared.

Again, little can be gained from cataloguing authors and titles. Until it abruptly ceased publication in June 1953 *Famous Fantastic Mysteries* retained a historical importance because of its wide selections, both American and British, some by well-known writers and some by obscure writers. Its choice ranged from frequent reprintings of the novels of John Taine, William Hope Hodgson, E. Charles Vivian, Murray Leinster and Jack London, for example, to largely unavailable titles which had had a single edition and were out of print, thereby being known only to those who had been able to afford the books. A few examples may suffice: Edward Shanks' "The People of the Ruins" (June 1947); C. T. Stoneham's "The Lion's Way" (October 1948); Edison Marshall's "Ogden's Strange Story" (December 1949); Arthur Stringer's "The Woman Who Couldn't Die" (October 1950); Arthur J. Rees's "The Threshhold of Fear" (March 1951); and Gilbert Collins' "The Valley of Eyes Unseen" (February 1952). Particularly valuable, of course, were those British titles which had had no American edition.

One may argue that these last years of *Famous Fantastic Mysteries* have an even greater historical importance than the early period, when it served as an outlet for Munsey reprints. By selecting works by authors from Jack London to Edison Marshall, *FFM* emphasized the fact that science fiction and fantasy had remained a viable form of modern literature not confined to the specialist magazines. In short, more than almost any of its contemporaries, *FFM* illustrated the ties between modern science fiction and the traditional body of American and British fantasy. It kept in print many works that might otherwise have been lost. Paradoxically, its importance may have caused its demise in that by reprinting older works, it gave its attention to themes and narrative techniques that had become dated and thus made the magazine less desirable to those readers who had been raised on the new, specialist periodicals.

Notes

1. Sam Moskowitz, "A History of the 'Scientific Romance' in the Munsey Magazines, 1912–1920," in *Under the Moons of Mars* (New York: Holt, Rinehart and Winston, 1970), pp. 291–433.

2. Virgil Finlay sold his first illustration to *Weird Tales* in 1935. He came to the attention of A. Merritt and worked on his staff at *American Weekly* for three years. He did twenty covers for *Weird Tales*, eight of them in 1939. Yet *FFM* probably gave him his widest audience, especially since it sponsored three folios by him during the 1940s— in 1941, 1943 and 1949. See Donald A. Tuck, comp., *The Encyclopedia of Science Fiction and Fantasy* (Chicago: Advent, 1974), "Volume 1: Who's Who A–L," p. 169.

3. During the 1940s Avon Publications issued at least three of Merritt's titles in digest-sized paperbacks in the Murder Mystery Monthly series. From 1928 to 1953 the New York firm of Liveright published a number of his novels in hardback. Mary Gnaedinger's

influence may be seen in that not only did *FFM* and *Fantastic Novels* feature his works, but for a short time in 1949 and 1950 Popular Publications issued *A. Merritt's Fantasy Magazine.**

4. William F. Nolan, *The Ray Bradbury Companion* (Detroit: Gale Research, 1975), p. 187. Originally published in *FFM*, this story was retitled ''R is for Rocket'' and was collected in the volume of that name (1962).

5. This was one result of Finlay's going into the army. He did the December 1946 cover, but thereafter, although he did a number of interior illustrations, Lawrence did most of the covers. Both artists had their army of fans in later years and had portfolios of their work issued by Popular.

Information Sources

BIBLIOGRAPHY:
Nicholls. *Encyclopedia.*
Tuck.
INDEX SOURCES: ISFM; MIT; SFM; Tuck.
REPRINT SOURCES:
  Reprint Editions: From August 1944 the Canadian *Super Science Stories** (subsequently retitled *Super Science and Fantastic Stories*) reprinted totally from *FFM*—see separate entry. An identical Canadian reprint of *FFM* with only back cover variations ran concurrently with the issues February 1948–August 1952 published by All-Fiction Field/Popular Publications, Toronto.
LOCATION SOURCES: Brigham Young University Library; M.I.T. Science Fiction Library; Northern Illinois University Library; Pennsylvania State University Library; Texas A&M University Library; University of Arizona Library; University of British Columbia Library; University of New Brunswick Library.

Publication History

TITLE: *Famous Fantastic Mysteries.*
VOLUME DATA: Volume 1, Number 1, September/October 1939–Volume 14, Number 4, June 1953. Six issues per volume, except Volume 5, which had five issues. After the first bi-monthly issue *FFM* was monthly from November 1939 to May/June 1940; bi-monthly to June 1942; monthly to December 1942; quarterly to December 1945 (no June 1943 issue); thereafter bi-monthly, but December 1950 issue slipped to January 1951 and September 1951 issue slipped to October. Total run: 81 issues.
PUBLISHER: The Frank A. Munsey Company, New York; September/October 1939–December 1942; All Fiction Field, Inc., a subsidiary of Popular Publications, New York, March 1943–June 1953.
EDITOR: Mary Gnaedinger.
FORMAT: Pulp; 128 pp., September/October 1939–August 1940; 112 pp., October 1940–April 1941; 128 pp., June 1941–April 1942; 144 pp., June 1942–March 1944; 132 pp., June 1944–October 1950; 112 pp., January 1951–June 1953.
PRICE: 15¢, September/October 1939–August 1940; 10¢, October 1940–April 1941; thereafter 15¢.

Thomas D. Clareson

FAMOUS SCIENCE FICTION

Famous Science Fiction, one of the Health Knowledge magazines, was a companion to *Magazine of Horror** and *Startling Mystery Stories.** It was conceived at a time when the publisher was having distribution problems and decided to diversify. The editor, Robert A. W. Lowndes, had had much experience with SF magazines (including *Science Fiction,** *Future Fiction,** *Science Fiction Quarterly** and *Dynamic Science Fiction**); when given the opportunity to start a new magazine, it was a natural choice to return to science fiction. The new magazine also helped ameliorate one of the problems with *Magazine of Horror*, where the readership was divided over whether SF should or should not be included. At least for a while Lowndes had a separate repository for these tales.

Lowndes had a limited budget for the magazine, and its contents were predominantly reprints. Fifteen of the forty-five stories presented during *FSF*'s short run were being published for the first time, though all were very short tales as compared to the much longer reprints. *Famous*'s policy was to reprint stories from before the Golden Age, or, more precisely, any that were published prior to 1938. In his opening editorial, in the Winter 1966/1967 issue, Lowndes claimed that this was to show that there were many still readable, if not necessarily respectable, stories from those days that had been overlooked by anthologists. He also intended the magazine to act as a bridging publication for young readers emerging from the comics who might find magazines like *Analog Science Fiction** and *Galaxy Science Fiction** too deep. In this way *Famous* was attempting to serve as a latter-day *Planet Stories.**

Because of Lowndes' restrictive budget he selected only those stories that he could obtain relatively cheaply and that did not involve too much trouble over copyright clearance. Thus he avoided, for the most part, the early *Amazing Stories** because these issues were still controlled by Sol Cohen, who was plundering the archives himself in his reprint magazines. But Lowndes also avoided stories from the Tremaine *Astounding Stories* (1933–1937), where the best of the pre-Golden Age stories appeared. While one can understand Lowndes' financial restrictions in selecting stories, that he did not reprint any of the classic stories of the 1930s was almost certainly the major mistake he made with *Famous*.

In effect, therefore, Lowndes limited himself to fiction from the Clayton *Astounding* (1930–1933) and Gernsback's *Wonder Stories,** plus pre-Gernsback publications. Within these limitations Lowndes selected wisely and certainly resurrected some readable stories generally unavailable to most readers during the 1960s. Examples are Clark Ashton Smith's "The City of Singing Flame" and its sequel, "Beyond the Singing Flame," in the first and third issues; "The Moon Menace" by Edmond Hamilton from *Weird Tales** in the second issue; "The City of Spiders" by H. Warner Munn in the fourth; "Plane People" by Wallace West in the fifth; "The Hell Planet" by Leslie F. Stone in the sixth; "Men of the Dark Comet" by Festus Pragnell in the seventh; "Dark Moon" by Charles Willard Diffin in the eighth; and "The Forgotten Planet" by Sewell Peaslee Wright in the ninth and last issue.

Significantly, through *FSF* Lowndes gave some latter-day recognition to the work of Laurence Manning, one of the better writers of the 1930s but one who since then had been largely forgotten. Lowndes had started to run some of Manning's "Stranger Club" stories in *Magazine of Horror* where he felt there was sufficient shiver among the science to warrant inclusion. *Famous* was the more obvious home for them, however, and Lowndes concluded the series in the first two issues with "Voice of Atlantis" and "Seeds from Space"—the story that may have been a subconscious inspiration for John Wyndham's *The Day of the Triffids*. Lowndes then ran complete Manning's Wellsian sequence, "The Man Who Awoke," in five consecutive issues (Numbers 3–7). This episodic novel of a man's series of progressions into the future had originally appeared in *Wonder Stories* during 1933, and only saw book publication in 1975. Though considerably dated, it is a perfect example as a source of the "sense of wonder" as well as being a typical example of Gernsback's ideal SF.

Generally Lowndes bypassed the opportunity to select examples of early SF. "The Last American" by J. A. Mitchell, recommended by Wallace West, dated from 1889 and is an amusing novelty piece about a Persian exploration of a derelict United States in the year 2951; it was the oldest story included. Sam Moskowitz selected and introduced Edward Olin Weeks' "Master of the Octopus," reprinted from the October 1899 *Pearson's Magazine*, and although Moskowitz and Robert A. Madle were subsequently listed as editorial consultants no other such items were forthcoming. In the last issue, however, Richard A. Lupoff introduced a turn-of-the-century story by John Kendrick Bangs with a brief essay about this "Forgotten Master of Fantasy."

The fifteen new stories published in *FSF* were mostly nonfamous and unmemorable, although the authors represented may raise an eyebrow or two. A. Bertram Chandler, for instance, was present with one of his Rim stories, "Rimghost" (Spring 1967), while Philip K. Dick had a slight story, "Not by Its Cover," in the Summer 1968 issue. That same issue included Robert Silverberg's mood story "The Fires Die Down," which was seeing its first U.S. publication, although strictly speaking it was a reprint, having first appeared in the Scottish magazine *Nebula Science Fiction** in 1958. Miriam Allen deFord, Burt K. Filer, Greg D. Bear, Edward D. Hoch and William F. Temple also appeared with new stories.

Perhaps one of the strongest features of *Famous* was its nonfiction. Starting in the second issue Lowndes presented a series of editorials on "Standards in Science Fiction," discussing, in turn, SF as instruction, as propaganda, and as delight. Although the series was intended simply to share with his readers some of the findings of Lowndes' many years as a devotee of SF, it showed considerable perception on his part and afforded a welcome insight into an editor's views of science fiction. The series was popular and was subsequently reprinted by the New England SF Association as *Three Faces of Science Fiction* in 1973. Lowndes wrote several other thoughtful editorials and gave space to articles by Robert A. Madle and Lester del Rey (a reprint of his Guest of Honor speech at the 1967 World SF Convention on the subject of "Art or Artiness?").

Distribution problems continued to plague, *FSF*, however; because of its perilously low circulation, it was finally withdrawn by the publisher, who decided instead to experiment with further horror titles (see *Weird Terror Tales**).

Information Sources

BIBLIOGRAPHY:
Lowndes, Robert A. W. "The Health Knowledge Years." *Outworlds* 28/29 (combined issue, October 1976): 1125–32.
Nicholls. *Encyclopedia*.
Tuck.
INDEX SOURCES: Marshall, Gene, and Carl F. Waedt, "An Index to the Health Knowledge Magazines," *Science-Fiction Collector*, No. 3 (1977): 3–42; ISFM-II; SFM; Tuck.
REPRINT SOURCES: None known.
LOCATION SOURCES: M.I.T. Science Fiction Library.

Publication History

TITLE: *Famous Science Fiction*.
VOLUME DATA: Volume 1, Number 1, Winter 1966/67–Volume 2, Number 3, Spring 1969. Six issues per volume. Quarterly. No issue for Winter 1969. Total run: 9 issues.
PUBLISHER: Health Knowledge Inc., Fifth Avenue, New York.
EDITOR: Robert A. W. Lowndes.
FORMAT: Digest (saddle-stapled), 128 pp.
PRICE: 50¢.

Mike Ashley

FANCIFUL TALES OF TIME AND SPACE

In 1936 Donald A. Wollheim and Wilson Shepard decided to produce a semi-professional magazine that they hoped would support itself by subscription-only sales. Both well-known fans of the period, Wollheim, from New York City, and Shepard, from Oakman, Alabama, were already involved in publishing *The Phantagraph*, the organ of a science fiction fan club. Shepard had some experience as a printer, and the two acquired a letterpress with high hopes. Significantly, they decided to issue the magazine, to be called *Fanciful Tales of Time and Space*, in a digest format, along the lines of the recently deceased *Marvel Times*.*

As editor, Wollheim secured the stories and artwork. The story headings were hand-carved on lino-block by Duane W. Rimel, while Wollheim paid Clay Ferguson, Jr., a small sum for the cover art. All the fiction was donated by the authors, despite the stature of the names. Wollheim was corresponding with H. P. Lovecraft, Robert E. Howard, August Derleth and David H. Keller, and there was no thought of payment. In the thirties writers customarily gave away material to fans upon request, receiving no payment other than a copy of the magazine in which it appeared.

In his editorial Wollheim proclaimed that it was his "intention to publish short stories of phantasy, weird fiction, science fiction, and that most elusive of all flights of fancy, Pure Phantasy." It is interesting to note that the spelling "phantasy" was used throughout the magazine.

With the calibre of the contributors, Wollheim had a reasonable likelihood of obtaining material of good quality, and some of the items make this small 200-copy magazine eminently collectable today. The lead story, taking up a third of the magazine, was "The Nameless City" by H. P. Lovecraft. Written in 1921, this had been the first of Lovecraft's tales to introduce the name of the mad Arab Abdul Alhazred. Dreadfully overwritten, it describes in typical Lovecraft fashion an eons-old city in the Arabian desert and the fate of a lone explorer.

One of the best stories in the issue was "The Typewriter" by David H. Keller, which is typical of his psychological stories. A bond salesman buys a typewriter, writes a best-seller, and finds that the soul of his heroine now inhabits the typewriter and controls him.

"The Man from Dark Valley" by August Derleth involves murder and vengeance by astral projection. A brief story, it may have been a plot outline never developed by Derleth or a reject from *Weird Tales*.*

The centerpiece of the magazine featured the first publication of Robert E. Howard's poem "Solomon Kane's Homecoming." A simple editorial comment inserted between the title and body of the poem read: "It is our sad duty to report the tragic death of Robert E. Howard." While it is virtually certain that the editors knew that Howard had killed himself, they clearly wished to avoid the sensational, and let the poem serve as a memorial.

The remaining contributions are minor, and little more than fanzine-fillers. They are Wollheim's own "Umbriel," a poorly developed story about alien worms; "The Forbidden Room" by Duane Rimel, a weak ghost story; "The Globe" by William S. Sykora, a single-page story that does no justice to its intriguing idea of a globe that sucks the life-essence from people, leaving them as withered husks; and "The Electric World" by Kenneth Pritchard, an unsuccessful attempt at humor.

Wollheim had clearly anticipated regular publication at the outset. The contents page boasts further material on hand by Robert Bloch, J. Harvey Haggard and Ralph Milne Farley. Under the alias "Braxton Wells," Wollheim used the forum of the "Discussions" column in *Amazing Stories*,* but by the time that letter appeared in the February 1937 issue, *FT* was already a thing of the past. Even before the magazine had been printed Shepard's interest had flagged, and he had paid a local linotype operator to finish the typesetting. He then decided to begin printing on a local basis and dropped out of SF fandom. Wollheim and Shepard dropped plans for future issues, cut their losses and parted company.

FT may well have developed into a historically significant magazine, but it was important in other respects. It gave Wollheim his first experience as a fiction editor and was a string to his bow when he went after an editorial job in 1940 (see *Stirring Science Stories**) that set him on the road to becoming one of the most important editors in the SF world.

Information Sources

BIBLIOGRAPHY:
Moskowitz, Sam. *The Immortal Storm*. Atlanta, GA: ASFO Press, 1954; Rpt. Westport, Conn.: Hyperion Press, 1974. P. 31.
Nicholls. *Encyclopedia.*
Tuck.
INDEX SOURCES: MT; SFM; Tuck.
REPRINT SOURCES: None known.
LOCATION SOURCES: M.I.T. Science Fiction Library.

Publication History

TITLE: *Fanciful Tales of Time and Space.*
VOLUME DATA: Volume 1, Number 1, Fall 1936. Only issue.
PUBLISHER: Wollheim/Shepard, Oakman, Alabama.
EDITOR: Donald A. Wollheim.
FORMAT: Digest, 48 pp.
PRICE: 20¢.

Howard DeVore

FANTASTIC

In 1950, when Howard Browne took over the editorship of *Amazing Stories** and *Fantastic Adventures,** he interested the publisher, Ziff-Davis, in converting *Amazing* to a slick magazine. The intervention of the Korean War caused the plans to be aborted, but a year later Ziff-Davis gave Browne the green light to prepare a sample issue of a new magazine.

Howard Browne did not like science fiction. It "bored the beJesus out of me," he later said.[1] But he did enjoy fantasy and so, naturally, the new magazine became *Fantastic*. "Now it can be told!" Browne declared in the editorial to the April 1952 *Amazing*. "Next month (on March 21st to be exact) a new and exciting kind of science-fiction and fantasy magazine will appear on the newsstands.... We've spared no expense, we've burned the midnight oil, we've read literally millions of words, we've talked ourselves hoarse with authors and artists."[2]

Browne was justifiably proud of his achievements with *Fantastic*—it was one of the more attractive magazines to appear during the SF boom years. Dated Summer 1952, the first issue was a 162-page digest magazine, not a pulp, selling for thirty-five cents, ten cents more than the companion pulps. The cover, printed in six colors, was by the popular new artist Barye Phillips; it portrayed a captivating witch and boasted a bevy of talented names. Browne provided no editorial, letting the contents speak for themselves. The issue led with "Six and Ten Are Johnny" by Walter M. Miller, Jr., magnificently illustrated by Virgil Finlay and one of Miller's most entertaining stories. Others included "What If" by Isaac Asimov, "The Smile" by Ray Bradbury, "The Opal Necklace" by Kris Neville and "And Three to Get Ready" by H. L. Gold, all sophisticated, modern stories, more in the tradition of *The New Yorker* than the pulps. But the item likely to attract the most attention and capture readers not normally drawn to a fantasy magazine was "Professor Bingo's Snuff" by Raymond Chandler. Browne, himself a writer of mystery fiction, had previously edited Ziff-Davis' *Mammoth Detective*, so it was not surprising that his own new dream magazine would contain work by writers in the thriller field. In turn, Chandler liked fantastic stories and actually worked out sketches for nearly a dozen, but only two were completed.[3] "Professor Bingo's Snuff" was also the only locked room story Chandler wrote, and its theme revolved around a unique snuff that turned people invisible. The story had first appeared in *Park East Magazine* the previous year and, though not one of Chandler's best, was an entertaining novelty.

To add to the "class" quality of the magazine, the back cover was a full-cover reproduction of Pierre Roy's "Danger on the Stairs," which was then on exhibition at the Museum of Modern Art. Hailed by Browne as "an acknowledged masterpiece of fantasy," the painting in fact simply portrayed a snake on a staircase, scarcely fantastic! It was intended as the first of a series of such paintings, and though it clearly added to the respectability of the magazine, its presence implied an air of misguided snobbery.

The response to the first issue was highly favorable: "so tremendous, in fact," Browne asserted, "that the magazine was changed from a quarterly to a bimonthly ten days after it hit the stands."[4] The next step was to add color interior artwork—only a two-tone variation and not especially attractive, but a further step away from the pulp image.

Browne kept the big names coming. The second issue included Truman Capote side by side with the field's own giants, Fritz Leiber ("I'm Looking for Jeff"), Eric Frank Russell ("The Sin of Hyacinth Peuch"), Anthony Boucher ("The Star Dummy") and Theodore Sturgeon ("The Sex Opposite"). The third issue, dated November/December 1952, led with a Mickey Spillane story, "The Veiled Woman"; it aroused certain hostility among the fantasy fans, and rumors began that the story had been ghost-written by Browne himself. That issue also contained stories by Cornell Woolrich, Richard Matheson and John Jakes, plus reprints of "The Cask of Amontillado" by Edgar Allan Poe and "The Celestial Omnibus" by E. M. Forster.

Impressive though the magazine was, there was a reaction from within the field against the use of reprints and the overt and nonsympathetic use of major names. Such arrows, however, echoed hollowly against Browne's defenses. He and his publisher were, after all, out to make *Fantastic* commercially viable, and the objections of a few hard-core fans were negligible. What's more, there was much to commend in the magazine. The January/February 1953 issue, for instance, led with "The Lighthouse," a hitherto unpublished and unfinished story by Poe which had been completed by Robert Bloch. That issue and later ones, carried "Mad House" by Richard Matheson, "The Sword of Yung Lo" by Maurice Walsh, "Root of Evil" by Shirley Jackson, "The Dark Room" by Theodore Sturgeon, plus stories by John Collier, John Wyndham, B. Traven, Jack Williamson and Alfred Bester.

The *Fantastic* experiment had clearly proved successful, highlighting what an editor can achieve when the publisher gives him a free hand and a reasonable budget. The publisher also had an eye to the future. All around, pulp magazines were folding. The future lay in the fields of television, the pocketbook and slick magazines. With the April/May 1953 issue *Amazing* was converted to a digest-size format. March 1953 saw the last issue of *Fantastic Adventures*. It was ostensibly combined with *Fantastic* with the May/June issue, but in truth the old pulp was dead.

But the changes also signaled that the experiment was over, and Ziff-Davis cut back its budget on both magazines. With the July/August 1953 issue the back cover art reproduction was discontinued; the next issue saw the last of the color interiors and the quality stock paper; the number of pages was reduced to 144 and again to 128 with the next issue. Browne's stock of quality stories was rapidly consumed, and as 1954 passed *Fantastic* regressed from one of the field's most impressive magazines to one of the most depressing. Moreover, the cover banner changed from declaring "The Finest in New Fantasy Fiction" to "Best New Fantasy and Science-Fiction," and though the letter column objected to SF being interspersed among the fantasy, by 1955 *Fantastic* had become predominantly a science fiction magazine with a dash of fantasy.

It is convenient to consider *Fantastic* during the years 1952–1954 as a separate entity, because, behind the pretentiousness, it was a good-quality magazine, on a par with *Beyond Fantasy Fiction*,* and carried some of the best fantasy stories available—be they humorous or chilling. An anthology of its best stories during these three years would be singularly impressive, but it is easy to overlook many of these issues by casting them in the same shadow that darkened the next three years.

Fantastic had been Browne's child at the outset. He selected all the stories and assembled the issues, leaving Lila Shaffer to handle *Amazing* and *Fantastic Adventures*. When the editorial budget was cut back, however, Browne grew disillusioned and turned his attention more to mystery fiction, eventually accepting an offer to write screenplays for Hollywood. In the meantime, however, he increasingly left the work of editing *Fantastic* to his new managing editor, Paul Fairman. By 1955 Fairman was more or less in full control and was putting into operation the new Ziff-Davis policy of salaried writers, whereby a number of "hack" writers were paid a regular stipend for a set wordage each month, often to agreed story titles, or around set cover paintings—mostly the work of art editor Ed Valigursky. This procedure is described in more detail in the entry for *Amazing Stories*, and it was the same team of writers who filled the pages of *Fantastic*—Robert Silverberg, Harlan Ellison, Randall Garrett, Henry Slesar, Milton Lesser and, for that matter, Fairman himself. Most of the stories, though, appeared under a variety of pseudonyms.

It was fortunate that the writers selected were all good ones. Most of them were still young and inexperienced, but they had vivid and versatile imaginations and a willingness to progress. The results, therefore, were not as bad as one might have expected, though they were far from good, as any of the writers would themselves readily attest. Nevertheless, while there was a certain predictability and even monotony about *Fantastic* during this period, some of the stories were surprisingly readable, due partly to the less restrictive policy of *Fantastic*, which gave the writers free rein on their ideas (limited only by common decency!), and due almost certainly to the numbing effect of so many similar stories prevalent in most of the magazines outside *Astounding* (*Analog Science Fiction**), *Galaxy Science Fiction** and *The Magazine of Fantasy and Science Fiction** during the 1950s where, in comparison, even average stories took on a semblance of grandeur. What is remarkable is that in 1957, at a time when *Fantastic* was at its lowest ebb, the publishers increased its schedule to monthly, which shows that somebody out there was buying it in sufficient quantities.

The depths to which *Fantastic* had sunk, however, became apparent in 1958 when Fairman, like Browne, abandoned Ziff-Davis to become a full-time writer and left the magazine in the hands of his assistant, the young Cele Goldsmith. Goldsmith had already been making her influence known on the magazine during 1957. Eric Frank Russell, for instance, who had always been fascinated by Fortean phenomena, began a series of articles on great world mysteries. The July 1958 issue marked, perhaps, the nadir of *Fantastic*'s quality, being devoted to a rediscovery of the Shaver Mystery, but thereafter everything started to improve, and from December 1958 Cele Goldsmith was in complete control.

The change was immediate. The house names vanished, and in their place came Robert F. Young, Arthur Porges, Gordon R. Dickson, Ron Goulart and Cordwainer Smith, most of whom would become mainstays. Hacksters Robert Silverberg and Randall Garrett remained, but under their own names and with nonformula stories. With the September 1959 issue *Fantastic* gained the subtitle "Science Fiction Stories," but the transition was never fully made and the qualification was dropped after thirteen issues.

With the November 1959 issue *Fantastic* did something no other American magazine had ever done. The issue was devoted to stories by one author—Fritz Leiber. Few today would deny that Leiber is one of the best fantasy writers of all time. In 1959 Leiber was making a comeback in the field after an absence of four years and had recently won the Hugo Award for his novel *The Big Time*. The five stories in the issue showed the five different facets of Leiber's writing talent and his mastery of them all. Most welcome was "Lean Times in Lankhmar," the first new Gray Mouser adventure in eight years. The Gray Mouser and Fafhrd thereafter became regulars in *Fantastic* and were just one of the many features that made the period between 1960 and 1965 a golden age for followers of fantasy fiction in the magazines.

Of major significance was the amount of new talent that *Fantastic* attracted. Cele Goldsmith acquired an enviable record for discovering new writers. The first wave, which followed immediately upon her accession to the editorial chair, included Jack Sharkey (with two stories in the March 1959 issue in two differing veins, with an editorial request for readers to select their preference), Phyllis Gotlieb ("A Grain of Manhood," September 1959) and Keith Laumer. Laumer had debuted in the sister magazine, *Amazing*, with "Greylorn" (April 1959), but in the January 1960 *Fantastic* "Diplomat-at-Arms" introduced the character of Jame Retief, one that Laumer went on to develop from this serious story to a series of humorous adventures in *If.**

Serials had hitherto been taboo in *Fantastic*, only one having appeared during the eight years of its existence. From the July 1960 issue, however, serials became a regular feature, starting with "The Crispin Affair" by Jack Sharkey and followed by "A Plague of Masters" by Poul Anderson, "Worlds of the Imperium" by Keith Laumer and "Second Ending" by James White.

Sam Moskowitz became a regular contributor from the May 1960 issue, initially with a series of articles on fantasy writers. The series was a continuation of those started in *Satellite Science Fiction,** which had folded a year earlier, and these essays were later collected into Moskowitz's volume *Explorers of the Infinite* (Cleveland: World, 1963). From the May 1961 issue Moskowitz began a regular selection of "Fantasy Classics," reprinting many lesser-known stories from rare or nongenre publications. The series began with "The Garden of Fear" by Robert E. Howard and continued for the next three years, resurrecting such tales as "Relic" by Eric Frank Russell, "The Creator" by Clifford D. Simak, "The Root of Ampoi" by Clark Ashton Smith, "The Mother" by David H. Keller, "The Human Zero" by Erle Stanley Gardner, "The Dragon of Iskander" by Nat Schachner, "The Titan" by P. Schuyler Miller, "The Singing Sands of Prester John" by H. Bedford-Jones, and Fritz Leiber's early Gray Mouser tale, "Adept's Gambit."

Other writers who had started their careers elsewhere now became regular contributors. David R. Bunch was perhaps the most controversial, with his lyrical fantasies that preempted the "new wave" explosion. Others included Daniel F. Galouye, Rosel George Brown and J. G. Ballard. A second and more powerful wave of new writers also began to appear: Roger Zelazny ("Horseman!," August 1962), Thomas M. Disch ("The Double-Timer," October 1962), Ursula K. LeGuin ("April in Paris," September 1962) and Piers Anthony ("Possible to Rue," April 1963), and there was redoubtable support from aspiring writers like Robert Rohrer, Albert Teichner and Neal Barrett, Jr.

The reason for this concentration of talent and entertainment was a simple one. Cele Goldsmith was receptive to good writing. Not having been an SF or fantasy fan before she became editor, she had no preconceived ideas but knew what she liked and assumed others would too. Her prompt and kindly responses to all contributors, big fish or little, did much to create an editor-writer rapport that is very valuable in a small magazine. Prompt payment plus constructive feedback is a powerful formula for success, yet so simple that many editors and publishers overlook it.

It was not only new writers that *Fantastic* attracted, but artists as well, both fresh and seasoned. By the early 1960s *Fantastic* was by far the most attractive magazine on the stands. A back cover illustration detailing another of the contents had been inaugurated with the May 1961 issue, and this frequently included the work of old *Weird Tales** favorites Virgil Finlay and Lee Brown Coye, both of whom also supplied many excellent interior illustrations. A variety of artists provided the eye-catching front covers, including Ed Emshwiller, Lloyd Birmingham, Vernon Kramer, Robert Adragna and Gray Morrow.

For the sword and sorcery buff, *Fantastic* was a haven. In addition to Leiber's Gray Mouser adventures, John Jakes had started his tales of Brak the Barbarian with "Devils in the Walls" (May 1963) and Roger Zelazny the chronicle of Dilvish the Damned with "Passage to Dilfar" (February 1965). The supernatural horror fan also had several treats. Fritz Leiber's classic "A Bit of the Dark World" appeared in the February 1962 issue and his equally chilling "Midnight in the Mirror World" in October 1964. The June 1963 issue featured Robert Arthur's "The Mirror of Cagliostro," while April 1964 saw "The Dunstable Horror," in fine Lovecraftian tradition, by the pseudonymous Arthur Pendragon.

Meanwhile, lovers of pure fantastic adventures could content themselves with "The Demon of the North" by C. C. MacApp, the new adventures of Lemuel Gulliver as chronicled by "Adam Bradford, M.D.," or the reprints of H. Bedford-Jones. Those whose special delight was for humorous fantasies would find plenty in the tales of Jack Sharkey and Ron Goulart, or in the reprints of Martin Armstrong or Robert Spencer Carr. Nor was there any shortage of straightforward science fiction, as evidenced by "The Kragen" by Jack Vance (July 1964), "Planet of Change" by J. T. McIntosh (September 1964), "Beyond the Ebon Wall" by C. C. MacApp (October 1964) and "The Unteleported Man" by Philip K. Dick (December 1964). And there was the just plain unclassifiable, as in "Paingod" by Harlan Ellison (June 1964), the stories by David R. Bunch and many of the vignettes by writers both unknown and/or pseudonymous, such as "I Am Bonaro" by John Starr Niendorff (December 1964).

For the period there was nothing else like it in the States. *Science Fantasy** in Britain came close, while by the late 1960s *The Magazine of Fantasy and Science Fiction* was of a similar vein, but both these publications lacked the artwork that helped make *Fantastic* under Cele Goldsmith the single greatest fantasy magazine since *Weird Tales* under Farnsworth Wright and *Unknown** under John Campbell.

And yet, despite its greatness, *Fantastic*'s circulation continued to dwindle. It is so often true that a public does not realize what it has until it has lost it, and that was the case with *Fantastic*. Ziff-Davis changed its publishing policy to exclude fiction magazines, and *Fantastic* and *Amazing* were sold to Sol Cohen's newly established Ultimate Publishing Company. With the titles, Cohen acquired the second serial rights to the stories that Ziff-Davis had acquired. Cohen now exercised this option by converting *Fantastic* into a nearly all-reprint magazine without further payment for the stories. An occasional new story appeared that had been in Goldsmith's inventory at the time of the sale, of which the most outstanding was Fritz Leiber's "Stardock," used in the first Ultimate issue, dated September 1965. Cohen hired Joseph Wrzos on a part-time basis as editor, and Wrzos reached an agreement that at least a few new stories could still be acquired.

Under Wrzos *Fantastic* remained readable, though it lacked the excitement of the earlier issues. He selected good-quality reprints not just from the early Browne issues, but also from *Fantastic Adventures* and even *Amazing*; but of more importance was the new fiction he acquired. This included a three-part serialization of the first of Keith Laumer's highly enjoyable novels of the adventures of Lafayette O'Leary in a parallel fantasy world, "Axe and Dragon"; a new Roger Zelazny Dilvish story, "The Bells of Shoredan"; and Avram Davidson's impressive "The Phoenix and the Mirror." Of special importance was a rare new story from Chad Oliver, "Just Like a Man."

Nevertheless, the budget was not adequate to acquire much new fiction, and Wrzos is to be congratulated for what he achieved under such circumstances. Furthermore, there was a limit to the quality reprints available, especially as the same vein was also being mined for several new reprint magazines that Cohen had launched (especially *Thrilling Science Fiction**). On one occasion Cohen used a reprint from a totally different source—*Weird Tales*. At the suggestion of Gerald Page, and at the start of the Conan boom, Cohen reprinted "The People of the Black Circle," by Robert E. Howard, in the January 1967 issue. Had more such experiments been attempted *Fantastic* might have remained a better magazine. For a period its circulation rose, but after 1968 it again fell. *Fantastic* became a shadow of its former self and a sad sight for fantasy fans.

The editorial problems encountered with the departure of Joseph Wrzos are fully recounted in the entry for *Amazing Stories* and require no further discussion here. Wrzos was succeeded by Harry Harrison, who had hopes of returning *Fantastic* to an all-new publication. This was not to be, but during his short tenure Harrison introduced a new book review column, "Fantasy Books," conducted by Fritz Leiber, and published the first story sale of James Tiptree, Jr., "Fault" (August 1968).

Harrison was followed by Barry Malzberg, who also had high hopes for the magazine, only to have them dashed. During his brief tenure Malzberg concentrated on acquiring a number of new but very short stories with an emphasis on the "new wave" experimentalism with writers like Thomas M. Disch, John Sladek and his own alter ego, K. M. O'Donnell.

Malzberg was followed in turn by Ted White. White had his roots firmly planted in fandom, and he approached the task with an enthusiasm not seen since Cele Goldsmith's day. It impressed Cohen enough to allow White a relatively free hand in the transformation of the two magazines, and an arrangement arose whereby the reprints would be phased out. Cohen now launched an armada of all-reprint magazines that flooded the market, the price that SF had to pay for an all-new *Amazing* and *Fantastic*.

Ted White was a firm believer in a magazine having a strong "family" feel with an identifiable editorial persona, a policy previously followed by Raymond Palmer and Robert A. W. Lowndes. White brought in long, chatty editorials—something not seen in *Fantastic* before—plus a lively letter column and extensive reviews. New fiction and new artwork suddenly transformed *Fantastic*, and there was a feeling that the golden days were about to return. If White never quite reached the level of Cele Goldsmith's golden issues, it was not through want of trying, and this period can be regarded as *Fantastic*'s silver age.

One of White's first achievements was the salvaging of Piers Anthony's unsold Arabian Nights adventure novel, *Hasan*, which was serialized to much acclaim from the December 1969 issue. With the April 1970 issue White was able to boast an original cover by Jeff Jones illustrating a new Fritz Leiber Fafhrd adventure, "The Snow Women." The same issue published "Dear Aunt Annie," the first story by Gordon Eklund, who became one of the exciting new talents of the 1970s.

Of major value over the next few years were *Fantastic*'s serials. These included "Always the Black Knight" by Lee Hoffman (June–August 1970), "The Shape Changer" by Keith Laumer (December 1970–February 1971), "Beyond the Resurrection" by Gordon Eklund (April–June 1972), "The Forges of Nainland Are Cold" by Avram Davidson (August–October 1972), "The Fallible Fiend" by L. Sprague de Camp (December 1972–February 1973) and "The Son of Black Morca" by Alexei and Cory Panshin (April–September 1973).

The last reprint appeared in the December 1971 issue, and thereafter Ted White had a totally free hand. He acquired a vast array of new stories covering the whole spectrum of SF and fantasy, illustrated by an equal variety of artists, many already established in the comic-book field. Mike Kaluta, Gray Morrow, Dan Adkins, Doug Chaffee, Mike Hinge, Esteban Maroto and Harry Roland all added to the magazine's appearance. Every effort was made to encourage new writers, and those who made their first or early sales to Ted White include Robert E. Toomey, Jr., Gerard F. Conway, Dennis O'Neil, Jack C. Haldeman II, Geo. Alec Effinger.

Fantastic celebrated its twentieth anniversary in August 1972 with a cover boasting a new Conan adventure, "The Witch of the Mists" by L. Sprague de Camp and Lin Carter. The Conan phenomenon had exploded in the mid-sixties with the saga's first paperback appearance in a sequence assembled by de Camp and published by Lancer Books. However, Lancer's financial problems had delayed the publication of the final volume, *Conan of Aquilonia*, and the four novelettes that made up that book thus appeared first in *Fantastic*. The others were "Black Sphinx of Nebthu" (July 1973), "Red Moon of Zembabwei" (July 1974) and "Shadows in the Skull" (February 1975). It was soon apparent that the issues containing the Conan stories or those with a strong fantasy cover sold better in certain areas, and with the April 1975 issue *Fantastic* changed its subtitle to "Sword & Sorcery and Fantasy Stories." Cohen also issued a *Sword & Sorcery Annual*.*

Thus *Fantastic*'s emphasis was on pure fantasy, a trend most readily evident in the serials, which had recently included Thomas Burnett Swann's "Will-o-the-Wisp" (September–November 1974). Lin Carter presented two new Thongor adventures with "Black Hawk of Valkarth" (September 1974) and "The City in the Jewel" (December 1975). He also completed a Robert E. Howard fragment in "The Tower of Time" (June 1975) and a Clark Ashton Smith fragment in "The Scroll of Morloc" (October 1975) and began a new fantasy chronology in "People of the Dragon" (February 1976). Fritz Leiber presented a new Gray Mouser tale in "Under the Thumbs of the Gods," and Juanita Coulson created a new fantasy world in "Wizard of Death" (February 1973) and "The Dragon of Tor-Nali" (February 1975).

A strong selling point were the covers by Stephen Fabian, who started with those for February and April 1975 and continued through 1976 and 1977. Fabian's style superbly captured the wondrous atmosphere of fantasy, be it sword and sorcery, as on the April 1975 cover for "Under the Thumbs of the Gods"; supernatural horror, as on the August 1976 cover, which chillingly captures the intent of Avram Davidson's "Bloody Man"; or humorous fantasy as on the June 1977 cover, which illustrated "The Flight of the Umbrella," one of the amusing series by Marvin Kaye.

Fantastic had much in its favor at a time when fantasy fiction was selling in vast quantities. And yet its circulation continued to dwindle. One reason given was the increase in the cover price, which rose to $1.00 from 75 cents in 1975. But this could not be the sole answer. Sales dropped so drastically that *Fantastic* was placed on a quarterly schedule from February 1975. Circulation, which had been 31,200 when White became editor in June 1969, was down to 17,400 by 1978, and this during a period when the quality of *Fantastic*'s content and presentation had been increasing. The $1.00 price tag was reasonable, since most paperbacks were already in excess of that. Instead, the blame must be laid firmly at the door of the magazine's distributor, who made no attempt to reach the right markets. Wherever *Fantastic* was displayed on sale it sold well, but this was mostly in specialist shops.

Ted White can only be congratulated on producing such a quality magazine against such odds. On several occasions he threatened to leave the magazine, and finally, in November 1978, with the retirement of Sol Cohen, White and *Fantastic* parted company. White's last issue was dated January 1979. As stories were only paid for on publication, Ultimate had no rights to those in the inventory, and Ted White returned them all to their authors.

The new editor, Elinor Mavor (initially masquerading under the name Omar

Gohagen), had to start from square one. The first of her issues, dated April 1979, was mostly reprint and mostly SF. The presentation was poor, with some illustrations that would have been rejected by a fanzine. The next issue showed signs of improvement, however, with the start of a new illustrated feature, "Daemon" by Stephen Fabian.

It was not until the January 1980 issue that the publisher and editor seemed to coordinate their efforts in a presentable format. A preponderance of new stories and a variety of artwork enlivened a promising issue. A number of reader departments had been established, and once again *Fantastic* began to acquire an identity. The April 1980 issue began a new fantasy serial, "The White Isle" by Darrell Schweitzer, and artist Gary Freeman helped to make the issue more attractive.

By October 1980 *Fantastic* looked as if it was back on the road to recovery. Marvin Kaye was present with a new James Phillimore adventure, "The Amorous Umbrella," and there were new stories by Wayne Wightman, Darrell Schweitzer and others. Yet it was the last issue. The publisher decided to concentrate his resources on one magazine, and *Fantastic* was merged with *Amazing* from November 1980.

Although *Fantastic* had a checkered career it was, on at least two occasions, the very best market for fantasy fiction. During Cele Goldsmith's editorship it helped popularize the sword and sorcery stories of Fritz Leiber, John Jakes and others at a time when fantasy did not sell. It is ironic that the magazine went under when the genre it helped establish was at the height of its popularity.

Notes

1. Howard Browne, quoted by Ron Goulart in *An Informal History of the Pulp Magazine* (New York: Ace Books, 1973), p. 192.

2. Howard Browne, "Editorial," *Amazing Stories*, April 1952.

3. Raymond Chandler, in *R. C. Speaking*, ed. Dorothy Gardner and Katherine Sorley (New York: Walker, Houghton Mifflin, 1962), p. 238.

4. Howard Browne, *Amazing Stories*, August 1952.

Information Sources

BIBLIOGRAPHY:

Nicholls. *Encyclopedia*.

Tuck.

INDEX SOURCES: IBSF; ISFM-II; MID; MT; NESFA; NESFA-II; NESFA-III; NESFA-IV; NESFA-V; NESFA-VI; NESFA-VII; SFM; Tuck.

REPRINT SOURCES:

British Edition: Eight issues released by Strato Publications through Thorpe & Porter, Leicester. Undated (December 1953–February 1955), bi-monthly; correspond to U.S. issues September/October 1953–December 1954.

Derivative Anthologies: Ted White, ed., *The Best from Fantastic* (New York, Manor Books, 1973), Introduction plus 10 stories from 1952–1964. Note also *Time*

Untamed (New York: Belmont, 1967), ed. Ivan Howard, which drew on stories reprinted in the Ultimate *Fantastic* regardless of origin, 8 stories.

LOCATION SOURCES: Eastern New Mexico University Library; MIT Science Fiction Society Library; Michigan State University Library; M.I.T. Science Fiction Library; Northern Illinois University Library; Pennsylvania State University Library; Red Wing, Minnesota, Public Library; San Francisco Public Library; Sarah Lawrence College Library; Temple University Library; Texas A&M University Library; Tulane University Library; University of Arizona Library; University of Colorado Library; University of Georgia Library; University of Texas-Austin Library; Western New Mexico Library.

Publication History

TITLE: *Fantastic*, Summer 1952–February 1955 and March 1958–August 1959; *Fantastic Science Fiction*, April 1955–February 1958; *Fantastic Science Fiction Stories*, September 1959–September 1960; *Fantastic Stories of Imagination*, October 1960–June 1965; *Fantastic* (on cover; spine read *Fantastic Stories*), September 1965–April 1971 (cover also read *Fantastic Stories* from February 1970 but masthead and indicia still read *Fantastic*); *Fantastic Science Fiction & Fantasy Stories* (on cover, but spine still *Fantastic Stories* and indicia still *Fantastic*), June 1971–February 1975; *Fantastic Sword & Sorcery and Fantasy Stories* (on cover and masthead only), April 1975–June 1977; *Fantastic Stories* (previous title still on masthead), September 1977–January 1979; *Fantastic Science Fiction* (on cover and masthead only), April 1979–October 1980.

VOLUME DATA: Volume 1, Number 1, Summer 1952–Volume 27, Number 11, October 1980. Volume 1, 3 issues, quarterly, Summer–Fall 1952; bi-monthly from November/December 1952. Volume 2, Number 1, January/February 1953–Volume 5, Number 6, December 1956, 6 issues per volume, bi-monthly (cover dates abbreviated to latter month from April 1954). Volume 6, Number 1, February 1957–Volume 13, Number 12, December 1964, 12 issues per volume (Vol. 6, 11 issues), monthly. Volume 14, 6 issues, monthly, January–June 1965. Volume 15, Number 1, September 1965–Volume 24, Number 6, October 1975, 6 issues per volume, bi-monthly (issues slipped a month for July to August 1968, June to July 1973, January to February 1975). Volume 25, 5 issues, bi-monthly, December 1975–February 1976; quarterly May–November 1976; Volume 26, 4 issues, quarterly, February, then June–December 1977. Volume 27, 11 issues, quarterly, April 1978–October 1980. Total run: 208 issues.

PUBLISHER: Ziff-Davis, New York, Summer 1952–June 1965; Ultimate Publishing, Flushing, New York, September 1965–January 1979; Ultimate Publishing, Purchase, New York, April 1979–October 1980.

EDITORS: Howard Browne, Summer 1952–August 1956; Paul W. Fairman, October 1956–November 1958; Cele Goldsmith, December 1958–June 1965 (Cele G. Lalli from July 1964); Joseph Ross, September 1965–November 1967; Harry Harrison, January–October 1968; Barry N. Malzberg, December 1968–April 1969; Ted White, June 1969–January 1979; Elinor Mavor, April 1979–October 1980.

FORMAT: Digest, 160 pp., Summer 1952–July/August 1953; 144 pp., September/October 1953; 128 pp., November/December 1953–June 1965 (except July 1960, 144 pp.); 160 pp., September 1965–November 1967; 144 pp., January 1968–December 1970; 128 pp., February 1971–October 1980.

PRICE: 35¢, Summer 1952–April 1963; 50¢, May 1963–October 1969; 60¢, December 1969–May 1974; 75¢, July 1974–August 1975; $1.00, October 1975–December 1977; $1.25, April 1978–January 1979; $1.50, April 1979–October 1980.

Mike Ashley

FANTASTIC ADVENTURES

Fantastic Adventures was a companion SF and fantasy magazine to *Amazing Stories.** The success of *Amazing* since its acquisition by the Chicago firm of Ziff-Davis in 1938 under the editorship of Raymond A. Palmer, coupled with the growing number of SF magazines on the bookstalls, was sufficient encouragement for the publisher to test the SF waters again.

Whereas with *Amazing* Palmer seemed to have done everything right, with *FA* he did just about everything wrong. As something of an experiment, and almost certainly at Palmer's suggestion, the new magazine was issued in the old large pulp size. Palmer had hoped this would appeal to the nostalgia of the fans who had first discovered SF in that format in *Amazing* in 1926. By 1939, however, few such magazines existed in the large pulp format (although, surprisingly, *Astounding* [*Analog Science Fiction**] would make just the same mistake in 1942). Perhaps Ziff-Davis also anticipated that the new size would give the magazine a better display on the bookstall. But it was soon discovered that tastes had changed. The appeal of the large-size magazine, which had been strong even as recently as 1933, had now waned.

More to the point, however, the contents of the first issue were poor. A strange mixture of lost-race adventures and juvenile SF by *Amazing* regulars like Arthur R. Tofte, Eando Binder, A. Hyatt Verrill, Harl Vincent and Ross Rocklynne did little to enamor the majority of SF devotees to the new infant. Palmer also instituted a number of departments, including a quiz page and a meet-the-author slot, and several illustrative features. These were possibly the best aspect of the new magazine, including "Fantastic Inventions" and "Fantastic Hoaxes," most written by Julius Schwartz and Willy Ley. The best innovation was a back cover illustration by Frank R. Paul. The first depicted "The Man from Mars" in all Paul's inimitable graphic detail, and was supported within the magazine by a description and analysis.[1] Paul's back cover feature became a popular part of the magazine and probably contributed to the sales, even though, of course, any potential purchaser had first to find the magazine and pick it up before the sight of the back cover had any sales advantage.

One feature in the first issue was an absolute disaster: a comic strip, "Ray Holmes, Scientific Detective," where, in twelve pictures, a crime was committed and the clues given, and the reader was given the chance of solving it. The feature lasted only the one issue and was dropped.

Palmer was not too sure whether *FA* was a science fiction or a fantasy magazine, although his editorial boasted that the magazine covered "every phase of science and fantasy, of mystery and unusual adventure, of strong action and plot, of good characterization and significance: we have given you all these."[2] Actually, it was debatable whether the issue contained any of these items, except "unusual adventure," but the rebellious robot portrayed on the cover and the blurb—"The Best in Science Fiction"—clearly indicated that the magazine was trying to appeal to the SF reading public rather than the *Weird Tales** or *Unknown** market, and in 1939 SF fans were very puritanical when it came to any SF/fantasy cross-breeding. And yet, promoting *FA* in the pages of *Amazing*, Palmer made it clear that *Amazing* would publish SF, and *FA* fantasy. "How any science fiction fan can keep from making his science fiction menu complete by reading this absolute coverage of the field will be hard to imagine," Palmer exclaimed.[3]

All this added to the general state of confusion in which *FA* was launched. Only by some good fortune, with the boom in SF starting to swell and fans naturally being curious to see the magazine, did the first issue sell well. Fortunately, the second issue marked an improvement. It also appeared to contain something of a scoop. The cover boasted "The Scientists' Revolt" by none other than Edgar Rice Burroughs. Almost certainly this must have attracted many of Burroughs' legion of fans, but they were to find the story disappointing. Burroughs' biographer Irwin Porges revealed that the story had started out in 1922 under the title "Beware."[4] It was then a routine story of intrigue centered upon an apparent crown prince of a mid-European country and was an attempt by Burroughs to get away from fantastic fiction. Rejection slips piled up, and although Farnsworth Wright did offer to buy it for *Weird Tales* in 1929, Burroughs rejected that offer. When the story came to Palmer in 1938 it was obviously unsuitable as SF, and so Palmer rewrote it, changing some of the characters and the time from the present day to the future. But the result did not fool SF devotees. Veteran fan Robert A. Madle wrote, "I was rather disappointed by Burroughs' 'The Scientists' Revolt.' It is not up to his usual standard." Nevertheless, Madle echoed the views of many when he went on to say:

I did not send my congratulations when the first issue of *FA* appeared because I was rather confused. I realized that you had every desire to please the average science fiction fan due to the fact that you had published a large-size magazine and featured Paul on the back cover. However, the stories, to be perfectly frank, were pretty lousy!

Then came the surprising second issue. It actually seems like a different magazine. First of all, the cover illustration, although sloppily drawn, is an improvement over that of the initial issue, if only because it covers the entire cover. Paul's back cover is just a wee bit better than his first one, which makes it very excellent.[5]

Apart from the Burroughs story, the issue featured "The Monster from Nowhere," a popular tale of other dimensions by Nelson S. Bond, and two stories by John Russell Fearn, "She Walked Alone" under his real name, and "The

Golden Amazon'' as "Thornton Ayre.'' Fearn wrote three other stories about superwoman Violet Ray before converting the series into a novel format for the Canadian paper *Star Weekly*, which he continued to write until his death in 1960. The original four novelettes were among the most popular stories published in the early issues of *FA*.[6]

The contents continued to improve with the third issue, which contained such solid, if derivative, adventure stories as "Horror out of Carthage" by Edmond Hamilton, "Golden Girl of Kalendar" by F. Orlin Tremaine and "City under the Sea" by Nathan Schachner. Eando Binder contributed one of his most interesting stories in "The Man Who Saw Too Late,'' about the victim of a scientific accident who has delayed vision—he sees events three minutes late. It could be said that this story presaged Bob Shaw's later "slow glass'' stories, but Binder failed to make much use of the idea beyond a routine adventure.

Of special interest, however, was Nelson S. Bond's whimsical story, "The Amazing Invention of Wilberforce Weems,'' about an elixir of genius. The title was probably foisted on Bond by Palmer, although Bond's obvious delight in humorous fantasies with daft titles had been evident since the prestigious *Scribner's* magazine had carried "Mr. Mergenthwirker's Lobblies'' in its November 1937 issue. Bond was an above-average pulp writer whose work has been sadly neglected in the field, probably because he seemed content to write less than his best. When given the challenge, as in *Unknown*, Bond could show his true abilities, and this professionalism was evident even in the humorous teasers he hurried out for Palmer. His true ability showed itself in the April 1940 issue of *FA*, which carried "The Judging of the Priestess,'' the second in his series of stories about Meg the Priestess, which had started in *Amazing* with "The Priestess Who Rebelled'' (October 1939) and which concluded in *Astounding* with "Magic City'' (February 1941). Bond was present in nine of the first eleven issues of *FA* with such zany stories as "The Fertility of Dalrymple Todd'' and his blundering space hero Lancelot Biggs, whose adventures began with "F.O.B. Venus'' (November 1939).

Bond, doubtless encouraged by Palmer, gave some personality to the otherwise shallow magazine by providing harmless, humorous entertainment. Here lay a possible route to success, and Palmer later played on it to excess. "Everyone likes to think and ponder and wonder at times,'' he later wrote, "but these stories must necessarily be in the minority, because it is the basic requirement that we entertain you.''[7] With Europe in the thick of World War II, and the future looking increasingly bleak, such tales came as welcome diversions. When Bond departed his place was taken to some extent by David Wright O'Brien and his friend William P. McGivern. Such titles as "The Strange Adventure of Hector Squinch'' (August 1940, by O'Brien) and "The Masterful Mind of Mortimer Meek'' (May 1941, by McGivern) are indicative of the trend. Although others would also take a turn at these fun-fantasies, the writer who capitalized on them was Robert Bloch, for whom *FA* was as ideal a market for his humorous writings as *Weird Tales* was for his macabre pieces. For *FA* Bloch created his memorable layabout Lefty Feep, who staggered through twenty-two adventures with such pun-ish titles as "Time Wounds All Heels" (April 1942), "The Little Man Who Wasn't All There" (August 1942), "The Chance of a Ghost" (March 1943) and "Tree's a Crowd" (July 1946).

Although these stories provided light-hearted diversion in *FA*, the magazine needed more substance if it was going to survive. An attempt at a scientific detective series was made by James Norman with "Oscar, Detective of Mars" (October 1940), about a Martian with a heightened sense of smell who becomes entangled in a plot to take over the United States through the use of a fear serum. Norman wrote four other Oscar stories, all rather shallow. Of greater potential was "The Prince of Mars Returns" (February–March 1940), a two-part serial marking the return to the SF magazines of Philip Francis Nowlan, the creator of Buck Rogers. Unfortunately, Nowlan died while the serial was running, on February 1, 1940, at age fifty-one. Whether he would have become another Palmer hack writer or whether he would have developed under Campbell's wing is a question which must remain unanswered.[8]

Perhaps the most memorable story from *FA*'s early days was "Jongor of Lost Land," a complete novel in the October 1940 issue. A solid adventure in the Edgar Rice Burroughs tradition, it met with considerable reader approval. Jongor was a Tarzan equivalent in a lost land in central Australia. The author, Robert Moore Williams, may have found his more immediate inspiration in the magazine *Jungle Stories*,* which featured another Tarzan-like hero, Ki-Gor. The similarities in name and plot bear consideration. Williams later produced two sequels, "The Return of Jongor" (April 1944) and "Jongor Fights Back" (December 1951); the three stories were sufficiently spaced out to avoid monotony of theme and to allow Williams a chance to create some freshness of plot. The three novels were reprinted by Paperback Library in 1970.

"Jongor of Lost Land" was indirectly responsible for saving *FA*. Although it had followed the successful *Amazing* into a monthly schedule with the January 1940 issue, it still lagged behind in sales. With the June 1940 issue it reverted to bi-monthly and was converted to the standard pulp format. Still circulation did not improve, and Ziff-Davis planned to fold the magazine after the October 1940 issue—the one featuring the first Jongor novel. Because of its obvious Burroughs connection, Ray Palmer had commissioned the foremost adventure pulp artist, J. Allen St. John, to paint the cover illustrating Jongor. Circulation doubled and *FA* lived to fight another day.

Publication was resumed with the January 1941 issue, and Palmer was quick to capitalize on the St. John success. He would later write, "It has been our experience that covers sell magazines—simply because they attract attention. The stories are what *keeps* those the covers attract."[9] During 1940 Palmer had clinched a deal with Edgar Rice Burroughs for a triple series of novelettes and, starting in the March 1941 *FA*, again heralded by a St. John cover, was "Slaves of the Fish Men," a new Carson of Venus adventure. Three more followed: "Goddess of Fire" (July 1941), "The Living Dead" (November 1941) and

"War on Venus" (March 1942), all with St. John covers, a combination that catapulted *FA*'s circulation. The four stories were subsequently published in book form as *Escape on Venus* (Tarzana: Burroughs, 1946).

FA now seemed to go from strength to strength. Monthly publication was resumed in May 1941, and in April 1942 the first of the bumper 240-page issues appeared. Despite the wartime paper shortages, these inch-thick issues continued to the end, and monthly publication was sustained until August 1943, when a bi-monthly and then quarterly schedule was forced on the magazine. Monthly publication did not resume until September 1947, by which time the page count had decreased significantly.

During this period *FA* was perhaps the most visually attractive magazine on the stalls, with arresting covers by St. John, Harold McCauley and Robert Gibson Jones, plus colorful back covers by Frank R. Paul and Malcolm Smith. The front covers are vividly characterized by danger, death and a healthy dash of sex, and it is the sex, particularly as embodied in McCauley's "Mac Girl," that one tends to remember. Palmer called McCauley "the Petty of the Pulps" and said that his "Mac Girl" was rivaling the Varga girl for public attention. Sheathed, bikini'd, and brass-bra'd girls—menaced by anything from robots to gorillas, but often with horses, snakes, tigers and polar bears as signs of their power—dominate the front covers. There was always some adverse criticism in the readers' letters about this display of sex, but the stories inside were quite innocuous.

In some ways this was indicative of *FA*, which promised much and delivered little. It concentrated more on quantity than quality, on brash sensationalism than subtlety. For although there was much light entertainment within its pages suitable for the period, there was little of enduring merit. William P. McGivern's stories are worthy of further consideration, however, especially the series that grew out of "The Enchanted Bookshelf" (March 1943), where the Three Musketeers come to life. Carlos McCune responded with a challenge to McGivern's story premise in "Caverns of Time" (July 1943), which caused McGivern to reply with "The Musketeers in Paris" (February 1944). He later wrote a further adventure, "The Wandering Swordsman" (April 1948). Another McGivern series featured Tink, a good-natured leprechaun, starting with "Tink Takes a Hand" (October 1941) and followed by three sequels.

Palmer's coterie of Chicago writers produced most of the stories under their own names or pseudonyms. In addition to McGivern, David Wright O'Brien, Don Wilcox, Chester S. Geier, Rog Phillips, Leroy Yerxa, Robert Moore Williams and Berkeley Livingston appeared in almost every issue. Robert Bloch, either under his own name or that of "Tarleton Fiske," was another regular. It was under the Fiske alias that his tender tale of an infant robot, "Almost Human" (July 1943), appeared. The majority of stories by these writers were routine adventures. Occasionally, however, Palmer would attract contributions by other, more serious fantasy writers, often *Weird Tales* regulars. August Derleth, for instance, had five stories in *FA*, of which "Carousel" (April 1945), a dark tale of a little girl and a carnival merry-go-round, was the best. Ray Bradbury had only one story in *FA*, but "Tomorrow and Tomorrow" (May 1947), about contact through time via a typewriter, was among the best stories *FA* published in the 1940s. Harold Lawlor, another Chicago resident who was a mainstay of *Weird Tales*, had five stories in *FA*, ranging from the light fantastic of "Dinky Winky Woo" (August 1943) to the dark fantastic of "The Manchu Coffin" (December 1942).

By the late 1940s, with the nuclear age having ushered in a more sophisticated type of SF, the contents of *FA* were of a respectable quality. This was almost certainly due to the fact that Palmer relinquished most of his editorial duties to William Hamling, who had an eye for a good fantasy. *FA* became an increasingly greater haven from the Shaver phenomenon, which dominated *Amazing* from 1945–1947. Although Shaver had a few stories in *FA*, of which "The Tale of the Red Dwarf" (May 1947) was possibly the best, the magazine remained relatively "sane" during this period. Nevertheless, Palmer could not resist one scoop: "The Secret of Elena's Tomb," in the September 1947 issue, purporting to be the entire and true story of Karl Tanzler von Cosel, the German scientist who in 1940 took the dead body of Elena Hoyos Mesa from the tomb and restored her to life, all told in von Cosel's own words. Needless to say, readers were not going to be drawn into two such sensations, and little else came of the von Cosel findings.

In the immediate postwar years *FA* contained several memorable stories. As J. W. Pelkie, Palmer wrote his own prehistoric adventure series about the caveman Toka, starting with "King of the Dinosaurs" (October 1945). Charles F. Myers began his series about the delectable dream girl Toffee in "I'll Dream of You" (January 1947), a story likened to the work of Thorne Smith. Raymond F. Jones contributed the chilling "The Children's Room" (September 1947), and Theodore Sturgeon appeared with "Largo" (July 1947), a powerful blending of music and fantasy. The story was attractively illustrated by Henry Sharp who, along with Rod Ruth, Malcolm Smith and Virgil Finlay, helped make *FA* one of the best-illustrated magazines around.

The strongest of the regular contributors in the late 1940s was Robert W. Krepps, who wrote under the alias Geoff St. Reynard. His best stories include "Androcles and the Buccaneer" (January 1947), "Five Years in the Marmalade" (July 1949) and "The Usurpers" (January 1950) and are told with the conviction of a born storyteller.

Although Hamling was largely responsible for *FA* from September 1946 on, Palmer still had overall control. The major change, however, came in 1949 when Palmer left, followed shortly by Hamling. Howard Browne, who had served as associate and managing editor on earlier issues but had recently left Ziff-Davis to write three mystery novels, was now called back as editor-in-chief. Browne preferred fantasy to SF (and favored mystery to both) and had as his managing editor Lila Shaffer, whom Browne recalls as "a very bright young woman and an excellent editor."[10]

Browne took over from the January 1950 issue, while Hamling still served as editor. He immediately strove to improve the magazine's quality, and the contrast was dramatic. Theodore Sturgeon's now classic novel, "The Dreaming Jewels," led the February 1950 issue, while L. Ron Hubbard's "The Masters of Sleep" was the feature story in the October 1950 issue. Both stories were reminiscent of the best of *Unknown*. L. Sprague de Camp contributed an exciting heroic fantasy in "The Eye of Tandyla" (May 1951). The last of Clifford D. Simak's City stories, "The Trouble with Ants," was in the January 1951 issue, while his " 'You'll Never Go Home Again!' " was in the issue for July 1951. Other authors included Walter M. Miller, Jr. ("Dark Benediction," September 1951), John D. MacDonald ("Vanguard of the Lost," May 1950), Fritz Leiber ("You're All Alone," July 1950, and "The Ship Sails at Midnight," September 1950), Lester del Rey ("When the World Tottered," December 1950) and William Tenn ("Medusa Was a Lady," October 1951), while Sturgeon returned with "Excalibur and the Atom" (August 1951).

Mack Reynolds entered the SF scene in 1950 with "Isolationist" (April 1950). A few months later "The Dreaming Trees" (November 1950), the first story by John W. Jakes, appeared. Future editor Paul W. Fairman had his second identifiable story, "The Broken Doll," in the July 1950 issue, although earlier contributions were hidden under house pseudonyms.

During its final years under Browne, *FA* was at its best. Even the old regulars found something extra with which to flavor their stories, although others found the standard hard to maintain. Browne had high hopes of converting *FA*, along with *Amazing*, into a deluxe up-market magazine, and Ziff-Davis had allowed him an increased budget that had enabled him to attract the major writers. The Korean War put a stop to these plans, and for most of 1952 the magazine's contents once again dropped in quality.

During 1952 Browne was given a second opportunity and brought out a superior digest-format *Fantastic*.* Its success was the death-blow for *FA*. For a year the two titles existed side by side until it was clear which was the greater commercial success. The March 1953 issue was *FA*'s last. It was combined with *Fantastic* for the May-June 1953 issue, but thereafter the name was dropped.

Fantastic cannot really be considered an extension of *FA*, although the mid-1950s issues exhibited some of the banality of the poorest of *FA*'s editions. In general *FA* was a light, harmless magazine with a superficial regard for quality and a penchant for escapist fun, frolics and adventure. At rare times, however, it contained fiction which rivaled the best that other magazines could offer in a package that was always bright, colorful and enjoyable.

Notes

The author wishes to thank Edward J. Gallagher for providing some of the information to help complete this essay.

1. This illustration was reproduced as the front cover for the September 1965 *Fantastic*.

2. Raymond A. Palmer, "The Editor's Notebook," *Fantastic Adventures*, May 1939, p. 4.

3. Raymond A. Palmer, "The Observatory," *Amazing Stories*, June 1939, p. 4.

4. Irwin Porges, *Edgar Rice Burroughs: The Man Who Created Tarzan* (New York: Ballantine Books, 1976), I: 558.

5. Robert A. Madle, letter in *Fantastic Adventures*, September 1939, p. 97.

6. The other three stories in *FA* were "The Amazon Fights Again" (June 1940), "The Golden Amazon Returns" (January 1941) and "Children of the Golden Amazon" (April 1943).

7. Raymond A. Palmer, *Fantastic Adventures*, May 1942, p. 236.

8. Nowlan had also just sold "Space Guards" to Campbell as the first of a new series. This was the only story completed; it appeared in the May 1940 *Astounding*.

9. Raymond A. Palmer, *Fantastic Adventures*, April 1944, p. 206.

10. Howard Browne, private communication to Mike Ashley, February 1982.

Information Sources

BIBLIOGRAPHY:

Gallagher, Edward J. *The Annotated Guide to Fantastic Adventures*. Mercer Island, Washington: Starmont House, 1985.

Nicholls. *Encyclopedia*.

Tuck.

INDEX SOURCES: IBSF; ISFM; SFM; Tuck.

REPRINT SOURCES:

Rebound Issues: Unsold issues of *FA* were rebound, 3 per volume, with a new cover and packaged as *Fantastic Adventures Quarterly*. Two series: Volume 1, Number 1, Winter 1941–Volume 2, Number 4, Fall 1943, 8 issues. Volume 6, Number 1, Summer 1948–Volume 9, Number 1, Spring 1951, 11 issues (no issue, Spring 1949).

Reprint Editions:

British: Two series. First series, 2 issues, undated [July and September 1946], released by Ziff-Davis, London. Pulp, 32 pp. Issues contained a small selection from wartime U.S. issues, but chiefly lead stories "Cult of the Eagle" (U.S. July 1946) by Berkley Livingstone in the first, and "The Giant from Jupiter" (U.S. June 1942) by Gerald Vance and Bruce Dennis in the second.

Second series, 24 issues, undated [June 1950–February 1954], released by Thorpe & Porter, Leicester. Pulp, 160 pp., decreasing to 128 pp. and 96 pp. First 2 issues unnumbered. Correspond to U.S. issues with some abridgment, as follows: [1], Mar 50; [2], Apr 50; 3, May 50; 4, Sep 50; 5, Oct 50; 6, Aug 50; 7, Feb 51; 8, Jan 51; 9, Feb 50; 10, Nov 50; 11, Dec 50; 12, Mar 51; 13, Apr 51; 14, May 51; 15, Aug 51; 16, June 51; 17, Sep 51; 18, Oct 51; 19, Apr 52; 20, Jun 52; 21, Jul 50; 22, Jan 53; 23, Dec 51; 24, Dec 52.

Reprint Magazines: See entry for *Fantastic Adventures Yearbook*. Specific issues of other Ultimate reprint magazines also relied heavily on contents from *FA*; see especially *Thrilling Science Fiction* 16 and 20, *Science Fiction Adventures* Jan 74, *Science Fantasy* (all 4 issues, 1970–1971), *The Strangest Stories Ever Told*, *Weird Mystery* (most issues).

Microform: Greenwood Press Periodical Series.

LOCATION SOURCES: Eastern New Mexico University Library; Florida International University Library; M.I.T. Science Fiction Library; Northern Illinois University Library; Pennsylvania State University Library; Texas A&M University Library.

Publication History

TITLE: *Fantastic Adventures*.

VOLUME DATA: Volume 1, Number 1, May 1939–Volume 15, Number 3, March 1953. Volume 1, 4 issues (bi-monthly, May–November 1939); Volume 2, 8 issues (monthly, January–June 1940; bi-monthly from August 1940); Volume 3, 10 issues (bi-monthly, January–May 1941; then monthly); Volume 4, 12 issues (monthly, January–December 1942); Volume 5, 10 issues (monthly to August 1943; bi-monthly from October); Volume 6, 4 issues (bi-monthly, February–June 1944; quarterly from October); Volume 7, 5 issues (quarterly, January–October 1945; then bi-monthly); Volume 8, 5 issues (bi-monthly, February–November 1946, but April issue slipped to May); Volume 9, 8 issues (bi-monthly, January–September 1947; then monthly); Volume 10, Number 1, January 1948–Volume 15, Number 3, March 1953, 12 issues per volume, monthly. Total run: 129 issues.

PUBLISHER: Ziff-Davis, Chicago and New York.

EDITORS: Editors-in-Chief: B. G. Davis, May 1939–January 1947; Raymond A. Palmer, March 1947–December 1949; Howard Browne, January 1950–March 1953. Managing Editors: Raymond A. Palmer, May 1939–January 1947; Howard Browne, March 1947–October 1947; William L. Hamling, November 1947–February 1951; Lila E. Shaffer, March 1951–March 1953.

FORMAT: Large Pulp, 96 pp., May 1939–May 1940; Pulp, 144 pp., June 1940–March 1942; 240 pp., April 1942–May 1943; 208 pp., June 1943–July 1945; 176 pp., October 1945–June 1948; 160 pp., July–August 1948; 156 pp., September 1948–May 1949; 144 pp., June–August 1949; 160 pp., September 1949–August 1950; 148 pp., September 1950; 130 pp., October 1950–March 1953.

PRICE: 20¢, May 1939–April 1942; thereafter 25¢.

Mike Ashley

FANTASTIC ADVENTURES QUARTERLY

Rebound copies of *Fantastic Adventures*. See FANTASTIC ADVENTURES, Reprint Sources.

FANTASTIC ADVENTURES YEARBOOK

Fantastic Adventures Yearbook was one of a number of yearbooks issued by Sol Cohen in 1970, relying on reprints from the back files of magazines acquired when he purchased the rights to *Amazing Stories** and *Fantastic** in 1965.

This *Yearbook* saw only one issue, in the summer of 1970, and reprinted six stories from *Fantastic Adventures** chosen from the period 1949–1952, with one exception, "The Empress of Mars" by Ross Rocklynne, from 1939. Unfortunately, they did not reflect the best examples of fiction published by that magazine, though of passing interest are "The Dark Balcony" by Emil Petaja, and

Lester del Rey's Nordic fantasy, "When the World Tottered," which had also been issued in book form as *Day of the Giants* (New York: Avalon, 1959; Airmont, 1964).

Information Sources

BIBLIOGRAPHY:
Nicholls. *Encyclopedia.*
INDEX SOURCES: ISFM-II; SFM.
REPRINT SOURCES: None known.
LOCATION SOURCES: M.I.T. Science Fiction Library.

Publication History

TITLE: *Fantastic Adventures Yearbook.*
VOLUME DATA: Unnumbered, 1970. Only issue.
PUBLISHER: Ultimate Publishing Co., Flushing, New York.
EDITOR: Sol Cohen (not identified within issue).
FORMAT: Digest, 128 pp.
PRICE: 60¢.

Mike Ashley

FANTASTIC NOVELS

After two of six scheduled installments of Austin Hall and Homer Eon Flint's "The Blind Spot" had been published in *Famous Fantastic Mysteries,** that serialization was abruptly terminated, and the entire story appeared in the first number (July 1940) of *Fantastic Novels*. The Frank A. Munsey Company wanted *Fantastic Novels* as a companion to *Famous Fantastic Mysteries* to serve as a vehicle for novel-length narratives. Mary Gnaedinger, who edited both, explained in a note about "The New Magazine" that it had come into being because everyone realized that "the longer stories would be delayed for years if they were published serially, even two at a time," in *Famous Fantastic Mysteries*. Although the older magazine had been issued monthly until this time, one effect of Munsey's decision was to place the companion periodicals on a bi-monthly schedule, each offered alternately. A second effect—perhaps unforeseen, perhaps resulting from the quantity of desirable novels—was that both magazines had the same format: a novel augmented either by a novelette or by one or two short stories.

The same editorial policy governed both; they were to reprint the "accepted classics" which had originally appeared in such magazines as *Cavalier, All-Story* and *Argosy** earlier in the century, especially during the period 1912–1920, when the Munsey chain had its greatest influence in shaping American fantasy and science fiction. In successive issues, *FN* followed "The Blind Spot" with Ray Cummings' "People of the Golden Atom" (1920), A. Merritt's "The Snake Mother" (1930), Ralph Milne Farley's "The Radio Beasts" (1925), and

A. Merritt's "The Dwellers in the Mirage" (1932). As in *Famous Fantastic Mysteries,* A. Merritt was the most frequent contributor; when an issue did not feature one of his novels, it included one of his short stories: "Through the Dragon Glass" (September 1940) and "People of the Pit" (January 1941). Significantly, the blurb for "The Dwellers in the Mirage" explained that this was "the original version of this great story, as it was first written by the author, and as the author prefers to have it concluded." The difference, however, between it and the "printed version in *Argosy* involves only the last two and a half pages of the story." More than any other magazine *FN* kept the work of Merritt before its audience and thus was instrumental in establishing him as one of the masters of American fantasy (one should not forget that in the late 1940s *FN*—not *Famous Fantastic Mysteries*—reprinted other novels by him). In like manner, except for the cover for "People of the Golden Atom," Virgil Finlay did the covers for these early issues of *Fantastic Novels,* as well as the interiors for the Merritt works, thereby strengthening his tie with Merritt.

In the April 1941 number, however, came the announcement that with its next issue *Fantastic Novels* would merge with *Famous Fantastic Mysteries.* Noting that the latter "is apparently the favorite title" and promising that the "combined magazine will continue to accommodate the novel length stories which have been so popular with the readers of both magazines," the "editors" gave no further explanation of the merger. Inasmuch as *Famous Fantastic Mysteries* stayed on a bi-monthly schedule until the latter half of 1942, just before Munsey sold it to Popular Publications, one can infer that in part, at least, the suspension of *Fantastic Novels* after five numbers resulted from problems related to World War II.

It resumed publication in March 1948. Amusingly, as though there had been no interruption, that issue was Volume 1, Number 6. Mary Gnaedinger remained its editor. Whereas Popular Publications had drastically altered the editorial policy of *Famous Fantastic Mysteries,* *FN* picked up where it had left off. In her initial editorial statement, "Between Us," Gnaedinger emphasized that it would "be used as a vehicle for the great stories from the renowned Munsey group of magazines, now owned by this company." That March issue featured A. Merritt's "The Ship of Ishtar." One may infer Gnaedinger's devotion to Merritt in that three of the next six issues contained major works by him: two reprinted stories that had appeared in early numbers of *Famous Fantastic Mysteries*—"The Moon Pool" (May 1948) and "The Conquest of the Moonpool" (September 1948), while another carried "Seven Footprints to Satan" (January 1949).

Another matter also gives insight into Gnaedinger, as well, perhaps, as raising questions about the decisions regarding Munsey materials. In the December 1942 issue of *Famous Fantastic Mysteries,* the last controlled by Munsey, Gnaedinger named the major stories scheduled for publication in subsequent issues. In 1948, as though there had been no interruptions in her plans, she immediately published in successive issues three of the works she had promised: "The Ship of Ishtar,"

J. U. Giesy's "Jason, Son of Jason," and Garrett P. Serviss' "The Second Deluge." Eventually, all but one of the titles she had mentioned saw publication: Tod Robbins' novelette, "The Toys of Fate" (March 1949), Charles B. Stilson's "Minos of Sardanes" (November 1949), George Allan England's "The Flying Legion" (January 1950) and Stilson's "Polaris and the Goddess Glorian" (September 1950).

Old favorites dominated her other choices: England, Cummings, Robbins, Victor Rousseau and Garret Smith. She even felt compelled to include Merritt's "The Dwellers in the Mirage" (September 1949). Surprisingly, Francis Stevens was represented by only two short stories—"The Elf-Trap" (November 1949) and "Friend Island" (September 1950). In contrast, three of her choices apparently involved first publication of the respective novels in a science fiction magazine: Eric North's "Three Against the Stars" (May 1950), C. L. Moore and Henry Kuttner's "Earth's Last Citadel" (July 1950) and Fred MacIsaac's earlier "The Hothouse World" (November 1950).[1] The selection of these titles may represent the attempt to recapture a faltering audience.

For suddenly, just as in 1941, *Fantastic Novels* was discontinued. The last issue (June 1951) featured a number of shorter works, among them Cummings' "The Girl in the Golden Atom" and Otis Adelbert Kline's "Spawn of the Comet." The decision must have come quickly, for Kline's "Maza of the Moon" was scheduled for the next issue.

With the disappearance of *Fantastic Novels*—and two years later of *Famous Fantastic Mysteries*—one period in American science fiction and fantasy definitely ended. In terms of themes, tone and narrative techniques, both magazines looked backward to the opening of the twentieth century. One must surmise that they became dated—especially with such a heavy reliance upon a comparatively small group of writers—and could no longer hold an audience dominated by *Astounding* (*Analog Science Fiction**) and the two new titles that were to revolutionize the field over the next two decades, *Galaxy Science Fiction** and *The Magazine of Fantasy and Science Fiction.** On the other hand, both magazines kept alive the reputations of a number of the earlier writers—Ray Cummings and A. Merritt in particular. And one can certainly argue that the influence that the Munsey group of magazines once had would not be so well remembered without *Famous Fantastic Mysteries* and *Fantastic Novels*.

Note

1. Donald Day's *Index* gives the appearance in *Fantastic Novels* as the only magazine publication of all three of these novels. Yet in the magazine each is assigned an earlier copyright date, all held by Popular Publications: North, "Three Against the Stars" (1938); Moore and Kuttner, "Earth's Last Citadel" (1943); and MacIsaac, "The Hothouse World" (1931). All three had previously been serialized in *Argosy*.

Information Sources

BIBLIOGRAPHY:
Dard, Roger. *Fantastic Novels: A Check List*. Perth, Australia: Dragon Press, 1957.
Ellis, James. "A Remembrance of FN." *Xenophile*, No. 20 (1976).
Nicholls. *Encyclopedia*.
Tuck.
INDEX SOURCES: IBSF; ISFM; MIT; SFM; Shaheen, Gary, "An Index to Fantastic
 Novels," *Xenophile*, No. 7 (1974); Tuck.
REPRINT SOURCES:
 Reprint Editions:
  Canadian: An identical Canadian edition with variations only in the back cover
  ran from September 1948 to June 1951, 17 issues, corresponding to the same
  U.S. numbers. Published by New Publications, Toronto.
  British: Two separate British editions were distributed by Thorpe & Porter on
  behalf of Pemberton's. The first, undated and unnumbered, released in March
  1950, was an exact reprint of the November 1949 issue. The second, confusingly
  numbered 1, undated, but released in June 1951, was an abridged (64 pp.) reprint
  of the May 1949 issue.
LOCATION SOURCES: M.I.T. Science Fiction Library; Pennsylvania State University
 Library.

Publication History

TITLE: *Fantastic Novels* for the first two issues (July and September 1940); thereafter
 Fantastic Novels Magazine.
VOLUME DATA: Volume 1, Number 1, July 1940–Volume 1, Number 5, April 1941;
 publication suspended. Revived Volume 1, Number 6, March 1948–Volume 5,
 Number 1, June 1951. Six issues per volume. Bi-monthly, but March 1941 issue
 slipped to April, and March 1951 issue slipped to April. Total run: 25 issues.
PUBLISHER: First series (July 1940–April 1941): The Frank A. Munsey Company, New
 York. Second series (March 1948–June 1951): New Publications, Inc., Kokomo,
 Indiana, an affiliate of Popular Publications, New York.
EDITOR: Mary Gnaedinger.
FORMAT: Pulp, 144 pp., July and September 1940; 128 pp., November 1940 and January
 1941; 112 pp., April 1941; 132 pp., March 1948–November 1950; 128 pp.,
 January 1951; 112 pp., April and June 1951.
PRICE: 20¢, July and September 1940; 10¢, November 1940–April 1941; 25¢, March
 1948–June 1951.

Thomas D. Clareson

FANTASTIC SCIENCE FICTION (1952)

Fantastic Science Fiction, a bedsheet-sized magazine billed as a quarterly,
ran only two issues. The first (August 1952) was published by Super Science
Fiction Publications, the second (December 1952) by Capitol Stories. (*FSF*
should not, as *The Science Fiction Encyclopedia* warns, be confused with *Fan-*

tastic,* also begun in 1952, which changed its title to *Fantastic Science Fiction* in April 1955.)[1] The editor, Walter Gibson, had edited *Tales of Magic and Mystery*,* a pulp magazine that ran for five issues in 1927–1928, and had written novels about the "invisible" detective, The Shadow. Gibson wrote the lead story for each issue under his own name plus a few of the short stories under pseudonyms. The remaining stories were the work of Edward Burkholder, who had arranged the contract between Gibson and the publishers.

Perhaps misled by the crudely cartoonlike illustrations by Al Fargo, Lou Morales, Frank Frollo, Dick Giordano and Stan Campbell, critics have erroneously referred to *FSF* as a "juvenile."[2] However, neither the advertisements (for such things as "French Lingerie" and a male girdle, the "Tummy Flattening Commander") nor the stories, with their violent, sometimes sadistic action, fantastically voluptuous women and bogus science, are for children.

In the first issue of *FSF*, Gibson wrote in an "Editor's Announcement":

When Jules Verne set the pace in fiction of the future, he dealt in plausibilities. From creations already in existence, he fashioned those that might or could be. He pushed his world ahead a trifle or sped up the development of some invention to show what the effects would be on things as they were. . . .

Nobody has ever proven for our money that fact is stranger than fiction and constant quoting of such a fallacy does not prove it. Fiction has always been jumps ahead of fact and will always stay there. Today fact is crowding fiction but not replacing it. It is up to fiction to set a still faster pace and this magazine intends to do just that.

We will show the things to come and leave it to others to shape them in actuality. All suggestions are welcome. Not even the sky is our limit.

This "Announcement" articulates Gibson's desire to exploit scientific wonder fictionally and his refusal to be confined by what persons with scientific training might consider possible. Besides stories featuring scientific inventions, *FSF* includes brief, nonfiction "Features" about aspects of outer space: for example, "Lost: One World: Join the Search for the Missing Planet Vulcan" and "Speeds Thru Space." In contrast to the hyperbolic tone of the science fillers, the book reviews consist of rather innocuous puffery of science fiction and popular science books.

The scientists and professors who people the *FSF* stories are evidence of the rather anti-intellectual tenor of the magazine. At best, they are eccentric in their single-minded concern with extending the frontiers of knowledge; at worst, the power of their inventions has rendered them dangerously maniacal.

Two stories in the first issue illustrate the magazine's penchant for out-and-out scientific howlers: Bruce Crandall's "Secret of the Locked Laboratory" and Wallace Smith's "The Lost City of the Sky." In "Secret of the Locked Laboratory," a scientist plots to rule the world with the aid of two inventions: a disintegrator ray and a "machine [that] can pick up the thoughts or words of any person anywhere in the world." The scientist plans to disintegrate everyone on earth except for a small number of sincere persons, whom he would govern, with the aid of the mind-reader to inform him of mutiny. Ultimately, the scientist is destroyed by one of his chosen sincere persons, Roger Channing. "Tall, blond, well-built, in his early thirties, with humorous, slightly irregular features," Channing represents another stereotype that is the staple of the *FSF* stories: the clean-cut, Anglo-Saxon man of action.

Culturally, though not fictionally, "The Lost City of the Sky" is more interesting, for it represents the preoccupation with atomic energy that characterized the fifties. With the aid of an "atomic ray" carried in an "oblong box," a professor discovers a lost race of Mayans, scientifically advanced but cut off from the outside world. "These people," the professor tells his down-to-earth sidekick, "have extracted atomic energy from the air. . . . They have a huge seismograph which records all the atomic waves and they know when atomic energy is anywhere in the world." Mayan soldiers shoot at the two men with "atomic guns," and the professor explains their remarkable escape in this way: "You will recall that I had you undress and wrapped that cloth around your body. For your information, that cloth, which you still wear, is made of special nylon with lead tissue. . . . That is why the atomic shots didn't kill us."

There are four other stories in the first issue. Gibson's novella, "The Day New York Ended," is the story of an attempt by an underground race of green men ("Our race crossed itself with vegetable and reptilian species long before your warm-blooded ancestors struggled out of their caves to seek a barbarous existence on the world's shriveled skin," an invader explains) to destroy "Surfacian" society with earthquakes and floods. Two other stories are derivative. George Moffatt's "The Nude in the Microscope" is a reworking of Fitz-James O'Brien's "The Diamond Lens" (1858). In "They Die on Mars," Phyllis L. Kaye has borrowed her setting from Bradbury's *The Martian Chronicles*, published two years earlier: a dying Mars, inhabited by an ancient race of golden-skinned, telepathic beings. Finally, the most original (by comparison, at least) but most incoherently written story is G. A. Lacksey's "The Black Planet." The scene shifts back and forth between a game of pool involving employees of Rocketways Incorporated and an astrophysicist, and the Black Planet, Infinito, whose inhabitants are threatened with destruction because the neighboring White Planet, Devolo, has been colliding with the other planets in the solar system. The billiard balls, it is revealed at the end, are inhabited worlds. Their motions during the game prove the generalizations the professor has been making about "curved space and limited universes." Unfortunately, not only is the writing exceedingly poor, but the illustrations give away the secret (that the balls are really planets) long before the end of the story.

In the second issue of *FSF*, also, most stories concern magical scientific inventions. The action, however, has become more violent and the characters more self-serving and heartless. Violence generally solves the problems raised by the plot, and the reader is expected to approve. The lead story, Gibson's "War of the Moons," is a tediously convoluted story about a war between the Grand Solar Alliance and the inhabitants of Titan. The plot features torture, acts of patriotism, and a hero, Len Ryder, given to unusually callous displays of machismo. Two tales of mad scientists are equally sadistic. In George Moffatt's "He Wouldn't Die," Professor Murillo toughens Pedro's skin with special baths so that he is immune to bullets and sends him out to rob banks. Pedro is so overworked that he kills the professor, but dies himself because he lacks the secret of the bath, which not only toughens his skin but keeps the pores open. In Phyllis Kaye's "The Murder Machine," Harcourt Dunwood has invented the Animaticus Electronicus, a machine that brings inanimate objects to life. Night after night, he murders secretaries working late by animating their office equipment. Predictably, he is killed by his own machine.

Two stories in this second issue are a departure from the theme of scientific invention and discovery. In Wallace Smith's weird tale, "She Was a Creature of Fire and Death," Mattie Hawkes, a toothless old hag, is made young and beautiful by a "Passion Diva" in exchange for her promise that she will be faithful to him. She keeps herself young by taking baths in the blood of men she murders, but makes the mistake of falling in love with an admirer. Though she kills the man she loves in the hope of staying young, the Diva destroys the spell and makes her an old hag again.

Bruce Crandall's "The Spidermen and the Cakes" is the only humorous story in either issue. Spidermen from Venus, bent on destroying the earth, attack a mother and daughter while they are getting ready for the daughter's birthday party. Accustomed to subsisting on synthetic vitamins, the Spidermen stuff themselves on birthday sweets to such an extent that they are easily defeated by police. Like Gibson's "The Day New York Ended," this story rather smugly assumes that Anglo-Saxon earthlings are superior to any alien.

FSF not only lacked literary merit; it did not even, like some pulp magazines, provide a training ground for young writers who were later to make a name for themselves in science fiction. The stories rather simplistically embody the belief that might makes right. Reticent, two-fisted Anglo-Saxon males are glorified, while dark-skinned humans and alien races, transparently symbolizing non-Caucasians, are defeated and ridiculed. Voluptuous, intellectually childlike women exist primarily to provide love interest. *FSF* is, in short, a mirror of prevailing social attitudes at the time it was written. If its stories are worth reading today, it is because they provide insight into racist and sexist assumptions that characterized the early fifties.

Notes

1. See "Fantastic" and "Fantastic Science Fiction," in *The Science Fiction Encyclopedia*, ed. Peter Nicholls (Garden City, N.Y.: Doubleday, 1979).

2. See "Gibson, Walter B.," in Donald H. Tuck, *The Encyclopedia of Science Fiction*

and Fantasy, Vol. I (Chicago: Advent, 1974); see also Michael Ashley, *The History of the Science Fiction Magazine 1946–1955* (Chicago: Contemporary Books, 1976), III: 83; and "Fantastic Science Fiction," in Nicholls, *Encyclopedia.*

Information Sources

BIBLIOGRAPHY:
Nicholls. *Encyclopedia.*
Tuck.
INDEX SOURCES: MIT; SFM; Tuck.
REPRINT SOURCES:
  Microfilm: Greenwood Press Periodical Series.
LOCATION SOURCES: Eastern New Mexico University, Golden Library (not available through interlibrary loan); Massachusetts Institute of Technology, MIT Science Fiction Society (not available through ILL); Michigan State University, Special Collections; Norther Illinois University Library, Rare Books and Special Collections (not available through ILL; partial photocopying of some issues *may* be possible); Ohio State University Libraries, Division of Special Collections; Pennsylvania State University Libraries, Special Collections; Queen's University, Special Collections (not available through ILL or microfilm); San Francisco Public Library, Literature Department, McComas Collection (not available through ILL); Temple University, Paskow SF Collection, Paley Library (not available through ILL); Texas A&M University, Special Collections; Toronto Public Libraries, Spaced Out Library (not available through ILL); University of British Columbia Library, Special Collections; UCLA, Special Collections (a microfilm may be produced, the negative remaining at UCLA, the patron to pay for negative and print); University of Georgia Libraries, Periodicals Department; University of Kansas, Spencer Research Library (December 1952 issue only).

Publication History

TITLE: *Fantastic Science Fiction.*
VOLUME DATA: Volume 1, Number 1, August 1952–Volume 1, Number 2, December 1952. Labeled quarterly. Total run: 2 issues.
PUBLISHER: Super Science Fiction Publications, Derby, Connecticut, first issue; Capitol Stories, Derby, Connecticut, second issue. Both imprints of Charlton Publishing Co.
EDITOR: Walter Gibson.
FORMAT: Large Pulp, 48 pp.
PRICE: 25¢.

Wendy Bousfield

FANTASTIC SCIENCE FICTION [STORIES] (1955–1960, 1979–1980)

See FANTASTIC. Also known as *Fantastic Science Fiction & Fantasy Stories* (1971–1975).

FANTASTIC STORIES

See FANTASTIC.

FANTASTIC STORY MAGAZINE

See FANTASTIC STORY QUARTERLY.

FANTASTIC STORY QUARTERLY

Standard Magazines had long taken advantage of its reprint rights to the stories in the early Gernsback *Wonder Stories** and its companions, which Ned Pines had acquired in 1936, first through the use of a Classic Reprint "Hall of Fame" department in *Startling Stories*,* and briefly in *Captain Future.** Many of the longer stories, however, would not fit into the Hall of Fame section, and so, when the postwar years indicated a favorable climate in the SF field, Pines issued *Fantastic Story Quarterly*, an all-reprint magazine fashioned to appeal to the nostalgia of the fans.

At the last moment it was decided to include at least one new story per issue though, to cut costs, they were usually short pieces by unestablished writers. Thus, the first issue, dated Spring 1950, which led with a reprint of Edmond Hamilton's 1929 novel "The Hidden World" and which also included "The Ideal" by Stanley G. Weinbaum, "Children of the Ray" by J. Harvey Haggard and "A Visit to Venus" by Festus Pragnell, also included "Trespass!," the first story by Gordon R. Dickson, written in collaboration with Poul Anderson.

FSQ presented some classic novels from the archives including "In Caverns Below" by Stanton A. Coblentz, "Vandals of the Void" by J. M. Walsh and "The Evening Star" by David H. Keller. Selections were not limited to the Gernsback days; indeed, from the Spring 1952 issue on, they came predominantly from the more recent issues of *Thrilling Wonder Stories* and *Startling Stories*. In one instance, *FSQ* even stepped outside its own archives to reprint A. E. van Vogt's "Slan" from *Astounding* (*Analog Science Fiction**), a sign of the formidable popularity of that novel.

Few of the new stories in *FSQ* were of lasting significance, although they include "Lazarus II" by Richard Matheson (July 1953) and "A Family Matter" by Walter M. Miller, Jr. (November 1952). *FSQ* was nevertheless extremely popular with the fans because SF was still hard to come by in paperback, and there was no other way of acquiring the old classics short of hunting around the second-hand bookstores. *FSQ* did not acquire an editorial personality as pronounced as some of the other magazines, although it had an editorial department, "Cosmic Encores," and a letter column, "Cosmograms," which was kept short.

FSQ later changed its title to *Fantastic Story Magazine* and even for a brief period increased its schedule to bi-monthly. It was attractively illustrated with work by Virgil Finlay, Vincent Napoli, Ed Emsh, Paul Orban and Earle Bergey.

However, when the blight settled on the pulp field in the mid-1950s, *FSQ* became one of many victims. After the Spring 1955 issue it was absorbed by *Startling Stories*, which was itself soon to perish.

Information Sources

BIBLIOGRAPHY:
Nicholls. *Encyclopedia.*
Tuck.
INDEX SOURCES: ISFM; IWG; MIT; SFM; Tuck.
REPRINT SOURCES:
  Reprint Editions: An identical Canadian edition was published simultaneously by Better Publications in Toronto corresponding to the first four U.S. editions, all titled *Fantastic Science Quarterly.*
LOCATION SOURCES: M.I.T. Science Fiction Library; Pennsylvania State University Library.

Publication History

TITLE: *Fantastic Story Quarterly*, Spring 1950–Winter 1951; thereafter *Fantastic Story Magazine.*
VOLUME DATA: Volume 1, Number 1, Spring 1950–Volume 8, Number 2, Spring 1955. Three issues per volume. Quarterly, Spring 1950–Fall 1952 (also dated September); bi-monthly, November 1952–September 1953; quarterly, Winter 1954–Spring 1955. Total run: 23 issues.
PUBLISHER: Best Books, Inc., Kokomo, Indiana, a subsidiary of Standard Magazines, New York.
EDITORS: Sam Merwin, Spring 1950–Fall 1951; Samuel Mines, Winter 1952–Fall 1954; Alexander Samalman, Winter–Spring 1955.
FORMAT: Pulp; 160 pp., Spring 1950–Winter 1951; 144 pp., Spring 1951–July 1953; 128 pp., September 1953–Fall 1954; 112 pp., Winter–Spring 1955.
PRICE: 25¢.

Mike Ashley

FANTASTIC UNIVERSE

Fantastic Universe was born at the height of the SF magazine boom in 1953, and perhaps the most surprising fact about it was that it survived the boom and appeared regularly throughout the rest of the 1950s. Because if *FU* had any distinguishing feature it was its remarkable lack of memorable or meritorious fiction. As with most magazines that ran for more than a few issues, it did publish at least some stories worthy of attention, but on the whole the quality was uneven and disappointing.

FU was published by Leo Margulies, one-time editorial director at Standard

Magazines and thus the man behind *Thrilling Wonder Stories* (*Wonder Stories**) and its companions. In 1952 he formed King-Size Publications in partnership with H. L. Herbert and issued *The Saint Detective Magazine* (first issue, Spring 1953) and then *Fantastic Universe*. Although the first issue was a bumper 192 pages, Margulies took a risk by setting the cover price at fifty cents, thus making it the most expensive SF magazine of its day. Most other titles were thirty-five cents, though a few remained at twenty-five. Margulies and Herbert obviously reconsidered this action as sales figures came in, for after the third issue the price dropped to thirty-five cents, with a corresponding decrease in size.

As his editor, Margulies had employed Sam Merwin, which brought together again the team that had worked so successfully on *Thrilling Wonder* and *Startling Stories** after the war, and would again on the first two issues of *Satellite Science Fiction.** Merwin only stayed as editor for the first three issues before joining Horace Gold at *Galaxy Science Fiction,** so in more ways than one these three maiden issues stand as a unit on their own.

Although it contained an impressive array of writers—Arthur C. Clarke, Frank Belknap Long, Philip K. Dick, Eric Frank Russell, Clifford D. Simak, Poul Anderson and others—there was little in the magazine that could not be found in its many rivals on the bookstalls. Worth singling out are two stories that highlight the fantasy side of the magazine, which, on the whole, was its best aspect. Both stories, coincidentally, were by British writers—''The Whispering Gallery,'' a ghost story with a time-cycle explanation by William F. Temple, and ''The Sepulchre of Jasper Sarasen,'' a good, solid supernatural story by that much overlooked master of the spectral, H. Russell Wakefield. On the SF side, perhaps the best story was the first issue's lead novelette, ''Nightmare Tower,'' by Sam Merwin writing as Jacques Jean Ferrat, featuring the characters Lynne and Rolf Marcein in a serious consideration of the future colonization of Mars. The story resulted in two sequels, ''The White Rain Came'' (May 1955) and ''Snowstorm on Mars'' (June 1956).

Beyond this, however, *FU* contained nothing special, and its ability to survive into a second year must have had some connection with its companion magazine, *Saint Detective*, which had proved immensely popular and secured a wide distribution. Distribution was the key factor to survival during the boom period, followed by retail display. If *FU* mastered that, it had a considerable chance of success. Thereafter, provided *FU* could continue to deliver a sufficient quota of good stories plus the occasional memorable item, it would survive.

And in this period, when *FU* remained generally dull, it produced one big scoop, Philip José Farmer's powerful prequel to ''The Lovers'': ''Rastignac the Devil'' (May 1954), a story that has been forgotten today but which at the time caused a stir.

It was a year before *FU* produced another worthy story, and this time it was the original short story that provided the kernel for Algis Budrys' now classic novel *Who?*, called, not surprisingly, ''Who?'' (April 1955). The years 1955 and 1956 were among *FU*'s better ones, partly because it started to publish some of the new Conan stories completed by L. Sprague de Camp from drafts and fragments left by Robert E. Howard. The other stories, though not outstanding, took on a fresh quality and became mildly different from those published in most other magazines. At this time appeared "Wednesday's Child" by William Tenn, "Sole Solution" by Eric Frank Russell, "Founding Fathers" by Robert Bloch, "So Bright the Vision" by Clifford D. Simak, "Blind Lightning" by Harlan Ellison, "The Pacifist" by Arthur C. Clarke and "First Law" by Isaac Asimov. Robert Bloch also contributed his homage to fandom, "A Way of Life," and there were regular contributions by Australians Frank Bryning and Dal Stivens.

Nevertheless, there was always an air of dullness about *FU*. It lacked interior artwork, the stories were presented with no frills or trimmings, and the only regular reader department was the book review column, "The Universe in Books," conducted with no flair by Robert Frazier. In October 1955, however, the column was taken over by Hans Steffan Santesson, who began to make a more regular contribution to the magazine. In 1956, when Margulies sold his share in King-Size to his partner to establish his own Renown Publications, Santesson took over as editorial director of the magazine.

Santesson is usually remembered with great fondness by those who knew him. Harry Harrison referred to him as a friend in need, and certainly he was an author's friend. In Harrison's case he thoughtfully allowed payment in advance against stories yet to be written, as was the case with many of the stories that went to make up Harrison's book *War with the Robots* (New York: Pyramid, 1962), starting with "The Velvet Glove" (November 1956).

Curiously, however, under Santesson *FU* did not improve. In fact, for a period, if anything, it deteriorated. In 1957 many of the SF magazines went through a flying-saucer phase, and *FU* was no exception. The February 1957 issue was almost entirely devoted to UFOs in fact and fiction. There were articles by Ivan T. Sanderson and Gray Barker, plus one by Dean McLaughlin on "How to Be a Saucer Author," and associated UFO stories by Harlan Ellison and George H. Smith. Then, starting in the March issue, Santesson ran a regular column of UFO news supplied by Alexander MeBane and Ted Bloecher of the group Civilian Saucer Intelligence. It ran for sixteen issues.

At length H. L. Herbert sold out his interest in King-Size, and both *FU* and *Saint Mystery* (as it had now become) were bought by Henry Scharf of Great American Publications, a considerably larger firm that concentrated on hot-rod publications for the teenage market. To keep all its magazines in a similar format, *FU* was enlarged to a neo-pulp size, and at last the magazine came alive. Santesson remained as editor and still kept his persona in the shadows, but nevertheless *FU* suddenly became a magazine of quality. Although the title remained the same, the identifying banner expanded to encompass "Science Fact & Fiction," taking a leaf from *Astounding*'s (*Analog Science Fiction**) book, although the science fiction was a little on the oblique side, starting with "Music for the Space Age" by Stephen Lloyd Carr (possibly a pseudonym of

Santesson's), and continuing with articles by Ivan T. Sanderson on the Abominable Snowman, and by Sam Moskowitz on the history of space travel in fiction, a short series which had been planned for *Satellite* before that magazine's demise.

The new *FU* was profusely illustrated, often by Virgil Finlay; a new column was added reviewing fanzines, "Fannotations," conducted by Belle Dietz; and, most important of all, *FU* now strove for quality fiction. The last seven issues probably contain as much good fiction as the rest of its entire run. Here first appeared Howard Fast's "The Large Ant"; Lester del Rey's "Mine Host, Mine Adversary"; John Brunner's "Curative Telepath" which, with "City of the Tiger," was later revised to form his Hugo-nominated novel, *The Whole Man*; Jorge Luis Borges' "The Rejected Sorcerer"; and L. Sprague de Camp and Fletcher Pratt's "Bell, Book and Candle." What's more, *FU* started a serial. During all its run it had avoided serials, but with the March 1960 issue appeared the first episode of Fredric Brown's "Mind Thing." Readers had to wait, however, for the Bantam paperback published in 1961 in order to finish the novel, because the March 1960 issue was the last *FU*. It was ironic that readers had managed to support a run-of-the-mill magazine for six years and then deserted it the moment it turned into a worthwhile publication. But it was more than that. The new publisher had a different distribution setup than that of King-Size, and its marketing arrangements did not suit a fiction magazine. *The Saint* survived the publisher, being taken over by another in 1961. During 1960 Great American tried to salvage *FU*. There were plans to issue a new magazine called *Summer SF* as a one-shot to use up the inventory of stories acquired for publication, but this never happened. Some of the stories almost certainly appeared in a short-lived companion, *Fear!*,* but by the end of 1960 Great American and *FU* were no more. A year earlier *FU*'s passing would have been no surprise, but now it was suddenly missed.

Information Sources

BIBLIOGRAPHY:
Nicholls, *Encyclopedia*.
SFM.
Tuck.
INDEX SOURCES: MIT; Tuck; Wood, Edward. *The Checklist to Fantastic Universe*. Published as a supplement to *Lore* 4 (1966). (Includes brief introductory history. Listing by issue only. Subsequent listings by author and title prepared but apparently not published.)
REPRINT SOURCES:
  Derivative Anthology: *The Fantastic Universe Omnibus* (New York: Prentice-Hall, 1960), ed. Hans Stefan Santesson, contains sixteen stories from the years 1956–1958, plus an introduction by Lester del Rey. A good selection.
LOCATION SOURCES: M.I.T. Science Fiction Library; Northern Illinois University Library; Pennsylvania State University Library.

Publication History

TITLE: *Fantastic Universe.*
VOLUME: Volume 1, Number 1, June/July 1953–Volume 12, Number 5, March 1960.
Six issues per volume, except Vols. 6, 10 and 12, which had only five. Bi-
monthly, June/July 1953–July 1954; monthly, September 1954–November 1958;
bi-monthly, January–July 1959; monthly, September 1959–March 1960. Total
run: 69 issues.
PUBLISHER: King-Size Publications, New York, June/July 1953–July 1959; Great
American Publications, New York, September 1959–March 1960.
EDITORS: Sam Merwin, June/July 1953–October/November 1953; Beatrice Jones, Jan-
uary–March 1954; Leo Margulies, May 1954–August 1956; Hans Stefan Santesson, September 1956–March 1960.
FORMAT: Digest, 192 pp., June/July 1953–October/November 1953; 160 pp., January–
July 1954; 128 pp., September 1954–September 1959; Pulp, 128 pp., October
1959–February 1960; 96 pp., March 1960.
PRICE: 50¢, first three issues; thereafter 35¢

Mike Ashley

FANTASY (1938–1939)

The first magazine with this title was a British pulp published by George
Newnes Ltd. In command was an aspiring young editor, Theodore Stanhope
Sprigg, who had joined Newnes in 1934 "with plans for a series of monthly
magazines I wanted to launch and edit for them. The first to appear was *Air
Stories*, and this was followed at intervals by *War Stories*, *Western Stories* and,
finally, *Fantasy.*"[1]

Fantasy's birth was not without its complications, however. Discussions over
the magazine did not begin until August 1935, and in February 1936 a Mem-
orandum of Requirements was issued "so restricting that it threw would-be
contributors into a complete tizzy."[2] After fifteen months and much indecision
the project was placed "in abeyance,"[3] though Sprigg confirmed that it was
always his "intention to launch it from the time I joined them."[4] It was only
after the clear success of *Tales of Wonder** that Newnes at last issued the
magazine in July 1938.

Sprigg's editorial made the now standard claim of publishing fiction "in the
Wells-Verne tradition."[5] He also claimed that *Fantasy* struck "a new note among
British magazines of popular fiction,"[6] even though *Tales of Wonder* was just
into its third issue. *Fantasy*'s chief artist was S. R. Drigin, who had illustrated
*Scoops.**

The cover illustrated the lead story, "Menace of the Metal Men" by Italian
naval engineer A. Prestigiacomo—actually a reprint from a 1933 British *Argosy.**
The remaining stories were new, including contributions from SF stalwarts John
Beynon (Harris), Eric Frank Russell and John Russell Fearn, and Newnes regulars

J. E. Gurdon and Francis H. Sibson. P. E. Cleator provided an article on interplanetary travel—a continuation of his *Scoops* series.

The second and third issues, which appeared months apart, followed much the same format—a reprint plus a few stories by SF regulars, and others by adventure writers who were giving it a try. Willy Ley had nonfiction articles in both. Because Newnes could pay a reasonable rate for fiction, the magazine attracted capable writers—and it is interesting to speculate what might have happened had World War II not intervened. A number of the stories saw later American publication: John Beynon's "Beyond the Screen" reappeared in the October 1939 *Amazing Stories** as "Judson's Annihilator"; Damon Knight reprinted Halliday Sutherland's "Valley of Doom" in the February 1951 *Worlds Beyond**; but most surprising of all was Eric Frank Russell's "Vampire from the Void" from the second issue, which resurfaced in the October 1972 *Fantastic** billed as "an exciting new novelet." When the story's origin was first revealed to editor Ted White, he replied: "Although it is possible that Russell reused the ideas in that story (I've not read it), I doubt very much that it was the same story we published under that title."[7] However, two issues later White had to concede that it was the same story, although Russell's agent, Scott Meredith, had sold it as new. This goes to show that Russell's fiction stood well the test of time and that *Fantasy* had some worthy stories in its three issues.

A fourth issue was prepared with the promise of a quarterly schedule when the war intervened. Stanhope Sprigg, a qualified pilot, enlisted in the RAF; with his influence gone and the threat of paper rationing looming, Newnes cut back on its magazines, and *Fantasy* was one of the first to go.

Fantasy's lifetime was too short to make a value judgment on its position in SF, but there is no denying that Sprigg had considerable editorial acumen and that *Fantasy* would no doubt have developed into a major magazine.

Notes

1. T. Stanhope Sprigg, private communication.
2. Walter Gillings, "Year of the Blast-off," *Vision of Tomorrow*, March 1970, p. 20.
3. Ibid., p. 22.
4. Sprigg, private communication.
5. Sprigg, "Fantasy" [editorial], *Fantasy*, No.1 (1938): 91.
6. Ibid.
7. Ted White, *Fantastic*, July 1973, in response to letter from John Carl, p. 127. See also *Fantastic*, November 1973, response to letter from Richard Brandt, p. 86.

Information Sources

BIBLIOGRAPHY:
Gillings, Walter. "Someting Old, Something New." *Vision of Tomorrow*, April 1970.
———. "Year of the Blast-Off." *Vision of Tomorrow*, March 1970.
Nicholls. *Encyclopedia*.
Tuck.
INDEX SOURCES: IBSF; ISFM; SFM; Tuck.

REPRINT SOURCES: None known.

LOCATION SOURCES: Beloit College Library; Brigham Young University Library; Chicago Public Library; Dallas Public Library; Denver Public Library; East Carolina University Library; Eastern New Mexico Library; Grand Valley State College Library; Harvard University Library; Idaho State University Library; Indiana State University Library; Michigan State University Library; Milton College Library; McGill University Library; New York Public Library; Northern Illinois University Library; Pennsylvania State University Library; Red Wing, Minnesota, Public Library; San Diego Public Library; San Diego State University Library; San Francisco Public Library; Southern Illinois University Library; S.U.N.Y.-Albany Library; Syracuse University Public Library; Temple University Library; Texas A&M University Library; Toronto Public Library; Tulane University Library; University of Arizona Library; University of California-Riverside Library; University of Kansas Library; University of Maryland-Baltimore County Library; University of Missouri-St. Louis Library; University of Southern California Library; University of Texas-Austin Library; University of Washington Library.

Publication History

TITLE: *Fantasy* (subtitled "Thrilling Science Fiction").

VOLUME DATA: No volume numbering; undated other than for year. Number 1, [July] 1938–Number 3, [June] 1939. Irregular. Total run: 3 issues.

PUBLISHER: George Newnes, Ltd., London.

EDITOR: T. Stanhope Sprigg.

FORMAT: Pulp, 128pp.

PRICE: 1/-.

Mike Ashley

FANTASY (1946–1947)

The second publication with this title was Britain's first digest-size SF magazine. Like its namesake, this one also saw only three issues, but apart from such contributors as Eric Frank Russell and John Russell Fearn, the two publications had nothing else in common.

Fantasy was edited by Walter Gillings, whose experience with *Tales of Wonder** as well as his vocation as a reporter showed in the professionalism of the magazine. It was more than competently edited, with something for everyone: new stories, the occasional reprint, speculative articles (these by Gillings in various guises) and a letter column, plus cameo illustrations.

In his request for submissions Gillings asked that writers avoid hackneyed themes and that they concentrate on how technological advances might affect individuals rather than whole populations. Gillings' initial request produced little response, but gradually a stockpile of manuscripts accumulated, enough, in fact, for nine issues, when the first issue appeared in December 1946.

The most popular story in the first issue—which led with Fearn's "Last Conflict" and reprinted Stanley G. Weinbaum's "The Worlds of If"—was

Arthur C. Clarke's "Technical Error." This was one of a number of stories Gillings had bought from Clarke a few years earlier, but the continuing paper restrictions delayed the appearance of *Fantasy* to the extent that Gillings returned some of the manuscripts and suggested Clarke try the American field. Thus, "Loophole" and the immortal "Rescue Party" heralded Clarke's fictional debut in *Astounding (Analog Science Fiction*)* instead of *Fantasy*.

Clarke was present, pseudonymously, in all three issues of *Fantasy*. Eric Frank Russell's only appearance was in the second issue, in April 1947, with "Relic," a memorable story of an ancient robot that returns to Earth to fulfill its destiny. Other contributors included Leslie V. Heald, P. E. Cleator, E. R. James and Norman C. Pallant, all with competent stories for the time.

Gillings reported that only 6,000 copies were printed and that these were a sellout. But the paper restrictions again took their toll, and after the third issue in August 1947, both the publisher and Gillings decided it was unprofitable to continue the magazine in the prevailing circumstances. When the time was more opportune Gillings revived it in much the same format as *Science-Fantasy (Science Fantasy*, 1950–1966*).

Information Sources

BIBLIOGRAPHY:
Gillings, Walter. "Pages in Waiting." *Vision of Tomorrow*, August 1970.
Nicholls, *Encyclopedia*.
Tuck.
INDEX SOURCES: Gillings, Walter, "Pages in Waiting," *Vision of Tomorrow*, August 1970; IBSF; ISFM; SFM; Tuck.
REPRINT SOURCES: None Known.
LOCATION SOURCES: M.I.T. Science Fiction Library; Pennsylvania State University Library.

Publication History

TITLE: *Fantasy* (subtitled "The Magazine of Science Fiction").
VOLUME DATA: Volume 1, Number 1, December 1946–Volume 1, Number 3, August 1947. Irregular. Total run: 3 issues.
PUBLISHER: Temple Bar Publishing Co., London.
EDITOR: Walter H. Gillings.
FORMAT: Digest (saddle-stapled), 96pp.
PRICE: 1/-.

Mike Ashley

FANTASY AND SCIENCE FICTION

See THE MAGAZINE OF FANTASY AND SCIENCE FICTION.

FANTASY AND TERROR

See THE LITERARY MAGAZINE OF FANTASY AND TERROR.

FANTASY BOOK (1947–1951)

Fantasy Book, edited by William Crawford and his wife under the pseudonym Garret Ford, appeared at irregular intervals from July 1947 to January 1951. There were eight issues in all, numbered but not dated, six in Volume 1 and two in Volume 2. *FB* was published in two editions, regular ($2.50 subscription price) and deluxe ($3.00), the latter with a higher grade of paper and different, though not always superior, cover illustrations.

In 1934 William Crawford, an active science fiction fan, edited and printed two semi-professional magazines, *Unusual Stories* and *Marvel Tales*.* These magazines failed because he was unable to secure newsstand distribution. From late 1935 to January 1937 Crawford printed *Fantasy Magazine*, taking that duty over from Conrad H. Ruppert. After the war, Crawford founded Fantasy Publishing Company, Inc. (FPCI), in Los Angeles, which published *FB* and, later, *Spaceway*.* Besides FPCI (usually referred to by the acronym), Crawford founded the Griffin Publishing Company. FPCI and Griffin were among the earliest companies to publish science fiction in book form, including anthologies of stories taken from *FB*.

The first *FB*, only forty-two pages long, was beset by difficulties with distribution. In "Editor's Notebook," Crawford explains:

> Prior to the publication of FB #1 the publishers had contacted a national distributor to handle the magazine. By the time the first issue was printed the distributor (the only national distributor on the West Coast) had suffered a business failure, and we were caught with a large supply of Fantasy Book #1.

Problems with distribution, Crawford goes on to explain, had continued to plague *FB*: "Since then we have developed some new outlets, but, as yet, only a fraction of what is needed to make FB into a major publication" (Vol. 1, No. 4). Long delays between issues resulted.

With the third issue, the format of *FB* changed from bedsheet to digest. Crawford explains: "The change in size may be inconvenient to some collectors—but it has become a question of a small FB or *no* FB at all." Critics of science fiction have, with some justification, found fault with both the artwork and the physical appearance of *FB*; and Crawford several times apologized editorially for both, blaming financial constraints. After discussing the change in *FB*'s size, Crawford goes on: "Since the illustrations used in FANTASY BOOK are rather expensive, and have received much unfavorable criticism, we shall cut down on the number per issue and try to present more attractive covers.'' In the last four issues of *FB*, interior illustrations were abandoned altogether.

While *FB*'s covers and illustrations tend to be amateurish, the best have the appealing quality of folk art. Indeed, in part because of its refreshing lack of slickness, the most attractive issue artistically is the first. Its cover, by ''Milo,'' illustrates ''The People of the Crater,'' the first published story of Alice Mary Norton (Andre Norton), printed under the pseudonym Andrew North. Limited to the colors pink and blue, the cover depicts Tharla, the captive princess, and her lizardlike companion. Although Milo depicts Tharla in stereotypical comic-book fashion with flowing hair and a revealing leotard, the cover has an engaging naïveté. ''People of the Crater'' also inspired pleasing interior drawings by Charles McNutt and R. K. Murphy. McNutt's illustrations for this issue are strikingly original. His best, for Bryce Walton's ''Strange Alliance,'' depicts the werewolf professor, facing a rifle pointed at him from a house. McNutt was soon to change his name and become internationally famous as writer Charles Beaumont.

The next two issues of *FB* are dominated by Lora Crozetti, whose illustrations, with one exception, are crude and uninspired. Crozetti's black and yellow cover for the deluxe, book paper edition of *FB*'s second issue purportedly illustrates fiction by Basil Wells and A. E. van Vogt, though the images are irrelevant to those stories. According to Michael Ashley, however, the cheaper newsstand edition carried a far better cover by Roy Hunt. Only one interior illustration in the second issue is noteworthy. For ''Little Johnny,'' by O. G. Estes, Jr., William F. Tanner evokes with a few details the courtyard of a medieval inn and a glowing, insectlike creature at the feet of a man.

The third issue of *FB* has another undistinguished Crozetti cover, illustrating ''Gifts of Asti,'' a second story by Andrew North (Andre Norton). Oddly, Norton's two early works, Edgar Rice Burroughs pastiches written in an oppressively lush, pseudo-archaic style, inspired *FB*'s best illustrations. The one illustration in which Crozetti's crudeness and naïveté appear charming rather than merely inept is her interior drawing of Norton's temple virgin in ''Gifts of Asti,'' disguised in a lizard suit, fleeing barbarian invaders.

One *FB* cover is truly outstanding. Depicting a scene from Cordwainer Smith's celebrated story, ''Scanners Live in Vain,'' the cover of the sixth issue is by Jack Gaughan, who was to win the Hugo awards for the best fan artist and best professional artist in 1967. His hand on a button in his chest, an angular Scanner (a human partially mechanized so as to withstand space exploration) stands surrounded by a tense crowd of other Scanners.

Besides fiction, *FB* published a column of innocuous book reviews called, first, ''The Fantasy Book Shelf'' (Vol. 1, No. 2) and, subsequently, ''The Book Shelf.'' In the third issue a poetry column, ''Songs of the Spaceways,'' was initiated, with Lilith Lorraine as poetry editor. *FB*'s poetry is uniformly serious and moral, concerned with man's warlike nature, greed and destruction of natural resources. A characteristic example is Enola Chamberlain's ''Recognition.''

In an "Introduction by the Editors" in the first issue, Crawford suggests that he is flexible about the point of view expressed in *FB*, requiring only that stories be thought-provoking:

> This is a liberal magazine—with no "thought-police" guiding its destiny. Our main requirements [*sic*] for stories is that they should be different— capable of stimulating a new line of thought. . . . A story may have almost any twist . . . and if it's good . . . well, that's the very thing we want. We believe that you will welcome the chance to get your reading out of the rut of the commonplace. . . . Naturally the fantasy, science-fiction or weird motif must be predominant.

Although only a handful of exceptional stories appears in the eight issues of *FB*, its fiction, like its art, is earnest and unhackneyed.

Besides Andre Norton, whose stories have been discussed in connection with their illustrations, the following are the writers best known today to contribute to *FB*: Forrest J Ackerman, Henry Hasse, Stanton A. Coblentz, L. Ron Hubbard, A. E. van Vogt, Isaac Asimov and Frederik Pohl. With a total of ten stories, Basil Wells appeared more frequently than any other writer. Festus Pragnell, John Taine and Murray Leinster contributed serials. Stories by Robert Bloch, Edsel Ford and Cordwainer Smith (Paul Myron Anthony Linebarger) deserve special recognition.

Two stories by the California fan, editor and collector Forrest J Ackerman appeared in *FB*: "Micro-Man" (Vol. 1, No. 1), under the pseudonym Weaver Wright; and "Dwellers in the Dust" (Vol. 1, No. 4). In the former, the insensitive though unmalicious narrator finds an almost microscopic man, whom he manipulates with stamp tweezers and then unwittingly crushes with a typewriter key. Though annoyingly loaded down with puns and word play, "Dwellers in the Dust" is more ambitious, attempting to demonstrate that all past times exist within any given moment. For no clear motive, George takes the narrator in his time machine into the last moments before the narrator's sister, Lori, is killed in a theatre fire, and then into the future to see the villainous Krebs, who had wronged Lori, killed hideously in biological warfare. Both stories expose the reader to unpleasant events with no clear justification.

Another California writer, Henry Hasse, contributed two stories, both depending for their effect on a reversal in the reader's expectations about humans and aliens. In "Walls of Acid" (Vol. 1, No. 1), the plucky Martians, who have won the reader's sympathy, turn out to be ants, and their loathsome enemy human beings. In "The Eyes" (Vol. 2, No. 2), a Martian stranded on Earth turns out to be a pregnant female. Stanton A. Coblentz's two stories, "Flight through Tomorrow" (Vol. 1, No. 1) and "The Universe Ranger" (Vol. 1, No. 6), both turn on scientific discoveries that enable man to move outside his physical body, transcending the limitations of time and space. L. Ron Hubbard, later the founder of Dianetics and scientology, contributed "Battle of the Wizards" (Vol.

1, No. 5), a smugly procolonialist story. In order to gain mining rights on a planet inhabited by a tribe of primitive humanoids, Angus McBane proves that science is stronger than magic. By substituting a robot for himself, he wins a contest with the local magician.

Stories by A. E. van Vogt, a characteristic mixture of flapdoodle and panache, appear in every one of *FB*'s first three issues. In "The Cataaaaa" (Vol. 1, No. 1), a professor receives a series of messages instructing him to come to a circus freak show to see "The Cat," exhibited by a high school acquaintance, Silkey Travis. The Cat explains that he is an alien, studying the races on various planets. When the professor tells him that religion is man's most characteristic quality, the Cat argues that it is self-dramatization ("Religion is self-dramatization before a god") and chooses the showman, Silkey, as his souvenir from Earth. Though its plot makes no sense whatsoever, "The Ship of Darkness" (Vol. 1, No. 2) has evocative, dreamlike imagery. A man takes a time machine 30,000 years into the past, where he finds a dark space platform on which naked people with burning eyes sit with no protection from the vacuum of space. He kisses a woman and as punishment is painlessly dissected, his organs cut out and replaced. Just before a battle with another space platform, he takes the woman in his space ship/time machine to Earth, where they will be the Adam and Eve of a new race. Van Vogt's third story, "The Great Judge" (Vol. 1, No. 3), concerns Douglas Aird, a scientist living under a cruel dictatorship. Douglas has just succeeded in transferring the nervous impulses of a chicken into the nervous system of a dog. Sentenced to die for criticizing the Great Judge, Douglas makes a series of exchanges of his own personality and body with the personalities and bodies of others. Eventually, the Great Judge is executed as Douglas, and Douglas in the Judge's body plans a more democratic government. In this very short story, the reversal of situation is handled adeptly.

"The Little Man on the Subway" by Isaac Asimov and James MacCreigh (pseudonym for Frederik Pohl) is the lead story in *FB*'s sixth issue. In the first volume of his autobiography, Asimov mentions that he and Pohl had collaborated on the story ten years before its appearance in *FB* and that Asimov had received $10 in payment. Depending for its humor on the flippant treatment of established religion and on the stereotyped Irish mannerisms of the main character, "The Little Man" concerns a subway conductor, Patrick Cullen, whose train is commandeered by a "god," Mr. Crumley. Crumley takes Cullen to one of his "factories" for disciples, where the Irishman is caught in a revolt, the discontented disciples having created a rival god to overthrow Crumley.

Under his own name and the pseudonym Gene Ellerman, Basil Wells contributed stories to every issue of *FB* except the first and third. Wells' contributions include both science fiction and weird tales. "Wall of Darkness" and "Prison Rats" are the least pretentious and therefore the best, lacking the sentimental relationships between men and women and the heavy-handed moral intent that mar other contributions. In "Wall of Darkness," the narrator buys a house that had belonged to a descendant of New England witches. When he tears the heavy covering off a wall, a black cloud begins to seep through, eating away his clothing and burning his flesh. Having closed the hole in time, the narrator vows that "mankind and the darkness must never meet again." In "Prison Rats," a seven-foot tall werewolf, imprisoned for murder, decides to escape by turning into a rat. He tarries to bite the guards, conscious that there are other rats with him doing the same thing. When he returns to human form, he is only five feet tall. The reader learns what happened to the rest of him when the scene shifts to the prison. A rat killed by a guard has been transformed into a tiny man. Wells' ten *FB* stories have been reprinted in *Planets of Adventure* (Los Angeles: FPCI, 1949).

FB published three serials. The first two, by the British writers Festus Pragnell and John Taine (Eric Temple Bell), respectively, are among the weakest stories *FB* published. Pragnell's "The Machine-God Laughs" (Vol. 1, Nos. 2–4) concerns a conflict between two mechanical super brains, invented by the United States and China in the midst of a war. The Asian brain, gruesomely constructed from the disembodied brains of Chinese intellectuals, is no match for the American brain, Frank (short for Frankenstein). Taine's "Black Goldfish" (Vol. 1, Nos. 4 and 5) fails largely because the villainous characters are grossly stereotyped. Klaup, an idiotic glutton, has underhandedly gained control of the Vesuvius Chemical and Drug Laboratories, previously owned by Jones. Jones has invented—and Klaup taken credit for—vitamins that turn people, physically and intellectually, into supermen. Traitorously, Klaup sells to a Latin American Communist nation, at war with the United States, what he believes to be the supervitamins. Actually, Jones has made sure that the Americans receive his invention, the enemy having been given sleeping pills.

In the third serial, "Journey to Barkut" by Murray Leinster (Vol. 2, Nos. 1 and 2), Tony Gregg finds a coin from an unknown Arab country, Barkut. A Syrian acquaintance tells him that the coin must be from a parallel world and that objects that stray into the wrong world are drawn back. Using flips of the coin to guide his life, Tony eventually arrives in an Arabian Nights land, inhabited by djinns and beautiful slave girls. Left incomplete when *FB* ceased publication, the story appeared in full in *Startling Stories** (January 1952) and in book form as *Gateway to Elsewhere* (Ace, 1954).

Three stories in *FB* should be singled out for special mention: Robert Bloch's "Black Lotus" (Vol. 1, No. 1), Edsel Ford's "Timeless" (Vol. 1, No. 5) and, of course, Cordwainer Smith's "Scanners Live in Vain." "Black Lotus," one of the few humorous pieces in *FB*, is a witty parody of Poe and H. P. Lovecraft. Genghir the Dreamer, a sultan devoted to experimenting with drugs, seeks the ultimate high from the Black Lotus. Bloch's word compounds and coinages ("benightmared brain," "enmausoleumed upon a slab," "Genii-beset progress") spoof Lovecraft; and his descriptions of Genghir's drug-induced visions borrow from Poe's "The Colloquy of Monos and Una" and "The Facts in the Case of M. Valdemar." Capturing the stylistic extravagances of both writers, "Black Lotus" delights through its pseudo-portentousness.

"Timeless" was contributed by Edsel Ford, an Arkansas regional poet not related to the automobile magnate. (Ford also contributed a poem, "Secret of the Sun," to Vol. 1, No. 4.) With a vague sense of wrongness, Foster leaves work early. He stops at Joe's Place for a doughnut, but finds the owner and customers unsmiling and remote. Waiting for a bus, Foster notices that the street is deserted and then realizes that he is unable to move. Time has stopped for him: "Because of the worry of his work and the burdens of life, he had deliberately forced himself out of the time and space of the ordinary mind." While Foster's recovery is too abrupt, his growing unease and alienation from his environment are superbly rendered.

If *FB* is remembered today, it is for having published Cordwainer Smith's "Scanners Live in Vain," the appearance of which, as Asimov states, made its author into "what was almost a cult object." The senses of the Scanners have been surgically blocked and their bodily functions mechanized so that they can govern spaceships in an environment deadly to ordinary mortals. Having achieved what the seventeenth-century religious poets longed for, the freeing of the spirit from the pains and demands of the body, the Scanners are revered by society. Yet, their renunciation of the life of the senses has been such a terrible price to pay that when they learn that Adam Stone has invented a means by which human beings can go into space without dying of the "Great Pain," the Scanners vote to kill him. A Scanner, Martel, saves the life of Smith, who has also invented a method by which the Scanners may be returned to their normal human state. The ritualized lives of the Scanners and their quaint argot (space is "the Up-and-Out") give the story a mystical quality.

The fiction in *FB* is still appealing today. *FB*'s stories are conspicuously lacking in triteness, cynicism, sadism and sexual exploitation. As the title might suggest, however, *FB*'s contributors treat science fiction as a subspecies of fantasy. Unconcerned with scientific credibility, they employ science fictional elements to conjure up exotic panoramas or to place the commonplaces of human nature in an alien perspective.

Information Sources

BIBLIOGRAPHY:
Nicholls, *Encyclopedia*.
Tuck.
INDEX SOURCES: ISFM; ISPF-2; MIT; SFM; Tuck.
REPRINT SOURCES:
   Derivative Anthologies: Both edited by William L. Crawford, the first anonymously, the second as Garret Ford. *The Machine-God Laughs* (Los Angeles: Griffin, 1949) contains the Pragnell title story and two short pieces; *Science and Sorcery* (Los Angeles: FPCI, 1953) contains fifteen stories, nine originating in *FB*.
LOCATION SOURCES: California State University–Fullerton, Special Collections (not available through interlibrary loan, but will photocopy articles upon request; Vol. 1, Nos. 3–6; Vol. 2, No. 1); Eastern New Mexico University, Golden Library (not available through ILL); Indiana University, Lilly Library (not available through

ILL, but will usually microfilm a work or photocopy short portions; Vol. 1, No. 1); Massachusetts Institute of Technology, MIT Science Fiction Society (not available through ILL); Ohio State University Libraries, Division of Special Collections (Vol. 1, No. 3–Vol. 2, No. 2); Pennsylvania State University Libraries, Special Collections (Vol. 1, No. 3–Vol. 2, No. 2); Queen's University, Special Collections (no ILL or microfilm; Vol. 1, No. 1); San Francisco Academy of Comic Art, Science Fiction Room (Vol. 1, Nos. 3, 5, 6); San Francisco Public Library, Literature Department (not available through ILL); Syracuse University, George Arents Research Library, Rare Books Division (Vol. 1, No. 1–Vol. 2, No. 1); Temple University, Paley Library, Paskow Science Fiction Collection (not available through ILL; Vol. 1, Nos. 1–2); Texas A&M University Library, Special Collections; Toronto Public Libraries, Spaced Out Library (not available through ILL; Vol. 1, Nos. 1–5); University of California–Los Angeles, Special Collections (a microfilm may be produced, the negative to remain at UCLA and the patron to pay for negative and print); University of California–Riverside, Special Collections; University of Georgia Libraries, Periodicals Department; University of Kansas, Spencer Research Library (Vol. 1, Nos. 1, 3, 5, 6); University of Kentucky, Special Collections (no ILL, but magazines may be microfilmed; Vol. 1, Nos. 1, 4); University of Maryland Baltimore County Library, Special Collections (no ILL, but sections of magazines may be photocopied).

Publication History

TITLE: *Fantasy Book*.

VOLUME DATA: Volume 1, Number 1, [July] 1947–Volume 2, Number 2, [January] 1951. Six issues to Volume 1. Irregular. Issues dated by year only. Brad Day lists intervening issues as appearing as follows: 2: Feb 48; 3: Jul 48; 4: Nov 48; 5: Jul 49; 6: Jan 50; 7: Oct 50. Total run: 8 issues.

PUBLISHER: Fantasy Publishing Co. Inc., Los Angeles, California.

EDITOR: "Garret Ford"—William and Margaret Crawford, with editorial assistance by Forrest J Ackerman. See Ackerman's answer to the question "Who is Garret Ford?" in *Lore*, Vol. 1, No. 5 (April 1966): 55–56.

FORMAT: Bibliographically confusing. Variant editions exist with up to three editions of each issue: subscriber's, collector's and newsstand, identified by quality of paper and slight variant in dimensions. In general: first two issues, Bedsheet, remaining issues Digest, although issues 6 Small Digest. Page runs: 1, 2: 44pp.; 3, 4: 68pp.; 5: 84pp.; 6: 112pp.; 7, 8: 82pp.

PRICE: Collector's editions 35¢; otherwise 25¢.

Wendy Bousfield

FANTASY BOOK (1981-)

Plans for a new *Fantasy Book*, in no way related to the earlier publication of the same name, but curiously also emanating from California, began in February 1981; by July the first issue was on sale (dated October). The intention was to fill a noticeable void in the market for a magazine devoted entirely to fantasy. Hitherto only *Fantastic** had filled that bill during most of the 1970s, but few all-fantasy magazines had succeeded since *Unknown*.* *FB* set out to cover the entire range of fantasy. "The horizon is limitless," wrote publisher Dennis Mallonee in the first issue. "High fantasy, light fantasy, heroic fantasy, horror stories, mystery stories, fairy stories, legends, fables, poems—all this and more will be grist for the *Fantasy Book* mill." Such a menu could adequately describe *The Magazine of Fantasy and Science Fiction*,* but it is true that that magazine does have a higher quota of science fiction, while *Fantasy Book*'s first issue went out of its way to emulate the old *Unknown*. This was especially evident from the cover by Cathy Hill, much in the style of Tim Kirk, portraying a showman shaking hands with a dragon in a sweatshirt. While later covers have been more serious in content, the first cover, which was also used in *FB*'s subscription campaign, evidently portrayed the image that the magazine wished to convey.

By the third issue, however, the editor, Nick Smith, was emphasizing that *FB* was not limiting itself to any single niche of fantasy, but was trying to appeal to all devotees from sword and sorcery to Lovecraftian horror. That third issue, for example, contained "The Return of Mad Santa" by Al Sarrantonio, which would not have been out of place in *Unknown*. It takes as its premise the simple fact that Santa Claus exists but poses the problem of what happens if once every 800 years his good side is overwhelmed by the cumulative impact of his evil side. "Mr. Hancock's Last Game" by David Kaufman is more in line with the type of story Horace Gold favored in *Beyond Fantasy Fiction** and shows the lengths to which some may go to win at chess. "A Shade of Jealousy" by C. Bruce Hunter would not have been out of place in the McIlwraith *Weird Tales** with its subtitle portrayal of revenge from the grave, while "The Summer's Garden" by Eric G. Iverson is a straightforward and rather timeless fable that could have come straight from the pages of a literary magazine of the 1890s complete with illustrations by Laurence Housman. Even science fiction was present in a poignant tale of the future as seen from the eyes of the world's oldest man, "Milk into Brandy" by Lil and Kris Neville.

FB has continued to present a sensible cross-section of most realms of fantasy and SF, and its staff are keenly aware of the pitfalls of trying to please all of the people all of the time. *FB* even carries a special classic reprint section where neglected fantasies can be resurrected for a new generation. As a large-format magazine it is taking advantage of the illustrative possibilities, and though some of the sketches and drawings have lacked professional polish, the covers have, for the most part, been particularly attractive, and interiors by Lynne Goodwin, Scott Hill and, of course, Stephen Fabian have greatly enhanced the overall feeling of the magazine. As of 1984 *FB* has become sufficiently established to incorporate a serial among its offerings.

FB has not gone for major distribution, perhaps wisely, but has taken the route originally followed by *Galileo** and *Unearth** in selling predominantly through the specialist dealers and by establishing a solid subscription list. Sales of the first issue were just over 4,000 against a print run of 10,000. Virtually all of that 4,000 was sold through dealers, and a 40 percent sales figure compares extremely favorably with *The Magazine of Fantasy and Science Fiction*, which sells about 18 percent of its print run through dealers, and *Isaac Asimov's Science Fiction Magazine*,* where less than 14 percent of its print run is shifted through newsstands. Both of these magazines have a very healthy list of subscribers, and this is the path that *FB* should follow in order to establish itself as a magazine with a future.

Information Sources

INDEX SOURCES: ISPF; ISPF-2; MT; NESFA-VIII; NESFA-IX; SFM.
REPRINT SOURCES: None known.
LOCATION SOURCES: M.I.T. Science Fiction Library.

Publication History

TITLE: *Fantasy Book*.
VOLUME DATA: Volume 1, Number 1, October 1981–. Bi-monthly for first three
    issues, quarterly from Number 4, May 1982.
PUBLISHER: Fantasy Book Enterprises, Long Beach, California.
EDITORS: Nick Smith, assisted on first two issues by Gavin Claypool as Consulting
    Editor, both under the direction of Dennis Mallonee as Publisher/Executive Editor.
FORMAT: Slick (saddle-stapled), 80pp.
PRICE: $3.00, changed to $3.95 as of December 1984.

Mike Ashley

FANTASY FICTION (1950)

This short-lived magazine was an early attempt to translate the successful format of the confession magazine from pulp to digest. It was an experiment that failed, as the future of the confession magazine lay in the glossy slick market that was rapidly acquiring impetus in the years after World War II.

Most of the stories published in *Fantasy Fiction*'s two 1950 issues were reprints with the titles changed for graphic effect. Thus, Theodore Roscoe's adventure story of biblical retribution, "On Account of a Woman," became "She Said 'Take Me If You Dare,' " while Irvin S. Cobb's superior story of the mystery of Lake Reelfoot—"Fishhead"—became "Blood-Brother of the Swamp Cats." The blurbs were equally lurid. The second issue contained supposed flying saucer revelations, the cover boasting: "Flying Saucer Secrets Blabbed by Mad Pilot."

Fantasy Fiction thus aimed itself at an audience more attuned to real-life confessions than to quality fantasy stories, and although the majority of the stories selected for reprinting were above average, they were delivered to the wrong readership. True fantasy fiction fans would have steered clear of covers displaying titles like "Her Lover Was Jungle Gold" (itself a mistitling of "Her Love Was Jungle Gold," a retitling of Theodore Roscoe's "Leopard Teeth") or "The Strange Loves of Beatrice Jervan" (a retitling of Max Brand's classic tale of reincarnation, "John Ovington Returns").

The first issue of *Fantasy Fiction* appeared in May 1950 on a quarterly schedule. The second issue, however, did not appear until November 1950 and was entitled *Fantasy Stories*. Both covers were the work of Bill Stone, a photographer who had also provided the first cover for *The Magazine of Fantasy and Science Fiction*,* and it may be that *Fantasy Fiction* was attempting to emulate that magazine, in format if not in content.

The magazine clearly intended to gravitate toward "true" stories. It requested readers to submit accounts of their true experiences and asked for help in finding the best haunted house in America for a film company. This may have been liaised through Forrest J Ackerman, who was present in the second issue with a quiz, "College of Scientifictional Knowledge."

The reprints came predominantly from issues of *Argosy** in the 1930s and are of the quality expected of that magazine, but the new stories were obviously written in response to an editorial policy of sensationalism and are of no significance.

Information Sources

BIBLIOGRAPHY:
Nicholls. *Encyclopedia.*
Tuck.
INDEX SOURCES: ASFI; ISFM; MT; SFM; Tuck.
REPRINT SOURCES: None known.
LOCATION SOURCES: M.I.T. Science Fiction Library; Pennsylvania State University
    Library.

Publication History

TITLE: First issue: *Fantasy Fiction*; second issue: *Fantasy Stories*.
VOLUME DATA: Volume 1, Number 1, May 1950–Volume 1, Number 2, November
    1950. Intended schedule, quarterly. Total run: 2 issues.
PUBLISHER: Magabook, Inc., Chicago. Editorial offices in New York (addresses differ
    for the two issues).
EDITOR: Curtis Mitchell (editor and publisher).
FORMAT: Digest, 128pp.
PRICE: 25¢.

Mike Ashley

FANTASY FICTION (1953)

See FANTASY MAGAZINE.

FANTASY MAGAZINE

Fantasy Magazine (later retitled *Fantasy Fiction*) was one of those ephemeral magazines that flowered and died during the boom period of the early fifties when more than a dozen science fiction and fantasy publications appeared for a few issues and then vanished. The four digest-size issues of *Fantasy Magazine* that appeared bi-monthly between March and November 1953 combined attractive appearance (striking Hannes Bok covers and interior illustrations by Ed Emsh, Paul Orban, Kelly Freas, Roy Krenkel and others) with above-average fiction by Poul Anderson, Algis Budrys, L. Sprague de Camp, Philip K. Dick, Robert E. Howard, Fletcher Pratt, John Wyndham and others. Responsibility for the high quality of the package—and certainly for the fiction—lies with Lester del Rey, who served as founding editor of *FM*, as he did (sometimes pseudonymously) for the other magazines in John Raymond's Future Publications group—*Space Science Fiction,** *Science Fiction Adventures** and *Rocket Stories.** Del Rey's tastes in fantasy ran to "modern" rather than "Gothic," with an admixture of humor and science fictional logic, as his editorials show:

> But there's no fun in rehashing all those old stories [in the Gothic tradition], nor even in simply lampooning them in an attempt to be funny. They have to be examined logically, and then put into a present-day setting in some way that makes them fit.
>
> . . .
>
> Our comedy of terrors requires a light touch—but one which goes into more logical extrapolation of the past into the present than might be thought. The old Gothic horror story is out—because it is dull. But given some good reasons and a few twists to make it consistent with present-day facts . . . well, why not?[1]
>
> . . .
>
> Fantasy, as we've been trying to point out, is a game of logic. Like fairy chess, it should be a game of logic where the basic rules are flexible, filled with some delightful surprise to twist the mind out of the rut, and must be played with consummate skill to be at all interesting. It requires a healthy, flexible mind to write or enjoy it.[2]

Thus, *Fantasy Fiction* belongs with Campbell's *Unknown Worlds (Unknown**), H. L. Gold's *Beyond Science Fiction** and del Rey's own later *Worlds of Fantasy** rather than with the eldritch terrors of *Weird Tales** or the primitive thrills of the horror pulps. Having promised readers stories that would be recognizable as fantasy but without repetitions of clichés and dead traditions, del Rey delivered a wide range: outright sword and sorcery in "The Black Stranger" and "The Frost Giant's Daughter," a pair of posthumous Robert E. Howard stories edited by L. Sprague de Camp; tales of alternate worlds where magic works in Bruce Elliott's " 'So Sweet as Magic . . . ' " and Katherine MacLean and Harry Harrison's "Web of the Worlds"; situation-comedy humor in Robert Sheckley's "The Demons" and Poul Anderson's "Ashtaru the Terrible." The largest group of stories, however, employs modernized, frequently humorous or ironic versions of supernatural or mythological themes along the lines described in the editorials. In Frank Robinson's "The Night Shift," a vampire tries to muscle in on the werewolves who control Chicago; in Stephen Arr.'s "The Apprentice Sorcerer," technological resourcefulness helps the hero defeat a "class A champion sorcerer" in a magical duel; in Fletcher Pratt's "Capital Expenditure," the cost-benefit economies of magic are revealed. Dragons, a Babylonian god, a griffin, Arachne and Leda's swan also make appearances in suitably renewed circumstances.

Despite its relatively strong fiction, *Fantasy Magazine*, like *Unknown Worlds* before it and *Beyond* and *Worlds of Fantasy* after it, stopped publication long before its potential was exhausted. The reason, in this case at least, is not that fantasy was not selling; del Rey has reported that all the Raymond magazines showed a profit.[3] Michael Ashley suggests that it was the publisher's attitude ("aggravating wall of ignorance" is the phrase he uses to describe the general situation) rather than lack of sales or quality.[4] After difficulties with the publisher over policy and payments to authors, del Rey resigned from Future Publications.[5] The fourth issue of *Fantasy Fiction*, assembled by del Rey, carried the ad hoc house pseudonym Cameron Hall;[6] a fifth issue was put together by Fletcher Pratt but never saw print.[7] Fifteen years later del Rey edited two and a half issues of another short-lived fantasy magazine, *Worlds of Fantasy*, and in 1976 became fantasy editor of Del Rey Books, where he has been responsible for a number of very successful books.

Notes

1. Lester del Rey, "A Comedy of Terrors," *Fantasy Fiction*, June 1953, pp. 4, 5.

2. Lester del Rey, "Non Multa, sed Multum," *Fantasy Fiction*, November 1952, p. 4.

3. In Michael Ashley, ed., *The History of the Science Fiction Magazine* (Chicago: Contemporary Books, 1977), III: 81.

4. Ibid., p. 82.

5. Del Rey in ibid., p. 81.

6. Del Rey, personal communication, June 1979.

7. Ashley, p. 81.

Information Sources

BIBLIOGRAPHY:
Ashley, Michael. "The Unsuccessful Successor." *Dark Horizons* 10 (Autumn/Winter 1974).
Nicholls. *Encyclopedia*.
Tuck.
INDEX SOURCES: Ashley, Michael, "The Unsuccessful Successor," *Dark Horizons* 10 (Autumn/Winter 1974); MIT; MT; SFM; Tuck.

REPRINT SOURCES: None known.
LOCATION SOURCES: M.I.T. Science Fiction Library.

Publication History

TITLE: *Fantasy Magazine*, first issue (February/March 1953); thereafter *Fantasy Fiction* (June–November 1953).
VOLUME DATA: Volume 1, Number 1, February/March 1953–Volume 1, Number 4, November 1953. Intended schedule bi-monthly, but intervening issues June and August. Total run: 4 issues.
PUBLISHER: Future Publications, Fifth Ave., New York.
EDITOR: Lester del Rey (last issue under alias Cameron Hall).
FORMAT: Digest, 160pp.
PRICE: 35¢.

Russell Letson

FANTASY STORIES

See FANTASY FICTION (1950).

FANTASY TALES

Fantasy Tales was the brainchild of two of the stalwarts of British fantasy fandom. The elder partner, Dave Sutton, had previously edited several horror anthologies as well as the fanzine *Shadow* and had been a founder, member and linchpin of the British Fantasy Society (BFS), editing many of its publications. Steve Jones had arrived on the scene in the early 1970s and became the prime motivating force behind the reorganization and redirection of the BFS in the mid seventies. Together they prepared *Fantasy Tales*, ''a Magazine of the Weird and Unusual,'' with the avowed aim ''to recreate the look and entertainment value of the pulp magazines of the 1930s and '40s, publishing fiction by established writers and newcomers to the horror/fantasy/weird genre.''

Fantasy Tales' debut in the summer of 1977 was spectacular, to say the least. A digest, perfect-bound forty-eight-page magazine with a color cover boasting contributions from Ken Bulmer, Michael Moorcock, Ramsey Campbell, Eddy Bertin and Brian Lumley shook the fantasy fanzine addicts, who had had, up till then, only the very infrequent *Anduril* to support their habit. That premier issue was accordingly awarded the BFS Award for 1977 in the Small Press Category. It was also nominated for a World Fantasy Award.

The next three issues followed regularly with only a slight variation in page count. The color covers were dominated by the work of Jim Pitts, although Stephen Fabian was featured on the third issue. Contents continued to boast a mixture of fiction and verse from established writers like Ramsey Campbell, Karl Edward Wagner, Adrian Cole, Brian Lumley, Denys Val Baker and H.

Warner Munn, plus talented newcomers like Steve Sneyd, Andrew Darlington, Patrick Connolly, Peter Coleborn, Joe Schifino, A. J. Silvonius and others. *FT* continued to be the "darling" of the British small press and was again given the BFS Award in 1978.

Fantasy Tales remained very true to its editors' aim, succeeding admirably in recreating the entertainment value of the pulps. But therein lay—and lies— perhaps its chief fault: that it has cast for itself too rigid a mold. There is no room for experiment or true originality, and as such the magazine turns out not to be as "unusual" as its subtitle might imply.

However, it continued successfully into 1979, when hard economic reality cast its long shadow. It was no longer feasible to produce *Fantasy Tales* with color covers, so with the fifth issue the editors nervously switched to black and white. They need not have worried, judging by the sombre power of that number's cover illustration by Dave Lloyd. Black and white could be just as effective. That issue's cover also announced "The Thing in the Moonlight" by H. P. Lovecraft and Brian Lumley, a two-part short piece that had appeared only once previously, ten years before in *The Arkham Collector.**

Since then *Fantasy Tales* has continued regularly in the same format and with the same kind of success. It won its third BFS Award in 1979 and its fourth in 1980 and received its second World Fantasy Award nomination in 1981. It reaped its major reward in 1984 when it at last received the World Fantasy Award in the nonprofessional category.

FT has grown in stature and now commands a large readership, having attracted many more professional writers, including Randall Garrett, Manly Wade Wellman, Hugh B. Cave, Denis Etchison, Darrell Schweitzer and Peter Tremayne. The magazine has a consistently high standard of illustration by such artists as Jim Pitts, Stephen Fabian, Jim Fitzpatrick, Alan Hunter, Dave Lloyd, Russell Nicholson, John Grandfield, Dave Carson, Randy Broecker and others.

Whatever its shortcomings, *Fantasy Tales* is very healthy and appears to be set for as long a life as its editors can sustain.

Information Sources

BIBLIOGRAPHY:
Nicholls. *Encyclopedia.*
INDEX SOURCES: ISPF; ISPF-2; MT; SFM.
REPRINT SOURCES: None known.
LOCATION SOURCES: M.I.T. Science Fiction Library.

Publication History

TITLE: *Fantasy Tales* (internal subtitle "A Magazine of the Weird and Unusual").
VOLUME DATA: Volume 1, Number 1, Summer 1977–. Latest issue sighted Volume 7, Number 14, Spring 1985. Two issues per volume. Issue numbering sequential and not limited by volume. Twice yearly (Summer and Winter). Total run to date: 14 issues.
PUBLISHER: Privately published, London.

EDITORS: Stephen Jones and David A. Sutton.
FORMAT: Digest (first four issues perfect bound; thereafter saddle-stapled). Pages as
    follows: Nos. 1–3 (Summer 1977–Summer 1978), 48pp.; No. 4 (Spring 1979),
    56pp.; Nos. 5 and 6 (Winter and Summer 1979), 44pp.; Nos. 7–11 (Spring 1981–
    Winter 1982), 48pp.; No. 12 (Winter 1983), 52pp.; No. 13 (Winter 1984), 56pp.
PRICE: First six issues, 60p.; 75p. until No. 13; 90p. thereafter.

Gordon Larkin

FEAR!

Fear! was the last involvement with the fantasy fiction field of Henry Scharf,
the publisher of *Fantastic Universe,** but without the knowledge or expertise of
the latter magazine's editor, Hans Stefan Santesson, *Fear!* was an aimless,
inconsequential magazine.

Unlike *Fantastic Universe*, the final issues of which had reverted to a neo-
pulp format, *Fear!* was a standard digest-size magazine of 128 pages. Clearly
the experiment with *Fantastic Universe* had not worked, though at the time of
Fear!'s first appearance in May 1960 it was not known that *Fantastic Universe*
had already taken its final bow.

Fear! was a borderline horror/mystery magazine and attracted contributions
by writers in both fields, Hal Ellson, John W. Jakes and Arthur Porges being
among the best known. A few of the contents may have been switched from
Fantastic Universe, such as "The Vandal" by Evelyn Goldstein (a regular
Fantastic Universe contributor), which told of an Earth converted into a Venusian
hell. Each issue also contained a classic reprint: "The Dream Woman" by Wilkie
Collins in the first, followed by "How Love Came to Professor Guildea" by
Robert S. Hichens, both of which upstaged the other contents.

With no editorial departments, and with pages set out as in a book rather than
in the two-column format traditional for magazines, *Fear!* appeared lifeless and
motiveless, and though some of its contents were marginally better than might
be expected, they were not good enough to enable the magazine to survive.

Information Sources

BIBLIOGRAPHY:
Tuck.
INDEX SOURCES: Cook, Michael L., *Monthly Murders*, Westport, Conn.: Greenwood
    Press, 1982; MIT; MT; SFM; Tuck.
REPRINT SOURCES: None known.
LOCATION SOURCES: M.I.T. Science Fiction Library.

Publication History

TITLE: *Fear!*
VOLUME DATA: Volume 1, Number 1, May 1960–Volume 1, Number 2, July 1960.
    Bi-Monthly. Total run: 2 issues.

PUBLISHER: Great American Publications, New York.
EDITOR: Joseph L. Marx.
FORMAT: Digest, 128pp.
PRICE: 35¢.

Mike Ashley

FIRESIDE GHOST STORIES

Fireside Ghost Stories, which probably appeared in 1937, was a single-issue magazine designed for Christmas reading, one of a number of publications loosely connected with the Master Thriller Series.* A straightforward collection of unpretentious ghost stories, it reprinted Charles Dickens' "The Signalman" and featured "The Haunted Ship" by Francis Stengreave. There were two stories by Hector Bolitho, "The Albatross" and "Crying Grate," both reprinted from his collection *The House on Half Moon Street and Other Stories* (London: Cobden-Sanderson, 1935), plus five short stories and sketches by R. Thurston Hopkins based on true ghost stories, which subsequently appeared in his Mitre Press collections published during World War II.

Information Sources

BIBLIOGRAPHY:
Tuck.
INDEX SOURCES: MT; Tuck.
REPRINT SOURCES: None known.
LOCATION SOURCES: None known.

Publication History

TITLE: *Fireside Ghost Stories*.
VOLUME DATA: Number 1, undated (probably December 1937).
PUBLISHER: World's Work, Kingswood, Surrey.
EDITOR: Not known, but may have been H. Norman Evans.
FORMAT: Pulp, 128pp.
PRICE: 1s.

Mike Ashley/Frank H. Parnell

FLASH GORDON STRANGE ADVENTURE MAGAZINE

In 1936 publisher Harold Hersey established the C.J.H. Publishing Company with the idea of blending the pulp field with the burgeoning field of the comic strip. He launched three magazines based on three popular picture strips—Dan Dunn the detective, Tailspin Tommy, and the best-known of them all, Flash Gordon. The original Flash Gordon script had been created by Alex Raymond in 1934, and its syndication through the Sunday and daily newspapers had led to a tremendous following. Seemingly, a magazine based on the character released at a time when the Flash Gordon film serial starring Buster Crabbe was on general distribution would be guaranteed success. A large-format pulp of only eighty pages, it boasted sixty-four pages with color illustrations, the first time ever in a pulp magazine, and appeared to be an attractive offering. The lead novel, "The Master of Mars," credited to James Edison Northford, was accompanied by three short stories. Two of these were the work of Russ Winterbotham, who had recently debuted in *Astounding* (*Analog Science Fiction*)* with "The Star That Would Not Behave" (August 1935).

Although the paper was of poor quality and the presentation shoddy, this should not have unduly deterred the readership at which it was aimed. The problem lay, however, in whether Hersey was aiming at the right market. Although there was an overlap, in general those who read the pulps did not read comic strips, and vice versa. Hersey was certainly in the vanguard of the comic strips, but he should have issued them in the comic-book format, which was then in its infancy but which shot into popularity in 1938–1939 with *Action Comics* and *Superman*. As was so typical with his career, Hersey had the right idea but went about it the wrong way. Had he persevered he might have been vindicated, but although a second monthly issue with the lead novel "The Sun Men of Saturn" was announced it never appeared. Sales figures on the first two issues of *Dan Dunn* and *Tailspin Tommy*, which had appeared in September and October 1936, must have indicated to Hersey that he was on the wrong track. *Flash Gordon* had the most potential of the three magazines, but it was struggling into life in the wrong medium.

Information Sources

BIBLIOGRAPHY:
Tuck.
INDEX SOURCES: SFM; Tuck.
REPRINT SOURCES: None known.
LOCATION SOURCES: M.I.T. Science Fiction Library.

Publication History

TITLE: *Flash Gordon Strange Adventure Magazine.*
VOLUME DATA: Volume 1, Number 1, December 1936. Intended schedule, monthly.
    Total run: 1 issue.
PUBLISHER: C.J.H. Publishing Co., New York.
EDITOR: Harold Hersey (Publisher; editor not specified).
FORMAT: Neo-pulp, saddle stapled, 80pp.
PRICE: 10¢.

Mike Ashley

FLYING SAUCERS FROM OTHER WORLDS

Interim retitling of *Other Worlds Science Stories*; later shortened to *Flying Saucers*, a nonfiction magazine. See OTHER WORLDS SCIENCE STORIES.

FORGOTTEN FANTASY

Forgotten Fantasy, which premiered in October 1970, is a perfect example of a magazine that is assembled and published with obvious love and dedication and then ruined by a distributor who has no interest in the field.

FF came about when writer and collector Douglas Menville got together with bookdealers Al and Joe Saunders. Menville had been buying books from them regularly for years, and they knew of his keen interest in SF. They also knew that there was considerable general interest in SF, so plans were made to publish a magazine. Nectar Press Inc. was formed by the Saunderses, who put up the capital. Menville became the editor, with his colleague Robert Reginald as associate editor. There was an attempt to call the magazine *Ray Bradbury's Fantasy Magazine*, in the vein of the old A. Merritt publication, but Bradbury politely—and wisely in Menville's view—declined. In the end the title *Forgotten Fantasy* was selected because Menville felt that too many of the great classics had been lost "in the mists of time, mouldering away in dusty libraries" that deserved to be dusted off and published so that modern readers could see "the quaint and fascinating concepts and imaginations of the men who shaped the course of today's imaginative fiction."[1]

Both Menville and Reginald had formidable knowledge of fantasy fiction and access to many lost and forgotten works. This was evident, not only from the content of the magazine, but from the editors' subsequent work as consultants for Arno Press' various reprint series, and in Robert Reginald's mighty bibliography, *Science Fiction and Fantasy Literature* (Detroit: Gale Press, 2 vols., 1979).

The magazine began with the first part of a four-part serialization of "The Goddess of Atvatabar," a hollow-earth adventure story by William R. Bradshaw, first published in 1892. George Barr had been commissioned to produce a cover painting illustrating the novel; but despite the artistic quality of the result, the distributor was against it: it lacked "punch." At a moment's notice local artist Bill Hughes had to produce another painting that fortunately appealed to the distributor. But this incident was a sign of the troubles ahead.

For the reader and devotee, however, *FF* was a delight. The magazine was filled with original illustrations from the book and magazine publications of the stories—which were all reprints—and otherwise empty spaces were decorated with reprinted art-noveau frills. Stories, many getting their first American publication, included "The Parasite" by Arthur Conan Doyle, "The Hollow Land" by William Morris—the subject of an effective cover debut by Tim Kirk—"A Lost Opportunity" by Tudor Jenks, and others by Algernon Blackwood, Edith Nesbit, H. G. Wells, Lord Dunsany and Mary Wilkins-Freeman.

Menville conducted a clever sequence of reader departments: "Excavations" was the editorial, "Calibrations" covered book reviews, "Articulations" was the letter column, and "Prognostications" announced the forthcoming news. Reader reaction was encouraging, and the third issue published a letter of support from Ray Bradbury himself.

With the first serial complete, *FF* began a two-part serialization of E. Douglas Fawcett's "Hartmann the Anarchist," but unfortunately readers were not able to finish it, because no further issues of *FF* appeared. "We found ourselves so badly ripped off in every way you could think of that we knew we would never make it to the 6th issue," recalled Menville.[2] The truth was that *FF* was a collector's magazine, not one for general readers. The distributor had no interest in it because it was clear that it would generate no profit for him, and the magazine was left to flounder. As subsequent years have shown, had the magazine been priced as a specialty publication, perhaps at three or four times its cover price, and sold through the specialist dealers, it might still have sold the same quota and made a passable profit. Instead, the publishers were losing money at an alarming rate, and to go on would have been suicidal. A few years later they began the Newcastle line of quality paperbacks, which has continued the policy of *FF* in resurrecting long-forgotten books.

Notes

1. Douglas Menville, "Excavations," *Forgotten Fantasy*, October 1970, p. 6.
2. Douglas Menville, private correspondence with Mike Ashley, August 1975.

Information Sources

BIBLIOGRAPHY:
Ashley, Michael. "The Forgotten Fantasy." *Dark Horizons* 12 (Autumn/Winter 1975). (Includes issue index.)
Nicholls. *Encyclopedia*.
INDEX SOURCES: Allen, Paul, "Forgotten Fantasy," *The Hyborian Scrolls* 1 (July 1977); reprinted in *The Science Fiction Collector*, No. 5 (1977); ISFM-II; MT; NESFA; SFM.
REPRINT SOURCES: None known.
LOCATION SOURCES: M.I.T. Science Fiction Library; Pennsylvania State University Library.

Publication History

TITLE: *Forgotten Fantasy*.
VOLUME DATA: Volume 1, Number 1, October 1970–Volume 1, Number 5, June 1971. Bi-monthly. Total run: 5 issues.
PUBLISHER: Nectar Press, Hollywood, California.
EDITOR: Douglas Menville.
FORMAT: Digest, 128pp.
PRICE: 60¢.

George Laskowski

FUTURE COMBINED WITH SCIENCE FICTION [STORIES]

See FUTURE FICTION.

FUTURE FANTASY AND SCIENCE FICTION

See FUTURE FICTION.

FUTURE FICTION

After testing the water with *Science Fiction*,* and with the crest of the SF wave still rising, publisher Louis Silberkleit decided to issue a companion magazine, *Future Fiction*. Charles D. Hornig again acted as editor. The first issue, dated November 1939, was in standard pulp format (though with fewer pages than most, at 112) and sold for fifteen cents.

Although Hornig was a keen science fiction fan, he put little thought or initiative into assembling each issue. They took him about a week to put together, working on a free-lance basis at home, and manuscripts were readily available from his friend, the literary agent Julius Schwartz. At this time John W. Campbell at *Astounding* (*Analog Science Fiction**) was rapidly casting out the old-guard SF writers who could not adapt to his policies, while Raymond A. Palmer at *Amazing Stories** was sufficiently satisfied with his stable of local Chicago writers. The writers from the first decade of magazine SF, therefore, had only the limited markets of *Thrilling Wonder Stories* (*Wonder Stories**) and its new companion, *Startling Stories*,* as well as *Marvel Science Stories** and Hornig's two magazines. Since Hornig's budget was very small, allowing him to pay only the lowest rates, he usually ended up with works rejected by the other publishers. Not surprisingly, therefore, the early issues of both *Science Fiction* and *Future Fiction* contained uninspired stories by writers who could not keep up with the changing trends in SF.

Future lacked even the excitement that was prevalent in *Wonder Stories* under Hornig's editorship only five years earlier. The stories were for the most part run-of-the-mill space opera, although the vivid imagination of John Russell Fearn was fuel to a small flame to warm that old sense of wonder. Fearn was the most prolific contributor to the early issues of *Future*, appearing under both his own name and a brace of pseudonyms like Dennis Clive, Dom Passante, John Cotton, Polton Cross and Ephriam Winiki. Most of the pseudonyms were invented by Charles Hornig, who had adopted a money-saving ploy of paying one cent a word to established authors if their real names appeared, but only half a cent to new authors or for work by known writers published under pen names. Thus, Earl and Otto Binder became John Coleridge, Edmond Hamilton became Robert Castle, and so on. Other old-timers present in the first issue were J. Harvey Haggard, Bob Olsen, Miles J. Breuer and Philip Jacques Bartel.

On this basis, and with the vantage of hindsight, the second issue, dated March 1940, would appear to have been a bargain. Apart from the inevitable Fearn presence, there were stories by Jack Williamson, Edmond Hamilton and Isaac Asimov. The stories, however, were of minor importance. Asimov sold two stories to Hornig: "Ring around the Sun" (March 1940) and "The Magnificent Possession" (July 1940). At the time of their publication Asimov was still a fledgling writer, and reference to *The Early Asimov* shows that those were his fifth and ninth completed stories. Asimov learned a lesson from his dealings with *Future*, as he recalls in his autobiography:

> This introduced me to two economic facts of life about fringe magazines. First, when a story is paid for on publication, there is no hurry to publish. "Ring Around the Sun" was published exactly a year and three days after it was bought. Second, payment on publication easily translates to payment long after publication . . . and then only after I had written a letter to a magazine called *Writer's Digest* to ask what one ought to do about it.[1]

Future was on only a thrice-yearly schedule, and by the time the fourth issue appeared in August 1940 (dated November), circumstances in the SF world and beyond had changed. In October 1940 Hornig was called upon to register for military service. Being a confirmed pacifist, he felt that he would have to register as a conscientious objector. Suspecting that the draft board interview might be more lenient in California than in New Jersey, he arranged to be in Los Angeles at the time it was due. There he remained for the next eighteen months before he was ordered to the Civilian Public Service Camp on the Columbia River. During that time it proved impractical to edit *Science Fiction*, *Future Fiction* and the new *Science Fiction Quarterly** long distance.

Silberkleit had been growing increasingly disenchanted with the free-lance arrangement, as well as being unhappy about the poor sales of the magazines. He offered the post of editor to Sam Moskowitz, who turned it down because of his friendship with Hornig. Donald Wollheim heard of this, however, and suggested to Robert W. Lowndes that he give the magazines a try. Wollheim advised Lowndes to contact the publisher of a new line of pulps without revealing that he knew him to be Silberkleit. "In the letter," Lowndes stated later, "I'd suggest that it might be a good idea to add a science fiction title to the list, offering my services as editor at a slightly lower price than Hornig was being paid, and also find fault with all the other sf titles presently out, but particularly with Hornig's."[2]

Silberkleit agreed to give Lowndes a trial, and in November 1940 he was appointed editor of *Future* and *Science Fiction Quarterly*. Hornig retained *Science Fiction* for a few more issues until it was combined with *Future* from the October 1941 number.

Although Lowndes had the same meager budget as had Hornig, it was the mark of a better editor that he provided more value for the money. Lowndes was a member of the New York-based fan group known as the Futurians that included Donald Wollheim, Cyril Kornbluth, John Michel, Richard Wilson, David Kyle and Hannes Bok. Following Wollheim's altercation with Hugo Gernsback in 1934, it was unlikely that he or his comrades would contribute to anything edited by Hornig, but with Lowndes it was another matter. Here was a vein of talent aching to be mined, and soon, under a legion of pen names, the Futurians were helping to fill the pages of *Future*.

Frederik Pohl and Cyril Kornbluth, for instance, graced Lowndes' first *Future* (dated April 1941, on sale in February) with ''A Prince of Pluto'' under the alias Paul Dennis Lavond. The same by-line appeared on the vignette ''Something from Beyond'' in the December 1941 issue, a joint work of Pohl, Lowndes and Dirk Wylie. Wollheim appeared regularly under pseudonyms like Martin Pearson, Lawrence Woods and Millard Verne Gordon. Kornbluth made a few appearances as S. D. Gottesman, while Lowndes hid his identity behind names like Carol Grey, Wilfred Owen Morley and Mallory Kent. Only James Blish, Richard Wilson and Damon Knight appeared in print under their own names.

Their stories were often short, and frequently little more than extended jokes, but there was a verve and sparkle to them that set them apart from the dull, uninventive and ironically immature stories that had filled the Hornig issues. The Futurians brought an identity to *Future* that Lowndes helped to mold into a personality. It was a strange irony that Lowndes preferred the chatty, informal editorial approach because this was what he had most appreciated about *Wonder Stories* in the mid-1930s, when the editor had been Charles Hornig. Hornig had kept the same informality with his new magazines, but this time, without the controlling hand of Hugo Gernsback, and without the first choice of manuscripts by writers like David H. Keller, Edmond Hamilton, Laurence Manning, Nathan Schachner and Stanley G. Weinbaum, Hornig's lack of editorial ability became apparent. Lowndes, on the other hand, had access to a fund of bubbling talent, and the ability to create. Although it cannot be said that anything of major importance appeared in *Future* during the next few years, it cannot be denied that the issues were enjoyable and did not insult the intelligence.

Of particular interest are the contributions by Hannes Bok, both as artist and writer. Internal illustrations aside, Bok provided the covers for October and December 1941 and for February and October 1942. He also appeared with his Merrittesque short stories—''The Alien Vibration'' (February 1942), ''Web of Moons'' (April 1942) and ''Beauty'' (October 1942)—and a novelette, ''Dusk on the Moon'' (February 1943).

As another budget-saver, Silberkleit made a deal with old-time author Ray Cummings to reprint his early stories; these became a regular feature in *Future*, starting in the October 1941 issue with ''The Man on the Meteor'' from *Science and Invention*.* Others were ''Around the Universe'' (December 1941) and ''Beyond the Stars'' (February 1942). ''Rain of Fire'' (August 1942), ''Patriotism Plus'' (February 1943) and ''The Man Who Saved New York'' (July 1943) were new stories, while the longer reprints appeared in *Science Fiction Quarterly*. While these were not exceptional as stories, Cummings was still legendary in SF circles at this time, and his early stories were not easy to locate. Reprints from the pre-Gernsback days were already proving popular in *Famous Fantastic*

Mysteries,* and there was no reason why they should not be received with similar approval in *Future*.

With the October 1942 issue *Future* was retitled *Future Fantasy and Science Fiction*. It was an experiment in combining fantasy and weird stories with SF and was not very successful. In hindsight, however, this proved to be *Future*'s best period, with such stories as "Storm Warning" by Wollheim (October 1942), "The Creator" by Ross Rocklynne and "The Leapers" by Lowndes (both December 1942).

In 1943 *Future* underwent another title change that has confused collectors ever since. It became *Science Fiction Stories* but was not a revival of the earlier companion, as the volume numbering continued that of *Future*. Only two issues appeared under this title; they are memorable for "The Great Secret" by L. Ron Hubbard (April 1943) and "Infiltration" by Clifford Simak (July 1943). By then the wartime paper shortage had taken its toll, and Silberkleit folded his SF magazines in favor of keeping the western and detective titles. Lowndes remained as editor, however, so that when, in 1950, it was considered timely to revive *Future*, Lowndes merely continued where he had left off seven years earlier.

The *Future* of the 1940s, however, was a different entity from that of the fifties. The Hornig issues contained little, if anything, that was memorable, while the Lowndes issues had a youthful and innocent exuberance about them. By the 1950s, however, SF had become decidedly serious, and with the advent of the atomic age it now wore a mantle of maturity (though in most quarters this was short-lived).

The first issue was entitled *Future combined with Science Fiction Stories*, a clumsy appellation used in order to retain rights to both the earlier titles. It was dated May/June 1950, and the numbering had reverted to Volume 1, to which extent it could be considered a new magazine. Retaining the standard pulp format, it was even slimmer than before, with only ninety-six pages, but it sold for just fifteen cents, the lowest price of any SF pulp at that time. (The price soon rose to twenty cents with the November 1950 issue.) Lowndes' budget was still small, but that did not stop him from acquiring average- to good-quality fiction both from the older generation of writers and from the new breed who had entered the field after the war. The first issue, for instance, displayed such names as James Blish, Lester del Rey, George O. Smith, Murray Leinster and Frank Belknap Long, and within a few issues Fritz Leiber, Judith Merril, H. Beam Piper and L. Sprague de Camp were added to the lineup. So there was certainly no shortage of talented writers. At the outset, *Future* had little serious competition, with only *Astounding*, *Thrilling Wonder*, *Startling Stories* and the new *Magazine of Fantasy and Science Fiction** as major contenders. Within a year, however, the situation would change dramatically, due to *Galaxy Science Fiction** and an ever-increasing number of new magazines entering the field, and to a new drive for respectability from Howard Browne at *Amazing*.

For the first three years, though, Lowndes, through his ability and integrity as an editor, managed to keep a slender hold on the better-quality manuscripts in the market. Between 1950 and 1953 *Future* ranked as one of the more readable of the profusion of magazines fighting for survival, and several of the stories have survived their initial printing by living on in anthologies, author collections and, more significantly, readers' memories, though many will have forgotten where the stories originally appeared. Among them are "Incomplete Superman" (March 1951) and "Honorable Enemies" (May 1951) by Poul Anderson, "Mind of Tomorrow" (May 1951) and "And There Was Light" (July 1951) by Lester del Rey, "Ultrasonic God" (July 1951) by L. Sprague de Camp, "If I Forget Thee, Oh Earth" (September 1951) by Arthur C. Clarke, "Testament of Andros" (January 1953) by James Blish, and "Liberation of Earth" (May 1953) by William Tenn.

Future could not be said to have a policy. Within his means Lowndes tried to obtain as good a selection of stories as possible and package them within an entertaining framework. A regular nonfiction article usually accompanied the stories, often the work of L. Sprague de Camp, who brought his usually scholarly technique to such items as "The So-called Fourth Dimension" (September 1951), "The Mystic Trance" (November 1951), "False Prophets Shall Rise" (January 1952), "The Mislaid Tribes" (May 1952) and "The Phantom Phoenicians" (September 1953). In addition, there was a lively book-review column—"Readin' and Writin' "—with contributions by James Blish, Damon Knight and Lowndes himself. From the September 1953 issue Robert Madle introduced his column of comment and nostalgia, "Inside Science Fiction."

Then, in 1954, confusion arose. Silberkleit was only too aware of the death knell tolling for the pulp magazine. As an experiment *Science Fiction Stories* was resurrected in a digest format, and two undated issues appeared in 1953 and 1954. Following the success of their sales, Silberkleit converted *Future* to digest size from the June 1954 issue. But sales proved less than encouraging and, suspecting the title to be at fault, Silberkleit changed *Future* to *Science Fiction Stories* from the January 1955 issue. The volume numbering continued that of *Future*, and the same reader departments appeared, so to all intents it was the same magazine. Confusion again arose when, a few months later, the title *Future Science Fiction* reappeared. The volume numbering could not continue as before, however, so this issue was identified as Number 28, since there had been twenty-seven issues of *Future* between the May 1950 and October 1954 numbers.

Future 28 served only as an experimental issue to test the market in the same unlimited way as the two undated issues of *Science Fiction* had in the previous two summers. Another *Future* appeared the following spring, and to further distinguish the two magazines *Science Fiction* was given the prefix "The Original . . . " to signify its link with the original 1939 magazine. *Future* was eventually given another chance, and in 1957 it reappeared, first quarterly, and then bi-monthly, but thereafter it always played second fiddle to *Science Fiction*.

Future published some good fiction during its final phase, perhaps the best known being Philip K. Dick's "Vulcan's Hammer" (No. 29, 1956) and Clifford Simak's "World's without End" (No. 31, Winter 1956), but on the whole it was not as enjoyable as its companion title, and even that was struggling. By the late 1950s science fiction had entered a period of doldrums, and good science fiction was scarce. What there was of it went to *Astounding*, *Galaxy* and *The Magazine of Fantasy and Science Fiction*, and the remaining magazines, of which there were still a good number, especially during the mini-boom of 1957, could only look on and fight for scraps.

Lowndes circumvented this to some extent by making *Future* appeal more to the SF enthusiast than to the casual reader. By doing this he clearly limited the magazine's appeal in general terms, although it always remained popular among the SF fraternity. Robert Silverberg probably best summed up the feeling about *Future* and *Science Fiction Stories* when he referred to them as "esteemed but impoverished."[3] Starting from the Summer 1957 issue, Lowndes began a series of editorials entitled "Yesterday's World of Tomorrow," where he looked back issue by issue at the SF magazines of 1927-1929 and discussed critically the merits or otherwise of the stories. Tied in with this was a "Science Fiction Almanac," which ran from the February 1958 issue, highlighting events in SF's history month by month.

In June 1958 Isaac Asimov began a series of science articles called "Point of View," which discussed the solar system from various vantage points. Thomas N. Scortia provided his own series on "The Race into Space" from the December 1958 issue. Other occasional articles surfaced from L. Sprague de Camp and Damon Knight, and there was always the lively letter column.

By October 1959, however, it was clear that *Future* was ailing. The color covers had given way to black and white, and Lowndes had been forced to institute a "second look" policy of reprints from *Future*'s first incarnation. The end came with the April 1960 issue, although there was no such indication from Lowndes' comments in the letter column (there was no editorial). The distributors had no further interest in pulp magazines, and Silberkleit's entire chain folded. Silberkleit himself continued with his main publishing venture in the Archie comics field, and Lowndes soon reappeared as editor of *Exploring the Unknown* and *Magazine of Horror*.*

Future stands as a testament of what a willing and capable editor can do with only the slightest of tools. Nevertheless, Lowndes must be viewed as something of an alchemist in the SF field, forever attempting to convert lead into gold, and it is remarkable how close he often came. Although the low budget never allowed *Future* much of a chance to shine, the passing of the years has failed to dull all that sparkles. *Future* had two brief heydays: 1941-1942 and 1950-1953, during which time Lowndes assembled issues that were better than his budget could have been expected to buy.

Notes

1. Isaac Asimov, *In Memory Yet Green* (Garden City, N.Y.: Doubleday, 1979), p. 262.

2. Robert A.W. Lowndes, private communication with the author, June 23, 1974.

3. Robert Silverberg, "Sounding Brass, Tinkling Cymbal," in *Hell's Cartographers*, ed. Brian W. Aldiss and Harry Harrison (London: Weidenfeld & Nicolson, 1975), p. 19.

Information Sources

BIBLIOGRAPHY:
Nicholls. *Encyclopedia*.
Tuck.
INDEX SOURCES: ISFM; MIT; SFM; Tuck.
REPRINT SOURCES:
  Reprint Editions: The British edition had two series. The first, released by Thorpe & Porter, Ltd., Leicester, ran for fourteen issues, undated, November 1951–June 1954. Pulp, 96pp., 1/6d. Nearly complete reprints of the U.S. issues, Nos. 1–5 and 8 were entitled *Future combined with Science Fiction*; Nos. 6, 7, 9–14 were *Future Science Fiction* and correspond approximately to the U.S. issues from March 1951 to March 1954 with some omissions. The second series was produced by Strato Publications, London, undated, November 1957–February 1960, eleven issues, digest, 128pp., 2/-. Contents correspond to the U.S. issues Summer 1957–August 1959 omitting February 1958.
  Derivative Anthologies: No single anthology consists of selections drawn solely from *Future SF*, but in the 1960s Ivan Howard assembled several volumes for Belmont Books, New York, which selected their contents entirely from the Columbia magazines. The following had a predominance of stories from *Future*: *The Weird Ones* (1962) with three; *Escape to Earth* (1963) with three; *Novelets of Science Fiction* (1963) with four; *Things* (1964) with three; and *Now and Beyond* (1965) with four. The anthology *Blue Moon*, ed. Douglas Lindsay (London: Mayflower Books, 1970), contains six stories from the August 1942 *Future* plus one from the Winter 1942 *Science Fiction Quarterly*.
LOCATION SOURCES: Eastern New Mexico University Library; M.I.T. Science Fiction Library; Pennsylvania State University Library; Texas A&M University Library; University of New Brunswick Library.

Publication History

TITLE:
  First Series: *Future Fiction*, November 1939–August 1941; *Future combined with Science Fiction*, October 1941–August 1942; *Future Fantasy and Science Fiction*, October 1942–February 1943; *Science Fiction Stories*, April–July 1943.
  Second Series: *Future combined with Science Fiction Stories*, May/June 1950–November 1951; *Future Science Fiction Stories*, January–May 1952; *Future Science Fiction*, July 1952; *Future Science Fiction Stories*, September 1952; *Future Science Fiction*, November 1952–October 1954. Name then technically changed to *Science Fiction Stories*, but *Future Science Fiction* was revived in 1955, and the title remained until April 1960.
VOLUME DATA:
  First Series: Volume 1, Number 1, November 1939–Volume 3, Number 5, July 1943. Six issues per volume. Schedule irregular until August 1941, thereafter bi-monthly. Initial run: 17 issues.
  Second Series: Volume 1, Number 1, May/June 1950–Volume 5, Number 3, October 1954 (numbering continued by *Science Fiction Stories*); six issues per volume. Bi-monthly. Recommended Whole Number 28 (no volume numbers hereafter),

[Winter] 1955–Number 48, April 1960. Schedule irregular until Number 31, Winter 1956/57. Quarterly until Number 34, Fall 1957. Bi-monthly, February 1958–April 1960. Total run: 17 + 48, 65 issues.

PUBLISHER: The editorial and executive offices remained in New York, but the office of publication changed as follows: Blue Ribbon Magazines, Holyoke, Massachusetts, November 1939; Double Action Magazines, Chicago, March–November 1940; Columbia Publications, Springfield and Holyoke, April 1941–April 1960.

EDITORS: Charles D. Hornig, November 1939–November 1940; Robert [A.]W. Lowndes, April 1941–April 1960.

FORMAT: Pulp, 112pp., November 1939–July 1943; 96pp., May/June 1950–March 1954; Digest, 128pp., June 1954–April 1960.

PRICE: 15¢, November 1939–April 1943; 20¢, July 1943; 15¢, May/June–September/October 1950; 20¢, November 1950–November 1952; 25¢, January 1953–March 1954; 35¢, June 1954–April 1960.

Mike Ashley

FUTURE SCIENCE FICTION [STORIES] (1952–1960)

Variant title used in 1950s for second series of magazine that started as *Future Fiction*. See FUTURE FICTION.

FUTURE SCIENCE FICTION (1953–1955)

Ronald Forster, operating as Frew Publications or Blue Diamond Publishing Company, ran a small publishing business in Sydney produing a multitude of magazines and comics. He had no great knowledge of science fiction, but there was clearly a market for it in Australia in 1953, with no less than seventeen British magazines being imported. One of the field's boom periods of frantic activity was at its height, and it was not yet obvious that there would follow a periodic slump.

Since the public evidently could not get enough science fiction it seemed a good proposition to add two more titles to the scene. Obtaining a batch of stories from an agent, Forster assembled two skimpy issues to launch the project. Some of the interior artwork used in the original American printings of the stories was appropriated, as were the two covers by Earle K. Bergey—whose work was deplored by serious scientifictionists.

The two magazines, *Future Science Fiction* and *Popular Science Fiction,** constituted a single operation, and any general remarks about one apply equally to the other. The format was the same for all issues. They were cheaply produced and looked it, even beside the British magazines of the time. The first issues' covers came out looking drab, and cover art was never good.

FSF 1 contained some established names, led by Henry Kuttner with ''The Infinite Moment,'' reprinted from the April 1942 *Thrilling Wonder* (*Wonder*

*Stories**). But whatever direction Forster might have taken, a new factor entered. Australia had a small body of SF enthusiasts who had suffered a long period when the country was cut off from most good science fiction. *Future Science Fiction* presented the first opportunity for anyone with any depth of knowledge in SF to influence local publishing.

Learning through a trade source of the impending new magazines, Vol Molesworth approached Forster and offered his expert advice. It was agreed that he would advise on the selection of stories and contribute a general-interest column of sorts. However, after the two second issues Vol withdrew because a new employment contract barred outside work, and handed the honorary position to Graham Stone.

Stone aimed to get new material, and Forster agreed that it was highly desirable, not only as a selling point, to distinguish the magazines among many competitors, but to make it possible to secure overseas distribution.

FSF used three new stories by Australians: "As We Were" by Norma K. Hemming, "Pass the Oxygen" by Frank B. Bryning and "The Long Sleep" by John A. Vile (all in issue 5), plus "The Twain Shall Meet" by the New Zealander D. C. McDonald (issue 6), who thus became the first resident of his country to be published in a science fiction magazine. In addition, *Popular Science Fiction* used another story by Hemming, "Symbiosis." It can now be recorded that in fact these were all the local manuscripts submitted, making a unique 100 percent acceptance rate!

Besides these, however, many unpublished manuscripts by Americans were submitted by the Ackerman Agency, and thirteen that were accepted and published are not known to have appeared elsewhere. Three are of special significance: "Mixpedition" by Norman E. Hartman (in *FSF*), "Expedition Void" by Jody McCarter and "The Square Peg" by M. Louis Moore (the first initial omitted by the printer; both in *Popular Science Fiction*). These authors appear to be unpublished elsewhere, at least in acknowledged outlets.

Molesworth's "Fandom's Corner" column was conceived as a topical department. The occasional nature of the publication schedule worked against that, and Stone's contributions on the inside covers of most issues are more like editorials, ruminating on what SF was about—a little naive in retrospect, but an innovation as far as Australian SF publishing was concerned.

The artist (or artists) who painted the covers received no credit and deserved none. The best were closely copied from American magazine covers by Frank R. Paul, Ed Emsh, Walter Popp, Malcolm Smith and Robert Gibson Jones. The original illustrations, however, began to show promise by the last issues.

Distribution was a problem, as many other publishers of science fiction have found, and while only two issues showed an actual loss, the sales were never much beyond what was required for bare survival. After two years, Forster felt that the magazines were not sufficiently profitable to keep them going. Stone's opinion was, and is, that they never became properly established. Appearing only three times a year, and planned on an individual basis with no long-term policy, the magazines had no chance to develop. They were still among the best SF magazines that Australia had to offer in the 1950s.

In 1967 another publisher somehow acquired the plates for issues 4 and 6 and reprinted them, numbered 1 and 2 on the covers only. New covers were painted by Keith Chatto, based closely on the original unsigned covers, the second in turn being copied from the work of Robert Gibson Jones.

Information Sources

BIBLIOGRAPHY:
Nicholls. *Encyclopedia*.
Tuck.
INDEX SOURCES: ASFI; IBSF; ISFM; MIT; SFM; Tuck.
REPRINT SOURCES:
   Reprint Editions: Issues 4 and 6, with the exception of Graham Stone's "In Future" column, which ran inside the front cover, were reprinted with new covers as *Future Science Fiction*, new series, Nos. 1 and 2, undated [April and June 1967], Digest, 64 pp., from Page Publications, Sydney.
LOCATION SOURCES: Futurian Society of Sydney Library; M.I.T. Science Fiction Library.

Publication History

TITLE: *Future Science Fiction*.
VOLUME DATA: All issues undated. Volume 1, Number 1 [July 1953]–Volume 1, Number 6 [March 1955]. Three times a year. Other issues published as follows: 2, November 1953; 3, March 1954; 4, July 1954; 5, December 1954. Total run: 6 issues.
PUBLISHER: Blue Diamond Publishing Co., Sydney.
EDITOR: Unidentified within issues. Ronald Forster was the Editorial Director, although Peter Grant handled most later issues. The contents of issue 2 were selected by Vol Molesworth, those of the remaining issues by Graham Stone.
FORMAT: Digest, 64pp.
PRICE; First two issues 1/3d, thereafter 1/6d.

Graham B. Stone

FUTURISTIC SCIENCE STORIES

In the summer of 1950 the London firm of John Spencer and Company prepared to issue four science fiction magazines. Apart from their titles there was nothing to distinguish *Futuristic Science Stories*, which appeared first, from *Tales of Tomorrow,* Worlds of Fantasy** or *Wonders of the Spaceways,** which followed over the next few months. The magazines were all pocketbook size, 128 pages (initially, though this fluctuated) and with lifeless, juvenile covers by Gerald Facey.

The magazines are for completist collectors only. Much of the fiction was by unknown writers, although a few, like Lan Wright and E. C. Tubb, contributed some of the better stories. *FSS* 6 (Winter 1952) carried the first story sale by R. Lionel Fanthorpe ("Worlds without End" as by "Lionel Roberts"); and within the next few years Fanthorpe would be writing the majority of the fiction for the magazines. His nearest rival was John S. Glasby, who first appeared in *FSS* 8 (Summer 1952) with "Moondust," under his best-known alias, "A. J. Merak." It was Glasby who created the notorious persona "Ray Cosmic."

Futuristic had to all intents folded after its fifteenth issue in 1954, but when Spencer introduced the Badger Books imprint in 1958 a sixteenth issue appeared consisting of stories written entirely by Glasby.

Information Sources

BIBLIOGRAPHY:
Ashley, Michael. *A Complete Index and Annotated Commentary to the John Spencer Fantasy Publications (1950–1966)*. Newcastle: Cosmos, 1979 (also contains index).
Nicholls. *Encyclopedia*.
Tuck.
INDEX SOURCES: Ashley, Michael, *A Complete Index and Annotated Commentary to the John Spencer Fantasy Publications (1950–1966)*, Newcastle: Cosmos, 1979; IBSF; SFM; Tuck.
REPRINT SOURCES: None known.
LOCATION SOURCES: M.I.T. Science Fiction Library.

Publication History

TITLE: *Futuristic Science Stories*, first fifteen issues; sixteenth issue *Futuristic*.
VOLUME DATA: No volume numbering. All issues undated. Number 1 [Summer 1950]– Number 16 [February 1958]. Irregular, approximately quarterly until fifteenth issue [Spring 1954]. Four-year gap until final issue. Total run: 16 issues.
PUBLISHER: John Spences & Co., London.
EDITOR: Credited as "John Spencer Manning." In reality Sol Assael and Michael Nahum, the publishers.
FORMAT: Pocketbook. Page count as follows: issues 1–4, 128pp.; 5–10, 112pp.; 11– 15, 128pp.; 16, 160pp.
PRICE: 1/6d. first fifteen issues; last issue 2/-.

Mike Ashley

FUTURISTIC STORIES

The first entry into the SF magazine field by Hamilton and Company (the firm that later published *Authentic Science Fiction**) produced two large-size companion magazines, *Futuristic Stories* and *Strange Adventures*,* indistinguishable from one another in their juvenile contents, and of no interest to other than a completist collector.

The contents were probably the work of gangster writer N. Wesley Firth, who is directly credited with the lead story of the first issue, "The Lords of Zorm," and may have been the man behind the other by-lines, Rice Ackman and Earl Ellison. It is possible, however, that editor Dennis Pratt, who had unsuccessfully submitted stories to Walter Gillings' *Fantasy** only months earlier, may have found a home for his stories in these ration- and quality-restricted pages.

Information Sources

BIBLIOGRAPHY:
Nicholls. *Encylcopedia.*
Tuck.
INDEX SOURCES: IBSF; SFM; Tuck.
REPRINT SOURCES: None known.
LOCATION SOURCES: M.I.T. Science Fiction Library.

Publication History

TITLE: *Futuristic Stories.*
VOLUME DATA: No volume numbering; undated. Number 1 [ca. October 1946]–
    Number 2 [ca. December 1946]. Total run: 2 issues.
PUBLISHER: Hamilton & Co., London.
EDITOR: Dennis H. Pratt.
FORMAT: Pulp; first issue, 48pp.; second issue, 32pp.
PRICE: First issue, 2/-; second issue, 1/-.

Mike Ashley

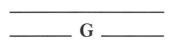

G

G-8 AND HIS BATTLE ACES

The most popular of the air-war single-character pulp heroes was G-8, the featured hero in *G-8 and His Battle Aces*. The creation of Robert J. Hogan, who penned 110 G-8 novels in the monthly magazine, G-8 was a master spy and ace flyer in World War I. Each month he fought a new German plot. The stories were pure hero pulp material, but there were large dashes of science fiction thrown in. Lead villains were pulp standbys and movie-serial creations. There was Herr Stahlmaske, a giant of a man whose steel mask hid a face destroyed in a bomb blast. Chu Lung was an oriental mastermind helping the German cause. Herr Grun was a voodoo priest who hated all normal men. Many of the menaces in the G-8 stories proved to be incredible deceptions by the Germans, such as the huge flying heads that had blazing eyes which destroyed allied planes. Supposedly the work of a master magician, the heads turned out to be merely balloons armed with machine guns. However, G-8 did have plenty of superscience, including giant tanks, rocket ships, giant bats, beast-men and more. It should be remembered, though, that the purpose of the SF in these stories was to provide plot devices for G-8 to defeat with his heroics; it added little to the stories. The novels, as with most long-running pulp series, were straight formula and varied little in content or style from month to month.

Much like *Dusty Ayres and His Battle Birds*,* most of the material appearing in *G-8* was written by Robert Hogan. However, these stories were not about future war but World War I, which G-8 refought in each issue. There was generally a story by "Greaseball Joe" (Hogan), as well. None of these stories had any fantasy or SF content; they were straight air-war adventures. The editorial department was also conducted by Hogan. Early issues of *G-8* contained columns by famous American and German fliers about their wartime experiences.

Information Sources

BIBLIOGRAPHY:
Bradd, Sidney H. "G-8, Flying Spy of the Pulps." *Xenophile*, No. 11 (1975).
Carr, Wooda N. *G-8, The Flying Spy.* Oak Lawn, Ill.: Pulp Press, 1978 (*Pulp Classics* No. 18).
Carr, Nick. "The Devil You Say." *Xenophile*, No. 3 (1974).
————. "The Subject Was Death." *Science-Fiction Collector*, No. 15 (1981).
Goulart, Ron. *Cheap Thrills.* New Rochelle, N.Y.: Arlington House, 1972, Chap. 7. Retitled *An Informal History of the Pulp Magazine.* New York: Ace Books, 1973.
Hern Schreiner, Herm. "Heroes of the Flying Pulps." *Xenophile*, No. 22 (1976).
Knight, Damon. "Knight Piece." In *Hell's Cartographers*, edited by Brian W. Aldiss and Harry Harrison. London: Weidenfeld & Nicolson, 1975.
Sullivan, John. "Nippy Weston: Girl Flyer." *Xenophile*, No. 11 (1975).
INDEX SOURCES: Weinberg, Robert, *The Hero Pulp Index*, Evergreen, Colo.: Opar Press, 1971 (lead novels only).
REPRINT SOURCES:
Novels: Eight of the lead novels were reprinted in paperback by Berkley Medallion, New York, as follows: No. 1 (1969), *The Bat Staffel* (orig. Oct 33); 2 (1970), *Purple Aces* (Nov 33); 3 (1970), *Ace of the White Death* (Dec 33); 4 (1971), *Bombs from the Murder Wolves* (Oct 43); 5 (1971), *Vultures of the White Death* (Apr 37); 6 (1971), *Flight from the Grave* (Jun 37); 7 (1971), *Fangs of the Sky Leopard* (Mar 37); 8 (1971), *The Mark of the Vulture* (Jun 42).
LOCATION SOURCES: San Francisco Academy of Comic Art.

Publication History

TITLE: *G-8 and His Battle Aces.*
VOLUME DATA: Volume 1, Number 1, October 1933–Volume 28, Number 2, June 1944. Monthly to April 1941, thereafter bi-monthly. Total run: 110 issues.
PUBLISHER: Popular Publications, New York.
EDITOR: Edythe Seims working under Rogers Terrill and then Alden H. Norton. William Fay also was editor at one point.
FORMAT: Pulp, 128 pp.
PRICE: 15¢, until 1936, when dropped to 10¢.

Robert Weinberg

GALAXY SCIENCE FICTION

With its first issue of October 1950, *Galaxy Science Fiction* magazine established itself as one of the three major SF magazines of its era, together with *Astounding* (later *Analog Science Fiction**) and *The Magazine of Fantasy and Science Fiction.** *Galaxy* set high standards of both editorial and authorial excellence for more than a quarter century and provided an alternative vehicle for many new authors whose stories did not fit into the pro-technology orientation and psi enthusiasms of John W. Campbell's *Astounding* or the fantastic preferences of Anthony Boucher and J. Francis McComas' *Magazine of Fantasy and*

Science Fiction. Perhaps as a result, *Galaxy* was perceived as occupying a middle ground between its two major competitors, claiming for itself that which is now termed soft science fiction with a satirical and sometimes irreverent approach to both scientific and social problems. The problem stories featured by *Galaxy*, therefore, tended to be social and ethical in character, and the solutions more often than not challenged conventional wisdom and the status quo. The realities of *Galaxy*'s relationship to the two other dominant SF magazines were far more complex than the traditional view because the same writers contributed to all three and there were few editorial restrictions that would place a story in one magazine rather than another. The big three overlapped in interests, contributors and, of course, readers. And yet the popular view does have the virtue of identifying a bias that has remained more or less consistent from the first issue to the most recent.

During the more than thirty years of its publication, *Galaxy* has been served by seven different editors and four publishers. It has been responsive to the changing currents and fortunes both inside and outside the genre which have shaped the publishing industry of the post-World War II period and especially the audience of subscribers on which *Galaxy* has depended for more than three decades. To a large degree, the success and influence of the magazine on the development of the genre since the fifties have been the result of the editorial and promotional skills of its editors. Although other factors of the marketplace must be taken into account, it is no serious exaggeration to say that *Galaxy*'s strength has been in its editors and conversely its weaknesses as well, as the following account will show.

H. L. Gold, founder and first editor of *Galaxy*, set the original course which the magazine was to follow for a quarter century. In the sixties Frederik Pohl dominated *Galaxy* as editor, author, promoter, counselor and all-purpose worker in a manner that surpasses Campbell's celebrated ascendancy as editor of *Astounding/Analog.* If we add James Baen to the list of influential editors and personalities who shaped the fortunes and charted the course of *Galaxy*, we may speak of the history of *Galaxy* in terms of its rise under Gold, maturity under Pohl, and revival under Baen before its long decline into bankruptcy.

Galaxy was started by Horace L. Gold, a writer of pulp fiction in the thirties and forties, who served as assistant editor of *Captain Future,* Startling Stories** and *Thrilling Wonder Stories (Wonder Stories*).* Later, Gold worked on the editorial staff of comic books and detective magazines and wrote for radio serials. His diversified background in popular entertainment and publishing gave him the experience he needed to form some conclusions on the production and management of pulp magazines. Like all successful editors, Gold knew his business from long apprenticeship and practical experience in every phase of the publishing operation from printing and proofing to sales and distribution. However, Gold was to work on *Galaxy* under a disability which he suffered as a result of his wartime experiences with the U.S. Army in the Pacific theatre of operations. His health was precarious for years, and his condition was aggravated by an agoraphobia which turned him into the Nero Wolfe of the industry. Treating him to some extent like the famous detective, the SF world came to his door or he reached it by telephone. Gold's disability and his increasingly complete retirement to his New York apartment with his wife gave him an insularity of viewpoint that contributed its share to Gold's dream of creating a SF magazine that would appeal to and be accepted by an adult, urban readership. His handling of the editorship of *Galaxy* reflects both the strengths and weaknesses of his New York, media-centered view of the world of science fiction. His aspirations for *Galaxy* were to produce a glossy SF magazine that would not be out of place on the coffee table or in the magazine rack alongside *Colliers* or *The Saturday Evening Post*. Although Gold never achieved his ambition of making *Galaxy* socially acceptable among the smart set, his magazine made a significant contribution to mainstreaming SF in the seventies.

As editor, Gold seems to have made as many enemies as friends from his notorious critical waspishness and from his practice of taking broad editorial liberties in making changes in manuscripts. These tendencies seemed to grow more pronounced as *Galaxy* prospered through the fifties and as his nerves began to fail under the strain of overwork and reclusive living. His editorial career came to a close following an automobile accident from which his recovery was prolonged and painful. Gold's achievement as the first editor of *Galaxy* deserves an additional recognition of the power of will overcoming otherwise crippling adversity.

The early success of *Galaxy* has been the subject of speculation among critics and popular historians. The traditional view is that *Galaxy* provided a fresh outlet for new and established writers, that there was a growing SF readership—enough to support a third major digest SF magazine—and that *Galaxy* began well by offering writers a higher rate of pay (three cents per word) than its competition. To these three more should be added. First, the magazine set a new tone in its editorials, stories and serialized novels: bright, inquiring, witty and skeptical. Second, Gold made overtures and repeated appeals for reader evaluation and suggestions for making the new *Galaxy* responsive to reader preferences in nearly every department from cover design and interior illustrations to frequency of serials, editorials and the questions of a "Letters" section. To Gold's astonishment, *Galaxy* readers disapproved of a "Letters to the Editor" section, and Gold therefore did not publish a regular letters feature, so dear to the hearts of economy-minded editors. There was, however, strong popular support for a feature Gold wished to avoid, namely, regular editorials, especially those addressed to the genre itself. Another feature that drew wide support was a regular science feature which under Willy Ley was to become a major attraction for nearly twenty years. Readers declared themselves opposed to a succession of serials in one issue after another, which is perhaps ironic since *Galaxy* is remembered as having been especially strong in this area. However, Gold set the policy of avoiding concurrently running serials and perhaps printed fewer serializations than he would have otherwise. The third point accounts in part for Gold's success in recruiting top name writers. Not only were his rates higher (although *Astounding* soon matched them), but his reprint arrangements and contract policies were also fairer to authors. *Galaxy* bought only first magazine rights, which meant that any reprinting of a story earned additional money for its author. Thus, enthusiasm for the magazine began at a high level among both readers and authors despite some early problems in production and distribution.

The original publisher, World Editions, Inc., was an Italian corporation seeking to expand into the U.S. market from its successful European operation, led by popular romance pulps. After the failure of its European headliner, *Fascination*, despite a major advertising campaign, World approached Gold for his assessment of potential publishing opportunities. Gold's contact was Vera Cerutti, a former employee during the early forties, and he recommended that World could reenter the American market successfully with the right kind of SF magazine. And so *Galaxy* was born with Vera Cerutti listed on the masthead as editor-in-chief but with the entire operation under the editorial control of Horace Gold. His original supporting cast included Washington Irving van der Poel, Jr., as art director, Groff Conklin as book reviewer, Jerome Bixby as assistant and Theodore Sturgeon as assistant in reading and screening manuscripts. Gold's major problems during the first year seem to have been production matters, especially in printing and distributing the magazine. World Editions grew cautious about the expense of the production upgrading recommended by Gold and about Gold's long-range plans, which included foreign language editions of the magazine, reprints of classic SF novels, publications of original novels, and an annual. Gold eventually got what he wanted, but World Editions decided to withdraw from a venture that was essentially outside the realm of its interest. After a year and beginning with its October 1951 issue, *Galaxy* was published by Galaxy Publishing Corporation, owned by Robert Guinn. The partnership continued through Gold's tenure as editor and that of Frederik Pohl, who succeeded him.

From Horace Gold's point of view, *Galaxy*'s first year was experimental; during it he developed a readership consensus on format and features and worked to win the support of important SF writers and to set up the Galaxy Publishing empire. He laid the foundations of the magazine's successful operation for the next two decades. It seemed that overnight the SF reader was presented with almost instant offspring of the vigorous new magazine in the Galaxy Reprints series; Galaxy Novels; and, later, the collected Best of Galaxy editions, leading eventually to foreign language editions; the "X Minus 10" radio program of the mid-fifties on the NBC Network with its *Galaxy* tie in; and the satellite digest magazines. During Gold's editorship, *Galaxy* had two running mates: *Beyond Fantasy Fiction*,* which ran only ten issues from 1953 to 1955, and *If*,* the original property of James Quinn Publishing, which had been edited by Paul Fairman and Damon Knight before Gold assumed the editor's post when Galaxy Publishing Co. acquired the magazine. Later editors of *If* moved up to the editorial chair of *Galaxy*: first Fred Pohl, then Ejler Jakobsson, and finally James Baen.

Although Gold made it clear that his early numbers were to be considered experimental and subject to reader approval, the format of Volume 1, Number 1 (October 1950) became the model on which Gold's *Galaxy* built its reputation. This edition included the first number of a Clifford Simak serial. "Time Quarry" (later printed as *Time and Again*); and novelettes including Sturgeon's "The Stars Are the Styx" and Katherine MacLean's "Contagion." Short stories were by Richard Matheson ("Third from the Sun"), Fritz Leiber ("Later Than You Think"), Fredric Brown ("The Last Martian") and Isaac Asimov ("Darwinian Pool Room"). Features included Gold's editorial, "For Adults Only" (from which the reader may easily infer the argument), Groff Conklin's book review, titled "Galaxy's Five Star Shelf" and a science feature by Willy Ley, "Flying Saucers: Friend, Foe, or Fantasy," which Gold had severely reduced in length because, he explained, he did not want to have anything to do with flying saucers. This balance of short fiction forms with a book serial and the nonfiction features became the standard format of *Galaxy* for the next twenty years.

Gold fulfilled both the letter and the spirit of his promise to his readers that *Galaxy* would constantly strive to improve its performance. Although the first issue featured a galaxy of SF stars, it had no top-notch fiction. The second number had the second part of the Simak serial together with more stories by Brown, Asimov and Leiber. Boucher and Knight also contributed. However, Leiber's contribution was the now classic post-holocaust story "Coming Attraction," with its warning of the long-term effects (on the human personality and on society) of limited or even victorious wars. The story caught the special tone that Gold was looking for and seemed to define the terms in which the new magazine would establish its special character as critical, satirical and clever. Its preference for the social and moral implications of technology and science encouraged dissent from the established values of society in the early fifties. The Leiber story was the first of an impressive list of *Galaxy* stories destined to become classics, many of them like "Coming Attraction" without the benefit of having won a prize. Gold's editorial in the second number seems to argue the point: "We have challenged writers to present themes that could not be sold elsewhere . . . themes that were too adult, too profound, or revolutionary in concept for other magazines to risk publishing." Under Gold, *Galaxy* would strive to be such a magazine—revolutionary, anti-establishment, but civilized.

Although *Galaxy* did not eschew hard and adventure SF on the one hand or fantastic SF on the other, it was to be the forum for "stories extrapolating possibilities not approving present trends" that grow out of conjectures about the future social impact of science and technology, as Gold put it in an editorial, "What Is the Purpose of SF?" (November 1951). Two stories cited as illustrating this view of SF as "fictional surmises based on present factors, scientific, social, political, cultural or whatever" were "Coming Attraction" and Ray Bradbury's "The Fireman" (February 1951), a shorter version of the later novel *Farenheit 451* (1953). The Bradbury piece illustrates another characteristic of the *Galaxy* story favored by Gold: the reversal of the conventional or familiar as a function of the conditional future mode of narrative. Bradbury's fireman, Montag, is a state-trained and state-employed arsonist whose purpose is to destroy cultural artifacts, especially books.

Volume 2 (April–September 1951) began to reflect the impact of reader responses to Gold's appeals. Cover designs were improved, as were color tones and sharpness. Gold was especially proud of the use of advanced and expensive printing techniques in the production of the magazine, much of which was mitigated, it must be admitted, by the standard stock paper on which the magazine was printed. Still, interior illustrations became more generous and more professional-looking. By this time the quality of the fiction throughout each issue had been improved, achieving the consistency associated with a leading publication but rarely achieved in the genre. There were few of the filler-calibre stories by big names that appeared in the earlier numbers. Beginning with Volume 2, Gold's *Galaxy* began to publish memorable stories and serials in almost every issue. It was rare that a number of *Galaxy* did not print a work with subsequent staying power, a track record maintained for nearly twenty years throughout the editorships of Gold and Pohl. Volume 2 introduced Cyril Kornbluth's "The Marching Morons" and Robert Heinlein's "The Puppet Masters" among numerous other familiar titles.

Once established, *Galaxy*'s features remained constant for the rest of the decade. Stability and continuity became accomplished facts. However, it was not until April 1952 that Willy Ley took up permanent residence as editor of the *Galaxy* "Science Department," suitably retitled "For Your Information," from which he held forth until his death in 1969. His column set a standard of excellence for its type, and he won two Hugos (1953 and 1956) for his work. Ley brought a wide-ranging curiosity and unquestioned scientific intelligence to his writing. During his tenure at *Galaxy*, he contributed more than any other writer. Perhaps it was no coincidence that the magazine enjoyed its greatest success during the period in which readers could count on finding "For Your Information" under the by-line of Willy Ley in each issue.

Groff Conklin, one of the deans of SF anthologists during the forties and fifties and a genre reviewer for mainstream book review columns, established his residency as *Galaxy*'s book reviewer with the first number. He also helped Gold acquire and evaluate manuscripts for the fledgling publication. He and Sturgeon did the initial screening, after which promising stories were sent on to Gold with their recommendations. Conklin stayed on as reviewer through October 1955. During his stay, Conklin wrote the feature fans most wanted, according to Gold's survey, but neither he nor Gold was ever able to use the kind of rating systems readers indicated they preferred. Floyd C. Gale replaced Conklin in November and tried to produce a more contemporary tone in the reviewing.

Horace Gold's editorials appeared regularly in every issue, fulfilling his pledge to honor reader preferences. He missed only twice during his years as editor. While the Gold editorials lack both the passion and the intelligence of Campbell's highly regarded efforts, they possess a sense of engagement and present a coherent and influential viewpoint. Gold's outlook was, as he defined it in an October 1951 editorial, democratic, liberal and pro-technology. His interest in soft science speculation probably exceeded his interest in hard science extrapolation, and that interest expressed itself in the character of the magazine. He saw the aim of SF as providing entertaining conjecture rather than prophecy. He expressed a preference for stories like "Coming Attraction," "The Fireman," and *Gravy Planet* (Pohl and Kornbluth's novel later retitled *The Space Merchants*) that extrapolated present trends to "extreme cases" and were implicitly critical of possible social trends stemming from the abuse of scientific technology. And yet, Gold was no Jonah. Early in 1952 Gold protested the current wave of "gloom and doom" stories, calling for more balance from authors, whom he exhorted to see positive trends also. In sounding this note, Gold also seemed intent on moderating the critical and ironic tone of his magazine; that balance was to remain consistently part of the *Galaxy* image until the late seventies. Pohl had sounded the same note in the sixties, as had his successors, Jakobsson and Baen, in the early seventies.

Gold's solution to the problems of the overcrowded SF magazine market in the early fifties was characteristic and revealing. He called for writers to revise their standards upward and for publishers to bring new authors into the field. Gold's own ability to encourage both was an important factor in *Galaxy*'s prosperity through the mid-decade collapse of the SF magazine bubble. Both Fred Pohl and James Gunn have testified that Gold, for all his asperity of manner, was an editor who got the most out of his writers.

Not all of *Galaxy*'s innovations were successful. Those that were not were dropped quietly from sight, silent lessons of literary Darwinism. For instance, Gold was an enthusiastic believer in the efficacy of contests in stimulating reader interest and identifying new talent. They never worked. Pohl recalls several instances (in *The Way the Future Was* [Ballantine, 1978]) of desperate pleas from Gold to ghostwrite an award winner from a new writer in order to salvage an unsuccessful contest for undiscovered writers. Fan support for rating stories in each issue was a tactic that Gold himself suppressed, an instance in which the editor clearly had his own views of what a SF magazine should be doing to accommodate the interests of its fans. It would have hopelessly compromised the editor's relationship with the authors. Willy Ley launched several unsuccessful contest schemes related to UFOs and aliens. Gold was not unhappy about the failures, being no supporter of alien or UFO mysticism. In April 1952 Gold proposed the Gernsbackian notion that *Galaxy* become a brokerage house for new, amateur scientific ideas until some legitimate, preferably official agency did the work. That idea died faster than it was born. Two years later, Gold planned another short story contest, this one in league with the American Humanist Association, to encourage college students to break into the world of SF—another noble effort failed for lack of interest. These and other failed experiments demonstrate the experimental spirit that Gold often brought to his work as editor.

Nevertheless, once Gold had trimmed his editorial sails and set the course in the early issues, *Galaxy* sailed smoothly during his career at the helm. Two events, both to some extent dictated by the marketplace, forced slight but significant deviations in plan. The first event was the failure of *Galaxy*'s stablemate fantasy magazine, *Beyond Fantasy Fiction*, in January 1955. As the editor of a fantasy magazine, Gold was publishing stories and authors who probably would not have been considered for *Galaxy*. However, after *Beyond*'s demise, Gold opened up the pages of *Galaxy* to writers whose work he had come to appreciate in his capacity as editor of *Beyond*. The result was that fantastic SF thereafter became a regular part of *Galaxy*'s content. Perhaps Alfred Bester, Fredric Brown, Edgar Pangborn, Robert Sheckley, Theodore Sturgeon and William Tenn had anticipated this movement in the early fifties, but following the *Beyond* debacle (a magazine that, like *Unknown,** deserved a better fate), Gold began including regularly in the pages of *Galaxy* titles by Evelyn E. Smith, Cordwainer Smith and Lloyd Biggle. The second course-changing event was the bi-monthly publication of *Galaxy*, beginning with the December 1958 issue. To compensate, the length of the magazine was expanded to 190+ pages, allowing for more and longer fiction, but there is no doubt that the bi-monthly schedule represented a retreat. Sales had slipped, and the SF short story seemed to be suffering through a less prosperous period. It seems ironic that the only short story to win a Hugo during Gold's editorial direction was Avram Davidson's "Or All the Seas with Oysters," published in May 1958. In addition to the above-mentioned woes, new competition was developing from mainstream publications interested in SF stories as well as from new, original paperback anthologies of unpublished, original stories. The marketplace was changing.

Galaxy prospered during Gold's editorship in part as the result of the many new writers it introduced to its readers together with the familiar faces. Among the new talents of the fifties identified with *Galaxy* were Robert Sheckley (who, in turn, did much to set the tone of the magazine), Richard Matheson, Cordwainer Smith, Gordon R. Dickson, Alan Nourse, Algis Budrys (who also served as an assistant editor), John Christopher, Evelyn E. Smith and Lloyd Biggle, Jr. Gold's editorial direction, of course, had much to do with developing new writers. The most celebrated instance of that was Gold's editorial direction of Bester's *The Demolished Man*, which almost amounted to a collaborative effort in writing. This was the positive side to the notorious editorial interference he was often justly accused of exercising.

Galaxy's bi-monthly schedule was an early sign of Gold's diminishing energies as well as his declining health. Pohl recalls that as the fifties came to a close, he did more and more of Gold's editorial work, including the ghosting of entire issues. In some ways this proved to be a fortuitous investment for the future. It certainly made the transition both easy and effective when Gold officially retired due to ill health with the November 1961 issue because, indeed, Pohl had been doing the editing for some time.

Galaxy practically swept the Hugos in 1953, tying with *Astounding* for best magazine, but receiving the awards for art and science features. These were the only awards that *Galaxy* itself was ever to win, even though its contributors consistently dominated the Hugo balloting. Despite its deserved reputation for excellence, the harvest of the Gold years is surprisingly light in award-winning fiction. As we have seen, only one *Galaxy* short story won a Hugo, and there were two winners in the novel category: Bester's *The Demolished Man* won the very first Hugo in 1952, and Fritz Leiber's *The Big Time* won it in 1958.

Although its stories won relatively few awards, *Galaxy* published an impressive list of titles that have since established themselves as classics. Of the novels, in addition to the Hugo winners above, there were Asimov's *Caves of Steel* (1953), Bester's *The Stars My Destination* (1956–57), Heinlein's *Puppet Masters* (1951), and Pohl and Kornbluth's *The Space Merchants* (as *Gravy Planet*, 1952). Among the memorable short fiction are Blish, "Surface Tension" (August 1952); Bradbury, "The Fireman" (February 1951); Heinlein, "The Year of the Jackpot" (March 1952); C. M. Kornbluth, "The Marching Morons" (April 1951); Miller, "Conditionally Human" (February 1952); Pohl, "The Midas Plague" (April 1954); Sheckley, "A Ticket to Tranai" (October 1955); C. Smith, "The Game of Rat and Dragon" (October 1955) and "The Lady Who Sailed the Soul" (April 1960); Sturgeon, "Baby Is Three" (October 1952; the centerpiece of *More Than Human*); and Kurt Vonnegut, "The Big Trip Up Yonder" (January 1954; later reprinted as "Tomorrow, and Tomorrow, and Tomorrow").

Frederik Pohl formally took the helm with the December 1961 issue. He had been named managing editor in June and had in fact been responsible for *Galaxy* since that time. Pohl's operational goals were to return *Galaxy* to a monthly schedule and to raise the payment rate back to the three cents a word minimum it had been when *Galaxy* began. If *Galaxy* had lost some of its prestige as a leader, Pohl was also determined to restore it to its former position. In so doing, Pohl had the added leverage provided by *If* magazine. Pohl was serving as editor of both *Galaxy* and *If* during this period, using *If* as the lower-paying vehicle for those stories that, although not quite up to the standards Pohl had set for *Galaxy*, were too good to go over to another publisher, as Pohl explained in *The Way the Future Was* (pp. 198–199). Pohl eventually succeeded in realizing these goals for *Galaxy*, despite his frustration and chagrin when *If* walked off with the awards.

Under Pohl *Galaxy* underwent no major course changes but rather developed the trends established under Gold. The magazine features changed little. Willy Ley continued his nonfiction column "For Your Information," observing and commenting on the fulfillment of many of his speculations of the fifties in the developing American space program of the sixties. Algis Budrys took over book reviewing in February 1965 after a hiatus of a year during which no reviews were published. Budrys made the book reviews witty, informative and insightful and gave them a status they had never before achieved.

Pohl's campaign to regenerate *Galaxy* followed the successful formula of its early years in reestablishing the respect and loyalty of the SF writer. Gold's fault-finding and truculence had alienated many, perhaps contributing to *Galaxy's* slump in the late fifties and early sixties. Pohl had established good personal relations with most of the professional SF community with the exception, possibly, of the leadership of the SFWA. Pohl's success with both old and new writers was notable, and during the sixties, *Galaxy* dominated the Hugo awards in its pages. Pohl published all the best SF writers, including Robert A. Heinlein, Cordwainer Smith, Harlan Ellison, Larry Niven, R. A. Lafferty, Fritz Leiber, and Jack Vance. Others who made significant contributions to *Galaxy* were Poul Anderson, Keith Laumer, Fred Saberhagen, Mack Reynolds, Roger Zelazny, Robert Sheckley, Harry Harrison, Edgar Pangborn, James Blish, Sydney Van Scyoc, and Algis Budrys.

That period also witnessed the resurrection of E. E. "Doc" Smith and Robert Silverberg. Silverberg wrote under a unique, exclusive agreement with Pohl that the editor had little reason to regret. Before Silverberg's association with *Galaxy* ended in 1974, he had written exclusively twenty-three stories and four novels.

The number of prize-winning short fiction pieces increased during Pohl's editorship from one (under Gold) to six. Ellison alone produced two: " 'Repent, Harlequin,' Said the Ticktockman" (December 1965—Nebula, 1965/Hugo, 1966) and "The Beast That Shouted Love at the Heart of the World" (June 1968—Hugo, 1969). Gordon Dickson's novella won a Hugo in 1965: "Soldier, Ask Not" (October 1964—expanded into a novel in 1967). Silverberg's novella "Night-Wings" (September 1968) won a Hugo in 1969; and Jack Vance won awards for "The Dragon Masters" (August 1962—Hugo, 1963) and the novella "The Last Castle" (April 1966—Nebula, 1966/Hugo, 1967). There were no award-winning novels.

Galaxy continued its tradition of publishing fiction that has become standard in the field. Among the short stories that distinguished the Pohl era were Poul Anderson's "My Object All Sublime" (June 1961) and "The Sharing of Flesh" (December 1968); P. K. Dick's "If There Were No Benny Cemoli" (December 1963) and "Precious Artifact" (October 1964); Dickson's "Home from the Shore" (February 1963); Philip José Farmer's "The Blasphemers" (April 1964); Damon Knight's "Auto-Da-Fe" (February 1961); R. A. Lafferty's "Thus We Frustrate Charlemagne" (February 1967); Larry Niven's "All the Myriad Ways" (October 1968), "The Organleggers" (January 1969) and "The Adults" (June 1967), later expanded into *Protector* (1967); Robert Sheckley's "Mindswap" (June 1965); and Robert Silverberg's "Hawksbill Station" (August 1967).

The most remarkable contributions to *Galaxy* during Pohl's tenure may have been the stories written by Cordwainer Smith: "A Planet Named Shayol" (October 1961), "The Ballad of Lost C'Mell" (October 1962), "The Boy Who Bought Old Earth" (April 1964), which eventually evolved into *Norstrilla* (1975), "The Dead Lady of Clown Town" (August 1964) and "Under Old Earth" (February 1966).

Serialized novels continued to set the tone of the magazine throughout the sixties. Although none of the novels of the sixties won a prize, many became

standards: Poul Anderson's *To Outlive Eternity* (June 1967–August 1967), re-
printed as *Tau Zero* (1970); Frank Herbert's *Dune Messiah* (July–October 1969);
Fritz Leiber's *A Specter Is Haunting Texas* (July–September, 1968); Clifford D.
Simak's *Here Gather the Stars* (June–August 1963), later *Way Station*; and Jack
Vance's *Star King* (December 1963–February 1964).

Under Pohl's direction, *Galaxy* continued to express its editorial viewpoint
primarily in the contents of the magazine. Pohl's editorials were more personal
than Gold's, and many of them were inspired by Pohl's participation in conventions and other events outside the New York area. This new mobility reflected
itself in the *Galaxy* editorial page. The tone of Pohl's editorials also differed
from Gold's. Gold had developed an editorial style that frequently employed
cosmopolitan small talk. Pohl, on the other hand, was more speculative and
wrote from a vantage point inside the genre. He explored the kinds of scientific
arguments on which stories might be based and confessed to an examined skepticism of UFOs. He also gave his readers an insider's view of SF writers and
fans. Pohl sought to be more entertaining than profound in his editorials, and
while he frequently addressed himself to genre questions, he did so in a familiar
and informal manner rather than as a lawgiver. Indeed, Pohl was dubious, and
has remained so, of the effects of both mainstreaming SF and its perhaps concomitant newly found academic respectability. Nevertheless, an editorial philosophy did emerge from Pohl's *Galaxy* that was to influence the future course
of the magazine. This philosophy may be viewed as either a further development
of the *Galaxy* viewpoint as articulated by Gold or as a new departure, depending
on how the reader perceives the kind of story and novel offered by Cordwainer
Smith, Vance, Lafferty, Ellison, Zelazny, Dick and Silverberg.

Pohl dealt with this question in a revealing editorial statement, ''The Day
After Tomorrow,'' in the October 1965 issue. He begins by establishing three
milestones of contemporary popular SF. The first was reached by John W.
Campbell, Jr., editor of *Astounding*, when he instructed his prospective contributors: ''Write your stories as though they were going to be printed as contemporary fiction in a magazine of the 22nd century.'' The second milestone
was Gold's addition of wit and relevance as characteristics of a good SF story.
The third milestone has been reached by writers like Smith and Vance who are
asking readers to see the future in new symbolic terms as belonging to itself
rather than perceiving it as a mere extension of the present. The future is conceived as more than a projection in which present-day types are placed because
the new writers show the ''people of the world of the future [operating] on their
own terms.'' The great message is that people of the future will differ from us,
differ in ways we may not even be able to guess. Pohl concludes that since we
do not know what the true future will be, we should be prepared to imagine as
many futures as we can. As a partial corrective to this rather indulgent view of
possibly fantastical extremes, Pohl offers a rather more orthodox argument for
the fundamental relationship between science and SF. The difference between
the two, Pohl proposes, is that SF makes accurate deductions from inaccurate

or presumably fanciful premises. This is a variant of what is called "The Game," and science plays it too. For Pohl the resemblance between science and SF is that "both are defined not by their subject matter but by their method of handling it." We may hear in this view distant echoes of those Gold expressed in an editorial of April 1958: "Resourcefully imaginative research and daringly creative extrapolation, these are two of the qualities that make SF a prime recruiter of future scientists, technicians and engineers." Gold's less sophisticated version of "The Game" is called "crag leaping," which Gold sees as "creative science, creative SF, both."

Pohl never won a Hugo for editing *Galaxy*. Ironically, he won three for editing *If*. The explanation may lie in the fact that his ambition was to make "good, gray *Galaxy*" the leader in its field once more, and he did. But editing *If* was just plain fun. If there was an important element missing from *Galaxy* during the Pohl years, perhaps it was that element of spontaneity, of playfulness—the sense of editorial sport. *Galaxy*, after all, had a reputation to live up to. Although he aspired to make *Galaxy* a leader again, Pohl's edition had fewer pretentions of capturing a share of the mainstream market than Gold's. Instead, Pohl seems to have nudged the magazine back toward the fan-reader, especially the young, college-educated reader for whom the reading of SF could be respectable fun if the magazine were *Galaxy*.

During 1968 Pohl got *Galaxy* back to monthly publication, and Lester del Rey joined the editorial staff as managing editor. By this time, Pohl was editing *If* and *Worlds of Fantasy** in addition to *Galaxy*. *Worlds of Tomorrow** had become absorbed into *If*, and Pohl's experimental *International Science Fiction** had folded after just two issues. In addition, Pohl was beginning to develop new creative interests, and his editorial duties had been interfering with his writing activities for some time. When Pohl returned from the World Science Fiction Symposium in 1969, he learned that the publisher, Bob Guinn, had sold *Galaxy* and its stablemates to Arnold Abramson's Universal Publishing and Distributing Corporation. Pohl opted to leave, remaining on the masthead as "editor emeritus."

The decade following Pohl's retirement as editor was unsettled. It began ominously with a missed June number as the transition between publishers and editors took place. Ejler Jakobsson became editor beginning with the July, 1969 issue. Jakobsson was a veteran contributor to pulp magazines in the thirties and served as an editor for Popular Publications in the forties. By coincidence Jakobsson had previously followed Pohl at both *Astonishing Stories** and *Super Science Stories** during World War II. This time he inherited both *Galaxy* and *If* as monthly magazines with comfortable backlogs of good material. Abramson tried reviving *Worlds of Tomorrow*, but it was to last only three more issues before folding in 1971. The title and some features were carried over, however, and combined with *If* to produce *Worlds of If*. This adventure foreshadowed an increasingly active publisher's presence in the fortunes and misfortunes of *Galaxy* during the seventies, which contributed in some measure to the magazine's decline and fall. Symptomatic of this change is the redesigned masthead of the magazine, listing the publisher, Arnold E. Abramson, at the head on a separate line above the editor. A small point, perhaps, but telling.

Under Jakobsson's editorship, *Galaxy* fluctuated from monthly to bi-monthly publication. Jakobsson introduced several unsuccessful changes in format and features that may have contributed to *Galaxy*'s slide. Three were probably management decisions as much as editorial ones. Cover designs, especially of the early Jakobsson issues, were poor. The quality of the paper and the printing were noticeably inferior, and there was a sudden blooming of obscure authors who have remained mercifully unknown ever since. *Galaxy* still attracted the better, newer writers just breaking in, and to Jakobsson's credit, many of the new stars of the seventies published first or early in the pages of *Galaxy*: George R. R. Martin, Joe Haldeman, Joanna Russ, David Gerrold, T. J. Bass and Ernest Taves. Jakobsson added Vaughn Bode's New Wave cartoon "Sunpot" in an attempt to make *Galaxy* more contemporary. It lasted four issues (November 1969–May 1970). While its sexually oriented drawings anticipated *Heavy Metal* in both treatment and style, the importance of "Sunpot" for *Galaxy* lay in its rather conscious attempt to breach the established slick image of the magazine in the name of relevance. It was to be the first of many such breaches, none successful. Vaughn Bode at least was a professional artist, but many of the later *Galaxy* anti-establishment innovations were simply the incorporation of fanzine amateurism into the pages of a growing red giant in the field.

Another change, not especially ominous but a departure from tradition, was the inclusion of a letters to the editor column beginning in late 1971 called "Directions." The column added a dimension of controversy perhaps appropriate to the times, created at least the sense of reader participation, even though a majority of the letters came from authors, and not incidentally made an inexpensive filler.

Algis Budrys was replaced as book review editor by Theodore Sturgeon in January 1972. Contrary to expectations, Sturgeon's reviews were not especially strong. Their main interest lay in the reflected light they threw upon their author. Willy Ley died in 1969 and was replaced as science editor by Donald H. Menzel. After a series of guest editorials, Jakobsson finally settled down to the grind of producing a regular editorial column, which he did competently, if without distinction, through 1973.

The strength of *Galaxy* remained in the publication of stories and novels of high merit, and the magazine won perhaps more than its share of both Hugos and Nebulas during Jakobsson's five years as editor. Sturgeon's "Slow Sculpture" deservedly won both the Hugo (1970) and Nebula (1971) awards. The other award winners were all serial novels: Asimov, *The Gods Themselves* (March/May 1972—Nebula, 1972/Hugo, 1973); the second part appeared in *If*; Clarke, *Rendezvous with Rama* (September/October 1973—Nebula, 1973/Hugo, 1974); and Silverberg, *Time of Changes* (March/May 1971—Nebula, 1971).

Helping *Galaxy* live up to Jakobsson's new subtitle—"The Best in Pertinent Science Fiction"—were several other strong entries: Ben Bova, *Exiled from*

Earth (January/February 1971); John Boyd, *The Doomsday Gene* (May/July 1973); John Brunner, *Web of Everywhere* (March/April 1974); Heinlein, *I Will Fear No Evil* (July–December 1970); Ursula LeGuin, ''Field of Vision'' (October 1973); Barry Malzberg, ''Gehenna'' (March 1971); Niven, ''Rammer'' (November 1971); and Silverberg, *Downward to Earth* (November 1969–March 1970) and *Dying Inside* (July/September 1972).

With *Galaxy*'s commercial fortunes sagging despite a dramatic showing in the quality of its novel serials, *If* was rejuvenated by James Baen. Thus, when Jakobsson stepped down in May 1974, Baen was his logical successor. Just before the transition, Jakobsson appointed Jerry Pournelle as the new science feature writer, a move that would produce an Indian summer under Baen's direction.

Under Baen's editorship *Galaxy* received a redesigned cover format that became standard over the succeeding forty months and improved illustrations both inside and out from Rick Sternbach and Stephen E. Fabian. In January 1975, *Worlds of If* was incorporated into *Galaxy*. The new arrangement was announced on the cover and masthead as well as in the redesigned format and in the kinds of stories and serials that began to appear. The serialization of Zelazny's *Sign of the Unicorn* (one of the Princes of Amber series) is a case in point. New features from the old *Worlds of If* also turned up: Dick Geis' ''The Alien Viewpoint,'' the ''Science Fiction Mart,'' and the ''Science Fiction Calendar,'' with their strong fan orientation. These were to set the direction in which *Galaxy* was later to move in search of a new, contemporary identity after at least tacitly abandoning the liberalism of Gold and Pohl.

Baen managed to blend the divergent interests now implied in the composite features of the new portmanteau magazine. The tone and direction of this new *Galaxy* were perceptibly more contemporary, more youth-oriented and diverse than in the past. Ascendant influences were to be found in the writing and personalities of Niven and Pournelle, although such *Galaxy* standbys as Sturgeon and Pohl continued a loose association with the magazine. Together with Baen, Niven and Pournelle brought ''good, gray *Galaxy*'' to life again by direct transfusions of enthusiastic support of hard science stories and in columns contributed by Pournelle and others on the speculative dimensions of present-day technology. The satirical tone of the original *Galaxy* under Gold, muted under Pohl, seems to have been replaced under Baen by an affirmative and positive belief in the ability of technology to solve its own problems, given proper faith and support, both moral and material, from people, industry and government. It seems a far cry from the social satire of Leiber's ''Coming Attraction,'' Bradbury's ''Fireman'' or the famous Ed Emsh cover illustration of June 1951 with its graphic commentary on mankind's persistent, self-destructive obsession with the development of weaponry. And yet, the manner is never entirely lost, remaining as a counterpoint in Geis' ''The Alien Viewpoint'' column and in stories by such veteran *Galaxy* contributors as Sheckley and Pohl and by newcomers J. J. Russ and John Varley. Indeed, by a twisted sort of logic, it is possible to see *Galaxy* as retaining its adversarial posture toward the spirit of the times; only the times had changed since the fifties, and over the years *Galaxy* had been a factor in those changes of values and attitude.

In addition to the new look and new features under Baen's leadership, guest editorials appeared that attempted to deal intelligently with meaty issues affecting both the world of science and SF. Subtly, perhaps, there was a shifting of the targeted audience that *Galaxy* was aiming at. Baen hoped to build a coalition out of fandom, the traditional adolescent or young adult subscriber, and the college-educated and professional reader.

The reading level of the magazine jumped substantially, particularly in its editorial features during these years. In addition to Pournelle's always challenging and well-written essays on theoretical science likely to become the underpinning of future SF stories, and to the other features mentioned, there was a series of essays written by SF authors giving interesting background information and discussion of their writing. The two most important were on *The Mote in God's Eye* and *Gateway*. Overall, the style and editorial outlook had changed, and the Baen *Galaxy* became bright, inquiring, informal, intellectual and collegiate. *Galaxy* remained pro-science and technology without losing its critical spirit. This trait was established by Gold and has been maintained ever since, but never, perhaps, as forcefully and convincingly as under Baen. His deliberate editorial echo of Heinlein's title "If This Goes On (and on, and on. . . .)" exhorts SF writers of the time (March 1975) to undertake what Baen calls "the next phase" in the growth of contemporary SF. Having contributed to raising consciousness on the dangers of overpopulation, genetic damage, ecologic degradation and the like, Baen argues that it is time to proclaim again the empirical credo in the hope and promise of science and technology to solve the problems it has helped create. A strong message, but one perfectly consistent with the *Galaxy* tradition of Gold and Pohl.

During the Baen editorship, *Galaxy* published only two prizewinners: LeGuin's "The Day before the Revolution" (August 1974—Nebula, 1974) and Pohl's *Gateway* (November/December 1976–March 1977—Nebula, 1977/Hugo 1978). Although it was losing its grip on the awards, *Galaxy* continued publishing work of good quality by new writers, like Lisa Tuttle's "Changelings" (March 1975) and Kevin O'Donnell, Jr.'s "In Xanadu" (November 1975). Among its stars were Charles Sheffield, who published stories in more than half the editions of 1977, and John Varley, whose four stories, all appearing in 1976, included "The Phantom of Kansas" (February 1976) and "Overdrawn at the Memory Bank" (May 1976). In addition, Baen published stories by Gene Wolfe, Saberhagen and Zelazny. Novels were serialized by Zelazny—*Sign of the Unicorn* (January–March 1975) and *The Hand of Oberon* (May–September 1976); Niven and Pournelle—*Inferno* (August–Sepbember 1975); Russ—*We Who Are About To* (January–February 1976); and Herbert—*Dorsadi Experiment* (May–August 1977). The notable nonfiction features included Baen's editorial "If This Goes On (and on, and on. . . .)" of March 1975; Zelazny, "Some Parameters of Science

Fiction. A Biased View'' (July 1975); and Poul Anderson, ''Our Many Roads to the Stars'' (September 1975). Baen's editorials were, on the average, several cuts above previous standards, and Pournelle's science features were easily the best in the field during that time. Sturgeon continued his book column in a workmanlike fashion through July 1975. He was replaced by Spider Robinson, who took over in August 1975, bringing a bright and personal informality to the reviews together with a clear and consistent viewpoint.

The Indian summer of *Galaxy* clouded over rather abruptly with Baen's departure for an executive position with Ace Books. The last Baen issue was October 1977. He was replaced by John J. Pierce, a friend of Lester del Rey and a SF fan well known and liked by conventioneers. Despite the fine showing under Baen, *Galaxy* had been having financial problems since 1966. Writers reported that payment was slower and less certain than usual (*Galaxy* still owed John Varley money for his stories five years after their appearance), and Baen seems to have had to survive on an issue-by-issue basis. When he left for a more secure position, *Galaxy*'s fortunes declined both as an SF magazine and as an influence in the field until its eclipse in 1979, after which only one issue appeared.

The deterioration in the quality of the magazine was as dramatic as the redesigned cover format. The amateurism of the artwork symbolized the coming hard times. Among the Baen feature writers, only Pournelle continued on as before, and that lasted only a few issues. Robinson was replaced as book editor by Paul Walker. *Galaxy* soon returned to bi-monthly publication, beginning in January/February 1978. Since that time, under Pierce, Hank Stine and Floyd Kemske, *Galaxy* has published only eleven issues, two under Stine and one under Kemske. During this period of decline and then fall, there have been a few bright spots: Cordwainer Smith's ''The Queen of the Afternoon'' made its posthumous appearance in Feburary 1978. The best novel serials have been C. J. Cherryh's *The Faded Sun: Kesrith* and Greg Benford's *The Stars in Shroud*, both in 1978, and Pohl's *Jem*, which ran for what must be a record two years in five parts under three different editors.

Critics have offered several reasons for the *Galaxy* decline. The most blame is heaped upon the publisher, Abramson, who could not or would not provide the necessary financial backing for the magazine. *Galaxy*'s payment rate dropped again, despite raging inflation, to a penny per word, hardly more than an honorarium. Increased postal rates and costs of paper, printing and production certainly helped undermine *Galaxy*'s position, together with competition from the paperback original anthology and the paperback magazine. Whatever market factors contributed to *Galaxy*'s fall, the magazine has simply failed to produce a competitive product. Stories of unpaid contributors quickly drove away almost every established writer except for Fred Pohl, who remained loyal to *Galaxy*. If fanzine amateurism became obvious in Pierce's *Galaxy*, it became the centerpiece of the Hank Stine issues of June 1979 and September/October 1979. Pohl's *Jem* continued doggedly on even though it had already appeared in book form, dwarfing the remaining contents of the two issues.

Abramson's UPD Publishing sold *Galaxy* to *Galileo** in late 1979. *Galileo*'s publisher, Vincent McCaffrey, appointed Floyd Kemske, review editor of *Galileo*, to preside over the intended resurrection of *Galaxy*; but *Galileo*'s vulnerable financial position doomed the plan. The intention was to renew *Galaxy* as a bimonthly publication, with four issues planned for 1980. The best that Galaxy Magazine, Inc. was able to do toward meeting its announced goal was the publication of one issue in August 1980. The issue was magazine-size rather than the familiar digest design. It had no newsstand distribution, and not even all *Galaxy* subscribers received copies due to lack of funds for postage. At this writing, *Galaxy* seems to be in publisher's limbo amid talk of possible revival by a new publisher.

At its best, *Galaxy* left a lasting imprint on the genre. Its great strength was in the leadership of its editors and, of course, in its authors. Although its editorial pages never achieved the kind of distinction attained by Campbell's *Astounding/Analog*, when it was at the top of its form, *Galaxy* did some things perhaps better. It promoted an editorial philosophy in both selection and production of materials that brought a new sophistication to the SF magazine. It promoted especially the social science fiction story in a way that made *Galaxy* the conscience, if not the mind and the heart, of the genre. At its best, under Gold, Pohl and Baen, it was never naive. Many writers have testified that Gold's *Galaxy* was important because it offered an alternative to *Astounding* and *The Magazine of Fantasy and Science Fiction*, and in so doing, it encouraged authors to write a type of story that otherwise may not have found a market. It was also frequently distinguished by artwork that was interpretive as well as decorative, and the magazine established new and better standards of production values for the genre.

Information Sources

BIBLIOGRAPHY:
Ashley, Michael. *The History of the Science Fiction Magazine*. Vol. 3. London: New English Library, 1978.
Carter, Paul Allen. *The Creation of Tomorrow: Fifty Years of Magazine Science Fiction*. New York: Columbia University Press, 1977.
Del Rey, Lester. *The World of Science Fiction*. New York: Ballantine, 1979.
Elliot, Jeffrey. "Interview: H. L. Gold." *Galileo* 13, July 1979.
Gold, H. L. *What Will They Think of Last?* Crestline, Calif.: IDHHB, Inc., 1976.
Gunn, James. *Alternate Worlds*. Englewood Cliffs, N.J.: Prentice-Hall, 1975.
Nicholls, Peter, ed. *The Science Fiction Encyclopedia*. Garden City, N.Y.: Doubleday, 1979.
Pohl, Frederik. *The Way the Future Was*. New York: Ballantine, 1978.
Pohl, Frederik, Martin H. Greenberg, and Joseph D. Olander, eds. *Galaxy*. 2 vols. New York: PEI Books, 1981.
Tuck.
INDEX SOURCES: IBSF; ISFM; ISFM-II; Metcalf, Norman, *The Index of Science Fiction Magazines: 1951–1965*, California: Stark, 1968; MIT; NESFA; NESFA-II; NESFA-III; NESFA-IV; NESFA-V; NESFA-VI; NESFA-VII; SFM; Strauss,

Erwin E., *Index to the S-F Magazines: 1951–1965*, Cambridge, Mass.: MIT SF Society, 1966; Tuck. An index is included in the Pohl, Olander, Greenberg *Galaxy* volume cited above.

REPRINT SOURCES:

British Edition: Released by Thorpe & Porter, and later Strato Publications, Leicester and London, starting with Volume 3, Number 1, corresponding to U.S. October 1952, but issued in U.K. in January 1953. Nine issues in 1953; monthly, but none for May, July or December. Thereafter monthly, January 1954–March 1959, Whole Number 72; thereafter bi-monthly, equal to the corresponding U.S. edition overprinted with number only. U.K. issues correspond to U.S. edition overprinted with number only. U.K. issues correspond to U.S. issues as follows: 3/1, Oct 52; 3/2, Sep 52; 3/3, Nov 52; 3/4, Dec 52; 3/5, Jan 53; 3/6, Feb 53; 3/7, May 53; 3/8, Jun 53; 3/9, Jul 53; 10, Aug 53; 11 to 29 equal Sep 54 to Mar 55; 30 to 35 equal Jun to Nov 55. (Note: No. 26 corresponds to July 1952 issue. The U.S. Dec 54 issue was not reprinted in U.K.) Nos. 36 to 71 equal Jan 56 to Dec 58. Continues to Number 79 corresponding to U.S. edition but released one month later in U.K. From Number 80, June 1960, U.S. volumes released. Price 1/6 to No. 25, 2/-, No. 26–71; thereafter 3/6d.

Second series issued by Gold Star Publications, London, equal to U.S. editions except for advertisements and redated and repriced covers, 3/6d. Five issues, U.K. equivalent to U.S. as follows: Jan/Feb 67 = Jun 66; Mar/Apr 67 = Aug 66; May/Jun 67 = Oct 66; Jul/Aug 67 = Dec 66; Sep/Oct 67 = Feb 67. Thereafter U.S. issues released with original cover dates.

Third series was released by Universal-Tandem Publishing Co. and was identical to the U.S. issue except for overprinted price (25p.) and issue number. Numbering was erratic and corresponded to U.S. issues as follows: Nos. 1–10 equal May/June 1972–October 1973; U.S. November and December 1973 issues were both numbered 11 in U.K.; U.S. January, February and March 1974 issues were all numbered 12 in U.K.; no issue 13. No. 14 equals U.S. April 1974; no issues 15 or 16. Nos. 17–25 equal to May 1974–January 1975. Thereafter U.S. issue released.

Foreign Editions: See the following entries in Section IV: Argentina—*Geminis* and *Más Allá*; Finland—*Aikamme Tieteis Lukemisto*; France—*Galaxie* (both series); Germany—*Galaxis*; Italy—*Galaxy*; Netherlands—*Galaxis*; Norway—*Tempo-Magasinet*; Sweden—*Galaxy*.

Derivative Anthologies: Edited by H. L. Gold: *Galaxy Reader of Science Fiction* (New York: Crown, 1952), 33 stories; *Second . . .* (Crown, 1954), 31 stories; *Third . . .* (Garden City, N.Y.: Doubleday, 1958), 15 stories; *The Fourth . . .* (Doubleday, 1959), 15 stories; *The Fifth . . .* (Doubleday, 1961), 15 stories; *The Sixth . . .* (Doubleday, 1962), 14 stories; *Five Galaxy Short Novels* (Doubleday, 1958); *The World That Couldn't Be and Eight Other Novelets from Galaxy* (Doubleday, 1959); *The Bodyguard and Four Other Short Novels from Galaxy* (Doubleday, 1960); *The Mind Partner and Eight Other Novelets from Galaxy* (Doubleday, 1961).

Edited by Frederik Pohl: *The Seventh Galaxy Reader* (Doubleday, 1964), 15 stories; *The Eighth . . .* (Doubleday, 1965), 12 stories; *The Ninth . . .* (Doubleday, 1966), 12 stories; *The Tenth . . .* (Doubleday, 1967), 11 stories; *The Eleventh . . .* (Doubleday, 1969), 10 stories; *Time Waits for Winthrop and Four Other Short Novels from Galaxy* (Doubleday, 1962).

By ''The Editors of Galaxy'': *The Best from Galaxy, Volume I* (New York: Award

Books, 1972), 13 stories; *Volume II* (Award, 1974), 12 stories.

Edited by Jim Baen: *The Best from Galaxy, Volume III* (Award, 1975), 10 stories, 2 articles; *Volume IV* (Award, 1976), 9 stories, 1 article; *Galaxy: The Best of My Years* (New York: Ace, 1980).

Edited by Frederik Pohl, Martin Harry Greenberg and Joseph Olander: *Galaxy Magazine: Thirty Years of Innovative Science Fiction* (Chicago: Playboy Press, 1980), 25 stories plus index.

LOCATION SOURCES: Beloit College Library; Brigham Young University Library; Chicago Public Library; Dallas Public Library; East Carolina University Library; Eastern New Mexico University Library; Harvard University Library; Johns Hopkins University Library; Northern Illinois University Library; Iowa Commission for the Blind Library; MIT Science Fiction Society Library; McGill University Library; New York Public Library; Pennsylvania State University Library; Red Wing, Minnesota Public Library; St. Louis University Library; San Diego Public Library; San Francisco Public Library; Sarah Lawrence College Library; SUNY– Albany Library; Syracuse University Library; Temple University Library; Texas A&M University Library; Toronto Public Library; Tulane University Library; University of Arizona Library; University of California–Riverside Library; University of Georgia Library; University of Kansas Library; University of Maryland– Baltimore County Library; University of Missouri–St. Louis Library; University of New Brunswick Library; University of Southern California Library; University of Texas–Austin Library; University of Wisconsin–Milwaukee Library.

Publication History

TITLE: *Galaxy Science Fiction*, October 1950–August 1958; *Galaxy Magazine*, September 1958–October 1962; *Galaxy* (on cover and spine only; masthead and indicia continued previous title), December 1962–December 1965; *Galaxy Science Fiction* (cover only; spine continues to read *Galaxy* while masthead and indicia read *Galaxy Magazine*), February 1966–September 1968; *Galaxy Science Fiction Magazine*, October 1968–January 1972 (on cover, and on masthead from November 1969; spine and indicia as before); *Galaxy Magazine* (cover and indicia only), March 1972; *Galaxy Magazine* (cover and indicia) and *Galaxy Science Fiction* (spine and masthead), May/June 1972–January 1973; *Galaxy* (on cover and spine only; still *Galaxy Magazine* on indicia), March/April 1973; *Galaxy* (on cover, spine and indicia, but *Galaxy Science Fiction* on masthead), May/June 1973–November 1973; *Galaxy Science Fiction* (on cover, but not spine or indicia), December 1973; *Galaxy* (on all but masthead), January 1974–January 1976; *Galaxy Science Fiction*, February 1976–October 1977; *Galaxy*, November 1977–January 1978; *Galaxy Science Fiction*, February 1978–October 1979; *Galaxy*, [Summer] 1980. The indicia and publisher's statement entitled the magazine *Galaxy, Incorporating Worlds of If* between January 1975 and October 1979.

VOLUME DATA: Volume 1, Number 1, October 1950–Volume 40, Number 1, [Summer] 1980. Volumes 1–16 (to October 1958), six issues per volume; monthly, but no Volume 7, Number 4 (3 followed by 5, followed by 5A), and no issue for December 1955. Volume 17, six issues; monthly, November–December 1958; bi-monthly from February 1959. Volume 18, Number 1, October 1959–Volume 25, Number 6, August 1967, six issues per volume; bi-monthly. Volume 26, six issues; bi-monthly, October 1967–April 1968; monthly from June 1968. Volume 27, six issues; monthly, August 1968–January 1969. Volume 28, six issues; monthly, but no issue for June 1969. Volume 29, six issues; monthly, but no issue for January 1970. Volume 30, six issues; monthly, April–July 1970; bi-monthly, August/September–October/November 1970. Volume 31, six issues, monthly, December 1970–April 1971; bi-monthly from May/June 1971. Volumes 32, 33, six issues each; bi-monthly, July/August 1971–May/June 1973. Volume 34, nine issues; began with Number 7, July/August 1973, Number 8, September, then Numbers 1–7 monthly to April 1974. Volume 35, eight issues, from Numbers 5–12, May–December 1974; monthly. Volume 36, nine issues; monthly, but none in May, November, December 1975. Volume 37, nine issues; monthly, but none in April, June, August 1976. Volume 38, nine issues; monthly, March–November 1977. Volume 39, eleven issues, December 1977/January 1978 issues combined; then monthly February–June 1978, followed by September 1978; then bi-monthly from November/December 1978, followed by March/April 1979, June/July and September/October 1979. Volume 40, one issue, released Summer 1980.

PUBLISHER: World Editions, Inc., New York, October 1950–September 1951; Galaxy Publishing Corp., New York, October 1951–June 1969; UPD Corp., New York, July 1969–March 1977; UPD, Scarsdale, New York, May 1977–September/October 1979; Avenue Victor Hugo, [Summer] 1980.

EDITORS: Horace L. Gold, October 1950–October 1961; Frederik Pohl, December 1961–June 1969; Ejler Jakobsson, July 1969–May 1974; James P. Baen, June 1974–October 1977; John J. Pierce, November 1977–March/April 1979; Hank Stine, June/July–September/October 1979; Floyd Kemske, [Summer] 1980.

FORMAT: Digest, 160pp., October 1950–December 1954; 144pp., January 1955–December 1958; 192pp., February 1959–May 1969; 160pp., July 1969–July 1970; 192pp., August/September 1970–April 1971; 176pp., May/June 1971–May 1974; 160pp., June 1974–June/July 1979; 128pp., September/October 1979; Large, 72pp., [Summer] 1980.

PRICE: 25¢, October 1950–April 1958; 35¢, May 1958–December 1958; 50¢, February 1959–October 1964; 60¢, December 1964–July 1970; 75¢, August/September 1970–March 1975; $1.00, April–July 1975; 79¢, Trial Offer, August 1975; 95¢, September 1975–March 1976; $1.00, May 1976–May 1977; $1.25, June 1977–September/October 1979; $1.50, [Summer] 1980.

Donald L. Lawler

GALILEO

Galileo was a courageous experiment that should have succeeded, and nearly did. Its fortunes, both good and bad, stand now as lessons in the field of magazine publishing.

Galileo was the brainchild of Boston publisher and bookdealer Vincent McCaffrey. McCaffrey ran the bookstore Avenue Victor Hugo, and since 1971 had been publishing a general magazine called, simply, *Fiction*. He had also branched out into book publishing on a small scale, and by 1975 felt that the time was ripe for issuing a select SF magazine. Preparations were drawn out, but the first issue eventually appeared on a quarterly basis in September 1976. The title, *Galileo*, had been chosen because that Renaissance scientist best represented what the magazine stood for, "that indomitable spirit, that undying quest for knowledge and sense of wonder that motivates all scientists, all honest seekers of truth."[1]

Unlike *Omni*,* which was launched only a year later with a multi-million-dollar campaign, *Galileo* started out with admirable restraint. Whereas *Omni* had financial backing, *Galileo* had to work for it. The first issue had a press run of 8,000 copies, of which 5,000 sold in the first two months. *Galileo* concentrated on selling only through the specialist bookstores and small distributors and building up a solid subscription list. By April 1977 the first issue had totally sold out, but still McCaffrey did not try to run before he could walk, and for the first year's issues he kept the print run low and ensured that the magazine broke even, with perhaps a marginal profit.

Despite this low-key launch, *Galileo* was no fanzine in slick's clothing, although a glossy exterior did hide interior pulp pages that allowed only mediocre reproduction of photographs and illustrations. Some of the artwork was amateurish, but the presentation was of reasonably good quality under the circumstances, and Tom Barber had supplied an arresting cover. The issue was able to boast such impressive names as Arthur C. Clarke and Ray Bradbury. The Bradbury piece, "Marvels and Miracles—Pass It On!," was an obscure reprint from 1955 and, while not nonfiction, was a hypothetical interview with Jules Verne. Clarke's "Communications in the Second Century of the Telephone" was a transcription of the speech he gave at the celebration of the first centenary of the telephone.

The stories came from less well known names, although some, like Robert Chilson, Damien Broderick and Ruth Berman, had been around for a few years. There was a pleasing balance between mood and action stories, and while nothing was outstanding, the result was a pleasant read.

On schedule, the second issue, again with a bold Barber cover, presented nonfiction by Hal Clement and stories by Alan Dean Foster, Arthur Jean Cox and Jacqueline Lichtenberg, among others. A letter column was introduced, and by now the other departments were becoming established, including the author profiles and extended book reviews. Andrew Adams Whyte took on the leviathan task of cataloguing all forthcoming books, something this bibliomaniac achieved with commendable thoroughness during the magazine's run.

By the third issue *Galileo*'s format was settled, and certainly there was a steady quality about its contents. The lead articles usually concentrated on scientific and literary aspects; the third issue, for example, included an excerpt from Carl Sagan's book *The Murmurs of Earth* on "The Naming of the Solar System," while Greg Bear looked at SF artwork and Brian Fraser interviewed Kelly Freas. There was usually room for a poem or two, in this issue "N" by Ray Bradury, and the stories were usually by a mixture of new and established writers, in this instance Lee Killough, Robert Chilson, Kevin O'Donnell, Jr., A. J. Giambra and Brian W. Aldiss.

The response among readers was more than encouraging. With the fifth issue, *Galileo* chanced a print run of 32,000, many of which went to subscribers, and that same issue printed the first episode in a serial, "Masters of Solitude" by Marvin Kaye and Parke Godwin, indicating that *Galileo* had now moved to a bi-monthly schedule. A statement of circulation printed in the special double issue in 1979 relating to 1978 sales showed a total paid circulation of 56,562 out of 68,000 printed, of which 52,900 were accounted for by direct subscriptions.

Everything seemed to be going right for *Galileo*. It was now publishing some excellent fiction; surprisingly, none was nominated for awards, although a few stories found their way onto the preliminary ballots for the Nebula. Issue 6 was especially commendable, with "Django" by Harlan Ellison, " . . . The Best Is Yet to Be" by M. Lucie Chinn, and a reprint of Cherry Wilder's "The Ark of James Carlyle." Unfortunately, *Galileo* insisted on including a comic strip called "Crosswhen" from the eighth issue, despite the fact that such ventures have never had much success in otherwise all-prose magazines, but it was an innocuous piece that could easily be overlooked. The concentration of features and articles by writers such as Robert Silverberg, James P. Hogan, Greg Benford, David Gerrold, Robert L. Forward and many others, along with revealing interviews of A. E. van Vogt, H. L. Gold and Greg Benford, and perceptive book reviews by C. J. Cherryh, Jack Williamson, George R. R. Martin and others gave the magazine considerable depth, and the circulation continued to rise.

At this point things started to go sour, and none of it was *Galileo*'s fault. With the high incidence of subscription sales, McCaffrey engaged a subscription agency that used a new computer system which failed miserably. Copies were lost, matters got rather out of hand, and issues were delayed in appearing while past issues were still being mailed out. This sudden eruption of irregularity in what had been an ordered and controlled magazine caused confusion among subscribers, who naturally enough withheld their subscriptions until they could see the outcome. As a result subscriptions dropped from 76 percent of the print run to 60 percent, and continued to dwindle.

This decline, despite the obvious popularity of *Galileo*, caused McCaffrey to seek a wider distribution, and he signed a deal with Dell Distributing for a nationwide network distribution of the magazine from the thirteenth issue. One hundred five thousand copies were printed against which Dell put up an advance of $28,000 per issue. This was based on a forecast sale potential of 40 percent of the print run. Since *Galileo* had hitherto been selling twice that without much difficulty, all seemed set for a very bright future, and *Galileo* made plans accordingly. As a major scoop they acquired serialization rights to Larry Niven's *The Ringworld Engineers*, sequel to his award-winning *Ringworld*. Another *Galileo* story contest was announced, and an increase in word rates was promised.

And then, just as suddenly, everything stopped. Sales, it was discovered, were not at the 40 percent level. They were not even at 20 percent. Dell cut back its advance and asked for repayment. Suddenly there was no money to print, or even to mail out past issues. Once the big new name in SF, *Galileo* was suddenly a disaster.[2]

The final scene has still to be played in the *Galileo*/Dell drama, but there seems very little likelihood of *Galileo* ever returning. It was a senseless and tragic loss. *Galileo* and McCaffrey had done everything right, but in the end they had become too entangled in the world of commerciality rather than staying in the safe, if potentially less prosperous world of specialist selectivity. There is much that is fresh and enjoyable in the pages of *Galileo*, and it was always a magazine worth acquiring. The sixteenth issue was never fully distributed and copies are virtually unobtainable, thus already increasing in value as collector's items. Future publishers will learn from McCaffrey's experiences, but at SF's loss.

Notes

1. Charles C. Ryan, "The Starry Messenger," *Galileo* 1, p. 8.
2. The story of *Galileo*'s demise has been the subject of several items in the news magazines, but of special interest are *Locus* 230 (February 1980): 1, news item headed "*Galileo* Retrenches"; *Locus* 233 (May 1980): 5, news item headed "*Galileo* in Trouble"; *Locus* 238 (October 1980): 1, news item headed "Galaxy, Galileo Go Under"; *Science Fiction Chronicle*, January 1981, p. 1, under headline "Galileo, Galaxy Suspend Publication, Seek Buyer."

Information Sources

BIBLIOGRAPHY:
Nicholls. *Encyclopedia.*
INDEX SOURCES: NESFA-V; NESFA-VI; NESFA-VII; Robinson, R. J. *An Index to Galileo.* Tamworth, U.K.: Diamond Press, 1981 (listings by issue, author, title, plus items reviewed and cover artists); SFM.
REPRINT SOURCES:
    Derivative Anthology: Charles C. Ryan, ed., *Starry Messenger: The Best of Galileo* (New York: St. Martin's Press, 1979), twelve stories.
LOCATION SOURCES: M.I.T. Science Fiction Library.

Publication History

TITLE: *Galileo* (subtitled "Magazine of Science & Fiction).
VOLUME DATA: Number 1, [September] 1976–Volume 2, Number 4 [Whole Number 16], January 1980. Quarterly, Number 1–Number 4, July 1977. Bi-monthly, Number 5, October 1977–Number 10, September 1978 (issue 6 dated January 1978). Issues 11 and 12 combined as an undated double issue [May 1979]. Thereafter bi-monthly, Number 13, July 1979–Number 16, January 1980. Issue 17 pasted-up and cover printed (see *Locus* 238) but never published. Total run: 16 numbered issues, but 2 issues combined, therefore 15 issues.
PUBLISHER: Avenue Victor Hugo, Boston, Massachusetts.
EDITOR: Charles C. Ryan.

FORMAT: Pulp (saddle-stapled); 80 pp., Number 1; 96 pp., Numbers 2–5; 112 pp.,
   Number 6; 96 pp., Numbers 7–10; 144 pp., Number 11/12; 96 pp., Numbers 13–
   16.
PRICE: $1.50, Numbers 1–10; $2.95, Number 11/12; $1.95, Numbers 13–16.

Mike Ashley

GAMMA

During its short and rather erratic life, *Gamma* displayed all the symptoms of
a split personality. "You've probably noticed by now that *Gamma* is not like
the other science-fiction magazines," William F. Nolan wrote in his first editorial. "In fact, we don't even refer to it on the masthead as a science-fiction
magazine. In this age when science-fiction and science-fact are so closely allied,
our aim is the only logical one, as spelled out for you on the table of contents
page in the subtitle: NEW FRONTIERS IN FICTION."

But what did that mean? If *Gamma* was trying so hard not to be a science
fiction magazine, then why did the cover of the first issue, for July 1963, boldly
display an American rocket leaving the moon? Why did the advertisement on
the page where one would expect to find an editorial refer to *Gamma* as "America's fabulous new science-fiction magazine"? Yet to counteract the obvious
space fiction image of Morris Scott Dollens' perfectly competent covers, the
covers also proudly display the names Tennessee Williams, Ray Bradbury, William Faulkner, Dorothy B. Hughes and even Shakespeare. The overriding impression was that here was a literary magazine trying to transcend its science fiction
content, and the result, instead, was something of a cuckoo in the nest. It was,
for the most part, ignored by the SF fraternity, perhaps because of its literary
pretentions, and yet it was also overlooked by the literary market at which it
was obviously aimed. It would seem that a blend of mispackaging, mismarketing
and the inevitable distribution problems soon put a noose around the neck of
what was, in fact, one of the better SF and fantasy magazines on the market.
The problem was that one first had to buy and read the magazine to appreciate
what it offered, and not enough people did. *Gamma* saw only five issues spaced
out over a period of two years, but there was a lot that was good in those issues.

The man behind *Gamma* was Charles E. Fritch, a sometime SF writer, though
better known in the crime fiction field where, for a while, he edited the detective
magazine *Chase*. Together with writer/editor and general all-rounder Jack Matcha
he planned to issue a new type of science fiction and fantasy magazine, although
to a great extent *Gamma* was a replay of *The Magazine of Fantasy and Science
Fiction** in its early years under Anthony Boucher and J. Francis McComas.
Because it was published in Hollywood, and because Managing Editor William
F. Nolan was closely associated with film scriptwriters, it was inevitable that
many of the contributors would have the same associations. In fact, the first
issue was overloaded with them: Charles Beaumont, Ray Russell, Rod Serling

(the subject of an interview), George Clayton Johnson, Richard Matheson, Ray Bradbury and Nolan himself. The stories were mostly slick, fast-action, almost like up-market screenplays written for a totally different audience than *Analog Science Fiction** or *Galaxy Science Fiction.** As a balance to these, however, were stories by A. E. van Vogt, Charles E. Fritch (an SF spoof, "Venus plus Three," which may have left non-SF initiates a little perplexed), Forrest Ackerman, and the first story sale of Tennessee Williams, "The Vengeance of Nitocris," from *Weird Tales** vintage 1928. There were a few novelties, such as a play by Fritz Leiber and poetry from Ray Bradbury; but this mixture, while readable, gave one the impression of being pulled in several directions at once.

Gamma 2 was much the same, although by now a pattern was starting to emerge. It was evident that by far the better stories were not SF, at least certainly not the serious SF items, but the fantasy and humorous SF spoofs. "The Granny Woman" by Dorothy B. Hughes, for instance, was a superb novelette about witchcraft. "Michael" by Francesca Marques was a beautifully moving fantasy about a blind child. Charles Beaumont's "Something in the Earth," SF by convention, was first and foremost a horror story, as was Charles Fritch's "Castaway," a terror tale of loneliness. Richard Matheson's "Deus ex Machina" can be seen simply as a robot story, but deep down it is a tale of growing madness. The issue was rounded off by Ray Bradbury's Hemingwayesque "Sombra y Sol." The power in these stories was formidable, and the novelty items in the same issue, such as Ib Melchior's clever juggling of Shakespeare's dialogue to produce a science fiction poem, were something of an intrusion.

Much of this power was sustained for the third issue, which included Patricia Highsmith's now classic horror story "The Snail Watcher" and equally meritorious vignettes by George Clayton Johnson, Miriam Allen deFord and Bernard Malamud. There was a stronger vein of humor in this issue that softened the punch that was otherwise promised, but it made *Gamma* a very worthwhile magazine. There was also an interview with a pseudonymous Russian editor about Soviet science fiction which threw a new light for the time on East-West views of SF.

Nolan left *Gamma* after the third issue, partly due to his workload, but possibly also because the direction in which he wanted to take the magazine was not the one favored by the publishers. *Gamma* had much latent quality within, but all the trappings of pulp fiction without. With Nolan's departure, Charles Fritch's influence is seen to greater effect. The fourth issue became a "Special Outer Space" number with a cover in the old tradition of a beautiful near-naked blonde being menaced by green, parrot-faced aliens—all well and good, if the readership attracted by such comic-book covers is likely to appreciate the real purpose of the magazine. The literary flavor had diminished in this issue, which was little more than a pretentious romp. Unfortunately, *Gamma* did not recover its composure for the fifth issue. Almost half of the issue was taken up by a short novel by Ron Goulart, "Nesbit," which would not have been out of place in *The Man from U.N.C.L.E. Magazine.** The rest of the issue had some good stories by

Beaumont, Matheson, Johnson, Bradbury and the up-and-coming Dennis Etchison, but the overall impression was that the wind had slackened in the sails. *Gamma* had become motiveless. This may have contributed as much as the lack of adequate financing to the fact that no further *Gamma*s appeared. There were rumors of an impending sixth issue for several months, and then even they died.

Nearly twenty years later we can learn much from *Gamma*. It was a worthwhile experiment that failed because of mismanagement. Had adequate finances been available, *Gamma* should have been issued in a slick format with up-market covers. It should have succeeded. In William F. Nolan's hands it showed promise. But if you want to sell something new, you don't wrap it in old boxes.

Information Sources

BIBLIOGRAPHY:
Nicholls. *Encyclopedia*.
Tuck.
INDEX SOURCES: MIT; MT; SFM; Tuck.
REPRINT SOURCES: None known.
LOCATION SOURCES: M.I.T. Science Fiction Library; Pennsylvania State University Library.

Publication History

TITLE: *Gamma* (subtitled "New Frontiers in Fiction").
VOLUME DATA: Volume 1, Number 1, [July] 1963–Volume 2, Number 5 [3], September 1965. Last two issues only carry an off-sale month. First two issues designated quarterly, last two issues bi-monthly, but all irregular. Issue 2: [November] 1963; 3: [June] 1964; 4: February 1965. Volume 1, 2 issues. Volume 2, 3 issues. Total run: 5 issues.
PUBLISHER: Star Press, Inc., North Hollywood, California.
EDITORS: First three issues, William F. Nolan; thereafter, Charles E. Fritch and Jack Matcha.
FORMAT: Digest (first two issues perfect bound, thereafter saddle-stapled), 128pp.
PRICE: 50¢.

Mike Ashley

GHOST STORIES

Ghost Stories has long been neglected by collectors of fantasy and science fiction for the simple reason that the magazine appeared to have little to offer. From its first issue in July 1926 it looked just like its companion magazines *True Story* and *True Detective Stories*, with stories concocted in a "confessions" format and accompanied by posed photographs to add an air of authenticity. Some stories bore bogus by-lines, as with "How I Tried to Cheat My Soul" by Arthur Keith as told to Philip Ashe.

As the contents concentrated solely on spooks and specters, it was ignored by most of the fantasy fraternity (although Robert A. W. Lowndes read it regularly), and only now is it being appreciated that *GS* carried several items of interest. It saw, for instance, the first American magazine publication of Agatha Christie's classic "The Last Seance" under the title "The Woman Who Stole a Ghost" (November 1926). It also was the first to publish fantasy writer Carl Jacobi, whose story "The Haunted Ring" appeared in the very last issue and beat his first sale, "Mive" (*Weird Tales,* * January 1932), into print by one month.

Also hidden in its sixty-four issues are single story contributions by Douglas M. Dold ("Prisoners of Fear," February 1931), Nictzin Dyalhis ("He Refused to Stay Dead," May 1927), Paul Ernst ("A Crystal Gazer's Crime!" June 1929), Frank Belknap Long ("The Man Who Died Twice," January 1927) and Robert E. Howard ("The Apparition in the Prize Ring" under the alias John Taverel, April 1929). Victor Rousseau was a regular contributor, as were Stuart Palmer and Robert W. Sneddon, all well known in the fantasy and mystery fields. This is not to say that their stories were of lasting quality. Written to a very restricting formula, they had none of the thrill or originality of the classic Victorian ghost stories, many of which were reprinted alongside them, such as "The Signalman" by Charles Dickens (May 1929) and "The Open Door" by Mrs. Oliphant (August 1926).

Also well represented with reprinted stories were H. G. Wells and Sir Arthur Conan Doyle. No less than six of Wells' stories appeared, including not only the more obvious ghost stories like "The Red Room" (April 1927) and "The Inexperienced Ghost" (August 1929), but less likely tales such as "A Moth—Genus Unknown" (October 1927) and "Pollock and the Porroh Man" (July 1930). Doyle was a more appropriate contributor following his conversion to spiritualism, and he was represented by both fiction ("The Captain of the Polestar," April 1931 and nonfiction ("Houdini's Last Escape," March 1930).

The magazine began as a large-size publication printed on coated paper, which allowed the reproduction of the photographs. After various changes the coated stock was replaced by the usual pulp paper, which brought an end to the "phantom photos," although the interior illustrations that took their place looked equally staged and wooden.

GS maintained a monthly schedule for most of its life but slipped to bi-monthly at the end. Although originally published by Bernarr MacFadden, it had been sold, in 1930, to Harold Hersey, the earlier editor of *The Thrill Book* * and subsequent publisher of *Miracle Science and Fantasy Stories.* * Hersey never had much success with his fantasy magazines, and *GS* saw only nineteen issues under his control. Its demise was inevitable, however, for if the Depression had not killed it, stagnation would have. The limited scope and variety offered readers by publishing solely ghost stories was leading to monotony and repetition. It was a mercy to let it die.

Information Sources

BIBLIOGRAPHY:
Moskowitz, Sam. "Neglected Repository of Supernatural Fiction." In *Stories of Ghosts*. Evergreen, Colo.: Opar Press, 1973.
Tuck.
INDEX SOURCES: MT; SFM; Sieger, James R. "Ghost Stories Index," *The Fantasy Collector*, January–May 1970, reprinted in *Stories of Ghosts*, Evergreen, Colo.: Opar Press, 1973; Tuck.
REPRINT SOURCES:
   Magazines: See entries for *Prize Ghost Stories* and *True Twilight Tales*.
LOCATION SOURCES: M.I.T. Science Fiction Library.

Publication History

TITLE: *Ghost Stories*.
VOLUME DATA: Volume 1, Number 1, July 1926–Volume 11, Number 4, December 1931/January 1932. Six issues per volume. Monthly until July 1931, thereafter bi-monthly. Total run: 64 issues.
PUBLISHER: Constructive Publishing Co., Dunellin, N.J., July 1926–March 1930; Good Story Magazine Co., New York, April 1930–December 1931/January 1932.
EDITORS: Exact issues not known. Believed to be: Harry A. Keller (1926–1927), W. Adolphe Roberts (1927–1928), George Bond (1928–1929), D. E. Wheeler (1929–1930), Arthur B. Howland (mid-1930), Harold Hersey (1930–1931).
FORMAT: Bedsheet (11½″ x 8½″), 96pp., July 1926–July 1928; Pulp, 128pp., August 1928–March 1929; Large Pulp, 96pp., April 1929–December 1929; Pulp, 128pp., January 1930–December 1931/January 1932.
PRICE: 25¢.

Mike Ashley

GHOSTS AND GOBLINS

Ghosts and Goblins, probably published in 1938, was one of the single-issue magazines associated with the Master Thriller Series,* although not numbered as such. Amusingly subtitled "Weird Tales, Quaint Conceits, Hair-Raising Happenings," it was a mixture of fiction and "fact," containing eighteen short items. The main contributor was R. Thurston Hopkins, whose lead story, "Sir Ralph's Agincourt Armour," was reprinted in Hopkins' wartime booklet *Weird and Uncanny Stories*. Also present was that popular contributor to the popular magazines of the thirties, Garnett Radcliffe, with "The Finger of Kali."

The other contributors are not as well known, and their names, which include Henry Rawle, Frank Clements, B. Wilmot Allistone and Frederick Graves, may be real or pseudonymous.

Information Sources

BIBLIOGRAPHY:
Tuck.
INDEX SOURCES: MT; Tuck.
REPRINT SOURCES: None known.
LOCATION SOURCES: None known.

Publication History

TITLE: *Ghosts and Goblins.*
VOLUME DATA: Undated, unnumbered (probably Christmas 1938).
PUBLISHER: World's Work, Kingswood, Surrey.
EDITOR: Not credited, but may have been H. Norman Evans.
FORMAT: Pulp, 128pp.
PRICE: 1s.

Mike Ashley

THE GIRL FROM U.N.C.L.E. MAGAZINE

The Girl from U.N.C.L.E. was a borderline magazine issued by Leo Margulies as a companion to *The Man from U.N.C.L.E. Magazine** as a natural tie-in to the television follow-up of the original series. It was identical in format and presentation to its big-brother companion.

Most of the plots of the lead novels, which were pseudonymously credited to "Robert Hart Davis" (Richard Deming, I. G. Edmonds, and Charles Ventura) have strong science fiction elements ranging from secret weapons to destroy the world, to an orbiting atom bomb, to a village of living dead. These novels were not reprinted in the paperback series of the same name.

While *GFU* did not reprint stories from the SF field, authors like Miriam Allen deFord ("The Kookhouse Murderer," December 1966) and Arthur Porges ("The Cunning Cashier," April 1967) were represented; both stories are mysteries.

The magazine is a minor contribution to the fantastic fiction field, being more of an adventure than an SF magazine, but the plots of the lead novels entitle it to a small niche in the field.

Information Sources

INDEX SOURCES: Cook, Michael L., *Monthly Murders*, Westport, Conn.: Greenwood Press, 1982.
REPRINT SOURCES: None known.
LOCATION SOURCES: Leo Margulies Collection, University of Oregon Library, Eugene, Ore.; Legal Department, MGM Studios, Culver City, Calif.; M.I.T. Science Fiction Library; Pennsylvania State University Library.

Publication History

TITLE: *The Girl from U.N.C.L.E. Magazine.*

VOLUME DATA: Volume 1, Number 1, December 1966–Volume 2, Number 1, December 1967. Six issues per volume. Bi-monthly. Total run: 7 issues.

PUBLISHER: Leo Margulies Corporation, New York.

EDITORS: The Editorial Director was Cylvia Kleinman (Mrs. Leo Margulies). Credited as Associate Editor was H. N. Alden for the first three issues and Holmes Taylor for the last four. Both these pseudonyms were a cover for Alden H. Norton.

FORMAT: Digest, 144pp.

PRICE: 50¢.

Grant Thiessen

GOLDEN FLEECE HISTORICAL ADVENTURE

Golden Fleece, first published in October 1938, was not a fantasy magazine. As its subtitle stated, it was a magazine of historical adventure, ranging from the days of legend to the recent past. But because the magazine contained stories by a number of fantasy writers, was illustrated by some of the same artists, and has been included in a number of fantasy bibliographies, *GF* has become so closely associated with the field that it demands an entry in this volume if only to set the record straight.

The magazine only lasted for nine issues, although, if the letter column is any indication (and it usually is not), it was very popular. It probably fell prey to distribution problems, coming as it did from the small Sun Publications offices in Chicago rather than from one of the major New York firms. Issues are now difficult to obtain, which has added to its prestige in the eyes of collectors. It was trying to compete with the major magazine *Adventure* and met too powerful an opponent.

The first issue led with "Roman Holiday" by the ever popular Talbot Mundy, and also presented the first of a short series by H. Bedford-Jones, "Coasts of Chance." *GF* ran no serials, but these three stories, which ran in consecutive issues, were the next best thing. Mundy only appeared once, but Bedford-Jones was a regular, appearing in six of the nine issues under his own name. Another regular was E. Hoffman Price, who succeeded in getting two stories in the December 1938 issue under his own name. The first, "Wolves of Kerak," was set at the time of the Crusaders, while the other, "Two Against the Gods," dealt with an incident during Pizarro's conquest of the Incas. Both stories were illustrated by Jay Jackson, then a regular artist for *Amazing Stories** and *Fantastic Adventures.** The mainstay artist for *GF*, however, was Harold Delay, whose work was competent and decorative and considerably more impressive than Jackson's. Harold McCauley made a few rare appearances, as did Margaret Brundage, who painted two of the covers.

Many of the adventures set in early days have an atmosphere of implied fantasy and certainly were created in that mood, even if supernatural events were not made explicit. Among such tales were "Eric of Aztalan" by Ralph Milne Farley; "Ariadne Speaks" and "The Bath of King Minos" by Clyde B. Clason; "Graah, Foiler of Destiny" by Pansy E. Black; and the short series by R. A. Emberg, "The Rune of Odin," "The Coming of the Goths" and "Over the Danube." Even Murray Leinster joined in the fray with "Swords and Mongols." For collectors perhaps the most interesting issues are those containing the work of Robert E. Howard: November 1938 with "Black Vulmea's Vengeance" and January 1939 with "Gates of Empire."

Golden Fleece was a rousing and unpretentious magazine. It can be read and enjoyed as historical adventure, but it was never intended to be a fantasy magazine, and despite the presence of so many associated names it never became one.

Information Sources

BIBLIOGRAPHY:
Tuck.
INDEX SOURCES: Cockcroft, IWFM; Day, IWFM; Tuck.
REPRINT SOURCES: *Derivative anthology: Golden Fleece* (Odyssey Publications, W. Newton, Mass., 1975).
LOCATION SOURCES: None known.

Publication History

TITLE: *Golden Fleece Historical Adventure Magazine* (full title as per contents page; abbreviated on cover and spine).
VOLUME DATA: Volume 1, Number 1, October 1938–Volume 2, Number 6, June 1939. Three issues in first volume. Monthly. Total run: 9 issues.
PUBLISHER: Sun Publications, Chicago.
EDITORS: A. J. Gontier, Jr., and C. G. Williams.
FORMAT: Pulp, 128pp.
PRICE: 20¢.

Mike Ashley

GREAT SCIENCE FICTION

When Sol Cohen took over publication of *Amazing Stories** and *Fantastic** in 1965 he decided to take full advantage of the legacy left by the former publisher, Ziff-Davis. It had purchased second serial rights to the stories, meaning that Cohen could reprint them without additional payment to the authors. He was able to cut costs further by printing directly from the original magazine copy, thereby lowering typesetting bills. With overhead cut to the bone, Cohen began to issue a series of all-reprint magazines. *Amazing* and *Fantastic*, which were edited by Joseph Wrzos, included one or two new stories each issue and reprints, selected by Wrzos, from the twenties and thirties. Cohen concentrated on selecting his reprints from the fifties and early sixties.

The first of the all-reprint magazines was *Great Science Fiction*, undated, but released in December 1965. The cover, which featured a small inset illustration reprinted from a 1940s issue, and which boldly displayed the names of the eight authors represented within, bore the full title of the magazine, *Great Science Fiction from Amazing*. Its contents were chosen from early Cele Goldsmith issues of 1959 through 1961 and were representative of *Amazing* at that time. They included Isaac Asimov's spoof on SF and sex, "Playboy and the Slime God," James Blish's tale of warning against meddling in native traditions on outpost planets, "A Dusk of Idols," and Robert Bloch's chilling tale of space exploration, "The Bald-Headed Mirage."

Cohen himself had selected the reprints. As a first issue it was of reasonably good quality, and the quality was maintained in the second issue, again undated, but released in March 1966. This time the title ran *Great Science Fiction from Fantastic*, with ten selections from *Fantastic*'s issues in 1959, 1960 and 1962. Arguably, the contents were superior to the first issue's because of the quality of *Fantastic* during this period, and certainly an issue that included "The Fife of Bodidharma" by Cordwainer Smith, "The Singing Statues" by J. G. Ballard and "The Hungry Eye" by Robert Bloch had much in its favor.

The magazine, however, betrayed signs of hasty compilation. The contents page of the first issue, for instance, had interchanged the stories by Jack Sharkey and J. F. Bone, while in the second issue Albert Teichner's story "The Thinking Disease" was misprinted as "The Thinking Machine." Clearly Cohen was not paying sufficient attention to the magazine even though, as Joseph Wrzos recalls, it was Cohen who "laid out these issues, decided on where the stories . . . would go, on how much art to use, on what the cover would be, the interior artwork, the heads and the advertisements."[1] Since Cohen was acting in this capacity on all the magazines, the result was errors and a deterioration in the general quality of the magazines. Therefore, Cohen decided that he needed more help and hired Herb Lehrman as an assistant editor. Together Cohen and Lehrman assembled the issues of *GSF* and the new companion magazines, *The Most Thrilling Science Fiction Ever Told* (*Thrilling Science Fiction**) and *Science Fiction Classics*.*

Cohen continued to choose *GSF*'s contents alternately from *Amazing* and *Fantastic* over the next few quarterly issues, taking stories from the 1958–1964 issues. Starting with issue 7 (the last undated number, released in Summer 1967) stories were integrated from both parent magazines (with the majority from *Amazing*), and the title was contracted to simply *Great Science Fiction*. On the face of it, *GSF* was progressing slowly but confidently.

Behind the scenes, however, matters were far from calm. Cohen had invoked the wrath of the newly formed Science Fiction Writers of America through his refusal to pay authors a reprint fee. The SFWA, under its president, Damon Knight, threatened to boycott the magazines, although a publication that relies on reprints is hardly going to be damaged by writers not submitting fiction, and the SFWA had no power to upset the already patchy distribution of the magazines. If there was any change it was that Cohen began to reprint older stories by writers who were not SFWA members or who had long since become lost to the SF field. This change, however, was more evident in the other magazines than in *GSF*, which continued to select stories from the fifties and sixties.

With the tenth issue (Spring 1968), the cover declared that the magazine was edited by Harry Harrison. Harrison had acted as arbitrator between Cohen and the SFWA and had subsequently agreed to edit *Amazing* and *Fantastic* on the understanding that all reprints be phased out. As a favor to help sales, Harrison agreed to have his name listed as editor of *GSF*, and he also wrote two editorials, but it was still Cohen who selected the stories and compiled the issues.

The continued use of reprints and the resultant changes in *Amazing* and *Fantastic* are described under the entries for those magazines. An echo of those changes, however, was felt in *GSF*. Peace between Cohen and the SFWA was eventually made during the presidency of Robert Silverberg, and it was Silverberg who recommended Ted White as editor of *Amazing* and *Fantastic*. In return, Cohen decided to assemble an all-Silverberg issue of *GSF*, reprinting stories from the 1956–1957 issues of the parent magazines. At the same time he changed the magazine title to *Science Fiction Greats*, effective from the thirteenth issue (Winter 1969). Cohen followed this with a special Harlan Ellison issue with stories chosen from the same period. Neither issue reflected the authors' best work, and certainly not the work by which they were becoming established in the 1960s. Nevertheless, for those interested in tracing the development of these authors' careers, the two issues provide an interesting selection of early tales. With the fifteenth issue *SFG* reverted to the original format and retained it for its final seven issues.

Of all the Ultimate reprint magazines, *SFG* is the most readable because the stories were selected from the best period of *Amazing* and *Fantastic*—the years under Cele Goldsmith's editorship. It was able to present SF of good quality by writers like Arthur C. Clarke, Ray Bradbury, John Brunner, Eric Frank Russell, Clifford D. Simak and Roger Zelazny, as well as artwork by Virgil Finlay. When Cohen dropped it in 1971, its format was continued with less effect by *Thrilling Science Fiction*.

Note

1. Private correspondence with Joseph Wrzos, March 1981.

Information Sources

BIBLIOGRAPHY:
Nicholls. *Encyclopedia*
Tuck.
INDEX SOURCES: ISFM-II; MIT; SFM; Tuck.

REPRINT SOURCES: None.
LOCATION SOURCES: M.I.T. Science Fiction Library; Pennsylvania State University
    Library.

Publication History

TITLE: *Great Science Fiction Magazine*, issues 1 (Winter-1965)–12, Fall 1968 [Note:
    issues 1, 3, 5 were *Great Science Fiction from Amazing* on the cover and spine;
    issues 2 and 4 were *Great Science Fiction from Fantastic*]; retitled *S. F. Greats*,
    issue 13, Winter 1969–issue 17, Spring 1970; retitled *S. F. Greats*, issue 18,
    Summer 1970–issue 21, Spring 1971.
VOLUME DATA: No volume numbering. Number 1 (undated, Winter 1965)–Number
    21, Spring 1971. Quarterly. No issue for Fall 1969, but issues 13 and 16 both
    dated Winter 1969.
PUBLISHER: Ultimate Publishing Co., Flushing, New York.
EDITOR: Not identified within issues, but Sol Cohen compiled all issues.
FORMAT: Digest, 128pp.
PRICE: 50¢, except final issue, which was 60¢.

Mike Ashley

GREAT SCIENCE FICTION FROM AMAZING

See GREAT SCIENCE FICTION.

GREAT SCIENCE FICTION FROM FANTASTIC

See GREAT SCIENCE FICTION.

GREAT SCIENCE FICTION STORIES

See TREASURY OF GREAT SCIENCE FICTION STORIES.

GRIPPING TERROR

In the years just after World War II, Britain was flooded with copies of
American magazines, either original editions or British reprint equivalents. Harry
Assael, one of the originators of the Panther pocketbook line, decided to jump
on the bandwagon by issuing a number of phony-American publications. *Gripping Terror* (undated, but probably published in late 1949 or early 1950) was
one such publication. The front cover declared that it was a "British Edition";
while this was true in a strict sense, the implication was that it was of American

origin. The stories did nothing to dispel that belief because they were all set in America, by Assael's special request. It is possible that the accompanying illustrations were actually lifted from American magazines.

The stories are of only borderline interest. The lead title, "When Churchyards Yawn" by Thornton Dale (which may be one of John Russell Fearn's unconfirmed pseudonyms), is a formula story of a young bride and her husband's sinister secret. "Murder Is Hell" is a straightforward murder story competently written by Norman Lazenby, while "Death Has No Boundaries" by Clarkson Waverley is a typical weird-menace yarn set in a lunatic asylum. Only the final story has any significance in the field: "Horror from the Swamps" by Richard Milne, about a menacing, slimy monster. Richard Milne was the pseudonym of Richard Milne Sharples who, ironically, is far better known in Britain as comedy writer Dick Sharples.

The remainder of the issue consisted of short nonfiction fillers about witches, werewolves and poltergeists. *GT* had a companion magazine, *Crime Detective*, but neither lasted more than one issue.

Note

The authors wish to thank Norman Lazenby for his help in the research on this article.

Information Sources

INDEX SOURCES: None known.
REPRINT SOURCES: None known.
LOCATION SOURCES: None known.

Publication History

TITLE: *Gripping Terror* (the cover punctuates the title with an exclamation mark, but this is not repeated on the spine or contents page).

VOLUME DATA: Unnumbered and undated. Norman Lazenby reports that he was commissioned to write his story in April 1949 and delivered it in June. Publication was therefore probably late 1949 or early 1950. Total run: 1 issue.

PUBLISHER: Hamilton & Co. (Stafford) Ltd., London.

EDITOR: Not identified within issue, but almost certainly Harry Assael.

FORMAT: Pulp, 64pp.

PRICE: 9d.

Mike Ashley/Frank H. Parnell

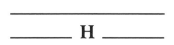

H

THE HAUNT OF HORROR

Haunt of Horror is one of those rare examples of a prose fiction magazine issued by a publisher of comic books, in this case Stan Lee's Marvel Comics Group. Gray Morrow's striking cover for the June 1973 issue (and Kelly Freas' equally commanding painting for the second issue, in August) ushered in a short run of fine horror and fantasy fiction. Editor Gerard Conway had gone a long way to select a variety of original and inventive material within the limits of his budget. Only one reprint featured in each issue, and though it took up most of the room, no one complained at the resurrection of Fritz Leiber's novel *Conjure Wife*, although Award Books had reprinted it as recently as 1968.

The new stories included "The First Step," one of the Dr. Warm investigations by associate editor Geo. Alec Effinger, published under the alias John K. Diomede; "Night Beat," a werewolf story impeccably plotted by Ramsey Campbell; and "Ghost in the Corn Crib," a flawless tale by R. A. Lafferty. Also present were David R. Bunch, Beverly Goldberg, A. A. Attanasio and Robert E. Howard (whose story, "Usurp the Night," had previously appeared in the small-circulation *Weirdbook**). There was an essay on modern horror by Dennis O'Neil and book reviews by Baird Searles, and the whole issue was rounded out with skilled artwork by Marvel's comic-book illustrators.

One item in the first issue reappeared in the second. This was Harlan Ellison's "Neon." On first printing, the last two pages of manuscript had been transposed, so the whole story was rerun with new illustrations, and in the right order. Also in the second issue were stories by Anne McCaffrey, Dennis O'Neil, Howard Waldrop, Ron Goulart, a further Dr. Warm story by Effinger and an article about Atlantis by Lin Carter.

The magazine showed signs of becoming a quality-content publication. The third issue promised to contain all-original material, with stories on hand by

John Jakes, R. A. Lafferty, Ramsey Campbell, Alan Brennert and George Ze-browski. The publisher, however, thought otherwise. Used to the higher and more immediate profits of the comics, he was unwilling to make a firm commitment to the magazine, and he gave it no opportunity to establish itself. Instead, it was converted into a bedsheet-sized black and white comic magazine, also called *The Haunt of Horror*. Gradually, this comic used up the purchased fiction inventory of the digest, and then converted to a straight comic magazine.

Information Sources

INDEX SOURCES: Cook, Michael L., *Monthly Murders*, Westport, Conn.: Greenwood
     Press, 1982; MT; NESFA-II. Schlobin, Roger C. "An Index to the Haunt of
     Horror." *The Age of the Unicorn*, Vol. 1, No. 1 (April 1979): 5; SFM.
REPRINT SOURCES: None known.
LOCATION SOURCES: M.I.T. Science Fiction Library.

Publication History

TITLE: *The Haunt of Horror*.
VOLUME DATA: Volume 1, Number 1, June 1973–Volume 1, Number 2, August 1973.
     Bi-monthly. Total run: 2 issues.
PUBLISHER: Marvel Comics Group, New York.
EDITOR: Gerard Conway.
FORMAT: Digest, 160pp.
PRICE: 75¢.

Grant Thiessen

HORROR STORIES (1935–1941)

Horror Stories, another of Popular Publications' successful mystery-terror magazines (see *Dime Mystery Magazine** for full details), first appeared in January 1935. The "horror" of the title was of the sadistic vengeance type rather than supernatural fantasy. Indeed, it became a trademark of the magazines to concoct increasingly bizarre circumstances which purportedly had supernatural origins only to have them explained away by human (or inhuman) agencies at the climax.

The most prolific contributors to *HS* were Ray Cummings, Wayne Rogers, Francis James, Arthur J. Burks and Paul Ernst, but although some of those names are known in the SF/fantasy fields, very few genuine fantasy stories appeared in the magazine.

A handful that are worth recording include Wyatt Blassingame's "The Horror at His Heels" (August/September 1936), set in a Mayan archeological excavation, where one of the party suffers from vengeance from the past. "Our Grave Is Waiting" by Robert C. Blackmon (July 1936) is set in an Arizona ghost town actually inhabited by ghosts. A rare example of science fiction of the mad scientist variety is "The Devil's Press Agent" (February/March 1937) by sometime SF writer John Hawkins. Using the time-honored theme from the hero pulps of a scientist bent on world domination, Hawkins weaves a few science-fictional devices into an otherwise typical terror tale.

The titles cited above are considerably more restrained than those most characteristic of *HS*, which are more in the vein of "Things That Once Were Girls," "A Mate for the Thing with a Tail" and the wonderful "Coming of the Unborn Things" by the later editor of *Galaxy Science Fiction*,* Ejler Jakobssen.

Note

The author wishes to thank Robert K. Jones for his help in the compilation of this essay.

Information Sources

BIBLIOGRAPHY:

Hardin, Nils. "An Interview with Henry Steeger." Xenophile, No. 33 (July 1977): 3–18.

———, and George Hocutt. "A Checklist of Popular Publications Titles 1930–1955." Xenophile, No. 33 (July 1977): 21–24.

Hersey, Harold, *Pulpwood Editor*. New York: Frederick A. Stokes Co., 1937.

Jones, Robert Kenneth. *The Shudder Pulps*. West Linn, Ore.: Fax Collector's Editions, 1975.

———. "The Weird Menace Magazines." *Bronze Shadows*, No. 10 (June 1967): 3–8; No. 11 (August 1967): 7–13; No. 12 (October 1967): 7–10; No. 13 (January 1968): 7–12; No. 14 (March 1968): 13–17; No. 15 (November 1968): 4–8.

Papalia, William. "John Newton Howitt, American Artist/Illustrator." *Xenophile*, No. 33 (July 1977): 87–88.

Weinberg, Robert. "Horror Pulps." In *Horror Literature*, ed. Marshall Tymn. New York: Bowker, 1981.

INDEX SOURCES: Austin, William N., *Macabre Index*, Seattle, Wash.: FAPA 59, 1952 (includes a nearly complete issue listing); Jones, Robert K., "Popular's Weird Menace Pulps," in *The Weird Menace*, ed. Camille Cazedessus, Jr., Evergreen, Colo.: Opar Press, 1972 (includes an author index); Day, Bradford M., ed, *The Complete Checklist of Science-Fiction Magazines*, New York: Science-Fiction & Fantasy Publishers, 1961.

REPRINT SOURCES: None known.

LOCATION SOURCES: None known.

Publication History

TITLE: *Horror Stories*.

VOLUME DATA: Volume 1, Number 1, January 1935–Volume 11, Number 1, April/May 1941. Four issues per volume. Monthly, January to December 1935 (but no issues for April or May); bi-monthly, February/March 1936–April/May 1941 (only five issues in 1940, no February or July issues). Total run: 41 issues.

PUBLISHER: Popular Publications, New York.

EDITOR: Overall editor, Rogers Terrill.
FORMAT: Pulp, 128pp.
PRICE: 15¢.

Mike Ashley

HORROR STORIES (1971)

See ADVENTURES IN HORROR.

I

IF

Although both Horace Gold and Theodore Sturgeon claim to have had the idea for a magazine named *If*,[1] in 1952 twenty-six-year-old Paul Fairman sold publisher James Quinn on a digest with such a title against the advice of Sturgeon, who thought the time not good for another such magazine.[2] Sturgeon was right: the boom years had produced a horde of digests, nine of which would go under the next year.[3] Yet *If* would survive many such crises until erratic distribution and inflation caused its absorption into *Galaxy Science Fiction** in 1974.[4] But in contrast to its coevals, *Galaxy* and *The Magazine of Fantasy and Science Fiction,* If* never was to receive a more explicit editorial direction than simply to be entertaining—a purpose that not only sustained it for twenty-two years but won it three Hugo awards as the best of the professional magazines.

Fairman was to last as editor for only four issues. The magazine that he produced was a hefty 160-page bi-monthly with a short novel, two novelettes, short stories and a wide range of features which would appeal to the fan of the day: a science-fact column; a regular editorial and guest editorials by such fellow editors as Sam Merwin and Lila Shaffer; several pages devoted to exchanging views with readers in "The Postman Cometh"; and biographies of such figures in fandom as Wilson Tucker, Ken Slater, James Taurasi and Raymond A. Palmer (who responded energetically in *Other Worlds Science Stories** to the essay on him).[5] Although he saw his magazine as innovative essentially in its features,[6] that structure was symptomatic of Fairman's previous association since 1950 with Ziff-Davis publications, often writing under the house pseudonym "Ivar Jorgensen." The fiction reflected the same association: he brought in such Ziff-Davis regulars as Milton Lesser; Howard Browne (currently editing *Amazing Stories** and *Fantastic Adventures**); Ray Palmer (former editor of these magazines) and Palmer's notorious protégé, Richard Shaver; and *Amazing* fan columnist Rog Phillips and his current wife, Mari Wolf.[7] But Fairman also secured good fiction from Sturgeon and L. Sprague de Camp, published three of Walter Miller, Jr.'s, early stories, and bought one of Philip Dick's first stories, thus beginning that prolific writer's use of *If* as one of his significant outlets.

Brief as his association with the magazine was, Fairman made an indelible mark on its character: he saw its stories simply as "entertainment and escape"; nor did he see science fiction as much more than a "background," unlike the "basic fiction pattern" of the love, mystery or puzzle stories for which it supplied a setting—though he was ambiguous on this point:

> Personally, I'd say a science fiction story is a fantasy in which the de-velopment is based on tangible gimmicks with at least a pseudo-scientific basis under them. I really feel, however, that the term denotes a background rather than a basis; just as the term western fiction is obviously a background.[8]

So the readers got love, mystery, and puzzle stories as well as fantasies inclining toward the weird, the alien encounter, and the psionic in tones ranging from humor to pathos. The response was cheering: his first issue brought in 624 letters,[9] and he soon ran out of copies of it.[10] But the pull of Ziff-Davis proved too strong: Fairman's new authority as an editor won him away from *If* to become Browne's associate editor at *Amazing*.[11]

Drawing essentially on his experience editing the occult "true story" maga-zine, *Strange*, publisher James Quinn ran *If* for three issues while hunting for Fairman's replacement; he approached Lester del Rey, who was currently be-ginning his editing career with *Space Science Fiction** (Del Rey was soon to regret turning down the offer).[12] Quinn reduced the page-count from 160 to 120 and dropped all features except the editorial, the letters pages and the science fact articles; but the fiction, as before, was by some of the Ziff-Davis people and Miller. He did acquire Gordon Dickson, Richard Matheson and the "new" Ziff-Davis regular "Ivar Jorgensen," whose short novel, *Deadly City*, was to make Fairman some extra money and prestige as the basis for the 1954 Allied film, *Target-Earth*.[13] Quinn's most laudable decisions concerned artists rather than writers: he hired a former Ziff-Davis assistant art director, Ed Valigursky, first to do half-tone space art for the inside covers and then as art director.[14] Immediately, Valigursky brought in a friend who was just beginning his career—Kelly Freas[15]—and bought work from Virgil Finlay, Ed Emsh and Paul Orban. Valigursky also hired Ken Fagg to do the spectacular wraparound covers adorning *If* until mid-1954.

Soon after he hired Valigursky, Quinn found his new editor, Larry Shaw. Shaw had been a fan for some time but his editorial experience was largely with *Auto Age*.[16] Shaw set out to make a magazine that would stun the fans. Leaving the format unchanged, he tackled the fiction. He regularly did the unexpected. He published authors for the first, and sometimes only time, thereby obtaining fine stories from such transients as Richard Stockham, Gavin Hyde and Tom

Leahy. He got five capable literary pieces from a *Planet Stories** regular, James McKimmey. He bought Mark Clifton stories the year before his novel, *They'd Rather Be Right*, won the Hugo. And ten years before the arrival of the drug culture, he bought Hunt Collins' extraordinary prophecy, *Malice in Wonderland*.[17] He introduced authors who would contribute to many later issues, among them James Gunn, Harry Harrison and Jack Vance. He obtained top-notch stories that would later find their way repeatedly into anthologies: Damon Knight's "Anachron," William Tenn's "The Custodian" and Arthur C. Clarke's "Jupiter V." His outstanding achievement was to publish the first half of James Blish's "A Case of Conscience," already turned down by no less perspicacious an editor than Lester del Rey.[18] Subjects ranged from drugs to religion, robots to rockets, planetary archeology to the occult—and there were startling stories smiling on prostitutes or frowning on anti-Communism. Lester del Rey describes the resultant conflict between Quinn and Shaw:

> Where Quinn wanted simply good story values by pulp standards, Larry felt it should have prestige stories that would start fan discussions, upset taboos, and generally be controversial. . . . But the readers who had followed the magazine for the pure story value Quinn had given were not adjusted to Shaw's brand of science fiction; and the new readers attracted by Shaw were dissatisfied with much of the rest of the magazine. The two characteristics could have been blended in time but the alteration was too rapid.[19]

A year after he was hired, Shaw left. For the next five years, Quinn would edit *If* by himself.

Del Rey was probably right. Quinn's interregnum between Fairman and Shaw was marked by pedestrian stories, pro-science and anti-Communist, set in scenes of future holocaust. But Shaw—or perhaps Quinn's new assistant, Eve Wulff—taught him lessons that soon emerged in *If* to help it survive. During 1954 and 1955 twenty science fiction magazines aborted.[20] But Quinn published *If* monthly until December 1955—probably because he did not employ American News as his distributor and because, working out of Kingston, New Jersey, with a small staff, he kept his overhead low.[21]

Quinn was to edit about one-fifth of *If*'s total run. He deserves more attention than he normally receives, the remarkable six issues of Shaw and three issues of Knight generally receiving the kudos. Del Rey describes him as "an honest and very decent man, aware of his ignorance of the field of science fiction, but determined to bring out a good magazine and to treat his authors fairly."[22] Thus he came across in his 1954–1955 editorials, rarely about science fiction, or even science: he was somewhat conservative politically (Oppenheimer was treated justly; labor unions needed to be controlled), liked small towns, believed that time travel and telepathy were possible, and was very optimistic about humanity's future. Interestingly enough, in connnection with this last point, he came down heavily on the holocaust stories that typified his first efforts.[23] He believed that science fiction "should be a medium of *entertainment* which advances worthwhile ideas and thoughts on the philosophy, inventions, conventions, and shenanigans of mankind." He decried gadget stories and space opera and was strong on simple plots working out a single idea "clearly and emphatically . . . and convincingly told in a straightforward manner."[24]

The result was a magazine made up almost entirely of novelettes, short stories and a few features: an editorial, a brief science-fact article and a quiz. During this period, he had a particularly poor idea: a $2,000 science fiction contest for college student writers and a resolve to print the top seven stories. As poor, as long, and as tedious as they were, he printed each story, issue after issue. But the contest did initiate the career of its first-place winner: Andy Offutt of Louisville, Kentucky, and also attracted entries from Harlan Ellison and Roger Zelazny.[25] The interior illustrations—and some of the covers—were superb under Valigursky's continued direction: the covers he assigned to a wide range of painters, the most prominent being Freas, Fagg, Anton Kurka and himself; but soon he limited the assignment of the ample interior illustrations to three very strong artists: Freas, Emsh and Orban.

Then came some changes in the magazine. *If* went bi-monthly in August 1955. There was a hiatus in the editorials. Mel Hunter succeeded Valigursky, did most of the covers himself, and exchanged Kelly Freas for Virgil Finlay as his third interior illustrator. For two months Forrest Ackerman wrote a gossip column on the science fiction scene. And by June 1956 Quinn began to make a science-fact article a major feature of each issue: research engineers on Project Vanguard, a Peenemunde scientist on extraterrestrials, an anonymous government scientist on runaway ICBMs (which brought comment from Isaac Asimov in a letter to the editor), Dr. Alan E. Nourse on the future of medicine, and so on. The letters pages had returned and, after a year's absence, so did Quinn with a much more professional editorial page split between brief reports on developments in science, thumbnail sketches of contributing authors and general observations in the Ackerman style.

Throughout both phases of Quinn's editorship, he and Eve Wulff consistently obtained stories ranging from the entertaining to the brilliant. The editorial watchwords were "variety and diversity."[26] Although Quinn's *If*s began with an emphasis on the holocaust and ended with an inclination toward space adventure, during the interim they ranged widely over psychological and sociological issues, engineering and science problem stories, and from alien invasion to alien anthropology, from love and sex to crime and horror, from psionics to matter transmission stories. And they were topical, embodying in their fantasies the Cold War, the civil rights movement, the economy, the automobile, television, juvenile delinquency, radiation, isolationism, conformity, the Skinner box—a kind of newspaper of the imagination. Quinn kept his previous editors' authors—Dick, Miller, Lesser, Phillips, Nourse, Clifton, Tenn, Gunn, Clarke, McKimmey—and he added new ones—Isaac Asimov, Poul Anderson, Tom

Godwin. He published not only Offutt's first story but those of William F. Nolan and David R. Bunch. Though he did not get their firsts, he recognized the abilities of Harlan Ellison and Robert Silverberg and regularly published their early work. Among the stories that have been oft-reprinted are Nolan's first story, "The Joy of Living"; Dick's "The Golden Man" and "Captive Market"; and Asimov's "Franchise" and "Feeling of Power." One of Quinn's major decisions was to avoid the serial, which was to become such a strong feature of Frederik Pohl's *If*; his monthly and his bi-monthly both emphasized the short story. Nor did he seriously explore the possibility of the series story that was to become *If*'s backbone in the Pohl period. But he did toy with the idea, publishing a few stories from each of several series: Gunn's *Station in Space*; Hospital Planet Earth stories by Nourse; one of Clarke's White Hart tales; some of Ellison's early Kyben space operas; two of Blish's *Seedling Stars* episodes.

Abruptly—with little change in *If* other than an inclination toward space adventure—Wulff left; and after giving the editorship to Damon Knight for three issues, Quinn sold *If*. Del Rey believed that Quinn found himself in a failing market; Pohl speculated that he simply "got tired of it."[27]

With Damon Knight as its editor, Quinn's *If* had an interesting death. Formerly editor of the short-lived but brilliant *Worlds Beyond*,* Knight retitled the first issue's table of contents "A Short History of Space Travel" and then sequentially dated each story from A.D. 1950 to A.D. 32,000,000. He eliminated all features except the letters page and added his own prestigious book review column, "In the Balance." Hunter and Finlay left; Valigursky and Freas returned. To Quinn's diversity Knight added excellence. Retaining a substantial number of the regulars, Knight introduced surreal fiction by Cordwainer Smith, David Bunch and George H. Smith. Currently publishing his stories with *The Magazine of Fantasy and Science Fiction* and *Astounding* (*Analog Science Fiction**), R. M. McKenna sold to *If* several of the stories that would represent his brief but brilliant foray into science fiction. Subsequent reprintings were given not only to Cordwainer Smith's stories but to those of Algis Budrys ("The Man Who Tasted Ashes"), Fritz Leiber ("Pipe Dream") and Marion Zimmer Bradley ("The Wind People," a haunting story that Knight would include in his own fine anthology of the best, *A Century of Science Fiction* [1962]); Judith Merril would pick Theodore R. Thomas' topical Cold War story, "Satellite," as one of her *Year's Best* and later reprint it in her *Best of the Best*. But none of it was enough. Quinn sold *If* to Robert Guinn. After nearly a half year off the stands, it reappeared as the stepsister of *Galaxy*.

If was not in good hands. Robert Guinn was a printing broker with a publishing sideline; he was not knowledgeable about science fiction and was penurious.[28] Horace Gold was in the last two years of his major editing career and was ailing; he published in *If* stories that he did not want for *Galaxy*.[29] The covers were pedestrian, but the sparse interior artwork was competently rendered by Finlay, Emsh and Jack Gaughan and by two artists who would make reputations with their comic books, Wally Wood and Gray Morrow. There was only one feature, a conscientiously thorough and ample book review column by Frederik Pohl.

Still a bi-monthly, *If* continued printing basically novelettes and short stories. But the fiction was different, perhaps because of Pohl's influence—he began to do most of the buying through the 1960s.[30] The stories were often space adventure and, more often than before, on psionics. Many of the topical stories were specifically satiric, sometimes even black humor. Short-shorts began to appear. And the surreal and experimental were more prominent than before: Philip Dick was back with psionic nightmares; Jim Harmon wrote surprising discontinuous pieces; and one of Pohl's "personal enthusiasms," R. A. Lafferty, was just beginning his career and developing with extraordinary speed. Returning to magazines after a hiatus in the late 1950s was Philip José Farmer. Fresh from writing *Flowers for Algernon* was Daniel Keyes. Robert Bloch published "Talent" and C. C. MacApp his first science fiction story. Especially prominent was well-written fiction by the talented Scot J. T. McIntosh. The magazine was still amorphous but very promising.

When Pohl took Gold's place on the masthead in 1961, the promise began to become a reality. Such writers as James Gunn would soon regard *If* as one of the better second-rank magazines: paying slightly better (2 cents a word), it tolerated the experimental and the literary.[31] The readers would hold *If* in even higher regard for reasons that would surprise even Pohl: making central to its issues a high-quality space opera that had been missing since such pulps as *Planet Stories* went out in the fifties.[32] Pohl received the kind of sudden success that would later reward the makers of *Star Wars*—*If* won three Hugos (1966–1968) as the best of the professional magazines.

But at the beginning Pohl's main problem with both *If* and his favored magazine, *Galaxy*, was a low budget. So he made ingenious use of his inventory, raised the rates for new stories from Quinn's 1 cent a word, and improved his relations with authors.[33] By mid-1962, he had hit upon his winning formula: the space adventure series and the serial leavened by literary experiment. He already had established the core series, Keith Laumer's *Retief*, stories of an adventurer reminiscent of James Bond. His first serial was Doc Smith's *Masters of Space* (the completion of a novel started by E. E. Evans). Doc's return to science fiction in the pages of *If* must have done much to shape its popularity and character. Pohl acquired other big names: Anderson, del Rey, Clarke, Leiber. And he continued to publish the experimental, adding even Kurt Vonnegut, Jr. He printed a regular column by Theodore Sturgeon, bought science-fact articles, printed an occasional cartoon and restored the editorial and letter pages. But he cut costs on artwork. By now *If* was in the black. Pohl pushed Guinn to make it a monthly—to expedite the serial—but instead Guinn and Sol Cohen, Guinn's appointment as publisher, decided that they would add a third magazine to Pohl's burden, *Worlds of Tomorrow*.*[34]

Until July 1964, *If* remained bi-monthly, but it got larger: Pohl added ten pages and used smaller type to gain the equivalent of another twenty-five; technically, *If* had gone from 120 to 155 pages. Thus, Pohl could continue to run serials: Heinlein's *Podkayne of Mars*, Anderson's *Three Worlds to Conquer*, and the first novel of *The Starchild Trilogy* he was to write in collaboration with Jack Williamson, *The Reefs of Space*. The series continued: Retief became regular, and Fred Saberhagen's first Berserker story appeared. He bought another short novel from Doc Smith and persuaded A. E. van Vogt to return to science fiction with "The Expendables" after a fourteen-year absence. He established the practice of publishing in each issue an "Ifirstory," the most spectacular discoveries being Alexei Panshin—who wrote for that issue the novelette that became *Rite of Passage*, "Down to the Worlds of Men"—and Larry Niven. Whereas he felt free to publish a short novel by Hal Clement, he also published the man who was to be the luminary of the British New Wave—J. G. Ballard. He brought back one of his own favorites, Cordwainer Smith, and obtained from Dick one of his most amusing pieces, the friendly spoof on Anderson, "Waterspider." Features remained about the same: Sturgeon wrote the bulk of the editorials, which leaned toward science-fact; the cartoons went; a crossword puzzle appeared for an issue. But the artwork improved considerably: covers by Paul Wenzel; covers and interiors by Norman Nodel, Gaughan, Emsh, Finlay— and a whole Finlay issue. The formula was firmly established: literate space adventure in the form of serials and series for the younger, less involved reader, but always with a touch of the unexpected—from hard science fiction to sophisticated literature—for *If* would be a good place to try out a whim, would be "easier to turn around" than would the more established *Galaxy* with its mature, sophisticated readership.[35]

When the magazine went monthly in July 1964, *If* entered the best years of its history—a five-year period that abruptly ended at its peak in May 1969 because of Guinn's business transactions. Its main success was literary, but the other departments contributed. The artwork remained at its usual level. Readers often objected, perhaps because of the "comics" look of Bode, Morrow, Wood and their imitators. But there were standard covers by Wenzel, McKenna, and Doug Chaffee. Finlay was omnipresent, and so was Jack Gaughan, who also would receive Hugos in 1967 and 1968. The features built slowly from an editorial and letters page: Lin Carter's column on national and international fandom enjoyed a two-year run and Lester del Rey's science-fact column another year; in addition there were guest editorials (Clarke, Gold, Asimov, etc.), interviews (Harrison, Ellison, del Rey, etc.), special features such as Sam Moskowitz on science fiction matriarchies, and a science fiction events calendar. Although staff were in continual flux, two important permanent additions were to carry *If* through in its third avatar: Judy-Lynn Benjamin was to become associate editor in June 1967, and Lester del Rey managing editor. Pohl described their relationship thus:

> While Judy-Lynn was working for me, she was a sort of general assistant doing everything that I didn't do. I did all the ms reading, and most of the copy-editing and proofreading. Judy-Lynn did the rest. Made up the

issues, kept the artists to deadlines, dealt with emergencies when I wasn't there (which was most of the time—I only went in to the office one day a week, working mostly at home).

Lester was primarily editor of Worlds of Fantasy. He also . . . helped out with occasional proofreading, etc., on the other magazines, on special projects . . . and from time to time with advice and counsel when needed. Generally speaking, we had pretty informal working arrangements.[36]

Through the rest of 1964 and 1965, Pohl ran strong serials: a violent Laumer spy-adventure novel, then Laumer's first Retief novelization; Pohl's own second novel in *The Starchild Trilogy*; Robert Heinlein's *Farnham's Freehold*. And, most extraordinary of all, he persuaded Doc Smith to complete his career by resuming the Skylark novels with *Skylark DuQuesne*. The series, of course, continued with Retief; Saberhagen began developing the Berserkers into an ongoing series; MacApp began his Gree series; and van Vogt wrote about Silkies. Although space adventure was in the foreground, Lafferty continued, Thomas M. Disch contributed "White Fang Goes Dingo," and Pohl himself knocked off a surreal parody, "Under Two Moons." The result: *If* won a Hugo in 1966.

Del Rey supposes that Pohl was surprised and a little puzzled. He had revived a longtime hero, Doc Smith, and the literature of his own youth for a new generation.[37] To embody it, he created a magazine for the younger and the less sophisticated but discovered that even the latter liked to have fun. Or, Pohl speculated, pondering the fact that the esteemed *Galaxy* never won him a Hugo, while *If* won him three, perhaps his fate was like that of another editor—"the less I do the better the readers like it."[38]

In 1966 Blish contributed a juvenile novel, Laumer and Rosel Brown collaborated on *Earthblood*, Chandler began publishing his Rim Worlds novels, McIntosh contributed another of his capable works, and Heinlein commanded five issues with *The Moon Is a Harsh Mistress*. Laumer, Saberhagen and MacApp were joined by Larry Niven when he wrote "Neutron Star" and began the "Tales of Known Space." But while Anderson and John Brunner contributed more space adventure, Lafferty reached a peak with "Nine Hundred Grandmothers," Silverberg upgraded his new literary reputation with such finely rendered stories as "Halfway House," Sladek contributed the opaque "The Babe in the Oven," and Offutt, Robert Margroff and Piers Anthony produced the strange alternate reality story, "Mandroid." Once more, *If* won a Hugo, as did *Moon* and "Neutron Star."

In 1967 the serialized novels ranged from space adventures by Budrys, Laumer, and Chandler to Hal Clement's substantial *Ocean On Top* to Blish's fantastic *Faust Aleph Null* (*Black Easter*) to a Philip José Farmer Riverworld episode— an extraordinary range owing to *If*'s absorption of its sister publication, *Worlds of Tomorrow*, Farmer's normal locus. The new fantasy spectrum reached from Andre Norton to Roger Zelazny. The big series continued as before. Such substantial writers as Asimov and Leiber appeared. By the middle of 1967, Pohl found himself taking sides against the New Wave as Judith Merril and her British friends were presenting it to him;[39] he protested that stylistic experimentation alone was neither new nor enough. Yet over this year and the next he was not to allow argument to obscure merit; some of the members of the American New Wave contributed their major stories, Ellison his "I Have No Mouth but I Must Scream" and Samuel Delany his "Driftglass." He also published more from the British New Wave: J. G. Ballard again and David Redd. When Zelazny's *Creatures of Light and Darkness* was published, part of it had already appeared in *If*, and part in *New Worlds*.* As correspondent Dean R. Koontz observed: "*If* is improving all the time. At first, I thought it was going to stand as the last bastion of the total science tale and the space opera (which all of us enjoy), but now I see it publishing both the new wave and the old and the wavelets in between. Good. Fine."[40] The Hugos for 1967 verified his judgment: *If* won for a third time, and Ellison's "I Have No Mouth" also received an award.

The 1968 *Ifs* made less of an impression among the Hugo nominators than among the Nebula nominators. Only Anthony's novelette "Getting through University" would receive a Hugo nomination. But Blish's *Black Easter* would receive Nebula's third place, Silverberg's *The Man in the Maze* second place, and a novel begun in *If* in 1964 first place—Panshin's *Rite of Passage. If* was gaining status among the writers. *If*'s readers had different priorities. In a contest with *Galaxy*, *If*'s stories by Niven, Silverberg, Pohl with Williamson, and Anthony won second, third, fourth and sixth places respectively.

A survey revealed that Pohl had attracted his readers with such writers as Heinlein, Anderson, Jack Vance, Doc Smith and Cordwainer Smith. Such diverse writers as Reynolds and Silverberg were most popular. Close were Niven on one side and Harlan Ellison on the other. And "a big part of the glue that kept the *If* readership sticking" were Laumer's Retief and Saberhagen's Berserkers.

Suddenly, Guinn sold *If* to Universal Publishing and Distribution Corporation—as the surprised Pohl learned upon returning from the World Science Fiction Symposium at Rio de Janeiro. It was not due to circulation problems but to "certain legal angles concerning the way in which a company can 'go public' with its stock."[41] The new publisher, Arnold Abramson, asked Pohl to stay on but insisted on nine to five hours. Anticipating the problems his successor would have with that situation, tired of the perpetual deadlines, and earning more money as a writer, Pohl decided to quit.[42]

Universal appointed as editor one of its employees, Ejler Jakobsson, who once before had succeeded Pohl, as editor of *Super Science Stories** in 1943.[43] With four magazines to manage and the distractions of the office, his "impossible load of work and the haste of transition" made *If* once more a *Galaxy* dumping-ground.[44] In the year of the transition, circulation dropped by 50 percent for *If* and 46 percent for *Galaxy*;[45] two issues were skipped for the first time in five years; readers began complaining about the subscription services breaking down; Gaughan now did all of the artwork—covers and interior illustrations—which suffered accordingly. The features diminished to three: Lester del Rey's book review column, the science fiction calendar and the letters page—which now printed letters about all Universal's science fiction magazines. On those pages Jakobsson got embroiled in the New Wave controversy and had to make the embarrassing confession that another writer had issued hard-line comments under his name.[46] In less than a year, *If* went bi-monthly.

Jakobsson employed the Pohl tactics but lost authors and stories. He kept publishing series, but Saberhagen, van Vogt and Niven temporarily disappeared from the pages. Readers began to complain about Retief; nor did they seem enthusiastic about Harrison's continuation of the Stainless Steel Rat episodes or new series by Chapdelaine, Larry Eisenberg and Young. There was more enthusiasm about such serials as Mack Reynolds' *The Towns Must Roll*, Frank Herbert's *Whipping Star*, the Gerrold-Niven fantasy *The Misspelled Magician*, Farmer's *The Fabulous Riverboat*, and, toward the end, Simak's *Our Children's Children* and two novels by the British writer Colin Kapp. The shorter fiction varied, as usual, in quality and kind. Asimov, Bloch, Pohl and Williamson appeared. Sturgeon contributed "Occam's Scalpel." Lafferty and Wolfe contributed regularly, and there were occasional appearances by Barry Malzberg and Norman Spinrad. The span between the two *If* stories nominated for Hugos in 1973 is suggestive of the range still exhibited by the magazine: Clifford Simak's scientifically conscientious "Construction Shack" and Michael Bishop's experimental collage, "Death and Designation among the Asadi." But a few months after the issue that contained these two pieces, the aging Jakobsson decided to retire.

The year 1974 was the last of *If*'s existence as an independent magazine. Then it "merged" with *Galaxy*, which inherited a few of its features and some of its typical stories. James Baen edited the last six issues. Del Rey observes:

> I wish that change had come earlier. Baen, I feel, was the right editor for the magazine. He began with every possible handicap, since he had to depend on manuscripts which were not considered right for *Galaxy*. But he began with the very great advantage of treating *If* as a potentially good magazine in its own right. He wanted it to be different from the more "sophisticated" magazines, to bring out the stories that were fun to read, to do the things that the field (other than in recent books) has been missing for too many years.[47]

Three space adventure novels were serialized: Leigh Brackett revived N'Chaka (born 1949) in *The Ginger Star*, the first novel of *The Book of Skaith* trilogy; Fred Saberhagen returned with a Berserker story and novel, *Berserker's Planet*, his first since the Pohl days; and Poul Anderson brought back Dominic Flandry (born 1951), space intelligence agent, in *A Knight of Ghosts and Shadows*. But, like Pohl, although Baen had his pronounced emphases, he was generous: "Here, off the top of my head are a few of my favorite authors: Robert Heinlein; Cordwainer Smith; Larry Niven; Roger Zelazny; James Blish; Theodore Sturgeon; Isaac Asimov; Ursula K. LeGuin; Poul Anderson; Kurt Vonnegut."[48] The point/counterpoint of hard/soft, scientific/literary, old/new in this list once again typified the magazine. Isaac Asimov appeared, but so did Robert Silverberg. Hal Clement contributed a well-realized "hard" lunar juvenile, but Norman Spinrad sold a biker fantasy, and Colin Kapp spanned both worlds with an extraordinary surreal fantasy deeply rooted in chemistry, "Mephisto and the Ion Explorer." Other stories came from Pamela Sargent and Chelsea Yarbro, Christopher Priest and Gordon Eklund, Fritz Leiber and James Schmitz, Larry Niven and Christopher Anvil. The magazine still needed focus, but the stories were of good quality as well as an interesting, fairly balanced variety.

By his third issue, Baen changed the appearance of the magazine considerably. Although Jack Gaughan did a cover and some interior illustrations, interior artists began to be credited; a special page, "Ars Gratia," was devoted to illustrations by new artists. Prominent among these were Wendy Pini and Stephen Fabian, who had just made his professional science fiction debut with *Galaxy* that year.[49] Baen retained the old features—editorial, letters, calendar, "Reading Room"— and added to them a guest editorial by Pohl; "(R)evolution," science-fact essays by Richard Hoagland and Robert Enzmann; and Richard Geis' controversial column, "The Alien Viewpoint."

Abruptly, all collapsed. Baen began the last issue by announcing the combination of *Galaxy* and *Worlds of If*, as of January 1975:

> The reason? A simple one: we ran out of paper—the kind of paper we can afford to buy, that is. We still have access to quantities sufficient for one magazine, but not two. (If we tried to put out a book with the next-higher grade we would go broke in nothing flat.)[50]

Lester del Rey added:

> The exigencies of publishing in a market of wildly increasing prices and erratic distribution have apparently forced this termination. I find it a sorry end to a magazine that has contributed a great deal to the field in twenty-two years—and which could have contributed a great deal more.[51]

The merger of the two magazines consisted of shifting Geis' column and the "SF Calendar" over and publishing in *Galaxy* some work that was to have appeared in *If*: "*Sign of the Unicorn*, a new *Amber* novel by Roger Zelazny . . . A new Mack Reynolds story. A new Chandler. A 'Berserker.' "[52] Though lower in circulation, *Galaxy* survived because of its prestige.[53] Thus, with its 175th issue fell *If*, victim perhaps of the questionable belief that readers prefer the prestigious to the pleasurable, perhaps simply because its publisher needed the money that month for another purpose.

Notes

1. Frederik Pohl, Interview (April 28, 1979), Conference on Teaching Science Fiction at Boca Raton, Fla.; Theodore Sturgeon, "The Other IF," *If*, Vol. 12, No. 2 (May 1962: 107.

2. Sturgeon, pp. 107–8.

3. Brian Ash, ed., "01. Program: 1953," in *The Visual Encyclopedia of Science Fiction* (New York: Harmony Books, 1977).

4. Lester del Rey, "Reading Room," *If*, Vol. 22, No. 8 (November-December 1974): 44.

5. Michael Ashley, *The History of the Science Fiction Magazine: 1946–1955* (Chicago: Contemporary Books, 1976), III: 78.

6. Paul W. Fairman, "A Chat with the Editor," *If*, Vol. 1, No. 1 (March 1952): 23.

7. Ashley, p. 78; Donald H. Tuck, various entries, *The Encyclopedia of Science Fiction and Fantasy*, Vols. 1-2.

8. Fairman, "Chat," *If*, Vol. 1, No. 3 (July 1952): 2–3.

9. *If*, Vol. 1, No. 2 (May 1952): 56.

10. "The Postman Cometh," *If*, Vol. 1, No. 4 (September 1952): 160. Perhaps the response was inspired by a contest for the best letter. First prize—an original manuscript for Issue No. 1—went to young Terry Carr of San Francisco.

11. Ashley, pp. 78, 330, 337.

12. Del Rey, p. 40.

13. Tuck, I: 163.

14. Ibid., II: 428.

15. Frank Kelly Freas, *Frank Kelly Freas: The Art of Science Fiction* (Norfolk, Va.: Donning, 1977), p. 30.

16. Tuck, II: 385.

17. Ibid., I: 234–35. Behind the pseudonym was S. A. Lombino, a contributor from the Fairman days and thereafter; a mystery writer also, he wrote *The Blackboard Jungle*, later made into the film of the same name, and as Ed McBain he wrote the "Eighty-Seventh Precinct" series.

18. Del Rey, p. 41.

19. Ibid., pp. 40–41.

20. Ash, "01. Program: 1954–1955."

21. Pohl, Interview.

22. Del Rey, p. 40.

23. James L. Quinn, "Chat," *If*, Vol. 3, No. 2 (April 1954): 2–3.

24. *If*, Vol. 4, No. 6 (February 1955): 4.

25. "*If*'s $2000 College Science Fiction Awards," *If*, Vol. 4, No. 3 (November 1954): 6.

26. James L. Quinn and Eve Wulff, eds., *The Second World of If* (Kingston, N.J.: Quinn Publishing,1958), inside front cover.

27. Pohl, Interview.

28. Frederik Pohl, *The Way the Future Was: A Memoir* (New York: Del Rey Books, 1978), p. 195.

29. Pohl, Interview.

30. Ibid.

31. James Gunn, *Alternate Worlds: The Illustrated History of Science Fiction* (Englewood Cliffs, N.J.: Prentice-Hall, 1975), pp. 186, 220.

32. Del Rey, p. 41.

33. Pohl, *Way the Future Was*, pp. 202–4.

34. Ibid., p. 204.

35. Ibid., p. 199; see also "Introduction," *The IF Reader of Science Fiction*, ed. Frederik Pohl (New York: Doubleday, 1966), pp. 10–11.

36. Pohl, Letter (May 11, 1979).

37. Pohl, Interview.

38. Pohl, *Way the Future Was*, p. 199.

39. Pohl, "Wiped Out," *If*, Vol. 17, No. 7 (July 1967): 4–5.

40. *If*, Vol. 17, No. 12 (December 1967): 162.

41. Del Rey, p. 42.

42. Pohl, *Way the Future Was*, pp. 245–46.

43. Ibid.

44. Del Rey, p. 43.

45. Anthony Lewis, "Annual Magazine Wrapup: 1974 Summary," *Locus*, No. 169 (February 16, 1975): 3.

46. Ejler Jakobsson, "Hue and Cry," *If*, Vol. 20, No. 2 (February 1970): 153.

47. Del Rey, p. 44.

48. James Baen, "On Building Walls," *If*, Vol. 22, No. 7 (September-October 1974): 94.

49. Gerry de la Ree, ed., *Fantasy by Fabian: The Art of Stephen E. Fabian* (Saddle River, N.J.: Gerry de la Ree, 1978), p. 6.

50. "Editorial," *If*, Vol. 22, No. 8 (November-December 1974): 6.

51. Del Rey, p. 44.

52. Baen, p. 6.

53. Lewis, *Locus*, No. 169, p. 3.

Information Sources

BIBLIOGRAPHY:
Nicholls. *Encyclopedia*.
Tuck.
INDEX SOURCES: IBSF; ISFM-II; MIT; NESFA; NESFA-II; NESFA-III; SFM; Tuck.
REPRINT SOURCES:

Reprint Editions:

British: Four series. First series, Strato Publications, Leicester, identical (with only minor changes) to U.S. editions. 15 issues, Digest, 128pp., 1/6d., undated, ran monthly November 1953–January 1955. Issues 1–6 correspond to U.S. March 1953–January 1954; issue 7 was U.S. January 1953; issues 8–15 equal U.S. March–October 1954.

Second series, Strato Publications, London, Digest, 128pp., 2/-. Correspond to U.S. issues, first issue reprinted, but thereafter original issues overprinted with number and price. 18 issues, bi-monthly from Number 2. Issue 1 [September 1959] corresponds to U.S. July 1959; thereafter issues consequential with U.S., January 1960–September 1962. Subsequent issues imported by Thorpe & Porter with their own symbol overprinting the cover, but with no physical changes.

Third series, Gold Star, London, identical to U.S. editions, Digest, 160pp. 3/6d., 11 issues, January–November 1967, corresponding to U.S. issues March 1966–January 1967. Thereafter, U.S. issues imported and overprinted.

Fourth series, identical to U.S. editions but carrying a U.K. cover number. 15 issues released by Universal-Tandem, London, correspond to U.S. May/June 1972–September/October 1974. (U.K. price 25p., but last three issues, 30p.) Cover numbers unnecessarily complicated, run in sequence 1 to 9, 11, 1, 13, 3, 4, 5.

Derivative Anthologies: Selections from the magazine by the editors have been as follows: James L. Quinn and Eve P. Wulff, *The First World of If* (New York: Quinn, 1957), 20 stories presented chronologically from issues from November 1952 to October 1956, and *The Second World of If* (Quinn, 1958), 9 longer stories in chronological order from issues June 1954–October 1956; Frederik Pohl, ed., *The Best Science Fiction from If* (New York: Galaxy, 1964), 12 stories selected from issues July 1960–September 1963; "The Editors of If" (Ejler Jakobsson and Judy-Lynn Benjamin), *The Best from If, Volume I* (New York: Award Books, 1973), 13 stories from issues in 1969–1971; *The Best from If, Volume II* (Award, 1974), 7 stories and a Guest Editorial from 1973–1974; Jim Baen, ed., *The Best from If, Volume III* (Award, 1976), 9 stories plus features from Baen's issues. Also in hardcover, Frederik Pohl, ed., *The If Reader of Science Fiction* (New York: Doubleday, 1966), 9 stories from 7 issues between May 1962 and December 1964, and *The Second If Reader of Science Fiction* (Doubleday, 1968), 10 stories selected between 1963 and 1967.

LOCATION SOURCES: Beloit College Library; Bowling Green State University Library; Brigham Young University Library; Dallas Public Library; Eastern New Mexico University Library; Michigan State University Library; M.I.T. Science Fiction Library; Pennsylvania State University Library; University of Arizona Library; University of California–Riverside Library; University of Georgia Library; University of Texas–Austin Library.

Publication History

TITLE: *If*. Note: The magazine was always entitled simply *If*, with a variant subtitle that began as *If: Worlds of Science Fiction* (March 1952–October 1958) and was then reduced on the cover to *If Science Fiction*. The contents page, however, was still headed with the full subtitle, and in March 1961 a new design for the contents page gave an altered emphasis to the subtitle so that it read *Worlds of If Science Fiction*. This design was translated to the cover logo with the November 1961 issue. Thus, even though the spine and the indicia still doggedly read *If Science Fiction*, and always would, for the period from November 1961 to July 1969 the magazine was usually thought of as *Worlds of If*, a title that was all the more obvious when the companion *Worlds of Tomorrow* and later *Worlds of Fantasy* were launched.

VOLUME DATA: Volume 1, Number 1, March 1952–Volume 22, Number 8, November/December 1974. Volumes 1 to 13, six issues per volume, although Volume 8, Number 1 (December 1957), misnumbered Volume 7, Number 6; Volume 9, Number 3 (July 1959), misnumbered Volume 8, Number 6. Bi-monthly, March 1952–January 1954; monthly, March 1954–June 1955; bi-monthly, August 1955–

February 1959, and July 1959–May 1964. Volume 14, seven issues, March–December 1964 (monthly from July, although September/October issues combined). Volumes 15–21, twelve issues per volume, except Volume 19 (1969), with ten issues. Monthly until May 1969; bi-monthly, July 1969; monthly, September 1969–April 1970; bi-monthly, May/June 1970–November/December 1974. Total run: 175 issues.

PUBLISHER: Quinn Publishing Co., Kingston, New York, March 1952–February 1959; Digest Productions, New York (a subsidiary of Galaxy Publishing), July 1959–May 1963; Galaxy Publishing Corp., New York, July 1963–May 1969; UPD Publishing Corp., July 1969–November/December 1974.

EDITORS: Paul W. Fairman, March–September 1952; James L. Quinn, November 1952–August 1958, with Larry T. Shaw as Associate Editor, May 1953–March 1954, and Eve P. Wulff as Assistant Editor, May 1954–April 1958; Damon Knight, October 1958–February 1959; H. L. Gold, July 1959–September 1961 (nominally, although Pohl had accepted more and more duties during 1960); Frederik Pohl, November 1961–May 1969; Ejler Jakobsson, July 1969–January/February 1974; James Baen, March/April–November/December 1974.

FORMAT: Digest, 160pp., March–September 1952; 120pp., November 1952–February 1959; 128pp., July 1959–August 1965; 160pp., September 1965–July/August 1970; 192pp., September/October 1970–March/April 1971; 176pp., May/June 1971–September/October 1974; 160pp., November/December 1974.

PRICE: 35¢, March 1952–January 1963; 40¢, March 1963–November 1964; 50¢, December 1964–July 1967; 60¢, August 1967–July/August 1970; 75¢, September/October 1970–November/December 1974.

E. F. Casebeer

IMAGINATION

Considering how long William L. Hamling's *Imagination* was published, the most striking thing about it may be how little of its fiction is worth mentioning. The first issue of *Imagination* was dated October 1950. Officially, the first two issues were edited by Ray Palmer and published by Clark Publishing Company, Hamling and his Greenleaf Publishing Company taking over with the third issue (February 1951). Actually, Hamling was editor and publisher from the beginning. The two men had worked together at Ziff-Davis, with Hamling assisting Palmer and ultimately taking over editorship of *Amazing Stories** and *Fantastic Adventures** in 1948, so when Hamling was unable to launch *Imagination* on his own because he was still officially an employee of Z-D, he asked Palmer to front for him until he departed Z-D, which occurred when the company's editorial offices were moved to New York.[1]

It is doubtful, however, whether the early issues of *Imagination* would have been different if Palmer actually had edited them. Having broken into the science fiction field under Palmer and having seen the success of *Amazing* and *Fantastic*

Adventures under him, Hamling echoed his mentor devoutly. In explaining his decision to return to basic adventure fiction in mid-1955, for example, Hamling proclaimed that

> the status of science fiction today is deplorable from an editorial standpoint. In a recent issue of *Fantasy-Times* Jim Quinn [then editor-publisher of *If**] and Ray Palmer agreed that too much intellectualism exists storywise. The good old days of action, adventure in science-fiction have been tossed out the window in favor of the so-called "adult" material. Fact remains that the heydey [*sic*] of the field—the forties—emphasized action and adventure, particularly in the case of *Amazing Stories* which had the highest sale of any science fiction book in history.[2]

This indicates the editorial policy that Hamling followed fairly consistently in *Imagination*, for he apparently truly believed that it was the way to attract new (that is, younger) readers to SF.

The magazine's covers were fairly consistent in stressing this juvenile slant. Most of them featured pretty girls in mild dishabille and considerable anguish. Many—though not necessarily the same ones—also featured monsters. But the one thing almost certain to be featured on an *Imagination* cover was destruction: fire, ray-gun blasts, collapsing buildings, explosions. Adolescence is a time of much uncertainty, hence much hostility; Hamling was fairly adept at exploiting that fact, giving the readers an obligatory hint of sex but a main serving of menace and mayhem.

In the case of *Imagination*, it is fair to judge a book by its cover. Most of the stories were melodramatic (as shown by the number of titles ending with an exclamation point, e.g., " 'Leave, Earthmen or Die!' " "Get Out of My Brain!," "Compete or Die!," "Bring Back My Brain!"). They tended to be rehashes of ideas that were thoroughly familiar to older SF readers; some, in fact, were even straight science fictional translations of history (the voyage of the *Titanic*, in "The Star Lord" by Boyd Ellanby, June 1953, or the American Revolution in "Revolt of the Outworlds" by Milton Lesser, December 1954). A typical issue of *Imagination* would contain a "complete novel" (20,000–30,000 words), a "novelette" (approximately 10,000 words) and an assortment of short stories. Generally, Hamling depended on a stable of writers who were often Midwesterners, usually known for regular production rather than originality, and always able to work the frustration-action vein. Several simply moved over to *Imagination* from *Amazing* and *Fantastic Adventures*. Regular writers included Chester S. Geier, Rog Phillips (pseudonym Roger P. Graham), Dwight V. Swain and Geoff St. Reynard (pseudonym Robert W. Krepps); very little of their work has been reprinted in book form, though this seems surprising only in the case of St. Reynard's consistently smooth fiction. *Imagination* also published early work by Daniel F. Galouye, Philip K. Dick and Robert Sheckley, and, in its later issues, Robert Silverberg and Harlan Ellison. Toward the end of its life, it published a string of short novels by Edmond Hamilton, who was able to do the kind of story Hamling desired with a great deal of professional polish.

To be fair, some good stories were scattered throughout *Imagination*'s run. The earliest issues, in particular, were sprinkled with occasional pieces by Ray Bradbury, Theodore Sturgeon and Richard Matheson. Perhaps the most noteworthy story in the magazine's run appeared in the third issue, "Revolt of the Devil Star" by Ross Rocklynne, the conclusion of the Devil Star series.[3]

The magazine was prosperous enough to go semi-monthly (published nine times a year) with the September 1952 issue, and monthly with the January 1953 issue, so Hamling was willing to experiment with his formula: he ran a longer story as a serial ("The Time Armada" by Fox B. Holden, October–November 1953), he used nonjuvenile covers from time to time (such as W. E. Terry's rocket and space station, illustrating Robert A. Heinlein's "Sky Lift," November 1953) and, as in his magazine *Imaginative Tales*,* he put more emphasis on humor.

In fact, starting at the end of 1954, Hamling seemed to be trying to upgrade the quality of the fiction generally, especially while George O. Smith's "Highways in Hiding" was serialized. As one sign of the magazine's new image, the covers of issues beginning December 1955 featured humorous pinups by Harold McCauley rather than the usual fire-and-fragments subject matter. Hamling evidently believed he could raise the level of sophistication a notch, gaining new readers while he held onto the old. It did not work. *Imagination* returned to bimonthly publication with the July 1955 issue, and Hamling returned to an uncomplicated action formula. Essentially, although he was willing to publish more sophisticated science fiction when he thought the market permitted, his heart was not in it. The only real change in *Imagination*'s contents for the rest of the magazine's run was a stress on science articles in its last, post-Sputnik issues; most of these were written by Henry Bott (pseudonym Charles Recour), *Imagination*'s book reviewer, now billed as "Research Engineer." The fiction continued at about the same level.

Despite all this, *Imagination* had a rather pleasant personality thanks to its relaxed and chatty departments and was affectionately known by its readers as "Madge." In particular, "Fandora's Box," a fan column conducted by Mari Wolf (Mrs. Rog Phillips), began in the fourth issue and ran until the April 1956 issue; Bob Bloch took it over then and continued it until the end of *Imagination*'s run. "Fandora's Box" was a friendly and leisurely column, and its extensive fanzine reviews provided a real service to prospective fans.[4] Hamling's editorials were rambling, consisting mainly of snippets of opinion and personal gossip. The letter column was fairly entertaining, too, though Bott's book reviews were sketchy. Hamling sometimes did some other audience-pleasing things, such as running word counts of the stories on the contents page and, in later issues, printing illustrations in crude color (a red or blue plate accompanying the black).

At its best, *Imagination* passed time effortlessly, like a routine TV adventure show. It is difficult, however, looking back over the magazine's history, to single out many truly outstanding stories—or, for that matter, to remember many that made it above the level of smooth mediocrity. Its survival for eight years, from October 1950 to October 1958, seems to indicate that there is a real market for this undemanding type of story. But Hamling lacked Palmer's screwball inventiveness. His affection for SF appears to have been genuine, but within the field he was a better merchandiser than originator. His talents probably were better used in his switch to soft-core (*Rogue*) and hard-core (Greenleaf Books) pornography, since porn thrives on repetition of familiar formulas.

Notes

1. Hamling explains this in "They Don't Hardly Write Them No More," *Inside and Science Fiction Advertiser* [fanzine], No. 8 (March 1955): 20; confirmed by Bea Mahaffey, Palmer's editorial assistant at the time, in a letter dated May 26, 1980.

2. "*Imagination* Goes Bi-monthly," *Fantasy-Times* [fanzine], No. 228 (First August 1955 issue): 2.

3. The case for ranking that story so highly is made by William L. Freeman in his essay review of *Imagination*, "She Ain't What She Used to Be," *Inside and Science Fiction Advertiser* [fanzine], No. 8 (March 1955): 12–14. For background on the Rocklynne series, see Terry Carr's introduction to "Into the Darkness," in *Classic Science Fiction: The First Golden Age* (New York: Harper & Row, 1978), pp. 62–67.

4. Hamling had come out of fandom himself, having been one of the supporting cast of Sam Moskowitz's *The Immortal Storm* (Atlanta: ASFO Press, 1954). He thus went out of his way to keep a good relationship with fans.

Information Sources

BIBLIOGRAPHY:
Nicholls. *Encyclopedia.*
Tuck.
INDEX SOURCES: ISFM; MIT; SFM; Tuck.
REPRINT SOURCES: None known.
LOCATION SOURCES: M.I.T. Science Fiction Library; Pennsylvania State University Library; University of New Brunswick (Canada) Library.

Publication History

TITLE: *Imagination* (subtitled "Stories of Science and Fantasy), October 1950–July 1955; *Imagination Science Fiction*, October 1955–October 1958. The table of contents, however, carried the original subtitle throughout.

VOLUME DATA: Volume 1, Number 1, October 1950–Volume 9, Number 5, October 1958. Number of issues per volume varied. Volume 1, two issues, October–December 1950, bi-monthly. Volume 2, five issues, February–November 1951, bi-monthly (August issue slipped to September). Volume 3, seven issues, January–December 1952, bi-monthly to September, thereafter six-weekly. Volume 4, eleven issues, January–December 1953, monthly (no March issue). Volume 5, twelve issues, January–December 1954, monthly. Volume 6, nine issues, January–December 1955, monthly to July, then bi-monthly from October. Volumes 7 and 8,

six issues per volume, February 1956–December 1957, bi-monthly. Volume 9, five issues, February–October 1958, bi-monthly.
PUBLISHER: First two issues, Clark Publishing Co., Evanston, Illinois. Thereafter Greenleaf Publishing Co., Evanston, Illinois.
EDITOR: William L. Hamling.
FORMAT: Digest, 160pp., October 1950–March 1954; 128pp., April 1954–October 1958.
PRICE: 35¢.

Joe Sanders

IMAGINATIVE TALES

As a staff member on the Ziff-Davis SF magazines under Ray Palmer, William L. Hamling became thoroughly familiar with the mingling of juvenile adventure and humor in *Amazing Stories** and *Fantastic Adventures.** Apparently he both liked that mixture and observed how well it sold. As editor/publisher of his own magazine, *Imagination,** beginning in 1950, Hamling put primary stress on action-adventure SF, but from time to time he included humorous SF and fantasy pieces among the short fiction. A few of the magazine's lead "novels" were humorous also, chiefly "The Vengeance of Toffee" by Charles F. Myers (February 1951), "Hell's Angel" by Robert Bloch (June 1951) and "No Time for Toffee!" by Myers (July 1952). Reader response evidently was favorable enough to encourage Hamling to make humor the main emphasis of the bi-monthly companion magazine he began during *Imagination*'s most prosperous period. In the editorial of the August 1954 *Imagination*, Hamling glowingly described the contents of *Imaginative Tales*' first issue (September 1954), consisting entirely of a Toffee novel by Myers:

> If you have ever been a fan of Thorne Smith you'll find Charlie Myers has deservedly been referred to as having taken up and worn well the mantle of the late master. TOFFEE stories have all the spice, humor, and clever science fantasy of the type of writing that Thorne Smith made world famous. So for an uproariously funny piece of science fantasy reading, don't miss the first issue . . . of IMAGINATIVE TALES.[1]

Key words here are "uproarious" and "spice." The novels by Myers—and by Bloch when he took over as writer of the lead novels for *Tales*—worked hard at being uproarious. They were wacky, rambling tales stretched to accommodate wild coincidence, slapstick and nonsequitur conversations. The spice consisted of an exaggerated pose of naughtiness. The erotic element actually did not go very far. Lack of clothing could be suggested, but naked bodies could not be described; characters could make coyly lustful declarations, but they always shriveled at the prospect of actually doing anything. It was hard to tell which was more prominent—the lure of sex or its panicky denial.

In the same editorial, Hamling also commented on the experimental format of *Tales*:

> We actually don't know whether it's a magazine or paperback in magazine form. Each issue we will publish a book-length novel or at most two shorter length novels. Each issue will contain the work of one author only. In this respect you might call IMAGINATIVE TALES a "pocket-book" except that the size and general format will be the same as IMAGINATION.[2]

Tales looked, in fact, very much like the Galaxy Novels series, with the magazine title displayed on the cover and spine, but with the title of the fiction receiving equal or greater emphasis. The number of each issue got more stress than the date, and no departments were used. Overall, *Tales* looked as much like a paperback book as a digest-sized magazine could. In any event, the policy remained intact for only two issues, two short pieces of fiction by other writers appearing along with Bloch's "Black Magic Holiday" in the January 1955 issue. In all, six issues consisted of or featured humorous novels, the first two filled by Myers and the next four led off by Bloch. In the fall of 1956, in the magazine's first editorial, Hamling announced:

> *An action story is more popular than any other type.* That's a positive statement if we ever heard—or made one! The funny thing is, it's true! . . . As you know we've been following a program of humorous-type fiction in *Tales*. Sadly enough—and we're not ashamed to admit it—sales figures were not encouraging enough to continue that policy. So, bowing to your wishes as readers, we make an abrupt about-face editorially. Action stories—the kind you can't put down until you're finished reading the entire piece—are the order of the day.[3]

From that time on, *Tales*' appearance and editorial policy were virtually indistinguishable from *Imagination*'s. The same energetic troupe of writers provided most of the fiction, with Geoff St. Reynard and (in late issues) Edmond Hamilton the most readable of the novelists. Along with editorials and letter columns much like *Imagination*'s, *Tales* featured one column of its own, Forrest J Ackerman's report of movie news, "Scientifilm Marquee," beginning in January 1956. *Tales* was definitely a poor relation, however. Unlike *Imagination*, the magazine never was published monthly and, except for the first issue, never got above the 128-page length. Its shorter fiction was undistinguished, lacking the occasional above-average piece found in *Imagination*. And it contained possibly the worst story published in either of Hamling's magazines, Ray Palmer's novel "The Metal Emperor" (November 1955).

In the apparent general interest in space that followed the launching of the Sputniks—at the same time Hamling was trying to give *Imagination* a serious, constructive image—he again tried to revamp *Tales*. Beginning with the July 1958 issue, the magazine was titled *Space Travel*, featuring an astronautical cover and blurb.[4] It was still bi-monthly, published in alternate months with *Imagination*. In fact, aside from articles by Henry Bott (who also wrote book reviews and science essays for *Imagination*) and Guenther Schmidt, the contents remained unchanged. If the magazine did attract new readers, they must have found it mindbending to read past restrained science articles into wild-eyed action-adventure fiction. The magazine staggered through only three issues under its new title, expiring before the end of 1958.

Except for its experimental beginning and the equivocal experiment of its last issues, *Tales* is essentially a footnote to the story of *Imagination*. It revealed little new about Hamling's taste or abilities, and it accomplished little in its own right.

Notes

1. "Editorial," *Imagination* 5 (August 1954): 4. Myers began writing Toffee stories for Hamling in 1947 for *Fantastic Adventures*. In fact, the person who first had the idea of comparing Myers to Smith was Hamling himself (reply to letter to the editor, *Imagination* 3 [June 1951]: 155).

2. "Editorial," *Imagination* 5 (August 1954): 4.

3. "Editorial," *Imaginative Tales* 2 (September 1955): 4.

4. " 'IMAGINATIVE TALES' FOLDS: 'SPACE TRAVEL' TAKES ITS PLACE," *Science-Fiction Times* [fanzine], No. 290 (First March 1958 issue): 1, 4.

Information Sources

BIBLIOGRAPHY:
Nicholls. *Encyclopedia*.
Tuck.
INDEX SOURCES: MIT; SFM; Tuck.
REPRINT SOURCES: None known.
LOCATION SOURCES: M.I.T. Science Fiction Library; Pennsylvania State University
    Library.

Publication History

TITLE: *Imaginative Tales*, September 1954–May 1958; *Space Travel*, July–November
    1958.
VOLUME DATA: [Volume 1], Number 1, September 1954–Volume 5, Number 6,
    November 1958. Six issues per volume, except Volume 2, two issues only (Sep-
    tember and November 1955). Bi-monthly. Total run: 26 issues.
PUBLISHER: Greenleaf Publishing Co., Evanston, Illinois.

EDITOR: William L. Hamling.
FORMAT: Digest, first issue 160pp., thereafter 128pp.
PRICE: 35¢.

Joe Sanders

IMPULSE

In 1965 Kyril Bonfiglioli, editor of *Science Fantasy*,* was so dissatisfied with that magazine's name that he resolved to change it. After considering *Caliban*, which publisher David Warburton convinced him was inappropriate, he finally settled on *Impulse* and, in order to sever all connections with *Science Fantasy*, he began *Impulse* anew with Volume 1, Number 1.

In so doing he committed two fatal mistakes. First, there was already a nonfiction magazine called *Impulse* on the stands, and this caused problems with the distributors. Bonfiglioli subsequently amended the title to *sf Impulse*, but by then the damage was done. Second, in treating *Impulse* as a new magazine, the publishers had to renegotiate a new distribution contract, and with all the attendant problems that created, Bonfiglioli discovered he had lost the bulk of his readership.

This was unfortunate, as the twelve pocketbook-sized issues of *Impulse* include some of the best SF and fantasy ever published in British magazines. For a start, the first issue is a collector's item. Bonfiglioli had hinted at the contents in the December 1965 *Science Fantasy* when relating the events after the 1965 World SF Convention (held in London) when a select group returned to Brian Aldiss' house in Oxford. "It was quieter by far, but no less festive and *Science Fantasy* profited exceedingly for, very late one night, those present agreed—in fact volunteered—to join in an all-star issue early next year with specially written stories round the theme of 'sacrifice.' "[1]

The impressive lineup included "The Circulation of the Blood" by Brian W. Aldiss, "High Treason," by Poul Anderson, "You and Me and the Continuum" by J. G. Ballard, "A Hero's Life" by James Blish, "The Gods Themselves Throw Incense" by Harry Harrison and "The Secret" by Jack Vance. Also present was "The Signaller,"the first story in the much acclaimed "Pavane" series by Keith Roberts. Other episodes appeared in later issues.

The second issue sustained the promise of quality. Apart from another Pavane story, there was a new "Traveller in Black" adventure by John Brunner, "Break the Door of Hell"; "A Light Feint" by John Rackham—a sequel to his popular "Room with a Skew" in an earlier *Science Fantasy*; and the first part of a serial, "Homecalling" by Judith Merril, a 36,000-word short novel originally published in *Science Fiction Stories* in 1956.

Although subsequent issues were not the equal of the first two, they were still above average in quality. Apart from the occasional reprint, Bonfiglioli was also giving new writers a start. Christopher Priest's first professional appearance, "The Run," was in the May 1966 issue. Chris Boyce, winner of the 1976

Sunday Times/Gollancz SF novel competition, also debuted here with "George" in the June 1966 issue.

Impulse also published two popular serials: "Make Room! Make Room!" (August–October 1966), Harry Harrison's frightening novel of future overpopulation, perhaps better known by its 1973 film title, *Soylent Green*; and "The Ice Schooner" (November 1966–January 1967), Michael Moorcock's stirring adventure set on a frozen Earth.

With the September 1966 issue Kyril Bonfiglioli bid farewell, stating that following the remarkable progress his magazine had made, the next step was to have "an internationally-known editor and a full-time Managing Editor. We now have them and it's time for me to bow myself out."[2] In truth, Bonfiglioli had made a killing in the antique art field and was now able to retire to Jersey, in the Channel Islands, where he has since established himself as a writer of humorous mysteries.[3]

The editor-in-chief was now Harry Harrison, who instantly brought a change to the magazine in making it less formal, instigating a letter column—something which Bonfiglioli had staunchly stood against. However, no sooner had Harrison assumed control than he was called away, first to Italy, then to the United States, so that while he still rustled for stories from leading writers, the main functions of reading and selecting manuscripts and assembling and illustrating the issues fell on the capable shoulders of Managing Editor Keith Roberts.

Impulse continued to include some memorable stories: "The Eyes of the Blind King" by Brian W. Aldiss and "The Roaches" by Thomas M. Disch (both November 1966); "Mantis" by Chris Boyce (January 1967); and, ironically, a high-class final issue which included "The Bad Bush of Uzoro" by Chris Hebron, "Inconstancy" by Brian M. Stableford, "The Number You Have Just Reached" by Thomas M. Disch, "It's Smart to Have an English Address" by D. G. Compton and "See Me Not" by Richard Wilson.

There was no indication that *Impulse* 12 was the last issue, but the dark cloud of insolvency was already threatening the publishers, as recounted in the entry on *New Worlds*.* Although both magazines made a profit, the problems caused by the name-change to *Impulse* meant that when the publishers decided to put out two interim issues of just one magazine, *Impulse* was not that magazine. It was absorbed with *New Worlds* for the March and April 1967 issues, but thereafter was dropped by the wayside.

Notes

1. Kyril Bonfiglioli, "Editorial," *Science Fantasy* 79 (December 1965), p. 2.

2. Bonfiglioli, "Editorial," *sf Impulse* 7 (September 1966), p. 2.

3. Brian W. Aldiss, *Billion Year Spree* (London: Weidenfeld & Nicolson, 1973), p. 302.

Information Sources

BIBLIOGRAPHY:
Aldiss, Brian W. *Billion Year Spree*. London: Weidenfeld & Nicolson, 1973.
Tuck.
INDEX SOURCES: ISFM-II; MT; SFM; Tuck.
REPRINT SOURCES: Oxford Microform Publications, MIT Science Fiction Society; Science Fiction Foundation.
LOCATION SOURCES: M.I.T. Science Fiction Library.

Publication History

TITLE: *Impulse*, March–July 1966; *sf Impulse*, August 1966–February 1967.
VOLUME DATA: Volume 1, Number 1, March 1966–Volume 1, Number 12, February 1967.
PUBLISHER: Roberts & Vinter, Ltd., London.
EDITORS: Kyril Bonfiglioli, March–September 1966; Harry Harrison and Keith Roberts, October 1966–February 1967.
FORMAT: Pocketbook, 160pp.
PRICE: 3/6d.

Mike Ashley

INFINITY SCIENCE FICTION

Infinity Science Fiction, edited by Larry T. Shaw, was introduced by Royal Publications in November 1955. It ceased publication, after twenty issues, in November 1958. Thus it spanned the second, lesser phase of the fifties' boom in the genre, the period between the collapse of more than a dozen science fiction magazines in 1954–1955 and the subsequent collapse of another dozen in 1958–1959. Except for the first issue, its covers were done by Ed Emsh, whose special emphasis on the female form made the magazines very attractive for the male readers. It appeared bi-monthly initially, went to a six-week schedule with its June 1957 issue, and attempted a monthly schedule (as an alternative to reverting to a bi-monthly one) with its October 1958 issue. Between December 1956 and June 1958, it had as a companion magazine Royal Publications' *Science Fiction Adventures*.*

During *Infinity*'s three years, it was notable for its book reviews by Damon Knight and for the publication of Arthur C. Clarke's "The Star," both of which received Hugo awards. It also included Harlan Ellison's first professional SF story, "Glow Worm" (February 1956), and some of the early work by Robert Silverberg.

Appearing in the last years when American science fiction still took its direction from its magazines and their editors, *Infinity* clearly reflects the attitudes and priorities of Larry T. Shaw. In his editorials, Shaw emerges as an editor of the middle echelon. He willingly promotes new authors, but is more inclined to accept than to cultivate their talent.[1] He is solicitous to draw the more intelligent range of fans into his readership and is disturbed by a tendency to promote the genre among a broader audience, feeling that such an increase would lower the genre's quality (2.1:111). Though he aims at diversity, his selection of material leans more toward science adventure and lightly humorous entertainment than toward the intellectually venturesome (4.2:4). Only in a few instances do the stories in *Infinity* rise significantly above the eclectic. In sum, Shaw defines science fiction more or less intuitively and according to his experience with it over the years, but he is not especially concerned to enlarge or refine that intuition (2.4:126).

In an editorial for *Infinity*'s third issue, Shaw cites "balance and story plausibility" as the two principal characteristics he wants the magazine to have (1.3:126). Most of the stories that Shaw selected demonstrate enough narrative competence to qualify as plausible within the premises they set themselves. And the cumulative contents suggest that Shaw did try to give his magazine's readers a fair range of styles and outlooks, from the garrulous irony of Robert Bloch's "Have Tux—Will Travel" (November 1955) to the grim retribution of Harlan Ellison's "Blank . . . " (June 1957).

At its best, *Infinity* included works like Arthur C. Clarke's "The Star" (November 1955) and Damon Knight's "Dio" (September 1957). In Clarke's cosmic scope or Knight's complex assessment of humanity, one finds the characteristics of excellent science fiction.

Infinity included works by other writers who were also capable of such excellence. Isaac Asimov and Clifford Simak were multiple contributors, as were more recently established writers like Robert Sheckley. The magazine gathered stories from Lester del Rey, L. Sprague de Camp, Poul Anderson, Algis Budrys, Gordon Dickson, William Tenn and Jack Vance. Few of these works, however, are the ones for which these authors will be remembered.

At the same time, reflecting the editor's regard for the fans among his readership, the magazine dipped into the output of the fanzines. Under the headline "Fanfare," it reprinted items from these publications as a regular feature.

Most typically in *Infinity*, though, the writers who appeared were among the younger or less well established professionals. These were writers like Richard Wilson, Edward Wellen, David Mason and Harlan Ellison—each of whom contributed at least five stories. This description also fits Robert Silverberg, whose output of stories (thirteen), analytical pieces (two) and—after Damon Knight moved on—book review columns (three) made him *Infinity*'s most frequent contributor. Especially in the magazine's last issues, Silverberg's work filled its pages; he used pseudonyms and published several stories in each.

In retrospect, Shaw's editorial work in *Infinity* appears as a foil to that of the magazine's other—and more formidable—critical intelligence, Damon Knight. Knight was *Infinity*'s book reviewer until August 1958, and the recurring phrase in his reviews is "science fiction at its best." When a work under his scrutiny failed to measure up to his conceptual ideal, he did not hesitate to detail its shortcomings. He criticizes Richard Matheson for having no plot sense (2.4:97),

William Tenn (Philip Klass) for blunting his perceptions in a commercial style which is self-conscious and mannered (2.4:99), and Frederik Pohl for idiotic characterization (2.6:109).

Such observations provoked some bitter rejoinders from *Infinity*'s readers, but unlike the more hostile of his own critics, Knight tended to offer balanced assessments in which the strengths and weaknesses of a work were given equitable notice. Against a lack of scientific credibility in a collection by Henry Kuttner and C. L. Moore, he weighs the skill which makes viable characters of robots (1.3:99). He overrides an awareness of Arthur C. Clarke's "painfully inadequate" characterization in *The Deep Range* with a tribute to his "abiding sense of the grandeur of creation" (2.5:100). He describes the style of Mervyn Peake as "images that are perfect nonsense and yet will chill your blood" (3.2:91). And of Robert Heinlein he shrewdly observes, "Almost invariably his most convincing and attractive characters are adolescents in one sense or another" (2.5:98).

Although Knight's reviews in *Infinity* do not provide the substance of a thoroughly worked out or logically consistent critical theory for science fiction, they do exemplify the discriminatory judgment which supports such theorizing. They also indicate a keenness for pushing science fiction toward higher standards and a greater audience. In his last review for *Infinity* (before going on to become editor of *If**), Knight surveys the genre as it seemed in 1958 and asserts, "There is not going to be another wide-open science fiction boom. What I hope to see happening next is more in the nature of a silent revolution: more and more novelists working for the general book public, rather than for the specialists alone" (3.5:99). Shaw, the magazine's editor, had insisted that "science fiction always has and always will be a specialized field appealing to a specialized audience" (2.1:111). Knight's sense of audience is more wide-ranging, his aim more ambitious.

By the last year *Infinity* was losing money, and Irwin Stein assembled the last two issues himself, having acquired the material as part of a package deal to cut costs, and changed printers. The result was depressing to say the least, and though Larry Shaw is listed as editor of those two issues, he has since felt inclined to disown them.[2]

Stein later started the Lancer Books paperback imprint, and in 1970 *Infinity* was revived as an original paperback series (see Section II).

Notes

1. Larry T. Shaw, "Tomorrowness," *Infinity*, January 1958, p. 53. Subsequent references to Shaw's editorials and to Knight's book reviews are included parenthetically within the text, using volume, number and page, thus: (3.2:53).

2. Larry T. Shaw, "Footnotes to Fan History," *The Alien Critic*, No. 11 (November 1974): 48–51.

Information Sources

BIBLIOGRAPHY:

Nicholls. *Encyclopedia.*

Shaw, Larry T. "Footnotes to Fan History." *The Alien Critic*, No. 11 (November 1974): 48–51.

Tuck.

INDEX SOURCES: ISPF-2; MIT; SFM; Tuck.

REPRINT SOURCES: None known.

LOCATION SOURCES: M.I.T. Science Fiction Library; Pennsylvania State University Library.

Publication History

TITLE: *Infinity Science Fiction.*

VOLUME DATA: Volume 1, Number 1, November 1955–Volume 4, Number 2, November 1958. Six issues per volume. Bi-monthly, November 1955–April 1957 (although first three issues irregular); six-weekly, June 1957–August 1958; monthly, October–November 1958.

PUBLISHER: Royal Publications, Inc., East 44th St., New York.

EDITOR: Larry T. Shaw.

FORMAT: Digest, 128pp.

PRICE: 35¢.

Joseph Marchesani

INTERNATIONAL SCIENCE FICTION

During the 1960s American readers were being made increasingly aware that science fiction existed in other countries, even those whose first language was not English. A number of Soviet stories had appeared in magazines and anthologies, along with several biting interviews. Some French and German stories and novels had been published in translation, and even some Japanese SF began to appear. Frederik Pohl, ever the cosmopolitan, suggested the idea to his publisher of bringing out a magazine composed entirely of stories by foreign writers. His publisher was not very keen on the idea, but the distributors were, so a sample issue of *International Science Fiction* was put together, dated November 1967. Stories were presented from Russia, Germany, France, Italy and the Netherlands, together with a few from England and Australia to save on translation costs.

The problem with some science fiction is that, for all its cosmic vision, it is often satirical of its own environment and thus does not always work in other surroundings. Add to that the difficulty of translating certain science fictional ideas, and the natural American reluctance to accept things that are non-American, and you have all the ingredients of a failure. A second issue did appear with additional countries—Poland, India and Chile—represented. There was even one story translated from Esperanto. But on the whole the quality of the stories was only average. Although interesting from a social study viewpoint, they had little to offer the general SF reader, who wants escapism, but also wants his heroes to be people he knows. Sales of *ISF* were disastrously low, and the idea was promptly dropped.

Information Sources

BIBLIOGRAPHY:
Nicholls. *Encyclopedia.*
Pohl, Frederik. *The Way the Future Was.* New York: Del Rey Books, 1979.
Tuck.
INDEX SOURCES: ISFM-II; SFM; Tuck.
REPRINT SOURCES: None known.
LOCATION SOURCES: M.I.T. Science Fiction Library; Pennsylvania State University
      Library.

Publication History

TITLE: *International Science Fiction.*
VOLUME DATA: Volume 1, Number 1, November 1967–Volume 1, Number 2, June
      1968. No schedule. Total run: 2 issues.
PUBLISHER: Galaxy Publishing Corporation, New York.
EDITOR: Frederik Pohl.
FORMAT: Digest, 128pp.
PRICE: 50¢.

Mike Ashley

INTERZONE

Interzone is something of an experiment in SF magazine publishing. Not a professional magazine in the full sense, neither is it a semi-professional magazine in the manner of *Whispers,** for example, which is produced more as a hobby, albeit an expensive one. *Interzone* is a nonprofit publication produced initially by an unpaid collective of eight people: John Clute, Alan Dorey, Colin Greenland, Graham James, Roz Kaveney, Simon Ounsley and in particular Malcolm Edwards, who served as the editorial address, and David Pringle.

Interzone is modeled very closely on *New Worlds** with the exception of the experimental graphics and the more extreme selections. The new magazine, first published in 1982, was intended to remedy the lack of a magazine "devoted to intelligent science fiction and fantasy—and to the other types of imaginative prose which lie on the borders of those genres." Certainly the contents have little in common with those to be found in other contemporary SF and fantasy magazines, with the possible exception of Keith Roberts' "Kitemaster" in the first issue, which is in much the same vein as "The Signaller" episode from *Pavane*, and Andrew Weiner's satire on alien invasions "The Third Test," in the second issue. On balance, the first issue was more like any standard mainstream quarterly of fiction—of which there are precious few. M. John Harrison's "The New Rays," for instance, is only qualifiable as SF by a token acceptance of a new method of medical treatment, and the real purpose of the story is a superb study of character disintegration in the same league as Daniel Keyes' "Flowers for Algernon." Similarly, the excerpt provided from Michael Moorcock's "The Brothel in Rosenstrasse" is blatantly not SF or fantasy, other than of the sexual variety, but is nevertheless pervaded with that atmosphere of one-step-beyond-reality that characterizes Moorcock's recent fiction.

While not disassociating itself from the SF fraternity—indeed, the majority of its charter subscribers were SF fans—*Interzone* clearly set out to align itself with the new establishment: names who were rebels in the 1960s but who are the alumni of today—Angela Carter, Michael Moorcock, Rachel Pollack, Thomas M. Disch. The result was stories that were, for the most part, extremely competent, polished and effective. But the magazine nevertheless gave the impression of taking itself too seriously. While the satires by John Sladek and Andrew Weiner, for example, work on their own levels, they have the effect of emphasizing *Interzone*'s deliberateness. As a consequence, at the outset *Interzone* lacked any real personality or identity. This was further hampered by the lack of interior illustrations and minimal front cover art. The effect in a large format magazine of two solid columns of print is daunting and created a claustrophobic atmosphere akin to long, dark, forbidding passages in a gothic castle.

The editorial collective, however, took cognizance of its readership and continued to learn and expand. After its first year *Interzone* began to acquire individuality. To some extent this personality drew it even closer to the Moorcock *New Worlds*, chiefly because of the interior illustrations and graphics that began to be featured. Nonetheless *Interzone* began to show a new confidence where before there had been trepidation, fuelled in part by the fact that the readership did respond with a renewal of subscriptions, and in part through financial aid granted by the Arts Council of Great Britain.

The breadth of *Interzone*'s imaginative fiction (as the cover declared) was no more evident than in the fifth issue (Autumn 1983), which included a highly atmospheric ghost story by Richard Cowper, "The Tithonian Factor," one of M. John Harrison's Viriconium gothic fantasies "Strange Great Sins," a hybrid new wave/old wave SF story "The *Flash!* Kid" marking the debut of Scott Bradfield, and "What Cindy Saw" by John Shirley, a piece so *sui generis* as to demonstrate that SF/imaginative fiction must be in the eye of the beholder.

Interzone has continued to strive and prosper although its editorial collective has shrunk so that at present it is now controlled primarily by Colin Greenland, Simon Ounsley and David Pringle. Although others of the collective still serve in an advisory capacity it is almost certain that this concentration of effort has resulted in a more cohesive publication that shows both substance and direction. The editors boldly stated their purpose in response to the magazine's second anniversary questionnaire published in issue 10 (Winter 1984/85):

If we deliberately courted popularity and followed this policy to its logical conclusion, the magazine would contain mainly stories about disinherited princes in pseudo-mediaeval fantasy lands. We don't want that either. We want to produce the kind of magazine we would like to read ourselves, and we want to attract the kind of readership who share our diverse tastes.

That is the right attitude and one that can only be held by a noncommercial magazine. By not courting popularity *Interzone* nevertheless commands respect and in future years may be regarded as the one true "science fiction" magazine of the eighties.

Information Sources

INDEX SOURCES: ISPF; ISPF-2; SFM.
REPRINT SOURCES: *Interzone: The First Anthology*, London: J. M. Dent, 1985, contains twelve stories from the first nine issues plus one new novelette.
LOCATION SOURCES: M.I.T. Science Fiction Library.

Publication History

TITLE: *Interzone*.
VOLUME DATA: Volume 1, 4 issues (Spring, Summer, Autumn 1982, Spring 1983); volume numbering thereafter discontinued. Number 5, Autumn 1983, thereafter quarterly.
PUBLISHER: Privately published under the Interzone imprint.
EDITORS: The original editorial panel was John Clute, Alan Dorey, Malcolm Edwards, Colin Greenland, Graham James, Roz Kaveney, Simon Ounsley and David Pringle. Graham James left after issue Number 2, Malcolm Edwards after Number 4, Roz Kaveney after Number 7, and John Clute with Alan Dorey after Number 9 (though they, with Kaveney, serve as advisory editors).
FORMAT: Slick; 28pp., Numbers 1 and 2; 32pp., Numbers 3 and 4; 36pp., Numbers 5 to 7; 40pp., Number 8; 48pp., Numbers 9–.
PRICE: £1.25

Mike Ashley

ISAAC ASIMOV'S SCIENCE FICTION MAGAZINE

This magazine, its first issue dated Spring 1977, evolved from an idea by Joel Davis, owner of Davis Publications, Inc., and the son of B. G. Davis the partner in Ziff-Davis, former publishers of *Amazing Stories*.* Davis's company publishes over thirty magazines, including *Ellery Queen's Mystery Magazine* and *Alfred Hitchcock's Mystery Magazine*. Davis wanted to expand into the science fiction field using the same technique of having a prominent name in the publication's title. He was already acquainted with Asimov through the latter's many stories in *Ellery Queen's* and on the firm basis that Asimov was one of the best known writers of science fiction, Davis proposed that his name appear on the new magazine.

After some reluctance, stemming mostly from fears that such an arrangement might interfere with his sales to other magazines, most notably his regular column of science fact in *The Magazine of Fantasy and Science Fiction*,* Asimov agreed to the use of his name. He became editorial director and a photograph of Asimov dominated the covers of the first three issues. Thereafter only a thumbnail picture of his face contained within the 'O' of Asimov adorned the cover and this was dropped after the March 16, 1981, issue. Every issue carries an editorial by Asimov and he responds to most of the letters printed in each issue, but the actual editorial work was done initially by George Scithers.[1]

The magazine was a quarterly for its first year, and sales were sufficiently encouraging for it to go bi-monthly during 1978. Late that year its sales per issue surpassed those of *Analog Science Fiction*, then the field leader. It was the first time any rival magazine had accomplished such sales since the Palmer days at *Amazing Stories*. By 1979 the magazine was a monthly and, in 1981, Davis increased the schedule to four-weekly, publishing thirteen issues a year.[2]

The magazine established a regular format from the start. Fiction aside, every issue included Asimov's editorials, book reviews (first by Charles Brown until April 1979, thereafter by Baird Searles), mathematical and logical puzzles by Martin Gardner, and a letter column whose rare critical entry did not do much to relieve a tone so determinedly upbeat as to strongly suggest Babbittry. Occasional articles about the SF field have appeared including pieces by James Gunn on the development of science fiction and interviews by Charles Platt. There is much poetry in the forms of limerick and haiku.

From the beginning the magazine did not accept serials—and serials have been the exception since—preferring instead very short stories, often under 2,000 words, many of them involving a joke, pun or surprise ending. Combined with the limericks these tended to give the issues a light-hearted, devil-may-care attitude, typical of Asimov's own writing, though not usually associated with science fiction which, during the 1970s, had become notoriously downbeat. It was this lightheartedness which certainly contributed to the success of the magazine, although its continuation since has become something of a joke within the field.

Scithers and Asimov openly encouraged new writers and, more than any other magazine at that time, *IASFM* presented a high quota of material by previously unpublished writers. Most notable among them were Somtow Sucharitkul and Barry Longyear.

The magazine was hospitable to series stories right from the outset. Most closely associated with the magazine are Longyear's Circus Planet of Momus stories which began with ''The Tryouts'' (November/December 1978) and Sucharitkul's Mallworld series starting with ''A Day in Mallworld'' (October 1979).

Generally the magazine concentrated on easily assimilable, light science fiction which could be appreciated by a wide readership. It was not averse to fantasy and in more recent years its quota of fantasy, and even horror fiction, has increased. Asimov's own popularity and the harmlessness of its fiction led to a magazine that could be read by the whole family, so that it came as rather a shock to some to encounter Frederik Pohl's "The Cool War" (August 1979) with its use of "strong" language. In response to one reader's complaint Asimov replied: "Fred's story was strong material, no doubt, and not everyone's cup of tea, but ask yourself—what was he trying to say? Forget the language and get to the core."[3] In a later issue Asimov further commented "Truthfully, George, Shawna and I are conservative in the matter of language; and you may be sure that we don't published 'these words' frivolously."[4]

Nevertheless following "The Cool War" and Pohl's subsequent serial "Like Until the Locust" (December 1979 to January 1980) one could never regard *IASFM* as innocuous and perhaps, by courtesy of Pohl, the magazine could be said to have matured.

From the start the magazine and its contents were frequently cited for awards. John Varley's "Air Raid" (Spring 1977 under the pseudonym "Herb Boehm") was nominated for both a Nebula and a Hugo. George Scithers won the 1978 and 1980 Hugos for Best Professional Editor. The 1980 Campbell Award for Best New Writer went to Barry Longyear, and in the following year went to Somtow Sucharitkul. Longyear's "Enemy Mine" (September 1979) won the 1980 Hugo for Best Novella, while Ken Duffin's "Meeting Place" (November 1980) won the 1981 Rhysling Award (voted upon by members of the Science Fiction Poetry Association) for the year's Best Short Poem.

This popularity, while partially the result of Asimov's fame, is also the product of a successful editorial judgment of the market for a mix of light humor, moderately "hard" science fiction and occasional fantasy and unclassifiable stories (such as Jonathan Fast's "Kindertotenlieder" in the first issue). Relatively few of the stories have downbeat endings reflecting not just Asimov's initial training in the science fiction field by John W. Campbell, Jr., but also Scither's editorial judgment of what readers prefer.[5] A rare exception to this upbeat approach was Tanith Lee's "The Thaw" (December 1979) which also violated Campbell's prejudice against showing humanity subjected to an alien species.

The year 1981, however, saw growing disenchantment at Davis Publications over the magazine. After the early high, sales and subscription renewals had slumped, though not drastically. Joel Davis was keen on having the editor of the magazine stationed in New York, whereas Scithers insisted on working from his home in Philadelphia. Although the parting was amicable Scithers finally resigned from the magazine. His place was taken ostensibly by Kathleen Moloney, a former executive editor at Bantam Books, although the work of reading and selecting manuscripts fell more to Managing Editor Shawna McCarthy. Moloney was acquainted with SF as a reader but not as an editor. Her immediate response to the lagging circulation was to include more Asimov in the magazine which took the shape of occasional brief stories. There was perhaps some slight movement away from accommodating the more "fannish" readers towards entertaining the more general SF reader—so that something like Charles Platt's profile of Alvin Toffler must have seemed rather a jolt to some. Nevertheless much of the former atmosphere of the magazine remained, along with the writers.

Moloney's stay with *IASFM* was short-lived. and in less than a year she had moved on as senior editor at Times Books. Shawna McCarthy now took over in total as editor maintaining a certain healthy continuity, as she had been associated with the magazine from its early issues. Her own plans were to drop some of the more ''cutesy'' humorous pieces and to aim for more character-oriented stories and ''hard'' science fiction. Nevertheless *IASFM* continued to be something of a maverick, its contents often unpredictable and impossible to categorize.

Public reaction to McCarthy's editorship was favorable. During 1983 subscriptions rose appreciably and in 1984 Shawna McCarthy won the Hugo Award for Best Professional Editor. Stories from *IASFM* continued to be nominated for and to win Hugo and Nebula Awards. Among them were ''Fire Watch'' by Connie Willis (February 15, 1982 issue; Hugo and Nebula Best Novelette Award 1983), ''Hardfought'' by Greg Bear (February 1983; Nebula Best Novella Award 1984), ''The Peacemaker'' by Gardner Dozois (August 1983; Nebula for Best Short Story 1984) and ''Speech Sounds'' by Octavia Butler (mid-December 1983; Hugo for Best Short Story 1984), while ''The Sidon in the Mirror'' by Connie Willis (April 1983), ''The Gospel According to Gamaliel Crucis'' by Michael Bishop (November 1983), ''Transit'' by Vonda McIntyre (October 1983) and ''Her Furry Face'' by Leigh Kennedy (mid-December 1983) were all award nominees.

IASFM is not the best presented of magazines, with a rather patchy feel about it, especially at the start, where editorial features, cartoons, reviews and quizzes outbid each other to push the fiction as far away from the front of the magazine as possible, but it is a magazine that attracts much reader involvement and, despite the boldness of the language in certain stories, has still retained a form of family atmosphere. There can be little doubt that unless Asimov himself falls soundly from grace, the future of the magazine can be assured.

Notes

1. See Isaac Asimov's editorial in *Isaac Asimov's Science Fiction Magazine*, Spring 1977, pp. 6–8, for the account of the founding of the magazine, Asimov's role and Scither's position. Asimov repeated his disclaimer of editorial control in the June 1980 issue, pp. 6–11, in an editorial discussing Davis's acquisition of *Analog*, ''Welcome Sibling,'' and again in May 1982, pp. 6ff, ''Farewell to George.''

2. Throughout 1981 and until March 15, 1982, each issue carried a weekly date. They reverted to month only in April 1982 (see Publication History). According to *Science Fiction Chronicle*, March 1982, p. 4, the Davis circulation department had found that magazines with a specific date, rather than just a month, stayed on newsstands a shorter time.

3. See letter column in issue for March 1980, p. 173.

4. See letter column in issue for August 1980, p. 174.

5. Personal conversation (Hamilton/Scithers) at Noreascon Two, September 1, 1980.

Information Sources

BIBLIOGRAPHY:
Asimov, Isaac. "Isaac Asimov's Science Fiction Magazine." In *In Joy Still Felt: The Autobiography of Isaac Asimov 1954–1978*. Garden City, N.Y.: Doubleday, 1980. Nicholls. *Encyclopedia*.
INDEX SOURCES: ISFM-III; NESFA-VI; NESFA-VII; NESFA-VIII; NESFA-IX; SFM.
REPRINT SOURCES:
   Foreign Editions: See the following entries in Section IV: Israel—*Cosmos* (1979); Japan—*SF Hoseki*.
   Derivative Anthologies: *IASFN* has been well mined by its own publisher for showcase anthologies. Initially whole issues with the nonfiction departments removed were issued by Davis Publications as paperback anthologies under the Dale Press imprint. Each bore the general heading *Asimov's Choice* and the main title as follows (together with the corresponding magazine issue): *Astronauts & Androids* (1977)— Fall 1977 issue; *Black Holes & Bug-Eyed Monsters* (1977)—Winter 1977 issue; *Comets & Computers* (1978)—March/April 1978 issue; *Dark Stars & Dragons* (1978)—May/June 1978 issue; *Extraterrestrials & Eclipses* (1978)—July/August 1978 issue. Subsequently fiction from two or more issues were combined and reissued in magazine format as *Isaac Asimov's Science Fiction Anthology* with a corresponding hardcover edition from Dial Press, New York, under a new title as follows: Volume 1, 1979 edition (reissued as *Masters of Science Fiction* [1978]); Volume 2, Fall/Winter 1979 (reissued as *Marvels of Science Fiction* [1979]); Volume 3, Spring/Summer 1980 (reissued as *Adventures of Science Fiction* [1980]); Volume 4, Fall/Winter 1980 (reissued as *Worlds of Science Fiction* [1980]); Volume 5, 1982 edition (reissued as *Near Futures and Far* [1982]). All of the above were published as edited by George Scithers. Volume 6, Fall/Winter 1982 (reissued as *Isaac Asimov's Wonders of the World* [1982]) edited by Kathleen Moloney & Shawna McCarthy; Volume 7, Spring/Summer 1983 (reissued as *Aliens & Outworlders* [1983]) edited by Shawna McCarthy. Volume 8, Fall/Winter 1983 (reissued as *A Space of Her Own* [1983]) edited by Shawna McCarthy is a departure from the earlier volumes being devoted to 22 stories by women writers from *IASFM*. (Note: a further anthology *Isaac Asimov's Tomorrow's Voices* by "the Editors of *Isaac Asimov's*" (New York: Dial Press, 1984) contains original material from the magazine's inventory purchased by the previous editor.)
   Derivative Magazine: Under license to Davis Publications and issued in vest-pocket size format was *Isaac Asimov's Science Fiction Stories* (New York: Bonomo Publications, 1979) edited by Julia Assante (5 stories).
LOCATION SOURCES: M.I.T. Science Fiction Library.

Publication History

TITLE: *Isaac Asimov's Science Fiction Magazine*
VOLUME DATA: Volume 1, Number 1, Spring 1977–. Volume numbering equates with each full calendar year: Volume 1, four issues, quarterly, Spring–Winter 1977; Volume 2, six issues, bi-monthly, January/February–November/December 1978; Volumes 3 and 4, twelve issues each, monthly, January 1979–December 1980; Volume 5 onwards, thirteen issues, four-weekly, January 19, 1981–. (The weekly

numbering was dropped from April 1982 and a monthly numbering continued with an additional mid-December issue each year.)

PUBLISHER: Davis Publications, New York.

EDITORS: Isaac Asimov serves as Editorial Director. Editors have been George Scithers, Spring 1977–February 15, 1982; Kathleen Moloney (as Executive Editor) March 15–mid-December 1982; Shawna McCarthy (Associate Editor January 1979–November 1980; Managing Editor December 1980–June 1982; Senior Editor July–mid-December 1982) January 1983–.

FORMAT: Digest, 192 pp., Spring 1977–November 1979; 176 pp., December 1979–. (Special issues in December 1982 and mid-December 1984 had 192 pp.)

PRICE: $1.00, Spring–Winter 1977; $1.25, January/February 1978–March 1980; $1.50, April 1980–November 1982; $1.95 December 1982 (special issue); $1.75, mid-December 1982–December 1984; $1.95 mid-December 1984; currently $2.00

Thomas W. Hamilton to 1982,

updated by Mike Ashley

J

JUNGLE STORIES

Two pulps were published under the title *Jungle Stories*. The first saw just three issues, in August, October and December 1931, and was a straight jungle adventure pulp. Published by William Clayton, it was a companion to *Astounding Stories (Analog Science Fiction*)* and *Strange Tales** and featured no significant fantasy stories. It did carry some stories by Douglas M. Dold, Murray Leinster and Gordon MacCreagh and was edited by H. A. McComas.

The second pulp under that title, one slightly more relevant to the fantasy field, appeared in 1939. It ran for considerably longer and featured the jungle heroics of Ki-Gor, the most popular of all the Tarzan imitations. Ki-Gor, the White Lord of the Jungle, was the only son of a Scottish missionary named Robert Kilgour. When his father was killed by unfriendly natives, the young Kilgour was left alone in the jungle to survive. In the first novel of the series society aviatrix Helene Vaughan crashes in the jungle near Ki-Gor's lair. Needless to say, Ki-Gor saves Helene from the same natives that killed his father, and the two then travel off into the jungle to return Helene to civilization. Subsequent novels continued their adventures until late 1940, when they were married. After that, stories featured no continuity but were one unconnected episode after another, with Ki-Gor and Helene battling one jungle menace or another.

Like the Tarzan series, the Ki-Gor stories contained a fairly high quota of science fiction. There were talking gorillas in "Ki-Gor and the Giant Gorilla Men" (Fall 1939) and dinosaurs in "Stalkers of the Dawn World" (Winter 1944). There were lost survivors from Atlantis, mad dictators with plots to rule all Africa, and voodoo monsters.

The first of the Ki-Gor stories—most of which were of novelette rather than novel length—was credited to John M. Reynolds, but thereafter they bore the house pseudonym John Peter Drummond. The identities of the writers have yet to be determined, though it is known that SF fan and writer Stanley Mullen wrote several of them. The magazine was primarily a quarterly and is a bibliographer's nightmare in that it reprinted covers, used the same titles on different novels and even reprinted novels under new titles.

While many blacks in the Ki-Gor stories were stereotypes, the adventures did have major black characters as heroes. More than anything else, the success of *Jungle Stories* pointed out the continued popularity of Tarzan and, indirectly, his imitators.

With the lead stories in *JS* seldom exceeding forty pages, there was plenty of room for other fiction. Frequent contributors included Armand Brigaud, Wilbur S. Peacock, Francis Gerard and Paul Selonke. Even fantasy fan Duane Rimel appeared in its pages with "Jungle Princess" (Winter 1944). Dan Cushman became a regular contributor in the mid-1940s with a series about Armless O'Neil, so named for one arm that had a hook instead of a hand. From time to time, pulpsters who also contributed to Fiction House's other pulps such as *Planet Stories** had work in *JS*, but none of the stories by Bryce Walton, Emmett McDowell or E. Hoffman Price had any fantasy elements. All fiction was strictly jungle adventure set in Africa.

Information Sources

BIBLIOGRAPHY:
Goulart, Ron. *Cheap Thrills*. New Rochelle, N.Y.: Arlington House, 1972. Retitled *An Informal History of the Pulp Magazine*. New York: Ace Books, 1973. Chapter 10.
Tuck.
INDEX SOURCES: Weinberg, Robert, *The Hero Pulp Index*, Evergreen, Colo.: Opar Press, 1971 (for lead stories only).
REPRINT SOURCES: A British edition was published in slim pulp format by Pembertons of Manchester during 1950. Five issues are known corresponding to U.S. issues as follows: Number 1, Fall 1949; Number 2, Winter 1950; Number 3, Spring 1950; Number 4, Summer 1950; and Number 5, Fall 1950.
LOCATION SOURCES: None known.

Publication History

TITLE: *Jungle Stories*.
VOLUME DATA: Volume 1, Number 1, Winter 1939–Volume 5, Number 11, Spring 1954. Twelve issues per volume. Quarterly, but no issue for Spring 1939, and no Summer issues in 1951, 1952 or 1953. Bi-monthly for two issues, February and April 1954. Total run: 59 issues.
PUBLISHER: Fiction House, New York.
EDITOR: Malcolm Reiss, Winter 1939–Winter 1949; Jerome Bixby, Spring 1949–Spring 1954.
FORMAT: Pulp, 128pp.
PRICE: 25¢.

Robert Weinberg

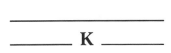

K

KADATH

There have been two magazines under the name *Kadath*. The more recent and certainly the better bargain, while it contains much in English-language material, is published and edited in Italy, and is dealt with under the entry for that country in Section IV.

The earlier publication to adopt the name from H. P. Lovecraft's famous novella was published as an annual by Lin Carter in 1974 but received such a hammering from critics and reviewers that it only saw one issue. It was a slim twenty-four-page booklet costing five dollars and printed in a very small press run, thus becoming an instant out-of-print collector's item. This was part of the critics' complaint, but it was also felt that the magazine contained little of merit, despite Carter's claims that it had cost $1,000 to produce. Stories included reprints of work by Lovecraft and Abraham Merritt, plus new stories by Lin Carter and Hannes Bok. The Bok story, "Jewel Quest," was subsequently anthologized by Carter in the first of his *Year's Best Fantasy Stories* (New York: DAW, 1975).

No doubt the cost of production and the lack of enthusiasm deterred Carter from attempting another annual, though it may be that, having secured an annual anthology from DAW Books, there was no longer any necessity to continue *Kadath*. It is now a rare collector's item.

Information Sources

INDEX SOURCES: ISPF; MT.
REPRINT SOURCES: None known.
LOCATION SOURCES: None known.

Publication History

TITLE: *Kadath.*
VOLUME DATA: Number 1, 1974 (advance copies released in April, most on general
   release in July).
PUBLISHER: Lin Carter, Queens, New York.
EDITOR: Lin Carter.
FORMAT: Booklet (saddle-stapled), 24 pp.
PRICE: $5.00.

Mike Ashley

KA-ZAR

An obvious Tarzan imitation, *Ka-Zar* appeared in 1936 from Manvis Publications, the parent company of Martin Goodman's Western Fiction, which would
soon start the SF magazine boom with *Marvel Science Stories.** Only three issues
appeared. All lead novels were written by Bob Byrd. In the first, "King of Fang
and Claw," a plane crash in the Congo kills John and Constance Rand, but their
infant son, David, is found and raised by the lion, Zar—hence the name Ka-
Zar. The hero, being raised by a beast, learns the languages of all the animals
of the jungle and can talk to them, like Mowgli in *The Jungle Book.* Ka-Zar
battles the men who were responsible for the death of his parents in the first
novel. In the second, "Roar of the Jungle," he fights a mad Arab despot intent
on setting up a kingdom of slaves in the jungle. The third and final novel tells
it all in the title, "The Lost Empire." The three novels were all clearly derivative
and showed no originality in either content or form.

   While the novels dominated the issues, the magazine found room for ten short
stories during its short life. All were straightforward jungle adventures with titles
like "Law of the Legion," "Jungle War," "Hades' Reef" and "Assassin's
Blood" and were by writers Anatole France Feldman, Rex Allen, Norman
Daniels and Beech Allen.

Information Sources

BIBLIOGRAPHY:
Goulart, Ron. *Cheap Thrills.* New Rochelle, N.Y.: Arlington House, 1972. Retitled *An
   Informal History of the Pulp Magazine.* New York: Ace Books, 1973.
Lupoff, Richard A. *Edgar Rice Burroughs: Master of Adventure.* New York: Ace Books,
   rev. ed., 1968. Chap. 18.
Tuck.
INDEX SOURCES: Tuck; Weinberg, Robert, *The Hero Pulp Index*, Evergreen, Colo.:
   Opar Press, 1971 (indexes lead novels only).
REPRINT SOURCES:
   Novels: The lead novel in the first issue, *King of Fang and Claw*, was reprinted in
      England under that title by Brown & Watson; London, 1937; The first issue was

reprinted by Odyssey Publications, Melrose Highlands, Massachusetts in 1976 in digest format (the issue was in facsimile, although the editorial and front-matter was replaced by an article by W. H. Desmond on jungle adventure fiction).

LOCATION SOURCES: San Francisco Academy of Comic Art.

Publication History

TITLE: *Ka-Zar*, October 1936–January 1937. Retitled *Ka-Zar the Great*, June 1937.

VOLUME DATA: Volume 1, Number 1, October 1936–Volume 1, Number 3, June 1937. First two issues quarterly, then irregular. Total run: 3 issues.

PUBLISHER: Manvis Publications, New York.

EDITOR: Charles Goodman.

FORMAT: Pulp, 128pp. (last issue 112pp).

PRICE: 10¢.

Robert Weinberg

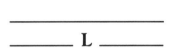

LAST WAVE

Last Wave is a small-press magazine, professionally typeset, which first appeared in October 1983. It was launched by editor Scott Edelman in the hope of recreating a market for the freestyle form of SF writing that had flourished during the "new wave" period of the mid-to-late sixties in such magazines as *New Worlds*.* The first issue showed a greater emphasis on fantasy than SF though this is not so surprising as most "new wave" SF reacts against the hardcore *science* fiction into outer realms of the speculative and bizarre. The names of the contributors are indicative of the content: Thomas M. Disch, Avram Davidson, John Sladek, Steve Rasnic Tem and Jessica Amanda Salmonson. It also contained a poem by Philip K. Dick, "My Life in Stillness: White as Day."

The center piece of the second issue was Thomas Disch's libretto for "Frankenstein: The Opera," backed up by individual stories by Ian Watson, Rachel Pollack and Ronald Anthony Cross.

By now Edelman was finding problems in obtaining fiction of the right quality. It seemed that there was no incentive to experiment in SF or fantasy. "Most of the obvious lessons of the sixties are so long forgotten now that it may well be that no new insights will surface before the new crop of writers suffers a repetition of the pain of disillusionment," Edelman commented in discussion at the World Fantasy Convention in 1984. As it stands at present *Last Wave* is a blend of anachronism and aspiration. Interestingly it has much in common with *Interzone** although the latter has been accepted more readily by the generally more liberal British than *Last Wave* has by its American market.

Information Sources

BIBLIOGRAPHY:
Fantasy Review No. 73 (November 1984), "The Editor's Notebook," p. 4.

INDEX SOURCES: ISPF-2.
REPRINT SOURCES: None known.
LOCATION SOURCES: M.I.T. Science Fiction Library.

Publication History

TITLE: *Last Wave*.
VOLUME DATA: Volume 1, Number 1, October 1983. Irregular; Number 2, Winter 1984; Number 3, Summer 1984; Number 4, Autumn 1984.
PUBLISHER: Private, Scott Edelman, Brooklyn, New York.
EDITOR: Scott Edelman.
FORMAT: Slick. Numbers 1 and 3, 32pp., Number 2, 48pp., Number 4, 40pp.
PRICE: $2.50.

Mike Ashley

THE LITERARY MAGAZINE OF FANTASY AND TERROR

The Literary Magazine of Fantasy and Terror was similar to many fan fiction magazines that appeared, flourished and withered in the early 1970s. The initial level of the fiction was poor to fair, but it slowly increased in competence.

The first issue appeared in 1973; it was issued in a loose-leaf format, though typeset throughout. Its editor, Amos Salmonson, possibly considered following the lead of Dale Donaldson's magazine *Moonbroth*, which consisted of volumes of loose-leaf sheets. The contents lived up to the magazine's name: a mixture of fantasy and terror fiction, plus poetry and music, accompanied by superficial illustrations. It was a mediocre affair, saved only by the editor's own contribution, a sword and sorcery story of the character Artonal which occupied the final third of the issue.

Salmonson later stated that *F&T* did not change throughout its life, although some may disagree with this view. The second issue differed from the first, not only in its standard magazine format, but also in the contents. It was oriented more toward fantasy than terror, and this emphasis continued for the rest of the magazine's life.

F&T lasted for seven issues, although the last was a triple issue. While from the second issue the menu did not change, the quality certainly did. For many magazines, the first few issues are a proving ground, and once having established their ability to survive, they will begin to attract more established writers. So it was with *F&T*, which had an advantage in that Salmonson was not only an able editor but a capable writer; this prompted others to contribute, not the least among them being Glen Cook, David C. Smith, Darrell Schweitzer, Eddy C. Bertin and Phyllis Ann Karr. Artwork throughout remained much as an afterthought, most pages being unrelieved by any form of design.

It was in the final issue that the editor officially reported her sex change from

Amos Salmonson to Jessica Amanda Salmonson. This period had been a trying time for Salmonson and even her openness about lesbianism did not totally liberate her. At length disillusioned with both the SF community and the world in general Salmonson attempted suicide. Fortunately it was not successful and in the ensuing months she began to gather herself together and start on the road that over the next few years would establish her as one of the better fantasy authors and anthologists of the eighties. However, this major personal disruption to her life left no time for amateur journalism and *F&T* folded. In retrospect it may be regarded as a good proving ground for new authors and it was competently edited.

Material left in the *F&T* inventory resurfaced in 1977 when Salmonson brought out a new amateur magazine called *Windhaven*. Subtitled "a matriarchal fanzine" it set out to bridge the gap between the women's press community and SF fandom. *Windhaven* ran for five issues and the sixth was lost when the feminist small press who had taken it over with the fifth issue fell foul of the police due to some illegal business totally unconnected with Salmonson. *Windhaven* was a provocative magazine containing much interesting material though progressively less fiction. It did contain some interesting *F&T* leftovers such as "The Great Cup" by Ron Nance in the first issue, "The Singing Drum" by Charles R. Saunders in the second and "The Great City" by David Madison in the third.

This was not the end of *F&T*. Despite her professional commitments, Salmonson still enjoyed the emotional and artistic outlet provided by small press publishing. At the end of 1983 she planned to issue a new magazine called *Golgoleth*. However she still wished to use a cover from the old *F&T* inventory by Judhe Fulkerson which had the original title worked into the illustration. As a consequence a new series of *F&T* was launched from January 1984. Much reduced in size and format from the original *F&T* it also showed a different emphasis over the first series, reflecting the editor's changing interests. Influenced to some extent by the amateur journals *Grimoire* and *Nyctalops*, *F&T* became a miscellany of prose and verse with an emphasis on necrophilia, the surreal, the bizarre and the supernatural. It included reprintings of many obscure tidbits hauled in from the editor's dredging of Victorian and turn-of-the-century periodicals and books. Little in the way of new fiction has appeared although there have been some notable ghost stories by Rosemary Pardoe (under the alias Mary Ann Allen).

In its new incarnation *F&T* is far more a self-indulgence than was the original series, and though at present it does not serve as a proving ground for new writers, it does allow for experimentation in areas where there are few attractive markets.

Information Sources

INDEX SOURCES: MT.
REPRINT SOURCES: None known.
LOCATION SOURCES: M.I.T. Science Fiction Library.

Publication History

TITLE: *The Literary Magazine of Fantasy and Terror* (first series); *Fantasy and Terror* (second series).

VOLUME DATA: Volume 1, Number 1, February 1973–Volume 2A, 1975. Six issues per volume. Irregular. Total run, first series: 7 issues. Second series, Number 1 (January) 1984-. Irregular.

PUBLISHER: First series: privately published, Zenith, Washington. Second series: Richard Fawcett, Uncasville, Connecticut.

EDITOR: Amos Salmonson/Jessica Amanda Salmonson (both series). Number 7, co-editor, Phyllis Ann Karr.

FORMAT: First series: Large-size (11″ x 8½″). Pages per issue: 1, 34pp., 2, 32pp., 3-5, 36pp., 6, 40pp., 7, 100pp. Second series: Digest; 1, 28pp., 2, 32pp., 3, 30pp.

PRICE: First six issues $1.50; Number 7, $4.50. Second series: $2.00.

Jon Harvey/Mike Ashley

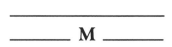

MACABRE

The first issue of *Macabre* appeared in 1957. Its origin and purpose may best be described by quoting from a brief editorial entitled "Macabre—An Introduction," which appeared in that rare first issue:

> With its issue of September 1954, *Weird Tales*,* the only magazine in the U.S. devoted exclusively to supernatural fantasy and horror went out of existence. . . . The gap has never been filled. . . .
>
> . . . supernatural stories, horror, the bizarre, the grotesque and the weird have virtually no present market in the U.S. *Macabre* . . . cannot replace *Weird Tales*. But it can do two things: it can work for the revival of that unique magazine, and it can, meanwhile, serve as a rallying place for all those devoted to horror and the supernatural.
>
> We hope to be something more than a fanzine; professional status will at least be the goal.

Macabre, unfortunately, did not achieve true professional status. It did not appear on the stands; it had no distributor. Nevertheless, published at irregular intervals, it survived for nearly twenty years, with a total of twenty-three issues. It counted among its subscribers established writers and major libraries.

Obstacles were legion: lack of ample free time; lack of ready cash; illness on the part of editor and publisher Joseph Payne Brennan; problems involving printers, most of whom had no interest in obscure, small-run magazines; and a relative scarcity of stories worth publishing.

In spite of all these obstacles, however, the magazine struggled on, and not without achievement. A respectable number of good stories were published, and a few outstanding ones. Contributors included Robert F. Young and Kit Reed, aside from Brennan himself, who had at least one story and poem in each issue, and occasionally articles. Of poetry there was an abundance in *Macabre*, in general of better than average quality. There were contributions by August Derleth, W. Paul Ganley and Sydney King Russell, as well as Lilith Lorraine, William J. Noble and David Park Barnitz.

Brennan and *Macabre* continued to work for the revival of *Weird Tales*. In the final issue, after the first (pulp format) *Weird Tales* revival had failed, Brennan suggested that the magazine should be issued in paperback as a quarterly. "In this format [it] would fit into the rack spaces of nearly all stands. The fact that it would be put out on a quarterly basis ought to insure its being left on the racks for a reasonable time." At length that is just what happened.

Brennan struggled on with *Macabre*, although by the twentieth issue in 1968 it was evident that the end was near. "We are sorry to report that the little magazine is not prospering," he wrote in that issue's editorial. "Subscription support is meagre." Somehow he brought out three more issues staggered over the next eight years, but since then the magazine has to all intents died. Brennan plans to keep the Macabre House imprint alive with books and pamphlets and hopes one day to publish an anthology of items from *Macabre*, to be entitled *Make Mine Macabre*. Brennan's reasons for discontinuing *Macabre* are logical. Finances and time aside, today there are a number of respected semi-prozines such as *Whispers** and *Weirdbook** which aim to continue what *Macabre* set out to do. In many ways *Macabre* was a pioneer in its field.

Today issues of *Macabre* are hard to locate. Even the editor's own set is missing a couple of issues!

Information Sources

BIBLIOGRAPHY:
Tuck.
INDEX SOURCES: MIT; MT; SFM; Tuck.
REPRINT SOURCES: None known.
LOCATION SOURCES: None known.

Publication History

TITLE: *Macabre*.
VOLUME DATA: Number 1, [Summer] 1957–Number 23, 1976. No regular schedule, although intention always semi-annual. Early issues sustained a Winter-Summer regularity, but this ceased in 1961.
PUBLISHER: Macabre House [Joseph Payne Brennan].
EDITOR: Joseph Payne Brennan.
FORMAT: Booklet (most $9^1/_2''$ x $6^1/_2''$, some $8^1/_2''$ x $5^1/_2''$). Pages varied. Originally mostly 24 pp., varied between 12 pp. and 34 pp.
PRICE: Originally 40¢, finally $1.25.

Joseph Payne Brennan

MAGAZINE OF FANTASY

See THE MAGAZINE OF FANTASY AND SCIENCE FICTION.

THE MAGAZINE OF FANTASY AND SCIENCE FICTION

In the autumn of 1949 a new quarterly, *The Magazine of Fantasy*, made its first appearance on the newsstand. New stories by Cleve Cartmill ("Bells on His Toes"), Theodore Sturgeon ("The Hurkle Is a Happy Beast") and Winona McClintic ("In the Days of Our Fathers") were balanced by selections from the works of Fitz-James O'Brien ("The Lost Room"), Guy Endore ("Men of Iron") and Oliver Onions ("Rooum"). In all, the initial issue printed eleven short stories.

Lawrence E. Spivak, named as its publisher, announced the rationale behind the basic editorial policy. Despite a long literary tradition, he explained, through-out "most of this century . . . fantasy has suffered neglect from critics and pub-lishers." He referred to "some two dozen anthologies of fantasy stories" published in the "past few years" and to "a dozen or more novels of the supernatural [which] have recently made their debut," as well as to "tales long buried in forgotten 'pulps' [which] are appearing in book form." Convinced that "there must be a public demand" for fantasy, he promised to print "the finest available material in stories of the supernatural." He went on to define the supernatural as "all the world of fantasy, from the thrilling to the chilling, from the comic to the cosmic—whatever our senses reject, but our imagination logically accepts."

As editors he had chosen Anthony Boucher and J. Francis McComas, the latter of whom he saluted as co-editor of "the definitive anthology of science-fiction, *Adventures in Time and Space*." Robert P. Mills was named managing editor, while Joseph W. Ferman was to be general manager. Citing the inclusion of O'Brien's "eerie masterpiece, long lost and underrated," as well as the "first published story by a distinctive new fantasy writer, Winona McClintic," Spivak announced that the magazine would offer "the best imaginative fiction, from obscure treasures of the past to the latest creations in the field." To emphasize this policy, the cover asserted that this was "an anthology of the best fantasy stories, new and old."

With its second issue (Winter-Spring 1950), it assumed the title *The Magazine of Fantasy and Science Fiction*, which it has retained to the present day. That change did not affect the basic editorial policy, for through March 1954 each issue announced that it contained "a selection of the best stories of fantasy and science fiction, new and old." Not until April 1954 did it declare that all stories were new, although the practice of reprinting classics continued, in the late 1960s designated for a while the "Special Reprint Feature."

In this practice *F&SF* echoed the efforts of Donald A. Wollheim in *Avon Fantasy Reader*,* and one must interpret it as a conscious effort of the editors to overcome any break—especially on the part of science fiction—with a con-tinuing literary tradition. Doubtless Spivak recalled the success of the short-lived *Unknown**/*Unknown Worlds*, to which Boucher had been an important contrib-utor. The emphasis on fantasy during its first several years disguises the fact that its appearance and success made *F&SF* the first periodical to challenge the domination of the field by John W. Campbell and *Astounding* (*Analog Science Fiction**).[1] Another factor that obscured that effect arose from the editors' policy of relying exclusively on short stories instead of the serials and novelettes which had long been a characteristic of magazine fantasy and science fiction. (Not until Cornell Woolrich's "Jane Brown's Body" appeared in October 1951 did *F&SF* publish a "short" novel, while the first serial was Poul Anderson's "Three Hearts and Three Lions" in September-October 1953.)

Significantly, subsequent commentary by the editors revealed that readers did not object to the length of Woolrich's story, although they were sharply divided as to its merit. In a recent article, one of the finer sketches of the history of American magazine SF, Algis Budrys has suggested that much of the early success of *F&SF* came from its drawing upon the talents of the writers associated with the so-called Futurians and from its being the field's "first entree into the market for American intellectual diversionary reading."[2] While these observations have merit, in themselves they play down two other factors that firmly established the place of *F&SF* as a leading periodical. First, the quality of the writing made the magazine distinctive. One hastens to include not only those authors who had turned out yesterday's "classics" or those authors who might be associated with a supposed "mainstream" or literary establishment—numbered among the latter were such figures as Andre Maurois, Idris Seabright, Oliver LaFarge, Agatha Christie, Robert Graves and Raymond Chandler—but also writers who have been primarily, if not solely, identified with magazine fantasy and science fiction—among them Damon Knight, L. Sprague de Camp, Fritz Leiber, Cyril M. Kornbluth, John Wyndham, Alfred Bester, Ray Bradbury and Theodore Sturgeon, to name only individuals who contributed to *F&SF* by the end of 1951. By the end of its first decade *F&SF* had attracted the great majority of those names who had fashioned the reputation of *Astounding* and shaped the essence of modern science fiction, as well as attracting the work of new writers such as Richard Matheson.

The significance of this to the field at large leads to the second factor which assured the importance of *The Magazine of Fantasy and Science Fiction*. Although, as Budrys has pointed out,[3] a tone of melancholy had entered modern science fiction with John Campbell's "Twilight" (1934), the essential quality of the field throughout the 1930s and 1940s reached toward the heroic. Whatever problem might face the protagonist, he could solve it. Robert Silverberg has suggested that SF of that period portrayed "galactic man";[4] that is, a linear projection of contemporary man and his technology triumphed throughout the galaxies, whatever the odds. This mood changed with *F&SF*, whether toward the comic, as in Damon Knight's "Not with a Bang" (Winter-Spring 1950) or toward the dreadful, as in Cyril Kornbluth's "The Silly Season" (Fall 1950). The authors made use of the same science fiction stage props, but their perspective changed. One might say that something of the pervasive mood of the fiction of H. G. Wells became more dominant. In short, neither man nor his inevitable progress was celebrated as certain of realization. One might well argue that much of the mood which manifested itself in the 1960s—perhaps most stridently in the so-called New Wave—could not have developed had not *F&SF* done much to break the old molds, perhaps especially its blurring of the sharp distinctions between fantasy and science fiction.[5]

Its impact was not, as noted, immediately recognized. Yet in retrospect three criteria measure its achievement. When the first Hugos were given at the World-con in Philadelphia in 1953, *Astounding* and *Galaxy Science Fiction** were named; from 1955 through 1957 *Astounding* was voted the best, with *F&SF* being nominated for the first time in 1957. From 1958 through 1960, however, *F&SF* was given the number one rating. (One wonders how much credit for this award should go to Robert P. Mills, who replaced Anthony Boucher as editor in September 1958; similarly, one wonders whether or not the failure of the companion magazine, *Venture Science Fiction,** and its absorption into *F&SF* influenced the decision.) Again in 1963 and from 1969 through 1972, after which fans no longer voted for the best magazine, *The Magazine of Fantasy and Science Fiction* won the award. Except for the three-year period between 1966 and 1968 when *If** received top rating during the tenure of Frederik Pohl as editor, either *Astounding/Analog* or *F&SF* won the Hugo for best magazine. Each received the prize eight times, and *F&SF* was disqualified in 1966 by the New York Worldcon Committee because some of its members were on the magazine's staff.

Second, although the majority of stories in *The Science Fiction Hall of Fame* (1970) came from *Astounding*, the second largest number came from *F&SF*. Chosen by the vote of the Science Fiction Writers of America, these stories had to be published before December 31, 1964 to be eligible. The earliest from *F&SF* was Richard Matheson's "Born of Man and Woman" (Summer 1950); others included Alfred Bester's "Fondly Farenheit" (August 1954), Damon Knight's "The Country of the Kind" (February 1956), Anthony Boucher's "The Quest for Saint Aquin" (reprinted January 1959), Daniel Keyes' "Flowers for Algernon" (April 1959) and Roger Zelazny's "A Rose for Ecclesiastes" (November 1963). No other magazine had so many selections taken from its fiction of the 1950s. In the voting, "Flowers for Algernon" (which was to receive the 1966 Nebula Award as best novel and, in its various forms, four Hugo nominations) finished in third place behind Isaac Asimov's "Nightfall" and Stanley G. Weinbaum's "A Martian Odyssey," while "A Rose for Ecclesiastes" finished in sixth place. Perhaps no two stories can better exemplify the change in tone that was to pervade science fiction. "Flowers for Algernon" moves toward pathos, if not tragedy, as it dramatizes the effects of the operation that fleetingly gives Charlie the I.Q. of a genius and then reduces him once more to the level of a retard. "A Rose for Ecclesiastes" overturns the convention of an Earthman's love for a Martian princess—a device going back through Edgar Rice Burroughs to Gustavus W. Pope—as the protagonist is used as a stud by the dying Martian culture whose males are sterile; he becomes the subject of a psychological study having strong Freudian overtones and is, finally, like Charlie, an anti-hero.

Finally, of course, the third criterion involves the numerous Hugos and Nebulas won by individual works from the magazine. This is not the place for a catalogue of authors and titles; that can be found elsewhere.[6] Suffice it to say here that *F&SF* won a Hugo as best magazine before any of its stories received awards. In 1959, however, not only did it repeat as best magazine, but nine of twenty-two story nominations went to works it had published, including the winning short story, Robert Bloch's "That Hell-Bound Train." In 1960 four of the five nominees for best short fiction came from *F&SF*; "'Flowers for Algernon" took the award. Even numbers are deceptive, however, for one should recall that the award-winning novel in 1961, Walter M. Miller's *A Canticle for Leibowitz*, originally appeared as three novelettes in *F&SF* during the late 1950s. When the first Nebulas were given in 1965, Brian Aldiss' "The Saliva Tree" (September) won as novella, while Zelazny's "The Doors of His Face, the Lamps of His Mouth" (March) took the award as novelette. There was seldom a year when multiple nominations from *F&SF* did not occur, especially in the categories for shorter fiction.

To avoid catalogues, perhaps the best procedure here is simply to sketch the history of *The Magazine of Fantasy and Science Fiction*, stressing those innovations which have made it one of the two strongest periodicals in the field.

F&SF remained a quarterly until December 1950; after that it went on a bi-monthly schedule until September 1952. From that issue it has remained a monthly. No changes occurred on the editorial staff until August 1954, when Joseph W. Ferman replaced Lawrence E. Spivak as publisher. In September Anthony Boucher became the sole editor, McComas assuming the role of advisory editor, while Robert P. Mills continued as managing editor, a position which he had held since 1949.

In January 1956 Ferman launched a companion magazine, *Venture Science Fiction*, with Mills as editor. It lasted for ten bi-monthly issues. In September 1958 Mills became editor of *F&SF*, although not until July 1959 did the masthead announce that *Venture* was included as part of *F&SF*. These dates indicate that *The Magazine of Fantasy and Science Fiction* was awarded the Hugo as the best in the field while *Venture* existed separately; in short, it did not gain the topmost position by absorbing its science fiction companion. In like manner, one cannot infer that some drastic change resulted from Mills' editorship which led to its recognition, for he had been part of the staff from the beginning.

Although Ferman remained the publisher, a number of personnel changes did occur during the next few years. Briefly, in the autumn of 1958 William Tenn was named consulting editor, Anthony Boucher book editor and J. Francis McComas advisory editor. For three months Edward L. Ferman became the editorial assistant. Then in February 1959 a consolidation took place. McComas remained as advisory editor; Isaac Asimov became the contributing science editor; and Ruth Ferman was named circulation director. Damon Knight became the book review editor in April, retaining that position until Alfred Bester replaced him in October 1960.

When Avram Davidson was named *F&SF*'s fourth editor beginning with the April 1962 issue, one of the duties he assumed was that of reviewer, so that he took over from Bester by July. Mills became consulting editor after Davidson's appointment. When Davidson left the magazine in November 1964, Joseph W. Ferman became editor and publisher; his son, Edward L. Ferman, had been named managing editor in November but was not appointed to the editorship until January 1966, although in a recent essay he suggests that he acted as editor from the autumn of 1964 after Davidson had returned from Mexico.[7] He himself became editor and publisher in November 1970. While these changes may seem a kind of shuffling—though they preserve an editorial continuity—they disguise the diversity, and the influence throughout the field, that *F&SF* has had. Among the book reviewers, for example, have been Judith Merril, Joanna Russ, John Clute, Alexei and Cory Panshin, Thomas Clareson and Algis Budrys. In addition, both Ted White and Andrew Porter served as assistant editors, in the early 1960s and 1970s, respectively.

One result of the editorial continuity was that from the outset *The Magazine of Fantasy and Science Fiction* made a number of innovations that assured its influence upon the field in general. To begin with, there was the matter of format. *F&SF* was the first science fiction magazine to abandon the traditional columns in favor of the book page. Even more important, it did away with interior illustrations (there was a single exception to that rule: Fred Kirberger illustrated Robert Heinlein's first novel, "Star Lummox," in 1954). This decision may have affected the quality of the covers. George Salter's early fantasy scenes were gradually replaced by more orthodox SF covers, most notably, perhaps, the extraterrestrial landscapes of Chesley Bonestell, beginning in December 1950. Ed Emsh, Kelly Freas and Jack Gaughan added their strengths as time went on. Most frequently, though not always, the cover captured a scene from a featured story, not always the lead novelette. In addition, from the beginning the editors collaborated on a "Recommended Reading" column that long remained the most catholic appraisal of the field because it considered fiction and nonfiction, fantasy and science fiction, new works and reprints; in addition, each year Boucher and McComas named the best books in the field for the previous year.

Two other factors shaped *F&SF* from the start. In the December 1950 issue C. Daly King did a special review of L. Ron Hubbard's *Dianetics*; he began his assessment by declaring that he found no "scientific evidence" to back up the "assertions and claims" made by Hubbard in his 400 pages. While one must observe that this was the period when Campbell became obsessed with Dianetics, the review has more importance than merely showing a disagreement between individuals. *The Magazine of Fantasy and Science Fiction* never took up a cause but remained open to all of the best fiction (and nonfiction) available to it. It stressed the fiction, not the science/technology. This may be seen through a number of items which satirized the conventions and attitudes thought by some to be so essential to the field. It did away with that holy of holies, the letters to the editor column, which Ron Goulart parodied in a delightful fashion in the

April 1952 issue. Equally important were the cutting edges of some of the "verse." In July 1953 Anthony Boucher described "The Model of a Science Fiction Editor," while in November of that year Randall Garrett's "I've Got a Little List" catalogued the clichés and types of authors which the field would never miss. In October 1954 Isaac Asimov outlined "The Foundation of S.F. Success." In many ways the spirit of this satire of the "traditional" field was perhaps best captured in the continuing series "Through Time and Space with Ferdinand Feghoot" by Grendel Briarton (a pseudonym for Reginald Bretnor); in sixty-eight episodes between February 1957 and January 1964, Feghoot transformed many of the timeworn plot/situation conventions into outrageously effective puns. Then, too, although cartoons had appeared as early as the 1950s, only after April 1965 did the wit of Gahan Wilson become an established feature (he is to science fiction what Charles Adams is to *The New Yorker*).

The extent to which *F&SF* refused to take any cause—including the field of SF itself—too seriously may be illustrated by its handling of a single subject. In January 1954 Miriam Allen DeFord did a serious study of "Charles Fort: Enfant Terrible of Science." Four years later Ron Goulart devastated the Fortean attitude by showing its ridiculousness in "A New Lo!" (January 1958).

This desire to curb the excesses of the enthusiasts did not mean, however, that the editors ignored science or scientific matters of topical interest. At the height of the Bridey Murphy controversy W. B. Ready wrote "Bridey Murphy: An Irishman's View" (August 1956). Robert S. Richardson's "The Day After We Land on Mars" (December 1955) drew retorts from Poul Anderson ("Nice Girls on Mars") and Miriam DeFord ("News for Dr. Richardson") in May 1956, although Richardson was permitted the last word in "The Facts about Life on Mars" (November 1957).

As editor Avram Davidson was to say, the magazine would not take sides in the UFO controversy, but as early as April 1956 it published "Unidentified Aerial Objects," written by the "United States Air Force"—a summary of the official report released late in 1955. In June 1956 Arthur C. Clarke argued that "The Planets Are Not Enough," while in January 1958 G. Harry Stine explained "Sputnik: One Reason Why We Lost." In December 1957 Isaac Asimov had written an article on strontium 90, "I Feel It in My Bones." In November 1958 he began his monthly "Science" column, which was to win him a special Hugo in 1963 for "adding science to science fiction."

Unquestionably the most controversial article that *F&SF* published was that by E. Brandis and V. Dmitrevskiy, "The Future, Its Promoters and False Prophets" (October 1965, translated by Theodore Guerchon), which appeared originally in *Kommunist*, the organ of the Central Communist Party of the Soviet Union. Its authors denounced the Western tendency to portray a dystopian future, berating American writers for not showing any concept "of the progressive development of society" but only "regression, decline, degeneracy, backwardness, and the destruction of mankind." The American writers who were directly attacked were given the opportunity to reply in the same issue: Asimov, Poul Anderson, Mack Reynolds and Ray Bradbury.

In its nonfiction, *F&SF* also gave attention to literary matters. It went far beyond its fine review column in exploring the history and nature of fantasy and science fiction. As early as 1955, before the revival of interest had begun, Martin Gardner published a two-part study of "The Historian of Oz" (January and February). Anthony Boucher followed with a "note" entitled "Jules Verne, Voyagiste" (September 1956), in which he advanced the now widely accepted thesis that Verne did not consciously write science fiction or realistic fiction but dealt with the *voyage extraordinaire*. During Damon Knight's tenure as book reviewer, he twice attacked H. P. Lovecraft. As late as May 1967 J. Vernon Shea defended the creator of the Cthulhu mythos in "H. P. Lovecraft: The House and the Shadows." The final episode in this running debate occurred when *F&SF* published L. Sprague de Camp's "Lovecraft: Failed Aristocrat" (January 1975), an excerpt from his biography of Lovecraft.

John Christopher wrote of "The Decline and Fall of the Bug-eyed Monster" (October 1956), while Sam Moskowitz told "How Science Fiction Got Its Name" (February 1957). During the same period Robert Bloch confessed that "Some of My Best Fans Are Friends" (October 1956), and one of the first articles to discuss the problem of language in SF was de Camp's "How to Talk Futurian" (October 1957). This interest in science fiction and its popular reception culminated in a special section, "Science Fiction and the University" (May 1972), the most extensive coverage that any magazine up to that time had given the encounter with academe in a single issue. William Tenn remained uncertain as to the benefit of academic attention in "Jazz Then, Musicology Now"; Thomas D. Clareson explored "SF: The Academic Dimension," appealing for cooperation among the various interested groups; and Darko Suvin seemed somewhat perturbed in "Against Common Sense: Levels of Science Fiction Criticism." The section was rounded off by the wise Dr. Asimov in "Science," writing about "Academe and I." The latest appraisal of the field came in the All British Issue (April 1978) when Brian W. Aldiss wrote of "The Gulf and the Forest," an assessment of contemporary SF in the United Kingdom.

One could mention the essays during the 1960s by Theodore L. Thomas on such topics as smog, and the scope of Sprague de Camp's essays is impressive, ranging from "Mammoths and Mastodons" (May 1965) and "The Falls of Troy" (March 1970) to "The Quarter Acre Round Table" (July 1970) and "The Decline and Fall of Adam" (November 1973). He has contributed verse, essays and fiction to *F&SF*, beginning as early as 1950, when he and Fletcher Pratt collaborated on the Gavagan Bar series of stories.

Perhaps one of *F&SF*'s most significant innovations came in the summer of 1955 with the appearance of Charles Beaumont's column, "The Science Screen." Although it soon disappeared, Samuel R. Delany undertook film reviewing in 1968 and 1969. Since December 1970, however, films have been the province of Baird Searles. He, Gahan Wilson and Asimov provide three of the personality cornerstone features of the magazine (the book review column has so often changed personnel, especially in the last decade or so, that one does not associate it with an individual).

These nonfiction elements may provide the parameters of *The Magazine of Fantasy and Science Fiction*, but ultimately it is the fiction itself that has given the magazine its flavor and continuing stature. There, too, it was innovative, for, perhaps more than any other magazine in the field, it featured translations of hitherto inaccessible stories. The first of these came in 1953 when Willy Ley translated Kurd Lasswitz's "When the Devil Took the Professor" (January) and "Aladdin's Lamp" (May). He presented a third Lasswitz story in 1955, "Psychotomy" (July). Meanwhile, Reginald Bretnor had given readers "The Cat, the Brahmin and the Penitent" by François Augustin Paradis de Moncrief (December 1954). No further translations were published until I. O. Evans' version of Jules Verne's "Gil Braltar" (July 1958). This was followed by Gerald Klein's "The Monster in the Park" (September 1961, translated by Virginia Kidd); Claude Veillot's "The First Days of May" (December 1961, Damon Knight); Shin'ichi Hoshi's "Bokko-Chan" (June 1963, Noriyoski Saito); and finally J. H. Rosny-aine's "The Shapes" (March 1968, Damon Knight). Before this, however, *F&SF* began its "Special Reprint Feature" with Rudyard Kipling's "Tomlinson" (March 1966). These, too, were limited in number, for if a single characteristic dominates the magazine, it is diversity within its fiction.

Normally an issue contained one to three novelettes and four to six short stories during the 1960s. As early as Ward Moore's "Bring the Jubilee" (November 1952), it had presented condensed versions of stories that were to become classic novels. As noted, the first serial was Poul Anderson's "Three Hearts and Three Lions" (1953). Although there were to be several exceptions, the serial became an annual feature. During the late 1950s Robert A. Heinlein published four in *F&SF*: "Star Lummox" (May–July 1954); "The Door into Summer" (October–December 1956), "Have Spacesuit, Will Travel" (August–October, 1958) and the controversial two-part "Starship Soldier," beginning in the tenth anniversary issue (October 1959). Theodore Sturgeon's "The [Widget], The [Wadget] and Boff" had appeared in November and December 1955, while Arthur C. Clarke's "Venture to the Moon" was published from December 1957 to January 1958. An added innovation came in 1957 when the text of Gore Vidal's play, *Visit to a Small Planet*, was presented in the April issue.

Gordon Dickson's "Naked to the Stars" saw publication in 1961 (October–November). It was followed by Robert Sheckley's "The Journey of Joenes" (October–November 1962); Heinlein's last novel in *F&SF*, "Glory Road" (July–August 1963); Damon Knight's "The Tree of Time" (December 1963–January 1964); Roger Zelazny's "And Call Me Conrad" (October–November 1965), the first serial to win a Hugo, though not the first to be nominated;[8] John Brunner's "The Productions of Time" (August–September 1966), the first to be nominated for the Nebula; John Christopher's "The Little People" (January–March 1967);

Piers Anthony's "Sos the Rope" (July–September 1968); and Poul Anderson's "Operation Changeling" (May–June 1969).

Thomas Burnett Swann's "The Goat without Horns" led off the 1970s (August–September 1970). Jack Vance, the only author to publish three consecutive serials in *F&SF*, followed with "The Faceless Man" (February–March 1971); his other titles were "The Brave Free Men" (July–August 1972) and "The Asutra" (May–June 1973). Roger Zelazny's "Jack of Shadows" (July–August 1971), which gained a Hugo nomination, marked the first time that two serials had been published in the same year.

After a longer than usual interval, Ferman scored a coup. Those familiar with the works of Philip José Farmer know that for a number of years he has incorporated famous characters into his own fiction, particularly as he constructed the genealogy of the Wold Newton family, which includes, among others, both Doc Savage and Tarzan, Lord Greystoke. Taking Kurt Vonnegut's Kilgore Trout, Farmer used that pseudonym for "Venus on the Half Shell" (December 1974–January 1975), which gained a Nebula nomination. Robert Silverberg followed with "The Stochastic Man" (April–June 1975), whose expanded form received both Hugo and Nebula nominations. Frederik Pohl's "Man Plus" (April–June 1976) won the Nebula. The policy of two serials a year continued with Algis Budrys' "Michaelmas" (August–September). In 1977 came Fritz Leiber's "The Pale Brown Thing" (January–February) and Charles N. Harness' "Wolfhead" (November–December).

The last two serials to be published as of this writing were Thomas Disch's distinguished "On Wings of Song" (February–April 1979) and the only four-part novel ever published in *F&SF*, although it was abridged from the book version: Robert Silverberg's "Lord Valentine's Castle" (November 1979–February 1980), which has been named by *Locus* as the best fantasy novel of 1980 and was a nominee for the Hugo Award.

A further innovation, though it was by no means an annual occurrence, devoted at least a section of an issue to one of the outstanding authors in the field. The first occasion marked one of the tragic moments in the history of the field: the death of Cyril M. Kornbluth. In the July 1958 issue Kornbluth's "Theory of Rocketry" was reprinted, and Anthony Boucher devoted the book column to a memorial bibliography. Not until September 1962 was Theodore Sturgeon honored. One can say that the full-blown format for these special issues came into being with this number. Sturgeon's novelette, "When You Care, When You Love," which received a Hugo nomination, was augmented by Judith Merril's "Profile" of him and by James Blish's critical essay, "Theodore Sturgeon's Macrocosm." Sam Moskowitz provided a bibliography.

In May 1963 the Ray Bradbury issue included his stories "Bright Phoenix" and "To the Chicago Abyss," while William F. Nolan contributed both an index to his works and an essay, "Ray Bradbury: Prose Poet in the Age of Space." Three years later L. Sprague de Camp's "You Can't Beat Brains" and a bibliography, valuable as both were, were overshadowed as Isaac Asimov provided the novelette "The Key"; a "Science" column devoted to "Portrait of the Writer as a Boy"; and a delightfully comic verse parody of Wordsworth, "The Prime of Life." A Gahan Wilson article capped off the issue.

The Charles Beaumont memorial issue (June 1967) included his story, "Gentlemen, Be Seated," as well as William F. Nolan's "Charles Beaumont: The Magic Man" and a bibliography. The Fritz Leiber issue (July 1969) contained his novelette "Ship of Shadows," which gained a Nebula nomination. Judith Merril once again did a "Profile," while Al Lewis provided the bibliography. Leiber also contributed some verse, but there was no critical appraisal of his work.

Poul Anderson's "The Queen of Light and Darkness" (April 1971) won both the Hugo and the Nebula as the best novelette of the year. Gordon R. Dickson did the "Profile," and James Blish provided the critical essay "Poul Anderson: The Enduring Explosion." There was, of course, a bibliography. Blish became the subject of the next special issue (April 1972), when he contributed "Midsummer Century," later expanded into a novel. Robert A. W. Lowndes wrote the "Profile," while Lester del Rey penned "The Hand at Issue," a tribute to Blish's critical work as well as his fiction. Mark Owings provided the bibliography.

Lester del Rey wrote "Frederick Pohl: Frontiersman" for the Pohl issue (September 1973), which featured the novelette "In the Pit." The bibliography was by Mark Owings. Carol Pohl added a special touch by doing the cover. The Robert Silverberg issue (April 1974) was built around his Nebula-winning novella, "Born with the Dead." Barry N. Malzberg did the "Profile," in which he called Silverberg the best writer in the field, if not in America. Thomas D. Clareson contributed a critical overview, "Robert Silverberg: The Compleat Writer," while Donald A. Tuck did the bibliography.

Damon Knight's "I See You" highlighted the November 1976 issue. Theodore Sturgeon wrote "Damon Knight: An Appreciation," and Vincent Miranda did the bibliography, but there was no critical appraisal of Knight's work. The July 1977 issue featured Harlan Ellison. Leslie Kay Swigart updated her bibliography of his work, Richard Delap provided "The Healing Art of Razorback Science Fiction," and Robert Silverberg drew upon his friendship to sketch "Harlan." Yet Ellison dominated the issue. His "Jeffty Is Five" won the Nebula and Hugo and other awards as the best short story of the year. In addition he contributed the stories "Alive and Well and on a Friendless Voyage" and "Working with the Little People," as well as the nonfiction piece "You Don't Know Me, I Don't Know You."

The above examples show the diversity, the variety of *The Magazine of Fantasy and Science Fiction*. Its successive editors constantly sought to obtain the best fiction; moreover, what these examples cannot show is the degree to which *F&SF* did not rely upon a small stable of writers, as had so many of its predecessors, disguising the individuals by a variety of house names. When Anthony Boucher died, the memorial editorial recalled how proud he was of the number of *first* stories by new writers which he had published during his career. One has only to go through the standard indexes of the SF magazines to see that his successors introduced the first or early work of many of the finest contemporary writers. Given certain fixed features—Wilson's cartoons, Asimov's science column, Searles' film reviews—to provide continuity, the respective editors were then able to vary the offering in fiction perhaps more than any of their contemporaries. That is to say, one never went to *F&SF* for a definite kind of story. Instead, one returned to its pages to find the innovative, sometimes the experimental, but always the science fiction and fantasy that represented the leading edge of the field at any given time. One has only to go to the history of the Hugo and Nebula Awards to find a listing of the nominations and winners that were annually published in *F&SF* (nor should one forget that from the mid-1960s onward, the novels which were nominated for and won awards increasingly were either published first in book form or, less and less frequently, were expanded from shorter works appearing in the magazines). Perhaps one of the high points attesting to the continued success of *The Magazine of Fantasy and Science Fiction* is that for more than thirty years it has retained the format and publication schedule which it developed during its first several years.

To mark the thirtieth anniversary of the magazine (October 1979) Ferman published a 320-page "retrospective issue"; in his editorial he hinted at the difficulties of selecting twenty stories from some 3,991 manuscripts accepted by the magazine during its history. His brief explanation and his report to those who advised him need not be dwelt upon here, except perhaps to note that the story receiving most votes was Richard Matheson's "Born of Man and Woman" and the author receiving most votes was Alfred Bester. A consideration of the stories reprinted in that issue emphasizes the variety and quality of the fiction published in *F&SF*:

Alfred Bester, "Fondly Farenheit" (1954), in *The Science Fiction Hall of Fame*.

Theodore Sturgeon, "And Now the News" (1956).

Damon Knight, "Not with a Bang" (1950).

Daniel Keyes, "Flowers for Algernon" (1959), winner of the Hugo as "Best Short Fiction" and of the Nebula as a novel, to say nothing of its other nominations in various forms.

Walter M. Miller, Jr., "A Canticle for Leibowitz" (1955), the first part of the Hugo-winning novel, which is one of the works most frequently used in academic courses dealing with SF.

Shirley Jackson, "One Ordinary Day, with Peanuts" (1955).

James Tiptree, Jr., "The Women Men Don't See" (1974), nominated for a Nebula.

Richard Matheson, "Born of Man and Woman" (1950), in *The Science Fiction Hall of Fame*.

Robert A. Heinlein, ''All You Zombies'' (1959).

Harlan Ellison, ''Jeffty Is Five'' (1977), winner of both the Hugo and Nebula awards.

Zenna Henderson, ''Ararat'' (1952), the first of her series about ''The People,'' which were collected into a book and made into a television play.

Robert Silverberg, ''Sundance'' (1969), Silverberg's most anthologized short story.

Reginald Bretnor, ''The Gnurrs from the Voodvork Out'' (1950), the first of his humorous series concerning Papa Schimmelhorn.

Isaac Asimov, ''Dreaming Is a Private Thing'' (1955).

Brian W. Aldiss, ''Poor Little Warrior'' (1958).

Philip K. Dick, ''We Can Remember It for You Wholesale'' (1966), nominated for the Nebula.

Avram Davidson, ''Selectra Six-Ten'' (1970), nominated for the Nebula.

Thomas M. Disch, ''Problems of Creativeness'' (1967).

Anthony Boucher, ''The Quest for Saint Aquin'' (1959), in *The Science Fiction Hall of Fame*.

In writing of his final choice, Ferman emphasized that ''this is a magazine, not a book, and we'll be back again next month and the month after that.'' For more than thirty years *The Magazine of Fantasy and Science Fiction* has come back each month with infinite vitality and quality. For more than a generation it has remained a leader in the field.

Notes

1. One must recall that *Galaxy Science Fiction* was not published until October 1950. It also challenged *Astounding* and was, under Herbert Gold and Frederik Pohl, one of the leaders of the field. But it has not survived the changing pressures of the publishing scene.

2. Algis Budrys, ''Paradise Charted,'' *TriQuarterly* 49 (Fall 1980): 47.

3. Ibid., p. 35.

4. Robert Silverberg, ''Introduction,'' *The Mirror of Infinity* (New York: Harper, 1970), p. 11.

5. I realize that the dystopian tone that dominated science fiction in the 1960s especially had had its foreshadowings in the tradition of Wells and even in *Astounding*, in such stories as Clifford D. Simak's ''City'' series and in the many tales that saw a post-atomic holocaust. Yet the maturity of the fiction in *F&SF* leads me to this admittedly debatable view.

6. Peter Nicholls, ed., *The Science Fiction Encyclopedia* (Garden City, N.Y.: Doubleday & Company, 1979). The entry for ''Magazine of Fantasy and Science Fiction, The,'' pp. 374–375, is confined to four columns—by necessity—a large part of which lists the award-winning stories.

7. Edward L. Ferman, "Preface," *The Magazine of Fantasy and Science Fiction* (Carbondale, Ill.: Southern Illinois University Press, 1981), p. ix. (This is a facsimile edition of the first issue that Ferman supposedly edited.)

8. Nominations for the Hugo included Heinlein's "Have Spacesuit—Will Travel" (1959), and "Glory Road" (1964). Expanded versions of Heinlein's "Starship Soldier" (entitled *Starship Troopers*) and Walter M. Miller's *A Canticle for Leibowitz* had won Hugos in 1960 and 1961, respectively, but in neither case was *F&SF* credited as publisher. In both cases credit went to the book publishers.

Information Sources

BIBLIOGRAPHY:
Budrys, Algis. "Paradise Charted." *TriQuarterly* 49 (Fall 1980): 5–75.
Nicholls. *Encyclopedia.*
Tuck.
INDEX SOURCES: ASFI; IBSF; ISFM; ISFM-II; ISFM-III; MIT; NESFA; NESFA-II;
    NESFA-III; NESFA-IV; NESFA-V; NESFA-VI; NESFA-VII; NESFA-VIII;
    NESFA-IX; SFM; Tuck.
REPRINT SOURCES;
    Foreign Editions: Most foreign editions have established an identity of their own, and have separate entries in Section IV. See Argentina—*Minotauro*; France—*Fiction*; Germany—*The Magazine of Fantasy and Science Fiction*; Israel—*Fantasia 2000*; Italy—*Fantascienza* and *Fantasia e Fantascienza*; Japan—*S-F Magazine*; Mexico—*Ciencia y Fantasia*; Norway—*Nova*; Sweden—*Jules Verne Magasinet* (second series).

    English Editions:

    Australia: 14 issues, undated, [November 1954–August 1958], published by Consolidated Press, Sydney. Digest (saddle-stapled); 128 pp., Nos. 1–6; 112 pp., Nos. 7–10; 96 pp., Nos. 11–14; 2/-. Irregular, but approximately quarterly. Contents selected from various issues at random with no corresponding sequence to U.S. edition. However, the final issue (No. 14) relates approximately to U.S. April 1957. See listing in Graham Stone's *Australian Science Fiction Index 1925–1967* (Canberra: Australian SF Association, 1968).

    British: 2 series.

    I: Mellifont Press, London. 12 issues, Volume 1, Number 1, October 1953–Volume 3, Number 4, September 1954. Monthly, 4 issues per volume. Digest, 128 pp., 1/6d. Contents not selected directly from corresponding U.S. issues, but relate approximately as follows: 1, various; 2, various; 3, Aug 53; 4, Jul 53; 5, Sep 53; 6, Oct/Nov 53; 7, Dec 53; 8, Jan 54; 9, various; 10, Feb/Mar 54; 11, Apr 54; 12, May 54. See Graham B. Stone's *Index to British Science Fiction Magazines: 1934–1953* (Sydney: Australian SF Association, 1977) and Durie index cited below.

    II. Atlas Publishing & Distributing Co., London. 55 issues, Volume 1, Number 1, December 1959–Volume 5, Number 7, June 1964. Monthly, 12 issues per volume. Digest, 128 pp., Dec 59–Dec 60; 112 pp., Jan 61–Nov 61; 128 pp., Dec 61–Feb 62; 112 pp., Mar 62–June 64. 2/-, Dec 59–Nov 61; thereafter 2/6. Contents not selected directly from single U.S. issues but correspond approximately to issues three or four months earlier (U.S. to U.K. cover date). Following the last issue reprints from earlier U.S. issues (pre-1959 in most cases) were included in the U.K. *Venture Science Fiction* (see entry). For details see A.J.L. Durie's *An Index to the British Editions of the Magazine of Fantasy and Science Fiction* (Windlesham, Surrey: Durie, 1965).

Facsimile Editions: The April 1965 issue has been reprinted, together with a new introduction by Edward Ferman and brief memoirs by authors included in the issue under the editorship of Martin H. Greenberg (Carbondale, Ill.: Southern Illinois University Press, 1981).

Derivative Anthologies:

> *Regular Series*: The *Best from Fantasy and Science Fiction*, edited as follows: Anthony Boucher and J. Francis McComas, eds., first volume [title as above] (Boston: Little, Brown, 1952); *Second Series* (Boston: Little, Brown, 1953); *Third Series* (New York: Doubleday, 1954); Anthony Boucher, ed., *Fourth Series* (New York: Doubleday, 1955); *Fifth Series* (New York: Doubleday, 1956); *Sixth Series* (New York: Doubleday, 1957); *Seventh Series* (New York: Doubleday, 1958); *Eighth Series* (New York: Doubleday, 1959); Robert P. Mills, ed., *Ninth Series* (New York: Doubleday, 1960); *Tenth Series* (New York: Doubleday, 1961); *Eleventh Series* (New York, Doubleday, 1962); Avram Davidson, ed., *Twelfth Series* (New York, Doubleday, 1963); *13th Series* (New York: Doubleday, 1964); *14th Series* (New York: Doubleday, 1965); Edward L. Ferman, ed., *15th Series* (New York: Doubleday, 1966); *16th Series* (New York: Doubleday, 1967); *17th Series* (New York: Doubleday, 1968); *18th Series* (New York: Doubleday, 1969); *19th Series* (New York: Doubleday, 1971); *20th Series* (New York: Doubleday, 1973); [for 21st Series, see 25th Anniversary volume below]; *22nd Series* (New York: Doubleday, 1977); *23rd Series* (New York: Doubleday, 1980); *24th Series* (New York: Scribner's, 1982).
>
> *Occasional Series*: Robert P. Mills, ed., *A Decade of Fantasy and Science Fiction* (New York: Doubleday, 1960), 25 stories from 1949–1959 not previously selected for the annual series; *Twenty Years of Fantasy and Science Fiction* (New York: Putnam, 1970), 20 stories with introduction by Isaac Asimov; eds. Edward L. Ferman and Robert P. Mills; Edward L. Ferman, ed., *Best from Fantasy and Science Fiction: Twenty-fifth Anniversary Anthology* (New York: Doubleday, 1974), lead stories, articles and bibliographies from six of the special author issues; *The Magazine of Fantasy and Science Fiction: A Thirty Year Retrospective* (New York: Doubleday, 1979), reprint of October 1979 issue less departments.
>
> *Other occasional anthologies*: Edward L. Ferman, ed., *Once and Future Tales from the Magazine of Fantasy and Science Fiction* (Jacksonville, Ill.: Harris-Wolfe, 1968), 9 stories from 1960–1966.

LOCATION SOURCES: Brigham Young University Library; Eastern New Mexico University Library; Indiana University Library; M.I.T. Science Fiction Library; Northern Illinois University Library; Pennsylvania State University Library; San Francisco Public Library; Texas A&M University Library; University of Arizona Library; University of California-Los Angeles Library; University of California-Riverside Library.

Publication History

TITLE: *The Magazine of Fantasy*, first issue. Thereafter *The Magazine of Fantasy and Science Fiction*. [Note: The spine and masthead have always carried the abbreviated *Fantasy and Science Fiction* from which the abbreviation *F&SF* is derived.]

VOLUME DATA: Volume 1, Number 1, Fall 1949–. The issue for December 1984 was Volume 67, Number 6. As a rule six issues per volume, except as follows. Volume 1, five issues (quarterly, Fall 1949–Fall 1950, then bi-monthly from December 1950); Volume 3, eight issues (bi-monthly, February–June 1952, then monthly from August 1952). The January 1958 issue was misnumbered Volume 13, Number 7 instead of Volume 14, Number 1, but the numbering was corrected with the next issue. Similarly, July 1960 should be Volume 19, Number 1 instead of Volume 18, Number 7, also corrected with the next issue. Monthly since August 1952. Total run as of December 1984 (Volume 67, Number 6): 403.

PUBLISHER: Fantasy House, Inc., Fall 1949–February 1958; Mercury Press, March 1958–. (Fantasy House was a subsidiary of Mercury Press. Lawrence Spivak was listed as publisher of *F&SF* from Fall 1949 to July 1954, when Joseph Ferman, a vice-president at Mercury Press, bought him out. He remained publisher until October 1970, when he was succeeded by his son, Edward L. Ferman. See Edward Ferman's obituary for his father in *F&SF*, May 1975, p. 5.)

EDITORS: Anthony Boucher, Fall 1949–August 1958 (co-editor with J. Francis McComas, Fall 1949–August 1954); Robert P. Mills, September 1958–March 1962; Avram Davidson (Executive Editor), April 1962–November 1964; Joseph W. Ferman, December 1964–December 1965; Edward L. Ferman, January 1966–. Details as per masthead, although recently Edward L. Ferman has stated that his first issue was April 1965. Of special interest is the role of Managing Editor, held as follows: Robert P. Mills, Fall 1949–August 1958, then post absorbed with Editor until March 1962; Edward L. Ferman, April 1962–December 1965, then absorbed again with Editor.

FORMAT: Digest; 128 pp., Fall 1949–October 1971 (except October 1959, 160 pp. ; 144 pp., November 1971–September 1972; 160 pp., October 1972– (except October 1974, 208 pp., and October 1979, 320 pp.).

PRICE: 35¢, Fall 1949–January 1959 (except October 1958, 40¢); 40¢, February 1959–December 1964 (except October 1959, 50¢); 50¢, January 1965–June 1969; 60¢, July 1969–October 1971; 75¢, November 1971–February 1975 (except October 1974, $1.00); $1.00, March 1975–February 1978; $1.25, March 1978–February 1980 (except October 1979, $2.50); $1.50, March 1980–September 1982; $1.75, October 1982–.

Thomas D. Clareson

MAGAZINE OF HORROR

In 1960, with the dissolution of the Columbia Publications pulp chain, which published *Future SF* (*Future Fiction**) and *Science Fiction Stories*, editor Robert A. W. Lowndes was hired by Health Knowledge Inc. to edit its two nonfiction magazines, *Real Life Guide* and *Exploring the Unknown*. By 1963, impressed at the success of the *Pan Book of Horror Stories*, the publisher, Louis Elson, suggested that a companion horror fiction magazine might work, and that summer saw the first issue of *Magazine of Horror*. The cover bore the more complete title, *Magazine of Horror and Strange Stories*, though this was later shortened.

In place of eye-catching art the magazine's cover merely listed the contents, as did its companion publications. This implied that all the magazines had a slim budget, which was further emphasized by the considerable use of reprints in all the issues. Lowndes' brief had been that he could start a new magazine provided costs were kept to a minimum. Thus, it was necessary to use as much out-of-copyright or "public domain" material as possible. Lowndes turned this to his advantage in his editorial sales talk: "We want to resurrect some memorable stories by authors who wrote this sort of material for the old 'pulps' because they enjoyed writing it, for editors who were not afraid to take an occasional story which did not follow the traditional formulas of pulp fiction."[1] However, he also added: "We want to offer an opportunity to today's writers, newcomer and old hand alike, to write the horror, strange, bizarre etc., story they'd like to write—and never mind the so-called policy."[2]

Health Knowledge allowed Lowndes a free hand to edit as he wished, and it was fortunate in having an editor with vast knowledge of the fantasy field and good judgment in his choice of old and new material. Furthermore, Lowndes enjoyed editing, and though he could be accused of self-indulgence in some of the issues, his enjoyment and enthusiasm were infectious. His magazines always radiated a "family" atmosphere, and their limited distribution and circulation gave the readers a sense of belonging to a very select club. This was openly encouraged in the reader-involvement departments that Lowndes ran, including the letter column. "We hope you will want to become associates," he stated in his first editorial.

In the first issue Lowndes touched on a point that would remain contentious throughout the magazine's existence. "Most science fiction is outside our orbit, but we have no 'keep out' sign posted here to flash before the eyes of the science fiction writer."[3] Later the magazine bore the subtitle "Strange Tales and Science Fiction," though reader protest caused this to change to "The Frightening: The Bizarre: The Gruesome." Science fiction, however, always formed a part of the contents. The first issue, for instance, reprinted Frank Lillie Pollock's "Finis," a story of the discovery of a vast central sun and the last day on Earth, which Lowndes retitled "The Last Dawn." Later issues included three of Laurence Manning's Stranger Club adventures from *Wonder Stories** before the formation of *Famous Science Fiction** brought a temporary solution to the science fiction controversy.

Through *Magazine of Horror* Lowndes performed several honorable services. First, though not foremost, he made available stories long out of print and available to none but the ardent collector. In this respect, *Magazine of Horror* was like a latter-day *Avon Fantasy Reader,** for Lowndes did not limit himself to the pulps (of which *Weird Tales** and *Strange Tales** were his main sources), but also selected stories from a wide variety of books by authors like Mary Wilkins-Freeman, H. G. Wells, S. Fowler Wright, Rudyard Kipling, Richard Marsh, R. W. Chambers and Ambrose Bierce. From the pulps he reprinted scarce stories by Robert E. Howard, Henry S. Whitehead, Clark Ashton Smith,

Hugh B. Cave and Arthur J. Burks. In addition, Sam Moskowitz unearthed several Victorian lost stories, which were presented along with Moskowitz's own introductions. Some, such as Robert Barr's "The Doom of London" (Spring 1967), were undeniably science fiction; others, like Frank Aubrey's "The Spell of the Sword" (Fall 1967), were fantasy.

Second, Lowndes brought into print for the first time stories by old-time writers that had hitherto remained unpublished for many years. This policy began in the first issue by rescuing "A Thing of Beauty" by Wallace West, a story rejected by Farnsworth Wright of *Weird Tales* as being too horrible. It was a policy that would soon bear fruit in a number of important areas. The sixth issue (November 1964) printed "The Life-After-Death of Mr. Thaddeus Warde" by Robert Barbour Johnson, which had been accepted by *Weird Tales*; however, that magazine had folded before it could be published. "Sacrilege" by Wallace West, in the June 1965 issue, had been purchased by Farnsworth Wright shortly before his death, and then rejected by Dorothy McIlwraith. The major service in this area, however, concerned the works of Robert E. Howard and David H. Keller.

In 1966 Howard was at the start of the current wave of his posthumous popularity, following the publication of the Lancer paperback editions of the Conan books. The first story to be rescued was "King of the Forgotten People" (printed as "Valley of the Lost" in the Summer 1966 issue), followed by a new Conan story confusingly titled "The Vale of Lost Women" (Spring 1967).[4] Other new non-Conan stories were "Dermod's Bane" (Fall 1967), "Out of the Deep" (November 1967) and "The Noseless Horror" (February 1970), plus several items of verse.

The first new Keller story appeared in the March 1969 issue. "The Oak Tree" was the beginning of a series of "Tales of Cornwall" which Keller had written back in the 1920s, of which only a handful of episodes had seen publication. *Magazine of Horror* now methodically printed them in correct chronological sequence. Unfortunately, *Magazine of Horror* came to an end before the series was completed.

Third, *Magazine of Horror* was a market for new writers, and Lowndes always tried to include one or two new stories per issue. Of the 250 or so stories *Magazine of Horror* published, nearly 30 percent were appearing for the first time— including those "lost" stories hitherto mentioned. It was not a reliable market, as stories might be delayed for a year or two before publication, and even then payment was only one cent per word. Nevertheless, several writers made their first or early sales to *Magazine of Horror*. These include Stephen Goldin, Joanna Russ, Janet Fox, Steffan B. Aletti and even Roger Zelazny. Zelazny had three stories in successive issues: "But Not the Herald" (No. 12, Winter 1965), "Divine Madness" (Summer 1966) and "Comes Now the Power" (Winter 1966). All three had been accepted long before their publication and were in keeping with Lowndes' no-holds-barred policy. Like the sales Zelazny had been making to *Amazing Stories** and *Fantastic,** they reveal the development of his unique talent.

Other more established writers who contributed new stories included August Derleth, Joseph Payne Brennan, Donald Wollheim, Emil Petaja and Robert Silverberg. Lowndes revised several of his own early stories for republication.

Lowndes conceded that its poor distribution meant that *Magazine of Horror* would have a small readership, but that the true collectors and lovers of the genre would hunt down each issue no matter what. Consequently, he tailored the magazine for the devotee, and to this end he succeeded admirably. Every issue of *Magazine of Horror* contained items for the collector whether they be long-lost stories, reminiscences by Lowndes in his editorials, story introductions and the letter column, or the reproduction of original illustrations, predominantly those by Virgil Finlay, which were frequently used for the front cover.

Magazine of Horror began on a bi-monthly schedule, but it seldom sustained that regularity at the start due in part to difficulties with the printer, lack of distribution, and the poor accounting system of the Acme Distribution Agency. Matters came to a head in 1965 when it was decided that each issue had to stay on sale for a longer display period. Only two issues appeared during 1966, but these were supplemented by two new companion magazines, *Startling Mystery Stories** and *Famous Science Fiction*, launched in the hope of obtaining a larger share of the distribution, and at the same time spreading the publisher's overhead over more titles. *Magazine of Horror* remained irregular until the end of 1967, when it returned to a bi-monthly schedule, which it maintained for the next two years. This stability allowed the magazine to print serials, and Lowndes selected Algernon Blackwood's John Silence investigation, "A Psychical Invasion" (May–July 1968), David H. Keller's "The Abyss" (September–November 1968), Seabury Quinn's "The Devil's Bride" (March–July 1969) and Paul Ernst's "The Duel of the Sorcerers" (February–May 1970). During this period a variety of companion magazines came and went, including nonfantasy titles like *World-Wide Adventures* and *Thrilling Western*. The intention was that Lowndes would be editing two titles per month, and with the emphasis on reprints, it increased the likelihood of supplementary income.

Two new horror magazines—*Weird Terror Tales** and *Bizarre Fantasy Tales**— were added to the list in 1969 and 1970, and all four fantasy titles were paying their way by autumn 1970, when Countrywide Publications took over Acme News, the owner of Health Knowledge Inc. Countrywide, however, decided that the four magazines were not paying their way, and they were promptly axed. *Magazine of Horror* survived the longest. The last issue appeared in February 1971 (dated April), and a subsequent issue was announced along with other plans, which indicates the abruptness of Countrywide's decision. Thirty years to the month after Lowndes had edited his first SF magazine, he left for other pastures.

Notes

1. Robert A. W. Lowndes' "Editorial," *Magazine of Horror*, 1, No. 1 (August 1963).
2. Ibid.
3. Ibid.

4. To further confuse matters, *Startling Mystery Stories* 4 (Spring 1967) printed "The Secret of Lost Valley." This was the story projected for the unpublished March 1933 *Strange Tales* and advertised as "Valley of the Lost." Glenn Lord found the manuscript of "King of the Forgotten People" and believed it to be the *Strange Tales* story. It was run under the title "Valley of the Lost" in the Summer 1966 *Magazine of Horror* before the real "Valley of the Lost" was discovered and printed in *Startling Mystery*.

Information Sources

BIBLIOGRAPHY:
Bates, Dave and Sue. "Health Knowledge Publications." *Collecting Paperbacks?*, Vol. 2, No. 3 (July 1980): 28.
Lowndes, Robert A. W. "The Health Knowledge Years." *Outworlds* 28/29 (October 1976): 1125–32. See also letter by Lowndes in *Science-Fiction Collector*, No. 8 (October 1979): 45–47.
Tuck.
INDEX SOURCES: Cook, Michael L., *Monthly Murders*, Westport, Conn.: Greenwood Press, 1982; ISFM-II; Marshall, Gene, and Carl F. Waedt, "An Index to the Health Knowledge Magazines," *Science-Fiction Collector*, No. 3 (1977): MIT; MT; NESFA; Tuck.
REPRINT SOURCES:
Derivative Anthologies: Thirteen out of the fifteen stories in Kurt Singer's *Tales of the Uncanny* (London: W. H. Allen, 1968) had appeared in the first twenty issues of *MOH*. Selections came from issues 2, 5, 6, 7, 10, 11, 12, 13, 16 and 20. Singer's anthology was reprinted in two parts by Sphere Books, London, as *The Oblong Box* and *The Plague of the Living Dead* (both 1970).
LOCATION SOURCES: M.I.T. Science Fiction Library.

Publication History

TITLE: *Magazine of Horror* (all issues, although the first three issues [August 1963–February 1964] used the longer *Magazine of Horror and Strange Stories* on the cover and masthead).
VOLUME DATA: Volume 1, Number 1, August 1963–Volume 6, Number 6, April 1971. Six issues per volume. Intended schedule and actual did not always match. Bi-monthly, issues 1–12, although this schedule not attained until issue 6 (November 1964) and then only patchily. Issues as follows: 1963: Aug [1], Nov [2]; 1964: Feb [3], May [4], Sep [5], Nov [6]; 1965: Jan [7], Apr [8], Jun [9], Aug [10], Nov [11], Winter [12]. Quarterly, issues 13–17, Summer 1966–Fall 1967 (no Fall 1966 issue). Bi-monthly, issues 18–32, November 1967–May 1970 (but November 1969 issue slipped to December, and April 1970 issue slipped to May). Quarterly issues 33–34, Summer–Fall 1970. Bi-monthly, issues 35–36, February–April 1971. Total run: 36 issues.
PUBLISHER: Health Knowledge Inc., Fifth Avenue, New York.
EDITOR: Robert A. W. Lowndes.
FORMAT: Digest, 128 pp.; first three issues perfect bound, thereafter saddle-stapled.

PRICE: 50¢, issues 1–31 (August 1963–February 1970); 60¢, issues 32–34 (May–Fall 1970); 75¢, issues 35–36 (February–April 1971).

Mike Ashley

THE MAGIC CARPET MAGAZINE

See ORIENTAL STORIES.

THE MAN FROM U.N.C.L.E. MAGAZINE

The Man from U.N.C.L.E. Magazine was published by Leo Margulies under license to tie in with and capitalize on the immense success of the television series of that name starring Robert Vaughn and David McCallum. Margulies was already publishing the relatively successful *Mike Shayne Mystery Magazine* and *Zane Grey Western Magazine*, and this was a useful addition. He later added a new companion, *The Girl from U.N.C.L.E. Magazine.**

MFU was launched with the issue dated February 1966. The editorial director was Cylvia Kleinman (Mrs. Leo Margulies), and the associate editor was ''H. N. Alden,'' an alias adopted by Alden H. Norton, who was at that time still an editor at Popular Publications.

Cover illustrations for all issues were stills from the television series, with further stills on the back cover. Interior illustrations were uncredited line drawings in a variety of single colors. Each issue featured a novel about the Men from U.N.C.L.E. attributed to ''Robert Hart Davis,'' a house pseudonym hiding the identities of several mystery writers. For example, during the first year, the lead novel was written alternately by Dennis Lynds (who also wrote the Belmont *Shadow* books as Maxwell Grant, and is better known under his alias Michael Collins) and Harry Whittington, a prolific writer of mystery and adventure paperbacks. It should be noted that the magazine novels were not reprinted in the twenty-three-volume paperback series, which was contracted separately. In addition to the lead novel, the first issue featured articles on the main characters in the television series, and there were also a variety of short stories.

The relevance of the magazine to the SF/fantasy field hinges on three points, of varying degrees of significance. First, the lead novels almost always set the U.N.C.L.E. agents against enemies and situations beyond the technological capabilities of the time, thus giving them a veneer of SF, much like the old hero pulps such as *Dusty Ayres and His Battle Birds** or *Doc Savage.** For example, ''The Moby Dick Affair'' (October 1966) involves a man-made tidal wave, while Frank Belknap Long's ''The Electronic Frankenstein Affair'' (July 1967) is about a robot that can read and destroy thoughts.

Second, a number of SF writers contributed short stories to the magazine. Unfortunately, few of these stories were SF, most being straight mystery or adventure. The closest to fantasy is "Dimension of Mind" by Robert Edmond Alter (October 1967), which involves ghosts, although there is an attempt at the end of the story to explain them as natural phenomena. However, among the other writers who appeared in *MFU* are Thomas Calvert McClary, Frank Belknap Long, Christopher Anvil, Tom Godwin, Barry Malzberg and Arthur Porges.

Finally, and perhaps most important, beginning in October 1966, the magazine featured a "Department of Lost Stories," in which SF stories of the past were reprinted, just as Margulies had seven years earlier in *Satellite Science Fiction.** In fact, John Christopher's "Doom over Kareeta" was resurrected from *Satellite.* Many of the stories came from *Weird Tales,** to which Margulies had acquired the rights. These included Robert Bloch's "Hell on Earth," Ray Bradbury's "The Lake," Robert Heinlein's "Our Fair City," Fritz Leiber's "The Dead Man" and C. L. Moore's "Hellsgarde," all excellent fantasy stories, but possibly out of place in what was ostensibly a modern-day superagent series.

The television series ran from 1964 to 1968, and inevitably its popularity ran its course. As interest waned, the sales of the magazine also declined, and it was dropped, with no prior warning, at the end of 1967 (issue dated January 1968).

Information Sources

INDEX SOURCES: Cook, Michael L., *Monthly Murders*, Westport, Conn.: Greenwood Press, 1982.
REPRINT SOURCES: None known.
LOCATION SOURCES: Legal Department, MGM Studios, Culver City, Calif.; Leo Margulies Collection, Library of the University of Oregon, Eugene, Ore.; M.I.T. Science Fiction Library; Pennsylvania State University Library.

Publication History

TITLE: *The Man from U.N.C.L.E. Magazine.*
VOLUME DATA: Volume 1, Number 1, February 1966–Volume 4, Number 6. January 1968. Monthly. Total run: 24 issues.
PUBLISHER: Leo Margulies Corporation, New York.
EDITOR: Cylvia Kleinman, assisted by Alden H. Norton under the pseudonyms H. N. Alden (February–November 1966) and Holmes Taylor (for the remainder).
FORMAT: Digest, 144 pp.
PRICE: 50¢.

Grant Thiessen

MARVEL SCIENCE FICTION

See MARVEL SCIENCE STORIES.

MARVEL SCIENCE STORIES

Premiering in August 1938, *Marvel Science Stories* was the first new professional all-SF magazine to be published in the United States since 1931. The last of the magazine's fifteen issues came out in May 1952, and publication had lapsed completely between April 1941 and November 1950.

Because its publication was interrupted, the magazine affords an opportunity for contrasting the state of science fiction pulp magazines in the late thirties and early forties with their state in the early fifties. Even in the late thirties, pulp magazines for most other genre fiction were disappearing; by the fifties, the locus even for magazine science fiction was shifting rapidly from pulps to a digest format. And—even in digest format—magazine science fiction was faced with increasing competition from publishers who were putting out science fiction books. Thus, *Marvel Science Stories*—with a break in publication longer than the two spans in which it did appear—illustrates the dying fall of the pulps and their tradition of more than fifty years in American science fiction.

In its effort to find an adequate audience, the magazine tried superficial variations, changing its name (several times) and its format. And it tried the bait of the lurid, an editorial attitude promoting stories with a sadistic cast that was sickly adolescent.

In its fifteen numbers, the magazine changed title four times. In the nine that appeared before the break in publication, it changed from *Marvel Science Stories* (five issues) to *Marvel Tales* (2 issues), and then to *Marvel Stories* (2 issues). After the break, it began again as *Marvel Science Stories* (3 issues) and then concluded as *Marvel Science Fiction*.

The changes in format ran across the changes in name. The magazine switched from pulp to digest with the last number called *Marvel Science Stories*. It kept that form for the first two numbers called *Marvel Science Fiction*, but reverted to pulp size for its last issue.

All of these changes bespeak an effort to attract an audience by manipulating the magazine's appearance. But the change from *Marvel Science Stories* to *Marvel Tales* also reflects the effort to attract an audience by reducing the scientific elements and replacing them with elements that were more erotic and more brutal. While even the first five numbers had included a substantial proportion of female characters whose principal function seems to have been to allow their clothes to be ripped away or shredded, the potential for maltreatment jumped notably in the two numbers called *Marvel Tales*. These were fond of story blurbs that leaned toward "passionate" or "lust-crazed" or "sin-lost," even for stories where there was more titillation in the packaging than in the package. But a high proportion of these stories—"Perfectionist Perdition," "Lust Rides the Roller Coaster," "World without Sex" and "Fresh Fiances for the Devil's Daughter" among others—were fabricated out of unpolished seductions, women entrapped, burned and otherwise maltreated, and whips cracking into use with uninventive frequency. The response of *Marvel*'s readers to this strategy remains conjectural, since the magazine's letter column was discontinued with the first number of *Marvel Tales*.

That *Marvel* attempted to attract a readership through such material suggests that its editor was unable either to grasp what John Campbell was doing with the genre at *Astounding* (*Analog Science Fiction**) or to match the resources with which he was working.[1] The combination of lust and the lash had apparently been applied with some success to other pulps in Western Publishing's stable (see *Uncanny Tales**). Its use in *Marvel*, though, reflects not only a crude sense of reader psychology but also a failure to imagine that the audience for science fiction might have been distinguishable from that for other pulps. Apparently, the combination did not attract the hoped-for readership. After trying it for two issues, the magazine became *Marvel Stories*, and its contents reverted to the mix of other-worldly adventure and superscience that had characterized the earlier numbers.

In maintaining this mix, *Marvel* remained a conservator of the pulp style in science fiction just when Campbell's *Astounding* was rising above the limitations in that style.[2] Throughout the prewar years, *Marvel*'s stories had plots whose driving energy was stronger than their sense of direction, settings which tapped wondrous improbabilities beyond the margins of established science, and characters whose most common motivation was an obsession with autocratic power. The more frequent contributors to the magazine in this period—Arthur J. Burks, Stanton Coblentz, John Russell Fearn, the early Henry Kuttner, D. D. Sharp and R. R. Winterbotham—display flashes of narrative vigor and a stolid innocence of stylistic grace. In "After World's End" and "The Iron God," Jack Williamson, however, does offer two promising treatments of the ambiguously superior androids in his later work.

In its postwar numbers, *Marvel* provides stories whose narrative construction is tighter and whose sense of characterization is both more varied and more subtle. Murray Leinster's "Skag with the Queer Head," Raymond Z. Gallun's "The Restless Tide" and Daniel Keyes' "Precedent" all move without wavering to their conclusions. The women in Milton Lesser's "Trans-Plutonian" and in Robert Moore Williams' "She Knew the Face of Evil" are not hapless victims. There are pathos and tenderness in Jack Vance's "The Golden Girl" and Cedric Walker's "The Guinea-Pig" and wit and irony in H. A. DeRosso's "Girl Who Practiced Aklat," Betsy Curtis' "The Ones" and L. Sprague de Camp's "In Group."

But if the quality of *Marvel*'s postwar stories is superior to that of the prewar ones, the quality of the competition had also increased in the interval. The contributors to *Marvel* in the fifties obviously benefited from the example that had been set by Campbell's *Astounding*. Only rarely does their sense of basic narrative craft falter. But even the best pieces in the magazine are not science fiction masterpieces. Contributors like Isaac Asimov, Richard Matheson and

William Tenn (Philip Klass) were placing superior work in *Galaxy Science Fiction** or *The Magazine of Fantasy and Science Fiction.** And in the end, even *Marvel*'s better was not good enough to preserve it.

Notes

1. For a detailed recollection of the conditions under which editors and writers for science fiction pulps worked at this time, see Frederik Pohl, *The Way the Future Was* (New York: Del Rey Books, 1979), pp. 96–107.

2. Mike Ashley, *The History of the Science Fiction Magazine, Vol. 2, 1936–1945* (London: New English Library, 1975), p. 52, describes *Marvel* as a product for the older of the two generations of science fiction readers in the late 1930s.

Information Sources

BIBLIOGRAPHY:
Nicholls. *Encyclopedia.*
Tuck.
INDEX SOURCES: IBSF; ISFM; MIT; SFM; Tuck.
REPRINT SOURCES:
> *Magazines*: See entry on *Skyworlds.*
> *Foreign Editions*: A British edition of the February 1951 issue was released in May 1951 by Thorpe & Porter, Leicester. Identical to U.S. edition except for cover and interior advertisements. Pulp, 128 pp., 1/6d. Brad Day lists a run of six British editions of the U.S. second series, but no other issues have been sighted and no others are listed in Graham Stone's *Index to British Science Fiction Magazines.*

LOCATION SOURCES: Brown University Library; Eastern New Mexico University Library; M.I.T. Science Fiction Library; Pennsylvania State University Library; Texas A&M University Library.

Publication History

TITLE: *Marvel Science Stories*, August 1938–August 1939. *Marvel Tales*, December 1939–May 1940. *Marvel Stories*, November 1940–May 1941. Reverted to *Marvel Science Stories*, February–May 1951. *Marvel Science Fiction*, August 1951–May 1952.

VOLUME DATA: Volume 1, Number 1, August 1938–Volume 2, Number 3, April 1941. Revived with Volume 3, Number 1, November 1950–Volume 3, Number 6, May 1952. Six issues per volume, although only three in Volume 2. First series irregular although intended schedule bi-monthly. Issues ran: Volume 1, August and November 1938, February, April/May, August and December 1939. Volume 2, May and November 1940, April 1941. Revived on a quarterly schedule for Volume 3, which it maintained. Total run: 9 + 6, 15 issues.

PUBLISHER: Postal Publications, Chicago, August–November 1938; Western Publishing, New York and Chicago, February 1939–April 1941. Revived by Stadium Publishing, New York, November 1950–May 1952. All issues published by Martin and Abraham Goodman.

EDITOR: Not credited in first series, but all issues edited by Robert O. Erisman. Daniel Keyes assisted as "Editorial Associate" from February to November 1951.

FORMAT: Pulp, 128 pp., August 1938–April/May 1939; 112 pp., August 1939–April
    1941. Revived Pulp, 128 pp., November 1950–February 1951; Digest, 128 pp.,
    May–November 1951; Pulp, 128 pp., May 1952.
PRICE: 15¢, August 1938–April 1941; 25¢, November 1950–May 1952.

Joseph Marchesani

MARVEL STORIES

See MARVEL SCIENCE STORIES.

MARVEL TALES (1934–1935)

In the wake of the growth of science fiction fandom out of the pages of the
letter columns in the professional magazines came a wave of amateur fan publications. The leading fan magazine was *Science Fiction Digest*, which benefited
from the services of Conrad H. Ruppert, who possessed a printing press and
was able to provide below-cost printing. The magazine was professional in every
respect except newsstand distribution, and it showed what quality fans could
achieve.

In 1933 the professional magazines, affected by the Depression, entered a
period of doldrums. *Astounding Stories* (*Analog Science Fiction**) folded, and
Amazing Stories* and *Wonder Stories** featured few works with originality. In
the autumn of that year William L. Crawford, who also possessed a printing
press (he would later succeed Ruppert as the printer of *Science Fiction Digest*—
then retitled *Fantasy Magazine*), mailed a circular to leading fans announcing a
new magazine to be called *Unusual Stories*:

> Science fiction should have a place in the literature of today. It does not
> occupy that position now, we believe, because of the restrictions placed
> on it by short-sighted editors and publishers. They use only tales which
> follow certain stereotyped forms. They avoid the "off-trail" story because
> it violates one or another of their editorial taboos, with the result that
> science fiction has been sinking into the mire of the commonplace.

Crawford's flyer almost certainly reached Charles D. Hornig, whose own
printed fanzine, *The Fantasy Fan*, had just been launched in September 1933
and who, within weeks, would become managing editor of *Wonder Stories* and
initiate the "new policy" for fiction. A copy may also have reached Desmond
Hall, who was just then resuming duties as assistant editor on the reborn *Astounding Stories* under F. Orlin Tremaine; the two were about to launch their
drive for "thought-variants." The year 1934 would see an avalanche of new
ideas which revolutionized science fiction, and it is possible that Crawford helped

to influence that change. In the pages of his magazine he planned to publish "taboo" SF that had been rejected by the magazines as being too risky, thus making *Marvel Tales* the spiritual grandfather of *Dangerous Visions*.

Following his circular Crawford prepared an advance issue of *Unusual Stories*. Dated March 1934, it was the first digest-sized science fiction magazine (as opposed to nonfiction, with *Science Fiction Digest* making the change in October 1933). The oddity of this "advance issue" was that it was mailed in two incomplete sections and the full issue never was published. Combined, the two sections included the story "When the Waker Sleeps" by Cyril G. Wates, a short biography of the author Richard Tooker and the start of his story "Tharda, Queen of the Vampires." The cover illustrated "The Titan" by P. Schuyler Miller, a story that had been announced in the earlier circular, but the actual text was not included.

It was a total surprise, therefore, that May 1934 should see the first issue of *Marvel Tales*, also digest-sized and with forty pages for ten cents. The contents included those announced for *Unusual Stories*, so it was fair to assume that *Marvel Tales* was the same magazine, retitled. Included in the first issue were "The Man with the Hour Glass" by Lloyd A. Eshbach, "Celephais" by H. P. Lovecraft and "Binding DeLuxe" by David H. Keller.

The second issue, dated July/August 1934, increased to sixty pages and was printed with three different covers in variant colors and paper stocks, thus making each a collector's item. Best remembered among the contents was Robert E. Howard's "The Garden of Fear."

It was not until December that the third issue came out, dated Winter 1934 and increased in size to sixty-eight pages. Here at last appeared part of P. Schuyler Miller's "The Titan" as the first episode in a four-part serialization. The same included "The Golden Bough" by David H. Keller and "Lilies," the first story in print by Robert Bloch.

The fourth issue, published in March 1935, was a giant. A full 108 digest-sized pages, it included that classic of science fiction, "The Creator" by Clifford D. Simak. Other stories were "The Doom That Came to Sarnath" by H. P. Lovecraft, "The Cathedral Crypt" by John Beynon Harris, part two of Miller's "The Titan" and part one of a new serial, "The Nebula of Death" by George Allan England. This had originally run in the *People's Favorite Magazine* during 1918 and had proved very popular. Its length implied that *Marvel Tales* was set for a long run.

Crawford had succeeded in gaining a limited newsstand distribution for this issue and had high hopes. Elated, he announced a series of books which, had they all materialized, would have included the first SF book by Andre Norton, *People of the Crater*.

To the surprise of many, at this point *Unusual Stories* appeared. The first issue, dated May/June 1935, contained forty-eight digest-sized pages and included the novelette "Waning Moon" by Robert A. Wait.

But Crawford had been overambitious, too early. His book publications sold poorly. The first had been *Mars Mountain* by Eugene George Key, perhaps not the most auspicious start, but it was followed by *The White Sybil and Men of Avalon*, a soft-cover binding of two stories by Clark Ashton Smith and David H. Keller, and then by *The Shadow over Innsmouth* by H. P. Lovecraft. Today these are both highly prized collector's items, but at the same time their sales were minimal.

This inevitably affected Crawford's other ventures. A Summer 1935 *Marvel Tales* appeared, followed by a Winter 1935 *Unusual Stories*, which bravely started a serial by Lowell Howard Morrow, "A Diamond Asteroid."

Plans were now afoot to publish *Marvel Tales* as a fully professional magazine with newsstand distribution. Large-size with sixty-four pages, and selling for fifteen cents, it was announced to appear late in 1936. It would carry the final installment of "The Titan" along with Lovecraft's "The Shadow over Innsmouth" and the two round-robin stories from *Fantasy Magazine*, both entitled "The Challenge from Beyond." Partial proofs of this issue were prepared, but the final product never materialized. Crawford's finances, affected by the poor sales of his other publications, were now drained beyond redemption, and he decided to cut his losses. It would be another eleven years before he issued another magazine, *Fantasy Book*,* and it was not until 1952 that patient fans could at last read Miller's "The Titan" in full when it was included as the title story in a collection of his stories published by Lloyd A. Eshbach's Fantasy Press. In the meantime, another publishing company took over the name *Marvel* for its *Marvel Science Stories.**

Marvel Tales was a worthwhile and exciting experiment that could have had a significant impact on the development of SF had it succeeded. It cannot be said that all its contents were taboo-breaking, since many of the stories probably did not find a place in the professional magazines because they were not very good. Others were probably donated by friends. However, by publishing Miller's "The Titan" and Simak's "The Creator" when he did, Crawford was able to prove that there are writers in science fiction who were prepared to challenge the establishment and not follow the rut of formula stories that has been the bane of science fiction for most of its magazine existence. With someone like Crawford willing to liberate SF, the genre could progress and evolve. Crawford has been overlooked in the history of SF, but one day he will be accorded his place beside pioneers F. Orlin Tremaine and John W. Campbell, as an editor who tried to shape the future of SF.

Information Sources

BIBLIOGRAPHY:
Moskowitz, Sam. Introduction to "The Titan." *Fantastic*, August 1962, pp. 17–18.
———. "William H. [*sic*] Crawford and His Contemporaries," Chap. 6 of *The Immortal Storm*. Westport, Conn.: Hyperion Press, repr. 1974.
Tuck.
INDEX SOURCES: MT; SFM; Tuck.

REPRINT SOURCES:
  Derivative Anthology: [William L. Crawford], *The Garden of Fear* (Los Angeles: Crawford Publishing House, 1945), contains five stories.
LOCATION SOURCES: M.I.T. Science Fiction Library.

Publication History

TITLE: *Marvel Tales*.
VOLUME DATA: Volume 1, Number 1, May 1934–Volume 1, Number 5, Summer 1935. Irregular. Other issues dated July 1934 [2], Winter 1934 [3] and March 1935 [4]. Total run: 5 issues. Advanced issue dated March 1934.
PUBLISHER: Fantasy Publications, Everett, Pennsylvania.
EDITOR: William L. Crawford.
FORMAT: Digest, first four issues; Large-size, fifth issue. Page counts: 1: 40 pp.; 2: 60 pp.; 3: 68 pp.; 4: 108 pp.; 5: 58 pp.
PRICE: First three issues, 10¢; thereafter 15¢.

Mike Ashley

MARVEL TALES (1939–1940)

See MARVEL SCIENCE STORIES. Not to be confused with the semi-professional magazine of the same name detailed in the previous entry.

THE MASTER THRILLER SERIES

This was an erratic series of assorted magazines with individual issues concentrating on different fields of fiction. The series was originally numbered sequentially but later the enumeration became sporadic with the result that it is not always clear whether some magazines form part of the series or not. The full listing together with approximate dates of publication appears below. Those magazines of fantasy interest are asterisked and are accorded separate entries.

1. *Tales of the Foreign Legion*, July 1933
2. *Tales of the North-West Mounties*, November 1933
3. *Tales of the Seven Seas*, March 1934
4. *Tales of Mystery and Detection*,* June 1934
5. *Tales of the Foreign Legion 2, September 1934*
6. *Tales of the Uncanny*,* December 1934
7. *Tales of African Adventure*, January 1935
8. *Tales of the Orient*, March 1935
9. *Tales of the Jungle*, May 1935

10. *Tales of the Foreign Legion 3*, July 1935

11. *Tales of the Sea*, September 1935

12. *Tales of Valour*, December 1935

13. *Tales of the Levant*, July 1936

14. *Tales of the Air*, September 1936 (?)

15. *Tales of the Foreign Legion 4*, November 1936 (?)

16. *Tales of Adventure*, February 1937 (?)

17. *Tales of Terror*,* April 1937 (?)

18. *Tales of East and West*, June 1937 (?)

19) *Tales of Wonder*,* July 1937

20. *Tales of the Uncanny 2*,* September 1937 (?)

21. *Tales of Crime and Punishment*,* November 1937 (?)

22) *Tales of the Uncanny 3*,* December 1937 (?)

23) *Fireside Ghost Stories*,* January 1938 (?)

24) *Ghosts and Goblins*,* December 1938 (?)

25. *Tales of the Great Dominion*, May 1939

26. *Tales of the Far Frontiers*, June 1939

27. *Tales of the Underworld*, July 1939

28. *The Far-Flung Coasts of Crime*, August 1939

29. *Tales of the Foreign Legion 5*, September 1939

30. *Tales of the Jungle* (2), October 1939

31. *Gangsters and 'G'-Men*, November 1939

32. *Tales of Ghosts and Haunted Houses*,* December 1939

Tales of Mystery and Detection split into a separate series of its own, entitled simply *Mystery and Detection*, while a companion series was *Mystery Stories*, which contained a number of weird stories in its twenty-issue run, especially in the last three issues published during 1938.

The editor of the series was not named, but research has shown that the early issues were compiled by H. Norman Evans, who may have remained the editor throughout.

See separate entries for publication history and other data. The series is indexed in MT.

Mike Ashley,
with the assistance of W. G. Lofts

MIDNIGHT SUN

Midnight Sun started life as a vehicle for and a tribute to Karl Edward Wagner and his anti-hero, Kane. As such it both succeeded and failed. It brought some attention to Wagner and his creation, attention any struggling new writer requires. However, the presentation did nothing to enhance the stories. The young editor, Gary Hoppenstand, had the necessary enthusiasm and finances, but not the experience. The first issue, though printed as a smart digest on expensive egg-shell-white gloss stock with full-color-separated covers, was a typesetting disaster. The text was produced with a manual typewriter that had seen better days. There were numerous typing errors, and the accompanying illustrations were inferior. Even the color covers were reminiscent of a child's gaudily crayoned picture. Despite the good stories by Wagner, the issue was a disappointment.

MS 2 was a great improvement. Although the presentation was less expensive, it was more effective. Gone were the glossy pages, and the text was more accurately typeset. The illustrations were still below par but were several steps above the first issue. The emphasis was still on Wagner, but almost half the issue was comprised of stories by David Drake, Robert Weinberg and Carl Jacobi.

The third issue was a complete departure from the earlier numbers. With Wagner not obtaining due recognition and concentrating his efforts in the professional field, Hoppenstand turned his attention to the late H. H. Hollis and published three of his stories. Although the quality of the artwork and the professional typesetting had improved the appearance of the magazine, the quality of the fiction had now deteriorated. Hollis was not a great author, and these three stories were not his best. Of all the issues of *MS*, Number 3 is the least satisfactory.

Number 4 followed within a few months. While billed as a C. L. Grant issue, it carried only two of Grant's stories, along with tales by Joseph Payne Brennan, Basil Copper and Richard K. Lyon. It was a well-balanced issue with material of reasonably good quality, and though it suffered from some inferior illustrations, these were much less in evidence. With promises of a regular bi-monthly publication, *MS* showed signs of developing into a quality magazine. Unfortunately, this was not to be. An unscrupulous printer charged twice his quotation for the fourth issue, and then the post office lost most of the issues mailed out to subscribers and bookshops. Hoppenstand had to reprint the issue to fulfill orders, which left him seriously in debt.

Some time later, by good fortune, Harlan Ellison enquired of Charles Grant why Hoppenstand had not produced an issue of *MS* of late. Grant explained, and Ellison sent Hoppenstand one of his own unpublished stories to help out.

Grant contributed two of his stories plus a review column, and these, along with stories by H. H. Hollis and Carl Jacobi, constituted the fifth and final issue. Hoppenstand recouped much of his loss, but, once bitten, he was not prepared to continued the magazine.

MS, after its editor had learned the ropes, had progressed well. It did have pretensions above its limitations, but it also printed some very good fiction. In all likelihood it would have continued to improve and become a highly respected magazine, but a printer and the postal service made certain that would never happen.

Information Sources

INDEX SOURCES: MT; NESFA-IV; NESFA-V.
REPRINT SOURCES: None known.
LOCATION SOURCES: M.I.T. Science Fiction Library.

Publication History

TITLE: *Midnight Sun*.
VOLUME DATA: Number 1, 1974–Number 5, 1979. Intervening issues dated: Summer/
    Fall 1975 [2], April 1976 [3] and August 1976 [4]. Total run: 5 issues.
PUBLISHER: Gary Hoppenstand, Columbus, Ohio.
EDITOR: Gary Hoppenstand.
FORMAT: Digest (first two issues perfect bound, thereafter saddle-stapled). Pages as
    follows: 1: 122 pp.; 2: 96 pp.; 3: 32 pp.; 4: 48 pp.; 5: 72 pp.
PRICE: First issue, not stated. Thereafter, 2: $3.98; 3, 4: $2.50; 5: $4.00.

Jon Harvey

MIND, INC.

One of the small but nevertheless frustrating mysteries of SF magazine collecting has been the question of the magazine *Mind, Inc.* Brad Day includes the title in his *Complete Checklist of Science-Fiction Magazines* and indicates a twenty-four-issue run from February 1929 to June 1931. He also states that the magazine was science fiction in content, with no further qualification, and yet the magazine is listed in no other reference work, bibliography or index. However, with the help of Canadian bookdealer, collector and publisher Grant Thiessen, and the Library of Congress catalogue, at least part of the mystery can now be solved.

The magazine was not a science fiction title. Its first issue was dated May 1929, not February, and was published by a quasi-religious organization called Mind, Inc. This was run by Robert Collier, a best-selling author of psychoreligious books, whose *The Secret of the Ages*, published as an educational part-work in 1926, had been one of the factors that led to the publication of the magazine *Tales of Magic and Mystery.** It replaced an earlier, somewhat similar magazine, called *How*.

The first issue included a twelve-page listing of all the stockholders in Mind, Inc., emphasizing that here was a company house organ and not a general-circulation magazine. Indeed, there was no overt salesmanship about its presentation. Initially in pocketbook form, there was no identification on the spine, so that when stacked on a shelf with other books, the magazine became all but invisible, which may well account for its apparent scarcity.

The magazine began with an approximately even mix of fiction and nonfiction, although the dividing line between them became increasingly more vague. The table of contents made no attempt to define the difference and merely listed the ten or twelve items that each issue averaged in order of appearance. Many of the articles were Bible-oriented. To illustrate the problem in distinguishing fact from fiction, an early example is "My Seven Minutes in Eternity" by William Dudley Pelley (May 1929), which details the author's out-of-body experiences and the hidden powers that are thus awakened. Its purpose was to teach rather than entertain, but it was arguably as much fiction as fact. In short, the magazine's purpose was to encourage self-improvement through God's power. What fiction it presented was merely to underline this dictum. To this end it did reprint many well-known stories, mostly in the supernatural fantasy vein. They include "Special Delivery" by Algernon Blackwood (May 1929), "A Great Rushing of Wings" by Emma-Lindsay Squier (October 1929), "Wonder of Woman" by Jack London (December 1929), "The Leather Funnel" by Sir Arthur Conan Doyle (November 1930) and others by Nathaniel Hawthorne, Washington Irving, L. Adams Beck and Oscar Wilde.

As issues progressed, the recognizable fiction decreased, until by 1932 it was virtually nonexistent, the magazine having been taken over by religious articles. In this guise it now changed its name, first to *Mind* and then to *Mind Magazine*, and also increased its size to digest, but saddle-stapled, so that the magazine was still not recognizable on a shelf. Its stated purpose in the September 1932 issue was to "become the finest medium of Christian metaphysics in the world."

By this stage it seems to have lost whatever contact it may have had with the SF world. *Mind, Inc.* can be regarded as a fantasy curiosity at first, and nothing else.

Information Sources

INDEX SOURCES: None known.
REPRINT SOURCES: None known.
LOCATION SOURCES: None known.

Publication History

TITLE: *Mind, Inc.*, May 1929–March 1932. Retitled *Mind* in April 1932, and *Mind Magazine* by October 1932.

VOLUME DATA: Volume 1, Number 1, May 1929–Volume 6, Number 5, March 1932.
     Presumably six issues per volume, but not all seen to verify. Magazine monthly
     until at least June 1933. Last issue (as *Mind Magazine*) listed in Library of Congress
     Catalogue as November 1939, but this is nonfiction.
PUBLISHER: Mind, Inc., with offices at 599 Fifth Avenue, New York.
EDITOR: Robert Collier.
FORMAT: Pocketbook, 96 pp., May 1929–September 1932; thereafter digest (saddle-
     stapled).
PRICE: Not known.

Mike Ashley/Grant Thiessen

MIND MAGAZINE

Nonfiction issues of the magazine which was originally titled *Mind, Inc.*, and
then briefly *Mind*. See MIND, INC.

MIND MAGIC MAGAZINE

Mind Magic, first published in June 1931, is a borderline fantasy/occult magazine that could not seem to make up its own mind what it was doing. A lack
of adequate financing is evident in the slim, sixty-four pages of low-grade pulp
adorned by poor, drab cover paintings. The prospect of a small circulation was
also clear from the high cover price. Planned at twenty-five cents, the publishers
obviously had second thoughts and released it at twenty cents; but at a time
when most pulps were only ten or fifteen cents and delivered twice as many
pages and more, it was clear that *MM* was aimed at a special, select audience
who would buy the magazine regardless of cost. That audience was those people
fascinated by the occult as manifested in astrology, psychometry, ouija boards
and all the paraphernalia of insincere spiritualism.

The magazine was a mixture of fiction and nonfiction. The articles were of a
nature that has appeared since the turn of the century and still appears today in
various guises: "Using the Subconscious," "Make Your Ideas Work," "Secret
of Riches" and so on. These were accompanied by accounts of so-called true
experiences.

In later issues, however, the emphasis was on fiction, or "Psycho-Mystic
Stories," as the cover proclaimed. Most were formula occult adventures when
they developed at all beyond vignettes of psychic experiences. The contents page
and story blurbs frequently referred to these items as "snappy," as if that were
something in their favor. What it meant was that they were slight, shallow stories
with undeveloped ideas. Anything that did approach normal story length was
serialized, as happened with Ralph Milne Farley's "The Man from Ouija Land,"
less than 10,000 words long but split into two parts for the July and August

1931 issues. This story, which tells of the escape of the hero from the police through the astral plane where he is pursued by the ancient Pack of Sekhet, was later reprinted in London by Benson Herbert as one of his American Fiction series under the title *Dangerous Love* (London: Utopian Publications, 1946).

Farley was one of a number of contributors who were well known in the SF and fantasy fields. The first issue, for instance, carried "Faithful Footsteps" by Manly Wade Wellman. August Derleth was in the second issue with a very brief story about a captain and his crew trapped in the Sargasso Sea, "Wraiths of the Sea." Also present in that issue was Rae King, a pseudonym known to have been used by Ray Cummings, but also the name of a real writer. King was a frequent contributor and started a series about the psychic adventures of Dorothea Deering just before the magazine failed.

Other contributors included Allen Glasser with "An Amulet from Egypt" (August 1931), Ed Earl Repp with "The Black Astral" (November 1931), Mary Elizabeth Counselman with "The Devil Himself" (November 1931) and Joe W. Skidmore with "Are You a Coward?"

With its fifth issue the magazine changed its name to *My Self*, perhaps in an attempt to attract a wider audience, but this did little to help. It continued to offer little that was not already supplied by other magazines, and asked twice the price for the privilege.

Information Sources

BIBLIOGRAPHY:
Nicholls. *Encyclopedia*.
Tuck.
INDEX SOURCES: MT.
REPRINT SOURCES: None known.
LOCATION SOURCES: None known.

Publication History

TITLE: *Mind Magic* (on the cover; *Mind Magic Magazine* on table of contents and indicia), June–September/October 1931; *My Self*, November–December 1931.
VOLUME DATA: Volume 1, Number 1, June 1931–Volume 1, Number 6, December 1931. Monthly, but September–October issues combined. Total run: 6 issues.
PUBLISHER: Shade Publishing Co., Philadelphia, Pennsylvania.
EDITOR: G. R. Bay (probably all issues, though not identified in first).
FORMAT: Pulp, 64 pp.
PRICE: 20¢.

Mike Ashley/Frank H. Parnell

MIRACLE SCIENCE AND FANTASY STORIES

By 1930 Harold Hersey, who had formerly worked as editor on *The Thrill Book** for Street and Smith, had established his own publishing company and was producing a number of magazines for the working man with titles such as

Gangster Stories, *Prison Stories*, *Detective Trails*, *Thrills of the Jungle* and *Murder Stories*. He had acquired *Ghost Stories*,* but this limited magazine had declined in sales, and Hersey folded it at the end of 1931. Nevertheless, as a companion fantasy magazine Hersey, early in 1931, decided to launch *Miracle Science and Fantasy Stories*, apparently encouraged by Elliott Dold, the popular artist on *Astounding Stories* (*Analog Science Fiction**).

Dold had a brother, Douglas, who was both an editor and a pulp writer, but he was also blind. Douglas is usually credited as the editor of *Miracle*, although some confusion has arisen. Donald H. Tuck and Peter Nicholls in their respective encyclopedias both refer to Douglas Dold as the editor, whereas in his biography, *Pulpwood Editor* (New York: F. A. Stokes, 1937), Hersey implies that Elliott did the work. This may be a misinterpretation of a single reference in the biography, so to set the matter straight, this is what Hersey recalled:

> My third venture was my own. It was entitled *Miracle Science*. . . . Elliott Dold, whose brother Douglas Dold had been our editor of an adventure magazine, the *Danger Trail*, encouraged me—not that I needed to be spurred, into publishing this periodical. Elliott Dold is one of the brilliant artists whose work now appears in many of the fantasy sheets. Unfortunately, serious illness prevented his continuing services as editor-artist-writer and I decided to put the magazine aside temporarily. I regret it has never been revived.

From this it is clear that Elliott was the editor, though in all probability Hersey, Douglas and Elliott all worked together. With only two issues, there was not much in the way of editing to be done, and Elliott had enough on his hands illustrating the magazine as well as writing for it.

The first issue, dated April/May 1931, appeared early in February and featured an impressive cover, frontispiece and interior illustrations by Elliott Dold. The lead novel, "Valley of Sin," was a rather poor piece by his brother Douglas. It shows signs of being assembled from previously rejected or incomplete fragments of other stories. It starts with a dying gangster, adds a note of mystery in the form of ancient Egyptian bricks containing secret messages and maps, shifts to rather minor jungle scenes and at length to the discovery of a hidden valley in deepest Africa. The valley contains a lake which, when drained, reveals an ancient Egyptian city. Our heroes battle various monsters, Egyptian priests and much more until they eventually return to the modern world.

This type of haggard Haggard remained unvaried for the second issue, dated June/July 1931. In this issue the lead novel was by brother Elliott, for all that any difference was noticeable. "The Bowl of Death" concerns our hero, who, engaged in aerial combat, crashes into the Mexican desert. There he discovers—yes, a hidden valley, an Aztec city, a fortune in gold and jewels, petrified soldiers from the days of Cortés, degenerated Aztec natives and the usual beautiful girl. After much derring-do fighting various monsters and priests, the two escape, repair the airplane, and fly off to be married. This story is apparently Elliott Dold's only attempt at fiction, for which we can be thankful. His illustrations for the second issue, however, were as fine as for the first.

Victor Rousseau was present in both issues. "Outlaws of the Sun" in the first is set on Circe, the outermost planet, where our protagonists face "monsters, giants, and walking cannibal plants." "Revolt on Inferno" is set on the prison planet Inferno, far beyond Pluto, where a group of men and women are banished by the dictator of Earth, much like the convicts to Botany Bay. Needless to say, our hero soon develops a secret weapon, conquers various monsters and the prison authorities, returns to Earth, defeats the dictator and frees the population.

The second issue carried a novelette, "Fish-Men of Arctica," by John Miller Gregory, a name that appeared only this once in the pages of the SF magazines, although he was probably a regular contributor to Hersey's other magazines. Certainly he had three stories in *Ghost Stories*, and equally certainly his idea of science fiction was little above the juvenile level, probably culled from reading a few issues of the Clayton *Astounding*. His story tells of a race of fish-men who have lived under the Arctic Ocean for millennia. They plan to use a magnetic ray to draw the moon back to its original position in the Arctic and thus enable the Arctic to bloom once more, although it will probably destroy the rest of the earth in the process. Our hero, Jim Fentress, along with a beautiful girl and a supersubmarine, travels to the Arctic to do battle with the fish-men.

Elliott Dold's illness was perhaps fortuitous in that it brought an end to a magazine that, had it continued, would have proved another of Hersey's failures. As it stands it can be reckoned an unresolved experiment. In all fairness, *Miracle* was no better and no worse than most other popular pulps at that time, and had Hersey attracted some of the better writers, the magazine might have developed. Today it is remembered primarily for its high-quality artwork and for its extreme rarity. Single copies are rarely offered by dealers, and when they do change hands they can command prices of $100. Complete sets are even more rare.

Information Sources

BIBLIOGRAPHY:
Hersey, Harold. *Pulpwood Editor*. New York: F. A. Stokes, 1937.
Nicholls. *Encyclopedia*.
Tuck.
INDEX SOURCES: ISFM; SFM; Tuck.
REPRINT SOURCES:
  Microform: Greenwood Press Periodical Series.
LOCATION SOURCES: M.I.T. Science Fiction Library.

Publication History

TITLE: *Miracle Science and Fantasy Stories*.
VOLUME DATA: Volume 1, Number 1, April/May 1931–Volume 1, Number 2, June/
    July 1931. Bi-monthly. Total run: 2 issues.
PUBLISHER: Good Story Magazine Co., Springfield, Massachusetts.

EDITOR: Elliott Dold (but see above essay).
FORMAT: Pulp, 144 pp.
PRICE: 20¢.

Howard DeVore

MODERN ELECTRICS

Technical magazine published by Hugo Gernsback which contained his first science fiction pieces. See SCIENCE AND INVENTION.

THE MOST THRILLING SCIENCE FICTION EVER TOLD

See THRILLING SCIENCE FICTION.

MY SELF MAGAZINE

See MIND MAGIC MAGAZINE.

THE MYSTERIOUS TRAVELER MAGAZINE

As a rule magazines generated by successful radio shows do not succeed in equal measure. *The Shadow** was the major exception, and perhaps in other fields there are other examples, but in the fantasy field all such magazines—*The Witch's Tales,* Suspense,* Tales of the Frightened**—came and went with startling rapidity.

The Mysterious Traveler Magazine, which first appeared in November 1951, was no exception. Inspired by the popular suspense programme "The Mysterious Traveler" from the Mutual Broadcasting System, the magazine concentrated on fiction in the same vein—mystery, suspense, detection, crime and the macabre. There was a token acknowledgment of science fiction, but it did not figure prominently in any issue. Even fantasy took a back seat. Ray Bradbury appeared in the first two issues, both stories being reprints. Murray Leinster, under his real name, Will Jenkins, was in the first issue, and Sax Rohmer figured in the third. One of William Hope Hodgson's Carnacki stories made the final issue. The magazine relied strongly on reprints. It was edited by Robert Arthur, who wrote many of the stories for the *Mysterious Traveler* radio series, most based on his stories from the pulps.

There was a noticeable lack of editorial presence in the magazine, which, along with the absence of illustrative material, gave it a rather bland, anonymous character. The magazine held no appeal for the SF or fantasy market. Despite many big names, such as John Dickson Carr, Edgar Wallace, Dorothy Sayers, Cornell Woolrich and Agatha Christie, it clearly held no appeal for the mystery market either, and this was probably due to the relative accessibility of many of the stories elsewhere. Later issues tried to coax reader response with a cover contest requesting stories to be written around the Norman Saunders covers. Over 400 entries were received for the first, but the story was never printed in the magazine. A point of interest is that among the honorable mentions was the name Edward Hoch, today a very prolific mystery writer and an occasional exponent of SF and fantasy.

Information Sources

BIBLIOGRAPHY:
Nicholls. *Encyclopedia.*
Tuck.
INDEX SOURCES: Cook, Michael L., *Monthly Murders*, Westport, Conn.: Greenwood
    Press, 1982; MIT; MT; SFM.
REPRINT SOURCES: None known.
LOCATION SOURCES: M.I.T. Science Fiction Library; Pennsylvania State University
    Library.

Publication History

TITLE: *The Mysterious Traveler Magazine*, November 1951–June 1952. Retitled *The
    Mysterious Traveler Mystery Reader*, issue 5, undated.
VOLUME DATA: Volume 1, Number 1, November 1951–Number 5, [September] 1952.
    Volume numbering ceased with issue 4, June 1952. First three issues bi-monthly,
    thereafter quarterly. Total run: 5 issues.
PUBLISHER: Grace Publishing Co., New York.
EDITOR: Robert Arthur.
FORMAT: Digest; 144 pp., first issue; 160 pp., January–June 1952; 128 pp., last issue.
PRICE: 35¢.

Mike Ashley

THE MYSTERIOUS TRAVELER MYSTERY READER

See THE MYSTERIOUS TRAVELER MAGAZINE.

THE MYSTERIOUS WU FANG

In an attempt to capitalize on the continued interest in "yellow peril" fiction, Popular Publications started *The Mysterious Wu Fang* in 1935. The lead character was clearly modeled on Sax Rohmer's Fu Manchu—a Mandarin with thoughts of world domination. Needless to say, his first line of attack is the United States, and New York City in particular. Aiding in Wu Fang's endeavors were all sorts of sinister orientals, dacoits, beast-men and turncoat occidentals. Wu Fang also controlled a horde of poisonous bugs, spiders and rodents, many of them unknown to modern science.

The novels were written by Robert J. Hogan, the author of the *G-8* series as well as other pulp material. During the run of *Wu Fang*, Hogan was averaging 130,000 to 150,000 words a month. He was given instructions to submit first drafts and not bother rewriting—deadlines had to be met! The Wu Fang novels featured a Nayland Smith imitation named Val Kildare who battled the sinister oriental with the aid of several assistants, including one youngster (to appeal to the younger pulp magazine readership). There was the obligatory mysterious female and plenty of torture. The novels continued issue after issue, but did feature changing characters and locations as Wu Fang was repeatedly thwarted.

In a further attempt to imitate the Fu Manchu series, Popular hired artist John Richard Flanagan, who had worked on the Fu Manchu magazine appearances, to illustrate Wu Fang. But an imitation was an imitation, and the magazine did not sell well.

Even the accompanying short stories were no saving grace. All were oriental villain stories written without much imagination or plot (most were less than ten pages long), and had few if any SF or fantasy elements. Most had typical pulp plots that could be used for whatever area the editor demanded with minimal rewriting—an oriental villain, a western outlaw, and so on. Most of them were written by Steve Fisher, Frank Gruber, O. B. Meyers and Frank Beaston.

After seven issues Popular decided to kill the magazine. It was a prompt decision since the cover for the next issue had been prepared. Instead, this was used on a new oriental villain pulp, *Dr. Yen Sin.**

Information Sources

BIBLIOGRAPHY:
Carr, Wooda Nicholas. "The Mysterious Wu Fang." *Doc Savage Club Reader*, No. 8 (1979): 5–8.
Gruber, Frank. *The Pulp Jungle*. Los Angeles: Sherbourne Press, 1967.
INDEX SOURCES: Weinberg, Robert, and Lohr McKinstry, *The Hero Pulp Index*, Evergreen, Colo.: Opar Press, 1971 (lists lead novels only).
REPRINT SOURCES:
  Novel: The first novel, *The Case of the Six Coffins*, was reprinted by Robert Weinberg as *Pulp Classics 8* (Oak Lawn, Ill.: Pulp Press, 1976).
LOCATION SOURCES: San Francisco Academy of Comic Art; University of California–Los Angeles Library (Vol. 1, No. 1 only).

Publication History

TITLE: *The Mysterious Wu Fang*.
VOLUME DATA: Volume 1, Number 1, September 1935–Volume 2, Number 3, March 1936. Four issues per volume. Monthly. Total run: 7 issues.
PUBLISHER: Popular Publications, New York.

EDITOR: Edythe Seims (under Rogers Terrill).
FORMAT: Pulp, 128 pp., September–November 1935; thereafter 112 pp.
PRICE: 10¢.

Robert Weinberg

MYSTERY ADVENTURE MAGAZINE

See MYSTERY ADVENTURES.

MYSTERY ADVENTURES

Mystery Adventures was a mid-1930s pulp that had no defined fiction policy. In each issue it presented a potpourri of pulp themes, usually an SF story, a weird-menace tale, an occasional fantasy and several nonfantasy adventures. It is generally acknowledged by SF collectors because of the October 1936 issue, which featured a Zenith Rand space adventure by sometime SF writer Richard Tooker. But the issue was not typical of the magazine's run; although other space stories did appear, they were no more regular than in other general adventure fiction pulps like *Argosy*.*

There were occasional weird fantasies, such as "Buried Alive" by Wayne Rogers (July 1936), about a wicked uncle's Svengali-like control of a young boy, and "Rescued by Satan" by Richard B. Sale (May 1936), which features a were-tiger, but again, they were not typical.

Today, the factor more likely to make the magazine a collector's item of peripheral interest to the SF fan is the early non-SF adventure stories by L. Ron Hubbard that appeared regularly in its pages.

Information Sources

BIBLIOGRAPHY:
Cook, Michael. *Mystery, Detective and Espionage Magazines.* Westport, Conn.: Greenwood, 1983.
Goulart, Ron. *Cheap Thrills.* New Rochelle, N.Y.: Arlington House, 1972.
Jones, Robert K. *The Shudder Pulps.* West Linn, Ore.: Fax Collector's Editions, 1975. Tuck.
INDEX SOURCES: Austin, William N., *Macabre Index.* Seattle, Wash.: FAPA 52, 1952 (incomplete issue listing); Cook, Fred, and Gordon Huber. "Index to *New Mystery Adventure/Mystery Adventure Magazine/Mystery Adventures Magazine* (Pt. 1)." *Xenophile,* No. 22 (1976), and "Pt. 2," *Xenophile,* No. 30 (1977); Tuck.
REPRINT SOURCES:
  Facsimile edition: October 1936 issue, reprinted by Odyssey Publications, Melrose Highlands, Mass., 1976.
LOCATION SOURCES: None known.

Publication History

TITLE: *Mystery Adventures*. Retitled *New Mystery Adventures* with the fourth issue, then *Mystery Adventure Magazine* from May to November 1936, then reverted to *Mystery Adventures*.

VOLUME DATA: The volume numbering is confusing. Volume 1, Number 1, February/ March 1935–Volume 5, Number 4, May 1937. Volume 1, four issues, bi-monthly, but fourth issue January 1936. Volume 2 continued the issue numbering of Volume 1, but then merged with Volume 3, which took its issue numbering from the start of *New Mystery Adventures*, hence Volume 3, Number 6, August 1936. Volumes 4 and 5, four issues per volume, monthly (but no April 1937 issue). Total run: 25 issues.

PUBLISHER: Pierre Publications, February/March 1935–December 1935/January 1936; Fiction Magazines Inc., February/March 1936–November 1936; Good Story Magazines, December 1936–May 1937.

EDITORS: A. R. Roberts, February/March 1935–December 1935/January 1936; W. W. Hubbard, February/March 1936–October 1936; H. D. Hubbard, November 1936; Harold Hersey, December 1936–May 1937.

FORMAT: Pulp, 112 pp.

PRICE: Volume 1, 20¢; thereafter 15¢.

Mike Ashley

MYSTIC MAGAZINE

Mystic Magazine should not be confused with the short-lived pulp, also called *Mystic Magazine*, that ran from November 1930 to April 1931 and was edited by August Derleth. That magazine laid an emphasis on occult articles; the last issue was retitled *True Mystic Crimes*, and Derleth resigned rather than compromise his principles with the publisher.

The 1950s *Mystic* had much the same policy, although the earlier issues had a stronger bias toward fiction. In 1953 Raymond A. Palmer was having financial problems with *Other Worlds Science Stories*.* In order to pay his printer he sold out his share in Clark Publishing to his partner Curtis Fuller, who thereby became the sole publisher of the nonfiction *Fate*. Palmer now incorporated himself as Palmer Publications, converted *Other Worlds* to *Science Stories*,* and brought out a new *Fate*-like magazine called *Mystic*.

While *Mystic* endeavored to establish itself, possibly with the intention of eventually going nonfiction (Palmer called for readers to submit their true occult experiences from the first issue), it published predominantly fiction. All was of the fantastic variety, with Palmer's own Shaver-and flying-saucer-influenced extravaganzas balanced by some readable stories by Randall Garrett, Robert Barbour Johnson, Joseph Payne Brennan and William Campbell Gault.

By the fourth issue, however, the nonfiction was starting to outweigh the stories, and even they took on a quasi-confessional slant with Rog Phillips writing Hindu fantasies as "Sanandana Kumara," plus a series of fictional essays by

Paul M. Vest about flying saucers. What had started out as a promising fantasy companion to *Science Stories* rapidly devolved into a nonfiction echo of *Fate*.

By the eighth issue in February 1955, fiction had all but disappeared. Of minor interest is the October 1955 issue, in which Palmer and Shaver discuss the Shaver Mystery at length.

Palmer retained the *Mystic* title for a further eight issues and then changed it to *Search* as being more relevant to the occult material he was publishing.

Information Sources

BIBLIOGRAPHY:
Tuck.
INDEX SOURCES: MT; SFM.
REPRINT SOURCES: None known.
LOCATION SOURCES: M.I.T. Science Fiction Library.

Publication History

TITLE: *Mystic Magazine*, November 1953–July 1956. Thereafter entitled *Search* and
    contents nonfiction.
VOLUME DATA: Number 1, November 1953–Number 16, July 1956; issue numbering
    was continued by *Search*. Last issue sighted Number 66, November 1965, but
    publication continued for several years afterward.
PUBLISHER: Palmer Publications, Evanston, Illinois.
EDITOR: Ray Palmer. (Bea Mahaffey is listed on the masthead of early issues, but
    Palmer selected all the material and assembled the issues.)
FORMAT: Digest, 128 pp.
PRICE: 35¢. (*Search* was still 35¢ in 1965.)

Mike Ashley

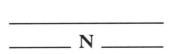

NEBULA SCIENCE FICTION

Nebula was somewhat unusual in the British SF magazine field in that it was the only publication to be based in Scotland. Yet it was also one of the most cosmopolitan of magazines, frequently featuring new stories by American and Australian writers.

Nebula was very much a one-man band, produced by its editor Peter Hamilton. It came about through a fortuitous set of circumstances. Hamilton was eighteen and had just left school (and not a nursing home, as he jokingly said in his first editorial) and was looking for work. His parents were proprietors of a printing firm at a time when work was sporadic, and they were considering going into some occasional publishing to fill in the times when the machinery was standing idle. Hamilton jumped at this opportunity and suggested at first a series of science fiction novels. The family at last agreed and plans went ahead, but when Hamilton visited the local wholesalers who would handle much of the distribution he was advised that a regular magazine would have more chance of success than an irregular pocketbook series. And so *Nebula* was born, with the first issue released with a cover date of Autumn 1952. Two novels had already been purchased for the projected pocketbook series, and these now formed the lead novels for the first two issues: "Robots Never Weep" by E. R. James, and "Thou Pasture Us" by F. G. Rayer.

Hamilton's family had not been prepared for a regular magazine, since the machinery had not lain idle all the time; therefore, *Nebula* was only given the go-ahead provided it fitted in with other commissions, and was not given priority. This contributed in part to *Nebula*'s erratic schedule in its early years.

The first issue, which was assembled with much help from Kenneth F. Slater, A. Vincent Clarke and especially John Brunner, included only two short stories aside from the novel: a vignette by new writer Peter J. Ridley and "Letter from the Stars,'' a reprint of A. E. van Vogt's 1949 story ''Dear Pen Pal.'' None of the stories was indicative of things to come; of more importance in this respect were the nonfiction departments, which showed Hamilton's leaning toward fandom and his determination to have reader involvement. He announced a competition for new short stories and novels, commissioned the Irish archfan Walt Willis to write a regular fan column and, starting in the second issue, carried a regular ''Scientifilm Preview'' by Forrest J Ackerman. Later issues featured a book review column by Kenneth Slater and a letter column.

Although the first issue had a mixed reception, the second received such an enthusiastic response that Hamilton planned to change his publication schedule from quarterly to bi-monthly. By the fourth issue he was able to boast that *Nebula* was now

the ''favourite'' of a large percentage of its readers and has a literary standard second to no other magazine in this country.

There are two reasons for this remarkable progress: firstly *Nebula* pays higher fees to authors than any other British science-fiction magazine (and naturally obtains correspondingly better stories) and secondly, *Nebula* is the only British magazine which actually gives the readers a say in editorial policy.[1]

Proof of the first fact was the number of leading writers—both British and American—whom *Nebula* attracted with new stories, in particular Eric Frank Russell, who had been selling exclusively to the States in recent years and who had ten stories in *Nebula*, five of which had not been published previously. Hamilton also acquired several stories from Robert A. Heinlein that had seen prior American publication, but not in the regular SF magazines. In *Nebula*'s last year, 1959, Hamilton acquired a new Heinlein novel for advanced serialization, but unfortunately the magazine folded before it could be published.

Hamilton's most impressive record must be in the number of new writers he launched in *Nebula*. He bought Brian W. Aldiss' first story, ''T,'' although he did not publish it for a few years. Aldiss recalls that Hamilton took great pains in encouraging his writing and with ''All the World's Tears'' (May 1957) published a story that attracted much reader response and thereafter made Aldiss a name to follow. Bob Shaw first appeared in print with ''Aspect'' (August 1954) and sold six stories in all to *Nebula* before withdrawing from SF for six years. Perhaps more remarkable was that Hamilton launched Robert Silverberg's career, publishing his first story, ''Gorgon Planet,'' in the February 1954 issue—paying him at the rate of four cents a word—higher than many American magazines.[2] He also published the first stories in Britain by John Brunner and the American Thomas Burnett Swann (who went on to make his name in another British magazine, *Science Fantasy**), and also bought the first story by Barrington J. Bayley, though he never published it.[3]

Nebula included a story-voting system much like *Astounding*'s (*Analog Science*

*Fiction**) "Analytical Laboratory," and an annual award for the most popular writer. In both cases the indisputable winner was E. C. Tubb, who also had more stories in *Nebula* than anyone else—thirty-one, including those under four pen names—most of novelette and novella length. Other writers who consistently rated high were William F. Temple, Kenneth Bulmer and Eric Frank Russell.

Hamilton also paid attention to illustrators, and *Nebula* featured the first covers by Eddie Jones and Ken McIntyre, plus a regular back cover illustration by Arthur Thomson who, along with Gerard Quinn and Alan Hunter, provided the best of the interior art. Hamilton made full use of the covers, the inside of the front and back covers being devoted to a series of short articles by "Kenneth Johns" (Kenneth Bulmer and John Newman) on matters scientific and astronomical—the higher-grade paper allowing better reproductions of the photographs used to illustrate the series.

After the twelfth issue problems between Hamilton and his family's printing firm were endangering *Nebula*'s future, and so Hamilton took over full responsibility for the magazine, eventually securing a new printer in Dublin. This allowed him to have more control over the magazine's publishing schedule. He soon brought *Nebula* onto a regular bi-monthly and then, from January 1958, monthly schedule. In his editorial in *Nebula* 24 (September 1957), Hamilton reported that the magazine's circulation now averaged 40,000 copies, ten times the sale of the first issue. All this gave Hamilton the confidence to acquire novels and *Nebula*'s first—and it so happened, last—serial, "Wisdom of the Gods" by Kenneth Bulmer, which ran from July to October 1958. Proclaiming the new serial in his editorial, Hamilton continued:

> But this is by no means the only innovation made possible by a dependable publishing schedule. Definite commissions can be offered to well known science-fiction authors and it is now possible for me to lay plans for the future of the magazine with greater confidence than at any other time in its history.[4]

But such plans did not come to fruition. *Nebula* relied heavily on its foreign circulation. Only 25 percent of its sales were in Britain. America accounted for about 33 percent, Australia another 25 percent and South Africa nearly ten percent. Import restrictions, first in South Africa and then in Australia, followed by crippling excise duties on other exports, suddenly left *Nebula* heavily in debt. With no capital behind him, Hamilton was unable to support the magazine, and there was no alternative but to cease publication. He subsequently established himself in the retail trade with a number of record shops, and even started a small recording company, but for twenty years he totally vanished from the SF scene. Recently, however, he has intimated that he would like to return, and if the opportunity presented itself, *Nebula* could even be revived.

Despite *Nebula*'s popularity, few of its stories are remembered today because, although they had immediate appeal, they soon became dated. Those with a more lasting quality include the thirteen contributions by Brian W. Aldiss, especially "Dumb Show" (December 1956), "Ten-Storey Jigsaw" (January 1958), "Legend of Smith's Burst" (June 1959) and the two already mentioned. A few other stories have resurfaced in author collections, and some were reprinted in American magazines, but unaccountably overlooked are John Brunner's "The Number of My Days" (December 1956), Eric Frank Russell's "Fly Away Peter" (April 1954) and James White's "Dark Talisman" (October 1958), as well as many of E. C. Tubb's contributions. *Nebula* was always an entertaining magazine, always friendly, and always hopeful. It was a sterling example of what one man can achieve and shows the kind of spirit that pervades the SF field as no other. Hamilton ranks with such people as William Crawford and Raymond Palmer who, despite all the odds, determined to and for a period successfully published their own SF magazines. It is this determination that makes SF and its fans such a force to be reckoned with.

Notes

The author wishes to thank Peter Hamilton for his assistance in the research and writing of this essay.

1. [Peter Hamilton], "Look Here . . . ," *Nebula* 4 (Autumn 1953): 2.

2. See Robert Silverberg's essay, "Sounding Brass, Tinkling Cymbal," in *Hell's Cartographers*, ed. Brian W. Aldiss and Harry Harrison (London: Weidenfeld & Nicholson, 1975), p. 15.

3. There remains some confusion over this story of Bayley's. Bayley himself is convinced it was never published. Hamilton recalls holding the story over for a while for technical reasons until there was a suitable moment to include it, but did not think that this would have been for any longer than a year, which would place it in 1956 or so. But the only story by Bayley published in *Nebula* was "Consolidation" under the alias John Diamond in the January 1959 issue.

4. [Peter Hamilton], "Look Here . . . ," *Nebula* 32 (July 1958): 2.

Information Sources

BIBLIOGRAPHY:
Nicholls. *Encyclopedia.*
Tuck.
INDEX SOURCES: IBSF; Jakubowski, Maxim, *Nebula: An Index*, Stourbridge, U.K.: B.S.F.A., 1963 (listing by issue, author and title, plus an appreciation by Brian W. Aldiss and an introduction by E. C. Tubb); MIT; SFM; Tuck.
REPRINT SOURCES: None known.
LOCATION SOURCES: McGill University Library; M.I.T. Science Fiction Library; Pennsylvania State University Library; University of New Brunswick Library.

Publication History

TITLE: *Nebula Science Fiction.*
VOLUME DATA: Volume 1, Number 1, Autumn 1952–Number 41, June 1959. Volume numbering ceased with Volume 2, Number 5 (whole issue 9). First three issues labeled quarterly, and bi-monthly from issue 4, but publication irregular, as fol-

lows: No. 1, Autumn 1952; 2, Spring 1953; 3, Summer 1953; 4, Autumn 1953; 5, September 1953; 6, December 1953; 7, February 1954; 8, April 1954; 9, August 1954; 10, October 1954; 11, December 1954; 12, April 1955; 13, September 1955; 14, November 1955; 15, January 1956; 16, March 1956; 17, July 1956; 18, November 1956; 19, December 1956; 20, March 1957; 21, May 1957; 22, July 1957; 23, August 1957; 24, September 1957; 25, October 1957; 26–39, monthly, January 1958–February 1959; 40, May 1959; 41, June 1959. Total run: 41 issues.

PUBLISHER: Crownpoint Publications, Autumn 1952–April 1955 (company name dropped from December 1953); Peter Hamilton, September 1955–June 1959.

EDITOR: Peter Hamilton.

FORMAT: Large Digest, 120 pp., Nos. 1–3; 128 pp., Nos. 4–6; 130 pp., No. 7; 136 pp., No. 8; 128 pp., Nos. 9–12; 112 pp., Nos. 13–41.

PRICE: 2/– for all issues but Nos. 40 and 41, at 2/6d.

Mike Ashley

NEW MYSTERY ADVENTURES

See MYSTERY ADVENTURES.

NEW WORLDS

The story of *New Worlds* is to a great extent the history of British science fiction in the postwar years. Most British writers of renown have appeared in its pages, many for the first time; in fact, its very existence resulted in the recognition of the depth of SF talent in Britain.

The history of *New Worlds* began in February 1939, but prior to that had existed a fanzine called *Novæ Terrae* (the link between the titles is obvious). *Novæ Terrae* had been founded in March 1936 by Maurice K. Hanson for the Nuneaton branch of the Science Fiction League run by *Wonder Stories*.*[1] Hanson subsequently moved to London, and when the Science Fiction Association (SFA) was established in 1937, *Novæ Terrae* became the official news organ.[2]

After twenty-nine issues, however, Hanson tired of his exceptional workload[3] and handed the magazine over to John Carnell, who retitled it *New Worlds* and reverted to Volume 1, Number 1 with the March 1939 issue.

Carnell, then twenty-six, had been associate editor of *Novæ Terrae* (along with Arthur C. Clarke and later William F. Temple) for the past two years, and as Hanson continued to help with the magazine, the shift in responsibility was only slight. The magazine was edited from the notorious "Flat" in Grays Inn Road, London, where all the celebrities of British SF of the 1930s appeared at least once.

New Worlds lasted for four issues until the outbreak of war in September 1939 curtailed the activities of the SFA.[4] However, during that year Carnell had made the acquaintance of W. J. Passingham, a sports and adventure fiction writer with a penchant for SF. Passingham had provisionally interested a publisher, the World Says Ltd., in issuing a science fiction magazine, and in January 1940 Carnell was given the go-ahead to prepare three issues.

> By early February the initial issue was beginning to round out. Harry Turner of Manchester . . . had submitted some magnificent cover lettering; artist Chester . . . had produced a number of cover roughs, and three other London artists . . . had been commissioned for illustrations as soon as the stories had been selected. . . .
> Unfortunately my records do not show the story line-up for that first issue . . . but I do remember that one novelette was Robert A. Heinlein's "Lost Legion" which later appeared under his pseudonym of "Lyle Monroe" in *Super Science Stories*.[*][5]

British writers John F. Burke, C. S. Youd (John Christopher) and David McIlwain (C. E. Maine) were asked for stories, and Americans like Jack Williamson, L. Sprague de Camp and Donald Wollheim had pledged their support. All seemed set when, in mid-March, the company suddenly collapsed amid internal squabbling and double-dealing, just weeks before the first issue was due to appear. So, even before its first official appearance in 1946, *New Worlds* had already had a checkered history—a foretaste of things to come.

From 1940 to 1946 Carnell served in the Royal Artillery. Demobilized in January 1946, he had a chance meeting with fan and writer Frank Edward Arnold that led to an introduction to Stephen D. Frances of Pendulum Publications. Frances (better known as "Hank Janson") had much faith in the future of SF, and *New Worlds* was again given the green light. This time everything went smoothly, and the first issue, undated, appeared in July 1946, pulp-sized with just sixty-four pages. The lead story was "The Mill of the Gods" by Maurice G. Hugi, but voted best by the readers and still considered one of his best early stories was "The Three Pylons" by William F. Temple.

Initial sales, however, were appalling—3,000 copies out of a print run of 15,000.[6] Yet the second issue, released in October, was a complete sellout due to a deliberate sales drive by the publisher. Carnell also suspected that the cover, which had been more impressive than Bob Wilkin's flat design for the first issue, had contributed to the success, and so the publisher rebound the first issue in a renumbered cover from the second issue. The result was another success. Completist collectors therefore should be aware of the two variant first issues.

The third issue appeared in October 1947, by which time the publisher was in all manner of difficulties. Pendulum went into receivership, and *New Worlds* was once again mothballed.

During 1946–1947, regular Thursday night meetings had been established at the White Horse Tavern in Fetter Lane, meetings immortalized in Arthur C. Clarke's *Tales from the White Hart*. At one meeting someone—alas, history does not record who—suggested that the regulars form their own company and publish *New Worlds*. The idea was taken up by Frank Cooper, who shaped the dream into reality. At the one-day convention held in London in May 1948, Carnell was able to inform attendees that the planned Nova Publications Ltd. was fast taking shape, and by early 1949 it was in business. *New Worlds* 4 appeared in April of that year, in a smaller, digest size, contents little changed from the planned fourth Pendulum issue. A fifth issue appeared in September, and by spring 1950 *New Worlds* was on a regular quarterly schedule. It had been taken to heart by the British fans and was an established success—a fact that was underlined by the appearance of a companion magazine, *Science Fantasy*,* in the summer of 1950.

Already *New Worlds* was presenting the best fiction by the core of British writers—Arthur C. Clarke, A. Bertram Chandler, John Beynon Harris, William F. Temple, F. G. Rayer, Peter Phillips—and as *New Worlds* was able to increase its schedule to bi-monthly and finally monthly, other writers were able to see that here was a regular, reliable magazine that made writing and experimenting with fiction worthwhile. By the end of 1952 Peter Hawkins, John Christopher, J. T. McIntosh, E. C. Tubb, Dan Morgan, Lan Wright, James White and John F. Burke had joined the ever-growing crowd of regular contributors.

Science fiction publishing entered a boom period in Britain in the early 1950s, but Carnell had very much cornered the market, his only serious rivals in the magazine field being *Authentic Science Fiction** and *Nebula*.* Carnell was also establishing himself as a literary agent and was at the very heart of the British SF scene. In 1952 he produced an anthology *No Place Like Earth*, with many of the stories selected from *New Worlds*, and endeavors such as this helped cement *New Worlds* firmly in position as Britain's premier SF magazine.

Perhaps one of Carnell's best discoveries at this time was artist Gerard A. Quinn, who first appeared in the Spring 1951 issue. His style was ideally suited to SF and was far superior to that of the magazine's other illustrators. His cover for the May 1952 issue (only his second) was one of the most advanced, and still one of the best covers to appear on any British SF magazine.

A number of external problems beset *New Worlds* in 1953, but the magazine's foundations were bolstered when Nova Publications was absorbed by the Maclaren Company.[7] The result was that when *New Worlds* reappeared in a slightly smaller format after a ten-month gap in April 1954, it was on a regular monthly schedule that was retained until 1964.[8]

It was from this issue that *New Worlds* really took shape. Kenneth Bulmer, Brian Aldiss, John Brunner and Arthur Sellings joined the ranks of its contributors, and Carnell began to include the occasional reprint of American stories that had appeared in publications not readily available to British readers. This was especially evident in the serials, which included "Take-Off" by Cyril Kornbluth and "Wild Talent" by Wilson Tucker in 1954, "The Time Masters" by Tucker in 1955, "Time out of Joint" by Philip K. Dick in 1959–1960, and "Venus plus X" by Theodore Sturgeon in 1961. Many of these novels might otherwise have appeared in the Nova SF Novels series that was also launched in 1953 with *Stowaway to Mars* by John Beynon, but it never survived the Maclaren merger.

With the solid reliability of *New Worlds* and *Science Fantasy* Britain was able to build a strong team of writers, and by the late 1950s—when J. G. Ballard, Colin Kapp, John Kippax, Donald Malcolm and Robert Presslie had been added to the lists—*New Worlds* could boast some of the finest SF anywhere. It is difficult to limit a selection to just a few examples to typify *New Worlds* SF during this heyday when there is such a wealth of choice. But one cannot ignore the pivotal stories by J. G. Ballard like "Build-up" (January 1957), "Track 12" (April 1958), "The Waiting Grounds" (November 1959), "The Voices of Time" (October 1960), "The Overloaded Man" (July 1961), "Billenium" (November 1961), "The Subliminal Man" (January 1963) and "The Terminal Beach" (March 1964). These were unlike anything else appearing in the SF magazines, and Carnell is to be commended for his foresight. He also was the first to publish Harry Harrison's controversial story "The Streets of Ashkelon" (September 1962)—although he had already rejected it once.[9] James White's very popular Sector General series appeared in *New Worlds* from 1957 onwards, as did many of Brian Aldiss' experimental stories, including "Psyclops" (July 1956), "Oh, Ishrael!" (April 1957), "The Pit My Parish" (January 1958), "Segregation" (July 1958), "The Towers of San Ampa" (February 1959), "Old Hundredth" (November 1960) and "Basis for Negotiation" (January 1962); and stories and serials like "Unit" by J. T. McIntosh (February 1957), "Tableau" by James White (May 1958), "A Man Called Destiny" by Lan Wright (December 1958– February 1959), "The Outstretched Hand" by Arthur Sellings (May 1959) and "Lambda 1" by Colin Kapp (December 1962).

New Worlds included "The Literary Line-up" as a regular feature. It looked forward to future issues and showed readers' votes on past issues—rather like *Analog Science Fiction*'s* "Analytical Laboratory." An analysis of the results reveals that authors who consistently won popular votes were Colin Kapp, James White, J. G. Ballard, E. C. Tubb and Lan Wright.

The "golden era' of *New Worlds* was certainly between 1956 and 1961. Thereafter the quality of fiction and the standard of presentation declined. Presentation had never been laudable. As early as August 1957 Carnell had taken the drastic step of omitting all interior artwork, except for fillers. "Art-work in the digest-size magazines is as out of date as a coal fire," he stated.[10] As a result the decorative and skillful illustrations of Gerard Quinn and Gordon Hutchings vanished, and artwork was only kept alive in the innovative covers by Brian Lewis and occasionally Quinn. More frequently from July 1962 onwards, the covers were a montage of author photographs; toward the end there was no cover art at all. Carnell's presence grew less evident as the magazine presented a series of guest editorials. The lack of enthusiasm in the blurbs and departments gave the impression that Carnell had become apathetic and disinterested. Even the title of his editorial for the March 1964 issue was "1964—A Dull Year," and that written even before the year had started!

The truth was that Carnell was convinced that SF's future did not lie in magazines. Throughout the early 1960s *New Worlds* had been suffering from steadily declining sales.[11] The companion magazine *Science Fiction Adventures** had folded in May 1963, and at a directors' meeting that September it was agreed to cease publication of both *New Worlds* and *Science Fantasy*. When readers learned the news letters poured in, including one from Michael Moorcock that suitably presented the case for *New Worlds*:

It is only of secondary importance that *New Worlds* and *Science Fantasy* are folding. The main tragedy is that the magazine is losing one of its most open-minded editors. As I have said elsewhere, sf often claims to be far-out when, in fact, it rarely is. It should be far-out—it needs editors who are willing to take a risk on a story and run it even though this may bring criticism on their heads.

You have published over the years a great many controversial stories and a great many good straight-forward ones. You have also published the early work of most of our best British writers. You have discovered, encouraged and advised scores of young writers. It is probably thanks to your early encouragement that we nowadays have so many good writers in this country. The magazines have had their ups and downs, suffering from the fact that the moment you have trained a writer up to a certain standard, he has left you for the more lucrative American markets. How, I wonder, is the potential to be found and trained in future?[12]

At the last minute *New Worlds* and *Science Fantasy* were saved. David Warburton of the publishers Roberts and Vinter was looking for a respectable magazine as a "front" to their more regular publications (which ironically included Hank Janson adventures), and he purchased the two titles.[13] Carnell recommended Moorcock to succeed as editor, as by now Carnell was contracted to edit the New Writings in SF series.

Moorcock was committed to a new approach from the outset. "The sf reader is an intelligent reader, dissatisfied, perhaps, with other forms of literary entertainment, who looks to sf for something more relevant to his own life and times. Also he wants variety of ideas, style, mood and plot. We intend to keep the contents of *New Worlds* both varied and stimulating."[14]

The revived *New Worlds* appeared in May 1964 in a pocketbook format as opposed to the more "slick" approach Moorcock had intended at first. While contents like Brunner's "The Last Lonely Man" and Aldiss' "Never Let Go of My Hand" could not be considered innovative, a clue to the direction in which Moorcock planned to go was evident in J. G. Ballard's essay on William S. Burroughs and Moorcock's associated editorial.

Within a few issues Moorcock was already making his presence felt, publishing stories that could not have appeared anywhere else. One of the most effective, and certainly most controversial, from this period was Langdon Jones' "I Remember, Anita . . . ," a powerful story of the near future. Jones was just one of a rapidly growing coterie of writers including George Collyn, Barry Bayley, John Hamilton, Charles Platt, David I. Masson and Michael Butterworth who would soon make *New Worlds* their home.

What was increasingly evident was the number of American writers who found a less restrictive market in *New Worlds*, most significantly Roger Zelazny and Thomas M. Disch. Zelazny's "Love Is an Imaginary Number" (January 1966), "For a Breath I Tarry" (March 1966) and "The Keys to December" (August 1966) all appeared first in *New Worlds*, as did Disch's "Invaded by Love" (September 1966), "The Squirrel Cage" (October 1966) and the novel "Echo Round His Bones" (December 1966–January 1967). When interviewed in 1968, Disch commented: "I couldn't have published *Echo Round His Bones* in America, although my agent tried. This is a very straight, and standard novel, perhaps too much so for the American magazines."[15] The rift between the British and American publications was becoming increasingly apparent.

Perhaps the most significant story published at this time was Moorcock's own "Behold the Man" (September 1966), which went on to win the Nebula Award for Best Novella of the year. A case could be made, however, for Moorcock's "Preliminary Data" (August 1965), the first of his Jerry Cornelius stories, a series that would typify the British "new wave" movement of the 1960s.

In the space of two years *New Worlds* had established itself as a controversial, thought-provoking and invigorating magazine which, while not to everybody's taste, was always full of surprises. But trouble was looming. Thorpe and Porter, distributors for Roberts and Vinter, went into receivership in July 1966. They owed Roberts and Vinter a considerable amount of money, and this setback meant that the publishers decided to concentrate on their more lucrative "girlie" magazines. Although *New Worlds* and *Impulse** were not making a loss, they were too borderline to chance.

It seemed that finally *New Worlds* would fold, and in its final issues Moorcock "fired off all the guns [he] had left,"[16] including publishing complete in one issue Aldiss' bizarre novel *Report on Probability A* and reprinting Ballard's experimental "The Assassination of John Fitzgerald Kennedy Considered as a Downhill Motor Race."

However, in the autumn of 1966 Brian Aldiss, acting on impulse, had contacted the Arts Council—a government body established to develop and improve the knowledge, understanding and practice of the arts, and to increase the accessibility of the arts to the public throughout Great Britain. Aldiss, with the support of stalwarts like Angus Wilson, J. B. Priestley, Kingsley Amis and Marghanita Laski, who rallied to the cause, succeeded in obtaining a grant of £150 an issue for the continued publication of *New Worlds*. David Warburton agreed to continue to publish the magazine under a new imprint; Langdon Jones accompanied

Moorcock as associate editor and Charles Platt as designer, responsible for the layout and production of the new format.

The first independent issue, dated July 1967, was impressive. It had grown from a pocketbook to a glossy slick. Inset on the bold blue cover was a fascinating piece of impressionist artwork by the Dutch artist M. C. Escher, the subject of Platt's interior article "Expressing the Abstract." Also clearly revealed on the cover was the new definition of SF. What was once science fiction had now evolved into speculative fiction, a far more liberal phrase that still remained enigmatic. It meant virtually what one wanted it to mean, and was the blank check Moorcock needed to break down all the barriers that had hitherto held SF in restraint.

There could be no clearer example of the breakthrough than the lead novel that opened the issue—"Camp Concentration" by Thomas Disch. It tells of shady political machinations to enhance the intelligence of political prisoners somewhere in America. Disch wrote the outline in Austria and sold the basic outline for the novel to Berkley Books in America, but an outline and the finished product are often two entirely different creations. Most evident in the final draft was the explicitness of the language used by the main character, Mordecai. As Disch recalled, "The sequence that opens book two, where he describes his ravings; this is something that I might not have done but for knowing that *New Worlds* was there. It wanted to see how far I could force the language, until I had to break off and return to ordinary narrative."[17]

The sudden appearance of four-letter words other than Mars and Moon in science fiction came as a traumatic shock to many a reader. Those acquainted with general "mainstream" literature were not so startled, nor were the younger readers. The new *New Worlds* came at an opportune time. The "underground" establishment in Britain was beginning to make itself heard. The year 1967 was the famous year of "flower-power" and "swinging London." In the arts— especially music and fiction—a revolution was under way. The newspaper of the underground, *International Times*, had appeared in October 1966, and this was followed by *Oz* and a host of imitations. While its approach was from another angle, *New Worlds* rapidly became associated with these underground magazines (they shared the same typesetter), and to the establishment, the underground meant nothing but immorality and indecency. *New Worlds* was treading on very dangerous ground.

Diehard *science* fiction fans were not impressed with the new *New Worlds* which, in their eyes, had impudently turned its back on tradition. Fantasy devotees were delighted with at least part of the issue, Roger Zelazny's "In the House of the Dead." This bizarre tale of gods from the Egyptian pantheon *in persona* was an episode from his forthcoming novel, *Creatures of Light and Darkness* (1969), and was in complete contrast with the rest of the issue, which included Pamela Zoline's "The Heat Death of the Universe," John Sladek's "1937 AD" and Ballard's "The Death Module." Fiction aside, the issue con-

tained analytical and critical essays on a variety of topics—not necessarily connected with fiction—and this trend grew in succeeding issues.

More American writers began to take advantage of the new British liberalism,
among them Gene Wolfe and James Sallis. Sallis soon joined the editorial staff,
later becoming co-editor.

The twenty-first anniversary issue in October 1967 could not have differed
more from the fledgling pulp that John Carnell had issued in 1946. The edition
represented a signpost in the direction SF would take in the next twenty-one
years and ranged from the first part of Brian Aldiss' novel *An Age* (also known
as *Cryptozoic!*) to Charles Platt's "The City Dwellers." The future appeared
bright by the close of 1967, as Moorcock reported in his April 1968 editorial:

> The interim period is now over and the next issue will complete the
> sequence of changes, when we increase our size (price remaining the same)
> and begin introducing colour to inside pages. We have new distributors
> trying hard to put *New Worlds* in the hands of those it will interest. . . .
> Since last November we have also had new publishers who stepped in with
> the necessary backing when we had almost lost hope of continuing
> publication.[18]

But just as Moorcock's venture was proving itself, fate struck again. The fuse
had been lit with the December 1967 issue, which had begun serialization of
Norman Spinrad's *Bug Jack Barron*. The novel concerns a highly successful
television program of the future where the public are allowed to air their griev-
ances, and centers on the complaint by a Negro that he was not allowed to apply
to the Foundation for immortality. Again, this was a straightforward SF plot,
but it was the approach that made the difference. Spinrad pulled no punches in
detailing the active sex life of Barron, and this was what caused a stir. Suddenly
readers and bookstall browsers, who thought *New Worlds* merely a "BEM-and-
blaster" pulp with literary pretensions, discovered that it was far more adult
than they dared to think. The question was even asked in the House of Commons
as to why the Arts Council was "sponsoring filth."

The immediate effect was that two of Britain's leading bookseller chains—
W. H. Smith and John Menzies—withdrew the March 1968 issue from sale. As
if this financial loss was not enough, it came at a time when the Arts Council
was considering renewing the grant. Feeling that they were handling something
too hot, the grant was nearly cancelled, but eventually—and reluctantly—it was
renewed. With the combined aid of advertising revenues, a number of private
donations and much of Moorcock's own money, *New Worlds* survived, but only
by the skin of its teeth. The magazine was now temporarily banned in South
Africa, New Zealand and Australia, reducing even more its shaky income.

The March 1968 issue had been no different from many preceding ones. The
cover portrayed the Maharishi superimposed on a sketch of a cavorting stripper,
all of which was intended to advertise Charles Platt's center article "Fun Palace—

Not a Freakout," about Keith Albarn's fun palace at Margate—hardly cause for a ban. The lead story was Langdon Jones' "The Eye of the Lens," an extremely effective and atmospheric piece of symbolic writing; and there was another episode of *Bug Jack Barron*.

The furor that followed the withdrawal of that issue put *New Worlds* in an entirely new perspective. It began to attract support and interest from the literati, while at the same time becoming more and more associated with the underground press. The situation emphasized the near-sightedness of many people in the bookselling trade. Here was a publication supported on one hand by government funds, and banned on the other hand by major booksellers. In addition, there was nothing in *New Worlds* that had not been in existence in general literature for decades. The difference was that books by D. H. Lawrence, James Joyce and Henry Miller sold and were profitable to stock. *New Worlds* appealed only to a select readership, and the profit margin for a bookdealer was small. The magazine was regarded as being of minor interest, and Menzies refused to stock it, while Smith's left it to the discretion of individual managers.

New Worlds was forced to survive on subscription and donation alone. Support from the SF fraternity decreased as the months passed. Moorcock was now sole publisher, but, not having formed a company, was responsible for all debts. Having to support both himself and the magazine, he turned again to writing and began to churn out fantasy novels at an alarming rate. It is a credit to his writing ability that these are still compelling and fascinating reading despite their conveyor-belt production.

This meant that the various editorial tasks fell into other hands, predominantly those of Charles Platt and Graham Hall. Langdon Jones, Graham Charnock and James Sallis all offered their services throughout the troublesome period. The results were often good, if somewhat erratic.

The November 1968 issue was a special edition for new writers, featuring fiction from Robert Holdstock, Graham Charnock, M. John Harrison and others. December 1968's issue included Samuel Delany's future award-winner, "Time Considered as a Helix of Semi-Precious Stones," while Harlan Ellison's award-winning "A Boy and His Dog" first appeared in the April 1969 issue. It was only when these stories were given wider book publication that they were accorded due praise. Their initial publication in *New Worlds* emphasized that here was a magazine determined to broaden the scope of science fiction and thereby widen the horizons of literature. But the SF fraternity accorded *New Worlds* increasingly less attention during 1969, with the result that in the August 1969 issue Charles Platt declared: "*New Worlds* is not a science fiction magazine."[19]

What then was it? In Moorcock's words: "New Worlds was to be a magazine that could produce a worthwhile synthesis of post-war art, science and ideas presented in the form of fiction, chiefly, also poetry and graphics, running features that reflected current concerns in arts and sciences."[20]

In short, *New Worlds* was a magazine of artistic and scientific comment and experiment. Had it started life as such, it is doubtful that anyone would have commented. But because it was originally a science fiction magazine that suddenly changed direction it was viewed as a wolf in the fold.

New Worlds ventured further from its SF base and began serialization of Jack Trevor Story's *The Wind in the Snottygobble Tree* from the November 1969 issue. That same month saw the debut of Ian Watson with ''Roof Garden under Saturn.'' A regular feature of *New Worlds* was cunningly constructed graphic poems, of which D. M. Thomas' ''Hospital of Transplanted Hearts'' (January 1969) and John Sladek's ''Alien Territory'' (November 1969) are the most ingenious.

Despite all opposition, *New Worlds* reached its two hundredth issue in April 1970. In his editorial Moorcock pointed out that *New Worlds* was still walking a knife-edge and its future was dependent on a number of factors, not least a renewed Arts Council grant.

In effect, *New Worlds* 200 was the last issue. The Arts Council grant was not renewed, but a greater blow was the discovery that the distributors had been withholding copies, and Moorcock was suddenly over £3,000 in debt. Clearly *New Worlds* could not continue on that basis, and Moorcock closed the magazine. But behind the scenes he was making arrangements to continue it in a new format—that of a quarterly paperback anthology. A final 201st issue was prepared and mailed to subscribers only. Labeled a ''Special Good Taste'' issue, it had a Victorian flavor featuring a Thomas Disch story, ''Feathers from the Wings of an Angel,'' and a reprint of a John Munro speculative article from the turn of the century. That issue is now extremely rare, and copies have been sighted on offer for £20 and more.

The *New Worlds* venture might at first seem a failure. It was certainly misunderstood, with many critics convinced that writers had gone overboard with sex for sex's sake. In several cases writers did push experimentalism to extremes, as anyone will go to excesses when confines are first removed. However, as a forum wherein writers could experiment with techniques and style it had no equal, and there can be no doubt that as a result of *New Worlds*, and the freedom it encouraged, science fiction and its allied forms gained tremendously.

What *New Worlds* did was open publishers' eyes to the possibilities of speculative fiction. Having achieved that, the book world began to adapt, and by 1969 *New Worlds* had served its purpose. The shape of things to come was clear from Langdon Jones' anthology *The New SF*, published by Hutchinson's as a hardback in November 1969. *The New SF* was no different from an issue of *New Worlds*. It featured new stories by the same authors, but lacked the artwork and critical essays. The book was generally well received and carried none of the controversy meted out to *New Worlds*' issues.

As a paperback anthology, *New Worlds* returned to much the same format and presentation as the Roberts and Vinter editions, only larger, retaining certain magazine features such as book reviews and criticism. Moorcock returned as editor, and in his introduction he set down his opinion of his critics and his intents:

In America, in particular, there have been a good many assumptions made about our policy and many people seem to have got hot under the collar about what they claim is our "destructive" attitude to sf. Those who have been angriest seem to be those who have been least familiar with *New Worlds*. Although identified with a so-called "new wave," we have always preferred to publish as wide a spectrum of speculative and imaginative fiction as possible. We have encouraged experiment, certainly, but we have not published unconventional material to the exclusion of all else. It would have been stupid to do so since we ourselves and, we assume, our readers enjoy all kinds of fiction.[21]

The *New Worlds* anthology issues carried some memorable stories: "The God House," "Weihnachtabend" and "The Ministry of Children" by Keith Roberts; "Angouleme" and "334" by Thomas M. Disch; "Thy Blood Like Milk" by Ian Watson; "The Bees of Knowledge" by Barry Bayley; and Moorcock's own "Pale Roses," "White Stars" and "Ancient Shadows."

After the sixth issue Moorcock handed over the editorship to Hilary Bailey, but after the eighth volume the British publisher, Sphere Books, cancelled the series. Corgi Books rescued it, but sales were so poor that it was dropped after only two more volumes. For the tenth time *New Worlds* was faced with the prospect of no future, but having survived so many upheavals, it seems the magazine will never die gracefully. Moorcock, in conjunction with M. John Harrison, John Clute and Charles Platt, and with the help of Charles Partington as printer, now reissued the magazine in a fanzine format, almost full circle to the original SFA organ. But there was a startling difference which made the new *New Worlds* totally original. The concept now was to make *New Worlds* the journal of an alternate world. "Essentially we are asking for news reports and pictures from imaginary versions of our own twentieth century."[22]

Although currently suspended, *New Worlds* is now as far removed from the original Carnell issues as it is possible to be, though it is no less entertaining or innovative. More recent issues have widened their scope to include conventional articles and stories, and provided sales are sufficient to cover the reduced overhead, there is every reason to assume that *New Worlds* will continue. The SF world needs it, as every group requires its rebel to act as a conscience and encourage it to analyze itself and not stagnate. As a consequence it may well be that *New Worlds* is (and has been since about 1956) the most significant and relevant of all SF magazines.

Notes

1. Sam Moskowitz, *The Immortal Storm* (Westport, Conn.: Hyperion Press, 1974), p. 97.

2. Ibid., p. 99.

3. [Maurice K. Hanson], "Finis . . . ," *Novæ Terrae*, Vol. 3, No. 5 (January 1939): 3–4.

4. In "The Magazine That Nearly Was," *Vision of Tomorrow*, Vol. 1, No. 9 (June 1970): 48, Carnell states that "three issues containing news, articles and fiction were published before the Association went into cold storage," but both *Fanzine Index*, ed. Bob Pavlat and Bill Evans (New York: H. P. Piser, 1965), p. 74, and *British Fanzine Bibliography* by Peter Roberts (U.K.: Privately printed, 1977), p. 7, list four issues.

5. Carnell, "Magazine That Nearly Was," p. 49.

6. John Carnell, "The Birth of New Worlds," *Vision of Tomorrow*, Vol. 1, No. 12 (September 1970): 62.

7. [Colin Lester], "Science Fiction Magazines," in *The Visual Encyclopedia of Science Fiction*, ed. Brian Ash (London: Pan Books, 1977), p. 308.

8. It missed a month in 1959 due to a seven-week printing dispute which caused the August and September issues to be combined. See "Apologies . . . and Plans" (editorial), *New Worlds* 86.

9. See Harry Harrison, "The Beginning of the Affair," in *Hell's Cartographers*, ed Brian W. Aldiss and Harry Harrison (London: Weidenfeld and Nicolson, 1975), p. 89.

10. John Carnell, "Traditions . . . ," *New Worlds* 62 (August 1957): 1.

11. See John Carnell, "Survey Report—1963," *New Worlds* 141 (April 1964): 3.

12. Michael Moorcock, *New Worlds* 141 (April 1964): 128.

13. Michael Moorcock, "New Worlds: A Personal History," *Foundation* 15 (January 1979): 6–7.

14. Michael Moorcock, "A New Literature for the Space Age," *New Worlds* 142 (May/June 1964): 3.

15. Thomas M. Disch, interviewed at the Second Brighton Arts Festival, May 1968, transcribed in *Vector* 51 (October 1968).

16. Moorcock, "New Worlds," p. 13.

17. Disch, interview, May 1968.

18. Michael Moorcock, "Lead-In," *New Worlds* 181 (April 1968): 2.

19. Charles Platt, "Lead-In," *New Worlds* 193 (August 1969): 1.

20. Michael Moorcock, *SF Writer's Bulletin*, published by the British Science Fiction Association, 1972.

21. Michael Moorcock, "Introduction," *New Worlds Quarterly* 1 (London: Sphere Books, 1971), p. 10.

22. Michael Moorcock et al., *New Worlds* 213 (Summer 1978): 2.

Information Sources

BIBLIOGRAPHY:

Aldiss, Brian W. "New Worlds and SF Horizons of the Sixties." *The Shape of Further Things* (London: Faber & Faber, 1970).

Carnell, John. "The Birth of New Worlds." *Vision of Tomorrow*, No. 12 (September 1970).

———. "The Magazine That Nearly Was." *Vision of Tomorrow*, No. 9 (June 1970).

Nicholls. *Encyclopedia*.

Moorcock, Michael. "New Worlds: A Personal History." *Foundation* 15 (January 1979). A condensed version of the introduction to *New Worlds: An Anthology* (London: Fontana, 1983). A shorter and slightly earlier version exists under the title "New Worlds—Jerry Cornelius" on pp. 144–55 of *Sojan* by Michael Moorcock (Manchester: Savoy Books, 1977).

Tuck.

INDEX SOURCES: Burgess, Brian, *A History and Checklist of New Worlds*, London: BSFA, 1959 (covers issues 1–55); IBSF; ISFM; ISFM-II; MIT; Moorcock, Michael, "Index to New Worlds," *New Worlds* 201 (March 1971) (covers issues 173–201); NESFA; SFM; Tuck. A complete issue index is included in *New Worlds: An Anthology*, London: Fontana, 1983.

REPRINT SOURCES:

Magazine Reprints: American edition, Volume 1, Number 1, March 1960–Volume 1, Number 5, July 1960, 5 issues, Digest, 128 pp. Great American Publications, New York. Editor, Hans Steffan Santesson. Reprinted predominantly from issues of *NW* during 1959, but with no corresponding sequence. One article was reprinted from the British *Science Fiction Adventures* and three items from earlier issues of *Fantastic Universe*. From British original Number 99, the original was released in the U.S. with a cover date one month later.

Anthology Reprints: The *NW* anthology format which ran 1971–1976 had an American edition as follows. U.K. *New Worlds Quarterly*, Numbers 1–4 had an identical edition from Berkeley Books, New York, Numbers 1–4 (1971–1972); U.K. Number 5 saw no U.S. edition. U.K. Number 6 became U.S. *New Worlds* 5 (New York: Avon-Equinox, 1974); U.K. Number 7 became U.S. *New Worlds* 6 (New York: Avon-Equinox, 1975). Thereafter U.S. series discontinued.

Derivative Anthologies: Edited by John Carnell: *The Best from New Worlds Science Fiction* (London: Boardman, 1955), 8 stories from 1949–1954, plus intro. by John Wyndham; *Lambda I and Other Stories* (New York: Berkley, 1964/London: Penguin, 1965), U.S. 7 stories, U.K. 8 stories from 1961–1963. Edited by Michael Moorcock: *The Best of New Worlds* (London: Compact Books, 1965), 15 stories from 1958, 1959, 1964 and 1965; *The Best SF Stories from New Worlds*, 8 volumes published by Panther Books, London/St. Albans, 1967–1974, and Berkley, New York (6 volumes only), 1969–1971. Stories selected from 1965–1967 predominantly but spread to 1962 and 1970 and also reprinted stories from *Science Fantasy* and *Science Fiction Adventures* from Number 4 onwards. A retrospective anthology of the Moorcock years is *New Worlds: An Anthology* (London: Fontana, 1983). Edited by Judith Merril: *England Swings SF* (Garden City, N.Y.: Doubleday, 1968) includes 15 items from *NW*. Abridged in U.K. as *The Space-Time Journal* (London: Panther, 1972), with 10 items from *NW*.

Rebound Copies: Unsold issues of *New Worlds* and *Science Fantasy* were rebound as *SF Reprise* in six volumes during 1966 by Compact Books, London. *NW* 144/145 became *SF Reprise 1*, *NW* 146/147 *SF Reprise 2*, *NW* 149–151 *SF Reprise 5*.

LOCATION SOURCES: SF Consultants; SF Foundation; MIT Science Fiction Library; Texas A&M University Library; Eastern New Mexico University Library; City of Toronto Public Library.

Publication History

Note: The following details exclude the fanzine period of *New Worlds*.

TITLE: *New Worlds*, [July] 1946–January 1953. *New Worlds Science Fiction*, March 1953–April 1964. *New Worlds SF*, May/June 1964–April 1967. Reverted to *New Worlds*, July 1967–March 1971. *New Worlds Quarterly*, June 1971–January 1973. *New Worlds*, September 1973–.

VOLUME DATA: Volume 1, Number 1, [July] 1946–Volume 51, Number 177, November 1967. Thereafter volume numbering ceased. Number 178, December 1967/
January 1968–Number 201, March 1971. Pocketbook editions (U.K.): Number 1
[202], [June] 1971–Number 10 [211], August 1976. Reverted to magazine, Number 212, Spring 1978–. Latest issue sighted Number 216, September 1979. At
present in limbo. The Carnell issues of *NW* ran three issues per volume, with
issue numbering continuous regardless of volume. First three issues intentionally
quarterly, but irregular: [July] 1946, [October] 1946 and [October] 1947. Issue
4, [April] 1949. Issue 5, [September] 1949. Quarterly, Issue 6, Spring 1950–
Issue 12, Winter 1951. Bi-monthly, Issue 13, January 1952–Issue 21, June 1953
(May 1953 issue slipped to June). Gap in publication, then monthly, Number 22,
April 1954–Number 141, April 1964 (August/September 1959, issue [86] combined). Under Moorcock *NW* initially ran twelve issues per volume but only five
issues in Volume 51 before volume numbering discontinued. Bi-monthly, Number
142, May/June 1964–Number 145, November/December 1964. Monthly, Number
146, January 1965–Number 172, March 1967. (Issue 171 was misdated March
1967 instead of February). Publication resumed Number 173, July 1967–Number
200, April 1970 (monthly, but no issues for Jan, May, Jun, Aug, Sep 68, or Sep
69). Subscribers only issue 201, March 1971. Anthology editions, quarterly,
Number 1 [202], [June] 1971–Number 4 [205], [April] 1972. Irregular, Number
5 [206], [January] 1973; 6 [207], [September] 1973; 7 [208], [December] 1974;
8 [209], [March] 1975; 9 [210], [November] 1975; 10 [211], [August] 1976.
Magazine format, irregular. Number 212, Spring 1978; Number 213, Summer
1978; Number 214, [Winter] 1978; Number 215, Spring 1979; Number 216,
September 1979. Total run: 216 issues as of September 1979.

PUBLISHER: Pendulum Publications, London, Number 1, [July] 1946–Number 3, [Oc-
tober] 1947. Nova Publications, London, Number 4, [April] 1949–Number 141,
April 1964. Roberts & Vinter, Ltd., London, Number 142, May/June 1964–
Number 172, March 1967. Moorcock/Magnelist Publications, London, Number
173, July 1967–Number 177, November 1967; Moorcock/Stonehart Publications,
Ltd., London, Number 178, December 1967/January 1968–Number 182, July
1968. Moorcock privately as New Worlds Publishing, London, Number 183,
October 1968–Number 201, March 1971. Sphere Books, London, Number 1
[202], [June] 1971–Number 8 [209], [March] 1975. Corgi Books, London, Number 9 [210], [November] 1975–Number 10 [211], [August] 1976. Coma Publications, Ltd., Manchester, Number 212, Spring 1978–.

EDITORS: John Carnell, Number 1, [July] 1946–Number 141, April 1964. Michael
Moorcock, Number 142, May/June 1964–Number 188, March 1969. Langdon
Jones, Number 189, April 1969–Number 192, July 1969. Charles Platt, Number
193, August 1969. Michael Moorcock, Number 194, September/October 1968.
Charles Platt and R. Glyn Jones, Number 195, November 1969. Graham Hall
and Graham Charnock, Number 196, December 1969. Charles Platt, Number 197,
January 1970–Number 200, April 1970. Michael Moorcock, Number 201, March
1971–Number 6 [207], [September] 1973. Hilary Bailey, Number 7 [208], [De-
cember] 1974–Number 10 [211], [August] 1976. Michael Moorcock, Number
212, Spring 1978. A consortium, headed by Charles Platt, R. Glyn Jones and
Richard Meadley, Number 213, Summer 1978–.

FORMAT: Pulp, 64 pp., Number 1, [July] 1946–Number 3, [October] 1947. Large
Digest, 88 pp., Number 4, [April] 1949; Large Digest, 96 pp., Number 5, [Sep-
tember] 1949–Number 20, March 1953. Digest, 128 pp., Number 21, June 1953–
Number 141, April 1964 (except Number 86, August/September 1959, 112 pp.).
Pocketbook, 128 pp., Number 142, May/June 1964–Number 159, February 1966;
160 pp., Number 160, March 1966–Number 170, January 1967; 128 pp., Number
171, February 1967–Number 172, March 1967. Slick, 64 pp., Number 173, July
1967–Number 192, July 1969. Slick, 32 pp., Number 193, August 1969–Number
200, April 1970. Printed A4, 20 pp., Number 201, March 1971. Pocketbook,
Number 1 [202], [June] 1971–Number 10 [211], [August] 1976. Pages as follows:
1, 176 pp.; 2, 192 pp.; 3, 208 pp.; 4, 224 pp.; 5, 280 pp.; 6, 272 pp.; 7, 216
pp.; 8 and 9, 224 pp.; 10, 240 pp. Printed A4, Number 212, Spring 1978–. Pages
as follows: 212, 8 pp.; 213, 32 pp.; 214, 56 pp.; 215, 48 pp.; 216, 44 pp.

PRICE: 2/-, Number 1–2; 1/6, Number 3, [October] 1947–Number 31, January 1955; 2/-,
Number 32, February 1955–Number 88, November 1959; 2/6, Number 89, December 1959–Number 133, August 1963; 3/-, Number 134, September 1963–
Number 141, April 1964; 2/6, Number 142, May/June 1964–Number 159, February 1966; 3/6, Number 160, March 1966–Number 176, October 1967; 5/-,
Number 177, November 1967–Number 192, July 1969; 3/6, Number 193, August
1969–Number 200, April 1970; 25 p., Number 201, March 1971–Number 1 [202],
[June] 1971; 30p., Number 2 [203], [September] 1971–Number 3 [204], [January]
1972; 35p., Number 4 [205], [APril] 1972; 40p., Number 5 [206], [January]
1973–Number 6 [207], [September] 1973; 50p., Number 7 [208], [December]
1974–Number 9 [210], [November] 1975; 60p., Number 10 [211], [August] 1976.
Free, Number 212, Spring 1978. 40p., Number 213, Summer 1978. 75p., Number
214, [Winter] 1978. £1.00, Number 215, Spring 1979–.

Mike Ashley

NEW WORLDS QUARTERLY

Paperback anthology/magazine of *New Worlds*. See NEW WORLDS.

NEW WORLDS SCIENCE FICTION

See NEW WORLDS.

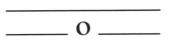

O

OCCULT

Occult was one of a number of booklets issued by Gerald Swan during the war years that can be regarded as much as paperback anthologies as magazines. Two issues of *Occult* appeared. The first, subtitled "a collection of stories of the supernatural," has been dated by George Locke as appearing in 1941, while both Donald Tuck and Robert Reginald give the date 1945. Dating of wartime publications is difficult, even with the British Museum registration system, because not all books were lodged at the time of publication, and with publishing hinging on paper supplies, some editions were reprinted one or more times as paper became available. Undated, these different reprintings may be a year or more apart. Swan, who had wisely stockpiled paper before the war, was able to publish regularly throughout the period, and so *Occult* could easily have first appeared in 1941 and then been reprinted in 1945 to coincide with the second volume.

Both issues contain extremely short supernatural vignettes with no room for character or even plot development. Some familiar names are present: W. P. Cockroft, Henry Rawle and John C. Craig, all of whom sold SF to Swan and other publications. Other contributors included are Alexander O'Pearson and John Body (believed to be a misprint for John Brody, who had four stories in the early issues of *New Worlds**).

Written and published for ephemeral wartime reading, the stories hold little interest today.

Information Sources

INDEX SOURCES: MT; SFM. Contents listings will be found in Tuck, pp. 13–14, under "Anonymous Anthologies," and in George Locke, *Ferret Fantasy's Christmas Annual for 1973*, London: Ferret Fantasy, 1974, p. 2.

REPRINT SOURCES:
  Derivative Anthologies: Unsold copies of the second volume, *Occult Shorts*, were rebound into *Four-in-One Weird and Occult Shorts* (London: Swan, 1949) together with *Weird Story Magazine* 2, and the nonfantasy *Racing Shorts* and *Detective Shorts* 4.
LOCATION SOURCES: None known.

Publication History

TITLE: First issue: *Occult: A Collection of Stories of the Supernatural*, followed by *Occult Shorts: 2nd Collection*.
VOLUME DATA: First issue unnumbered. Undated (see essay above). 1945, possibly as early as 1941.
PUBLISHER: Gerald G. Swan.
EDITOR: Unidentified, probably Gerald Swan.
FORMAT: Pocketbook (saddle-stapled), 36 pp.
PRICE: 7d.

Mike Ashley

THE OCTOPUS

The Octopus was a single-character pulp magazine that appeared in 1939 and lasted only one issue, despite the confusing numbering as Volume 1, Number 4.[1] *The Octopus* had first been conceived as *The Scorpion*, but was altered to *The Octopus* at the last minute. All this confusion emphasizes the unsureness of the publishers, determined to capitalize on the continuing success of the many hero pulps, but groping for something original and with immediate appeal. After the single issue of *The Octopus*, a new magazine was started carrying the second novel in the series, but now entitled *The Scorpion*.* Since that also lasted only one issue, Popular Publications clearly decided that it was barking up the wrong tree.

The lead story, "The City Condemned to Hell," was written by Norvell Page (who also wrote the Spider novels) under the house name Randolph Craig and revised by Edith and Ejler Jakobsson. The hero was Jeffrey Fairchild, who had two alternate identities. One was the kindly Dr. Skull, the other a relentless vigilante in the tradition of The Spider called the Skull Killer. Fairchild battled The Octopus, a criminal who threatened New York City with ghastly death and destruction. He and his minions operated secretly out of a New York hospital where they broadcast a ray that changed normal people into monsters. There were numerous subplots in what was a very complicated novel. Page, who wrote three novels for *Unknown*,* was adept at using science fiction ideas as part of fast-paced, illogical thrillers. On close examination, the logic of "The City Condemned to Hell" displayed glaring holes, but the fast pace kept disbelief at bay until long after the story was concluded.

The novel was accompanied by three short stories, the works of Donald G.

Cormack, Russell Grey and Arthur Leo Zagat. All three were of the weird-menace variety that proliferated in Popular's other horror magazines: stories with seemingly supernatural happenings which are resolved at the end as being the diabolical machinations of some evildoer. This issue also contained a short editorial, "The Purple Eye," and a brief feature, "Horrors of History."

Note

1. See explanation under volume data.

Information Sources

BIBLIOGRAPHY:
Hardin, Nils. "An Interview with Henry Steeger." *Xenophile*, No. 33 (July 1977): 3–20.
Hardin, Nils, and George Hocutt. "A Checklist of Popular Publications Titles 1930–1955." *Xenophile*, No. 33 (July 1977): 21–24.
Hickman, Lynn. "The Pulp Collector." *The Pulp Era*, No. 75 (Spring 1971): 6–11.
Jones, Robert Kenneth. *The Shudder Pulps*. West Linn, Ore.: Fax Collector's Editions, 1975.
Tuck.
Weinberg, Robert. *Pulp Classics 11*. Oak Lawn, Ill.: Pulp Press, 1976.
INDEX SOURCES: SFM; Tuck; Weinberg, Robert, and Lohr McKinstry, *The Hero Pulp Index*, Evergreen, Colo.: Opar Press, 1971.
REPRINT SOURCES:
  Novels: The lead novel, *The City Condemned to Hell*, was reprinted by Robert Weinberg as *Pulp Classics 11* (Oak Lawn, Ill.: Pulp Press, 1976).
LOCATION SOURCES: San Francisco Academy of Comic Art.

Publication History

TITLE: *The Octopus*.
VOLUME DATA: Volume 1, Number 4, February 1939. The *Octopus* is a retitling of the *Western Raider* magazine, which ran 3 issues, numbered Volume 1, Numbers 1-3.
PUBLISHER: Popular Publications, New York.
EDITORS: Ejler and Edith Jakobsson.
FORMAT: Pulp, 112 pp.
PRICE: 10¢.

Robert Weinberg

ODYSSEY

The mid-seventies, during which *Odyssey*'s two issues appeared, were characterized by contradictory events in the science fiction periodical market. Between 1974 and 1977, the pages of *Locus: The Newspaper of the Science Fiction Field* carried stories about long-established magazines such as *Galaxy Science Fiction,* *Amazing Stories* and *Fantastic* experiencing financial and circulation problems, and about the folding of *If** and *Vertex** (the latter after only two years), as well as announcements of the establishment of new magazines—*Odyssey*,* *Galileo*,* *Isaac Asimov's Science Fiction Magazine** and *Cosmos Science Fiction and Fantasy Magazine*.* Of the latter four, all launched in 1976, three employed variations on the established formula (*Odyssey*, large format; *Galileo*, large format and subscription-only distribution; *Cosmos*, large format and color interiors), while *Isaac Asimov's* stayed within the conventions, even harkening back to the Campbell *Astounding* (*Analog Science Fiction**) in editorial policy. One might have expected that *Isaac Asimov's*, with its traditional story values and the Asimov name, would survive; that *Cosmos*, with excellent packaging and high-quality fiction, would do well; that *Galileo*, lacking newsstand exposure and name contributors, would go the way of other little-magazine projects; and that *Odyssey*, with solid fiction and a commercially shrewd editor, would fall in behind *Cosmos*. In fact, for a period, *Galileo* increased its circulation, went on to newsstand distribution, and published major writers such as Larry Niven, and *Isaac Asimov's* has flourished, winning a Best Editor Hugo for George Scithers. *Cosmos* ran four issues, succumbing to bad planning by the publishers in 1977; *Odyssey*, after only two issues, collapsed in mid-1976. The magazine furnishes a case study in some of the factors that can contribute to a publication's failure.

Locus stories in September and October 1975 supply the essential facts about the founding of *Odyssey*: Roger Elwood (who had been extremely active in the original anthology market for several years) would edit the large-format quarterly; the first issue would carry a book review column by Robert Silverberg, a fanzine column by Charles Brown (editor of *Locus*), an article by Theodore Sturgeon, and fiction by Jerry Pournelle, Frederik Pohl, Barry Malzberg, Robert Bloch, Thomas Scortia and Joseph Green.[1] Unfortunately, problems developed. Distribution, a crucial factor in a magazine's survival, was poor—in February 1976, Charles Brown reported in *Locus* that *Odyssey* "had limited distribution in the midwest only as of today" and that he had not yet seen a copy himself (this from a contributing editor).[2] Similarly, fanzine editor Richard Geis reported that he had seen only fifteen copies in a local (Portland, Oregon) supermarket, and that these were pulled in two weeks.[3]

The trouble went beyond distribution. Geis also reported that even the copies that got to his supermarket did not sell—"Fifteen copies—fourteen copies off!"[4] *Odyssey*'s shoddy appearance worked against it—coarse, pulpy paper, confession-magazine advertisements ("Dial Your Destiny!" "Be a Locksmith"), and a contents page strewn with exclamation points and hype ("3 Important New Novellas!" "4 Exclusive New Features!"). The first cover, by Kelly Freas, was irrelevant but not offensive, but the second was accurately described by Geis as "a pink and blue disaster."[5] In the eyes of fanzine editors Brown and Geis, these cosmetic defects contributed significantly to *Odyssey*'s failure, and Geis writes of the first issue that "the material is better than the magazine's appearance suggests."[6] The result was poor sales and subsequent cessation of publication.

The question of responsibility in a case such as this is an interesting one—who can break (or make) a periodical? There are suggestions that the editor was not to blame. Geis writes: "Roger Elwood, the editor, obviously has no control over these matters [of layout and appearance]. He is charged with buying so much wordage for the magazine and after that . . . "[7] A *Locus* report in July 1976 indicates some tension between editor and publisher: "Elwood cited poor sales figures on the first issue, poor production values and slow payments from the publisher as reasons for his hesitation for continuing even if the publisher is willing."[8] And in the "SF Magazine Summary for 1976," Brown coyly refers to *Odyssey* as being " 'edited' " by Elwood.[9]

The fiction, nevertheless, is reasonably strong. Larry Niven's "The Magic Goes Away" mixes science fictional logic with heroic fantasy conventions in an appealing way; Barry Malzberg's "Impasse" is a well-written bit of ironic, metafictional SF; R. A. Lafferty's "Love Affair with Ten Thousand Springs" is a strange, half-allegorical fantasy about the nature of nature; Frederick Pohl's "The Prisoner of New York Island" affords corner-of-the-eye glimpses of a future America of dead metropolises and rural communes. Where the fiction is weak (as in Robert Bloch's in-jokey "ETFF" or Thomas Scortia's telegraphed-surprise-ending "Someday I'll Find You"), it is no worse than the filler material in other SF magazines. It was not the fiction that killed *Odyssey*, but bad management, a sloppy appearance and inadequate distribution.

Notes

1. "Another New Magazine," *Locus* 179 (September 27, 1975): 1; "Odyssey Science Fiction," *Locus* 180 (October 27, 1975): 1.
2. "Editorial Matters," *Locus* 185 (February 29, 1976): 1.
3. "The Alter-Ego Viewpoint," *Science Fiction Review* 17 (May 1976): 45.
4. "Prozine Notes," *Science Fiction Review* 18 (August 1976): 30.
5. Ibid.
6. "Alter-Ego Viewpoint," p. 45.
7. "Prozine Notes," p. 30.
8. "Magazine Problems," *Locus* 191 (July 31, 1976): 2.
9. *Locus* 200 (March 1977): 4.

Information Sources

BIBLIOGRAPHY:
Brown, Charles N., ed. *Locus, The Newspaper of the Science Fiction Field* [Nos. 1–207], 2 vols. (Boston: Gregg Press, 1978).
Nicholls. *Encyclopedia*.
Science Fiction Review 17 (May 1976)–18 (August 1976).
INDEX SOURCES: NESFA-V; SFM.
REPRINT SOURCES: None known.
LOCATION SOURCES: M.I.T. Science Fiction Library.

Publication History

TITLE: *Odyssey.*
VOLUME DATA: Volume 1, Number 1, Spring 1976–Volume 1, Number 2, Summer
1976. Quarterly. Total run: 2 issues.
PUBLISHER: Gambi Publications, Inc., Brooklyn, New York.
EDITOR: Roger Elwood.
FORMAT: Bedsheet (saddle-stapled), 80 pp.
PRICE: $1.00.

Russell Letson

OMNI

In the puffery of the business, *Omni* has been called "the trail-breaking
magazine of science and science fiction."[1] The first three years of *Omni*, including the promotional buildup as well as the controversy prior to its first issue,
dated October 1978, can best be seen as an experiment to determine if the mass-
market periodical business can maintain the intelligence, the flexibility and the
individuality of the more specialized markets in which science fiction has flourished. There is no question that *Omni* has blazed commercial trails; the recent
appearance of a new science magazine published by Time Inc. is directly attributed in *Locus, The Newspaper of the Science Fiction Field* to the fast commercial pace set by *Omni.*[2] The question is, however, whether or not the mix
of expensive advertising, features on current fads, and compartmentalized news
on current happenings in science and technology supports the science fiction that
is published in the magazine. It is perhaps a significant indicator that the imitator
from Time Inc. does not publish fiction, and the best of the more than 100 pieces
of short fiction that *Omni* has published constitute the more complex and demanding reading in the magazine. In other words, the depth of tone and meaning
in recent science fiction may not coincide exactly with the requirements of the
magazine. The new fiction editor, Ellen Datlow, is quoted in *Locus* (August
1981) explaining a reduction in the role of fiction in the future plans of *Omni*:
"[Four pieces of fiction per issue have] been cut back to an average of two. . . .
'*Omni* is not a fiction magazine. The non-fiction and pictorials are very popular.' "[3]

Omni was originally to be titled *Nova Magazine* and was to be introduced in
a special science fiction issue of *Penthouse* on September 1, 1978. But the
Boston PBS television station WGBH obtained an injunction against the publishers of *Penthouse* on the use of the word "Nova" on the grounds that their
widely acclaimed show of the same name was too close to the aims of the new
magazine—mass-media communications in the science field. Penthouse International, rather than risking a delay in the appearance of the magazine by a
lawsuit, substituted the name *Omni*, which looked similar in the layout that had
been designed and had the same number of letters.[4] That first summer of development for the new publishing venture also saw quick and possibly confusing

adjustments in the editorial staff. On the evidence of subsequent congratulatory comment in editorials, one learns that Bob Guccione designed the original concept. Kathy Keeton, who by the second anniversary issue was president of Omni Publications International, writes:

> Framed on a wall in this magazine's offices is a series of pencil sketches by Bob Guccione. They represent *Omni*'s moment of inception, the first visualization of a concept so powerful it would precipitate a whole new era in magazine publishing. Few believed that these bold and imaginative drawings would evolve into the world's next major publication, and fewer still, that it could be accomplished with something as dry and detached and non commercial as science.[5]

During that first summer of 1978, Keeton had the position of associate publisher. The executive editor of the magazine for its first year was Frank Kendig, who had held editorial positions and other publications that popularize science. The first science editor was Trudy Bell, who had worked for NASA and for *Scientific American*. The position of fiction editor changed hands three times in those early months. Judith McQuown was the first fiction editor for the project. She was followed by Diana King, who held the position for only some three weeks. Finally Ben Bova, who had just left *Analog Science Fiction*,* became fiction editor as of August 15. By early 1980, Bova had become executive editor of the magazine, and Robert Sheckley was hired as fiction editor. Sheckley resigned in the summer of 1981 to return to full-time writing and was replaced by Datlow.

The consistently optimistic and ''gee whiz'' editorial stance of the magazine, as characterized by Keeton above, has always been at odds with the complexity of tone and meaning of the better stories published behind the editorials. For example, in the first anniversary editorial Guccione writes rather eloquently about the dangers in our rapidly progressing technological society of pausing to speculate about lost simplicities or the complexities of developing from one Golden Age to the next:

> And all the while we hear pleas for a return to the ''simple life''—a legendary state of being that occurred before the advance of technology, before pollution, and before the so-called energy crisis. These inane protestations prove one thing—that the ultimate fallibility of man is his curious need to rationalize history.[6]

Speculation about the fallibility of man and about the strange curvatures in development by which the past may be more ''golden'' than the future, however, obsesses modern science fiction writers. Both Robert Silverberg's ''Our Lady of the Sauropods'' (September 1980) and Orson Scott Card's ''Saint Amy's Tale'' (December 1980) defy the straightline positivism of science and its popularizers, and both stories have been nominated for awards. In addition to the

Golden Age/Iron Age paradoxes and complexities that concern the fictionists of *Omni*, dystopian wit and pathos often appear in the magazine next to the glossy advertisements for the latest technology of our time. Norman Spinrad's "Prime Time" (November 1980—it was a good autumn for pessimistic science fiction) challenges well, in his favorite manner, the shallow optimism of the whole communications industry that brings his work to a wide audience. Spinrad's story is also a nominee. Similarly, the popular pictorials in the magazine, which are often introduced by well-known science fiction writers, carry a depth of complexity and often a comic tone that belie the more positivistic representations of actual science and technology. Alien life-forms and cleverly imagined alien technology are more fantastic and more thought-provoking in effect than the most fantastic images from science. Thus, the mixture of effect in *Omni* between the popularization of science and the fantastic reflections on science has seemed so far to be uneasy, if exciting.

But Guccione and Keeton were correct in their hunch that science had become uptown and could be made big business. What *Playboy*, *Penthouse* and others had done with sexual fantasy, *Omni* has done with science. The magazine looks and feels expensive and sexy, and it has worked right from the start. According to *Locus*, the first issue sold 850,000 copies, and the magazine was called "the most successful new venture in decades."[7] After a year and a half, a book-length collection entitled *The Best of Omni Science Fiction* was published that sold over 300,000 copies by the summer of 1980. By the fall of 1980, the magazine was claiming that market measurements showed almost 4 million readers for each issue of *Omni*.[8] *The Best of Omni Science Fiction No. 2* appeared in 1981; it was actually a "spinoff magazine" since it contained original pieces as well as reprints. Another spinoff in the big business of popular science was the projected nationally broadcast television program produced by Omni Productions International, *Omni: The New Frontier*, premiered in the fall of 1981.[9]

Many of the best writers of science fiction and fantasy today have appeared in *Omni* because, in part, it pays the highest rates; and both Nebula and Hugo awards went to fiction that first appeared in the magazine in 1979. Nevertheless, *Locus* described the fiction in the early issues as "minor"; and its report of an interview with Bova about the time the magazine was starting suggests part of the problem with the fiction that Bova has published: "He's looking for less hard core and gimmicky SF and more characterization and color."[10] It is not that the gimmicks of science fiction are valid in themselves (no mere formula writing is very exciting); but the genre has developed a character of its own in the imaginative use of its conventions that *Omni* seems to be bending toward a conformity with other slick magazine fiction. One might argue that the more urgently a Sturgeon or a Walter Tevis or a Thomas Disch (all have appeared in *Omni*) is enticed to write fiction that sounds like—and looks like in the way it is published alongside slick graphics—the fiction in *Playboy* or even *The New Yorker*, the more his writing loses in science fiction character. Even though some of our best writers may have marketed less than memorable work in *Omni*'s slick pages and even though the science fiction conventions seem harder to recognize next to all the expensive graphics, the fictional expressions of complex pathos and pessimism are often effective, as in the stories by Silverberg and Card mentioned above. Similarly, some of the other matter in the magazine is often done best by the leading science fiction writers—Arthur C. Clarke on science or Ursula K. LeGuin in a "Last Word" (October 1979) that is funnier than the work of professional humorists in the same isue. In short, *Omni* has been good for science fiction writers; and science fiction writers have published some good things in *Omni*.

The first three pieces of fiction from *Omni* to win awards or place second or third were "Unaccompanied Sonata" by Orson Scott Card (March 1979), "The Way of Cross and Dragon" by George R. R. Martin (June 1979), and "Sandkings," also by Martin (August 1979). Card's short story was runner-up for the Nebula Award. Martin's novelette "Sandkings" was the winner of both Nebula and Hugo awards, and his short story won the Hugo Award and placed third in the Nebula competition. "Sandkings," which seems the most memorable of the winners, is an engrossing fantasy of decadent and neurotic cruelty that may remind the reader of Poe and that is part of the general strain of pessimism running counter to the optimism of popular science in the magazine. In summary, then, the questions of tone and complexity in the science fiction material or material related to science fiction as it resides in the slick magazine package of *Omni* and alongside an editorial policy of unbridled optimism seem the most problematic. It is an unlikely marriage, but thus far not an unproductive one. Readers will have to wait for more fiction to be published, however, to see if this symbiosis eventually produces an important body of fiction or if commercial pressures and problems of tone tend to yield a more forgettable body of work.

Notes

1. See the dustjacket to Ben Bova's *Kinsman* (New York: Dial Press, 1979).
2. *Locus* 233 (May 1980): 5.
3. *Locus* 247 (August 1981): 13.
4. *Locus* 213 (August 1978): 1.
5. Kathy Keeton, "First Word," *Omni*, October 1980, p. 6.
6. Bob Guccione, "First Word," *Omni*, October 1979, p. 6.
7. *Locus* 220 (April 1979): 6.
8. Kathy Keeton, "First Word," *Omni*, October 1980, p. 6.
9. *Locus* 245 (June 1981): 1.
10. *Locus* 214 (September 1978): 21.

Information Sources

INDEX SOURCES: NESFA-VI; NESFA-VII; NESFA-VIII; NESFA-IX; SFM.
REPRINT SOURCES:
  British Edition: Identical to U.S. edition except for cover price. From March 1980
    issue date dropped in favor of volume/issue numbering.

Derivative Magazine: Omni: Book of the Future, a part-work subtitled "The Weekly Library of Scientific Fact and Speculation," published by Eaglemoss Publications, Ltd., London. Five weekly parts only issued in selected parts of Britain (not nationally) during November 1981 and again in January 1982. Sales proved disappointing and it was discontinued. Editor, Jack Schofield. Slick, 32 pp., 75p. Reprinted articles plus one story per issue from an assortment of U.S. *Omnis*.

Derivative Anthology: An annual *The Best of Omni Science Fiction* has been issued by the same publisher in 1980, 1981 and 1982, reprinting articles for *Omni*. In the first volume fiction was reprinted, but Volume 2 featured one new story, and Volume 3 contained four new stories.

LOCATION SOURCES: Widely available.

Publication History

TITLE: *Omni*. The subtitle "The Magazine of Science Fact, Fiction, and Fantasy" was introduced from March 1980.

VOLUME DATA: Volume 1, Number 1, October 1978–. Twelve issues per volume. Monthly.

PUBLISHER: Omni Publications International, Third Avenue, New York.

EDITORS: [Executive] Frank Kendig, October 1978–December 1979; Ben Bova, January 1980–August 1981; Dick Teresi, September 1981–. [Fiction] Ben Bova, October 1978–December 1979; Robert Sheckley, January 1980–September 1981; Ellen Datlow, October 1981–.

FORMAT: Slick, 176 pp., October 1978–December 1981; 128 pp., January 1982–.

PRICE: $2.50.

Donald M. Hassler

OMNI: BOOK OF THE FUTURE

A British derivative magazine, based on *Omni*. See OMNI, Reprint Sources.

OPERATOR #5

Operator #5 was the perfect blend of the single-character pulp and the science fiction magazine. Unfortunately, it was presented entirely as a hero pulp and has been ignored and forgotten by the science fiction field. The magazine was a pioneer publication in presenting realistic and well-planned menace novels featuring excellent extrapolation based on the known science of the day. *Operator #5* showed what a skilled writer could produce using a strong blend of scientific data and a trained imagination. Only its formula plot heroics and lead characters consigned it to oblivion.

The magazine went through two identifiable periods. The first, and most successful, both financially and artistically, was from the first issue, April 1934, through November 1935. The magazine appeared monthly, and the novels were the work of Frederick C. Davis. The second period, from December 1935 to the last issue, November/December 1939, saw the magazine alternating between monthly and bi-monthly publication. The novels were the work of two men: Emile C. Tepperman until March 1938, followed by Wayne Rogers to the end.

The Davis novels were the best examples of how SF and the pulp hero concepts could be blended. Each month, Operator #5, Jimmy Christopher of the American Secret Service, battled some threat to the United States. Usually the menace was from some overseas nation or group plotting to conquer America. Other novels featured criminal forces or secret organizations intent on taking over the government. No matter what the menace, each group used some form of new threat based on known science to further its aims. Davis provided copious footnotes to all of his novels detailing the basis for each menace. In the first novel, "The Masked Invasion" (April 1934), a sinister cabal tries to overthrow the U.S. government by using a device that causes massive power blackouts. "Blood Reign of the Dictator" (May 1935) features a power-hungry governor who becomes president and tries to establish a dictatorship, complete with a guillotine for public executions. In "The Army of the Dead" (March 1935) a madman uses the latest medical techniques to revive the recent dead. The oriental villains in "Invasion of the Crimson Cult" (September 1935) use sonic waves to create panic as well as devastate buildings, while in "Scourge of the Invisible Death" (November 1935) the weapon is a ray much like a laser that cuts a hole in the ionosphere, letting in deadly solar radiation and cosmic rays.

Other, less superscientific novels by Davis include "The Yellow Scourge" and "The Invasion of the Yellow Warlords" (June 1934 and June 1935) wherein Japan attacks the United States, while in "Legions of Starvation" (December 1934) sinister industrialists buy up food supplies during the dust-bowl conditions and try to impose their will on the country through control of the grain market. Stories such as these used the tried and tested SF theme of "if this goes on."

Davis wrote his novels (as did Tepperman and Rogers) under the house name of Curtis Steele. He later became well known for detective novels published under his own name. Perhaps if he had received some recognition for his Operator #5 novels he might eventually have become equally famous in the SF field.

When Davis left *Operator #5* so that he could write on a less rigid schedule, his replacement was Emile Tepperman. In an unusual move, Tepperman started what was to be a thirteen-part novel published in sequence in the magazine. Starting with "Death's Ragged Army" (June 1936), the Purple Invasion series had America invaded by the Purple Empire, a world-conquering force much like the Black Invaders used in *Dusty Ayres and His Battle Birds** from the same publisher. Each novel in the sequence had Jimmy Christopher and his band of freedom fighters battle the invaders in a Second War of Independence. Each novel was complete in itself but also formed a part of the larger story. Tepperman made the narratives believable through the same technique as had Davis—footnotes—but this time, the footnotes were long quotes from imaginary books written in the future detailing the long struggle for independence.

Wayne Rogers took over the *Operator #5* series in 1938 and continued the idea of sequential novels. Though the Purple Invasion had been beaten in the March 1938 novel, "The Siege That Brought the Black Death," Rogers continued with the rebuilding of America and the repeated threats from other nations. In 1939 a new sequence began as the Japanese invaded the West Coast under the leadership of "The Yellow Vulture." This last sequence was never concluded; the final issue of the magazine left the series unresolved, with American cities being destroyed by Japanese atom bombs.

While bound by the restrictions of the single-character pulp format, the *Operator #5* novels offered a perfect example of what could be done if SF and spy fiction were combined. They predated and predicted the many postwar spy novels that were to offer the same mixture but rarely as well as their pulp predecessors.

As befitted a magazine featuring a secret service agent, the short stories in *Operator #5* were also spy adventures, but unlike the lead novel, the shorter pieces were little more than fast-action yarns with a minimum of plot. There were several series including Red Finger, the mysterious Secret Service Agent, written by Arthur Leo Zagat; and John Vedders, another Secret Service Agent series by Frank Gruber. In the department "The Secret Sentinel," The Chief warned readers of the terrible dangers that threatened America, while "Secret Sentinel Reports" carried letters from readers telling what they were doing to combat the foreign menaces. With World War II rumbling in the background, the columns were not as paranoid as they seem on rereading today. The authors of the *Operator #5* novels usually wrote the Secret Sentinel, although Moran Tudry later took over the chore.

Information Sources

BIBLIOGRAPHY:
Carr, Nick. "The Subject Was Death." *Science-Fiction Collector*, No. 15 (1981).
Carr, Wooda N. *America's Secret Service Ace*. Oak Lawn, Ill.: Pulp Press, 1975.
Goodstone, Tony. *The Pulps*. New York: Chelsea House, 1970.
Goulart, Ron. *Cheap Thrills*. New Rochelle, N.Y.: Arlington House, 1972.
Grennell, Dean A. "Jumping Jimmy Christopher." *Xenophile*, No. 30 (1977).
Tuck.
INDEX SOURCES: Weinberg, Robert, and Lohr McKinstry, *The Hero Pulp Index*,
    Evergreen, Colo.: Opar Press, 1971 (covers lead novels only).
REPRINT SOURCES:
    Novels: Three series of *Operator #5* novels have been reprinted in the United States.
        The first, published in San Diego by Corinth Books in 1966, ran: 1: *Legions of
        the Death Master* (Jul 35), 2: *The Army of the Dead* (Mar 35), 3: *The Invisible
        Empire* (May 34), 4: *Master of Broken Men* (Sep 34), 5: *Hosts of the Flaming
        Death* (Aug 35), 6: *Blood Reign of the Dictator* (May 35), 7: *March of the Flame
        Marauders* (Apr 35), 8: *Invasion of the Yellow Warlords* (Jun 35). The second
        series, published in New York by Freeway Press in 1974, ran: 1: *The Masked
        Invasion* (Apr 34), 2: *The Invisible Empire* (May 34), 3: *The Yellow Scourge* (Jun

34). All novels were by-lined Curtis Steele and were the work of Frederick C. Davis. The third came from Dimedia, Inc., all in 1980, and ran *Cavern of the Damned*, *Legions of Starvation* and *Scourge of the Invisible Death*.

LOCATION SOURCES: San Francisco Academy of Comic Art.

Publication History

TITLE: *Operator #5*.

VOLUME DATA: Volume 1, Number 1, April 1934–Volume 12, Number 4, November/ December 1939. Four issues per volume. Monthly, April 1934–April 1936; bi-monthly, June 1936–December 1936; monthly, January–March 1937; bi-monthly, April/May 1937–November/December 1939. Total run: 48 issues.

PUBLISHER: Popular Publications, New York.

EDITOR: Rogers Terrill.

FORMAT: Pulp, 128 pp., April 1934–September 1935; thereafter 112 pp.

PRICE: 10¢.

Robert Weinberg

ORBIT SCIENCE FICTION

In 1953, when the SF magazine boom was at its height, it was easy to overlook one or more of the many titles that appeared and, with startling rapidity, disappeared. One such title perhaps unnecessarily overlooked was *Orbit Science Fiction*. Although the magazine lacked an editorial persona, with no editorial or reader departments, it published some fiction of reasonably good quality that was no worse—and at times a little better—than much of what was appearing elsewhere at the time.

It was a slim digest magazine. The editor was credited as Jules Saltman, a name unknown in the SF field. However, the presence of the two by-lines Martin Pearson and David Grinnell may have given astute readers a clue to the real editor of the magazine, as both names were pseudonyms used by Donald A. Wollheim. Wollheim, who was then in his first year of editorship at Ace Books, having only recently left Avon, where he had edited its fantasy and SF readers, had been put in touch with publisher Morris Latzen by a literary agent who had heard that Latzen was planning to launch an SF magazine to cash in on the current genre popularity. Wollheim explains what happened:

> Latzen's full-time professional editor was a man named Jules Saltman. I knew him slightly. A good man and a real pro. Saltman told me that he knew nothing at all about science fiction and wanted me to become the "literary" editor of *Orbit*. By this, he meant that I would find and buy the entire contents of each issue. They paid $1\frac{1}{2}$ cents a word (not bad for those days) and I would receive a flat fee over that for my efforts.
>
> The material in all five of the numbers was entirely of my purchase, and many of the titles were my changes. However, Saltman was the editor.

He did the layouts, arranged the illustrations, the cover, the order in the magazine, etc. Once I turned over the copy, I knew nothing further until the magazine appeared.[1]

Such arrangements were becoming increasingly common throughout the magazine publishing world, as it was cheaper and less of a risk for the publisher to engage an editor on a free-lance issue-by-issue basis than incur further overhead costs by employing another full-time house editor. It was also more convenient for the editor, as he retained his independence. Such practices will be found over and over again, and not just with little magazines. It was under this system that Boucher and McComas edited *The Magazine of Fantasy and Science Fiction** with Robert P. Mills doing the in-house work in New York, and in the same way Harry Harrison edited *Impulse** as he traveled, with Keith Roberts acting as managing editor. The difference was that in most other cases the editor was credited, while on this occasion, because of his position at Ace Books, Wollheim remained anonymous. He thus avoids the brickbats associated with failure, but also loses out on the roses of success. For *Orbit* has had little consideration in the history of SF and should at last be accorded its due place.

The first two issues of *Orbit* were experimental. Bearing no cover dates, they were left on the stands to attain maximum exposure, in much the same way that Louis Silberkleit released two experimental issues of *Science Fiction Stories* (*Science Fiction**) at this time. Both carried ten short stories; the second added a feature titled "Science Notes." Both issues carried a Tex Harrigan story by August Derleth. Derleth was at that time writing a series of stories about Harrigan, a reporter with a penchant for finding odd people, and Wollheim arranged to publish the stories as they were written. Derleth was planning on publishing them as a collection, but in the event they did not appear until after his death, as *Harrigan's File* (Sauk City, Wis.: Arkham House, 1975). A Harrigan story appeared in every issue of *Orbit*. Competent they were, but on the whole unspectacular, although "The Penfield Misadventure," in the fifth issue, which told of a young lad who claimed that he could travel in time, has a brooding, sombre atmosphere that lingers in the memory.

Also in both the issues were Charles Beaumont and Mack Reynolds but, once again, despite the stature of the names (although both were still neophytes), there is nothing especially memorable about the stories, even though they are well written. In fact, only one story really stands out in the first two issues, and that was by Wollheim himself: "Asteroid 745: Mauritia" under the Martin Pearson alias. It is a rare combination of SF and the supernatural and is a genuine SF ghost story. Set on an asteroid, it tells of three prospectors and the harsh ship's captain who claims to be a descendant of Hitler. While the three men are out prospecting, the captain is visited by a fourth—one who does not require a spacesuit.

Nevertheless, despite the general blandness of the two issues by today's standards, their sales, even at the height of the boom, must have been sufficiently encouraging for Latzen to chance a regular bi-monthly schedule. The first of these retained the same blend of competent but unmemorable stories, although Charles Beaumont's deal-with-the-devil story, "Hair of the Dog," had an amusing punch line; Bryce Walton's "The Passion of Orpheus" was an unusual (for the period) treatment of the post-nuclear holocaust theme and is worthy of a second reading; and Mack Reynolds's "Paradox Gained . . ." is one of those inevitable time travel tangles that are good brain-teasers if nothing else.

The fourth issue led with Alfred Coppel's "The Last Night of Summer," a short disaster story of a temporary solar distortion that would raise the Earth's temperature to two hundred degrees for only a short time, but long enough to exterminate life. The treatment had much in common with Frank Lillie Pollock's early "Finis" and Richard Matheson's recent (1953) "The Last Day," and the story may have been derivative of both, though it is just as likely that it was a coincidence. The best stories in the issue were "Beast in the House" by Michael Shaara, a neat story of alien observers, and "Adjustment Team" by Philip K. Dick, an intriguing story of a mistake in time.

Dick was present in the fifth and final issue, which also included such names as Chad Oliver, Gordon R. Dickson and Jack Vance, plus the Derleth story already mentioned. Yet such an array of talent once again failed to produce anything special.

And yet this would not have led directly to *Orbit*'s fate. Taken in the context of the year it appeared, *Orbit* offered stories that were no worse than others in *Galaxy Science Fiction,** Future Fiction,** Astounding* (*Analog Science Fiction**) or *Startling Stories.** They published little that was memorable during a period when the market for SF was so glutted that the talent and quality were spread thin. Most of the magazines edited by good editors, of which Wollheim was most definitely one, attracted a little of that quality, in ratio to that magazine's prestige and regularity as seen by the writers and their agents. *Orbit* was able to catch only a very few good stories, and the rest were average. But, allowing for individual tastes, few readers will find a bad story in *Orbit*, and that is not the case with many other magazines. Every story is worth reading, but most will soon be forgotten. Such is the penalty for being a small fish in a momentarily vast sea.

As for the reason for *Orbit*'s demise, it is probable that the magazine entered the field too late, and although early issues sold well, by the time a regular schedule was established the SF wave had crested, and distributors and wholesalers were no longer interested in the small fry. Latzen had had his momentary dabble with SF and moved on to pastures new.

Note

1. Quotation from private communication with Donald A. Wollheim, October 1981.

Information Sources

BIBLIOGRAPHY:
Nicholls. *Encyclopedia*.
Tuck.
INDEX SOURCES: ASFI; MIT; SFM; Tuck.
REPRINT SOURCES:
  Reprint Editions: An Australian edition of the first issue (minus the Grinnell story),
    misleadingly numbered '10', was issued in April 1954 (undated) by Consolidated
    Press, Sydney; pulp, 64 pp., 2/-. Some of the remaining stories appeared in the
    Australian Satellite Series of anthologies issued simultaneously in 1958.
LOCATION SOURCES: McGill University Library; M.I.T. Science Fiction Library;
    Pennsylvania State University Library.

Publication History

TITLE: *Orbit Science Fiction* on cover and spine, but always *Orbit: The Best in Science
    Fiction* on the masthead and simply *Orbit* on the indicia.
VOLUME DATA: First two issues undated. Volume 1, Number 1, [Fall] 1953–Volume
    1, Number 5, November/December 1954. First two issues quarterly (Number 2,
    [Spring] 1954). Bi-monthly, July/August 1954. Total run: 5 issues.
PUBLISHER: Hanro Corporation, New York. Last two issues identified as "A Sterling
    Publication."
EDITOR: Jules Saltman, but Donald A. Wollheim selected the stories (see above essay).
FORMAT: Digest, 128 pp.
PRICE: 35¢.

Mike Ashley

ORIENTAL STORIES

Although this magazine's title implies that the contents consisted solely of
Far Eastern adventures, *Oriental Stories*, and more especially its subsequent
incarnation as *The Magic Carpet Magazine*, contained a large quota of fantasy
and even some measure of science fiction, as well as featuring many writers
who are closely associated with the fantasy field.

OS was the companion title to *Weird Tales** and was similar to that legendary
magazine in many respects, except longevity. While *Weird Tales* saw 279 issues
during a period of thirty-one years, *OS* saw only 14 issues in forty months. It
was launched in October 1930 with the intention of featuring stories with an
Eastern flavor, ranging from the Arabian Nights to drug-smuggling in China.
Needless to say, Frank Owen was present in that first issue, with two stories.
Owen was a popular contributor to *Weird Tales* with his own special brand of
oriental stories depicting a China more of legend than of reality, and the new
magazine was tailor-made for him. Surprisingly, therefore, he had only eight
stories in the magazine during its short run. These included one of his best
known, "Della Wu, Chinese Courtesan" (February/March 1931), which was

the title story to his collection of Eastern tales published by Lantern Press in New York that same year. Owen also used the name Richard Kent on certain stories, plus the alias Hung Long Tom on a variety of poems that were scattered through the fourteen issues.

Also present in that first issue was another popular *Weird Tales* writer who became a mainstay in *OS*, Robert E. Howard. His first contribution, "The Voice of El-Lil," told of the lost city of Eridu in Mesopotamia. Later stories included two of the stirring adventures of Cormac FitzGeoffrey, "Hawks of Outremer" (April/May/June 1931) and "The Blood of Belshazzar" (Autumn 1931). Four of his historical swashbucklers were later collected as *The Sowers of the Thunder* (West Kingston, R.I.: Donald M. Grant, 1973).

Otis Adelbert Kline began his association with the magazine with the first in a series of stories related by an old dragoman, Hamad the Attar, recounting tales of his youth. "The Man Who Limped" (October/November 1930) later served as the title to a collection of five of seven of these stories published by the small press firm Saint Enterprises in 1946.

Other popular fantasy writers who appeared in the magazine were E. Hoffman Price, Frank Belknap Long, G. G. Pendarves, Paul Ernst, August Derleth and David H. Keller. Dorothy Quick, who would later become a regular contributor to *Weird Tales* and *Unknown*,* made her first appearance in *OS* with "Scented Gardens" (Spring 1932). Perhaps of even greater importance, that story was illustrated on the cover by a new artist who would soon establish herself as synonymous with the *Weird Tales* of the 1930s—Margaret Brundage.

OS did attract writers from other fields, most notably S.B.H. Hurst, James W. Bennett and Warren Hastings Miller, who regularly contributed straightforward jungle and Eastern adventures, but the magazine was filled mostly by those well known in the fantasy genre.

Initially bi-monthly, *OS* slipped to a quarterly schedule after only four issues; and following the Summer 1932 issue it had, by all accounts, folded. Farnsworth Wright had rethought the magazine's policy and, presumably considering it too limited, relaunched it in a reduced format (and cover price) in January 1933 as *The Magic Carpet Magazine* with the idea of including stories from all distant lands and even other worlds. This now made the magazine a market for science fiction, and Edmond Hamilton began a series in the tradition of Edgar Rice Burroughs featuring a John Carter-style hero called Stuart Merrick who is projected by matter transmitter to "Kaldar, World of Antares" (April 1933).

Many of the same regular contributors remained, but a few more of *Weird Tales*'s coterie now added their weight to the magazine, among them Seabury Quinn and Hugh B. Cave (whose earlier contributions had been masked behind the alias "Geoffrey Vace"). Of greater import, however, was the appearance of H. Bedford-Jones. A popular writer of adventure stories in leading pulps like *Argosy*,* *Blue Book* and *Adventure*, Bedford-Jones had ignored the lower-paying genre pulps, so that the publication of "The Master of Dragons" in the first issue of *Magic Carpet* was a scoop for Wright, for all that the story was probably a reject from elsewhere. Bedford-Jones had two further stories in *Magic Carpet* but did not become a regular contributor to *Weird Tales* until the 1940s through his association with its stepsister magazine, *Short Stories*.

It was to be Farnsworth Wright's bane that he could not attract other leading writers with Bedford-Jones's selling power, such as Edison Marshall, Talbot Mundy or Harold Lamb. *Magic Carpet* was up against such established competition as *Adventure* and had insufficient financing to gain a foothold. Eventually, after just five issues, Wright cut his losses and folded the magazine. Stories still in stock were used in *Weird Tales*, where the third tale in Edmond Hamilton's series "The Great Brain of Kaldar" appeared in December 1935.

Information Sources

BIBLIOGRAPHY:
Tuck.
Weinberg, Robert. "Collecting Fantasy." *Fantasy Newsletter*, No. 36 (May 1981): 14–16.
INDEX SOURCES: Cockcroft, IWFM; T.G.L. Cockcroft, *Index to the Verse in Weird Tales*, Lower Hutt, New Zealand: Privately printed, 1960; Day, IWFM; SFM; Tuck.
REPRINT SOURCES:
　　Derivative Anthologies: *Oriental Stories* (Melrose Highlands, Mass.: Odyssey Publications, 1975) and *The Magic Carpet* (Melrose, Mass.: Odyssey Publications, 1977).
LOCATION SOURCES: M.I.T. Science Fiction Library.

Publication History

TITLE: *Oriental Stories*, October/November 1930–Summer 1932. Retitled *The Magic Carpet Magazine*, January 1933–January 1934.
VOLUME DATA: Volume 1, Number 1, October/November 1933–Volume 4, Number 1, January 1934. Six issues, Volume 1, bi-monthly until February/March 1931, then quarterly. Volume 2, three issues, quarterly. Volume 3 (as *MCM*), four issues, quarterly. Volume 4, one issue only. Total run: 9 + 5, 14 issues.
PUBLISHER: Popular Fiction Co., Chicago, Illinois.
EDITOR: Farnsworth Wright.
FORMAT: Small Pulp; 144 pp. as *OS*, 128 pp. as *MCM*.
PRICE: 25¢, October/November 1930–Summer 1932; 15¢, January–July 1933; 25¢, October 1933–January 1934.

Mike Ashley

THE ORIGINAL SCIENCE FICTION STORIES

Mistaken form of title for *Science Fiction Stories*, itself a retitle for the second series of *Science Fiction*. See SCIENCE FICTION.

OTHER TIMES

Other Times, its first issue dated November 1975/January 1976, was an ephemeral "underground" magazine that defined itself as "an international *speculative* quarterly." In style and format it was similar to the large-size *New Worlds*,* and this was echoed in editorial acknowledgments to Christopher Priest, Hilary Bailey and Michael Moorcock. The magazine included a variety of prose and visual experiments, including a tribute to artist Mal Dean and fiction by Barry Malzberg, John Sladek, Michael Moorcock, Ed Bryant and David Bischoff. Distribution was poor, however, and despite the assistance of the Greater London Arts Council, *OT* soon experienced the same fate as its inspirational predecessor.

Information Sources

INDEX SOURCES: None known.
REPRINT SOURCES: None known.
LOCATION SOURCES: None known.

Publication History

TITLE: *Other Times*.
VOLUME DATA: Volume 1, Number 1, November 1975/January 1976–Volume 1, Number 2, [February] 1976. Intended schedule, quarterly. Total run: 2 issues.
PUBLISHER: P. P. Layouts (Publishers) Ltd., London.
EDITORS: Andrew Ellsmore, first issue (credited as Mr. E); Leo Bulero, second issue.
FORMAT: Slick (saddle-stapled), 48 pp.
PRICE: 60p.

Mike Ashley

OTHER WORLDS SCIENCE STORIES

Other Worlds, which premiered in November 1949, was the first fully professional science fiction magazine published by a die-hard science fiction fan, a true godson of Hugo Gernsback, Raymond A. Palmer. And likewise, *Other Worlds* could be called the godson of the Shaver Mystery that had so devastated *Amazing Stories** in the mid-1940s. As described in the entry for *Amazing*, the Shaver story began in 1944 and culminated in June 1947 with the all-Shaver special issue. Palmer realized that he had discovered a vast and highly receptive market; it had responded vociferously, even fanatically, to the mystical and bizarre aspects of the Shaver phenomenon, and it was clearly a market to tap.

Palmer was an enterprising man of action. Full of ideas and never afraid to gamble, he had a successful record behind him, both in fandom, where he had been one of the earliest active fans, and as a professional editor, where he had increased *Amazing*'s circulation tenfold. It was inevitable that the day would come when he would want to be his own boss, and in 1947 he started to put those plans into action. Ziff-Davis, the publishers of *Amazing*, though happy with the magazine's thriving circulation, became increasingly concerned over the criticism levied against it by the literary press and by letters complaining about the unscientific aspects of the Shaver Mystery, so they asked Palmer to soft-pedal it.

Instead, Palmer channeled Shaver out of *Amazing* and into his new nonfiction magazine, *Fate*. Palmer, in partnership with Curtis Fuller, had formed the Clark Publishing Company in North Clark Street, Chicago, expressly to concentrate on books and magazines dealing with the strange and unusual. *Fate*, a slim, digest magazine selling for twenty-five cents, was an immediate success, and Palmer was soon able to switch from a quarterly to a bi-monthly schedule. Because he was still employed by Ziff-Davis as editor (although William Hamling covered for him), Palmer adopted the pseudonym Robert N. Webster under which to edit *Fate*. It was obvious to anyone acquainted with *Amazing*, however, that Palmer must have had a connection with the magazine, if only because of the frequent references and advertisements for Shaver and UFO material. In addition, *Amazing*'s regular artist, Malcolm Smith, provided many of the illustrations, and several of the contributors had also appeared in *Amazing*, from Vincent H. Gaddis and Palmer's own alias, G. H. Irwin, to the Navaho "Oge-Make," who had featured in the January 1948 issues of both *Amazing* and *Fantastic Adventures** with the Indian legend "The Fire-Trail" and who now appeared in the September 1949 *Fate* with "Tribal Memories of the Flying Saucers."

All the clues were there to implicate Palmer, and he made no real attempts to hide his identity from SF fans. Attending the World SF Convention held at Cincinnati in September 1949, Palmer announced that he had left Ziff-Davis and was now publishing his own SF magazine, *Other Worlds*. The first issue, dated November 1949, had been delayed by the printer, otherwise Palmer would have distributed free copies to the fans. While at the convention Palmer met twenty-three-year-old fan Bea Mahaffey and hired her as his assistant. She took up her duties officially with the fourth issue, dated May 1950.

Other Worlds was a 160–page digest magazine printed on hefty pulp stock; it was the thickest magazine on the stands, which helped assuage the relatively high cover price of thirty-five cents. Malcolm Smith had painted an extremely eye-catching cover to illustrate Richard Shaver's lead story, "The Fall of Lemuria." In his editorial, written over the Webster by-line, Palmer claimed that *OW* would present "the best of each type of science fiction being published today."[1] To emphasize this claim he surveyed the leading SF magazines and highlighted the type of SF provided by each one.

> Let's take the magazine called *Astounding Science Fiction* [*Analog Science Fiction**]: we've read it for a long time, and we've enjoyed a great many of its stories. We like its editor, John W. Campbell, and we think he's tops when it comes to putting up-to-the-minute science in the stories

in his magazine. He can weave a powerful scientific punch into a story, and he's always careful to be 100% accurate in his science data. We like that, and we know you do too. So, you'll get at least one story each issue of *Other Worlds* which we might call the best *ASF* type.[2]

In like manner, Palmer covered *Amazing*, *Planet Stories** and *Thrilling Wonder* (*Wonder Stories**), and highlighted a story in his first issue which related to each magazine. The *Astounding* story was "The Miracle of Elmer Wilde" by Rog Phillips, which had in fact been rejected by Sam Merwin at *Thrilling Wonder*.[3] A controlled tale of a man with unfailing predictive powers, the story might well have appealed to Campbell, but if it had appeared in *Astounding* there is no doubt that Campbell would have encouraged Phillips to make more of the idea than the routine thriller that the author produced, but then Phillips had probably not written it with *Astounding* in mind. Nevertheless, the story did present SF with the following immortal line. Following the suggestion that Elmer Wilde did not possess ESP but was instead a unique individual who always guessed correctly, a character remarks: "I think you've hit it. I think that's the answer to a lot of things in history: Napoleon, Hitler, J. P. Morgan, and even you, Elmer."[4] Despite this, readers apparently voted it their favorite story in the issue.

The story representative of *Amazing* was, predictably, Shaver's "The Fall of Lemuria," which he still claimed to be truth veiled as fiction. Shaver also wrote the *Planet Stories* yarn "Where No Foot Walks" under the house name G. H. Irwin. It was an enjoyable, unpretentious adventure and probably the best story in the issue despite readers' votes.

With the second issue *OW* began to hit its stride, with examples of the full variety of SF and fantasy that Palmer (who now declared his involvement in print) wanted to publish. These ranged from such quasi-fictional items as Gustavus Meyrinck's "The Fatal Word," purported to be the report of the findings of an expedition into mysterious Tibet, to such genuine SF as "To Give Them Welcome" by Melva Rogers, wherein Earth becomes a haven for two alien eggs.

In his editorial Palmer laid down a challenge:

We hereby invite Ray Bradbury, L. Sprague de Camp, John W. Campbell, Jr. (oops, he's an editor, but allasame, we like his stories), Theodore Sturgeon, Jack Williamson, Lester del Rey, A. E. van Vogt—in fact, any writer who thinks he can write a story which is so unusual most editors wouldn't dare to publish it—to let us see same.[5]

Throughout his editorials and the letter columns of all the early issues, Palmer promoted his liberal policy, claiming that he wanted to publish a magazine that contained only what the readers wanted and was not hindered by publishing taboos—something Palmer was in a unique position to achieve. The result was that *OW* published some of the better stories of the early 1950s, and the first important issue was that dated May 1950—the first in which Bea Mahaffey's services were evident. Malcolm Smith's cover strikingly illustrated Eric Frank Russell's "Dear Devil," which tells of a lone Martian, utterly repulsive to human eyes, who remains behind after an exploratory mission to Earth, and who slowly wins the confidence and affection of a young boy. In his chapter on Eric Frank Russell, Sam Moskowitz tells us that Russell had submitted the story to *Astounding*, but when Campbell returned it for revision, Russell sent it to Palmer. The story was apparently unofficially nominated as the best novelette of the year.

Also in the same issue were "War of Nerves," one of A. E. van Vogt's Space Beagle adventures, and "Portrait of a Narcissus," a very readable story by Raymond F. Jones about a creature, native to Earth, that takes on the forms that others wish to see.

This level was sustained in the next issue, which featured Ray Bradbury's "Way in the Middle of the Air," a story that had been written for, but had failed to sell to, *Harper's*. Included in *The Martian Chronicles*, it was a pointed look at the American race problem with the Negroes' mass emigration to Mars. The same issue included "Enchanted Village" by A. E. van Vogt, considered by many to be his best short story. As these stories had already been in Palmer's inventory at the time of his challenge, we can see here another example of his salesmanship.

Yet, although many of these stories had good claims to being among the best stories of 1950, they were not typical of the contents. There was, for instance, a monotonous preponderance of stories about Mars—and even these classics echo that. The remaining stories were competent and readable, but forgettable—even the promised blockbusters like S. J. Byrne's Colossus sequence. A youthful Harlan Ellison laid it on the line in a letter published in the January 1952 issue. He listed 21 out of the 103 stories published in the fourteen issues of *OW* up to October 1951 that he regarded as excellent. These included, aside from some already mentioned, "Punishment without Crime" by Ray Bradbury, "Forget-Me-Not" by William F. Temple, "The Living Lies" by John Beynon, "Test Piece" by Eric Frank Russell and, believe it or not, "Journey to Nowhere" by Richard Shaver. "Now," Ellison continued, "is that using the potential that you've got? I ask you? Seriously, I'd like a good, down to Earth answer. None of this 'we're trying' routine. Cold, hard facts. Show us what is coming up."[6]

This good, but not quite good enough, quality characterized *OW* for its entire existence, even in the early years when it was at its best. Palmer tried hard, but he had his own problems. Palmer had fallen down the stairs in his basement in June 1950 and was paralyzed. Doctors were convinced that it was permanent, but Palmer fought back, and in only four months he was hobbling up the aisle as best man at the wedding of Rog Phillips and Mari Wolf. All this time he kept his finger on the pulse of the magazine, despite the capable work of Bea Mahaffey.

Rap's influence on the magazine was always predominant, even while he was in the hospital after his fall. . . . As his employee, my decisions were naturally based on what I believed were his intentions; as he began recovering, I kept him up on what was happening and he gave any necessary guidance. While he very generously gave me a lot of credit for keeping *OW* going during this time, it was a joint venture still.[7]

Palmer was also troubled by finances. *Other Worlds* had been launched in the wake of *Fate*'s success and in the heightened postwar awareness of the potential of science fiction, but the magazine's steep thirty-five cent cover price must have limited its appeal to only the more devoted SF readers. Palmer was nevertheless able to increase the magazine's frequency from bi-monthly to six-weekly in 1950, but then *OW* hit the problem of competition.

OW was one of the earliest digest magazines, and also the first to decry editorial taboos. It had first appeared in the same month as *The Magazine of Fantasy*,* and a year later came *Galaxy Science Fiction*.* The corner of the market that Palmer had hoped to call his own was now filled by two magazines that could afford top-class names and high-quality stories, without the stigma that was still attached to Palmer as a result of his work at *Amazing*. Palmer, as an independent publisher operating on a narrow budget, could not match their rates and had to be content with what he could attract by way of his policy—which was to always publish something new and daring. This did not mean that it was necessarily good, but in his own way Palmer, who had done so much to blacken the name of SF through his sensationalism in *Amazing*, was now trying to make amends. As Moorcock would with *New Worlds** and Harlan Ellison with *Dangerous Visions* in the mid-1960s, so Palmer tried to be innovative in the early 1950s.

If measured by this yardstick, rather than by its quality, *OW* was a success, certainly during the period 1950–1953. Despite the fact that Palmer still included flying-saucer articles and stories in the magazine, the science fiction was always challenging. "The Tin You Love to Touch" by Robert Bloch (June/July 1951), for instance, was a humorous story which highlighted the possible problems that attractive female robots could cause in future marital relationships. Robots also featured in "Robot Unwanted" (June 1952), where Daniel Keyes explores the problem of racial equality by showing man's reaction to a "free robot." Both "Act of God" by Richard Ashby (serialized December 1951–January 1952) and "These Are My Children" by Rog Phillips (serialized January–March 1952) challenged readers' views of God. Then there were "Somewhere a Voice" (January 1953), Eric Frank Russell's savage story of survival on an alien planet; Fritz Leiber's "The Seven Black Priests" (May 1953), a Gray Mouser tale at a time when fantasy was unpopular; "Tedric" (March 1953), another fantasy and a controversial volte-face for the superscience master E. E. Smith; and "Myshkin" by David V. Reed (April 1953), a 60,000–word novel published complete in one issue.

But these were the exceptions, not the rule. Attractive though the magazine was, with both front and back cover artwork by Malcolm Smith, Robert Gibson Jones, Harold McCauley and Hannes Bok, the bulk of the fiction was overblown superscience by Stuart J. Byrne and Richard Shaver that tried to stagger the reader through vastness of concept and in so doing lost touch with reader involvement and interest.

Palmer's position was perhaps best indicated by a comment he let slip in one of the letter columns, while talking about Alfred Bester's *The Demolished Man*, serialized in *Galaxy* during 1952 and regarded today as one of SF's greatest novels:

> Frankly we would have rejected Al Bester's story, although Al is a really top writer! Reason, we have an unreasoning objection to carrying a yarn with gimmicks! And it was hard to read. . . . The story might be good, we don't know—and we'll never know—because we couldn't read it.[8]

If this was typical of Palmer's attitude it would seem that the memorable stories published in *OW* appeared through Bea Mahaffey's involvement, not through any action by Palmer. Where Palmer's strength lay was in his own personality, which overflowed the editorial and letter columns of the magazine. No other editor would freely discuss and recommend stories published in rival magazines or openly admit to his errors of judgment. In *OW* Palmer laid bare his soul, and it gave the magazine a unique, impious quality.

Aside from Palmer's presence, the occasional outstanding story and the attractive covers, the best aspect of *OW* during its early life was a series of articles by L. Sprague de Camp under the general title "Lost Continents," condensed from his book *Lost Continents: The Atlantis Theme in History, Science and Literature* (New York: Gnome Press, 1954), serialized in the issues from October 1952 to July 1953.[9]

By 1952 the SF boom made it possible for *OW* to risk monthly publication. Already, however, the issues were growing weaker, with the apparent scarcity of quality material now being shared over a far greater market.

Then, suddenly, *Other Worlds* vanished, and in its place was *Science Stories*.* In effect, it was the same magazine. *OW*'s full title was *Other Worlds Science Stories*, and Palmer merely dropped the main title. The first issue of *Science Stories* was the August 1953 *Other Worlds* in a different jacket, but Palmer had designated the issue as Number 1, and it thus has a separate entry in this volume.

The decision to drop *OW* had been made at a moment's notice—not untypical of Palmer—because of financial problems, which indicated that sales of the magazine had suffered during the boom. Now Palmer was trying another gamble. He had had an offer from a Chicago businessman to edit a new magazine which would be independently financed. The magazine was to be called *Universe Science Fiction*,* and to keep his involvement suitably disguised, Palmer invented a new persona, George Bell. A new company, Bell Publications, was formed, and both *Universe* and *Science Stories* were published under its imprint.

The businessman's interest was short-lived, however, so Palmer bought him out. In order to do this, Palmer sold his interest in Clark Publications, thus losing his connection with *Fate*, and established the new Palmer Publications, which not only continued to publish *Universe* and *Science Stories*, but also launched a new magazine, along the lines of *Fate*, called *Mystic Magazine*.*

But after four issues, *Science Stories* ceased as suddenly as its predecessor, and *Universe* suddenly metamorphosed into *Other Worlds*, this time with a duplicate numbering system continuing the old *OW* sequence alongside that of *Universe*'s. Palmer had somehow resolved his financial problems (he claimed, "I dumped $40,000 on *OW*")[10] and was now set on a new future. In a response to a reader's letter that was almost as long as his editorial, Palmer explained that materialistic SF was past its heyday, "washed-up." The future lay in "psychic-SF," and that was the road *OW* was to follow.

The new *OW* was a pale version of its earlier self. Black and white covers had replaced the previous attractive paintings, although occasional interior artwork from Lawrence was some recompense. Most of the big-name authors were absent, although Theodore Sturgeon and Robert Bloch maintained a presence with inferior stories. Palmer continued "The Club House" by Rog Phillips, which had been revived in *Universe*, but this had limited appeal beyond the few loyal fans who still followed Palmer.

The ensuing issues saw the return of color covers, reprinted from earlier editions, but the magazine still conveyed a drab, almost pathetic quality. By now Palmer had closed his Evanston offices and was operating from his farm at Amhurst, Wisconsin. Bea Mahaffey moved back to her home in Cincinnati and continued to edit by mail. All this time Palmer was losing money, and though always the fighter, his editorials took on a disillusioned tone: "Brother, what a come down from ZD days! We used to have a $50,000.00 inventory to pick from, now we are begging stories from authors. Goes to prove what a sap we really are."[11]

Yet still he experimented, going against the grain if necessary. By 1955 all the pulp magazines, with the single exception of *Science Fiction Quarterly*,* had gone the way of the dinosaur. Yet, with the November 1955 issue, Palmer converted *OW* to a slim pulp format. The paper was of a slightly better quality than the standard pulp stock, which meant that the magazine had less bulk. Palmer hoped it would make *OW* stand out among the digests on the stands. He also reprinted a J. Allen St. John cover, whose work in the past had helped save *Weird Tales** and *Fantastic Adventures*. It was to be his final fling. In response to a letter written by Joe Gibson, Palmer laid it on the line:

And Joe, this is the end, if it doesn't go. If *Other Worlds* is a bad job, it will be because Palmer is what you say he is. And we won't be too proud to throw in the sponge, and leave the field to better men. We haven't any more money to lose—we've lost it all. If nobody reads *Other Worlds* with what I'll put into it in the next year, the printer won't be paid, and nothing

I can do will keep *OW* alive. But if the readers enjoy what they find in the next year, nothing I can do will keep the magazine from going ahead— and I promise you one thing Joe, whatever comes in in cash, will go right back out for more and better science fiction. It's up to the readers, Joe. *OW* can outsell even the old *Amazings* and certainly *Galaxy* and *ASF*, if what I've just said is the truth.[12]

Palmer also instigated another challenge to the estate of Edgar Rice Burroughs, proposing that they nominate a successor to Burroughs to continue the adventures of all his favorite characters. Palmer already had someone in mind, as Stuart Byrne had completed a 110,000–word novel, *Tarzan on Mars*. He needed the authorization of the Burroughs estate, however, before he could publish the novel, and he had every faith that it would be a best-seller and pull *OW* out of the red.

But he was fighting a losing battle on both counts. C. V. Rothmund, the business manager for the Burroughs estate, would not grant permission, and Byrne's novel remains unpublished to this day.

While sales dropped by 6 percent with the change to pulp, Palmer stubbornly persisted because what letters he did receive were encouraging. Despite what he continued to say in his editorials about true science fiction, Palmer now published out-and-out adventure fiction, entertaining but shallow. Hal Annas, Robert Donald Locke and Don Wilcox were his chief contributors, and *OW* presented only two or three stories per issue. He encouraged new writers Evelyn Martin and Barry P. Miller. The May 1957 issue featured Marion Zimmer Bradley's "Falcons of Narabedla," but of more import was that had the magazine continued Palmer would have published the first of Bradley's famed Darkover series with "The Sword of Aldones," which he had had on hand from at least 1956.[13] Instead, the novel was returned and eventually appeared as a separate book from Ace in 1962.

During 1956 Palmer found himself billed for additional local taxes, and he had to tell Bea Mahaffey that he could no longer pay her. Thereafter *OW* became a one-man operation: "Lots of midnight oil is burned. For instance, we do all our own layouts, planning covers, and even doing the artwork! If a set of cover plates have to be made, we don't have an artist to do it. We get out brushes, paints, pens, inks, drawing board, and go to it."[14] And all this from a man who was semi-paralyzed.

In the end, though, Palmer knew when he was beaten. Despite his claim in the May 1957 editorial that "with one big smash" *OW* had "attained all its goals," Palmer was admitting defeat. He had one last experiment. With the June 1957 issue he was going to change the emphasis of the magazine to feature news and articles about flying saucers. But so as not to totally burn his bridges, he retained the *Other Worlds* format for SF with alternate issues. By doing this he hoped to attract a wider readership and also trick the wholesalers into believing that there were two magazines and thus leave them on display longer. Palmer was nothing if not crafty.

Thus, the June issue was entitled *FLYING SAUCERS from Other Worlds* while the July issue became *Flying Saucers from OTHER WORLDS*. But the direction was clear. The SF magazines were going through a black period, and although there was a mini-boom in 1957 associated with the launch of the first artificial satellites, within a few years the field was down to just a handful of magazines. Palmer had predicted this in his July 1957 editorial: "Not that all sf magazines will die—perhaps a group of 4 or 5 will remain." On the other hand, there were no magazines devoted to flying saucers, and once Palmer had the evidence that sales of the UFO issues were more encouraging than those for the SF numbers, he made the break.

From the November 1957 issue the magazine permanently became *Flying Saucers*. Palmer would start other magazines, but from here on he concentrated on nonfiction and successfully continued with them until his death in 1977.

Although the passing of *Other Worlds* was no loss to the SF field, the departure of Raymond A. Palmer removed just a little of the sparkle.

Notes

1. Robert N. Webster [Raymond A. Palmer], "Editorial," *Other Worlds*, November 1949, p. 3.

2. Ibid., p. 2.

3. See *Other Worlds*, January 1950, p. 4.

4. Rog Phillips, "The Miracle of Elmer Wilde," *Other Worlds*, November 1949, p. 115.

5. Raymond A. Palmer, "Editorial," *Other Worlds*, January 1950, p. 5.

6. Harlan Ellison, letter in *Other Worlds*, January 1952, pp. 155–56.

7. Bea Mahaffey, private communication, January 1982.

8. Raymond A. Palmer in response to a letter from Edward J. McEvoy published in *Other Worlds*, October 1952, p. 144. Bea Mahaffey's own rejoinder to the letter was "I disagree about 'The Demolished Man' which I thought an exceptionally good story!"

9. The book had originally been planned to be published by Prime Press in 1952, and this credit was given in the early episodes of the book.

10. Raymond A. Palmer in response to a letter from Jack Hunter published in *Other Worlds*, May 1955, p. 120.

11. Raymond A. Palmer in response to a letter from George W. Earley published in *Other Worlds*, September 1955, p. 111.

12. Raymond A. Palmer in response to a letter from Joe Gibson published in *Other Worlds*, November 1955, p. 97.

13. Raymond A. Palmer listing forthcoming novels in response to a letter from Deen A. Warren in *Other Worlds*, June 1956, p. 98.

14. Raymond A. Palmer, "Editorial," *Other Worlds*, September 1956, p. 5.

Information Sources

BIBLIOGRAPHY:
Nicholls. *Encyclopedia.*
Tuck.

INDEX SOURCES: ISFM; MIT; SFM; Tuck.
REPRINT SOURCES: None known.
LOCATION SOURCES: M.I.T. Science Fiction Library; Pennsylvania State University
　　　Library; Sarah Lawrence College Library.

Publication History

TITLE: *Other Worlds Science Stories*, November 1949–July 1953, and May 1955–May
　　　1957 (see also *Science Stories*); *Flying Saucers from Other Worlds*, June 1957–
　　　May 1958; thereafter *Flying Saucers*, nonfiction.
VOLUME DATA: Volume 1, Number 1, November 1949–Volume 5, Number 7, July
　　　1953. Volumes 1 and 2, four issues per volume, bi-monthly to September 1950,
　　　thereafter six-weekly. Volume 3, six issues (January–December 1951), six-weekly
　　　(September 1951 issue labeled both Vol. 3, No. 5 and Vol. 4, No. 1). Volume
　　　4, nine issues (January–December 1952), six-weekly to October 1952, then monthly.
　　　Volume 5, seven issues (January–July 1953), monthly. Converted to *Science
　　　Stories*. Total run at this stage, 31 issues.
　　　Revived, May 1955. No volume numbering; continued sequence of both *Universe*
　　　and earlier *Other Worlds*. Issue 11 [32], May 1955–Issue 22 [43], May 1957, bi-
　　　monthly (May 1957 issue mislabeled 21 [42] inside). June–November 1957, un-
　　　numbered. Thereafter numbering followed *Flying Saucers* sequence, counting June
　　　1957 as Number 1. Total run of fiction issues in second series, 14 issues. Therefore,
　　　total run: 45 issues.
PUBLISHER: Clark Publishing Co., Evanston, Illinois, November 1949–July 1953 (ad-
　　　dress changed from August 1952); Palmer Publications, Evanston, Illinois, May
　　　1955–November 1957.
EDITOR: Raymond A. Palmer (all issues—first two as Robert N. Webster). Managing
　　　Editor: Bea Mahaffey, May 1950–November 1955.
FORMAT: Digest, 160 pp., November 1949–July 1953; 128 pp., May–September 1955;
　　　Pulp, 96 pp., November 1955–November 1957.
PRICE: 35¢.

Mike Ashley

OUT OF THIS WORLD

Out of This World, a short-lived companion to *Supernatural Stories** containing the same blend of weird fiction, was first published in 1954. Although
published by the firm of John Spencer and Co., which was noted for some of
the poorest SF magazines (among them *Futuristic Science Stories**), *OOTW* is
surprisingly readable, and this is because the two standard issues of the magazine
were written entirely by John Glasby. Glasby, a great fan of weird fiction, ranging
from H. P. Lovecraft to M. R. James, produced fiction at great speed but nevertheless had an ability to create atmosphere and a surprising variance of plot,
even though, from necessity, most of the plot-lines are derivative. The first issue,
for instance, includes "The Nightmare Road," which bears the ludicrous pen

name "Ray Cosmic" yet is a gripping tale of a man who slips suddenly from the normal world into one of unreality and ultimate death.

Only two issues proper of *OOTW* were published on a bi-monthly basis. Three years later, when the Supernatural Series was appearing in a regular pocketbook format, four issues were entitled *Out of This World* on the cover and spine, but were still identified as *Supernatural Stories* on the contents page and indicia, and are thus dealt with under that entry.

Information Sources

BIBLIOGRAPHY:
Ashley, Mike. *Fantasy Reader's Guide* 1. Wallsend, U.K.: Cosmos, 1979.
Tuck.
INDEX SOURCES: Ashley, Mike, *Fantasy Reader's Guide* 1, Wallsend, U.K.: Cosmos, 1979; MIT; MT; SFM; Tuck.
REPRINT SOURCES:
 Reprint Magazines: The full contents of Number 1 were reprinted in *Supernatural Stories* 34, and those of Number 2 in *Supernatural Stories* 36.
LOCATION SOURCES: M.I.T. Science Fiction Library; Pennsylvania State University Library.

Publication History

TITLE: *Out of This World*.
VOLUME DATA: Issues undated. Volume 1, Number 1, [November 1954]–Volume 1, Number 2, [January 1955]. Bi-monthly. Total run: 2 issues.
PUBLISHER: John Spencer & Co., London.
EDITORS: Sol Assael and Michael Nahum (not credited within issues).
FORMAT: Digest, 128 pp.
PRICE: 1/6d.

Mike Ashley

OUT OF THIS WORLD ADVENTURES

Out of This World Adventures, a pulp magazine scheduled for bi-monthly publication, ran for two issues, July and December 1950. Earlier that year, Avon's printer, J. W. Clement, had suggested to Joseph Meyers, publisher of Avon Books, a pulp magazine with a special folio of comics inserted. Intrigued by the idea, Meyers instructed Donald A. Wollheim, Avon's executive editor, to prepare three titles with this format in different categories. Besides *OOTWA*, there were *Pioneer Western* (lasting one issue) and *Sparkling Love Stories* (one issue). The time was late for new pulp magazines, and advance sales showed strength only in *OOTWA*. As Meyers lost interest and sales were insufficient, *OOTWA* died after its second issue.[1]

In the introduction to the first issue, Wollheim indicated that the stories would be primarily interplanetary adventures: "We tend to stress the celestial frontiers rather than the mundane background, in the feeling that space flight will prove to be the most exciting stimulant to adventure and progress yet to come.'' Hyperbolically, he described the comics section as ''an innovation in the realm of science-fiction. It combines the modern techniques of the full-color pictorial story with the best of the established fiction-magazine presentation, to achieve a new effect in fantasy.'' Wollheim also announced a letter department, inviting readers to ''write to the editor and tell him your thoughts on the first number and your suggestions for improvement.''

The letters printed in ''Mail from Planet Terra'' (December issue) were almost all unfavorable to the comics experiment. ''A reputation for good stories will sell far more copies than 'Hey Kids! They got funnies in the middle,' '' was a typical response. Interesting today primarily as period pieces embodying outdated social attitudes and science fictional motifs, the three comics adventures included in each issue were, nevertheless, written and illustrated by persons with some reputation in the science fiction field. John Michel, one of the leaders of the Futurians,[2] wrote the lead comics stories in each issue, both complicated inter-planetary adventures with hard-hitting, John Carter-like heroes. Gardner Fox (who had contributed to the early Superman comics) wrote and John Giunta (a highly respected comic and science fiction magazine artist) illustrated two con-secutive stories about ''Crom the Barbarian,'' Conan pastiches. Under the pseu-donyms Edward Bellen and E. J. Bellen, respectively, John Michel wrote ''The Man-Eating Lizards'' (July) and a supernatural story, ''Dead Man's Tale'' (De-cember). The former represents a kind of masculine wish-fulfillment prevalent in the pulps. Three tough, cool, wise-cracking GIs crash land on a Pacific island, where green-skinned savages attempt to sacrifice them to giant carnivorous liz-ards. The women of the tribe fall in love with the GIs, rescue them, and feed the male savages to the lizards instead.

Although *OOTWA*'s fiction, including the comics, were Wollheim's respon-sibility, the interior art and covers were the work of Avon's art director. Provided for the most part by William McWilliam and ''Martin,'' from Avon's comics office, the interior illustrations are rather conventional, often exaggerating the sexual attributes of female characters. (A few illustrations, like McWilliams' depiction of a little boy in pajamas watching the bearded ''Shipwrecked Bogey Man'' of Lloyd Williams' story, are unusually appealing.) A unique artistic feature of *OOTWA* is that the initial letter of each story is embellished with a weird or science fictional motif. The tables of contents of both issues are dec-orated with tableaus of weird images: in the July issue, for example, a snake's coils are intertwined with a skull-faced man, a frog-like alien and a spaceship with a needle in front resembling a hypodermic. While arresting, these designs suggest misleadingly that the stories that follow are weird tales rather than interplanetary adventures.

Unfortunately, the unsigned covers of the two issues, both featuring assaults on provocatively dressed women, are pure exploitation. Presumably depicting one of the Nazi-like Martians from Ray Cummings' ''The Planet Smashers,'' the cover of the July issue shows a gray-skinned entity strangling a blonde in a low-cut evening dress.[3] Illustrating a scene from A. Bertram Chandler's "Raiders of the Solar Frontier," the cover of the December issue shows a woman in a bikini and metal bra who has stabbed another woman, similarly clad. Incongruously, a man nearby is wearing a space helmet (neither woman is so equipped) but is naked to the waist.

Ray Cummings and A. Bertram Chandler, whose stories are depicted on *OOTWA*'s covers, contributed the longest stories in both issues. Besides the comics adventures already discussed, Cummings wrote "The Planet-Smashers" (Novelette) for the July issue. While the pleasure-loving Venusians enact a yearly fertility ritual, Martians, apparently out of sheer arrogance and love of destruction, attempt to blow up Venus. Chandler's violent "Raiders of the Solar Frontier" (Complete Novel), which concerns a battle between spiderlike alien invaders disguised as humans and the inhabitants of a prison planet, has elements of the western. ("His hand went automatically to his belt. But the spacesuit he was wearing had no belt, neither had it holster and the pistol that for so long had seemed part of himself.")

Chandler's "Terror of the Mist-Maidens" (Novelette) is remarkable because the alien threat is only a part of a battle waged between the sexes. Female mist-creatures have alienated human men from women of their own kind. The problem is solved when the male mist-creatures are released from the cylinder imprisoning them; but even after the human men have recovered from their infatuation, fear and hostility exist between the sexes: "For generations they [the men of the planet] would pay for the wrong that they had done the women, and for generations the women would crack the whip." While hostility toward women is not as overt in the other Cummings and Chandler stories in *OOTWA*, they stereotype women in ways that make uncomfortable reading today. Similarly, Cummings' and Chandler's stories are dated by their unabashed militarism and failure to recognize that alien invaders might be motivated by anything more complex than a lust for power and destruction.

Cummings and Chandler were, of course, enormously popular during the 1940s. The first issue of *OOTWA* is impressive for the other eminent writers who contributed: A. E. van Vogt, Lester del Rey, William Tenn, Mack Reynolds and Kris Neville. With the exception of Chandler, the contributors to the second issue are less well known.

The stories by William Tenn and Mack Reynolds, both concerned with man's helplessness in the face of older alien civilizations, are among the best in the magazine. In Tenn's "The Puzzle of Priipiirii" (July), an expedition from earth is investigating a Martian labyrinth sacred to Priipiirii, the god, we learn, of puzzles. Since the maze and the puzzles it contain are too intricate for the earthmen's mental powers, one by one they kill one another or go insane. The attributes of the Martian god, as revealed in the artifacts decorating the labyrinth, are skillfully unfolded. Reynolds' "The Discord Makers" (July) is based on the assumption that man's self-destructive behavior is so extreme that it can be explained only by alien subversion. An agent from the Department of Security discovers that aliens manipulate man to act against his own best interests: "Long after war has become ridiculous, they see to it that we remain warlike; they nurture our superstitions and our intolerances; they keep us divided into nations, classes, races, different religious groups." Predictably, when the agent submits his report, he is liquidated by the aliens, who control the Department of Security.

Not surprisingly, given *OOTWA*'s emphasis on space opera, the stories that are most successful today tend to be humorous or whimsical. A. E. van Vogt's witty story, "Letter from the Stars" (July), unfolds through letters from an alien to his earth pen pal. The earthman realizes that the alien is plotting to take over the earth and cleverly immobilizes him. Len J. Moffatt's "Alpha Centauri Curtain Call" (December) is narrated by a vaudeville performer, who tells of performing his routine before hostile aliens and literally "knocking them dead." What begins as a dramatic monologue of the Ring Lardner type becomes a shaggy dog story. Already mentioned for its charming illustration, Lloyd Williams' "Shipwrecked Bogey Man" (July) is the story of an alien, stranded on earth, who enlists the help of a little boy. With the child's toys, he attempts to rig a device for returning to his planet.

The focus of *OOTWA* is on interplanetary adventure. While quite a number of the stories transcend the escapism that often characterizes stories of this type, others are marred by a simplistic treatment of good and evil, militaristic glee, and females that are stereotypically helpless and voluptuous. The first issue of *OOTWA* contains the works of now important writers. An appealing feature of the second issue is the letter department, with enthusiastic and self-consciously witty remarks from readers and Wollheim's dialogue with them.

Notes

1. For accounts of Wollheim's tenure as executive editor of Avon Books, see Damon Knight, *The Futurians* (New York: John Day, 1977), pp. 180–182; and Michael Ashley, ed., *History of the Science Fiction Magazine, 1946–1955* (Chicago: Contemporary Books, 1977), III: 51–52. Facts about the publication and contents of *OOTWA* were provided in a letter from Donald A. Wollheim to the author.

2. See Knight, *The Futurians*; and Frederik Pohl, *The Way the Future Was: A Memoir* (New York: Ballantine, 1978).

3. This cover is reproduced in James Gunn, *Alternate Worlds: The Illustrated History of Science Fiction* (A & W Visual Library, 1975), p. 196.

Information Sources

BIBLIOGRAPHY:
Nicholls. *Encyclopedia*.
Tuck.
INDEX SOURCES: ISFM; SFM; Tuck.
REPRINT SOURCES: None known.
LOCATION SOURCES: California State University–Fullerton Library, Special Collections (Vol. 1, No. 1 only); Eastern New Mexico University, Golden Library (not

available through inter-library loan); Massachusetts Institute of Technology, MIT Science Fiction Society (not available through ILL); Northern Illinois University Library, Rare Books and Special Collections (no ILL or microfilm, but partial photocopying of some issues *may* be possible); Ohio State University Libraries, Division of Special Collections; Pennsylvania State University Libraries, Special Collections (Vol. 1, No. 1 only); San Francisco Academy of Comic Art, Science Fiction Room; San Francisco Public Library, Literature Department; Syracuse University, George Arents Research Library, Rare Book Division; Temple University, Paley Library, Paskow Science Fiction Collection (not available through ILL); Texas A&M, Special Collections; Toronto Public Libraries, Spaced Out Library (not available through ILL); University of California–Los Angeles, Special Collections (a microfilm may be produced, the negative to remain at UCLA and the patron to pay for negative and print); University of California–Riverside, Special Collections (Vol. 1, No. 1 only); University of Georgia Libraries, Periodicals Department (Vol. 1, No. 1 only); University of Kansas, Spencer Research Library; University of Maryland Baltimore County Library, Special Collections (not available through ILL, but will photocopy selections from the magazines, provided the material is not too fragile).

Publication History

TITLE: *Out of This World Adventures*.
VOLUME DATA: Volume 1, Number 1, July 1950–Volume 1, Number 2, December 1950. Intended schedule, bi-monthly. Total run: 2 issues.
PUBLISHER: Avon Periodicals, New York.
EDITOR: Donald A. Wollheim.
FORMAT: Pulp, 128 pp.
PRICE: 25¢.

Wendy Bousfield

OUTLANDS

At first appearance *Outlands* in no way resembled a science fiction magazine. Subtitled "A Magazine for Adventurous Minds," it sported a blue cover with an inset pastoral scene. A slim, digest publication of only forty pages, it could have passed as a church parish magazine almost anywhere.

Outlands was edited by Liverpudlian fan Leslie J. Johnson, co-founder of the British Interplanetary Society. He had sunk most of his RAF gratuity into forming a company with Leslie J. Heald and together with Ernest L. Gabrielson (who provided the cover and the magazine's title) launched *Outlands* in October 1946.

Its contents were not special. John Russell Fearn provided the lead story, "Pre-Natal," while Leslie V. Heald (as "Charnock Walsby") and Ernest Gabrielson (as "John Gabriel" and "Antony Cotrion") helped complete the issue. If any historical significance can be attached to it, it is that it contained both a first and a last. "Strange Portrait" was the first published story by Sydney J. Bounds, soon to become a well-known name in British SF circles. It had been used at the last minute to replace "Hully Gee," a fantasy by Eric Frank Russell that had been withdrawn due to disagreements between author and editor. "Rival Creators," on the other hand, was the last published story by George C. Wallis, a grand old name on the British scene who had published SF in the popular periodicals since the 1890s in one of the longest careers in SF.

The stories and articles showed a strong bias toward psychic fantasy rather than SF: stories the editor called "outlandish." Soon after publication Johnson discovered that copies were being returned without being distributed; he promptly decided to cut his losses, and the magazine folded.

In 1979, however, young fan Stephen Holland decided to revive the magazine with Johnson's blessing, and has attempted to assemble a second issue with as many of the original planned stories as possible, plus new stories by authors included in the first issue. Publication of this novelty item is still awaited.

Information Sources

BIBLIOGRAPHY:
Johnson, Leslie J. "The Story of Outlands" (unpublished, but planned for *Outlands* 2).
Nicholls. *Encyclopedia*.
Tuck.
INDEX SOURCES: SFM; Tuck.
REPRINT SOURCES: None known.
LOCATION SOURCES: None known.

Publication History

TITLE: *Outlands*.
VOLUME DATA: Labeled only First Issue, Winter 1946. Intended schedule, quarterly.
        Total run: 1 issue.
PUBLISHER: Outlands Publications, Liverpool.
EDITOR: Leslie J. Johnson (not directly credited within issue).
FORMAT: Digest (saddle-stapled), 40 pp.
PRICE: 1/6d.

Mike Ashley

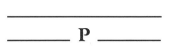

PHANTASY DIGEST

Wayne Warfield encountered William Hall, Jr., shortly after parting company with the Robert E. Howard fanzine *Cross Plains*. Together, Hall and Warfield decided to produce a series of small-press items culminating in a regular magazine. Warfield would be the editor/designer, while Hall would remain the "silent" publisher. All of the items that Hall Publications produced leaned toward the Howard style.

While the one-off items were somewhat hurried in construction, the magazine, *Phantasy Digest*, which appeared three times in 1976 and 1977, showed a greater investment of time and care. Typeset throughout in a pleasing face, it lacked the cluttered appearance typical of other A5 semi-prozines.

His work on *Cross Plains* had supplied Warfield with many contacts. This was evident from the first issue of *PD*. Among its contents were "The Undying Druids," an article by Andrew Offutt, and "The Place of Stones," the story that traced the origin of Charles R. Saunders' popular hero Imaro. Robert E. Howard was present with a reprint of his 1936 *Thrilling Mystery** story, "Graveyard Rats," introducing the detective Steve Harrison. The artwork, while sparse, was of good quality, with contributions by Gene Day, John Stewart and Jim Pitts.

The second issue continued in the same vein, except that it was predominantly reprint. There was a second Steve Harrison story by Howard, and a John Jakes Brak the Barbarian tale, accompanied by an interview with Jakes. The quality of the artwork, sadly, declined. Artwork improved by the third issue, which gave pride of place to a Nifft the Lean novelette by Michael Shea, rumored to have been a reject from *The Magazine of Fantasy and Science Fiction.**

It is difficult for a magazine to mature significantly in a short life of three issues, but *PD* showed considerable promise. The magazine would no doubt have developed had it continued, but, inexplicably, Wayne Warfield departed from the fantasy scene, and the magazine ceased publication.

Information Sources

INDEX SOURCES: MT.
REPRINT SOURCES: None known.
LOCATION SOURCES: M.I.T. Science Fiction Library.

Publication History

TITLE: *Phantasy Digest*.
VOLUME DATA: Volume 1, Number 1, 1976–Volume 1, Number 3, 1977. Schedule irregular. Total run: 3 issues.
PUBLISHER: Hall Publications, Perryville, Maryland.
EDITOR: Wayne Warfield.
FORMAT: Digest (saddle-stapled). Pages as follows: 1, 80 pp.; 2, 74 pp.; 3, 66 pp.
PRICE: $4.00.

Jon Harvey

PHANTOM

Phantom, which began publication in 1957, was the only regular magazine devoted to weird fiction ever published in Britain, yet it has frequently been overlooked by researchers, and today issues are becoming increasingly scarce. Attempts to locate its editor, Leslie Syddall, and its art director, Cliff Lawton, who later resurfaced as editor of *A Book of Weird Tales*,* have been unsuccessful. *Phantom* by name is rapidly becoming phantom by nature.

Its early issues were unexceptional. They were filled with short stories that lacked any development of plot and characterization and were merely the relation of some spooky incident. They were not dissimilar to the narratives of true tales of hauntings, and in fact a number of the contributors were collectors and afficionados of such facts, especially Greta Briggs, whose name will be familiar to tourists in the north of England, where her many booklets on various local hauntings are still available.

A change became noticeable with the fourth issue, which began to introduce American reprints, the first being "The Last Grave of Lill Warren" by Manly Wade Wellman, from *Weird Tales*.* This was followed in the next issue by two reprints from August Derleth and Merle Constiner, both from *Weird Tales*. Derleth's involvements at this early stage may indicate that he was in fact working with Leslie Syddall on the selection of American reprint material. Derleth was always actively involved in British publishing affairs on the weird fiction scene, and it is unlikely that he did not at least offer some suggestions. However, all the stories reprinted at this stage had been available in British editions of *Weird*

Tales only a few years earlier, and it may be that Syddall had simply requested reprint rights through Thorpe and Porter. There is a third possibility. By the time Lawton was editing *A Book of Weird Tales* he was collaborating with Forrest J Ackerman, who suggested most of the contents. It is quite likely that Lawton and Syddall had already made contact with Ackerman at this early stage to clear rights. Whatever the circumstances—and it could be a combination of all three—it was noticeable that from the fifth issue, and more so from the twelfth, *Phantom* became a regular home for weird fiction by American writers, not just for reprinted stories but for new tales as well. The sixteenth and final issue is perhaps the best example. It contained new stories by Bob Olsen and Andre Norton, possible reprints from Idella Stone, Rice Arden and Tigrina, and reprints from Sophie Wenzel Ellis, Robert Barbour Johnson and Gene Hunter (from sources all but inaccessible to British readers). The inclusion of Tigrina and stories selected from *Fantasy Book** make Forrest Ackerman's involvement at this stage almost a certainty.

British authors were not neglected, though it is ironic that the only appearance of H. Russell Wakefield, probably the best British writer of ghost stories active in the 1950s, was with a story reprinted from *Weird Tales*—"The Third Shadow." A few names from the SF field made sales: Lionel Fanthorpe had two contributions, John S. Glasby had one under the alias Alan Thorndyke, and Peter Baillie and Anthony Williamson had a couple of stories, but no major names appeared. The only other regular British contributors besides Greta Briggs was Thomas H. Martin, equally well known for his detective stories and for some of his weird fiction under the house name Peter Saxon, who had four stories under the alias Martin Thomas.

The British contributions, however, were minor pieces, and the strength of *Phantom* for British readers lay in its presentation of work from America. The fact that the last issue was written entirely by Americans demonstrates that British writers were not making sufficient use of the market, and that what contributions were coming in were poor. It may also indicate that *Phantom* was in financial trouble, reprints being more economical.

For a while *Phantom* had a companion nonfantasy magazine, *Combat*, and the same publisher also distributed the one-shot *Screen Chills and Macabre Stories.** Efforts to trace the original publishers have shown that they existed in name only and had certainly gone out of existence by 1958. Just why *Phantom* folded is not clear. "The circumstances which have brought about this magazine's death have been a surprise to us all, and they have been completely outside our control," wrote the editor in the last issue. At the time it was hoped that it would be only a temporary hiatus, but *Phantom* never was revived.

Information Sources

BIBLIOGRAPHY:
Tuck.
INDEX SOURCES: Cook, Michael L., *Monthly Murders*, Westport, Conn.: Greenwood Press, 1982; MIT; MT; SFM; Tuck.

REPRINT SOURCES: None known.
LOCATION SOURCES: None known.

Publication History

TITLE: *Phantom*.
VOLUME DATA: Volume 1, Number 1, [April] 1957–Volume 1, Number 16, July
1958. Monthly. Total run: 16 issues.
PUBLISHER: Dalrow Publications Ltd., Bolton, Lancs., issues 1–12; Pennine Publi-
cations, Ltd., Bolton, issues 13–16.
EDITOR: Leslie Syddall.
FORMAT: Large Digest, 112 pp., issues 1–12; 104 pp. thereafter.
PRICE: 2/-.

Mike Ashley

PLANET STORIES

From the moment that he or she saw the cover, the reader knew what to
expect: *Planet Stories*: "Strange Adventures on Other Worlds—the Universe of
Future Centuries." Its cover illustrations reinforced the impression. Allen Anderson's leggy, beautiful women (not always Earthlings, for one of *Planet*'s
specialties was lovely princesses from Venus or Mars or some "unknown/lost"
world) were constantly threatened by BEMs. Throughout its history—from Winter 1939 through Summer 1955, a total of seventy-one issues—although its
subeditors were frequently changed, its basic makeup was not. Usually each
number featured one or two novels, whose blurbs emphasized the promise of
melodramatic action as well as declaring anything from "A Terrific Novel of
Outer-Space Worlds" (Winter 1939) or "A Barbarians World Story" (July 1951)
to "A grimly-stirring novel of weird adventure on an alien world" (Winter 1943)
or simply "A Novel of the Lost Ones" (Fall 1949).

In 1974, in the introduction to what was to have been the first of a series of
paperbacks entitled *The Best of Planet Stories*, Leigh Brackett acknowledged
that the magazine, "unashamedly, published 'space opera,' " which she defined
as "a story that has an element of adventure." She then argued eloquently that

the tale of adventure—of great courage and daring, of battle against the
forces of darkness and the unknown—has been with the human race since
it first learned to talk. It began as part of the primitive survival technique,
interwoven with magic and ritual, to explain and propitiate the vast forces
of nature with which man could not cope in any other fashion. The tales
grew into religions. They became the Mabinogion and the Ulster Cycle
and the Voluspa. They became Arthur and Robin Hood, and Tarzan of
the Apes.

Then she asserted that "the so-called space opera is the folk-tale, the hero-tale of our particular niche in history." What she said may not please all of today's critics, with their love of narrow definitions and restricting elitism, but Leigh Brackett defined well not only her own works but the body of fiction published by *Planet Stories* (as well as many of its contemporaries). Nor is her 1974 statement a belated effort to gain favor with modern critics and defend her fiction, for as early as January 1943 she remarked, "I believe in science-fiction and fantasy as a definite form, entitled to dignified consideration," although one should remember that it is written "as entertainment and not as propaganda." Here, then, once again, in a magazine notorious in some circles because of its emphasis upon action, the present-day reader finds that one of *Planet*'s most frequent and most distinguished contributors links together science fiction and fantasy as a single form. Nor should one overlook her mention of "the hero-tale."

Leigh Brackett was one of a comparative handful of writers whose fiction sustained *Planet Stories* during its lifetime and has given it literary and historical significance since its demise. Her first contribution to *Planet* was the story "Stellar Legion" (Winter 1940); her second, "The Dragon-Queen of Jupiter" (Summer 1941). From the Spring 1944 issue, in which her novel "The Jewel of Bas" appeared, Brackett's novels and novelettes were regularly featured, including the three that created Erik John Stark, perhaps her most famous protagonist-hero: "Queen of the Martian Catacombs" (Summer 1949), "The Enchantress of Venus" (Fall 1949) and "The Black Amazon of Mars" (March 1951). In all, she published seventeen titles in *Planet*, although one for which she is probably best remembered is the collaboration with Ray Bradbury, "Lorelei of the Red Mist" (Summer 1946), the idea for which originated with her.

The number of her contributions to *Planet* should not be regarded as unusual. Many magazines had a small number of authors upon whom they depended and without whom they could not have existed—at least without a radical change in identity. For example, if one looks at the first twenty-four issues of *Planet Stories* (the two volumes published between 1939 and 1945), one finds that the first two issues featured novels by John Murray Reynolds, disguising one of the publisher's house writers. After that, taking into consideration longer fiction only, Nelson Bond wrote eight lead novels or novelettes, as well as two stories in verse—"The Ballad of Blaster Bill" and "The Ballad of Venus Nell." Ray Cummings was featured ten times; Ross Rocklynne, four. These writers established the distinctive flavor of *Planet* in its early years: if—because of Cummings especially—the magazine seemed to look backward toward the 1930s and earlier, that impression is reinforced by the fact that the majority of interior illustrations for the lead novels and novelettes were done by Paul, whom one associates with Gernsback and the earliest science fiction magazines.

The middle and late 1940s belonged to Leigh Brackett and Ray Bradbury, along with such now little-known writers as Albert dePina, Erik Fennel and Emmett McDowell. Better-known names include Alfred Coppel, Henry Hasse and Gardner F. Fox. These authors all belong almost exclusively to *Planet*'s middle period, with only a handful of stories overlapping into the early 1950s.

From 1950 until the magazine folded, Poul Anderson became the newest writer featured by *Planet*, but he was so prolific and widely published that he cannot be as closely identified with the magazine as the others.

As one examines the seventy-one numbers that make up the complete run of *Planet Stories*, one realizes that any narrowly defined concept of space opera must be broadened considerably to take into account the bulk of the magazine's offerings. True, Earth itself is often threatened—by some past revolt of Venusians and Martians which has been defeated so that the truth may now be told, as in Ray Cummings' "Space-Liner X87" (Summer 1940), or by a present menace, as in Eando Binder's only novel, "One Thousand Miles Below" (Winter 1940). On occasion—and note the date—the story celebrates an organization such as the U.S. Rocket Service, taking "pride in the men of Terra," as in Keith Bennett's "The Rocketeers Have Shaggy Ears" (Spring 1950), but on occasion the civilization (democracies) of Earth is defeated, as in Nelson Bond's "The Ultimate Salient" (Fall 1940), whose narrator broods over a manuscript supposedly from the future as he watches Western Europe destroyed by tyranny, Mussolini's troops prepare for action and Japan make advances against the Indies, while Russia looks on silently.

Most often the revolts or wars are on other worlds, and an Earthman is thrust unwittingly into a struggle which is not his own. Perhaps the most famous—and typical—of this variation remains Leigh Brackett and Ray Bradbury's "Lorelei of the Red Mist." Certainly beleaguered Amazons and fair princesses abound, as do the beautiful, power-hungry temptresses like Rann of "Lorelei." Significantly, many of these stories take place in primitive, sometimes barbarian worlds which now bring to mind many of the worlds of "sword and sorcery." This emphasis upon women, good or evil—however stereotyped—indicated a sexuality in the fiction whose presence many editors and writers have denied except in the fiction of Philip José Farmer or Theodore Sturgeon. One may question the maturity of treatment, but that sexuality was present in such a story as Carl Selwyn's "Venus Has Green Eyes" (Fall 1940), which reaches its climax only when the protagonist seizes and kisses the Venusian princess who has declared her hatred of mankind. One must acknowledge that even as she succumbs to his embrace, she does slap him. One of the most amusing letters to the editor came from a man who was "ashamed to see" that *Planet* had accepted and printed "Lorelei of the Red Mist"; he needed a "pint of Listerine to wash the dirty taste out of my mouth" and pleaded with the editor to "please remember it is the younger readers" (Fall 1946).

Whatever patterns dominate the stories as a whole, *Planet* did give Leigh Brackett and Ray Bradbury the opportunity to find and explore their own idioms. One says this while realizing that both authors had published elsewhere, Bradbury especially. Yet a close examination of his contributions is particularly rewarding, for in them one may trace his development from just another writer who skillfully handles the conventional materials of fantasy and science fiction, as in "The Monster Maker" (Spring 1944), "The Creatures That Time Forgot" (Fall 1946) to the master capable of "Zero Hour" (Fall 1947)—in which the invasion of Earth by aliens is accomplished with the aid of the very young children who play the required game—and the two episodes collected in *The Martian Chronicles*: "The Million Year Picnic" (Summer 1946) and "Mars Is Heaven" (Fall 1948). In the pieces published in *Planet* glimpses of that artistry may perhaps be seen first in "Morgue Ship" (Summer 1944) and "Lazarus Come Forth" (Winter 1944), stories built around the idea of collecting dead bodies drifting in space after the various battles of a 300-year-long war between Earth and Mars. His central theme that technology has advanced too rapidly is fully enunciated in "Rocket Summer" (Spring 1947), in which the President attempts to resist public pressure demanding the launching of a spaceship. The last stories by Bradbury that *Planet* issued were "The Golden Apples of the Sun" (November 1953), apparently its first magazine publication, and "A Sound of Thunder" (January 1954), reprinted from *Collier's* for June 28, 1952. It seems to be the one reprint *Planet Stories* used.

While the authors already mentioned may be regarded as the core of contributors who gave the magazine its identity, *Planet* did publish a number of selections by other important science fiction writers. One of the earliest examples is Isaac Asimov's "The Black Friar of the Flame" (Spring 1942), rejected by *Astounding* (*Analog Science Fiction**). Clifford Simak's "Mr. Meek, Musketeer" (Summer 1944) met with sufficient favor to warrant inclusion of its sequel, the novelette "Mr. Meek Plays Polo" (Fall 1944). Other contributors included Frank Belknap Long, Donald A. Wollheim, Henry Kuttner, James Blish and Gordon Dickson. A noteworthy inclusion was that of Theodore Sturgeon's "The Incubi of Planet X" (September 1951), in which alien invaders have cast Earth's women into a parallel world. It was not reprinted until its appearance in *Sturgeon in Orbit* (1964).

Damon Knight's two novels, "The Third Little Green Man" (Summer 1948) and "The Star Beast" (Spring 1949), mark another high point, although there are those who will argue that the classic story published by *Planet* was Fredric Brown's delightfully comic "Star Mouse" (Spring 1942). Its sequel, "Mitky Rides Again," did not appear until November 1950.

During its final years perhaps *Planet*'s major contribution to the field came when it published five stories by Philip K. Dick. His first commercial sale was "Beyond Lies the Wub" (July 1952); his second of four sold that year was "The Gun" (September 1952), the same month that "The Skull" appeared in *Worlds of If* (*If**). *Planet* also included "The Infinites" (May 1953), "The Crystal Crypt" (January 1954) and "James P. Crow" (May 1954). Of the five, "The Infinites" has importance because of its handling of the theme of altered neural reactions which lead to mutation and chains in the brain which free the mind from the body. Historically, "James P. Crow" has an even greater significance in that it foreshadows the direction that science fiction was to take in social criticism in the 1960s and 1970s. It explores the place of humans in a robot-dominated world and focuses upon a protagonist who refuses to be a second-class citizen.

Two other features of *Planet Stories* deserve notice. In "The Vizigraph" it maintained one of the strongest letters to the editor columns of any science fiction magazine. Its often lengthy entries indicate how emotionally involved the readers became with the fiction. More important, historically at least, it reveals the extent to which an active fandom was developing into a lasting subculture. For example, Bob Madle periodically reported the activities of PSFS (the Philadelphia Science Fiction Society). Chad Oliver is one of the writers of the 1950s whose letters appeared almost a decade earlier. And a priceless remark occurs in a letter from Robert Silverberg (Summer 1950), in which he acknowledges that Ray Bradbury "certainly gets some original ideas, if not good ones."

Finally, *Planet* was one of the few magazines to give recognition to its artists. Significantly, Paul, as noted, did many of the illustrations for the featured novels and novelettes, as did Hannes Bok. Allen Anderson did many of the covers, but in its last few years Frank Kelly Freas frequently took on that task. Possibly the best yet most underrated artist was Leydenfrost, whose graphic creations epitomized much of what *Planet Stories* represented in the 1940s.

One cannot definitely say why *Planet Stories* ceased publication with the Summer 1955 issue. From the beginning it had been a quarterly, always wanting to go bi-monthly. It did so for two issues (March and May) in 1943, but wartime shortages cut short that venture. It did, however, remain bi-monthly from January 1951 through May 1954. Then once again it went quarterly. It was one of a chain of magazines published by Fiction House and one can only surmise that its publishers decided that the pulp field was no longer sufficiently profitable. One should recall that the first so-called boom enjoyed by the field had ended by the mid-1950s. A second reason may lie in the fact that, editorially, it seemed to look backward at the very time when other magazines such as *Galaxy Science Fiction** began to explore the themes and narrative techniques that so changed much of science fiction in the 1950s. In the final analysis, *Planet Stories* made at least two contributions to the field in general: first, it provided a market for the story of heroic adventure at a time when psychological and sociological "realism" were becoming increasingly important to the field; second, it permitted such writers as Leigh Brackett and Ray Bradbury to develop much of their artistic maturity.

Information Sources

BIBLIOGRAPHY:

Nicholls. *Encyclopedia*.

Stevens, Milton F. "Visit to a Pulpy Planet." *Science-Fiction Review*, No. 2 (1975).

Tuck.

INDEX SOURCES: IBSF; ISFM; MIT; O'Malley, Robert, "An Index to Planet Stories,"
    Xenophile, Nos. 20–22, 26 (1976); SFM; Tuck.

REPRINT SOURCES:

Reprint Magazine:

British: Twelve issues, undated [March 1950–September 1954], first published by Streamline Publications, London; remainder by Pembertons, Manchester. A scarce thirteenth issue is rumored to exist but has not been sighted. First four issues irregular [March, July 1950; January, April 1951], remainder bi-monthly from June 1953. Correspond to U.S. editions, abridged, as follows: 1, Fall 49; 2, Spr 50; 3, Sum 50; 4, Jan 51; 5, Fall 50; 6, Jul 53; 7, May 53; 8, Sep 53; 9, Nov 53; 10, Mar 53; 11, Jan 54; 12, Mar 54. Issues 7 and 8 carried nonfiction reprinted from *Startling Stories* and *Thrilling Wonder Stories*. Pulp, 64/66 pp., 1/- (first two issues 9d.).

Canadian: Twelve issues corresponding to U.S. run Fall 1948–March 1951; by American News Co., in Toronto.

Derivative Anthology: Leigh Brackett, ed., *The Best of Planet Stories #1* (New York: Ballantine Books, 1975), contains 7 stories from period 1942–1952.

Reprint Magazine: See entry for *Tops in Science Fiction*.

Microform: Greenwood Press Periodical Series.

LOCATION SOURCES: Brigham Young University Library; Florida International University Library; M.I.T. Science Fiction Library; Northern Illinois University Library; Pennsylvania State University Library; Texas A&M University Library; University of Arizona Library; University of British Columbia Library; University of Montana Library; University of New Brunswick Library; University of Washington Library.

Publication History

TITLE: *Planet Stories*.

VOLUME DATA: Volume 1, Number 1, Winter 1939–Volume 6, Number 11 (misnumbered 12 on spine), Summer 1955. Twelve issues per volume. Quarterly, Winter 1939–Fall 1950 (although Summer 1943 issue came out one month earlier, dated May); bi-monthly, November 1950–Summer 1954; quarterly, Fall 1954–Summer 1955. Total run: 71 issues.

PUBLISHER: Love Romances, Inc., New York.

EDITORS: Malcolm Reiss was in overall editorial control throughout. He was designated Editor, Winter 1939–Summer 1942; Managing Editor, Fall 1942–Summer 1944; General Manager, Winter 1944–January 1952; Managing Editor, March 1952–Summer 1955. Other supporting editors were: Wilbur S. Peacock, Fall 1942–Fall 1945; Chester Whitehorn, Winter 1945–Summer 1946; Paul L. Payne, Fall 1946–Spring 1950; Jerome Bixby, Summer 1950–July 1951; Jack O'Sullivan, March 1952–Summer 1955.

FORMAT: Pulp; 128 pp., Winter 1939–Fall 1950; 112 pp., November 1950–May 1954 (except March 1952, 96 pp.); 96 pp., Summer 1954–Summer 1955.

PRICE: 20¢, Winter 1939–Fall 1950; 25¢ thereafter.

Thomas D. Clareson

POPULAR SCIENCE FICTION

Popular Science Fiction, first published in 1953, was one of a pair of indistinguishable companion magazines, and both its policy and history are discussed in the entry for *Future Science Fiction*.*

All issues were in a slim, digest format, cheaply produced. Most of the content was of American origin, though some stories saw their first and only publication here. The only Australian writer present was Norma K. Hemming with "Symbiosis!" A. Bertram Chandler did have one story, "The Viscous Circle," reprinted from the first issue of *Fantastic Universe*,* but at this time he was still based in London.

"Expedition Void" by Jody McCarter, in the fourth issue, and "The Square Peg" by M. Louis Moore (his first initial dropped by the printer), in the sixth, are of interest as the only known appearances by these two American writers.

The magazine ceased publication in March 1955. But in 1967 another publisher acquired the plates of Numbers 4 and 6 and reprinted them, with renumbered covers. These were painted by Keith Chatto based closely on the originals, the second being in turn inspired by Frank R. Paul's cover for the February 1933 *Wonder Stories*.*

Information Sources

BIBLIOGRAPHY:
Nicholls. *Encyclopedia.*
Tuck.
INDEX SOURCES: ASFI; Day, IWFM; Tuck.
REPRINT SOURCES:
  Reprint Editions: Issues 4 and 6 were reprinted with new covers as *Popular Science Fiction* NEW SERIES, Nos. 1 and 2, undated [August and November 1967], Digest, 64 pp., from Page Publications, Sydney.
LOCATION SOURCES: Futurian Society of Sydney Library; Pennsylvania University Library.

Publication History

TITLE: *Popular Science Fiction.*
VOLUME DATA: All issues undated. Volume 1, Number 1, [July 1953]–Volume 1, Number 6, [March 1955]. Three times a year. Other issues published as follows: 2, Nov 53, Mar 54; 4, Jul 54; 5 Dec 54. Total run: 6 issues.
PUBLISHER: Blue Diamond Publishing Co., Sydney.
EDITOR: Unidentified within issues. Ronald Forster was the Editorial Director, although Peter Grant handled most later issues. The contents of issue 2 were selected by Vol Molesworth, those of the remaining issues by Graham Stone.
FORMAT: Digest (saddle-stapled), 64 pp.
PRICE: First two issues, 1/3d; thereafter 1/6d.

Graham B. Stone

PRIZE GHOST STORIES

Prize Ghost Stories was a reprint magazine that selected its stories from the 1920s magazine *Ghost Stories*.* Accompanied by fake photographs and sensationalized title changes (for example, "The Leopard" had become "Voodoo and the Virgin''), the magazine was clearly aimed at the readership that bought confessions magazines but also liked a touch of the occult.

Only one issue, dated 1963, is known, but others may have appeared. It had a companion publication, *True Twilight Tales,** which see for full details.

Information Sources

BIBLIOGRAPHY:
Tuck.
INDEX SOURCES: MT; Tuck.
REPRINT SOURCES: None known.
LOCATION SOURCES: None known.

Publication History

TITLE: *Prize Ghost Stories.*
VOLUME DATA: Unnumbered and undated, except 1963.
PUBLISHER: League Publications, Inc., New York.
EDITOR: Not identified within issue, but probably Helen Gardiner.
FORMAT: Large Pulp, 96 pp.
PRICE: 50¢.

Mike Ashley

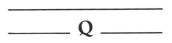

QUESTAR

Questar began life in 1978 as a glossy semi-professional fanzine that combined interests in SF in the cinema and comic books; as a result the contents were a mixture of articles, comic strips and the occasional amateurish piece of fiction. Packaged with care and imagination, the production was a labor of love for its co-editors. It had zeal, energy and novelty, and these survived through the second issue, only to be tragically lost in the third.

It was the third issue that introduced interior color to artwork and photographs, but along with this came a more commercial attitude. While some fiction remained, the emphasis slid to a concentration on the cinema, which was undergoing a popular revival. Sadly, though, this coverage grew increasingly condescending in attitude until the reviews became little more than press handouts.

Questar settled into a long period of stagnation. Contents of each issue were predictable: an interview with a science fiction writer, plus another with someone in the film industry, and occasionally a third with an actor or actress. Fiction became almost superfluous, and there was a totally "bad" comic strip, "Just Imagine: Jeanie." Occasional artist profiles and portfolios were of interest, but the whole impression was one of inferior material given a glossy respectability.

With the thirteenth issue, however, and the change in title to *Quest/Star*, there was a dramatic change in emphasis and presentation. In the previous issue Horace Gold had been drafted as fiction editor, and his presence was felt with this latest issue, reprinting stories by Robert Silverberg and Richard Matheson and selecting a new story by David Curtis. Sales of the issue were good, but the whole venture was undercapitalized and suffered from too rapid growth too soon. There were insufficient finances to publish and distribute the fourteenth issue, and the magazine had to be suspended, pending refinancing.

Information Sources

INDEX SOURCES: None known.
REPRINT SOURCES: None known.
LOCATION SOURCES: None known.

Publication History

TITLE: *Questar*, Spring 1978–June 1981; *Quest/Star: The World of Science Fiction*, October 1981.

VOLUME DATA: Volume 1, Number 1, Spring 1978–Volume 4, Number 1, October 1981. Four issues per volume. Initially quarterly, and later six-weekly, but usually irregular, as follows: 1, Spring 1978; 2, Summer 1978; 3, March 1979; 4, August 1979; 5, November 1979; 6, February 1980; 7, June 1980; 8, August 1980; 9, October 1980; 10, December 1980; 11, February 1981; 12, June 1981; 13, October 1981.

PUBLISHER: M. W. Communications, Inc., Pittsburgh, Pennsylvania.

EDITOR: William G. Wilson, Jr.

FORMAT: Slick, 40 pp., Spring 1978; 44 pp., Summer 1978; 64 pp., March 1979–February 1980; 72 pp., June 1980–October 1980; 76 pp., December 1980; 84 pp., February–June 1981; 68 pp., October 1981.

PRICE: $2.00, Spring 1978–February 1980; $1.95, June–August 1980; $2.25, October 1980–June 1981; $2.50, October 1981.

Jon Harvey/Mike Ashley

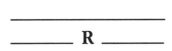

R

RIGEL SCIENCE FICTION

Rigel Science Fiction followed the path mapped out by *Unearth** and *Galileo** and also being trod by *Fantasy Book** and *Interzone,** bypassing the distributors with their requirements of minimum print runs too large for specialist and under financed magazines, and concentrating on sales by subscription and through specialist dealers. Alas, while *Fantasy Book* and *Interzone* have continued to survive, *Rigel* found the going rough and with rising costs and irregular cash flow the magazine was forced to fold after eight issues.

Although *Rigel* cannot claim to have published anything astounding it presented an enjoyable and entertaining blend of fannish and professional aspirations. It was able to attract fiction from such stalwarts as Alan Dean Foster, Michael Bishop, Richard Lupoff, Jack Wodhams and Stanley Schmidt. It was edited by Eric Vinicoff, a frequent contributor to *Analog,** and to some extent *Rigel* could be compared to a second-string *Analog* which, alas, by the 1980s was not such a compliment as it would have been a decade or two earlier. *Rigel* contained many stories by *Analog* regulars such as Timothy Zahn, Marcia Martin, Tom Easton, Joseph Green and, as already mentioned, the editor Stanley Schmidt. The stories were thus more oriented toward *science* fiction and though this made *Rigel* the major semi-professional market for that end of the spectrum it was probably also the cause of its downfall. Hard-core SF lends itself more to novel-length works where it satisfies much of its readership, and is also well-catered for in *Analog* and to some extent *Omni** for short fiction. There were apparently not enough readers to support financially the magazine's printing costs, and there was negligible income from advertising.

Some of the better stories in *Rigel*, all reflecting the editor's preference for stories in the traditional vein of SF, were ''Still Fall the Gentle Rains'' by Joseph Green and Patrice Milton (issue 2), ''The Hand of Strange Children'' by Mark

J. McGarry (issue 4), "Pet" by Jack Wodhams (issue 6) and "The Easy Way" by Stanley Schmidt (issue 8).

Of special interest among the regular departments (which included a film review column by Alan Dean Foster) was a series of interviews. The first issue, true to *Rigel*'s affinity with *Analog*, carried an interview with former *Analog* editor Ben Bova which contains useful behind-the-scenes revelations about *Analog* and *Omni* and an insight into the problem of magazine distribution. The other interviews were Jack Williamson (conducted by Richard Lupoff and Larry Davidson) in issue 2; Anne McCaffrey (by Richard Wolinsky and Larry Davidson) in issue 3; Alan Dean Foster (by Darrell Schweitzer) in issue 4; Poul Anderson (by Larry Davidson) in issue 6; Michael Moorcock (by Richard Lupoff) in issue 7, and Barry Longyear (by Darrell Schweitzer) in issue 8.

Information Sources

INDEX SOURCES: ISPF; ISPF-2; NESFA-VIII; NESFA-IX; SFM.
REPRINT SOURCES: None known.
LOCATION SOURCES: None known.

Publication History

TITLE: *Rigel Science Fiction*.
VOLUME DATA: Number 1, Summer 1981–Number 8, Summer 1983. Quarterly. (No issue for Summer 1982.)
PUBLISHER: Aesir Press, Richmond, California.
EDITOR: Eric Vinicoff.
FORMAT: A5 (saddle-stapled), 64 pp.
PRICE: $1.75 issues 1–4; $2.50 issues 5–8.

Mike Ashley

ROCKET STORIES

Rocket Stories is another product of the inexperienced publishers' scramble for the science fiction market in the early 1950s. A "girlie" magazine publisher, John Raymond, launched four moneymaking science fiction and fantasy digests in little over a year: *Space Science Fiction** (May 1952), a successful combination of science fiction and sword and sorcery; *Science Fiction Adventures** (November 1952), proposed as a juvenile adventure magazine but soon surpassing this goal; an important vehicle for such fantasy as L. Sprague de Camp's continuation of the Conan series, *Fantasy Magazine** (March 1953); and *Rocket Stories* (April 1953), a *Planet Stories** imitation—robust space opera for the juvenile reader. The secret of Raymond's success was Lester del Rey, who went to the publisher's office to sell a novelette and found himself—with some apprehension and reluctance—launched upon an editorial career.[1]

Rocket Stories is clearly a minor episode in the history of science fiction magazines, but it is of some interest, as were all of the early del Rey productions. Among its short stories regularly appeared one novel and two novelettes. Two-thirds of its writers were established or about to begin lucrative careers; among them were Poul Anderson, Algis Budrys, Irving Cox, James Gunn, John Jakes, Milton Lesser and George O. Smith. Ornamented by such artists as Ed Emsh, Paul Orban and Kelly Freas, the stories were lively, dramatic, uninhibited escapist fiction—sometimes more than competently written. The scene was galactic rather than solar, and the parent genre more often than not was the western. In fact, in the persona of Wade Kaempfert (pronounced "Kemfer"),[2] del Rey recruited two western writers, Noel Loomis[3] and H. A. DeRosso;[4] bullied his young discovery Budrys into writing the energetic space western, *Blood on My Jets*;[5] and made the link in his editorials:

> We aren't calling the magazine science fiction, for the same reason that stories of the old west were never called science or invention fiction. Colt, in inventing the revolver, made that west possible, and the men who are working on the rockets will make our future possible.[6]

And yet, despite the juvenile intent and western slant, *Rocket* published a few stories of lasting quality. In the first issue, for example, was John Jakes' powerful "Jackrogue Second," a story that could almost have been written by Harlan Ellison. "Picnic" by Milton Lesser, in the second issue, was a chilling space story beautifully illustrated in Finlayesque style by Joseph Eberle, while in the third issue was Harry Harrison's emotive "An Artist's Life."

Unfortunately, *Rocket*'s engines were silenced early when, following a disagreement with Raymond, del Rey quit. Harry Harrison stepped in as editor, but by then Raymond had had enough of the SF field and pulled out. All of the del Rey/Raymond magazines are worth exploring, and *Rocket Stories* contains far more than its covers and title might imply.

Notes

1. Michael Ashley, *The History of the Science Fiction Magazine* (Chicago: Contemporary Books, 1976), III: 78–80.
2. Lester del Rey, *Rocket Stories*, July 1953, p. 99.
3. Donald H. Tuck, *The Encyclopedia of Science Fiction and Fantasy* (Chicago: Advent, 1974), I: 281.
4. Del Rey, *Rocket Stories*, July 1953, p. 125.
5. Ibid.
6. Ibid.

Information Sources

BIBLIOGRAPHY:
Nicholls. *Encyclopedia*.
Tuck.

INDEX SOURCES: MIT; SFM; Tuck.
REPRINT SOURCES: None known.
LOCATION SOURCES: Pennsylvania State University Library.

Publication History

TITLE: *Rocket Stories*.
VOLUME DATA: Volume 1, Number 1, April 1953–Volume 1, Number 3, September
    1953. Bi-monthly, but issue 2 July. Total run: 3 issues.
PUBLISHER: Space Publications, New York.
EDITORS: "Wade Kaempfert": Lester del Rey, first two issues; Harry Harrison, last
    issue.
FORMAT: Digest, 160 pp.
PRICE: 35¢.

E.F. Casebeer

ROD SERLING'S *THE TWILIGHT ZONE* MAGAZINE

Perhaps the most popular of all television fantasy series was *The Twilight Zone*, which ran from 1959 to 1964, guided by the capable hands of writer and presenter Rod Serling. Serling died in 1975, but his name and that of his series have not been forgotten, and they still held sufficient impact for a magazine launched in 1981 to meet with an encouraging response from a market not noted for taking weird fiction magazines to its heart. With the possible exception of *Unknown*,* it may be correct to say that, in terms of sales, *Rod Serling's The Twilight Zone Magazine* is the most popular weird fiction magazine yet published.

It owes its reception not just to its title. It is intelligently edited, attractively presented, and contains an above-average quota of competent and even excellent fiction. Published in the standard flat saddle-stapled format with bold, arresting covers, *TZ* has adopted a policy of trying to present something new and different to a readership that has been turned on to the possibilities of horror fiction through the best-selling works of Stephen King and Peter Straub, in the same way that Rod Serling's original television series attracted audiences twenty years earlier.

The extent of its success can be measured in the response to its first short story contest, which brought over 9,000 manuscripts into the editorial offices. That indicates the enormous potential among the readership, even though Harlan Ellison, who served as one of the contest judges, considered almost all of the entries to be "derivative, silly, illiterate, hackneyed or outright plagiarized."[1] Perhaps it indicates even more the obvious need for an intelligent magazine of this kind and that, with the proper distribution, *TZ* could reach an audience equal in scale to that of *Omni*.* By 1982 *TZ* had a paid circulation of only about 60,000, although a change in distributor after the first nine months was already resulting in a marked increase in newsstand sales. However, to realize its potential *TZ* also has to maximize its subscription list. *TZ* comes from the same publisher as the successful men's magazine *Gallery*, which sells almost exclusively through newsstands, and it will take a while for its managers to realize that the readers of weird fiction are a different market and will willingly subscribe to such a magazine.

Nevertheless, *TZ* is able to benefit from the financial backing of its parent company to the extent that it can pay competitive rates to its contributors and thus attract many of the major names. Already *TZ* has published stories by Stephen King, Peter Straub, Gary Brandner, Joan Aiken and Robert Bloch, all major names recognizable to the general reading public. On top of that, the cream of the core of genre writers has also been represented in full—Fritz Leiber, Robert Silverberg, Ron Goulart, Robert Sheckley, Tanith Lee, Ramsey Campbell, Richard Matheson, Harlan Ellison, Frank Belknap Long—names that it is very hard for even the least excitable of weird fiction enthusiasts to ignore.

Apart from its fiction, *TZ* presents a number of regular features. At the outset Gahan Wilson served as film critic and Theodore Sturgeon looked at books, but soon Stephen King was commenting on the silver screen, Robert Sheckley and then Thomas Disch followed in Sturgeon's wake, and Jack Sullivan started an equivalent series reviewing music. A regular center feature looked at new horror or fantasy films, while at the end of each issue was a continuing show-by-show guide to the *Twilight Zone* television series, plus the printing of a teleplay. Later *TZ* inaugurated a classic reprint section presenting some of the gems of yesteryear, accompanied by biographical profiles of leading writers of the past such as M. R. James, Sheridan Le Fanu and Arthur Machen.

TZ is edited by Ted Klein, himself an occasional writer of horror fiction with a deep knowledge of the field. Carol Serling, Rod's widow, who retains the rights to *The Twilight Zone*, acts as Editorial Consultant, but is far from just a figurehead and does have a say in the magazine's policy and content.

In a drive to increase sales *TZ* was forced to drop to a bi-monthly schedule in 1983 but circulation has risen and the magazine remains buoyant. In order to survive, however, it has had to sell itself more and more to the fantasy/horror film enthusiasts and the followers of Stephen King. Consequently the covers usually herald film features or articles about or fiction by King. Fortunately Klein has managed to retain a large quota of the magazine for fiction and *TZ* continues to include a variety of bizarre and outre tales.

Notes

1. Harlan Ellison, "Hard Truths for Would-be Writers," *Fantasy Newsletter* 47, April/May 1982, p.5.

Information Sources

INDEX SOURCES: MT; NESFA VIII; NESFA IX; SFM
REPRINT SOURCES: *Great Stories From Rod Serling's 'The Twilight Zone' Magazine*
    1983 Annual, edited by T.E.D. Klein, reprinted 15 stories and other features in

magazine format. *Twilight Zone Special, Number 1: Night Cry,* edited by Klein (TZ Publications, 1984) reprinted 20 stories in digest magazine format.

LOCATION SOURCES: None known.

Publication History

TITLE: *Rod Serling's The Twilight Zone Magazine.*

VOLUME DATA: Volume 1, April 1981–March 1982, 12 issues, monthly; Volume 2, April 1982–February 1983, 10 issues, monthly to December 1982, then bi-monthly (there was no Volume 2, Number 9 as for copyright reasons that number was allotted to the 1983 Annual cited above. The ten issues were thus numbered up to Number 11). Volumes 3 and 4, six issues per volume, bi-monthly, April 1983–.

PUBLISHER: TZ Publications Inc., New York.

EDITOR: T.E.D. Klein.

FORMAT: Flat (saddle-stapled), 104 pp. April–July 1981; 100pp., August 1981 and thereafter, although June 1982 104 pp., and Feb 1984 116pp.

PRICE: $2.00 April 1981–December 1982; $2.50 February 1983–. (February 1984 special issue $3.50.)

Mike Ashley

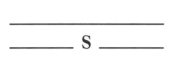

S

SATELLITE SCIENCE FICTION

Satellite Science Fiction was an appropriate name for a magazine in the late 1950s, although it was launched in 1956, a year before the first artificial satellite, Sputnik I, was put into Earth orbit. *Satellite* was the brainchild of Leo Margulies, who had recently left his partner at King-Size Publications, where he had published and edited *Fantastic Universe*.* Margulies established a new company, Renown Publications, issuing not only *Satellite*, but also *Mike Shayne Mystery Magazine* and later the long-established *Short Stories*, to which he had acquired the rights (along with *Weird Tales*,* which he also planned to revive, though this did not happen until 1973).

The idea behind *Satellite* was simple: to publish a complete novel per issue and back it up with a few short stories. This was scarcely new in science fiction, but it was not common in the digest magazines, where the description of "novel" had been deflated to describe stories of 15,000 words or more. Margulies, on the other hand, meant what he said. Most of the novels published in *Satellite* were around the 40,000–word mark, a few even longer. Margulies was, of course, competing head on with the blossoming paperback market, where a number of publishers, especially Ace Books, were issuing SF novels for the same price as the magazines. Since novels were always more popular than short stories and were a good selling point of the magazines, the paperbacks were luring away potential magazine readers. Margulies' gimmick for *Satellite*, therefore, was to call it "The Magazine That Is a Book!," a slogan that featured in all his advertisements.

Since an average issue of *Satellite* usually ran to about 53,000 words, a 40,000–word novel naturally dominated the issue and left precious little room for short stories—and even less when Margulies added a regular nonfiction feature. The stories were thus, of necessity, seldom more than short squibs, brief stories spun around a clever idea or joke punch-line. Typical was "Four-Billion Dollar Door" by Michael Shaara (December 1956), which tells of the first manned trip to the moon (which Shaara correctly forecast would be followed by TV cameras) during which the spaceship's door freezes shut and proves unopenable. Another is Isaac Asimov's "A Woman's Heart" (June 1957), which is in fact neither SF nor fantasy. It looks at the shallowness of women when one particular woman, who has been granted perfect beauty, asks her three suitors to name the one wish they would want granted if they wanted her to be permanently happy. She chooses the man who wishes that all her machines, created to take away household drudgery, remain in perfect working order. A third example is "The Last Day" by Helen Clarkson (April 1958), a poignant story of the end of mankind and of the last human and the last songbird alive. A few writers were regular contributors of these short items, among them Arthur C. Clarke and the Australian Dal Stivens, who wrote a series of tall stories.

Margulies avoided regular reader departments, writing only the briefest of editorials and offering no letter column. The latter would have provided useful feedback in later issues when Sam Moskowitz became a regular contributor, as he did in later issues of *Amazing Stories** and *Fantastic.** Margulies had been impressed with Moskowitz when they met in 1956, and Moskowitz became the magazine's book reviewer from the third issue with his column "The Science Fiction Collector." However, this soon developed into something far larger. Margulies had been scouting around for an article about artificial satellites, and Moskowitz suggested that one be done on the development of the satellite in SF. The article, "The Real Earth Satellite Story," appeared in the June 1957 issue and led to Moskowitz writing a series on the progenitors of science fiction, which in turn formed the basis of his book *Explorers of the Infinite* (Cleveland: World, 1963). While most of the essays were revised and updated for book publication, the subsequent version lacks some of the advantages of the originals, notably illustrative material. The article on earth satellites, for instance, included a facsimile reproduction of Hugo Gernsback's editorial in the April 1930 *Air Wonder Stories** on "Stations in Space," while the one on H. G. Wells repro-duced the 1908 cover for *The War in the Air*. This enhancement of the articles was best exemplified when they moved to *Fantastic Universe* following *Satel-lite*'s demise. Moreover, one of the essays in *Satellite* was not reprinted in any of Moskowitz's books because of its minor importance, namely, "Tennessee Williams, Boy Wonder," which looks at that playwright's very first story sale to *Weird Tales*. It does contain, however, one fundamental flaw, common to many entries on Williams, in that Moskowitz gives his date of birth as 1914 instead of 1911. As a sideline to his articles Moskowitz also suggested short stories that might be reprinted. To accompany his essay on Fitz-James O'Brien, for instance, the magazine ran "How I Overcame My Gravity," which had not been reprinted since its publication in 1864. The story, furthermore, was illus-trated by Frank R. Paul. Elsewhere, Moskowitz reprinted the chapter "The Further Vision," excised from the book version of H. G. Wells' *The Time*

Machine, where his time traveler voyages millions of years into the future. This time the extract was illustrated by Leo Morey, who featured prominently in *Satellite*.

The features and short stories, however useful or entertaining they may have been, were the trimmings of the magazine. The main meat was the lead novel. Here the quality of Margulies' selection can be measured by the number of novels subsequently published in book form, but this has two riders. First, a number of his choices had already appeared in book form in England, and the magazine version marked the first American publication. Second, one could more readily measure *Satellite*'s success by highlighting how many of the novels are still in print. In fact, only one of them has remained fairly regularly in print since its first appearance: Jack Vance's *The Languages of Pao* (December 1957; New York: Avalon, 1958), which Peter Nicholls in his *Science Fiction Encyclopedia* has called "one of the most intelligent uses in genre sf of the idea that the worldview of different races is reflected in . . . the language they speak" (p. 358).

Most of the lead novels were sophisticated space opera loaded with cosmic intrigue. The first issue featured "The Man from Earth" by Algis Budrys (*Man of Earth* [New York: Ballantine, 1958]) where our hero, in a transformed body, finds himself on Pluto. "A Glass of Darkness" by Philip K. Dick (*The Cosmic Puppets* [New York: Ace, 1957]), in the second issue, takes place in what had once been a sleepy town in the Virginia hills, but what is now a battleground for cosmic forces which have taken control of the town and its inhabitants. "Planet for Plunder," in the third issue, has not seen subsequent book publication, perhaps because it was something of an experimental novel, although it was an intriguing production. Hal Clement had submitted the story as a short novel to the magazine; it told the story of an alien's mission to Earth totally from the viewpoint of the alien. The story was too short to serve as a lead novel, but too long to fill in as a supporting story. Rather than reject it, however, *Satellite*'s maiden editor, Sam Merwin, wrote a parallel story of the events from the human viewpoint, and this was integrated in alternate chapters. Clement's original story remained intact, therefore, and could be read with the odd-numbered chapters. The result was not as uneven as might be expected.

The fourth issue also featured a collaborative novel, "Operation: Square Peg" by Irving W. Lande and Frank Belknap Long, unique in that it provided the stimulus for what must stand as Ed Emsh's worst cover for any SF magazine. Long, who later served as associate editor on the magazine, contributed another, better novel, "Mission to a Distant Star" (*Mission to a Star* [New York: Avalon, 1964]) in the February 1958 issue, although by today's standards it is rather weak.

Of the original novels published in *Satellite* the strongest were the first three. Thereafter they lapsed into variants on invasions from space, although the one exception, aside from the Vance novel, was "The Million Cities" by J. T.

McIntosh (August 1958 [New York: Pyramid, 1963]), set in the distant future when Earth was one vast city.

The reprint novels began with "The Year of the Comet" (August 1957), one of John Christopher's competent "Managerials" series, which had been published by Michael Joseph in London in 1955 and would later be published as a paperback by Avon Books in the United States in 1959. Others included "Wall of Fire" by Charles Eric Maine (originally *Crisis 2000* [London: Hodder & Stoughton, 1955]), "The Resurrected Man" by E. C. Tubb (London: Scion, 1954) and, possibly the best, "The Man with Absolute Motion" by Noel Loomis. Although Loomis was an American writer, this novel about the search for new power as the universe runs out of energy was first published in London by Rich and Cowan in 1955 bearing the alias Silas Waters.

For its first fourteen issues, during which time *Satellite* was a highly readable if at times predictable magazine, it took little care over its appearance. The covers were usually satisfactory, especially those by Alex Schomburg, although they have a monotonous similarity if viewed in sequence, but the interiors had rather mediocre illustrations, mostly by Leo Morey.

From the February 1959 issue, however, all this changed. In a drive that was intended to make *Satellite* more prominent on the newsstands, the magazine was converted from a digest to large-size, a complete reversal of the trend at the start of the 1950s. The new look was superficially attractive, although internally the magazine was indistinguishable from the large-size pulp magazines. At the same time *Satellite* increased to a monthly schedule and there was a change of policy. The novels were dropped in favor of a short novel and more stories. The Moskowitz articles remained, but in addition there was now a "Department of Lost Stories" where Margulies resurrected old, overlooked stories by popular demand, starting with "Abductor Minimi Digit" by Ralph Milne Farley from the January 1932 *Weird Tales*, requested with nostalgic fondness by Theodore Sturgeon.

Many of the short squibs remained, but now *Satellite* had lost its backbone. Its one weapon against the paperbacks had been its full-length novels, but now it became just like other magazines, except that it lacked reader departments and still delivered little attractive interior artwork. The large-format change was also a mistake, for rather than being noticed on the stands, it became an outcast. Once the sales records for the first monthly issue came in, Margulies could see his mistake. Rather than gamble by returning to a digest format, he promptly axed the magazine. The June 1959 issue had already been printed in proof form, but was never published, although a handful of the proof copies exist and are thus rare collector's items.

Nevertheless, *Satellite* served at least two purposes. It published a number of British novels that might otherwise not have seen American publication, and it gave Sam Moskowitz his first regular professional market for his articles.

Information Sources

BIBLIOGRAPHY:
Nicholls. *Encyclopedia.*
Tuck.
INDEX SOURCES: ASFI; MIT; SFM; Tuck.
REPRINT SOURCES: None known.
LOCATION SOURCES: M.I.T. Science Fiction Library; Pennsylvania State University
    Library.

Publication History

TITLE: *Satellite Science Fiction.*
VOLUME DATA: Volume 1, Number 1, October 1956–Volume 3, Number 6, May
    1959. Six issues per volume. Bi-monthly, October 1956–December 1958. Monthly,
    February–May 1959. Total run: 18 issues.
PUBLISHER: Renown Publications, New York.
EDITOR: Sam Merwin, October–December 1956; Leo Margulies, February 1957–De-
    cember 1958; Frank Belknap Long, February–May 1959. Cylvia Kleinman [Mrs.
    Leo Margulies] was Managing Editor/Editorial Director on all issues.
FORMAT: Digest, 128 pp., October 1956–December 1958; Large Neo-Pulp, 64 pp.,
    February–May 1959.
PRICE: 35¢.

Mike Ashley

SATURN, THE MAGAZINE OF SCIENCE FICTION

Saturn was spawned during a minor boom in SF publishing, when several outside publishers wanted to get magazines onto the stands rapidly. Robert Sproul, *Saturn*'s editor of record, was publisher of *Cracked* and other magazines; he also was the son of Joe Sproul, then manager of the Ace News Company, distributor for Ace Books (and wholly owned by the same management, A. A. Wyn). Joe Sproul had used his influence to get his son into magazine publishing; and when the decision was made to produce an SF magazine, it was only natural for the younger Sproul to contact Donald A. Wollheim, editor of Ace Books. Thus, Wollheim was hired to put together the magazine for a flat fee per issue, and he was responsible for all the magazine's contents, though the table of contents listed him only as "Editorial Consultant."[1]

Despite its frequent variations in title—three different subtitles in its five issues—*Saturn* consistently reflects Wollheim's tastes and skills as an editor, as well as showing the limitations within which he was forced to work. It was a rather provocative magazine, despite some severe weaknesses. The bland cover of the first issue, dated March 1957, was by Leo Summers; interior illustrations were by John Giunta, the art director, who did all the magazine's interior artwork until the final issue. The contents were presented with some high-level hype (a "New Find" short novel by Jules Verne) and some low-level hype (a story about reincarnation titled "The Bridey Murphy Way"). Under all this, the stories were varied and readable.

All these traits persisted throughout *Saturn*'s brief life. The hype became shriller in later issues, as the magazine's financial situation worsened. For instance, the cover of the post-Sputnik final issue featured a Russian spaceship on the moon, cosmonauts in the foreground raising the hammer and sickle flag; this illustrated an impassioned lead article warning SF fans to work to prevent a "Red Flag Over the Moon." Otherwise, however, *Saturn*'s contents were surprisingly interesting. Wollheim explains that he actively "solicited contributions from authors and submissions from agents."[2] That effort shows in the range of stories. Finding stories by Cordwainer Smith *and* by H. P. Lovecraft and August Derleth in the same issue of an SF magazine, as a reader of the second issue of *Saturn* could, is jarring but distinctly intriguing. And this range was characteristic of *Saturn*. For two more examples, the third issue began with a story by Gordon R. Dickson, followed immediately by one by Jules Verne, and the fifth included one by Ray Cummings (his last original appearance in an SF magazine) next to one by Marion Zimmer Bradley. Other writers of note published in *Saturn*'s five issues included John Brunner, John Christopher, Harlan Ellison, Robert Heinlein, Damon Knight, James Schmitz, Robert Silverberg, Clark Ashton Smith and Jack Vance: a varied list indeed. To be sure, the stories did not represent the best of which those authors were capable. Those by the most famous writers gave the suggestion of being dragged out of the back corner of some desk drawer. Nevertheless, many of *Saturn*'s stories were surprisingly fresh, and the combination added up to more than the sum of the parts.

The SF boom, unfortunately, proved illusory, and *Saturn* found itself in trouble from the beginning. The first two issues each contained 128 pages, but this was cut by 16 pages beginning with the third issue.[3] Although officially bi-monthly until the end, the fourth issue was one month behind schedule (redated accordingly), and the fifth was dated five months later. At that point, Sproul transformed the magazine entirely. As *Saturn Web Detective Stories*, it specialized in crime tales of an extremely sadomasochistic variety. Wollheim explains that Sproul kept *Saturn* as part of the title only "to keep his postal registration valid."[4] With the September 1959 issue, however, the magazine became simply *Web Detective Stories*, and all but passes from our concern.[5]

An avid collector who scanned the bookstalls for any likely item, however, would have witnessed a further transformation in 1962 when the detective stories, which already emphasized the sadistic side of life, tipped the scale even further and brought back the old-style terror magazines of the 1930s with a further title change to *Web Terror Stories* in emulation of the old pulps like *Terror Tales** and *Horror Stories.** The first issue under this title featured stories by John Jakes—"My Love, the Monster!"—and, perhaps more surprisingly, Marion Zimmer Bradley, whose "Treason of the Blood" was a readable if formula-patterned tale of revenge upon a vampire. The issue even contained a bona fide science fiction story, "Orbit of the Pain-Masters" by Arthur P. Gordon, which was dreadful even by old pulp standards.

Science fiction, or even the supernatural, did not form a standard part of *Web Terror*'s contents, which relied on various ways of torturing women as the main theme and used no imagination in inventing new plots. *Web Terror* appeared erratically for the next three years and eventually folded, through lack of interest either from the public or the publisher, who thereafter concentrated more on film monster magazines.

If we forget *Saturn*'s later transmogrifications and remember the original magazine, while it would be stretching the point to claim that it left a vacant place when it was prematurely stifled, it had not been published for long enough to establish a place for itself.[6] But there is reason to believe that it could have done so had it been given the chance.

Notes

1. Wollheim, personal letter, May 14, 1980. This editorial arrangement caused some confusion. The first *Fantasy-Times* story was titled "Wollheim to Edit New Mag Called 'Saturn'!" (No. 255 [Second September 1956 issue], 1, 7); however, Sproul was the source of all further information about the magazine: " 'Saturn' Delayed One Month," *Science-Fiction Times* [fanzine]: No. 277 (Second August 1957 issue): 5, and "Saturn Science Fiction Delayed," *Science-Fiction Times* [fanzine], No. 286 (First January 1958 issue): 3.

2. Wollheim, May 14, 1980.

3. It thus became the smallest professional SF magazine published in America up to that time ("Two Mags Cut Pages, Indicating 'Boomlet' Has Cracked," *Science-Fiction Times* [fanzine], No. 271 [Second May 1957 issue]: 1).

4. Letter.

5. " 'Saturn' Disappears from 'Detective' Edition," *Science-Fiction Times* [fanzine], No. 14 (Second June 1959 issue): 1–2. Presumably the change in content caught the Science Fiction Book Club by surprise, since their ads continued to appear on *Web*'s back cover.

6. Readers in the *Science-Fiction Times* Poll, for example, voted *Saturn*'s short stories overall into second place, behind *The Magazine of Fantasy and Science Fiction* but ahead of *Astounding*, *Venture* and *Infinity*. (" 'Astounding' Wins 'S-F Times' 1958 Poll," *Science-Fiction Times* [fanzine], No. 294a (First June 1958 issue): 1).

Information Sources

BIBLIOGRAPHY:
Nicholls. *Encyclopedia.*
Tuck.
INDEX SOURCES: MIT; SFM; Tuck.
REPRINT SOURCES: None known.
LOCATION SOURCES: M.I.T. Science Fiction Library; Pennsylvania State University
    Library.

Publication History

TITLE: *Saturn, The Magazine of Science Fiction*, March 1957. Retitled *Saturn, Magazine of Fantasy and Science Fiction*, May 1957. Retitled *Saturn, Science Fiction and Fantasy*, July 1957 (on cover and spine, but variations on masthead and indicia. To all intents during this period the magazine was simply *Saturn*.)–March 1958. Retitled *Saturn Web Detective Stories* (on cover, but variants on spine, masthead and indicia), August 1958–April 1959. Retitled *Web Detective Stories*, September 1959–(?) 1961. Retitled *Web Terror Stories*, August 1962–June 1965.

VOLUME DATA: Volume 1, Number 1, March 1957–Volume 5, Number 2, June 1965. *Saturn* ran from Volume 1, Number 1, March 1957 to Volume 1, Number 5, March 1958. *Web Terror Stories* ran from Volume 4, Number 1, August 1962 to Volume 5, Number 2, June 1965. All volumes ran six issues per volume. Schedule always indicated as bi-monthly but all issues irregular. Total run: 26 issues, of which *Saturn* ran for 5, and *Web Terror Stories* ran for 8.

PUBLISHER: Candar Publishing Company, Holyoke, Massachusetts. Editorial offices at Madison Avenue, New York, during 1957, then to West 48th Street from 1958 to 1961, then West 45th Street from 1962 to 1965.

EDITOR: Donald A. Wollheim (all issues of *Saturn*); thereafter not credited.

FORMAT: Digest. Page count as follows: 128 pp., March–May 1957; 112 pp., July 1957–(?) 1965; 160 pp., June 1965.

PRICE: 35¢, except last issue, 50¢.

Joe Sanders/Mike Ashley

SCIENCE AND INVENTION

Science and Invention, although essentially a nonfiction magazine, has become justifiably famous in the history of science fiction because of its August 1923 issue, which was a special "Scientific Fiction" number, qualifying as possibly the first English-language science fiction issue of a magazine. *S&I*, however, was the successor to a magazine that first appeared in 1908 and that played a large part in the development of SF.

The progenitor was entitled *Modern Electrics*. The first issue, dated April 1908, contained thirty-four pages and sold for ten cents. Its publisher was Hugo Gernsback, then only twenty-three years old but already a veteran of four years' self-employment in the dry battery and electrical importing business. Gernsback had designed the first home radio set in 1905 and began to issue a radio catalogue that year.[1] This evolved into a radio magazine, and *Modern Electrics* was born. It was instantly accepted, and its circulation soon leveled at around 100,000.[2]

For the first three years the magazine carried no fiction, although several articles, especially those by Gernsback, were of an extrapolative nature. The story goes, however, that early in 1911 Gernsback lacked enough material to complete the April issue and so wrote what proved to be the first installment of *Ralph 124C 41+*, subtitled "A Romance of the Year 2660." The novel has since become a landmark in the history of SF for, though by no means a great work of fiction, it is an astonishing catalogue of predictions and inventions. The serial continued for twelve monthly issues and attracted so much comment that when it ended Gernsback found it necessary to make at least one SF story a regular part of the content. Gernsback's first "discovery" was Jacque Morgan, already a contributor of nonfiction, who began the Scientific Adventures of Mr. Fosdick, a humorous series that started in the October 1912 issue with "The Feline Light and Power Company Is Organized" and ran for five issues. The first three stories were reprinted in the June, July and August 1926 issues of *Amazing Stories.**

In 1913 Gernsback sold *Modern Electrics* and launched a new magazine, *The Electrical Experimenter*. It was not a title change, as Moskowitz and others have reported, but a completely new magazine in a totally different format, large-size, rotogravured of only sixteen pages, selling for five cents. Both the page-count and the price rose steadily over the next few years. Nevertheless, the policy of publishing a regular SF story was retained, the first new piece being "Mysterious Night" by Thomas W. Benson (June 1914). Benson and George F. Stratton became regular contributors over the next few years. "Story" is perhaps too generous a term for these items. Most were extrapolative articles with fictional frills. This approach was continued by Gernsback in his own thirteen-part series, "Baron Munchhausen's New Scientific Adventures," which began in the May 1915 issue.

Of more import was a new illustrator that Gernsback introduced in the magazine in 1914, Frank R. Paul, who became a mainstay thereafter. The magazine continued to present stories about silly inventions and bogus science by writers Charles Magee Adams and John T. Dwyer until 1920 saw a change in emphasis to a stronger story line. The first writer to exploit this new approach was Charles S. Wolfe, who first appeared in the March 1920 issue with "Whispering Ether" and contributed regularly thereafter. He created a series around the character of a scientific detective, Joe Fenner, and although the plots still hinged on a new invention of sorts (e.g., a rifle fired by remote control in "The Phantom Arm," June 1920), they invited more reader involvement.

The June 1920 issue carried as a subhead "Science and Invention," and with the August 1920 issue this had supplanted *The Electrical Experimenter* as the official title of the magazine. With the new name came a new policy. Now the magazine would run two or more SF stories per issue, and to stoke the fire Charles Horne presented an article entitled "Jules Verne, the World's Greatest Prophet" (August 1920), followed by an article on the work of Luis Senarens in "The American Jules Verne" (October 1920).

To accompany Wolfe as a regular contributor came Clement Fezandié, who wrote more fiction for *S&I* than anyone else. Fezandié was a French-American in the powder-pigment business. Gernsback called him an "idea genius" and recalled that "he wrote for fun only and religiously sent back all checks in payment of his stories!"[3] Fezandié had been writing SF since at least 1898, when his story *Through the Earth* (New York: Century, 1898) had been serialized in the children's *St. Nicholas Magazine*. He had appeared briefly in the July 1920 *Electrical Experimenter*, but his real claim to fame began in the May 1921 *S&I* with "The Secret of Artificial Reproduction," the first of forty-three humorous tales of Dr. Hackenshaw's Secrets. In true Gernsbackian tradition Fezandié chronicled a variety of inventions and discoveries that must have been a source of wonder and inspiration to many of the magazine's youthful readers. He explored such subjects as suspended animation (October 1921), robots (June 1922), matter transmission (September 1922), television (October 1922), earthquakes (May 1923), perpetual youth (February 1924), dream machines (August 1924), perpetual motion (November 1924) and atomic energy (May 1925). The series ended in *S&I* with a four-part serial, "A Journey to the Center of the Earth" (June–September 1925), although two further stories appeared in *Amazing Stories*. Although little more than scientific lectures in a fictional format, the stories were enjoyable and epitomized Gernsback's desire to educate through science fiction.

By 1923 it was clear that Gernsback was expanding further into the SF field and had his eye on a wider market. He reprinted two stories by H. G. Wells— "The New Accelerator" (February 1923) and "The Star" (March 1923)—and was fortunate to acquire a new story by George Allan England, possibly second only to Edgar Rice Burroughs in popularity at that time as a fantasist in the adventure pulps (see *Argosy**). His story "The Thing from—Outside" had been rejected by *Argosy/All-Story*, but appeared in the April 1923 *S&I* and remains arguably the best single story ever published in that magazine.

Gernsback's intentions were clear by the July 1923 issue, which boasted the first episode in a six-part serialization of "Around the Universe" by Ray Cummings; the next issue was the special "Scientific Fiction Number." Apart from the second episode of "Around the Universe" and Fezandié's Dr. Hackenshaw tale, "The Secret of the Super-Telescope," it contained "Advanced Chemistry" by Jack G. Huekels, "Vanishing Movies" by Teddy J. Holman, "The Electric Duel" by Hugo Gernsback and "The Man from the Atom" by G. Peyton Wertenbaker, which provided inspiration for the remarkably realistic (for the period) cover by Howard V. Brown. Wertenbaker, then only sixteen years old, became a regular contributor to the early *Amazing Stories* before branching out into other realms of writing.

Fezandié and Cummings dominated *S&I* during 1924, Cummings with a new serial, "The Man on the Meteor" (January–September 1924). That serial was followed by "The Living Death" (October 1924–June 1925) by John Martin Leahy, then establishing himself as a popular contributor to *Weird Tales.** This was followed in turn by one of Cummings' best-known novels, "Tarrano the Conqueror" (July 1925–August 1926).

This serial was thus in full battle order when Gernsback launched *Amazing Stories* in April 1926. It was obvious that much of the fiction would be siphoned from *S&I* to its new companion, but a regular serial and an occasional story remained. Ironically, Ray Cummings, who was rapidly becoming one of SF's most popular writers, never appeared in *Amazing* with a new story at this time. "Around the Universe" was reprinted in the October 1927 issue, but Gernsback retained all Cummings' new stories for *S&I*, evidently to keep those readers who might otherwise also be siphoned to *Amazing*. At this time the total circulation of Gernsback's technical magazines exceeded 1 million copies, with *Radio News* (which also carried a regular SF item) accounting for 400,000 copies a month.[4]

In 1927 Gernsback acquired Abraham Merritt's revised version of *The Metal Monster* (the original had run in *Argosy* during 1920), and it was serialized in *S&I* as "The Metal Emperor" from October 1927 to August 1928. With its conclusion, science fiction, as a rule, passed from *S&I*. The magazine reverted to its original format as a technical magazine, although the prognosticative articles remained.

When Gernsback lost control of the Experimenter Publishing Company in 1929, *S&I* passed with *Amazing* to the new owners and did not fold, as some authorities maintain. It continued until August 1931, when it merged with its companion magazine, *Popular Mechanics*.

There can be no denying the importance of *S&I* (and its predecessors) in the history of science fiction. Writers like Charles S. Wolfe and Clement Fezandié encouraged others to consider the potential of science, and Gernsback himself in both fiction and forecast showed the possibilities of future technology. The success of the stories in *S&I* led directly to Gernsback issuing *Amazing Stories* and thus to the birth of the SF magazine. That such a magazine would have evolved by another route along the trail already blazed by *Argosy*, *The Thrill Book** and *Weird Tales* is more than probable, but it was Gernsback who made that decision and thereby made history.

Today we can look back over the history of SF and consider whether that decision was right. An all-SF magazine was an inevitability by the 1920s, and few can argue against its necessity, certainly for the subsequent advancement of SF in the guiding hands of F. Orlin Tremaine and John W. Campbell. But in Gernsback's case it may well have been the wrong decision. Other editors experienced in the pulp field, especially Harold Hersey, had also considered the potential of SF and would doubtless have experimented with such a magazine at some time. Gernsback, however, was first and foremost a scientist and inventor, not a storyteller, and the mixture provided in *S&I* was correct for that readership. Had he expanded the SF content of *S&I* instead of launching *Amazing*, the history of SF may well have been considerably different. For in basic concept and intent there is little to distinguish *S&I* from *Omni,** once one removes all the gloss and glitter that modern-day technology and money can provide. *Omni* has proved one of the biggest success stories of recent years, and Gernsback had the same formula sixty years earlier and found it equally successful.

Notes

1. Sam Moskowitz, "Hugo Gernsback: Father of Science Fiction" in *Explorers of the Infinite* (Cleveland: World, 1963), pp. 231–32.
2. Hugo Gernsback, *Evolution of Modern Science Fiction* (New York: Gernsback, 1952).
3. Hugo Gernsback, guest editorial in *Amazing Stories*, April 1961, p. 7.
4. Gernsback, *Evolution*.

Information Sources

BIBLIOGRAPHY:
Tuck.
INDEX SOURCES: Cockcroft, T.G.L., *Index to Fiction in Radio News and Other Magazines*, Lower Hutt, New Zealand: Privately printed, 1970. (This is an index by author and title that relies heavily on two earlier indexes which listed fiction only by issue: "The Gernsback Forerunners" by William H. Evans [New York: Julius Unger (?), 1944] and *Evolution of Modern Science Fiction* (New York: Gernsback, 1952); Tuck.
REPRINT SOURCES: None known.
LOCATION SOURCES: None known.

Publication History

TITLE: *Modern Electrics*, April 1908–December 1913. *The Electrical Experimenter*, May 1913–July 1920. Retitled *Science and Invention*, August 1920–August 1931.
VOLUME DATA:
   Modern Electrics: Volume 1, Number 1, April 1908–Volume 6, Number 9, December 1913. Twelve issues per volume. Monthly. Total run: 69 issues.
   The Electrical Experimenter/Science and Invention: Volume 1, Number 1, May 1913–Volume 19, Number 4, August 1931. Twelve issues per volume. Monthly. Total run: 220 issues.
EDITORS: Hugo Gernsback, April 1908–April 1929; thereafter, not known. H. Winfield Secor was Managing Editor for many issues. Arthur H. Lynch probably assumed full editorship after April 1929.
FORMAT:
   Modern Electrics: Quarto; 34 pp. first issue; thereafter 64 pp.
   The Electrical Experimenter/Science and Invention: Large Pulp; 16 pp., May 1913–February 1915; 32 pp., March–September 1915; 72 pp., October 1915–April 1919; 96 pp., May–September 1919; 144 pp., October 1919 onwards. (Details not known after April 1929.)
PRICE:
   Modern Electrics: 10¢.
   The Electrical Experimenter/Science and Invention: 5¢, May 1913–March 1915; 10¢, April 1915–June 1916; 15¢, July 1916–October 1918; 20¢, November 1918–January 1920; 25¢, February 1920 onwards. (Details not known after April 1929.)

Mike Ashley

SCIENCE FANTASY (1950–1966)

By 1950 the newly formed company Nova Publications Ltd. was sufficiently established to plan a companion magazine to *New Worlds*.* The result was *Science-Fantasy*, edited by Walter Gillings (the title was hyphenated until 1954). A few years earlier Gillings had edited *Fantasy** and had acquired a considerable backlog of stories that seemed fated never to see the light of day when that magazine folded after only three issues. Gillings was now, however, able to select the cream of these, and the first issue included "Time's Arrow" by Arthur C. Clarke and "Monster" by Christopher Youd (better known as John Christopher). The lead story was "The Belt" by J. M. Walsh, a popular writer in both the SF and detective fiction fields.

Gillings' policy was all-encompassing. In his first editorial, which went to great lengths in rationalizing the disparate terms "science" and "fantasy," Gillings stated that "in this new magazine we shall be concerned with it [science-fantasy] in all its forms: with its significant ideas, its surprising prophecies, its sheer fictions, its evolution as a fascinating literature."[1]

What was refreshing about the first two issues of *Science-Fantasy* was the balance between fiction and nonfiction, something lacking from most earlier British SF magazines. In the three years since the demise of *Fantasy* Gillings had been privately publishing a very professional magazine, *Fantasy Review* (first issue March 1947). With the sixteenth issue in autumn 1949 it was retitled *Science Fantasy Review*, and with the nineteenth issue in summer 1950 it was incorporated as a department within *Science-Fantasy*. *Science-Fantasy* included several pages of news and intelligent reviews of the SF field, mostly by Walter Gillings under a number of pseudonymous guises, but also by John Aiken (son of the noted poet Conrad Aiken).

Disputes in the printing industry delayed the appearance of the second issue until the winter of 1950–1951, and although a third was promised in March,[2] because of paper rationing it did not appear until the following December. Readers of the Autumn 1951 *New Worlds* were advised of the delay with the following announcement: "Our companion magazine *Science-Fantasy* was hard hit by the paper situation, but we have redesigned the third issue and increased the size to that of *New Worlds*. The issue, expected in September, contains new stories by some of our top authors, with the accent upon *fantasy* with a scientific theme."[3]

What the announcement did not reveal were the internal disagreements that had been occurring within Nova Publications. The third issue was indeed revised, as reference to the back cover advertisement on *New Worlds* 10 will attest. The planned Summer 1951 *Science-Fantasy*, still priced 1/6d., was to include stories by A. Bertram Chandler, F. G. Rayer, Robert Wright, E. E. Evans, J. T. McIntosh and others. When it finally appeared (now priced 2/-) Chandler's story had been replaced by John Wyndham's "Pawley's Peepholes" and the Robert Wright story ("Dhactwhu—Remember?" by Robert Lowndes and Forrest Ackerman) was dropped.

The reason for the rearranging was a change of editors. At a board meeting the directors had decided that it was uneconomical to keep two editors, and Gillings had been outvoted in favor of John Carnell. Gillings supplied an editorial to the third issue, but thereafter he faded from the forefront of British SF for nearly twenty years (see *Vision of Tomorrow**). The emphasis was now on fiction, and the enlightening departments that Gillings had introduced were all dropped.

With one editor in control it was possible to ensure that *Science-Fantasy* and *New Worlds* did not conflict in either policy or content. Although for the first few issues under Carnell there was little to distinguish one from the other, gradually *Science-Fantasy* began to acquire a personality all its own. The transformation really took shape with the seventh issue, which appeared after a delay of over a year caused by printers' strikes and the reorganization of Nova Publications. A slightly smaller format, increased pages and a reduction in cover price (back to 1/6d.) were the immediately obvious results of the change, along with a regular bi-monthly publication schedule. The internal policy—of a strong lead novelette supported by several short stories and a guest editorial—remained much the same for the rest of Carnell's editorship. The stories were still basically science fiction, but there was an increased tendency toward including stories with a greater fantastic element. The first classifiable fantasy of the *Unknown** tradition to appear was William F. Temple's "Eternity" in the February 1955 issue, wherein thousands of people suddenly acquire haloes. Despite the final extraterrestrial rationale, the story was evidently of a kind that would not suit *New Worlds'* policy. Similarly, Dal Stivens' "Free Will" in the same issue (which subsequently appeared in *Fantastic Universe**) had robot ghosts as its theme.

But *Science Fantasy* really came into its own with the lead novelettes by Kenneth Bulmer, and more especially John Brunner, starting with Brunner's "The Talisman" in the September 1955 issue. Over the next few years Brunner's contributions included "Death Do Us Part" (November 1955), about a ghost wanting a divorce; "Proof Negative" (February 1956, as Trevor Staines), a Christmas fable; 'This Rough Magic" (May 1956), involving black magic; "A Time to Rend" (December 1956), an alternate-world fantasy; "The Kingdoms of the World" (February 1957); "Lungfish" (December 1957), set on a generation starship; "Earth Is But a Star" (June 1958; published in book form as *The 100th Millennium*); "City of the Tiger" (December 1958) and its sequel, "The Whole Man" (April 1959; in book form as *Telepathist*); "Echo in the Skull" (August 1959); "The Gaudy Shadows" (June 1960); and "Imprint of Chaos" (August 1960), the first of his Traveller in Black fantasies. There was not a dud among them.

At the same time Kenneth Bulmer was providing stories like "The Bones of Shosun" (October 1958), "Castle of Vengeance" (November 1959), "Strange Highway" (April 1960) and "The Map Country" (February 1961). Brian Aldiss also made an early mark in *Science Fantasy*, which published his first novel, "Non-Stop" (February 1956), and several experimental stories like "The Flowers of the Forest" (August 1957) and "Faceless Card" (April 1960).

Although *Science Fantasy* used predominantly new stories, Carnell was not averse to selecting reprints, and these often reflected the true nature of the magazine—"Web of the Norns" by Harry Harrison and Katherine MacLean, "The Graveyard Reader" by Theodore Sturgeon, "Space-Time for Springers" by Fritz Leiber, and "Little Jimmy" by Lester del Rey.

It was evident that Carnell was taking special care with *Science Fantasy*. In 1956 he deliberately delayed an issue for two months "through lack of suitable material" rather than release something substandard.[4] Consequently, standards in *Science Fantasy* were high; this was reflected in the frequent selection of stories from its pages for Judith Merril's annual *SF: Year's Greatest* anthologies. In time *Science Fantasy* was frequently short-listed for the Hugo Awards, though, alas, it never won.

By 1959 the occasional article had found its way back into the magazine, and from 1959 to 1961 it printed Sam Moskowitz's series, "Studies in Science Fiction," which were eventually incorporated in his book *Explorers of the Infinite* (1963).

The incidence of pure fantasies in *Science Fantasy*, as opposed to weird-SF, had increased so much by 1960 that the December edition was labeled a "Special Weird Story" issue. It contained two novelettes—"All the Devils in Hell" by John Brunner and "The Black Cat's Paw" by John Rackham; Sam Moskowitz's essay on H. P. Lovecraft; and a short story, "The Painter," by American writer Thomas Burnett Swann.

It was only Swann's second story in *Science Fantasy*, yet in a few issues his name would be synonymous with the magazine. His triumph came with the publication of his beautiful retelling of the myth of Romulus and Remus, "Where Is the Bird of Fire?," in the April 1962 issue. Carnell prefaced the story with the following blurb: "Outstanding fantasy stories are all too rare these days— *Science Fantasy* is the sole outlet for authors who still love this medium—so that when we received Thomas Burnett Swann's latest novelette we felt privileged to be its publisher."[5] Three issues later Carnell was proclaiming that "Where Is the Bird of Fire?" "received more praise than any other [novelette] in recent years."[6] It would be four years before Swann finally found recognition in his homeland, and it is sobering to wonder what might have become of his fiction without John Carnell and *Science Fantasy*.

Swann, with his rare brand of historical fantasy, was the third corner of the triangle of writers whose work symbolized *Science Fantasy* in the early 1960s, following Brunner and Bulmer in the late 1950s. The other two were J. G. Ballard and Michael Moorcock.

Ballard had first appeared in the December 1956 issue with "Prima Belladonna" (one of his Vermilion Sands stories). As his stories grew more surreal, so *Science Fantasy* became the ideal medium for them, and the early 1960s saw such enigmatic yet refreshingly original stories as "The Sound Sweep" (February 1960), "The Last World of Mr. Goddard" (October 1960), "Studio 5, the Stars" (February 1961), "Mr. F. Is Mr. F." (August 1961), "The Watchtowers" (June 1962), "Minus One" (June 1963) and "Time of Passage" (February 1964).

Michael Moorcock's fantasy hero Elric first appeared in the June 1961 *Science Fantasy* in "The Dreaming City," with the prince himself represented on the cover by Brian Lewis. Thereafter Moorcock was in almost every issue of *Science Fantasy* for the next three years, usually with an Elric adventure. Moorcock also provided a four-part survey of the fantasy field in "Aspects of Fantasy" (October 1963–April 1964) and an appreciation of Mervyn Peake in the same issue (August 1963) that contained one of Peake's rare short stories, "Same Time, Same Place."

The editorial in that August 1963 issue announced that "we are planning on making *Science Fantasy* a monthly publication just as soon as possible."[7] This had been written shortly after the folding of the companion magazine *Science Fiction Adventures** at a time when the fortunes of Nova Publications were showing a consistently downward trend. The monthly schedule never materialized, and in 1964 *Science Fantasy* (along with *New Worlds*) was sold to the firm of Roberts and Vinter Ltd.

The Carnell *Science Fantasy* and the subsequent magazine under Oxford art dealer Kyril Bonfiglioli were two very different publications. The Carnell editions, with their long lead novelettes and effective and creative covers by Gerard Quinn and Brian Lewis, had an air of freshness and uniqueness about them. Michael Moorcock summarized the situation in the final part of his "Aspects of Fantasy" series:

> *Science Fantasy* has published a proportionately higher number of good stories than any other magazine to date. The comparative freedom allowed to the writer for this magazine has been greater than anywhere else. I only wish I could have written better stories for it while I had the chance.
>
> It was not only my opinion that *Science Fantasy* was achieving a more literary and less prosaic tone in its choice of material. To some extent it had always possessed a more literary "image" than any of its competitors.
>
> In recent years with the publication of stories like "The Watchtowers," "Where is the Bird of Fire?," "Same Time, Same Place," "Skeleton Crew" and many others, it has shown the uses to which Fantasy can be put, has done something more than entertain on an escapist level.
>
> Perhaps this is why it was beginning to be thought, in this country and the States, the best of all the current magazines.[8]

The new *Science Fantasy*, dated June/July 1964, was in pocketbook format with an unprepossessing cover design by Roger Harris. For no obvious reason there had been a reduction in cover price (from 3/- to 2/6d.). Of the six stories in the issue, three were by Brian W. Aldiss, with two under pen names. When Bonfiglioli assumed control he was desperate for quality material. In his first editorial he admitted, ''I have just read through a quarter of a million words of ms and half of it was so bad it made be blush.''[9] Naturally he had turned to his fellow Oxfordian and asked if he had any spare stories. ''Yes,'' replied Aldiss, ''but they were written before I got the hang of things. They're no damned good.'' ''They can't possibly be worse than the rubbish that's being submitted,'' Bonfiglioli replied, and Aldiss conceded on the proviso that Bonfiglioli invent some pseudonyms to disguise them.[10] Thus the alter egos John Runciman and Jael Cracken were born to help tide Bonfiglioli over until he had sufficient quality fiction to support the magazine. ''Science Fiction for Grown-Ups!'' he declared in his editorial,[11] at the same time striking a sideways blow at fiction in the vein of Edgar Rice Burroughs and Robert E. Howard. He posed a competition with a first prize of £50 for the best new story written by a professional, qualified scientist—though no more was heard of it. Bonfiglioli's intentions were clear from the outset. He wanted an adult, literary magazine where the stories were considered as fiction first, and SF or fantasy only as an afterthought.

He soon attracted a number of new writers, of whom the most impressive and significant was Keith Roberts. He debuted with two stories in the same issue (September/October 1964): ''Escapism'' (a simple time-travel story) and ''Anita,'' the first of an enjoyable series about a young witch. This same issue, Bonfiglioli's third, showed the first signs that he was coming to grips with the situation. It included bizarre stories by Johnny Byrne and Thom Keyes, stories that would never have appeared in a Carnell magazine, but also included the first episode in *Science Fantasy*'s first serial, fittingly Thomas Burnett Swann's ''The Blue Monkeys'' (published in book form as *The Day of the Minotaur*). By the final episode, *Science Fantasy* was sufficiently solvent to risk a monthly schedule, giving Bonfiglioli more opportunity to experiment.

Several new writers were now appearing, including Robert Wells, Philip Wordley, Patricia Hocknell, Josephine Saxton and Brian Stableford (disguised in pseudonymous collaboration as Brian Craig). Keith Roberts, however, seemed set to all but take over the magazine. He appeared in almost every issue either under his own name, under his alias Alistair Bevan, or in his role as illustrator, providing many of the covers. With the last issue Roberts became associate editor.

All along Bonfiglioli disliked the title *Science Fantasy*. ''I felt—and still feel— that this title promised the worst of both worlds.''[12] His final choice was *Impulse*,* and its appearance in March 1966 with a revised volume numbering firmly brought an end to *Science Fantasy*.

Bonfiglioli had been a patchy editor with stubborn attitudes to SF and a number of blind-spots, but under him *Science Fantasy* was always readable, though the aura of the issues of the early 1960s had long since faded.

Notes

1. [Walter Gillings], "Fantasies and Facts," *Science-Fantasy* 1 (Summer 1950): 3.
2. [Walter Gillings], "Going Your Way," *Science-Fantasy* 2 (Winter 1950): 2.
3. [John Carnell], "Space Opera . . . ," *New Worlds* 11 (Autumn 1951): 39.
4. [John Carnell], "Editorial-in-Brief," *New Worlds SF* 53 (November 1956): 20.
5. [John Carnell], *Science Fantasy* 52 (April 1962): 58.
6. [John Carnell], *Science Fantasy* 55 (October 1962): 71.
7. [John Carnell], "Editorial," *Science Fantasy* 60 (August 1963): inside back cover.
8. Michael Moorcock, "Aspects of Fantasy," Part 4, *Science Fantasy* 64 (April 1964): 124.
9. Kyril Bonfiglioli, "Editorial," *Science Fantasy* 65 (June–July 1964): 2.
10. Brian W. Aldiss, private correspondence.
11. Bonfiglioli, "Editorial," p. 3.
12. Kyril Bonfiglioli, "Editorial," *Science Fantasy* 81 (February 1966): 2.

Information Sources

BIBLIOGRAPHY:
Nicholls. *Encyclopedia*.
Tuck.
INDEX SOURCES: IBSF; MIT; MT; SFM; Tuck.
REPRINT SOURCES:
   Derivative Anthology: Eight of the ten stories in *Weird Shadows from Beyond*, ed. John Carnell (London: Corgi Books, 1965), came from *SF*.
   Microform: Oxford Microform Publications.
LOCATION SOURCES: M.I.T. Science Fiction Library; Pennsylvania State University Library.

Publication History

TITLE: *Science-Fantasy*, Summer 1950–Spring 1953; *Science Fantasy*, [Spring] 1954– February 1966.
VOLUME DATA: *Science-Fantasy*, Volume 1, Number 1–Volume 2, Number 6; *Science Fantasy*, Volume 3, Number 7–Volume 24, Number 81. Total: 81 issues.
PUBLISHER: Nova Publications Ltd., Summer 1950–April 1964; Roberts and Vinter Ltd., June–July 1964–February 1966. Both publishers operated in London.
EDITORS: Walter Gillings, Summer–Winter 1950; John Carnell, Winter 1951–April 1964; Kyril Bonfiglioli, June–July 1964–February 1966.
FORMAT: Digest, 96 pp., Number 1, Summer 1950–Number 2, Winter 1950/51; Large Digest, 96 pp., Number 3, Winter 1951/52–Number 6, Spring 1953; Digest, 128 pp., Number 7, [Spring] 1954–Number 35, June 1959; 112 pp., Number 36, August 1959–Number 63, February 1964; 124 pp., Number 64, April 1964; Pocketbook, 128 pp., Number 65, June/July 1964–Number 81, February 1966.
PRICE: 1/6d., Numbers 1–2; 2/-, Numbers 3–6; 1/6d., Numbers 7–10; 2/-, Numbers 11– 45; 2/6d., Numbers 45–60; 3/-, Numbers 61–64; 2/6d., Numbers 65–81.

Mike Ashley

SCIENCE FANTASY (1970–1971)

Science Fantasy was one of the many reprint digest magazines issued by Sol Cohen in 1970 that drew on the back files of *Amazing Stories** and *Fantastic Adventures*;* it is not to be confused with the British *Science Fantasy.**

This magazine was launched as a yearbook in 1970 when Cohen was experimenting with a number of titles. The stories came mostly from the years 1950–1952, and the first issue is worth noting for a rare appearance of Theodore Sturgeon's Arthurian fantasy "Excalibur and the Atom." A second issue followed in the fall, also leading with a Sturgeon novella, "The Dreaming Jewels." Two further issues appeared, both with lead novellas. Edmond Hamilton's "The Quest of Time" in the third issue was weak by comparison, but the fourth issue featured William Tenn's "Medusa Was a Lady," though this had only recently been issued in paperback by Belmont as *A Lamp for Medusa* (New York, 1968).

The remaining short stories were of variable quality, as one might expect in a magazine where stories are selected as much by their length as for merit. Many were enhanced by Virgil Finlay illustrations.

Information Sources

INDEX SOURCES: ISFM-II; NESFA; SFM.
REPRINT SOURCES: None known.
LOCATION SOURCES: M.I.T. Science Fiction Library.

Publication History

TITLE: *Science Fantasy* (this title remained on the indicia and masthead throughout. The cover of the first issue read *Science Fantasy Yearbook–1970*, while the spine read *1970 Science Fantasy Yearbook*).
VOLUME DATA: No volume numbering; numbered and dated on cover and spine only. *Yearbook* unnumbered and dated only by year (released Summer 1970); Number 2, Fall 1970–Number 4, Spring 1971. Quarterly. Total run: 4 issues.
PUBLISHER: Ultimate Publishing Co., Flushing, New York.
EDITOR: Sol Cohen (not identified within issues).
FORMAT: Digest, 128 pp.
PRICE: 60¢.

Mike Ashley

SCIENCE FANTASY YEARBOOK

See SCIENCE FANTASY (1970–1971).

SCIENCE FICTION

The growing popularity and success of the science fiction pulps in the late 1930s, especially the revamped *Amazing Stories** and *Thrilling Wonder Stories* (*Wonder Stories**) along with the new *Marvel Science Stories,** encouraged other publishers to test the waters. Among them was Louis Silberkleit, who had established the Winford Publishing Company in 1934. Silberkleit had been an employee of Hugo Gernsback in the 1920s, and the two had remained close friends. It was not that much of a surprise, therefore, that Silberkleit's first magazine should include many of the elements that had featured in the Gernsback magazines, right down to the title—*Science Fiction*—a term coined by Gernsback. Although *Astounding Stories* (*Analog Science Fiction**) had changed its title to *Astounding Science-Fiction* in 1938 with the obvious intention of phasing out the ''Astounding,'' *Science Fiction* preempted Campbell's plan and became the first magazine to use the term solely as a title.

The first issue was dated March 1939. Gernsback provided a guest editorial, but the actual editor was Charles D. Hornig, who had formerly edited *Wonder Stories*. Hornig had visited Silberkleit at Gernsback's suggestion and had been promptly hired as a free-lance editor, operating almost entirely from his home in New Jersey. Silberkleit allowed Hornig only a small budget for the purchase of stories, and Hornig took the easy way out by acquiring manuscripts from his friend, the literary agent Julius Schwartz. Most of these were rejects from the other magazines, so that even though the authors' names may have held promise, the stories were of questionable quality. In fact, Hornig even reduced the sale potential of authors' names by publishing many of the stories under pen names. This was a direct result of his poor budget. He paid one cent a word to a big-name author if the story appeared under his own name, but only half a cent if it appeared under an alias. Schwartz would not sell stories by his authors for less than one cent a word if their real names were used. To some extent the authors may have been glad of the cloak of pseudonymity. Stories like Earl and Otto Binder's ''Martian Martyrs,'' Raymond Z. Gallun's ''The Machine That Thought'' and John Russell Fearn's ''Leeches from Space,'' all published under pseudonyms, seemed aimed at a very juvenile readership indeed.

The second issue, however, marked an improvement. Binder's ''Where Eternity Ends'' was fast-paced despite the simplistic revenge argument used to justify genocide; Henry Kuttner (under the pseudonym Paul Edmonds) contributed ''Telepathy Is News!,'' an exciting story with some interesting if insufficiently developed insights into the conflict between the rights of the individual and of society; while Edmond Hamilton, writing as Robert Castle, produced an interesting idea when he envisaged the galaxy as the atoms of a superbrain in ''Short-Wave Madness,'' but he failed to do anything with it.

That second issue also contained a letter from eighteen-year-old Ray Bradbury, still a couple of years away from his first story sale. Bradbury was a friend of Hornig, so it is not surprising that he praised *Science Fiction* to embarrassing extremes. ''There have been many new science-fiction mags out lately, but I can truthfully say that your mag leads the race by miles.'' He went on to say, ''Don't let the mag ever degenerate to the kindergarten class—let it grow with the minds of the fans,'' an obvious swipe at the new polces of *Amazing* and *Thrilling Wonder*, to which Hornig's response was, ''I'm trying to give the magazine an appeal to mature minds,''[1] but this never became evident. By the third issue Hornig was proclaiming that his policy was to provide ''more entertainment—less technicalities of science. . . . the authors have cleverly camouflaged science facts in the midst of thrilling escapades.''[2]

What this meant too often was stories that were little more than a series of loosely connected adventures, such as Neil R. Jones' rambling Burroughsian ''Swordsmen of Saturn.'' They frequently featured scientists with beautiful daughters (or sisters) for the dauntlessly active hero to marry after various encounters with snarling villains. They soon grew tedious. Even the better stories, like Binder's ''The Life Beyond,'' Ed Earl Repp's ''Destiny Made to Order'' and Bob Olsen's ''The Scourge of the Single Cell,'' suffered from the failure to explore the implications of the events narrated. Probably the best tale in the magazine was ''Proxies on Venus'' in the June 1940 issue, a poignant account of robots acquiring emotions, told with a carefully controlled point of view by Nelson S. Bond. However, it was but a solitary spark of light in the pervading gray of mediocrity.

Science Fiction was originally scheduled as a bi-monthly, but seldom appeared regularly, a situation that was only aggravated by the appearance of two companion titles, *Future Fiction** and *Science Fiction Quarterly,** a sign which clearly indicated Silberkleit's view that the science fiction field was worthy of investment provided one spread one's risk.

In October 1940, however, Hornig moved to Los Angeles, where he felt that he had a better chance to register as a conscientious objector rather than enter military service. It meant that Hornig was now editing the magazines long distance, an arrangement that soon dissatisfied the publisher. Donald A. Wollheim, a leading member of the talented group of budding writers and editors known as the Futurians, learned of this, and he prompted Robert W. Lowndes, a fellow Futurian, to write to Silberkleit, as related in the entry on *Future Fiction.* The result was that Lowndes became editor of *Future Fiction* and *Science Fiction Quarterly,* and Hornig retained *Science Fiction.*

This arrangement was short-lived, however. *Science Fiction*'s sales remained poor, and after the September 1941 issue it was combined with *Future Fiction* under the editorship of Lowndes.

In 1943 *Future Fiction,* which underwent several title changes, was briefly retitled *Science Fiction Stories,* but the volume numbering continues that of *Future Fiction,* and the issues are considered under that entry.

The demise of the first incarnation of *Science Fiction* was no loss to the field, for it opened no new vistas and developed no new talents. It relied too heavily upon inferior material from veterans like Repp, Hamilton, Binder and Fearn, whose best work was either behind them or appearing elsewhere; even the covers by Frank R. Paul were poor examples of his art. The result was that much material appeared in print that would have been better discarded. Had Hornig been as energetic about improving fiction content as he was in responding companionably to letters, spreading his enthusiasm for Esperanto, and writing pacifist editorials,[3] he might have achieved more impressive results. As it was, *Science Fiction* from 1939 to 1941 was unmemorable.

Silberkleit retained the rights to *Science Fiction*, and when *Future Fiction* was revived in 1950 it appeared under the cumbersome safeguard title of *Future combined with Science Fiction Stories*. Over the next two years that title was contracted to *Future Science Fiction*, and in 1953 the original title was revived and *Science Fiction Stories* was issued as a one-shot digest-size experiment. (*Future Fiction* was still pulp-sized.)

The new magazine bore neither date nor number. The SF boom was at its height and the bookstands were saturated with magazines. *Science Fiction* had some thirty rivals in the SF field alone, of which 60 percent were in digest-size format. Many were on monthly or bi-monthly schedules, though others were still feeling their way and appeared irregularly. Silberkleit decided to test *Science Fiction* on title and content alone under a prolonged display rather than have the retailer withdraw the issue once the cover date had passed. This experiment was tried twice, in the summers of 1953 and 1954, and sales were encouraging in both instances. The contents did not differ much from those of many other magazines, and certainly not from those of *Future SF*, which featured the same type of action story by the same writers, such as Algis Budrys, Poul Anderson, Noel Loomis and Philip K. Dick—all capable of producing quality fiction.

The success of the two experimental issues had to be for one or more of three reasons: the duration of sale display, the digest format or the title. As for the sales period, this obviously helped, but it was ridiculous for a publisher to sell a regular magazine on such a basis. By the end of 1954 the SF boom had faded, which gave the survivors a larger share of the market. The possibility existed, therefore, for a new bi-monthly publication.

But of greater import were the title and format. The day of the pulps was over. The new generation of postwar readers was after magazines with a more sophisticated and mature appeal than the brash roughness of the pulps. The 1950s would see the rise of the pocketbook, television and slick magazines which appealed to the greater part of the public. The young readers who had once bought many of the juvenile adventure pulps were now being accommodated by the comic books, so the digest magazine catered to the more discriminating reader. Silberkleit was aware of the situation and converted *Future* to a digest

Finally, reader reaction had intimated that *Science Fiction* had a greater sales potential as a title than *Future SF*, so with the January 1955 issue *Future SF* was retitled *Science Fiction Stories* and the volume numbering of *Future* was continued. In effect, therefore, the revived *Science Fiction Stories* was a continuation of *Future SF*, and had nothing else changed would always have been considered as such. Confusion arose later in 1955, however, when Silberkleit decided the market could support an additional title and *Future SF* reappeared on an experimental basis. It bore no cover date, but continued its old numbering sequence, converted to a whole number instead of using issue and volume. At the same time, ostensibly to help clarify the situation, the title *Science Fiction Stories* was prefixed on the cover by ''The Original. . . . '' This was to show that the magazine was a continuation of the original 1939 title, and the prefix was never officially part of the title. Nevertheless, it led to much confusion, with readers believing that it was a new magazine called *The Original Science Fiction Stories*. In fact, because of the various incarnations of the two magazines, it is wiser to regard *Future Fiction* and *SFS* as two sides of the same coin, especially since *SFS* never returned to its own numbering system but retained that of *Future Fiction*. Lowndes commented on this in a later issue:

> I am often asked whether *Future SF* October 1954 Volume 5 Number 3 should be followed by Volume 5 Number 4 (*Science Fiction Stories* January 1955) or by *Future SF* No. 28. To this I reply that you may have it either way, or, in this instance, both ways! Really, I don't see why science fictionists, who can absorb alternate time tracks etc. with the utmost aplomb, should be confused.[4]

Future SF itself would later be revived as a regular bi-monthly, but from 1955 till its demise in 1960, after thirty-six issues, *Science Fiction Stories* was always the senior partner and featured the more mature stories. *Future SF's* contents became weighted more toward the general fan, *SFS*'s toward the general reader. Both magazines followed the same format—a long lead story supported by several short stories, an article and reader departments. For a period during 1958–1959, when *Science Fiction* was issued on a monthly basis, it carried two serials. The first was L. Sprague de Camp's ''The Tower of Zanid'' (May–August 1958), one of his cycle of future histories, telling of the exploits of an English adventurer and a Polish archeologist as they attempt to discover the secret of the eponymous tower set against de Camp's meticulously structured society of Krishna. The novel was subsequently published by Avalon Books, for which Lowndes was also the editor, later in 1958. The second serial was the nearly forgotten ''Caduceus Wild'' by Ward Moore and Robert Bradford (January–May 1959), which did not see book publication until 1980, two years after Moore's death. It portrays an oppressed society, governed by the rule of the ''caduceus''—the doctors— and follows the inevitable bid for freedom by the ''mallies,'' or maladjusted.

Both novels emphasized the individual in society, a theme that was common in SF in the 1940s and 1950s, especially in the years of recovery after the McCarthy ''witch-hunts.'' Neither novel, however, was outstanding, and this was true for much of *Science Fiction*'s content. Working with a limited budget, Lowndes was unable to attract much first-rate work, relying instead on rejects from the leading magazines plus work by new writers, or the overspill from such prolific wordsmiths as Robert Silverberg and Randall Garrett, for whom even the major markets were not sufficient. There was another factor. Lowndes was a much respected editor; there was no stigma attached to his magazines as there was to some other titles, such as *Other Worlds** or *Imaginative Tales.** In retrospect the stories in *Science Fiction* were never below, but seldom above, average.

Clifford Simak provided two especially worthy stories. "Full Cycle" (November 1955) looks at a nomadic society where the city as an institution has passed away, where farms have become corporations and where people live in trailers rather than houses. "Galactic Chest" (September 1956) was again typical Simak, with a newspaper reporter discovering that the brownies and little folk of legend are in fact aliens, and that now they are back for a second visit. Raymond F. Jones provided one of his most intriguing stories in "The Non-Statistical Man" (May 1956). Beginning in a small way with a sudden rush of insurance claims on recent policies, it leads to the discovery of how intuition can be used as a precision tool to predict the future. *SFS* also saw the first magazine appearance of James Blish's "Giants in the Earth" (January 1956), which was the basis for his novel *Titan's Daughter* (New York: Berkley, 1961), but as it had previously appeared under the title "Beanstalk" in Kendall Foster Crossen's anthology *Future Tense* (New York: Greenberg, 1952) it cannot truly be claimed as a feather in Lowndes' cap.

Robert Silverberg had a story in virtually every issue after his first appearance in May 1956 with "The Dessicator." He contributed eighteen stories in all, most appearing under either his own name or the alias Calvin M. Knox. Although most have since reappeared in several of Silverberg's collections, only one has been deemed of sufficient merit for anthologization, "Sunrise on Mercury" (May 1957). As examples of early Silverberg, these stories must be considered among the better portion—a mixture of aspiring ideas and embryonic characters mishandled by inexperience, but made readable by his infectious enthusiasm. For instance, in "Why?" (November 1957) one overlooks the comic-book way in which the two-man exploration team discovers and investigates new planets because of the question posed by Silverberg: "Why do the characters continue to operate as they do?," and the reader is compelled to find the answer. To some extent, this is the appeal of *SFS*. For the most part its fiction had sufficient zest to imbue the reader with a sympathetic enthusiasm without insulting his intelligence.

This reflected the aptitude of Robert A. W. Lowndes as an editor, a fact that was also evident from his thoughtful editorials. In *Science Fiction* these sometimes rivaled John W. Campbell's for their provocativeness. In "Job for a Superman" (September 1957), for instance, Lowndes considers the question, "Is it likely that we will see great works of literature in the form of science fiction?," and he reminds fans that many have a too blinkered attitude to their chosen field. "One cannot rationally proclaim science fiction as true English Literature (in the British and American tradition), then simultaneously call *Slan* and *Grey Lensman* great novels—to name just a pair of examples—and expect to be taken seriously."[5] This was the approach taken by Damon Knight and

James Blish in their book review columns (some of which Lowndes published), and it was refreshing to see an editor with the same view.

In "Disciplined Imagination" (May 1958), Lowndes offered this basic advice on the writing of science fiction, and it holds good today:

There are two fundamental laws for good science fiction.

1) It must conform to the discipline of fiction in general. No idea, no gadget, no cosmic marvel can atone for a story which does not "convince" because of shoddy plot-structure or unbelievable characters.

2) It must conform to the basic elements of the physical sciences. No amount of magnificence in plot and character portrayal, and "sense of wonder" can make good science fiction if the story is befouled by the author's ignorance of high school physics, chemistry, biology, etc.[6]

These editorials underline Lowndes' ability as an editor, and one can only wonder at what he might have achieved had he been allowed a larger budget. As it is, most issues of *Science Fiction* are still readable today—which cannot be said for many of its contemporaries—and although their production left much to be desired, this was the fault of the publisher and his printer, not the editor. Lowndes acquired good interior artwork from Virgil Finlay, Kelly Freas, Ed Emsh and Paul Orban, but the covers were far from memorable.

Among the writers who owe their first story sale to Robert A. W. Lowndes is R. A. Lafferty, who debuted in *Science Fiction* with a tongue-in-cheek catastrophe story about a new Ice Age, "Day of the Glacier" (January 1960). *Science Fiction* also carried a variety of reader departments, including a lively letter column, and occasional news and reminiscences by Robert A. Madle in "Inside Science Fiction," a column that appeared erratically in most of the Lowndes magazines at some time in the 1950s. Most of the early issues featured a nonfiction article. L. Sprague de Camp provided a brief series on myths and legends, and there were other items by Frederik Pohl and Isaac Asimov.

Science Fiction was a well-balanced magazine that always showed promise. But instead of allowing Lowndes more money, Silberkleit tightened the purse strings, so that in the final issues Lowndes had to rely on reprints from the 1940s issues and cannibalized old illustrations for the cover. It was a sad sight to see *Science Fiction* withering before one's eyes, and mercifully the magazine was put out of its misery after the May 1960 issue, when the whole of Silberkleit's magazine chain was dropped by the distributor. The end nevertheless came abruptly, with no indication in the final issue.

The rights to the title were sold to longtime fan James V. Taurasi, who in December 1961 issued a flyer announcing the continuation of the magazine on a semi-professional basis and available by subscription only. Two issues appeared, dated Winter 1962 and Winter 1963 respectively, printed in a fanzine format and running to fifty-two pages. They featured only minor fiction, although Sam Moskowitz was present in both issues, with the column "Inside SF" in the first, and a story, "Outcasts of Light," in the second. But response was minimal, Taurasi lost interest, and finally *Science Fiction* was allowed to pass away.

Notes

1. *Science Fiction*, Vol. 1, No. 2 (June 1939):126. Letter from Ray Bradbury plus editorial comment by Charles D. Hornig.

2. *Science Fiction*, Vol. 1, No. 3 (August 1939):117.

3. Hornig's opinions were reflected not only in his editorials but also in some of the stories he printed, for example, Repp's "Wisdom of the Dead." As an absolute objector to all forms of wartime service Hornig was ordered to the Civilian Public Service Camp at Cascade Locks, Oregon, in March 1942. Discovering the hypocrisy of the camp system, Hornig went AWOL and was subsequently sent to trial and imprisoned in 1943.

4. *Science Fiction Stories*, Vol. 8, No. 3 (November 1957):125. Comment by Robert A. W. Lowndes in response to a letter from Milton Stevens.

5. Robert A. W. Lowndes, "Job for a Superman," *Science Fiction Stories*, Vol. 8, No. 2 (September 1957):96.

6. Robert A. W. Lowndes, "Disciplined Imagination," *Science Fiction Stories*, Vol. 8, No. 6 (May 1958):128.

Information Sources

BIBLIOGRAPHY:
Lowndes, Robert A. W., Article in *Pulp Era*, May–June 1967.
Nicholls. *Encyclopedia*.
Tuck.
INDEX SOURCES: ISFM; SFM; Tuck.
REPRINT SOURCES:
Reprint Editions:
British: Two series. Two abridged but direct reprints of the October and December 1939 U.S. issues complete with volume numbering were released by Atlas Publications, London. Pulp, 96 pp. Second series was reprinted by Strato Publications, London. Undated, it ran for twelve issues from October 1957 to May 1960, digest, 128 pp., 2/-. Abbreviated from U. S. originals as follows: 1, Sep 57; 2, Nov 57; 3, May 58; 4, Jun 58; 5, Jul 58; 6, Aug 58; 7, Nov 58; 8, Jan 59; 9, Feb 59; 10, Mar 59; 11, May 59. Issue 12 was the May 1960 issue overprinted with U.K. cover price.
See also separate entry on Canadian edition.
Derivative Anthologies: Ivan Howard assembled several anthologies in the 1960s, drawing their contents entirely from the Columbia magazines. No single anthology consists solely of stories from *SFS*, but *Masters of Science Fiction* (1964) contained three, *Now & Beyond* (1965) four, *Rare Science Fiction* (1963) four, and *6 and the Silent Scream* (1963) three. All were published in New York by Belmont Books.
Microform: Greenwood Press Periodical Series.
LOCATION SOURCES: M.I.T. Science Fiction Library; Pennsylvania State University Library.

Publication History

TITLE: First Series: *Science Fiction*, March 1939–September 1941; thereafter combined with *Future Fiction*, of which the two issues dated April and July 1943 were retitled *Science Fiction Stories*. Revived as *Science Fiction Stories* in 1953, and title retained. The prefix "The Original . . . " was added with the September 1955 issue but was not part of the official title.

VOLUME DATA: The publication history is complicated, and the reader may want to refer to Lowndes' own detail on the facts in the issues for November 1957 (pp. 123–125) and further corrected and clarified in May 1958 (pp. 125–126). The numbering runs: Volume 1, Number 1, March 1939–Volume 2, Number 6, September 1941. Six issues per volume. First volume schedule intentionally bi-monthly but issues dated 1939: Mar, Jun, Aug, Oct, Dec; 1940: Mar. Second volume quarterly, but issues dated 1940: Jun, Oct; 1941: Jan, Mar, Jun, Sep (see also *Future Fiction* entry). An unnumbered, undated issue appeared in the summer of 1953, followed by Number 2, also undated, in the summer of 1954. The second series began as a retitled continuation of *Future Science Fiction* with that magazine's volume numbering: Volume 5, Number 4, January 1955–Volume 11, Number 2, May 1960. Six issues per volume, but Volume 8, seven issues. Bi-monthly until May 1958 (Vol. 8, No. 6); monthly, May 1958–March 1959 (no issues in October or December 1958); thereafter bi-monthly. Total run: First Series, 12 issues; Intermediary Series, 2 issues; Second Series, 36 issues. Total: 50 issues.

PUBLISHER: *SF/S* has always been published by Louis Silberkleit by one company under a variety of imprints. Blue Ribbon Magazines, of Holyoke, Massachusetts, and Hudson Street, New York, March–December 1939; Double Action Magazines, Chicago and New York, March 1940–January 1941; Columbia Publications, Springfield and Holyoke, March–September 1941. The Columbia Publications imprint remained from 1953 to May 1960, registered at Holyoke, and with editorial offices at Church Street, New York.

EDITORS: Charles D. Hornig, March 1939–September 1941 (the last issue was also worked on by Lowndes; Robert [A.] W. Lowndes, April–July 1943, 1953–May 1960.

FORMAT: Pulp, 132 pp., March 1939–December 1939; Pulp, 116 pp., March 1940–September 1941 (and April–July 1943); Digest, 128 pp., 1953–November 1955; Digest, 144 pp., January 1956–May 1957; Digest, 128 pp., July 1957–May 1960.

PRICE: 15¢, March 1939–September 1941 (and April–July 1943); 35¢, 1953–May 1960.

Mike Ashley/Raymond H. Thompson

SCIENCE FICTION (Canadian)

The Canadian edition of *Science Fiction* proudly proclaimed that it featured stories by Canadian authors, though in fact it reprinted its entire contents from the American magazines *Science Fiction,* Future Fiction** and *Science Fiction Quarterly,** selecting from a variety of issues. The only Canadian presence was in the artwork; stories were provided with new illustrations, and artists like John Hilkert and Edwin Shaw painted new covers. The editor of the magazine was credited as William Brown-Forbes. Ray Cummings' "The Man on the Meteor," which had been reprinted in the October 1941 *Future Fiction*, was serialized in three parts in the Canadian magazine, in the issues from January to March 1942.

Most of the Canadian wartime pulps are now scarce collector's items, but of them all, the Canadian *Science Fiction* is possibly the rarest.

Information Sources

BIBLIOGRAPHY:
Tuck.
INDEX SOURCES: None known.
REPRINT SOURCES: None known.
LOCATION SOURCES: None known.

Publication History

TITLE: *Science Fiction*.
VOLUME DATA: Volume 1, Number 1, October 1941–Volume 2, Number 4, June
     1942. Monthly, but no issues for December 1941 or April and May 1942. Total
     run: 6 issues.
PUBLISHER: Superior Magazines, Toronto, first two issues; thereafter Duchess Printing
     & Publishing, Toronto.
EDITOR: William Brown-Forbes.
FORMAT: Large Pulp, 64 pp.
PRICE: 25¢.

Mike Ashley

SCIENCE FICTION ADVENTURE CLASSICS

See SCIENCE FICTION CLASSICS.

SCIENCE FICTION ADVENTURES (1952–1954)

During the 1950s the science fiction magazine field reached its peak, with thirty-four different magazines being published in the United States alone. Generally containing inferior fiction and geared to the adolescent male, most of these magazines, though quite popular, would fold due to poor circulation before the decade was over. *Science Fiction Adventures* was an unusual exception to the rule.

Science Fiction Adventures was one of four publications edited by Lester del Rey and published by John Raymond's Science Fiction (later Future) Publications. Conceived to satisfy a magazine distributor's desire for an SF magazine, *SFA* was to be a more juvenile version of the earlier del Rey-edited *Space Science*

*Fiction.** Instead, del Rey stressed well-written stories with characters expressing human emotions, much like those published by *Astounding* (*Analog Science Fiction**) and *Galaxy Science Fiction.** In the first issue he stated his feelings:

> We also feel that science fiction isn't meant to be educational. It is primarily fiction, not a discourse on science. The science in the stories should be acceptable, of course—otherwise they might as well be labeled fairy tales. But the problems of the people in the stories must be stressed more than the gadgets they use. Fiction is concerned with the reactions of human believable characters in unusual predicaments. The fact that the character is a robot or a man from Sirius, and the predicament is one which can only exist in the future or on another world, doesn't change that; it only gives a freshness or gives added punch to a story.[1]

The first issue, dated November 1952, looked very similar to both *Astounding* and *Galaxy*. The magazine had solid borders, usually yellow, across the top and down the left side, much like the early issues of *Galaxy*. The last names of the major authors in the issue ran across the top of the illustration. The editor was listed as Philip St. John, a pseudonym used by del Rey. The publisher was R. Alvarez, del Rey's real name.

The contents of the first issue showed the care with which del Rey selected the stories that appeared in *SFA*. The feature novel was "The Fires of Forever" by Chad Oliver, which details the search to save Earth from certain demise. There were also top-notch stories from L. Sprague de Camp, Wilmar H. Shiras and Ross Rocklynne, three regular writers from *Astounding*; C. M. Kornbluth's "Make Mine Mars" also appeared. To round the issue out, del Rey had a nonfiction article under his own name entitled "How Phonetic Can You Get?" which prompted so much critical reaction that del Rey responded in the letters section. This is a perfect example of del Rey writing a letter to himself and also answering it!

The quality of the magazine improved with each issue. In the March 1953 issue, readers were treated to two outstanding stories. The first was a four-part serial entitled "Police Your Planet" by Erik Van Lhin, another of del Rey's many pen names. The second was the issue's feature novel, "Ten to the Stars" by Raymond Z. Gallun, which was voted by the reders as the best story printed in *SFA*.

There was also an early minor story by Algis Budrys called "Recessional," which was a typical interstellar war story. Chad Oliver and Roger Dee, who appeared in the first issue, also made an appearance in the second. The letter column, called "The Chart Room," began, highlighted by a humorous letter from Isaac Asimov.

The May 1953 issue continued Van Lhin's serial. There was also a humorous story by Robert Sheckley, "What Goes Up," which showed how one man's greed could be his own downfall. The feature novel in this issue was Theodore

R. Cogswell's "The Other Cheek," a minor interstellar story involving such characters as Prince Tarz and Captain Klag. The most unusual feature of the issue was the introduction of a department called "Among the Fen." It contained articles about the various science fiction fan clubs in existence at the time. The first article, written by Robert A. Madle, was about the Philadelphia Science Fiction Society. Madle's article chronicled the PSFS from its inception in 1934 to the upcoming World Science Fiction Convention to be held in Philadelphia in 1953. Incidentally, membership for that convention was only one dollar.

The July 1953 issue contained the third installment of "Police Your Planet." Raymond Z. Gallun contributed the feature novel, entitled "Legacy from Mars." Poul Anderson was represented by his novelette "The Nest." Damon Knight's book review column was also present in this issue. By this time *SFA* had settled comfortably into a set combination of short stories, novelettes, feature novels and serials.

For the remainder of its existence *Science Fiction Adventures* for the most part printed generally interesting but unexceptional stories. There were exceptions, of course. The January and March 1954 issues serialized C. M. Kornbluth's classic novel "The Syndic." Thomas H. Scortia's first magazine appearance, "The Prodigy," was in the March 1954 issue. Irving E. Cox, Jr., published three stories about earthmen marooned on Venus and how they evolved a new civilization. The first story, "On Streets of Gold," appeared in the May 1953 issue, the second, "Semantic Courtship," in the July 1953 issue, and the last, "The Venusian," was part of the September 1953 number.

The highlight of *SFA*'s later issues was William Tenn's article "The Fiction in Science Fiction." In it Tenn stated that science fiction stories "like all good fiction are essentially stories of human relationships, individually and communally, and no misstatements of scientific fact can rob them of this quality nor can dozens of validating footnotes add to their stature."[2] Tenn also felt science fiction to be the most revolutionary form of literature to appear in a long while and that it would eventually become the most important form of fiction. Tenn's article was one of the first to treat science fiction as a serious form of literature rather than viewing it as a curiosity enjoyed by a few.

The list of artists contributing their talents to *SFA* was practically a who's who of science fiction artists of the 1950s. H. R. Van Dongen, now a major cover artist for Del Rey and DAW books, contributed several covers. Ed Emshwiller, Alex Schomburg and Mel Hunter also drew covers for *SFA*.

The interior illustrators were even more illustrious. Kelly Freas contributed several excellent drawings. Paul Orban, one of *Astounding*'s major artists, was a regular contributor. Roy G. Krenkel, who later became a major science fiction artist with his covers for the Ace editions of Edgar Rice Burroughs, was represented with a fine illustration.

It would be quite logical to suppose that with such strong literary and artistic foundations *Science Fiction Adventures* was one of the major science fiction publications of the 1950s. The magazine lasted only nine issues. This was not caused by circulation problems but by lack of interest on the publisher's part.

The publisher, John Raymond, had no real idea of what to do with *SFA*. One day he would decide that the magazine would go monthly. The next day he would change his mind. He would decide on the spur of the moment when copy was due for the latest issue. *SFA* also paid the writers upon publication. As a result del Rey never kept an inventory of stories. He would contact agents or even write a story himself. It was not the best atmosphere in which to publish a magazine.[3]

In spite of all this, *SFA* was successful. It sold more than enough copies to show a profit. But instead of using the profits to improve the magazine, Raymond used the money elsewhere.[4]

Del Rey severed his relationship with *SFA* when, contrary to his understanding that Raymond would upgrade the magazine, the publisher decided to reduce the rate of payment to authors, cut the page count to 144 and eliminate illustrations from contributors. Harry Harrison took over for the last few issues. Raymond stopped publication with the May 1954 issue.

Science Fiction Adventures was one of the more interesting and better edited SF magazines to appear in the 1950s. It was a shame that the publisher did not care about the magazine; *Science Fiction Adventures* could have been one of the most successful magazines of the 1950s.

Notes

1. Philip St. John (pseudonym of Lester del Rey), "An Editorial Introduction," *Science Fiction Adventures* 1 (November 1952):2.

2. William Tenn, "The Fiction in Science Fiction," *Science Fiction Adventures* 2 (February 1954):72.

3. Michael Ashley, *The History of the Science Fiction Magazine, Volume 3* (Chicago: Contemporary Books, Inc., 1976), p. 80.

4. Ibid., p. 81.

Information Sources

BIBLIOGRAPHY:
Nicholls. *Encyclopedia.*
Tuck.
INDEX SOURCES: MIT; SFM; Tuck.
REPRINT SOURCES: None known.
LOCATION SOURCES: Eastern New Mexico University Library; M.I.T. Science Fiction
    Library; Pennsylvania State University Library; University of New Brunswick
    Library.

Publication History

TITLE: *Science Fiction Adventures.*
VOLUME DATA: Volume 1, Number 1, November 1952–Volume 2, Number 3, May
    1954. Six issues per volume. Bi-monthly, but second issue dated February 1953,

followed by March. Volume 2 runs December 1953, February/March 1954, May 1954. Total run: 9 issues.
PUBLISHER: Science Fiction Publications, New York, for first issue, thereafter Future Publications, New York.
EDITOR: Lester del Rey under alias Philip St. John for Volume 1 (November 1952–September 1953); Harry Harrison for Volume 2.
FORMAT: Digest, 160 pp.
PRICE: 35¢.

Ted Krulik/Bruce Tinkel

SCIENCE FICTION ADVENTURES (1956–1958)

In 1955 Irwin Stein's Royal Publications launched two new magazines, both with a first issue cover date of November. *Infinity Science Fiction** was a science fiction title which was a modest but immediate success, its first issue featuring Arthur C. Clarke's "The Star," which went on to win a Hugo Award. Its companion was *Suspect Detective Stories*; though at the outset it was expected to be the profit-maker, it instantly bombed. After five flagging issues Stein decided to drop the magazine, but rather than sacrifice his much-coveted second-class mailing permit, he merely retitled *Suspect* and brought forth a new SF magazine, *Science Fiction Adventures*. The first issue continued the number of *Suspect* and was thus identified as Volume 1, Number 6. The postal authorities refused to sanction this practice, so that with the next issue *SFA* became Volume 1, Number 2. The numbering of that first issue, however, caused considerable consternation in the SF field, because only two years earlier Lester del Rey had been editing a *Science Fiction Adventures** and many thought that this was a revival of the magazine; however, del Rey's title had seen nine issues.

SFA was to be the junior companion to *Infinity* and would contain basic, enjoyable SF, with the intention of restoring that much needed "sense of wonder," as editor Larry Shaw confided in his editorial. The emphasis was on long stories, two or three an issue, misleadingly labeled as novels, though usually less than 20,000 words; they would concentrate on adventure—nothing cerebral, just good solid entertainment. As an example, the first issue carried three "Complete *New* Action Novels," the cover, by Ed Emsh, depicting one of his usual well-endowed ladies being liquidated by a green alien while another alien lies at her feet. It illustrated "Secret of the Green Invaders" by Robert Randall (Robert Silverberg and Randall Garrett in tandem) and showed "Earth ground under the heel of the Khoomish rulers." The story was, in fact, the not uncommon one of Earth dominated by savage aliens, and how a small group of survivors fights back. There was some similarity of theme, on a more cosmic scale, in "Battle for the Thousand Suns" by Calvin Knox and David Gordon, perhaps not so surprising since these names also masked the team of Silverberg and Garrett. The lead novel, however, "The Starcombers," was by veteran Edmond Hamilton and was a slighly less exuberant, more sober study of aliens and their fight for survival.

In like manner *SFA* continued for most of its twelve issues, usually fitting three long stories into each issue. Robert Silverberg provided most of them, and he even ran a short-lived book review column in the last three issues. It was in *SFA* that Silverberg's noted "Chalice" series appeared, under the alias Calvin M. Knox, telling of the search for a mythical treasure and the serendipitous discovery of old Earth. The three stories, "Chalice of Death" (June 1957), "Earth Shall Live Again" (December 1957) and "Vengeance of the Space Armadas" (March 1958), were subsequently published in book form as *Lest We Forget Thee, Earth* (New York: Ace Books, 1958), credited to Knox. Another regular contributor was Harlan Ellison, whose stories included "Assassin!" (February 1957), which was subsequently incorporated with the story "The Sound of a Scythe" in *Amazing Stories** to form the novel *The Man with Nine Lives* (New York: Ace, 1960).

Other writers who contributed only one novella include Cyril M. Kornbluth with "The Slave" (September 1957), Algis Budrys with "Yesterday's Man" (June 1957) and Harry Harrison with "The World Otalmi Made" (June 1958). On the whole, these and other novellas followed a basic format of Earth re-covering either from self-destruction or alien invasion and coming good in the end, or alternatively hard-hitting space adventures not far removed from alien "cowboys and Indians," or slightly more sophisticated space espionage.

The magazine carried few outstanding stories, however, and with the final few issues resorted to using more short stories, an indication that longer stories of reasonably good quality were hard to find. In fact, two of the short novels had been siphoned over to *Infinity* by the publisher in an attempt to boost the flagging sales of that magazine. In the event, sales of neither magazine improved, and *SFA* was the first to go.

Information Sources

BIBLIOGRAPHY:
Nicholls. *Encyclopedia.*
Tuck.
INDEX SOURCES: MIT; SFM; Tuck.
REPRINT SOURCES: See *Science Fiction Adventures* (1958-1963).
LOCATION SOURCES: M.I.T. Science Fiction Library; Pennsylvania State University Library.

Publication History

TITLE: *Science Fiction Adventures.*
VOLUME DATA: Volume 1, Number 5 (no Number 1; see above essay), December 1956–Volume 2, Number 6, June 1958. Six issues per volume. Bi-monthly, December 1956–June 1957; six-weekly, August 1957–June 1958. Total run: 12 issues.
PUBLISHER: Royal Publications, New York.

EDITOR: Larry T. Shaw.
FORMAT: Digest, 128 pp.
PRICE: 35¢.

Mike Ashley

SCIENCE FICTION ADVENTURES (1958–1963)

The British *Science Fiction Adventures* started life as a reprint edition of the
American *Science Fiction Adventures* (1956–1958)* edited by Larry Shaw. Plans
had been afoot since editor John Carnell had met Shaw and publisher Irwin Stein
at the World SF Convention in New York in September 1956, when the first
issue of the American edition was already printed. Carnell did not release the
news, however, until the end of January 1958, when in his editorial in the
February 1958 *New Worlds** he stated:

> For more than two years now we have been considering an additional title
> to the Nova list—we knew that the market *needed* a magazine of quality
> that would appeal primarily to newer readers—but all the necessary factors
> failed to come together until the end of 1957. During the past ten years
> science fiction in general has gained in popularity and acquired a measure
> of respect in literary circles, but in Europe and Australasia at least there
> has been no magazine published which would serve as an introductory
> medium. The gap between the stories published in the long established
> magazines and such so-called science fiction as published in other literary
> mediums is so great that the former are often incomprehensible to casual
> readers.
>
> *Science Fiction Adventures* will very adequately bridge that gap by
> stimulating, thought-provoking stories packed with action—stories which,
> to newer readers, are filled with exciting possibilities as they come across
> the concepts for the first time.[1]

The first issue, dated March 1958, went on sale on February 14 and reprinted
three novelettes from the June and September 1957 American issues. As a debut,
Carnell could not have selected three better stories. The lead was Cyril M.
Kornbluth's "The Slave," followed by "Chalice of Death" by Calvin M. Knox
(Robert Silverberg) and "Yesterday's Man" by Algis Budrys—a selection that
would stand together in any modern anthology. The issue also reprinted Larry
Shaw's editorial in the first U.S. edition bemoaning the loss of that "sense of
wonder" and welcoming its return in *Science Fiction Adventures*.

While the American edition featured both short stories and novelettes, Carnell
planned to limit *SFA* to the longer stories, as the shorter pieces were well catered
for in *New Worlds* and *Science Fantasy*.* However, scarcely had the third bi-
monthly issue appeared when news came that the American edition had fallen

into distribution problems and was to cease publication. Normally the British edition would also have folded, but this time that did not happen. Its circulation was increasing rapidly and it showed all the signs of a healthy magazine. It had met with a jubilant response, and Carnell saw no reason to discontinue it. So, with the American contract now cancelled, Carnell commissioned new stories which, he claimed, were "probably better than the original American material published in our previous issues."[2]

The last reprint issue, Number 5, appeared in October 1958 (dated November), and two months later came the first all-new issue.[3] Carnell blew a fanfare for the new magazine in both the reprint edition and *New Worlds*, acclaiming in particular James White's novella "Occupation: Warrior," which led the second all-new issue in March 1959. "Occupation: Warrior" set the standard for the magazine—a fast, action-packed adventure, well-plotted and laced with originality. White, one of Britain's best writers, had developed the idea of armies composed entirely of cowards into a clever and intriguing story.

The new *SFA* had a mixed but mostly favorable reception. Some readers preferred the old reprint edition, but New York fan Carl Frohmayer noted the essential difference between the reprint and new editions:

> I must say how much I liked all the stories although your policy seems to be somewhat different from the old *SFA*. Different inasmuch as although you still have the action-adventure type of plot there seems to be something more mature about your approach to these themes.[4]

Carnell still used the occasional U.S. reprint (now mostly from *Fantastic Universe**), but the remaining twenty-seven issues were composed almost entirely of new stories by British and Australian writers. The magazine was never pretentious but simply presented what its title implied, and many of the contents can be enjoyed as much today on that same basis. The few that saw subsequent book publication include William F. Temple's novella 'A Trek to Na-Abiza" (July 1961), reprinted as *The Three Suns of Amara* (Ace, 1962), Kenneth Bulmer's short novel "Of Earth Foretold" (May 1960), reprinted as *The Earth Gods Are Coming* (Ace, 1960), J. G. Ballard's *The Drowned World* (January 1962; Berkley, 1962) and John Brunner's "Society of Time" series, published as *Times without Number* (Ace, 1962; revised 1969).

Many of the most popular stories, however, have not been reprinted, and these include Australian Wynne Whiteford's "Shadow of the Sword" (January 1959) and its sequel, "Distant Drum" (July 1959); the stories by Nelson Sherwood (Kenneth Bulmer), especially "Scarlet Denial" (May 1962) and its sequel, "Scarlet Dawn" (September 1962); "Galactic Destiny" (October 1959) by E. C. Tubb; and the two stories by John Ashcroft, "The Lonely Path" (January 1961) and "No Longer Alone" (July 1961) which, with "This Wonderful Birthday" (*New Worlds*, May 1961), form a trilogy on the colonization of Mars and the search for a lost civilization.

SFA concentrated on fiction and only irregularly included science articles or editorial departments. Readers were therefore not made aware of the declining sales of the magazine in the early 1960s until May 1963, when those who had just completed Michael Moorcock's "The Blood Red Game" would have encountered a footnote stating: "This is the last issue we shall be publishing, at least for the time being. Well-liked though the magazine is in certain circles, sales no longer warrant keeping it on our lists."[5]

Carnell's optimism was well meant. By sacrificing *SFA* he hoped that its companion magazines would prosper and that in time *SFA* would be revived, but economic circumstances did not make that possible.

Science Fiction Adventures was unique: it was the only U.K. reprint magazine to survive its mother publication and assume an identity of its own. Although it was regarded by many as the poor sister in Nova Publications, in retrospect it contained a greater percentage of more enjoyable and memorable stories than any other British magazine.

Notes

1. [John Carnell], "Bridging the Gap," *New Worlds Science Fiction* 68 (February 1958):2.

2. [John Carnell], "The Editor's Space," *Science Fiction Adventures* 6 (January 1959):4.

3. The fiction was "new" in that it was not reprinted from the American edition, although Wynne Whiteford had sold the U.S. serial rights of his lead story "Shadow of the Sword" to *Fantastic Universe*, where an edited version had appeared in the October 1958 issue.

4. [Carl Frohmayer], "The Reader's Space," *Science Fiction Adventures* 16 (September 1960):111.

5. [John Carnell], "Special Notice . . . ," *Science Fiction Adventures* 32 (May 1963):69.

Information Sources

BIBLIOGRAPHY:
Nicholls. *Encyclopedia*.
Tuck.
INDEX SOURCES: Peyton, Roger, *A Checklist of Science Fiction Adventures*, Birmingham, U.K.: Peyton, [1966]; SFM; Tuck.
REPRINT SOURCES: None known.
LOCATION SOURCES: M.I.T. Science Fiction Library; Pennsylvania State University Library.

Publication History

TITLE: *Science Fiction Adventures*.
VOLUME DATA: Issue numbering continuous, thus: Volume 1, Number 1, March 1958–Volume 6, Number 32, May 1963. Six issues per volume. Bi-monthly, but no September 1959 issue (dated October). November 1959 issue followed by December. February 1960 issue followed by May. Total run: 32 issues.
PUBLISHER: Nova Publications, London.

EDITOR: John Carnell. Larry T. Shaw listed as U.S. editor on first five issues.
FORMAT: Digest, 112 pp. (all issues except No. 21, July 1961, 116 pp.).
PRICE: 2/-, issues 1–18 (March 1958–January 1961), thereafter 2/6d.

Mike Ashley

SCIENCE FICTION ADVENTURES (1973–1974)

See SCIENCE FICTION CLASSICS.

SCIENCE FICTON ADVENTURES YEARBOOK

Science Fiction Adventures Yearbook was one of the many digest-sized reprint magazines issued by Sol Cohen in 1970 with contents selected from back issues of *Amazing Stories.** *SFAY* appeared in the winter of 1970 and could be regarded as a continuation of *Science Fiction Classics*,* a regular quarterly magazine which had changed its title to *Science Fiction Adventure Classics* with its eighth issue in the fall of 1969 but which had since ceased to appear.

SFAY contained eight stories ranging from as early as the January 1930 *Amazing* with "The Sword and the Atopen"—an early example of a story about biological warfare—by Taylor H. Greenfield, to nothing more recent than "Who Sows the Wind," Rog Phillips' lead story fron the June 1951 *Amazing*, which, at 25,000 words, took up over half the issue. In general the stories were as readable as one would expect given the era of their origin. Thus, Festus Pragnell's "Warlord of Mars" reflects the juvenile idiocies of the early Palmer *Amazing*, "Beyond the Universe" by Stanton A. Coblentz reflects the dryness of the post-Gernsback *Amazing*, while "The Children" by Chester S. Geier is typical of the inventiveness of the Howard Browne *Fantastic Adventures.** None of the stories, however, could be said to have stood well the test of time.

There was no second *Yearbook*, but a companion *Fantastic Adventures Yearbook** was published.

Information Sources

INDEX SOURCES: ISFM-II; SFM.
REPRINT SOURCES: None known.
LOCATION SOURCES: M.I.T. Science Fiction Library.

Publication History

TITLE: *Science Fiction Adventures Yearbook.*
VOLUME DATA: Unnumbered, dated only 1970 (released January).
PUBLISHER: Ultimate Publishing Co., Flushing, New York.
EDITOR: Sol Cohen (unidentified within issue).

FORMAT: Digest, 128 pp.
PRICE: 60¢.

Mike Ashley

SCIENCE FICTION CLASSICS

In 1965, after leaving *Galaxy Science Fiction*,* Sol Cohen formed the Ultimate Publishing Company and bought *Amazing Stories** and *Fantastic** from Ziff-Davis, the publisher of *Amazing* since 1938. This transaction included the second serial rights to all stories previously published by these magazines (including *Fantastic*'s predecessor, *Fantastic Adventures**). Cohen was thus able to cut costs by converting both *Amazing* and *Fantastic* to near-reprint, and by issuing three new magazines composed entirely of reprints, the profits from which would help subsidize the parent magazines. The first two magazines were *Great Science Fiction** and *The Most Thrilling Science Fiction Ever Told* (*Thrilling SF**), but the third, *Science Fiction Classics*, did not claim itself as one of the fold. For the first five issues, Jack Lester is noted as the editor and Ralph Adris as managing editor, and later issues are without editorial credit. In fact, the magazine was introduced at the suggestion of Herb Lehrman, whom Cohen had brought in as assistant editor to help with the selection of reprints in the other magazines. Because of the growing conflict with the Science Fiction Writers of America over nonpayment of reprint fees, *Science Fiction Classics* was launched under a new Cohen imprint, Magazine Productions, while Cohen masqueraded as Jack Lester and Herb Lehrman as Ralph Adris.

Despite its title, *SFC* was primarily composed of stories by relatively obscure writers from the Hugo Gernsback and T. O'Conor Sloane days of *Amazing*. A few minor stories by more popular authors were reprinted, but the overall quality of the publication was unimpressive, the "classics" of the title referring more to age than excellence. The first six issues contain stories originally published between 1926 and 1933, and include stories by John Campbell, Edmond Hamilton, David H. Keller, Murray Leinster and A. Hyatt Verrill. From the viewpoint of the occasional reader, most of these stories would have appeared quaint and dated. More serious devotees, however, would have welcomed the opportunity to sample stories by authors often cited in reference books but whose early work was hard to obtain. The first issue, for instance, reprinted "The Eggs from Lake Tanganyika" by Curt Siodmak and "Politics" by Murray Leinster. Later issues revived "When the Atoms Failed," the first published story by John W. Campbell, Jr., "The Gostak and the Doshes" by Miles J. Breuer, and "The Death of the Moon" by Alexander M. Phillips.

In the winter of 1968/1969, with the seventh issue, the title was changed to *Science Fiction Adventure Classics*, and the format changed for this one issue to feature work by just one writer—Edmond Hamilton. This policy was also being tested with *Great Science Fiction* and *Most Thrilling Science Fiction*, but was not repeated. Instead *SFC* now entered a complicated phase.

In place of an eighth issue, subscribers received copies of an entirely new magazine, *Strange Fantasy*,* which began with Number 8. But a few months later an eighth issue of *SFAC* appeared, possibly originally planned as one of the mass of annuals and yearbooks Cohen was assembling. This issue did not require much planning, as it was a straight reprint of the fiction contents of the April 1956 *Amazing*, themselves all reprints.

Anyone expecting *SFAC* 9, however, instead received a copy of *Space Adventures* (*Classics*) 9, another new magazine. This time the issue was clearly originally planned as *SFAC* 9 because all the even pages are headed *S-F Adventure Classics*. This was also true of the next three issues, and for this period it is easy to assume that *Space Adventures* was a new title for *SFAC* as a result of a new contents policy, since these issues were reprinted from the early Palmer *Amazings* and thus had even less claim to classic status than the earlier selections.

The only problem with this theory is that it did not work in practice. No sooner had the twelfth issue of *Space Adventures* appeared than a twelfth issue of *SFAC* hit the stands. This means that there were no issues numbered 9, 10 or 11, and the corresponding issues of *Space Adventures* do fill that gap. With the twelfth issue, however, Cohen probably felt that *SFAC* was a strong enough title to stand on its own, possibly following satisfactory sales of *Science Fiction Adventures Yearbook** and *Science Fiction Classics Annual.** *SFAC* 12 is, in fact, a continuation of the ploy adopted with the *Annual* by reprinting stories previously included in *Amazing*'s "Classic Reprint" section in the early 1960s, with stories selected by Sam Moskowitz and accompanied by an informative introduction. These introductions were also reprinted, and may well have contributed to the success of the *Annual* and the revival of *SFAC*. Whether the issue had been intentionally or mistakenly numbered 12 is now academic, because a thirteenth issue of both *SFAC* and *Space Adventures* followed, meaning that the two magazines now had a separate existence.

With *SFAC* 13, the magazine now adopted a policy that remained fairly consistent for the rest of its existence, that of reprinting stories from the early Palmer days. While the previous selections from the Gernsback and Sloane days may not have been literary wonders, they did have a certain historic, almost archeological interest, as examples of primordial magazine SF. Not so the subsequent reprints, which were mostly hack work churned out by a stable of writers to Palmer's editorial order. Although some of them have a lighthearted competence, they lack depth or conviction, and few stand up to a first reading, let alone second. As an example of restrained and ordered writing, there is William F. Temple's "Mr. Craddock's Amazing Experience" (Number 14, Summer 1971), and as an example of a developing writer there is "The Man Who Walked Through Mirrors" by Robert Bloch (same issue). Temple's "The 4–Sided Triangle," of justifiable classic status, was included in the March 1972 issue. But most of the stories were either by John Russell Fearn under various pseudonyms or by writers like Festus Pragnell, Don Wilcox, Ed Earl Repp, Neil R. Jones and Leroy Yerxa. The September 1972 issue varied from the path by including several earlier reprints by Keller, Stanton Coblentz, Isaac R. Nathanson and G. Peyton Wertenbaker, offset by Richard Shaver's "Invasion of the Micro-Men," but such incursions into the earlier days were rare.

The final days of *SFAC* saw the magazine's title fluctuating between *Science Fiction Adventures* and the ungainly *Science Fiction Adventures: Classics*. It would clearly have been better to have left "Classics" off all together, as Cohen's definition of the word is questionable. It is unlikely that more than a half dozen or so stories of possible classic status were reprinted during the whole run of the magazine, whereas it is certain that much that should never have been published in the first place was resurrected for a new generation of readers.

Information Sources

BIBLIOGRAPHY:
Nicholls. *Encyclopedia*.
Tuck.
INDEX SOURCES: ISFM; NESFA; NESFA–II; NESFA–III; SFM; Tuck.
REPRINT SOURCES: None known.
LOCATION SOURCES: Pennsylvania State University Library.

Publication History

TITLE: *Science Fiction Classics*, [Summer] 1967–Fall 1968; *Science Fiction Adventure Classics*, Winter 1969–November 1972; *Science Fiction Adventures*, January 1973–May 1973; *Science Fiction Adventures: Classics*, July 1973–July 1974; *Science Fiction Adventures*, September 1974–November 1974.

VOLUME DATA: First issue undated. Numbering ceased after issue 19, July 1972. Number 1, [Summer] 1967–November 1974. No issues numbered 9, 10 or 11 (see *Space Adventures*). Quarterly, [Summer] 1967–Winter 1969 (issues 1–7); issue 8, Fall 1969; quarterly, issue 12, Winter [1971]–Fall 1971; bi-monthly, January 1972–November 1974. If issue numbering had continued the last issue would have been Number 33, but because of the three "missing" issues, the total run is 30 issues.

PUBLISHER: Magazine Productions, Long Island, New York, Number 1, [Summer] 1967–Number 3, Winter 1967; Ultimate Publishing, Long Island, Number 4, Spring 1968–Number 8, Fall 1969; thereafter Ultimate Publishing, Flushing, New York.

EDITOR: Herb Lehrman, Number 1, [Summer] 1967–Number 8, Fall 1969 (pseudonymously as Ralph Adris on first five issues, then not credited); Sol Cohen thereafter.

FORMAT: Digest, 128 pp.

PRICE: 50¢, issues 1–12 (Summer 1967–Winter 1971); 60¢, Spring 1971–May 1974; 75¢, July–November 1974.

Mike Ashley

SCIENCE FICTION CLASSICS ANNUAL

One of the many digest-sized reprint magazines issued by Sol Cohen during 1970, *Science Fiction Classics Annual* is directly related to *Science Fiction Classics*,* which had seen an eighth issue in fall 1969 but had to all intents suspended publication. The *Annual* reprinted nine stories from the Gernsback and Sloane issues of *Amazing Stories*,* all of which had previously been selected by Sam Moskowitz in his "Classic Reprint" department in *Amazing* in the early 1960s. The stories were accompanied by Moskowitz's earlier introductions.

This format was followed for one issue only. The stories were a good selection supported by Moskowitz's knowledgeable introductions, and included "The Cosmic Express" by Jack Williamson, "The Last Evolution" by John W. Campbell, Jr., "Devolution" by Edmond Hamilton and "I, Robot" by Eando Binder.

Information Sources

BIBLIOGRAPHY:
Nicholls. *Encyclopedia*.
INDEX SOURCES: ISFM; SFM.
REPRINT SOURCES: None known.
LOCATION SOURCES: None known.

Publication History

TITLE: *Science Fiction Classics Annual*.
VOLUME DATA: One issue, unnumbered, released Fall 1970.
PUBLISHER: Ultimate Publishing Co., Flushing, New York.
EDITOR: Sol Cohen (unidentified within issue).
FORMAT: Digest, 128 pp.
PRICE: 60¢.

Mike Ashley

SCIENCE FICTION DIGEST (1954)

In 1954, a few months after his *Vortex** folded, presumably because of difficulty obtaining the great amount of short fiction it required, Chester Whitehorn launched *Science Fiction Digest*. In both of its issues he apologized for the title: he emphatically did not—as did *Readers Digest*—propose to condense the science fiction and science-fact articles that he had collected from magazines printed over the last six years. The most interesting aspect of the project was these sources: although he drew from some standard American science fiction magazines, he located most of his material in such places as *Woman's Day*, Standard Oil's *Lamp*, Macfadden's *Climax, Esquire, Ballyhoo* and *Man's Magazine* as well as Britain's *New Worlds** and Scotland's *Nebula*.*

But the result was unimpressive. Visually, the magazine consisted of tiny

Chester Matin sketches and movie stills. The stories were routine alien encounters, space adventures with a strong admixture of telepathy, trips in time and
other dimensions, teleportation, magic and mysticism—all short or short-short
stories as in *Vortex*. The features and science-fact articles were perhaps of greatest
interest to Whitehorn. Commanding much of the magazine's space, the features
included ESP experiments, science-fact notes and book and film reviews, while
the first issue's science-fact articles ranged over meteorology, lunar travel, bioen-
gineering, research techniques and prophecies for 1977. The ESP experiment
involved Whitehorn's telepathically transmitting a phonograph record title each
day for a week at 11 P.M., EST, starting on January 31, 1954, although the
issue did not make it to the stands until February. In the second issue Whitehorn's
inclination toward the occult became even more pronounced. Among articles on
telepathy, levitation and the Renaissance soothsayer John Dee was a specially
commissioned article by Eartha Kitt on her one clairvoyant experience. Features
and fiction produced an uneasy combination of *Fate* and *Planet Stories.** There
was no third issue.

Information Sources

BIBLIOGRAPHY:
Nicholls. *Encyclopedia.*
Tuck.
INDEX SOURCES: MIT; SFM.
REPRINT SOURCES: None known.
LOCATION SOURCES: Pennsylvania State University Library.

Publication History

TITLE: *Science Fiction Digest.*
VOLUME DATA: Volume 1, Number 1, [February] 1954–Volume 1, Number 2, [May]
       1954. Neither issue dated by month. No schedule indicated at first, but should
       have gone bi-monthly from the second issue.
PUBLISHER: Specific Fiction Corp., a subsidiary of Authentic Publications, New York.
EDITOR: Chester Whitehorn.
FORMAT: Digest, 160 pp.
PRICE: 35¢.

E. F. Casebeer

S. F. DIGEST (1976)

When the signs were clear that sales of *Science Fiction Monthly** were rapidly
dwindling, New English Library decided to cut production costs and issue a
more conventional magazine, *S. F. Digest*. The first issue appeared just one
month after the final *S. F. Monthly* and was a superior production. It contained
fiction by Robert Silverberg, Michael G. Coney and Brian W. Aldiss, plus
interesting features by Maxim Jakubowski, John Brunner and Christopher Evans

(the subject of an interview). As a projected quarterly it should have succeeded, but it came too late. NEL had already decided to drastically reduce its magazine output, and *SFD* was promptly scrapped. Many copies were not even distributed.

Information Sources

BIBLIOGRAPHY:
Nicholls. *Encyclopedia.*
INDEX SOURCES: NESFA–V; SFM.
REPRINT SOURCES: None.
LOCATION SOURCES: None known.

Publication History

TITLE: *S. F. Digest.*
VOLUME DATA: Number 1, undated [June 1976].
PUBLISHER: New English Library, London.
EDITOR: Julie Davis.
FORMAT: Slick, 44 pp.
PRICE: 50p.

Mike Ashley

SCIENCE FICTION DIGEST (1981–1982)

The latest magazine by this name used the name more literally than its pred-ecessors. In the tried and tested digest format it set out to present excerpts from forthcoming books—mostly novels, but, where appropriate, nonfiction, as in the first issue (dated October/November 1981), which presented an extract from Isaac Asimov's forthcoming *Asimov on Science Fiction.* The novels were not condensed or rewritten in any form, but episodes that were as nearly self-supporting as possible were presented for their own merit. Just what market *Science Fiction Digest* hoped to corner is not quite clear. Certainly it served as an aperitif to whet the appetite for the forthcoming book, but with books almost always outselling magazines, it is questionable that many readers were likely to buy the magazine for the sole purpose of reading an extract from a book that in all likelihood they would purchase anyway. The question was answered when *SFD* folded after four issues.

SFD was a companion to *Isaac Asimov's Science Fiction** and *Analog Science Fiction** and was published as part of a promotional drive by Joel Davis who, as publisher of *Ellery Queen's Mystery Magazine*, was also launching a *Crime Digest* in the hope of establishing, or perhaps reestablishing, the digest magazine as a viable alternative to the paperback novel, or at least, as an equal to the paperback. With sensible trepidation, the magazine was issued as a bi-monthly, and with the faces of Isaac Asimov and Stephen King on the first two issues good sales were almost certainly guaranteed. Thereafter, however, sales flagged. What would have been the fifth issue was combined with number four into a double issue and the magazine's future rested on its sales. They proved insufficient to warrant continuing the magazine.

SFD did not present solely science fiction or related nonfiction. The cover blurb boasted "the best in current fantasy, horror, occult, speculative and science fiction," proving the title was not literal. Although the first two issues were an attractive offering, editor Shawna McCarthy realized that the magazine also required additional features in the form of film, book and record reviews and interviews to give the magazine extra depth.

Information Sources

INDEX SOURCES: NESFA–VIII; NESFA–IX; SFM.
REPRINT SOURCES: None known.
LOCATION SOURCES: None known.

Publication History

TITLE: *Science Fiction Digest*.
VOLUME DATA: Volume 1, 4 issues: October/November 1981, January/February, May/
    June and September/October 1982. Designated quarterly.
PUBLISHER: Davis Publications, New York.
EDITOR: Shawna McCarthy.
FORMAT: Digest, 192 pp. Last issue, 288 pp.
PRICE: $1.50 first issue, then $1.95. Last issue, $2.95.

Mike Ashley

SCIENCE FICTION FORTNIGHTLY

See AUTHENTIC SCIENCE FICTION.

SCIENCE FICTION GREATS (1969–1970)

See GREAT SCIENCE FICTION.

S. F. GREATS (1970–1971)

See GREAT SCIENCE FICTION.

SCIENCE FICTION LIBRARY

Science Fiction Library, published in 1960, marked the last appearance in the SF field of publisher Gerald Swan, and his departure was no loss. In the 1940s Swan had stockpiled a vast backlog of manuscripts, many of which are still unpublished. This final short series of three digest issues scarcely grazed the surface. Only five new stories were used, including "The Man Who Stole St. Pauls" by Maurice Hugi. Hugi had been a regular contributor to the Swan publications, but as he died in 1947, we have some yardstick whereby to measure the story's age.

The remaining stories were reprints from the Robert W. Lowndes'–edited Columbia magazines, in particular the January 1941 *Science Fiction** and the Spring 1942 *Science Fiction Quarterly.** The only tales worthy of attention are "Saknarth" by "Millard Verne Gordon" (Donald A. Wollheim) and "Crisis!" by "Cecil Corwin" (Cyril Kornbluth). On the whole, however, they were poor-quality magazines of little interest. A companion series of slightly greater read-ability was *Weird and Occult Library.**

Information Sources

BIBLIOGRAPHY:
Nicholls. *Encyclopedia.*
INDEX SOURCES: ASFI.
REPRINT SOURCES: None known.
LOCATION SOURCES: None known.

Publication History

TITLE: *Science Fiction Library.*
VOLUME DATA: Number 1–Number 3, undated but during 1960.
PUBLISHER: Gerald G. Swan, Ltd., London.
EDITOR: Not identified, but under the general control of Gerald Swan.
FORMAT: Small Digest, 64 pp.
PRICE: 1/-.

Mike Ashley

SCIENCE FICTION MONTHLY (1951)

See AUTHENTIC SCIENCE FICTION.

SCIENCE-FICTION MONTHLY (1955–1957)

Atlas Publications of Melbourne issued a varied range of magazines using both imported and original content, and editor-in-chief Michael Cannon was interested in trying new ideas, in contrast to the timidity and conservatism of the Australian publishing industry in the 1950s (or any other time, discounting superficial trendiness in the seventies). His experiments in science fiction were innovative, though their success was limited. The Science-Fiction Library pa-perback series was doomed from the outset by poor choice of books. Six of the eight produced, though not particularly bad, had been on sale in British Panther editions in the previous two years and obviously did not attract enough new readers to pay their way.

Science-Fiction Monthly, which debuted in 1955, was better planned, however, and the concept was unusual. Cannon acquired reproduction rights from a number of American magazines, but what he produced was not a simple local edition of any one of them, but a quite distinct new magazine. A given issue usually presented stories from one or two issues of an American magazine of a few years earlier. Thus, the first four issues were mostly abridged versions of Hugo Gernsback and Sam Moskowitz's *Science-Fiction Plus*,* dropping most of the nonfiction and some of the interior artwork. Numbers 5 to 8 were based on the short-lived *Cosmos Science Fiction and Fantasy Magazine** of L. B. Cole, with a few shorts from *Science-Fiction Plus*. Numbers 9 to 11 represented three issues of W. L. Hamling's *Imagination*.* Numbers 12 to 18 recast six issues of the popular adventure magazine *Planet Stories*,* incidentally overlapping with the earlier British edition, which cannot have helped sales. Occasional stories from other sources were included, and even two original stories.

A broad spectrum of writing was represented, but there was a trend toward lower-quality fiction through the magazine's life; the decline was not consistent, however, reflecting the varying quality of the sources it drew upon. A number of notable authors appeared. Early figures such as Harry Walton, Richard Tooker and John Scott Campbell appeared in the first few issues. Murray Leinster's "Nightmare World" continued and rounded out his series showing humanity in reduced circumstances in a world dominated by outsized insects, which had started with "The Mad Planet" in 1920. Ray Bradbury's "The Golden Apples of the Sun" is one of the more successful of his unusual views of space flight. Eric Frank Russell's "Postscript" is a classic insight into the question of non-human intelligence. Other names of importance included Clifford D. Simak, Philip K. Dick, Raymond Z. Gallun and Jack Vance. It was a magazine with much to recommend it.

The format was modest, a 96–page digest typical of local popular magazines of the time and slight in comparison to the British competition. It was increased to 112 pages with Number 12, and the extra 16 pages were devoted to its most unusual feature, the "Science Fiction Scene" department, which appeared in the last seven issues.

Independently edited and written in part by Graham Stone, "Science Fiction Scene" was a miscellany of nonfiction items related to science fiction in general. Some were reprinted from amateur or obscure publications, but most were newly written. There were book reviews, film notes, reports on events, interviews and information about authors and essays on scientifictional topics. Little discussion and background material was readily available at the time, especially in Australia, and the seven issues provided a useful body of work.

The magazine was a moderate success, but when Cannon left the firm at the end of 1956 it was dropped in a general policy reorganization—meaning, no doubt, that though the magazine was established and took little effort to continue, no one else had enough interest or knowledge of science fiction to take it over. He said at the time that he hoped to try again with a more original publication with higher standards, but *Science-Fiction Monthly* was moderately successful within its terms of reference: a magazine of popular entertainment.

Information Sources

BIBLIOGRAPHY:
Nicholls. *Encyclopedia.*
Tuck.
INDEX SOURCES: ASFI; Tuck.
REPRINT SOURCES: None known.
LOCATION SOURCES: Futurian Society of Sydney Library; Michigan State University
    Library.

Publication History

TITLE: *Science-Fiction Monthly.*
VOLUME DATA: Issues undated. Number 1, [September 1955]–Number 18, [February
    1957]. Monthly. Total run: 18 issues.
PUBLISHER: Atlas Publications, Melbourne.
EDITOR: Michael Cannon (not credited within issues).
FORMAT: Digest, 96 pp., increased to 112 pp. with issue 12 [August 1956].
PRICE: 2/6d.

Graham Stone

SCIENCE FICTION MONTHLY (1974–1976)

An entirely new approach in science fiction magazine publishing came in 1973 from New English Library. NEL published a popular line of science fiction paperbacks (including Frank Herbert and Robert Heinlein), and was especially proud of its covers. Many readers wrote in requesting copies of the original paintings (minus the book title and blurb). This gave NEL the idea of issuing a poster magazine, and one thought led to another. By mid-1973 it was decided to make it a combined poster/SF monthly, but with the emphasis on art rather than fiction.

Called *Science Fiction Monthly*, it appeared as a large-size tabloid at the end of January 1974. Patricia Hornsey was responsible for the format and arrangement of the magazine, although the direct editorial duties fell to Aune Butt. The magazine appeared at a propitious moment. Interest in fantastic art was mushrooming, and the imminent publication of Anthony Frewin's *One Hundred Years of Science Fiction Illustration* (1974), along with the growth of artistic record album sleeves—especially the work of Roger Dean—made SF art a very salable commodity. At first *SFM* struck gold and sales were very pleasing.

However, it soon became clear that once the novelty of the availability of the art began to decline, *SFM* needed something else to bolster its circulation.

Because of the format there were restrictions on word length and the number of stories. None of the major name authors took much notice of the magazine, and consequently its fiction came from aspiring new authors of varying degrees of talent. Among the best were Ian Watson and Terry Greenhough. On the nonfiction front, Walter Gillings supplied a regular succinct essay on "Masters of Science Fiction," tied in with a choice reprint of the authors' stories, and Michael Ashley and Peter Weston provided a variety of articles on the SF field.

But it was soon clear that *SFM* was on the decline. Its new editor, Julie Davis, tried to inject a spark of vitality into the magazine, but she was "running to stand still." *SFM* was slipping between two factions: those who wanted the art did not want the fiction, and vice versa. Later appearances by Bob Shaw, Harlan Ellison, Jack Williamson and Keith Roberts were not sufficient to sustain interest. Because of its high production costs, *SFM* required a far larger circulation than a typical digest, so when it was realized that readership was down to the 20,000 level and dwindling, the axe fell.

New English Library did make a last-ditch effort with a new magazine, *S. F. Digest*,* but it only lasted one issue.

Information Sources

BIBLIOGRAPHY:
Nicholls. *Encyclopedia*.
INDEX SOURCES: NESFA-III; NESFA-IV; NESFA-V; SFM.
REPRINT SOURCES:
   Reprint Editions: A French edition entitled *Science-Fiction Magazine* in identical format but with several new items saw seven issues from November 1976 to May 1977. Published by Editions de France, S. A., Paris, Tabloid, 44 pp., 8F.
   Derivative Anthology: Janet Sacks, ed., *The Best of Science Fiction Monthly* (New English Library, 1975), containing eighteen stories.
LOCATION SOURCES: M.I.T. Science Fiction Library.

Publication History

TITLE: *Science Fiction Monthly*.
VOLUME DATA: Volume 1, Number 1, [February] 1974–Volume 3, Number 4, [May] 1976. Twelve issues per volume. Monthly. Total run: 28 issues.
PUBLISHER: New English Library, London.
EDITORS: Aune Butt, Volume 1, Number 1, [February] 1974–Volume 1, Number 4, [May] 1974; Julie Davis, Volume 1, Number 5, [June] 1974–Volume 3, Number 4, [May] 1976.
FORMAT: Large Tabloid (16" x 11"), 28 pp.
PRICE: 25p., Vol. 1, No. 1, [February] 1974–Vol. 1, No. 8, [September] 1974; 30p., Vol. 1, No. 9, [October] 1974–Vol. 2, No. 3, [April] 1975; 35p., Vol. 2, No. 4–Vol. 2, No. 11, [December] 1975; 40p., Vol. 2, No. 12 [January] 1976–Vol. 3, No. 2, [March] 1976; 50p., Vol. 3, No. 3, [April] 1976–Vol. 3, No. 4, [May] 1976.

Mike Ashley

SCIENCE-FICTION PLUS

Science-Fiction Plus was Hugo Gernsback's last attempt to preach the gospel of science fiction in a popular magazine format. He had retired as an SF editor after his *Wonder Stories** was sold to Standard Publications in 1936, but as president of Gernsback Publications he continued to publish scientific journals. Perhaps encouraged by the success of *The Magazine of Fantasy and Science Fiction** and *Galaxy Science Fiction** in 1950 and to some extent provoked by the emergence of the many new SF magazines after the war, Gernsback re-entered the lists in March 1953 with a glossy, folio-format magazine of sixty-five pages which proclaimed by its very appearance that SF had at last come of age and had earned a place on the magazine stand beside *Colliers*, *The Saturday Evening Post* and *Liberty Magazine*. *Science-Fiction Plus* ran for only seven issues through the remainder of 1953, closing out with Volume 1, Number 7 in December 1953. The brief career of Gernsback's magazine set no particular trends and established no special milestones. It did call out of retirement several SF writers of the thirties and forties, however, and published several good works of fiction by then younger writers. Above all, the magazine was the expression of the editor-publisher's idealism and the fan enthusiasm of its managing editor, Sam Moskowitz.

Science-Fiction Plus was a magazine produced by true believers for the already converted who shared Gernsback's rather Victorian ideas of the ministry of SF in the modern world and Moskowitz's hero worship of the pulpsters of the previous generation. *Science-Fiction Plus* made few concessions to the SF trends of the day, and perhaps its failure should be attributed in part to its fundamental orientation to the past in tone and emphasis. In reality, the magazine was an anachronism. The writing, the authors, the illustrations, the editorial policy and the tone were the products of a bygone era and of an idealism of science that seemed more characteristic of the twenties than of the post-atomic fifties. But then again, these very qualities were the essence of the charm of Gernsback's last crusade. There is a kind of *noblesse oblige* underlying this venture, the last of the great proprietary SF magazines. There have been other noble experiments since *Science-Fiction Plus* in which the publishers offered the SF readership a slick, glossy alternative to the traditional pulps on the strength of the new maturity (that is, popularity) of the genre, but none has been as committed to SF evangelism. Perhaps Gernsback's sin was not so much that he preached but how he chose to do so. He was simply unrelenting. The reader was given the gospel of science according to Gernsback in editorial pages and in at least one of the featured stories of each issue. But despite all the drum-beating for future science, despite the originality of some departments and features, and despite the enthusiasm of Gernsback and Moskowitz for the cause, the awful truth is that *Science-Fiction Plus* was dull from first issue to last. The only relief in addition to a handful of good stories was unintentional comedy that proceeded from Moskowitz's zeal and Gernsback's incurable amateurism.

It was Gernsback who began the SF pulp industry in 1926 with the publication of *Amazing Stories*,* a fact recalled by Gernsback in his first editorial for *Science-Fiction Plus*, called "The Impact of Science-Fiction on World Progress." He began by banishing "the fairy tale brand, the weird or fantastic type of what mistakenly masquerades under the name of Science-Fiction today!" Only the "truly scientific, prophetic Science-Fiction with the full accent on SCIENCE" wins Gernsback's endorsement. He was to return to this theme of true versus false SF several more times in later editorials. It is a distinction that did not always apply to the fiction that appeared in the magazine in future issues, especially the stories of Philip José Farmer.

Gernsback recounts the plight of SF in the early twentieth century until he began to publish *Amazing Stories*. He never suspected that he himself may have been one of the causes of the Babylonian captivity which American SF suffered through for most of the present century. In his editorial, Gernsback presses the claims of SF literature as both a source of potential inspiration for science and as the vehicle for providing "valuable hints to the engineer or industrialist . . . leading to future material benefits" for all; but not, alas, Gernsback lamented, for the SF writer. Therefore, he calls for a patent reform so that writers of true SF can benefit from their ideas. Ever the one for seals, shields and the trappings of heraldry, Gernsback suggests that SF stories containing forecasts of potentially workable schemes be identified by a distinctive mark so as to alert future patent readers, who are urged to include SF routinely in their search of scientific literature prior to granting U.S. patents. Gernsback just happened to have such an official device handy, a five-pointed star on top of a sphere bearing the letters SF. For those with iconographic interests, Gernsback translates the symbolism: SF is the star that enlightens the world! The first story in the magazine to earn the star and globe award was "Exploration of Mars" by Hugo Gernsback, a characteristic self-tribute. Readers are advised on the title page that "this design, symbolizing science-fiction, is displayed with all stories of a serious scientific-technical trend. Such stories contain new ideas which are certain to be realized in the future."

Gernsback ended his first editorial in characteristic fashion with an appeal to the conscience of his readers from the self-proclaimed "father of science-fiction": "Since the public is beginning to take Science-Fiction seriously . . . let us treat Science-Fiction with the seriousness and the dignity this great endeavor is everlastingly entitled to."

The layout of the first issue served as the model for all subsequent ones. There were novelettes, one of which was sure to be in the style of a speculative, future magazine feature story, typified by Gernsback's own "Exploration of Mars." It was an interesting fictional idea that failed because the fiction depended so heavily on labored exposition. One or more of the short stories included in each issue would be contributed by a name out of the past like Eando Binder, Raymond Z. Gallun or Frank Belknap Long. Although these were to be new stories, each was more characteristic of the thirties than the fifties. In this we can see the passion of Sam Moskowitz for SF nostalgia rather than a real contemporary critical sensibility.

Balancing the fiction, and indeed often overbalancing it, were articles on various wonder and awe-evoking aspects of science, written by one of Gernsback's staff of scientists. The first issue contained an article on "Rapid Wonder Plants" by Dr. Gustav Albrecht and "The Evolution of the Space Ship" by Leslie R. Shepherd, Ph.D., and A. V. Cleaver, F.R.As.S. The titles helped establish Gernsback's claim that he was publishing a serious SF magazine. Among the other features of the magazine in addition to the inevitable Gernsback editorial were rather comprehensive "Science News Shorts," a "Book Review" by Moskowitz, a "Stranger Than Science-Fiction" vignette, "Science Questions and Answers" and a "Science Quiz."

Clearly, Gernsback and Moskowitz had launched a noble experiment in publishing a glossy, folio-format magazine that would please in order to instruct. In the second issue Gernsback queries earnestly and perhaps somewhat accusingly, "What Type of Science-Fiction Do You Read?" The reader well may tremble before such stern orthodoxy. "Good Science-Fiction," we are instructed, "must be based on true science—science as interpreted and understood by responsible scientists. In other words, the story should be within the realms of the possible." If the hapless reader fears that he may have strayed from the true path, Gernsback reassures him that there will be no pseudo-SF printed in *Science-Fiction Plus*. Such writers are compared by Gernsback, and none too favorably, with charlatans and other practitioners of criminal fraud who make use of scientific appearances to exploit their foolish victims. But then the world is full of snares for the unwary, as we know, and despite, or perhaps because of, Moskowitz's best efforts at recruiting SF All-Americans from the past, by the third issue Gernsback was able to field only one story that merited the star-and-globe symbol.

In the fourth issue Gernsback tackled the matter of "Skepticism in Science-Fiction," dealing manfully with the embarrassing contempt in which the genre was held among so many real, live scientists. Writing from the pangs of unrequited love, Gernsback blamed this obduracy on the ravages of pseudo-SF and on the failure of many scientists themselves to keep up with the new SF that was emerging from a new and more scientific age. It goes without saying that Gernsback was himself missing the point.

The fifth issue's editorial deserves some notice as an unintended self-parody epitomizing the tone of fervent amateurism that pervades so much of the nonfiction of the magazine. Gernsback addresses himself seriously to the need for a more correct—that is to say, more scientific sounding—terminology for both popular science and SF. In "Science-Fiction Semantics," Gernsback proposes the following as household words of the future: "spatiology," "orbitemp" (for the time it takes a planet to revolve around its primary instead of the more provincial word "year"), "light unit" (for the unscientific "light year") and "solex," "ulvio" and "corsar" for sources of radiation. This same issue was to be the last of the glossies, and it contained one gem by Clifford Simak, "Spacebred Generations," a story that also won a star-and-sphere symbol from the delighted editor.

The sixth issue switched from glossy paper to the less expensive pulp. If one could have accused Gernsback of a perverse sense of humor, a connection might be argued between the switch to pulp paper and the contents of the issue, which boasted stories by Jack Williamson, Eric Frank Russell and Philip José Farmer and the debut of Anne McCaffrey. Farmer's short novel, "Strange Compulsion," marked the high point in story quality for the entire run.

The next issue, Number 7, proved to be the last. Ironically, it was also the best-balanced issue, containing a short novel by Harry Bates and stories by Murray Leinster, Frank M. Robinson and Eric Frank Russell. In his editorial Gernsback assessed the effects of too much fan influence on the field in general and on magazine circulation in particular. It is the statement of a confused man who finds himself no longer in control of a field he once, quite mistakenly, regarded as his own. Fans are criticized, finally, for developing a more sophisticated taste that has "driven the art to higher accomplishments" (which is good) but has contributed to what Gernsback perceives as the alienation of the genre from the masses. It has led, Gernsback complains, to a preference for "high brow" stories at the expense of the popular story told in "simple language so that it is not over the heads of the masses." In his disappointment at the declining fortunes of *Science-Fiction Plus*, Gernsback has created a curious scapegoat indeed: "Modern science-fiction today tends to gravitate more and more into the realm of the esoteric and sophisticated literature, to the exclusion of all other types." Just what Gernsback has specifically in mind is not clear beyond a general disenchantment with a readership that has failed to support the cause of a true science fiction according to Gernsback. Kicking the dust symbolically from his shoes, Gernsback ends his career with the following words: "At present, science-fiction literature is in its decline—deservedly so. The masses are revolting against the snob dictum 'Let 'em eat cake!' They're ravenous for vitalizing plain bread."

Whatever grain of truth there may have been in Gernsback's complaint, history has proven him a poor prophet. The last editorial rings instead with the frustration, confusion and pain of a man for whom the cause of a lifetime has ended in a defeat he must suffer without understanding. While admitting that fans are the sole arbiters of taste, Gernsback fails to interpret correctly the nature of their judgment on his own understanding of SF literature.

Although changes were made in the composition and balance of the last two issues, it seems clear that Gernsback never appreciated fully the tedium that was finally produced by his own incessant earnestness, pulpit mannerism, and obsession with instructing and improving his readers. Moreover, Gernsback's sense of literary style and tone had hardly changed from the early days of *Modern Electrics* in which his novel *Ralph 124C 41+* appeared under his own editorship. In the years between *Amazing* and *Science-Fiction Plus* (which seems to have taken its addition sign from the novel of 1911), science fiction stories had grown more sophisticated; but as the field changed and matured, Gernsback did not, either as an editor or as an amateur scientist-watcher. He remained all his life the lover of science-related hobbies and crafts; but it had become obvious by the early fifties that the new ideas and science were not coming out of the backyard or basement labs of contemporary Tom Edisons, more's the pity. Science was being generated instead by high-powered government and university laboratories in which Gernsback's amateurism would have been unwelcome and out of place. Shirtcuff calculations were out, computers were in. Moreover, Hiroshima had forever changed at least one side of the face of science. It was impossible for the world of the 1950s to believe in science as the salvation of the race.

It is a fair estimate to say that *Science Fiction Plus* (subtitled "Preview of the Future") is truly representative of its publisher in both its strengths and weaknesses. If the father of science fiction has turned out in the end to be more like Don Quixote than Lear, perhaps that is to the benefit of his "child."

Information Sources

BIBLIOGRAPHY:
Nicholls. *Encyclopedia.*
Tuck.
INDEX SOURCES: MIT; SFM; Tuck.
REPRINT SOURCES:
  Magazine: No formal foreign edition was published, but early issues of the Australian *Science Fiction Monthly* draw heavily on *Science Fiction Plus*.
LOCATION SOURCES: M.I.T. Science Fiction Library; Pennsylvania State University Library.

Publication History

TITLE: *Science-Fiction Plus* (designated as *Science Fiction* + on the indicia and spine); subtitled "Preview of the Future."
VOLUME DATA: Volume 1, Number 1, Mach 1953–Volume 1, Number 7, December 1953. Monthly to June, then bi-monthly. Total run: 7 issues.
PUBLISHER: Gernsback Publications, Philadelphia and New York.
EDITOR: Hugo Gernsback, with Sam Moskowitz as Managing Editor.
FORMAT: Slick, first five issues; thereafter Large Pulp (same dimensions); 64 pp. all issues.
PRICE: 35¢.

Donald Lawler

SCIENCE FICTION QUARTERLY

Science Fiction Quarterly was the third of the magazines issued by publisher Louis Silberkleit during the period of the science fiction boom that swept America in the years before World War II. It followed *Science Fiction** and *Future*

Fiction* and, like those magazines, was edited by Charles Hornig. A trial issue was released in July 1940 (dated Summer), with the second issue following six months later, but thereafter it remained on a quarterly basis except for one missed issue for Fall 1941.

Hornig approached the magazine much as he did the two others, his choice of fiction hampered to some extent by his limited budget, but more so by his general lack of editorial ability. *Science Fiction Quarterly*, however, had one advantage over its companion magazines in that it aimed at presenting a complete novel in each issue, always a favorite with readers in the years when paperbacks did not proliferate. *SFQ* to some extent, therefore, was issued to emulate the original quarterlies issued by Hugo Gernsback a decade or more earlier. During the Depression years the bulky quarterlies, which were always more expensive than the monthlies, had gone out of fashion, but Silberkleit felt that the time was ripe for a revival. *SFQ* could not compete with the earlier quarterlies for sheer size, but it could bring back the flavor and atmosphere of those old giants in the hands of a competent editor. The magazine was helped on its way as the result of a deal Silberkleit made with his old employer, Hugo Gernsback, to reprint the lead novels from the first two issues of *Science Wonder Quarterly* (*Wonder Stories Quarterly**) in 1929: *The Moon Conquerors* by R. H. Romans and *The Shot into Infinity* by Otto Willi Gail. These two alone would have been worth the twenty-five cent price of admission to each issue and almost certainly helped establish them. However, the remainder of the two issues consisted of the usual poor-quality items, predominantly rejects from other magazines, and published for the most part under pseudonyms. If any story stands out above this mediocrity it is "Double Destiny" by Helen Weinbaum, sister of the late Stanley G. Weinbaum. Although dreadfully overwritten, it has a curious power all its own, telling of a villainous superscientist and his double from an advanced civilization in the past. A topical story, it is preoccupied with the ominous health hazards of nuclear radiation and with the plans of Fascists to dominate the world.

By the time the second issue was published Hornig had moved to California and Robert W. Lowndes had succeeded him as editor of *Future Fiction* and *SFQ*. Lowndes's first issue, dated Spring 1941, was transitional, as he used up some of the items in Hornig's inventory, but he found room to include some stories by his fellow Futurians. Donald Wollheim, writing as Martin Pearson, was present with an implausible but effective mood story, "Cosmos Eye," while Cyril Kornbluth and Frederik Pohl combined as Paul Dennis Lavond with "Callistan Tomb," a grim but well-contrived story of a cave-in down a radium mine on Jupiter's moon Callisto. Here too was one of James Blish's early stories, a simple time paradox, "Weapon out of Time."

With the fourth issue, *Science Fiction Quarterly* could be said to have established its policy. Louis Silberkleit made a deal with Ray Cummings to reprint a number of his early stories, and five of his novels appeared in *SFQ*, starting with "Tarrano the Conqueror" in the Summer 1941 issue. This had originally been serialized in *Science and Invention* in 1925 but had also appeared in hardcover from McClurg in 1930. The other Cummings novels reprinted in the *SFQ* were "Into the Fourth Dimension" (Winter 1941/1942), "The Shadow Girl" (Spring 1942), "Brigands of the Moon" (Fall 1942) and "Wandl the Invader" (Spring 1943). Arthur J. Burks provided the other lead novels—neither being a reprint—"The Great Mirror" (Summer 1942) and "The Far Detour" (Winter 1942). Both the Burks stories were good, solid pulp adventures, while the Cummings novels, though now woefully dated, retain their sense of wonder.

The remainder of the issues were almost entirely filled by tales from the Futurians, ranging from short squibs like Donald Wollheim's "Bomb" (Winter 1942, as Millard Verne Gordon), where the far side of the moon is discovered to contain a long fuse, to long Merrittesque adventures in "Starstone World" by Hannes Bok (Summer 1942). The Futurians brought a fresh breath of excitement to science fiction and occupied a middle range between the serious and mature work appearing in *Astounding* (*Analog Science Fiction**) and the juvenile, immature stories appearing in most other magazines. At times their own stories could be deadly serious, as in "The Year of Uniting" by John Michel (Winter 1941/1942, as Hugh Raymond). Michel was, by political persuasion, a Communist, and he looks forward to after World War II, when a Science Government has been established in America, bringing about a society with no poverty, no unequal distribution of goods and services, no insecurity and . . . no freedom.

Science Fiction Quarterly saw ten issues in its first incarnation. The last seven are all collectable and readable and, though of variable quality, still show that verve and sparkle that helped raise the magazine above the level of many of its contemporaries.

Science Fiction Quarterly ceased publication after the Spring 1943 issue. Eight years later it reappeared, a slightly thinner 128 pages, but still in pulp format and still edited by Robert W. Lowndes. The first issue of the second series, dated May 1951, was renumbered Volume 1, Number 1, so in this respect it was a new magazine, although much of the old policy remained. The intention was still to publish longer than average stories that would not fit into *Future Fiction* (which had also been revived), but the so-called feature novels were seldom more than novelettes with the occasional exception. This time, however, there were no reprints. All stories were new.

The Futurians were not present in any great numbers. Although several of them were now establishing themselves as writers, especially Frederik Pohl, Cyril Kornbluth, Isaac Asimov and Damon Knight, few of them appeared in Lowndes' magazines during the 1950s with other than the occasional story or article. Instead, the contents were provided by many of the new generation of writers who had established themselves after the war, such as Poul Anderson, William Tenn, Arthur C. Clarke and Milton Lesser, plus a few of the older generation, such as George O. Smith, Lester del Rey, Wallace West and L. Sprague de Camp. Lowndes, in fact, obtained quality names for the magazine, but because his budget seldom allowed first pickings, he did not always obtain quality fiction. Nevertheless, writers had to write, and they could not always please John Campbell, Horace Gold or Anthony Boucher, and at this time the next market from a prestige point of view was either the Lowndes magazines or the Wonder group; and with the number of SF writers growing all the time, it is quite likely that Lowndes was not always faced with having to select from previous rejects. Furthermore, there was a certain reliability about *SFQ*. During the SF boom of 1951–1954 SF magazines came and went, and even *Future Fiction* and *Science Fiction* were erratic, but every March, June, September and December *SFQ* appeared without fail. (The cover dates for these issues were, respectively, May, August, November and February). Not only that, but when most other magazines converted to digest and the remaining pulps folded, *Science Fiction Quarterly* remained in the pulp format. By 1956 the magazine was the last surviving pulp—*Other Worlds Science Stories** had converted from a digest to a pulp in 1955, but *SFQ* remained unaltered throughout the great dying, and even outlasted *Other Worlds*. Silberkleit's belief had been that a digest quarterly would not have had the same feeling as a pulp, and he stood by this decision until 1957, when falling circulation at last proved that the magazine was no longer viable.

SFQ published little fiction of lasting quality, although a few stories remain memorable. Foremost among them is "Second Dawn" by Arthur C. Clarke (August 1951), one of the most poignant and powerful of the warning stories in the immediate postnuclear years. L. Sprague de Camp contributed his humorous tale of the exploits of a twenty-first-century actor back in Saxon England, "Rogue Princess' (February 1952). Eric Frank Russell appeared with one of his typical tongue-in-cheek satires, "The Timeless Ones" (November 1952), and Isaac Asimov asked "The Last Question" in the November 1956 issue. *SFQ* also published one of James Blish's best stories, "Common Time" (August 1953).

If anything, *Science Fiction Quarterly* was more memorable for its nonfiction, certainly among the SF devotees as opposed to the general readers. James Blish presented a four-part series on "Science in Science Fiction" (May 1951–May 1952), and this was later continued by Dr. Richard H. Macklin (August 1956– August 1957). Robert Madle looked at the progenitor of science fiction in "Edgar Allan Poe—Ancestor" (May 1953) and teamed up with Sam Moskowitz to pose the question "Did Science Fiction Predict Atomic Energy?" (November 1952). The ubiquitous L. Sprague de Camp contributed a number of articles including "The Lost Continents of Fiction" (August 1954), while the equally ubiquitous Isaac Asimov maintained a presence with a couple of articles, "Anxious for Everybody" (August 1957) and "The Clock Paradox" (November 1957).

Robert A. W. Lowndes evoked the same family atmosphere in *SFQ* that he did in all his magazines, with encouraging reader departments and editorials. But his presence was less noted in *SFQ*, which did not develop the same personality as *Future Fiction* and *Science Fiction*, perhaps because of the gap between issues. By the end of its run it had become an anachronism in format though not in content, and at the close of 1957 Silberkleit released the final issue, dated February 1958. It carried complete Robert Silverberg's novel "We, the Marauders,'' subsequently published by Ace Books as *Invaders from Earth* (1958), and for once looked more the part of the old quarterlies. But rather than change the image and convert it to a digest, Louis Silberkleit decided to fold it, and so passed *Science Fiction Quarterly*, the last of the science fiction pulps.

Note

The author wishes to thank Wendy Bousfield for her help in the research for this entry.

Information Sources

BIBLIOGRAPHY:
Nicholls. *Encyclopedia.*
Tuck.
INDEX SOURCES: ISFM; MIT; SFM; Tuck.
REPRINT SOURCES:
  British Editions:
    First series: Gerald Swan selected liberally from Silberkleit's various publications for his own books and magazines. The Summer 1940 *SFQ* had two separate British editions. First, four of the five short stories, minus the lead novel, appeared as *Yankee Science Fiction* No. 3 in February 1942. Then the whole issue, under the uncredited title of *The Moon Conquerors*, was published as a 176–page paperback in 1943. The same year the fifth issue was published as *Into the Fourth Dimension and Other Stories* as a 128–page paperback.
    Second series: Ten undated issues, 128 pp., 1/-, published by Thorpe & Porter, Leicester, appeared between February 1952 and August 1955 corresponding to abridged versions of the following: 1, May 1951; 2, August 1951; 3, February 1952; 4, November 1952; 5, August 1952; 6, May 1953; 7, February 1954; 8, November 1953; 9, February 1953; 10, May 1954.
  Derivative Anthologies: No single anthology is derived entirely from *SFQ*, but three of the eight stories in *Rare Science Fiction*, ed. Ivan Howard (New York: Belmont, 1963), date from 1957 issues.
  Microform: Greenwood Press Periodical Series.
LOCATION SOURCES: Brigham Young University, HBL Library (Vol. 1 [1951/2]); Vol. 2, No. 1 [1952]; Vol. 4, No. 3 [1956]); California State University–Fullerton, Library, Special Collections (No. 9, Winter 1943; Vol. 1, Nos. 1–5, Summer 1951–Summer 1952; Vol. 2, Nos. 1–6, Fall 1952–Spring 1954; Vol. 3, Nos. 1–5, Summer 1954–Summer 1955; Vol. 4, Nos. 1–3, Fall 1955–Summer 1956; Vol. 5, No. 4, Spring 1958); Dallas Public Library (Nos. 1–10, 1940–1943, microfilm); Eastern New Mexico University, Golden Library; Indiana University, Lilly Library (May 1954–August 1957, as follows: Vol. 3, Nos. 1, 3, 4, 6; Vol. 4, Nos. 3–6; Vol. 5, No. 2); Massachusetts Institute of Technology, MIT Science Fiction Society; Michigan State University, Special Collections (Vol. 1, No. 1, May 1951–Vol. 2. No. 6, February 1954; Vol. 3, No. 5, May 1955; Vol. 4, No. 1, Nov. 1955–Vol. 5, No. 1, May 1957; Vol. 5, No. 4, Feb. 1958; Northern Illinois University Library, Rare Books and Special Collections (Vol. 1, No. 1–Vol. 5, No. 4 [May 1951–Feb. 1958]); Ohio State University Libraries, Division of Special Collections (Nos. 1–10 [1940–1943]; Vols. 1–5 [1951–1958]); Pennsylvania State University Libraries, Special Collections (Nos. 1–4, Summer 1940–Summer 1941;

Nos. 6–10, Spring 1942–Spring 1943; Vol. 1, Nos. 1–6, May 1951–August 1952; Vol. 2, Nos. 1–6, Nov. 1952–Feb. 1954; Vol. 3, Nos. 1–6, May 1954–August 1955; Vol. 4, No. [?] 1955–Feb. 1957; Vol. 5, Nos. 1, 2, 4, May 1957–Feb. 1958); Queen's University, Special Collections; San Francisco Academy of Comic Art, Science Fiction Room ("have many issues"); San Francisco Public Library, Literature Department (Vols. 1–5, No. 4; 1940–1958); Syracuse University, George Arents Research Library, Rare Book Division (Nos. 1–7 [1940–1942]; Vol. 1, Nos. 1, 3, 5, 6; Vol. 2, Nos. 1–6; Vol. 3, Nos. 1–6; Vol. 4, Nos. 1, 3–6; Vol. 5, Nos. 1–4 [1951–1957]); Temple University, Paley Library, Paskow SF Collection (Vol. 1, No. 1–Vol. 5, No. 4 [1951–1958]); Texas A&M University, Special Collections; Toronto Public Libraries, Spaced Out Library; University of British Columbia Public Library Special Collections (Vol. 2, No. 4, August 1953); University of California–Los Angeles, Special Collections; University of California–Riverside, Special Collections (Nos. 1–8, 10 [1940–1943]; Vol. 1, Nos. 1–6; Vol. 2, Nos. 1–2; Vol. 3, Nos. 1, 4, 6; Vol. 5, No. 1); University of Georgia Libraries, Periodicals Dept.; University of Kansas, Spencer Research Library; University of Maryland-Baltimore County Library, Special Collections; University of New Mexico, General Library, Special Collections; Yale University Library (Nos. 1–10, Summer 1940–Spring 1943).

Publication History

TITLE: *Science Fiction Quarterly*.

VOLUME DATA: First series: Number 1, Summer 1940–Number 10, Spring 1943 (no volumes). Second series: Volume 1, Number 1, May 1951–Volume 5, Number 4, February 1958. Six issues per volume. Quarterly. Total run: 10 + 28, 38 issues.

PUBLISHER: First issue, Double Action Magazines, Holyoke, Mass.; the remainder, Columbia Publications, Holyoke, with editorial offices in New York.

EDITORS: Charles D. Hornig, Number 1, Summer 1940–Number 2, Winter 1941; Robert [A.]W. Lowndes, Number 3, Spring 1941–Volume 5, Number 4, February 1958.

FORMAT: Pulp; 144 pp., Summer 1940–Spring 1943; 128 pp., May 1951–August 1953; 96 pp., November 1953–May 1957; 128 pp., August 1957–February 1958.

PRICE: 25¢, Summer 1940–May 1957; 35¢, August 1957–February 1958.

Mike Ashley

SCIENCE FICTION STORIES (1943)

See FUTURE FICTION.

SCIENCE FICTION STORIES (1953–1960)

Title used by *Science Fiction* in its second series. Also known as *The Original Science Fiction Stories*. See SCIENCE FICTION.

SCIENCE FICTION YEARBOOK

Science Fiction Yearbook was a continuation of the *Treasury of Great Science Fiction Stories** series of anthologies issued in neo-pulp magazine format by Popular Library, which had acquired the rights to *Thrilling Wonder Stories* (*Wonder Stories**), and *Startling Stories** from Better Publications. Commencing in 1967, it reproduced stories and illustrations in facsimile from the original issues of those magazines and featured such authors as Murray Leinster, Ray Bradbury, Leigh Brackett, L. Sprague de Camp, L. Ron Hubbard and John Russell Fearn, all of whom had been prominent contributors. *SFY* also reprinted early work by Philip José Farmer ("Sail On! Sail On!" in Number 4), Gordon R. Dickson and Philip K. Dick. The issues were enhanced by the reproduction of a number of illustrations by Virgil Finlay.

The contents were, on the whole, of good quality, having been selected from the better years of the parent magazines under Samuel Merwin and Samuel Mines. *SFY* lacked any editorial or reader departments. The series should not be confused with the various yearbooks issued in 1970 by Sol Cohen.

Information Sources

BIBLIOGRAPHY:
Tuck.
INDEX SOURCES: NESFA; SFM; Tuck.
REPRINT SOURCES: None known.
LOCATION SOURCES: M.I.T. Science Fiction Library.

Publication History

TITLE: *S-F Yearbook: A Treasury of Science Fiction* (No. 1); thereafter *Science Fiction Yearbook*.
VOLUME DATA: Number 1, 1967–Number 5, 1971.
PUBLISHER: Popular Library, New York.
EDITORS: Helen Tono, issues 1–4; Anne Keffer, issue 5.
FORMAT: Neo-pulp, 96 pp.
PRICE: 50¢.

Mike Ashley

SCIENCE STORIES

Science Stories, a bi-monthly, digest-sized magazine, ran for four issues: October and December 1953, and February and April 1954. Its relationship to two other titles, also published and edited by Raymond A. Palmer, is complex. After resigning from Ziff-Davis as editor of *Amazing Stories** in September 1949, Palmer, who had already established his own publishing company, Clark Publications, in Evanston, Illinois, brought out *Other Worlds Science Stories,** with Bea Mahaffey as assistant editor. For financial reasons, Palmer discontinued

Other Worlds in July 1953 and, with Mahaffey, published and edited a replacement, *Science Stories*, which was shorter and less expensive to produce. Also in 1953, Palmer initiated another new magazine, a companion to *SS* called *Universe Science Fiction*.* Subscribers to the discontinued *Other Worlds* were given the choice of receiving the issues to which they were entitled from either *SS* or *Universe Science Fiction*. When *Other Worlds* was revived in May 1955, it succeeded *Universe Science Fiction*, continuing the numbering of that magazine.[1]

In the second issue of *SS*, dated December 1953, Palmer explains why *SS* was substituted for *Other Worlds*:

> This is the second issue of SCIENCE STORIES. The first issue was tossed in your lap with little or no ceremony, and even less explanation. For a variety of reasons—and let's be honest, most of them were financial—we had to make a spur-of-the-moment decision to discontinue OTHER WORLDS and replace it with the magazine you are now reading. We phoned the typesetter, halted work on the August OW, and lifted the editorial and stories we needed for SCIENCE STORIES No. 1 from OW material on hand.

Palmer goes on to apologize for the corners he has been obliged to cut. *SS* has no back cover picture and thirty-two fewer pages than *Other Worlds*, hence fewer pages devoted to editorials, letters and personals.

SS includes no memorable fiction, but the quality of the cover art and many interior illustrations is high. The cover of the first issue (October 1953), by Hannes Bok, depicts in violet tones an alien landscape with a girl, dressed only in a wreath of flowers, feeding flowers to a dinosaur. In "The People Who Write Science Stories" (adapted from "The People Who Make Other Worlds" in the parent magazine), Jack Williamson explains that he was sent a photostat of the Bok picture and asked to write a story that fit. In "Hocus-Pocus Universe," a man who paints his high school sweetheart in the setting depicted on the cover eventually travels with her to the planet he had visualized.[2] Bok also provided for the same story an arresting black and white illustration of a powerfully muscled nude male, flying superman fashion with one arm raised.

Illustrating John Bloodstone's "Potential Zero," the cover of *SS*'s second issue is by Virgil Finlay. Though not as evocative as the black and white interior drawings he contributed to *SS*, the cover painting appealingly depicts flying saucers cascading like golden rings onto an alien planet and the nebulous images of a man and woman superimposed on the sky. For the same story, Finlay provided a magnificent black and white drawing of a nude woman running across a field toward a man, the ringlike saucers overhead.

The cover of the third issue, dated February 1954, is by Albert A. Nuetzell, who also contributed the autobiographical sketch for that month's "The People Who Write Science Stories." In his editorial for that issue, Palmer explains that, as a way of developing new talent, *SS* would pay $500 for the best story that fit Nuetzell's painting: "A space ship, obviously damaged, some men, its crew, outside it. And hovering over it is a 'something,' a shadow, a shapeless shape, clutching menacing. . . . '' Since the subsequent issue was *SS*'s last, the winning story was not announced.

Perhaps *SS*'s most appealing cover is its last (April 1954) by Robert Gibson Jones, illustrating Frank Patton's "The Secret of Pierre Cotreau": two lumberjacks in knitted caps discover a tiny woman lying unconscious in the forest. Patton's forgettable story of a beautiful Martian held captive by a brutal logger also inspired a graceful drawing by Virgil Finlay of a diminutive female with pointed ears. Finlay, who contributed the April 1954 "The People Who Write Science Stories," provided all the interior illustrations for that issue. His finest drawing illustrates T. P. Caravan's "Problem in Geometry": the yang and yin in the form of two spaceships. While Finlay's drawings are consistently far more impressive than the stories that he illustrates in *SS*, Finlay does not go outside the world the author has created for his images.

Few writers represented in *SS* are well known today. While *SS* employed house names and pseudonyms, Frank Robinson is the only noted contributor to appear pseudonymously. As Robert Courtney, Robinson contributed "One Thousand Miles Up" (April 1954). A space station, armed with nuclear weapons, is manned by a Russian, a Chinese, an Italian, an Englishman and an American. All vie for control until the American blackmails them into cooperating. Courtney has been attributed as a pen name of Harlan Ellison although both Robinson and Charles Beaumont used the name. Richard S. Shaver, under the pseudonym Richard Dorot, contributed "She Was Sitting in the Dark" (December 1953). Shaver, a protégé of Palmer, had contributed a highly controversial cycle of stories, allegedly based on fact, to Palmer's *Amazing*. Shaver's contribution to *SS* is both silly and sexist, mingling pseudo-medieval magic with science fictional elements.

Besides Robinson, the only writers represented in *SS* likely to be recognized today are Jack Williamson, whose "Hocus-Pocus Universe" has been discussed, and Mack Reynolds. Reynolds' "Optical Illusion" (December 1953) is a slight story, the plot of which turns on a trick last sentence. A child, belonging to a race with powers superior to man's, masquerades as a midget to escape detection. When the narrator guesses the truth, the child tries to hypnotize him into forgetting but fails because, as we discover at the very end, the narrator is blind.

Two types of fiction predominate in *SS*: short, humorous tales and stories with lively, often violent action. *SS*'s humor is often of the shaggy dog variety, depending on an absurd last line or final revelation. In Ralph Sloan's "The Treason of Joe Gates," a janitor at the White House explains, from his prison cell, that he stayed late one night to clean up after a meeting between government officials and a man in a "diving suit." The hungry janitor eats what he thinks is a piece of Roquefort cheese, left on the table, but is arrested because it is actually "a chunk of moon real estate." Other humorous stories in *SS* poke fun at the improbabilities of science fiction. In T. P. Caravan's "Problem in Geometry'' (April 1954), a spaceship is lost in overdrive because of a malfunction in the computer. Eddie, a little boy, wonders why the captain doesn't act like his space hero, Killer Mike, and save the ship by pressing a button.

Palmer was partial to stories with lively physical action. John Bloodstone's "Last Days of Thronas," taking up 107 pages of the 130–page February 1954 issue, concerns two tribes of barbarians, anachronistically engaging in swordplay and slaughter at a time when interplanetary flight is routine. Robert Moore Williams, who contributed an autobiographical sketch to the October 1953 issue, states that the western is the model for his own science fiction: "There is a kind of bold challenge about the old West, where a man went in by the skin of his teeth, his wits, his guts, his heart, and a gun, and made something for himself out of a wilderness that I like." Williams' "Battle in the Sky" in the same issue concerns an attempt by the Tethanni, brutal aliens with German accents, to take over Earth's settlements on Venus. While SS includes fewer pure examples of space opera than might be expected, the problems raised in most of the stories are solved by physical prowess.

Despite the reduced space devoted to editorials, Palmer makes his presence and tastes felt in SS, not only through his choice of stories, but through commentary embellished with exclamation points and italics. Palmer's fondness for self-promotion may be seen in the prominent advertisements for the book he co-authored with Kenneth Arnold, *The Coming of the Saucers*. Among SS's numerous cartoons on science fictional subjects is one in which Palmer as the Invisible Man—suit, glasses and pipe, but no visible body—sits in the *Other Worlds* office. One man tells another, "You'll like Palmer—he's real gone, and so's his magazine" (February 1954).

In his editorial in SS's final issue, Palmer suggests: "We'd like science fiction writers to begin building some spiritual and moral values into our magazine, and subject the gadgets to them." While the stories published in SS, by and large, respect traditional moral codes, Palmer would surely have become impatient with writers who dwelt upon the subjective or introspective. Palmer interrupts Edward Wellen's autobiographical sketch (December 1953): "*Editors' note*. Sorry Herr Professor, but because of a space warp we have to delete that long psychoanalytic reply. Be brief and breezy. You heard us, Professor. *Nein!*" Palmer, as this deletion and his choice of stories suggest, was committed to entertainment of the most lively and undemanding sort.

Notes

1. Information about the interrelationship of the magazines Palmer edited during this period was taken from the following: Michael Ashley, ed., *History of the Science Fiction Magazine, 1946–1955* (Chicago: Contemporary Books, 1976), III: 46–49, 88, 106; "Science Stories," in *The Science Fiction Encyclopedia*, ed. Peter Nicholls (Garden City, N.Y.: Doubleday, 1979).

2. This cover is reproduced in James Gunn's *Alternate Worlds: The Illustrated History of Science Fiction* (Prentice-Hall, 1975), p. 202.

Information Sources

BIBLIOGRAPHY:
Nicholls. *Encyclopedia.*
Tuck.
INDEX SOURCES: MIT; SFM; Tuck.
REPRINT SOURCES: None known.
LOCATION SOURCES: California State University–Fullerton, Special Collections (not available through interlibrary loan, but will photocopy articles upon request); Eastern New Mexico University, Golden Library (not available through ILL); Massachusetts Institute of Technology, MIT Science Fiction Society (not available through ILL); Michigan State University Library, Special Collections; Northern Illinois University Library, Rare Books and Special Collections (no ILL, but partial photocopying of some issues *may* be possible); Ohio State University Libraries, Division of Special Collections; Pennsylvania State University Libraries, Special Collections (Nos. 1, 3 and 4 only); Queen's University, Special Collections (no ILL or microfilm); San Francisco Academy of Comic Art, Science Fiction Room; San Francisco Public Library, Literature Department (not available through ILL); Syracuse University, George Arents Research Library, Rare Book Division; Temple University, Paley Library, Paskow Science Fiction Collection (not available through ILL); Texas A&M University, Special Collections; University of California–Los Angeles, Special Collections (a microfilm may be produced, the negative to remain at UCLA and the patron to pay for negative and print); University of California–Riverside (No. 1 only); University of Georgia Libraries, Periodicals Department; University of Kansas, Spencer Research Library; University of Maryland Baltimore County Library, Special Collections (no ILL, but sections of magazines may be photocopied); Toronto Public Libraries, Spaced Out Library (no ILL; Nos. 1, 2 and 3 only).

Publication History

TITLE: *Science Stories.*
VOLUME DATA: Number 1, October 1953–Number 4, April 1954. Bi-monthly. No volume numbering. Total run: 4 issues.
PUBLISHER: Bell Publications, Chicago, first issue; thereafter Palmer Publications, Evanston, Illinois.
EDITORS: Raymond A. Palmer and Bea Mahaffey.
PRICE: 35¢.

Wendy Bousfield

SCIENCE WONDER QUARTERLY

See WONDER STORIES QUARTERLY.

SCIENCE WONDER STORIES

See WONDER STORIES.

SCIENTIFIC DETECTIVE MONTHLY

Early in December 1929, followers of Hugo Gernsback's *Science Wonder Stories* (*Wonder Stories**) and *Air Wonder Stories** found a full-page ad in the new January 1930 issues announcing: "And NOW we present *Scientific Detective Monthly*." Most of the page was occupied by a black and white reproduction of the cover for the first issue, dated January 1930 and scheduled to go on sale December 15. The format was the same as that of the two Wonder magazines: 100 pages, 8½ by 11⅝ inches, printed on rather stiff pulp stock with enough bulk to make the magazine look somewhat bigger than it actually was. Readers were told: "SCIENTIFIC DETECTIVE MONTHLY, *the first national detective monthly with a scientific background* will have as its Editorial Commissioner Mr. Arthur B. Reeve, the foremost science fiction writer and author of the world-read 'Craig Kennedy' series. . . . A brand new Craig Kennedy story, and many other scientific detective stories written by such famous authors as Dr. David H. Keller, Captain Meek, U.S.A., etc." would appear in that first issue, as well as "The Bishop Murder Case," by S. S. Van Dine.

Precisely what role Reeve played in the magazine, apart from writing one new story, agreeing to the reprint of nine other Craig Kennedy tales, and either writing an article on the "best" detective stories or agreeing to the reprint of an article published earlier, was obscure at the time and remains so now. Hugo Gernsback was listed as "Editorial Chief," and, as with all his other magazines, nothing appeared therein that he had not read and okayed. Hector Grey (who had a solid background in criminology) was listed as the "Editorial Deputy," which meant that, like David Lasser on the Wonder magazines, he was the managing editor: he did the main editorial work. However, no one working under Hugo Gernsback had the final say on whether any story or article would be accepted, though we can be sure that Gernsback approved a majority of the material passed on to him with a recommendation for acceptance.

As with nearly all of his other publications, *Scientific Detective Monthly* was designed to be instructive as well as entertaining. The first sentence in his January editorial states the purpose of the magazine: "In the firm belief that science in its various applications will become one of the greatest deterrents to crime, SCIENTIFIC DETECTIVE MONTHLY has been launched." In the course of well-written mystery and crime stories, the readers would learn how criminals are detected through the use of various scientific instruments.

In nearly all of the stories in *SDM*, the devices used to detect crime already existed, although they may not have actually been used in the same way that the fictional detective uses them. Only in a minority of the stories (seldom more than one in each issue) is there a description of a machine or device of some kind that did not already exist (although its existence may have been theoretically possible), which made the tale science fiction. On the whole, *Scientific Detective Monthly* was not a science-fiction magazine at all.

Each issue contained factual material as well as fiction and editorial and reader departments. In the January issue (all dates are 1930) the following lineup appeared: Fiction: "The Mystery of the Bulawayo Diamond" by Arthur B. Reeve; "The Campus Murder Mystery" by Ralph W. Wilkins; "The Fast Watch" by Edwin Balmer and William MacHarg; "The Perfect Counterfeit" by Captain S. P. Meek, U.S.A.; "The Eye of Prometheus" by R. F. Starzl; and part one of "The Bishop Murder Case" by S. S. Van Dine—with no indication of how many installments it would run. Nonfiction: "Science vs. Crime" (editorial) by Hugo Gernsback; "What Are the Great Detective Stories and Why?" by Arthur B. Reeve; "A Message from the Ultraviolet" by H. Ashton-Wolfe. Departments: "How Good a Detective Are You?"; "Questionnaire"; "Detective Play Reviews"; "Science-Crime Notes"; "Book Reviews"; and "The Reader's Verdict."

The cover was by Jno Ruger, illustrating a scene in "The Fast Watch." We see red-headed Luther Trant taking notes on a dial reading; a suspect grips the device, which is supposed to measure his reactions electronically while the front page of a newspaper is shown to him. One gathers that he is at least startled. Ruger also did the interior illustration for that story. Frank R. Paul illustrated the Starzl story, Walter Edward Blythe the Philo Vance serial, and Winter the other stories.

While Philo Vance discourses on Riemannian geometry, among other learned matters that would be of interest to science fictionists, nothing that could be called science fictional has anything to do with the solution to the mysterious "Mother Goose" murders—unless one insists that Vance's use of psychology might be called that. However, Vance does arrive at his conclusions through psychology, so there is some justification for Gernsback's reprinting it.

In the Reeve story, the bolometer, a heat-measuring device, is used to detect a black girl blushing—which gives Craig Kennedy the lead he needs. In the Wilkins tale, the victim is quick-frozen and his body dropped from a height simultaneously with an explosion, so that it appears that he has been blown up. In the Luther Trant story, electronic measurement of a suspect's palm-sweat reveals the truth. And in the Starzl story, the murder method requires the use of a certain catalyst. Captain Meek's story alone (one of the Dr. Bird series, which ran in all three science fiction monthlies of the period) is science fiction: it is the first time we see the use of a matter-duplicating machine—which explains why the counterfeit bills are indeed perfect.

The department titles pretty much explain themselves. At the time the first issue was being made up, a couple of mystery plays were running off Broadway. "How Good a Detective Are You?" is an observation test: the readers were supposed to study an illustration of the scene of a crime for two minutes, then answer thirty-five questions about it. But no deduction is required; it's all there in the picture. The questionnaire followed the pattern of questionnaires in the Wonder magazines (to see if the reader had picked up any scientific information from the stories) and the science-crime notes corresponded to science or air news of the month.

"The Readers Verdict" is, of course, letters from the readers. Such letters were always genuine in the Gernsback magazines, in the sense that none were staff-written. How did he manage to get real letters in the very first issue? Elementary: advance notices of the magazine were sent to people on the subscription lists for other titles, and they were invited not only to subscribe but to write suggestions for future issues and state their opinions of the policy as outlined in the prospectus.

That pattern of presentation continued throughout the magazine's run. The February issue has another laboratory-like scene by Ruger, and the same artists illustrate the stories. ("Winter" in *Scientific Detective Monthly*, however, was not the same as "Lumen Winter," whose artwork appeared in *Wonder Stories* from 1934 to 1936.)

Two stories in the February issue are worth mentioning: "A Scientific Widowhood' by David H. Keller and "The Man with the Silver Disc" by L. A. Eshbach. Keller's story is in his Taine of San Francisco series, and goes back to his very first case, wherein he discovers that the victims have been subjected to prolonged exposure to a concealed x-ray machine and turns the tables on the culprit. Eshbach, who would have a number of stories in the regular magazines, and would later become the publisher of Fantasy Press, offers a science fiction crime story: the "silver disc" is a brain implant through which the subject can be controlled.

The March issue is the only one with a cover that looks like science fiction; it shows a robot, and "The Robot Terror" is a one-machine crime wave, controlled remotely by radio. The author, Melbourne Huff, was a one-shot writer so far as the Gernsback and science fiction magazines are concerned. Craig Kennedy and Luther Trant appear again, as they would in each issue up to the next to last. Several of the Trant stories had been reprinted in *Amazing Stories** earlier.

The April cover is by Paul, with a scene from a two-part serial, "Rays of Death" by Tom Curry, who also appeared in *Astounding Stories of Super Science* (*Analog Science Fiction**). It hardly belonged in the magazine, being little more than a thriller dealing with stolen radium, used to bring lingering death to the subject of the culprit's revenge plot.

There is one memorable story: "The Invisible Master," by Edmond Hamilton, which appears to be science fiction (it deals with a means of producing invisibility) but proves to be a hoax; the author rings in a second surprise that makes the tale vivid even today.

In the May issue, Ruger is back on the cover, illustrating "The Electrical Man" by Neil R. Jones, who would later become well known to science fiction fans for his Professor Jameson series, among others. This can pass as science fiction, since the hero has a wired suit to which electricity is broadcast, and anyone who touches him when the power is on gets at least a severe shock. Bullets will not penetrate the suit, and a knife will deliver a lethal charge to its user. The story is an action-thriller, and while Jones points out the weaknesses of the device, he overestimates its values.

There is an announcement that, with the next issue, the title of the magazine will be changed to *Amazing Detective Tales*. Hugo Gernsback removed the word "science" from *Science Wonder Stories* and combined that title with *Air Wonder Stories* at the same time. Obviously the three magazines were not selling very well, and he suspected that the word "science" turned people away rather than attracting them.

The magazine did not change otherwise, except that Hector L. Grey was replaced by David Lasser as managing editor with the July issue. Perhaps Grey resigned in protest at the apparent "cheapening" of the magazine; perhaps he was let go as an economy move.

The May issue had another excellent scientific murder mystery by Edmond Hamilton, "The Murder in the Clinic," in which the reader is given a fair chance to solve the puzzle. That was rare in *SDM*. The real "scientific" detective stories were usually based on technological details of which the average reader knew nothing.

Once one gets by Ruger's June cover—this was a cover contest issue, and prizes were offered for the best short-short stories written around it—*Amazing Detective Tales* looks no different. What difference there was lay in there being even less real science in the new fiction.

There is another Taine story by Keller, which hints at science fiction: in "Burning Water" a power source is purportedly derived from the atom. It can also be a tremendous explosive. Taine manages to set it off, wiping out the culprits and most of the building (there are no radiation side effects), but Keller hedges by suggesting that an anarchist group on a lower floor was also out to blow up the building at the same time. In "The Gland Murders" (Dr. Bird again) Captain S. P. Meek's culprit sets off a wave of homicides by poisoning whiskey with special gland extracts, which arouse homicidal mania. It was close enough to science fiction to have appeared in one of the regular SF magazines.

Someone named Jay Gould (whose style differed from that of J. Fleming Gould in *Astounding Stories*) joined the art staff with the July issue. And the art in that issue is interesting for another reason: Ruger's cover gives away the secret of "Horror House" by Walter Livingston Martin, and Winter's illustration solves "The Mystery of the Phantom Shot" by Amelia Reynolds Long, effectively spoiling what otherwise would have been a good puzzle, just barely "scientific."

Two stories are definitely science fiction. In "The Grey Shadow" by W.F. Hammond we have real, rather than phony, invisibility used to bring justice upon malefactors otherwise untouchable by the law; "The Mind Machine" by Eugene George Key, who had appeared in *Air Wonder Stories*, centers around a fantastic invention, which involves mind control, death rays, and so on.

The August cover was the most attractive of the entire run. (And the least gaudy—we just see the head and shoulder of an attractive blonde woman, and a hand pouring some sort of gas which gives off a green vapor into a dish on her bedside table.) It illustrates "Vapours of Death," one of the better Luther

Trant stories, which were all superior to the Reeve tales. There was no signature on the cover and no identification inside; it does not look like Ruger's work. A new artist named Romaine appears inside, along with the regulars, but most of the artwork is by Gould—and not especially attractive.

Nothing can be called science fiction in this issue aside from the stories by Kennedy and Trant, but two other stories have a solid scientific background: "The Painted Murder" by Eugene De Reszke is very well written and deals with little-realized aspects of anatomy; "The Vanishing Man" by Ralph Milne Farley outlines a practical way in which a man can change his face almost instantly.

Ruger is back on the September cover with what has been called "an extreme picture of a bad Chinaman"; it illustrates "Menacing Claws" by Keller, wherein Taine disguises himself as a Chinese and invades San Francisco's Chinatown to deal with the insidious Ming Kow, suspected to be behind the elimination of several investigators who died rather mysteriously of tetanus.

Eugene George Key is back with another story in the same unspecified future depicted in "The Mind Machine." "The Temple of Dust" deals with chemical possibilities and anarchists. Ed Earl Repp's serial "The Carewe Murder Mystery" vies with Tom Curry's serial as the poorest and silliest overextended stories in the magazine's lifetime. The blurb reads "Did death come through the Nth Dimension to strike down the eminent Dr. Carewe?" By the end of the first installment it is clear that the Nth Dimension has nothing to do with the laughable melodrama that makes up the case. "Winged Death" by O. L. Beckwith (who had appeared in *Science Wonder Stories* and *Air Wonder Stories*) deals effectively with experiments on mosquitoes, making them lethal rather than irritating.

Readers did not know, of course, when they picked up the October issue, with what may be a Ruger cover for C. R. Sumner's overdone but fairly interesting "The Flower of Evil" (it has hypnotic effects), that they were looking at the final issue of *Amazing Detective Tales*. As in the October issue of *Wonder Stories*, there is no editorial: the page is given over to an announcement that the next issue would be published in regular pulp format: 7 by 10 inches.

Two science fiction tales were announced for the November issue: "The Man of Bronze" by A. L. Fierst, and "The Murders on the Moon Ship" by George Beattie. The former appeared later in *Wonder Stories Quarterly** (Winter 1931) and the latter in *Wonder Stories* (February 1931).

Other fiction in the October issue was "Death in a Drop" by Ralph Wilkins; "The Clasp of Doom" by Eugene De Reszke; "Shadows of the Night" by Neil R. Jones; "The Man Who Was Dead" by Arthur B. Reeve; "Murder in the Fourth Dimension" by Clark Ashton Smith; "The Man in Room 18" by Otis A. Kline; "The Man No One Could Lift" by Fred Ebel; and the conclusion of the Ed Earl Repp serial. There was an article, "The Most Dangerous of Forgeries" by Edmund Locard, billed as "a scientific authority," and the usual departments. Mark Marchioni, who had just started doing work for *Wonder*

Stories, illustrated the Wilkins, Jones, Reeve, Sumner and Kline stories; Gould did the De Rezke tale and the serial; the other two had no artwork.

Luther Trant is missing; also missing is nearly everything that could justify the stories being described as "scientific detective," with the exception of those by Reeve, De Reske and Wilkins. The Smith story is a crime biter-bit tale, in a fourth-dimensional setting: the culprit has found a means to go into the fourth dimension, lures his victim to take a trip with him, kills him—then finds that he can not get back and is marooned with the corpse of his victim. The De Reske story has genuine chemical scientific methods, and the Wilkins story can pass as science fiction chemistry, while the Jones tale is a pale prequel telling about an earlier exploit of Miller Rand, who became the "electrical man" in the first story.

Nonetheless, *Amazing Detective Tales* was mostly enjoyable reading, more lurid and less stuffy than *Scientific Detective Stories*. In better times it might have lasted longer. But even then it could not have sustained the level on which it started. Arthur B. Reeve's clue in his article in the first issue proved to be prophetic: he said that he himself had stopped writing "scientific" detective stories because he believed that their time had passed.

More than that: Hugo Gernsback's original presentation was designed to appeal to technological-minded readers who also liked mystery fiction. (He had run that type of story in *Science and Invention** and *Radio News*, and the readers had approved.) But at first, *SDM* had very little newsstand appeal to the not-already-hooked Gernsback-magazine follower. He did not even try to attract science fictionists by putting titles and names of stories by science fiction authors on the first two covers—there were no titles or names at all. And those first two covers looked like those of a technical magazine, not a fiction magazine. Later, when he tried to provide newsstand appeal, the covers were too gaudy for his technological audience, except for those who already read magazines with lurid covers.

Some of the stories in *SDM/ADT* that qualify as science fiction might have appeared in *Wonder Stories* or *Amazing Stories*. Some of the later straight detective stories could easily have appeared in *Real Detective Tales*, a rival which did run some mildly "scientific" mystery stories. The true-fact articles were interesting and nonsensational, much like popular books by criminologists one could find in libraries at the time.

The cover contest announced in the June issue never came off. One entry was published a few years later in *Fantasy Magazine*, the leading fan magazine of the period.

Nevertheless, *Scientific Detective Monthly/Amazing Detective Tales* was unique. Hugo Gernsback spoke truly when he said that nothing like his new magazine had ever appeared before, and there has never been another like it. The atmosphere remained to the end; it was a fascinating experiment, even though it failed.

Information Sources

BIBLIOGRAPHY:

Moskowitz, Sam. "From Sherlock to Spaceships." In *Strange Horizons*. New York: Scribner's, 1976.

Tuck.

INDEX SOURCES: ISFM; SFM; Tuck.

REPRINT SOURCES: None known.

LOCATION SOURCES: M.I.T. Science Fiction Library.

Publication History

TITLE: *Scientific Detective Monthly*, January–May 1930. Retitled *Amazing Detective Tales*, June–October 1930. Later retitled *Amazing Detective Stories* but in this incarnation was a strict detective magazine.

VOLUME DATA: Volume 1, Number 1, January 1930–Volume 1, Number 10, October 1930. Monthly. Volume 2 continued as *Amazing Detective Stories*, non-SF. Total run, SF issues: 10 issues.

PUBLISHER: Techni-Craft Publishing Co., New York, a subsidiary of Stellar Publications. Volume 2 (*Amazing Detective Stories*) was published by Fiction Publishers, Inc., New York.

EDITORS: Hugo Gernsback was Editor-in-Chief and Arthur B. Reeve was Editorial Consultant. Managing Editors were: Hector Grey, January–June 1930; David Lasser, July–October 1930.

FORMAT: Large Pulp, 96 pp.

PRICE: 25¢.

Robert A. W. Lowndes

SCIENTI-SNAPS

Fanzine issues of a magazine that later turned semi-professional for one issue under the title *Bizarre*. See BIZARRE.

SCOOPS

Scoops holds the dubious honor of being Britain's first all-SF magazine. It was also the first and only weekly English-language SF magazine the field has had. It is unfortunate, therefore, that *Scoops* is now looked back upon as a dismal failure and mistake. Walter Gillings described it as "the biggest blunder British science fiction ever made,"[1] yet no full appraisal of its existence has been made till now even though the magazine has become a collector's item.

Scoops was published by the established firm of C. Arthur Pearson, Ltd., which also published the monthly *Pearson's Magazine*, noted for the SF stories it had carried by H. G. Wells, A. Conan Doyle and George Griffith. In 1933 the rival company of Odhams had converted the weekly *The Passing Show* into a glossy family magazine, serializing the Venusian novels of Edgar Rice Burroughs. Such fantastic adventures had always been popular in the boys' magazines, so Pearson's, feeling that the climate was favorable, decided to chance a weekly fiction paper to bridge that gap—*Scoops*. It was a tabloid, priced at twopence and subtitled "The Story Paper of Tomorrow." The first issue, dated February 10, 1934, was issued on Thursday, February 8, and it appeared every Thursday for the next nineteen weeks.

The editorial explained the magazine's title and purpose:

> To a newspaper man everything that is different, out of the ordinary, something others haven't got, is a scoop.
>
> Here, then, is a paper full of good stories—all scoops. They are scoops because they *are* different, because they look ahead with the vision of Jules Verne and H. G. Wells, whose fiction stories of wonder and science, declared impossibilities at the time of publication, are now fact.
>
> *Scoops* is a paper for all. It has the thrill of adventure and mystery and will transport its readers from the everyday happenings into the future, with all its exceptions of development and discovery.
>
> As a story paper, *Scoops* stands in a class of its own. It arrives at a time when all the world is wondering what the next new and amazing discovery will be. In its stories *Scoops* will endeavour to anticipate the marvels of the age in which we live.
>
> Thus will it justify its claim as the story paper of tomorrow.[2]

There can be no doubt that, while the term was not used, *Scoops* was intended as a science fiction magazine. Furthermore, it called itself "a paper for all," and indeed, although prizes in its first competition included penknives, mouth organs and magnetic compasses, they also included cigarette holders, cufflinks and shaving mirrors, showing that while its fiction was aimed primarily at the young readers, the editors hoped also to interest the fathers.

Where they failed at the outset was in the selection of writers. The managing editor responsible for policy decisions (though probably not the selection of fiction) was Haydn Dimmock, editor of *The Scout* from 1918 to 1954 and the originator of the notorious annual "Bob-a-Job" week. It was Dimmock who had planned the magazine as "a paper for youth,"[3] not realizing that adults had any serious interest in SF.

The authors commissioned to write stories—most of which were serialized in short episodes—were noted as boys' adventure writers. Although most stories appeared anonymously, the researches of W. G. Lofts have identified several of them. The lead serial, for instance, "Master of the Moon," was the work of Bernard Buley, editor of Hulton's *Boys Magazine*, which had specialized in scientific adventures and had folded only three weeks before *Scoops* was launched. "The Striding Terror"—the continuing story of a once weak and ailing child now turned fifty-foot monster—was by Reginald Thomas, who wrote thousands of stories for the boys' papers.

To give the paper some respectability, the only author identified at the outset, with a serial starting in the second issue, was Professor A. M. Low, one of Britain's most distinguished scientists and inventors of the period, credited with inventing the first guided missile in 1917. His novel *Space* was serialized in ten episodes and subsequently appeared in book form in 1937 as *Adrift in the Stratosphere*.

The general tenor of the magazine changed little for the first twelve issues until the initial batch of serials had run their course. By then Haydn Dimmock and his editorial staff had discovered—mostly through the efforts of devotees like Walter Gillings, John Russell Fearn and P. E. Cleator—that there was an adult audience for a serious SF magazine. Already it was known that circulation was dwindling, and the decision was made to change the magazine's appeal.

The cover received a face-lift; most stories were now credited with by-lines, and the new feature serial was Sir Arthur Conan Doyle's "The Poison Belt," which, although a reprint (*The Strand*, 1913), was of considerably greater literary value than the earlier serials. As a rule, however, the boys' fiction writers, such as George E. Rochester and Stuart Martin, filled most of the magazine. Only in its last few issues did any of the specialist SF writers find a market. P. E. Cleator, the co-founder of the British Interplanetary Society—who in an earlier issue had responded to Sir James Jeans' article "Shall We Ever Travel to the Planets?" with "We Shall Travel to the Planets"—began a regular column, "To the Planets," while John Russell Fearn, Maurice Hugi and W. P. Cockroft supplied some of the more readable fiction. Cockroft's story "Cataclysm," in November 12, was especially popular, and a sequel, "City of Mars," was demanded.

However, serials like "Death Broadcasts" and "The Black Vultures" remained the more standard fare, and though these appealed to a certain market, Dimmock confirmed that "demand was not sufficient to give us confidence for the future."[4]

Scoops ended with the twentieth issue, dated June 23, 1934. Three years later Pearson's issued a 160–page large-size volume, *The Boys' World of Adventure*, reprinting five stories from *Scoops* along with Serge Drigin's illustrations, plus eight new stories. But that was the end of the experiment.

Notes

1. Walter Gillings, "The Impatient Dreamers, Part 4: Science Fiction Weakly," *Vision of Tomorrow* 4 (January 1970):30.

2. [Haydn Dimmock], "Here's a Scoop," *Scoops*, February 10, 1934, p. 15.

3. Haydn Dimmock, letter to Walter Gillings.

4. Ibid.

Information Sources

BIBLIOGRAPHY:
Gillings, Walter. "Science Fiction Weakly." *Vision of Tomorrow* 4 (January 1970):30ff.
Nicholls. *Encyclopedia.*
Tuck.
INDEX SOURCES: IBSF; SFM.
REPRINT SOURCES:
  Derivative Anthology: The Boys' World of Adventure (London: Pearson, 1937), no
      editor credited, contains five stories from *Scoops* plus eight previously unpublished
      but possibly bought for the magazine originally.
LOCATION SOURCES: None known.

Publication History

TITLE: *Scoops.*
VOLUME DATA: Volume 1, Number 1, February 10, 1934–Volume 1, Number 20,
      June 23, 1934. Weekly. Total run: 20 issues.
PUBLISHER: C. A. Pearson, Ltd., London.
EDITOR: Haydn Dimmock.
FORMAT: Tabloid (12½" x 9¼"), 32 pp.
PRICE: 2d.

Mike Ashley

THE SCORPION

Published in 1939 shortly after *The Octopus*,* *The Scorpion* continued the adventures of the Skull Killer against the evil, purple-eyed minions of a master criminal, the Scorpion. While both novels featured different villains (though evidently they began with the same villain who was changed by editorial demands), they featured the same hero and the same supporting characters. However, neither story made any reference to the other, and they were mutually independent. The novel, "Satan's Incubators," was again written by Norvell Page using the Randolph Craig house name. Again, it was marginal SF, with a supercriminal trying to take over New York City through a reign of terror. As with *The Octopus*, the novel was fast-paced and easy reading but had glaring gaps in logic. Filled with violence and torture, "Satan's Incubator" was the type of story that gave the pulps, and indirectly SF, a bad name for years to come.

The Scorpion featured three short stories in the weird-menace tradition by Wyatt Blassingame, Donald Dale and William Hines. All read as if they had been scheduled for one of Popular Publications' other horror magazines (*Horror Stories** or *Terror Tales**) and were used as space-fillers in *The Scorpion*. There was also an editorial, "When the Scorpion Strikes," a short illustrated feature, "Horrors of History," and "The Crypt," which previewed things to come, somewhat abortively, as there were no more issues.

Information Sources

BIBLIOGRAPHY:
Tuck.
Weinberg, Robert. *Pulp Classics 11*. Oak Lawn, Ill.: Pulp Press, 1976.
INDEX SOURCES: SFM; Tuck; Weinberg, Robert, and Lohr McKinstry, *The Hero Pulp Index*, Evergreen, Colo.: Opar Press, 1971 (lead novel only).
REPRINT SOURCES:
  Reprint Novels: *Satan's Incubator* was included in *Pulp Classics 11* (Oak Lawn, Ill.: Pulp Press, 1976).
LOCATION SOURCES: San Francisco Academy of Comic Art.

Publication History

TITLE: *The Scorpion*.
VOLUME DATA: Volume 1, Number 1, April 1939.
PUBLISHER: Popular Publications, New York.
EDITORS: Ejler and Edith Jakobssen.
FORMAT: Pulp, 112 pp.
PRICE: 10¢.

Robert Weinberg

SCREEN CHILLS AND MACABRE STORIES

Screen Chills and Macabre Stories was one of the first magazines to capitalize on the popularity of the horror and monster films of the 1950s, beating *Famous Monsters of Filmland* into print by a couple of months. The idea behind the magazine was a good one: to bring the best of the current crop of horror films to the readers in story form, together with new macabre stories. The first and only issue featured uncredited fictionalizations of *Dead That Walk* and *I Was a Teenage Werewolf*, both of which were released in November 1957. Both stories were accompanied by stills from the films.

What makes the issue a collector's item today, however, is the third story, "Them Ones" by Robert Bloch, which comes within the purview of his Lovecraftian tales. Presented as a new story, this was actually an unauthorized reprint of his 1951 *Weird Tales** story, "Notebook Found in a Deserted House."

Although further issues were promised, no more appeared. It is probable that the magazine suffered from distribution problems. It was distributed by the company that published *Phantom,** and it may have been advantageous at the time to concentrate more on the all-fiction title. It is equally possible that Leslie Syddall edited this magazine as well, though there were no credits.

Information Sources

BIBLIOGRAPHY:
Tuck.
INDEX SOURCES: MT.

REPRINT SOURCES: None known.
LOCATION SOURCES: None known.

Publication History

TITLE: *Screen Chills and Macabre Stories.*
VOLUME DATA: Volume 1, Number 1, undated (probably November 1957).
PUBLISHER: Pep Publishers, Croydon, Surrey.
EDITOR: None credited. May have been Leslie Syddall.
FORMAT: Small Pulp (9¾" x 7½") (saddle-stapled), 32 pp. (numbered from 12 to 42).
PRICE: 1/6d.

Mike Ashley

SECRET AGENT 'X'

Secret Agent 'X', its first issue dated 1934, was one of the early American single-character magazines and the only one published by Periodical House to run more than a single issue. Each number featured a novel-length exploit of Secret Agent 'X', a nameless crime fighter whose principal talent was his ability to assume any disguise successfully, whether that involved impersonating someone or creating fictitious identities, of which he possessed several. A former World War I intelligence officer, he was employed by the United States government after the war to stamp out crime. Despite his title, partially inspired by the X-shaped wound on his torso, Secret Agent 'X' is not so much a secret agent as an officially unrecognized crime fighter. He is assisted by several aides: Jim Hobart, Harvey Bates and a reporter, Betty Dale. His nominal superior is Ronald Holme, otherwise known as K9.

Although the Secret Agent 'X' novels were published under the by-line Brant House, there were several writers who used that name, principally Paul Chadwick, Emile C. Tepperman and G. T. Fleming-Roberts. Throughout its run, the Secret Agent 'X' novels were brooding, atmospheric stories in which physical horror predominated. While the authors often created situations which implied supernatural horror, these were almost always explained away in rational terms. However, a number of stories legitimately belong to the fantasy and science fiction fields. "Devils of Darkness" (March 1935) involves attacks on New York City by criminals who possess a ray that temporarily blinds anyone exposed to it. In "Ringmaster of Doom" (November 1935), a criminal named Thoth transforms ordinary people into Neanderthals and sets them on a crime rampage. Most of these novels, such as "Brand of the Metal Maiden" (January 1936), "Horde of the Damned" (October 1935) and "Plague of the Golden Death" (December 1937), feature ghoulish murder methods in which people die, variously, by accelerated aging, petrification or the rapid softening of their skeletons.

By and large, *Secret Agent 'X'* started as something of a crime/horror magazine whose secondary features included Frederick C. Davis' occult-powered investigator, Ravenwood, but by later issues the stories concerned detectives and G-men almost exclusively. Most of the supporting stories were by Norman A. Daniels, Emile C. Tepperman and G. T. Fleming-Roberts.

Information Sources

BIBLIOGRAPHY:

Johnson, Tom. "Lady X." *Age of the Unicorn* 6 (February 1980).

―――. "The Leopard Lady." *Doc Savage Club Reader* 8, (1979).

―――. "Madame Death." *Doc Savage Club Reader* 11, (1980). The same issue also includes Tom Johnson's "Erlik, Daughter of Satan."

―――, and Will Murray. *Secret Agent 'X'—A History*. Chicago: R. Weinberg, 1980.

Murray, Will. "The Unknown Brant Houses." In *Secret Agent 'X'* (facsimile of September 1934 issue). Greenwood, Mass.: Odyssey, 1977.

Tonik, Albert. "Tracing Through the Torture Trust." *Cloak and Pistol* 1 (Fall 1981).

Tuck.

Ven, These. "Solution for 'X'." *Xenophile* No. 42 (September/October 1979).

INDEX SOURCES: Robert Weinberg's and Lohr McKinstry's *The Hero Pulp Index* (Oak Forest, Ill.: 1974) and Johnson and Murray's *Secret Agent 'X'—A History* (Chicago: R. Weinberg, 1980) both index the lead novels; Tuck.

REPRINT SOURCES:

Reprint Novels: The following seven novels (with original publication dates) were all issued by Corinth Books, San Diego, in 1966: *The Torture Trust* (February 1934), *Servants of the Skull* (November 1934), *Curse of the Mandarin's Fan* (February 1938), *City of the Living Dead* (June 1934), *The Death Torch Terror* (April 1934), *Octopus of Crime* (September 1934), *The Sinister Scourge* (January 1935). Also *Brand of the Metal Maiden* ([orig. January 1936] Oak Forest: Weinberg, 1974) and *Octopus of Crime* (West Newton, Mass.: Odyssey, 1977).

LOCATION SOURCES: San Francisco Academy of Comic Art.

Publication History

TITLE: *Secret Agent 'X'* throughout, but the subtitle varied as follows: "The Man of a Thousand Faces" (February 1934–October 1935), "Detective Mysteries" (November 1935–October 1936), "G-Man Action Adventures" (December 1936–April 1937), "G-Man Action Mysteries" (June–December 1937), "Detective Mysteries" (February 1938–March 1939).

VOLUME DATA: Volume 1, Number 1, February 1934–Volume 14, Number 3, March 1939. Six issues per volume for first six volumes, thereafter four issues per volume. Monthly (but no issue for February to April 1936); bi-monthly, June 1936–June 1938; quarterly, September 1938–March 1939. Total run: 41 issues.

PUBLISHER: Periodical House, New York.

EDITORS: Rose Wynn to 1937; Harry Widmer thereafter.

FORMAT: Pulp, 128 pp., later dropping to 96 pp.

PRICE: 10¢.

Will Murray

SELECTED SCIENCE-FICTION MAGAZINE

By the time that *Selected Science-Fiction Magazine* commenced in 1955, Malian Press had been producing the monthly paperback series *American Science Fiction [Magazine]** for over three years and must have felt confident that it was sufficiently well established in the field to branch out.

Unlike *American Science Fiction, SSFM* featured its title unmistakably on the cover, and the issues were visibly numbered, if not dated; but the thirty-two-page flimsy digest format was the same, and it was simply no competition for the many British magazines (mostly abridged versions of the better-known U.S. originals) on sale in Australia in 1955, all of which were clearly better values. Had *Selected* appeared a few years earlier it might have worked, but both *Selected* and the original series ended abruptly after five months.

All five of the featured stories in *SSFM* had appeared in the Year's Best Science Fiction Novels series edited by Everett Bleiler and Ted Dikty (New York: F. Fell. 1952–1954). "Flight to Forever" by Poul Anderson was perhaps the most outstanding and filled the second issue completely; but all were good contemporary works by recognized writers. Artwork was limited to the covers by Stanley Pitt, which were quite appealing.

The Malian Press publications stand out among the Australian ventures using imported material as the most worthwhile to the reader in the standard of fiction presented. Unfortunately, they were on too small a scale to encourage support.

Information Sources

BIBLIOGRAPHY:
Nicholls. *Encyclopedia*.
Tuck.
INDEX SOURCES: ASFI.
REPRINT SOURCES: None known.
LOCATION SOURCES: Futurian Society of Sydney Library.

Publication History

TITLE: *Selected Science-Fiction Magazine*.
VOLUME DATA: All issues undated. Number 1, [May 1955]–Number 5, [September 1955]. Monthly. Total run: 5 issues.
PUBLISHER: Malian Press, Sydney.
EDITOR: Not identified.
FORMAT: Digest (saddle-stapled), 32 pp.
PRICE: 9d.

Graham Stone

SF IMPULSE

See IMPULSE.

THE SHADOW

The Shadow, first published in 1931, was the first of the trend-setting pulp magazines built around a single character, much in the way that the earlier dime novels had featured the continuing adventures of such characters as Nick Carter and Buffalo Bill. Indeed, the magazine owes its origins to the natural evolution of the dime novel. The beginnings of the single-character pulps were in the dime novels of the nineteenth century. These cheaply printed adventure novels were developed originally as spinoffs of the literary newspapers but soon developed into a major market, selling to the general populace. Beadle and Adams was the first dime novel publisher, but it was soon pressed by Street and Smith. Favorite characters included Ned Buntline, Deadwood Dick and Nick Carter, and there was even a regular science fiction series devoted to the adventures and inventions of Frank Reade, Jr. Each book was cheaply printed on wood pulp paper, featured a color cover and contained a complete novel selling for five or ten cents.

When Frank A. Munsey developed the pulp magazine market (see *The Argosy**) the lessons of the dime novels were not forgotten. Continued characters were featured in many of the magazines. In fact, it was not uncommon for a pulp of the 1920s to feature five or six different stories, each detailing the latest adventure of a continued character.

One such pulp was *Detective Story Magazine*, published by Street and Smith. Ironically, the magazine had itself evolved from the remnants of its dime-novel *Nick Carter Weekly*. In July 1930 a new radio show was started to help push sales of the magazine. A story from the next issue was read over the air by a narrator known as "The Shadow." It was from that radio show, and narrator Frank Readick, that came the immortal line, "The Shadow Knows."[1]

This experiment in selling pulps by radio proved to be an enormous success, and soon listeners began to ask for "that Shadow magazine" when they really meant *Detective Story*. Realizing that a character so popular was bound to be imitated, Henry Ralston, circulation manager of Street and Smith, acted to protect his character in the easiest way possible. A new magazine was started, *The Shadow*, featuring a complete novel about a mysterious denizen of the night, The Shadow, in his fight against crime. The magazine was launched as a quarterly, and Walter Gibson, a newspaperman, ghostwriter and magician (and former editor of *Tales of Magic and Mystery**) was given the job of writing the first novel as well as several subsequent ones. No one expected much from the magazine, as evidenced by the fact that no new cover was painted for the first issue; instead, an old cover from the Street and Smith warehouse, featuring a Chinaman and his shadow, was used. No matter that Gibson had no such character in his story—a quick rewrite added a Chinese element to the mystery.

The first issue sold out; so did the second. The magazine progressed rapidly from its quarterly schedule to monthly and then twice-monthly, with an incredible twenty-four issues a year, every issue featuring a complete novel about The Shadow. Although the by-line on the lead novels was Maxwell Grant, they were primarily the work of Walter Gibson, who was helped out at times by Theodore Tinsley, Bruce Elliott and even Lester Dent, the legendary chronicler of Doc Savage's escapades.

The first novel, "The Living Shadow," introduced the nebulous, almost supernatural detective whose true identity was unknown, but who often took the identity of millionaire Lamont Cranston. For the first six years of the series, until 1937, The Shadow was a mysterious crime fighter possessing the deductive powers of Sherlock Holmes, the skill of a western gunfighter, and the abilities of a magician. However, Gibson also often invested his character with attributes that verged upon the supernatural. Criminals died when they gazed upon his true face; his ability to sway people and animals was greater than hypnotic, and he often made intuitive leaps that went beyond deduction. Gibson never addressed these matters directly and, after he revealed that The Shadow was World War I spy Kent Allard, in "The Shadow Unmasks" (August 1, 1937), they were entirely forgotten.

While the series belongs overwhelmingly to the detective and mystery genre, Gibson often explored areas of science fiction. One early novel, "Six Men of Evil" (February 15, 1933), is a lost race story in which The Shadow discovers an unknown tribe of Aztecs in Mexico. A later story, "The Devil Monsters" (February 1, 1943), is a fantasy wherein the villain, named Monstradamus, summons up dinosaurs and creatures of mythology to do his bidding.

Most of the science fiction in *The Shadow* involves scientific discoveries perverted to evil ends. "The Black Hush" (August 1, 1933) tells of a ray that blacks out whole cities. Death rays abound in the series, with disintegrating rays of all kinds featuring in "Atoms of Death" (July 15, 1935), "The Sledge-Hammer Crimes" (August 1, 1936), "Double Death" (December 15, 1938) and "The Crime Ray" (September 1, 1939). "The Dark Death" (February 15, 1935) is more novel in that its death ray only kills people with dark skin.[2] "Charg, Monster" (July 1, 1934) is a clever novel of robots controlled by a master criminal, and "The Robot Master" (May 1943) is a less successful variation on that theme.

Other novels containing SF overtones include "The Death Sleep" (October 15, 1934), "The Dead Who Lived" (October 1, 1938), "The Strange Disappearance of Joe Cardona" (November 15, 1936), "The Silent Death" (April 1, 1933), "The Death Giver" (May 15, 1933), "The Green Terror" (January 15, 1941), "Syndicate of Death" (February 1944), "The Thunder King" (June 15, 1941) and "Crime under Cover" (June 1, 1941).

Perhaps the high point of the fantastic as manifested in *The Shadow* was the quartet of novels pitting The Shadow against Shiwan Khan, the supernaturally powered descendant of Genghis Khan. In these stories—"The Golden Master" (September 15, 1939), "Shiwan Khan Returns" (December 1, 1939), "The Invincible Shiwan Khan" (March 1, 1940) and "Masters of Death" (May 15, 1940)—occultism, telepathy, reanimation of the dead, scientific discoveries and a kind of provisional invisibility were all introduced into the mix.

The Shadow was considered a detective pulp by Street and Smith, and the batches of short stories that supported each issue's lead novel were all in that vein, with no SF or fantasy among them. Contributors included Norman Daniels, William G. Bogart, John D. MacDonald, Steve Fisher and Frank Gruber. There were, in addition, several departments, including one on codes, a letter column and a Shadow Club.

When *The Shadow* ended with the Summer 1949 issue, it had published a total of 325 Shadow novels, of which perhaps 25 might be called SF or fantasy. That number is small only in proportion to the amazing quantity of Shadow novels produced by Walter Gibson, but considered alone is no mean SF output for one man. In fact, it was Gibson's use of SF and fantasy elements in *The Shadow* that led to his selection as editor of the short-lived *Fantastic Science Fiction** in 1952.

Notes

1. The first radio Shadow was once believed to be James La Curto, but recent research indicates that it was Frank Readick.
2. Despite what the plot synopsis might imply, this story was decidedly not racist. Street and Smith was the only pulp publisher to go out of its way not to be racist.

Information Sources

BIBLIOGRAPHY:
Eisgruber, Frank, Jr. *Gangland's Doom*. Oak Lawn, Ill.: Weinberg, 1974.
Gibson, Walter B. *The Shadow Scrapbook*. New York: Harcourt Brace, 1979.
Murray, Will. *The Duende History of the Shadow Magazine*. Greenwood, Mass.: Odyssey, 1980.
"Out of the Shadows—Walter Gibson" [Interview]. *Duende* 2 (April 1977).
Sampson, Robert. *The Night Master*. Chicago: Pulp Press, 1982.
Tuck.
INDEX SOURCES: No complete index exists, but the lead novels are listed in *The Hero Pulp Index* by Robert Weinberg (Opar Press, 1971) and *The Duende History of the Shadow Magazine* by Will Murray (Odyssey, 1980), and the full contents of the digest-sized issues are listed in *Monthly Murders* by Michael Cook (Westport, Conn.: Greenwood Press, 1982).
REPRINT SOURCES:
    Novels (Fantasy/SF only): *Charge, Monster* (1977), *The Silent Death* (1978) and *The Death Giver* (1978), all published by Jove Books, New York.
LOCATION SOURCES: Nearly complete set, Street and Smith collections, George Arents Research Library, Syracuse University.

Publication History

TITLE: *The Shadow* (subtitled "A Detective Magazine"), April–July 1931; subtitle amended to "A Detective Monthly" for October and November 1931 issues; *The Shadow Detective Monthly*, December 1931–September 1932; *The Shadow Magazine*, October 1, 1932–August 1, 1937; *The Shadow*, August 15, 1937–January

1947; *Shadow Mystery*, February/March 1947–August/September 1948; *The Shadow*, Fall 1948–Summer 1949.

VOLUME DATA: Volume 1, Number 1, April 1931–Volume 55, Number 1, Summer 1949. Six issues per volume. Quarterly, April and July 1931; monthly, October 1931–September 1932; twice monthly, October 1, 1932–March 1, 1943; monthly, April 1943–December 1946; bi-monthly, January 1947–September 1948; quarterly, Fall 1948–Summer 1949. Total run: 325 issues.

PUBLISHER: Street & Smith, New York.

EDITORS: Frank Blackwell, 1931; Lon Murray, 1931–1932; John L. Nanovic, 1932–1943; Charles Moran, 1943; William de Grouchy, 1944–1946; Babette Rosmond, 1946–1948; William de Grouchy, July–September 1948; Daisy Bacon, Fall 1948–Summer 1949.

FORMAT: Pulp, 128 pp. for all issues except December 1943–September 1948, when digest, 128 pp.

PRICE: 10¢, April 1931–March 1, 1943; 15¢ until February/March 1947; thereafter 25¢.

Will Murray/Robert Weinberg

SHAYOL

One of the most attractive and "professional" of the nonprofessional magazines, *Shayol* grew out of the publisher's previous magazine, *Chacal*.* According to editor/publisher Arnold Fenner and his executive editor, Pat Cadigan, they were concerned that *Chacal* was too closely associated with the Robert E. Howard/swords and sorcery image that it had inherited from *REH: Lone Star Fictioneer*, despite its inclusion of several off-beat fantasy items. *Shayol* was a further step toward reaching a wider audience and presenting material of far greater scope. They also wanted to give their contributors the best possible market in which to appear, and to make a showcase for new talent.

The first issue, dated November 1977, was a good indication of their intent. There was a top-quality story by Howard Waldrop, "Dr. Hudson's Secret Gorilla," which was subsequently nominated for the British Fantasy Society Award for best short story. There was an excerpt from Tom Reamy's then unpublished novel *Blind Voices* entitled "Wonder Show," together with a lengthy interview with Reamy. Lisa Tuttle had a story, "A Piece of Rope," and there were further contributions from Karl Edward Wagner, Michael Bishop, Marc Laidlaw, Jim Fitzpatrick and Steven Utley.

The second issue contained that same blend of quality material, but it was evident that readers would have to wait for the privilege of reading *Shayol*, as it became a highly irregular publication. Indeed, it is a magazine sans schedule, but with every new issue it occludes all other magazines in the field. There were stories by Harlan Ellison and Tom Reamy, poetry by Steve Utley, an interview with Tim Kirk, art portfolios by Robert Haas and Vikki Marshal. Pat Cadigan's story "Death from Exposure" won the 1979 Balrog Award for Best Short Story, and *Shayol* was nominated for a World Fantasy Award in the Special Non-Professional category in 1979.

It was over a year before the third issue appeared, but was worth the wait. Tom Reamy was again present with the story "Blue Eyes" which he had hoped to develop into his second novel before his untimely death. There was fiction from Lisa Tuttle, Steve Utley, Michael Bishop, Tanith Lee, C. J. Cherryh and Howard Waldrop; an interview with Stephen King, plus the, by now expected, fine artwork from the brushes of Clyde Caldwell, Hank Jankus, Stephen Fabian and others. Again *Shayol* was nominated in the nonprofessional categories for both the World Fantasy Award and the Balrog Award.

By now the format for *Shayol* had been fixed. Stunning cover artwork together with beautiful interior illustrations would emblazon features on writers and artists and fiction from a fairly regular stable that included Michael Bishop, Steve Utley, Howard Waldrop and Charles L. Grant. The quality of the fiction was not always high but it was always inventive. Following the fourth issue *Shayol* at last received the World Fantasy Award in the nonprofessional category in 1981.

Maintaining the quality of production in *Shayol* requires not only considerable finances but also a strong editorial and artistic drive. By the fourth issue *Shayol* had achieved all that its editors had set out to achieve. It was also proving very expensive. All the time producing it was enjoyable, the finances could be coped with, but once that urge to produce had gone the lustre faded. Two more issues of *Shayol* appeared, both up to usual standards, and then publisher Arnie Fenner announced that was the end. Gone was that challenge to produce a beautiful magazine. In its place other challenges had risen: Pat Cadigan had turned more to writing, while Arnie Fenner to production and design. A seventh issue of *Shayol* was prepared though as of December 1984 it has not been published. *Shayol* will remain as a landmark, indeed a pinnacle, in the field of semi-professional fantasy magazines.

Information Sources

INDEX SOURCES: ISPF; MT.
REPRINT SOURCES: None known.
LOCATION SOURCES: M.I.T. Science Fiction Library.

Publication History

TITLE: *Shayol*
VOLUME DATA: Volume 1, Number 1, November 1977–Volume 2, Number 2, Winter 1982. Six issues. Irregular. Other issues: February 1978, Summer 1979, Winter 1980 and Winter 1982. (Both issues 5 and 6 were dated Winter 1982, Number 5 issued in January, Number 6 in November.)
PUBLISHER: Flight Unlimited, Kansas City, Missouri (first two issues) moving to Kansas City, Kansas, with issue 3.
EDITOR: Patricia Cadigan.

FORMAT: Slick. Page-count varies: Number 1, 64 pp., 2, 68 pp., 3, 60 pp., 4, 52 pp., 5, 52 pp., 6, 48 pp.
PRICE: $3.00 issues 1–5; $3.95 issue 6.

Gordon Larkin

SHEENA, QUEEN OF THE JUNGLE

Sheena was Fiction House's female counterpart to its Tarzan imitation, Ki-Gor, who appeared regularly in *Jungle Stories*.* Sheena was a blonde jungle goddess, a white woman who was left orphaned in the African jungle upon the death of her father, an explorer. She was subsequently raised by N'bid Ela, witch woman of the Abamas, to be their white queen. Innocent of civilization, Sheena kept the peace between warring tribes and natives and European explorers and settlers.

Originally, Sheena was a comic-book character created in 1938 for Fiction House's *Jungle Stories* counterpart, *Jumbo Comics*. The firm maintained many comic-book versions of its established pulp titles, most of which, by the time *Sheena* was published in 1951, were more popular than their older sister publications. Usually, pulp characters were adapted into comic form, but with *Sheena*, the reverse was true. The first and only issue of *Sheena* contained not one lead Sheena novelette, as was the case with the Ki-Gor tales in *Jungle Stories*, but three. The titles were "The Slave-Brand of Sleman Bin Ali," "Killer's Kraal" and "Sargasso of Lost Safaris," all by-lined James Anson Buck, an obvious pen name. Most probably Fiction House's intention was to publish a regular *Sheena* magazine with one Sheena novelette per issue, but, after having several such stories written, the plans were changed and the three stories (along with some others) were packaged as a one-shot magazine. Three years later a fourth Sheena novelette, "Sword of Gimshai" by Joseph W. Musgrave, appeared in the final issue of *Jungle Stories*, dated Spring 1954.

The Sheena stories are only marginally fantasy, and only in regard to their premise of a white woman raised in the African jungle who becomes a friend to animals and natives and an enemy to criminals.

Information Sources

BIBLIOGRAPHY:
Carr, Nick. "Mistress of Violence." *Xenophile* No. 22 (March/April 1976).
Tuck.
INDEX SOURCES: None known.
REPRINT SOURCES: None known.
LOCATION SOURCES: None known.

Publication History

TITLE: *Sheena, Queen of the Jungle.*
VOLUME DATA: Volume 1, Number 1, Spring 1951.
PUBLISHER: Glen-Kel Publishing Co., Stamford, Connecticut, a subsidiary of Fiction
    House, New York.
EDITOR: Not stated, but probably Jerome Bixby under Malcolm Reiss.
FORMAT: Pulp, 96 pp.
PRICE: 25¢.

Will Murray

SHOCK

There have been three magazines that have employed *Shock* as the main part
of their title. The first, simply called *Shock*, saw three, thin pulp-sized issues in
1948, but concentrated on off-trail weird-mystery stories and is of no interest to
the fantasy fan. Similarly, *Shock Mystery Tales*, which saw a few irregular issues
between 1961 and 1962, and which was an indirect successor to the magazine
covered below, was, like *Web Terror Stories*, a throwback to the terror pulps
of the 1930s.

The only one that concerns us is the *Shock* that saw three bi-monthly issues
during 1960. All fiction, most of the contents were reprints but were well received. Selections came from all sources and included Theodore Sturgeon's
"Bianca's Hands," Henry Kuttner's "Graveyard Rats," Stanley Ellin's "Specialty of the House," John Collier's "Green Thoughts" and Ray Bradbury's
"The Emissary" as well as "Yours Truly, Jack the Ripper" by Robert Bloch,
"Moon-Face" by Jack London, "A Bottomless Grave" by Ambrose Bierce
and, perhaps inevitably, "The Monkey's Paw" by W. W. Jacobs.

The editor remained anonymous, always being represented both on the cover
and interior as a Cro-Magnon-like beast-man, with his pet tarantula, Lulubel.
A strain of sardonic humor ran throughout the editorials and introductory blurbs
for the three issues. This was also reflected in the choice of new fiction, which
included stories by Robert Bloch (one published under the alias Will Folke),
Avram Davidson, Edward D. Hoch and Miriam Allen deFord.

Shock had a companion mystery magazine called *Keyhole Mystery*, and both
were companions to the successful nonfiction magazine *Space World*, edited by
Otto Binder.

Just why *Shock* failed after three issues is not known, but it is after the third
issue that circulation figures for the first issue are fully known, and, as with so
many magazines, they were probably too low to support a magazine that relied
on sales and not advertising for its revenue.

Information Sources

BIBLIOGRAPHY:

Tuck.

INDEX SOURCES: Cook, Michael L., *Monthly Murders*, Westport, Conn.: Greenwood Press, 1982 (contains issue and author index); MIT; MT; SFM.

REPRINT SOURCES: None known.

LOCATION SOURCES: M.I.T. Science Fiction Library; University of California–Los Angeles Library (Vol. 1, Nos. 1, 3).

Publication History

TITLE: *Shock*, subtitled "The Magazine of Terrifying Tales."

VOLUME DATA: Volume 1, Number 1, May 1960–Volume 1, Number 3, September 1960. Bi-monthly. Total run: 3 issues. (Note: *Shock Mystery Tales* continued the volume numbering with at least four issues, Volume 2, Number 1, December 1961–Volume 2, Number 4, July 1962, published by Pontiac Publishing, New York.)

PUBLISHER: Winston Publications, Inc., New York.

EDITOR: Not identified within issue.

FORMAT: Digest, 128 pp.

PRICE: 35¢.

Mike Ashley

SKYWORLDS

Of all the new magazines that appeared (and disappeared) during the 1970s, *Skyworlds* was, without any shadow of a doubt, the worst. A digest magazine of only eighty pages, the first issue, dated November 1977, contained five stories, all of which had first appeared in either the February or August 1951 issues of *Marvel Science Fiction (Marvel Science Stories*)*. Some of the original illustrations were also reprinted, but elsewhere—including the cover—publicity photographs from NASA were inserted, often quite incongruously. The stories bore an impressive set of by-lines: "The Last Spaceman" by Lester del Ray (*sic*), "This Joe" by A. E. van Vogt, "Seed" by Raymond F. Jones, "Skag with the Queer Head" by Murray Leinster and "Trans-Plutonian" by Milton Lesser. The stories, however, were far from their authors' best output and had become badly dated in the intervening twenty-six years. Newcomers to the field, however, not appreciating the origins of the stories, must have had a distorted view of the contents.

Skyworlds was published by Humorama Inc., under the management of Abraham Goodman. Abraham and his brother Martin had been the publishers of *Marvel Science Stories* back in 1937, as well as of other pulps such as *Uncanny Tales** and *Mystery Tales*, and had later established the lucrative Marvel Comics line. *Skyworlds* was an odd throwback to the early days and was clearly produced by men who had no knowledge of or respect for the SF market. The editor was Jeffrey Stevens, who maintained that "the stories were choice bits of nostalgia, and written so that the average reader interested in sf would have an easy understanding."[1]

The issues continued to appear on a quarterly basis. The February 1978 issue reprinted from the May 1952 *Marvel*, May 1978 from the November 1950 issue (although it did include Harold Lawlor's "Mayaya's Little Green Men" from *Weird Tales*,* an indication, as promised by the editor, that he was expanding his sources). All stories were reproduced directly from the original magazines, complete with illustrations and blurbs. Production was poor, although the editor was "certain that an improvement will be found in the August 1978 issue."[2] That issue was the worst of them all. Apart from two further stories from the November 1950 *Marvel* and a number of fillers, the issue was dominated by an appalling comic strip, "Hell on Astra 6," whose perpetrators remained sensibly anonymous.

Mercifully, it was the last issue. "The acceptance was disappointing," confessed Abraham Goodman, "and with the extra high cost of publishing today, we saw no way to continue."[3]

Normally it is a sad day when a science fiction magazine folds. In the case of *Skyworlds* it was a sad day when it appeared. That it could have survived for four issues is a poor reflection on the public that could sustain it and yet not support such magazines as *Cosmos Science Fiction and Fantasy Magazine** or *The Haunt of Horror*.*

Notes

1. Jeff Stevens, private correspondence, March 1978.
2. Ibid.
3. Abraham Goodman, private correspondence, May 1979.

Information Sources

BIBLIOGRAPHY:
Nicholls. *Encyclopedia.*
INDEX SOURCES: NESFA–VI; SFM.
REPRINT SOURCES: None known.
LOCATION SOURCES: M.I.T. Science Fiction Library.

Publication History

TITLE: *Skyworlds* on indicia of first issue, but *Sky Worlds* on cover (and in private correspondence). Subtitle was "Classics in Science Fiction" on first issue and "Marvels in Science Fiction" thereafter. Title misprinted *Skywords* on indicia of May 1978 issue.

VOLUME DATA: Volume 1, Number 1, November 1977–Volume 1, Number 4, August 1978. Quarterly. Total run: 4 issues.

PUBLISHER: Humorama Inc., Rockville Centre, New York.
EDITOR: Jeff Stevens (not identified within issues).
FORMAT: Digest (saddle-stapled), 80 pp.
PRICE: 75¢.

Mike Ashley

SOMETHING ELSE

It is rare for a science fiction/fantasy magazine to aim for an exclusive image, though some have had exclusiveness thrust upon them. *Something Else*, first published in 1980, has a delightfully carefree air of being unconcerned with worldly success that could just succeed. In any event, it forms an antidote to the commercialism rampant elsewhere.

Charles Partington, the editor, is also printer and publisher of *Something Else*. He can therefore afford to some extent to consult his own tastes. He says, ''I imagine there are very few editors outside the amateur press field who are able to indulge their personal tastes completely, without having to keep an anxious eye on distribution and sales figures. I have that freedom—and what a delicious freedom it is—or I would never have considered producing the magazine.''

Partington is quite well known in England as a writer, with some of his best stories appearing in *New Writings in SF*, although his name does not appear in either Tuck's *Encyclopedia of Science Fiction and Fantasy* or in R. Reginald's *Science Fiction and Fantasy Literature*. With his partner, Harry Nadler, he earlier issued a one-shot semi-professional magazine, *Alien Worlds*.*

Something Else was designed to fill a gap in British SF publishing. Following the demise of such intermittently brilliant magazines as *New Worlds** and *Science Fiction Monthly*,* there have been few outlets for indigenous British stories. Even the somewhat staid *New Writings in SF* is now defunct. To a large degree *Something Else* has been overtaken in this respect by *Interzone*.*

What *Something Else* has to offer, judging by its first issue, is good-quality production, a fashionably ''period'' presentation, and honorable intentions toward authors and artists as well as the readers. The authors present include Michael Moorcock (a story featuring Jerry Cornell), M. John Harrison (an extract from a forthcoming novel), Brian W. Aldiss, and the editor, with an interesting macabre story, ''Nosferatu's Ape.'' Artwork is by James Cawthorn, Eddie Jones and others.

The intention was that the magazine would run quarterly, but after the two issues labeled Spring 1980 and Winter 1980, printing difficulties intervened. Production of the magazine was relegated to a spare-time hobby and it would be over three years before the next issue appeared.

The most interesting feature of *SE*, and the one that promises best for the future, is that it continues a well-defined indigenous tradition. Short-lived recent

British magazines such as *Ad Astra** and *Vertex** have tended to throw away past developments and go for cranky new prescriptions. *SE* continues along the lines of John Carnell's *Science Fantasy** and *New Writings*, with a dash of the yeast of *New Worlds* for buoyancy. This seems to be the prescription which offers best hopes for successful stories. The first two issues were well received on a small scale.

Part of the unity of *SE* lies in the way the editors themselves carry through most of the processes. The pasteups, negatives, color separation, plates, printing and finishing are all their own work. William Morris would have been proud of them. He would probably have enjoyed most of the contents too.

Information Sources

INDEX SOURCES: MT.
REPRINT SOURCES: None known.
LOCATION SOURCES: None known.

Publication History

TITLE: *Something Else*.
VOLUME DATA: Number 1, Spring 1980. Number 2, Winter 1980. Number 3, Spring 1984.
PUBLISHER: Pan Visuals, Manchester, England.
EDITOR: Charles Partington.
FORMAT: Slick, issues 1–2, 48 pp., issue 3, 52 pp.
PRICE: Issues 1–2, 90p., issue 3 £1.50. (U.S. price $2.50, all issues.)

Brian W. Aldiss

SORCERER'S APPRENTICE

The Sorcerer's Apprentice, like *Ares*, is a fantasy wargaming magazine that contains a fair quota of fiction and fantasy-oriented articles. The fiction has been both new and reprint, and has included a steady reprinting of the Dilvish stories by Roger Zelazny, together with a new adventure, "Garden of Blood" (Summer 1979). Other issues contained new stories, "The Squire's Tale" by Tanith Lee (Summer 1980) and Manly Wade Wellman's new John the Balladeer story, "Can These Bones Live?" (Summer 1981).

A slim but very attractive magazine, *SA* places a necessary emphasis on features related to wargaming but has proved a valuable new market for fantasy fiction and artwork.

Information Sources

INDEX SOURCES: None known.
REPRINT SOURCES: None known.
LOCATION SOURCES: None known.

Publication History

TITLE: *The Sorcerer's Apprentice*.
VOLUME DATA: Number 1, Winter 1978– . Quarterly. Issues 9 and 10 combined as
    double issue, Spring 1981.
PUBLISHER: Flying Buffalo, Inc., P.O. Box 1467, Scottsdale, Arizona.
EDITOR: Ken St. Andre.
FORMAT: Slick, 32 pp. (issue 9/10, 64 pp.).
PRICE: $2.00, issues 1–4; thereafter $2.25 [double-issue 9/10, $3.50].

Mike Ashley

SPACE ADVENTURES

Space Adventures was one of two reprint magazines published by Sol Cohen
that had no chance to evolve (the other was *Strange Fantasy**). Instead, it
appeared, fully formed, with issue Number 9 in the winter of 1970. Keen eyes
would have noticed that the banner at the top of every even page, however, read
S-F Adventure Classics, and it did not take long to deduce that *Space Adventures*
was a continuation of the former magazine of that title, which had already seen
eight issues.

What had apparently happened was that the original *Science Fiction Classics**
had been the brainchild of Herb Lehrman and had kept a form of independence
from Cohen's other magazines by being allotted a separate special imprint and
being assembled by Lehrman at his own home. Lehrman left to pursue other
matters in 1968, however, and Cohen, rather than continue *Science Fiction
Classics*, first varied the title to *Science Fiction Adventure Classics* to absorb it
into his fold, and then changed the title to *Space Adventures*, with a concurrent
change in policy to reprinting stories from the Ray Palmer period of *Amazing
Stories'** history.

This was fine for three issues; then, presumably following the success of an
annual and a yearbook, Cohen decided that more mileage could be gained from
the *Science Fiction Adventure Classics* title, and he relaunched it with the twelfth
issue. Since there was also a *Space Adventures* 12, there was now no alternative
but to consider the two magazines as independent entities.

In the event, *SA* saw only two more issues. Sales must have indicated that it
was no longer viable, and it was dropped. Cohen thereafter concentrated on only
two reprint magazines (see *Thrilling Science Fiction**).

SA is of little interest to anyone other than the completist collector. All the
stories come from the Palmer days and are of little value, though a few are
superficially interesting. These are mostly from the late 1940s and include early
stories by Mack Reynolds and Kris Neville, and a surprisingly good example
by Paul W. Fairman, "Strange Blood" (from the March 1952 *Amazing*, under
Howard Browne). The original illustrations are also reprinted, which affords an

opportunity to see some of Virgil Finlay's work. On the whole, though, the issues are unmemorable, and it is better to seek out the original issues of the parent magazines than these meager offsprings.

Information Sources

BIBLIOGRAPHY:
Nicholls. *Encyclopedia.*
INDEX SOURCES: ISFM–II; NESFA; SFM.
REPRINT SOURCES: None known.
LOCATION SOURCES: California State University–Fullerton, Special Collections; Eastern New Mexico University, Golden Library (No. 9, Winter 1970–No. 12, Winter 1970; No. 14, Summer 1971); Massachusetts Institute of Technology, MIT Science Fiction Society; San Francisco Academy of Comic Art, Science Fiction Room; Texas A&M University Library, Special Collections; Temple University, Paley Library, Paskow Science Fiction Collection (Nos. 9, 10, 11); Toronto Public Libraries, Spaced Out Library; University of Kansas, Spencer Research Library (Nos. 9–10, 12–14).

Publication History

TITLE: *Space Adventures* (on the first two issues (*Classics*) is added as an afterthought).
VOLUME DATA: Number 9, Winter 1970–Number 14, Summer 1971. No issues 1–8 (see *Science Fiction Classics*). Quarterly (but no Fall 1970 issue). Total run: 6 issues.
PUBLISHER: Ultimate Publishing Co., Flushing, New York.
EDITOR: Sol Cohen (not identified in issues).
FORMAT: Digest, 128 pp.
PRICE: 50¢, issues 9–12 (Winter 1970–Winter 1970/71); thereafter, 60¢.

Mike Ashley

SPACE AND TIME

It is rare for a fan magazine devoted almost entirely to fiction to have a long life. In the SF field the availability of professional SF in many forms is sufficient for most readers, and few will continually support a magazine of fan fiction for more than perhaps one or two sample issues. This lethargy soon affects the editor, who in turn finds new avenues for his efforts. The weird fiction field fares marginally better because of the general lack of other markets.

Space and Time is therefore something of an anomaly. It is an amateur magazine containing predominantly fiction, and it has been published for two decades. For most of that time it has been on a regular schedule, quarterly and even bimonthly. It started in early 1966 when three high school students, John Eiche, Larry Lee and Gordon Linzner, purchased a second-hand mimeograph and, with Nestor Jaremko, put out the first issue, crudely printed, as a showcase for their stories (and those of friends who could be persuaded to contribute). After two years, active interest in producing *S&T* waned in all except Linzner, who had by then discovered fandom at large and was receiving contributions from strangers by mail.

Although early issues suffered from poor artwork, presentation soon improved with work by Clyde Caldwell, Jim Garrison, Gene Day and others. The regular schedules prompted interest from both aspiring and professional writers, and by 1974 Linzner was making nominal payments for stories and artwork. Recently Linzner has retrenched to a twice-yearly schedule to allow for greater concentration on each issue. Circulation is low (between 400 and 500 copies), but *S&T* nevertheless remains an impressive showcase for developing writers and artists and for off-beat stories that professional magazines avoid.

Writers who have appeared in *S&T* include Charles de Lint, Janet Fox, Wayne Hooks, Richard K. Lyon, the late David Madison, Ardath Mayhar, Andrew J. Offutt, Jessica Amanda Salmonson, Charles R. Saunders, Darrell Schweitzer, David C. Smith (first publication), Steve Sneyd, Steve Rasnic Tem, Richard L. Tierney, and Eric Vinicoff and Marcia Martin. Many of these owe much to *S&T* for providing a regular market for their experimental writing; no professional magazine could afford to maintain such a forum. *S&T* also has a lively letter column where critics pull no punches in their praise or condemnation of stories.

No better example of the success of *S&T* can be cited than by referring to the anthology *Swords Against Darkness III* (New York: Zebra Books, 1978). Although the cover boldly claims "Never Before Published!" three of the stories had previously appeared in *S&T*. The editor, Andrew Offutt, explained what happened:

> I only just discovered it in April of '77 . . . and immediately obtained all of its then forty-four issues I could (thirty-eight). I read everything in them while appreciating the whole lot of interior art. Three stories were outstanding: different. They deserve wider readership. (So do others in *S&T*, but they aren't hf [heroic fantasy].) Hence one day all three of those guys opened their mail to find Surprises: letters asking if they'd mind terribly selling their stories professionally for ducal sums.

Further stories from *S&T* made their way into the next volume of *Swords Against Darkness*, and that volume also carried Gordon Linzner's first professional appearance, "The Ballad of Borrell."

While the SF field does not need to be saturated with regular fan magazines, *S&T* shows that not only is there room for at least one such publication, but that it can be a yellow brick road to prodom.

Information Sources

INDEX SOURCES: ISPF; ISPF–2; MT.
REPRINT SOURCES: None known.
LOCATION SOURCES: M.I.T. Science Fiction Library.

Publication History

TITLE: *Space and Time*.

VOLUME DATA: Number 1, Spring 1966– . Latest issue as of writing, Number 67, Winter 1984/5. Quarterly, Nos. 1–17, although schedule only maintained in 1972. Issues dated as follows: 2, Fall 67; 3, Spring 68; 4, Winter 68; 5, Spring 69; 6, Summer 69; 7, August 69; 8, February 70; 9, July 70; 10, March 71; 11, April 71; 12, June 71; 13, September 71; 14, February 72; 15, May 72; 16, August 72; 17, November 72. Bi-monthly, Nos. 18–45, May 1973–November 1977; quarterly, Nos. 46–60, January 1978–July 1981; bi-annual, No. 61, Winter 1981/82–.

PUBLISHER: Gordon Linzner, New York; partnered by Nestor Jaremko, John Eiche and Larry Lee on issue 1, by Nestor Jaremko on issue 2, and by Rebecca Linzner, issues 9–14.

EDITOR: Gordon Linzner.

FORMAT: 8 1/2" x 11" (stapled), issues 1–4; Digest (saddle-stapled), issues 5– . Pages as follows: 1, 20 pp.; 2, 54 pp.; 3, 28 pp.; 4, 24 pp.; 5–10, 20 pp.; 11–44, 40 pp.; 45–60, 60 pp.; 61– , 120 pp.

PRICE: 1, 35¢; 2–4, 50¢; 5–10, 25¢; 11–20, 50¢; 21–27, 60¢; 28–37, 75¢; 38–44, $1.00; 45–52, $1.50; 53–60, $2.00; 61– , $4.00.

Mike Ashley/Gordon Linzner

SPACE—FACT AND FICTION

One of the many Gerald Swan semi-reprint magazines, *Space—Fact and Fiction*, large-size with only thirty-two pages, ran for eight issues in 1954. All the fiction in the fifth and eighth issues was reprinted, predominantly from 1941/1942 issues of *Future Fiction** and *Science Fiction Quarterly.** Only eight new stories appeared, of which one—"Forced Landing on Elvarista," by Edwy Searles Brooks under the alias Reginald Browne, in the first issue—deserves serious consideration as the worst SF story ever written. Other contributors included John Russell Fearn, John Brody and John Craig under various pseudonyms. The magazine is of minor interest only.

Information Sources

BIBLIOGRAPHY:
Nicholls. *Encyclopedia*.
Tuck.
INDEX SOURCES: IBSF; Tuck.
REPRINT SOURCES: None known.
LOCATION SOURCES: None known.

Publication History

TITLE: *Space—Fact and Fiction*.

VOLUME DATA: Volume numbering included on last two issues only. Last four issues undated. Number 1, March 1954–Volume 1, Number 8, [October 1954]. Monthly. Total run: 8 issues.

PUBLISHER: Gerald G. Swan, London.
EDITOR: Not identified.
FORMAT: Small Pulp, 32 pp.
PRICE: 6d.

Mike Ashley

SPACE SCIENCE FICTION

In 1952 John Raymond, chiefly a publisher of "girlie" magazines, was advised by one of his distributors that there was a rising wave of SF magazines that he might do well to cash in on. Fortunately for the world of SF, Lester del Rey, through his agent, heard of Raymond's intentions and at length became editor of a new magazine, *Space Science Fiction*. Because of del Rey, *SSF* became one of the better SF magazines of the boom years, and also because of del Rey and his principles, it was one of the short-lived titles as well.

Although *SSF* later acquired three companion magazines, it remained the prestige publication of the group, aimed at a discerning and modern (that is, postwar) readership. In his first editorial del Rey emphasized that the title did not mean that the magazine would deliver a monotonous diet of space fiction, although he agreed that "there are as many stories to be written of man against space as there are worlds out there waiting for us." He took the broadest definition of "space," "extension in all directions," as the key to the magazine's contents, even leaving the door open for an occasional fantasy to appear (although the later companion *Fantasy Magazine** became the forum for these). "Our sole aim," del Rey further specified, "will be to bring you a varied selection of first-rate fiction, and our only taboo will be against dullness," and by and large del Rey kept his word.

The first issue led with del Rey's fast-action story of psi powers, "Pursuit"; also included were Isaac Asimov's "Youth" and Henry Kuttner's humorous "The Ego Machine," one of his inimitable treatments of robots.

Another del Rey story, "Moon-Blind," led the second issue, this time under his alias Erik van Lhin. It told of the first moon landing in 1948 and of the hero's return to an Earth that knew nothing about it. Of special significance in the second issue, however, was the publication of "The God in the Bowl" by Robert E. Howard, the first of the new Conan discoveries, slightly edited by L. Sprague de Camp. The deluge of further Conan stories seems unstoppable, and this initial magazine publication is of further interest because de Camp introduces the story with his own notes on the discovery of the manuscript as well as comments on the story by H. P. Lovecraft. The story later appeared in *The Coming of Conan* (New York: Gnome, 1953), and subsequently in the paperback *Conan* (New York: Lancer, 1968). The magazine and paperback versions differ slightly.

Also in that issue were stories by Clifford D. Simak, Murray Leinster, Fletcher

Pratt, Theodore L. Thomas, John Jakes and Robert W. Lowndes (as Michael Sherman), none of which would be out of place in a modern anthology. In this issue also began what was to become a regular feature. Del Rey devoted his editorial to a particular topic, in this instance telepathy. There was a book review column by George O. Smith, and issues featured occasional science articles. The most regular artist was Paul Orban, whose work was attractive and competent. Kelly Freas, Peter Poulton and Alex Ebel were among *SSF*'s other illustrators, while cover artists also included Earle Bergey and Hannes Bok.

Although *SSF* kept rather erratically to its bi-monthly schedule, del Rey chanced three short serials. The first, "Ullr Uprising" (February–March 1953) was an abridged version of H. Beam Piper's "Ullr Uprising," one of his Terran Federation sequence, which had first appeared in Fletcher Pratt's anonymously edited anthology *The Petrified Planet* (New York: Twayne, 1952). It was followed by "Cue for Quiet" (May–July 1953), a scoop for del Rey, as it was the first appearance in six years of T. L. Sherred, who had made such a big name for himself with just one story, "E for Effort," in the May 1947 *Astounding (Analog Science Fiction*).

The third serial was not so fortunate. "The Escape" by Poul Anderson began in the September 1953 issue, which also turned out to be the last, following a disagreement between del Rey and Raymond over payments to authors. This story, still one of Anderson's most intriguing, eventually appeared complete in book form as *Brainwave* (New York: Ballantine, 1954).

In only eight issues del Rey managed to publish a great many good-quality stories. Aside from those already mentioned, there were "The Adventurer" by Cyril Kornbluth (May 1953), a story about a future President of the United States that twenty years later took on a timely relevance; "Second Variety" by Philip K. Dick (May 1953); "Breaking Point" by James E. Gunn (March 1953); "The Worshippers" by Damon Knight (March 1953); and "Walk to the World" (November 1952), the first story by Algis Budrys.

The magazine did not acquire a personality, but del Rey edited it faultlessly. Even now it remains a very readable publication. Thirty years ago it was considerably more so.

Information Sources

BIBLIOGRAPHY:
Nicholls. *Encyclopedia.*
Tuck.
INDEX SOURCES: IBSF; MIT; SFM; Tuck.
REPRINT SOURCES:
  Reprint Magazine: A British edition was issued by The Archer Press, Ltd., London. Issues undated, but according to Brad Day and Graham Stone run Vol. 1, No. 1, December 1952–Vol. 2, No. 3, August 1953 (five issues per volume). The first issue corresponded to the second U.S. issue and then continued sequentially reprinting the entire issue in most cases. The last U.K. issue reprinted the first U.S. issue. However, if the issue dates are correct the U.K. Vol. 2, No. 2, which

corresponds to the U.S. Vol.2, No. 2 (last issue), appeared first, in July 1953, the U.S. issue not following until September. This would seem unlikely, especially as the same applies to the previous issue. U.K. edition Digest, 128 pp., 1/6d.

LOCATION SOURCES: M.I.T. Science Fiction Library; Pennsylvania State University Library.

Publication History

TITLE: *Space Science Fiction.*

VOLUME DATA: Volume 1, Number 1, May 1952–Volume 2, Number 2, September 1953. Bi-monthly, most issues, though issues labeled monthly February–May 1953. Actual run: 1952, May, Sep, Nov; 1953, Feb, Mar, May, Jul, Sept. Total run: 8 issues.

PUBLISHER: Space Publications Inc., New York.

EDITOR: Lester del Rey.

FORMAT: Digest, 160 pp.

PRICE: 35¢.

Mike Ashley

SPACE SCIENCE FICTION MAGAZINE

Space Science Fiction Magazine, digest-sized and billed as a bi-monthly, was published by Republic Features.[1] *SSFM* and a companion magazine, *Tales of the Frightened*,* both ran for two issues, Spring and August 1957. Although Lyle Kenyon Engel is listed as sole editor on the masthead of both magazines, Michael Avallone carried out many editorial responsibilities. In a letter to the author, Avallone, an editor for Republic Features from 1956 to 1958, describes his role in *SSFM*, *Tales of the Frightened* and another Engel magazine, *American Agent*. Of *SSFM*, he writes:

> I was writer-editor for Engel on all his mags and was never listed on the masthead because my own material was used many times. So specifically, I read, selected and approved all stories for SPACE, wrote descriptions for the artists to follow for the illos, ditto the covers, did all the blurbs and copy—indicia *et al.* Engel was the Brains Producer, I was the Working Stiff—and I loved it.

While *Tales of the Frightened* includes stories by Avallone, *SSFM* published no fiction under his name or any pseudonym attributed to him.

The covers by Tom Ryan and the interior illustrations, attributed to Bruce Minney, are unremarkable. The May 1957 cover depicts warrior women in abbreviated white tunics brandishing spears at terrified, space-suited men.[2] In the cover story, Adam Chase's "New World to Conquer," the women on an Earthlike planet, having rebelled years ago against men's wars, keep the males imprisoned in a "drone building." Predictably, when astronauts from Earth arrive, the glamorous Amazons fall in love with them, throw down their weapons and promise henceforth to live as "normal men and women." Chase's story is a classic example of the stock science fictional plot that was made to seem both offensive and ridiculous by James Tiptree, Jr., in "Houston, Houston, Do You Read?" and Joanna Russ in *The Female Man*.

The August 1957 cover illustrates Steve Frazee's novelette "Flying Saucers Do Exist," in which skeptical townspeople hound a timid man to death when the local newspaper prints the story of his ride in a flying saucer. Ryan's stock images of two saucers and the planet Earth in space, irrelevant to a story that takes place entirely in a small town, might serve as an illustration for virtually any outer space adventure. *SSFM*'s interior illustrations are half-tones with low-contrast, innocuous images.

Engel and Avallone, both writers and editors of all genres of popular fiction, did not seek an intimate relationship with readers of science fiction. Lacking editorial commentary, reviews, science facts and letters, *SSFM* consists entirely of stories and illustrations. *SSFM* contains a mixture of humor, weird tales and science fantasies, some of which, though by no means the majority, are markedly sentimental or didactic. It is nevertheless difficult to generalize about the types of stories or points of view favored by *SSFM*'s editors.

By far the oddest of the didactic stories is Winston K. Marks' "King Bee" (Spring). A gigantic bee informs the U.S. Secretary of State that the arms race must stop before humans and animals alike are destroyed. The bees bring the representatives of major nations into telepathic communication by stinging them. After sharing one another's thoughts, the diplomats can no longer practice nuclear brinksmanship. Rather inconsistently, the bees are the occasion for a heavy-handed anti-Communist message. The bees' "distressingly Communistic ideas" are deplored, and one character even proposes that Senator Joe McCarthy should investigate the apiaries. The King Bee himself suggests that the bees' telepathic rapport makes them inferior to humans: "Humans bicker and bitch among selves alla time, but got privacy of own opinions no matter how hard somebody beats on outside to make think different."

Russ Winterbotham, a Kansas writer of science fiction and westerns, and Mack Reynolds contributed stories to both issues of *SSFM*. In Winterbotham's "The Individualist" (Spring), Hudu, owner of a Martian cafe, boasts that no one leaves unhappy. He tells a man and woman that he has a machine that can discover the purpose of death. While the two puzzle over the huge, noisy contraption, the machine's real purpose—bringing two lonely people together—is accomplished. Winterbotham's "An Experiment in Gumdrops" (August), like "King Bee," concerns the hazards of nuclear power, a theme common in magazine science fiction of the 1950s. A man brings a digging creature from an ice planet to mine uranium in Antarctica, rewarding it with gumdrops. Imagining that the locked chamber containing the uranium is full of his favorite sweet, the greedy creature kills his master and breaks into the chamber. He sets off a chain reaction that destroys him and his wives.

Reynolds' three contributions to *SSFM* are short, with uncomplicated plots and characters. Published under the pseudonym Mark Mallory, "Posted" (Spring), a story of about 400 words, concerns a man from 1,000 years in the future who travels to 1956 to prevent aliens from enslaving Earth. "Obedience Guaranteed," in the same issue, also deals with a threat to freedom. An evil politician, traveling by rocketship to a meeting, plans to force his fascist ideas on the galactic league. When he irritably tells the ship's robot to "get lost," the literal-minded machine loses the rocket in outer space, making sure that his dangerous passenger will not make his power play. In Reynolds' third story, the comic fantasy "Slow Djinn" (August), a movie script-writer, while drunk, accepts the gift of a djinn so stupid that he misinterprets every order. The writer solves the problem by putting the djinn to work on the set of a biblical movie, flooding Death Valley to represent the Sea of Galilee and bringing in mountains and pyramids.

Among *SSFM*'s better-known contributors are Charles Eric Maine (pseudonym for David McIlwain), Raymond F. Jones, Jack Vance, Arthur C. Clarke, Carl Jacobi and John Jakes. In both Maine's "Reverse Procedure" (Spring) and Jones' "The Star Dream" (August), twentieth-century Earthmen have had identities in societies in other times and places, to which they return after death. In "Reverse Procedure," Dr. Paul Levison, experimenting with a narcotic, aphinine, travels during his trances to an island inhabited by the Lanoans, a magnificent, bronze-skinned race, threatened by the disease, thrayn. Levison learns that he is actually a Lanoan, sent into the future to discover a cure. Convinced that aphinine will counteract the thrayn, he commits suicide with an overdose and returns to the Lanoans with this information.

In "The Star Dream," Joel Nygren believes that before birth he had lived on an idyllic planet with a girl, Nahlia. Hoping to return, he works to develop a faster-than-light space drive. His wife, fearful of losing him, hires an engineer to sabotage the rocket, with the result that the men engaged in the project are poisoned by radiation. On his deathbed, Joel forgives his wife and prepares to rejoin Nahlia. Both Maine's and Jones' versions of a stock plot are sentimental and unconvincing.

Jack Vance and Arthur C. Clarke have contributed amusing trivia. In Vance's "A Practical Man's Guide" (August), the editor of *Popular Crafts Monthly*, Ralph Banks, tests a process outlined in an article recently submitted. Following the instructions, which call for such homey props as glasses, six pins and a steel knitting needle, Banks vanishes. Shortly thereafter, the author calls to say that he has omitted the last two pages of the article, which presumably would have informed Banks how to regain visibility.

In Clarke's "Critical Mass" (August), a group of scientists (including one named John Wyndham) are relaxing in a bar. When a truck crashes nearby, its driver and two bicyclists take off at a run. The crates in the truck have broken and are surrounded by an aura resembling gas. Believing that he is risking his life, the narrator investigates, but finds that the crates contain not chemicals but bees.

The two best stories to appear in *SSFM* are Carl Jacobi's weird tale, "The Martian Calendar" (Spring), and John Jakes' space western, "The Devil Spins a Sun-Dream" (Spring). In Jacobi's story, Hathaway believes that a neighbor is attempting to steal a Martian artifact, a calendar containing valuable crystals. Just as the neighbor falls into the booby-trap Hathaway has set for him, Hathaway breaks the calendar and thus is forced to reenact the murder again and again.

In "The Devil," Jakes skillfully brings together in a Martian setting both the frontier society of the old West and the legend of the Seven Cities of Cibola. Like other prospectors on Mars, Case Barrows is searching for the fabled Sun-Metal City. With a map his dying partner has given him, Case finds the city; but he is attacked by Aka Hasp, a treacherous half-breed (half-Martian, half-human) who has followed him. While the city is unimaginably lovely ("seven delicate spidery buildings, tall and graceful as upreaching female hands . . . "), it is a trap. A huge, amoeba-like creature lurking there devours Aka. Resolving to give up prospecting for a normal life, Case returns to his wife. Jakes ironically depicts an alien environment, which Earthmen believe they are exploiting, but which really manipulates them.

While Jacobi's and Jakes' stories have substance and originality, most other contributors are not represented by ambitious works. One misses, also, in *SSFM* the persona created by many editors of science fiction magazines and the dialogue they carried on with science fiction fans. Nevertheless, most of *SSFM*'s fiction, especially the humor, makes pleasant light reading today.

Notes

1. *SSFM* should not be confused with two earlier magazines with similar titles: *Space Science Fiction** (May 1952–September 1953), published by Space Publications and edited by Lester del Rey; and *Space Stories** (October 1952–June 1953), published by Standard Magazines and edited by Samuel Mines.

2. This cover is reproduced in James Gunn's *Alternate Worlds: The Illustrated History of Science Fiction* (Englewood Cliffs, N.J.: A & W Visual Library, 1975), p. 207.

Information Sources

BIBLIOGRAPHY:
Nicholls. *Encyclopedia*.
INDEX SOURCES: MIT; SFM.
REPRINT SOURCES: None known.
LOCATION SOURCES: Eastern New Mexico University, Golden Library (not available
    through interlibrary loan); Massachusetts Institute of Technology, MIT Science
    Fiction Society (not available through ILL); Michigan State University, Special
    Collections; Northern Illinois University Library, Rare Books and Special Col-
    lections (no ILL or microfilm, but partial photocopying of some issues *may* be
    possible); Ohio State University Libraries, Division of Special Collections; Penn-
    sylvania State University, Special Collections; Queen's University, Special Col-
    lections (no ILL or microfilm); San Francisco Academy of Comic Art, Science
    Fiction Room; San Francisco Public Library, Literature Department (not available

through ILL); Syracuse University, George Arents Research Library, Rare Books
Division; Temple University, Paley Library, Paskow Science Fiction Collection
(not available through ILL); Texas A&M University Library, Special Collections;
Toronto Public Libraries, Spaced Out Library (not available through ILL); Uni-
versity of California—Los Angeles, Special Collections (a microfilm may be
produced, the negative to remain at UCLA and the patron to pay for negative and
print); University of California—Riverside, Special Collections (Vol. 1, No. 2);
University of Georgia Libraries, Periodicals Department; University of Kansas,
Spencer Research Library; University of Maryland Baltimore County Library,
Special Collections (no ILL, but sections of magazines may be photocopied).

Publication History

TITLE: *Space Science Fiction Magazine.*
VOLUME DATA: Volume 1, Number 1, Spring 1957–Volume 1, Number 2, August
    1957.
PUBLISHER: Republic Features Syndicate, New York.
EDITOR: Michael Avallone (not credited in issue; Editorial Director was Lyle Kenyon
    Engel).
FORMAT: Digest, 128 pp.
PRICE: 35¢.

Wendy Bousfield

SPACE STORIES

Space Stories, a pulp magazine edited by Samuel Mines for Standard Magazines, ran from October 1952 to June 1953. *SS* has five issues in all, three in
Volume 1 and two in Volume 2.[1] Mines had joined Standard Magazines in 1942
as an editor of westerns. He worked mainly on Standard's non-science-fiction
pulps until Sam Merwin, Jr., editor of *Thrilling Wonder Stories (Wonder Sto-
ries*), Startling Stories,* Fantastic Story Magazine (Fantastic Story Quarterly*)*
and *Wonder Story Annual,** left the company in 1951. Mines became editor of
these magazines, as well as *SS*, which was added the following year as a companion.[2] A general decline in the pulp magazine industry, suffering from distribution problems and from the powerful competition of the new digests, *Galaxy
Science Fiction** and *The Magazine of Fantasy and Science Fiction,** was surely
a factor in *SS*'s early demise.[3]

Mines' lively editorial commentary and repartee with *SS*'s readers are the most
appealing features of the magazine. In the first issue (October 1952), Mines
explains that *SS* will be devoted to space opera, stories less intellectually demanding than those found in its companion magazines:

While *SS, TWS* and *FSM* will continue to range the entire field, SPACE
STORIES will be edited for you who want action and thrills, strange and
exotic backgrounds, weird and wonderful adventures—all the gorgeous,

colorful miracles which man's imagination may entice from the vast
unknown.

That coldly mental story, the complex parable, the tale of social significance is not for us. We offer warmth, excitement, color, action. We
build upon science fiction's greatest asset: its imagination-stirring concepts
of tremendous distances, colossal speeds, vast empty sweeps of space,
unknown, mysterious worlds, unguessable forms of life behind strange
murky atmospheres.

In "Flashes from Our Readers," a letter column initiated in the second issue,
it is evident that *SS*'s professed anti-intellectual bias struck a responsive chord,
especially among teenage readers. In the third issue (February 1953), a fan
writes:

> And may I make a suggestion for the forthcoming letter column? As you
> say, "The coldly mental story, the complex parable, the tale of social
> significance is not for us." How about readers remembering that and not
> harping on religion, sex, world population and repopulation? There are
> three good mags for that; so here, let's just talk space-opera.

In other letters as well Mines' description of the type of fiction *SS* would eschew
is quoted enthusiastically by fans.

Characterized by complicated and self-conscious witticisms, impassioned evaluations of stories, and abbreviations ("Febish" for February issue, for example)
intended to mark the writer as an insider to science fiction fandom, the letters
printed in *SS* seem to be written by younger fans. Mines accompanies each letter
with a joking response. In "Flashes" (February 1953), a fan suggests: "It is
not logical, to my mind, to assume that because on this planet a bipedal, upright
life-form is dominant, the same will hold true elsewhere; especially should we
consider that the dominant life form is apt to have more than two hands. Do I
get a nibble, or are all of us too firmly convinced of the same thing? Very likely
life on other worlds won't even be based on carbon." Mines replies: "As an
ammonia-silicon being, with four hands, three pedal membranes and a purple
goatee, I can say only that if you should come to New York and visit us you
will definitely get a nibble. . . . Earthmen taste *so* good." Since the aliens in
SS's fiction are depicted anthropomorphically (many are capable not only of
communicating in English with humans but of interbreeding with them), the
writer has made a valid criticism. It is, however, characteristic of Mines that he
refuses to be drawn into serious dialogue. Though Mines confines his own
remarks to light banter, he does allow fans to use the letter column as a soap
box for their own points of view. Most important, "Flashes from Our Readers"
was a *Gemeinschaft*, which gave fans the pleasant sense of belonging to an elite
in-group.

Besides letters and stories, *SS* has a variety of features. The first issue contains

"When Did It Happen? A Quiz": a list of scientific discoveries that must be matched with the correct dates. The first two issues contain brief essays on scientific wonders: "Perils of Empty Space," for example, describes the meteors and "mysterious cosmic rays" that may endanger space travelers (October 1952). In the last three issues, the scientific essays are replaced by a column, "Science Bulletins, Facts and Oddities." The fourth issue contains "Science-Fiction Bookshelf" (a feature that does not reappear in *SS*'s final issue), including reviews of new books by Chad Oliver and Arthur C. Clarke. In the last issue cartoons appear for the first time. One, for example, shows Martians cleaning their flying saucers in an Earth-style washing machine.

Artists well known in the science fiction magazine field contributed *SS*'s cover art; and there are fine interior illustrations by Peter Poulton, Paul Orban, Alex Schomburg, Virgil Finlay and Ed Emsh. Emsh painted the first, third and fifth covers; Earle K. Bergey the second; and Walter Popp the fourth. As is the case with all *SS*'s covers except the last, Emsh's first cover painting (October 1952) bears no relationship to any of the stories. Red-uniformed men with guns in hip holsters rush up an escalator and enter a massive rocket ship with brilliantly yellow tail fins.[4]

Emsh's garishly colored cover for the third issue (February 1953) invokes the triangle stereotypically associated with science fiction pulp art: the spaceman, the voluptuous blonde and the threatening bug-eyed monster (BEM). Recoiling in fright, a man and woman watch through the window or viewing-screen of their spacecraft as a pink crablike monster breaks through the red, cratered surface of the planet on which they have landed. This cover provoked a teenager to complain in the letter column that "dames" on the covers of science fiction magazines are an embarrassment: "Most teen-agers like to read their zines in school or on the trolley going to school, so why do this to us? . . . So, why not use good space scenes on your covers or some space-men fighting a BEM? Don't you see any other possibilities than scared femmes?" (June 1953). With the unabashed sexism still possible in the early 1950s, Mines replies: "There's only one good reason for putting dames on the covers, George, they dress it up so." Mines' suggestion that women's function in science fiction is purely decorative applies to *SS*'s fiction as well as its art.

The only *SS* cover to illustrate a particular story is Emsh's depiction of a scene from Sam Merwin, Jr.'s novel, "The Dark Side of the Moon," for the final issue (June 1953). UN rockets, with the same yellow fins found on the spacecraft in Emsh's first *SS* cover, are firing at alien "water pirates," who are attempting to rip the Antarctic ice cap away from the Earth. Beneath the battle, its continents in silhouette, is the planet Earth. Emsh also provided the interior illustrations for this story. For the same issue, he contributed comic pictures of the pear-shaped aliens in Roger Dee's "The Enemy Time" and of a robot bringing coffee on a tray for Charles Foster's "Red Alert."

Earle K. Bergey, an illustrator for Standard Magazines, is best known for initiating the trend in pulp covers away from scientific gadgetry to women in "brass brassieres" threatened by BEMs.[5] His cover for *SS*'s second issue, however, totally lacks the sensuality that fans expected of him. A woman dressed in what an annoyed letter-writer describes as "long green woolen underwear" aims a pistol at two red men running from a spaceship, to which a lighted fuse is attached.[6] Answering the criticism this cover received in the letter column, Mines states that Bergey had recently died: "Still, this was Earle Bergey's last cover for us—it wasn't one of his best, but no one knew that it was going to be his last."

The least distinguished of *SS*'s five covers is the fourth (April 1953) by Walter Popp. The breath of a provocatively dressed woman forms a bubble containing a futuristic city.[7]

Most of *SS*'s short stories, like its nonfiction features, are attributed to writers who are untraceable in science fiction's biographical sources or dictionaries of pseudonyms. The number of unfamiliar names prompted one letter-writer to ask whether the authors of the "shorts" are "pen-names numbers nineteen, twenty, and twenty-one for Kuttner." Characteristically, Mines' response is witty but evasive: "You've got it mixed up. Vance isn't Leinster. He's Judy Merril and Leinster is Ray Bradbury. Bradbury, of course, is Bryce Walton and Walton is Leigh Brackett" (June 1953). While most of *SS*'s short stories by unknowns are fillers, three are worth special mention: two because they are unusually original and one because it provides such a pure example of the sexism that characterizes magazine science fiction of the time.

In Charles Foster's story of male wish fulfillment, "The Satyr Stratagem" (April 1953), representatives of a corporation wishing to secure a contract to mine thoralite, a mineral necessary for space flight, land their spaceship on a little-known planet. Upon leaving the ship, a party of men are embraced by voluptuous women bearing flowers. The dictatorial captain jails the men for unfitting conduct: but Red Harrington, a maverick space-trader whom the crew had picked up en route, negotiates the contract on his own, convincing the natives that the miners will provide sorely needed husbands. Almost twenty years later, Joanna Russ in *The Female Man* and James Tiptree, Jr., in "Houston, Houston, Do You Read?" would expose the absurdities of this stock science fictional situation: a world inhabited by love-starved women who are restored to joyful normality by the arrival of male Earthmen.

"Expedition to Earth" (April 1953), by another unknown, Robert Zacks, is one of *SS*'s wittiest short stories. Wishing to see whether human beings would be more useful "as servants, laborers, or for amusement or medical research," alien nasties open a "science fiction restaurant," where their unearthly forms are perceived as costumes. Because the restaurant has a neon light of a color unknown on Earth, a scientist deduces that the aliens are genuine and forces them to evacuate Earth. The story unfolds in a series of newspaper stories, which amusingly treat alien wonders as promotional gimmicks.

"The Toy Tiger," a short story attributed to Phyllis Sterling Smith, is told from the point of view of a sensitive narrator-observer, who makes the reader care about the tragedy that befalls a mother and son. The narrator's friend claims to have developed a new breed of cat, the Toy Tiger, which is actually a real tiger, shrunk by a diet of ''Reductisone.'' When the woman temporarily runs out of the compound, the tiger grows prodigiously in both size and intelligence. Thinking to raise the IQ of her retarded son by the same method, the woman shrinks him with Reductisone and then allows him to grow to eight feet in height. When the mother shoots the tiger, now uncontrollable, her enormous son, still a child emotionally, kills her in revenge for the loss of his pet.

Despite the demeaning treatment of women in much of *SS*'s fiction, the magazine has four feminine contributors. Besides the unknown but presumably female Phyllis Sterling Smith, Margaret St. Clair and Miriam Allen deFord contributed short stories and Leigh Brackett a novel. St. Clair, perhaps better known by her pseudonym, Idris Seabright, wrote ''Continued Story'' (October 1952). Belonging to the paranoid or conspiracy subgenre of science fiction, this work concerns beings from the future who have planted a toy shop in our present. The shop stocks kits promising science fictional games: robot, makeup kit, moon experience. Through these kits, a future race manipulates individuals into violent actions so as to have entertaining stories to follow. Another exceptional illustration by Peter Poulton shows two men in spacesuits and fish-bowl helmets, presumably enacting the ''moon experience,'' on a cratered landscape. Watching in the sky are a beautiful woman and a head that seems to be sculpted of wire.

In the same issue is Miriam Allen deFord's amusing short story, ''The Whatsits.'' When human beings land on a planet inhabited by a gigantic humanoid life-form, they are placed in a laboratory for study. The story's humor arises from the mock-academic style of the laboratory reports by various alien scientists. Ed Emsh has provided a witty picture of the aliens examining with complicated instruments a tiny human.

While many other short stories are forgettable, *SS*'s novels and novelettes are ambitious works by well-known names. Like Standard's *Startling Stories*, also edited by Mines, *SS* had one novel in each issue. Every issue except the fourth contains one or two novelettes.

Gordon R. Dickson contributed novelettes to the first and third issues of *SS*, both of which recreate the frontier society of the American West on another planet. In ''The Invaders'' (October 1952), Hector McGarrity, a military commander, comes to the aid of settlers on the planet Lamia, about to be attacked by evil aliens, the spindle-shippers. Tica Smith, a government observer, at first disapproves of Hector's ruthlessness, but subsequently falls in love with him. After Hector saves Lamia, a dying settler points out the moral to Tica: ''When a woman starts going by how she thinks instead of how she feels, she goes all wrong. That's how come you've been so mixed up. From now on you let the commander do the thinking and you do the feeling.''

A more sensitive story, lacking the macho bullying glorifed in ''The Invaders,'' is Dickson's ''The Bleak and Barren Land'' (February 1953). Kent Harmon is the Colonial Representative on Mordor, where a few prospectors from Earth live in harmony with the Mordorians, who resemble the American Indians in their reverence for the land. When Earth sends a colony of settlers, Maker, the oldest of the "Wild Mordorians," creates vibrations in an attempt to destroy the settlement with an earthquake. Although the Earthmen stabilize the area with countervibrations, Kent is forced to kill Maker. While the advance of civilization is deemed inevitable, the Mordorians are depicted with respect. Schomburg has provided a realistically detailed illustration of the prospectors attempting to run off the settlers.

Bryce Walton's novel in the first issue, "Man of Two Worlds" (October 1952), is set in a future in which humans on Earth have been destroyed in atomic war, while those remaining on Mars are being wiped out by a cruel dictatorship. A man and woman escape into an earlier period in Mars' history, which corresponds to Greek mythology. After battling such supernatural beings as the Minotaur and the giant Talos, the two make their way to a prehuman Earth, where they will begin the human race.

More interesting than the story itself is a long, patronizing, precious letter from nineteen-year-old John Brunner (April 1953). Brunner condemns Walton's story for

> containing everything but the kitchen sink. As I leaf through it, I run across: universal teleportation, a lost Martian civilization, racial memory, interplanetary colonization, corrupt police and righteous rebels, mutation, transtemporal ego exchange, four-dimensional awareness, the atomic devastation of Earth, a dragged-in so-called scientifictional rewrite of the Cretan-Minoan mythos involving the following hunks of ham: the soul-stealers, aliens masquerading as human beings, religion and magic on a scientific basis, considerable swordplay, a malignant robot, considerable sadism lifted from Shaver, . . . heroic self-sacrifice (by Conan!), the "origin" of the Norse god Thor (this apparently as an afterthought): a closed time-cycle, and once again the items at the head of the list.

Brunner continues this exercise in overkill with ironic praise for SS's anti-intellectualism: "However, push on! I'm all for the non-cerebral type of story because it makes for an occasional mindless hour. I shall buy SS as religiously as I do the TWinss." Hinting that SS must have low standards for its contributors, Brunner offers his services: "And I intend this very night to start (or tomorrow) on a novel for you, which I can always sell to someone later."

Jack Vance's "Planet of the Damned" (December 1952) is SS's second novel. Roy Barch works for Markel, a member of an alien race called Lekthwans, which has brought advanced technology to Earth. He falls in love with Markel's daughter, Komeitk Lelianr, but smarts under her cultural superiority. When Barch and Komeitk are kidnapped by wicked aliens, the Klau, and taken to a prison planet, Barch shows a drive and inventiveness that the Lekthwans lack. Reunited on Earth after having escaped, Barch and Komeitk marry.

In the letter column of the fourth issue (April 1953), Vance's now dated adventure is much praised. One letter-writer, however, asks astute questions about the characters' motivation. Did the Klau empire, he asks, "come into existence as the result of overpopulation, of a power drive, or a desire for wealth on the part of the Klau?" The letter-writer questions especially the plausibility of the ending:

> But it is in striving after a happy ending that Jack Vance pulls a real howler. No where's are we told that Kometik Lelianr really loved Barch. . . . Kometik Lelianr had deserted Barch before. There was no convincing proof that she ceased to regard him as inferior. Yet Vance would have us believe that after Kometik Lelianr had let Barch make love to her from force of circumstances and had run out on him before, she would turn around and become his wife for no sufficient reason. T'ain't convincing!

The letter-writer is pointing out the absurdity of a convention employed in other *SS* stories as well: a beautiful woman is a prize bestowed on a man who successfully carries out heroic exploits. Mines, however, dismisses the letter as "a bit of choice G.I.-type griping."

Like Dickson's "The Invaders," "The Big Jump," a novel by Leigh Brackett in the February 1953 issue, wearies the reader with a succession of fistfights, shootings, and macho swaggerings. Having lost his buddy, Paul Rogers, on a voyage to Barnard's star, Comyn muscles his way into the Cochrane clan, which owns the corporation conducting the space exploration. Accompanying the Cochranes on a second journey to the planet, Comyn finds that it is inhabited by starlike beings, who have transformed the members of the previous expedition into joyous savages, enjoying perfect health and no longer needing human hardware and speech. Comyn is almost transformed himself, but is taken away before the process is complete.

William Morrison (pseudonym for Joseph Samachson) contributed the novel "The Gears of Time" to *SS*'s April 1953 issue. On Earth and its colonies, two kinds of metabolic abnormalities have occurred: there are persons whose metabolism is ten times faster than normal, and who thus age and move with unusual speed, and persons who move and perceive ten times more slowly than normal. Fast, slow and normal humans are at war. Because new drugs enable individuals to speed or slow their metabolism and time perception for extended periods, the hero is able to convince leaders of the three societies that they can cooperate with one another.

Morrison's earlier contribution to *SS*, a short story, "Revenge" (December 1952), is more interesting than his novel in terms of both its characters and its perspective on society. Lawson, in the fashion of Poe's madmen, plots revenge on Trotter, who has caused the suicide of Lawson's wife by callously seducing and abandoning her. On Mars, where the two are stationed, the swinish Trotter kills two Martians, but is rescued from the angry crowd by Lawson, who wishes to be singlehandedly responsible for Trotter's death. The mother of the dead Martians, a physiologist and psychologist, transforms Trotter and Lawson into duplicates of her sons. By following the dictates of Martian justice, she has received complete reparation for her losses and has bloodlessly rid society of two sociopaths. Orban provided an effective illustration.

In conclusion, while the lively physical action of *SS*'s unpretentious fiction still entertains, its social attitudes and literary conventions are often dated. The swaggering and fistfighting of *SS*'s heroes may be offputting to modern readers, and aliens and women are often treated insensitively. Reflecting the Cold War phobia of a monolithic Communist threat, evil aliens are motivated solely by a lust for destruction. Beyond providing traditional love interest, female characters generally have little to do. Clearly, however, the young fans who honed their critical tools in *SS*'s letter column cared passionately about the magazine's fiction. Through the forum he provided for science fiction fans and through the wit and gusto of his own comments, Samuel Mines gave *SS* enormous vitality.

Notes

1. *Space Stories* should not be confused with two magazines with similar titles: *Space Science Fiction** (May 1952–Sept. 1953), edited by Lester del Rey for Space Publications; and the later *Space Science Fiction Magazine** (Spring and August 1957), edited by Lyle Kenyon Engel for Republic Features.

2. For Samuel Mines' editorial involvement with *SS* and other science fiction magazines, see "Mines, Samuel" and "Space Stories," in *The Science Fiction Encyclopedia*, ed. Peter Nicholls (Garden City. N.Y.: Doubleday, 1979); and "Mines, Samuel," in *The Encyclopedia of Science Fiction and Fantasy Through 1968*, comp. Donald H. Tuck (Chicago: Advent, 1978).

3. Mines, Samuel," in *Science Fiction Encyclopedia*; and *The History of the Science Fiction Magazine, 1946–1955*, ed. Michael Ashley (Chicago: Contemporary Books, 1976), III: 83.

4. This cover has been reproduced in Brian Aldiss, *Science Fiction Art* (New York: Bounty Books, 1975), p. 44; and in James Gunn, *Alternate Worlds: The Illustrated History of Science Fiction* (A & W Visual Library, 1975), p. 200.

5. "Bergey, Earle K.," in *Science Fiction Encyclopedia*.

6. A black and white picture of this cover accompanies the entry on "Space Stories" in *Science Fiction Encyclopedia*.

7. This cover has been reproduced in black and white in Aldiss, p. 126.

Information Sources

BIBLIOGRAPHY:
Nicholls. *Encyclopedia*.
Tuck.
INDEX SOURCES: Cook, IWG; MIT; SFM.
REPRINT SOURCES: None known.
LOCATION SOURCES: Bowling Green State University Library; Brigham Young University, HBL Library (not available through interlibrary loan; Vol. 1, Nos. 1 and 2); California State University—Fullerton, Special Collections (not available through

ILL, but will photocopy articles upon request); Eastern New Mexico University, Golden Library (not available through ILL); Massachusetts Institute of Technology, MIT Science Fiction Society (not available through ILL); Michigan State University, Special Collections; Northern Illinois University Library, Rare Books and Special Collections (no ILL or microfilm; partial photocopying of some issues *may* be possible); Ohio State University Libraries, Division of Special Collections; Pennsylvania State University Libraries, Special Collections; Queen's University, Special Collections; San Francisco Academy of Comic Art, Science Fiction Room; San Francisco Public Library, Literature Department (not available through ILL); Syracuse University, George Arents Research Library, Rare Books Division; Temple University, Paley Library, Paskow Science Fiction Collection (not available through ILL); Texas A&M University Library, Special Collections; Toronto Public Libraries, Spaced Out Library (not available through ILL; Vol. 1, Nos. 1 and 2; Vol. 2, Nos. 1 and 2); University of California—Los Angeles, Special Collections (a microfilm may be produced, the negative to remain at UCLA and the patron to pay for negative and print); University of California—Riverside, Special Collections; University of Georgia Libraries, Periodicals Department; University of Kansas, Spencer Research Library (Vol. 1, Nos. 1–3; Vol. 2, No. 2); University of Maryland Baltimore County Library, Special Collections (no ILL, but sections of magazines may be photocopied).

Publication History

TITLE: *Space Stories*.
VOLUME DATA: Volume 1, Number 1, October 1952–Volume 2, Number 2, June 1953. Three issues per volume. Bi-monthly. Total run: 5 issues.
PUBLISHER: Standard Magazines, Kokomo, Indiana.
EDITOR: Samuel Mines.
FORMAT: Pulp, 128 pp.
PRICE: 25¢.

Wendy Bousfield

SPACE TRAVEL

See *Imaginative Tales*.

SPACEWAY

William Crawford had a determined though fated career as a science fiction publisher and editor. Through *Marvel Tales*,* *Unusual Stories* and *Fantasy Book** plus such volumes as H. P. Lovecraft's *The Shadow over Innsmouth*, Crawford strove for adequate newsstand distribution without success.

In 1953 it looked as if his luck might change. At that time Hollywood was undergoing a science fiction film boom inspired by the success of *Destination Moon* (1950), produced by George Pal. Pal had gone on to a second triumph with *When Worlds Collide* (1951) and was next at work on *War of the Worlds*. Through the agency of Forrest J Ackerman plans were made to launch a new SF magazine, *George Pal's Tales of Space Conquest*. Crawford was engaged as editor, and a national distributor was found. An issue of the magazine was linotyped and made up for publication when the distributor decided that the boom was over and withdrew.

Though left high and dry, Crawford persevered and, with a new title, launched *Spaceway* (itself inspired by a British film released in 1953, *Spaceways*). It was a bad time to release a new magazine without solid financial backing and distribution. It was the height of the SF boom and the field was saturated with titles. Newsstand space was limited, and in many instances magazines were not even unpacked from their cartons unless someone specifically requested an issue, and who would know about a new magazine? Thus, many magazines were stifled at birth.

As a West Coast magazine, *Spaceway* stood a moderate chance since most of the SF magazine publishers were concentrated in New York and Chicago. But Crawford still needed to acquire good material, and, with major authors able to command high rates and a regular market with the leading titles, he had to content himself with what remained. Much the same situation had prevailed when he published *Fantasy Book* only a few years earlier, and yet Crawford had still acquired a few reasonably good stories, including the classic "Scanners Live in Vain" by Cordwainer Smith. But such opportunities do not come every day. Crawford had to rely on material supplied by Ackerman through his agency, and the first issue led with a serial, "The Osilans" by Arthur J. Burks. Other stories were by Stanton Coblentz, Gene Hunter, Clyde Beck and Charles Eric Maine, on whose original radio script the film *Spaceways* had been based. Presentation was poor, due mostly to the less than satisfactory artwork by Paul Blaisdell and others.

Little of interest appeared in the first four bi-monthly issues, although the second reprinted L. Ron Hubbard's "Battle of Wizards" from *Fantasy Book*. The fiction was otherwise uninspired and poor, an irony from a publisher who twenty years earlier had planned to rid the SF world of just such chaff with *Marvel Tales*. Equally ironic was that what proved to be Crawford's poorest publication was the only one to achieve relatively good distribution and a British edition.

Financial and distribution problems delayed the fifth issue until December 1954, and although presentation had not improved, the story content had. A new serial, John Taine's "Cosmic Geoids," began, and there were stories by Charles Eric Maine ("The Festival of Earth") and Arthur J. Burks ("The City of Ind"). Three more bi-monthly issues appeared, all with some stories of interest, such as "The Towers of Silence" by George H. Smith (February 1955), "Riddle of the Rim" by Jack Lewis (April 1955) and "Curtain Going Up" by Harry Warner, Jr. (June 1955). The eighth and final issue began two new serials, "Stairway to Mars" by E. Everett Evans and "The Radio Minds of Mars" by Ralph Milne

Farley. After this issue Crawford lost his distribution and decided to cut his losses and fold the magazine.

Crawford remained out of touch with the SF field from 1956 to 1968, during which time he became a real estate agent and did some commercial printing. Then, fired with nostalgia, he revived *Spaceway*, with the first new issue dated January 1969. Most of the contents were reprints from the earlier *Spaceway* or stories held in the inventory at the time the magazine folded. Forrest Ackerman provided a column, "A Letter from Mr Sci-Fi," and the serial "The Radio Minds of Mars" was relaunched.

Still digest-sized, the new *Spaceway* was saddle-stapled and featured a cover by Morris Scott Dollens, who provided all the covers for the new series. All were infinitely superior to those on the original run. The revived *Spaceway* only lasted for four issues, but at least the Farley serial reached its conclusion. Not so the next serial, which, to the surprise of many, was by Andre Norton: "Garan of Yu-lac." This had been one of two stories that Norton had delivered to Crawford in 1935 for *Marvel Tales*, but that venture ceased without their seeing print, and they remained in the inventory. "People of the Crater" made it into *Fantasy Book*, but "Garan" had to wait for thirty-five years, and even then fate struck. It was intended as a three-part serial, but only two episodes saw print, and readers did not get to see the story in its entirety until Crawford published it with other stories in book form as *Garan the Eternal* (Los Angeles: FPCI, 1972).

With the help of Gerald Page, Crawford issued two special editions of *Spaceway*. The third, dated September 1969, was in keeping with the first manned lunar landing and reprinted two stories from Britain's *Tales of Wonder*,* including William F. Temple's 1938 story of the first manned moon trip, "Lunar Lilliput."

The fourth and last issue was in many ways the best. An attractive Dollens cover heralded a special Martian issue which contained only one reprint. Gerald Page contributed an article on the "Many Worlds of Edgar Rice Burroughs" plus two stories, "The City in the Syrtis" as Carleton Grindle, and "Farewell, Mars" in collaboration with Hank Reinhardt. Other stories were by Emil Petaja, Thomas Cleary and Max Sheridan.

Although fans were pleased to see the revival of *Spaceway*, and many vouched support for a reborn *Fantasy Book*, the magazine had limited financial backing, and Crawford was forced to suspend publication. At that time, however, he took over the subscription list to *Coven 13** and wanted to reorganize his publishing before launching *Witchcraft and Sorcery** as a joint venture. There was no room for *Spaceway* in the new framework, and the title was suspended.

Information Sources

BIBLIOGRAPHY:
Nicholls. *Encyclopedia*.
Tuck.
INDEX SOURCES: ISFM-II; MIT; SFM; Tuck.

REPRINT SOURCES:
  British Edition: The first four issues were released with minor changes between April
    1954 and February 1955 by Regular Publications, London, same format, 1/6d.
LOCATION SOURCES: Eastern New Mexico University Library; M.I.T. Science Fiction
  Library; Pennsylvania State University Library; Texas A&M University Library.

Publication History

TITLE: *Spaceway*, December 1953–June 1954; expanded to *Spaceway Science Fiction*,
  December 1954–June 1955, and retained for second series.
VOLUME DATA: Volume 1, Number 1, December 1953–Volume 3, Number 2, June
  1955. Recommenced Volume 4, Number 1, January 1969–Volume 5, Number 1,
  May/June 1970. Three issues per volume, where complete. First series bi-monthly,
  though June 1954 issue followed by December 1954. Second series planned as
  bi-monthly but irregular. Cover dates: January 69, June 69, October 69, June 70.
  Total run: 8 + 4, 12 issues.
PUBLISHER: Fantasy Publishing Co., Inc., Alhambra, California.
EDITOR: William L. Crawford.
FORMAT: Digest (first series perfect bound, second series saddle-stapled); 160 pp.,
  December 1953–April 1954; 128 pp., June 1954–June 1955 and January 1969–
  May/June 1970.
PRICE: First series, 35¢; second series, 50¢.

Mike Ashley

THE SPIDER

The first issue of *The Spider* appeared in October 1933 and was written by
R. T. M. Scott, a well-known mystery and thriller writer of the time. The
character was based heavily on Scott's own earlier creation, Secret Service Smith,
a gentleman detective and crime solver. The Spider was a wealthy man-about-
town, Richard Wentworth, who went after criminals that the law could not touch
or could not punish. Wentworth, in the name of The Spider, killed crooks and
branded their foreheads with a tiny stamp of a spider. In the first two novels of
the series, both written by Scott, Wentworth is little more than a gentlemanly
vigilante battling normal criminals. This ended with the third issue, when the
novels began to appear under the house name of Grant Stockbridge.

Most of the novels for the next ten years were the creation of Norvell Page,
though a number of the stories were written by Emile C. Tepperman, Wayne
Rogers and other Popular Publications regulars. Page transformed The Spider
from a gentleman crook battling normal crooks to a dedicated avenger battling
unbelievable criminal menaces that threatened New York and oftentimes the
entire country.

Science fiction played a major role in many of the Spider novels, serving as
the focus for the menace of the stories. Usually, little more than a brief notation
or statement was made to justify the plausibility of the inventions or devices,

but the machines and menaces themselves were well thought out and well integrated into the plot. In one novel, the villain was a science fiction pulp author who masqueraded as a Beast-Man from Mars to perform his crimes. Science fiction menaces used in *The Spider* included a virus that ate metal in "The City Destroyer" (January 1935); a disease that changed men into nearly unkillable monsters in "The Grey Horde Creeps" (March 1938); giant robots controlled by human operators in "Satan's Murder Machines" (December 1939); and a lost race of Neanderthal men in "Hordes of the Red Butcher" (June 1935). Norvell Page spent long hours working on the Spider novels, and his efforts showed. The stories were fast-paced and well written. Page was familiar with the science fiction field and even sold three novels to *Unknown*.* His work for *The Spider* reflected a strong blend of the single-character pulp hero concept and science fiction menaces. *The Spider* was one of the most popular of the hero pulps and foreshadowed the rise of the ruthless spy and vigilante paperback heroes of the 1970s.

The Spider frequently ran short stories to accompany the lead novel, but they were detective-oriented. They reflected Popular's format of the 1930s and had a strong emphasis on gruesome crimes and horrible deaths. Series appearing most often were the Doc Turner stories by Arthur Leo Zagat (featuring an elderly pharmacist in a run-down neighborhood of New York, who monthly battled extortionists and killers who preyed on the poor and elderly) and the Masked Marksman stories by Emile Tepperman, featuring Ed Race, a juggler who was a superior marksman (he used his guns as props) and solved mysteries in his spare time. None of these stories had any SF notions, and even the smallest fantasy elements implied in the Doc Turner stories were explained at the end to be part of some mad scheme.

Information Sources

BIBLIOGRAPHY:

Carr, Nick. "The Pulp Reincarnation." *Xenophile*, No. 10 (1975).

Murray, Will. "The Top Ten Spider Novels—and One Stinker." *Megavore*, No. 13 (March 1981). A symposium with contributions by Murray, Bob Sampson, Al Grossman, Michael Avallone, Bob Weinberg and Joseph Lewandowski.

Sampson, Bob. "The Pulp Library." *Xenophile*, No. 30 (1977).

Tuck.

Weinberg, Robert. "The Man from the East." *Pulp*, No. 4 (1972).

INDEX SOURCES: Weinberg, Robert and Lohr McKinstry, *The Hero Pulp Index*, Evergreen, Colo.: Opar Press, 1981 (lists lead novels only).

REPRINT SOURCES:

Novels: Berkley Medallion Books, New York, reprinted at least the first four novels in 1969: *The Spider Strikes!* (orig. Oct. 33), *The Wheel of Death* (Nov 33), *Wings of the Black Death* (Dec 33) and *City of Flaming Shadows* (Jan 34). Pocket Books subsequently issued *Death Reign of the Vampire King* (orig. Nov 35), *Hordes of*

the Red Butcher (Jun 35) and The City Destroyer (Jan 35); in 1980 Dimedia Inc.,
issued a limited edition quality paperback edition of Builders of the Black Empire
(Oct 34), Master of the Death Madness (Aug 35) and Overlord of the Damned
(Oct 35); and in 1984 Dimedia issued Satan's Death Blast (June 1934) and Corpse
Cargo (July 1934).

LOCATION SOURCES: M.I.T. Science Fiction Library; San Francisco Academy of
Comic Art; University of California–Los Angeles Library (1933–1942, 5 issues).

Publication History

TITLE: The Spider.

VOLUME DATA: Volume 1, Number 1, October 1933–Volume 30, Number 2, December 1943. Four issues per volume. Monthly until March 1943, followed by June
1943 and thereafter bi-monthly. Total run: 118 issues.

PUBLISHER: Popular Publications, New York.

EDITORS: Rogers Terrill, October 1933–early 1940s; Robert Turner, 1943; Ryerson
Johnson, December 1943.

FORMAT: Pulp; 128 pp., October 1933–March 1936, thereafter 112 pp.

PRICE: 10¢.

Robert Weinberg

STAR SCIENCE FICTION

The digest *Star Science Fiction* was an attempt by Ballantine Books to convert
into a magazine Frederik Pohl's popular *Star* anthologies, the first major episode
in the history of the original story anthology following Raymond J. Healy's *New
Tales of Time and Space* (1951).[1] Ian Ballantine began his fruitful involvement
with science fiction when he decided during the 1953 boom to publish Pohl and
Cyril Kornbluth's *Gravy Planet* as *The Space Merchants*; but making it to the
paperback racks one month before the novel was *Star Science Fiction Stories*.
The anthology was to keep the publishing house's "image bright in the memories
of all science fiction writers" to expedite Ballantine's resolve to publish one
such writer every month. Pohl had the idea for the anthology, Ballantine for
publishing original stories,[2] for which he proposed to pay the lavish sum of five
cents a word.[3] Between March 1953 and January 1955, Ballantine published
three issues of *Star* and one of *Star Short Novels*. Each anthology featured
excellent stories by familiar authors, many of whom were writing for Ballantine.[4]
Then the project ceased until November 1958.

Between the first and second series of *Star* anthologies appeared the only issue
of *Star Science Fiction* magazine, conceived as a quarterly digest which would
be a "logical development" of the books.[5] The format was basically the same
as the one used in the anthologies—novelettes and short stories—plus a newsy
Pohl editorial, "A Pinch of Stardust." Ballantine's paperback cover artist, Richard Powers, produced a stylish abstract painting and a series of abstract sketches
for interior illustrations.[6] But the only current Ballantine writer that the magazine

might have been promoting was Poul Anderson; of the others only Algis Budrys had a book with the house, but he wrote for the magazine under his "John Sentry" pseudonym. The range was wider than the previous books': from the "Golden Age" writer Chan Davis to a "first" from a young Irishman, Gavin Hyde, discovered by Ray Bradbury on his trip to that country;[7] in between were Isaac Asimov, Robert Bloch and Brian Aldiss. Naturally, the Asimov story, "S as in Zebatinsky," has been reprinted at least once. More surprisingly, Aldiss's story, the first of his American appearances, "Judas Dancing," was reprinted five times as "Judas Danced";[8] appearing the next decade in Harry Harrison's *SF: Authors' Choice* and *Best Science Fiction Stories of Brian W. Aldiss*, it seemed to be one of the author's favorites. A brief announcement informed the reader that the magazine would be back in three months with novelettes and short stories by Kornbluth, Henry Kuttner, Miriam Allen deFord, and Lester del Rey (an omnipresent *Star* author).

When *Star* reappeared—eleven months later—it was as an anthology, not a magazine. By then Kornbluth and Kuttner were dead. Prefaced by the "Pinch of Stardust" editorial and introduced by memorial essays, their stories appeared as promised, but in a paperback book. It seemed that the 1950s war between paperbacks and pulps was over, and the magazines were not the victor.

Notes

1. James Gunn, *Alternate Worlds: The Illustrated History of Science Fiction* (Englewood Cliffs, N.J.: 1975), pp. 220–21.

2. Frederik Pohl, *The Way the Future Was: A Memoir* (New York: Del Rey Books, 1978), p. 161.

3. Gunn, p. 220.

4. Pohl, *Star Science Fiction Stories No. 2* (New York, 1953), p. 98.

5. *Star Science Fiction*, Vol. 1, No. 1 (January 1958), inside front cover.

6. Ibid.

7. Pohl, "A Pinch of Stardust," *Star Science Fiction*, Vol. 1, No. 1 (January 1958):5.

8. In the same month, *Fantasy and Science Fiction* published "The New Father Christmas."

Information Sources

BIBLIOGRAPHY:
Nicholls. *Encyclopedia*.
Tuck.
INDEX SOURCES: MIT; SFM.
REPRINT SOURCES: None known.
LOCATION SOURCES: M.I.T. Science Fiction Library; Pennsylvania State University Library.

Publication History

TITLE: *Star Science Fiction*.
VOLUME DATA: Volume 1, Number 1, January 1958. Intended schedule, quarterly, but only one issue published.

PUBLISHER: Ballantine Magazines, Derby, Connecticut.
EDITOR: Frederik Pohl.
FORMAT: Digest, 128 pp.
PRICE: 35¢.

                                                                E. F. Casebeer

STARDUST (1940)

During the era of hectographed and mimeographed fan magazines, *Stardust*, which was published in 1940, was unusual. It was a printed magazine on slick paper. The contents were primarily fiction rather than fan-oriented material, and while not in competition with the professional magazines, it was an interesting supplement to them.

The editor and publisher was eighteen-year-old W. Lawrence Hamling, one of the core of fans active in Chicago, and later involved with *Amazing Stories** and *Fantastic Adventures** before becoming publisher of his own *Imagination** in the 1950s. Most fans were astounded that such a high-quality publication could be financed in a day when most eighteen- or nineteen-year-olds had little money, and many thought Hamling must have been a rich man's son.

Hamling went into production of the magazine in a big way. Serving as assistant editor was Neil de Jack, while Chester S. Geier was listed as literary editor, Howard Funk as business manager and Harry Warner, Jr., as editorial adviser. The first issue was large-size with just twenty pages and sold for twenty cents. It was a neatly presented, rather handsome production and boasted fiction by L. Sprague de Camp, Malcolm Jameson, Robert Moore Williams and Chester S. Geier plus nonfiction by Ralph Milne Farley, Charles D. Hornig and Henry Bott. In his history of fandom, *The Immortal Storm*, Sam Moskowitz suggests that *Stardust* was one of the cards that Hamling was playing in his bid to hold the 1940 World SF Convention in Chicago, a bid that was successful, though more through the rival actions of Mark Reinsberg and Erle Korshak. Nevertheless, *Stardust* was a prestigious production for fandom and could have been significant in the future of SF had not other factors intervened.

The purpose of *Stardust*, as explained in the first issue, was to bridge the gap between the small number of active fans and the large number of passive fans; consequently, some fan material appeared among the fiction. A "Meet the Fan" department was included from the third issue, and a regular letter column began in the second issue. The fourth issue included a piece by Sam Moskowitz entitled "Future Fandom," while there was a typical Ray Palmer piece in the fifth issue, "Palmer Tears His Hair."

But the real focus of *Stardust* was its fiction, which included work by many of the big names. Amelia Reynolds Long was present in the second issue with "Justice in Time," and L. Sprague de Camp and Robert Moore Williams were well represented. Probably the best-known stories from *Stardust* were the two by Jack Williamson, "Crystal of Death" in the third issue and "Ashes of Iron" in the fifth. It was evident that the stories were rejects from better-paying markets, but the might of the names lent much to the prestige of the magazine.

Prestige, however, did not convert into cash. With the fourth issue Hamling cut the size of the magazine to six by nine inches with added pages, but it was clear that without sufficient subscriptions the costly production could not be sustained. But perhaps the purpose of the magazine had already been served. The Chicago World Convention was held in September 1940 when the fourth issue went on sale at a reduced fifteen cents, but only one more issue appeared. The eventual demise was probably a combination of financial limitations and insufficient fannish response. *Stardust* had not been the first of the semi-professional fiction magazines (*Marvel Tales** and *Fanciful Tales of Time and Space** preceded it), but it did have the most potential and was an indication of the lengths to which fans would go for their favorite fiction.

Information Sources

INDEX SOURCES: None known.
REPRINT SOURCES: None known.
LOCATION SOURCES: None known.

Publication History

TITLE: *Stardust*
VOLUME DATA: Volume 1, Number 1, March 1940–Volume 1, Number 5, November 1940. Bi-monthly, though July issue dated August. Total run: 5 issues.
PUBLISHER: W. Lawrence Hamling.
EDITOR: W. Lawrence Hamling.
FORMAT: Large: size (8½" x 11"), 20 pp., March–August 1940; Medium Octavo (6" x 9"), 28 pp., September 1940; 36 pp., November 1940.
PRICE: 20¢, March–August 1940; 15¢, September–November 1940.

Robert A. Madle/Mike Ashley

STARDUST (1975–)

Stardust is the only Canadian semi-prozine devoted to science fiction, although there are a number dedicated to fantasy (*Dragonfields,** for example). It is also the only one currently published in English. (French readers have their choice of two, the slick *Solaris* and the scholarly *Imagine . . .* , both published in Quebec.)

Stardust was named after Perry Rhodan's first spaceship. Edited and published by Forrest Fusco, Jr., a naturalized Canadian, it reflects the editor's personal tastes, publishes largely unknown new writers, and appears irregularly in varying formats, but it manages to pay contributors one cent a word for stories, poems, articles, reviews and even puzzles.

Better-known writers who have found themselves in *Stardust* include Darrell Schweitzer with "The Story of Obbok" in the second issue; Judith Merril, reprinted in the eighth issue; Phyllis Gotlieb, reprinted in the ninth issue; and John Robert Colombo with the reprint of a talk on "Four Hundred Years of Fantastic Literature in Canada." Regular contributors include Natalia Mayer, Julian Dust, Dena Bain and Judith Quinlan.

The writing tends to be amateurish, but its quality and the general editing of the magazine are of less importance than the continued appearance of the publication which, in "solitary splendor," is the first periodical since the Canadian pulps of the 1940s and early 1950s to publish original SF by Canadian writers.

Issues appear only when Fusco can afford to publish them, so *Stardust* clearly relies on its subscribers. Whatever its future, and whatever its current quality, it should be encouraged because it is a sole voice in a wilderness.

Information Sources

INDEX SOURCES: None known.
REPRINT SOURCES: None known.
LOCATION SOURCES: None known.

Publication History

TITLE: *Stardust*; carried subtitle "The Canadian SF Magazine" from issue 4.
VOLUME DATA: Volume 1, Number 1, [August] 1975– . Latest issue sighted Volume 3, Number 2, Spring 1981. Volume 1, four issues undated, but numbers 2 and 3, 1976. Volume 2, three issues, all undated but during 1978–1980. Volume 3, two issues to date. Total run so far: 9 issues.
PUBLISHER: Stardust Publications, Toronto, Canada.
EDITOR: Forrest Fusco, Jr.
FORMAT: Digest, except for issues 2 and 3 which were vest-pocket sized (6¾" x 4"). Pages: issue 1, 48 pp., issues 2 and 3, 80 pp., issues 4 to 7, 56 pp., issue 8, 88 pp., issue 9, 72 pp.
PRICE: First issue unpriced, thereafter $1.50 until issue 8, then $1.95.

John Robert Colombo

STARTLING MYSTERY STORIES

Startling Mystery Stories was launched at a time when Health Knowledge, Inc., the publishers of *Exploring the Unknown, Real Life Guide* and *Magazine of Horror*,* experiencing distribution problems, felt that it would be more beneficial to both themselves and the distributor to have a greater concentration of titles on the market. Thus, editor Robert A. W. Lowndes took it upon himself to assemble two more regular titles in the same saddle-stitched digest format. *Startling Mystery* appeared in May 1966 (with a cover date Summer) and five months later *Famous Science Fiction** was launched.

Startling Mystery had a wide editorial range. "Mystery both natural and unnatural is our province," wrote Lowndes in his first editorial. "The only restriction in the 'natural' section is that it be truly *unusual*."[1] *Startling Mystery* was therefore a hybrid detective/fantasy magazine. Science fiction, though not directly excluded, took a distant back seat.

As with *Magazine of Horror*, Lowndes strove for a mixture of new and reprint material, though the proportion of reprinted fiction was higher in *Startling Mystery* (78 out of 105 stories). Unlike *Magazine of Horror*, the reprints came predominantly from the pulps, and there was a high concentration of character series. Most prominent were the Jules de Grandin stories by Seabury Quinn, which appeared in thirteen of the eighteen issues. There was also a two-part chronological listing of the de Grandin stories accompanied by samplings of relevant *Weird Tales** covers in the Summer and Winter 1969 issues. Other series characters featured were the Dr. Satan stories by Paul Ernst; Simon Ark, created by Edward Hoch; and Taine of San Francisco, created by David H. Keller.

The nearest the reprints came to science fiction was in such stories as "The Game of Chess" (Summer 1967) by Robert Barr, resurrected by Sam Moskowitz from the March 1900 issue of *Pearson's Magazine*, and the "Darkness" series by Murray Leinster. Three of these stories, originally published in *Argosy** in 1929/1930 and subsequently difficult to obtain, were reprinted as follows: "The Darkness on Fifth Avenue" (Summer 1967), "The City of the Blind" (Spring 1969) and "The Storm That Had to Be Stopped" (March 1971). Not all of the reprints selected by Lowndes had stood the test of time, but he usually showed good judgment in his choice and often honored requests from readers. Lowndes regarded his readership as select because of the limited distribution of the magazine, and considered that a high percentage were devotees rather than general readers. Thus, he did not always choose his reprints solely on story merit, but took into consideration scarcity, novelty and popularity.

The new stories published by Lowndes are, in hindsight, perhaps more significant, as they include the first two sales by Stephen King. Lowndes prefaced the first, "The Glass Floor" (Fall 1967), with the following: "Stephen King has been sending us stories for some time, and we returned one of them most reluctantly, since it would be far too long before we could use it, due to its length. But patience may yet bring him his due reward on that tale."[2] Reader reaction was promising, and in "The Cauldron" (the magazine's letter column) in *Startling Mystery* 8, Lowndes asked King to resubmit his story; it appeared as "The Reaper's Image" in the Spring 1969 issue.

Other new stories in the magazine included "The Scar" by Ramsey Campbell (Summer 1969); "The Cleaning Machine," the first story sale by F. Paul Wilson, who later went on to establish himself in *Analog Science Fiction** (March 1971); "The Men in Black" by John Brunner (Fall 1966); and "The Man Who Collected Eyes" by Eddy Bertin (Summer 1970). Lowndes also revised two of his own early stories, "The Other" (Winter 1966) and "The Long Wall," retitled "Settler's Wall" (Fall 1968), and slipped in two others under the alias Jay Tyler.

Collectors will also find much of interest in Lowndes' editorials. These covered a variety of subjects in the detective fiction field with considered character analyses of such fictional sleuths as Sherlock Holmes, C. August Dupin, Nero Wolfe, Solar Pons and Hercule Poirot.

Startling Mystery was suddenly chopped in 1971 after the parent company, Acme News, was taken over by Countrywide Publications. It would be an exaggeration to say that the magazine had influenced the course of horror fiction by reviving interest in the works of Seabury Quinn and discovering Stephen King, but it cannot be denied that it has earned its niche in the history of the horror genre.

Notes

1. Robert A. W. Lowndes, "Introduction," *Startling Mystery Stories* 1 (Summer 1966):4.
2. Robert A. W. Lowndes, in his blurb to "The Glass Floor," *Startling Mystery Stories* 6 (Fall 1967):23.

Information Sources

BIBLIOGRAPHY:
Lowndes, Robert A. W., "The Health Knowledge Years." *Outworlds* 28/29 (combined; October 1976).
———. Letter in *Science-Fiction Collector* 8 (October 1979):45–47.
Tuck.
Weinberg, Robert. "Startling Mystery." In *Horror Literature*, ed. Marshall B. Tymn. New York: R. R. Bowker, 1981.
INDEX SOURCES: Cook, Michael L., *Monthly Murders*, Westport, Conn.: Greenwood Press, 1982; ISFM–II; Marshall, Gene, and Carl F. Waedt, "An Index to the Health Knowledge Magazines," *Science-Fiction Collector* No. 3, 1977; MT; NESFA; SFM; Tuck.
REPRINT SOURCES: None known.
LOCATION SOURCES: M.I.T. Science Fiction Library.

Publication History

TITLE: *Startling Mystery Stories*.
VOLUME DATA: Volume 1, Number 1, Summer 1966–Volume 3, Number 6, March 1971. Six issues per volume. Quarterly to Fall 1970, but no Fall 1969 issue. Planned as bi-monthly from March 1971, but no further issues appeared. Total run: 18 issues.
PUBLISHER: Health Knowledge, Inc., Fifth Avenue, New York.
EDITOR: Robert A. W. Lowndes.
FORMAT: Digest (saddle-stapled), 128 pp.
PRICE: 50¢, Summer 1966–Spring 1970; 60¢, Summer 1970–Fall 1970; 75¢, March 1971.
[Note: *Startling Mystery Stories* should not be confused with the earlier terror pulp *Startling Mystery*, which specialized in weird-menace stories as in *Horror Stories* and *Terror Tales*. It saw two issues in February and April 1940 and had a com-

panion magazine, *Sinister Stories*, March, April and May 1940. Both magazines came from the Popular Publications, Fictioneers Inc. imprint and were edited by Costa Caroussa. Both were 112 pp. and cost 15¢. Neither carried any fantasy or SF.]

Mike Ashley

STARTLING STORIES

In January 1939, Standard Magazines brought out a companion magazine to *Thrilling Wonder Stories (Wonder Stories*)*, appropriately called *Startling Stories*, in keeping with Standard's policy of prefixing its titles with attention-getting adjectives. *Startling* was pulp-size, 132 pages, and was designed to carry a lead novel of 45,000–60,000 words and a classic "Hall of Fame" reprint. Standard, with the rights to *Wonder Stories*, could present the old "classics" to a group of new readers, some of whom were too young to read when *Wonder Stories* was first published.

To lead off the first issue, Mortimer Weisinger, the first editor, acquired the rights to *The Black Flame* by Stanley G. Weinbaum, who had become a cult figure after his untimely death in 1935 cut short a brilliant career.[1] Any new work by Weinbaum would attract readers to a new magazine, but Weisinger had not plunged blindly into this new venture. In the Feburary 1938 issue of *Thrilling Wonder Stories*, Weisinger had asked for readers' reactions and suggestions regarding a companion magazine and had received a favorable response.

The initial reprint, complete with the original illustration by Frank R. Paul, was "The Eternal Man" by D. D. Sharp from the August 1929 *Science Wonder Stories*. The uncredited cover illustrated an action-packed scene from Eando Binder's short story, "Science Island." Otis Adelbert Kline wrote the first of a series of guest editorials, and Otto Binder presented a tribute to Weinbaum. Features included a pictorial article by Jack Binder on Albert Einstein entitled "They Changed the World," a "Science Question Box" and a crossword puzzle. Weisinger himself instituted a set of thumbnail sketches on famous scientists called "Thrills in Science," which rapidly became very popular. A letter column, "The Ether Vibrates," was started, and a review of fanzines, giving prices and addresses, became a regular feature.

Startling's format of novel and reprint was sufficiently different from *Thrilling Wonder Stories* for readers to want to purchase both magazines. In these early years the magazine was slanted toward a juvenile audience, and the novels were mostly interplanetary adventures written in pulp style by Eando Binder, Oscar J. Friend, Edmond Hamilton, Henry Kuttner, Manly Wade Wellman and Jack Williamson.

Among these were some novels quite daring in concept, and Wellman wrote two of them in the first two years.[2] In "Giants from Eternity" (July 1939), a blight from outer space is destroying all life on Earth. Two scientists discover a method to resurrect the bodies of the great scientific minds of the past—Pasteur, Newton, Darwin, Edison and Curie—to combat the menace. Probably Wellman's finest work in this period, illustrated by Virgil Finlay, was "Twice in Time" (May 1940), popular enough to be reprinted a decade later in *Fantastic Story Quarterly*.* Like Twain's Hank Morgan in *A Connecticut Yankee in King Arthur's Court*, Leo Thrasher, a modern time traveler, is thrown back into fifteenth-century Italy as Leonardo da Vinci.

Edmond Hamilton also wrote three novels in this early period which are worth remembering. The earliest was "The Prisoner of Mars" (May 1939), in which Martians invade Earth for its water. The first anniversary issue (January 1940) featured "The Three Planeteers," a space opera which Hamilton later claimed was the seed of the Captain Future series. The most compelling of the three was "A Yank at Valhalla" in the second anniversary issue (January 1941), a lost-race yarn with the original premise that the ancient Norse gods were actually men with advanced scientific knowledge.

One more novel from this early period deserves recognition for its advanced theme—Henry Kuttner's "A Million Years to Conquer" (November 1940). An ancient astronaut waits millions of years in orbit in suspended animation for Homo sapiens to evolve, making a number of forays to Earth during its history to search for a proper mate to rebuild the astronaut's race.

The choice of reprints was soon turned over to well-known fans, and the policy of reprinting the original artwork with the story was continued. Most of Weinbaum's stories found their way into the "Hall of Fame" ("A Martian Odyssey" was revived the first year, in November 1939), as well as old favorites by Clark Ashton Smith and David H. Keller.

The interior illustrations in this prewar period were capably drawn by Hans Wesso, Mark Marchioni and Alex Schomburg, with an occasional guest appearance by Virgil Finlay. Rudolph Belarski and Howard Brown painted most of the early covers, but in 1942 Earle K. Bergey became the exclusive cover artist until his death in 1952. His smooth, sensual covers featuring half-dressed women in brass brassieres established a pulp image that is often blamed for the unsavory reputation of SF during the forties.

When Oscar J. Friend became editor in 1941, most of the regular novelists had gone to war. Friend stayed on until 1944 and brought the inane Sergeant Saturn character over from *Thrilling Wonder Stories* to "The Ether Vibrates." On the whole, *Startling*'s quality during the war was maintained at a higher level than *Thrilling Wonder*, probably because of its format of longer novel and reprint. The magazine was forced to go quarterly in 1943 until late 1946.

When *Captain Future** was dropped, his adventures were continued in *Startling*. Captain Future was easily assimilated, for many of the novels were straight pulp SF adventure. But occasionally the usual offerings were leavened with a fantasy or weird tale. Prolific pulpster Norman A. Daniels wrote two of these light fantasies, for which Bergey did two of his finest covers: "Speak of the

Devil'' (March 1943), a pseudo-scientific apology for the existence of Satan, and "The Great Ego" (Spring 1944). Two more worthy weird fantasies were the Lovecraftian "Strangers on the Heights" (Summer 1944) by Manly Wade Wellman, a tale unearthing cult worship of alien creatures in the Andes, and Leigh Brackett's own polished brand of interplanetary sword and sorcery in "Shadow over Mars" (Fall 1944).

Perhaps influenced by the real Holocaust raging in the world, a number of catastrophe novels appeared during the war years. Writers imagined such disasters as dwarf stars peeling off the atmosphere and the oceans, leaving a desert world (except for America, of course) in Jack Williamson's "Gateway to Paradise" (July 1941); giant atoms out of control in Malcolm Jameson's "The Giant Atom" (Winter 1944); or gravity clouds and plagues sent by aliens from the future—as in Ross Rocklynne's "The Day of the Cloud" (November 1942) and Joseph J. Millard's "The Gods Hate Kansas" (November 1941).

One of the more imaginative pieces in this wartime interregnum was former western writer Noel Loomis' "City of Glass." Three time travelers are warped into the desolate distant future of 800,000 A.D., where a race of silicon humans has evolved. Loomis later wrote a sequel about another species, "The Iron Men" (Winter 1945).

With the Winter 1945 issue, Sam Merwin became editor. With the help of the enormously prolific team of Henry Kuttner and C. L. Moore and the frequent appearances of such stars from *Astounding (Analog Science Fiction**)* as A. E. van Vogt, George O. Smith and Murray Leinster, the quality of the fiction steadily improved.

From 1946 to 1949 the Kuttners, as Henry Kuttner and Keith Hammond, contributed seven of the lead novels. According to James Gunn, the Kuttners produced 300,000 words for *SS* and *Thrilling Wonder Stories* between 1947 and 1952.[3] Most of these works could be classified as science fantasy, a type of writing very common today but then very rare. Kuttner evoked praise from such ardent fans as Marion Zimmer [Bradley]. She and other readers especially liked "The Dark World" (Summer 1946), a Merrittesque parallel-worlds fantasy which had elements of Norse, Welsh, and Greek mythology and included werewolves, vampires, witches and talking trees. Kuttner followed up with "Lands of the Earthquake" (May 1947), a medieval fantasy set during the Crusades, and "Lord of the Storm" as Keith Hammond (September 1947), a tale set in the far future.

In the very popular "The Mask of Circe" (May 1948), the Kuttners recast the Greek myth of Jason and the Golden Fleece. Jay Seward, doing psychological research on ancestral memories, unleashes the memories of Jason and is plunged into a battle between Hecate, the last of a race of alien beings who became gods on Earth, and Apollo, a machine created by the gods to draw atomic power from the sun. Though these tales are fantasy and are sometimes written in a lush style reminiscent of A. Merritt, the Kuttners often contrived a pseudo-scientific rationale for their mysteries.

The Kuttners also wrote a number of shorter gems: "Absalom" (Fall 1946), a child-father conflict of superpowers, one of Kuttners' "generation gap" stories about children; and the incomparable "Don't Look Now" (March 1948), now called "The Third Eye."

Startling increased its size to 180 pages in November 1948, and in this same year two novels appeared in successive issues which have become standards in the field. In September came Fredric Brown's complex comic novel of alternate worlds, "What Mad Universe," and in November, Arthur Clarke's "Against the Fall of Night," which later was expanded into his famous *The City and the Stars*. Also in November was Ray Bradbury's first Martian Chronicle for *SS*, "The Visitor," and a filler lineup of A. E. van Vogt, Jack Vance and John MacDonald.

Throughout 1949 and 1950, this postwar trend toward excellence was escalated. Kuttner continued to lead the parade with a straight SF novel, "The Time Axis," in the tenth anniversary issue (January 1949), but returned to fantasy in September 1949 with "The Portal in the Picture." Newer authors like Charles L. Harness—"Flight into Yesterday" (May 1949)—and John MacDonald—"Wine of the Dreamers" (May 1950)—took over the lead spots. Old-timer Edmond Hamilton returned in the July 1950 issue with "City at World's End," a fine social SF novel about the aftermath of atomic war.

Merwin had built *Startling* into the best quality magazine of the period apart from *Astounding*. A list of the novelettes and short stories reads like a "best of Clarke and Bradbury" anthology: Arthur Clarke's "History Lesson" (May 1949), "Transience" (July 1949) and "The Fires Within" (September 1949); Bradbury's "Marionettes, Inc." (March 1949), "The Lonely Ones" (July 1949) and "Purpose" (July 1950); Jack Vance's Magnus Ridolph series; the Conquest of Space series by L. Ron Hubbard as Rene Lafayette; and other fine stories by C. M. Kornbluth, Fritz Leiber, Clifford Simak, William F. Temple and John Wyndham.

While its competitors like *Astounding* and *Galaxy Science Fiction** were reduced to digest size, *Startling*'s larger pulp size favored illustrators. The Bergey covers were sometimes awful, but with interior illustrations by Finlay and Stevens, *SS* and *Thrilling Wonder Stories* were among the best-illustrated magazines on the market, although there was a tendency to highlight scantily clad, curvaceous females.

The features also improved, except perhaps for the reprints, which began to come from the *Thrilling Wonder* of the thirties. The reprints were finally dropped with the November 1950 issue. Jerome Bixby now edited the fanzine column, and a book review column was added. Long before, Merwin had mercifully discontinued Sergeant Saturn in "The Ether Vibrates" and was receiving letters of praise and encouragement from such fans as Marion Bradley Zimmer, Chad Oliver, John Jakes and Robert Silverberg.

Samuel Merwin left the magazine in 1951 and later became a frequent contributor of fiction. *SS*, like other pulps, was feeling the increased competition from new magazines like *Galaxy* and *The Magazine of Fantasy and Science Fiction*.* In response, the new editor, Samuel Mines, instituted a policy of printing experimental, realistic fiction. In an editorial in "The Ether Vibrates" (August 1952), he proclaimed a new direction for *Startling*: "Science fiction must be good fiction as well. It must contain the basic requirements of drama, it must be well told, it must depict real people, it must be sincere in its emotional values as in calculating the speed of a spaceship operating on ultra-galactic drive."

Probably nothing was more startling in *Startling* than the publication of the now famous taboo-breaking "The Lovers" by Philip José Farmer in this same issue, which showed how sex could be used in an SF story without being obscene. Originally rejected by John W. Campbell at *Astounding* and Horace L. Gold at *Galaxy*, "The Lovers" is mild by modern New Wave standards. On a planet of humanoids metamorphosed from insects, the females called *lalitha* can only breed by mating with a human. After pregnancy, the mother dies and the young live off her flesh. One of the humans, in love with a lalitha, assumes that she is addicted to a drink which prevents pregnancy. Inadvertently, he dilutes the drink and the lalitha conceives and dies. The story is poignantly told and won Farmer a Hugo for "most promising new author" in 1953. A less memorable sequel demanded by the readers, "Moth and Rust," appeared in the August 1953 issue. Meanwhile, Farmer contributed a much better known story, "Sail On! Sail On!" (December 1952).

Startling had something for every taste and did not specialize in one type of story, as did *Astounding* and *Galaxy*. It varied from space opera—George O. Smith's "Hellflower" (May 1952)—to sociological SF—Jack Vance's "Big Planet" (September 1952), in which a variety of social systems coexist on a huge Earthlike world (an ancestor to Robert Silverberg's Majipoor). There was humor from Sprague de Camp, Kendall Foster Crossen and Anthony Boucher, and even an Arthurian fantasy by old-timer Fletcher Pratt, "The Spiral of the Ages" (Summer 1954).

Other stars of the fifties like Poul Anderson, Isaac Asimov, R. Bretnor, Miriam Allen deFord, Damon Knight, Judith Merril and Theodore Sturgeon appeared regularly, along with newer talents Philip K. Dick, Gordon Dickson, Frank Herbert, Walter Miller, Jr., and Robert F. Young.

In January 1952 the boom was under way, and *Startling* went monthly with the July 1952 issue, proof that *SS* was more popular than *Thrilling Wonder Stories*, the first and only time that a companion magazine started after the parent magazine was considered the superior title. (Even when *If** kept winning Hugos, *Galaxy* was still regarded as a "big sister.")

Mines completely changed the look of the magazine. He exchanged the lightning-shaped letters of the cover logo for more sedate block letters and revised the contents page. With Bergey's death in 1952, the covers were now painted by Alex Schomburg, Ed Emshwiller, Walter Popp and Jack Coggins. The breast-plated girls had been replaced by scenes of machines, spaceships or alien land-scapes, almost a return to the *Wonder Stories* days.

On the interiors, Virgil Finlay was unparalleled. Some of his finest work was done during the fifties for the larger-size Standard magazines, and capable artists like Schomburg, Emsh and Kelly Freas also graced its pages.

The pretense of printing a "book-length" novel was dropped, and the new format consisted of a long novelette or novella, two or three shorter companion novelettes, and several short stories. Science articles became a regular feature once again, and even an occasional cartoon appeared.

But even with a new format and improved quality, the fate of the pulps could not be long delayed for *Startling*. In June 1953 Mines announced that he was having trouble getting enough good material. In August 1953 the magazine went bi-monthly again, and in January 1954 turned quarterly. With the Spring 1955 number, the "novel" was officially dropped for the first time in the magazine's history, and *Startling*, now the only magazine left in the Standard group, absorbed *Thrilling Wonder Stories* and *Fantastic Story Quarterly*.

Only nine months after its companion, *Thrilling Wonder Stories*, disappeared from the market, *Startling Stories* passed into oblivion with the Fall 1955 issue. Its last issue included a novella, James Gunn's "The Naked Sky" (which later became part of *The Joy Makers*), illustrated by Virgil Finlay; shorter fiction by Mack Reynolds, Margaret St. Clair and Bryce Walton; and a cover by Ed Emsh. Ironically, *Startling Stories* had declined only a little from its peak under Merwin, publishing its share of the superb stories written during the fifties, when it ceased publication one short of its hundredth issue.

Notes

1. Weinbaum's original version, *Dawn of Flame*, had been rejected. He then wrote a much longer sequel, *The Black Flame*, which was again rejected because it did not have enough action for regular pulp readers.

2. Wellman actually wrote a third novel, "Sojarr of Titan" (March 1941), a pulpish adventure about a young Tarzan marooned on Saturn's largest moon.

3. James Gunn, "Henry Kuttner, C. L. Moore, Lewis Padgett *et al.*," in Thomas D. Clareson, ed., *Voices for the Future* (Bowling Green, Ohio: Bowling Green University Popular Press, 1976). I:211.

Information Sources

BIBLIOGRAPHY:
Nicholls. *Encyclopedia*.
Tuck.
INDEX SOURCES: ISFM; IBSF; IWG; MIT; SFM; Tuck.
REPRINT SOURCES:
   British Editions: Published irregularly by Pemberton's, Manchester, undated, but re-leased June 1949 to Summer 1954, 18 issues. Pulp, 64 pp., 1/-. Abridged editions of U.S. consisting mostly of lead story plus one or two shorts. U.K. issues correspond to U.S. as follows: 1, Win 46; 2, Mar 46; 3, Sum 46; 4, Sep 50; 5,

May 51; 6, Jul 51; 7, Sep 51; 8, May 51/Apr 52; 9, May 52; 10, Oct 52; 11, Nov 52; 12, Dec 52; 13, Jan 53; 14, Jan 53 (also); 15, Feb/Jun 53; 16, Dec 52 [*sic*]; 17, Jan 54; 18, Spr 54.

Foreign Editions: See *Enigmas* in the article on Mexico in Section IV.

Derivative Anthologies: Leo Margulies and Oscar J. Friend, *From off This World* (New York, Merlin: 1949), reprints 18 stories originally reprinted in *SS* as the "Hall of Fame" classics.

Microform: Greenwood Press Periodical Series.

LOCATION SOURCES: Brigham Young University; Eastern New Mexico University; Northern Illinois University; Pennsylvania State University; Texas A&M University; University of Arizona; University of California–Riverside; University of New Brunswick; University of Texas–Austin; University of Washington; University of Wisconsin-Milwaukee.

Publication History

TITLE: *Startling Stories*.

VOLUME DATA: Volume 1, Number 1, January 1939–Volume 33, Number 3, Fall 1955. Always three issues per volume. Bi-monthly, January 1939–March 1943; quarterly, June 1943–Fall 1946, although a March 1946 and a Spring 1946 issue were both released; bi-monthly, January 1947–November 1951; monthly, January 1952–June 1953; bi-monthly, August–October 1953; quarterly, January 1954–Fall 1955. Total run: 99 issues.

PUBLISHER: Better Publications, Chicago, January 1939–Winter 1955; Standard Magazines, New York, Spring–Fall 1955.

EDITORS: Mortimer Weisinger, January 1939–May 1941; Oscar J. Friend, July 1941–Fall 1944; Samuel Merwin, Jr., Winter 1945–September 1951; Samuel Mines, November 1951–Fall 1954; Alexander Samalman and Herbert D. Kastle, Winter-Fall 1955, last four issues. (In R. Reginald's *Science Fiction and Fantasy Literature*, Vol. 2, p. 957, Herbert D. Kastle claims to have "officiated over the death of *Startling Stories*.")

FORMAT: Pulp; 128 pp., January 1939–Spring 1944; 112 pp., Summer 1944–Spring 1945; 96 pp., Summer 1945–Winter 1946; 112 pp., March 1946–January 1948; 144 pp. March–September 1948; 176 pp., November 1948–January 1949; 160 pp., March 1949–May 1951; 144 pp., July 1951–August 1953; 128 pp., October 1953–Summer 1954; 112 pp., Fall 1954–Fall 1955.

PRICE: 15¢, January 1939–January 1948; 20¢, March–September 1948; 25¢, November 1948–Fall 1955. (Note: In March 1948 issue, masthead shows 15¢, but cover shows 20¢.)

Robert Ewald

STIRRING SCIENCE STORIES

The appearance of *Stirring Science Stories* and its companion, *Cosmic Stories*,* among the many magazines that proliferated during the early years of World War II marked the start of Donald A. Wollheim's long career as a professional editor. Spotting a magazine called *Stirring Western-Detective*, he wrote in the fall of 1940 to the publishers, Albing, to ask if they wanted to put out a *Stirring Science-Fiction*. They invited him over. Wollheim describes the interview as follows: "It was a father and son, . . . operating out of a desk in the corner of an advertising office, and what they had was credit from one of the news companies [distributors], . . . and they said, 'We don't have any capital, but if you can put the magazine together for nothing, we can go up to fifteen bucks for art, and we can do it. If the magazine succeeds, then we'll be able to pay you a regular salary after the third issue.' My attitude was that at least I'd be getting the experience, and something was better than nothing."[1]

The name finally given the magazine was *Stirring Science Stories*, but it was doomed from the outset by the lack of funds, since the writers too were promised payment only if the magazine succeeded. F. Orlin Tremaine, editor of another newcomer to the field, *Comet*,* expressed his anger to Isaac Asimov that "Wollheim was getting stories for nothing and, with these, could put out magazines that would siphon readership from those magazines that paid."[2] However, Asimov reports that John Campbell at *Astounding (Analog Science Fiction**), was unperturbed at competition from a magazine that could "only print stories that were unsalable in any professional market (What other stories would be given without payment?)."[3] This prognosis proved correct. Three issues of the magazine appeared in 1941, dated February, April and June (*Cosmic Stories* was published in the alternate months). Then, long after everyone had assumed its demise, a fourth issue, in larger format with fewer pages, came out in March 1942. The publishers had meanwhile become Manhattan Fiction Publications, and they promised monthly publication. Wollheim proclaimed in an editorial that the magazine had been revived in response to popular demand for what had become a leader in fantasy, and he announced that the next issue would feature "The Millionth Year" by Arthur C. Clarke. It never appeared, however, for the magazine went out of business once again.

Considering the severe financial handicaps under which he labored, Wollheim did a surprisingly good job. He had considerable experience with fanzines such as *The Phantagraph*, and together with Wilson Shepard had even edited a promising semi-professional magazine, *Fanciful Tales of Time and Space*,* though it managed only one issue, in 1936. Moreover, like Frederik Pohl, editor of *Astonishing Stories** and *Super Science Stories*,* he was able to draw upon the resources of his fellow Futurians, that talented group of fans already in the process of making their indelible mark upon science fiction. They were eager to get into print and willing to help a friend, and so their submissions, under their own names and a variety of pseudonyms, made up the bulk of each issue. James Blish, Walter Kubilius, David Kyle, Robert W. Lowndes, John Michel and Wollheim himself all contributed, sometimes in confusing collaborations, and Damon Knight's first story was published in the February issue. Entitled "Resilience," it was a humorous account of mankind's demise at the hands of tiny aliens, but its impact was unfortunately limited by a misprint that rendered the story incomprehensible. Under the pseudonym Hugh Raymond, Michel published what is probably his finest story, "Spokesman for Terra," in which a series of farcical intrusions gleefully deflates the romantic idealism of the situation.

However, the most notable contributions, in terms of both quantity and quality, came from Cyril Kornbluth under a variety of pseudonyms. As S. D. Gottesman, he wrote rambling but fast-paced adventures; as Kenneth Falconer, he produced a couple of suitably chilling tales, including "The Words of Guru," which proved very popular with the readers. His greatest success, however, was as Cecil Corwin. "Thirteen O'Clock" is, as Knight remarks, "a delightful screwball fantasy, full of demons, warlocks, lava nymphs with Brooklyn accents, etc."[4] although the novelty palls in the sequel, "Mr. Packer Goes to Hell." "The Golden Road" shows the author in a more philosophical mood: he weaves an appropriate atmosphere of phantasmagoria in a story of experience after death that makes a penetrating comment upon the struggle between good and evil.

Of stories by non-Futurians, two particularly merit attention: David Keller's "Key to Cornwall" and Clark Ashton Smith's "The Coming of the White Worm" were compelling fantasies, written with a stylistic and technical control that were too often painfully lacking in the newcomers. Wollheim was able to coax imaginative and fast-paced adventure stories from his friends, but they lacked the experience and financial incentive to produce better-crafted work for him. As a result the stories usually suffered from stereotyped characterization, trite dialogue, weak plot structure and a failure to develop theme.

Despite these weaknesses, however, *Stirring Science Stories* is worth remembering for several reasons. For a start, Wollheim hit upon the innovative idea of dividing the magazine into two parts, connected by an editorial section called "The Vortex": the first, subtitled "Stirring Science-Fiction," was devoted to "hard" science fiction; the second, subtitled "Stirring Fantasy-Fiction," contained stories of fantasy, and it was here that the best tales were found, perhaps because the competing market for fantasy was smaller.[5] Furthermore, the artwork of Hannes Bok, which appeared on the covers of the last three issues, was well above the average encountered in magazines and deservedly won the approval of the readers; the magazine also served as a useful training ground both for aspiring young authors, several of whom went on to impressive careers, and for Wollheim himself, who has proved to be one of the great science fiction editors; and finally, it provided some of the most lively reading in the field. For a magazine operating on next to nothing, these achievements were certainly stirring!

Notes

1. Damon Knight, *The Futurians* (New York: John Day, 1977), p. 87.
2. Isaac Asimov, *In Memory Yet Green* (Garden City, N.Y.: Doubleday, 1979), p. 283.
3. Ibid., p. 285.
4. Knight, *Futurians*, p. 88. The Cecil Corwin stories were later collected and edited by James Blish in *Thirteen O'Clock and Other Zero Hours* (New York: Dell, 1970).
5. Of the titles cited above only the two stories by Knight and Michel did not appear in the fantasy section.

Information Sources

BIBLIOGRAPHY:
Knight, Damon. *The Futurians*. New York: John Day, 1977.
Nicholls. *Encyclopedia*.
Tuck.
INDEX SOURCES: ISFM; MT; SFM; Tuck.
REPRINT SOURCES:
  Microform: Greenwood Press Periodical Series.
LOCATION SOURCES: Pennsylvania State University Library.

Publication History

TITLE: *Stirring Science Stories*.
VOLUME DATA: Volume 1, Number 1, February 1941–Volume 2, Number 1, March 1942. Three issues per volume. First three issues bi-monthly. Total run: 4 issues.
PUBLISHER: Albing Publications, New York, February–June 1941; Manhattan Fiction Publications, New York, March 1942.
EDITOR: Donald A. Wollheim.
FORMAT: Pulp, 128 pp., first three issues; Large Pulp, 6 pp., final issue.
PRICE: 15¢.

Raymond H. Thompson

THE STORYTELLER

Title given to final pocketbook version of *Copper Toadstool*. See COPPER TOADSTOOL.

STRANGE ADVENTURES

The first incursion into the SF magazine field by Hamilton and Co. (the firm that later published *Authentic Science Fiction**) produced two large-size companion magazines—*Futuristic Stories** and *Strange Adventures**—indistinguishable from one another in their poorly written, juvenile-oriented contents, and of no interest to anyone other than the completist collector. Two undated issues of *SA* appeared; the first was probably published in late 1946.

The contents were almost certainly the work of gangster writer N. Wesley Firth under various pen names, though editor Dennis H. Pratt may have found a home for one or two of his rejects from Walter Gillings' *Fantasy*.*

Information Sources

BIBLIOGRAPHY:
Nicholls. *Encyclopedia*.
Tuck.
INDEX SOURCES: IBSF; SFM; Tuck.

REPRINT SOURCES: None known.
LOCATION SOURCES: None known.

Publication History

TITLE: *Strange Adventures* (first issue entitled *Amazing Adventures* on contents page).
VOLUME DATA: Issues undated. Number 1 [ca. November 1946]–Number 2 [ca. January 1947]. 2 issues.
PUBLISHER: Hamilton & Co., London.
EDITOR: Dennis H. Pratt.
FORMAT: Large Pulp; 48 pp., first issue, 32 pp., second issue.
PRICE: 2/-.

Mike Ashley

STRANGE FANTASY

During the years 1969 and 1970 Sol Cohen experimented with a variety of magazine titles and contents, partly to test the market, but mostly to make full use of the reprint rights to stories published in *Amazing Stories** and *Fantastic** and acquired by Cohen when he purchased the magazines from Ziff-Davis in 1965. Cohen had crossed swords with the Science Fiction Writers of America over the payment of reprint fees, and part of the final resolution was to phase the reprints out of *Amazing* and *Fantastic*. As a counterbalance, however, Cohen issued nine different reprint titles in addition to the three already launched (*Great Science Fiction,** *Most Thrilling Science Fiction Ever Told* [*Thrilling SF**] and *Science Fiction Classics**).

The experiments resulted in a number of surprises, one of which was the first issue of *Strange Fantasy*, dated Spring 1969, but issued as Number 8. It was mailed to subscribers to *Science Fiction Classics* and followed the seventh issue of that magazine, but it was clearly not meant as a substitute for that title. The contents were totally different, and in fact an eighth issue of *Science Fiction Classics* followed soon after. Cohen was simply using the slot with his distributor to test a new magazine that could use some of the fantasy-oriented stories not suited to his other titles. The issue contained four stories, all with an SF connection, and including "Some Fabulous Yonder" by Philip José Farmer and "Nine Starships Waiting" by Roger Zelazny.

With the next issue, *Strange Fantasy* settled into the format that would remain—shorter stories and articles culled mostly from the early 1960s issues of *Fantastic*. Authors included Fritz Leiber, Harlan Ellison, Roger Zelazny, Ursula K. LeGuin, Robert Bloch and J. G. Ballard, but the names do not reflect the quality of the fiction, only one or two stories per issue being worthy of resurrection. The best issue was also the last. Dated Fall 1970, it included Fritz Leiber's chilling "Midnight in the Mirror World," John Brunner's "Elixir for the Emperor," Ursula K. LeGuin's early fantasy "The Word of Unbinding" and an early episode in the life and death of Roger Zelazny's Dilvish the Damned, "Thelinde's Song."

The content of *SF* was continued to some extent by *Weird Mystery*.*

Information Sources

BIBLIOGRAPHY:
Nicholls. *Encyclopedia*.
INDEX SOURCES: ISFM-II; MT; SFM.
REPRINT SOURCES: None known.
LOCATION SOURCES: None known.

Publication History

TITLE: *Strange Fantasy*.
VOLUME DATA: Number 8, Spring 1969–Number 13, Fall, 1970. [No issues 1–7.]
     Quarterly, issues dated Spring, Summer, Fall (no Winter). Total run: 6 issues.
PUBLISHER: Ultimate Publishing Co., Flushing, New York.
EDITOR: Sol Cohen (not identified within issues).
FORMAT: Digest, 128 pp.
PRICE: 50¢.

Mike Ashley

STRANGE LOVE STORIES

Strange Love Stories was one of several booklets published by Benson Herbert's Utopian Publications, some of which, including *Strange Tales** and *Thrilling Stories*,* are borderline magazine/anthologies that because of continued wartime restrictions had to be issued in book form. *SLS* was one of the last of the fantasy booklets and carried three stories, by E. Hoffman Price, Edmond Hamilton and Jack Williamson from *Strange Stories*,* *Weird Tales** and *Argosy*,* respectively. The stories were difficult to obtain at the time, and the booklet is now a rare collector's item.

Two further booklets followed that could easily have borne the *SLS* title but instead carried the title of the lead (or only) story: *Dangerous Love* by Ralph Milne Farley and *Romance in Black* by Gans T. Field (Manly Wade Wellman). The three booklets should be regarded, if not as a short magazine series, certainly as an anthology triplet.

Information Sources

BIBLIOGRAPHY:
Gillings, Walter. "Topless in Utopia." *Vision of Tomorrow*, July 1970, pp. 62–63.
INDEX SOURCES: Gillings, Walter, "Topless in Utopia," *Vision of Tomorrow*, July
     1970, pp. 62–63.
REPRINT SOURCES: None known.
LOCATION SOURCES: None known.

Publication History

TITLE: *Strange Love Stories*.
VOLUME DATA: Unnumbered, undated, but released April 1946.
PUBLISHER: Utopian Publications, London.
EDITOR: Benson Herbert (not identified in issue).
FORMAT: Digest (saddle-stapled), 74 pp.
PRICE: 1/-.

Mike Ashley

STRANGE STORIES

The first major boom in science fiction and fantasy publishing took place from 1939 through 1941, when well over a dozen new magazines were launched by ambitious publishers looking for new markets. It was not that science fiction had become a major force in pulp publishing, but that the entire pulp publishing field experienced a major boost in sales due to a recovery in personal finance as the Depression ended and war approached. Standard Magazines was one of those chains that started a number of new magazines. Standard (or Better Publications) already was the publisher of *Thrilling Wonder Stories*.* In 1939 it launched *Startling Stories** and *Strange Stories* and followed those with *Captain Future** in early 1940.

Strange Stories was a fantasy magazine in the vein of *Weird Tales*.* Unfortunately, that similarity was its major problem through its three-year existance. The magazine had little personality or character of its own, and most of the stories read like rejects recycled by authors who sold their best material to *Weird Tales*. With the science fiction boom, authors had a variety of markets to submit their work to. *Unknown*,* supported by the giant Street and Smith publishing chain, could afford the best and attracted the best new fantasy with good rates. *Weird Tales* had begun an economy move under new ownership but still was a long-established market with loyal authors. *Strange Stories* thus started with two strikes against it. Adding to these problems was the magazine's format.

Each issue of *Strange Stories* promised thirteen stories. In a pulp that was never more than 128 pages, and later was only 96 pages (including ads), there was little room for long stories. In keeping with the policy of Standard at the time, no serials were permitted. There was little room in such a magazine for stories that allowed the author to develop character, plot or mood. Most were short weird or horror pieces with twists or unusual endings—not the type of material to build a strong and loyal readership for a sales base.

While some attempt was made to feature well-known fantasy authors, many hacks who did work for other Better Publications magazines were often featured in *Strange Stories*. Thus, issues might carry work by headliners Robert Bloch and August Derleth side by side with stories by pedestrian authors like Maria Moravsky and Don Alviso. Not helping matters any was a group of dreadful covers, among the worst ever seen on any pulp, by Standard staff artists Rudolph Belarski and Earle Bergey.

Not everything published in *Strange Stories* was second-rate. Too much of it was, though, for the magazine to succeed. Robert Bloch had a dozen stories in the magazine (under his own name and the pseudonym Tarleton Fiske) but only a few were on the level of his work in *Weird Tales*. August Derleth, not noted for consistently high quality in his weird fiction, had sixteen stories in the magazine published under his own name, two under pseudonyms and two in collaboration with Mark Schorer. Of those stories, only one was of any note— ''Logoda's Heads,'' perhaps Derleth's best weird fantasy for any magazine. Manly Wade Wellman contributed several good stories to the early issues of the pulp. Eric Frank Russell and C. L. Moore both had one story each in *Strange Stories*, and they were among the highlights of the magazine's history. Seabury Quinn, E. Hoffman Price and Henry Kuttner each had several stories in the thirteen-issue run; all were less than spectacular.

Strange Stories had an ambitious beginning but sank into mediocrity within a few issues. When, in August 1940, the magazine dropped its price from fifteen cents to ten cents and the page count dropped from 128 to 96, discerning readers must have sensed that the end was in sight. The magazine struggled along for three more issues and then folded.

As with most competitors of *Weird Tales* that tried to copy the original, *Strange Stories* had little influence on the fantasy field. It offered nothing new, and except for publishing a few noteworthy stories did not have any effect on the genre. *Weird Tales* was already in financial difficulty when *Strange Stories* began, and it was the huge glut of magazines that soon followed that hurt ''the Unique Magazine'' more than any one competitor. *Strange Stories* was a typical mass-produced pulp title, an imitation doomed before it ever began.

Information Sources

BIBLIOGRAPHY:
Nicholls. *Encyclopedia*.
Tuck.
Weinberg, Robert, *The Weird Tales Story*, West Linn, Ore: Fax Collector's Editions, 1977.
INDEX SOURCES: Cockcroft, IWFM; Day, IWFM; MT; SFM; Tuck; Weinberg, Robert. *The Weird Tales Collector* 6. Chicago, Ill.: Pulp Press, 1980 (gives listing by issue).
REPRINT SOURCES: None known.
LOCATION SOURCES: None known.

Publication History

TITLE: *Strange Stories*.
VOLUME DATA: Volume 1, Number 1, February 1939–Volume 5, Number 1, February 1941. Three issues per volume. Bi-monthly. Total run: 13 issues.
PUBLISHER: Better Publications, New York.

EDITOR: Not identified within issues, but probably Mort Weisinger.
FORMAT: Pulp, 128 pp., February 1939–June 1940; 96 pp., August 1940–February
     1941.
PRICE: 15¢, February 1939–June 1940; 10¢, August 1940–February 1941.

Robert Weinberg

STRANGE TALES

Two small British booklets appeared after the war reprinting stories from
American magazines, predominantly *Weird Tales.** Although in format these
could be regarded as anthologies, and legally that is all they were, in intent they
were magazines. Labeled as first and second "selections," the two issues could
not be classified as magazines because immediate postwar restrictions did not
allow new magazines to begin without a lot of form-filling and red tape, and it
was unlikely that a small, new magazine such as *Strange Tales* would be granted
an additional quota of paper.

And so these two issues of a magazine were a real wolf in sheep's clothing.
The editor, who remained uncredited, was Walter Gillings, former editor of
*Tales of Wonder** and, to all intents, the father of British magazine SF. With
his usual impeccable editorial acumen he selected a very readable cross-section
of stories by writers such as Jack Williamson, Robert Bloch, Clark Ashton Smith,
Ray Bradbury (purportedly his first publication in Britain) and H. P. Lovecraft.

Apparently, however, copies were slow to sell, because, so the distributor
believed, there was such a glut of horror titles on the market. As a result the
third issue, which was ready to go to press, never appeared. Today, issues are
extremely rare and command high prices. Had *ST* continued there is no doubt
that it would have become one of the best sources in Britain of rare and inaccessible American fantasy.

Information Sources

BIBLIOGRAPHY:
Gillings, Walter. "Topless in Utopia." *Vision of Tomorrow*, July 1970, pp. 61–62 (also
     includes index).
Nicholls. *Encyclopedia.*
Tuck.
INDEX SOURCES: Cockcroft, IWFM; Day, IWFM; IBSF; MT; Tuck.
REPRINT SOURCES: None known.
LOCATION SOURCES: None known.

Publication History

TITLE: *Strange Tales.*
VOLUME DATA: Labeled First Selected and Second Selection. Undated, but issued
     February and March 1946.
PUBLISHER: Utopian Publications, London.

EDITOR: Walter Gillings (not credited in issue).
FORMAT: Digest, 64 pp.
PRICE: 1/-, first issue; 9d., second issue.

Mike Ashley

STRANGE TALES OF MYSTERY AND TERROR

Strange Tales of Mystery and Terror, which debuted in 1931, was the only magazine published as direct competition to *Weird Tales** that offered that magazine a serious challenge; not only was its policy much the same and its contents written by many of the same authors, but, unlike the later *Unknown** and the terror pulps, *ST* was aimed at the same readership. The magazine was a companion to Clayton's *Astounding Stories* (*Analog Science Fiction**) and was likewise edited by Harry Bates. It was published on a thicker stock cheap pulp paper, and thus, while it contained about the same number of pages as *Weird Tales*, it actually look thicker.

Bates was an experienced editor and had definite ideas about what he wanted for his magazine. He was not as catholic in his taste as Farnsworth Wright, preferring fast-paced action stories over anything else. However, he knew good writing and paid two cents a word for the best material, a rate that *Weird Tales* could not match. Bates was thus able to attract many authors who would not have contributed to *Weird* and was also able to obtain some of the better stories by that magazine's regulars. The result was a magazine that, while it only lasted for seven issues, contained, measure for measure, a far greater quantity of good stories than would be found in *Weird Tales* or, for that matter, any other magazine of the time with the possible exception of *Unknown*.

One way that Bates achieved better quality was by publishing long stories complete in one issue. *ST* published no serials, which often lessen the impact, but allowed authors to experiment more with story and character development. Every one of the seven issues featured a long lead story, and all are worthy of reprinting. The first issue, dated September 1931, featured "The Dead Who Walk" by Ray Cummings, about lost souls who have returned to Earth and taken over the bodies of the recently dead. The lead story for November 1931 was Arthur J. Burks' tale of Aztec mystery, "Guatemozin the Visitant," followed by perhaps the best long story *ST* published, "Wolves of Darkness" by Jack Williamson (January 1932). This novella is really science fiction, telling of evil creatures from another dimension that take possession of humans and animals. It gave Hans Wessolowski a chance to produce possibly his best cover for *ST*.

The March 1932 issue presented Paul Ernst's "The Duel of the Sorcerers" as the feature story, a powerful variant on the vampire theme, though by far the best vampire story in *ST* appeared in the last issue: "Murgunstruum" by Hugh B. Cave, a vampire story with a difference. The title, incidentally, refers to a dwarf who feeds off human flesh, which gives some idea of the lengths to which

ST's authors went to supply something out of the ordinary. The other two feature stories in *ST* were "The Great Circle" by Henry S. Whitehead, one of his popular West Indian stories about the secret of a strange circular clearing in the forest, and "The Curse of Amen-Ra" by Victor Rousseau, a rather typical and disappointing tale of Egyptian revenge.

In spite of *ST*'s short life, a number of writers became regular contributors. Henry Whitehead was present in all but the first issue, and four of his stories were narrations by Gerald Canevin, including "Cassius" (November 1931), possibly the best of them all, and "The Trap" (March 1932), a story of other dimensions and a strange mirror. Clark Ashton Smith nearly equalled Whitehead, with five contributions, starting in the first issue with his oft-reprinted "Return of the Sorcerer." Others included "The Door to Saturn" (January 1932) and "The Nameless Offspring" (June 1932), though the best was probably "The Hunters from Beyond," the cover story for the October 1932 issue.

Both Smith and Whitehad were, of course, also *Weird Tales* regulars, as were Arthur J. Burks, Victor Rousseau, August Derleth, Edmond Hamilton and Robert E. Howard, all of whom published one or more stories in *ST*. S. P. Meek would later sell one story to *Weird*, but in 1931 he was better known as a science fiction writer. His two contributions to *ST* therefore showed that he had an equal flair for the supernatural, especially in the first issue with "Nasturtia," which used the theme of reincarnation. Other Clayton regulars who appeared in *ST* include Charles Willard Diffin, who had two stories including the pseudo-scientific "The Dog That Laughed" in the first issue, Sewell Peaslee Wright with "The Dead Walk Softly" (October 1932) and adventure writer Gordon MacCreagh, who contributed two excellent stories about Dr. Muncing the exorcist. The third story was advertised but never appeared because *Strange Tales* was one of the first Clayton pulps to fold as the Depression years squeezed William Clayton's finances beyond the limit.

The passing of *ST* was a sad loss. In many ways it was the equal of *Weird*, for although it did not carry some of the more bizarre and esoteric tales that made *Weird* so exceptional, it also avoided many of the dull, repetitious and routine stories that made *Weird* so predictable. We shall probably never know why Street and Smith did not revive *Strange Tales* when it acquired rights to the title along with *Astounding* in 1933. Had it been allowed to develop under Desmond Hall and F. Orlin Tremaine in like manner to *Astounding*, it is almost certain that the magazine would have bettered *Weird Tales*. But it might also have meant that *Unknown* would never have come into being, and we must, in the final analysis, admit that that would have been an even greater loss.

Information Sources

BIBLIOGRAPHY:
Jones, Bob. "Masterpieces of the Macabre." *Xenophile*, No. 42 (1979):127–30.
Tuck.
INDEX SOURCES: Cockcroft, IWFM; Day, IWFM; MT; SFM; Tuck.

REPRINT SOURCES: The first four issues were reprinted in their entirety in various issues of the Health Knowledge magazines (*Magazine of Horror, Startling Mystery Stories, Weird Terror Tales* and *Bizarre Fantasy Tales*), as were most of the fifth and sixth issues.

Derivative anthology: Strange Tales (Melrose Highlands, Mass.: Odyssey, 1976).

LOCATION SOURCES: None known.

Publication History

TITLE: *Strange Tales of Mystery and Terror* (usually referred to simply as *Strange Tales*).

VOLUME DATA: Volume 1, Number 1, September 1931–Volume 3, Number 1, January 1933. Three issues per volume. Bi-monthly, September 1931–March 1932; quarterly, June 1932–January 1933 (middle issue October 1933). Total run: 7 issues.

PUBLISHER: Clayton Magazines, New York.

EDITOR: Harry Bates.

FORMAT: Pulp, 144 pp.

PRICE: 25¢.

Robert Weinberg

THE STRANGEST STORIES EVER TOLD

The Strangest Stories Ever Told was one of the many digest magazines issued by Sol Cohen in 1970 that reprinted stories from the files of *Amazing Stories** and *Fantastic Adventures.** This magazine saw only one issue and formed a brief weird fiction companion to *The Most Thrilling Science Fiction Ever Told.** It contained only seven stories, chosen from the 1949 issues of *Amazing Stories* and the 1951 issues of *Fantastic Adventures*. The stories were of little merit except for William P. McGivern's macabre "Fix Me Something to Eat."

Information Sources

INDEX SOURCES: ISFM-II; MT; SFM.

REPRINT SOURCES: None known.

LOCATION SOURCES: None known.

Publication History

TITLE: *The Strangest Stories Ever Told*.

VOLUME DATA: Number 1, Summer 1970. Only issue.

PUBLISHER: Ultimate Publishing Co., Flushing, New York.

EDITOR: Sol Cohen (not identified within issue).

FORMAT: Digest, 128 pp.

PRICE: 50¢.

Mike Ashley

SUPER SCIENCE AND FANTASTIC STORIES

See SUPER SCIENCE STORIES (Canadian).

SUPER-SCIENCE FICTION

By the mid-1950s, Frederik Pohl has estimated, there were in existence thirty-eight different periodicals more or less describable as science fiction magazines.[1] By the end of 1959, there were only nine. *Super-Science Fiction*, first published late in 1956, was, deservedly, one of the casualties. A digest-size magazine from a publisher and editor both new to the science fiction field,[2] it managed to limp through eighteen bi-monthly issues of six numbers each before expiring.

Published by Headline Publications and edited by W. W. Scott, an editor experienced in pulp magazine fiction but unable to tell good science fiction from bad,[3] *Super-Science Fiction* filled its issues with stories and short science and pseudo-science articles by the "fiction factory" writers of the time, chiefly Robert Silverberg. Of the 120 stories and novelettes published in its eighteen issues, thirty-six were by Silverberg, writing under his own name and the pseudonyms Dirk Clinton, Calvin M. Knox, Dan Malcolm, Alex Merriman, Eric Rodman, and Richard F. Watson, and ten were by Harlan Ellison, writing under his own name and the pseudonyms Cortwainer Bird and Ellis Hart. In the seventeenth issue, the magazine's next to last, the novelette "Planet of the Angry Giants" by Dirk Clinton and three of the seven stories—"The Horror in the Attic' by Alex Merriman, "Monsters That Once Were Men" by Eric Rodman and "Which Was the Monster?" by Dan Malcolm—were by Silverberg, who had won a Hugo Award in 1956 as "most promising new author" and later said of this period in his life, "I often wrote 10,000 words a day."[4]

The first issue, dated December 1956, featured a striking cover by Kelly Freas, portraying a spaceman shaking his fists in defiance at the stars, and an editorial by W. W. Scott declaring that the theme of the new magazine would be "people." "In our time, science is becoming super-science," wrote Scott. "But the way this coming super-science will affect people, human character, is the whole idea of SUPER-SCIENCE FICTION. . . . The Man of The Future is going to conquer the universe with fist and fury. . . . His intelligence and his determination, his brains and his courage will conquer the stars."

This optimistic credo was contradicted by the contents of the magazine. Witness the first issue: in the Robert Silverberg story "Catch 'Em All Alive" spacemen land on a planet and wind up as displays in its zoo; in "Who Am I?" by Henry Slesar a spaceman turns schizophrenic; and in "Psycho at Midpoint" by Harlan Ellison a young spaceman, after fifteen months in space, goes mad and murders his crewmates.

The cover painting by Ed Emsh for the second issue (February 1957) shows a giant mummified inhabitant of the planet on which a spacewoman has landed coming to life to destroy her and features a novelette, "Every Day Is Christmas" by James E. Gunn, set in a dystopian Earth future in which the hero shoots Santa Claus and is incarcerated in an asylum, a novelette, "Mission: Hypnosis" by Harlan Ellison, in which the leading spacemen characters are killed; and a story, "Death of a Mutant" by Charles V. De Vet, in which a boy with "strange

and wonderful powers'' is slain by the police. In almost every story it is the
environment that triumphs, not the hero.

In its third issue, the magazine began to publish bug-eyed monster stories
(''Galactic Thrill Kids'' by Robert Silverberg), which by the fifteenth issue,
announced on the cover as ''Special Monster Issue,'' had taken over almost
completely. The cover of the sixteenth issue bore the label ''Second Monster
Issue,'' the issue after that ''Third Monster Issue'' and the eighteenth and final
issue ''Weird Monster Issue.''

The titles of the stories in these issues show the descent of the magazine from
its original bold editorial proclamations: in issue 15, novelettes ''Mournful Monster'' by Dan Malcolm (Silverberg) and ''Vampires from Outer Space'' by
Richard F. Watson (Silverberg) and stories ''The Abominable Creature'' by
F. X. Fallon, ''The Huge and Hideous Beasts'' by James Rosenquest and ''A
Cry for Help'' by Eric Rodman (Silverberg); in issue 16, the novelette ''Beasts
of Nightmare Horror'' by Richard F. Watson (Silverberg) and the stories ''Terror
of the Undead Corpses'' by Russell Thompson, ''Creatures of Green Slime'' by
James Rosenquest and ''The Day the Monsters Broke Loose'' by Robert Silverberg; in the eighteenth and final issue, the novelette ''The Loathsome Beasts''
by Dan Malcolm (Silverberg) and the stories ''The Monsters Came by Night''
by Abraham Stern, ''Asteroid of Horror'' by James Rosenquest and ''The Insidious Invaders'' by Eric Rodman (Silverberg). The last story was summarized
on the contents page with the words ''Can a more inclusive form of life swallow
up man?,'' a sad ending for a magazine which had proclaimed in its first editorial
to be about man's conquering the universe.

Among the writers published in *Super-Science Fiction* were Isaac Asimov,
Lloyd Biggle, Jr., Robert Bloch (whose name was misspelled ''Block'' on the
cover), Evelyn E. Smith, Jack Vance and Robert F. Young, but none with their
best work. ''Though it used material by established writers,'' was the verdict
by Brian Stableford on the magazine, ''its contents were mediocre.''[5]

Notes

1. Paul A. Carter, *The Creation of Tomorrow: Fifty Years of Magazine Science Fiction*
(New York: Columbia University Press, 1977), p. 275.

2. Michael Ashley, *The History of the Science-Fiction Magazine. Part 4, 1956–1965*
(London: New English Library, 1978), p. 21.

3. Ibid., p. 21.

4. Mike Ashley. *The Illustrated Book of Science Fiction Lists* (London: Virgin Books,
1982), p. 100.

5. Peter Nicholls, ed., *The Science Fiction Encyclopedia* (New York: Doubleday,
1979), p. 585.

Information Sources

BIBLIOGRAPHY:
Nicholls. *Encyclopedia.*
Tuck.
INDEX SOURCES: MIT; SFM; Tuck.

REPRINT SOURCES: None known.
LOCATION SOURCES: Pennsylvania State University Library.

Publication History

TITLE: *Super-Science Fiction.*
VOLUME DATA: Volume 1, Number 1, December 1956–Volume 3, Number 6, October
     1959. Six issues per volume; bi-monthly. Total run: 18 issues.
PUBLISHER: Headline Publications, Inc., Holyoke, Massachusetts. Editorial offices:
     New York City.
EDITOR: W. W. Scott.
FORMAT: Digest, 128 pp.
PRICE: 35¢.

Milton Subotsky

SUPER SCIENCE NOVELS MAGAZINE

See SUPER SCIENCE STORIES.

SUPER SCIENCE STORIES

Super Science Stories was one of the two science fiction magazines set up
under the editorship of the nineteen-year-old Frederik Pohl at the beginning of
World War II.[1] From the outset (the first issue was dated March 1940) the
magazine was planned to carry longer fiction, while its companion, *Astonishing
Stories,** concentrated upon shorter material. This focus led to a title change in
the seventh issue, which appeared in March 1941 as *Super Science Novels
Magazine*; but after only three appearances under this new name it reverted to
the original title. This issue marked an editorial change also, as Alden H. Norton
replaced Pohl. However, having responsibility for several magazines, Norton
soon rehired his predecessor as associate editor, in which capacity Pohl continued
as the major influence upon *Super Science Stories* until he joined the Air Force
in April 1943.

Although owned by Popular Publications, the magazine was part of a subsidiary known as Fictioneers, Inc., which paid only half the regular market rate of
a penny a word. With so tight a budget Pohl was forced to scramble for material
to fill his pages. Fortunately he was one of a group of young science fiction
enthusiasts known as the Futurians, who were not only eager to write stories,
but went on to prove that several of them could do it very well indeed. In their
first year alone Pohl's two magazines published fifteen stories by Futurians,
notably Isaac Asimov, Donald Wollheim, James Blish, Richard Wilson, Cyril
Kornbluth and Pohl himself, sometimes in a confusing variety of collaborations.
When mixed with the productions of veterans like Leigh Brackett, John Russell

Fearn, Frank Belknap Long, Ross Rocklynne and Raymond Gallun, and seasoned with some nonetheless respectable rejects from John Campbell's *Astounding* (*Analog Science Fiction**) written by Robert Heinlein, Clifford Simak and Jack Williamson, the result was one of the better magazines of the day.

If many of the stories seem less than the authors' best efforts, some are worthy by any standard. Wollheim, under the pseudonym Martin Pearson, produced a poignant little mood piece about the aftermath of war in "A Planet Called Aquella" (November 1942); Damon Knight, writing as Stuart Fleming, created strong suspense in "New Day on Aurora" (May 1943); and Asimov supplied a humorous yarn about robots called "Victory Unintentional" (August 1942). Most notable, however, was Blish's "Sunken Universe" (May 1942), which creates a very believable alien world. Written under the pseudonym Arthur Merlyn, this is the first of the Pantropy series; resumed in 1952, the stories were finally brought together in the outstanding *The Seedling Stars* (1957). *Genus Homo* (1950) by P. Schuyler Miller and L. Sprague de Camp is another novel developed from a fine novelette which was first published in the pages of *Super Science Stories* (March 1941). Pohl's keen eye for talent was further evidenced by his publishing the first sales of Bob Tucker and Ray Bradbury. Despite such successes, the economics of the wartime paper shortage doomed *Super Science Stories* along with its companion, *Astonishing*, once Pohl left. Ejler Jakobssen stepped in to assist Norton with the last issue, dated May 1943.

Popular Publications had started a Canadian edition of *Super Science Stories** in August 1942, reprinting material from all their science fiction magazines, and they continued this until December 1945. However, when the second boom swept through the field of science fiction, the publishers decided that the time was opportune for a revival of the magazine.

Norton was now the associate publisher at Popular, and he appointed as editor Ejler Jakobssen, who had helped him when Pohl left. Damon Knight later joined as assistant editor. *Astonishing* and *Super Science Stories* had been the first science fiction magazines to attempt serious literary criticism in their book reviews, and this tradition was revived, fittingly enough by Pohl himself, in a column called "The Science Fictioneer." Pohl's astute reviews won praise in the readers' letters, though his unenthusiastic response to Orwell's *Animal Farm* and *1984* in the November 1949 issue suggests that his judgment had its biases. The revived *Super Science Stories*, which appeared in January 1949, was published simultaneously in Canada and the United States; in fact, both editions were printed in Canada initially. The lead novelette was Henry Kuttner's "The Black Sun Rises," and this choice signaled the direction which the magazine was to take during its last years.

For a start, the novelette was a reprint from the Canadian edition of June 1944. Indeed, the entire issue was made up largely of reprints. They continued to appear and were instituted as a regular feature during the last year. Readers grumbled about this policy in their letters, although, as one lamented, part of his annoyance arose at finding Blish's "Sunken Universe" superior to the contemporary stories. This link with the past was reinforced by stories like Neil R. Jones' resurrected saga of Professor Jameson and the robotmen, which had started in *Amazing Stories** back in 1931 and continued in *Astonishing* during the war. The readers still enjoyed it, but they were less patient with Cummings' "Fragment of Diamond Quartz" (January 1950), which at least one recognized as yet another tired variation upon the story of a microscopic world first explored by the author over thirty years earlier in "The Girl in the Golden Atom."

Although it recalled the past traditions of science fiction, both good and bad, "The Black Sun Rises" also looked to the future and a new era in science fiction writing. It was not just a well-paced adventure story, but went on to explore the conflict between personal loyalties and humane ideals. Although it suffered from being too short to deal satisfactorily with the problems raised, it did serve to give notice of the magazine's willingness to explore new directions, even if the results sometimes fell short of expectations. The second issue contained "Dhac-twhu—Remember?" by Robert Lowndes and Forrest Ackerman writing under pseudonyms, but the evocative and dreamlike atmosphere is unfortunately wasted on a trite story. This was Bradbury's territory, and he demonstrated his mastery of it in a series of stories, including "I, Mars" in the same issue, and the haunting "Impossible" (November 1949), which is a comment upon man's attempts to realize his conflicting hopes and dreams. The story was later collected as part of the author's *Martian Chronicles* (1950), under the title "The Martian." Ironic reversals were popular in many stories, though nowhere exercised with finer skill than in Arthur C. Clarke's "Exile of the Eons" (March 1950), where a power-mad dictator seeking to escape into the future is killed, even though execution has long been rejected as barbaric.

Faces new to the field also appeared: the mystery writer John D. MacDonald contributed regularly, and Chad Oliver, an inveterate letter-writer, made his first appearance in fiction with "The Land of Lost Content" (November 1950). The most impressive newcomer to appear in *Super Science Stories*, however, was Poul Anderson, and it was ironic that the last issue carried his "Terminal Quest" (August 1951), which recounts the last day in the life of the sole survivor of a troll-like race, callously exterminated when humans seize their planet. The story is sentimental but channels this emotion to deliver a powerful indictment against intolerance and selfishness that is impossible to forget.

Super Science Stories was one of the most interesting magazines to appear during the 1940s. Its artwork was never distinguished: it improved substantially over the amateurish efforts that marked its earlier years, but even in the hands of Virgil Finlay and Stephen Lawrence its covers never lost their preoccupation with spacesuited heroes rescuing lithesome damsels in improbably scanty garb from the grasp of menacing robots or grotesque aliens. However, the literary merits of the magazine belied its garish covers. Writers of the stature of Anderson, Blish and Bradbury wrote first-class tales for *Super Science Stories*, and if others seemed to give less than their best, few of the major writers of the era failed to supply memorable stories. As Michael Ashley has perceived, the magazine "acted as the necessary link between *Astounding* and the new breed of magazines to follow. It provided that needed refresher course wherein authors had a chance to rethink their style and approach in preparation for what was to come."[2]

It is regrettable that *Super Science Stories* ceased publication just as it was making significant strides toward establishing a distinctive voice. Yet it had served its function: during the war it proved a valuable training ground for burgeoning young talents, and later served as an equally vital point for new departures in style and approach; with its early companion, *Astonishing*, it introduced literary criticism into book reviews. However, the links with the past, reinforced by the policy of reprints, were possibly too strong and restrictive. The decision to cease publication was economic, but it served the science fiction field better than many might have imagined at the time. Its writers were now ready for the new magazines, less hampered by the past. But it was no accident that *Galaxy Science Fiction*,* most successful of the newcomers, should have been guided through its greatest years by Frederik Pohl, applying the lessons he had learned so well as the first editor of *Super Science Stories*, to coax award-winning work from former regulars like Poul Anderson. *Super Science Stories* had served the future well indeed.

Notes

1. For a description of what took place see the entry for *Astonishing Stories*.
2. Michael Ashley, *The History of the Science Fiction Magazine, Part 3* (London: New English Library, 1976), p. 36.

Information Sources

BIBLIOGRAPHY:
Nicholls. *Encyclopedia*.
Tuck.
INDEX SOURCES: ISFM; MIT; SFM; Tuck.
REPRINT SOURCES:
  Reprint Editions: See entry on *Argosy Special*.
  Foreign Editions: See separate entry on Canadian edition. See also separate entry on U.K. magazine *Cosmic Science Stories* (1950). Two separate British reprint series appeared. The first ran for three issues, undated, unnumbered [October 1949, February and June 1950], issued by Thorpe & Porter, Leicester, pulp, 96 pp., 1/-. Correspond to U.S. issues Jan and Nov 49 and Jan 50. Second series issued by Pemberton's of Manchester, undated, fourteen issues [September 1950–June 1953]. First eight issues approximately quarterly, thereafter bi-monthly. Pulp, 64 pp., 1/-. First seven issues equate to abridged editions of U.S. originals Apr 49, Sep and Nov 50, Jan, Apr, Jun and Aug 51. Issues 8–14 select from first U.S. series corresponding predominantly as follows: 8, May 43; 9, Feb 43; 10, Aug 42; 11, Nov 42; 12, May 42; 13, Mar 41; 14, Nov 41. Issue 13 [April 1953] only is entitled *Super Science Novels Magazine* on cover.
LOCATION SOURCES: Brigham Young University Library; Pennsylvania State University Library; Texas A&M University Library.

Publication History

TITLE: *Super Science Stories*, March 1940–January 1941; *Super Science Novels Magazine*, March 1941–August 1941. Reverted to *Super Science Stories*, November 1941–May 1943 and January 1949–August 1951.

VOLUME DATA: Volume 1, Number 1, March 1940–Volume 8, Number 3, August 1951. Four issues per volume. Bi-monthly, March 1940–May 1941; quarterly, August 1941–May 1943, and again January–April 1949; bi-monthly July 1949–January 1951 and April–August 1951.

PUBLISHER: Fictioneers, Inc. (a subsidiary of Popular Publications), March 1940–May 1943; Popular Publications, New York, January 1949–August 1951.

EDITORS: Frederik Pohl, March 1940–August 1941; Alden H. Norton, November 1941–May 1943; Ejler Jakobssen, January 1949–August 1951.

FORMAT: Pulp; 128 pp., March 1940–January 1941; 144 pp., March 1941–February 1943; 128 pp., May 1943 and January 1949–January 1951; 112 pp., April–August 1951.

PRICE: 15¢, March 1940–January 1941; 20¢, March 1941–February 1943; 25¢, May 1943 and January 1949–August 1951.

Raymond H. Thompson

SUPER SCIENCE STORIES (Canadian)

When the Canadian government imposed a ban on the import of pulp magazines in February 1941, it provided an impetus to American publishers to bring out editions of their magazines north of the border. The most ambitious of these ventures was mounted by Popular Publications, which brought out three reprint issues of *Astonishing Stories** during the first half of 1942, then switched to *Super Science Stories** in August 1942. Although the magazines ceased publication in the United States in April and May 1943, respectively, the Canadian edition of *Super Science Stories* survived until December 1945, by which time twenty-one bi-monthly issues had been printed in Toronto.

Most of the stories were reprinted from Popular's American magazines, initially from earlier issues of *Super Science Stories* and *Astonishing Stories*. The contents of the first Canadian issue were drawn from the February 1942 American edition of *Super Science Stories*, those for the second from the June 1942 *Astonishing Stories*; this pattern of taking material from single issues of the two magazines alternately, though never reprinting the entire contents of any one issue, continued with little variation until these sources were depleted. The eleventh issue, which appeared in April 1944, included not only tales from a variety of earlier issues of both American magazines, but also two original stories that had been purchased but remained unpublished when they ceased publication. The next issue contained no less than six of these original stories, and three more appeared in later issues, but the magazine thereafter filled its pages with material from *Famous Fantastic Mysteries*,* which Popular had taken over from the Munsey chain in 1941. This magazine, itself devoted largely to reprints of earlier "classics," was more oriented toward fantasy than had been Popular's other two publications, and this change in the contents of the Canadian magazine was signaled by a title change to *Super Science and Fantastic Stories* for the last six issues.

The stories reprinted from *Super Science Stories* included some notable performances, such as Isaac Asimov's "Victory Unintentional" and Ross Rocklynne's "Abyss of Darkness," as well as exciting adventure yarns like E. E. Smith's "The Vortex Blaster Makes War." However, by failing to reprint material from most of the earlier issues of both magazines, the publishers ignored such striking stories as "Sunken Universe" (May 1942), written for *Super Science Stories* by James Blish under the pseudonym Arthur Merlyn.

That this exclusion resulted from publishing convenience rather than from a desire to spare Canadian readers dated material is apparent from the choice of reprints from *Famous Fantastic Mysteries*. These included such venerable stories as Murray Leinster's "The Mad Planet" (December 1944), which had first appeared in *Argosy** on June 12, 1920, to say nothing of A. Merritt's "The Moon Pool" (December 1945) and Ray Cummings' "The Girl in the Golden Atom" (October 1945), both from the pages of *All-Story Weekly*, the former on June 22, 1918, the latter on March 15, 1919. Despite their age, these were effective stories, although the merits of the last were unfortunately dimmed by the author's own too-frequent imitations of the idea of a microscopic world. Indeed, one of them, "A Fragment of Diamond Quartz," had already been published under the pseudonym Ray Shotwell in the August 1944 issue of the Canadian magazine. Stories of more recent vintage were also reprinted: Robert W. Chambers' "The Yellow Sign" (April 1945), which first appeared in *Famous Fantastic Mysteries* in September 1943, was typical of that magazine's penchant for the weird; George Michener's "Last Stop—Earth" (June 1945), first printed in *Argosy* on March 7, 1942, was equally typical, though as in many such tales the conflict which the protagonist experiences between the urges of love and duty gains poignancy from its wartime relevance; however, Ray Bradbury's account of the disillusionment that follows attaining a childhood dream in "King of the Gray Spaces" (August 1944), reprinted from the December 1943 issue of *Famous Fantastic Mysteries*, was powerfully evocative despite its sentimentality.

The handful of original tales also included some strong performances, notably James Blish's sardonic account of political leapfrog in "The Bounding Crown" (December 1944) and Ray Bradbury's brief but chilling "And Then—the Silence" (October 1944).

Once the war ended and the ban on pulps was lifted, the magazine ceased publication. No real attempt had been made to establish a Canadian identity; even letters in "Viewpoint" were reprinted from the American magazines. Some of the artwork was new, presumably by Canadians, but most of it was borrowed: Stephen Lawrence's cover for the final issue, for example, had appeared on *Famous Fantastic Mysteries* in September 1945.

However, the magazine's Canadian exile was not quite over, for when it was revived in January 1949 with its original title, *Super Science Stories*, not only was it published simultaneously in Canada and the United States but both editions were in fact printed in Canada initially. This issue was composed mainly of reprints from the original stories in the Canadian edition and featured Henry Kuttner's fine novelette, "The Black Sun Rises," which had appeared in June 1944. Notwithstanding these promising signs, the Canadian dimension to the revival remained, as before, an arrangement of financial convenience. The decision to cancel publication of the joint Canadian and American edition in anticipation of a recession in the market for pulps was reached, fittingly, in New York, not Toronto. Despite its northern ventures, *Super Science Stories* was always an American magazine, run from New York under the editorship of Alden H. Norton during the war (initially assisted by Frederik Pohl), then by Ejler Jakobssen; its disappearance after the August 1951 issue was neither more nor less significant to Canadians than might have been that of any of its American rivals.

Information Sources

BIBLIOGRAPHY:
Thiessen, J. Grant. "Super Science Stories [Canadian Series]," *The Science-Fiction Collector* No. 4, July 1977, available from J. Grant Thiessen, Box 54, Neche, N.D. 58265.
Tuck.
INDEX SOURCES: SFM; Thiessen, J. Grant, "Super Science Stories [Canadian Series]," *The Science-Fiction Collector* No. 4, July 1977; Tuck.
REPRINT SOURCES: None known.
LOCATION SOURCES: The Spaced-Out Library, Toronto.

Publication History

TITLE: *Super Science Stories*, August 1942–October 1944; *Super Science and Fantastic Stories*, December 1944–December 1945.
VOLUME DATA: Volume 1, Number 1, August 1942–Volume 1, Number 21, December 1945. Bi-monthly. Total run: 21 issues.
PUBLISHER: Popular Publications, Toronto.
EDITOR: Edited from New York by Alden H. Norton.
FORMAT: Pulp; 96 pp., Numbers 1–10; thereafter 80 pp.
PRICE: 15¢

Raymond H. Thompson

SUPERNATURAL STORIES

Supernatural Stories is one of those oddities of weird fiction. It began life in 1954 as a simple small digest publication of surprisingly readable quality considering that it was published by John Spencer and Company, whose earlier track record with SF magazines (for example, *Futuristic Science Stories**) was less than admirable. It then vanished for nearly two years and reemerged as a regular pocketbook publication. In another two years the series took on a double identity. Alongside the regular story collection was published simultaneously a complete novel. The novels were numbered sequentially as part of the series, and on the whole alternated with the collection.

SS therefore is arguably not a magazine, certainly not in its second incarnation, but a regular companion novel and story collection. Since the contents of the collections were usually written by a single hand—mostly Lionel Fanthorpe, but also John Glasby—little editing was necessary. The publishers never referred to the series as a magazine, not even in its first incarnation. It was always a ''bimonthly pocket book.'' Nevertheless, its regularity and its feature of short stories under different by-lines have caused most collectors to regard it as a magazine, in much the same way that some of the hero pulps, also written entirely by one writer (*G-8 and His Battle Aces*,* for instance), are seen as ''magazines.''

Most of the first series of *SS*, which ran for eight issues, was written by John Glasby under such pseudonyms as A. J. Merak, Randall Conway, Michael Hamilton, Max Chartair and even Ray Cosmic. Despite the pace at which they were written, the stories are readable and even enjoyable. Glasby had a natural talent for producing weird fiction, and it is even possible that the fast pace helped generate moods and emotions. Although many of the plots are derivative and the characterizations weak, the stories, if read selectively, still carry a certain power. Certainly many are the equal of the stories that had appeared in the final issue of *Weird Tales*,* which had seen a British edition at about the same time.

The ninth issue of *SS* appeared eighteen months later, in the spring of 1957, still in the small-digest format. This time the entire issue was the work of E. C. Tubb. The stories lack some of the verve of the Glasby tales, but are still readable.

With the tenth issue *SS* was converted to pocketbook format, and so it remained. This issue and the next were both the work of John Glasby, but with the twelfth issue Lionel Fanthorpe started his long but surprisingly quick route to becoming the world's most prolific writer of SF and fantasy. Fanthorpe was also producing the new companion Science Fiction series of novels, as well as the later Supernatural Series novels, and as he also held down full-time employment, the stories and novels were created at white-heat with no revision and precious little time for plotting or character development. Fanthorpe, however, is a born storyteller; provided one does not read too many of his stories at one sitting, and once one gets used to his flippant treatment of stock characters and settings and keys into his in-jokes, the stories can become quite enjoyable. They are, however, not a patch on Glasby's for the creation of a supernatural atmosphere or even an element of conviction. There can be no reader involvement in Fanthorpe's stories, whereas there can be in Glasby's.

Fanthorpe filled forty-eight of the *SS* collections and thirty-five of the *SS* novels; the remainder were predominantly by Glasby. Fanthorpe's issues are easily identifiable by his bizarre use of pseudonyms, most of them being partial anagrams of his full name, Robert Lionel Fanthorpe. Thus, we are presented with such alter egos as Lionel Roberts, Pel Torro, Bron Fane, Terbor Thorpe, Leo Brett, and, as issues passed, more exotic variants like Rene Rolant, Erle Barton and Olaf Trent. Under the Bron Fane alias, Fanthorpe presented a series about an occult investigator, Val Stearman, and his wife, La Noire; at times these are among the better stories, although they frequently pall. Fanthorpe was certainly better at short stories than novels, which allowed him room to be more flamboyant but show little development over the shorter works. Instead they are packed with padding, lengthy dialogues that get nowhere, and some interminable poetry.

In order to fill some issues at this breathtaking pace (some of the collections were put together in less than twenty-four hours), Fanthorpe used stories by friends, and these are among the better items, simply because they were not written to a publishing deadline. The best are those under the alias Noel Bertram, which hide the work of Noel Boston, an East Anglian vicar who had privately published a short volume of stories called *Yesterday Knocks* (Dereham: Colby, 1954). Somewhat in the tradition of M. R. James, these stories convey a rather more homely but no less positive ecclesiastical chill, from a man who had formidable background knowledge of matters mysterious. Two other writers for whom Fanthorpe fronted were Harry Mansfield and Ernest Kemp, whose stories are scattered throughout the issues under a variety of pseudonyms, none specific. Mansfield, for instance, wrote "The Chinese Lustre Vase" (*SS* 87, as Phil Nobel), "The Lady Loves Cats" (*SS* 91, as Thornton Bell) and "In a Glass Darkly" (*SS* 93, as Robin Tate), among others.

A few of the stories, by both Glasby and Fanthorpe, come within the framework of the Cthulhu Mythos of H. P. Lovecraft, although they have not been generally recognized. These include "The Sorcerer's Cave" by Fanthorpe as Trebor Thorpe (*SS* 12) and "Solitude" by Glasby as Michael Hamilton (*SS* 79).

The series came to an abrupt end in 1967 when Spencer sensed that the market was drying up and turned to producing a series of technical books. It is still in operation, the only one of the hack publishers to survive the blight that devastated the field in the mid-1950s.

Information Sources

BIBLIOGRAPHY:
Ashley, Mike. *Fantasy Reader's Guide* 1. Wallsend, U.K.: Cosmos, 1979.
Tuck.
INDEX SOURCES: Ashley, Mike, *Fantasy Reader's Guide* 1, Wallsend, U.K.: Cosmos, 1979; MT.
REPRINT SOURCES: None known.
LOCATION SOURCES: Pennsylvania State University Library.

Publication History

TITLE: *Supernatural Stories*. This title always applied to the story collections; although issues 13, 15, 17 and 19 bore the cover and spine title *Out of this World* (a former companion to *SS*), they are still part of the *SS* sequence. The novels were headed "Supernatural Special" but continued the numbering of the series.

VOLUME DATA: The entire run was designated Volume 1 until issue 85; thereafter the volume and issue number were united. All issues undated. Number 1, [May 1954]– Number 109, [Summer 1967]. Bi-monthly, Nos. 1–8 [May 1954–Autumn 1955]; No. 9 [Spring 1957]; bi-monthly, Nos. 10–18 [June 1957–October 1958]; monthly, Nos. 19–27 [November 1958–July 1959]; bi-monthly, Nos. 28–33 [September 1959–May 1960]; monthly, Nos. 34–36 [June–August 1960]; No. 37 [November 1960]; monthly, Nos. 38–42 [January–March 1961]; thereafter on a six-weekly schedule until No. 81 [September 1963]; bi-monthly, Nos. 82–93 [November 1963–September 1964] and Nos. 94–103 [February 1965–Spring 1966]; quarterly, Nos. 104–109 [Summer 1966–Summer 1967]. Issue 108 has not been sighted and may not have been released. The above sequence includes the companion novels, which were usually published simultaneously. The novel series numbers run: 29, 32, 35, 40, 42, 44, 46, 48, 50, 52, 54, 56, 58, 60, 62, 64, 66, 68, 70, 72, 74, 76, 78, 80, 82, 84, 86, 88, 90, 92, 94, 96, 98, 100, 102, 104, 106, plus 108 if published. Total run: novels, 37 [or38]; collections, 71.

PUBLISHER: John Spencer & Co., London.

EDITORS: Sol Assael and Michael Nahum (unidentified in issues, but credited to John Spencer Manning in some).

FORMAT: Issues 1–8, Small Digest, 128 pp.; issue 9, 160 pp.; issues 10–109, Pocketbook, 160 pp., except issues 33, 34, 36, 41, 43, 144 pp.

PRICE: Issues 1–8, 1/6d.; issues 9–36, 2/-; issues 37–99, 2/6d.; issues 100–109, 3/6d.

Mike Ashley

SUSPENSE MAGAZINE

Suspense, first published in 1951, has only a passing relevance to the SF field, although it is of greater interest to the weird fiction and mystery fan. Inspired by the CBS radio and television series of the same name, and including a reprint of an episode in script form in each issue, *Suspense* was a general fiction magazine presenting stirring adventures in the crime, mystery, fantasy, SF and adventure fields. The selection included both new and reprint stories.

Science fiction was probably included because the genre was starting to experience a boom, and the publisher felt that it should have at least token representation. Included were stories by some of the field's best writers—Theodore Sturgeon, A. E. van Vogt, William Tenn, Ray Bradbury—but on closer examination one learns that many are reprints and others are more in the weird fiction vein, such as Sturgeon's "Ghost of a Chance." The same might be said of a contribution by H. L. Gold, "Love Ethereal," which is closer to his writings for *Unknown** than to the stories he was purchasing for *Galaxy Science Fiction.** The magazine did mark the first American publication of John Wyndham's "Pawley's Peepholes," but under the title "Operation Peep."

On the fantasy side reprints were once again dominant, with stories from William Hope Hodgson, Ambrose Bierce, Sir Arthur Quiller-Couch and Mary

Elizabeth Counselman. A surprise appearance, however, and one that now makes the Fall 1951 issue a collector's item, was the publication of a hitherto unpublished Gray Mouser story by Fritz Leiber, "Dark Vengeance."

The final issue carried no SF and precious little weird fiction. By then the wave of SF magazines had yet to crest, but *Suspense* had decided not to ride that wave. Its attempt to refocus itself as a mystery and crime story magazine, however, did not sustain it.

Information Sources

BIBLIOGRAPHY:

Nicholls. *Encyclopedia*.

Tuck.

INDEX SOURCES: Cook, Michael L., *Monthly Murders*, Westport, Conn.: Greenwood Press, 1982 (lists by issue and author); MIT; MT; Tuck.

REPRINT SOURCES: None known.

LOCATION SOURCES: Pennsylvania State University Library; University of California–Los Angeles Library.

Publication History

TITLE: *Suspense Magazine*.

VOLUME DATA: Volume 1, Number 1, Spring 1951–Volume 1, Number 4, Winter 1952. Quarterly. Total run: 4 issues.

PUBLISHER: Farrell Publishing Co., Chicago, Illinois, with editorial offices in New York. General Manager was Arnold Abramson, who later became the publisher of *Galaxy*.

EDITOR: Theodore Irwin.

FORMATR: Digest, 128 pp.

PRICE: 35¢.

[Note: This magazine should not be confused with two British mystery magazines of similar title. *Suspense Stories* saw three issues (undated and unnumbered) between July and November 1954, published by Curtis Warren, London, and contained only a minimum of fantasy if one stretches one's imagination. Then there was *Suspense*, from Fleetway Publications, which saw thirty-two monthly issues between August 1958 and April 1961 and contained fantasy of a better quality; although it published more fantasy than the earlier magazine, the amount was still minimal. Finally, there was an earlier American magazine called *Suspense, The Mystery Magazine* from Suspense Magazine, Inc. in Los Angeles, which saw four issues between November 1946 and March 1947. This one also claimed to be based on the CBS radio show of the same name, but even with Leslie Charteris as editor was short-lived. It contained no recognizable fantasy.]

SWAN AMERICAN MAGAZINE

Non-SF series which included two SF issues. See YANKEE SCIENCE FICTION.

SWAN YANKEE MAGAZINE

See YANKEE SCIENCE FICTION and YANKEE WEIRD SHORTS.

SWORD & SORCERY ANNUAL

The last fling Sol Cohen had with reprint magazines came in the winter of 1974/75 when he issued the nonfiction *U.F.O. Annual* and the *Sword & Sorcery Annual*. The latter had arisen because of the increase in sales in issues of *Fantastic*,* which contained a new Conan story.

Cohen went to the expense of acquiring reprint rights to an original Robert E. Howard Conan story, "Queen of the Black Coast," which had first appeared in the May 1934 *Weird Tales** and was therefore not available to Cohen through his back files. The story had also been included in the 1969 Lancer paperback *Conan of Cimmeria*. Cohen printed a new painting by Steve Fabian for the cover and included new Fabian illustrations in the story; thus, the *Annual* was far superior in appearance to the other Cohen reprint magazines.

Fortunately the contents were also good, being selected from the golden age of *Fantastic* under editor Cele Goldsmith in the early 1960s. They were "The Pillars of Chambalor," a Brak adventure by John Jakes; "Master of Chaos" by Michael Moorcock; "The Mirror of Cagliostro" by Robert Arthur; "The Cloud of Hate," one of Fritz Leiber's Fafhrd and Gray Mouser tales; "The Masters" by Ursula K. LeGuin; and "Horseman!," an apocalyptic vignette by Roger Zelazny. There was also a reprint of Sam Moskowitz's article on the writings of L. Sprague de Camp.

For a period thereafter *Fantastic* bore the subtitle "Swords & Sorcery and Other Fantasies," but the *Annual* was never repeated.

Information Sources

BIBLIOGRAPHY:
Nicholls. *Encyclopedia*.
INDEX SOURCES: MT; NESFA; SFM.
REPRINT SOURCES: None known.
LOCATION SOURCES: None known.

Publication History

TITLE: *Sword & Sorcery Annual* (bannered "Fantastic Stories Special—1975").
VOLUME DATA: One issue, undated, released Winter 1974/75.
PUBLISHER: Ultimate Publishing Co., Flushing, New York.
EDITOR: Sol Cohen.
FORMAT: Digest, 128 pp.
PRICE: 75¢.

Mike Ashley

TALES OF CRIME AND PUNISHMENT

Despite the misleading title, *Tales of Crime and Punishment* (Number 21 in the World's Work's Master Thriller Series*) contains much of interest to the fantasy fan. This relates more to the range of the contributors than the fiction, although the lead story, "The Enthroned Goat of Ballycarry" by F. W. Murray, had fantasy connections. Of slightly greater interest is a story by Benson Herbert, "Hand of Glory." Herbert had sold several stories to *Wonder Stories** in the early 1930s and in the 1940s would set up his own company, Utopian Publications, which published *Strange Tales.**

Of greater interest is "Egyptian Episode," a forgotten story by one of SF's greats, Eric Frank Russell. Also of interest is "The Shot That Told" by Arlton Eadie. Eadie is remembered as a prolific contributor to *Weird Tales** during the 1930s and it is easy to forget that he was in fact a British writer who contributed regularly to the popular periodicals of the day. Eadie, whose real name was Leopald Eady, had died in 1935, and "The Shot That Told" was probably his last published story.

Information Sources

BIBLIOGRAPHY:
Tuck.
INDEX SOURCES: MT.
REPRINT SOURCES: None known.
LOCATION SOURCES: British Library.

Publication History

TITLE: *Tales of Crime and Punishment*.
VOLUME DATA: Number 21 in the Master Thriller Series. Undated, but published around November 1937.

PUBLISHER: World's Work, Kingswood, Surrey.
EDITOR: Not named, but possibly H. Norman Evans.
FORMAT: Pulp, 128pp.
PRICE: 1/-.

Mike Ashley/Frank H. Parnell

TALES OF GHOSTS AND HAUNTED HOUSES

Although only a minor magazine, *Tales of Ghosts and Haunted Houses* is important as being the only one of the Master Thriller Series* to bear a cover date—December 1939. Because of the entry of Britain into World War II it is probable that this was also the last title in the series—Number 32.

It contained ten stories, and most of the contributors are unknown, with the exception of Henry Rawle, whose name appears frequently in both the Master Thriller Series and several of the Gerald Swan magazines. The stories are mostly squibs, relating spooky incidents, although the lead story, ''The Curator Chats'' by J. Ennarke, is of novelette length.

Information Sources

BIBLIOGRAPHY:
Tuck.
INDEX SOURCES: MT.
REPRINT SOURCES: None known.
LOCATION SOURCES: None known.

Publication History

TITLE: *Tales of Ghosts and Haunted Houses.*
VOLUME DATA: Number 32 in the Master Thriller Series, December 1939.
PUBLISHER: World's Work, Kingswood, Surrey.
EDITOR: Not credited but may be H. Norman Evans.
FORMAT: Pulp, 96pp.
PRICE: 1/-.

Mike Ashley/Frank H. Parnell

TALES OF MAGIC AND MYSTERY

Tales of Magic and Mystery was a short-lived magazine which specialized in true tales and articles about magic and the occult, mixed in with a number of short stories. It has achieved a certain fame because it published a story by H. P. Lovecraft, ''Cool Air,'' one of the few to appear outside the pages of *Weird Tales** at that time. But until now little has been written of the history of TOM&M and of its eventual demise.

It came about in 1927 when the firm of Personal Arts, a subsidiary of the mighty corporation International Correspondence Schools, was pleased at the success indicated by one of its mailings on "The Secrets of the Ages," and was looking about for further suggestions. Publisher Bill Kofoed, who produced the magazine *Brief Stories* for another of ICS's subsidiaries, Haddon Press, together with writer and magician Walter Gibson, came up first with the idea of a series on miracles, to be called *Book of Secrets*, and then with the idea of a magazine which would combine magical and mystical fact and fiction—*Tales of Magic and Mystery*.

A dummy issue was prepared, and production estimates indicated an extremely favorable proposition. Kofoed questioned the costs but was reassured, and the magazine went ahead on a monthly basis.

Walter Gibson edited the magazine and wrote the nonfiction. This included a series on mysterious people of the past and present under the pen name Alfred Maurice; a piece about the trick of bullet-catching under the alias Bernard Perry, illustrated by Earle K. Bergey—later to become famous for his SF pulp covers; a series of semi-factual articles about incidents in the life of the famous American magician Howard Thurston, published under Thurston's name; and a variety of fillers. The Thurston series was all that was ever promoted on the front cover, indicating the sales potential in the magician's name. The series included such episodes as "The Miracle Man of Benares," "The Girl Who Was Burned Alive" and "Among the Head-Hunters of Java," all with a kernel of truth but suitably embellished by Gibson.

Gibson also wrote a series under his own name on the feats and special tricks of the great Harry Houdini, whom Gibson knew as well as if not better than anybody. Whether it was the Houdini connection that drew Lovecraft's attention to *TOM&M* is not clear. Houdini had died in 1926, and only a few years earlier Lovecraft had ghostwritten one story for Houdini for *Weird Tales*. Since Gibson was also ghostwriting some books on magic for Houdini at the time of the escapologist's death, it is likely that Lovecraft knew of Gibson and thought *TOM&M* might be less of a risk than most of the other pulps outside *Weird Tales*. Since not long before Lovecraft had had an altercation with Gernsback over payment for "The Colour out of Space," it was probably not his practice to submit a story directly to another magazine without some background knowledge. Another factor was that *TOM&M* was edited in Philadelphia and not New York, which may have brought it more into Lovecraft's favor.

"Cool Air" is not one of Lovecraft's best stories, but it is far from his worst. In theme it is a reworking of Poe's "The Facts in the Case of M. Valdemar," except that the hapless victim is kept alive not by mesmerism, as in Poe's tale, but by refrigeration.

A few other recognizable names appeared in the magazine. Frank Owen, another regular in *Weird Tales*, had two stories. "The Yellow Pool," one of his earliest, had originally appeared in Kofoed's *Brief Stories* and was reprinted in the second issue. His others were "The Black Well of Wadi" (December 1927) and "The Lure of the Shrivelled Hand" (April 1928). "The Yellow Pool" had, in fact, also been reprinted in *Weird Tales* (October 1925), which implies that Owen had probably kept control of the reprint rights to the story. Whether he sanctioned its publication in *TOM&M* is questionable. Gibson recalled that most of the fiction "was material that had been offered to *Brief Stories* or that Bill Kofoed acquired through regular contacts,"[1] but Gibson may not have known the full circumstances. Miriam Allen deFord also had a story in the magazine, "Ghostly Hands" (January 1928), but when Sam Moskowitz reprinted that story in *Weird Tales* fifty years later, it brought this response from the author:

> Believe me, "Ghostly Hands" is a greater mystery than you know! I never heard of *Tales of Magic and Mystery*. The story was originally called "The Neatness of Ann Rutledge" . . . and it appeared in a defunct magazine called the *Westminster* sometime about 1924. *Tales of Magic and Mystery* apparently just swiped it without notifying them or me—or paying for it.[2]

Just how many other stories were reprinted in this manner has yet to be ascertained, but if some were rerun without payment it would help explain why the preliminary cost estimates had been so favorable, although Kofoed was in for a rude awakening on that score. Just after the fifth issue had been released it was discovered that Haddon Press, which had prepared the estimates, had forgotten to include the cost of the paper. Whereas the magazine had seemed to be making a comfortable profit, it was in fact making a shattering loss. Needless to say, it was promptly wound up.

With the emphasis on magic in the magazine, the fiction took second place, but on the whole it was of reasonably good quality. The Lovecraft, Owen and deFord stories aside, there were contributions from Charlton L. Edholm with "Tomorrow's Paper," the plot being amply summarized by the title; Archie Binns with a ghost story, "The Magic Cart"; Carl M. Rosenquist with "The Onyx Vase"; and the probably pseudonymous Peter Chance with a serial set in a lost land in Turkestan, "The Black Pagoda."

Gibson and Oursler kept the inventory to *TOM&M*, and some of the stories probably surfaced in MacFadden's *True Strange Stories*, which Gibson briefly edited. That magazine, which saw just eight issues between March and November 1929, laid a much greater emphasis on true experiences, with a confessions slant, and is thus not accorded an entry in this volume. It was a companion to *Ghost Stories*.*

Copies of *TOM&M* are today very rare and have become collector's items, mostly due to the Lovecraft connection. As an episode in the fascinating life of Walter Gibson, they are of even greater importance. But as repositories of weird and fantasy fiction, they are of only average interest.

Notes

The author wishes to thank Walter Gibson for his help on the above essay, and Frank H. Parnell for providing the bibliographic data.

1. Walter B. Gibson, from a first draft of a chapter in Gibson's projected series of memoirs.

2. Miriam Allen deFord, in a letter quoted in "The Eyrie," *Weird Tales*, Summer 1974, pp. 95–96.

Information Sources

BIBLIOGRAPHY:
Tuck.
INDEX SOURCES: Day, IWFM; MT; Tuck.
REPRINT SOURCES: None known.
LOCATION SOURCES: None known.

Publication History

TITLE: *Tales of Magic and Mystery*.
VOLUME DATA: Volume 1, Number 1, December 1927–Volume 1, Number 5, April 1928. Monthly. Total run: 5 issues.
PUBLISHER: Personal Arts Company, Camden, New Jersey, with editorial offices at Drexel Buildings, Philadelphia.
EDITOR: Walter B. Gibson, associate editor with William Kofoed.
FORMAT: Pulp (saddle-stapled), 64pp.
PRICE: 25¢.

Mike Ashley

TALES OF MYSTERY AND DETECTION

Despite the title, this pulp, which was Number 4 in World's Work's Master Thriller Series,* contained a large quota of supernatural fiction. The lead story was "Sapper" 's "The Horror at Staveley Grange," and also present were such reprints as "The Moth" by H. G. Wells, "The Pikestaffe Case" by Algernon Blackwood, "The Token" by May Sinclair, and stories by Dorothy L. Sayers, Sir Arthur Quiller-Couch, R. Austin Freeman, H. R. Wakefield and G. K. Chesterton.

Following this sample issue, which appeared in June 1934, a few independent numbers were published, not part of the Master Thriller sequence, and entitled simply *Mystery and Detection*. At least three appeared, and there was a quota of fantasy in each one, but full details are not known.

Information Sources

INDEX SOURCES: MT.
REPRINT SOURCES: None known.
LOCATION SOURCES: None known.

Publication History

TITLE: *Tales of Mystery and Detection*, first issue; thereafter *Mystery and Detection*.
VOLUME DATA: All issues undated. First, Number 4 of the Master Thriller Series,
    June 1934. Remaining issues, probably 1938.
PUBLISHER: World's Work, Kingswood, Surrey.
EDITOR: Not identified, but probably H. Norman Evans.
FORMAT: Pulp, 128pp.
PRICE: 1/-.

Mike Ashley/Frank H. Parnell

TALES OF TERROR

Tales of Terror was Number 17 in the Master Thriller Series* published by
World's Work during the 1930s. Only one issue under this title exists, undated,
but published during the summer of 1937. It contained six stories and they give
some indication of the variety of sources from which this series selected.

The lead story was "The Phantom Killer" by C. V. Tench. Tench is known
from the standard SF magazine bibliographies for his solitary appearance in the
first issue of *Astounding Stories* (*Analog SF**) with "Compensation." But Tench
also appeared in the Canadian *Uncanny Tales** and he had a story, "The Toothless Killer" in issue 366 of the British weekly detective fiction tabloid *The
Thriller*. The similarity of titles may indicate this story is a reprint or a sequel
to "The Phantom Killer." It seems likely that Tench was either a British or
Canadian writer.

The second story was "Cracky Miss Judith" by Hector Bolitho, reprinted
from his 1935 collection *The House on Half Moon Street* published by Cobden-
Sanderson in London.

Other contributors included the prolific John Creasey, the ubiquitous Edmund
Snell and the relatively unknown Walter Rippinger. So far as can be ascertained
all contents were reprints but this has yet to be verified.

Information Sources

BIBLIOGRAPHY:
Tuck.
INDEX SOURCES: MT.
REPRINT SOURCES: None.
LOCATION SOURCES: None known.

Publication History

TITLE: *Tales of Terror*.
VOLUME DATA: Number 17 in the Master Thriller Series; undated but published during
    Summer 1937.

PUBLISHER: World's Work, Kingswood, Surrey.
EDITOR: Not identified, but probably H. Norman Evans.
FORMAT: Pulp, 128pp.
PRICE: 1/-.

Mike Ashley/Frank H. Parnell

TALES OF TERROR FROM THE BEYOND

A large-size, neo-pulp magazine, *Tales of Terror from the Beyond*, published in 1964, consisted predominantly of reprints, and chiefly of stories by Stanton Coblentz. Some originated in *Weird Tales*,* while others may possibly have been new. Certainly a reprint was Stanley Ellin's "Specialty of the House," which rounded out the issue. A mixture of routine ghost stories and macabre mysteries, *Tales of Terror* must have failed to find a large enough readership, as no further issues are known. Seventeen years later the same publisher had marginally better success with *Chillers.**

Information Sources

BIBLIOGRAPHY:
Tuck.
INDEX SOURCES: MT; SFM.
REPRINT SOURCES: None known.
LOCATION SOURCES: None known.

Publication History

TITLE: *Tales of Terror from the Beyond.*
VOLUME DATA: Volume 1, Number 1, Summer 1964. Listed as quarterly, but no
       further issues known.
PUBLISHER: Charlton Publications, Inc.
EDITOR: Patrick Masulli.
FORMAT: Large Pulp, 80pp.
PRICE: 50¢.

Mike Ashley/Frank H. Parnell

TALES OF THE FRIGHTENED

In 1956 Michael Avallone was establishing himself in the thriller field with his Ed Noon private eye novels. At the same time, under several aliases, he was writing for and editing a variety of men's magazines. In 1957 he found himself writing short tales to be read by Boris Karloff in a new radio series, *The Frightened*. Publishing agent Lyle Kenyon Engel arranged a magazine tie-in with the series called, inevitably, *Tales of the Frightened*, and Michael Avallone ghost-edited it. (He also ghost-edited the companion magazine, *Space Science Fiction*,* issued to take advantage of the distribution outlet.)

The magazine saw only two issues, neither of major importance. The best-remembered story is Avallone's own quasi-autobiographical "The Man Who Thought He Was Poe" in the second issue. Avallone had the lead story in the first issue under his own name ("The Curse of Cleopatra"), plus a story in each issue as "Mark Dane." He also wrote the two vignettes as related by Boris Karloff.

Surprisingly, the magazine acquired several stories from leading SF writers, which gives the two issues some value for collectors. Included in the first were "Alias Napoleon" by John Jakes, "But a Kind of Ghost" by John Wyndham and "The Gardener" by John Christopher; in the second were "Mr Tiglath" by Poul Anderson, "Dead End" by Mack Reynolds and "The Window" by A. Bertram Chandler.

Although billed as a bi-monthly, the second issue, which lacked a cover illustration, did not appear for five months. There were no editorial departments, and the magazine was not missed—in fact, it was scarcely noticed in the first place. In 1963 Michael Avallone compiled a volume of stories from the radio series collected as *Tales of the Frightened* (New York: Belmont, 1963), which included the two vignettes from the magazine.

Information Sources

BIBLIOGRAPHY:
Tuck.
INDEX SOURCES: MIT; MT; SFM.
REPRINT SOURCES: None known.
LOCATION SOURCES: M.I.T. Science Fiction Library; University of California–Los
    Angeles Library (Vol. 1, No. 1).

Publication History

TITLE: *Tales of the Frightened*.
VOLUME DATA: Volume 1, Number 1, Spring 1957–Volume 1, Number 2, August
    1957. Listed as bi-monthly. Total run: 2 issues.
PUBLISHER: Republic Features Syndicate, New York.
EDITOR: Michael Avallone (not credited within issues). Lyle Kenyon Engel is listed as
    Editorial Director.
FORMAT: Digest, 128pp.
PRICE: 35¢.

Mike Ashley

TALES OF THE UNCANNY

At least three issues of this rare English magazine are known, and there may possibly be more. Number 1 was actually Number 6 in the World's Work Master Thriller Series,* and the second issue was Number 20 in that series. The third issue was unnumbered.

The first issue, which appeared undated in 1934, was a bonanza of classic reprints compiled, uncredited, by H. Norman Evans. The lead story was Algernon Blackwood's notable "The Willows," the story of an island in the River Danube that forms a link to other-dimensional beings. It was followed by "The Inexperienced Ghost," one of H. G. Wells' more humorous stories; "Honolulu," a tale of South Sea magic by Somerset Maugham; "The Wind in the Portico" by John Buchan; "A Pair of Hands," an oft-reprinted ghost story by Sir Arthur Quiller-Couch; "Mrs. Lunt," another ghost story by Hugh Walpole; "Old Man's Beard" by H. R. Wakefield; and other stories by Oliver Onions, Mrs. Belloc Lowndes and Michael Arlen. It was a good solid selection that would still make a fine ghost story anthology today.

The second number, which was subtitled "Weird Tales of the Supernatural," appeared about thirty months later. This time the names were nearly all new, although a number were regular contributors to the Master Thriller Series, such as R. Thurston Hopkins and Douglas Newton. Another contributor, named as Francis H. Gibson on the title page, was probably Francis H. Sibson, a regular writer for British magazines who published a story in the first issue of *Fantasy** and who had his 1933 novel *Unthinkable* reprinted in *Famous Fantastic Mysteries.**

The third issue is subtitled "Midwinter Nights Entertainment," from which we might deduce that it was published in December 1937. It was a mixture of reprint stories, such as Oliver Onions' "Hic Jacet" and Sydney Horler's "Black Magic," and possibly new stories, such as J. Russell Warren's "The Cat." Hector Bolitho's "Taureke's Eyes" was another reprint from his 1935 collection *The House on Half Moon Street.*

Information Sources

BIBLIOGRAPHY:
Tuck.
INDEX SOURCES: MT.
REPRINT SOURCES: None known.
LOCATION SOURCES: None known.

Publication History

TITLE: *Tales of the Uncanny.*
VOLUME DATA: Three unnumbered, undated issues. Master Thriller Series Numbers 6 and 20. Third, unnumbered. Publication dates probably December 1934, Summer 1937, and Winter 1937/38.
PUBLISHER: World's Work, Kingswood, Surrey.
EDITOR: First issue, H. Norman Evans; later issues probably also compiled by Evans.
FORMAT: Pulp, 128pp.
PRICE: 1/-.

Mike Ashley/Frank H. Parnell

TALES OF TOMORROW

Tales of Tomorrow was one of four indistinguishable SF pocketbook magazines of poor-quality fiction issued by John Spencer and Company in the early 1950s. It is of no interest to collectors except for tracing the development of writers like E. C. Tubb and John S. Glasby. For details, see the entry on *Futuristic Science Fiction.**

Information Sources

BIBLIOGRAPHY:
Ashley, Michael. *Fantasy Readers Guide 1*. Wallsend, U.K.: Cosmos, 1979.
Nicholls. *Encyclopedia*.
Tuck.
INDEX SOURCES: Ashley, Michael, *Fantasy Readers Guide 1*, Wallsend, U.K.: Cosmos, 1979; IBSF; MIT; SFM; Tuck.
REPRINT SOURCES: None known.
LOCATION SOURCES: M.I.T. Science Fiction Library.

Publication History

TITLE: *Tales of Tomorrow.*
VOLUME DATA: All issues undated. Number 1, [Autumn 1950]–Number 11, [Summer 1954]. Irregular, though approximately quarterly. Total run: 11 issues.
PUBLISHER: John Spencer & Co., London.
EDITOR: Sol Assael and Michael Nahum (not credited within issues).
FORMAT: Pocketbook; first three and last four issues, 128pp.; issues 4–7, 112pp.
PRICE: 1/6d.

Mike Ashley

TALES OF WONDER

Although *Scoops** had appeared in 1934, most SF afficionados prefer to think that *Tales of Wonder* was Britain's first real SF magazine. It appeared initially as a one-shot issue in June 1937, as part of the World's Work Master Thriller Series.* This had already included *Tales of Mystery and Detection** and *Tales of the Uncanny*,* so when Walter Gillings approached the publishers with the idea of including an SF title they were instantly receptive, and *Tales of Wonder* was born.

For the first time a magazine composed of stories written entirely by British "science-fictioneers" was assembled. There were eight stories by six writers. John Russell Fearn was present with both the cover story, "Superhuman," and "Seeds from Space." Festus Pragnell also contributed two stories, while W. P. Cockroft, Eric Frank Russell, Maurice Hugi and John Beynon Harris completed the issue.

Tales of Wonder sold sufficiently well, and Gillings was told to assemble a second issue; he was soon given the green light for a quarterly schedule. The popularity of *Tales of Wonder* is evident in that it was the only publication in the Master Thriller Series to become a regular magazine—attributable in part to the determination of its editor.

Gillings did not push for original SF concepts in the fiction, because he wanted to attract readers who had not become attuned to the progress in American SF. Nevertheless, he hoped his contributors would learn from the state of the art in the United States. As a "pointer" to British writers, Gillings chose to reprint at least one American story each issue, starting with David H. Keller's "Stenographer's Hands."

Initially, Gillings was able to include a significant percentage of new stories by British writers. Chief among the contributors were Eric Frank Russell, William F. Temple and, in later issues, George C. Wallis. Among Russell's contributions was "I, Spy!" (Autumn 1940)—an early SF detective story that later appeared in *Weird Tales** as "Venturer of the Martian Mimics"; but the most memorable story in the magazine was William F. Temple's "The Smile of the Sphinx" (Autumn 1938), wherein cats are revealed as alien infiltrators. Damon Knight resurrected the story for the December 1950 *Worlds Beyond.**

Gillings was also able to encourage new writers, of whom he thought the most promising were Charles F. Hall and D. J. Foster. Hall, however, only submitted two stories before World War II intervened, and Foster was reported dead or missing while serving in the R.A.F.

A number of Britain's SF writers were committed to the war effort, and many new manuscripts lacked quality. As a result Gillings found he had to rely more and more on reprint material. He placed the emphasis on reprinting stories by British writers from U.S. magazines, but did not neglect the American writers and actually published some new stories by them: "The Horror in the Telescope" by Edmond Hamilton (Summer 1938), "Out of the Past" by Lloyd A. Eshbach (Autumn 1938) and "The Mentality Machine" by S. P. Meek (Spring 1939). In selecting his reprints Gillings spread the net wide. A popular writer in the early years of the century was Australian R. Coutts Armour, who wrote as Coutts Brisbane. His "The Planet Wrecker" in the Winter 1939 issue had first appeared as "Beyond the Orbit" in *The Red Magazine* back in 1914, and his other contributions were from the same era except "The Big Cloud," which was new.

Perhaps most important was that *Tales of Wonder* carried the first professional pieces by Arthur C. Clarke, "Man's Empire of Tomorrow" (Winter 1938) and "We Can Rocket to the Moon—Now!" (Summer 1939). Gillings encouraged speculative articles and fillers from fans including such features as the "Search for Ideas" department where fans conjectured on such points as "Are We Martians?," "The Future of Man" and "If Hitler Had Laid Claim to Luna." Professor A. M. Low and I. O. Evans also supplied articles.

Tales of Wonder was a lively, entertaining and enjoyable magazine, and World's Work had sufficient faith to continue the magazine into the war years even though paper rationing ate away at the contents, reducing it from 128 to

72 pages by 1941. By then Gillings had to rely almost entirely on reprints. In the sixteen issues that appeared until Spring 1942, *Tales of Wonder* published ninety-six stories; forty-three were new, fifty-two were reprints, and only eight of those new stories appeared in the last eight issues. In the end paper rationing took its toll. Moreover, by the final issue Gillings had been drafted into the army even though he was a conscientious objector.

Tales of Wonder remains a collector's item today. Despite the criticisms levied against him by keen SF fans for his use of reprints, Gillings nevertheless showed the general readership in Britain that the adult SF short story existed beyond the pages of Wells and Doyle.

Information Sources

BIBLIOGRAPHY:
Gillings, Walter. "Something Old, Something New," *Vision of Tomorrow*, April 1970.
————. "Year of the Blast-Off." *Vision of Tomorrow*, March 1970.
Nicholls. *Encyclopedia*.
Tuck.
INDEX SOURCES: IBSF; ISFM; SFM; Tuck.
REPRINT SOURCES: None known.
LOCATION SOURCES: M.I.T. Science Fiction Library.

Publication History

TITLE: *Tales of Wonder*.
VOLUME DATA: First issue unnumbered, first two issues undated, [Number 1, Summer 1937]–Number 16, Spring 1942. Quarterly from second issue, but no issues for Summer 1941 or Winter 1942. Total run: 16 issues.
PUBLISHER: World's Work Ltd., Kingswood, Surrey.
EDITOR: Walter H. Gillings.
FORMAT: Pulp; 128pp., issues 1–8; 96pp., issues 9–11; 80pp., issues 12 and 13; 72pp., issues 14–16.
PRICE: 1/-.

Mike Ashley

TEN STORY FANTASY

Ten Story Fantasy, a pulp-sized magazine billed as a quarterly, was published simultaneously in New York and Canada by Avon Publications. Its first and only issue appeared in Spring 1951. Misleadingly titled, *TSF* contains thirteen works of fiction—three novelettes and ten short stories.

The editor of *TSF*, Donald A. Wollheim, had been executive editor of Avon Books since 1947. In 1950, at the suggestion of Joseph Meyers, owner of Avon, Wollheim had edited three pulps: *Out of This World Adventures** (lasting two issues), *Pioneer Western* (one issue), and *Sparkling Love Stories* (one issue). These had died because of insufficient sales. The following year, however,

Meyers asked Wollheim to try again because J. W. Clement, Avon's printer, had offered Meyers a special bargain rate for pulp magazines. The result was *TSF*, which died after a single issue because of the poor distribution pulp magazines were receiving.

In fiction and interior artwork, *TSF* is a more distinguished work than its predecessor, *Out of This World Adventures*. The stories in both magazines are originals. *TSF* contains stories by now famous authors of science fiction and fantasy: John Beynon (better known by the pseudonym John Wyndham), L. Sprague de Camp, A. E. van Vogt, Fritz Leiber, C. M. Kornbluth, August Derleth and Lester del Rey. Like *Out of This World Adventures*, the table of contents of *TSF* is decorated with a striking arabesque design, here an insectlike creature growing out of a tree trunk. Also, as in the earlier magazine, the initial letter of each story is embellished with a weird or science fictional motif. William McWilliam and "Martin," artists employed by Avon's comics office, provided most of the internal black and white illustrations. Also, four artists of some standing among science fiction magazine illustrators contributed to *TSF*: Leo Morey, Vincent Napoli, John Giunta and Hannes Bok.

Unfortunately, from the gaudy, sadomasochistic cover, no potential reader would have guessed that *TSF* was a respectable artistic effort. Supplied by Joseph Meyers (not approved by Wollheim, who had free play only with the internal artwork), the cover depicts a muscular hero in a green cape rescuing a voluptuous woman from a whip-wielding villain. The cover ostensibly illustrates John Beynon's story, "Tyrant and Slave-Girl on the Planet Venus." (The sensational and misleading title was also supplied by Meyers). Curiously, while the artist invented the bikini-clad blonde, the scene relates to an actual event. Beynon's hero, Bert, kills an overseer in the manner suggested in the picture because he is beating, not a woman, but a Griffa, a furry humanoid native to Venus. Furthermore, in Beynon's story, Griffas are not only used as slave labor in the mines but killed for their silver fur. That the woman's bikini and the overseer's boots and tunic are trimmed with fur suggests that the anonymous artist is attempting to incorporate details of the story at the same time that he is deliberately misrepresenting a key event.

Most of the thirteen stories, divided about evenly between fantasy and science fiction, read well today. Perhaps the two weakest are A. E. van Vogt's "Haunted Atoms" and de Camp's "Getaway on Krishna." "Haunted Atoms" is a confusing story of a couple who own a house on top of an ancient but still dangerous nuclear plant. Implausibly, they spend most of the story explaining to one another the energy sources ("nuclearicity," "nucleonite") of their postnuclear holocaust world. "Getaway" concerns the perils of two Earthmen, fleeing from the natives of the planet Krishna, an adventure story marred by an extremely unsympathetic protagonist, Singer. Although at the end he humbles himself to his Eskimo companion, who has brought them both safely through Krishna's arctic wastes, Singer's brutal and swinish behavior makes the story unpleasant. "Getaway" also suffers from wooden and incredible dialogue: "Oh, great lord, you mock a poor mountain maid." Vincent Napoli has, however, provided a spirited illustration of the two Earthmen fighting antennaed Krishnans who have surprised them in a tunnel.

Two more stories depend upon motifs that from the perspective of the 1980s seem overworked. Like "Getaway on Krishna," Beynon's "Tyrant and Slave Girl" is a space opera, which takes its inspiration from the Anglo-American conquest of the western Indians. Earth has blown up. Earthmen have settled either on Mars, the spent planet of Bradbury's *Martian Chronicles*, or on Venus, a young, wet planet, with a cruel frontier society based on slave labor. Transported to Venus, Bert engages in a series of adventures, then returns to Mars to marry a native girl. Like the Krishnans, Beynon's Martians are idealized versions of American Indians.

If alien noble savages are no longer fresh subjects for fiction, neither are robots. In "Uneasy Lies the Head," Lester del Rey explores, as Isaac Asimov had been doing during the past decade, the capacity of a robot to experience human emotions and assume human responsibilities. Jason, a benevolent dictator, rules a future society in which mankind has been rendered "weak and submissive" by twelve decades of war. Knowing that no human can replace him, Jason has built a robot of himself, which he implants every night with his memories. When Jason dies of a heart attack, his doctor activates the robot Jason. Since the robot secretary, Nema, has displayed worry about her boss's health, the doctor is convinced that the robot Jason is capable of becoming fully human.

Some of the most successful stories in the magazine concern animals or alien life-forms. Franklin Gregory's supernatural tale, "The Poisonous Soul," is remarkable for the extraordinarily knowledgeable detail about snakes it incorporates. Cheever, a young man who, we learn, is able to control poisonous snakes and to become a snake himself, gets a job at a zoo snake house. Cheever kills eminent biologists, thus absorbing their knowledge of snakes. The scientist narrator ends this scourge by killing all the zoo snakes, including Cheever in his snake form. John Giunta has illustrated this story with a tableau of fiendish faces and a striking snake.

"The Woodworker" by Gene A. Davidson (a pseudonym for David Lesperance) concerns a vegetable brain, which has come into being on a deserted farm. The "Woodworker" protects itself from hunters using it for target practice by extruding four-inch-long wooden insects armed, first, with sharp thorns, then, as it observes the hunters more closely, with tiny wooden rifles. Hannes Bok has provided a fine illustration of a man holding an enormous insect in his hand.

In K. W. Bennett's "Who Builds Maos Traps?," one of three bachelor roommates has been given a "maos trap," which he believes is for mice until it begins catching exotic, unearthly lizards. The roommates leave the trap under the bed of an evil political boss, who is subsequently eaten, along with his flunky, by purple lizards. The story includes a parody of pulp fiction; for while these bizarre creatures are appearing, the narrator, a pulp fantasy writer, is trying to complete a serial, *Death Among the Icecakes*: "A wolf pack had Griff ringed in and he had only three shells in his thutty-thutty." The breezy, stiff-upper-lip, masculine dialogue seems dated today; but the story is a witty variation on the idea that truth is stranger than fiction.

Best of the alien life-form stories is C. M. Kornbluth's grimly ironic "Friend to Man." A callous murderer, dying of thirst on the sands of Mars, is nursed back to health by a large insectlike alien. The murderer's cold heart is touched, and he resolves to live a better life. The Martian Samaritan, we learn, however, is fattening him up to serve as a host for its parasitic young.

Two stories in *TSF* whimsically explore the idea that other worlds coexist with ours. Although attitudes toward women are stereotyped and the elements in the story never quite gel, August Derleth's "The Other Side of the Wall" is still amusing. Pincus Hawk inherits a house with a windowless, seemingly unfinished wall. From time to time, Pincus finds that he can pass through the wall to a world of chicken-footed beings, comically depicted by the artist, H. W. Kiemle. Pincus wants desperately to get away from his dreary job selling women's shoes: "listening to a lot of gabbing women whine about this and that, and pretend they were two sizes less than what their feet called for." Learning that in the other world positions are decided entirely by aptitude tests, Pincus studies engineering and disappears into what is presumably an all-male utopia.

"Private World" is a delightful fantasy written by Donald A. Wollheim under the pseudonym Martin Pearson. A rich hobbyist, Mr. Budd, has ordered large numbers of remarkably detailed soldiers and armaments from Meteor Miniatures. On a visit to Budd, the Head of the Special Orders Department drinks a glass of strong wine and passes out. He awakes in the middle of a battle fought by identical-looking soldiers in the uniforms of the miniatures his company had made for Budd. The story's charm lies in details, including a dragon general who plays chess, that suggest that this is a toy world. Hit by a cannon, the businessman comes to at Budd's house. Budd tries to convince the businessman that he has been dreaming; but the latter does not believe him, especially since he finds in his pocket a toy soldier with his own face.

Clarke's "Sentinel of Eternity," Fritz Leiber's "Cry Witch!" and Kris Neville's "Seeds of Futurity" are the most provocative stories in *TSF*. Subsequently reprinted as "The Sentinel," Clarke's story is the basis of the film and novel, *2001: A Space Odyssey*. It corresponds to the episode in which the exploration team to the moon breaks the monolith that is transmitting signals to a distant planet, thus informing its inhabitants that man has achieved space flight.

In "Cry Witch!," a delicious tale of the supernatural, a man in a remote village loves a girl who is immune to death. While he sleeps, she places a dead hand in his grasp so that he will imagine she is still there, then visits the other village men, to whom she represents the same ideal.

Nevill's "Seeds of Futurity" resembles Hawthorne's "Earth's Holocaust" in its prophetic rendering of the consequences of the information explosion. Descriptions of humanity drowning in paper are poetic and insightful:

> There was a baffling array of data; there were giant stands of virgin statistics; there was chaos. No one could even be sure where the past experimenters had left off; no one knew in which direction lay the unexplored fields and unseen vistas. In fact, in any scientific field formerly considered a meaningful specialty, a lifetime of study was needed to push forward to the frontier; all energy expended in encompassing the known, no residue remaining to supplement it.

To save the species, Edward Barnett raises a group of children on an uninhabited island, not even teaching them human speech. When these innocents have reached the age of eleven, Barnett takes them to another planet to continue the race. The interest of this remarkable story lies less in the plot than in the descriptions of a world so smothered by dead knowledge that humanity's initiative and will to live have been sapped.

TSF was begun, unfortunately, at a time when pulp magazines were no longer economically feasible. Furthermore, despite the skilled direction of its editor, Donald A. Wollheim, it lacked a sustained commitment from its publisher. The one issue that did appear is, however, remarkable for the quality of both its art and fiction. Besides Clarke's classic "Sentinel of Eternity," there is an unusual number of stories by now eminent writers, which stand up well to changing tastes.

Information Sources

BIBLIOGRAPHY:
Nicholls. *Encyclopedia*.
Tuck.
INDEX SOURCES: MIT; SFM; Tuck.
REPRINT SOURCES: None known.
LOCATION SOURCES: California State University–Fullerton, Special Collections (not available through interlibrary loan, but will photocopy articles upon request); Eastern New Mexico University, Golden Library (not available through ILL); Massachusetts Institute of Technology, MIT Science Fiction Library; Northern Illinois University Library, Rare Books and Special Collections (no ILL, but partial photocopying of some issues *may* be possible); Pennsylvania State University Libraries, Special Collections; San Francisco Academy of Comic Art, Science Fiction Room; San Francisco Public Library, Literature Department (not available through ILL); Texas A&M University, Special Collections; Toronto Public Libraries, Spaced Out Library (not available through ILL); University of California–Los Angeles, Special Collections (a microfilm may be produced, the negative to remain at UCLA and the patron to pay for negative and print); University of California–Riverside, Special Collections; University of Georgia Libraries; University of Kansas, Spencer Research Library.

Publication History

TITLE: *Ten Story Fantasy*.
VOLUME DATA: Volume 1, Number 1, Spring 1951. Quarterly, but only one issue
    published.
PUBLISHER: Avon Periodicals, New York.
EDITOR: Donald A. Wollheim.
FORMAT: Pulp, 128pp.
PRICE: 25¢.

Wendy Bousfield

TERENCE X. O'LEARY'S WAR BIRDS

Another attempt to revive a dying pulp, *Terence X. O'Leary's War Birds* was
the last gasp of Dell's air-war pulp, *War Birds*. O'Leary had been appearing in
War Birds for years as the hero of an endless stream of air adventures. However,
in 1935, he was suddenly changed from a modern-day hero to a futuristic pilot
battling the Ageless Men, a group of evil immortals from the lost city of Atlantis
who desire world domination. The three O'Leary novels were written by Arthur
Guy Empey and were filled with wild action and improbable plots. There were
flying belts, force pistols, futuristic airplanes and more, but the quality of the
science fiction was scarcely a step above the comic book. While good writing
was not a prerequisite for success in the pulps, terrible writing usually doomed
a magazine. The transformed *War Birds* only lasted three issues.

Happily, there were few short stories in *TXO'LWB* as the lead novel filled
most of the magazine, leaving room for a few departments such as "The Cockpit"
(a big meeting for War Birds!), "Is That a Fact?" and a cash contest for $50
that was probably never awarded.

Information Sources

INDEX SOURCES: SFM; Weinberg, Robert, *The Hero Pulp Index*, Evergreen, Colo.:
    Opar Press, 1971 (lists lead novels only).
REPRINT SOURCES: *Terence X. O'Leary's War Birds* by Arthur Empey (Melrose
    Highlands, Mass.: Odyssey Publications, 1974).
LOCATION SOURCES: M.I.T. Science Fiction Library.

Publication History

TITLE: *Terence X. O'Leary's War Birds*.
VOLUME DATA: Continued the numbering of *War Birds*, with issue numbering se-
    quential. Volume 30, Number 84, March 1935–Volume 30, Number 86, May/
    June 1935. Monthly. Individual run: 3 issues.
PUBLISHER: Dell Publishing Co., New York.

EDITOR: Carson Mowre.
FORMAT: Pulp, 128pp.
PRICE: 15¢.

Robert Weinberg

TERROR TALES

Following the success of its new policy for mystery-terror stories in *Dime Mystery Magazine*,* Popular Publications brought out a full fledged weird menace magazine, *Terror Tales*, in 1934. As with *Dime Mystery*, the emphasis was on bizarre crimes, murder and mayhem, and, increasingly, lust and depravity; but although many of the perils seemed to be caused by some supernatural agency, their origins were usually rationalized at the end by some equally fantastic but totally mundane explanation.

TT is, on the whole, therefore, of little interest to the purist weird fiction devotee. Of peripheral interest is the fact that a number of writers noted in the SF and fantasy fields contributed stories in vast quantities to *TT* and its companions. Leading contributors were Wayne Rogers, Wyatt Blassingame, Ray Cummings, Paul Ernst, Arthur Leo Zagat and Arthur J. Burks, while other contributors included Hugh B. Cave, Carl Jacobi, Henry Kuttner, Mindret Lord, Norvell Page, Wilbur S. Peacock, Earl Pierce, Jr., Nat Schachner and E. Hoffman Price, sometimes with only one or two stories.

Occasional stories that fit within the SF framework did appear, and the most often-quoted is "Test-Tube Frankenstein" by W. Wayne Robbins (May 1940), wherein a scientist creates a protoplasmic blob that eventually overcomes him and takes over his human form. This protean monster then continues to absorb others and transmute into their forms in a story that may owe much to John Campbell's "Who Goes There?" The denouement of the story, however, is something that would have shocked SF readers of the day, though it would not have been out of the ordinary for the terror pulps. The blob eventually absorbs and takes the form of the hero's fiancee, and in assuming this alluring shape is able to tempt other men to their destruction. But because the monster had not seen the girl unclothed it was not able to form a perfect duplicate, and the hero realizes this when at the last he perceives, as keen-eyed as ever, that the breasts have no nipples!

Carl Jacobi's one contribution to *TT*, "Satan's Roadhouse" (October 1934), was a fantasy, dealing with voodoo in New Orleans. Paul Ernst's "Man into Monster" (August 1935) concerns an ancient Egyptian ritual which the villain uses against his employer to turn him into an ape. *TT* carried a couple of stories by the Belgian writer Jean Ray under the Anglo-Saxon alias John Flanders. "If Thy Right Hand Offend Thee" (November 1934) is reminiscent of W. F. Harvey's "The Beast with Five Fingers" in having a dismembered hand seeking

revenge, but it adds a new twist to the theme by following further the consequences of the plot.

Such contributions were rare, however, and purist devotees of supernatural
fiction should approach *TT* with caution.

Information Sources

BIBLIOGRAPHY:
Jones, Robert K. *The Shudder Pulps*. West Linn, Ore.: Fax Collector's Editions, 1975.
Tuck.
Weinberg, Robert. "Horror Pulps." In *Horror Literature*, ed. Marshall Tymn, New
     York: Bowker, 1981.
INDEX SOURCES: Austin, William N., *Macabre Index*, Seattle, Wash.: FAPA 59,
     1952 (contains an incomplete issue listing); Jones, Robert Kenneth, "Popular's
     Weird Menace Pulps: Essay and Index," in *The Weird Menace*, ed. Camille
     Cazedessus, Jr. Evergreen, Colo.: Opar Press, 1972.
REPRINT SOURCES:
  British Edition: Three undated unnumbered issues were released during 1948–1950.
     Details unknown.
  Derivative Anthologies: *The House of Living Death* and *Death's Loving Arms*, both
     ed. Jon Hanlon (both San Diego: Corinth, 1966), selected stories from the first
     and second issues, although both included a non-*TT* story.
LOCATION SOURCES: None known.

Publication History

TITLE: *Terror Tales*.
VOLUME DATA: Volume 1, Number 1, September 1934–Volume 13, Number 3, March/
     April 1941. Four issues per volume. Monthly, September 1934–June 1936, there-
     after bi-monthly. Total run: 51 issues.
PUBLISHER: Popular Publications, New York.
EDITOR: Rogers Terrill.
FORMAT: Pulp, 112–128pp.
PRICE: 15¢.

Mike Ashley

THE THRILL BOOK

The Thrill Book was a short-lived magazine that saw sixteen twice-monthly
issues during 1919. In later years a myth grew that it was the first science fiction
magazine, much as *The Black Cat* (1895–1923)* acquired a reputation as a
supernatural magazine. This belief probably stems from the fact that several of
the leading contributors to the magazine later established themselves in the SF
and fantasy fields—notably Murray Leinster and Greye La Spina—or, indeed,
were already noted for their fantasy in other magazines, as were Tod Robbins
and Francis Stevens. But if one were to seriously analyze the 107 stories and

serials, then in all probability the proportion of SF and fantasy would be no greater than that in the other adventure pulps such as *The Argosy* and *All-Story*.*

The intention was clear during the magazine's gestation that the contents were to be "strange, bizarre, occult, mysterious tales,"[1] thus suggesting that it was to be a precursor of *Weird Tales** rather than *Amazing Stories*.* The maiden editor of *TTB*, Harold Hersey, when looking back over his career, remarked: "It seems that I enjoy a reputation as editor and publisher in the fantasy field far out of proportion to my just deserts. I failed miserably with *The Thrill Book* in 1919, a pulp that included many excellent pseudo-science yarns by Murray Leinster and others . . . but which was not entirely devoted to this type of story."[2]

In point of fact, Hersey gets his facts wrong on another score. He calls *The Thrill Book* a pulp magazine, which in time it became, but during the period of his editorship it was in a larger, saddle-stapled format similar to the dime novel which Street and Smith had published for the last half-century.

Science fiction was not as prominent in *TTB* as was fantasy. Murray Leinster may be the name best known to later generations of SF readers, but he had only three stories in the magazine, of which one, "Juju," in the final issue, was a straightforward jungle adventure. He did not in fact appear in the magazine until its life was half over, and then with nothing of particular merit. "A Thousand Degrees Below Zero" (July 15) was one of the early scientific menace stories that would become a trademark of his work in the 1920s and 1930s. In a similar vein, "The Silver Menace" (September 1–15) told of minute organisms that reproduce at an alarming rate and threaten to smother the Earth's surface.

The fantasy content of *TTB* is better gauged from the work of Greye La Spina, the most regular contributor to the magazine. She had seven stories published in all, including three under pseudonyms, and her very first story was the cover story to the first issue. Entitled "Wolf of the Steppes," it was a werewolf story with a slight difference. Over subsequent issues of the magazine La Spina was present with a variety of supernatural stories covering most of the time-honored themes, as evidenced by the three stories published under her Isra Putnam alias: "The Broken Idol" (March 15), "The Inefficient Ghost" (May 1) and "The Wax Doll" (August 1).

Tod Robbins was noted as a writer of fantasy stories, and he had six stories in *TTB*, ranging from "The Bibulous Baby" (July 1), about a baby that was born an old man and thereafter grew younger, to "Crimson Flowers" (October 1), a mood piece about an old man who cuts flowers in his garden as symbols of the thoughts of his son, who is buried there. None of Robbins' contributions have been reprinted because, rather than being solid stories, they are little more than shallow mood sketches.

Seabury Quinn was present with one story, "The Stone Image" (May 1), which, because it includes a "walk-on part" for the character Dr. Trowbridge, has always been regarded as a forerunner of Quinn's famous Jules de Grandin occult detective series in *Weird Tales*, even though Quinn later declared that he had not even thought of de Grandin at that stage.[3]

Probably the most important science fiction story in *TTB* was Francis Stevens' serial "The Heads of Cerberus," which saw a specialty press hardcover edition thirty-three years later (Reading, Pa.: Polaris Press, 1952). A rather dated story by today's standards, the novel is justifiably regarded as a classic, being one of the first to suggest the possibilities of alternate time tracks. Set in Philadelphia in the year 2118 A.D., it is a bizarre study of an anti-utopian society.

In the fantasy vein, the most intriguing series in *TTB* did not survive the magazine but is perhaps worthy of revival. Under the general heading of "Tales of the Double Man," Clyde Broadwell contributed a series of five stories (July 15–September 15) about a doomed New York stockbroker, William Gray, who has an exact psychic counterpart on the other side of the globe in Cape Town, South Africa, namely, Arthur Wadleigh. At twelve hourly intervals Wadleigh and Gray exchange identities. The story relates the attempts by Gray to establish his own identity and to rid himself of this dual life.

Other writers present in *TTB* known for their fantasy include Perley Poore Sheehan, Edward Lucas White (whose "The House of the Nightmare" was in the September 15 issue), William Wallace Cook, Don Mark Lemon, Robert W. Sneddon and H. Bedford-Jones. Bedford-Jones created a bibliographic puzzle with his story "Mr. Shen of Shensi," the cover story of the October 1 issue. Only two years earlier he had had a story with exactly the same title in the August 18, 1917 *All-Story Weekly*, and it had been assumed that the two stories were the same. Bibliophile Thomas Moriarty has confirmed, however, that they are completely different.[4]

TTB also carried a profusion of verse, much written by Hersey himself under pseudonyms. It is rumored that this was a leading reason for Hersey's replacement as editor after the eighth issue by Ronald Oliphant. Hersey later admitted that had Oliphant been editor from the start, *TTB* might have lasted far longer, and certainly Oliphant selected more stories of a science fictional and fantasy flavor than had Hersey. But it seemed that *TTB* had started on the wrong foot and was unable to establish itself thereafter. After a further eight issues it folded. The decision must have been abrupt, for future stories were announced in the final issue, and with a fortnightly schedule this issue had probably gone to press no later than early September. One thing is certain: had *The Thrill Book* lasted into the 1920s its increased longevity would have debunked the myth that here was the first fantasy magazine.

Notes

The author wishes to thank Robert K. Jones for his help in the compiling of this essay.

1. Harold Hersey, *Notice to Authors*, issued prior to publication of *TTB*, and reprinted in part in Sam Moskowitz, *Under the Moons of Mars* (New York: Holt, Rinehart and Winston, 1970), p. 425.

2. Harold Hersey, *Pulpwood Editor* (New York: F. A. Stokes, 1937), p. 188.

3. See introduction to Quinn's "The Cloth of Madness," in *Magazine of Horror* 10 (August 1965): 24.

4. See letter by T. M. Moriarty in *Lore* 5 (April 1966): 59.

Information Sources

BIBLIOGRAPHY:

Jones, Robert K. "The Thrill Book," *WSFA Journal*, March–November 1970; reprinted and revised in *Xenophile* (March 1977): 4–10.

Moskowitz, Sam. "A History of 'The Scientific Romance' in the Munsey Magazines, 1912–1920." In *Under the Moons of Mars*. New York: Holt, Rinehart & Winston, 1970.

Tuck.

INDEX SOURCES: Cockcroft, IWFM; Day, IWFM; Evans, William H., "The Thrill Book," *Fantasy Commentator*, Fall 1947; Jones, Robert Kenneth, "The Thrill Book," *WSFA Journal*, March–November 1970 (reprinted and revised in *Xenophile*, No. 30, March 1977, pp. 4–10); MT; SFM.

REPRINT SOURCES: None known.

LOCATION SOURCES: Smith and Street Collection, Syracuse University Library.

Publication History

TITLE: *The Thrill Book*.

VOLUME DATA: Volume 1, Number 1, March 1, 1919–Volume 3, Number 2, October 15, 1919. Volume 1, eight issues; Volume 2, six issues. Semi-monthly (1st and 15th). Total run: 16 issues.

PUBLISHER: Street & Smith, New York.

EDITOR: Harold Hersey, March 1–June 15, 1919; Ronald Oliphant, July 1–October 15, 1919.

FORMAT: Large-size (10¾" x 8"), 48pp., March 1–June 15, 1919; Pulp, 160pp., July 1–October 15, 1919.

PRICE: 10¢, March 1–June 15, 1919; 15¢, July 1–October 15, 1919.

Mike Ashley

THRILLER

At least three magazines have borne the title *The Thriller* or simply *Thriller*, and unfortunately the one that has the closest connection with the fantasy field is also the one least worthy of that name. For the record, the first to bear the title was the magazine *The Black Cat*,* which changed its name in 1919. The second was a British weekly tabloid of crime thrillers where the title was justified. It ran for 589 issues between February 1929 and May 1940 and is covered in Michael Cook's *Mystery, Detective and Espionage Magazines* (Westport, Conn.: Greenwood Press, 1983).

The third, simply titled *Thriller*, saw only three issues in mock-slick format, though they were only neo-pulp. Like the confession magazines, *Thriller* filled its pages with posed photographs concentrating on ladies in various stages of deshabille, all purporting to be witches, vampires, or more usually, victims of some menace or other. Today they are nothing but laughable, as in fact are most of the contents. A trip through the first issue, dated February 1962, will soon prove that.

After the contents page which, incidentally, carries the best piece of artwork in the whole issue, we encounter our first piece of fiction, "The Vampire Is a Sucker!" credited to "Siral" and blurbed as "A Classic Second Look at a Horror Tale Guaranteed to Shock!" There was a further editorial note to the effect that if you suffer from a nervous ailment, do not read the story (wise advice no matter what you suffer from). Whether the story is a reprint is not easy to check, and certainly not worth checking. It is a timeworn tale of a man who discovers that his family are vampires. The next story, "Fiend of the Future," is labeled "From the Best of Science Fiction by John Baskerville" and tells of the survivors of an atomic war, both human and monstrous. John Baskerville is listed as one of the staff writers. "The Werewolf Lover" by Geoffrey Van Loan, Jr., another staff writer, is billed as a true story, and the winner of the Thriller Fact Horror Award, no less. "Bored to Death" is the next thrilling yarn, revealing the ills of dabbling with devil worship. It comes, we are told, "from the pen of one of the masters of horror, Sir John Catalpa." The story was apparently "reprinted from a manuscript willed to us upon his recent sudden death."

Such baloney continues with the next item, "Dream-Time, Scream-Time," a tale of growing madness, which we are told was first published in "Masters of the Occult" in 1895, even though the story includes a psychiatrist and a policeman calling the narrator "Buddy." The editors tell us that they located the manuscript in a trunk in the attic of a reputedly haunted house. "Since then the house has been demolished and in its place is a cemetery. And in the cemetery is the author, Sir David Leeds."

And so it continues for the rest of the issue and the two that follow. We are treated to such gems as "The Damned Spot" by the Master of Horror Writers, Harry Schreiner (who is also the magazine's editorial director); "The Secret Horror of Mr. Hyde," an award-winning classic by Sandor Szabo; "The Girl and the Monster," a classic reprint by Victor Hugo; "The Jelly Fiend from Hell," another classic reprint by Thomas Beecham; the useful "How to Spot a Vampire" by Baron Von Monster; and so much more.

The magazine is so obviously fraudulent that it is hard to believe that the publisher was being serious or that he felt his readership was so gullible. The fact that the magazine lasted only three issues is an indication that the readers did regard the magazine as rubbish and ceased to buy it. The third issue carried a letter column with contributions clearly written by the magazine's staff, but it included one sensible comment, credited to "Bill Travers": "The best part of your alleged magazine is the little subtitles written under the story names on the contents page. I read those and then throw the magazine away"—sound advice.

Note

The author wishes to thank Frank H. Parnell for his assistance with this essay.

Information Sources

BIBLIOGRAPHY:
Tuck.
INDEX SOURCES: MT.
REPRINT SOURCES: None known.
LOCATION SOURCES: None known.

Publication History

TITLE: *Thriller*.
VOLUME DATA: Volume 1, Number 1, February 1962–Volume 1, Number 3, July
    1962. Bi-monthly (but second issue May). Total run: 3 issues.
PUBLISHER: Tempest Publications, New York.
EDITOR: Harry Schreiner (Editorial Director).
FORMAT: Slick, 64pp.
PRICE: 35¢.

Mike Ashley

THRILLING MYSTERY

Success always breeds imitation, and soon after Popular Publications had
launched its weird-menace pulps *Dime Mystery Magazine*,* *Terror Tales** and
Horror Stories,* Ned Pines at Standard Publications decided to add his contribution to the genre with *Thrilling Mystery*. It was launched with a certain amount
of consternation, as in April 1935 Popular had issued its fourth title, *Thrilling
Mysteries*. Pines, however, felt that he had a prior claim to the prefix "Thrilling,"
which he used in his pulps *Thrilling Detective*, *Thrilling Love* and *Thrilling
Adventures*; and so Popular dropped its pulp, and *Thrilling Mystery* appeared.

As with the other terror pulps, *TM* offered little in the way of genuine supernatural fiction, or even science fiction. Nevertheless, *TM* featured many stories
by regular SF writers, even before Pines bought *Wonder Stories** from Hugo
Gernsback and converted it to *Thrilling Wonder*. Contributors included Arthur
K. Barnes, Arthur J. Burks, Hugh B. Cave, Ray Cummings, Paul Ernst, John
Russell Fearn, Edmond Hamilton, Robert E. Howard, Carl Jacobi, Henry Kuttner, Frank Belknap Long, Mort Weisinger and Jack Williamson. Most of the
regular SF writers appeared with stories that had all the trappings of science
fiction, but had natural explanations. Williamson's "The Devil in Steel" (July
1937), for instance, leads the reader to believe that the menace is a rogue robot,
but it turns out to be a human villain dressed up in a tin can.

There was less of an emphasis on sex and sadism in *TM* than in other terror
pulps, and as a result the stories had greater originality, although they are not
necessarily of better quality. Some, however, are especially memorable. "Satan's
Kite" by Carl Jacobi (June 1937) is a clever story set in Borneo, where a man
and his family suffer from a curse as a result of stealing a rare silk from a

forbidden temple. Robert E. Howard contributed two stories about detective Steve Harrison, beginning with "Graveyard Rats" (February 1936), not to be confused with Henry Kuttner's like-named story in *Weird Tales*.* Arthur J. Burks contributed a particularly powerful yarn with no natural explanation in "Devils in the Dust" (December 1935).

When the terror boom faded at the end of the 1930s, *Thrilling Mystery* converted to a more conventional detective pulp, and though contributors still included Fritz Leiber, Fredric Brown, Seabury Quinn and Robert Bloch, the later issues are of no specific interest to SF/fantasy readers.

Information Sources

BIBLIOGRAPHY:
Jones, Robert K. *The Shudder Pulps*. West Linn, Ore.: Fax Collector's Editions, 1975. Tuck.
Weinberg, Robert. "Horror Pulps." In *Horror Literature*, ed. Marshall Tymn. New York: Bowker, 1981.
INDEX SOURCES: Austin, William N., *Macabre Index*. Seattle, Wash.: FAPA 59, 1952 (incomplete issue index); Jones, Robert Kenneth, "Popular's Weird Menace Pulps: Essay and Index," in *The Weird Menace*, ed. Camille Cazedessus, Jr. Evergreen, Colo.: Opar Press, 1972; Tuck. (Both T.G.L. Cockcroft and Virgil Utter have been working on indexes.)
REPRINT SOURCES: None known.
LOCATION SOURCES: University of California-Los Angeles Library (Vol. II, No. 3 only).

Publication History

TITLE: *Thrilling Mystery*, October 1935–Fall 1945; thereafter *Thrilling Mystery Novel Magazine*, a straightforward detective pulp.
VOLUME DATA: As *Thrilling Mystery*, Volume 1, Number 1, October 1935–Volume 22, Number 2, Fall 1944. Three issues per volume. Monthly, October 1935–August 1937 (but no November 1935 issue); bi-monthly, September 1937–March 1943; quarterly, June 1943–Fall 1944. Weird-menace pulp up to November 1941 [Volume 17, Number 3] only. Thereafter a detective fiction pulp. Total run: weird-menace, 51 issues; overall run, 74 issues.
PUBLISHER: Standard Magazine/Beacon Magazines, New York.
EDITOR: Overall editor Leo Margulies (not credited in issues) but contents indicate Mort Weisinger assisted on many issues.
FORMAT: Pulp, 112pp.
PRICE: 10¢.

Mike Ashley

THRILLING SCIENCE FICTION

Hot on the heels of *Great Science Fiction*,* publisher Sol Cohen issued another all-reprint magazine, initially modestly entitled *The Most Thrilling Science Fiction Ever Told*. The first issue, undated, was released in the summer of 1966.

Just as with *Great Science Fiction*, Cohen took advantage of the great store of SF published by Ziff-Davis, the publishers of *Amazing Stories** since 1938, who had purchased second serial rights to the stories. The issues were assembled at minimal cost, with the stories reproduced directly from the original copy. Cohen acted as editor on all of the issues, though possible reprints were suggested at first by Herb Lehrman, and subsequently by such fans as Gerald W. Page, Arnie Katz, and Grant Carrington.

The first three issues were among the more readable, with stories selected from *Amazing* and *Fantastic*'s* best period—1959–1964, under the editorship of Cele Goldsmith. The first issue, for instance, reprinted James E. Gunn's "Donor," one of the stories in his series about the Immortals, and Keith Laumer's first adventure of Jame Retief, the uncharacteristically serious "Diplomat-at-Arms." The second issue included one of SF's peculiarities, the round-robin story "The Covenant," where Poul Anderson, Isaac Asimov, Robert Sheckley and Murray Leinster had taken turns to further complicate the plot of this 1930s-style fantasy, leaving it to Robert Bloch to find a conclusion.

These first two quarterly issues were both 160 pages long, but with the third issue the magazine was reduced to 128 pages, and so it remained. For the first couple of years it maintained the quarterly schedule, and on the whole selections were readable, with occasional lapses into reprinting stories from the days of Paul Fairman's tenure as editor of *Amazing* and *Fantastic*.

With the ninth issue (Summer 1968), Harry Harrison's name appeared on the cover as editor, but this was merely a favor by Harrison to help sales. He also contributed two editorials, but Cohen continued to select the fiction and assemble the issues.

From the tenth issue (Fall 1968), *TSF* underwent a policy change, and for three numbers it published two complete short novels per issue. The first two were by Murray Leinster, to commemorate his fiftieth anniversary as a writer. "Long Ago, Far Away" (1959) was a complex and intriguing time-travel puzzle, while "Planet of Dread" (1962) was a traditional "space explorer versus the environment" adventure. The next issue selected work by two authors: Alan E. Nourse's "Gold in the Sky" (which had seen book publication as *Scavengers in Space*) and Henry Slesar's "The Goddess of World 21." Neither was up to the standard of the Leinster novellas. The twelfth issue was better, reprinting "Beacon to Elsewhere" by James H. Schmitz and "The Kragen" by Jack Vance. With the abundance of long stories published in *Amazing*'s history, this might have seemed a fruitful policy to pursue, but sales must have indicated otherwise, for with the thirteenth issue (Summer 1969) *TSF* returned to the original format with a reasonable selection of short stories from the late 1950s and early 1960s.

At this point *TSF* underwent another transformation. It was retitled *Thrilling Science Fiction Adventures*, and the stories were selected from the late 1940s and early 1950s. To all intents it was a different magazine, and only the issue numbers betrayed the continuity. For four issues *TSF* presented such skeletons from SF's cupboard as "The Iron Men of Venus" by Don Wilcox, "Invaders from the Monster World" by Edmond Hamilton, "The Wee Men of Weehen" by Lester Barclay, "The Metal Monster" by E. K. Jarvis, "Swamp Girl of Venus" by H. H. Harmon and many others that should have been allowed to rest in peace and not paraded like zombies in a world of science fiction that was alien to them.

There was a temporary lapse with the Winter 1970 issue, which once again resumed the identity of *The Most Thrilling Science Fiction Ever Told* and presented stories from the years 1954 to 1965. The next five issues, however, revert to the Howard Browne years, with stories selected more for their length than for their merit as fiction. By the law of averages some of them were still readable, such as Alfred Coppel's story of android wives, "Death Is Never Final"; Fredric Brown's chilling tale of alien infiltration, "From these Ashes . . . "; and Rog Phillips' touching story of a changed Earth, "The World of Whispering Wings"; but they were few among many. The stories were enhanced by several of Virgil Finlay's excellent illustrations, but beyond this the magazine had little to offer.

Clearly, however, Cohen was convinced that this was the direction to follow. After a boom of reprint titles in the period of 1970–1971, in which Cohen published more new titles than any other SF publisher before or since and whereby he tested the market, he settled down to two reprint titles, *Science Fiction Adventure Classics (Science Fiction Classics*)* and *Thrilling Science Fiction*. *TSF* became bi-monthly from December 1971, and from June 1972 the story selection reverted to the Cele Goldsmith period, and the quality substantially improved, even though many of the best stories had already been reprinted. Cohen even began reprinting stories from his own early issues. The February 1973 *TSF* carried "On the Sand Planet" by Cordwainer Smith, "Mute Milton" by Harry Harrison and "Two Days Running Then Skip a Day" by Ron Goulart, all from post-Ziff-Davis issues.

Thereafter *TSF* continued to reprint from the Goldsmith period, with occasional forays into the Fairman days, and the quality was as uneven as one would expect from a reprint magazine with no policy. Articles were also reprinted, although most had lost the impact that their original publication had intended.

With the April 1975 issue, *TSF* absorbed *Science Fiction Adventures* and thereafter intended to include one "famous classic" alongside the more recent reprints. Cohen also announced that new stories and an editorial would feature from the next issue, "if the readers agree to submit suitable material." Cohen thereupon requested readers to submit stories up to 3,000 words and an editorial of about 500 words, to be paid for in subscriptions to the magazine.

Whatever the outcome, only one more issue of *TSF* appeared, and that was all-reprint. Its passing was scarcely noticed.

Information Sources

BIBLIOGRAPHY:
Nicholls. *Encyclopedia.*
Tuck.

INDEX SOURCES: ISFM-II; NESFA; NESFA-II; NESFA-III; SFM; Tuck.
REPRINT SOURCES: None known.
LOCATION SOURCES: M.I.T. Science Fiction Library; Pennsylvania State University Library.

Publication History

TITLE: *The Most Thrilling Science Fiction Ever Told*, Number 1–Number 13; *Thrilling Science Fiction Adventures*, Number 14–Number 17; *The Most Thrilling Science Fiction Ever Told*, Number 18; *Thrilling Science Fiction*, Number 19–[Number 42], July 1975. Issues 9 and 18 both bore the title *Thrilling SF* on the spine.

VOLUME DATA: No volume numbering. First six issues undated; last seventeen issues unnumbered. Number 1, [Summer 1966]–[Number 42], July 1975. Quarterly, issues 1–21, Fall 1971 (but no Winter 1969 issue); bi-monthly, Number 22, December 1971–December 1974; quarterly, April–July 1975. Total run: 42 issues.

PUBLISHER: Ultimate Publishing Co., Flushing, New York.

EDITOR: Sol Cohen (not identified within issues).

FORMAT: Digest, 160 pp. (first two issues), thereafter 128 pp.

PRICE: 50¢, Number 1–Number 18, Winter 1970; 60¢, Number 19, Spring 1971–June 1974; 75¢, August 1974–July 1975.

Mike Ashley

THRILLING SCIENCE FICTION ADVENTURES

See THRILLING SCIENCE FICTION.

THRILLING STORIES

Thrilling Stories, released in January 1946, was one of a series of booklets issued by Benson Herbert's Utopian Publications at the end of World War II, some of which were arguably magazines (especially *Strange Tales** and to some extent *Strange Love Stories**), but which because of wartime paper restrictions had to be published in the guise of books.

Thrilling Stories contained only two items: "Cat's Eye" by Harl Vincent, from the April 1934 *Amazing Stories*,* and "The Master of the Genes" by Edmond Hamilton, from the January 1935 *Wonder Stories*.* Poor sales may have indicated that the title was not sufficiently strong, for Herbert's follow-up booklet was *Strange Love Stories*.

Information Sources

BIBLIOGRAPHY:

Gillings, Walter. "Topless in Utopia." *Vision of Tomorrow*, July 1970, p. 62 (also includes index).

Tuck.

INDEX SOURCES: IBSF.
REPRINT SOURCES: None known.
LOCATION SOURCES: None known.

Publication History

TITLE: *Thrilling Stories*.
VOLUME DATA: Unnumbered, undated, but released January 1946.
PUBLISHER: Utopian Publications, London.
EDITOR: Benson Herbert.
FORMAT: Digest (saddle-stapled), 36 pp.
PRICE: 1/-.

Mike Ashley

THRILLING WONDER STORIES

See WONDER STORIES.

THRILLS

Thrills was a borderline fantasy magazine consisting of reprints from the William Clayton magazines, which include *Ranch Romances*, *Ace-High*, *Jungle Stories*,* *Clues* and, of course, *Strange Tales** and *Astounding Stories* (*Analog Science Fiction**). The origins of the stories were not noted within the magazine, which gave every indication of being a British original. The first issue (which probably appeared in 1939) contained five stories from an assortment of magazines, and only the lead story, which took up over half of the issue, was fantasy—"The Duel of the Sorcerers" by Paul Ernst, from the March 1932 *Strange Tales*. Also in the issue was an oriental adventure, "The Spirit of France" by S.B.H. Hurst, whose name also figures in *Strange Tales*, though this was not a fantasy.

Thrills promised a second monthly issue which would contain "Wolves of Darkness" by Jack Williamson and "By the Hands of the Dead" by Francis Flagg, but this issue has not been sighted and may have been a victim of the wartime paper restrictions.

Thrills also had three companion magazines—*Stirring Stories*, *Swift Action Stories* and *Exciting Fiction*—which probably had the same blend of fantasy and adventure that characterized the Clayton magazines, but these issues have not been sighted.

Information Sources

BIBLIOGRAPHY:
Tuck.
INDEX SOURCES: None known.

REPRINT SOURCES: None known.
LOCATION SOURCES: None Known.

Publication History

TITLE: *Thrills*.
VOLUME DATA: Number 1, undated, probably 1939.
PUBLISHER: Atlas Publishing & Distributing Co., London.
EDITOR: Not identified, but may have been Paul Imbush.
FORMAT: Pulp, 96 pp.
PRICE: 9d.

Frank H. Parnell

THRILLS INCORPORATED

Thrills Incorporated was a minor project of a diversified Australian publishing organization with a wide range of interests. Some significant science fiction magazines have operated in such an environment with satisfactory results; but it seems a valid generalization that a periodical with specific and unconventional requirements needs a standard of planning and constant attention only to be expected when its proprietors see it as an important and challenging venture.

Thrills obviously began with sketchy planning and a confused concept of what it was meant to be, unsupported by research. One's impression on looking at its early issues (the first, undated, was the March 1950 issue) is that those responsible must have heard about science fiction but never read any. The artwork supports the impression, though in fact the first cover suggests that someone had seen at least one American magazine.

It used to be a common joke in criticism of less-than-ideal science fiction that the author was trying to convert a mundane piece of popular fiction into science fiction by changing the setting and disguising familiar elements as future or interplanetary equivalents. Thus, a story in the western tradition might be re-worked, with the same kind of conflicts of interest, disorderly frontier conditions and so on, by converting Indians to Martians and so on. Ordinary stories of adventure, mystery and intrigue could be dressed up with exotic details. And in the 1930s some writers did something of the sort. When space piracy was imagined its practitioners were often suspiciously like the buccaneers of tradition.

But it was left to *Thrills* to make this lazy man's way to write bad SF an officially supported procedure. "When *Thrills* began we had no science fiction writers," editor Alister Innes said. "We had only a team of western and detective writers, and so we had to create a formula, not necessarily a good one, but at least a functional one, for the writing of science fiction . . . to take any story and put it forward (say) 2,000 years, adapting plot and environment as the author went along."

Since this is precisely how *not* to write science fiction, which begins with a scientific concept and imagines a consequent setting and story possibilities, it is no surprise that the resulting fiction was terrible. It was spiritless hack work, as devoid of human interest and spontaneity as of prophecy. Scientific background was nonexistent: stories allegedly set in interplanetary space showed no grasp of the simplest facts of astronomy, and future technology was vague and unrealistic. Future society, business, warfare, crime, and personal relationships and conflicts were usually transplanted unchanged from the present or the past as conventionally viewed in popular fiction. But there were some attempts to imagine future social changes here and there.

On the other hand, there were stories that plainly revealed that the author had read some overseas science fiction. "We were . . . hoodwinked by unscrupulous writers who plagiarised American SF stories," Innes admitted. "As soon as this was pointed out we sacked those writers." Not content with imitation, they had simply typed out a few stories, changing no more than the title. But if the editor (not being familiar with the field) did not recognize Clifford Simak, William Tenn, Murray Leinster, Charles Harness, Ray Bradbury and even Hal Remson, there were readers who did.

"Our present policy," Innes said in the second half of *Thrills'* life, "is to give an author a title and an illustration and get him to write a story around them. This may not produce fiction on the level of *Astounding* [*Analog Science Fiction**] but at least it ensures an original story." This is of course *another* classic wrong way to write science fiction, the dubious originality being offset by even thinner content.

Innes went on to claim:

We have also had to educate our readers as we went along, and although we have been far less scientific than our American cousins, this has been for the very good reason that the general reading public in Australia is far less advanced in the field of science fiction than is the U.S. reading public. There may be a small group of regular readers who want higher-quality science fiction, but the bulk of our readers must be educated to it.

Educated!

The pity of it was that, even then, there was no more Americanized country than Australia, which had a well established following for *Astounding* because through the 1940s the emaciated British edition of it had been the only science fiction readily available. No doubt there was a place for something more like *Planet Stories** or *Startling Stories,** but what *Thrills* offered was many steps further down the scale. It was no match for the British imports (mostly extensions of the U.S. magazines) that were building up sales in Australia by 1952. As with other Australian attempts, in quality as well as quantity it was a case of too little, too late.

The physical standard of the magazine did not help it. It was a cheap, shoddy looking production, a thin forty-eight pages at best, unattractively packaged.

The size varied noticeably from one issue to the next, between 9¼ and 11 inches for the first twelve, between 7 and 8 inches for the rest. With the change to octavo came a change of cover layout, the feature story providing the main title and giving it the appearance of a booklet rather than a magazine.

Little can be said about *Thrills'* group of authors. Norma Hemming wrote under her own name, as did the team of G. C. Bleeck and Alan Yates (better known in detective fiction as Carter Brown) and Durham Garton. Stanford Hennell probably contributed, and a writer who remains anonymous wrote a substantial amount. Most of the names were obvious pseudonyms, and some no doubt were house names used by anyone as convenient. The magazine failed to create either a significant body of writing or a sizable group of writers.

Remarkable as Australia's first attempt, for editorial policy that has to be called unorthodox, and for its unusual lack of merit, *Thrills Incorporated* is not one of science fiction's worthier products.

Information Sources

BIBLIOGRAPHY:
Nicholls. *Encyclopedia*.
Tuck.
INDEX SOURCES: ASFI; Tuck.
REPRINT SOURCES:
Magazines: See *Amazing Science Stories*.
LOCATION SOURCES: Futurian Society of Sydney Library; M.I.T. Science Fiction Library.

Publication History

TITLE: *Thrills Incorporated*.
VOLUME DATA: All issues undated. Number 1 [March 1950]–Number 23 [June 1952].
    Monthly issues 1–9 [March–November 1950] and issues 14–23 [August 1951–
    June 1952, missing December 1951]. Number 10 [January 1951], 11 and 12 [both
    April 1951] and 13 [June 1951]. Total run: 23 issues.
PUBLISHER: Associated General Publications, Sydney. Company name changed to
    Transport Publishing from issue 13.
EDITOR: Not identified within issues. *TI* was produced with many other publications,
    and several staff members may have worked on it, but Alister Innes was mainly
    responsible.
FORMAT: Varied, but in general: Pulp, 48 pp., Numbers 1–5; Large Pulp, 48 pp.,
    Numbers 6–12; Digest, 32 pp., Numbers 13–23.
PRICE: 9d, Numbers 1–5; 1/-, Numbers 6–12; 8d, Numbers 13–23.

Graham Stone

TOADSTOOL WINE

Toadstool Wine, published in 1975, was not an independent magazine but a single sampler of contents from six other semi-professional magazines: *Fantasy and Terror,* * *Moonbroth, Space and Time,* * *Weirdbook,* * *Whispers* * and *Wyrd*.

Such samplers are relatively common in the fanzine field, where they are known as "combozines," and might be assembled for a convention, with the costs shared between the respective publishers, but such samplers are all but unknown in the professional field and are equally rare in the semi-pro field.

What made *Toadstool Wine* a worthwhile publication was that, apart from the *Whispers* section, all other contents were new and not reprints. There was an introductory article by Fritz Leiber on "The Literature of Cosmic Dread" which led into representative soupçons from the six magazines, running to about eight pages apiece. From *Fantasy and Terror* comes fiction by David C. Smith and an article by Charles R. Saunders; from *Moonbroth* comes fiction by Douglas Justice and an article by Tredennick; *Space and Time* has two short stories and a comic strip; *Weirdbook* has three items of fiction, *Whispers* another two, and *Wyrd* two more. For the remainder there is a pleasant admixture of artwork— including Gary Kato, Lee Brown Coye, William Church and Gene Day—and poetry—by Stephanie Stearns, Joseph Payne Brennan, Robert E. Howard and John Bredon.

Paul Ganley, the editor of *Weirdbook*, took on the responsibility of coordinating and publishing the sampler, and the overall result gives a very good idea of the kind of material published by the other magazines. Because it contains so much new material, however, it must be regarded as an extension of all of those publications, with a little bit extra, in combining so many alternative approaches to what is good fantasy.

Information Sources

INDEX SOURCES: MT.
REPRINT SOURCES: None known.
LOCATION SOURCES: M.I.T. Science Fiction Library.

Publication History

TITLE: *Toadstool Wine.*
VOLUME DATA: Unnumbered; published in 1975.
PUBLISHER: W. Paul Ganley, Buffalo, New York.
EDITORS: Coordinating editor, W. Paul Ganley. Individual editors for each section: Dale Donaldson, *Moonbroth*; Gordon Linzner, *Space and Time*; Jessica Amanda Salmonson, *Fantasy & Terror*; Stuart Schiff, *Whispers*; Greg Stafford, *Wyrd*.
FORMAT: A4, printed; 64 pp.
PRICE: $2.95.

Mike Ashley

TOPS IN SCIENCE FICTION

This *Planet Stories** reprint magazine is most noteworthy as a symptom of the rise of the digest and the decline of the pulp. Following the current reprint trend, publisher Malcolm Reiss directed Jack O'Sullivan to serve as editor of a magazine that would reprint in pulp some of *Planet Stories*' better work, from the early and mid-forties: an early Leigh Brackett interplanetary sword and sorcery novelette, "Citadel of Lost Ships"; a Nelson Bond novelette with the humorous approach of his Biggs series, "Castaways of Eros"; one of Isaac Asimov's earliest pieces, "Black Friar of the Flame"; Ray Bradbury's first *Martian Chronicles* story, "The Million Year Picnic";[1] and the sole published story of the then noted fan personality Raymond Van Houten, "The Last Martian."[2] Notable among the artists was Kelly Freas, at the beginning of his career, with full-page interior illustrations for the Brackett and van Houten stories.

But 1953 was not only the year of a reprint trend, it was a year in which the digests seriously would threaten the pulps; eventually American News, the major distributor, would refuse to handle the latter. So Reiss became editor himself and converted *Tops*' second issue to a digest. He used a better quality of paper, shrank the size, and introduced a new style of artwork by Freas and Ed Emsh. Replacing the girl-devouring phallic bug-eyed monster of A. Leydenfrost was a stylish symbolic cover by Freas for the Bradbury/Brackett "Lorelei of the Red Mist." It and the related interior illustrations impressed the artist himself:

> The Lorelei apparently shook me up as much as she did the hero. She generated a whole new cover format (I did the logo-type too, and I'm still pleased with it). But she also generated a lovely set of interiors in a style brand new, and still unique: I was never quite able to repeat it. A hex, of course.[3]

But the contents were similar to those of the first issue: the Brackett/Bradbury reincarnation of Conan, in "Lorelei"; a comic piece by another major *Planet Stories* writer, Fredric Brown; a 1943 story by Horace Gold writing as Harold C. Fosse, "Grifters' Asteroid," a possibly ironic demonstration that one of the major editors of the modish digests was once a writer of interplanetary juveniles himself.

But it was not enough for *Tops* simply to look like a digest. The atomic age had brought with it a new world, and, for a while at least, magazines like *Planet Stories* were an anachronism. *Tops* was thus an echo of an anachronism in the fifties, a reflection of the mirage of the forties, and it could not survive in a world for which it was not meant.

Notes

1. Donald H. Tuck, *The Encyclopedia of Science Fiction* (Chicago: Advent, 1974), I: 61.

2. Tuck, II: 429.

3. Frank Kelly Freas, *The Art of Science Fiction* (Norfolk, Va.: 1977), pp. 36–37.

Information Sources

BIBLIOGRAPHY:
Nicholls. *Encyclopedia.*
Tuck.
INDEX SOURCES: MIT; SFM.
REPRINT SOURCES:
> British Edition: Three issues, Digest, 128 pp., 1/6d., published by Top Fiction Ltd., London; undated, but released Autumn 1954, Winter 1955, Summer 1956. First two selected from Spring 53 U.S., the third from Fall 53 U.S.

LOCATION SOURCES: M.I.T. Science Fiction Library; Pennsylvania State University Library.

Publication History

TITLE: *Tops in Science Fiction.*
VOLUME DATA: Volume 1, Number 1, Spring 1953–Volume 1, Number 2, Fall 1953.
> Intentional schedule, quarterly, but only 2 issues.

PUBLISHER: Love Romances Pub. Co., Stamford, Connecticut.
EDITORS: Jack O'Sullivan, Spring 1953; Malcolm Reiss, Fall 1953.
FORMAT: Pulp, 128 pp., Spring 1953; Digest, 128 pp., Fall 1953.
PRICE: 25¢, Spring 1953; 35¢ Fall 1953.

E. F. Casebeer

TREASURY OF GREAT SCIENCE FICTION STORIES

Although in a magazine format and reprinting stories in facsimile, this reprint annual, which first appeared in 1964, should really be regarded as a paperback anthology. It followed the facsimile reprint of *Wonder Stories,** which had appeared in 1957 and had been reissued with slight changes in 1963. Sales were sufficiently encouraging for the anthology to be issued on an annual basis. Stories came from the pages of *Thrilling Wonder*, *Startling Stories** and *Space Stories** accompanied by their original illustrations, which provided an opportunity to see more of the work of Virgil Finlay.

The stories were chosen wisely, aided by the fact that *Thrilling Wonder* and *Startling* were at their best in the late 1940s with authors like Ray Bradbury, Leigh Brackett, Murray Leinster, Henry Kuttner, L. Sprague de Camp, Jack Vance and Arthur C. Clarke, all of whom featured prominently in the *Treasury* series. The three Bradbury stories, for instance, come from his Martian Chronicles sequence. Also reprinted were stories not so easily accessible, such as "Hero" by H. L. Gold, "Messenger" by Theodore Sturgeon and "A Condition of Beauty" by John D. MacDonald.

The publications lacked any editorial departments and were otherwise featureless, but the quality of the stories made it a series worth acquiring. With the third issue the series was retitled *Great Science Fiction Stories*, but this clashed with Sol Cohen's *Great Science Fiction.** With the next issue, therefore, the series was completely revamped as *Science Fiction Yearbook*,* with the issue sequence reverting to Number 1. Although a clear continuation of the *Treasury*, it had a new editor and can be regarded as a separate publication.

Information Sources

BIBLIOGRAPHY:
Nicholls. *Encyclopedia.*
Tuck.
INDEX SOURCES: ISFM-II; MIT; SFM.
REPRINT SOURCES: None known.
LOCATION SOURCES: M.I.T. Science Fiction Library.

Publication History

TITLE: *Treasury of Great Science Fiction Stories*, first two issues; thereafter *Great Science Fiction Stories.*
VOLUME DATA: No volume numbering. Number 1, 1964–Number 3, 1966.
PUBLISHER: Popular Library, Inc., New York.
EDITOR: Jim Hendryx, Jr.
FORMAT: Pulp, 96 pp.
PRICE: 50¢.

Mike Ashley

TRUE TWILIGHT TALES

True Twilight Tales was a companion title to *Prize Ghost Stories*,* both of which relied for their contents on reprinting items from the 1920s *Ghost Stories*.* The publisher, League Publications, was a subsidiary of MacFadden-Bartell, which owned the rights to the original title. The stories had their titles changed, which, in the case of those reprinted in the original *Ghost Stories*, meant a further retitle. Thus Algernon Blackwood's innocuous title, "The Woman's Ghost Story," which had become "The Specter That Asked for a Kiss" in the July 1929 *Ghost Stories*, was now pepped up as "Ghost Who Begged 'Kiss Me! Love Me!' "— an indication of the changing tastes of readers. New illustrations accompanied the stories, though they followed the same style as the originals and included a few fake photographs. The magazine was clearly intended to appeal to the same readership that bought the various confessions magazines with a spiritualistic leaning—in fact, exactly the same audience targeted forty years earlier.

Two issues of *TTT* are known, dated Fall 1963 and Spring 1964; as they are unnumbered, however, there may have been more. Collectors will be interested to know that these two issues reprinted stories by E. and H. Heron, Everil Worrell, Erckmann-Chatrain and Sophie Wenzel Ellis.

Information Sources

BIBLIOGRAPHY:
Tuck.
INDEX SOURCES: MT.
REPRINT SOURCES: None known.
LOCATION SOURCES: None known.

Publication History

TITLE: *True Twilight Tales.*
VOLUME DATA: Unnumbered. Issues sighted dated Fall 1963 and Spring 1964.
PUBLISHER: League Publications, Inc., New York.
EDITORS: Helen Gardiner, Fall 1963; John M. Williams, Spring 1964.
FORMAT: Large Pulp, 96 pp.
PRICE: 50¢.

Mike Ashley

THE TWILIGHT ZONE MAGAZINE

See ROD SERLING'S THE TWILIGHT ZONE MAGAZINE.

TWO COMPLETE SCIENCE-ADVENTURE BOOKS

A companion to *Planet Stories,** *Two Complete Science-Adventure Books* came from Wings Publishing Company. Appearing three times a year (dated Spring, Summer and Winter), it ran as a pulp for eleven issues between winter 1950 and spring 1954.

In that short time, the magazine had three editors. The first, Jerome Bixby, who had been editing *Planet Stories* at the same time, left *Two Complete Science-Adventure Books* after the third issue (Summer 1951), when he became an assistant to Sam Mines at Standard Publications. Malcolm Reiss, who had been the original editor of *Planet Stories*, headed the next six issues (Winter 1951–Summer 1953). And for the magazine's last two issues, Katherine Daffron was the editor. Only under Bixby did the magazine print readers' letters, and none of the three provided an editorial column.

Initially, *Two Complete Science-Adventure Books* was designed as a reprint magazine, intended to provide readers with two recently published works in an inexpensive format. A periodical with the same idea, *Two Complete Detective Books Magazine*, had been tried by *Planet Stories'* publisher in the 1930s. The first issue of *Two Complete Science-Adventure Books* contained Isaac Asimov's "Pebble in the Sky" (1950) and L. Ron Hubbard's "The Kingslayer" (1949). Among works reprinted in later issues were Edmond Hamilton's "The Star Kings," H. G. Wells' "The Time Machine," Jack Williamson's "The Humanoids,'' and Anson MacDonald's (Robert A. Heinlein's) ''Beyond This Horizon.''

With the second issue, however, the magazine began to include previously unpublished work, and for the next two years the contents were split—one reprint and one original in each issue. Some of the late issues contained only original material.

Especially in its original material, *Two Complete Science-Adventure Books* imitated *Planet Stories* and leaned heavily toward action-oriented science fiction. Much of this original material, in fact, might be described more accurately as derivative space opera. Typical stories in *Two Complete Science-Adventure Books* project a hero from Earth into some battle to save an alien world or galactic empire from rebellious invaders. Another favored story line keeps the human hero on his home planet, where he must thwart some alien effort—usually covert—to subjugate the Earth. The protagonist of James Blish's ''Sword of Xota,'' for example, finds himself acting as the long-prophesied instrument of an alien deity; the hero of Poul Anderson's ''Silent Victory'' discovers that a devastating war between Mars and Earth has really been a cover for an invasion by metamorphic aliens from the Sirian system.

Among writers less conscientious than Blish or Anderson, scientific plausibility founders amid the adventures. In one egregious instance (''Survivor of Mars''), a traveler at ''twice'' the speed of light requires an hour to get from Mars to Venus. More often, as the writers pour out their wonders, they do not even encumber themselves with explanations of such precise illogicality.

Even so, two early pieces—one by John Brunner and another by Arthur C. Clarke—contain some promise of situations and themes which each writer later develops more effectively. Thus, the ambiguity of legitimizing authority in Brunner's ''The Wanton of Argus'' does offer a garish and unresolved version of questions which arise in works like *Shockwave Rider* and *Stand on Zanzibar*. And in Clarke's ''Seeker of the Sphinx,'' the brooding anomolous sphinx and the impact of the superior culture on Earth's inhabitants point toward the more profound handling of the pyramid in *The Sentinel* and the overlords in *Childhood's End*.

By 1954, however, the increased competition of paperback novels made *TCSAB* less a viable concern, and with the general collapse of the pulp empire, it was one of the first to go.

Information Sources

BIBLIOGRAPHY:
Nicholls. *Encyclopedia.*
Tuck.
INDEX SOURCES: MIT; SFM; Tuck.
REPRINT SOURCES: None known.
LOCATION SOURCES: M.I.T. Science Fiction Library; Pennsylvania State University
      Library.

Publication History

TITLE: *Two Complete Science-Adventure Books.*

VOLUME DATA: Volume 1, Number 1, Winter 1950–Volume 1, Number 11, Spring 1954. Thrice yearly. Total run: 11 issues.

PUBLISHER: Wings Publishing Co., New York (first six issues) and Stamford, Connecticut (last five issues).

EDITORS: Jerome Bixby, Winter 1950–Summer 1951; Malcolm Reiss, Winter 1951–Summer 1953; Katherine Daffron, Winter 1953–Spring 1954.

FORMAT: Pulp; 144 pp., Winter 1950–Summer 1951; 128 pp., Winter 1951; 112 pp., Spring 1952; 96 pp., Summer 1952–Summer 1953; 128 pp., Winter 1953–Spring 1954.

PRICE: 25¢.

Joseph Marchesani

UNCANNY STORIES

Uncanny Stories, a single issue of which appeared in April 1941, was the last science fiction pulp magazine to be born before World War II decimated the field. Ironically, it came from the same stable as *Marvel Science Stories*,* which to all intents had sparked off the SF boom when it appeared in 1937. Unfortunately, it also came from the same publisher, noted more for its terror magazines, like *Mystery Tales* and *Uncanny Tales*,* than for its science fiction. *Uncanny Tales* had occasionally featured SF of a weird-menace variety, and had last appeared in May 1940, after five issues, but so erratic were the Goodman pulps that many could be forgiven for thinking that *Uncanny Stories* was merely a continuation of the former pulp with a title change. (See the entry for *Marvel Science Stories* to see how frequently that pulp changed titles.) Certainly the cover did little to dispel that belief. The work of Norman Saunders, it portrayed a scene from Ray Cummings' lead story, "Coming of the Giant Germs," but just such girl-in-peril covers had adorned *Uncanny Tales*. In all probability the one-shot was using up stories in the inventory for *Marvel* and the other pulps as the publishers were placing a greater emphasis on the comic-book field.

On the whole, the story titles were more restrained than the usual "Blood-Brides of the Lusting Corpses" fare, but editor Robert Erisman still felt it necessary to pep up some of them; for example, David H. Keller's "The Chestnut Mare" became "Speed Will Be My Bride." Other stories in the issues were "The Earth-Stealers" by F. A. Kummer, Jr., "Beyond Hell" by R. DeWitt Miller and "The Man from the Wrong Time-Track" by Denis Plimmer who, by a strange coincidence, was a regular contributor to the Canadian pulp *Uncanny Tales*,* which otherwise had no connection with this title.

US offered nothing new to the SF reader and little else to others who normally purchased the terror pulps. It is notable today only for the fact that it was so obscure even when published that it became a hard-to-find collector's item for the SF magazine completist.

Information Sources

BIBLIOGRAPHY:
Nicholls. *Encyclopedia*.
Tuck.
INDEX SOURCES: ISFM; MT; SFM.
REPRINT SOURCES: None known.
LOCATION SOURCES: M.I.T. Science Fiction Library; Pennsylvania State University
    Library.

Publication History

TITLE: *Uncanny Stories*.
VOLUME DATA: Volume 1, Number 1, April 1941. Only issue.
PUBLISHER: Manvis Publications, New York.
EDITOR: Robert O. Erisman.
FORMAT: Pulp, 112 pp.
PRICE: 15¢

Mike Ashley/Robert Weinberg

UNCANNY TALES

One of the profusion of sex-and-sadism pulps that erupted in the 1930s in the wake of the success of *Horror Stories** and *Terror Tales,** *Uncanny Tales* (not to be confused with the Canadian pulp of the same name, or the later magazine *Uncanny Stories**) was a companion to *Marvel Science Stories,** which would soon change its identity to *Marvel Tales* and go in for the same kind of sex-ploitation tales that *UT* offered.

Regular contributors included Arthur J. Burks, Ray Cummings, Russell Gray and Donald Graham, but few of the known fantasy writers offered supernatural stories. In the first known issue (dated April/May 1939)—which is notable, if for nothing else, for Donald Graham's "Revelry in Hell," which Robert Weinberg regards as "probably the most sadistic torture story ever featured in the horror pulps"—there was a restrained attempt at fantasy in "Nameless Brides of Forbidden City" by Frederick C. Davis, which is set in Lhasa and hints at reincarnation. A bolder attempt at the supernatural came in the second issue with "Open the Dead Door" by Alexander Faust, which involves a witch-woman and an exchange of personalities. By the third issue there was even a science fiction cover with space-helmeted aliens threatening a bikini-clad damsel while the hero comes to the rescue with a ray-gun.

This was the extent to which *UT* featured SF and fantasy. There was no serious intent to utilize these themes; they were merely a convenient device whereby to change the milieu or rationale of a story that otherwise followed a very basic and already aging plot of terror and revenge. The titles say it all: "Lovely Bodies for the Butcher," "Blood-Brides for the Lusting Corpse," "Fresh Blood for My Bride" and "Blood Is My Bride." *UT* came in the final days of the terror pulps and attempted to plunder the field to excess. Fortunately, it was short-lived and forgettable.

Information Sources

BIBLIOGRAPHY:

Jones, Robert, K. *The Shudder Pulps*. West Linn, Ore.: Fax Collector's Editions, 1975.
———. "The Weird Menace Magazines." *Bronze Shadows*, No. 10 (June 1967): 3–8; No. 11 (August 1967): 7–13; No. 12 (October 1967): 7–10; No. 13 (January 1968): 7–12; No. 14 (March 1968): 13–17; No. 15 (November 1968); 4–8.

Nicholls. *Encyclopedia*.

Tuck.

Weinberg, Robert. "The Horror Pulps." In *Horror Literature*, ed. Marshall Tymn. New York: Bowker, 1981.

INDEX SOURCES: Austin, William N., *Macabre Index*, Seattle, Wash.: FAPA 59, 1952; MT; SFM.

REPRINT SOURCES:

Derivative Anthology: Robert Weinberg, ed., *Revelry in Hell* (Oak Lawn, Ill.: Weinberg, 1974), contains five stories.

LOCATION SOURCES: University of California–Los Angeles Library (*Real Mystery*, Vol. 1, No. 1 only).

Publication History

TITLE: *Uncanny Tales*.

VOLUME DATA: Possibly took over from another magazine's sequence. No issues exist before Volume 2, Number 6, April/May 1939. Last issue Volume 3, Number 4, May 1940. Listed as bi-monthly, but irregular. Other issues August/September 1939, November/December 1939 and March 1940. Total run: 5 issues.

PUBLISHER: Manvis Publications, New York.

EDITOR: Robert O. Erisman (not credited within issue).

FORMAT: Pulp, 112 pp.

PRICE: 15¢.

Mike Ashley

UNCANNY TALES (1940–1943)

Uncanny Tales is the longest-running example of that rarest of publications, an indigenous Canadian science fiction magazine. Single issues, let alone complete runs, are scarce, and its origin and existence has been one of the enigmas of the fantasy field.

The first issue appeared in November 1940. It was a thin, sixty-four page digest-size publication with the contents printed in green ink. The emphasis was on weird fiction, and Canadian writer Thomas P. Kelley, who was known from his contributions to *Weird Tales*,* dominated the issue with the lead story, "Murder in the Graveyard," and the first episode in a five-part serial, "The Talking Heads." Because of Kelley's close association with the magazine, as a contributor of both fiction and nonfiction, it has been conjectured that he also edited it. It is quite possible that he served as an associate editor or first reader, but the editor was someone else. Donald A. Wollheim recalls:

> I attended a little gathering of writers and professional journalists in New York some time after the demise of *Stirring* [*Science Stories**] and *Cosmic* [*Stories**] but during the War. I met a Canadian journalist there named, as far as I can recall, Colby. He was working on a newspaper in Toronto but had been augmenting his salary by acting as editor for a little publisher putting out magazines, one of which was *Uncanny Tales*.[1]

The meeting with Wollheim changed the course of the magazine.

> Colby heard that I was a science fiction expert and he asked if I could suggest sources for stories he could get very cheap. I said the stories in *Stirring* and *Cosmic* were available, never having been distributed in Canada and being controlled entirely by the authors—all friends of mine for whom I could speak. We struck a deal. I would supply him copy for the magazine. He would pay 1/4 cent a word. Great. It worked out without much problem. We sent him tear-sheets, we sometimes changed titles, we threw in one or two original stories we wanted to see in print for the fun of it.[2]

Wollheim's involvement was not noted until the sixth issue, when he was present with a short story of his own, "The Thought Monsters." Prior to that the magazine consisted of minor stories and articles by Canadian writers, most of them unknown and many of the names possibly pseudonyms for Thomas P. Kelley. The only other recognizable names were Leslie A. Croutch, who occasionally appeared in the American magazines, and Oliver Saari, a Finnish-born American fan who had started to sell stories to *Astounding* (*Analog Science Fiction**) in 1937. The fiction was predominantly supernatural, with a bias toward allegedly true stories.

With the fifth issue the magazine changed its format dramatically, to pulp size, with ninety-six pages, and the sixth issue added a letter column, "Around the Cauldron."

It was the seventh issue that first fully reflected the Wollheim connection. Four of the stories had been supplied by Wollheim from various recent issues of *Stirring Science Stories*. "Bones," "The Strange Return" and "Cosmophobia" were the work of Wollheim himself, while "The Gray One" had been written by Robert W. Lowndes. These two, plus Cyril M. Kornbluth, became the main contributors to the ensuing issues, and in time Wollheim included most of the Futurians. Thirty-seven of the stories have been identified as originating in either *Stirring* or *Cosmic*, and there were possibly others, retitled. A few stories were reprinted that had not been supplied by Wollheim, as for a very short period Sam Moskowitz also became involved. Moskowitz's "The Way Back" from *Comet** appeared in the February 1942 issue, and soon after Stanton Coblentz's novel *After 12,000 Years* was serialized.

Of greater significance, however, are the new stories in *Uncanny Tales*, and these came from two sources: from Wollheim or through direct submissions to the magazine. Wollheim had three new stories published: "The Hat" (November 1941), "The Coming of the Comet" (December 1942) and "The Drums of Reig Rawan" (February 1942); John Victor Peterson had "The Magic Touch of Mozart" (February 1942); and Robert W. Lowndes had two stories, "Lure of the Lily" (January 1942) and "Blacklist" (May 1942). The former was considerably revised and was retitled "Lilies" for its publication by Lowndes in the Spring of 1967 *Magazine of Horror*.*

The February 1942 issue also included a story by the well-known American fan James V. Taurasi, "Magician of Space." This had probably been supplied by Moskowitz and is Taurasi's only professionally published SF.

The Canadian stories were less notable. Some may have been the work of Kelley writing under pseudonyms. Canadian fan Bob Gibson has also suggested that several of the stories seem to be plagiarisms and rewrites of other people's work. An irregular contributor was Denis Plimmer, who appeared with eight stories starting with "The Coming of Darakk" (December 1941). He had earlier appeared with "The Green Invasion" in the November 1940 *Weird Tales* (which was reprinted in the April 1942 *Uncanny Tales*), and by one of the strange quirks of fate was one of a handful of contributors to the single issue of the American *Uncanny Stories*,* which, despite the similarity in the name, had no connection with the Canadian magazine.

Another curiosity concerns C. V. Tench, hitherto noted in the SF field solely as the author of "Compensation," an unmemorable story from the very first issue of *Astounding Stories* in January 1930. That story resurfaced in the December 1941 *Uncanny Tales*, but then Tench appeared twice subsequently with "The Kiss of Bohaana" in the May 1942 issue and "The Spot of Blood" in the September/October 1943 issue. This may indicate that Tench was a Canadian author.

Uncanny Tales was clearly a miscellany of curiosities, and well worth serious study. While the quality of the stories was not particularly high, the lack of any large body of indigenous Canadian magazines has inflated the value of the magazine out of proportion to its importance in the field as a whole. Nevertheless, it was an attempt at a mature contribution to the SF magazine field and has been overlooked unnecessarily by historians and bibliographers. Although it started out as a weird fiction magazine, it soon became a blend of science fiction and fantasy and was a bona fide part of the field.

The magazine was able to maintain a monthly schedule for most of its existence, although wartime paper restrictions forced it to go bi-monthly in July 1942 and eventually stifled it. There was a gap of nine months between the twentieth issue and the final one in September 1943.

Notes

1. Donald A. Wollheim, private communication, October 1981.
2. Ibid.

Information Sources

BIBLIOGRAPHY:
Nicholls. *Encyclopedia*.
Tuck.
INDEX SOURCES: Lien, Dennis, "Uncanny Tales" (Canadian), *The Science-Fiction Collector/Megavore* 9 (June 1980), available from J. Grant Thiessen, Box 54, Neche, N.D. 58265; MT; SFM; Tuck.
REPRINT SOURCES:
   Reprint Magazines: See entry on *Brief Fantastic Tales*.
LOCATION SOURCES: M.I.T. Science Fiction Library.

Publication History

TITLE: *Uncanny Tales*.
VOLUME DATA: No volume numbering. Number 1, November 1940–Number 21, September/October 1943. Monthly, issues 1–17 (November 1940–May 1942, but no issues for February or April 1941); Number 18, July 1942; 19, September 1942; 20, December 1942. Total run: 21 issues.
PUBLISHERS: Adam Publishing Co., Toronto, Numbers 1–17; Norman Book Co., Toronto, Numbers 18–21.
EDITOR: Melvin R. Colby (not credited in issues). Stableford in Nicholls's *Encyclopedia* suggests Lyle Kenyon Engel was editor but this is refuted by both Donald Wollheim and Sam Moskowitz. Engel had nothing to do with the magazine.
FORMAT: Digest, 64 pp., Number 1–Number 4, March 1941; Large Pulp, 96 pp., Number 5, May 1941–Number 20, December 1942; 128 pp., Number 21.
PRICE: 15¢, all issues except final, 25¢.

Mike Ashley/Grant Thiessen

UNEARTH

Unearth was a Boston-based magazine created specifically to publish and promote the work of new writers and artists. It published eight digest-sized issues between 1977 and 1979.

Unearth was founded as a somewhat indirect result of a science fiction workshop taught by Hal Clement at the Boston Center for Adult Education in late 1976. When the workshop concluded, three of its members, John Landsberg, Jonathan Ostrowsky-Lantz and Craig Gardner, decided to keep meeting on an informal basis. Through their experiences with the workshop and in writing and submitting stories in the year following, the three found that they were less than totally satisfied with the reaction they were getting from the existing science fiction markets. Manuscripts which the group believed had merit were being returned with form rejections, or with cryptic and often contradictory replies. Conversation often turned to this topic in the meetings, and one day Landsberg casually remarked that there must be many writers with real potential who could not find a market for their work. Wouldn't it be great, he added, if someday they could put out a magazine to publish just those writers? Ostrowsky-Lantz asked why they should wait. The need for the magazine was there; why not start it now?

So, with tremendous enthusiasm and very little experience, *Unearth* was born, with Landsberg and Ostrowsky-Lantz as its co-editors. Even without experience, the editors knew it would be virtually impossible to sell a magazine with nothing but the work of unpublished writers. Large amounts of time in the planning stages of the magazine were spent contacting established science fiction writers to see if they would be willing to contribute something to this idealistic enterprise.

A number of professionals agreed to help. With the first issue, Hal Clement would contribute a column on the science in science fiction. With the second, Harlan Ellison would add a column on writing science fiction. With the addition of Ellison's name, the magazine became a viable proposition.

With the first issue the editors also instituted a ''First Sale'' department. The magazine would reprint the first published story of a ''name'' science fiction writer, with a new introduction by that author on how the story had been written and sold. Harlan Ellison contributed the first of these, and later issues featured the first sales of Clement, Algis Budrys, Norman Spinrad, Kate Wilhelm, Roger Zelazny, Damon Knight, Poul Anderson, Philip K. Dick, Michael Moorcock and Fritz Leiber. Essays were also written by Theodore Sturgeon and Charles Platt to lend additional ''name'' value.

The original intention of *Unearth* was to publish fiction only by previously unpublished writers (with the added provision that those writers could continue to sell new stories to *Unearth*, no matter how many stories they then sold elsewhere). The magazine held to this policy for the first six issues. However, a number of new writers in the field, who had made one or two story sales and then found it impossible to place anything else, complained to the editors. These writers were far from being established in the field. Shouldn't *Unearth* promote them as well?

Editor Jonathan Ostrowsky-Lantz addressed this issue in an editorial in the fifth issue of *Unearth*:

> Another possible change concerns editorial restrictions. . . . Our concern is
> that we may not be helping enough writers. In addition to previously-
> unpublished writers, there are many authors who have only made one or
> two sales in the genre. These writers are themselves hardly ''established'';

yet we exclude them from consideration. It's important to make a rule and stick to it; the question is, what should the nature of that rule be?...We would appreciate your comments and suggestions.

Opinion was overwhelmingly in favor of expanding *Unearth*'s eligibility requirements. With the seventh issue, the line "by writers who have made no more than three prior sales in professional SF markets" was added to the manuscript submission information at the bottom of the contents page.

A second change was announced in the eighth issue but never implemented (this issue, dated Winter 1979, was the last to see print). Landsberg and Ostrowsky-Lantz had felt the SF market to be incredibly restrictive when they began the magazine. Two years later, more magazines had appeared on the market, but the short fiction field remained basically unchanged. (One of the newcomers, *Isaac Asimov's Science Fiction Magazine*,* had an even narrower focus than many existing magazines.) They therefore offered a new department, the "Unearth Special." According to Ostrowsky-Lantz's editorial in the Winter 1979 issue: "The Special represents the first time we will have offered original fiction by established writers. Ideally, these stories will be somewhat less conservative and traditional than current standard magazine fare; almost a dozen years after *Dangerous Visions*, formula and convention are still too often the rule."

The first "Special" was to be a Michael Moorcock story, never before published in the United States. With the "Special," the editors hoped to publish good new fiction outside the norm, and to add yet another name to help sell the new fiction without compromising the spirit of the magazine.

Unearth was produced on a shoestring, with a staff that rarely exceeded half a dozen people. Just as the magazine was getting under way, Landsberg was accepted at Albany Medical School, and most of the actual day-to-day work of running the magazine was taken on by Ostrowsky-Lantz. The third member of the original workshop, Craig Gardner, refused an equal editorial position offered by the other editors (a move which would have created three equal editors on the masthead), afraid that too much involvement in the magazine would take away from his writing. Gardner did have more production experience than the two primary editors during the magazine's inception, however, and remained in an advisory position as consulting editor.

A pair of art directors helped give the magazine its continually improving "look": Steve Gildea in the first four issues, Wayne Dewhurst in the final four. Writers and artists were always paid, but the staff usually was not. All profits from the magazine went back into improving its appearance. *Unearth*'s first issue was ninety-six pages stapled in a black and white cover drawn by Gildea. Its eighth issue was 192 pages, perfect bound, with a new logo and a four-color illustration by Clyde Caldwell, an *Unearth* "discovery" who went on to illustrate for *Heavy Metal* and a number of SF paperback publishers.

Throughout it all, *Unearth* never sent a form rejection. (During the last few months of the magazine's existence, a form was used that listed some common problems with many of the manuscripts being received, but it was always accompanied by some personal comments by one of the editors.) All but the most amateur manuscripts were read in full, and every submission received a personal reply, usually from Ostrowsky-Lantz. This commitment often led to eighty-hour work weeks, but both editors felt that the personal contact was central to the purpose of the magazine.

Most issues of the magazine also carried a contributors' page, listing short biographies of authors and artists, while the seventh issue featured an ''Update'' department which listed other markets *Unearth* writers had since sold stories and novels to.

Never well financed, *Unearth* found itself running out of money by its seventh issue. Paper and postage costs were rising, and some distributors who were supposed to pay in three months took nine, if they paid at all. The new issues were more expensive to produce, and, while they bore a higher cover price, it would take most of a year to recoup the losses.

The editors waited six months to publish the eighth issue, to wait for sufficient cash flow to fund the issue and to give time to search for more substantial financial backers. With that issue, though, backing had been found with a new but growing publishing concern. As the issue's editorial boasted, it was only a matter of time before the magazine went bi-monthly.

But backing vanished at the last minute; the corporate heads above those negotiating decided that the money could be spent better elsewhere. Landsberg and Ostrowsky-Lantz were forced to suspend publication before *Unearth* went any deeper in debt.

Unearth, in its short existence, was able to showcase the work of thirty-five new writers and a dozen new artists, many of whom have gone on to publish elsewhere. The two biggest success stories for *Unearth* alumni so far are Somtow Sucharitkul, who won the John W. Campbell Award for best new science fiction writer; and Rudy Rucker, who later had his second novel, *Spacetime Donuts* (partially serialized in *Unearth*), published by Ace as part of a multibook contract. Others who have published elsewhere, many extensively, include D. C. Poyer, Timothy R. Sullivan, Craig Shaw Gardner, Richard Bowker, Steve Vance and Keith Justice. Two successful SF artists, Clyde Caldwell and Barclay Shaw, were also introduced by *Unearth*.

Co-founder John M. Landsberg plans to revive the magazine sometime in the future.

Information Sources

INDEX SOURCES: NESFA-II; NESFA-VII; SFM.
REPRINT SOURCES: None known.
LOCATION SOURCES: M.I.T. Science Fiction Library.

Publication History

TITLE: *Unearth*, subtitled "The Magazine of Science Fiction Discoveries."
VOLUME DATA: Volume 1, Number 1, Winter 1977–Volume 2, Number 4, Winter
    1979. Four issues per volume. Quarterly, but no issue for Fall 1978. Total run:
    8 issues.
PUBLISHER: Unearth Publications, Boston, Massachusetts.
EDITORS: Jonathan Ostrowsky-Lantz and John M. Landsberg.
FORMAT: Digest (first three issues saddle-stapled, thereafter perfect bound); 96 pp.,
    Winter 1977–Summer 1977; 128 pp., Fall 1977; 176 pp., Winter 1978; 128 pp.,
    Spring–Summer 1978; 192 pp., Winter 1979.
PRICE: $1.00, Winter–Fall 1977; $1.50, Winter 1978; $1.25, Spring–Summer 1978;
    $2.00, Winter 1979.

Craig Shaw Gardner

UNIVERSE SCIENCE FICTION

Universe Science Fiction was an episode in the history of Raymond A. Palmer's Chicago-based magazine *Other Worlds Science Stories*.* That magazine had increased to a monthly schedule with a cut subscription rate just at the time that the market broke in 1953. Palmer found himself unable to meet his printing costs and legally evaded the problem by changing that magazine's name to *Science Stories*.* At this same time a Chicago businessman who had a desire to publish a new science fiction magazine offered Palmer a chance to help him out. Palmer promptly grabbed the opportunity, and with the newly established Bell Publications, he launched both *Universe* and *Science Stories*. *Universe*, financed fully by the businessman, was edited under the alias George Bell, but it was still a Palmer magazine. Hardly had the first issue appeared when the businessman lost interest in the venture. Palmer sold out his half-interest in Clarke Publications (which had formerly published *Other Worlds* and the more profitable *Fate*), established Palmer Publications, and took over *Universe* under his own name and imprint.

Curiously, SF historians have regarded the first two issues as having a certain merit, discarding the remainder as infected with the Palmer stigma. If one seriously considers the issues, however, it is easy to see that, while the first two Bell issues are worthy of consideration, the best issues are the middle run under Palmer before financial problems brought a drop in quality.

The first two issues do seem surprisingly un-Palmerlike because he was keeping his profile low, leaving Bea Mahaffey to assemble the issues. Included were stories by Murray Leinster, Mark Clifton and Mack Reynolds as well as Robert Bloch's "Constant Reader" and, most significantly, Theodore Sturgeon's bold treatment of homosexuality in "The World Well Lost," which caused a considerable uproar at the time. The second issue had less impact, though it contained a fine story by Sylvia Jacobs, "Up the Mountain or Down," which put human-kind firmly in its own place in the universe.

While its fiction was of reasonably good quality, *Universe* was not initially an especially attractive magazine, with erratic monochromatic interior color splashes that detracted from rather than enhanced the quality of the drawings, and washy covers. When Palmer assumed full control, the magazine improved considerably, publishing some superior illustrations by Virgil Finlay, Lawrence Stevens, Joseph Eberle and even Edd Cartier. The "first" Palmer issue, December 1953, is a fine example. Apart from a rather poor, rather clearly sales-worthy cover by Mel Hunter and Malcolm Smith on "Sunbathing in Space," there was a fine Lawrence illustration to L. Sprague de Camp's fantasy "The Hungry Hercynian"; a charming Cartier picture for Poul Anderson and Gordon R. Dickson's Hoka story, "The Adventure of the Misplaced Hound"; and a stunning Finlay drawing for "Mr. Peavey's Tiger" by Holly Wolcott, which lingers far longer in the memory than does the story. This issue also included Isaac Asimov's "Everest," itself memorable if for nothing else other than the incredible mistiming of its publication, appearing not long after Everest was climbed for the first time and thus totally ruining the story.

Finlay and Lawrence alone continued to make *Universe* a must, but Palmer did not rest on his laurels. In the March 1953 *Other Worlds* he had included a heroic fantasy story by that superscience sagaman, Doc Smith. Now the March 1954 *Universe* presented another episode in the life of "Lord Tedric," much to the fans' consternation. But, although the illustrations continued to highlight the magazine, there were definite signs that quality was tapering off after this issue.

As always Palmer's personality overwhelmed the magazine, and he turned it more and more into a publication for the fans, reintroducing Rog Phillips' "The Club House," which had been dropped from *Amazing Stories** in the sixth issue in July 1954. There was the usual letter column, plus various fan features and Palmer's inimitable editorials. In fact, in the ninth issue there were two editorials.

With the last three issues presentation deteriorated rapidly. Palmer instituted some muddy black and white covers, purportedly to imitate *Time Magazine*, but in reality to cut costs, while interior artwork all but vanished. Stories were of mediocre quality, and all the flair and sparkle had gone.

The tenth and last issue (March 1955) had as a cover a photographic reprint of a Finlay painting and had two interior illustrations; it devoted half its pages to a Margaret St. Clair sword and sorcery novel and the rest to newcomers—except for Palmer's own short story justifying the cover; and beneath photographs of Palmer and Mahaffey appeared the unsurprising announcement that *Universe* had expired. Instead, *Other Worlds* was reborn, and the final days of the magazine are covered under that entry.

Information Sources

BIBLIOGRAPHY:
Nicholls. *Encyclopedia.*
Tuck.

INDEX SOURCES: MIT; SFM; Tuck.

REPRINT SOURCES: None known.

LOCATION SOURCES: City of Red Wing, Minnesota Public Library; M.I.T. Science Fiction Library.

Publication History

TITLE: *Universe Science Fiction*.

VOLUME DATA: No volume numbering. Number 1, June 1953–Number 10, March 1955 (numbering sequence continued by *Other Worlds* in tandem with its own sequence). Designated bi-monthly, but first four issues quarterly, June 1953–March 1954; thereafter bi-monthly. Total run: 10 issues.

PUBLISHER: Bell Publications, Chicago, June–September 1953; Palmer Publications, Evanston, Illinois, December 1953–March 1955.

EDITORS: Raymond A. Palmer and Bea Mahaffey (all issues; first two under alias George Bell).

FORMAT: Digest, 128 pp.

PRICE: 35¢.

E. F. Casebeer

UNKNOWN

Founded as a vehicle for fantasy fiction by editor John W. Campbell, Jr., *Unknown* (later *Unknown Worlds*) was published simultaneously with *Astounding Science-Fiction* (*Analog Science Fiction**) from the spring of 1939 to the fall of 1943. In its brief history, *Unknown* had a major impact on the development of the fantasy genre and, perhaps more so, on the broader field of science fiction.

In the February 1939 issue of *Astounding*, Campbell announced the founding of *Unknown*, describing it as a quality magazine devoted entirely to fantasy:

> It has been the quality of the fantasy you have read in the past that has made the very word anathema. . . . *Unknown* will be to fantasy what *Astounding* has made itself represent to science-fiction. It will offer fantasy of a quality so far different from that which has appeared in the past as to change your entire understanding of the term.[1]

He went on to explain that although he had been planning the magazine for some time and gathering material for it, the receipt of the British writer Eric Frank Russell's manuscript for *Sinister Barrier* had "finally started in motion the already-laid plans" for the new magazine. Comparing Russell's novel to E. E. "Doc" Smith's first *Skylark* story, Campbell promised that it would be a "classic referred to for another decade to come." Russell, a devotee of Charles Fort, had based the novel upon the concept that mankind is owned by an alien race. Thus, *Sinister Barrier* became the lead novel in the first issue of *Unknown* in March 1939. The importance of its theme, human possession by aliens, is reflected by its recurrence, for example, in Robert Heinlein's "They" (1941), one of three stories he wrote for *Unknown*, and as late as 1967 in Robert Silverberg's "Passengers."

Considering the impact of *Unknown* on the field at large, its publishing history is far too brief. In July 1940 its cover abandoned the often garish paintings associated with the pulps for an almost scholarly listing of its contents, with brief synopses of each story. Just as Campbell had changed the title of *Astounding Stories* to *Astounding Science-Fiction* in March 1938, so, too, in December 1940 he added to *Unknown* the subtitle "*Fantasy Fiction.*" With the October 1941 issue, as though to aid the readers even more, the title was changed to *Unknown Worlds* and the subtitle retained. As Campbell often explained, from the first sales were poor; rumor had it that some dealers did not display the magazine because they did not understand what category, if any, it fit into. From February 1941 it was published bi-monthly until it ceased publication with the October 1943 issue. Whatever its other problems, however, *Unknown* was undoubtedly a casualty of the wartime paper shortage, and one must infer that Campbell was willing to sacrifice the magazine so that *Astounding* would have adequate paper to appear monthly.

In all, there were thirty-nine issues of *Unknown/Unknown Worlds*. Despite its commercial failure, no one commenting substantively on the magazine has called its success less than meteoric. David Kyle asserted that with its demise, "a void was left which was never really filled."[2] When in 1948 Campbell brought out a single 8½ by 11 inch, magazine-format anthology called *From Unknown Worlds: An Anthology of Modern Fantasy for Grownups*—complete with a garish cover depicting gnomes, a skull and a snake by Edd Cartier, who had done much of the artwork for the magazine—he furnished in a special foreword his most complete rationale for supporting a magazine devoted to fantasy:

> The old "Unknown Worlds" believed that fantasy was intended for fun; it used the familiar creatures of mythology and folklore, but treated them in a most disrespectful fashion. Fantasy—and the Things of fantasy—are, we felt, much more fun than anything else, if you'll just take off those traditional wrappings of the "grim and gharstly." . . .
>
> It's perfectly true that the fantasy chiller has a place; we agree to that, and you'll find them with us, too. But not, please, the gloom and terror spread on with a trowel, driven in with a mallet, and staked out with an oak stave through its heart. Horror injected with a sharp and poisoned needle is just as effective as when applied with the blunt-instrument technique of the so-called Gothic Horror tale.

The above suggests also that John Campbell took science fiction more seriously than fantasy. He expressly rejects the Gothic tradition (one recalls how important to the beginnings of science fiction were Mary Shelley's *Frankenstein* and the works of Edgar Allen Poe), and, more immediately, he attacks the "grim and gharstly" tone which had grown up around the most famous modern pulp mag-

azine of fantasy, *Weird Tales*,* founded in 1923, and around which grew the
H. P. Lovecraft cult. The emphasis upon the supposed humor of *Unknown/
Unknown Worlds* was continued by Les Daniels when he declared that "the
typical tale recognized the humorous incongruity of the supernatural in urban
life and demonstrated that even magical intervention in the affairs of men was
unlikely to relieve the frustration of the human condition."[3] (Note the phrases
"urban life" and "frustration of the human condition"; they may have particular
importance in explaining the nature and success of contemporary fantasy, whatever its medium.)

Such judgments do injustice to the spectrum of fiction in *Unknown/Unknown
Worlds*. At one end lie the horrors of Russell's *Sinister Barrier*, Theodore
Sturgeon's "It" (1940), and L. Ron Hubbard's *Fear* (1940); at the other, the
rollicking "Magical Misadventures of Harold Shea," the collective efforts of
L. Sprague de Camp and Fletcher Pratt. Somewhere in between range such tales
as the apparently humorous but open-ended terror of Henry Kuttner's "A Gnome
There Was" (1941) and the two sword and sorcery novels of Norvell W. Page
(who, as Grant Stockbridge, wrote 93 of the 118 *Spider** novels). The solo
efforts of de Camp also enjoyed great success: *Lest Darkness Fall* appeared in
1939, and stories from his collection *The Wheels of If* were published in both
Astounding and *Unknown* between 1938 and 1942.

Significantly, as with so many of Campbell's authors, de Camp published in
both magazines. In the autumn of 1939, Theodore Sturgeon had stories in both
Astounding and *Unknown*; he was to publish twenty-four in the former and sixteen
in the latter. As early as 1938 a story by Hubbard had been accepted for *Astounding*; in the early 1940s he wrote an outstanding series of novels for *Unknown*, and after its demise he returned to *Astounding* and the tangled web of
Dianetics. Not only did Campbell publish Jack Williamson's *Legion of Time* in
Astounding in 1938, he also included Williamson's fine novel on lycanthropy,
Darker Than You Think, in *Unknown* in 1940. Examples abound. While both
Henry Kuttner and C. L. Moore (of "Shambleau" fame) appeared in *Unknown*,
all their collaborations as Lewis Padgett were published in *Astounding*. But
ignoring the question of timing, the core of the problem that developed may be
seen in the fact that Fritz Leiber's classic *Conjure Wife* headed *Unknown Worlds*
for April 1943, while his *Gather Darkness*—which also emphasized witchcraft—
appeared in *Astounding* the following month.

As becomes apparent, Campbell gathered around him a group of highly talented writers who made both *Astounding* and *Unknown* top magazines of the
period.[4] One infers that a given story often could have been published as easily
in one magazine as in the other. In his "Foreword" to *The Wheels of If* (1948),
L. Sprague de Camp wrote:

[These stories] can all be called fantasies in the broad sense; that is,
" 'tain't so" stories. In a strict sense they are science-fiction stories: that
is, stories based upon scientific or pseudoscientific assumptions, as opposed
to fantasies in the strict sense: stories based upon mythological or supernatural assumptions.[5]

In a way, this observation by one of Campbell's most accomplished writers measures Campbell's success in establishing and continuing, however briefly, *Unknown/Unknown Worlds*. His accomplishment, to begin with, was to destroy not only the prevalent narrative tone but also most of the trappings that had dominated fantasy from *The Castle of Otranto* and *The Monk* through the nineteenth century to *Weird Tales*. More than any other editor, Campbell infused fantasy into the mundane streets of the modern world and into the future(s) that technology might make possible. And this had wider ramifications: for simultaneously, in expanding the vistas of fantasy, he also broke down many of the conventions that had governed science fiction wrriting, even in *Astounding Science-Fiction*. Perhaps without realizing it, through *Unknown/Unknown Worlds* he did much to change that linear movement with which so much of earlier science fiction's belief in progress had been concerned. He opened the gates, so to speak.

Through Fritz Leiber, with his Gray Mouser stories, and to some extent Norvell Page, Campbell gave strength to sword and sorcery; his writers expanded the concept of multiple worlds and, generally, emphasized that anything might happen. Two specific examples may suffice: without the precedent of *Unknown*, one cannot imagine that Peter Phillips' "Dreams Are Sacred" (1948), in which the mind of the protagonist is projected into the imaginings of a supposedly crazed writer of "science fiction, fantasy," would have found its way into *Astounding*.[6] (Intriguingly, echoes of the dream/fiction occur in the reality to which the protagonist returns.) More important, without *Unknown*, one cannot be sure that Campbell would have accepted all but one of the stories which were to compose Clifford D. Simak's *City*.

Unknown/Unknown Worlds provides a turning point for the entire field of science fiction. One may assert that both in tone and in content it led to *Galaxy Science Fiction** and *The Magazine of Fantasy and Science Fiction*,* magazines which skillfully combined elements of science fiction and fantasy. In this regard it seems highly appropriate that the first number of the Galaxy Science Fiction Novel series was Eric Frank Russell's *Sinister Barrier*.

Notes

1. [John Campbell], "Unknown," *Astounding Science-Fiction* 22 (February 1939): 72.

2. David Kyle, *A Pictorial History of Science Fiction* (London: Hamlyn, 1976), p. 113n.

3. Les Daniels, *Living in Fear: A History of Horror in the Mass Media* (New York: Charles Scribner's Sons, 1975), p. 146.

4. There were, of course, exceptions. Jane Rice published ten stories and novelettes in *Unknown* and *Unknown Worlds* and then seemingly disappeared from the literary scene. There is no entry for her in Donald H. Tuck's *The Encyclopedia of Science Fiction and Fantasy* (Advent, 1978). In some ways more puzzling, Robert Bloch, that master of fantasy, published only three stories in *Unknown* and nothing in *Astounding*.

5. L. Sprague de Camp, "Foreword," *The Wheels of If* (Chicago: Shasta, 1948), p. vii. [One might add that there are those, among them Howard DeVore, who consider *Lest Darkness Fall* science fiction instead of fantasy. A close examination of the stories

included in *Unknown* and *Astounding* will reveal how much the two fields overlap and, perhaps, how pointless it is to try to establish succinct definitions, as some recent scholars have attempted.]

6. Peter Phillips, "Dreams Are Sacred," *Astounding Science Fiction* 42 (September 1948): 52. [Note that in the 1930s Campbell used a hyphen in "Science-Fiction" but did not do so later.]

Information Sources

BIBLIOGRAPHY:
Carter, Lin. "The Mathematics of Magic: Imaginary World Fantasy in *Unknown*." In *Imaginary Worlds: The Art of Fantasy*. New York: Ballantine, 1973.
Nicholls. *Encyclopedia*.
Tuck.
INDEX SOURCES: Hoffman, Stuart, *An Index to Unknown and Unknown Worlds*, Black Earth, Wis.: Sirius Press, 1955 (contains a foreword by Robert Bloch, an index by author, by title [which also cites locale and principal characters], and an index by character); ISFM; Metzger, Arthur, *An Index & Short History of "Unknown,"* Baltimore, Md.: T-K Graphics, 1976 (contains a short history, indices by author and title, plus a brief listing of important reprint sources); MT (which also indexes British edition); Murray, Will, "The Unknown Unknown," *Xenophile*, No. 42 (1979); SFM; Tuck.
REPRINT SOURCES:
Foreign Editions:
   British: The British reprint edition had an erratic life longer than that of the U.S. original. Published by Atlas Publishing & Distributing Co., London, the first six U.S. issues were imported and distributed as normal. With the start of the war, a British edition, slightly abridged, began following the U.S. volume numbering. It also followed the U.S. edition on a monthly basis, hence Volume 2, Number 1 (U.K.) was dated September 1939 and ran to Volume 4, Number 5 (U.K.), February 1941. Issues erratic for next four years: Volume 4, Number 6 dated July 1941, followed by Volume 5, Number 5, March 1942; Volume 6, Number 1, June 1942; Number 3, October 1942; Number 4, February 1943; Number 5, May 1943. Volume and issue numbering ceased for four issues, October 1943, January 1944, May 1944, Autumn 1944. Thereafter began new volume numbering treating the first U.K. edition (September 1939) as being Volume 1, Number 1, thus Volume 3, Number 4, Spring 1945–Volume 4, Number 5, Winter 1949, thrice yearly [Spring, Summer, Winter, but no issues for Summer 1945 or Spring 1946], twelve issues per volume. Total run: 41 issues. Entitled *Unknown* to July 1941, thereafter *Unknown Worlds*.
   Derivative Anthologies: John W. Campbell, Jr., *From Unknown Worlds* (New York: Street & Smith, 1948), published in large pulp format. It is often treated as a reprint magazine issue. Contained 14 stories plus verse. A British edition, minus one story, came from Atlas in 1952 in pulp format. D. R. Bensen, *The Unknown* (New York: Pyramid, 1963), 11 stories plus foreword by Isaac Asimov; D. R. Bensen, *The Unknown 5* (New York: Pyramid, 1964), 5 novelettes; George Hay, *Hell Hath Fury* (London: Neville Spearman, 1963), 6 stories plus 1 novella.
LOCATION SOURCES: M.I.T. Science Fiction Library; Pennsylvania State University Library; Street and Smith Collection, Syracuse University Library; University of New Mexico Library.

Publication History

TITLE: *Unknown*, March 1939–August 1941; *Unknown Worlds*, October 1941–October 1943. The subtitle "Fantasy Fiction" was introduced from the December 1940 issue.

VOLUME DATA: Volume 1, Number 1, March 1939–Volume 7, Number 3, October 1943. Six issues per volume. Monthly until December 1940, thereafter bi-monthly. Total run: 39 issues.

PUBLISHER: Street and Smith Publications, New York.

EDITOR: John W. Campbell, Jr.

FORMAT: Pulp, 164 pp., March 1939–August 1941; Large Pulp, 130 pp., October 1941–April 1943; Pulp, 164 pp., June–October 1943.

PRICE: 20¢, March 1939–August 1941; thereafter 25¢

Thomas D. Clareson

UNKNOWN WORLDS

See UNKNOWN.

UNUSUAL STORIES

Companion magazine to *Marvel Tales*. See MARVEL TALES (1934–1935).

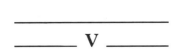

VANGUARD SCIENCE FICTION

In 1958, James Blish wrote as preface to his new magazine, *Vanguard*:

We hope to print authentic science fiction, the pure stuff, of which we have seen all too little in recent years. . . . We subscribe to Theodore Sturgeon's: *A good science-fiction story is a story with a human problem, and a human solution, which would not have happened at all without its science content.*

He saw his magazine as a rival to *Astounding* (*Analog Science Fiction**):

The fact that the most successful magazine in this field prints the highest proportion of stories of this kind (although not as many as it used to) indicates to us that most science fiction readers share our preference for the genre. It is that preference, and that audience, that VANGUARD hopes to satisfy.

For Blish, it was a time for personal optimism. He was at the peak of his career, having just seen entering into print the conclusion of his Cities in Flight series, *The Triumph of Time*, as well as his enlargement of *A Case of Conscience*, which would win him the Hugo Award the following year.

Naming his magazine after Project Vanguard, the Earth Satellite Project, "man's first real step into space," he commissioned a cover from Ed Emsh, an interior illustration from Kelly Freas, a science-fact article from L. Sprague de Camp, a book review column from Lester del Rey, and five pieces of fiction: the magazine began with a Bertram Chandler novelette and a James Gunn short story on planetary colonization and anthropology; there followed a Raymond F.

Jones story based on metallurgy; and an impeccable Richard Wilson short-short story prefaced a final powerful novelette from Blish's friend, C. M. Kornbluth, "Reap the Dark Tide"—later to be anthologized at least five times as "Shark Ship." Blish prefaced each story with a succinct but substantial biocritical note. Excepting Jones's contribution, the stories were stronger on human problems than science content.

To follow were to be stories and novelettes by Chandler, del Rey, Nourse, and Blish's collaborator, Damon Knight. But *Vanguard* emulated its namesake: although to be acclaimed, it was killed before it even took off, its proposed future contents to go to *Fantastic Universe*,* *Fantastic Science Fiction Stories* (*Fantastic**), *The Magazine of Fantasy and Science Fiction** and *New Worlds**—none to *Astounding*. Thus, *Vanguard* went the way of its coeval, Pohl's one-issue *Star Science Fiction*,* the only other magazine to appear in 1958. Blish probably put his finger on the cause on Vanguard's last page, a warning to purchasers to subscribe:

> The withdrawal of American News Company from magazine distribution last year caused a lot of confusion on the newsstands, some of which is still with us. . . .
>
> VANGUARD's distributor is one of the biggest remaining in business, and we expect to get good service from him; but neither he nor anyone else can absolutely guarantee that VANGUARD will be on your local newsstand regularly. The situation is still too shifty to make such guarantees possible.

That year six other magazines would fold, and Quinn was ready to sell *If** to *Galaxy Science Fiction*'s* publisher, Guinn. The magazine boom that began in the early 1950s was definitely over.

Information Sources

BIBLIOGRAPHY:
Blish, James. *The Issue at Hand*. Chicago: Advent, 1973.
Nicholls. *Encyclopedia*.
Tuck.
INDEX SOURCES: MIT; SFM.
REPRINT SOURCES: None known.
LOCATION SOURCES: M.I.T. Science Fiction Library.

Publication History

TITLE: *Vanguard Science Fiction*.
VOLUME DATA: Volume 1, Number 1, June 1958.
PUBLISHER: Vanguard Science Fiction Inc., New York.

EDITOR: James Blish.
FORMAT: Digest, 128 pp.
PRICE: 35¢.

E. F. Casebeer

VARGO STATTEN BRITISH SCIENCE FICTION MAGAZINE

See VARGO STATTEN SCIENCE FICTION MAGAZINE.

VARGO STATTEN SCIENCE FICTION MAGAZINE

In 1950 the firm of Scion, Limited, in London had issued a new science fiction paperback novel, *Operation Venus*, which introduced the name "Vargo Statten" to the SF world. The name was a pseudonym of prolific writer John Russell Fearn, though it had been concocted by Scion's managing editor, Maurice Read. A second Statten novel, *Annihilation*, soon followed, and before long they were appearing at the rate of one a month. In all fifty-two Vargo Statten novels appeared, and amid the welter of cheap and mediocre SF that proliferated in paperback in the early 1950s Vargo Statten stood head and shoulders above the rest in popularity and quality.

So popular were the novels that in 1953 Scion decided to issue a regular magazine, which was launched in January 1954. It was deliberately aimed at a junior readership and was shaped in the pulp format, but with only sixty-four pages. Every effort was made to cater to fandom with regular columns—"Fanfare and Suchlike" by "Inquisitor" (A. Vincent Clarke) and a "Who's Who in Fandom"—while advance notification of the magazine had been sent to all the leading SF groups in Britain in October 1953 so that the "Rocket Mail" letter column in the first issue was filled with good wishes from fans like Kenneth F. Slater, Terry Jeeves and Dave Cohen. These letters revealed that while "Vargo Statten" was credited as editor, the man at the helm was Alistair Paterson.

Needless to say, Fearn was present in the first issue with three stories, although the serial, "The Inevitable Conflict," was the work of E. C. Tubb. Indeed, Fearn and Tubb were the only well-known writers to appear regularly in the magazine, although Kenneth Bulmer contributed a few stories as "Chesman Scott" and Jonathan Burke made a solitary appearance. Brian Aldiss found that his submission to the early issues was rejected and declined to try again.

Instead the magazine became a market for fans and newcomers. Barrington J. Bayley's first appearance in print, "Combat's End," was in the May 1954 issue (although he had earlier sold a story to *Nebula Science Fiction** that never appeared), but he was the only debutant to survive the magazine and reach greater glory.

After the third issue, in April 1954, there was an internal upheaval when Scion was absorbed by another company. In the chaos that ensued the "Vargo Statten" magazine and novels were handed over as partial payment for debts to Dragon Press. Paterson remained at Scion, and Fearn now became editor of the magazine, which was retitled *The British Science Fiction Magazine*. The magazine had already converted to a large digest-size with the fourth issue in May 1954, and under Fearn's editorship there was a determined effort to raise the standard of the contents. The proposed Vargo Statten Fan League was dropped, and the number of nonfiction fillers increased.

Fearn, however, worked under the handicap of a reduced budget, being able to pay authors only half of what other magazines offered. One cannot buy quality at 12/6d. per thousand words, and Fearn was forced to fill issues by reprinting his own stories from prewar U.S. magazines. A standard cover design was adopted for further economy, and the magazine shrank to pocketbook size.

After nineteen issues, the magazine finally folded in February 1956, its end hastened by a printing strike. Ironically, many of the rival pocketbook publishers also collapsed at the same time. It is true to say, therefore, that "Vargo Statten" had not only started the British SF pocketbook boom, but had also ended it.

Information Sources

BIBLIOGRAPHY:
Harbottle, Philip. *The Multi-Man*. Wallsend, U.K.: Privately printed, 1968.
Nicholls. *Encyclopedia*.
Tuck.
INDEX SOURCES: MIT; SFM; Tuck.
REPRINT SOURCES: None known.
LOCATION SOURCES: M.I.T. Science Fiction Library.

Publication History

TITLE: *Vargo Statten Science Fiction Magazine*, Volume 1, Number 1, January 1954–
      Volume 1, Number 3, [April 1954]; *Vargo Statten British Science Fiction Magazine*, Volume 1, Number 4, [May 1954]–Volume 1, Number 5, [July 1954]; *The British Science Fiction Magazine*, Volume 1, Number 6, [September 1954]–
      Volume 1, Number 12, [April 1955]; *The British Space Fiction Magazine*, Volume 2, Number 1, [June 1955]–Volume 2, Number 7, [February 1956].
VOLUME DATA: Volume 1, Number 1, January 1954–Volume 2, Number 7, [February 1956]. Last two issues undated. Earlier issues dated only by internal reference. No cover or masthead date. Volume 1, twelve issues. Intended schedule, monthly, but no issues for 1954: March, June, August, October; 1955: May or November; 1956: January. Total run: 19 issues.
PUBLISHERS: Scion, Ltd., London, January–April 1954; Scion Distributors, Ltd., London, May–November 1954; Dragon Publications Ltd., Luton, December 1954–February 1956.
EDITORS: Alistair Paterson, first seven issues (January–November 1954); John Russell Fearn thereafter.

FORMAT: Fluctuation in size between issues, but in general: Pulp, 64 pp., January–
April 1954; Digest, 128 pp., May 1954–January 1955; Pocketbook, 128 pp.,
February 1955–February 1956.
PRICE: 1/6d.

Mike Ashley

VENTURE SCIENCE FICTION (1969–1970) (1957–1958)

Founded by publisher Joseph W. Ferman as a companion to *The Magazine of Fantasy and Science Fiction*,* with emphasis on action/adventure science fiction, *Venture Science Fiction* was published concurrently with its companion for ten bi-monthly issues from January 1957 to July 1958. From 1958 to the spring of 1969, *Venture* was combined wtih *Fantasy and Science Fiction*, then revived as a separate entity for six quarterly issues until the summer of 1970, when the magazines again merged. Though *Venture* had a short life in both of its incarnations, it will be remembered for long-running features that began with the magazine and for others that were revived there, as well as for several stories.

In the first issue of *Venture* (January 1957), Ferman described the reasoning behind this new "venture" in the magazine field:

This first issue of *Venture Science Fiction* offers, we think, a pretty fair example of the kind of strong stories of action and adventure that future issues will contain. And we believe there is room in the field for such a magazine.

Science fiction offers to the storyteller a diversity of subject matter and an imaginative scope not equalled in many other fields of literature. And the types of science fiction are rich and varied, ranging from comic strip simplicity up through H. G. Wells-Huxley-Orwell inspiration and profundity. In the magazine field, the range is almost as great. We are proud of the solidly established quality reputation of *Fantasy and Science Fiction*, and we are now publishing *Venture SF* in the belief that we can make it another fine sf magazine—with a substantially different approach.

There will be two prime requisites for *VENTURE* stories: In the first place, each must be a well told story, with a beginning, middle and end; in the second place, each must be a strong story—a story with pace, power, and excitement. This does not mean that pace will be substituted for sense, cardboard for characters, or improbability for excitement. It does mean, we think, first-rate entertainment, and a worthy sister magazine for *FANTASY AND SCIENCE FICTION*.[1]

Ferman envisioned *Venture* as a blending of the literary style of its companion magazine and the pulp magazine style of the late *Planet Stories*.* But he hoped to avoid stereotyped characters, implausible plots, and stories with pace and little else, thereby creating another *Fantasy and Science Fiction* with more emphasis on science fiction. And there was room for a magazine of adventure science fiction. With the demise of *Planet Stories* in 1955, only a revived *Science Fiction Adventures** had arisen to take its place, so that another SF adventure magazine was not crowding the field.

In addition to sharing the same publisher as *Fantasy and Science Fiction*, *Venture* also had the same editor, Robert P. Mills, as well as having *Fantasy and Science Fiction*'s Anthony Boucher as an advisory editor. Also, for eight of the ten issues, Ed Emshwiller (or Emsh) contributed his artwork to the covers, thereby adding a feeling of *Fantasy and Science Fiction* to *Venture*.

The original plan for *Venture* was to publish a short novel per issue, or two or three novelettes in each issue, along with several short works and, later, special features. The January 1957 issue began with a short novel by Poul Anderson ("Virgin Planet") and also contained stories by Isaac Asimov, Theodore Sturgeon, Judith Merril (as Rose Sharon) and Charles Beaumont. In short, *Venture* drew upon much the same pool of authors as *Fantasy and Science Fiction*, except that these authors' adventure stories were frequently chosen for *Venture*. Other authors who contributed to *Venture* included Clifford Simak, Avram Davidson, Marion Zimmer Bradley, Robert Silverberg, Damon Knight, James Gunn, Lester del Rey, Gordon Dickson, Edmond Hamilton and Algis Budrys. In addition, H. Beam Piper contributed "The Keeper" in the July 1957 issue, and Tom Godwin, known primarily for "The Cold Equations," had two stories in *Venture*: "Too Soon to Die" (March 1957) and "The Harvest" (July 1957). C. M. Kornbluth contributed several stories to *Venture* before his death in 1958, including "The Education of Tigress MacArdle" (July 1957), "Virginia" (March 1958) and "Two Dooms" (July 1958).

Of particular interest were some stories that did not fit the mold of adventure fiction. Included were Walter M. Miller's story of a mother's revenge for the death of her child, "Vengeance for Nikolai," which appeared in the March 1957 issue; Leigh Brackett's commentary on racism against the backgroup of alien contact on Earth, "All the Colors of the Rainbow" (November 1957); Theodore Sturgeon's sociological SF "Affair with a Green Monkey" (May 1957) and Sturgeon's look at telethons and their sponsors, "The Comedian's Children," in the May 1958 issue. All four stories could be considered as episodes in the adventure of life, but they are not typical adventure stories. Instead, they have fairly strong characters, strong themes, and solid plotlines, thereby exemplifying the type of story Ferman described in his publisher's note in the first issue.

In addition to the stories that appeared in *Venture*, there were three features in the magazine's first ten issues. In the first issue appeared "Venturings," Robert Mills' column of anecdotes, commentary and insights on the stories in each issue. Usually the column was humorous, even to the inclusion of a "mascot" for two issues.[2] But in the final issue of the first series Mills turned the column over to Fred Pohl and Theodore Sturgeon for obituaries for C. M. Kornbluth and Henry Kuttner. This column was not an editorial page per se, but it served a similar purpose—to pass along information from the editor to the readership, as well as to impart some opinions.

The second major feature began in the July 1957 issue: a book review column. The inclusion of a book review column was not unusual, though the contributor was: Theodore Sturgeon. This column was Sturgeon's first book review column in a science fiction magazine, and he showed much the same style that would popularize his later column in *Galaxy Science Fiction*.* Sturgeon's *Venture* reviews were concise and entertaining, and they did offer a fairly good insight to the books considered. The Sturgeon column ran through July 1958, and eventually Sturgeon became the *Galaxy* book reviewer, as well as a contributor to the *New York Times Book Review*.

The third major feature began with the January 1958 issue of *Venture* and continued through July 1958. The feature, a 1,200-word science column entitled "Fecundity Limited" (subject: population control) by Isaac Asimov, was the prototype of a new science column for *Venture*. Though it was similar to a series of science articles Asimov wrote for *Astounding* (*Analog Science Fiction**) a few months earlier, this column was meant to be the first of an ongoing series of science articles with emphasis on the layperson's viewpoint. A second column, "The Atmosphere of the Moon," appeared in the March 1958 issue, and "The Big Bang" ran in May 1958. All three columns were brief and filled with technical information that was easily understandable, but they did not yet include the anecdotal introductions of Asimov's later columns. A fourth column, "The Clash of Cymbals" (subject: colliding galaxies), was the final "Science" column for *Venture*, appearing in July 1958 (the last 1950s issue). But with the cancellation of *Venture*, the next Asimov "Science" column appeared in the November 1958 issue of *Fantasy and Science Fiction*, where it has become a permanent fixture.[3]

The first run of *Venture* ended with the July 1958 issue. The probable causes of its demise were its less than spectacular sales and a large number of competitors, which divided the audience and thereby hurt sales of new magazines. However, in light of the many SF magazines in this period that lasted merely one, two or three issues or only one year, *Venture*, though not a spectacular success, was not quite a complete failure. Soon after the cancellation of *Venture*, *Fantasy and Science Fiction* changed its contents page masthead to read "including *Venture Science Fiction*," thus protecting the rights of Fantasy House/ Mercury Press to the title. For the next eleven years, the title existed only as part of *Fantasy and Science Fiction*'s masthead in the United States.[4] But in 1969, probably due to increased interest in science fiction (thanks to *2001: A Space Odyssey* and the Apollo missions), Mercury Press revived *Venture* with the May 1969 issue.

The revived *Venture* had the same cover logo as before, and a similar emphasis on adventure/action science fiction, but there were a few changes. The magazine was published on a quarterly basis rather than bi-monthly, and the covers were done by Bert Tanner. (These new covers were like pencil sketches overlaid by a single color rather than paintings, as in the earlier *Venture*. The covers were not as impressive as the earlier ones and could have hurt sales.) There was a return to the original format, with an abridged novel beginning each issue, followed by several short stories, a book review column by Ron Goulart, and, occasionally, a film review. There was also a greater emphasis on humor in this series of *Venture*, as each issue contained an "episode" of the revived feature "Through Time and Space with Ferdinand Feghoot" by Grendel Briarton (Reginald Bretnor), the pun series that ran in *Fantasy and Science Fiction* from 1956 through the early 1960s. Also, most issues contained a Larry Eisenberg story in his series concerning the "unique" inventor, Duckworth. This time around there were no science columns by Isaac Asimov or anyone else.

Novels in this series of *Venture* included Gordon Dickson's "Hour of the Horde," Julius Fast's "League of Grey-Eyed Women," Harry Harrison's "Plague Ship," Keith Laumer's "The Star Treasure," Edward Wellen's "Hijack" and Dean Koontz's "Beastchild." Other authors represented in the new *Venture* were K. M. O'Donnell (Barry Malzberg), Bill Pronzini, Greg Benford, Vonda McIntyre, Ron Goulart, James Tiptree and Christopher Anvil. Though the novels were fair, the short fiction was not particularly memorable, save Tiptree's "The Snows Are Melted, the Snows Are Gone."

After six quarterly issues, this second series of *Venture Science Fiction* succumbed to poor sales and suspended publication with the August 1970 issue. A few months later, "including *Venture Science Fiction*" returned to the masthead of *Fantasy and Science Fiction*, where it remains to the present. There have been no new efforts to revive the magazine.

Though *Venture* lasted only sixteen issues altogether, it deserves to be remembered as an attempt to blend the best of the pulp tradition with an emphasis on characters and themes. It should also be remembered for instituting two long-running features (Asimov's and Sturgeon's columns), as well as reviving the "Ferdinand Feghoot" series. It was also one of the few magazines to return from suspension, though it did not become a success the second time. *Venture* did not change the face of science fiction in the magazines, but it does deserve a bit more than a footnote in the history of SF.

Notes

1. Joseph W. Ferman, "Publisher's Note," *Venture Science Fiction* 1 (January 1957):2.

2. Venture's mascot made his first appearance in the September 1957 "Venturings" column. The creation of Ed Emsh, "Venchy," as he was called, was a rather tough-looking cherub with a crew-cut, three-day beard and space helmet. He also sported a ray-gun rather than the traditional bow and arrow, and he smoked a cigar. The next issue was Venchy's final appearance. (Supposedly, the wife of a contributing author thought that Venchy bore too close a resemblance to her husband and she refused to contribute any more stories to *Venture*, or so Mills' story went.)

3. Asimov's first column for the magazine, "Dust of Ages," which appeared in the November 1958 issue, was originally the fifth *Venture* column. The length of the columns

fluctuated for a time, until Asimov finally settled on the length and style of introduction that marks his present ''Science'' columns.

4. There was a British edition of *Venture* from September 1963 to December 1965. See separate entry.

Information Sources

BIBLIOGRAPHY:
Asimov, Isaac. *In Joy Still Felt*. Garden City, N.Y.: Doubleday, 1980.
Nicholls. *Encyclopedia*.
Tuck.
INDEX SOURCES: Bishop, Gerald, and Bob Leman, *Venture SF: A Checklist*, Exeter: Aardvark House, 1970 (covers first series and first three issues of second series); ISFM-II; MIT; SFM; Tuck.
REPRINT SOURCES:
Magazines: The British edition of *Venture Science Fiction* (1963–1965) selected stories from both *Venture* and *The Magazine of Fantasy and Science Fiction*. See separate entries.
LOCATION SOURCES: M.I.T. Science Fiction Library.

Publication History

TITLE: *Venture Science Fiction*.
VOLUME DATA: Volume 1, Number 1, January 1957–Volume 2, Number 4, July 1958. Revived Volume 3, Number 1, May 1969–Volume 4, Number 3, August 1970. Volume 1, six issues, bi-monthly. Volume 2, four issues, bi-monthly. Volumes 3 and 4, quarterly, three issues per volume. Total run: 10 + 6, 16 issues.
PUBLISHERS: First series, Fantasy House, Concord, New Hampshire; second series, Mercury Press, Concord, New Hampshire.
EDITORS: First series, Robert P. Mills; second series, Edward L. Ferman.
FORMAT: Digest, 128 pp.
PRICE: First series, 35¢; second series, 60¢.

Nicholas S. De Larber

VENTURE SCIENCE FICTION (1963–1965)

Starting in December 1959 the London firm of Atlas Publishing and Distributing Limited began a British edition of *The Magazine of Fantasy and Science Fiction*.* Stories were not selected from concurrent issues; initially the selection was haphazard, but by November 1960 the time lapse was approximately four months, with stories juggled for length. Atlas also published a British edition of *Analog Science Fiction*,* but with the lifting of import restrictions these editions were rapidly becoming unnecessary. The last British *Analog* appeared in August 1963, and to replace it Atlas started a new magazine—*Venture Science Fiction*.

Venture Science Fiction had been the title of *Fantasy and Science Fiction*'s companion magazine, which had appeared during 1957–1958. The British edition, however, did not reprint solely from *Venture*. Since a British *Fantasy and Science Fiction* had not been published in those years, the greater selection of stories came from the late 1950s issue of that magazine. Stories from more recent issues that had been squeezed out of the British *Fantasy and Science Fiction* were also included, so that one could regard *Venture* as a form of safety net.

With *Venture* established, Atlas now folded the British *Fantasy and Science Fiction*, with the last issue, dated June 1964, selected from the February 1964 U.S. edition. Following the January 1964 issue *Venture* discontinued pictorial covers in favor of a standard format merely listing authors present in each issue and the feature story. Only the two-tone coloring varied. Combined with the booklike presentation of the text in single-column pages with minimal artwork, it gave *Venture* a dull appearance that may well have harmed sales.

Venture lasted for twenty-eight issues, folding in December 1965. The publishers explained that this was "due to the expiration of available material," but this must have been only part of the story. There were still sixteen stories from the original U.S. *Venture* unreprinted, plus stories from earlier *Fantasy and Science Fiction* issues. The final British *Venture* had reprinted from 1964 issues of *Fantasy and Science Fiction*, but these were now being regularly imported into Britain. It was the regular availability of the real article plus failing sales that had really sounded the death knell for *Venture*.

Information Sources

BIBLIOGRAPHY:
Tuck.
INDEX SOURCES: Bishop, Gerald, *Venture SF: A Checklist*, Exeter, U.K.: Aardvark House, 1970 (also includes first U.S. series and part of second U.S. series); SFM; Tuck.
REPRINT SOURCES:
  Reprint Editions: The Australian edition was dated two months ahead of the UK cover date and hence ran November 1963 – February 1966. Issues identical.
LOCATION SOURCES: M.I.T. Science Fiction Library; Pennsylvania State University Library; Texas A&M University Library.

Publication History

TITLE: *Venture Science Fiction*.
VOLUME DATA: No volume numbering. Number 1, September 1963–Number 28, December 1965. Monthly. Total run: 28 issues.
PUBLISHER: Atlas Publishing & Distributing Co. Ltd., London.
EDITOR: Ronald R. Wickers (not identified within issues).
FORMAT: Digest; 128 pp., first four issues, thereafter 112 pp.
PRICE: 2/6d. for first ten issues, thereafter 3/-.

Mike Ashley

VERTEX

Vertex was arguably one of the more interesting and theoretically more successful experiments of the 1970s though, ironically, it started almost by accident. Donald Pfeil, who edited several magazines for Mankind Publishing in California, mentioned to his publisher that "it sure would be nice if we could put out a good science fiction magazine—like no other magazine on the stands. A real slick, quality product."[1] Although it was said more as a joke than anything else, a week later the publisher gave Pfeil the green light, and he had only thirty-three days in which to assemble the first issue.

Dated April 1973, that first issue is a remarkable achievement in just under five weeks. The shortage of time meant that Pfeil relied on a few reprints to help fill the issue, although these three stories alone are among the best of the seventies: William Rotsler's "Patron of the Arts"—originally from the anthology *Universe 2*, it had been nominated for a Nebula that year; "The Dance of the Changer and Three," Terry Carr's powerful story of contact with a totally alien life-form; and Robert Silverberg's gnawingly satirical "Caught in the Organ Draft."

But of more import than the fiction was the magazine's format. Designed by art director Andrew Furr and further augmented by William Rotsler, who served in an unpaid capacity as visual coordinator, *Vertex* was a fully fledged slick, the first proper such magazine in the SF field. There had been earlier attempts, from the disastrously lavish fan-financed *The Vortex* (1947)* through Hugo Gernsback's *Science-Fiction Plus** to John Campbell's *Analog Science Fiction.**[2] Curiously, these last two magazines had turned slick at ten-yearly intervals, and *Vertex* followed on schedule in 1973. But *Science-Fiction Plus* and *Analog* were little more than pulp magazines with a slick veneer, and they made no serious inroads into the up-market slick magazines which, by 1973, were dominating the newsstands.

Vertex, on the other hand, was a genuine and serious slick magazine, with a cover that emphasized the serious aspects of both SF and science, and a cover price that reflected the up-market target. At $1.50 *Vertex* was by far the most expensive SF magazine on the stands. By comparison *Analog*, *Galaxy Science Fiction** and *The Magazine of Fantasy and Science Fiction** had just increased their cover price to seventy-five cents, and some critics felt that *Vertex* would price itself out of the market. In hindsight, however, it seems that *Vertex* was doing what the SF field should have done long before. Science fiction expected to be treated as adult fiction, therefore it needed to aim at the adult market, with more sophisticated layout and the feeling of prestige that a higher cover price gave. Gone were the gosh-wow, space rocket covers of its rivals. Those for *Vertex* were usually symbolic, and though not necessarily artistic were certainly sufficiently unusual to catch the eye, which is the primary purpose of a cover.

All these factors worked so that by the fourth issue Pfeil was able to boast that "it appears that our upcoming ABC audit will show [*Vertex*] to be outselling any other SF magazine on the market."[3]

From the start *Vertex* adopted a format that appealed to the core of its readership. Each issue would feature seven or eight stories of varying lengths, the bi-monthly schedule precluding serials (although one was presented at a later stage); a potpourri of short-story stories; five or six scientific or speculative articles, extensively illustrated with photographs and diagrams; an interview with a leading author or SF personality; plus news and book reviews. Throughout, the magazine was attractively illustrated; mostly through the auspices of William Rotsler, *Vertex* became a vehicle for fan artists. It featured prominently the work of Tim Kirk at an early stage of his career, and there were regular contributions by George Barr and Alicia Austin. Nevertheless, obtaining the right variety and quality of artwork was difficult. Even as late as June 1974 Rotsler—who only worked for *Vertex* in an unofficial capacity—was saying:

> We are *desperate* for covers and I don't think this will change much in the future. . . . I would like a GIANT number of artists available to us, from those capable of "every-rivet-showing-on-the-gleaming-ship" style to the wildest and most abstract. I would like the artist mated to the work, style to style, but I can only do that if I have competent artists available.[4]

Vertex was always striving to be visually appealing. It never had the financial wherewithal that *Omni** could subsequently boast, and it never presented any color interiors—though it did feature some attractive back cover paintings instead of saving that area as a lucrative advertising outlet, as is usual with most slicks— but it was always experimenting, which is what every genuine SF magazine should do.

This applied equally to the fiction, even though Pfeil admitted he was "old-fashioned." He believed that writing had two aims. One was to make money for the author, but marginally more important was "to please and entertain the reader,"[5] and it was with this intent that he compiled *Vertex*. Although he acquired fiction from many of the leading SF names, including Harry Harrison, Larry Niven, Jerry Pournelle and even Robert A. Heinlein, he also gave ample space to new writers. The August 1974 issue carried "Scoreboard," the first story to appear in print (though not the first sale) by John Varley. *Vertex* helped Alan Brennert, Spider Robinson, George R.R. Martin and Steven Utley learn the writing trade. William Carlson, another newcomer, was the only author to have a story from *Vertex* make the final ballot for the Nebula Award with his novella "Sunrise West," serialized in the October and December 1974 issues. In fact, as is often the case, it was the new writers striving to establish themselves who provided most of the better fiction in *Vertex*, rather than the better-known authors whose names may have lent the magazine some respectability, but whose stories seldom lived up to expectations. Of the new stories by major authors, possibly only "Bleeding Stones" by Harlan Ellison (April 1973) and "In the

House of the Double Minds'' by Robert Silverberg (June 1974) are worthy of reprinting, while in almost every issue were one or more memorable stories by lesser-known names, including "Experiment" by William Carlson (August 1973), "Door to Malequar" by Kathleen Sky (July 1975), "To the Waters and the Wild" by Mildred Downey Broxon (July 1975) and "Little Brother" by Fletcher Stewart (June 1975)—and this but skims the surface.

Unaccountably—though the cover price may have had some effect—*Vertex* never attracted a strong SF fan following, and this was reflected to some extent in the poor level of subscriptions the magazine received—a little over 4,000, or about 5 percent of the print run. *Vertex* relied almost solely for its circulation upon newsstand sales, and here it was phenomenally successful, selling around 60 percent of its print run for most of its first year, and increasing to nearly 80 percent in its second year. Lack of distribution is the major cause of death for magazines—especially fantasy ones—but *Vertex* had clearly circumvented this hurdle. It had the advantage of being published in California, while all other major SF magazines emanated from the East Coast. Previous West Coast magazines, however, had all died prematurely, but these (such as *Spaceway** and *Forgotten Fantasy**) had suffered from being produced by a minor publisher. *Vertex* was handled by a major publisher that published several lucrative magazines and thus was able to reach a viable local readership.

Vertex, therefore, should have been the success story of the seventies, but it fell foul of the one plague that SF should have predicted but did not. The early seventies was a period of chronic paper shortages. During 1974 *Vertex* had to change its paper stock on several occasions, sometimes using even more expensive paper simply because that was all that was available. By early 1975 the paper situation was becoming critical, and Mankind Publishing made a conscious but ill-conceived decision to switch *Vertex* from a slick to a tabloid format. The result was a disaster. Although the quality of the fiction in its final three issues was, if anything, superior to the slick issues, the format was visually abysmal, and the magazine bombed.

The tabloid approach had been a token effort by the publisher to sustain the magazine, but even before sales figures were in, *Vertex*'s fate was sealed. Mankind just could not obtain sufficient paper to publish all of its magazines, and what paper it acquired was used for the more lucrative titles. With the August 1975 issue—which through poor editorial judgment had started to serialize a Flash Gordon comic strip—*Vertex* folded. Within a year the paper shortage that had killed it was over, and in another year more and more magazines were adopting the slick format. *Cosmos Science Fiction and Fantasy Magazine* (1977)* and *Odyssey** failed in turn, and it was not until 1979 that the financial power of Bob Guccione was able to launch the ultimate science/SF slick, *Omni*, but there is no denying that *Vertex* had been on the right road. Had it outlived the paper crisis—which had also contributed to the demise of *If**—it might well have become one of the major forces in the SF magazine field.

Notes

1. Donald J. Pfeil, "Editorial," *Vertex*, April 1973, p. 5.
2. By coincidence *Vertex* was originally going to be called *Vortex*, but the name was changed at the last minute so as not to clash with the earlier *Vortex* published in 1953 (not the fan magazine of 1947).
3. Don Pfeil, letter to *The Alien Critic*, No. 7 (November 1973): 15.
4. Bill Rotsler, letter to *The Alien Critic*, No. 10 (August 1974): 27.
5. Pfeil, "Editorial."

Information Sources

BIBLIOGRAPHY:
Nicholls. *Encyclopedia*.
INDEX SOURCES: NESFA-II; NESFA-III; NESFA-IV; SFM.
REPRINT SOURCES: None known.
LOCATION SOURCES: M.I.T. Science Fiction Library.

Publication History

TITLE: *Vertex*.
VOLUME DATA: Volume 1, Number 1, April 1973–Volume 3, Number 4, August 1975. Bi-monthly, April 1973–April 1975 [Volume 3, Number 1]. Monthly, June–August 1975. Total run: 16 issues.
PUBLISHER: Mankind Publishing Co., Los Angeles, California.
EDITOR: Donald J. Pfeil on all issues, although Lawrence Neal named as editor on the August 1973 issue.
FORMAT: Slick, 96 pp., April 1973–April 1975; Tabloid, 48 pp., June 1975; Tabloid, 32 pp., July and August 1975.
PRICE: $1.50 on all slick issues; £1.00 on tabloid.

Mike Ashley

VISION OF TOMORROW

In 1969 Australian businessman Ronald E. Graham, owner of one of the largest personal SF collections outside the United States, contacted British fan and collector Philip Harbottle. They had a mutual interest in promoting the works of John Russell Fearn, among the most prolific of all SF writers. Graham's other businesses were successful enough to allow him to sink considerable money into financing a new magazine with the expectation of only breaking even. The new venture was planned as a pocketbook series to start in June 1969, but as is so often the case the distributors dictated the terms. They insisted that the magazine be in a large-size, glossy format, but this caused all manner of trouble with the printers, who had prepared the plates and were not geared to such a change. Harbottle found he was doing much of the work himself, and it was this confusion that led to the first issue being patchily printed, with vacant spaces at the end of stories.

The first issue, dated August 1969, featured a mixture of material from British writers like Kenneth Bulmer and William Temple and Australian authors Damien Broderick, Jack Wodhams and Lee Harding. There was also a short piece from Stanislaw Lem, one of his first to see print in English. This balance continued through later issues, although a ban by Graham on using any American material meant that Harbottle was restricted in the major names he could use. It also harmed sales because the American writers were more marketable in both countries. As a consequence Harbottle was forced to rely on John Carnell's brigade of writers and leading Australians.

The original printers were still causing trouble over the second issue, with the result that Harbottle went ahead with a new printer. Far more efficient, they produced the third issue before the second was completed; thus, the third issue, with a hastily changed cover date, was released first. The fates were certainly against Harbottle, and *Vision* could not have started with much more of a handicap.

Nevertheless, Harbottle overcame these odds, and *Vision* settled into a monthly schedule. Harbottle had also changed distributors, and the new firm was completely disorganized in its accounting. Initial returns showed that sales were as low as 12,000, itself a critical and worrisome figure. But then in May 1970 came the shocking news that sales were sometimes as low as 5,000. To continue under those circumstances was suicidal, and immediately all other plans were in a state of turmoil. The first issue of a new fantasy magazine to be edited by Kenneth Bulmer, *Sword and Sorcery*, all set for September 1970, was quashed. So was a companion reprint magazine, *Image of Tomorrow*.

Momentary plans to convert *Vision* into a paperback anthology, as originally intended, were also aborted. There appeared to be no way around the disaster, and Graham and Harbottle found they were at opposite poles of opinion. As a result, with the September 1970 issue *Visions of Tomorrow* ceased. Since by then *New Worlds** had also vanished, Britain was without an SF magazine for the first time in twenty-two years.

Vision of Tomorrow was an extremely handsome magazine, often featuring full-page interior color paintings from the brush of David Hardy. Harbottle struggled to obtain good-quality stories, but with his publisher's restrictions was hard pressed. Nevertheless, his efforts bore fruit, as *Vision* received the Australian Ditmar Award as the world's best SF magazine, beating *Analog Science Fiction** convincingly. He unearthed some previously unpublished Fearn material, but the original purpose of the magazine—to promote Fearn's work—was never accomplished. For nonfiction fans the most memorable aspect of *Vision* was the regular series "The Impatient Dreamers," which was a running history of SF activity in Britain from the earliest days. It was started by Walter Gillings, who in April 1969 had just returned to the SF field, after nearly twenty years, when he issued his neatly printed booklet *Cosmos*. William Temple, John Carnell and Gordon Landsborough all wrote episodes for the series, but it remained incomplete when *Vision* folded.

Vision proved useful in advancing the career of Eddie Jones. He was brought onto the salaried staff of the magazine as art editor, which allowed him time to produce good work of his own. It was the stepping-stone he needed to establish himself in the field.

On the fiction side, *VOT* published one of the early stories by Brian Stableford, "Prisoner in the Ice" (November 1969), and other early work by Christopher Priest, Richard Gordon and Eddy C. Bertin. One of its best-known stories was "The Bitter Pill" (June 1970) by A. Bertram Chandler, which formed the basis of his later novel of the same title, and which won the Australian Ditmar Award. Bob Shaw, Michael Moorcock and John Brunner were all represented by at least one story, but E. C. Tubb, Sydney J. Bounds, Kenneth Bulmer and William F. Temple supplied most of the stories from England, while Lee Harding, Damien Broderick, Frank Bryning and Jack Wodhams flew the Australian flag.

VOT is remembered as a unique example of a collaborative magazine edited in England and financed by an Australian. For collectors the last issue is of special note. Lost by the distributors, copies are now rare.

Information Sources

BIBLIOGRAPHY:
Nicholls. *Encyclopedia*.
INDEX SOURCES: ISFM-II; Stone, Graham B., *Australian Science Fiction Index Supplement 1968–1975*, Sydney: Australian SF Association, 1976; SFM.
REPRINT SOURCES: None known.
LOCATION SOURCES: M.I.T. Science Fiction Library.

Publication History

TITLE: *Vision of Tomorrow*.
VOLUME DATA: Volume 1, Number 1, August 1969–Volume 1, Number 12, September 1970. Monthly, but September issue rescheduled to December 1969. No issue for October 1969. Issue 3 dated November. (December 1969 issue numbered 2). Total run: 12 issues.
PUBLISHER: Ronald E. Graham, Yagoona, New South Wales.
EDITOR: Philip Harbottle, Newcastle, England.
FORMAT: Slick, 64 pp., except Number 2, 66 pp., and Number 11, 68 pp.
PRICE: 5/-.

Mike Ashley

VOID SCIENCE FICTION & FANTASY

Australia has not been noted for its SF magazines. Most have been reprints of U.S. magazines in distorted formats, and what few original stories were included were usually best forgotten. That was in the 1950s. Yet by the 1960s Australia had a growing cadre of good writers such as Lee Harding, Jack Wodhams, Damien Broderick and ex-Briton A. Bertram Chandler, only they had no SF magazine of their own. Their stories appeared at times in British and American magazines, but even when in 1969 Ronald E. Graham financed an Anglo-Australian SF magazine, *Vision of Tomorrow*,* it was edited in England.

Void thus stands as something of an exception: the only worthwhile and original Australian SF magazine. There is the small matter that its editor, Paul Collins, was born in England and raised in New Zealand, and had only been resident in Australia since he was eighteen, but it is apparently the closest Australia is going to get.

Void was launched at the most opportune moment in 1975, when the World SF convention was held in Melbourne, Australia. *Void* was not a prestige publication. A small booklet, although professionally printed, it looked like a quality fanzine—although even this was streets ahead of Australia's former magazines. Collins was both editor and publisher, although originally Dennis Stocks had been intended to serve as editor. Collins was new to the SF scene, and the magazine received a rather hostile reception from the SF fraternity. The first issue included mostly reprints from America by Robert Silverberg, Leigh Brackett, J. F. Bone, Howard Goldsmith and even Ralph Milne Farley, and what Australian writers were present were represented predominantly by short squibs or joke stories. The illustrations by Diana Buckman and Kevin MacDonnell left much to be desired, and the overall impression left by the first issue was one of misguided effort.

With the second issue, everything started to change. Collins had patched up his differences with Australian fandom, and his solid determination had brought much support from both Australia and America. Presentation and production had improved, including the artwork, with a marked improvement in MacDonnell's work, which continued throughout the magazine's life. Most of the stories were new or had not previously been printed in a major publication, and included work by Australians Jack Wodhams, Frank Bryning, Bertram Chandler, Gregory FitzGerald and Paul Harwitz and Americans Edward Bryant and Karl Hansen. The stories no longer carried an undertone of insincerity, and it was clear that all concerned were taking *Void* seriously.

The third issue, confusingly unnumbered, had a few fannish elements, but on the whole maintained the trend toward greater quality. American Darrell Schweitzer had now involved himself with the magazine, which printed one of his Sir Julian fantasy adventures in each of the next three issues. Under the alias Theodore Butler, Schweitzer also conducted an "Out of the Vault" department where he resurrected old stories. These included "The Planet," an anonymous story from an 1853 issue of *Knickerbocker's Magazine*, "Lindenborg Pool" by William Morris and "The Haunted Ships" by Allan Cunningham. The final three issues of *Void* continued to present new stories by Australian and American writers; not all were of top quality, but at least there was a determined effort to achieve respectability.

After the fifth issue, however, *Void* took a totally new direction. Collins, now boosted by the Literature Board of Australia, converted *Void* into an anthology series. The contents planned for the sixth, seventh and eighth issues became, instead, a hardcover volume, *Envisaged Worlds* (St. Kilda: Void, 1977), and this was followed on an approximately annual basis by *Other Worlds*, *Alien Worlds* and *Distant Worlds*. Each volume contained an original foreword by such respected members of the SF world as Christopher Priest, Roger Zelazny and Joe Haldeman, and sales were sufficiently encouraging for Collins to establish his own literary agency and publishing imprint. Australia had long been a void when it came to a central publication for science fiction. How ironic that it required a *Void* to fill it.

Information Sources

BIBLIOGRAPHY:
Nicholls. *Encyclopedia*.
INDEX SOURCES: NESFA-IV; NESFA-V.
REPRINT SOURCES: None known.
LOCATION SOURCES: M.I.T. Science Fiction Library.

Publication History

TITLE: *Void Science Fiction & Fantasy*.
VOLUME DATA: Issues undated, other than copyright by year. Also unnumbered except by cryptic references. Identification and publication dates as follows. Number 1, "Special Aussiecon Edition," August 1975; Number 2, "The Second Void," November 1975; Number 3, "Copyright 1976," February 1976; Number 4, "The Fourth Dimension," May 1976; Number 5 [no identification, but inside front cover advertises the First Sydney SF Film Fest in April 1977], February 1977. First four issues, quarterly. Total run: 5 issues. Thereafter continued as original annual anthology series.
PUBLISHER: Void Publications, St. Kilda, Australia.
EDITOR: Paul Collins.
FORMAT: Digest (saddle-stapled), 80 pp.
PRICE: $1.00.

Mike Ashley

THE VORTEX (1947)

The Vortex was the first postwar attempt to launch a semi-professional magazine from a fan base, and it barely survived the first issue, which probably appeared in the fall of 1947. The editors and publishers set their sights high but were rather too ambitious. The first issue was a prestigious publication, eighty pages thick, printed on quality china stock and professionally printed. Unfortunately, none of the names was well known outside of a tiny circle of fans, and indeed some were probably pseudonyms of the editors, George Cowie and Gordon Kull. As an opening offer, which was if anything suicidal, *The Vortex* would be given free to any who requested it at the outset. Later copies would sell for twenty cents. In all probability the only people interested in the magazine acquired it while the offer lasted, and subsequent sales must have been minimal.

Somehow the editors managed to issue a second number, but it was now little more than a fanzine. All but five pages were mimeographed. The five insets, being printed on the original coated stock, were either hangovers from the first issue or the first pages prepared for the second issue before Cowie and Kull realized that they would have to substantially cut costs. These pages were for the most part title pages to the stories, with handsome illustrations by D. Bruce Berry and Roy Hunt.

The contents showed considerably greater promise than those in the first issue, and it is surprising that the editors did not go for some of the bigger names initially. Included were stories by Forrest J Ackerman, David H. Keller, E. Everett Evans and Stanley Mullen, plus verse by Clark Ashton Smith and an article by James Taurasi. Other items were by the editors, including an article on "Burg Frankenstein" that was illustrated by an interior photograph and a photographic cover.

Evidently response must have been minimal and expenditure astronomic, because no further issues appeared.

Note

The author wishes to thank Paul Spencer for his help with this essay.

Information Sources

BIBLIOGRAPHY:
Warner, Harry, Jr. *All Our Yesterdays*. Chicago: Advent, 1969.
INDEX SOURCES: Issues are listed in *Fanzine Index*, ed. Bob Pavlat and Bill Evans (Flushing, N.Y.: Piser, 1965); MT.
REPRINT SOURCES: None known.
LOCATION SOURCES: None known.

Publication History

TITLE: *The Vortex*.
VOLUME DATA: Number 1, 1947–Number 2, 1947. Exact dates unknown but possibly Spring and Fall. Intended schedule bi-monthly. Total run: 2 issues.
PUBLISHER: Fansci Pubafi, San Francisco.
EDITORS: Gordon M. Kull and George R. Cowie.
FORMAT: Digest, 80 pp., first issue; Large Digest, 88 pp., second issue. First issue professionally printed and bound; second issue mimeographed and stapled.
PRICE: First issue, 20¢; second issue, 25¢.

Mike Ashley

VORTEX (1977)

Vortex was a handsome large-size magazine with full-color covers by Eddie Jones and Rodney Matthews and many colored interior paintings. Its editor, Keith Seddon, was an aspiring writer with little grounding in editing. Confusingly subtitled "The Science Fiction Fantasy," *Vortex* attempted to present the whole spectrum of fantastic fiction, but the editor was working against unenviable odds. Art agencies refused to forward material because they had little faith in the publisher's reputation, and the publisher's insistence that the magazine be packed with colored illustrations sent production costs soaring. Seddon had secured serialization of Michael Moorcock's *The End of All Songs* to launch the magazine, although the remaining fiction was of average quality. There were signs that it was improving when the publisher decided to stop publication. Circulation had settled at the 12,000 mark, far too low to support a magazine with such high costs. *Vortex* had seen just five monthly issues, and with its passing in May 1977 Britain was again without a science fiction magazine.

Information Sources

BIBLIOGRAPHY:
Ashley, Mike. "Magazines." Section 7 in *The International SF Yearbook*, ed. Colin
        Lester. Pierrot, 1978.
INDEX SOURCES: None known.
REPRINT SOURCES: None known.
LOCATION SOURCES: None known.

Publication History

TITLE: *Vortex*.
VOLUME DATA: Volume 1, Number 1, January 1977–Volume 1, Number 5, May
        1977. Monthly. Total run: 5 issues.
PUBLISHER: Cerberus Publishing Ltd., Hertfordshire (copyright in their name but other
        imprints identified on indicia).
EDITOR: Keith Seddon.
FORMAT: Slick, 48 pp.
PRICE: 45p.

Mike Ashley

VORTEX SCIENCE FICTION

Editor Chester Whitehorn's new idea was to produce a digest that would have "more stories than any magazine of its kind." So he filled 160 pages with twenty to twenty-five stories by excluding novelettes, novels, serials and features. Actually, his first issue, which appeared in the summer of 1953, fell somewhat short of his goal: Alfred Coppel, Milton Lesser, and Lester del Rey dominated a third of the space with stories running from 7,000 to 12,000 words. The issue was well received, according to Whitehorn; half of its mass was occupied by known authors, and three of their stories subsequently were anthologized: Charles E. Fritch's "The Honeymoon," Jack Vance's "The Mitr," and Lester del Rey's compelling "Stability." That Whitehorn was once a *Planet Stories** editor showed: about half the stories involved space opera and alien encounters with a light admixture of humor and holocaust, most of it competently illustrated by the cover artist, Chester Martin.

It was not until his second issue that Whitehorn realized his goal. He raised the story count from 20 to 25 and kept the word range between 600 and 5,000, nearly half the stories staying at 2,500. But nine of the writers were appearing for the first time and the remainder were just beginning two- to ten-story careers, the most established and prolific of them being Gene Hunter and L. Major Reynolds. The *Planet* emphasis remained strong—inflected now by a very large group of murder mysteries.

Nothing more was heard from Chester Whitehorn until *Science Fiction Digest*.* Perhaps he should have listened to the critics that he quoted:

You'll never find enough *good* short pieces to fill 160 pages. There just aren't that many around. There just isn't the talent there used to be. The field is too crowded with magazines. Production costs are too high. Look at your break-even point on sales. Man, are you in trouble!

But the ill-fated second issue ranged widely enough to make history in a small way: it published the first two stories of Marion Zimmer Bradley.

Information Sources

BIBLIOGRAPHY:
Nicholls. *Encyclopedia.*
Tuck.
INDEX SOURCES: MIT; SFM.
REPRINT SOURCES: None known.
LOCATION SOURCES: M.I.T. Science Fiction Library; Pennsylvania State University
    Library.

Publication History

TITLE: *Vortex Science Fiction.*
VOLUME DATA: Issues undated. Volume 1, Number 1, [Summer 1953]–Volume 1,
    Number 2, [Winter 1953]. No schedule indicated. Total run: 2 issues.
PUBLISHER: Specific Fiction Corp., a subsidiary of Authentic Publications Inc., New
    York.
EDITOR: Chester Whitehorn.
FORMAT: Digest, 160 pp.
PRICE: 35¢.

E. F. Casebeer

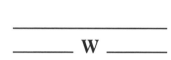

WEB TERROR STORIES

Final incarnation of a magazine that started life as *Saturn, The Magazine of Science Fiction*. See SATURN, THE MAGAZINE OF SCIENCE FICTION.

WEIRD AND OCCULT LIBRARY

Weird and Occult Library, which ran for three issues in 1960, was a curious collection of vignettes which marked the swan song of Gerald Swan in the publishing field. Preparing for retirement, Swan appeared to have sorted through his inventory and at last brought to print stories acquired up to twenty years earlier during his wartime publishing. Three issues featured old stories by Ernest L. McKeag, John Russell Fearn, John Body (probably a misprint for John Brody), A. M. Burrage, Henry Rawle, Norman Pallant (misprinted Jallant), Kay Hammond and other Swan regulars.

The stories were written for a less sophisticated readership than that of the 1960s and were unoriginal in plot and characterization. Most relate little more than spooky incidents. Even so, the stories are marginally better than those in the short-lived companion publication, *Science Fiction Library*.*

Information Sources

BIBLIOGRAPHY:
Nicholls. *Encyclopedia*.
Tuck.
INDEX SOURCES: MIT; MT; SFM.
REPRINT SOURCES: None known.
LOCATION SOURCES: None known.

Publication History

TITLE: *Weird and Occult Library.*
VOLUME DATA: Undated. Number 1 [Spring 1960]–Number 3 [Autumn 1960].
PUBLISHER: Gerald G. Swan, London.
EDITOR: Not identified but may be Walter Swan.
FORMAT: Pocketbook, 64 pp.
PRICE: 1/-.

Mike Ashley

WEIRD MYSTERY

One of the fourteen reprint digest magazines issued by Sol Cohen during the early 1970s, *Weird Mystery* relied mostly on stories from the late 1940s issues of *Fantastic Adventures*,* although the second issue (Winter 1970) selected stories from the Cele Goldsmith *Fantastic** and was more like an issue of *Strange Fantasy.**

WM presented a lead novella supported by short stories. The quality varied because issues were assembled with few, if any, editorial criteria, but a few interesting stories were revived. Of the more recent stories were "Darkness Box" by Ursula K. LeGuin and "Solomon's Demon" by Arthur Porges, while the older items included "Make Yourself a Wish" by Geoff St. Reynard and "The Dead Don't Die" by Robert Bloch. The magazine demonstrated that the stories from *Fantastic Adventures* did not date as rapidly as those from *Amazing Stories.**

Information Sources

BIBLIOGRAPHY:
Cook, Michael L. *Monthly Murders.* Westport, Conn.: Greenwood Press, 1982 (features
    an issue and author index).
INDEX SOURCES: ISFM-II; MT; NESFA; SFM.
REPRINT SOURCES: None known.
LOCATION SOURCES: M.I.T. Science Fiction Library.

Publication History

TITLE: *Weird Mystery.*
VOLUME DATA: No volume numbering. Number 1, Fall 1970–Number 4, Summer
    1971. Quarterly. Total run: 4 issues.
PUBLISHER: Ultimate Publishing Co., Flushing, New York.
EDITOR: Sol Cohen (not identified within issues).
FORMAT: Digest, 128 pp.
PRICE: 50¢, first two issues; thereafter 60¢.

Mike Ashley

WEIRD POCKET LIBRARY

Weird Pocket Library was a borderline magazine/pocketbook anthology, one of a number issued by Gerald Swan during World War Two (see *Occult** for full details). A slim booklet, *WPL*, probably published in 1943, contained only two short macabre mystery stories, "The Dark City" by Kay Hammond and "Milky Throws a Boomerang" by Trevor Dudley-Smith. The latter was the real name of the popular thriller writer Elleston Trevor, now best known under his alias Adam Hall. Kay Hammond was the name used by Kay H. Davies, who wrote a number of romances for Swan's.

Information Sources

BIBLIOGRAPHY:
Tuck.
INDEX SOURCES: MT.
REPRINT SOURCES: None known.
LOCATION SOURCES: None known.

Publication History

TITLE: *Weird Pocket Library*.
VOLUME DATA: Undated, unnumbered. Possibly 1943.
PUBLISHER: Gerald G. Swan, London.
EDITOR: Not identified. May be Gerald's brother, Walter Swan.
FORMAT: Pocketbook, 48 pp.
PRICE: 4d.

Mike Ashley

WEIRD SHORTS

Weird Shorts, one of a number of pocketbook anthology/magazines issued by Gerald Swan during World War II, was probably published in 1945. Although fully identified as *Weird Shorts—First Selection*, no second issue has been sighted. However, bookdealer and bibliophile George Locke has unearthed an issue of crime and mystery stories published under the same title and cover; such were the exigencies of wartime publishing.

The weird fiction issue contains seven vignettes bearing by-lines known in other Swan publications, including the SF ones: Henry Rawle, Trevor Dudley-Smith, Dallas Kirby, W. P. Cockroft and even I. O. Evans. The Evans contribution is "The Kraken."

Stories possibly intended for future issues, all of which were probably first acquired for *Yankee Weird Shorts,** eventually turned up fifteen years later in *Weird and Occult Library.**

Information Sources

BIBLIOGRAPHY:
Locke, George W. *Ferret Fantasy's Christmas Annual for 1973*. London: Ferret Fantasy, 1974.
INDEX SOURCES: MT.
REPRINT SOURCES: None known.
LOCATION SOURCES: None known.

Publication History

TITLE: *Weird Shorts—First Selection.*
VOLUME DATA: Undated, probably 1945.
PUBLISHER: Gerald G. Swan, London.
EDITOR: Not identified but may be Walter Swan.
FORMAT: Pocketbook, 36 pp.
PRICE: 7d.

Mike Ashley

WEIRD STORY MAGAZINE

Weird Story Magazine had two separate incarnations from the same publisher, Gerald G. Swan. It was one of a number of ephemeral publications issued by Swan during World War Two when Swan's business acumen had led him to stockpile paper just before it was rationed.

The first issue of *WSM* was dated August 1940—one of the few of Swan's magazines to bear a cover date. Published in pulp format its contents were written almost entirely by William J. Elliott, a former actor who became a prolific writer of thrillers and historical romances during the 1930s. He would later complete a science fiction novel for Swan's, *To-morrow's Spectacles* (1946). His contributions to *WSM*, under such anagrammatical pseudonyms as Leopold J. Wollett, L.T.J. Wilte and W. E. Tillot, include brief vignettes like "Doctor Doom, Ghost Detective" and "So This is Death." Other by-lines were Basil Herbert, James Bruce and Henry Retlaw (the latter may be another Elliott alias or may be the same writer as Henry Rawle). The magazine also carried an anonymous comic-strip "Dene Vernon, Ghost Investigator."

WSM's second incarnation was not until the end of the War when two undated issues appeared in slim pocketbook format. These were more in line with Swan's other wartime publications (see *Occult** and *Weird Shorts**) and contained short unimaginative stories and articles by Swan regulars like W. P. Cockroft, John Body, A. C. Bailey and Henry Rawle. The second issue is of slightly more interest than the first by virtue of the presence of the prolific but short-lived writer of gangster stories N. Wesley Firth.

Not one of the issues is especially memorable, being aimed at a wartime readership starved of regular material. *WSM* is for completist collectors only.

Information Sources

BIBLIOGRAPHY:
Tuck.
INDEX SOURCES: Locke, George W., *Ferret Fantasy's Christmas Annual for 1973*, private, 1974; MT; Tuck.
REPRINT SOURCES: The second issue was rebound into *Four-in-One: Weird and Occult Shorts* (London: Swan, 1949) together with unsold copies of *Occult Shorts 2** and the nonfantasy *Racing Shorts* and *Detective Shorts 4*.
LOCATION SOURCES: British Library.

Publication History

TITLE: *Weird Story Magazine* (both series).
VOLUME DATA: First series, Number 1, August 1940. Second series, undated, 2 issues, probably 1946.
PUBLISHER: Gerald G. Swan, London.
EDITOR: Not identified, but may have been Walter Swan.
FORMAT: First series, Pulp, 96 pp. Second series, Pocketbook, 36 pp.
PRICE: First series, 7d; second series, 6d.

Mike Ashley

WEIRD TALES

Early in 1922, Jacob Clark Henneberger and J. M. Lansinger formed Rural Publications Inc. to publish magazines in the flourishing pulp field. Henneberger was already a successful magazine publisher with his two collegiate-oriented magazines, *College Humor* and *The Magazine of Fun*. Looking for new worlds to conquer, Henneberger was impressed by well-known Chicago authors who were looking for a market for off-trail material that no magazine would accept. It was with these authors in mind that Henneberger stated many years later, "I must confess that the main motive in establishing *Weird Tales* was to give the writer free rein to express his innermost feelings in a manner befitting great literature."[1] Thus, early in 1923, *Weird Tales*, subtitled "The Unique Magazine," was begun. Rural Publications also established *Real Detective and Mystery Stories* at the same time. Editing both magazines was Edwin Baird, a Chicago newspaperman and author. *Weird Tales* started slowly and went downhill from there. The authors that Henneberger had hoped to attract to his new publication, such as Ben Hecht and Emerson Hough, showed no interest in submitting to the pulp. The magazine began in standard 6 by 9 inch pulp format with unattractive three-color covers. After its second monthly issue, *Weird Tales* switched to an even more dismal looking 8½ by 11 inch bedsheet size, with fewer pages and even worse covers. The magazine remained a monthly but skipped an issue in August 1923 and December 1923. A delay of several months after its April 1924 issue suggested that the magazine was on shaky financial ground. A thick 192-

page anniversary issue, dated May/June/July, was the last issue to be seen for months.

Weird Tales was in deep financial trouble. It was a losing proposition from the start, the uninspired editing of Baird coupled with the bland look of the magazine generating poor sales and massive debts. Deciding to keep "The Unique Magazine" alive at any cost, Henneberger split with Lansinger, giving him control of *Real Detective* (already a money-maker). Baird, who had edited the detective pulp as well as *Weird Tales*, stayed wtih Lansinger, and the first reader for *Weird Tales*, Farnsworth Wright, took over as editor of *Weird Tales*. The first issue of the revived pulp appeared in November 1924, and the publication slowly inched toward respectability.

The thirteen issues of *Weird Tales* edited by Baird were not totally without merit. For one, he featured the first stories by H. P. Lovecraft to be published in something more than a semi-professional or small circulation magazine. Baird also published good stories by Anthony Rud, Frank Owen and Seabury Quinn, as well as poetry by Clark Ashton Smith. However, in general the editorial tone of the magazine was anything but unique. Baird envisioned *Weird Tales* as primarily a ghost story magazine, and so it was. Stories were short and mainly traditional in tone. Little was surprising or original. Illustrations and cover art were of low quality.

Under the gifted editorial guidance of Farnsworth Wright, the magazine improved noticeably with each issue. The format reverted to standard pulp size, and the magazine maintained a strict monthly schedule. Four-color covers began appearing and by the end of 1925 were regularly featured. Interior art began to make itself felt, though most was crude and not very weird in nature. More important, the contents of the magazine improved dramatically.

While Baird left some good material when he departed as editor, it was Wright who discovered and encouraged new writers that were to become the mainstay of the magazine. During the first few years of Wright's tenure as editor, the first stories by Robert E. Howard, E. Hoffman Price, Donald Wandrei, Frank Belknap Long, Nictzin Dyhalis, H. Warner Munn, Arthur J. Burks and Edmond Hamilton appeared in *Weird Tales*. Wright was an early exponent of science fiction and published superscience epics not only by Hamilton but also by J. Schlossel and Otis Adelbert Kline. H. P. Lovecraft, while constantly complaining in letters to friends about Farnsworth Wright's editorial whims, became a steady contributor.

Not only did Wright find and nurture a new talent, he also encouraged and obtained established writers in the fantasy genre to contribute to his magazine as well. Seabury Quinn, who had been writing fantasy fiction since 1919, and who had done several nonfiction pieces for Baird, became a regular and very popular contributor of fiction under Wright's editorial control. Greye La Spina's novel *Invaders from the Dark* had been rejected by Baird. Wright asked to see it again and bought it. The werewolf novel proved to be extremely popular and a definite boost to the magazine's circulation. Ray Cummings, an extremely popular writer of the kind of scientific romance published in *The Argosy and*

*All-Story** contributed a number of stories to Wright's magazine. Wright even obtained a short story from A. Merritt, "The Woman of the Wood," the only story by that immensely popular author not to appear in a Munsey publication.

Wright's editorial policies kept *Weird Tales* growing and provided a healthy (if low-paying) market for new authors to expand and grow. Wright paid his more popular authors better rates and constantly offered good advice to his newer contributors. Robert E. Howard sold nearly all of his early fiction to *Weird Tales*, and Edmond Hamilton made his mark in that magazine long before he became a regular in the science fiction pulps of the day. Both Arthur J. Burks and E. Hoffman Price were regular contributors to *Weird Tales* for years before they branched out into other pulp fields.

Variety and diversity made *Weird Tales* something special among pulps, fulfilling some of Henneberger's dreams. Under Wright's editorial guidance, *Weird Tales* drew away from publishing ghost stories and developed into "The Unique Magazine." There were stories of torture and diabolical revenge with no trace of the supernatural. There were science fiction space operas and strange mood pieces that defied conventional categorization. It was only in *Weird Tales* that one could find such a gruesome story as "The Copper Bowl" by Major G. F. Elliot, Lovecraft's "The Call of Cthulhu," Seabury Quinn's "The Jest of Warburg Tantavul" (about incest between a brother and sister), and Howard's seminal sword and sorcery epic, "The Shadow Kingdom."

Weird Tales continued to grow successful throughout the 1920s and early 1930s, even with the Depression cutting into most magazine sales. Priced at twenty-five cents, the magazine represented a sizable investment in bad times. A sudden bank closing, freezing nearly all of the magazine's cash assets late in 1930, brought about a minor crisis early in 1931. *Weird Tales* was forced to go bi-monthly from February through July 1931 (for three issues). However, the magazine soon righted itself and was back on an even keel by August of that year. The appearance of a long, very popular serial by Otis Adelbert Kline, who was at the peak of his popularity during these years, was a considerable boost to the pulp. Even without the Kline serial, though, *Weird Tales* probably would have managed to continue. The magazine, under Wright's excellent editorial policies, had developed a superior stable of top fantasy authors whose only market was "The Unique Magazine." Wright continued to offer a steady diet of Lovecraft, Robert E. Howard, Otis Adelbert Kline and Seabury Quinn to his readers. By the 1930s he had added the unusual talents of Clark Ashton Smith, C. L. Moore, David Keller, Jack Williamson, Paul Ernst and a host of others, some discoveries made by Wright from the slush piles, and others from the SF and adventure pulps, looking for a market where they could work unrestrained by the usual pulp formulas.

The death of Howard and Lovecraft in 1936 and 1937, respectively, did some damage to the magazine, but not as much as some critics claimed. A great deal of Lovecraft material had originally been published in fanzines, and Wright managed to use such material for the next few years, offering more Lovecraft fiction and poetry after his death than before! Howard's Conan was missed somewhat more as there was little of his unpublished material available, but other writers, most notably Henry Kuttner (another *Weird Tales* discovery) helped filled the gap.

The sale of the magazine in late 1938 to William J. Delaney spelled hard times for Farnsworth Wright. Delaney, a former advertising salesman, also owned *Short Stories*, a much more successful, general pulp fiction magazine, and he expected the weird fiction magazine to make a profit as well. *Weird Tales* had always been marginal at best, so changes were made. Editorial offices were moved from Chicago to New York to be combined with the offices of *Short Stories*. Dorothy McIlwraith, editor of *Short Stories*, also served as Wright's assistant and began taking on many of his duties. In February 1939 the magazine went from 144 pages to 160 pages in a move to try to boost circulation. When that effort failed, the page count was dropped to 128 in September 1939 and the price lowered to fifteen cents.

In January 1940 the magazine switched from monthly to bi-monthly. Wright, who had been in bad health for many years, stepped down as editor in May 1940, and Dorothy McIlwraith took over. The magazine continued with marginal success as a bi-monthly through September 1954, when it finally folded.

Under the editorial directorship of Dorothy McIlwraith, *Weird Tales* continued to publish excellent fantasy and horror fiction. However, much of the uniqueness of the magazine was gone. Humor was introduced, much of it reading like rejects from the better-paying *Unknown*.* Swords and sorcery material virtually vanished, as did serials and longer stories. There was a great deal less variety to the magazine.

There were still many memorable stories. Robert Bloch, who had been a regular contributor since his first story had appeared in *Weird Tales* in 1935, continued to write for the magazine. Ray Bradbury had a number of excellent early stories in the pulp, and Manly Wade Wellman, who had been a steady contributor in the late 1930s, became a regular name with his tales of John Thunstone. Seabury Quinn and August Derleth both continued to work for "The Unique Magazine," as did Edmond Hamilton.

It was *Short Stories*, however, that commanded most of the budget for the two magazines, and the difference showed in *Weird Tales*. As science fiction grew in popularity, the magazine shrank increasingly in page count as the price continued to rise. September 1953 saw it reduced to a digest magazine at thirty-five cents an issue, and September 1954 saw its last regular publication.

Weird Tales, during its original run of 279 issues, was the most important and influential of all fantasy magazines. Not only did it offer a long-term market for supernatural and fantasy fiction, but it provided an outlet for stories that would never have been published otherwise. It was in *Weird Tales* that Lovecraft published nearly all of his important work. The Cthulhu Mythos, starting with "The Call of Cthulhu" and "The Dunwich Horror" and progressing through "The Whisperer in Darkness" and "The Case of Charles Dexter Ward," all appeared in *Weird Tales*. Swords and sorcery became a major pulp genre with the works of Robert E. Howard, the most important of which appeared in *Weird Tales*. King Kull, Solomon Kane, Bran Mak Morn and Conan were all creations that owed their life to *Weird Tales*. And after Howard's death, it was *Weird Tales* that kept the genre alive with Kuttner's Elak and Clifford Ball's Duar the Accursed until *Unknown* gave it new life when it published the Gray Mouser series by Fritz Leiber.

It was *Weird Tales* that provided a home for Jules de Grandin, Seabury Quinn's popular supernatural sleuth, who used modern science to battle traditional horrors. It is doubtful that Catherine Moore's unusual tales of Northwest Smith or Jirel of Joiry would ever have seen print if it had not been for *Weird Tales*. Nor is it likely that Clark Ashton Smith's tales of Hyperboria and Averoigne would ever have been published in any other magazine.

It was in the pages of *Weird Tales* that science fantasy artwork made itself a force worth noting. The first work of Virgil Finlay, Hannes Bok and Lee Brown Coye appeared in *Weird Tales*. It was in "The Unique Magazine" that Finlay made science fiction fans aware of what could be done even with the limitations of pulp paper and brought about a renaissance in science fiction illustration. It was the work of Bok and Coye that had brought style to fantasy artwork where before all there had been was substance and form.

It was *Weird Tales* that provided most of the reprints for the first collections of modern fantasy and horror fiction done in book form from both large and small publishers. It was *Weird Tales* material that formed the bulk of the fiction and poetry published by Arkham House and brought that company into existence. It was stories from *Weird Tales* that provided most of the weird fiction for early radio shows devoted to modern horror and fantasy stories, including the classic "Stay Tuned for Terror." Later, stories from *Weird Tales* were adapted for numerous movies and for TV shows including *The Twilight Zone*, *Alfred Hitchcock* and, most notably, *Thriller*. *Weird Tales* gave the fantasy field a solid foundation, a huge body of work to be drawn upon for both stories and ideas.

Most important, it was the policy and nature of the magazine that influenced the entire spectrum of fantasy and SF publishing. It was in *Weird Tales*, not the early SF magazines, that traditions were broken. It was in *Weird Tales* that unusual writing and poetry was featured. The outrageous and the ordinary mingled side by side in the magazine, and it was *Weird Tales* that was studied by the editors of the *Year's Best Short Stories* and not the other fantasy magazines or SF publications. It was a magazine where anything might find a home. Not everything published in *Weird Tales* was a classic—much of it was standard pulp fiction. But, at the same time, much of the material in "The Unique Magazine" was important, seminal literature from which modern fantasy had developed. It was a unique magazine in every sense of the word. Without it swords and sorcery, Lovecraft's Cthulhu Mythos, or the outré worlds of Clark Ashton Smith might never have reached fruition, or have been lost forever.

In 1973, under the editorial guidance of Sam Moskowitz, *Weird Tales* was revived for four pulp-size issues by Leo Margulies. The magazine featured an interesting jumble of contents, ranging from reprints from the turn of the century to new stories by contemporary authors. Most prominent were several rare William Hope Hodgson stories discovered by Moskowitz, along with Moskowitz's biography of that author. The magazine folded after four issues due to poor distribution, lackluster sales and lack of a strong financial base that would enable it to develop a strong following.

In 1981 the magazine was again revived under the editorial hand of Lin Carter, this time as a paperback quarterly. Published by Zebra Books with the assistance of the current title owner, Robert Weinberg, *Weird Tales* in its new format went through four issues until business and contractual problems brought the series to an end. The issues featured a combination of new material—usually stories by old-time contributors to *Weird Tales*, some rescued from old amateur magazines—and reprints. The major criticism of this series was too much reliance by Carter on the old names like Lovecraft, Howard and Smith by reprinting mediocre material with a slim novelty value. New writers were not sufficiently encouraged although there were good stories from Ramsey Campbell, Tanith Lee, Steve Rasnic Tem and a first sale by John Brizzolara.

Once the contractual problems had been resolved plans were afoot for further issues of *Weird Tales*, but further problems arose. What seemed most bizarre was that two individuals were serving separately as editors—Gil Lamont and Forrest Ackerman. Lamont's selection of fiction had been set up in galley-form while the cover for the projected July/August 1984 issue referred to Ackerman's contents.[2] A Fall 1984 issue finally appeared in early 1985.

Notes

1. J. C. Henneberger, in Robert Weinberg, *The Weird Tales Story* (West Linn, Oregon: Fax Collector's Editions, 1977), p. 3.

2. See news item "*Weird Tales* in Limbo" in *Locus* 285, October 1984, p. 4, which also reproduces the cover and contents line-up.

Information Sources

BIBLIOGRAPHY:

The major reference work on *WT* is *The Weird Tales Story* by Robert Weinberg (West Linn, Ore.: Fax Collector's editions, 1977), which contains a potted history of the magazine plus a detailed survey of the stories and artwork, reminiscences by many of the contributors and excerpts from "The Eyrie," plus other sundry items. This book is itself an expansion (and a major one) of Weinberg's *WT 50* (Oak Lawn, Ill.: Weinberg, 1974), which also contains a history and reminiscences, and other items besides, plus five stories in the *WT* tradition. The items below will also be of interest, and readers should refer to the introductions to the Haining and Margulies' anthologies listed under Reprint Sources.

Bloch, Robert. "In Memoriam: W. T." *Isomar* 2 (September 27, 1955). Reprinted in *The Eighth Stage of Fandom*. Chicago: Advent, 1962.

de Camp, L. Sprague. *Lovecraft: A Biography*. Garden City, N.Y.: Doubleday, 1975 (gives extensive detail on *WT*).

Hillman, Arthur F. "Twenty-Five Years of Weird Tales." *Fantasy Review* (February/ March 1948).

Moskowitz, Sam. "Weird Tales Creator," *Luna Monthly* 8 (January 1970). Obituary of J. C. Henneberger.

Price, E. Hoffman. Price probably knows more about *WT* than anyone else living. His many articles ooze with information and behind-the-scenes anecdotes. See his series "The Jade Pagoda" in *Witchcraft & Sorcery*. Also his pieces "Farnsworth Wright," *The Ghost*, July 1944, and "Weird Tales: Cradle of Fantasy," *Lethe*, July 1946.

Smith, Reginald. *Weird Tales in the Thirties*. Santa Ana, Calif.: Smith, 1966. Reprinted in part in *WT 50*.

Tuck.

Witter, Richard. "From the Bygone Days of Weird Tales." *Fantasy Commentator* (Summer 1945).

See also specialist magazines *The Weird Tales Collector*, edited by Robert Weinberg (detailed in Section III) and *The Diversifier*, of which issues 20 and 21 (May and July 1977) were devoted to *WT* and contain stories and reminiscences.

INDEX SOURCES: The major index to *WT* is Cockcroft, IWFM, which lists contents by author and title, plus other bibliographic data. Cockcroft also published *Index to the Verse in Weird Tales* (1960). An issue index was included in *An Index on the Weird and Fantastica in Magazines*, compiled and published by Bradford M. Day (New York, 1953), complete to the November 1953 issue. A complete issue index, including the Moskowitz issues, was run in issues 1–5 of *The Weird Tales Collector* (1977–1979). IWFM; MIT; MT; NESFA-II; NESFA-III; NESFA-VIII; SFM; Tuck.

REPRINT SOURCES:

Magazines:

Canadian: First series, June–July 1936, 128 pp., 25¢, monthly, abridged from concurrent U.S. editions, but some covers displaying nudes suitably expurgated with well-placed announcements.

Second series, May 1942–November 1951. Followed format of U.S. editions but with all new artwork (until March 1945) and frequent reorganization of stories both within issues and between issues. In general Canadian issues from May 1942 to January 1945 correspond to the U.S. issues January 1942 to September 1944 (with variant volume numbering). There was no Canadian edition of the U.S. November 1944 issue. Canadian issues from March 1945 to January 1948 generally correspond to U.S. issues January 1945 to November 1947. There was no Canadian edition of the U.S. January 1948 issue. Issues from March 1948 to November 1951 identical to U.S. originals. The Canadian *WT* printed a few stories prior to their appearance in the U.S. issues, reprinted some items from the U.S. *Short Stories* not included in the U.S. *WT*, and also reprinted some stories and verse from U.S. issues under bogus pen-names. See full details in Parnell's *Monthly Terrors* and article by Mike Ashley "That Other *Weird Tales*" in *Etchings & Odysseys* 5, 1985. Total run: 14 + 58 = 72 issues.

British: First series, 3 issues, unnumbered and undated but released early 1942 by Gerald G. Swan, London. 48 pp./64 pp./48 pp., 6d. Correspond to abridged versions of U.S. issues September and November 1940 and January 1941.

Second series, 1 issue, unnumbered and undated but released in late 1946 by William Merrett, London, 36 pp., 1/6d. Three stories selected from U.S. October 1937 issue.

Third series, 23 issues, undated (first issue unnumbered), released during November 1949 and December 1953 by Thorpe and Porter, Leicester. 96pp., 1/- (except issues 11 to 15, 1/6d). Corresponds to U.S. issues July 1949–May 1953 (September 1949 U.S. not reprinted, and March and May 1953 issues reprinted in reverse order.

Fourth series, continues from third series by Thorpe & Porter, but corresponds to U.S. digest issues September 1953–May 1954, issued in U.K. as Volume 1, Number 1 (November 1953)–Volume 1, Number 5 (July 1954) bi-monthly. (Issue 3 confusingly mislabelled Volume 3, Number 1.) Total run: 3 + 1 + 23 + 5 = 32 issues.

Reprint Magazines: A number of magazines have drawn extensively upon *WT* for reprints. A special section in both *Satellite Science Fiction* and *The Man from U.N.C.L.E. Magazine* used many *WT* stories, as did the British magazine *Phantom*, and the Lowndes reprint magazines *Magazine of Horror*, *Startling Mystery Stories*, *Weird Terror Tales* and *Bizarre Fantasy Tales*. See also *Shock* and *Avon Fantasy Reader*.

Derivative Anthologies: Many anthologies have selected from *Weird Tales*, but the following have special relevance:

Asbury, Herbert. *Not at Night!*. New York: Macy-Macius, 1928. Twenty-five stories with twenty-four from *WT*. Selected from C. C. Thomson series (see below).

Ashley, Mike. *Weird Legacies*. London: Star Books, 1977. Nine stories, all from *WT*, plus introduction by Robert Bloch.

Haining, Peter. *Weird Tales*. Jersey: N. Spearman, 1976. Twenty-six items, facsimile reproduction from *WT* with historical introduction by Haining. The paperback editions lacked the facsimile reproduction and are inferior.

Margulies, Leo. *The Unexpected*. New York: Pyramid Books, 1961. Eleven stories mostly from late 1940s. *The Ghoul Keepers* (New York: Pyramid Books, 1961) 9 stories, mostly from 1940s. *Weird Tales* (New York: Pyramid Books, 1964) 8 stories, mostly from 1930s. *Worlds of Weird* (New York: Pyramid Books, 1965) 7 stories with important historical introduction by Sam Moskowitz who in fact ghost-edited this and the previous volume.

Stong, Philip D. *The Other Worlds*. New York: Funk, 1941. Regarded as a major landmark anthology because it was the first prestige anthology to select its contents from the pulp magazines. Twenty-five stories of which eleven came from *WT*— the single largest representative.

Thomson, Christine Campbell. CCT's "Not at Night" series was regarded as an unofficial British edition of *WT* in the 1920s. On a few occasions it published the stories before their U.S. appearance. Not all the series drew from *WT*, but the major titles are: *Not at Night* (1925), all 15 stories; *More Not at Night* (1926), all 15 stories; *You'll Need a Night Light* (1927), 14 out of 15 stories; *By Daylight Only* (1929), 15 of 20 stories; *Switch on the Light* (1931); *At Dead of Night* (1931), 8 of 15; *Grim Death* (1932) and *Keep on the Light* (1933), both 7 of 15; *Terror by Night* (1934), 9 of 15. The reprint *Not at Night Omnibus* (1937) contained 35 stories, of which 20 came from *WT*. There have been derivative paperback reprints. See also Asbury item above.

Weinberg, Robert. *Far Below and Other Horrors*. West Linn, Ore.: Fax Collector's Editions, 1974. Nine of eleven stories mostly from the Wright period. Also Weinberg's Lost Fantasies series has drawn almost exclusively from *WT*.

[Wright, Farnsworth]. *The Moon Terror*. Indianapolis: Popular Fiction, 1927. Four stories, published by *WT* itself (see above essay).

LOCATION SOURCES: Brown University Library; East Carolina University Library; Eastern New Mexico University Library; Grand Valley State College Library; M.I.T. Science Fiction Library; Pennsylvania State University Library; Temple University Library; Texas A&M University Library; University of Arizona Library; University of California-Los Angeles Library; University of Kansas Library; University of New Brunswick Library; University of Texas-Austin Library.

Publication History

TITLE: *Weird Tales*.

VOLUME DATA: Volume 1, Number 1, March 1923–. Latest issue at time of writing Volume 48, Number 4, 1982. Three series.

First series: Volume 1, Number 1, March 1923–Volume 46, Number 4, September 1954. Volume 1, four issues, monthly. Volume 2, four issues, monthly, but July/August 1923 issues combined. Volume 3, four issues, monthly, January–April 1924. Volume 4, three issues (but now Number 1). May/June/July issues combined. Then monthly, November and December 1924. Volume 5, Number 1, January 1925–Volume 16, Number 6, December 1930, six issues per volume, monthly. Volume 17, four issues, January–June/July 1931, bi-monthly from February/March issue. Volume 18, Number 1, August 1931–Volume 34, Number 6, December 1939, six issues per volume, monthly, except Volumes 18, 28 and 33 with five issues; August/September 1936 issues combined, as were June/July 1939 issues. Volume 35, ten issues, January 1940–July 1941, bi-monthly. Volume 36, twelve issues, September 1941–July 1943. Volumes 37 and 38, September 1943–July 1945, six issues per volume, bi-monthly. Volume 39, September 1945–September 1947, thirteen issues (both May and July 1947 issues numbered 11), bi-monthly. Volume 40, Number 1, November 1947–Volume 43, Number 6, September 1951, six issues per volume, bi-monthly. Volume 44, eight issues, November 1951–January 1953, bi-monthly. Volumes 45 and 46, March 1953–September 1954, six issues and four issues, respectively; bi-monthly. Total run: 279 issues.

Second series: Volume 47, Number 1, Summer 1973–Volume 47, Number 4, Summer 1974. Quarterly (but no Spring 1974 issue).

Third series: Volume 48, Number 1, Spring 1981–. Both issues 1 and 2 are dated Spring 1981 and were issued in December 1980. Issue 3 dated Fall 1981. Issue 4 dated Summer 1983.

Fourth Series: Volume 49, Number 1, Fall 1984.

Total run: 279 + 4 + 5 (to date), 288 issues.

PUBLISHERS: Rural Publications, Chicago, March 1923–May/June/July 1924; Popular Fiction Publishing Co., Chicago, November 1924–October 1938; Weird Tales, Inc., New York (a subsidiary of Short Stories, Inc.), November 1938–September

1954; Weird Tales, Los Angeles (a subsidiary of Renown Publications), Summer 1973–Summer 1974; Kensington Publishing Corp., New York, Spring 1981–Summer 1983; Weird Tales, c/o 8555 Sunset Blvd., Suite D, Los Angeles, Calif. 90069, Fall 1984–.

EDITORS: Edwin Baird, March 1923–April 1924; issue for May/June/July 1924 assembled by Jacob Henneberger and Otis A. Kline from dummies assembled by Baird; Farnsworth Wright, November 1924–March 1940; Dorothy McIlwraith, May 1940–September 1954 (with associates Henry A. Perkins, May 1940–September 1942; Lamont Buchanan, November 1942–September 1949); Sam Moskowitz, Summer 1973–Summer 1974; Lin Carter, Spring 1981–Summer 1983; Gil Lamont, 1984–.

FORMAT: Pulp, 192 pp., March–April 1923. Large Pulp, 64 pp., May 1923–April 1924; 192 pp., May/June/July 1924. Pulp, 144 pp., November 1924–December 1938; 160 pp., February–August 1939; 128 pp., September 1939–March 1943; 112 pp., May 1943–March 1944; 96 pp., May 1944–July 1953. Digest; 128 pp., September 1953–September 1954. Pulp, 96 pp., Summer 1973–Summer 1974. Pocketbook, 272 pp., Spring 1981 (both issues); 320 pp., Fall 1981; 288 pp., Summer 1983. Slick, 70 pp., Fall 1984.

PRICE: 25¢, March 1923–April 1924; 50¢, May/June/July 1924; 25¢, November 1924–August 1939; 15¢, September 1939–July 1947; 20¢, September 1947–March 1949; 25¢, May 1949–July 1953; 35¢, September 1953–September 1954; 75¢, Summer 1973–Summer 1974; $2.50, Spring 1981–Fall 1983; $2.95, Summer 1983; $2.50, Fall 1984.

Robert Weinberg

WEIRD TERROR TALES

At the close of the 1960s Health Knowledge Inc., the publisher of *Magazine of Horror*,* was striving to establish a large number of new titles in the magazine field in an effort to spread its overhead over a greater area and also to attain better distribution. The intention was that the editor, Robert A. W. Lowndes, would compile two magazine issues per month. So when two titles were dropped in 1969 (*Famous Science Fiction** and *World-Wide Adventures*) two new ones were created (*Weird Terror Tales* and *Bizarre Fantasy Tales**).

In the first issue, Lowndes tried to explain how the contents of the two magazines would be distinct, though he was forced to admit that almost any story in *Weird Terror* could appear in *Magazine of Horror*. Indeed, there was nothing to distinguish the format or general contents of either magazine other than that Lowndes featured at least one long story in each issue of *Weird Terror*.

The three issues that appeared contained mostly reprints, although one new story appeared each issue: "The Whispering Thing" by Eddy Bertin (which had previously been published in the United Kingdom), "The Laundromat" by Dick Donley and "The Cellar Room" by Steffan B. Aletti. The reprints came predominantly from *Weird Tales** and *Strange Tales** and included such scarce stories as "Dead Legs" by Edmond Hamilton, "Stragella" by Hugh B. Cave, "The Trap" by Henry S. Whitehead and "The Wheel" by H. Warner Munn.

In 1970 the parent publishing company, Acme News, was taken over by Countrywide Publications, which already published *Weird Comics* and *Terror Comics*. To avoid possible conflict and confusion over the titles, *Weird Terror Tales* was dropped.

Information Sources

BIBLIOGRAPHY:
Lowndes, Robert A.W. "The Health Knowledge Years," *Outworlds* 28/29.
————. Letter. *Science-Fiction Collector*, No. 8 (October 1979): 45–47.
INDEX SOURCES: Cook, Michael L., *Monthly Murders*, Westport, Conn.: Greenwood Press, 1982; Marshall, Gene, and Carl F. Waedt, "An Index to the Health Knowledge Magazines," *Science-Fiction Collector*, No. 3 (1977): 3–42; MT; SFM; SFM-II.
REPRINT SOURCES: None known.
LOCATION SOURCES: M.I.T. Science Fiction Library.

Publication History

TITLE: *Weird Terror Tales*.
VOLUME DATA: Volume 1, Number 1, Winter 1969/70–Volume 1, Number 3, Fall 1970. Quarterly. No Spring 1970 issue.
PUBLISHER: Health Knowledge Inc., Fifth Avenue, New York.
EDITOR: Robert A. W. Lowndes.
FORMAT: Digest, 128 pp.
PRICE: 50¢, Number 1, Winter 1969/70; 60¢, Number 2, Summer 1970–Number 3, Fall 1970.

Mike Ashley

WEIRD WORLD

Weird World was a short-lived British magazine of reasonably good quality for the period. It came from Gannet Press, originally a London-based firm and an offshoot of Scion, Ltd., the original publisher of *Vargo Statten Science Fiction Magazine.** Having gone bankrupt in 1954, Gannet was taken over by its printers, Merseyside Press, who operated under the name Gannet Press (Sales) Ltd. At this time Gannet was producing a number of risqué magazines like *Zest*, *Brash*, *Saucy*, *Hot* and *Gorgeous* which may have contributed to its demise. *Weird World* was probably among the last publications it issued when, in February 1956, it was hit by a printer's strike. The second issue is considerably more rare than the first.

Attractively illustrated by Roger Davis, the first issue carried all new stories. It is possible that most were pseudonymously written, but their quality was not an insult to the reader. "The Man Who Loved Cats," for instance, by Konstantin Faber, tells of a painter whose models, unaware of the fate of past models, become acquainted with the truth about his cats.

The second issue reprinted Poe's "The Fall of the House of Usher" and included stories of slightly lower quality. "Man Wanted" by Richard James, for example, is a science fiction tale of a man returning to Earth after five years in space only to find civilization destroyed by a nuclear war and a feudal society established. Somehow, though, the idea of "the terrible holocaust of Worthing" (a resort on the south coast of England) drags the story down into farce.

Nevertheless, *WW* could well have developed into a good magazine. There were plans for a companion title, *Fantastic World*, and the second issue announced a short story competition. But none of this came to pass.

Information Sources

BIBLIOGRAPHY:
Nicholls. *Encyclopedia*.
Tuck.
INDEX SOURCES: MIT; MT; SFM.
REPRINT SOURCES: None known.
LOCATION SOURCES: None known.

Publication History

TITLE: *Weird World*.
VOLUME DATA: Issues undated. Volume 1, Number 1, [October 1955]–Volume 1, Number 2 [January 1956].
PUBLISHER: Gannet Press, Birkenhead, England.
EDITOR: Not identified; may have been B. Z. Emmanuel, the original director of Gannet.
FORMAT: Small Pulp (saddle-stapled), 48 pp.
PRICE: 1/-.

Mike Ashley/Stephen Holland

WEIRDBOOK

Editor Paul Ganley recalled the origins of *Weirdbook* thus:

In 1967 I was bored. I'd taken a new job, teaching at Wilson College in Pennsylvania; I had gotten settled into the routine. I was restless. I bought an MGB convertible. I took flying lessons. I found a few new girlfriends. I went to a World SF Con for the first time in 13 years. I figured out what was wrong. I wasn't publishing anything. So I decided to start a magazine and call it *Weirdbook* (after *Redbook* and *Bluebook*). I got stories from Joseph Payne Brennan, H. Warner Munn and Robert E. Howard, but most of the rest I either wrote myself or dredged up from my old mimeographed fanzine of the early 1950s.

Weirdbook was generally ignored in its early days because of its grotesquely bad covers and its flat, uninspired interiors, broken only by small illustrations that rivaled the covers as base designs. Paul Ganley has never made any concerted effort to ''present'' the material he publishes—it stands or falls on its own merits, or lack of them. This has remained true throughout *Weirdbook*'s existence. However, much of the material has merits, as an ever increasing number of fans have learned. It is because of Ganley's lack of blatant showmanship that *Weirdbook* has become so respected by readers and contributors alike.

By the fourth issue all reprints and pseudonymously penned fiction by Ganley had disappeared. It cannot be said that *Weirdbook* matured over the issues, as it has always had a latent maturity. The fiction it has published, a mixture of horror, the bizarre and weird fantasy, has never been of classic standard, but all has been good, readable fare. It has featured stories by Brian Lumley, Adrian Cole, Joseph Payne Brennan, Darrell Schweitzer, Janet Fox, H. Warner Munn, Charles Saunders, William Scott Home, Michael Bishop, C. L. Grant, Tanith Lee and many others. Poetry has also featured strongly in *Weirdbook*, with Munn and Brennan being joined by L. Sprague de Camp, Robert E. Howard and a host of others.

With the upsurge of interest in fantasy fiction in the early 1970s, *Weirdbook* started to take notice of itself, and Ganley improved the layout and presentation. Covers by Roy Krenkel, Steve Fabian and D. Bruce Berry brought about a radical improvement, and the issues increased in thickness, hinting at much promise. By this time Ganley was expanding his own publishing enterprises. Having been the general coordinator for *Toadstool Wine*,* he now launched a companion magazine, *Eerie Country*, which was an overflow magazine to use up those stories too long in the inventory. He also published his first hardcover book, *Hollow Faces, Merciless Moons* (Buffalo: Weirdbook Press, 1977) by longtime contributor William Scott Home. The next year Ganley followed it by a hardcover edition of the tenth anniversary issue of *Weirdbook* (issue 13), a bumper number which included Michael Bishop's impressive ''Within the Walls of Tyre'' and H. Warner Munn's ''The Stairway in the Sea.''

Some magazines have been more impressive and shown more promise than *Weirdbook* but have overreached themselves and rapidly faded. Slowly but surely *Weirdbook* has established itself as one of the most reliable sources of weird fiction, and should continue for as long as Paul Ganley's enthusiasm lasts.

Information Sources

INDEX SOURCES: ISPF-2; MT.
REPRINT SOURCES: None known.
LOCATION SOURCES: Brown University Library; M.I.T. Science Fiction Library.

Publication History

TITLE: *Weirdbook*.
VOLUME DATA: No volume numbering. Issue 1, [Summer] 1968–. Latest issue sighted Number 16, [March] 1982. First ten issues constitute Series 1. Number 11, [Spring]

1977 began Series 2. Schedule irregular. Initially annual; a semi-annual schedule
was attempted in 1977. Two issues appeared in 1973. No issue for 1980. Latest
issue sighted is Number 19, Spring 1984.

PUBLISHER: Paul Ganley, Chambersburg, Pennsylvania, Numbers 1–5 (1972); thereafter at Buffalo, New York.

EDITOR: W. Paul Ganley.

FORMAT: A4 Printed; 32 pp., Numbers 1–10; 64 pp., Numbers 11 and 12; 96 pp.,
Number 13; 64 pp., Numbers 14 to 19; 64 pp., Number 15 only, 68 pp.

PRICE: 75¢, Numbers 1–7; $1.00, Numbers 8–10; $3.00, Numbers 11 and 12; $5.00,
Number 13 [$15.00 in hardcover]; $3.00, Number 14; $4.50, Numbers 15 and
16; $5.00 Numbers 17 to 19.

Jon Harvey/Mike Ashley

WHISPERS

As editor Stuart David Schiff explained in the first issue, dated July 1973,
Whispers arose out of Schiff's suggestion of assuming the editorship and publication of *The Arkham Collector*,* which had folded with the death of August
Derleth in 1971. The magazine was originally to be titled *Whispers from Arkham*,
but it was shortened to *Whispers* to avoid any conflict with the legal position of
Arkham House. In hindsight this was a blessing, as it allowed *Whispers* to
develop its own identity while still acting in tribute to Arkham House and its
authors.

Schiff cited three main goals for *Whispers* at the outset, all aimed primarily
at collectors: first, to present all the current news in the horror, fantasy and
macabre fiction fields; second, to publish articles of bibliographic importance;
and third, to present new fiction.

Whispers has succeeded reasonably well in accomplishing the first of these
aims, although trying to keep news current while maintaining an irregular publishing schedule meant that even with a loose-leaf news supplement insertion
with each issue several important items were nevertheless overlooked. The articles were occasionally of a scholarly nature, but the majority were nostalgic
reminiscences by *Weird Tales** and Arkham House authors. Portfolios by artists
such as Stephen Fabian, Lee Brown Coye and Frank Utpatel have been featured,
but a number of the ''spot'' illustrations have left a lot to be desired.

Whispers' main strength, however, lay in its fiction and, as a paying market,
it has attracted top-flight authors. This did not always work in the magazine's
favor—big-name writers do not always produce quality fiction—and this has
occasionally caused some rancor among *Whispers*' readers. Nevertheless Karl
Edward Wagner's ''Sticks'' (March 1974) went on to win the British Fantasy
Award for that year's Best Short Fiction and, two years later, *Whispers* itself
received the World Fantasy Award in the non-professional category. A second
British Fantasy Award went to Fritz Leiber's ''The Button Moulder'' from the
special Leiber issue (October 1979).

Other issues have laid special emphasis on certain aspects of fiction. The July 1974 issue contained an article by Leiber on H. P. Lovecraft's story "The White Ship" which led to a portfolio of pictures inspired by the story with contributions by Frank Utpatel, Lee Brown Coye, Alan Hunter, Vincent diFate and others, and was rounded out by a holograph of Lovecraft's original manuscript of the story.

The magazine appeared fairly regularly at first but Schiff's employment as a dentist in the U.S. army and his resultant postings have caused delays. Schiff's energies have also been channelled into his own Whispers Press producing quality edition hardcovers, and he also edits a regular *Whispers* anthology series.

In recent years Schiff has concentrated on producing special 'double' issues of *Whispers* with sections dedicated to certain writers. Manly Wade Wellman was the first author under the spotlight in the October 1978 issue followed by Leiber in October 1979. Subsequent issues have concentrated on Ramsey Campbell (March 1982), Stephen King (August 1982) and Whitley Strieber (October 1983). Harlan Ellison and Charles L. Grant issues are planned.

Information Sources

BIBLIOGRAPHY: None.
INDEX SOURCES: ISPF; ISPF-2; MT; NESFA-IV; NESFA-V.
REPRINT SOURCES:
Magazines: See *Toadstool Wine*.
Derivative Anthologies: Stuart D. Schiff, *Whispers* (Garden City, N.Y.: Doubleday, 1977), *Whispers II* (Garden City, N.Y.: Doubleday, 1979), *Whispers III* (Garden City, N.Y.: Doubleday, 1981), *Whispers IV* (Garden City, N.Y.: Doubleday, 1983), contain both stories from the magazine and originals.
LOCATION SOURCES: Brown University Library; M.I.T. Science Fiction Library.

Publication History

TITLE: *Whispers*.
VOLUME DATA: Volume 1, Number 1, July 1973–current. Latest issue Volume 6, Number 1/2, December 1984. Four issues per volume, but four issues combined. Volume 2, Number 2/3, June 1975; Volume 3, Number 3/4, October 1978; Volume 4, Number 1/2, October 1979; Volume 4, Number 3/4, March 1982. Volume 5, Number 1/2, August 1982; Volume 5, Number 3/4, October 1983. Original schedule quarterly, but soon became irregular. There was also a nonsequence issue 8½, August 1976. Issues now number 22, but because of combined issues, total run is 15 (plus one-half).
PUBLISHER: Stuart David Schiff, at Fayetteville, N.C., Numbers 1–8; Chapel Hill, N.C., Number 9; Brown Mills, N.J., to Number 13/14; Binghamton, N.Y., thereafter.
EDITOR: Stuart David Schiff.
FORMAT: Digest (saddle-stapled and then perfect bound). 64 pp., Numbers 1–5; 132 pp., Number 6/7; 64 pp., Number 8; (12 pp., Number 8½); 68 pp., Numbers 9 and 10; 132 pp., Number 11/12; 128 pp., Number 13/14; 176 pp., Number 15/16 on.

PRICE: $1.50, Numbers 1–4; $1.75, Number 5; $3.50, Number 6/7; $2.00, Number 8;
    (50¢, Number 8½); $2.00, Numbers 9 and 10; $4.00, Numbers 11/12 and 13/14;
    $5.00 thereafter.

Jon Harvey/Mike Ashley

WITCHCRAFT & SORCERY

New version of a magazine which started as *Coven 13*. See COVEN 13.

THE WITCH'S TALES

Street and Smith had had enormous success when it issued a single-character pulp magazine in 1931 to tie in with its radio program introduced by The Shadow. That did not mean that such success could necessarily be repeated, but over the next fifty years a number of radio programs spawned magazines, though few have lived to tell the tale.

One of the earliest was *The Witch's Tales*, inspired by a radio program of the same name which had been broadcast since May 1931. The magazine, a thin, bedsheet publication, went on sale on September 23, 1936, cover dated November. The cover had a painting by Elmer Stoner portraying the old crone Nancy who related the stories and a borderfiller of her cat, Satan. Inset was a photograph of Alonzo Deen Cole, who scripted the radio series and was purportedly editor of the magazine. Cole, who later had two stories in *Weird Tales*,* did little work for *TWT*, however. He probably wrote the lead story in the first issue, "The Madman," but his contribution in the second issue, "Mrs. Hawker's Will," had been adapted to story form by Laurence D. Smith from the original radio script. The managing editor of the magazine, and the man who actually assembled the issues, was Tom Chadburn.

TWT is an odd publication in that apart from the Witch's tales themselves, and a few pages of true strange experiences, plus a story by Laurence Smith in his own right, the remainder of the contents were probably all reprints. The researches of Sam Moskowitz have found that at least three of the stories originated in the American edition of the British *Pearson's Magazine* at the turn of the century. "Phantom of the Links," a ghostly golfing story by John C. Haywood, had originally appeared as "The Gray People" in the March 1906 issue. "The Death-Trap" by George Daulton, about a monster in the New York sewers, was in the March 1908 issue, and "The Monster of Lake LaMetrie" by Wardon Allan Curtis, a quite remarkable story about the transplanting of a man's brain into the body of a prehistoric creature, came from the September 1899 issue. In addition, it is known that William Hamilton Osborne, who appeared with "Fountain of Youth" in the first issue, had been a prolific contributor to *The Black Cat** twenty years earlier, but whether this story originated there has yet to be established. The sequel to "Fountain of Youth," entitled "The Habit of Death," was promised for the second issue but was not published. All illustrations for the magazine were by Elmer Stoner, and a few were in two-tone, but in general were rather hasty sketches.

Significantly, the second issue carried no announcements of forthcoming stories, although it did solicit submissions for the true experiences column. It is unlikely that the publishers would have known at that time how the first issue had been selling, and it is likely that other factors contributed to the magazine's demise.

The reprints selected were of high quality, though it is probable that they would not have appealed to the general reader of American pulp magazines in the mid-1930s. The strong action implied by the cover of the second issue was not delivered in the contents, and it may be that though the magazine appealed to readers of *Weird Tales* and devotees of the radio series, distribution problems did not enable *TWT* to reach its true audience.

Information Sources

BIBLIOGRAPHY:
Jones, Bob. "The Witch's Tales," *WSFA Journal*.
Moskowitz, Sam. Introduction to "The Gray People." *Startling Mystery Stories* 8 (Spring 1968): 31–33. Much of this information is repeated in Moskowitz's introduction to "The Monster of Lake LaMetrie," in *Science Fiction by Gaslight* (Cleveland: World Pub., Co., 1968), p. 177.
Tuck.
INDEX SOURCES: *Fantasy Collector*, No. 119; MT; SFM.
REPRINT SOURCES: None known.
LOCATION SOURCES: M.I.T. Science Fiction Library.

Publication History

TITLE: *The Witch's Tales*.
VOLUME DATA: Volume 1, Number 1, November 1936–Volume 1, Number 2, December 1936. Monthly. Total run: 2 issues.
PUBLISHER: The Carwood Publishing Co., New York.
EDITOR: Tom Chadburn.
FORMAT: Bedsheet, 48 pp.
PRICE: 15¢.

Mike Ashley/Frank H. Parnell

WONDER STORIES

The founding of the Wonder Stories group reflected the business acumen and resilience of Hugo Gernsback. With the future of *Amazing Stories** in the balance, and with bankruptcy proceedings filed against him, Gernsback and his brother Sidney defiantly formed Stellar Publishing. Within weeks the initial issue (dated

June 1929) of the new *Science Wonder Stories* (*SWS*) was in production, to be followed shortly thereafter by *Air Wonder Stories** and *Science Wonder Quarterly* (*Wonder Stories Quarterly**). *SWS* was large-size, 96 pages, printed on glazed pulp paper of good quality with smooth edges, and was stacked with the slicks on the newsstands. It sold for 25 cents, partly on the theory that the higher the price, the better the quality.

SWS flourished. It was from very much the same mold as *Amazing*, with Frank R. Paul serving as art director and providing all of the covers and most of the interiors. As managing editor, however, Gernsback no longer had the aging T. O'Conor Sloane. Instead, he employed the twenty-seven-year-old David Lasser, fifty years Sloane's junior. Lasser was the complete opposite of Sloane, not just in age but in attitude. Whereas Sloane had grave doubts that man would ever climb Everest, let alone get into space, Lasser was one of the driving forces behind the formation of the American Rocket Society in March 1930, acting as its first president. He also wrote one of the first nonfiction books on rocketry, *The Conquest of Space* (New York: Penguin, 1931). Lasser thus brought a verve and dedication to *SWS* that was missing from *Amazing* except in Gernsback's editorials.

The magazine's masthead boasted an impressive list of names. Apart from Gernsback, Lasser and Paul, there were two associate editors, M. E. Dame and C. P. Mason. Dame was more involved with *Air Wonder Stories* and left when it merge with *SWS* a year later. Mason was associated more with Gernsback's technical magazines but helped out on *SWS* by providing answers for the "Science Questions and Answers" column and contributing to the "Science News of the Month." In addition, there were eighteen "Associate Science Editors" whose function, according to the magazine, was to "pass upon the scientific principles of all stories." They covered the fields of astronomy, botany, chemistry, electricity, entomology, mathematics, medicine, physics, psychology, radio and zoologoy. Probably the best-known name among them was Dr. Lee deForest, the man who made radio possible, but the list also included Donald H. Menzel, a noted astronomer, friend of science fiction and enemy of UFOs, and David H. Keller, possibly the most popular SF writer at that time, but also a medical authority and physician. It is not known to what extent the services of all these people were used, although Keller, who was easily accessible, was often consulted.

The editorial system was the same as it had been at *Amazing*. Lasser would read the incoming manuscripts and select those he thought had merit, passing them to Gernsback, who made the final decision on acceptance. With guidelines from Gernsback, Lasser would then assemble the issues with other staff helping sort out the various scientific and letter columns.

Many of the same authors who had debuted in *Amazing* continued with *SWS*. Curiously, Edmond Hamilton, who appeared regularly in the companion magazines, had no stories in *Science Wonder Stories* during its first year, but Miles J. Breuer, Francis Flagg, Harl Vincent, Stanton Coblentz, Fletcher Pratt and David H. Keller were all represented. For the first issue Gernsback fell back on

H. G. Wells as a selling power, reprinting "The Diamond Maker"; otherwise the stories were new.

Aware that many of the magazine's readers were youngsters, and knowing the growing reputation of the pulps, Gernsback emphasized in his first editorial that all of the stories were "clean" and that the only thing they would stimulate was the imagination. He also underlined the scientific aspect of the content, maintaining that the stories were educational. "Prophetic Fiction Is the Mother of Scientific Fact" was the slogan on the editorial page. It was rather contradictory, therefore, that later issues would bear the banner MYSTERY—ADVENTURE—ROMANCE along the top of the magazine.

Science fiction in magazine form was still in its infancy in 1929 and was continuing to attract new writers, establishing the first real post-Wellsian generation of SF authors. One of the first was Ed Earl Repp, who had a double debut with "Beyond Gravity" in the August 1929 *Air Wonder Stories* and his short novel "The Radium Pool," serialized starting in the August *SWS*. Repp soon became a regular Gernsback author and contributed prolifically to the SF magazines during the 1930s and early 1940s. The Merrittesque "Radium Pool" is probably his best work. Raymond Z. Gallun also had a double debut in the November 1929 issues of the two magazines, and *Wonder Stories* remained his main market for the next four years until he established himself in *Astounding Stories (Analog Science Fiction*)* in 1934 as one of the major names in SF. Less known today but a writer of enjoyable stories at the time was Drury D. Sharp, who made his SF debut with "The Eternal Man" (August 1929), which was so popular on its first publication that a sequel appeared in the *Quarterly* in the following year. Other writers who first appeared in the pages of *SWS* include Gawain Edwards, John Scott Campbell and Frank Brueckel, but the real era of discovery would come in a few more years.

During *SWS*'s first year Gernsback introduced American readers to stories translated from the French and German, a policy he continued throughout *Wonder*'s existence. Among his first selections was a nonfiction work, *Problem der Befahrung des Weltraums*, translated by Francis M. Currier and published as "The Problems of Space Flying" in three parts in the July to September 1929 issues. The author was the Austrian Captain Potocnik who used the alias "Herman Noordung." Sam Moskowitz states that the cover for the August 1929 issue, which illustrated Noordung's article, was the first color representation of an earth satellite ever published. Another such piece was "Can Man Free Himself from Gravity" by the German Dr. Wolff, published in the February 1930 issue. Perhaps this association attracted direct contributions from foreign writers and thereby introduced the ephemerally popular Hendrik Dahl Juve.

SWS's dominant writer was David H. Keller, who appeared in ten of the twelve issues. In the very first issue appeared "The Threat of the Robot," believed to be the first story to use the word "robot" in its title, and following Keller's usual theme of a warning against uncontrolled automation. Then came a rather weak example of Keller's work, "The Boneless Horror," but the next issue saw his short novel "The Feminine Metamorphosis" (August 1929), a rather daring story for the period dealing with an independent group of literally misanthropic women who undergo treatment to become male in the long-term hope of ridding the world of men. These three stories were followed in quick succession by three serials, the popular if controversial "The Human Termites," "The Conquerors," and its sequel "The Evening Star." Thereafter Keller became so swamped by his editorial and writing activities with Gernsback's medical publications that his appearances in *Wonder* decreased rapidly; he had only eight more stories published there over the next six years plus a further adventure of the Conquerors completed by David Lasser and serialized as "The Time Projector" (July–August 1931).

What was most evident in *SWS*, was the rapid growth in organized fandom. Gernsback, of course, promoted contact between readers in the letter columns of his magazine and was always instituting competitions. One such, launched in the Spring 1930 *Science Wonder Quarterly*, had been "What I Have Done to Spread Science Fiction." The winner was Raymond A. Palmer, who would soon establish himself as one of the leading SF fans and who had already sold his first story, "The Time Ray of Jandra," to Gernsback. It was originally scheduled for the April 1930 *SWS*, but its length caused it to be squeezed out. Palmer's debut was thus in the June 1930 issue of the newly titled *Wonder Stories*. Runner-up in the competition was Conrad H. Ruppert, who suggested the idea of a science fiction week. Gernsback took this idea to heart and promoted it in the May 1930 *SWS*, suggesting that March 31 to April 7 be set aside for just such an occasion. The purpose of the week, Gernsback explained, was "to induce every true lover of science fiction to spend this allotted time in educating friends and acquaintances, and others, in the merits of science fiction." Promoting SF almost like a religion, Gernsback went on to say: "Not only is science fiction an idea of tremendous import, but it is to be an important factor in making the world a better place to live in, through educating the public to the possibilities of science and the influence of science on life."

It is ironic, however, that in the same issue that Gernsback was lauding the virtues of science fiction and science, he had to admit that "it has been felt for some time that the word 'Science' has tended to retard the progress of the magazine, because many people had the impression that it is a sort of a scientific periodical rather than a fiction magazine" (p. 1099). For that reason Gernsback had placed the seemingly out-of-place MYSTERY—ADVENTURE—ROMANCE banner atop the front cover, and had been fading out the word "Science" from the title by the use of a light yellow ink, much to the consternation of the readers. From the June issue the word had vanished completely and *Wonder Stories* (*WS*) was born. There was no difference otherwise in the magazine. Surprisingly, the readers approved of the changes.

The old *Science Wonder Stories* was the first periodical to use the term "science fiction," coined by Gernsback in an effort to disassociate himself further from his old magazine and thus the term "scientifiction" that he had used there. The term ''science-fiction'' (with a hyphen) had earlier been coined by William Wilson, a totally forgotten Victorian writer, in a book entitled *A Little Earnest Book upon a Great Old Subject* (London: Darton, 1851). It would be over 120 years before anyone rediscovered that book, during which time Gernsback and *Wonder Stories* had popularized the term independently.

The title change was only one aspect of the changing face of *Wonder Stories*. Gernsback was obviously aware of a new rival to his publications in the shape of *Astounding Stories of Super Science*. There was no real competition from *Amazing Stories* since that and *Wonder* had the same policy and looked the same. *Astounding*, however, was a pure pulp adventure magazine costing five cents less than *Wonder* and offering many of the big names in SF, including Murray Leinster and Ray Cummings, neither of whom featured in Gernsback's new magazines. After only five issues of the new *Wonder Stories*, therefore, Gernsback converted *WS* from large to pulp size. This brought a general outcry from the readers, who hated to see their magazine degraded in this fashion. Gernsback kept *WS* in pulp format for a year before switching back to the large format. By then the Depression had begun, and Gernsback probably felt he would be safer if his magazine was associated more with the technical and slick magazines. Gernsback gave as the reason, however, the simple fact that in this format the magazine could be saddle-stapled and thus could lie open flat without having to be held open. At the same time Gernsback reduced the cover price to fifteen cents, thus undercutting *Astounding* by five cents. This price reduction only lasted until the March 1933 issue, after which it returned to twenty-five cents. Gernsback had also drastically cut the number of pages in *WS* but now restored them. The year 1933, however, in the depth of the Depression, was a bleak year for *WS*, and by June the magazine had slipped to bi-monthly publication. Eventually, in November, *WS* once again went pulp, a format it retained thereafter. By that time the worst of the Depression had passed and, as 1934 showed signs of a revival, *WS* entered a brighter phase of existence.

Despite the rivalry of *Astounding* until 1933, *WS* was almost certainly the best magazine on the stalls for the sheer inventiveness in the stories. *Astounding* relied predominantly on adventure fiction with scientific connotations. *Wonder*, however, now bannered itself alternatively ADVENTURES OF FUTURE SCIENCE and THE MAGAZINE OF PROPHETIC FICTION, and still concentrated on the application of scientific inventions or discoveries in the future, present and past. Moreover, *WS* openly encouraged new writers, usually by way of competitions, and thus helped the field grow and establish itself. Although *Astounding* was not closed to new writers, it was more accessible to those who had already established themselves in the field or in other forms of pulp fiction.

Thus the majority of the writers who debuted in SF in the years 1930 to 1933 made the breakthrough in *Wonder Stories*, even though they may have gone on to make a name for themselves elsewhere. One such writer was Charles R. Tanner, who had made it into print with a gimmick story, ''The Color of Space,'' in the March 1930 *SWS*. This story had been the winner of the cover contest in the November 1929 issue. Tanner soon reappeared with a longer and far more adventurous interplanetary story, "The Flight of the Mercury." He never again appeared in *WS* but two years later immortalized himself in *Amazing* with the story "Tumithak of the Corridors."

Another contest winner was P. Schuyler Miller, who first appeared in print in the July 1930 *Wonder* with "The Red Plague," the winner of the February 1930 cover contest. Although Miller's best stories appeared elsewhere, mostly in *Astounding*, he did not desert *WS*. He made six contributions in all, of which the best remembered—perhaps because Isaac Asimov included it in his *Before the Golden Age* anthology—is "Tetrahedra of Space" (November 1931).

John Beynon Harris was the first major find of 1931. A British writer, later to become world renowned under the alias John Wyndham, Harris debuted in the May 1931 issue with an intriguing time puzzler, "Worlds to Barter." Harris had seven more stories in *WS*, including "The Venus Adventure" (May 1932) and "Wanderers of Time" (March 1933), but ironically his best story of the period, "The Lost Machine," appeared in *Amazing Stories*.

The month after Harris' debut saw the first appearance of Frank K. Kelly, then only sixteen years old, with "The Light Bender." Kelly is all but forgotten today, but in the early 1930s he was a very popular writer. He deserted the field to follow his chosen career as journalist. Kelly showed commendable restraint in his fiction and was not carried away by youthful exuberance. Indeed, in his most powerful story, "The Moon Tragedy" (October 1933), Kelly portrays the death of the early moon colonists with a poignancy that was years ahead of its time.

The best-known discovery of 1931, however, was Clifford D. Simak who, though having earlier sold a story to *Amazing*, nevertheless debuted in the December *Wonder* with a Wellsian time travel tale, "The World of the Red Sun." Simak sold two other stories to *Wonder* before temporarily deserting the field, returning in 1938 to establish himself as one of the major names in the pages of *Astounding*.

The year 1931 had also seen a number of stories from the writing team of Nat Schachner and Arthur Leo Zagat. The pair had first appeared in the magazine in the September 1930 issue with "In 20,000 A.D.," an astonishing tale that had demanded a sequel in "Back to 20,000 A.D." (March 1931). Schachner, who is also forgotten today, was one of the most popular SF writers in the 1930s and was extremely prolific, in both the SF and terror pulps. He soon split from Zagat and wrote on his own. Although he subsequently established himself in *Astounding*, he served a solid apprenticeship in *Wonder*.

The year 1933 was the year of technocracy for Hugo Gernsback. For a while he suspected that it marked the way for the future, and in the Depression years it was but one of many straws at which drowning men clutched. Gernsback put out two issues of *Technocracy Review* and told of the "Wonders of Technocracy" in his editorial for the March 1933 *WS*. At the same time he published a series of articles in *Everyday Science and Mechanics*. By now, however, Gernsback had decided that technocracy was a bad idea, and he soon phased out all mention of it in the magazine. However, he had commissioned a series of stories from Schachner on technocracy, and these ran their course. There were two preludes to the series, "The Eternal Dictator" in the February 1933 *WS*, followed by "The Robot Technocrat" in March. Then came a three-part sequence under the general heading of "Revolt of the Scientists," which showed the scientists rebelling against the absurdities of authorities and establishing rule themselves over industry and commerce. Schachner continued the story in "The Great Oil War" and "The Final Triumph" in the May and June 1933 issues. He presented a convincing argument in favor of technocracy and doubtless influenced many young readers, among them Ray Bradbury, who was supporting technocracy in his late teens. Technocracy remained a favored ideal of the 1930s, but its following was dispersed during the war years.

Schachner was one of the most popular contributors to *Wonder* during Lasser's editorship, but possibly the best writer during those years and the one most closely associated with the magazine was Canadian Laurence Manning, who had become a close friend of Gernsback. Manning had first appeared in the May 1930 *SWS* in collaboration with Fletcher Pratt on "The City of the Living Dead." He next reappeared in the *Quarterly* with his downbeat but realistic story of Martian exploration, "The Voyage of the *Asteroid*." Its sequel, "The Wreck of the *Asteroid*," ran as a three-part serial starting in the December 1932 *Wonder Stories* and was regarded by many as the best story of the year. Immediately following the conclusion of the serial, Manning began a new series of stories of Wellsian scope, starting with "The Man Who Awoke" (March 1933), which takes Norman Winters, through suspended animation, two thousand years into the future. Later stories in the series followed each month as Winters progressed on through the millennia, culminating in "The Elixir" where, in 25,000 A.D., Winters seeks the secret of complete immortality. The idea was far from new in science fiction, but Manning was one of those rare creatures in early SF—a good writer—and the series proved extremely popular. Over forty years later, just after Manning's death, the series appeared for the first time in book form as *The Man Who Awoke* (New York: Ballantine, 1975).

Established writers who furthered their career in *Wonder Stories* included Clark Ashton Smith. Smith appeared in more issues of *WS* than any other contributor apart from Laurence Manning, with twelve stories, from "Marooned in Andromeda" in October 1930 to "The Visitor from Mlok" in May 1933. Far less scientific than the other fiction but containing imagery that is a blend between Merritt and Lovecraft, Smith's stories are, in hindsight, among the most fascinating in the magazine. Only Clark Ashton Smith could describe the dust on Mars as being "ferruginous" as he does in "Dweller in Martian Depths" (March 1933), one of his most atmospheric contributions. Another was "The Invisible City" (June 1932), where an archeological expedition to the Middle East discovers an alien ultraviolet city in the desert. But without a doubt his best was "The City of the Singing Flame" (July 1931), which has remained popular to this day. Its immediate success led to the inevitable sequel, "Beyond the Singing Flame" (November 1931).

Edmond Hamilton did not appear in the pages of *WS* until the April 1931 issue, but that marked one of his most impressive early stories, "The Man Who Evolved," where Hamilton explores the concept of cyclical evolution. Later contributions include the cautious "A Conquest of Two Worlds," which considers the consequences of the clash of a scientifically advanced civilization with one less so.

One of the big SF names to appear in *WS* at this time was the mathematician Eric Temple Bell, who wrote under the pseudonym John Taine. Most of his SF appeared directly in book form, a rarity in those days, so that the serialization of "The Time Stream" in three parts starting in the December 1931 issue was something of an event. Brian Stableford, writing in the revised edition of Neil Barron's *Anatomy of Wonder* (New York: Bowker, 1981), has called this "the best of Taine's novels . . . more sober in tone than his extravagant stories . . . [it] . . . is by no means simply an imaginative display of spectacular violence."

Taine was Scottish by birth, and *WS* was a regular home for SF from beyond the United States. British contributors apart from John Beynon Harris, already mentioned, included Festus Pragnell, Benson Herbert, J. M. Walsh, and later Philip Cleator, H. O. Dickinson and W. P. Cockroft. From Australia came Arthur G. Stangland and later Alan Connell, and from Germany and France came a host of translations. The most frequent European contributor was Otfrid von Hanstein, one of science fiction's few nonagenarians (he died in 1959 at age ninety). After two novels were published complete in the *Quarterly*, three were serialized in *WS*: "Utopia Island" (May–June 1931), "In the Year 8000" (July–August 1932) and "The Hidden Colony" (January–March 1935). Hanstein was an imaginative writer whose work survived well in translation (even though four different translators worked on these three novels). Less successful were some of the French works by Eugene Thebault and Conrad de Richter which appeared in later issues.

At this time there were a few women SF writers, and Gernsback, being far from the misogynist that history has painted him, welcomed their work in his magazines. Clare Winger Harris and M. F. Rupert were two earlier writers, while one of the regulars in *WS* was Leslie F. Stone. She had five stories in the magazine, starting with "The Conquest of Gola" (April 1931). Of merit were "The Hell Planet" (June 1932)—one of SF's rare visits to the hypothetical planet of Vulcan that was once suspected of existing sunward of Mercury—and "Gulliver, 3000 AD" (May 1933), a long story set on Jupiter.

Always fond of experimenting, Gernsback tried a new contest in the form of a round-robin story, "The Moon Doom," started in the February 1933 issue by Nathaniel Salisbury. It was a typical disaster (and for that matter disastrous) story of the moon being dislodged from its orbit following collision with a rogue asteroid, and its spiralling inwards to Earth. Readers were invited to send in their continuation of the story, which had to be delivered within ten days. Just how this contest was judged and how the stories were fitted into the next issue in time is still something of a mystery. The episodes, which were painfully amateur, bore the hallmark of all "good" serials: the cliff-hanger ending.

Many SF fans sent their own fanzines to Gernsback, and seventeen-year-old Charles D. Hornig was no exception. He had just started *The Fantasy Fan* (see the article in Section III) with the first issue, dated September 1933, circulated in July. Gernsback was impressed and sent a telegram to Hornig asking him to visit the *Wonder Stories* offices. It so happened that David Lasser was now so involved with the Socialist movement and workers' unions that he could not devote any more of his time to editing, and Gernsback was looking for a new editor. Although a little shaken at Hornig's youth, Gernsback hired him, and Hornig became the youngest professional SF editor, starting his duties with the November 1933 issue. Hornig immediately instituted a "new policy" for stories, a drive for new ideas and a fresh treatment to bring vitality back to SF, which, Hornig believed, had grown stale in the last few years. His drive coincided with the "thought-variant" policy that Tremaine and Hall instigated at *Astounding* in the same month.

The year 1934 was probably *Wonder*'s best year, and 1935 was a close second. For although its stories could not compete with those in *Astounding*, it was in *WS* that Stanley G. Weinbaum first appeared, and it was the July 1934 issue that featured "A Martian Odyssey." As Isaac Asimov remarked, "A Martian Odyssey" was the first story to be published in the SF pulps that withstood the test of time. Weinbaum had only five other stories published in *WS* as he was soon lured away by *Astounding*.

Nothing else *WS* ever published can compare with "A Martian Odyssey." Perhaps the best that *WS* could offer was a new series of stories by Laurence Manning, which told of the individual exploits of members of the Stranger Club. There were five stories in all, one of which, "Seeds from Space" (June 1935), may have given John Wyndham the idea for *The Day of the Triffids*

Both stories may in turn owe something to "The Spore Doom" by the brothers Earl and Otto Binder, who wrote as Eando Binder. Published in the February 1934 issue, "The Spore Doom" told of Earth in the midst of biological warfare in 1975 and of the results when one side unleashes a new strain of fungus which, in time, takes over the whole surface of the planet. Eando Binder had been a regular by-line in *WS* ever since "The Moon Mines" (April 1933), but the best contributions were the two serials "Enslaved Brains" (July–September 1934) and "Dawn to Dusk" (November 1934–January 1935).

Among the regulars who continued to appear were Edmond Hamilton, Leslie F. Stone and Stanton A. Coblentz. But the new writers were bringing the best works to *WS*, though none with such a force as Weinbaum. Emma Vanne, who may have been related to E. J. Van Name, had three stories in earlier issues of *WS* under the alias Jim Vanny. Australian writer Alan Connell had first appeared with a fairly straightforward time travel story, "The Reign of the Reptiles"

(August 1935), but followed it with possibly the strangest story to appear in the magazine, "Dream's End" (November 1935).

Another new writer was Donald A. Wollheim. Better known today as an editor and as the publisher of his own line of DAW Books, Wollheim made his fictional debut with "The Man from Ariel" in the January 1934 issue. Wollheim had only one other story in the magazine, "The Space Lens" (September 1935), which appeared under the alias of Millard Verne Gordon, but Wollheim's involvement with the magazine is significant for two other reasons.

The first was that Wollheim knew his own mind and was not to be treated lightly. Gernsback's habit of not paying his authors was common knowledge by 1935, and he had not changed his ways in the ten years he had been publishing SF magazines. Wollheim, however, went further than most. He banded together other writers who had not been paid for stories published in *WS* (including Henry Hasse, Arthur K. Barnes, Chester Cuthbert and even Stanley G. Weinbaum) and hired a lawyer to secure payment. A settlement was eventually reached, but it did not enhance Gernsback's reputation with either fans or writers. This was not an isolated incident. Earlier, Jack Williamson had utilized the services of the Fiction Guild's attorney to recover some $300 that was long overdue. Even David H. Keller, at one time science fiction's most popular author, was owed money by Gernsback, but his son-in-law was an attorney and he was able, eventually, to recover all the money owed him. But by then Keller felt he had been taken advantage of, and he refused to write for Gernsback again.

Wollheim's other involvement is perhaps equally if not more significant, but to appreciate it we must review another aspect of *WS*. Gernsback, satisfied with the success of the Short Wave Radio League, which he had launched in one of his radio magazines, suggested to Hornig that a Science Fiction League be established to provide a forum for fans, to enhance the popularity of science fiction and to increase the number of its followers. At the same time Gernsback hoped that it would provide a steadily growing readership for the magazine, but the idea was not entirely financially inspired. Fans had only to apply for membership and, if granted, they received a certificate designed by Frank R. Paul and could acquire special stationery and badges. If three or more fans combined they could put forward a proposal to form a Chapter of the League.

Each month *WS* carried a special section on the league's activities listing newly formed and proposed chapters, reports on fans' special suggestions, results of science fiction tests and other news. Many names well known in the field today will be found listed in the tiny print of the Science Fiction League's news column, including James Blish, Milton Rothman, Sam Moskowitz, Frederik Pohl, Robert W. Lowndes, Leslie Flood, Donald A. Wollheim, Bob Tucker and Oswald Train.

The league did more for science fiction fandom than anything before or since. It showed fans what they could achieve when they organized. As Frederik Pohl commented in his autobiography, the discovery that he was member 490 meant that there were at least another 489 like himself, whereas hitherto he had thought there were just a handful. It gave fandom a drive and a purpose, but it also brought about internecine rivalry. The main cause of this rivalry was Donald A. Wollheim.

In 1934 Wollheim, along with Wilson Shepherd, had formed the Terrestrial Fantascience Guild, which soon merged with the International Cosmos Science Club, formed the year before by John Michel, William Sykora, Edward Gervais and Walter Kubilius. The union renamed itself the International Scientific Association, and in principle it opposed the Science Fiction League. In later years Wollheim looked back on the crisis that was brewing: "Their stand was that only an independent organization could develop fandom to maturity and greatness—that a pro club, by its very nature, must be commercial and would hamper the free flow of criticism. Finally, the greatest evil in science fiction at that time was the bad financial policy of the sponsoring magazine, *Wonder Stories*, which was alienating writers everywhere."

The resulting feud split fandom, but in the end, in the September 1935 issue Hornig announced that three members of the league had been expelled for working against it—Wollheim, Sykora and Michel. In a series of clashes at meetings of the New York League chapters, Wollheim and Sykora succeeded in wresting the chapters away from the league and establishing them as independents. The Independent League for Science Fiction (ILSF) was now formed, and other chapters began to withdraw their Science Fiction League chartership and apply for membership with the ILSF. Although it was not reported in the pages of *Wonder Stories*, the Science Fiction League was crumbling. And much to the pleasure of many in the ILSF, *Wonder*'s days were numbered.

The magazine had been suffering from a dwindling circulation throughout 1935. Although it had presented much readable fiction, it had failed to capitalize on its greatest asset, Stanley G. Weinbaum. If Gernsback had paid authors reasonable sums, Weinbaum would probably not have been lured away to *Astounding*. Writers like Gallun, Schachner and Vincent had deserted the magazine for one that paid an honest one cent a word promptly upon publication, and sometimes earlier. To the same end *Astounding* was presenting stories by Campbell, Wandrei, Leinster and others who had never contributed to *Wonder*.

Gernsback's first move was to drop the cover price of *Wonder* to fifteen cents, five cents cheaper than *Astounding*; this action failed to increase *Wonder*'s circulation and only reduced vital revenue. There was little Gernsback could do to combat *Astounding*. Gernsback had Paul as cover artist, but Paul was no longer the draw he had been ten years before. *Astounding* had Howard Brown providing some excellent covers, and Elliot Dold the interiors. Even Mark Marchioni, who had once illustrated stories with *Wonder*, was now in *Astounding*. *Wonder* had discovered Charles Schneeman, but he was not yet the draw he would be when he later worked with Campbell at *Astounding*.

In the end, therefore, Gernsback had to take more drastic measures. Circulation had evidently dropped to well below 50,000, and Gernsback was planning to withdraw the magazine from the newsstand. In the April 1936 issue he wrote a scathing editorial in which he accused the distributors and retailers of criminal acts in selling off coverless copies of unsold magazines instead of returning them to the publisher.

As an alternative Gernsback proposed selling *Wonder Stories* by subscription only. Readers had simply to send in a coupon cut from the issue and for a year they would be sent issues of *Wonder* with no payment in advance. On receipt of each issue, accompanied by a bill, readers had only to dispatch fifteen cents within the week. But the response was dismal, and Gernsback put *Wonder Stories* up for sale. It was purchased by Ned Pines, whose Standard Magazine group was growing and prospering.

The last issue of *Wonder Stories* appeared exactly ten years after the first issue of *Amazing*. Those were the Gernsback years. Although Gernsback returned briefly in 1939 with *Superworld Comics* and again in 1953 with *Science Fiction Plus*,* he had now lost control of the science fiction field. While he did more to further science fiction than any other editor with the single exception of John W. Campbell, he had no real idea how to edit a science fiction magazine. His sole interest was in promoting science, and he felt that as the pioneer in this field he could rely on the loyalty of his readers. He was wrong. The readers were not as interested in the promotion of science as in the escapism of the fiction. When the readers discovered that Tremaine and Hall at *Astounding* were offering something new and exciting, they soon changed allegiance. It was now Gernsback's time to stand aside and let the real professionals take over.

In August 1936, with the sale of Gernsback's *Wonder Stories* to Standard Magazines, the magazine was reissued as *Thrilling Wonder Stories*. The editor-in-chief of the Standard chain was Leo Margulies, who, as a former literary agent, was well acquainted with many authors. Margulies eventually appointed Mort Weisinger as editor. Weisinger had been the agent for Stanley G. Weinbaum, Earl and Otto (Eando) Binder, H. P. Lovecraft, David H. Keller and Edmond Hamilton. He had been employed by Margulies as a reader and assistant editor and since he was the only one who knew anything about science fiction, Weisinger was the logical choice for editor of *TWS*.[1]

TWS had all the same departments as the old *Wonder*: the Science Fiction League, the lively letter column "The Reader Speaks," "Science Questions and Answers" and "Test Your Knowledge." It introduced a new feature, "The Story behind the Story," in which the authors of the lead stories would chat about their inspirations for their stories, a thrill to juvenile readers who felt that through this feature they "knew" the authors.

The first editorial paid lip-service to Gernsback's canon of scientific plausibility, but at 15 cents, the cheapest price on the market, Margulies and publisher Ned Pines were aiming at the teenage market. "Blood and thunder" pulp action and adventure, based on antique plots but mostly life-and-death combats with alien life-forms, comprised the bulk of the stories. In the first issue, a moon colony of Earthlings is attacked by Martians (Ray Cummings' "Blood on the Moon"), a mad scientist threatens to conquer the world by creating "gland-men,'' specialized human beings with hormone imbalances (Eando Binder's ''The Hormone Menace''), and a group takes a journey to the center of the earth in a metal cylinder to fight off monsters made of limestone (Paul Ernst's ''Death Dives Deep''). Early on, the humorous story also became a regular offering.

The first two issues featured posthumous works by Weinbaum and an even rarer find—two short stories by famous fantasy writer A. Merritt, ''The Drone Man'' and ''Rhythm of the Spheres,'' both reprinted from Weisinger's semi-pro fanzine, *Science Fiction Digest*. To further establish the magazine's juvenile slant, the first eight issues ran a comic-strip serial called ''Zarnak'' by Jack Binder. When the fans protested, it was interrupted in midplot.

Under Weisinger's editorship, the quality of the fiction showed some improvement. Reader interest may have helped. In the April 1938 ''Reader Speaks,'' long-time fan Robert W. (Doc) Lowndes begrudgingly admitted that *TWS* had improved during the last year (1937), and in February 1939, Sam Moskowitz lavishly praised the previous issue. Later (March 1940), Moskowitz called Eando Binder's ''The Three Eternals'' a ''classic.'' In almost every issue, faithful fans like Charles Hidley and D. B. Thompson wrote regularly in ''The Reader Speaks,'' criticizing every story and feature, and Weisinger began publishing the favorite story of the past issue selected by the readers.

A group of writers from the old *Wonder* continued to contribute to *TWS*: Eando Binder, Stanton A. Coblentz, Ray Cummings (who had a story in almost every issue), Raymond Z. Gallun, Edmond Hamilton, Clifford Simak and Jack Williamson. But from 1938 to 1941, a newer group of writers began to appear regularly in its pages, led by Henry Kuttner and including Nelson S. Bond, Malcolm Jameson, Frederic Arnold Kummer, Jr., William Morrison and Robert Moore Williams. As early as November 1937 Kuttner began his prolific output for Standard's SF magazines with ''When The Earth Lived,'' a fascinating story about alien rays focused on the Earth bringing inanimate objects to life.

In April 1939 *TWS* began running a contest for the best amateur short story. Most of the writers have happily passed into oblivion except for the very first prizewinner, Alfred Bester, who submitted ''The Broken Axiom.'' In a recent interview, Bester claims that Weisinger and another editor, Jack Schiff, showed him how to revise the story into acceptable form.[2]

With bi-monthly publication, serials were not considered practical. *TWS* only published complete stories and leaned toward the story series, either short stories or novelettes of interplanetary adventure featuring the bizarre types of flora and fauna first pioneered by Weinbaum. In December 1936, John W. Campbell began a series of adventures about two interplanetary fugitives, Penton and Blake, with ''The Brain Stealers of Mars.'' Five Penton and Blake tales subsequently appeared, ending with ''The Brain Pirates'' in October 1938.

In 1937, three new series started. Beginning with ''Via Etherline'' in October, ''Gordon A. Giles'' wrote the Via series, stories written in journal form from an expedition pursuing pyramidal artifacts from planet to planet in the solar system. Also in October, Ray Cummings revived his series about Tubby (originally in Munsey's *Argosy*), a humorous fellow whose fictional adventures ran until 1946. In June, the Gerry Carlyle series by Arthur K. Barnes had begun and was an instant success with the readers. Gerry Carlyle, a kind of female interplanetary Frank Buck, roamed the solar system capturing zoo animals.

In 1938, Henry Kuttner introduced the Hollywood on the Moon series starring Tony Quade, ace cameraman for a moon-based filmmaker, who could create special effects for any planet in the solar system. Also in the same year, Eando Binder began his popular Anton York series about an immortal man who returns regularly from his interstellar wanderings to save the solar system.

In 1939, Kuttner and Barnes again collaborated, using the pen name Kelvin Kent, on the long-running series of humorous yarns about Pete Manx, a time-traveling gangster.

As early as February 1938 (and perhaps in response to teachers' concern about their students reading anything as garish as *TWS*), *TWS* published an article by Sir James Jeans, British mathematician and cosmologist, on "Giant and Dwarf Stars," and in the very next issue (April 1938), British astronomer Sir Arthur Eddington initiated readers into the mysteries of "Eclipses of the Sun." Jeans and Eddington were the Carl Sagans of their time, and each had written several books popularizing science. In addition, there were regular "science-fact" articles by rocket expert Willy Ley and others.

During this period, *Thrilling Wonder Stories* reached its peak with the tenth anniversary issue in June 1939. The table of contents included such stars as Stanley G. Weinbaum's "Dawn of Flame," the original novella on which "The Black Flame," the lead novel in the first issue of *Startling Stories*,* was based; E. E. Smith's "Robot Nemesis"; and John Taine's "The Ultimate Catalyst," with Finlay illustrations. The shorter fiction was equally stellar, with stories by Otis Adelbert Kline, Eando Binder, Jack Williamson, the two sons of Edgar Rice Burroughs, John Coleman and Hulbert, and the return of David H. Keller. With this issue, *TWS* began featuring "novels" (actually long novelettes) at the back of the magazine in finer print. Of particular historical value in this issue are the six pages of profiles of authors and artists with accompanying photographs.

The artwork, especially the gaudy covers frequently displaying varied monsters, placed a distinctive stamp on the magazine. Howard V. Brown painted most of the earlier issues, but beginning with the September 1940 issue, Earle K. Bergey became the exclusive cover artist for *TWS* and its companions until his death in 1952. He, more than any other artist, became associated with the BEM (bug-eyed monster) stigma attached by the general public to science fiction.[3] He loved monsters and giants, but his favorite scene was a brass-bra'd female floating in outer space (sans space suit) being snatched by a BEM—often while a male helplessly looks on. Bergey must be credited with using more realistic human beings on his covers, moving away from the gadgetry and machines popularized by Frank R. Paul in the early *Wonder Stories*.

Inside, the illustrations were competently done by Hans Wesso, Mark Marchioni, Leo Morey and the young Alex Schomburg; after 1939, Virgil Finlay and Frank R. Paul made frequent appearances, often illustrating the novels.

In December 1939, *TWS* went monthly, and earlier that year Standard had begun a bi-monthly companion magazine, *Startling Stories*, carrying "book-length" novels and reprints of "classics" from the early *Wonder Stories*. A third magazine, *Captain Future*,* written by Edmond Hamilton and featuring super-hero Curt Newton saving the universe in every issue, appeared quarterly in 1940. A fourth magazine, *Strange Stories*,* devoted to weird and supernatural fiction in competition with *Weird Tales*,* came out in 1939 but lasted only thirteen issues.[4]

In June 1941, Mort Weisinger left Standard Magazines to become editor of the various Superman comic books.[5] He was replaced by Oscar J. Friend, a forty-three-year-old western writer who had turned his hand to SF and had published some popular stories under his own name and as Owen Fox Jerome in *TWS* and *Startling*. Friend remained until 1944 and was responsible for the silly "Sergeant Saturn" character in the editorials and letter columns, rating stories in "jugs of Xeno" and referring to his readers as "kiwis."

In that same month, *TWS* returned to bi-monthly publication, alternating with *Startling* throughout 1942. With the August 1943 issue, *TWS* went quarterly until late 1946. Despite the war, *TWS* continued to print occasionally good stories by Fredric Brown, the indefatigable Ray Cummings, John Russell Fearn (and as Polton Cross), Frank Belknap Long (his series on John Carstairs, a twenty-first-century botanical detective, was well received) and Ross Rocklynne. Leigh Brackett came over from *Planet Stories** with her polished blend of space opera and sword and sorcery. One of her finest was "The Veil of Astellar" (Summer 1944), a dark, haunting tale of a man who plays a Judas goat, regularly betraying his own people for the love of an alien.

The February 1943 issue featured Ray Bradbury's first solo professional sale, "The Piper." Jack Vance made his first appearance anywhere with "The World Thinker" (Summer 1945).

During these war years, an occasional weird tale was added for variety. The readers liked "The Devil's Fiddle" (June 1943) by N. R. deMexico and "Call Me Demon" (Fall 1946) by Henry Kuttner. Much of the fiction in these years was hackwork and sometimes propagandistic. Quite a number of the stories were set in the war zone with Nazis and Japs as villains, for example, Ross Rocklynne's "Exile to Centauri" (August 1943) and Henry Kuttner's "A God Named Kroo" (Winter 1944). The artwork began to show the influence of the "pin-up" girl so popular with the armed forces—the women were drawn much sexier, revealing deeper cleavage and a glimpse of thigh above the stocking top, usually the kind of illustrating found in the "Spicy" pulps.

The war took its toll on the Science Fiction League. Friend had continued Weisinger's practice of appending the SFL chapter news and activities to the letter column. But the column grew shorter and shorter, and with a final complaint that there was no news to report, the printing of the membership application form was discontinued with the Fall 1945 issue.

Friend left Standard at the end of 1944, and Samuel Merwin, Jr., at age thirty-four, took over with the Winter 1945 issue. Merwin was virtually unknown to the fans except for one story, "The Scourge Below" (October 1939), and two articles about aircraft. Merwin had his own ideas about changing the magazine but had to wait until the war was over. (Mercifully, he discontinued Sergeant Saturn as soon as possible.)

TWS resumed bi-monthly publication with the December 1946 issue. Merwin responded to John Campbell's competition at *Astounding* and strove to alter the juvenile image of *TWS* by improving both story quality and presentation. Even Bergey's covers improved. He replaced the brass bras with diaphanous, form-fitting costumes, and his humans were painted even more realistically.

Merwin began to purchase fiction from *Astounding*'s stable of writers. Murray Leinster (Will F. Jenkins) had a story in almost every issue from 1944 to 1949 and started several series, the Bud Gregory series as William Fitzgerald and the Kim Rendell series under the Leinster name. George O. Smith and L. Ron Hubbard wrote hard science stories, and Theodore Sturgeon's "The Sky Was Full of Ships" (June 1947) was nominated by the readers as one of the best ever printed in *TWS*. Even Robert Heinlein contributed a story—"Jerry Is a Man" (October 1947). Some of Ray Bradbury's finest stories, later to be included in *The Martian Chronicles*, were published: "And the Moon Be Still As Bright" (June 1948), "The Naming of Names" (August 1949), and "Payment in Full" (February 1950).

In this period, the contribution of the Kuttners (by this time Kuttner and Moore were a team) to both *TWS* and *Startling* was immeasurable. They wrote many fine stories under the Kuttner name and numerous pseudonyms: Keith Hammond, Hudson Hastings, C. H. Liddell and Woodrow Wilson Smith. In a single issue, there might be several stories by the Kuttners; the August 1947 issue carried a novelette by Kuttner, "Atomic!," and two short stories, "Noon" by Hudson Hastings and "Dark Dawn" by Keith Hammond. They ran the gamut from humor to Merrittesque fantasies, which, however, tried to retain a pseudo-scientific rationale.

In 1948, the size of the magazine was increased—to 144 pages in February and to 176 pages in October. Many excellent "filler" stories were penned by Fredric Brown, L. Sprague de Camp and detective story writer John MacDonald. The newcomers included James Blish, Charles L. Harness, William Tenn and Margaret St. Clair, one of the new generation of women writers who entered SF after the war. Old-timers from *Wonder* also began to contribute again: Raymond Z. Gallun, Lloyd Arthur Eshbach, A. G. Stangland, Wallace West and especially Fletcher Pratt.

Without a doubt, 1949 was the best year under Merwin's masthead. The February issue featured A. E. van Vogt's sequel to the Weapon Shop series first published in *Astounding*, "The Weapon Shops of Isher"; Ray Bradbury's "The

Man," a daring religious theme which describes a spaceship landing on another world only to discover that Christ had come just the day before; short fiction by Sturgeon; and the combination of Damon Knight and James Blish. The June issue carried Leigh Brackett's finest ancient Mars novel, "The Sea Kings of Mars" (later published as *The Sword of Rhiannon*), and Fredric Brown's "Mouse." In August came Arthur C. Clarke's famous parable, "The Lion of Comarre," and in October, Ray Bradbury's poignant tale of men dying in space, "Kaleidoscope." To close the year in December, James Blish led off with "Let the Finder Beware" (later published as *Jack of Eagles*); that issue also contained Clarke's "Thirty Seconds—Thirty Days" and Bradbury's "A Blade of Grass."

In addition to Bradbury, Blish and Clarke, Jack Vance remained a mainstay over these postwar years, especially adept at interstellar adventures like the Magnus Ridolph series. Like Kuttner, he included fantasy elements in his backgrounds written in a colorful, almost exotic style.[6]

In the early fifties, the boom continued. Clarke contributed "Earthlight," his famous story about a lunar colony; de Camp, "The Continent Makers," a Viagens Interplanetaria story set on his invented planet Krishna; Blish, "There Shall Be No Darkness," one of the few attempts to rationalize lycanthropy since Jack Williamson's *Darker Than You Think*; and MacDonald's frequently anthologized short story, "Spectator Sport." Kendall Foster Crossen, former editor of *Detective Fiction Weekly*, started the amusing and satirical Manning Draco series about the dealings of an interstellar salesman. In addition, there were more fine fillers by Anthony Boucher, H. B. Fyfe, Richard Matheson, Walter M. Miller, Jr. and John Wyndham.

Under Merwin, the features improved, too. In June 1951 James Blish began a series of ten articles on "Our Inhabited Universe," and occasional book reviews and movie reviews appeared. Jerome Bixby edited the fanzine column and even contributed one of his rare short stories, "Sort of Like a Flower" (August 1952). Marion Bradley Zimmer (she called herself "Astra"), John Jakes, Robert Silverberg, A. J. Budrys and other writers-to-be sent long, thoughtful fan letters to "The Reader Speaks," testifying to the magazine's improved quality.

TWS and its companions were probably the best illustrated magazines of any of the pulps. Since no magazine could pay enough to claim him exclusively, Merwin was able to feature regularly the talents of Virgil Finlay, probably the finest black and white artist of the period, who was going strong until the magazine expired. Under Finlay's influence, the illustrations generally displayed exquisitely drawn, undressed females discreetly covered at the appropriate places (what Brian Aldiss referred to as The Great Nipple Shortage).[7] When Finlay was not available, other fine imitators—Lawrence Stevens, Astarita and Peter Poulton—were on hand.

In 1952, Earle Bergey died, but a new coterie of cover artists—Alex Schomburg, Ed Emshwiller and Jack Coggins—took over with their own unique talents and styles and gave the magazine a completely different look. BEMs and undressed females were replaced by space scenes and alien landscapes.

Samuel Mines, probably one of the most broad-minded of editors, succeeded Sam Merwin as editor in December 1951. Mines challenged writers to be more experimental, to use more daring themes and to create more realistic characters. The result was such milestones as Philip José Farmer's "Mother" (April 1953), with its incestuous overtones, and Edmond Hamilton's "What's It Like Out There?" (December 1952), a grim and realistic treatment of a spaceman's return from Mars. According to Leigh Brackett, Hamilton had originally written this story in 1933 but considered it unfit for his audience. He then rewrote the much shorter, modern version with less action, a more oblique and restrained viewpoint, and more humanity, "touching the heart without ever faltering into sentimentality."[8]

Others, less daring but unusual in theme, were Katherine MacLean's "The Diploids" (April 1953) and Theodore Sturgeon's "The Golden Helix" (Summer 1954). Offbeat stories by John Christopher, Philip K. Dick, Kris Neville, Robert Sheckley and William Tenn sprinkled the pages of *TWS* during these closing days.

Yet a change to more realistic fiction and the finest artwork could not stave off the inevitable collapse of the magazine. In November 1953 *TWS* was forced to appear quarterly, and in the very next issue (Winter 1954) the logo was changed to a more dignified block lettering similar to that of its competitors.

TWS survived long enough to celebrate its twenty-fifth anniversary in the Spring 1954 issue. Three issues later, with the Winter 1955 number, *TWS* ceased publication. (*Startling Stories* hung on a few months longer until October 1955.) The final issue contained "Name Your Pleasure" by James Gunn (later included in *The Joy Makers*), a science fantasy by Margaret St. Clair and a short story by Isaac Asimov.

By the end of 1955, the *Wonder Stories* group was gone, all vanished within the space of one year because no one was interested in distributing them anymore. An era that had begun with Hugo Gernsback twenty-six years before and that had been responsible for making science fiction a popular genre with a much larger audience than ever before had come to an end.

Notes

1. In the Statement of Ownership in the first issue, the editor is listed as "Harvey Burns," and no name is cited as managing editor.

2. "Alfred Bester," in *Speaking of Science Fiction: The Paul Walker Interviews* (Oradell, N.J.: Luna Press, 1978), p. 306. When Weisinger and Schiff left Standard, Bester went to work for them writing comic scripts.

3. In protest, some readers formed a mythical society, the SFTPOBEMOTCOSFP (Society for the Prevention of Bug-Eyed Monsters on the Covers of SF Publications).

4. *TWS* even went Hollywood. A story by Will Garth (Henry Kuttner), "Dr. Cyclops" (June 1940), about a mad scientist who shrank human beings, was simultaneously released by Paramount Pictures as a fairly popular B movie starring Albert Dekker.

5. Another loss was Eando Binder when Otto Binder deserted to the comics. Eando

was the pseudonym of brothers Earl and Otto Binder, but Earl had long since stopped collaborating in 1935.

6. Some of the fans were convinced that Vance and Kuttner were the same person despite editorial protests to the contrary. The heresy had even spread to Europe: Damon Knight (*In Search of Wonder*, p. 219) quotes from an SF anthology printed in German: "Lewis Padget: Pseudonym für Henry Kuttner (anderes Pseudonym: Jack Vance)."

7. Brian W. Aldiss, *Science Fiction Art* (New York: Bounty Books, 1975), p. 98.

8. Leigh Brackett, ed., *The Best of Edmond Hamilton* (Garden City, N.Y.: Nelson Doubleday, Inc., 1977), p. xv.

Information Sources

BIBLIOGRAPHY:
Ashley, Michael, ed. *The History of the Science Fiction Magazine, Volume 2: 1936– 1945*, and *Volume 3: 1946–1955*. Chicago: Henry Regnery Company, 1976.
Moskowitz, Sam. *Seekers of Tomorrow*. Cleveland, Ohio: World Publishing Company, 1966.
Nicholls. *Encyclopedia*.
Tuck.
INDEX SOURCES: Cook, IWG; ISFM; MIT; SFM; Tuck.
REPRINT SOURCES:
Reprint Editions: *Wonder Stories*, 2 issues. A digest, 128 pp. anthology reprinting 8 stories from the *TWS* years was issued in 1957. It included "Shadow on the Sand" by John D. MacDonald, "All the Time in the World" by Arthur C. Clarke, "The Sound of Thunder" by Ray Bradbury and "Thanasphere" by Kurt Vonnegut. It continued the *TWS* numbering as Volume 45, Number 1. In 1963 it was reissued in pulp facsimile format with many of the original illustrations by Virgil Finlay. Although numbered Volume 45, Number 2, it carried identical contents, but "Spacemate" by Walt Sheldon was deleted and "The Hunters" by Sheldon and "Robert" by Evan Hunter were added. The success of this issue caused the publishers to publish a regular reprint annual—see entries for *Treasury of Great Science Fiction Stories* and *Science Fiction Yearbook*.
British Editions: Two series. First series, 10 issues [1 volume], undated but issued irregularly between December 1949 and Summer 1953 by Atlas Publishing, London. 64 pp., 1/- (later 9d.). Abridged versions of U.S. editions usually consisting of lead story plus two or three shorts, not always from the same U.S. issue. U.K. issues correspond approximately as follows to U.S. originals: 1, Aug 49; 2, Dec 49; 3, Oct 49; 4, Feb 50; 5, Apr 52; 6, Oct 51; 7, Jun 52; 8, Dec 51; 9, Aug 52; 10, Dec 52. Second series, continuation of above by Pemberton's, Manchester, 4 issues numbered 101 to 104, undated, released quarterly between Autumn 1953 and Summer 1954. Pulp, 64 pp., 1/-. Abridged, as above, equal to U.S. as follows: 101, Aug 53; 102, Nov 53; 103, Win 54; 104, Spr 54.
Foreign Editions: No formal foreign editions, but the Mexican *Enigmas* and *Los Cuentos Fantasticos* relied heavily on *TWS*. See entries under Mexico in Section IV.
Derivative Anthologies: No specific volume, but a number of selections from *TWS* turn up in *My Best Science Fiction Story* (New York: Merlin, 1949) and *Giant Anthology of Science Fiction* (Merlin, 1954), both edited by Leo Margulies and Oscar J. Friend.

Microform: Greenwood Press Periodical Series.

LOCATION SOURCES: Brigham Young University Library; Florida International University Library; Indiana University Library; M.I.T. Science Fiction Library; Pennsylvania State University Library; Syracuse University Library; Texas A&M University Library; University of Texas-Austin Library; University of Wisconsin-Milwaukee Library.

Publication History

TITLE: *Science Wonder Stories*, June 1929–May 1930 [Volume 1]; *Wonder Stories*, June 1930–March/April 1936 [Volumes 2–7]; *Thrilling Wonder Stories*, August 1936–Winter 1955 [Volumes 8–44].

VOLUME DATA: Volume 1, Number 1, June 1929–Volume 44, Number 3, Winter 1955. Volumes 1 to 4, twelve issues per volume, monthly. Volume 5, ten issues, no issues for July or September 1933, otherwise monthly. Volume 6, twelve issues, monthly. Volume 7, eight issues, monthly, June to October 1935; bi-monthly, November/December 1935 to March/April 1936. Thereafter three issues per volume. Bi-monthly, August 1936 to December 1939; monthly, January 1940 to April 1941; bi-monthly, June 1941 to August 1943; quarterly, Fall 1943 to Fall 1946; bi-monthly, December 1946 to August 1953; quarterly, November 1953 to Winter 1955. Total run: *SWS*, 12 issues; *WS*, 66 issues; *TWS*, 111 issues. Total: 189 issues.

PUBLISHERS: Stellar Publishing Corporation, New York, June 1929–October 1933; Continental Publications, Inc., Springfield, Massachusetts, November 1933–March/April 1936; Beacon Magazines, New York, August 1936–June 1937; Better Publications, Inc., Chicago, August 1937–August 1943; Standard Magazines, Inc., New York, Fall 1943–Winter 1955.

EDITORS: David Lasser, June 1929–October 1933; Charles D. Hornig, November 1933–March 1936; Mortimer Weisinger, August 1936–June 1941; Oscar J. Friend, August 1941–Fall 1944; Samuel Merwin, Jr., Winter 1945–October 1951; Samuel Mines, December 1951–Summer 1954; Alexander Samalman, Fall 1954–Winter 1955. Theron Raines and Herbert D. Kastle may have had some involvement with the final issue. Note: Hugo Gernsback was editor-in-chief from June 1929 to April 1936 and had the final say on content; Leo Margulies was editorial director from August 1936 to Fall 1944 and had a similar power of veto.

FORMAT: Large-size, 96 pp., June 1929–October 1930; Pulp, 144 pp., November 1930–October 1931; Large-size (saddle-stapled), 96 pp., November 1931–November 1932; 64 pp., December 1932–March 1933; 96 pp., April–October 1933; Pulp, 128 pp., November 1933–Spring 1944; 112 pp., Summer 1944–Spring 1945; 96 pp., Summer–Fall 1945; 112 pp., Winter 1946–February 1948; 144 pp., April–August 1948; 176 pp., October–December 1948; 160 pp., February 1949–April 1951; 144 pp., June 1951–August 1953; 128 pp., November 1953–Summer 1954; 112 pp., Fall 1954–Winter 1955.

PRICE: 25¢, June 1929–October 1932; 15¢, November 1932–March 1933; 25¢, April 1933–May 1935; 15¢, June 1935–February 1948; 20¢, April–August 1948; 25¢, October 1948–Winter 1955.

Robert Ewald/Mike Ashley

WONDER STORIES QUARTERLY

When, in 1929, Hugo Gernsback lost control of his pioneer SF magazines *Amazing Stories** and *Amazing Stories Quarterly,** it was inevitable that when he established a new company and issued *Science Wonder Stories* (*Wonder Stories**) that he would also issue a bulky companion quarterly. *Science Wonder Quarterly* duly appeared, the first issue dated Fall 1929.

Science Wonder Quarterly followed the same policy as Gernsback's earlier quarterly in publishing one or two full-length novels each issue, plus two or three short stories. After three issues, at the time when Gernsback felt that the word "science" in his magazine titles might be having a deleterious effect on sales, he retitled the magazine *Wonder Stories Quarterly*. He could justifiably have retitled it *Interplanetary Stories Quarterly* because the main thrust of the contents was toward the stars, reflecting what was probably the most popular theme in science fiction. In fact, Gernsback made the Winter 1931 issue an all-interplanetary number, and with the next issue he sponsored a competition for original ideas to be made into space stories. Thereafter the magazine bore a banner declaring "Interplanetary Stories" as a feature of the magazine.

This deliberate policy may not have been just a publishing ploy by Gernsback. As his managing editor he had selected David Lasser, an engineer in his late twenties. Lasser was the founding president of the American Interplanetary Society, inaugurated in March 1930 and still in existence today as the American Rocket Society. He also edited the society's *Bulletin*. Members of the society included R. F. Starzl, Nathan Schachner, Fletcher Pratt, C. P. Mason, William Lemkin and G. E. Pendray (who wrote SF as Gawain Edwards). Many of these were also members of the German Society for Space Travel, created in 1927, and vice-president of that organization in 1929 was Willy Ley. Starzl had sent Ley the first issue of *Science Wonder Quarterly*, and it had converted Ley instantly. Ley also corresponded with Gawain Pendray, who reported Ley's news of German rocketry experiments in the *Bulletin of the American Interplanetary Society*.

This parallel organization and development helps put the contents of *Science Wonder Quarterly* in perspective. Combined with Hugo Gernsback's own European origin (and the fact that European fiction could be acquired for translation at moderate rates), it is hardly surprising that the *Quarterly* carried so many interplanetary stories by French and German writers. The first issue led with "The Shot into Infinity" by German writer and rocket expert Otto Willi Gail, originally published in 1925. Gail was the first to transfer many of the seminal ideas of the remarkable Hermann Noordung into fiction. The novel includes, for instance, such modern-day concepts as the three-stage rocket,[1] while its sequel, *The Stone from the Moon* (printed in the Spring 1930 issue), goes into great detail on the subject of a space station.[2]

Other German writers appearing in translation were Otfrid von Hanstein with "Electropolis" (Summer 1930), surprisingly not an interplanetary novel but set in a wonderful new city built in the Australian desert, and ''Between the Earth and the Moon'' (Fall 1930); Bruno H. Burgel, whose ''The Cosmic Cloud'' (Fall 1931) took a lead from Conan Doyle's *The Poison Belt* by studying the effects on the Earth as it passes through a cloud in space; and Ludwig Anton, whose ''Interplanetary Bridges'' (Winter 1933) concerned the first space flight to Venus.

French writers were not ignored. R. H. Romans had two novels in the early issues: ''The Moon Conquerors'' (Winter 1930), which looks at some remarkable engineering possibilities on the moon, and ''The War of the Planets'' (Summer 1930). British writers also waved the flag, especially J. M. Walsh, who had an interplanetary triad: ''Vandals of the Void'' (Summer 1931), about war with Mercury; its sequel, ''The Struggle for Pallas'' (Fall 1931); and the popular ''Vanguard to Neptune'' (Spring 1932), about the first exploratory expedition.

American writers also appeared in great numbers. Stanton A. Coblentz was quick to make use of the discovery of the planet Pluto in 1930 with ''Into Plutonian Depths'' (Spring 1931), which looked at a hivelike society within the planet. Soon after came John Scott Campbell, who took us ''Beyond Pluto'' (Summer 1932), although the novel started on Earth with the discovery of an alien city. In the meantime Richard Vaughan had decided to add yet another new planet to the solar system, this time between Neptune and Pluto. In the highly improbable ''The Woman from Space'' (Spring 1932) he postulates a world where the men have died out and where the women attain a high scientific prowess, sufficient that they learn how to move their planet from its far-out orbit into an orbit nearer Earth, where by some fluke a cosmic disaster has wiped out nearly all the women. The two planets thus succeed in reaching more than friendly terms.

Planets full of women is not an uncommon theme in SF, though for its day Don Mark Lemon's ''The Scarlet Planet'' (Winter 1931) went a little too far for its readers, who howled in protest at the idea of a shipload of spacemen having a good time on this wanton world. Fifty years ago most SF readers preferred their sex in test tubes.

This is not to say that the *Quarterly* featured only space stories, though they certainly dominated it. As already mentioned, ''Electropolis'' is set in central Australia, and Edmond Hamilton's ''The Hidden World'' (Fall 1929) takes place within the hollow Earth. M. F. Rupert's ''Via the Hewitt Ray'' (Spring 1930) is set in the fourth dimension, while David H. Keller's ''The Moon Rays'' (Summer 1930) is set very solidly on Earth and uses Keller's psychiatric background to look at lunacy and the effect that a concentrated nationwide study of the moon has on the mass populace.

Other contributors included P. Schuyler Miller, Fletcher Pratt, Manly Wade Wellman and John Beynon Harris, whose ''Exiles on Asperus'' in the last issue has a good claim to being the best novelette from the magazine. More recently reprinted in Sam Moskowitz's *Three Stories* (Garden City, N.Y.: Doubleday, 1967; retitled for U.K. publication as *A Sense of Wonder* [London: Sidgwick &

Jackson, 1967] and for U.S. paperback publication as *The Moon Era* [New York, Curtis, 1969]), it looks at the discovery of the descendants of an expedition lost in space many years earlier. The descendants have been enslaved by the masters of the planet and are now so conditioned to this state that they would rather die than be freed by their potential saviors.

Perhaps the best single novel published in *WSQ* was "The Voyage of the Asteroid" by Laurence Manning in the Summer 1932 issue. Instead of glamorizing space travel he concentrated on its harsh realities and gave a relatively modern depiction of the exploration of Mars. The sequel, "The Wreck of the Asteroid," did not appear in the *Quarterly* but was serialized in *Wonder Stories*. This was not a last-minute decision because the serial was announced in advance, but it was a fairly clear indication that Gernsback had already decided to cease publication of the *Quarterly*. From the harsh realities of Mars, Gernsback had to face up to the equally harsh realities of the Great Depression, and in 1932 there were not many readers who could buy the regular monthly SF magazines and afford a further fifty cents each for the two quarterlies. As a last-ditch effort Gernsback reduced the price of *WSQ* to twenty-five cents with a corresponding reduction in size, but to little avail. At this time David Lasser was turning his own efforts away from rocketry to the very worldly subject of workers' unions. He would leave Gernsback's employ within the year, and with all things considered it was the most opportune time to suspend the magazine. Gernsback's fortunes continued to fail during the mid-1930s, and *WSQ* was never revived.

Apart from serving as a lively forum for the fictional flights of fancy of enthusiasts and supporters of American rocketry and space exploration, *WSQ* does have one other significant claim to fame. The Fall 1929 issue published the first fan letter by Forrest J Ackerman, who went on to become the number one science fiction fan, "Mr. Science Fiction" himself.

Notes

1. See Paul Carter, *The Creation of Tomorrow* (New York: Columbia University Press, 1977), pp. 38–39.

2. See Richard H. Macklin, "Satellites in Fact and Fiction," *Science Fiction Stories*, May 1958, pp. 58–61; and Sam Moskowitz, "The Real Earth Satellite Story," *Explorers of the Infinite* (Cleveland: World, 1963), p. 102.

Information Sources

BIBLIOGRAPHY:
Nicholls. *Encyclopedia*.
Tuck.
INDEX SOURCES: Cook, IWG; ISFM; SFM; Tuck.
REPRINT SOURCES:
    Microform: Greenwood Press Periodical Series.
LOCATION SOURCES: M.I.T. Science Fiction Library; Pennsylvania State University
        Library.

Publication History

TITLE: *Science Wonder Quarterly*, Fall 1929–Spring 1930. Retitled *Wonder Stories Quarterly*, Summer 1930–Winter 1933.

VOLUME DATA: Volume 1, Number 1, Fall 1929–Volume 4, Number 2, Winter 1933. Four issues per volume. Quarterly. Total run: 14 issues.

PUBLISHER: Stellar Publishing Corporation, New York.

EDITOR: Hugo Gernsback with Managing Editor David Lasser.

FORMAT: Large Pulp, 144 pp., Fall 1929–Summer 1932; thereafter Pulp, 96 pp.

PRICE: 50¢, Fall 1929–Summer 1932; 25¢, Fall 1932–Winter 1933.

Mike Ashley

WONDER STORY ANNUAL

A bumper reprint magazine, *Wonder Story Annual* came from the same stable as *Thrilling Wonder Stories* (*Wonder Stories**) and *Startling Stories*,* and was a companion to a similar reprint magazine, *Fantastic Story Quarterly*.* Whereas the latter concentrated on short novels and stories, *WSA* went boldly for full-length novels. Its four issues, published between 1950 and 1953, resurrected such now forgotten wonders as "The Onslaught from Rigel" by Fletcher Pratt, which had first appeared in the Winter 1932 *Wonder Stories Quarterly*,* and "The Death of Iron" by French writer, S. S. Held, which had been serialized in *Wonder Stories* in 1932. Of greater significance was Manly Wade Wellman's "Twice in Time" from the May 1940 *Startling Stories*, and Jack Williamson's "Gateway to Paradise" from the July 1941 *Startling*. Williamson's shorter novel, "The Alien Intelligence," was also reprinted.

Among the shorter contents worthy of resurrection were D. D. Sharp's "The Eternal Man," Henry Kuttner's "Call Him Demon," John W. Campbell's "The Brain-Stealers of Mars," Fredric Brown's "Nothing Sirius" and Ray Bradbury's "The Irritated People."

On the whole *WSA* was well received, especially its first issue, which was a bumper 196 pages, though later issues shrank a little. The idea of a regular *Annual* and *Quarterly* brought back echoes of the 1920s and appealed to the ever-present nostalgia of the fans. The publishers, Standard Magazines, were also aware of the steadily growing rivalry of the paperback novels and anthologies, and so made *WSA* a tempting offer. In fact, the magazine was arguably a hybrid anthology, and, indeed, later issues declared themselves as "America's Best Science Fiction Anthology," just another indication of the war that was going on behind the bookstalls.

It was the paperbacks that would be the victors, however. By 1953 the blight was already settling on the pulp field, and *WSA* was one of the first to succumb.

Information Sources

BIBLIOGRAPHY:
Nicholls. *Encyclopedia.*
Tuck.
INDEX SOURCES: Cook, IWG; ISFM; MIT; SFM.
REPRINT SOURCES:
    Reprint Magazine: A Canadian edition identical to the first issue only was released by Better Publications in Toronto.
LOCATION SOURCES: M.I.T. Science Fiction Library; Pennsylvania State University Library.

Publication History

TITLE: *Wonder Story Annual.*
VOLUME DATA: Undated other than by year. Volume 1, Number 1, [Summer] 1950– Volume 2, Number 1, [Spring] 1954. Annual. 1951 edition issued in summer, 1952 edition in spring. Total run: 4 issues.
PUBLISHERS: Better Publications (an imprint of Standard Magazines), Chicago and New York, 1950 edition; thereafter, Best Books, New York.
EDITORS: Sam Merwin, 1950–1951; Sam Mines, 1952–1953.
FORMAT: Pulp, 196 pp., 1950; thereafter, 160 pp.
PRICE: 25¢.

Mike Ashley

WONDERS OF THE SPACEWAYS

Wonders of the Spaceways was one of four indistinguishable SF pocketbook magazines of poor quality fiction issued by John Spencer and Company in London in the early 1950s. On balance *WOTS* contained moderately better fiction than the others, with a number of contributions by fans as opposed to hack writers in other fields, but the margin of improvement was minimal. Later issues carried stories by Lionel Fanthorpe and John S. Glasby. See *Futuristic Science Stories** for further details.

Information Sources

BIBLIOGRAPHY:
Ashley, Michael. *Fantasy Readers' Guide Number 1.* Wallsend, U.K.: Cosmos, 1979.
Nicholls. *Encyclopedia.*
Tuck.
INDEX SOURCES: Ashley, Michael, *Fantasy Readers' Guide Number 1*, Wallsend, U.K.: Cosmos, 1979; IBSF; MIT; SFM; Tuck.
REPRINT SOURCES: None known.
LOCATION SOURCES: M.I.T. Science Fiction Library.

Publication History

TITLE: *Wonders of the Spaceways.*
VOLUME DATA: No volume numbering. Issues undated. Number 1 [February 1951]–
    Number 10 [Spring 1954]. No regular schedule, issue 2 appearing in January 1952
    and thereafter approximately quarterly. Total run: 10 issues.
PUBLISHER: John Spencer & Co., London.
EDITORS: Sol Assael and Michael Nahum (not credited within issues).
FORMAT: Pocketbook; Number 1, 128 pp.; Number 2, 96 pp.; Numbers 3–6, 112 pp.;
    Numbers 7–10, 128 pp.
PRICE: 1/6d.

Mike Ashley

WORLDS BEYOND

If *Worlds Beyond* had served no other purpose, it justified its existence by
helping to increase the going rate for science fiction stories in 1950 from two
to three cents a word. As Frederik Pohl tells the story, Damon Knight wanted
more authority than was offered by the job that Pohl had helped him get at
Popular Publications[1] as assistant editor of *Super Science Stories.*[*2] Pohl suggested that he convince Alex Hillman, owner of a magazine chain, to add a
science fiction digest to his line. Successful, Knight returned to Pohl to ask him
how he could get a look at the stories going to Horace L. Gold and John W.
Campbell. Pohl's reply was "Pay more than they do." After Hillman granted
Knight a budget that enabled him to pay three cents a word, Pohl used the fact
to manipulate first *Galaxy Science Fiction** and then *Astounding* (*Analog Science
Fiction**) to follow suit—"the two-cent line had been broken."[3]

Knight spent his money well, purchasing both high-quality reprints and new
stories ranging widely under the heading he gave them—"science-fantasy fiction":

> a blend of two forms of imaginative writing: science-fiction and fantasy.
> . . . The "pure" science-fiction story is almost nonexistent; it has acquired
> the flavor and the freedom of fantasy. "Pure" fantasy is equally doomed
> by the new attitudes and knowledge that science has introduced; but at the
> same time the principles of science-fiction writing have given it new life.
>
> The hybrid (and if you doubt that it exists, read C. M. Kornbluth's *The
> Mindworm*, in this issue!) is as strongly alive as any form of modern
> fiction. It's our aim to do everything possible to strengthen it further and
> to aid its growth.
>
> You won't find "wiring-diagram" science-fiction stories here, or Gothic
> horror-fantasy either. But the whole field in between is our meat.[4]

Although half of each issue's stories were reprints, they were unusual—for
example, Franz Kafka's "The Hunter Gracchus," Philip Wylie's "An Epistle
to the Thessalonians," Graham Greene's "The End of the Party," E. B. White's

"The Supremacy of Uruguay." He drew strongly upon the British writers for further reprints to create a marked element of literate fantasy in his magazine: Lord Dunsany, Rudyard Kipling, R. E. Morrough, and William F. Temple. Finally, the reprint feature allowed Hillman to promote one of his company's new novels, Jack Vance's *The Dying Earth*,[5] from which Knight selected an episode from "Liane the Wayfarer."

Knight cut costs on features and artwork. The only feature was his book review column, "The Dissecting Table," the one element to survive the demise of *Worlds Beyond*—it was to continue in Lester del Rey's *Science Fiction Adventures** and finally establish him as one of the field's major book reviewers.[6] The covers were uninteresting efforts by Paul Calle and H. R. Van Dongen. The interior illustrations were sparse and small, but destined to find distinction in a different direction was one of the artists—Harry Harrison. A commercial artist at the time and a member of the Hydra Club, to which belonged nearly every important science fiction writer in the New York area, in the magazine's last issue he published his first short story—"Rock Diver."[7]

But most of Knight's new stories were from established writers. Original and individual pieces came from a wide range of talents—from Cleve Cartmill and Lester del Rey to C. M. Kornbluth and William Tenn to Katherine MacLean and Judith Merril. Within this group was a contingent simultaneously experiencing considerable success in the detective novel: Fredric Brown, Wilson Tucker, even John D. MacDonald.[8] The quality of the new stories is attested to by the fact that two-thirds subsequently appeared in anthologies, notably William Tenn's "Null-P" (four times), Judith Merril's "Survival Ship" (five times) and C. M. Kornbluth's "The Mindworm" (eight times).[9]

But Alex Hillman clearly saw matters differently. Although the second and third issues were already produced and the reception of the first issue was enthusiastic, he killed the magazine because its initial sales were inadequate; nor did he reverse his decision when the prepared issues made better money.[10] Perhaps he was rankled to learn that he had raised science fiction writers' wages by a half.

Notes

1. Frederik Pohl, *The Way the Future Was: A Memoir* (New York: Del Rey Books, 1978), p. 153.

2. Michael Ashley, "Appendix C: Glossary of Magazine Editors," in *The History of the Science Fiction Magazine (1946–1955)* (Chicago, 1976), III: 334.

3. Pohl, pp. 153–54.

4. Damon Knight, "Science Fantasy Fiction," *Worlds Beyond*, Vol. 1, No. 1 (December 1950): inside back cover.

5. Ashley, p. 58.

6. Ibid., pp. 79–80.

7. Knight, "Contributors," *Worlds Beyond*, Vol. 1, No. 3 (February 1951): inside back cover.

8. *Worlds Beyond*, Vol. 1, No. 1 (December 1950): inside front cover; also see Donald

H. Tuck, *The Encyclopedia of Science Fiction and Fantasy* (Chicago, 1978), II: 426. In this connection, it is illuminating to read in Knight's ''The Dissecting Table'' of the same issue the following: ''van Vogt is not, strictly speaking, a science-fiction writer. . . . he had been writing crime-suspense novels, with a dollop each of science-fantasy background ever since *Slan*'' (p. 115).

9. Data derived from William Contento, *Index to Science Fiction Anthologies and Collections* (Boston, 1978).

10. Ashley, p. 58.

Information Sources

BIBLIOGRAPHY:
Nicholls. *Encyclopedia.*
Tuck.
INDEX SOURCES: ISFM; MIT; MT; SFM.
REPRINT SOURCES: None known.
LOCATION SOURCES: M.I.T. Science Fiction Library; Pennsylvania State University
        Library.

Publication History

TITLE: *Worlds Beyond*, subtitled ''Science-Fantasy Fiction.''
VOLUME DATA: Volume 1, Number 1, December 1950–Volume 1, Number 3, February
        1951. Monthly. Total run: 3 issues.
PUBLISHER: Hillman Periodicals, Chicago. Editorial offices in New York.
EDITOR: Damon Knight.
FORMAT: Digest, 128 pp.
PRICE: 25¢.

E. F. Casebeer

WORLDS OF FANTASY (1950–1954)

Worlds of Fantasy was the second of four indistinguishable SF pocketbook magazines of poor-quality fiction issued by John Spencer and Company in the early 1950s. The first few issues carry possibly some of the worst SF Spencer ever published, and its standards were low to begin with. However, the balance was subsequently evened, and the seventh issue, which carries two stories by E. C. Tubb and others by John S. Glasby and Alfred Hind, is moderately readable. All stories, however, were plagued by slipshod, inept writing and totally unimaginative plots which usually involved the invasion of Earth by Moon-men or Martians. Readers wishing to sample the range in writing quality of the Spencer magazines could do no better than read the first (Summer 1950), seventh and final (fourteenth) issues of *WOF*. See *Futuristic Science Stories** for further details.

Information Sources

BIBLIOGRAPHY:
Ashley, Michael. *Fantasy Readers Guide* 1. Wallsend, U.K.: Cosmos, 1979.
Nicholls. *Encyclopedia*.
SFM.
Tuck.
INDEX SOURCES: Ashley, Michael, *Fantasy Readers Guide* 1, Wallsend, U.K.: Cosmos, 1979; IBSF; MIT; MT; Tuck.
REPRINT SOURCES: None known.
LOCATION SOURCES: Grand Valley State College Library; M.I.T. Science Fiction Library; Pennsylvania State University Library; University of Georgia Library.

Publication History

TITLE: *Worlds of Fantasy*.
VOLUME DATA: All issues undated. Number 1 [Summer 1950–Number 14 [Summer 1954]. Schedule irregular, but approximately quarterly. Total run: 14 issues.
PUBLISHER: John Spencer & Co., London.
EDITORS: Sol Assael and Michael Nahum (not credited in issues).
FORMAT: Pocketbook; Issues 1–3, 128 pp.; Issue 4, 96 pp.; Issues 5–10, 112 pp.; Issues 11–14, 128 pp.
PRICE: 1/6.

Mike Ashley

WORLDS OF FANTASY (1968–1971)

Worlds of Fantasy was the third magazine (after *Worlds of Tomorrow** and *International Science Fiction**) added to Robert Guinn's Galaxy Publishing line during the nine-year tenure of Frederik Pohl with that company. Pohl chose Lester del Rey to edit the magazine,[1] but after the sale of the Galaxy group to Arnold Abramson's Universal Publishing and Distributing Corporation in 1969, del Rey became associate editor under Ejler Jakobsson (who also took over *Galaxy Science Fiction,* If,** and *Worlds of Tomorrow*).[2] The cover of the undated (but copyright 1968) first issue carries an arresting Jack Gaughan painting of a green mer-creature bottle-feeding a human infant, and promises material by L. Sprague de Camp and Robert E. Howard. A starburst and a spine copy line assure the reader, "All Stories New," perhaps to distinguish *Worlds of Fantasy* from the increasing number of reprint fantasy magazines. The Gaughan covers and interior illustrations continued in subsequent issues, as did the names of prominent genre writers displayed on the cover and contents page: Gordon Dickson, James Gunn, Ursula LeGuin, Andre Norton, Frederik Pohl, Clifford Simak, Theodore Sturgeon, Robert F. Young. Nevertheless, after four issues spread across more than two years, UPD, apparently dissatisfied with its economic performance, dropped *Worlds of Fantasy* in the spring of 1971.

Del Rey assembled Numbers 1 and 2 and acquired about half the material for

Number 3, the point at which UPD's Jakobsson assumed control.[3] Despite the changes in control, del Rey set the tone for the magazine. As with his earlier work on *Fantasy Magazine*,* the emphasis was on the modern, *Unknown Worlds* (*Unknown**) rather than the Gothic, *Weird Tales** strain of fantasy, with a strong infusion of adventure. In his inaugural editorial, "Fads and Fantasies," del Rey repeats attitudes and preferences voiced fifteen years earlier—that fantasy is fun, entertainment, as is all literature, but that modern fantasy makes special demands: "A vampire isn't at all funny or entertaining—until it is displaced into modern anachronistic times or until its character is displaced by the introduction of some purely human attitudes."[4] He cites Tolkien's work as the "most successful of all recent fantasy" in its juxtaposition of "the displaced against that which remains firmly anchored in our own reality."[5] Fantasy's "displacement," says del Rey, encourages "the flexibility that seems to me the most desirable of mental attitudes."[6]

The influence and popularity of the fantasy adventure, from literate, Tolkienian pseudomedievalia, through science fantasy, to pulpy, Robert E. Howard sword and sorcery, is apparent in the longer fiction published in *Worlds of Fantasy*: of the five "complete novels," four are sword and sorcery or action stories (Simak's science fantasy "Reality Doll" qualifies as the latter), and the fifth is Ursula LeGuin's Earthsea novel, "The Tombs of Atuan." Add to this two novelettes (a Carter–de Camp Conan pastiche and Gordon Dickson's science fantasy "Walker between the Planes") and five out of twenty-three short stories (including an authentic, unpublished Howard story), and the total reveals that more than half of each issue belongs to the heroic fantasy/sword and sorcery/fantasy adventure family.

Most of the remaining stories pursue the *Unknown Worlds* tradition of modernizing or ringing changes on established supernatural motifs: in Robert Silverberg's "As Is," a used car's trunk magically produces emergency gear; psychic cannibalism and traditional vampirism figure in Frederik Pohl's "Call Me Million" and Bill Warren's "Death Is a Lonely Place" respectively; Mack Reynolds' "What the Vintners Buy" and Frank S. Robinson's "Kerman Widens Lead in Poll" provide yet another pair of variations on the deal-with-the-devil theme. Some of the most memorable stories, however, do not fit this pattern— Sonya Dorman's "Me-Too," a science fictional portrait of an alien; Naomi J. Kahn's "Funny Place," with its Coney Island setting; and early stories by Michael Bishop ("If a Flower Could Eclipse") and James Tiptree, Jr. ("The Man Doors Said Hello To").

In literary quality and commercial appeal, *Worlds of Fantasy* falls somewhere between *The Magazine of Fantasy and Science Fiction** and Cele Goldsmith's *Fantastic*.* The magazine had attractive packaging, famous names, and a strong mix of popular fantasy subgenres. Its discontinuation, like those of *Unknown*, *Beyond Fantasy Fiction** and *Fantasy Fiction* before it, should not be attributed to any literary failure, but to the unpredictable and often irrational forces of the magazine publishing world.

Notes

1. Frederik Pohl, *The Way the Future Was* (New York: Del Rey Books, 1978), p. 235.
2. Lester del Rey, private communication, June 1979.
3. Ibid.
4. *Worlds of Fantasy* 1 (1968): 4, 130.
5. "Fads and Fantasies," *Worlds of Fantasy* 1 (1968): 130.
6. Ibid.

Information Sources

BIBLIOGRAPHY:
Nicholls. *Encyclopedia.*
Pohl, Frederik. *The Way the Future Was.* New York: Del Rey Books, 1978.
Tuck.
INDEX SOURCES: ISFM-II; NESFA; SFM.
REPRINT SOURCES: None known.
LOCATION SOURCES: M.I.T. Science Fiction Library.

Publication History

TITLE: *Worlds of Fantasy.*
VOLUME DATA: Volume 1, Number 1, [September] 1968–Volume 1, Number 4, Spring
    1971. No schedule, but final three issues approximately quarterly. Total run: 4
    issues.
PUBLISHER: First issue, Galaxy Publishing Corp., New York. Thereafter Universal
    Publishing & Distributing Corp., New York.
EDITORS: Lester del Rey, Number 1, [September] 1968–Number 2, [Fall] 1970; Ejler
    Jakobsson, Number 3, [Winter] 1970/71–Number 4, Spring 1971.
FORMAT: Digest; first issue, 128 pp.; thereafter 192 pp.
PRICE: 60¢, first issue; thereafter 75¢.

Russell Letson

WORLDS OF IF

Variant title by which *If* became conveniently known during the 1960s, although the formal title was still *If, Worlds of Science Fiction.* See *IF*.

WORLDS OF THE UNIVERSE

A single-issue magazine, *Worlds of the Universe*, probably published in 1953, has always been something of a mystery to SF researchers. The unnamed editor betrayed a clear knowledge of the SF field and opened his editorial with the admission that he regarded himself as an SF *fan*, but his identity was never disclosed. The artwork was signed "Marcus," but the style is undoubtedly that of Norman Light, who produced some of the better covers for the John Spencer magazines and became a popular comic artist. The publishers were Gould-Light, and the inference is that Norman Light was also the editor. Light had established his own publishing house to produce comics, a field to which he turned totally when *Worlds of the Universe* failed.

WOTU contained three stories. The lead, attributed to "Mark Denholm," was by John Russell Fearn. Another, attributed to "Manning Stern" on the contents page, was credited to Thomas W. Wade in the interior. (Wade was also a regular contributor to the John Spencer magazines). The third was credited to the unknown "John Sylvassey." All three were rather routine adventure stories showing little imagination.

Light had high hopes for his magazine. The editorial looked forward to a letter column and a serial in future issues. Just what happened is not known, but no further issues appeared, and the magazine has since become a collector's curio.

Information Sources

BIBLIOGRAPHY:
Nicholls. *Encyclopedia*.
Tuck.
INDEX SOURCES: None known.
REPRINT SOURCES: None known.
LOCATION SOURCES: None known.

Publication History

TITLE: *Worlds of the Universe*.
VOLUME DATA: Undated. Number 1 [probably late 1953].
PUBLISHER: Gould-Light Publishing Co., London.
EDITOR: Not identified in issue, but probably Norman Light.
FORMAT: Pocketbook, 102 pp.
PRICE: 1/6d.

Mike Ashley

WORLDS OF TOMORROW

Worlds of Tomorrow, which debuted in 1963, came as a surprise not only to the readers—it was the first new genuine SF magazine since 1958, and with the blight that had settled on the field in 1960, it came as a sign of fresh hopes—but also to its editor, Frederik Pohl. Pohl had been striving to increase bi-monthly schedules of *If** and *Galaxy Science Fiction** to monthly, but each time he convinced publisher Sol Cohen and proprietor Robert M. Guinn, they had second thoughts and his hopes were dashed. Thus the sudden suggestion to publish a totally new SF magazine and issue it as a monthly left Pohl somewhat speechless. In the end *WOT* also appeared as a bi-monthly, but within the year his wishes were granted and *If* became monthly.

WOT's first two issues seemed to lack direction, and in answer to readers' requests, in the third issue Pohl stated that his lack of editorial guidance had been deliberate to test whether or not *WOT* could stand up for itself. In effect, though, Pohl had enough on his hands structuring *Galaxy* and *If* and, if the truth were known, there was not much else he could do with *WOT*. As a result *WOT* could be called the magazine without a policy. *Galaxy* was always the big sister, presenting the bolder SF concepts and hoping to appeal to a more sophisticated SF reader. *If* was the fun magazine, appealing to adventurous minds and also catering more to the SF fan as opposed to the general reader. *Worlds of Tomorrow* fitted somewhere between the two, presenting stories that did not seem right for the other magazines but that were too good to reject. Actually, most of the stories in *WOT* could easily have fitted into either of the other titles, but on the whole they were less polished than the *Galaxy* stories, and yet perhaps a little too out of the ordinary for *If*. "*Worlds of Tomorrow* will not—repeat, *not*—specialize in any one kind of science-fiction story," Pohl told his readers in the third issue, in the hope that it would encourage writers to experiment and not feel restricted by publishing policies.[1] This same no-holds-barred approach applied to the non-fiction. Pohl did not want a regular scientific article in each issue, but instead encouraged articles that looked at new aspects of future science and how they might be reflected in SF. The results of this package were entertaining, to say the least. Although *WOT* always remained third fiddle to *Galaxy* and *If* it was nevertheless a magazine worth checking out each issue, and by and large there was something rewarding to be found.

WOT concentrated on longer stories, although it also published serials and short pieces. The first issue, for instance, released in February 1963 and dated April, carried the first episode of a new serialized novel by Arthur C. Clarke, "People of the Sea," subsequently published in book form as *Dolphin Island* (New York: Holt, 1963). It was a juvenile adventure novel about a teenage boy and his experiences with dolphins, and certainly inferior work by Clarke's standards. Elsewhere in the issue were competent stories by such old-timers as Murray Leinster and Miriam Allen deFord and newcomer Keith Laumer, but in hindsight perhaps the most important story, and one indicative of *WOT*'s significant liberality, was "To See the Invisible Man" by Robert Silverberg. As Silverberg relates in his autobiographical essay, "Sounding Brass, Tinkling Cymbal" (1975), Pohl had offered him total creative freedom to write whatever he chose. This story was the first result. Inspired by Jorge Luis Borges, the story was entirely different from anything Silverberg had previously written in SF, and he himself regarded it as "a mature, complex story."[2] In simple terms it told of an outcast to society whose punishment is to go totally unnoticed by everyone for the period of one year.

The second issue presented a further challenging item, this time nonfiction. It was an abridgment of R. C. W. Ettinger's "The Prospects of Immortality," which had hitherto been published only in a limited, spiral-bound edition by the author. Following its publication in *WOT* and the ensuing excitement it provoked, a much enlarged version was published by Doubleday (1964). Ettinger put forward the suggestion that corpses could be frozen immediately after death and before any brain damage began until the time when technology was sufficiently advanced to revive the body and restore it to life and health. Ettinger's plans were eventually put into action, and quite a few "corpsicles" are supposed to exist. *WOT* became a small forum for news on immortality through freezing. The August 1966 issue reprinted a discussion that took place on Long John Nebel's radio program on WNBC, New York, between Ettinger and Pohl, together with Dr. Joseph Lo Presti, Shirley Herz and Victor Borge. The following issue, November 1966, contained a further article by Ettinger, updating the information.

On the fiction side, *WOT* now became a fairly regular home for writers like Cordwainer Smith, Roger Zelazny and, most especially, Keith Laumer, all of whom had something new to offer. R. A. Lafferty appeared with his unique brand of SF, and Brian W. Aldiss offered something of a surprise in "The Dark Light-Years" (April 1964) about the first meeting between the human race and a race mentally superior but physically repugnant. It delights in wallowing in "filth of a certain rich consistency made up chiefly of mud and excrement."

However, if *Worlds of Tomorrow* is to go down in history for any one reason, it will be because it published the first of Philip José Farmer's immensely popular Riverworld series. Farmer had originally written a long novel, *I Owe for the Flesh*, at white heat in 1953 for a contest. The novel had won but was never published. Ten years later Farmer took the novel, then about 150,000 words, and sent it to Frederik Pohl. Pohl "read it, and he thought it was a terrific idea, but he thought it'd be a lot better if I were to write a series, because he said actually the concept was really too big to be put into one novel."[3] And so the Riverworld series was born, starting with "Day of the Great Shout," which led the January 1965 issue and was decorated with some powerful Virgil Finlay illustrations. A year later the second part appeared, simply titled "Riverworld" (January 1966). The two were subsequently interwoven, with much rewriting, into Farmer's Hugo-winning novel, *To Your Scattered Bodies Go* (New York: Putnam, 1971), along with "The Suicide Express" (March 1966).

Also to *WOT* goes the distinction of publishing Larry Niven's first novel, "World of Ptavvs" (March 1965), subsequently published in a much enlarged form by Ballantine Books (1966). *WOT* also published two novels by Philip K. Dick, "All We Marsmen" (August–December 1963; published in book form as *The Martian Time-Slip* [New York: Ballantine, 1964]) and "Project Plowshare" (November 1965–January 1966; in book form as *The Zap Gun* [New York: Pyramid, 1967]).

Starting with the November 1965 issue *WOT* took over publication of Sam Moskowitz's series of articles on themes and personalities in SF, which had hitherto run in *Amazing Stories** until a change in publisher. Moskowitz covered the lives and works of such people as Virgil Finlay and Willy Ley as well as dealing with such themes as racialism in SF and the history of the SF detective. Some of these articles, along with others published when the series was absorbed by *If*, were subsequently included in Moskowitz's book *Strange Horizons* (New York: Scribner's 1976).

But now there were signs that *WOT* was ailing. Its bi-monthly schedule was dropped to quarterly, ostensibly to try to fit a new magazine into the schedule. That new magazine, *International Science Fiction,** did not appear for a year, and when it did *WOT* was dropped completely. The decision was clearly sudden, for the May 1967 issue announced further stories as forthcoming. These subsequently appeared in *If*, the August 1967 issue of that magazine bearing the additional subtitle "combined with Worlds of Tomorrow," which remained on the cover until the change of publisher in 1969. The reason for *WOT*'s decline, according to Pohl, was the lack of adequate distribution, a disease rife in SF magazines. In its latter days *WOT* had become an increasingly exciting magazine, thriving in the wake of *If*'s success. One of the last major stories it published was Samuel R. Delany's "The Star Pit" (February 1967), which was also Delany's first appearance in any SF magazine.

It was not the end of *WOT*, however. When *Galaxy* and *If* were taken over by new publisher Arnold Abramson there were immediate announcements that both *Worlds of Fantasy** and *Worlds of Tomorrow* would be revived. First distribution and then printing technicalities delayed the day of resurrection for a year, but eventually, in the summer of 1970, the new *Worlds of Tomorrow* appeared. In many ways it would have been better had it remained a memory. At this time the Galaxy group of magazines were at their most shoddy. Overloaded with the four magazines, Jack Gaughan poured out hasty line drawings which failed to enhance the appearance of the magazine. The covers were certainly no better, and the contents held little merit. The covers were certainly no better, and the contents held little merit. The editor, Ejler Jakobsson, seemed to be responding to the newfound sexual freedom in SF prevalent at the end of the sixties. It found its way into at least three of the stories, "In the Land of Love" by George H. Smith; "The State vs Susan Quod" by Noel Loomis, perhaps the best story in the issue, relating the events leading up to a court case between husband and android; and "The Bridge" by Piers Anthony, where a man finds he has to have intercourse with a nine-inch alien beauty in order to save another civilization.

Most of the stories, many of them short, were mediocre, with only Neal Barrett, Jr.'s "Greyspun's Gift" and William Rotsler's "Epic" in later issues showing promise. *WOT* now lacked any personality or sincerity. It looked and felt just like an overflow magazine, assembled with no real feeling or diligence. The consensus of opinion was clear. Within three issues *WOT* had once again folded, this time for good.

Notes

1. Frederik Pohl, "Hindsight and Foresight," *Worlds of Tomorrow*, August 1963, p. 4.

2. Robert Silverberg, "Sounding Brass, Tinkling Cymbal," in *Hell's Cartographers*, ed. Brian W. Aldiss and Harry Harrison (London: Weidenfeld & Nicolson, 1975), p. 28.

3. From an interview with Philip José Farmer conducted by David Kraft and Mitch Steele in June 1972 and published in *Science Fiction Review*, No. 14 (August 1975): 11.

Information Sources

BIBLIOGRAPHY:
Nicholls. *Encyclopedia*.
Tuck.
INDEX SOURCES: ISFM-II; MIT; NESFA; SFM; Tuck.
REPRINT SOURCES:
  Reprint Editions: A British edition was released by Gold Star Publications, London, identical to U.S. edition except for interior cover advertisements and redated. Four issues, 3/6d., corresponding to U.S. as follows: U.K. Spring 1967 = U.S. August 1966; U.K. Summer 1967 = U.S. November 1966; U.K. Autumn 1967 = U.S. February 1967; U.K. Winter 1967 = U.S. May 1967.
  Derivative Anthologies: Issued in magazine format, *The Best Science Fiction from Worlds of Tomorrow*, ed. Frederik Pohl (New York: Galaxy, 1964), selected stories from the first six issues.
LOCATION SOURCES: Bowling Green State University Library; Harvard University Library; M.I.T. Science Fiction Library; Pennsylvania State University Library; State University of New York-Albany Library.

Publication History

TITLE: *Worlds of Tomorrow*.
VOLUME DATA: Volume 1, Number 1, April 1963–Volume 5, Number 3, Spring 1971. Volumes 1 and 2, six issues per volume, bi-monthly (except October 1964 issue became November and schedule adjusted by one month). Volume 3, seven issues, bi-monthly. Volume 4, four issues, quarterly. Combined with *If* after May 1967 issue. Revived with Volume 5, three issues, quarterly, as follows: [Summer] 1970, Winter 1970, Spring 1971. Total run: 26 issues.
PUBLISHERS: The first issue (April 1963) was issued by the Barmaray Co., Inc., a subsidiary of Galaxy Publishing Corp., which published all issues June 1963–May 1967; UPD Publishing Corp., [Summer] 1970–Spring 1971.
EDITORS: Frederik Pohl, April 1963–May 1967; Ejler Jakobsson, [Summer] 1970–Spring 1971.
FORMAT: Digest, 160 pp., April 1963–May 1967 and [Summer] 1970; 192 pp., Winter 1970–Spring 1971.
PRICE: 50¢, April 1963–May 1967; 60¢, [Summer] 1970; 75¢, Winter 1970–Spring 1971.

Mike Ashley

WU FANG

See THE MYSTERIOUS WU FANG.

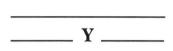

YANKEE SCIENCE FICTION

One of the most enterprising of wartime publishers in Britain was Gerald G. Swan. He had established his own small publishing company in 1938, but at the outset he stockpiled his books rather than having them distributed. "By the time World War II had started," discovered researcher W. G. Lofts, "he had three large warehouses full of paperbacks. By this uncanny foresight, when paper became severely rationed . . . he was still able to 'get in on the market' to his great advantage."[1] Indeed, Swan virtually cornered the magazine market and released hundreds of publications in all fields of fiction.

His first venture into science fiction was in producing the British edition of Columbia's *Science Fiction*,* more specifically the October and December 1939 issues. Swan made a deal with publisher Louis Silberkleit which Swan sustained for twenty years. He would still be reprinting from the early 1940 Columbia magazines in 1960 (see *Science Fiction Library**). In 1941 Swan began to issue a series of *Yankee* magazines. They ranged the whole spectrum of fiction and were released at a varying rate averaging one a week. Numbers 3, 11 and 21 of the series were entitled specifically *Yankee Science Fiction*, while issues 6, 14 and 19 were *Yankee Weird Shorts.**

It was fortunate for Swan that no Trades Description Act existed, since the majority of the contents were by British writers. Apart from *YSF* 3—which reprinted four stories from the Summer 1940 *Science Fiction Quarterly**—and one story in *YSF* 11, all stories were by homegrown talent. These included W. P. Cockroft, Gerald Evans and John Russell Fearn, but of special interest is the author of "Invasion from Venus" in *YSF* 21—Paul Ashwell. In the 1950s this writer became better known in the pages of *Astounding* (*Analog Science Fiction**) under the pseudonyms Paul Ash and Pauline Ashwell, but her first story is hidden away in this obscure British magazine.[2]

Yankee Science Fiction followed the format of all of Swan's magazines at this time, large-size, slim (about thirty pages on poor-quality paper) and atrociously printed. After the war Swan recommenced the series with the slightly more refined title of *Swan American Magazine*. Issues 11 and 15 were partial reprints of the December 1942 *Future Fantasy and Science Fiction (Future Fiction*)* and the Winter 1942 *Science Fiction Quarterly*.

Notes

1. W. G. Lofts, "Memories of Gerald G. Swan—Publishers," *Collector's Digest*, November 1970; reprinted in *Bill's Amusement Alley* 2 (Spring 1976).
2. Her real name was Pauline Whitby.

Information Sources

INDEX SOURCES: IBSF.
REPRINT SOURCES: None known.
LOCATION SOURCES: None known.

Publication History

TITLE: *Yankee Science Fiction*.
VOLUME DATA: Numbers sequential in *Swan Yankee Magazine* series, Number 3 (February 1942), Number 11 (April 1942), Number 21 (July 1942).
PUBLISHER: Gerald G. Swan, Ltd., London.
EDITOR: Not identified within issue.
FORMAT: Pulp, 32 pp.
PRICE: 10¢ on front cover, 3d on back cover.

Mike Ashley

YANKEE WEIRD SHORTS

Three 1942 issues of the *Swan Yankee Magazine* were devoted specifically to weird fiction, just as another three featured science fiction. Although Gerald Swan gave every impression that the magazine was a U.S. import, or possibly reprint, all of the stories were British in origin. They included contributions from W. P. Cockroft, Kay Hammond, John Maxwell (probably an alias of Ernest L. McKeag) and Gerald Evans. The stories were all featureless vignettes aimed at a story-starved wartime readership and of transient importance. Stories not used in the series surfaced in *Weird Shorts** a few years later and in *Weird and Occult Library** nearly twenty years later.

Information Sources

INDEX SOURCES: MT.
REPRINT SOURCES: None known.
LOCATION SOURCES: None known.

Publication History

TITLE: *Yankee Weird Shorts*.

VOLUME DATA: Numbers sequential in *Swan Yankee Magazine* series, Number 6 (March 1942), Number 14 (May 1942), Number 19 (June 1942).

PUBLISHER: Walter G. Swan, London.

EDITOR: Not identified within issue, but probably Gerald Swan.

FORMAT: Pulp, 32 pp.

PRICE: 10¢ on front cover, 3d. on back cover.

Mike Ashley

Section II

ASSOCIATIONAL ENGLISH-LANGUAGE ANTHOLOGIES

ANALOG ANNUAL/ANALOG YEARBOOK

An extension of the monthly magazine. See ANALOG in Section I.

ANDROMEDA

Andromeda was a short-lived British anthology series edited by Peter Weston, editor/publisher of the respected fanzine *Speculation* (formerly *Zenith*). It came about as a result of a meeting between Anthony Cheetham of Futura Publications and Weston with Rog Peyton, proprietor of the Andromeda Bookshop in Birmingham, England, and the shop lent its name to the series. Weston's intention was simply to bring together the best-quality science fiction he could find. There was no deliberate annual schedule, and certainly no restrictive editorial policy. He admitted, however, that trying to find good-quality stories that lived up to all his criteria had been difficult. For this reason the *Andromeda* series appeared erratically, but it contained some very fine stories. The first volume came out in May 1976 and included among its ten stories "Seeing" by Harlan Ellison, "An Infinite Summer" by Christopher Priest, "A Beast for Norn" by George R. R. Martin and stories by Naomi Mitchison, Bob Shaw, Brian W. Aldiss and Robert Holdstock.

Weston took more of a gamble with the second volume by presenting stories mostly by unknown or relatively new writers, Bob Shaw being the only name recognizable to general readers. He completed the blend with the third volume, which included a memorable nightmare, "Black Glass" from Fritz Leiber, "Flare Time" from Larry Niven, and items from such new names as William Wu, Tom Allen and David Langford.

The third volume, however, found Weston writing words of advice to would-be new writers, and the impression was that it was hard going. Worthily, Weston had set his limits for quality high, and the *Andromeda* series is a good addition to any library; but apparently the general readership were not so convinced, as sales were insufficient to keep the series alive.

Publication History

TITLE: *Andromeda.*
VOLUME DATA: Number 1, [May] 1976; Number 2, [June] 1977; Number 3, [September] 1978.
PUBLISHER: Orbit Books, an imprint of Futura Publications, London.
EDITOR: Peter Weston.
FORMAT: Pocketbook, 206 pp., Numbers 1 and 2; 240 pp., Number 3.
PRICE: Number 1, 65p.; Number 2, 80p.; Number 3, 90p.

Mike Ashley

AVON FANTASY READER and AVON SCIENCE FICTION READER

Two paperback anthology series that have always been regarded as reprint magazines and are thus accorded an entry in Section I.

CHRYSALIS

In 1977 Roy Torgeson, an editor at Zebra Books, set himself the goal of publishing an anthology series that ran to a million words of the best original science fiction he could buy. Thus was born *Chrysalis*, a series that soon attracted much attention from readers and writers, not only because of the rapid appearance of its early volumes, but also because of the surprising quality of its stories, many of which were written by new and unestablished writers. The series name was perhaps significant here. A chrysalis is "something in the stage of development," and Torgeson was clearly becoming increasingly experienced as the series evolved from one volume to the next.

Initially Theodore Sturgeon supplied the introductions, but Torgeson eventually took over himself. The first seven volumes appeared as paperback originals, but thereafter Doubleday published a hardcover edition first. Torgeson concentrated on obtaining fascinating and entertaining stories, putting quality before names. As a result the second issue contained something of a blockbuster in "The Works of His Hand, Made Manifest," the first story sale by Karen Jollie, which caused Sturgeon to honor it with the statement that it "is one of the finest short stories I have ever read anywhere."

The early volumes crammed in an amazing number of stories of all lengths. Surprisingly, few were nominated for awards, perhaps because few stories were outstanding in any one volume when compared to the other contents—in other words, the evenness of quality prevented many of the meritorious stories from standing out. Apart from the new names Torgeson also published the last story by Ward Moore as well as items by Philip José Farmer, R. A. Lafferty, Charles L. Grant, Thomas F. Monteleone and Michael Bishop, but it was increasingly evident that the better stories came from the new recruits, fresh and untainted, bursting to reveal their talents. Stories to link with Jollie's as outstanding examples are "Comets and Kings" by Somtow Sucharitkul in the fifth volume and "The Wizard of Shensi Province" by Glenn Chang in the sixth. Orson Scott Card, who became a regular contributor, also provided some memorable stories, especially "A Cross-Country Trip to Kill Richard Nixon" in the seventh volume.

A companion series to *Chrysalis* was *Other Worlds*.

Publication History

TITLE: *Chrysalis*.

VOLUME DATA: Volume 1, August 1977; Volume 2, August 1978; Volume 3, December 1978; Volume 4, February 1979; Volume 5, September 1979; Volume 6, October 1979; Volume 7, November 1979; Volume 8, September 1980; Volume 9, September 1981; Volume 10, April 1983.

PUBLISHER: Zebra Books, an imprint of the Kensington Publishing Corp., New York, through Volume 7. Thereafter hardcover edition first from Doubleday, Garden City, N.Y.

EDITOR: Roy Torgeson.

FORMAT: Pocketbook, 288 pp. with slight variations. Hardcover edition introduced from Volume 8.

PRICE: Volumes 1–7, $1.95; Volume 8, $9.95; Volume 9, $10.95; Volume 10, $11.95.

Mike Ashley

DESTINIES

Destinies was founded by Ace Books as part of an agreement with James Baen, whereby he became editor of its science fiction line and of *Destinies*.[1] According to Baen, he wanted to have a magazine to edit, as well as Ace Books' line of paperbacks, and thus *Destinies* was created.[2] It was given a paperback book format to take advantage of Ace Books' printing facilities and in order to capture readership among those who purchase science fiction books, but not magazines. Whether or not this strategy was successful, it does not seem to have converted significant numbers of book buyers into purchasers of the other science fiction magazines.

The first issue was announced by Ace Books' publicity department for July 1978 but finally appeared with a date of November-December 1978.[3] This issue sold out an initial printing of 150,000 copies, and a second printing of 35,000 was ordered. These carry the line "second edition" on the copyright page but are otherwise identical to the first printing.

The second issue was dated January-February 1979 on the cover, but February-March on the title page. This was the result of a change in planned frequency made after the covers were printed. Baen commented that while a monthly publication would be appreciated by readers, he would have to cut back to a quarterly schedule due to the press of business in maintaining the book line.[4]

The third issue read April-June on both cover and title page, but still said "published six times a year" on the title page. The fifth issue continued the bibliographic confusion. It read October-December 1979 and Volume 1, Number 5 on the cover, but "published four times a year." The next issue was February-March 1980 on the cover, but "the Spring issue" inside. After that things settled down, except that the final issue (Vol. 3, No. 2) carried no date. Logically it should be Winter 1981, but that was the preceding issue, there being no Autumn 1980 issue.

Baen had a decided orientation toward scientism as editor of *Galaxy Science Fiction* and carried this over as editor of *Destinies* in even more pronounced form. Thus, he usually placed major emphasis on selection of stories he regarded as "hard" science fiction (see comments below on Poul Anderson's series of articles), and those aimed at solutions of current or potentially near-term problems.[5] This should not be taken as indicating a uniformly serious publication. Each issue tried to include at least one humorous story; Larry Niven's farce "Assimilating Our Culture, That's What They're Doing" appeared in the first issue, and Gregory Benford's satirical "Time Guide" in the second. Of a unique psychological character is the paranoid fantasy "The Story Writer" by Robert Wilson. The final issue had no humor and had an unusual amount of downbeat material—perhaps appropriate for a final issue.

We might note here a Poul Anderson story in the second issue, "The Ways of Love," which is a sequel to a story that appeared twenty years earlier in *Analog*, "We Have Fed Our Sea." Anderson was also represented in the early issues of *Destinies* by a five-part series on the relationship between science and science fiction, "Science Fiction and Science." Baen gave the first section, subtitled "Reality, Fiction, and Points Between," the blurb "Serendipititiously [*sic*], Poul has precisely outlined the editorial philosophy of this magazine." The series discussed how various sciences (physical, social, biological) are adapted into fiction, drawing on stories by Anderson and many others for its points. Anderson was back with autobiographical notes in the last issue. Prepublication excerpts from Robert Heinlein's "Expanded Universe" appeared in the Summer 1980 issue. After the completion of the Anderson series, there was a series, which ran through the final issue, by Dean Ing on how to survive a nuclear war. *Destinies* never carried any fiction serials.

In its brief life *Destinies* attracted some attention from the various awards in the science fiction field. Gordon Dickson's "Lost Dorsai," the cover story for February-March 1980, placed eighth in the *Locus* poll of novellas, was nominated for a Nebula, and won the 1981 Hugo for best novella.[6] Baen rated sixth in polling for the Hugo for best editor in 1980, and third in 1981.

Baen took Jerry Pournelle as a science columnist with him from *Galaxy*,* as well as some of his favorite authors, such as Larry Niven and Gregory Benford. Each issue except the last carried book reviews, initially primarily by Spider Robinson, and later mostly by Norman Spinrad. The second issue carried a retrospective by Frederik Pohl on his career. Much of this is devoted to his experiences as an editor for thirty-nine years, his opinions on what makes a good editor, and changes in the status of the editor in the science fiction field over the years.

Since Baen feels that our culture is doomed unless it expands into space, the articles were generally even more oriented toward this theme than was the fiction, although the story "Spirals" by Niven and Pournelle explicitly dealt with that theme. The story also took a sly dig at academicians with perfect hindsight. The Spring 1980 issue featured an attack on the proposed Moon Treaty which, as part of a national campaign, may have helped defeat any chance for that United Nations-sponsored agreement to win passage in the United States.

In the final issue Baen said, "*Destinies* has had a level of sales comparable to a 'hot' anthology or a mid-range novel, while it has required a degree of editorial effort equal to what six or eight novels call for." He felt only a "magazine-editing junkie" (such as himself) could rationalize the misallocation of a book publisher's time, energy and enthusiasm. His departure from Ace Books meant the demise of *Destinies* after all the material he had purchased for it was used. Baen put out the last two issues (Vol. 3, Nos. 1 and 2) as a free-lance contractor for Ace.[7]

These two issues did not exhaust the purchased material, although they did exhaust the last of Baen's interest. The remaining stories were published with some additional material in a 1981 anthology entitled *Proteus: Voices for the 80's*, edited by Richard S. McEnroe. His editorial was entitled "The *Destinies* That Isn't." The cover, using the *Destinies* format, carried the line "A Destinies Special," and the frontispiece called it "a special *Destinies* edition." This should have convinced loyal followers to buy it, but those who enjoyed the nonfiction in Baen's version would have been disappointed by the lack of any nonfiction except McEnroe's brief editorial in *Proteus*. There was no indication of any plan to publish a second issue of *Proteus*.

Notes

1. Baen was editor of *Galaxy Science Fiction* from 1974 to 1977, before that serving as managing editor of *Galaxy*.

2. Comments by James P. Baen at Apricon 2, held at Columbia University on February 28, 1979.

3. "Destinies Announced," *Locus* 205 (October 1977): 1.

4. Comments by Baen at Apricon 2.

5. See especially Baen's editorial in the third issue, "The Plot," *Destinies*, Vol. 1, No. 3 (April-June 1979): 6–7.

6. *Locus* 246 (July 1981). *Locus* bills itself as the monthly newspaper of the science fiction field. It annually polls its readers for their choices of best editor, novel, short

story, and so on. The Nebula is awarded by the professional authors' organization, the Science Fiction Writers Association. The Hugos are voted on by members of the annual World Science Fiction Convention.

7. "Baen Quits Ace," *Locus* 237 (September 1980): 1.

Information Sources

INDEX SOURCES: NESFA-VI; NESFA-VII; NESFA-VIII; SFM.

DERIVATIVE ANTHOLOGIES: *The Best of Destinies* (New York: Ace, 1980), ed. James P. Baen, includes 9 stories and 4 articles. See also *Proteus: Voices for the Eighties*, ed. Richard S. McEnroe (New York: Ace, 1981), labeled "A Destinies Special," which contained stories purchased mostly for *Destinies* but which subsequently did not equate with the "hard science" image that the series projected.

Publication History

TITLE: *Destinies*, subtitled "The Paperback Magazine of Science Fiction and Speculative Fact."

VOLUME DATA: Volume 1, Number 1, November/December 1978–Volume 3, Number 2, [August] 1981. Volume 1, five issues, bi-monthly to issue 3, April/June 1979, thereafter quarterly. Volume 2, four issues, quarterly. Total run: 11 issues.

PUBLISHER: Ace Books, New York.

EDITOR: James Baen.

FORMAT: Pocketbook; page counts vary each number.

PRICE: $1.95, Number 1; $2.25, Numbers 2–7; $2.50, Numbers 8–10; $2.75, Number 11.

T. W. Hamilton

THE GIRL WITH THE HUNGRY EYES

Some alternate universe somewhere contains one SF pulp magazine that shone for the quality of its stories in what was, mysteriously, only a single-issue magazine. In this reality, however, that magazine eventually took shape in 1949 as a paperback anthology, and thus is frequently overlooked in the histories of the field.

The Girl with the Hungry Eyes started life when Donald A. Wollheim, then editor at Avon Books, was asked by publisher Joseph Meyers to acquire some quality stories for a new pulp magazine, occasioned by a new printing outlet. Wollheim acquired the stories, but then the outlet never eventuated. Rather than waste good material, Wollheim issued the anthology anonymously under the title of the lead story, written by Fritz Leiber. The cover was aimed at attracting male readers with a promise of more than science fiction, Leiber's story as well as William Tenn's "Venus and the Seven Sexes" suggesting a variety of sexual connotations.

The volume has been called the first original science fiction anthology, and this is certainly true of the adult market. That it originated as a science fiction magazine only emphasizes the close link between the magazine and the original anthology.

Every one of the six stories is a winner, the others being "Mrs. Manifold" by Stephen Grendon, "Daydream" by P. Schuyler Miller, "Maturity Night" by Frank Belknap Long and "Come into My Parlor" by Manly Wade Wellman. All were mature, polished stories reminiscent of the best in *Unknown* and *Astounding*, and a credit to Wollheim as editor.

Publication History

TITLE: *The Girl with the Hungry Eyes and Other Stories.*
VOLUME DATA: Unnumbered [but Avon Books, 184], copyright 1949.
PUBLISHER: Avon Publishing Co., New York.
EDITOR: Donald A. Wollheim (not credited in issue).
FORMAT: Pocketbook, 128 pp.
PRICE: 25¢.

Mike Ashley

INFINITY

Infinity is one of the best examples of the affinity between the magazine and original anthology fields. The series, which appeared beginning in 1970 as original paperback publications from Lancer Books, was a direct descendant of the magazine *Infinity*, published in the late 1950s. Indeed, Robert Hoskins, the editor at Lancer, had talked Irwin Stein, Lancer's publisher, and the former publisher of *Infinity Science Fiction* into considering the possibility of reviving the magazine. Budget estimates, however, showed that for the magazine to be economically feasible it would have to sell 50 percent of its 100,000 print run, which was not viable.

So instead *Infinity* was launched as a paperback anthology. The cover blurbed it as "New Writings in Speculative Fiction," a subtitle that remained throughout the series, but the title page of the first issue declared that *Infinity* was "a magazine of speculative fiction in book form." Furthermore, as an additional link to magazine SF, and in particular its namesake, the first volume reprinted "The Star" by Arthur C. Clarke, which had concluded the first issue of *Infinity Science Fiction* and had gone on to win the Hugo Award. It was the only story to be reprinted in the anthology series.

Such were *Infinity*'s claims to be a magazine in book form. Unlike the later *Destinies*, however, *Infinity* concentrated solely on fiction and carried none of the features traditionally associated with magazines such as review columns, nonfiction departments and editorials. Robert Hoskins provided a brief, reflective introduction and a "Notes from Infinity" section which gave capsule comments on the contributors, but all else was fiction. In his introduction, "The Future of the Future," in the fourth volume, Hoskins made the observation that magazines were becoming increasingly specialized and that the future outlet for short fiction could be in the paperback anthology market. This was a view prevalent in the early 1970s, but there is as yet no evidence that this is happening.

While at the time none of the stories published in *Infinity* ended up on the final ballot forms for the Hugo or Nebula awards, the passing years have added a further dimension to the significance and relevance of several of the contents. The first volume, for instance, also marked the first appearance of George Zebrowski with his sensitive story "The Water Sculptor of Station 233." The second volume included not only Robert Silverberg's convoluted "In Entropy's Jaws," subsequently selected by Terry Carr as being among the year's best stories, but also Edward Bryant's "The Road to Cinnabar," one of the key threads in Bryant's later important volume *Cinnabar* (New York: Macmillan, 1976). In the same vein, the third volume included "A Time of the Fourth Horseman" by Chelsea Quinn Yarbro, an integral sequence to her own first novel of the same title (New York: Doubleday, 1976).

There was a consistency of readability in all five volumes and much evidence that Hoskins was willing to encourage new talent. Aside from those already mentioned, fledgling writers like Alan Brennert, Grant Carrington, Michael Fayette, Anthony Warden and Scott Edelstein all made first or early sales to *Infinity*, and of special relevance here is Anthony Weller, who ranks as the youngest SF writer ever; he was a month short of thirteen when he sold "Antiquity" to Hoskins in 1970, and still only fourteen when the story appeared in *Infinity 3*.

Side by side with the newcomers were such established names as Fritz Leiber, Clifford D. Simak, James E. Gunn, Arthur C. Clarke, Poul Anderson and Ron Goulart. Hoskins gave the writers free rein to produce whatever they wanted, which resulted not just in some original ideas, but in such experimental pieces as Silverberg's "The Science Fiction Hall of Fame," William F. Nolan's "Kelly, Fredric Michael: 1928–1987" and the items by Barry Malzberg/K. M. O'Donnell.

Infinity 6 was completed and scheduled for publication in December 1973, but as Lancer Books' future looked bleak, Hoskins retrieved the manuscript and returned the stories.

Publication History

TITLE: *Infinity*, subtitled "New Writings in Speculative Fiction."
VOLUME DATA: Five volumes. Number 1, 1970; Number 2, 1971; Numbers 3 and 4, 1972; Number 5, 1973.
PUBLISHER: Lancer Books, New York.
EDITOR: Robert Hoskins.
FORMAT: Pocketbook: page count varies.
PRICE: Number 1, 75¢; thereafter, 95¢.

Mike Ashley

NEW DIMENSIONS

New Dimensions, *Orbit* and *Universe* represented the Big Three anthology markets of the 1970s much as *Galaxy*, *The Magazine of Fantasy and Science*

Fiction and *Analog* had for magazines in earlier years. By the time *ND* appeared in 1971 the magazine field was going through a bad patch, and the anthology market was being glutted with collections containing both new and reprint stories. Where did editor Robert Silverberg expect to find a new niche? "I decided to start *New Dimensions* because I felt the magazines were paying insufficient attention to craftsmanship and literary technique," Silverberg wrote in a private letter in 1977, "whereas the original anthologies of the day seemed overly concerned with experimentation at the expense of narrative values." In the editorial to the first volume, Silverberg maintained that *ND* was taking a "middle course" between the old established pulp tradition and the new avant-garde literary experimentalism. Moreover, Silverberg used as his model for *ND* Frederik Pohl's *Star Science Fiction* series of the 1950s, which he felt had the same concern for both quality of writing and genuine SF thinking.

That Silverberg was on the right road might be measured by the number of stories that either received or were nominated for Hugo or Nebula awards. The first volume, for instance, while it carried off no awards, had three nominees among its contents, including Ursula K. LeGuin's evocative story of explorers and a vast planetary entity, "Vaster Than Empires and More Slow." The second number included R. A. Lafferty's disturbingly simple "Eurema's Dam," which was co-winner of the Hugo Short Story Award, while the third volume contained another winner in LeGuin's "The Ones Who Walk Away from Omelas," plus a powerful nominee in James Tiptree's "The Girl Who Was Plugged In." So the roll call continued, only the sixth and seventh volumes failing to get at least one story on the final award ballot sheets, and, with Volume 11, finding another winner in "Unicorn Tapestry" by Suzy McKee Charnas.

This enviable record suggests an interesting line of thought. That these same stories would have sold to other markets had *ND* not existed is undeniable, and that they would also have won awards is a certainty tempered only by the possibility that different publishing schedules may have brought some into competition with each other. And yet, when the Hugo Award for Best Editor was established, Silverberg, whose unerring ability to select potential award-winning stories had made *ND* such a prestigious series, frequently did not make the final ballot in the editor category and never won the award, although he was runner-up on two occasions. This also applies to Damon Knight and Terry Carr, and the inference is that while these editors are capable of selecting exceptional stories on a once-a-year basis, the consistency with which a magazine editor can produce collections of readable if in general less distinguished stories gives rise to a greater popularity.

After the tenth volume, Silverberg stepped aside as editor, remaining in a consulting capacity, and the series was taken over by Marta Randall. That Randall's first volume contained the award-winning "Unicorn Tapestry" by Suzy McKee Charnas is an indication that the series is again in safe hands.

Information Sources

DERIVATIVE ANTHOLOGY: *The Best of New Dimensions*, ed. Robert Silverberg (New York: Pocket Books, 1979), eighteen stories and a new retrospective editorial.

Publication History

TITLE: *New Dimensions.*
VOLUME DATA: Annual from 1971.
PUBLISHER: Volumes 1–3, Doubleday, Garden City, N.Y. (Number 3 in hardcover as for the Science Fiction Book Club); Volume 4, Signet Books, New York; Volumes 5–10, Harper & Row, New York; Volume 11–, Pocket Books, New York.
EDITORS: Robert Silverberg, Volumes 1–10; Marta Randall, Volumes 11–.
FORMAT: Hardcover followed by a paperback reprint. No hardcover editions for Volume 4 or Volume 11–.

Mike Ashley

NEW WORLDS [QUARTERLY]

The paperback incarnation of the magazine *New Worlds*. See NEW WORLDS in Section I.

NEW WRITINGS IN S.F.

This, the longest-running original anthology series, grew out of the magazine *New Worlds SF* when edited by its founder, John Carnell. Sales of *New Worlds* were ailing and Carnell felt that the future lay in the paperback market, not the magazines. Before it was known that the magazine would be taken over by a new publisher, Carnell had made a deal with Corgi Books and Dennis Dobson to produce a regular quarterly of new science fiction, much in the vein of *New Worlds*, but with the potential of reaching a wider audience. Its success cannot be measured by awards because few American readers were aware of the series at the outset, but the fact that the first volume was fairly rapidly reprinted was an indication that Carnell had found the audience he sought.

In his editorial to the first number, dated August 1964, Carnell underlined the fact that the SF magazines were becoming more and more specialized in favor of the afficionado and that it was up to the original anthology market to pave the way for the general reader unacquainted with all the paraphernalia of science fiction but nonetheless interested in the medium. Carnell used much the same blend that he had in earlier issues of *New Worlds*, except that he had the chance to use longer stories and had the money to buy some of the bigger names. The first number led with "Key to Chaos" by that typically British author Edward Mackin, with one of his humorous stories about cyberneticist Hek Belov, who this time had invented a rejuvenation machine. Headmaster Douglas R. Mason, writing as John Rankine, introduced a character who became a regular in his later stories and novels, Dag Fletcher, in the stock SF situation of a stranded survey team in "Two's Company." The satire and adventure stepped aside for grim speculation in Brian W. Aldiss' "Man on Bridge," but we are back into the alien unknown in "Haggard Honeymoon" by Americans Joseph Green and James Webbert. Finally, Australian Damien Broderick looked at the theme of cyclic progression on a galactic scale in "The Sea's Furthest End." It was a well-balanced and entertaining volume; none of the stories would have been out of place in the Nova *New Worlds* and would certainly have appeared there had Carnell remained as editor. *New Writings*, therefore, has to be considered a child of *New Worlds*, in effect the first born.

Carnell had always been something of a British John Campbell, and the emphasis was much the same, an optimistic view of the potential of science with an occasional dash of pessimism. But the natural divide between British and American SF was still very evident in the work in *New Writings*, where the last vestiges of colonialism as opposed to frontiersmanship remained, and where inventions were still the product of individuals more than corporations.

Perhaps the strongest contributors to the early *New Writings* and the ones who best displayed and molded its character were Colin Kapp, James White and Keith Roberts. Roberts, who had first appeared in *Science Fantasy*, nevertheless owed his first sale to Carnell, who held onto two of his stories before giving him a double debut in Volume 3. "Manipulation" (under the alias John Kingston) was the first of a number of powerful psi-power stories that Roberts would write; they included his later "The Inner Wheel" in *New Writings 6*, which formed the basis of his novel of the same name. "Boulter's Canaries," on the other hand, was a slightly humorous look at a scientific explanation for poltergeists that nevertheless made a convincing story. It introduced the character of Alec Boulter, who has made a few other appearances in Roberts' subsequent stories. Aside from "The Inner Wheel," probably Roberts' best story in *New Writings* has been "Synth" (in Volume 8), which looked in detail at the future problems of female androids; but other worthy contributions include "Sub-Lim" in Volume 4 and "High Eight" in the same volume (as "David Stringer"), which looked at a new type of alien being created inadvertently through modern technology.

Volume 3 launched Keith Roberts and also presented "The Subways of Tazoo" by Colin Kapp, which brought back the ingenious team of Unorthodox Engineers who had proved so popular in *New Worlds*. These stories are in the best tradition of scientific fiction in the Hal Clement vein, involving a peculiar but totally scientific problem which has to be solved, often by unconventional means. Kapp had three of these stories in *New Writings*, of which perhaps the most intriguing was "The Pen and the Dark" (Volume 8). While "Hunger over Sweet Waters" (Volume 4) was not part of the series, it was still from the same mold. However, other stories by Kapp, such as "Which Way Do I Go for Jericho?" (Volume 20) and "The Cloudbuilders" (Volume 12), testify to the writer's versatility.

James White had long ago established himself as one of the most popular writers in *New Worlds*, especially with his medical stories of the Sector General. This series continued in *New Writings* beginning with "Invader" (Volume 7) and including "Vertigo" (Volume 12), "Blood Brother" (Volume 14), "Meatball" (Volume 16) and the stunning "Major Operation" (Volume 18), where the team operates on an entire planet. This later formed the basis of the novel of the same name published by Ballantine in 1971.

Other regulars at this time included John Baxter, Sydney J. Bounds, Michael G. Coney, Joseph L. Green, Lee Harding, H. A. Hargreaves, Vincent King, R. W. Mackelworth, John Rackham, Gerald W. Page, William Spencer and Arthur Sellings, which shows that though *New Writings* concentrated on British writers, it did not ignore Australian, Canadian or American contributors. Nor did Carnell avoid the opportunity of reprinting the occasional story if he felt that it was not readily available to British readers. Thus Dennis Etchison made his British debut with "Odd Boy Out" (Volume 2), and there were stories by Frederik Pohl, Isaac Asimov and William Tenn, all from nongenre sources. Keeping the flavor as international as possible, Carnell also reprinted a story from the Spanish in "The Song of Infinity" by Domingo Santos (Volume 14).

The use of series stories, and the selection of stories with a polished finish, brought a consistency of both quality and entertainment to *New Writings* that made the series very popular. However, even the best laid plans may soon start to crumble, and publishing difficulties with the hardcover edition caused volumes to appear at greater intervals, even though Carnell tirelessly assembled each number on a quarterly and then tri-annual basis. By the tenth volume, the paperback was actually appearing first, and though the hardcover reasserted its prerogative with the thirteenth volume, by now the series was only appearing twice yearly, and with no set schedule. This erraticism clearly contributed to a reduction in sales, previously sustained by the dogged regularity of the series.

Carnell continued to edit the series until his death in 1971. At that stage a new hardcover publisher, Sidgwick and Jackson, had been found, and Sidgwick wished to continue the series. Kenneth Bulmer, who had curiously contributed only one story to the series so far, in Volume 19, stepped in as editor, and his first effort, Volume 22, was assembled as a tribute to Carnell. It included stories by E. C. Tubb, Arthur C. Clarke, Harry Harrison, Brian W. Aldiss, James White (a new Sector General episode), John Kippax, Christopher Priest and even Donald A. Wollheim, all of whom owed their careers to or had had some association over the years with Carnell.

Bulmer continued the series in much the same tradition as Carnell, including works by many of the same authors, but perhaps also encouraging more new writers than before, and also introducing work by women writers, who were always noticeably lacking in Carnell's numbers. Holding the banner high for women writers was Cherry Wilder, whose "The Ark of James Carlyle" in Volume 24 proved extremely popular. Wilder made two other worthy appearances in the series. Other new writers included Charles Partington, David Langford, Leroy Kettle, Michael Stall, Martin Ricketts, Ian Watson, Bryn Fortey and Robert P. Holdstock, not all with their first stories, but all producing works which would help establish their hold on the SF field.

Unfortunately, the continuing trend by British publishers away from short story collections toward novels now made itself felt on *New Writings*. While a market for short fiction continues to exist, publishers find it increasingly difficult to target that audience and prefer the easy solution of concentrating on novels. Thus, more as a result of publishing trends than audience appreciation, the sales of *New Writings* fell, and following Volume 30 it was suspended. While Bulmer had at least the next two volumes prepared and delivered, the likelihood that they will ever appear has receded.

New Writings accomplished for the SF market in the mid-1960s what *New Worlds* had in the early 1950s; it provided a foothold for new writers in the field and became a regular showcase for British talent. Unfortunately, the same factors that led to the failure of Carnell's *New Worlds*—its lack of regularity and the continuing change in publishing attitudes—brought about the demise of *New Writings*.

Information Sources

AMERICAN REPRINT EDITION: U.K. Volumes 1–6 reprinted by Bantam Books, New York as follows: 1, 1966; 2, 1966; 3, 1967; 4, 1968; 5, 1970; 6, 1971. U.S. Volume 7 (1971) selected from U.K. Volumes 7, 8, 9; U.S. Volume 8 (1971) selected from U.K. Volumes 10, 11, 12; and U.S. Volume 9 (1972) selected from U.K. Volumes 12–15. Thereafter U.S. edition ceased.

DERIVATIVE ANTHOLOGIES: *The Best from New Writings in S-F: First Selection*, ed. John Carnell (London: Dobson, 1971), reprinted 11 stories from the first four volumes. Carnell's death precluded a further selection, but in 1975 Sidgwick & Jackson issued a *New Writings in S-F Special 1*, which reprinted in full the contents of Volumes 21 and 23.

Publication History

TITLE: *New Writings in S.F.*

VOLUME DATA: First publication dates as follows: 1, Aug 64; 2, Oct 64; 3, Feb 65; 4, May 65; 5, Jul 65; 6, Oct 65; 7, Jan 66; 8, Jun 66; 9, Aug 66; 10, Aug 67 [paperback]; 11, Dec 67 [paperback]; 12, May 68 [paperback]; 13, Sep 68; 14, Jan 69; 15, Jun 69; 16, Jan 70; 17, Apr 70; 18, Mar 71 [paperback]; 19, Jun 71; 20, Jan 72 [paperback]; 21, Aug 72; 22, Apr 73; 23, Nov 73; 24, Apr 74; 25, Apr 75; 26, Aug 75; 27, Mar 76; 28, Jul 76; 29, Nov 76; 30, Sep 78 [paperback copyright 1977 but not issued in hardcover].

PUBLISHER: Hardcover: Dennis Dobson, Volumes 1–20; thereafter Sidgwick & Jackson.
   Paperback, Corgi Books (all London).
EDITOR: John Carnell, Volumes 1–21; thereafter Kenneth Bulmer.

Mike Ashley

NOVA

Nova, a short-lived anthology series edited by Harry Harrison, first appeared in 1970. The name arose because Harrison felt it to be a brief, compact term that nevertheless conveyed both an association with science, and hence science fiction, and the suggestion that the contents were new. The name may have subconsciously lingered from an editorial he wrote for *Great Science Fiction* two years earlier, "Novas and the Steady State" (Summer 1968), which had considered that issue's contents in the light of how its writers had burst novalike on the SF scene in their respective years. *Nova* was instigated as a series because Harrison felt that the other anthology series, in particular Damon Knight's *Orbit*, were not sufficiently covering all areas of SF. He also hoped that authors, writing for a book market rather than a magazine, would feel freed from some of the taboos that have traditionally fettered the genre. Moreover, freed of the burden of a monthly deadline, Harrison hoped that the time spent on each volume of *Nova* would yield a higher-quality content.

One of the areas that Harrison explored with *Nova* was the realm of humor, highlighted with the very first story, "The Big Connection" by Robin Scott [Wilson]. It was developed further in the second volume with several whimsical stories and two memorable spoofs, "The Sumerian Oath" by Philip José Farmer and "The Steam-Driven Boy" by John Sladek. Harrison, however, did not let the humorous occlude the serious potential of SF, as best evidenced in Farmer's "Sketches among the Ruins of My Mind" in the third issue and Tom Reamy's "Beyond the Cleft" in the fourth. Between these two extremes, Harrison selected some good nonsensational SF stories such as "Jean Duprès" by Gordon R. Dickson, "I Tell You It's True" by Poul Anderson, "Now + n . . . Now − n" by Robert Silverberg and "The Whole Truth" by Piers Anthony. Regular contributors included Brian W. Aldiss, Naomi Mitchison and Barry N. Malzberg.

A number of writers made their first story sales to *Nova*, although only one, Tom Reamy, whose "Beyond the Cleft" has already been mentioned, can be said to have made any mark subsequently on the field.

Nova came to an end when Harrison found himself once again devoting more time to writing. The four volumes, while containing nothing outstanding, can claim to have a high quota of entertaining stories.

Publication History

TITLE: *Nova*.
VOLUME DATA: Four volumes. Number 1, 1970; Volume 2, 1972; Volume 3, 1973; Volume 4, 1974 (but actually published January 1975).

PUBLISHER: Hardcover editions: Number 1, Delacorte Press, New York; thereafter Walker & Co., New York. Paperback editions: first three volumes, Dell Books, New York; Volume 4, Manor Books, New York. [Note: Number 3 was later reissued by Dell under the new title *The Outdated Man*, 1975].

EDITOR: Harry Harrison.

BRITISH EDITIONS: Hardcover editions from Robert Hale, London, in 1976/77; paperback editions from Sphere Books, London, 1975/76.

Mike Ashley

ORBIT

Orbit was arguably the most important of all the original anthology series and possibly even the most significant publishing event in SF during the 1960s, though history has yet to set it alongside *Dangerous Visions* and *New Worlds* in true perspective.[1]

Orbit, first published in 1966, was not the first such series—Frederik Pohl's *Star Science Fiction* and John Carnell's *New Writings* both preceded it; but unlike those two series, both of which published some excellent SF, *Orbit* actually set a trend. It arrived at a time when the SF field was moribund, and though Frederik Pohl, Harlan Ellison and Michael Moorcock would each play their part as editors in upheaving the past and establishing a new status quo, in the long term it was Damon Knight with *Orbit* that had the major effect, partly in its revision of attitudes toward SF; partly in opening up a vast new market in original anthologies and thus paving the way for *New Dimensions*, *Universe* and a whole catalogue of others; and partly in breaking down some of the last vestiges of editorial and publishing taboos that limited the field and thus allowing more freedom of expression for its writers.

If *Orbit*'s success were to be measured purely by the number of awards and nominations its contents garnered, or by the number of new writers it helped establish, then there would be success enough, even if one discounted the general entertainment value of the series, although it could at times be infuriating and idiosyncratic. In all these areas it is possibly the first ten volumes of *Orbit*, or essentially half of the series, that were the most rewarding.

The first volume, for instance, was still firmly rooted in traditional SF, with solid contributions from Poul Anderson, James Blish, Keith Roberts, Kate Wilhelm and Virginia Kidd. Nevertheless, one of them, ''The Secret Place'' by Richard M. McKenna, was nominated for both the Nebula and Hugo awards, carrying off the former.

Although there were no award winners in *Orbit 2*, there were two nominees: ''The Doctor'' by Theodore L. Thomas and ''Baby, You Were Great'' by Kate Wilhelm. Of greater significance, however, was the debut in that number of Gene Wolfe with ''Trip, Trap.'' Wolfe went on to become a regular *Orbit* contributor with stories in virtually every edition, among them ''The Fifth Head of Cerberus'' (No. 10) and ''Alien Stones'' (No. 11).

Orbit 3 further cemented the preeminence of the series by containing not just one, but two future award winners, ''Mother to the World'' by Richard Wilson and ''The Planners'' by Kate Wilhelm. Knight was demonstrating that with the time to select quality manuscripts unhampered by magazine editorial taboos and deadlines, and with a reasonable budget arising from both hardcover and paperback editions, an experienced editor could assemble an anthology of new stories that would be, measure for measure, of greater merit than any magazine.

The consistency remained. *Orbit 4* contained the Nebula winner ''Passengers'' by Robert Silverberg, and another nominee, ''Shattered Like a Glass Goblin'' by Harlan Ellison, while *Orbit 5*, missing out on the winners, still had two nominees in Norman Spinrad's ''The Big Flash'' and Ursula K. LeGuin's ''Winter's King,'' related to her later award-winning *The Left Hand of Darkness* (New York: Ace, 1969).

*Orbit*s 6 and 7, however, proved beyond a shadow of a doubt the significance of the *Orbit* series. Although only two of the stories (both in No. 7) made the final Hugo ballot, they dominated the Nebula ballot, and yet, ironically, received no awards. There was a controversy over the voting in the short story category, where it was felt that Gene Wolfe's ''The Island of Dr. Death and Other Stories'' (No. 7) should have won, while ''Continued on Next Rock'' by R. A. Lafferty (No. 7) was in strong contention for the best novelette award, and ''April Fool's Day Forever'' by Kate Wilhelm (also No. 7) was in the running for the best novella award. In fact, of the twelve stories in *Orbit 7* five were nominated for the Nebula, an enviable quota for any anthology. There were another five in the running from *Orbit 6* (which had had fifteen stories in all).

However, thereafter *Orbit*'s stranglehold on the awards was weakened by the appearance of *Universe* and *New Dimensions*, where both Terry Carr and Robert Silverberg showed they were the equal of Knight in their editorial abilities. It was perhaps also significant that when Gene Wolfe won the Nebula for ''The Death of Doctor Island,'' of deliberate derivation, it had been published in *Universe* and not in *Orbit*. In fact, no further awards would go to stories from *Orbit*, although a number still made the final ballots, most noticeably ''Shark'' by Edward Bryant (No. 12) and ''Seven American Nights'' by Gene Wolfe (No. 20).

But there were other important events in *Orbit*'s later years. ''Tin Soldier'' in *Orbit 14* marked the first appearance of Joan D. Vinge, while ''Under the Hollywood Sign'' was one of the early sales, though not the debut, of Tom Reamy. *Orbit 15* carried ''Where Late the Sweet Birds Sang'' by Kate Wilhelm, which formed the basis for her subsequent award-winning novel of the same name. Wilhelm figured prominently in the *Orbit* series, and while this might be lightly excused as a consequence of her marriage to Damon Knight, the fact remains that a great number of her stories received award nominations, and all are significant in their exploration of new areas of SF with refreshingly new treatments. Another regular contributor was R. A. Lafferty, whose stories have always remained individualistic, but who helped create the general unreal atmosphere that pervaded *Orbit*, especially in the later volumes.

Strangely, although *Orbit 1* was clearly in the direct tradition of SF, within a few numbers *Orbit* had almost established a subgenre of its own, and some of its stories are pure fantasy, while others are *sui generis*. This was, in part, what Knight had set out to achieve, but the results brought the inevitable criticisms from the SF traditionalists. Nevertheless, the record speaks for itself. By the mid-1970s, however, the SF climate had changed, and *Orbit*, far from being the exception, was becoming the norm. The field had broken free of the stagnation of the sixties, and with such new editors as Ben Bova, George Scithers, Silverberg, Carr and a more experienced Edward Ferman, the magazines and rival anthologies had taken over the niche *Orbit* carved for itself.

After a change in publisher, but a continued decline in sales, *Orbit* made it to a twenty-first volume and then ceased.

Note

1. See introductions to *The Best From Orbit* and *Orbit 21*; index to first ten volumes in *Orbit 10*.

Information Sources

BRITISH REPRINT EDITION: First 8 volumes published in hardcover by Rapp & Whiting, London, between 1969 and 1974; first 4 volumes only in paperback from Panther Books, 1969–1972.
DERIVATIVE ANTHOLOGIES: *The Best from Orbit*, ed. Damon Knight (New York: Berkley, 1975), 28 stories from first 10 volumes.

Publication History

TITLE: *Orbit*.
VOLUME DATA: Volume 1, 1966; 2, 1967; 3, 1968; 4, 1968; 5, 1969; 6, 1970; 7, 1970; 8, 1970; 9, 1971; 10, 1972; 11, 1972; 12, 1973; 13, 1974; 14, 1974; 15, 1974; 16, 1975; 17, 1975; 18, 1976; 19, 1977; 20, 1978; 21, 1980.
PUBLISHERS: Hardcover: G. P. Putnam's, New York, Volumes 1–13; Harper & Row, New York, Volumes 14–21. Paperback: Berkley Books, New York, Volumes 1–13 only.
EDITOR: Damon Knight.

Mike Ashley

PERRY RHODAN

The longest-running SF series in the world concerns the adventures of Perry Rhodan, Overlord of the Universe, who has now been the hero of over a thousand short novels published not only in his native Germany, but in most West European countries. In 1969 the first English-language translations were published in America by Ace Books. The series came under the general editorship of archfan Forrest Ackerman, with translations by his wife Wendayne.

To test the market the first three books, reprinting the first six novels, were issued simultaneously. Ackerman supplied an editorial to the first number, but otherwise they stood alone. Their success led to two more editions in 1970 and then, in 1971, they began to appear on a regular basis, monthly publication later becoming fortnightly for a brief period. With the sixth volume, Ackerman brought some individuality to the publication by creating a "magabook." In fact, *Perry Rhodan* was a magazine in pocketbook form, although it has always been treated as a paperback. Under the excruciating alias of Forry Rhodan, and with pages littered with puns and neologisms, Ackerman provided a regular editorial to each number plus a film review column, "Scientifilm World," and a letter column, "The Perryscope." Only one short novel was featured each issue, though on occasion the original German sequence was accelerated by summarizing certain episodes.

It was with Volume 16 in August 1972 that Ackerman expanded the magabook into a museum of nostalgia. To bolster the Rhodan novel, Ackerman now included a continuing serial and a "shock short," both usually reprints. The first serial was Garrett P. Serviss' "Edison's Conquest of Mars," originally published in 1898, but now appearing in a slightly pruned and edited version. The first shock short was "The Swordsmen of Varnis" by Clive Jackson, which had originated in Walt Willis' fanzine *Slant*. Thereafter the series carried a variety of vignettes and even articles culled from Ackerman's archives, mostly from obscure fan publications, but there was the occasional new story. Perhaps the greatest surprise was that Steven Utley, who has since established himself as a worthy writer in the field, owed his first sale to Ackerman; he debuted in *PR 20* with "The Unkindest Cut of All," while George W. Proctor also made a sale with "Paper Work" (in *PR 25*).

PR was clearly aimed at a juvenile readership, and even Ackerman's zeal became overbearing at times. Nevertheless, for SF historians the series held a certain appeal in the items that Ackerman chose to reprint, either as serials or in the "Time Vault" slot. Of special service was the reprinting of the classic round-robin story "Cosmos," which ran in the fanzine *Science Fiction Digest* from 1933 to 1935. Seventeen episodes in all, with writers including Edmond Hamilton, E. E. Smith, A. Merritt, P. Schuyler Miller and John W. Campbell, the serial was reprinted in *Perry Rhodan* starting with Number 32 (October 1973) and concluding in Number 60. Starting in Number 61 was a totally new serial, "New Lensman," written by William B. Ellern as a sequel to E. E. Smith's great series.

The American series eventually ceased with Number 118, although there was a brief merger with Rhodan's companion series *Atlans*, which also saw a few U.S. translations. The series had, by then, however, reverted to a twin-novel format and had little resemblance to a magazine.

Publication History

TITLE: *Perry Rhodan*.
VOLUME DATA: Number 1, [May] 1969–Number 118, August 1977. Not always a
regular schedule, though for the most part monthly.
PUBLISHER: Ace Books, New York.
EDITOR: Forrest J Ackerman.

Mike Ashley

PROTEUS

Mop-up anthology for the *Destinies* series. See DESTINIES.

QUARK/

Quark/, subtitled "A Quarterly of Speculative Fiction," resembled a magazine
in book form. It had been initiated in 1970 by the publishers, Paperback Library,
in the hope of attracting new talent to their company, and they had commissioned
Marilyn Hacker and Samuel R. Delany to edit it. The series selected not just
fiction but poetry, articles and graphics, and it included work not just by new
writers, but by such established names as A. E. van Vogt and Fritz Leiber. On
the whole the content was experimental, with the usual early 1970s overreaction
to the new freedom of SF and the new wave. Not surprisingly, contributors
included Charles Platt, Christopher Priest, Hilary Bailey, Joanna Russ, Josephine
Saxton, Thomas M. Disch and the ever-indefinable R. A. Lafferty. There were
graphics from Russell Fitzgerald, Steve Gilden, Roger Penney, Nemi Frost and
Robert Lavigne, plus verse from Marilyn Hacker, Helen Adam, Marco Cacchioni
and Sonya Dorman, and much else besides.

In the perspective of hindsight it is easy to brand *Quark/* as overpretentious.
The first issue was presented with all the names in lower case, and authors were
credited at the end of the story, not at the beginning. Beyond the affectations,
however, lay a readable and pertinent series. Of special relevance was Delany's
own article in the first number, "Critical Methods: Speculative Fiction," which
takes an unblinkered view at science fiction and its place in art. The stories, for
the most part, stand up well a decade later, and some of the more memorable
include "A Trip to the Head" by Ursula K. LeGuin (No. 1), "Fire Storm" by
Christopher Priest (No. 1), "Gold, Black and Silver" by Fritz Leiber (No. 2),
"Encased in Ancient Rind" by R. A. Lafferty (No. 3), "Ring of Pain" by M.
John Harrison (No. 3), "Voortrekker" by Michael Moorcock (No. 4) and "The
Fourth Profession" by Larry Niven (No. 4).

At the time, *Quark/* received a number of hostile reviews from the fan and
literary press, which, while praising Delany and Hacker, crucified Paperback
Library. Since the series had been initiated by the publisher and had been a

deliberate nonprofit venture, they considered this flack too much of an insult and discontinued the series. When the sales figures were considered, it was seen that the series had sold moderately better than expected.

Publication History

TITLE: *Quark/*.
VOLUME DATA: Four issues, quarterly; 1970: November; 1971: February, May, August.
PUBLISHER: Paperback Library, a subsidiary of Coronet Communications, New York.
EDITORS: Samuel R. Delany and Marilyn Hacker.
FORMAT: Paperback, 240 pp.
PRICE: $1.25.

Mike Ashley

STAR SCIENCE FICTION STORIES

Star Science Fiction Stories, first published in 1953, was the father of all the original anthology series and the direct inspiration for *New Dimensions*, subliminally for *New Writings in S.F.*, and paternally for *Stellar*. The series had been devised between Frederik Pohl and Ian Ballantine; the latter was establishing his new line of Ballantine paperbacks, which was to have a strong element of science fiction.[1] *Star* thus formed a kind of showcase for new talent. While there had been isolated original anthologies prior to *Star*, there had not been an attempt at a preconceived series. *Star* was the first real sign that the paperback anthology could be a viable rival to the magazines, which at the time *Star* first appeared were undergoing a painful metamorphosis from pulp to digest, a change so traumatic that few survived. *Star* can itself be considered as having undergone a transformation, its two paperback series having been hyphenated by a single magazine issue, indicating that throughout the 1950s the whole future of magazine and paperback publishing was unsure. That one magazine issue in 1958 is considered in Section I, and might otherwise have been *SSF 4* in another continuum.

Pohl's previous opportunities as an editor had been limited by his own youth, and thus inexperience, and his budget. Now, a decade later, he was able to give more evidence of his abilities. Although no story from *Star* won an award, it is significant that many stories from the series have seen subsequent reprintings. From the first volume, for instance, amid stories by Clifford Simak, Isaac Asimov, Ray Bradbury and Cyril Kornbluth, one could single out Arthur C. Clarke's "The Nine Billion Names of God," from the second "It's a *Good* Life" by Jerome Bixby and from the third "It's Such a Beautiful Day" by Isaac Asimov. Other memorable stories were "Country Doctor" by William Morrison, "Contraption" by Clifford D. Simak, "Disappearing Act" by Alfred Bester and "Whatever Happened to Corporal Cuckoo?" by Gerald Kersh.

After the third volume and a companion *Star Short Novels*, there was a hiatus in the series, and *Star* might reasonably, though prematurely, have been considered dead. Then, in 1957, came the decision to revive it as a magazine. Soon thereafter *SSF 4* appeared, back in the paperback format, but his experiment shows that, apart from a few magazine features such as illustrations and departments (and not all magazines have these), there is little to distinguish a digest magazine from a pocketbook.

SSF 4 contains several stories that have since remained regularly in print: "Space-Time for Springers" by Fritz Leiber, "The Advent on Channel Twelve" by Cyril M. Kornbluth and "Idiot Stick" by Damon Knight. It was something of a memorial issue since Kornbluth had died in March 1958 while the volume was still being assembled, and Henry Kuttner, whose "A Cross of Centuries" opened the number, had died in February.

Two further numbers appeared, containing such stories as "Adrift on the Policy Level" by Chan Davis and "Star Descending" by Algis Budrys, before Pohl's duties as a writer and managing editor of *Galaxy* and *If* took him away from *Star*. Pohl used the opportunity of a paperback market to open up the field to writers beyond the pulp tradition, so that among the works of Simak and Asimov were stories by Gerald Kersh, Robert Crane, Howard Koch and Elizabeth Mann Borgese. This same movement was under way in *The Magazine of Fantasy and Science Fiction*, always intended as the most literary of the genre magazines, but it was not as evident elsewhere in the field, and Pohl helped accelerate the trend. In more than a small way *Star* helped chip away at the barriers between the SF world and beyond.

Note

1. See Frederik Pohl, *The Way the Future Was* (New York: Del Rey, 1978), pp. 187–190.

Information Sources

BRITISH REPRINT EDITION: First two volumes only reprinted in hardcover by T. V. Boardman, London, 1954 and 1955.

DERIVATIVE ANTHOLOGIES: *Star of Stars*, ed. Frederik Pohl (Garden City, N.Y.: Doubleday, 1960), 14 stories plus introduction. U.K. edition retitled *Star Fourteen* (London: Whiting & Wheaton, 1966).

Publication History

TITLE: *Star Science Fiction Stories*.

VOLUME DATA: Number 1, February 1953; Number 2, January 1954; Number 3, December 1954; Number 4, November 1958; Number 5, May 1959; Number 6, December 1959.

PUBLISHER: Ballantine Books, New York.

EDITOR: Frederik Pohl.

FORMAT: First three volumes, simultaneous hardcover and paperback; last three volumes, paperback only.

PRICE: Paperback, all 35¢.

Mike Ashley

STELLAR

Stellar is really a showcase anthology with little affinity with the SF magazines, and is included here because it was a deliberate though uncredited successor to *Star Science Fiction*, albeit a decade and a half later. *Star* had been published by Ian Ballantine, and when Judy-Lynn del Rey became SF editor at Ballantine Books and desired to start a showcase anthology, it was a relatively short step to revive *Star*, but with a variant title, *Stellar*.

Stellar, which debuted in 1974, had one simple criterion—to entertain and bring back some of the enjoyment to science fiction. Thus, while some critics have looked down on the series as taking a backward step and offering little, the stories do live up to their name. Indeed, with the second number Isaac Asimov's "The Bicentennial Man" went on to win both Hugo and Nebula awards, giving some indication of the popularity and quality of the series.

There is nothing pretentious about *Stellar*. Produced with the immaculateness one associates with Ballantine Books, the series has presented entertaining if predictable stories by Clifford D. Simak, Larry Niven, Hal Clement, Jack Chalker, James P. Hogan, Charles Sheffield, Jack Williamson, Anne McCaffrey and many more. Just as with *Star*, there was a companion *Stellar Short Novels* (1976), and indeed a number of the stories in *Stellar* are unusually long. Volume 4, for instance, had a rare short story from Stephen R. Donaldson, "Animal Lover," which ran to over 20,000 words, while "The Sword of Damocles" by James P. Hogan, in Volume 5, was of almost equal length.

While there is a touch of all forms of SF in *Stellar*, the emphasis has been on the science, as the above catalogue of contributors implies, and, critics aside, the series remains popular.

Publication History

TITLE: First volume simply *Stellar*; thereafter *Stellar Science-Fiction Stories*.

VOLUME DATA: Number 1, September 1974; Number 2, February 1976; Number 3, October 1977; Number 4, May 1978; Number 5, May 1980; Number 6, January 1981; Number 7, August 1981.

PUBLISHER: Random House, New York. The first two volumes appeared under the Ballantine Books imprint, and thereafter Del Rey Books.

EDITOR: Judy-Lynn del Rey.

FORMAT: Paperback.
PRICE: $1.25, Number 1; $1.50, Number 2; $1.95, Numbers 3–5; $2.25, Number 6; $2.50, Number 7.

Mike Ashley

SUPERNATURAL STORIES

Paperback series of alternating novels and collections which started life in the guise of a magazine. See SUPERNATURAL STORIES in Section I.

UNIVERSE

Universe and *New Dimensions* are the sole survivors of the rash of original anthology series that mushroomed in the early 1970s in the wake of the success of *Orbit*. It originated in 1971 with Ace Books while Terry Carr was still that publisher's SF editor, and it allowed him to add a few extras not common with most anthologies. The cover, for instance, illustrated one of the stories—a common, almost obligatory practice with magazines, but not so with books. Moreover, each story was illustrated with a sketch by Alicia Austin. These innovations lasted for only the first two numbers, when *Universe* changed publishers.

Carr made it clear at the outset that *Universe* was a science fiction series, publishing only the occasional fantasy when he could not bring himself to reject it. Speculative fiction was out, for, unlike many editors in the field, Carr felt that labels helped a reader know what he was buying. This, of course, did not mean that Carr was imposing editorial restrictions, because his own views and definitions of science fiction were wide.

Just as with *Orbit* and *New Dimensions*, *Universe* soon made itself felt, its stories being nominated for and winning awards. From the first number, a Nebula went to Robert Silverberg's ''Good News from the Vatican,'' while ''Poor Man, Beggar Man'' by Joanna Russ and ''Mount Charity'' by Edgar Pangborn were on the final ballot. *Universe 2*, although it had no winners, boasted a clutch of nominees in ''Patron of the Arts'' by Bill Rotsler, ''On the Downhill Side'' by Harlan Ellison and ''When We Went to See the End of the World'' by Robert Silverberg—three of the twelve stories in that volume.

Universe 3 claimed only one nominee, but it won the Nebula: ''The Death of Doctor Island'' by Gene Wolfe. Carr pulled off the same trick in the following year with ''If the Stars are Gods'' by Gordon Eklund and Greg Benford from Volume 4. That volume had led with a long story by Jack Vance, ''Assault on a City,'' which received a Hugo nomination.

Universe then entered a lull, for despite the excellence of many of its stories, a revitalized magazine field was at last serving up quality competition. Hence such stories as Ursula K. LeGuin's delightful "Schrodinger's Cat" (No. 5), Brian W. Aldiss' "Journey to the Heartland" (No. 6), Carter Scholz's "The Ninth Symphony of Ludwig van Beethoven and Other Lost Songs" (No. 7), Michael Bishop's "Old Folks at Home" (No. 8) and Bob Shaw's "Frost Animals" (No. 9) could go unnoticed. One story that refused to go unrecognized through its pure unconventionality was "Custer's Last Jump" by Steven Utley and Howard Waldrop (No. 6), a bold finger-in-the-eye poke at the theme of alternate realities.

Universe proved itself again, though, with the tenth volume; it contained "The Ugly Chickens" by Howard Waldrop, which went on to win both the Nebula and the World Fantasy Award, showing how fragile are the barriers between the genres.

Despite three changes in publisher, *Universe* has maintained a regular annual appearance and a consistency of quality that has established it today as probably the leading original anthology series.

Publication History

TITLE: *Universe*.
VOLUME DATA: Annual, 1971–. Volume 13, 1983.
PUBLISHER: Hardcover, from Volume 3 only, Random House, New York, until Volume 5; thereafter by Doubleday, Garden City, N.Y. Paperback: Ace Books, New York, Volumes 1 and 2; thereafter Paperback Library.
EDITOR: Terry Carr.
BRITISH EDITION: Hardcover edition from Dobson Books, London, starting in 1975, of Numbers 1–9 (excluding 4).

Mike Ashley

WEIRD HEROES

Weird Heroes, first published in 1975, undeniably considered itself a magazine. It even advertised itself on the cover as "A New American Pulp" and went out of its way to emulate the old hero pulps of the 1930s, while also nodding in acknowledgment to the comic-book field.

WH was an experiment in blending together science fiction, the hero pulps and graphic art. It was a bold and exciting experiment which produced some fascinating results. Designed, rather than simply edited, by Byron Preiss, it relied heavily on integrated artwork by such talents as Esteban Maroto, Jeff Jones, Jim Steranko, Alex Nino, Tom Sutton, Stephen Fabian, Neal Adams and Stephen Hickman. It also called upon those writers who clearly associated themselves with the hero pulps and comic books to produce new hero-fiction. Thus, Philip José Farmer created Greatheart Silver, Zeppelin captain and daring adventurer, in a friendly spoof on all pulp heroes in "Showdown at Shootout." Ron Goulart created the enigmatic Gypsy in "There's Coming a Time." Harlan

Ellison gave substance to his alter ego Cordwainer Bird, and Ted White fathered Doc Phoenix, billed as the new Doc Savage.

The first two issues of *WH*, which actually were one volume split in half, carried a number of other features, including nonfiction reminiscences and interviews, but with the third volume things developed apace. Having established several new heroes, the intent now was to give them a whole novel in which to display their talents. Ron Goulart's Gypsy thus occupied all of Number 3 with *Quest of the Gypsy*. The fourth volume introduced a new and mysterious heroine, mistress of magic, Nightshade, in *Terror, Inc.*, written by Tappan King and Beth Meacham, while Doc Phoenix took on a novel-length adventure in *The Oz Encounter*, in Volume 5. Ted White's outline was completed by Marv Wolfman.

Volume 6 saw the return to the magazine format with a new hero in the slithery-shape of Shinbet, masterminded by Ron Goulart, while Ben Bova created a new and rather fantastic superman in the form of Orion. *WH 7* was a full-length Gypsy novel, *Eye of the Vulture*, but *WH 8* presented another collection. Alongside a new Orion adventure were two stories about Kamus of Kadizar, a clever blending of fantasy, SF and detective fiction by J. Michael Reaves; one, "The Big Spell," was nominated for the British Fantasy Award.

At this point *WH* ceased; an afterword, while not directly saying this was the end, hinted as much. Clearly the series had initially been successful, since the first two volumes were reprinted. How much sales tapered thereafter is not clear, but the likelihood is that the series did not fit into the new schedules set up when Jove/Harcourt Brace Jovanovich took over Pyramid Books in 1977. Almost certainly there is a place for a hero series such as *WH*, and no doubt its appointed time will come.

Publication History

TITLE: *Weird Heroes*.

VOLUME DATA: Magazine issues only: Volume 1, October 1975; Volume 2, December 1975; Volume 6, April 1977; Volume 8, November 1977. Volumes 3, 4, 5 and 7 all novels.

PUBLISHER: Volumes 1–6, Pyramid Books, New York; thereafter Jove/Harcourt Brace Jovanovich.

EDITOR: Byron Preiss.

FORMAT: Pocketbook.

PRICE: Volumes 1–5, $1.50; Volume 6, $1.75; Volume 7, $1.50; Volume 8, $1.75.

Mike Ashley

WEIRD TALES

Recent incarnation in paperback form of the legendary weird fiction magazine. See WEIRD FICTION in Section I.

Section III

ACADEMIC PERIODICALS AND MAJOR FANZINES

This section lists various magazines containing material that could be useful to both the amateur and professional enthusiast of fantastic literature: raw news; information about specific authors, subgenres, publishers, or other topics; comprehensive reviews; or fan/academic criticism.

One intimidating aspect of science fiction and fantasy is the mass of writing that readers in these fields have produced. In addition to the academic journals, fanzines (amateur magazines issued by enthusiasts) have published huge amounts of informative and critical material. Not all this writing is equally valuable, of course, and it tends to shade off into reflections on other subjects or personal nattering. Still, one can be virtually certain that *any* writer, book, magazine, or movement in SF/fantasy has received written attention somewhere, sometime. A scholar-critic should remember that this is all part of the exchange of ideas that underlies fandom—and criticism. He also should remember that he ignores any source of confirmation or challenge at his own risk. Annotations in the following list should help him decide how important it is to check a given publication.

To avoid getting bogged down in a most ambiguous area, the annotation makes no absolute distinction between professional journals and fanzines. Such a distinction may be impossible to draw. Some "amateur" magazines are larger and more attractive than some "professional" magazines. A few points associated with the two ends of the publication spectrum may be useful to note, though, since they affect the material's availability. Fanzines tend to be published by one individual rather than a group; if a group is responsible for a fanzine, it tends to be an unstructured and spontaneous assortment of people, changing membership and function at the members' pleasure. This means that a fanzine usually directly reflects the tastes of one person and that the "zine" waxes and wanes with that person's enthusiasm, work schedule, and so on. Also, fanzines tend to be published in smaller press runs than the professional journals, since the method of reproduction (often dittograph or mimeograph until recent years) and the editor's finances prevent running off many spare copies. Finally, fanzines tend to be circulated directly by mail, information about them being spread by word of mouth or by reviews in other fanzines; it is unusual for a fanzine to advertise itself in generally circulated magazines, still more unusual for it to be circulated to the entire membership of a large organization or sold in stores. These factors can vary greatly—they do, from zine to zine—but they are more reliable guides than size or appearance in distinguishing the nature of a publication.

But understanding the nature of a publication helps one to plan how to locate it—and to avoid unnecessary desperation if it does not turn up in a preliminary search of "normal" sources. Fanzines do tend to be more evanescent and much harder to locate than professional periodicals. In the list that follows, I indicate when a magazine of any type has been reprinted, and I also list fanzine holdings in libraries. For each magazine, I also list the name of the editor and the address of those currently (early 1984) being published. A letter of inquiry, with a stamped, self-addressed envelope, would be advisable before sending money for a subscription or back issues. Libraries should be queried about the extent of holdings in a given title.

At the same time, individual items in fanzines are difficult to locate. There is no overall, comprehensive index of critical material on SF/fantasy. Schlobin and Tymn's annual survey (see *Extrapolation*), valuable as it is, leaves out many fanzines, although it tries to keep up with the major titles. Hal Hall's book review index includes more but is more narrowly focused. There is not even a reliable index of what zines have been published or are being published. Under the circumstances, this section may be regarded as a tentative introduction to SF/fantasy critical periodicals and as an invitation to anyone able to undertake a fuller study. Under the circumstances, however, the list of magazines given here shows the limitations not only of my judgment but of my information. The fanzines listed, for example, do tend to be of recent vintage—a fact that should make them much easier for an interested scholar to locate.

In choosing which titles to include, I have tried to be as selective as possible for the needs of the scholar-critic, and I have indicated the magazines that *consistently* are worth an effort to check. The publications listed here contain a strong, continuing body of material or at least one solid, continuing feature that I consider really valuable to the serious student of SF and fantasy. I have left out magazines (such as *Hyphen*) that are delightful to read but of only tangential interest to the scholar; one-shots (such as *Who Killed Science Fiction?* or *A Sense of FAPA*) that would be apart from the regular runs of magazines; magazines (such as *Habbakuk* or *Starling*) that published material of interest in scattered issues; or magazines (such as Ellison's *Dimensions* or Silverberg's *Spaceship*) that were produced by youngsters who later became important writers.

Because of the frequent title changes of fanzines, I have listed most under the earliest name; in confusing cases, cross-references will lead to the full entry. Editors are listed chronologically, their tenure discussed in the annotation when relevant. Information on awards is taken from Franson and Devore's *A History of the Hugo, Nebula, and International Fantasy Awards*, rev. ed. (Dearborn, Mich.: Misfit Press, 1981) and from *Locus*. In a few cases—*The Acolyte, Fanewscard, Fantasy Commentator, The Pulp Era*, and *Science Fiction Digest*—the listing is based not on personal inspection but on one of the three book-length histories of SF fandom— Sam Moskowitz's *The Immortal Storm* (Atlanta: ASFO Press, 1954), Harry Warner, Jr.'s *All Our Yesterdays* (Chicago: Advent, 1969) and Warner's *A Wealth of Fable* (Lighthouse Point, Fla.: Fanhistorica, 1977)—hereafter cited as Moskowitz,

Warner 1 and Warner 2. I have annotated magazines when necessary; that is, the title of *The Mervyn Peake Review* requires little elaboration; on the other hand, *Yandro* is not exactly self-explanatory. In general, annotation is as full as seems necessary and as my information permits.

My thanks to Sandra Miesel and to Buck and Juanita Coulson for giving me access to their fanzine collections. Paul C. Allen, Roger C. Schlobin and Joe Siclari offered basic suggestions and general criticism. Individual entries were checked and verified by people associated with the various publications: Carl B. Yoke, Paul C. Allen, Charles Platt, Erwin H. Bush, Ian Myles Slater, SF-3, Neil Barron, Dick Lupoff, Richard E. Geis, George Scithers, Jeffrey Smith, Robert M. Philmus, Robert Coulson, J. Grant Thiessen, Doug Fratz, A. L. Searles, F. M. Busby, Terry Carr, Lisa Cowen, David Pringle, John Watney, Andrew Porter, Donald L. Miller, Charles N. Brown, Bruce Gillespie, Brian Aldiss, Michael Kaplan, Gordon Larkin and Geoff Rippington. The overall coverage was edited and enlarged by Mike Ashley, whose contributions are indicated by his initials.

Joseph L. Sanders

Note on Library Collections of Fanzines:

In addition to the libraries listed at the end of each description, the following have fanzine holdings; however, the librarians either have not catalogued the fanzines or are too busy to circulate a list of holdings through the mail: Ohio State University; Spaced-Out Library, Toronto Public Libraries; Texas A&M; University of Maryland, Baltimore Campus; and University of Sydney, Australia. In addition, Colin Lester's *The International Science Fiction Yearbook* (New York: Quick Fox, 1978) lists the following libraries, none of which responded to my queries as owning fanzines: British Fantasy Society; Brown University; Michigan State University; SSF Library; and University of Kansas. Of private collections, the most notable probably is that of Forrest J Ackerman, who "wrote the first article on the first page of the first sci-fi fanzine, *The Time Traveller*, Feb. 32," claims a virtually complete file from there until 1950, and "recently bought the 1950–80 fanzine files of a major collector." Ackerman describes the first twenty years of zines as being arranged alphabetically, but explains that he has not been able to have the rest catalogued in any fashion.

THE ACOLYTE

Dates: Fall 1942–Spring 1946.
Editors: Frances T. Laney and Duane W. Rimel, later joined by Sam Russell.
The *Acolyte* began as a Lovecraft-centered fanzine, but after the first five issues it expanded its contents to include all weird fiction and some SF. In later issues, fiction and poetry were reduced in amount as Laney chose to concentrate on nonfiction. The magazine included material by Fritz Leiber, Anthony Boucher, Sam Moskowitz, and so on; columns included Forrest J Ackerman on fantasy films and Harold Wakefield on little-known fantasy writers.
Source: Laney's own *Ah, Sweet Idiocy* and the *1946–1947 Fantasy Review*, edited by Joe Kennedy.

ALGOL/STARSHIP

Dates: 1963–Winter-Spring 1984.

Editor: Andrew Porter.

Growing from a dittoed fanzine to a glossy semi-prozine with full-color covers, *Algol* changed its name to *Starship* to attract a larger audience, beginning with the Winter 1978–79 issue. Under either title, *Algol/Starship* was a dazzling production. Porter was one of the few fan editors who could reflect on his "slowly-developing sense of esthetics" without appearing pretentious. The outstanding appearance attracted major contributors such as Susan Wood, Ursula K. LeGuin, Gregory Benford, Frederik Pohl and others. Of special note are Dick Lupoff's long-running book review column and the frequent publication of criticism otherwise not easily available, such as Sandra Miesel's introductions to Gregg Press books. The magazine's high production costs made it especially vulnerable to shrinking revenue from advertising during the recession of the early 1980s, and after becoming sporadic in schedule, it finally ceased publication with its "Twentieth Anniversary Issue."

Hugo Nominee: 1973, 1974, 1975, 1976, 1981.

Winner: 1974.

Library Collections: Porter indicates "too many to list (50–100)"; including California State University, Fullerton.

Microfilm available from University Microfilms.

THE ALIEN CRITIC

See SCIENCE FICTION REVIEW.

AMRA

Dates: 1956–.

Editors: George R. Heap/George H. Scithers, Box 8243, Philadelphia, Pa. 19101.

George Heap founded *Amra* as the mimeographed newsletter of the Hyborean Legion in 1956. With Scithers' first issue in January 1969, it became a multilithed general magazine, centered on the Conan stories by Robert E. Howard but branching out into anything connected with sword and sorcery fiction: early weapons and military tactics, the work of other S&S authors, verse, and both straight and parody fiction. Contributors include L. Sprague de Camp, Fritz Leiber, Poul Anderson and others. By far the most literate and attractive S&S fanzine, it is the source of several anthologies of essays.

Hugo Nominee: 1962, 1964, 1968.

Winner: 1964, 1968.

Library Collections: Bowling Green State University; California State University, Fullerton.

Microfilm: 1969–1979 available from University Microfilms.

ANDURIL

Dates: January 1972–1980.

Editor: John Martin.

Anduril, for a while, rated as the British equivalent of *Amra*, devoted to articles and dissertations on fantasy plus the occasional story. *Anduril* had started life as the official bulletin of the British Tolkien Society, and in that incarnation there exists an issue Number 0, but very soon the society reshaped, its bulletin now titled *Amon Hen* and the journal titled *Mallorn*. Editor John Martin took *Anduril* in his own direction and soon developed an intelligent if irregular magazine that attracted letters and contributions from Lin Carter, Marion Zimmer Bradley, L. Sprague de Camp, Robert Bloch, Ramsey Campbell and other professionals. On the fiction side it is most noted for its series about Thula by Pat McIntosh, each part of which was subsequently selected by Lin Carter for his *Year's Best Fantasy* volumes. *Anduril* reached its zenith with the sixth issue, which was attractively printed and adorned by beautiful artwork, much of it by Russ Nicholson. That issue won the British Fantasy Award in the small press category in 1976. Unfortunately, the cost of producing the issue and the lack of financial return coupled with the editor's moving home and job brought a temporary suspension of the magazine, and only one further issue has appeared since.

Winner: British Fantasy Award, 1976.

M.A.

ARENA SF

Dates: 1976–1982.

Editor: Geoff Rippington.

Arena SF was a determinedly controversial magazine of reviews, critical essays and interviews, especially notable for featuring multiple approaches to an author, for example, an interview with a major writer such as Kurt Vonnegut or John Brunner coupled with a critical essay about or by the same writer. In this, as in the controversy, the intent was to encourage readers to think with some depth about what they were reading. The editor remarked in a letter, "It is too easy a road to publish material that is an enjoyable read, but has no depth."

Library Collections: Bowling Green State University; The British Council; British Library; Foundation Library; Niedersachische Staats-Und Universitatsbebliothek, Gottingen, Germany; Spaced Out Library, Toronto Public Libraries; Texas A&M.

AURORA

See JANUS/AURORA.

AUSTRALIAN SCIENCE FICTION REVIEW

Dates: June 1966–June 1969.
Editor: John Bangsund.

A magazine that helped establish Australia as a major center for serious writing about SF, *Australian Science Fiction Review* offers essays and reviews. Bangsund tried determinedly to make the magazine cosmopolitan in tone and contents, but the major contributors were solid local critics like John Foyster, George Turner, Lee Harding and Bruce Gillespie.

Hugo Nominee: 1967, 1968.
Library Collections: California State University, Fullerton.

THE BAUM BUGLE

Dates: June 1957–.
Editors: David L. Green/Fred M. Meyer, 1620 First Avenue South, Escanaba, Mich. 48929.

Published by the International Wizard of Oz Club (Box 95, Kinderhook, Ill.), this journal covers not only the Oz stories but other fiction by the pioneering American fantasist. It also discusses the context of Baum's work with information on publishing, promotion, adaptations and other related subjects. It is detailed and factual, despite its fundamental admiration for Baum.

THE BULLETIN OF THE SCIENCE FICTION WRITERS OF AMERICA

Dates: 1965–.
Edited by members of SFWA: Damon Knight/Terry Carr/Alexei Panshin/Barry N. Malzberg/George Zebrowski/Stephen Goldin/John F. Carr/Richard Kearns/ and others.
Editor: David Brin, 5081 Baxter St., San Diego, Calif. 92117.

The *Bulletin* is SFWA's public magazine, as opposed to its more freeswinging

Forum, which is circulated to members only. Basically a vehicle for market tips and for news of current writing and publishing projects, it nevertheless offers a constant exchange of professionals' opinions on SF writing as well as occasional critical articles.

Library Collections: Bowling Green State University; California State University, Fullerton.

Microfilm: available from 1974 on from University Microfilms.

CINEFANTASTIQUE

Dates: Fall 1970–.

Editor: Frederick F. Clarke, P.O. Box 70, Oak Park, Ill. 60303.

Some periodicals dealing with SF and fantasy films, such as *Castle of Frankenstein*, *Starlog* and *Starburst*, have occasionally been valuable; many have been juvenile dreck. *Cinefantastique* is far and away the best magazine in the field. It features at least one very detailed article per issue, concentrating on a movie or the work of one creator, along with lively and well-reasoned film reviews. At one time its attitude was criticized as rather pretentious, but this has changed in recent years. The graphics are extremely attractive, with many photos reproduced on high-quality paper.

CRY [OF THE NAMELESS]

Dates: January 1950–1970.

Editors: G. M. Carr/Wally Weber and Burnett R. Toskey/*Cry* in 1954–1955 entered a brief period of rotating editorship which ended with the magazine in the editorial hands of Weber, Toskey (who departed the editorial chair in 1959) and F. M. and Elinor Busby/Weber, E. Busby and Vera Heminger.

Cry began as a brief recap of news of Seattle's fan club, The Nameless Ones, and it carried Wally Weber's zany reports of Nameless Ones meetings through its life; however, after 1959 the magazine was called simply *Cry*. As it prospered and waxed fat, *Cry* was basically a fannish zine, with lots of humorous essays and a very uninhibited letter column. It is of interest to people concerned with criticism, however, because of the column of chiefly prozine reviews by Renfrew Pemberton (F. M. Busby) that ran from the mid-fifties until the end of the decade, when Busby switched to a wider-ranging column. Busby's comments on magazine SF are not as concentrated as James Blish's, but they are comprehensive, perceptive and pungently expressed. However, when Boeing sent Wally Weber to Alabama for two years, *Cry* announced its own demise in issue 174 (March 1964). Later, under the editorship of Weber, Elinor Busby and Vera Heminger, the magazine was revived, but with a somewhat different emphasis. Between late 1968 and early 1970, an additional twelve issues were published.

Hugo Nominee: 1959, 1960, 1962. In 1961, says Busby, "the magazine was disqualified by the World SF Committee because the *Cry* staff (Editors plus helpers) *was* the Committee, but it still came in second in the nominations." Winner: 1960.
Library Collections: University of Washington, Seattle; California State University, Fullerton.

CYPHER

Dates: June 1970–November 1974.
Editor: James Goddard (and initially Mike Sandow).
    Running for twelve issues, *Cypher* was the leading serious British SF fanzine in the early 1970s, thus forming a link between *Speculation* and *Arena SF*. Goddard acquired mature if occasionally self-indulgent articles that concentrated on the works of specific writers. It was significant as the first British SF fanzine to receive a publication grant from an official body, in this case the Southern Arts Council. Of special interest was issue 9 (March 1973), which featured an interesting four-way interview between the editor, Harry Harrison, Leon Stover and Brian Aldiss. Other highlights of the magazine were an interview/conversation between Aldiss and James Blish, and a probing interview with Edmund Cooper. An unpublished thirteenth issue had planned to study the state of SF in Britain in the mid-1970s, and manuscripts were apparently completed by Christopher Priest, John Brunner, James Blish, Mark Adlard and others; none, however, made it into print.

M.A.

DARK HORIZONS

Dates: 1971–.
Editors: Rosemary Pardoe (Nos. 1–4), Trevor Hughes (5), Adrian Cole (6), Dave Sutton (7), Darroll Pardoe (8), Steve Jones (9–15), Geoffrey N. Smith (16–17), John Heron (18), Mike Chinn and John Merritt (19–22), Dave Sutton (23–), The British Fantasy Society, c/o Rob Butterworth, 79 Rochdale Road, Milnrow, Rochdale, Lancs. OL16 4DT, England.
    Dark Horizons is the official magazine of the British Fantasy Society, linked with the *B.F.S. Bulletin*, which concentrates on news and reviews. *DH* contains both fiction and nonfiction and has varied considerably in quality from editor to editor. The best issues were those under Pardoe, and especially Steve Jones, and the current editor Dave Sutton, who has brought to the magazine the tried and tested blend which proved so successful with his fanzine *Shadow*. The magazine is notable for its wide range of subject matter; besides written fantasy, essays deal with films, music and occult lore. Issue 14 (Summer 1976) was a

special Brian Lumley issue. Issue 15 (Winter 1976) was all-fiction and in some ways was a precursor to the editor's *Fantasy Tales* (see Section I). Steve Jones published an index to issues 9–15, and *DH* is also indexed in ISPF-2.

M.A./J.S.

DELAP'S F&SF REVIEW

Dates: April 1975–March-April 1978.
Editor: Richard Delap.

Delap's F&SF Review was a valiant attempt to cover all SF and fantasy published (including hardbound and paperback, adult juvenile, foreign, media-related, and recorded), in compact but relatively thorough reviews. After its first two small, thin issues, *Delap's* blossomed into a large, attractive magazine, with photos of the book covers accompanying each review. In addition to reviews, it included a list of all titles published each month. Delap used a relatively small crew of reviewers—he contributed a substantial percentage of the reviews himself—but they included competent fans and academics, as well as such pros as Michael Bishop, Marion Zimmer Bradley and Harlan Ellison. However, the number of books published and the length of the reviews meant that the magazine fell farther and farther behind in coverage, even as a monthly. An altercation between Delap and his publisher, Fred Patton, disrupted publication from mid-1977 to early 1978, and *Delap's* expired soon after.

Library Collections: Bowling Green State University.

DESTINY

Dates: Spring 1950–Fall 1954.
Editors: Malcolm Willits and Jim Bradley/Malcolm Willits and Earl Kemp.

Through most of its life, *Destiny* was largely a vehicle for short-short amateur fiction. It did publish some notable nonfiction, however, especially beginning with Number 4–5 (Summer-Fall 1951), which began printing the inherited backlog of Don Day's *Fanscient*. When Earl Kemp replaced Bradley (with the Spring 1953 issue), the magazine became of even more interest to the scholar-critic, culminating with the last issue, which was subtitled "Tales of Science & Fantasy" but which actually was a detailed index of SF publishing for 1953 by Ed Wood and Earl Kemp, covering magazines and books and including Wood's commentary on publishing trends. Earlier issues included articles on films, debate on space travel, and a running series of autobiographical sketches by people such as Walter M. Miller, Jr., Leigh Brackett and Fritz Leiber.

EISFA/YANDRO

Dates: February 1953–.
Editors: Juanita Wellons and Beverly J. Amers/Robert ("Buck") and Juanita (Wellons) Coulson, Route 3, Hartford City, Ind. 47348.

Yandro (originally *EISFA*) grew out of the clubzine of a college group, the Eastern Indiana Science Fiction Association. In January 1956 the Coulsons renamed it after the haunted mountain in a folk song and made it one of the most popular monthly general fanzines of the mid-1950s and 1960s. Juanita supervised mimeographing, including superior stenciling of illustrations; Buck handled most of the written material, in his role of bristling curmudgeon. Contributors have included Ted White, Sandra Miesel, Marion Zimmer Bradley and Gene De Weese. Contents have tended toward straight humor or SF-satirical, with a lively letter column. However, of special interest to scholars are the review columns. Buck Coulson's book reviews are generally succinct and consistent—a researcher has the advantage of encountering the same reviewer throughout; they also are startlingly comprehensive. (One also can use the reviews, during the years *Yandro* was on a regular monthly schedule, to assign dates to otherwise elusive paperbacks.) Its fanzine reviews are valuable for similar reasons. *Yandro*'s publishing schedule has become irregular in recent years, beginning around 1968, as the Coulsons' writing careers have flourished, but the quality of the contents has remained high.

Hugo Nominee: 1959, 1960, 1961, 1962, 1963, 1964, 1965, 1966, 1967, 1968.
Winner: 1965.
Library Collections: California State University, Fullerton.

ENERGUMEN

Dates: February 1970–May 1973.
Editors: Mike Glicksohn/Michael and Susan (Wood) Glicksohn.

One of the hardest things for nonfans to comprehend is how people can expend large amounts of time, energy and concern on such ephemeral, low-circulation publications as fanzines. It seems futile. Yet at the same time fanzine writing is immediately exciting and rewarding in its quick interchange of ideas, and the results are sometimes valuable to scholar-critics who happen by later. *Energumen* is a beautiful example of such a magazine: lovingly produced, informal, yet full of direct, personal interest. Science fiction is *one* of the things that interested *Energumen*'s editors and contributors; though the proportion of SF-centered material is not great, the quality is high. Especially useful is Sandra Miesel's criticism of current books, a rare mixture of erudition and perception.

Hugo Nominee: 1971, 1972, 1973.
Winner: 1973.

ERBANIA

Dates: April 1956–.
Editor: D. Peter Ogden, 8001 Fernview Lane, Tampa, Fla. 33615.
Longest-lived and most impressive of the currently active fanzines centered on the works of Edgar Rice Burroughs, *Erbania* was begun by Ogden in England, continued in Canada, and is now published in Florida. Contents have included discussions of Burroughs' work, including different media such as radio, television, motion pictures and comic strips. It also features articles on the different artists who have illustrated his work, reviews of new books in the field, and so on. Occasionally articles appear on other authors who have written "heroic fantasy," such as Robert E. Howard, Otis Adelbert Kline, C. T. Stoneham and Philip José Farmer.
Library Collections: New York Public Library; University of Louisiana; University of Louisville.

ERB-DOM

Dates: May 1960–?.
Editors: Alfred Guillory and Camille "Caz" Cazedessus.
Of the fanzines rooted in love of Edgar Rice Burroughs' perennially popular wish-fulfillment fantasies, *Erb-dom* stands out as valuable even for readers who do not adulate the writer. It gives many background and bibliographical details of Burroughs' work as it has appeared in magazines, books, comic strips and movies. Some material is reprinted, some new.
Hugo Nominee: 1964, 1966.
Winner: 1966.
Library Collections: Brigham Young University; California State University, Fullerton.

EXTRAPOLATION

Dates: December 1959–.
Editors: Thomas D. Clareson/Associate Editors: Carl B. Yoke and Mary T. Brizzi, The Kent State University Press, Kent, Ohio 44242.
Extrapolation was the first of the academic critical journals. Clareson began it as a twice-yearly "Newsletter of the Conference on Science Fiction of the MLA" in an effort to give SF some visibility and respectability in the academic world. With the December 1971 issue, it became "The Journal of the MLA Seminar on Science Fiction, also serving the Science Fiction Research Association," a change reflecting how successful Clareson's efforts had been. For most of its life, *Extrapolation* has been a one-man operation; Clareson handled all

editorial and production chores in the early issues, except during his college leave in 1966–1967, when Tom Bowman filled in. In the Spring of 1979, publication of the journal was assumed by Kent State University Press. It was increased to a quarterly, graphics and design were improved, and Yoke and Brizzi were added to the editorial staff. Contents have kept much the same emphasis: mildly theoretical essays on the nature of SF; studies of specific works, both historical and modern; essays and source information of value to teachers of SF. Of special interest are the bibliographies of critical material on SF begun by Clareson and continued annually by Roger Schlobin and Marshall B. Tymn as "The Year's Scholarship in Science Fiction and Fantasy," until 1982, when they became a separate publication of the KSU Press.

Reprint Editions: Volumes 1–13 were republished by Johnson Reprint Corporation (Vols. 1–10, 1970; Vols. 11–13, 1973). Gregg Press also issued a reprint of Volumes 1–10 in 1978.

Library Collections: California State University, Fullerton; Wooster College, Wooster, Ohio (complete run).

Microfilm: all issues available from Greenwood Press.

FANEWSCARD

Dates: July 3, 1943–January 1948.

Editors: Bob Tucker/Frank Robinson and Ed Connor/Walt Dunkelberger.

Begun as a weekly postal card publication, *Fanewscard* went through several formats, policies and editors for a total of 339 issues. According to Warner, "It gave the most thorough coverage of fandom and prodom of any newszine in history" (Warner 1). Tucker's later publication *The Bloomington News Letter*, later called *Science Fiction Newsletter*, "never skimped on fannish news, but its professional coverage was unexcelled in any newszine until the much later arrival of *Locus*" (Warner 1, 2). Though they overlap *Science Fiction Times*' lifespan, these publications also might supply valuable information.

THE FANSCIENT

Dates: September 1947–Spring/Summer 1951.

Editor: Donald B. Day for the Portland SF Society.

According to Harry Warner, Jr., this magazine was one of the leading serious publications of its period. It provided "an enormous amount of material about the most important professional writers of fantasy and their works, some good fiction, and articles with principally serious slants" (Warner 1). The main feature was "Author! Author!" which contained autobiographical sketches by noted authors such as Jack Williamson, Murray Leinster, Ray Bradbury, Anthony Boucher and David H. Keller, accompanied by complete bibliographies of their work. Much of this served as basic groundwork for Don Day's seminal *Index to the Science-Fiction Magazines 1926–1950*. The magazine ran for thirteen issues (the last issue a double-numbered 13/14), initially in octavo format and then halved to a compact thirty-two-page booklet.

FANTASIAE

Dates: April 1973–July 1980.
Editor: Ian M. Slater.

Subtitled "The Monthly Newsletter of the Fantasy Association," *Fantasiae* was designed to spread information about any and all writers within the broad field of fantasy, from classical legend and mythology through J.R.R. Tolkien up to Marion Zimmer Bradley and Larry Niven. It appeared on a fairly regular schedule and ranged from eight to twenty-four pages. Contents included news, special essays and lengthy reviews, written with special emphasis on literary, historical and mythological background and connections.

Library Collections: British Fantasy Society, Lancaster; British Library, Aldermaston; Brooklyn Public Library; California State University, Fullerton; Fairfax County Library, Fairfax, Va.; Falvey Public Library, Villanova University; Fantasy Foundation, Los Angeles, Calif.; Indiana State University; Masao W. Satow Library, Gardena, Calif.; National Library of Australia; New York Public Library; Northern Illinois University; Portland State University; Spaced Out Library, Toronto; Stark County District Library, Canton, Ohio; Texas A&M University; Toronto Public Library, Palmerston Branch; University of Calgary; University of California–Riverside; University of Colorado; University of Sydney; University of Tennessee; University of Waterloo, Canada; Ward Chipman Library, University of New Brunswick; Wheaton College.

FANTASY ADVERTISER/SCIENCE FICTION ADVERTISER/INSIDE AND SCIENCE FICTION ADVERTISER/INSIDE

Dates: April 1946–June 1963.
Editors: Norman E. "Gus" Willmorth/Roy Squires/Ron Smith/Jon White.

This publication, most important in its years as *Inside and Science Fiction Advertiser*, began as a means for collectors to acquire and dispose of material; within a year, however, Willmorth had added book and fanzine review columns, and he later published critical and bibliographical essays to leaven the mass of advertisements. When Squires took over, with the January 1950 issue, he continued this policy, changing the name to *Science Fiction Advertiser* with the January 1952 issue and steadily increasing the amount of written material. The

March and July 1952 issues, for example, offered a major two-part essay on A. E. van Vogt by Arthur J. Cox. By late 1954, *SFA* was essentially a magazine of essays and reviews, with a few ads mixed in. Meanwhile, in 1953, California fan Ron Smith had begun publishing *Inside*, bubbling with enthusiasm and ambition. Tired of the drudgery of publishing, Squires handed his magazine over to Smith, who built the combined publication into an impressive blend of current reviews, critical essays and exchanges of opinion about the writing and publishing of SF. *Inside and SFA* also featured original fiction and humor, especially parodies of SF writers and magazines. As *Inside and SFA* grew larger and more elaborate, however, its schedule became increasingly infrequent, and it ceased publication in 1958. Jon White edited two issues of *Inside* in 1962 and 1963, largely pieced together from material left over from Smith's files. After that, the name changed to *Riverside Quarterly*—such a radically different magazine that it has a separate entry in this section.

Hugo Nominee: 1956, 1957.

Winner: 1956.

Library Collections: California State University, Fullerton.

FANTASY COMMENTATOR

Dates: December 1943–1952; Fall 1979–.

Editor: A. Langley Searles, 48 Highland Circle, Bronxville, N.Y. 10708.

    Fantasy Commentator focused largely on books, in anti-stuffy style. It serialized Sam Moskowitz's *The Immortal Storm*, but is best known, according to Warner, for "an imposing series of bibliographies of fantasy fiction in many mundane magazines, scholarly and literate articles about the writers of fantasy, and original material by almost all of the most famous pros of the era—Merritt, Kuttner, Keller, Lovecraft, and Hodgson, for instance" (Warner 1). *Fantasy Commentator* resumed publication in 1979 as an annual with the same policy. It also publishes SF verse. Recent issues have concentrated on studies of the writers Edward Lucas White and Algernon Blackwood, together with the serialization of Sam Moskowitz's history of early SF.

THE FANTASY FAN

Dates: September 1933–February 1935.

Editor: Charles D. Hornig.

    The Fantasy Fan is one of the legendary magazines of the 1930s. It would be notable if only because as the result of seeing the first issue Hugo Gernsback interviewed Hornig and on that basis made him the managing editor of *Wonder Stories* at the age of seventeen. But it was also an extremely consistent and reliable magazine, its sixteen pages, printed by Conrad H. Ruppert, appearing on a regular monthly schedule. After the first issue, Hornig changed the policy of the magazine to concentrate chiefly on weird fiction, and it is in this respect that the magazine is best remembered. It published some first-run fiction by H. P. Lovecraft, Clark Ashton Smith, David H. Keller, Eando Binder and others. It also ran the revised version of Lovecraft's "Supernatural Horror in Literature," although this was incomplete when the fanzine ceased publication. *The Fantasy Fan* also featured the first writings of Bob Tucker and Robert Bloch, while researchers will be interested in the news column "Weird Whisperings" compiled by Mort Weisinger and Julius Schwartz.

M.A.

FANTASY MACABRE

Dates: November 1980–.
Editors: Dave Reeder and Dave Carson. Published by Richard Fawcett, 61 Teecomwas Drive, Uncasville, Conn. 06382.

Fantasy Macabre is published occasionally as a showcase for aspiring writers in the field of macabre fantasy, in the *Weird Tales* tradition. It publishes stories along with some poetry; a central feature is its bibliographies of prominent writers. Issues 2 and 3 contain the most complete checklist of the work of David H. Keller yet published. *FM* also includes interviews and essays. After issue 4 (July 1983) pressure of work upon Reeder as editor of the revived British horror film magazine *Halls of Horror* led to his relinquishing his editorship of the magazine, and publisher Richard Fawcett passed the editorship to Jessica Amanda Salmonson, whose first issues appeared in 1985. *FM* is indexed in ISPF-2.

M.A.

FANTASY MAGAZINE.

See SCIENCE FICTION DIGEST/FANTASY MAGAZINE.

FANTASY MEDIA

Dates: March 1979–September 1980.
Editors: Jon M. Harvey, Stephen Jones, Gordon Larkin, David A. Sutton.

Fantasy Media reported extensively all aspects of fantasy and science fiction in all media, especially films. In addition to news and reviews, *FM* published interviews with leading authors and film directors (Anne McCaffrey, Nigel Kneale, Stephen King, George Romero and others) and special articles on subjects like German SF, the birth of Virgin Books, and so on. Spiraling costs and diminishing advertising revenue, coupled with a static circulation, caused the magazine's collapse in the autumn of 1980.

FANTASY NEWSLETTER/FANTASY REVIEW

Dates: June 1978–.
Editors: Paul Allen/Paul and Susan Allen/Robert A. Collins, College of Humanities, Florida Atlantic University, Boca Raton, Fla. 33431.

Allen began *Fantasy Newsletter* as a "no-frills" eight-page monthly newsletter to circulate news of current and forthcoming publications so that collectors would not miss anything of interest. At that time, the journal briefly covered specialty publishers, trade publishers, paperbacks, the fan press and the British scene, plus miscellaneous news. Allen soon added news on magazines and began running photos of writers and samples of artwork from the books and magazines mentioned. In January 1980 *FN* became a full-fledged magazine, adding book and movie reviews, original essays and interviews, and columns in alternating months by Karl Edward Wagner and Fritz Leiber. Expanded previews of written material were especially comprehensive and valuable. Despite all this, *FN* failed to attract enough buyers to be viable, and it ceased publication with Number 41, October 1981. It was immediately revived by Robert Collins, director of the International Conference on the Fantastic in the Arts, held at Florida Atlantic University. In this incarnation, *FN* mixed whimsy and controversy with the regular features and with essays and commentary by various writers. At the beginning of 1984, the magazine merged with the *Science Fiction and Fantasy Book Review* edited by Neil Barron and published by the Science Fiction Research Association. The title changed to *Fantasy Review*. Henceforth, Collins announced, the section of reviews would be expanded considerably under Barron's editorship, while the contents otherwise would remain unchanged.
Hugo Nominee: 1983.
Library Collections: California State University, Fullerton.

FANTASY REPORTER

See SCIENCE FICTION TIMES.

FANTASY REVIEW/SCIENCE FANTASY REVIEW

Dates: March 1947–Spring 1950.
Editor: Walter Gillings.

Fantasy Review was the title Gillings gave to his postwar revival of *Scientifiction*. Professionally printed as a neat twenty-page booklet (later growing to thirty-two and even forty pages), it was edited with Gillings' usual polish. Gillings also wrote most of the contents, often under such pen names as Thomas Sheridan and Geoffrey Giles, and the magazine contains an immense amount of news of all kinds, as well as intelligent reviews and criticism. *FR* was certainly the most mature news magazine British fandom had produced, and is still one of the most elaborate of its kind. After eighteen issues, Gillings incorporated the magazine as a supplement in his new professional magazine *Science-Fantasy*, but the review supplement was dropped when Gillings lost control of the magazine.

M.A.

FANTASY TIMES

See SCIENCE FICTION TIMES.

FOUNDATION: THE REVIEW OF SCIENCE FICTION

Dates: March 1972–.
Editors: Peter Nichols/Malcolm Edwards/David Pringle, The SF Foundation, North East London Polytechnic, Longbridge Road, Dagenham, RM8, 2AS, U.K.

Of the three major academic journals, *Foundation* is the closest to a good, informal, but serious fanzine. A fair share of the articles are by active SF writers—for instance, a long-running feature on ''The Profession of Science Fiction'' gives writers a chance to express opinions or vent spleen. Another important feature of *Foundation* is the large amount of space given to reviews of current SF; these contain some of the most perceptive and well-written criticism appearing anywhere. It is published three times a year.

Reprint Editions: Numbers 1–8 (March 1972–March 1975) were reprinted by Gregg Press in 1978.
Library Collections: California State University, Fullerton.
Microfiche: available from Oxford Microform Publications.

THE FUTURIAN/PSEUDO-FUTURIAN/FUTURIAN WAR DIGEST/THE NEW FUTURIAN

Dates: 1938–1958.
Editor: J. Michael Rosenblum.

The Futurian is perhaps the most legendary of British fanzines. It grew out of the *Bulletin of the Leeds SF Society*, edited by Harold Gotliffe. Rosenblum turned it into a chatty fanzine which, while informal, conveyed much news and information on books of the day. Rosenblum's personal SF collection was already enviable, and he was able to provide information on books little known elsewhere. A neat, booklet-sized printed fanzine, it ran for six issues before the war occluded publication. Rosenblum registered as a conscientious objector, and though he was conscripted to do farm work he still managed to remain the core of British SF fandom during the war. Two unnumbered issues of *The Futurian* were duplicated before Rosenblum merged the magazine with *War Digest*, a two-page publication put out by Leslie Heald and Ron Holmes. The new magazine was called *Futurian War Digest* and was the main voice of British fandom during the war years, running for thirty-nine issues and surviving despite harsh paper restrictions (most issues were only three or four sheets, but sometimes crept as high as nine or ten sheets, occasionally on paper provided by American fans). Contributors included Sam Youd (John Christopher), David McIlwain (C. E. Maine), Ken Bulmer and the noted bibliophile Dr. George Medhurst, whose reviews and columns of chatter are packed with facts and details of bibliomania. The magazine was much loved and earned the nickname "Fido." Rosenblum encouraged other fans to produce wartime fanzines, and these were often bound with Fido, resulting in a reasonably sizable package. Such titles included John F. Burke's *Moonshine*, Terry Overton's *Galaxy* and John Carnell's *Sands of Time*.

Fido eventually ceased publication in March 1945, but Rosenblum was prevailed upon to relaunch the magazine, which appeared as *The New Futurian* in the spring of 1954, running for eight issues until 1958. Many of the same writers continued to contribute, but the series is most notable for Walter Gillings' series of articles, "The Clamorous Dreamers," which looked back over the history of British fandom. The series was later revised as "The Impatient Dreamers" in *Vision of Tomorrow*. *The New Futurian*, or "NuFu," as it was inevitably christened, was perhaps the most academically oriented of the fanzines of the 1950s.

In fond remembrance, ten years after NuFu's demise Michael Rosenblum's son, Howard, launched *Son of New Futurian*, although this fannish zine was anything but academic.

M.A.

FUTURIAN WAR DIGEST

See THE FUTURIAN/PSEUDO-FUTURIAN . . .

GOTHIC

Dates: June 1979–1981.
Editor: Gary William Crawford, Gothic Press, 4998 Perkins Road, Baton Rouge, La. 70808.

Published semi-annually, *Gothic* defines Gothicism as "a spirit or impulse

that variously influence[d] literature in the nineteenth- and twentieth-centuries,'' especially showing "the darker side of human existence.'' The magazine alternated new fantasy stories and scholarly articles on the Gothic impulse in literature. It also contained an annual annotated bibliography of criticism in the field, which, since the demise of *Gothic*, has been continued as a separate publication.
Library Collections: California State University, Sacramento; Indiana University; University of Florida; University of Guelph; University of Illinois.
Microfilm: available from University Microfilms.

INSIDE AND SCIENCE FICTION ADVERTISER

See FANTASY ADVERTISER/SCIENCE FICTION ADVERTISER . . .

JANUS/AURORA

Dates: Fall 1975–.
Editors: Janice Bogstad and Jeanne Gomoll/SF-3 (a cooperative group), SF-3, Box 1624, Madison, Wis. 53701.
An exception to the general rule that group-edited zines falter and die without accomplishing much, *Janus* is a fascinating hodgepodge of cartoons, essays, reviews, interviews and other material. Its basic emphasis is serious and feminist, and it studies SF in order to widen the consciousness of readers. Special emphasis is placed on female SF writers, such as Elizabeth A. Lynn, Octavia E. Butler, Joan Vinge and Suzette Hayden Elgin. Recent issues feature material on a common theme: Number 18 on postholocaust feminist fiction, for example, and Number 19 on communication.
Hugo Nominee: 1978, 1979.
Library Collections: Madison Public Library, Wis.

THE JOURNAL OF SCIENCE FICTION

Dates: Fall 1951–1953.
Editors: Charles Freudenthal, Edward Wood and (issue 1 only) Lester Fried.
Ostensibly the official organ of the University of Chicago Science Fiction Club, *The Journal of Science Fiction* was anything but the typical club publication. It ranks as one of the most mature and important fanzines of the 1950s. Offset-lithoed in a neat saddle-stapled A5 format, this magazine is every bit as professional as any major publication, as was the intention of the editors. They were attempting to provide the field with a serious, central annual which surveyed the field of SF. The magazine had to be reader-supported and pay its way. It was not financed by the club. In this respect it failed, and with the fourth issue

the editors announced, "If a publication fails to satisfy the needs and desires of its time, it deserves to die." In fact *JOSF* was a critical success, but it was the right approach at the wrong time, failing to reach its full readership. Highlights of the magazine were lengthy articles by authors such as Robert Bloch and Hugo Gernsback, plus Edward Wood's surveys of the SF published in magazines for 1951 and 1952. It is an invaluable aid to any researcher.

M.A.

KHATRU

Dates: February 1975–February 1978.
Editors: Jeffrey D. Smith; Jeffrey D. Smith and Jeffrey A. Frane.

A continuation of *Phantasmicom* (edited by Donald G. Keller and Jeffrey D. Smith, from 1969 to 1974), *Khatru* is an altogether exemplary informal but serious SF fanzine. The magazine stressed the fast exchange of ideas in brief essays, but it included longer works by Douglas Barbour, Jeff Clark and Smith himself. It is also notable for continuing contributions by Alice Sheldon (James Tiptree, Jr.). The combined issue 3 & 4 contains a massive symposium on women in science fiction; participants include Suzy McKee Charnas, Samuel R. Delany, Virginia Kidd, Ursula K. LeGuin, Vonda N. McIntyre, Joanna Russ, James R. Tiptree, Kate Wilhelm and Chelsea Quinn Yarbro.

LIGHTHOUSE

Dates: 1958–1967.
Editors: Peter Graham and Terry Carr; Terry Carr.

After helping create one of the definitive fanzines (*Innuendo*) and the definitive fannish newzine (*Fanac*), Carr turned his talents to another type of fanzine. *Lighthouse* is one of the apparently informal, strongly personal fanzines that wind up showing much more about the nature of SF and the interests of its creators than anyone would imagine while leafing through an issue. It featured very high-powered contributors; for example, the August 1967 issue contains contributions by Carr himself, Samuel R. Delany, Gahan Wilson, Fritz Leiber, Damon Knight, Thomas M. Disch, Dick and Pat Lupoff, Joanna Russ and Harlan Ellison—not an atypical lineup. Other contributors during *Lighthouse*'s life in-cluded Ted White, Philip K. Dick, Gregory Benford, Alexei Panshin and Donald A. Wollheim.
Library Collections: California State University, Fullerton.

LOCUS

Dates: April 1968–.

Editors: Charles N. Brown, Ed Meskys, Dave Vanderwerf/Charles and Marsha Brown/Charles Brown/Charles and Dena Brown/Charles Brown, Locus Publications, P.O. Box 13305, Oakland, Calif. 94661.

From a bi-weekly, scrappy looking, mimeographed newszine, *Locus* has developed and expanded until it fully deserves its subtitle, "The Newspaper of the Science Fiction Field." It is the basic source of raw news about SF during the years it has been published. In addition to news, *Locus* has run columns on writing SF by Algis Budrys and Norman Spinrad, selective book reviews, a best-seller list, a monthly list (beginning in 1974) of the books actually published in America, an annual tabulation of books published, and an annual survey of the personal data and tastes of its readership. Such features, along with extensive news coverage in an average forty-four-page monthly issue, make it absolutely indispensable.

Hugo Nominee: 1970, 1971, 1972, 1973, 1974, 1975, 1976, 1977, 1978, 1980, 1981, 1982, 1983.

Hugo Winner: 1971, 1972, 1976, 1978, 1980, 1981, 1982, 1983, 1984.

Reprint Editions: Numbers 1–207 plus two preliminary issues and one special issue were reprinted in two volumes by Gregg Press in 1978 (o.p.).

Library Collections: Bowling Green State University; Brigham Young University; California State University, Fullerton.

LORE

Dates: 1965–1969.

Editor: Gerald W. Page.

Lore was launched as a forum for disseminating information, inspired when editor Page was asked if he knew anything about the author William L. Chester and had to confess he had never even heard of him. Each issue of *Lore* revolved around questions sent in by all and sundry and answers provided by any who could respond. In addition there were articles and reviews, often inspired by questions, plus a few bibliographies ranging from the SF and fantasy of H. Bedford-Jones to Edward Wood's issue index of *Fantastic Universe*. Of special interest was issue 7 (September 1966), an index to fantasy pseudonyms compiled by Donald Franson that was the best available until the publication of Barry McGhan's volume. The compiling and publishing of *Lore* was too time-consuming for Page, who in the end let the publication fade away. Hidden among the hundred or more questions and answers are many gems of information unavailable in any other form and of immense value to the dedicated researcher.

M.A.

LOVECRAFT STUDIES

Dates: Fall 1979–.
Editors: S. T. Joshi; Marc A. Michaud, 101 Lockwood Street, West Warwick, R.I. 02893.

The most academic of the journals dealing with Lovecraft, *Lovecraft Studies* insists on careful attention to scholarly form, strict attention to textual authority, and so on. In addition to critical essays, it publishes Lovecraft material difficult to locate otherwise; it is also willing to reprint articles on Lovecraft from obscure sources.

LUNA/LUNA MONTHLY

Dates: June 1969–Spring 1977.
Editor: Anne F. Dietz.

This magazine was a successor to *Luna*, edited by Frank M. Dietz, Jr., which was published briefly (1962–1963?) as a repository for transcripts of taped presentations from the programs of SF conventions. The later *Luna* was notable for the regularity of its appearance in its earlier years, and for its impeccable appearance. Contents included Paul Walker's series of interviews with major SF writers (*Luna* interviews make up the bulk of Walker's collected interviews, *Speaking of Science Fiction* [New York: LUNA Press, 1978]), columns on the international scene, comprehensive book reviews (including a section on juvenile books) and lists of books published each month.
Library Collections: Brigham Young University; California State University, Fullerton.

LUNA MONTHLY

See LUNA/LUNA MONTHLY.

MEGAVORE

See THE SCIENCE FICTION COLLECTOR/MEGAVORE . . .

THE MERVYN PEAKE REVIEW

Dates: 1974–.
Editors: G. Peter Winnington/John Watney, Flat 36, 5 Elm Park Gardens, London SW10 9QQ, U.K.

This is the official publication of the Mervyn Peake Society, dedicated to rescuing fugitive material by Peake and to spreading information about and criticism concerning the man and his work.

Library Collections: Bibliothèque Cantonale and Universitaire, Lausanne, Switzerland; Bibliothèque Nationale, Berne, Switzerland; Birmingham Public Libraries, Birmingham, U.K.; Library of Congress; Library of the University of Iowa; Manchester Polytechnic, Manchester, U.K.; University of London; DMS Watson Library, University College, London; Niedbersaechsische Staats-und Universitaets Bibliothek, Gottingen, West Germany; St. David's University College, Dyped, Wales; State University of New York at Buffalo; University of Sydney; York University Libraries, Ontario; University of Exeter; Bodleian Library, Oxford; The British Library; Cambridge University Library; National Library of Scotland; National Library of Wales; Trinity College, Dublin.

MYTHLORE: A JOURNAL OF J.R.R. TOLKIEN, C. S. LEWIS, CHARLES WILLIAMS, GENERAL FANTASY AND MYTHIC STUDIES

Date: 1969.

Editor: Glen H. Goodnight, 740 South Hobart Boulevard, No. 4, Los Angeles, Calif. 90005.

Mythlore is the major, longest-lived quarterly journal in the scholarly study of high fantasy, combining explication and discussions of the writers' literary and philosophical backgrounds. It incorporated Ed Mesky's impressive *The Tolkien Journal* (1965–1972) after that magazine's fifteenth issue.

The Mythopolic Society (P.O. Box 4671, Whittier, Calif. 90607) also publishes *Mythprint* (1969–), a monthly newsletter with book reviews, branch discussion reports and news; and *Mythellany* (1981–), an annual fiction/poetry magazine. Past publications include the philological journal *Parma Eldalamberon* (1971–1976).

Library Collections: The Mythopolic Society's secretary reports that "nearly 100 college and public libraries subscribe to *Mythlore*; many have a complete set."

NEW FRONTIERS

Dates: December 1955–August 1960.

Editor: Norman Metcalf.

This small but high-quality magazine featured essays giving background on SF (on the planet Krishna by L. Sprague de Camp, on planet building by Poul Anderson) and polemics by Mark Clifton.

THE NEW FUTURIAN

See THE FUTURIAN/PSEUDO-FUTURIAN . . .

NIEKAS

Dates: June 1962–January 1969; 1977–.
Editors: Ed Meskys/Ed Meskys and Felice Rolfe/Felice Rolfe and Jerry Jacks/
Ed Meskys with Charles and Marsha Brown/Ed Meskys with Sherwood Frazier,
Rafe Foch-Pi, and Margaret Shepard/Mike Bastraw, Sherwood C. Frazier, and
Ed Meskys. (Subscriptions) RFD #1 Box 63, Center Harbor, N.H. 03226.

Niekas began as a small zine published by Meskys for an amateur press
association, the continuation of *Polhode*, Meskys' earlier "apazine." However,
Niekas soon expanded, especially after Meskys read *The Lord of the Rings* and
decided to feature Tolkien-related material in every issue. The enthusiasms of
Meskys and various co-editors produced bulky but sometimes rather shapeless
issues; however, the magazine contained material of real merit, such as the
glossaries of Middle-Earth by Al Halevy and Robert Foster (Foster's more elaborate work was later published in book form by Mirage Press and by Ballantine
as *The Complete Guide to Middle-Earth*). Newly revived, under its current
editorial board *Niekas* continues its emphasis on high/heroic fantasy but with
tighter focus, especially in special sections or issues devoted to dragons, Conan,
Lewis Carroll, and so on.
Hugo Nominee: 1966, 1967.
Winner: 1967.

NYCTALOPS

Dates: 1970–.
Editor: Harry O. Morris, Jr., Silver Scarab Press, 502 Elm Street SE, Albu-
querque, N.M. 87102.

Nyctalops is described by its editor as "a journal devoted to the serious study
of H. P. Lovecraft and related authors and subjects," though that policy is broad
enough to include essays on films, Dunsany's plays, Saki's fiction, and other
topics. Each issue includes considerable fiction and poetry, illustrated by often
surrealistic drawings, photographs and collages. It is an extremely attractive,
sometimes disconcerting magazine.
Library Collections: Brown University Library.

OAK LEAVES

Dates: Fall 1970–Autumn 1979).

Editor: David Anthony Kraft.

Oak Leaves is devoted to the life and writing of Otis Adelbert Kline (1891–1946), with many letters to and by Kline. A writer who worked the same vein of popular romance as Edgar Rice Burroughs, Kline is of debatable importance personally; nevertheless, this material is valuable for information on the pulp writing industry.

Reprint Editions: Facsimile reprint of all twelve issues was published in 1980 by Fictioneers, Inc., of Clayton, Ga.

OUTWORLDS

Dates: January 1970–Spring 1976.

Editor: William L. Bowers.

Bowers had been co-editor of a large zine, *Double-Bill*, with Bill Mallardi, and in fact had published a first issue of *Outworlds* in Summer 1966. The new *Outworlds*, beginning with a new first issue, went all out in terms of experimental, lavish production, the zine's appearance sometimes varying wildly from issue to issue. It soon became one of the major general fanzines of the early 1970s with a long-running column on SF by Robert A. W. Lowndes and frequent columns by Piers Anthony, Bob Tucker, Poul Anderson and Ted White. Other contributors included Sandra Miesel, Douglas Barbour and Gregory Benford. It also featured some vicious, pertinent feuds.

Hugo Nominee: 1971, 1974, 1975, 1976, 1977.

Library Collections: Bowling Green State University; California State University, Fullerton.

POE NEWSLETTER/POE STUDIES

Dates: April 1968–.

Editor: G. R. Thompson, Washington State University Press, Pullman, Wash. 99164.

Poe Newsletter began as a semi-annual, sixteen-page newsletter intended to help give direction to studies in the life and work of Edgar Allan Poe. As its size increased, it took on more of the assurance of a magazine after its title change (December 1970). The magazine features both reviews of scholarship (publications, dissertations, papers and lectures) and new essays. There is some discussion of the contexts of Poe's work; its policy is broad enough to cover all of Gothic and grotesque literature, and even some contemporary works. It is still published semi-annually, but its size has expanded to sixty-four pages per issue.

POE STUDIES

See POE NEWSLETTER/POE STUDIES.

PSYCHOTIC

See SCIENCE FICTION REVIEW.

THE PULP ERA

Dates: 1959-1960?–1975-1976?
Editor: Lynn Hickman, 413 Ottokee, Wauseon, Ohio 43567.

This publication was actually an outgrowth of Hickman's long-running fanzine *JD-Argassy*, which had touched on Hickman's many interests, including pulp magazines. *JD-A* 59 was subtitled ''The Pulp Era,'' and that title (and focus) took over the magazine with Number 61. Articles covered the history of the pulps and the writers and artists whose work appeared in the pulps, with frequent special attention to fantastic literature. Articles were written by knowledgeable enthusiasts, including August Derleth on *Weird Tales* and Redd Boggs on *Wild West Weekly*.
Source: Lynn Hickman.

RICHARD E. GEIS

See SCIENCE FICTION REVIEW.

RIVERSIDE QUARTERLY

Dates: August 1964–.
Editor: Leland Sapiro, Box 1763, Hartville, S.C. 29550.

Riverside Quarterly may have begun with the publication of *H. P. Lovecraft: A Symposium*, a transcript distributed in place of the third issue of *Inside*, which editor Jon White had failed to produce, and *RQ* itself carried the label ''(formerly *Inside*)'' for a few issues; actually *RQ* was a distinct break from the relatively relaxed genzine (general topics magazine) *Inside* subscribers were used to. Finally, in the third issue, Sapiro included an editorial note explaining that his choice of title and policy was intended "to emulate the *Hudson Review*, possibly the best literary magazine, and perform the same office for fantasy and science fiction that the *HR* does for literature in general." Like its model, *RQ* publishes fiction and poetry as well as critical essays and reviews. *RQ* was the most academic of the sixties fanzines, and Sapiro drew as much criticism for the formality of his writing as he did praise for his exacting dedication. The magazine is notable for its willingness to serialize long essays over several issues. Always a struggling publication, *RQ* resumed publication in 1977 after a several-year lapse.

Hugo Nominee: 1967, 1969, 1970.

Library Collections: Brigham Young University, California State University, Fullerton.

Microfilm: available from University Microfilms.

THE ROMANTIST

Dates: 1977–.

Editors: John C. Moran, with Don Herron and Steve Eng, The F. Marion Crawford Memorial Society, Saracinesca House, 3601 Meadowbrook Avenue, Nashville, Tenn. 37205.

The Romantist is an annual publication that avoids the early, personal and subjective "romantics" to concentrate on writers like F. Marion Crawford who stress "the Idea and Imaginative." Much stress is placed on authors who have written at least some fantasy; essays have focused on Algernon Blackwood, Arthur Machen, Robert W. Chambers, Russell Kirk, Montague Summers, H. Warner Munn and others. *The Romantist* is especially valuable for essays on obscure writers and works that nevertheless deserve attention.

Library Collections: Arizona State University; Bibliothèque Nationale; Bowdoin College; Brown University; Huntington Library; Iowa State University; National Library of Scotland; New York Public Library; Newberry Library; Portland State University; Princeton University; Stanford University; Texas Woman's University; Universidad Nacional Autonoma de Honduras; University of California, Berkeley; University of Mississippi; Vanderbilt University.

SCIENCE FANTASY REVIEW

See FANTASY REVIEW/SCIENCE FANTASY REVIEW.

SCIENCE FICTION: A REVIEW OF SPECULATIVE LITERATURE

Dates: June 1977–.
Editor: Van Ikin, Centre for Studies in Australian Literature, Department of English, University of Western Australia, Nedlands, W.A. 6009.

Science Fiction is more slender (in size and substance) than the other academic periodicals, but steadily improving. It features a mixture of articles, interviews and short stories—usually one of each per issue—with various reviews and commentary. Though some foreign writers have appeared in the magazine, it is largely locally written and is oriented toward local writers or those who have had a major impact on the Australian SF scene. With issue 13, it took over the unused material of Bruce Gillespie's *Science Fiction Commentary* and indicated that it would welcome more of the reader participation that helped make that publication so lively.

SCIENCE FICTION ADVERTISER

See FANTASY ADVERTISER/SCIENCE FICTION ADVERTISER . . .

SCIENCE FICTION & FANTASY BOOK REVIEW

Dates: February 1979–December 1983.
Editor: Neil Barron.

Appearing shortly after the demise of *Delap's*, the *Review* aimed at comprehensive coverage of both new and reprinted SF/fantasy books and selected non-print materials published in the United States as well as selected British and European books. Reviews were carefully edited for concision and ranged from 50 to 800 words. Each sixteen-page issue included sixty to seventy reviews. The reviews were written by a large number of people, though Barron personally handled most bibliographical works. Despite the restrictions on length and the large number of reviewers, the magazine could not keep up with the flood of material published. It proved economically unviable too. Barron, along with the *Review*'s publisher, Robert Reginald of Borgo Press, announced that published and unpublished reviews would be collected in *Science Fiction and Fantasy Annual*; this volume never materialized, although Borgo lists a microfiche comprehensive edition as forthcoming.

The Science Fiction Research Association voted in 1981 to fund a book review with the same title but with coverage limited to original books plus selected hardcover reprints, approximately 400 titles annually. The first issue appeared in January 1982. Actually, the magazine's index shows that by 1983 it was covering over 600 titles a year. At the beginning of 1984, however, the *Review* merged with *Fantasy Newsletter*; Barron became review editor for the newly titled *SF and Fantasy Review*.

SCIENCE FICTION CHRONICLE

Dates: Winter 1978-79–.

Editor: Andrew Porter, S.F. Chronicle, P.O. Box 4174, New York, N.Y. 10163.

Begun as a department in *Algol/Starship* to test the waters, and first published separately in June 1979, *Science Fiction Chronicle* is now established as the chief rival of *Locus* as a source of news. Porter was not exactly a neophyte as a newszine editor, having published *SF Weekly* (an outgrowth of his *Degler*) from July 1964 to May 6, 1968; he had even published a brief tryout called *Chronicle* in 1973. After that, he devoted his attention to building *Algol/Starship* into an outstanding magazine. Thus, when he returned to *Science Fiction Chronicle*, Porter was able to draw on considerable experience in design; as a result *SFC* is extremely attractive. Compared to *Locus* in content, *SFC* covers more subjects than print SF (including films and other media) and publishes comprehensive market report listings.

Hugo Nominee: 1981, 1982, 1983.

Library Collections: Porter indicates "too many to list."

THE SCIENCE FICTION COLLECTOR/MEGAVORE: THE JOURNAL OF POPULAR FICTION (combination of THE SCIENCE FICTION COLLECTOR and AGE OF THE UNICORN)/THE SCIENCE FICTION COLLECTOR (including AGE OF THE UNICORN)

Dates: October 1976–1981.

Editor: J. Grant Thiessen.

Along with dealers' and collectors' advertisements, this magazine contained interviews and reviews, but its real center was detailed bibliographic articles and checklists, sometimes organized by publisher (e.g., Harlequin), author (e.g., Philip José Farmer) or category (e.g., SF/fantasy erotica). Thiessen's policy was extremely eclectic, covering "science fiction, fantasy, horror, mystery, pulps, old paperbacks, etc." A static subscription list led to the magazine's abrupt demise following an experiment in a tabloid format.

SCIENCE FICTION COMMENTARY

Dates: January 1969–February 1980.

Editor: Bruce Gillespie.

Gillespie began this journal of reviews and essays with the straightforward, serious intention of improving SF. Although more recent issues exposed more of Gillespie's personal drives and ponderings, *Science Fiction Commentary* held fast to that purpose. One example of Gillespie's extreme dedication is his reprinting, in issue 19, the run of John Foyster's fanzines *Journal of Omphalistic Epistemology* and *Exploding Madonna*—a total of 131 pages—simply because he believed they deserved wider circulation. Other issues varied widely in size, contents and frequency of publication. In addition to good local critics like George Turner, Gillespie drew on highly serious European critics like Franz Rottensteiner and Stanislaw Lem. Though it actually ceased publication several years before, it remained theoretically alive until the thirteenth issue of Van Ikin's *Science Fiction*, which contained Gillespie's note that *SFC* was dead; Ikin announced that unpublished *SFC* material would be run in "a special 'Last *SFC*' issue of *Science Fiction*."

Hugo Nominee: 1972, 1973, 1975.

Library Collections: Bowling Green State University; California State University, Fullerton.

SCIENCE FICTION DIGEST/FANTASY MAGAZINE

Dates: September 1932–January 1937.

Editors: Maurice Ingher/Conrad H. Ruppert/Jules Schwartz (with unofficial aid of Mort Weisinger).

Science Fiction Digest has been described by Sam Moskowitz as "unsurpassed in the history of fandom . . . for all-around quality." In addition to original fiction by leading authors, including several round-robin stories, the *Digest* featured biographical and autobiographical information on leading writers, artists and editors, reviews and gossip, and "solid, interesting, factual articles." After the January 1934 issue, the magazine was renamed *Fantasy Magazine*, becoming even broader in appeal but maintaining the same high quality. It merged eventually with *Science Fiction Correspondent*, with an abrupt change in policy that emphasized amateur fiction and removes the magazine from our concern.

M.A.

SCIENCE FICTION REVIEW (a.k.a. PSYCHOTIC, RICHARD E. GEIS, and THE ALIEN CRITIC)

Dates: 1955; 1967–.

Editor: Richard E. Geis, P.O. Box 11408, Portland, Ore. 97211.

The publishing history of *Science Fiction Review* is much more complicated than the brief heading above suggests. In the mid-1950s, Geis published twenty issues of *Psychotic*—a general interest fanzine containing much fannish controversy but considerable emphasis on SF—before he suddenly limited the contents to SF-centered material and changed the title to *Science Fiction Review* for three issues and then dropped out of fandom with the October-November 1955 issue. Twelve years later, in November 1967, Geis returned to fanzine publishing with *Psychotic* 21 (he chose not to count the three issues of *SFR*) and continued with that title for a few issues before switching to *SFR* again. In 1971 he killed *SFR* yet again, but in 1972 he began *Richard E. Geis*, an intimate personalzine, which became *The Alien Critic: An Informal Science Fiction & Fantasy Journal* with issue 4; when he later returned to the *SFR* title still again, Geis maintained the same numbering. Through most of this, *SFR* has featured much the same contents: many book, film and magazine reviews by the editor and others; interviews; news; contentious essays and speech transcripts. Underlying and unifying it all is Geis himself: infuriatingly self-assured, stating extreme positions and daring any reader to knock them down; curious, asking rude but pertinent questions; smooth, clear and funny whatever he's writing—the ideal person to provoke a violent response, which in turn triggers other reactions and sometimes a violent response, which in turn triggers other reactions and sometimes manages to generate some light along with the waves of heat. Geis explains, in a letter, that "the value of controversy is in the facts and viewpoints it brings into the field; controversy is a tool to blow minds and expand consciousnesses." At its best, under whatever title, *SFR* has been an outstanding lightning rod for controversy in *SF*.

Hugo Nominee: 1968 (*Psychotic*), 1969, 1970, 1971, 1974 (*Alien Critic*), 1975 (*Alien Critic*), 1976, 1977, 1978, 1979, 1980, 1981.

Winner: 1969, 1970, 1974 (*Alien Critic*), 1975 (*Alien Critic*), 1976, 1977, 1979.

Library Collections: Bowling Green State University; California State University, Fullerton; New York Public Library; University of California–Los Angeles; University of Southern California; Yale University.

Microfilm: *Alien Critic*, 1973–1974, is available from University Microfilms; *Science Fiction Review*, 1975–, is also available from University Microfilms.

SCIENCE FICTION STUDIES

Dates: Spring 1973–.

Editors: R. D. Mullen and Darko Suvin/Robert M. Philmus and Charles Elkins, with Marc Angenot, Arts Building, McGill University, 853 Sherbrooke Street West, Montreal, Quebec H3A 2T6, Canada, or c/o English Department, Concordia University, 7141 Sherbrooke Street W, Montreal, H4B IR6, Canada.

Third among the major academic periodicals dealing with SF, *Science Fiction Studies* usually has reflected the interests of its first co-editors, Mullen and Suvin—historical and theoretical respectively—though its new editors are willing to accommodate a somewhat wider range of topics. It has gained a reputation as the most fiercely scholarly of the periodicals and is sometimes criticized for

stiffness in writing. However, it has found a niche by its willingness to labor in areas the other journals leave less thoroughly explored. Especially noteworthy are efforts to make available information on SF in other countries and to run original work or at least translations of essays by foreign critics; also, *SFS* is frequently willing to devote entire issues to the work of one writer, such as Philip K. Dick or Ursula LeGuin, or to topics such as "Science Fiction Before Wells," "The Sociology of Science Fiction," "Science Fiction on Women—Science Fiction by Women," and "Science Fiction and the Non-Print Media." Reprint Editions: Selected essays from *SFS* Numbers 1–13 have been published in two volumes by Gregg Press, 1976 and 1978.
Library Collections: Concordia University; McGill University; most major U.S. universities.

SCIENCE FICTION TIMES
(a.k.a. FANTASY REPORTER, FANTASY TIMES)

Dates: September 1941–March 1969?
Editors: James V. Taurasi/Sam Moskowitz/Taurasi again/James Ashe/Anne F. Dietz.

Science Fiction Times was the successor to Taurasi's *Fantasy News*, after Will Sykora had taken over responsibility for the latter. Moskowitz edited the zine when Taurasi went into the service during World War II, then dropped it; Taurasi revived it after the war. The title changed back and forth over the years. Despite these vagaries, *SFT* is the standard source of raw news through the mid-sixties. In newspaper format, it reported on authors' and editors' intentions, publishers' plans, and sometimes anticlimactic outcomes. *SFT* is not basically concerned with criticism (James Blish *very* briefly reviewed books for it because he blurted some rude truths about the books under review), but it gives valuable information about the production of SF/fantasy. In the late 1950s, however, the zine went from a dependable bi-weekly schedule to monthly or even less frequent; several issues were published and mailed simultaneously to give the illusion of regularity. It went officially monthly in 1962. Taurasi relinquished it to a new team, editor James Ashe and publisher Frank Prieto, Jr., in December 1966, and Anne F. Dietz took over in March 1968. By then, however, the first issue of *Locus* had appeared. (*SFT* is not to be confused with *Science Fiction Times* [edited by Hans Joachim Alpers, fl. 1969], a German fanzine of reviews and Western European news, or with *Science Fiction Times* [1979?–1980], a tabloid outpost of the equally ephemeral *Galileo* publishing empire.)
Hugo Nominee: 1955, 1957, 1959, 1960.
Winner: 1955, 1957.
Library Collections: Bowling Green State University; California State University, Fullerton.

SCIENTIFICTION

Dates: January 1937–March 1938.
Editor: Walter Gillings.

Scientifiction is still one of the most important fanzines ever produced in Britain and is now an invaluable source of news about prewar SF. Moskowitz called it "a superb effort," while Warner considers it "one of the most ambitious fanzines in history." With his expertise as a journalist, Gillings was able to produce a highly readable magazine useful both to those inside and outside SF. Apart from news and reviews presented in professional newspaper style, the magazine also contained interviews, photographs and critical articles. It is an essential reference aid for the serious researcher. *Scientifiction* ran for seven issues on its own before Gillings' increased work load as editor of *Tales of Wonder* caused him to merge the magazine with Doug Mayer's equally professional *Tomorrow*, and the combozine ran for three more issues until finances ran out.

M.A.

THE SF&F JOURNAL

See THE WSFA JOURNAL/THE SF&F JOURNAL.

SF AND FANTASY REVIEW

See FANTASY NEWSLETTER/SF AND FANTASY REVIEW.

SF HORIZONS

Dates: Spring 1964–Winter 1965.
Editors: Harry Harrison and Brian W. Aldiss.

SF Horizons was a short-lived (two issues) but impressive effort at a readable but serious magazine of SF commentary and criticism. It carried essay reviews, articles and interviews; of special interest are Aldiss' own pioneering examination of J. G. Ballard's work and the only existing interview with C. S. Lewis on the subject of SF.

Reprint Editions: Arno Press, 1975.
Library Collections: California State University, Fullerton.

SHADOW

Dates: 1968–1974.
Editor: David A. Sutton.

Shadow was one of the few fanzines to appear in Britain that gave serious consideration and analysis to the supernatural in fiction. (*Gothique*, the other major British horror fanzine, concentrated predominantly on films.) Most of the early issues, which appeared with surprising regularity, were written by David Sutton himself with the help of Eddy Bertin and Brian J. Frost and included brief but useful studies of Poe, Charles Birkin and Jean Ray. With each issue, however, *Shadow* grew in confidence and ambition. The seventh issue (September 1969) was devoted to a study of the work of H. P. Lovecraft. Highlights of subsequent issues include Brian Frost's studies of the works of M. P. Shiel and on the development of the werewolf and vampire themes in fiction; Eddy Bertin's series on European horror writers; David A. Riley's analysis of the work of M. R. James; Sutton's look at the life and writings of Shirley Jackson; Martin Ricketts' analysis of the work of Robert Aickman; and R. Alain Everts' seminal study of the life of William Hope Hodgson, accompanied by the first publication anywhere of two of Hodgson's short stories. Sutton sustained *Shadow* for six years and twenty-one issues before deliberately ceasing publication.

M.A.

SKYRACK/SKYRACK NEWSLETTER

Dates: April 1959–April 1968.
Editor: Ron Bennett.

Over nearly ten years Ron Bennett put out ninety-five issues of a short but snappy four- to eight-page newsletter that was the only reliable source of news on the SF scene in Britain. Bennett managed to squeeze a vast amount of news into his brief monthly broadsheet, and it is invaluable to the researcher, especially on the British scene. Toward the end, the magazine became the *Skyrack Trader* as Bennett enlarged his postal bookdealing business; with his temporary removal to Singapore, Bennett dropped publication of the newsletter, subsequently resuming publication of the *Trader* as a catalogue only.

M.A.

SPECULATION

See ZENITH SCIENCE FICTION/ZENITH SPECULATION/ SPECULATION.

STARSHIP

See ALGOL/STARSHIP.

THRUST—SCIENCE FICTION IN REVIEW

Dates: Fall 1972–.
Editor: Douglas Fratz, 8217 Langport Terrace, Gaithersburg, Md. 20877.

Beginning as the organ of the University of Maryland Science Fiction Society, *Thrust—Science Fiction in Review* was the standard genzine mixture of fiction, interviews, essays and reviews. When Doug Fratz made it an independent publication in 1977, he scrapped the fiction and emphasized the magazine's role as critical commentator on current SF. A typical issue is built around a core of often argumentative columns by people like Ted White, John Shirley, Dave Bischoff, Michael Bishop and Charles Sheffield, but it also includes one or two interviews and a large number of medium-length reviews.

Hugo Nominee: 1980.

VECTOR

Dates: Summer 1958–.
Editors: E. C. Tubb (No. 1), Terry Jeeves (2–4), Roberta Wild (5), Roberta Gray and Mike Moorcock (6–7), Jim Groves (8–15), Ella Parker (16–17), Jim Groves (18), Archie Mercer (19–25), Rog Peyton (26–39), Steve Oakey (40), Ken Slater and Doreen Parker (41–42), Doreen Parker (43), Darroll Pardoe (44), Phil Muldowney (45–46), Tony Sudbery (47), Tony Sudbery and Vic Hallett (48–49), Michael Kenward (50–55), Bob Parkinson (56–58), Malcolm Edwards (59–68), Chris Fowler (69–83), David Wingrove (84–94), Mike Dickinson (95–97), Alan Dorey, Joseph Nicholas and Kevin Smith (98), Kevin Smith (99–107), Geoff Rippington (108–). The British Science Fiction Association, c/o Sandy Brown, 18 Gordon Terrace, Blantyre, Lanarkshire, Scotland.

The official journal of the BSFA has, in recent years, followed a fairly standard format, publishing transcripts of speeches, long interviews with major writers (such as J. G. Ballard, Harlan Ellison and Robert Silverberg) and extensive reviews. Historically, *Vector* may have certain interest because of the early involvement of Mike Moorcock, but the magazine was of variable quality until Rog Peyton's editorship in the mid-1960s, when he produced a run of consistently readable and valuable issues with mature essays and reviews. For the next few years *Vector*'s quality plunged under a series of stop-gap editors, and it was not until Malcolm Edwards and Chris Fowler took over that quality or respectability returned. Recent contributors have included Ursula K. LeGuin, Brian Stableford and Ian Watson.

M.A.

THE WEIRD TALES COLLECTOR

Dates: Fall 1977–.

Editor: Robert Weinberg, 15145 Oxford Dr., Oak Forest, Ill. 60452.

Focusing primarily on the pioneering American fantasy magazine and its cohorts, *The Weird Tales Collector* includes issue-by-issue listings of the contents of different pulps. In addition, the editor reports that "all issues contain articles on the weird fiction magazines along with interviews and articles about the people who wrote for them, dealing with both personal experiences as writers and circumstances of publishing."

WORLD SF NEWSLETTER

Dates: 1980–.

Editor: Elizabeth Anne Hull, World SF, c/o Dr. E. A. Hull, 1502 Seven Pines Road, Schaumburg, Ill. 60193.

The *World SF Newsletter* is the publication of a new organization trying to connect everyone anywhere connected with SF. It is potentially valuable for news from outside the relatively small geographic area covered by *Locus* and *Science Fiction Chronicle*.

THE WSFA JOURNAL/THE SF&F JOURNAL

Dates: March 1965–.

Editor: Donald L. Miller, 12315 Judson Road, Wheaton, Md. 20906.

In the early 1960s, a few members of the Washington Science Fiction Association produced *Speculative Review*, a slender but neatly produced journal of magazine and book reviews. Later, different people in the WSFA began *The WSFA Journal* to publish minutes and club news. This small monthly clubzine was expanded by members' participation in postal *Diplomacy* games and by their willingness to contribute more general material. Highlights, according to Miller, included "Mark Owings' 'The Electric Bibliograph' series author bibliographies, Bob Jones' series on the thriller pulps . . . , and Thomas Burnett Swann's series of semi-autobiographical essays." *The WSFA Journal* also included numerous reviews by a huge number of people. For a time, frequency of publication increased to bi-weekly, but *The WSFA Journal* soon became too bulky to produce easily. To use up surplus energy and to bridge the lengthening gap between issues, *Son of the WSFA Journal* was begun as a bi-weekly "news supplement" in late 1969, later printing reviews as well, changing its name to *The Journal Supplement*, and finally being incorporated into the *Journal*. By Number 84 (December 1974) the official staff listed Miller as editor-in-chief and publisher; four major staff members, five section editors, eleven staff reviewers, and others. Like a dinosaur, the *Journal* was outgrowing its resources and losing its ability to move. Shortly thereafter, it collapsed as a group effort. The quantity of the remains is impressive, containing much material of interest if it can be located; the *Journal*'s own system of classification and indexing is formidably complicated. Beset by ill health and the defection of co-editors, sometimes with the accompanying loss of material, Miller has continued publishing the magazine under its new title, *The SF&F Journal*, on an erratic schedule since Number 87 (February 22, 1976).

Library Collections: California State University, Fullerton.

XENOPHILE (Combined with the Fantasy Collector): AN ADVERTISOR & JOURNAL DEVOTED TO FANTASTIC AND IMAGINATIVE LITERATURE

Editor: Nils Hardin, P.O. Box 9660, Kirkwood Branch, St. Louis, Mo. 63122.

A wide-ranging magazine dealing with "Fantasy, Mystery, Weird Tales, Thrillers, Detectives, Pulp Magazines, Science Fiction, Supernatural Horror," and anything else the editor wishes, *Xenophile* focuses especially on SF in the pulp magazines. It is notable for biographical and bibliographical articles on writers (such as Henry Kuttner and Leigh Brackett), artists and publishers who are connected with SF among other fields.

Library Collections: California State University, Fullerton.

XERO

Dates: 1960–1963.

Editors: Dick and Pat Lupoff.

The Lupoffs began *Xero* with the idea of producing a big zine for a limited time, outdoing themselves every issue during that period. They succeeded. *Xero* was especially noted at the time for its experimental graphics (mostly the work of Robert Stewart) and its willingness to publish lengthy works. Its biggest influence, however, may have been bringing fandom in touch with the serious study of popular culture. Fans had mentioned comic art from time to time, for example; however, *Xero*'s feature "All in Color for a Dime" ran long, detailed essays on Captain Marvel and other superpowered heroes and villains. Such essays make it possible for anyone so inclined to begin thinking about the relations between written and visual SF. Other essays discussed fantastic serials, movies and stage plays. *Xero* also included considerable discussion of SF, especially controversy concerning how market factors affect the quality of writing. And there was room for plenty of fannish hijinks, too. In its ten issues, plus an additional letter-column and index issue, *Xero* contributed something of interest to almost every area of fandom. It also was the source of at least four books: Dick Lupoff and Don Thompson's *All in Color for a Dime* and *The Comic-Book Book*, Lin Carter's *Tolkien: A Look Behind the Lord of the Rings* and Norman Clarke's study of fantastic theatrical spectacles.

Hugo Nominee: 1963.

Winner: 1963.

Library Collections: California State University, Fullerton.

YANDRO

See EISFA/YANDRO.

ZENITH SCIENCE FICTION/ZENITH SPECULATION/ SPECULATION

Dates: October 1963–1973.

Editor: Peter E. Weston.

At birth, *Zenith Science Fiction* was a genzine mixing writing about SF and fandom (especially Walt Willis' "Fanorama") with original fiction. In 1966, however, the name changed to *Zenith Speculation*, and later simply to *Speculation*, and the editorial policy concentrated entirely on nonfiction. The magazine specialized in long essay-reviews by Brian Stableford, Bruce Gillespie, Tony Sudbury and others, and in essays by people like James Blish, Alexei Panshin, John Brunner, Frederik Pohl, Brian Stableford, Michael Moorcock and David Mason. In particular, the participants enthusiastically debated "New Wave" versus "Old Guard" SF, editor Weston later commenting that "Speculation was the first, I think, to begin the serious discussions about the nature of SF which have taken place in the last few years" (Editorial in fifth anniversary issue, September 1968). The publication is an extremely valuable, intensely serious effort.

Hugo Nominee: 1965, 1966, 1970, 1971.

Winner: 1970.

Library Collections: Bowling Green State University; California State University, Fullerton.

Section IV

NON-ENGLISH-LANGUAGE MAGAZINES, BY COUNTRY

Just as the development of science fiction in the United States and Great Britain was fostered by the existence of a dynamic group of magazines, the development of science fiction as a well-defined genre around the world was nurtured by a variety of active magazines. The magazines provided a pivot around which science fiction revolved and developed in most countries, yet the lack of significant magazine publishing in a country did not mean that the genre would necessarily fail to develop there.

The challenges and difficulties of identifying and gathering data on non-English-language magazines are considerable, particularly since few of the titles are represented widely in the United States. Bibliographic data and descriptions of the magazine are rare and sometimes contradictory. The few existing collections are widely separated and sometimes not freely accessible to the scholar. This section covers over 160 titles, identifying the classic science fiction magazines (prozines, in the fan vernacular) from twenty-three countries. Some additional titles are included to clarify their status or to correct previous errors in reportage.

If the quantity of titles is noteworthy, so also is the diversity of quality. Several students of science fiction have commented on the exceptional quality of some titles, among them *Nueva Dimension* (Spain), *Robot* (Italy), *Fiction* (France) and *Galaktika* (Hungary). At their best, these titles equal the best of the American and British magazines and have a following of fans as dedicated and devoted as those of *Analog* or *The Magazine of Fantasy and Science Fiction*. These four titles are classic SF magazines, featuring excellent fiction, attractive art and perceptive critical commentary. Just as in America and Britain, however, there are titles which were poorly planned and badly produced, with substandard fiction, poor translation and substandard art. These titles frequently managed one or a few issues before ceasing.

Historically, the non-English-language magazines had close ties to American and British SF magazines. More often than not, they were first associated with an American or British title, either as a non-English-language edition of the magazine, or selecting stories from several sources. From that starting point, as reader interest and involvement grew, the magazines frequently shifted to using more material from their own country, with a corresponding decrease in translated fiction. Even after such a shift occurred, close ties were maintained with the American and British sources, and most issues used up to 50 percent translated material. Serious study of the history of the SF magazines is hampered by the lack of available resource material and by sometimes formidable language barriers.

The identification of the "first science fiction magazine" is a topic that has been discussed at some length in the literature, but it is not a pivotal issue. Classically, this distinction has gone to Hugo Gernsback's *Amazing*, but in the last decade claims have been advanced for other titles as "the first," such as *Hugin* (Sweden, 1916), *Mir Prikliuchenni* (U.S.S.R., 1910) and *Der Orchideengarten* (Germany, 1919). Definition has been part of the problem: what is the definition of "science fiction"? How does it differ from "fantasy," "weird" and "horror"? Consultants to this chapter have identified both *Hugin* and *Der Orchideengarten* as more nearly fantasy than any other category, just as *Weird Tales*, although it frequently featured SF writers and carried stories indistinguishable from those in the SF magazines, is rarely identified as a science fiction magazine. What is both clear and significant is the existence of stories which are identifiable with science fiction in a world-wide setting in the late 1800s and early 1900s and the development of an interest among the reading public in such fictional extrapolations. The proper question is not "What was the first?" but "What was the breadth and depth of this interest, what fostered the interest, and how did the interest spread both within a country and internationally?"

Defining the subset "magazine" in the world framework is sometimes difficult. Publishing practices vary from country to country, as does the cultural matrix in which the publishing occurs. In some cases, it is impossible to determine whether a title is a magazine or not. We have identified some titles previously cited as magazines which are actually the equivalent of the old "dime novels" in America. Even though these titles are not magazines, they serve as the functional equivalent of magazines in some countries. Likewise, some countries have a host of numbered and dated series which may be mistaken for magazines until examination reveals otherwise.

This section was developed with the help of consultants from most of the countries represented. These consultants are identified at the beginning of each country's listing. Even with the expert help of these consultants, however, data on many titles are sketchy. This annotated listing represents the first step toward a comprehensive world bibliography of science fiction magazines and series. Additions and corrections will be welcome, and should be sent to the compiler: H. W. Hall, 3608 Meadow Oaks Lane, Bryan, Tex. 77801, USA.

Hal W. Hall
Mike Ashley

ARGENTINA

Consultant: *Hector R. Pessina*

GEMINIS

Dates: July–August 1965 (2 issues).
Editor: H. G. Oesterheld.

Publisher: Ediciones H.G.O., Cangallo.

Geminis was planned as a fortnightly magazine, but only two issues were published. A digest magazine of 128 pages, it featured stories reprinted predominantly from *Galaxy*, but also some stories of indigenous origin, mostly by the editor. The artwork was by Argentine illustrators but also included poorly reproduced photographs of the U.S. space program. The second issue included a translation of Howard Koch's script for the noted Orson Welles production of H. G. Wells' *La Guerra de los Mundos* (The War of the Worlds) under the title ''La Gran Invasión.''

HOMBRES DEL FUTURO

Dates: August-October 1947 (3 issues).
Editor: Not known.
Publisher: Editorial El Tabano.

This little-known pulp magazine contained reprints from U.S. sources.

MÁS ALLÁ

Dates: June 1953–June 1957 (48 issues).
Editor: Julio Portas.
Publisher: Editorial Abril, Buenos Aires.

This was the key Argentinian SF magazine of the 1950s. Digest-sized, 128 pages, it featured reprints mostly from *Galaxy* and some British magazines, but in later issues also included occasional fiction by South American authors. It also carried a photographic scientific supplement, a science question and answer column, and a letter column. It was influential in generating a healthy fan following.

MINOTAURO

Dates: September 1964–June 1968 (10 issues).
Editor: Ricardo Gosseyn.
Publisher: Ediciones Minotauro, Buenos Aires.

The Argentine edition of *The Magazine of Fantasy and Science Fiction*, its full title was *Minotauro fantasía y ciencia-ficción*. Stories were selected from various issues of the American magazine, rather than reprinting complete issues.

NARRACIONES TERRORIFICAS

Dates: (April?) 1939–January 1950 (72 issues).
Editor: Not known.
Publisher: Not known.

A pulp magazine concentrating on reprints from various U.S. sources, it apparently contained mostly horror and fantasy with some science fiction. A monthly schedule was hampered by the war. Monthly publication was resumed temporarily in 1945, but it soon became irregular.

EL PÉNDULO

Dates: 1980 (4 issues).
Editor: Not known.
Publisher: Not known.

The full title is *Péndulo entre la Ficcion y la Realidad* (Pendulum between Fiction and Reality). It began as a supplement to a magazine called *Humor*, but its success caused the publishers to issue it separately. It was an attempt to bridge the gap between the early Argentine SF magazines of the 1950s and the sporadic publications of the 1960s and 1970s. Each eighty-page issue featured fiction, mostly translated from American sources, detailed reviews, a comic strip, and an article about SF literature or about an author. The title ceased publication, but was revived a year later, in 1981.

EL PÉNDULO

Dates: (May?) 1981–1984 (10 issues).
Editor: Andrés Casioli.
Publisher: Ediciones de la Urraca, Buenos Aires.

El Péndulo featured stories, articles, columns and a comic strip in each issue. Stories and articles were frequently translated from English, but other languages were also featured. Issues consisted of 130 pages, well-designed and printed, with excellent color covers.

PISTAS DEL ESPACIO

Dates: May 1957–April 1959 (14 issues).
Editor: A. Bois.
Publisher: Editorial Acme, S.A.C.I.

Pistas del Espacio reprints American and British novels with occasional short stories as fillers. Digest-sized, ninety-six pages, it was originally published monthly, but became irregular.

LA REVISTA DE CIENCIA FICCION Y FANTASIA

Dates: October 1976–February 1977 (3 issues).
Editor: Marcial Souto.
Publisher: Ediciones Orión, Buenos Aires.

This 160–page digest magazine reprinted stories from various sources, mostly *Galaxy* and *Analog*. It also featured new fiction by South American writers and included a book review column by Pablo Capanna.

UMBRAL TIEMPO FUTURO

Dates: November 1977–?
Editors: Nahuel Villegas, Fabio Zerpa.
Publisher: Cielosur Editora S.A.C.I., Buenos Aires.

Sometimes cited as a science fiction magazine, this title concentrated mostly on flying saucers and other unknown phenomena, the special interest of publisher Fabio Zerpa. All the contents were of Argentine origin.

URANIA

Dates: October/November–December 1953 (2 issues).
Editor: Julio A. Echevarria.
Publisher: Selecciones Argentinas, Rosario.

The Argentine edition of the Italian magazine *Urania*, it offered no original Argentine fiction. It also contained lessons in English, and in chess!

AUSTRIA

Consultants: *Franz Rottensteiner and Uwe Luserke*

Austria has no true science fiction magazines, even though *Star-Utopia* and *Uranus* are reported as magazines in some sources. These two titles are more nearly modern equivalents of the old dime novels, usually saddle-stitched "booklets," softbound, of thirty-two or sixty-four pages each, containing a single story. Occasionally a second short item is included. Frequently, the booklets are part of a series with a single hero. *Star-Utopia* was published by Josef-Maria Steffek, Vienna, and appeared in 10 issues in 1957–1958.

KOKAIN

Dates: 1925 (5 [?] issues).
Editor: Not known.
Publisher: Not known.
  Kokain featured fantasy and weird fiction by well-known German and Austrian authors, illustrated with black and white drawings. At least five issues appeared, published in Vienna, in 1925.

MAGAZIN DES GRAUENS

Dates: 1950 (1 issue).
Editor: Robert Baraniecki.
Publisher: Zemann Verlag, Vienna.
  Magazin des Grauens was a weird-fiction magazine which featured six stories in its only issue. One story was Poe's ''The Fall of the House of Usher''; the others were originals by unknown writers. The magazine was approximately six by nine inches, with forty-eight pages.

BELGIUM

Consultant: *Eddy C. Bertin*

ANTICIPATIONS

Dates: September 25, 1945–May 1946 (14 issues).
Editor: Not known.
Publisher: Not known.
  Published in French, this was the first postwar magazine on the European continent. Originally published twice a month under the title *Collection Antic-ipations*, it became *Anticipations Magazine* with Number 8, then skipped an issue in March 1946, making up for it with a double issue, Number 13/14, in April 1946. The last issue, Number 15, is actually the fourteenth physical issue to appear. Contents were selected predominantly from the British *Tales of Wonder*, and thus it included translations of both British and American prewar SF, published under by-lines that were so distorted as to make identification very difficult.

APOLLO

Dates: May 1972–November 1973 (20 issues).
Editor: A. Van Hageland.
Publisher: De Schorpioen/De Vrijbuiter, Strombeek-Bever.

Apollo was a monthly magazine printed on cheap paper and containing about fifty pages per issue. Two issues (Nos. 8 and 9) were released in December 1972, and Number 15 was a 100–page double issue. Each issue carried a first publication (in Belgium or Holland) of an abridged SF novel from an English, American or French writer. On some occasions original novels by Belgian writers were substituted. Each issue also contained a short horror or supernatural story, most by Belgian writers. It was a joint venture by a Belgian and Dutch publisher.

ATLANTA

Dates: January 1966–December 1967 (12 issues).
Editor: Michael Grayn.
Publisher: Michael Grayn.

Originally a fanzine, *Atlanta* went to professional status in 1966, though it remained a slim, digest-sized offset magazine of twenty–thirty pages. It contained short articles and very short stories in French.

CLUB

Dates: March 1958–1961 (15 science fiction issues).
Editor: Not known.
Publisher: Castrum, Gent.

Published every three weeks, *Club* alternated between issues of westerns, thrillers and science fiction novels, usually supported by a comic strip and a short story. Most contents were translated either from German or American sources. The science fiction issues were Numbers 2, 6, 10, 14, 16, 18, 21, 23, 31, 36, 40, 48, 54 and at least two others.

HORROR

Dates: January 1973–May 1974 (28 issues).
Editor: Not known.
Publisher: Not known.

This was a horror fiction companion to *Apollo* from the same publishing cooperative. It usually appeared twice monthly, but some months saw three issues, others only one. Every issue had fifty pages and contained one abridged horror novel by an English, American or French writer. Two original Belgian novels were published; "Oogg van de Vampier" by Eddy Bertin and a novel by Hilda Bouters (pseudonym of Andreas Haegland) in issue 21. There were no supporting short stories or departments. The same publisher issued a soft-pornography magazine, *Maxi-Hoho*, which regularly featured SF, fantasy and horror short stories and occasional serials.

UTOPIA

Dates: June 1961–May 1963 (24 issues).
Editor: Albert Van Hageland.
Publisher: De Schorpioen, Strombeek-Bever.
A novel-magazine of forty-eight pages per issue, featuring translations and abridgments of American, British and German novels, *Utopia* featured color covers based on film stills, but of poor quality.

BRAZIL

GALAXIA 2000

Dates: February 1968–?
Editor: Not known.
Publisher: Not known.
This magazine is mentioned in Walter Martin's "Sao Paulo Letter," *Amazing Stories*, September 1968, page 136, but no further information has been located.

MAGAZINE DE FICCAO CIENTIFICA

Dates: 1970–?
Editor: Not known.
Publisher: Not known.
This is a Portuguese edition of *The Magazine of Fantasy and Science Fiction*. No other details are known. The cover for issue 7 for October 1970 is reproduced on the back cover of the December 1971 issue of *The Magazine of Fantasy and Science Fiction*.

CANADA

Note: English-language Canadian magazines are covered in Section I. The following title was published in French.

LES ADVENTURES FUTURISTES

Dates: March 1–September 1949 (10 issues).
Editor: Not known.
Publisher: Not known.

Les Adventures Futuristes is a very rare French-Canadian magazine, published in Montreal. It is believed to have featured a lead novel which told of the adventures of two superscientist heroes. It appeared bi-weekly for the first six issues, then monthly.

DENMARK

Consultants: *Frits Remar and Carsten Schiøler*

MANADENS BEDSTE SCIENCE-FICTION

Dates: September 1975–April 1977 (16 issues).
Editor: Frits Remar.
Publisher: Schroder Publications, Copenhagen.

The title translates as "The Best Science Fiction of the Month." The magazine presented mostly American and British fiction translated for the first time into Danish. The editor planned to establish the magazine first by relying on the accepted names in SF. He then hoped to introduce the "new wave" writers and open the way for new stories by Danish writers, but the magazine never achieved this goal. Sales had to top 10,000 to break even, and the average circulation was only 5,000. The magazine was monthly for the first twelve issues (with a July/August 1976 issue because of traditionally poor summer sales) and was large-sized, with 100 pages. It was suspended for economic reasons, then re-launched in January 1977 for its final four issues, which were reduced in size to sixty-eight pages.

PLANETMAGAZINET

Dates: Undated, ca. January–June 1968 (6 issues).
Editor: Knud Erik Andersen.
Publisher: Skrifola, Copenhagen.

This 100-page digest magazine featured reprints predominantly from *Astounding*. It serialized Arthur C. Clarke's *Exploration of Space*.

PROXIMA

Dates: October 1974–?
Editor: Carsten Schiøler, plus other members of the Danish SF Circle.
Publisher: Danish SF Circle.

Proxima was a semi-professional quarterly published by the Danish SF Circle in a run of 500 to 700 copies. The first three issues were reprinted. It contained mostly nonfiction, with one short story each issue. The short stories included both translations and originals.

SCIENCE FICTION MAGASINET

Dates: June 1977–?
Editors: Henry Madsden, Bent Irlov, Ove Hoyer and Neils Søndergaard.
Publisher: not known.

This magazine featured both new and reprinted material.

FINLAND

Consultant: *Jari Koponen*

AIKAKONE

Dates: Fall 1981–.
Editor: Jari Koponen.
Publisher: Ursa Astronomical Association.

Aikakone is the only Finnish magazine devoted to all aspects of good SF literature. Fandom and pulp SF are excluded. Each quarterly issue contains at least one foreign and one original Finnish short story, but the weight is on factual articles. Regular columns deal with SF news, SF movies and Finnish SF literature. Correspondents from all over the world keep the readers well informed about the international scene.

AIKAMME TIETEIS LUKEMISTO

Dates: August–December 1958 (5 issues).
Editor: Mary A. Wuorio.
Publisher: Viikkosanomat Oy.
This was a Finnish edition of *Galaxy*.

ISAAC ASIMOV'S SCIENCE FICTION VALIKOIMA

Dates: Spring 1981–.
Editor: Kari Lindgren.
Publisher: Viihdeviikarit Oy.
This is the Finnish edition of the U.S. magazine minus the editorial departments. Issued as a bi-monthly pocket book, it is not technically a magazine.

POORTI SCIENCE FICTION

Editor: Raimo Nikkonen.
Publisher: Not known.
Poorti features translated stories, Finnish science fiction stories, reviews, articles, and lists of new books. Each issue includes an English summary of contents.

FRANCE

Consultant: *Pascal J. Thomas*

ARGON

Dates: April–October 1975 (7 issues).
Editor: Daniel Lamy.
Publisher: Alain Detallante.
Argon was a semi-professional magazine containing predominantly new French material in the "new wave" style.

AU DELÀ DU CIEL

Dates: March 16, 1958–February 1961 (40 issues).
Editors: Cesare Falessi and Armando Silvestri.
Publisher: E. Silvestri, Rome.

A French edition of the Italian magazine *Oltre il Cielo*, it was published concurrently in Rome by the original publisher. It featured two short novels and a variety of stories by English, American and Italian writers but also included some original French material and some scientific articles.

L'AUBE ENCLAVÉE

Dates: 1970–1972 (6 issues).
Editor: Henri-Luc Planchat.
Publisher: Planchat.
Initially a fanzine, which began with issue 0, this became a semi-professional magazine with issue 3. Intended as a quarterly but irregularly issued, it printed modern SF by English, French and Spanish writers.

CHRONIQUES TERRIENNES

Dates: May 1975 (1 issue).
Editors: Herve Designe and Lionel Hoebeke.
Publisher: Librairie "Parallèles."
A proposed quarterly "new wave" magazine, *Chroniques Terriennes* was composed chiefly of French material plus one story by John Brunner. The quality was poor.

CONQUÊTES

Dates: September 1939 (2 issues).
Editor: Georges H. Gallet.
Publisher: Société des périodiques illustrés du *Petit Parisien*.
A proposed weekly publication, it was launched at the worst possible time. Editor Georges Gallet had made an arrangement with Walter Gillings to use British and American material from *Tales of Wonder* although the magazine was to emphasize scientific and technical articles.

FICTION

Dates: October 1953–.
Editors: Nos. 1–279, Alain Dorémieux; Nos. 280–?, Daniel Riche; Nos. ?–, Alain Dorémieux.
Publisher: Editions OPTA until December 1977; then Les Nouvelles Editions OPTA.

Fiction ranks as one of the premier SF magazines in the world. Originally created as a French edition of *The Magazines of Fantasy and Science Fiction*, it still uses translations for about two-thirds of its fiction. Issues generally carry book reviews, articles about SF, and news notes about the field. The back issues of the magazine are a particularly important source of French critical material. For this reason alone, *Fiction* should be a part of all SF research collections. The magazine ran as a monthly from March 1954 (with the first three issues bi-monthly) to June 1977, skipping only September 1968, when there were nationwide strikes. After issue 283, the publisher became bankrupt, but the magazine was relaunched in early 1978. Alain Dorémieux left the editorship of *Fiction* in late 1984. For details of the significance of *Fiction* in the development of new French talent, see Maxim Jakubowski's introduction to his *Travelling towards Epsilon* (London: New English Library, 1977).

FUTURS

Dates: June–December 1978 (7 issues).
Editors: Gérard Klein, Philippe Curval, Grichka and Igor Bogdanoff and J.-C. Mézières.
Publisher: Futurs Presse Editions S.A.

This magazine featured original and translated stories, regular columns, criticism and book reviews.

FUTURS

Dates: March–May 1981 (3 issues).
Editor: Pierre Delmotte.
Publisher: Idemedia.

A poorly managed effort, this title collapsed quickly.

GALAXIE

Dates: (First Series) November 1953–April 1959 (65 issues).
Editors: Nos. 1–11, Irina Orloff; Nos. 12–27, Jacqueline Boissy; Nos. 28–65, Jeannine Courtillet.
Publisher: Editions OPTA, Paris.

Galaxie was a French edition of *Galaxy*. Editorial expertise was not shown in this series, however, which merely reprinted truncated versions of the original, in poorly translated issues. Declining sales forced the title to be dropped.

GALAXIE

Dates: (Second Series) May 1964–August/September 1977 (158 issues).
Editors: Nos. 1–67, Alain Dorémieux; Nos. 68–158, Michel Demuth.
Publisher: Editions OPTA, Paris.

The *Fiction* team acquired the French serial rights to *Galaxy* and showed what could be done with proper editorial direction, with the result that *Galaxie* eventually outsold *Fiction*. It contained much the same blend of translated and new material, with a greater emphasis on French authors from the November 1974 issue on. *Galaxie* was terminated by Editions OPTA because of declining sales.

HORIZON 3000

Dates: July 1976 (1 issue).
Editor: Alain Tremblay.
Publisher: Not known.

A proposed monthly magazine, *Horizon 3000* was of poor quality. It consisted of SF adventure material, apparently aimed at UFO fans.

HORIZONS DU FANTASTIQUE

Dates: Late 1968–1976 (37 issues).
Editors: Nos. 1–26, Dominique Besse; Nos. 27–35, Marianne Leconte.
Publisher: Editions EKLA (Dominique Besse).

A fanzine for three issues, *Horizons du Fantastique* quickly shifted its emphasis from the occult to SF stories and articles, usually from French writers. For a while it was seen as France's "third" SF magazine (after *Fiction* and *Galaxie*). During its life, it served as a launching pad for various French writers.

OPZONE

Dates: March 1979–? (8 issues).
Editor: Francis Valéry.
Publisher: Opzone S. A./Jacky Goupil.

Opzone published fiction from well-known French writers as well as translations of American material and carried a wide variety of articles, ranging from SF and mysteries to films.

PIRANHA

Dates: March 1977–1980?
Editor: Yann Menez.
Publisher: Piranha/Jean Mesnais (aka Yann Menez).
This bi-monthly magazine featured SF, fantasy, comic strips and film material.

SATELLITE

Dates: January 1958–December 1962 (47 issues).
Editors: Nos. 1–29, Hervé Calixte; Nos. 30–47, R. Volney.
Publisher: Satellite, Paris; Editions Scientifiques et Littéraires, Paris.

For the first twenty-four issues, *Satellite* was similar in quality to *Fiction*, but thereafter it became irregular in both publication and quality, with innumerable typographical errors and stories translated twice under different titles. It is regarded by Pierre Versins as more of a fan magazine professionally printed. (M.A.)

SCIENCE FICTION

Dates: 1984– (1 issue).
Editor: Daniel Riche.
Publisher: Denoel.

Science Fiction is a book-format magazine scheduled for three issues per year. The premier issue featured three stories, an interview with J. G. Ballard, an autobiographical sketch of Ballard reprinted from *Foundation*, book reviews, and a list of recently published books. The editors plan to stress inclusion of good critical material.

SCIENCE FICTION MAGAZINE

Dates: 1953 (1 issue).
Editor: Not known.
Publisher: Not known.

A large-sized, very slim (eighteen-page) magazine, it contained translated stories and science articles.

SCIENCE FICTION MAGAZINE

Dates: November 1976–May 1977 (7 issues).
Editor: Jean-Louis Ferrando.
Publisher: Editions de France, S.A.

A French edition of the British *Science Fiction Monthly*, in the same tabloid format, it has considerably more photographic material and some original French material.

SPIRALE

Dates: June 1975–October 1976 (6 issues).
Editors: Fermin Gonzalez, Pierre Grimaldi, André Colié, Richard D. Nolane and Karl Johns.
Publisher: Slan Club/André Colié/Fermin Gonzalez.

This semi-professional but extremely attractive magazine was published by the Slan Club. The first issue was a fanzine in intent, titled *Fantasmagoria*, retitled *Spirale* with issue 2 in February 1976. It retained bi-monthly scheduling, but failed financially in 1976. Contents included SF and fantasy from France and in translation.

UNIVERS

Dates: June 1975–Fall 1979 (19 issues).
Editor: Yves Frémion.
Publisher: J'ai Lu, Paris.

Initially launched in a pocketbook format, *Univers* set out to champion the English and American new wave SF in France. It also included reviews, articles and news notes. In 1980 *Univers* became an annual anthology edited by Jacques Sadoul and is still published in that format.

GERMANY

Consultants: *Franz Rottensteiner and Uwe Luserke*

Note: Germany has many continuously numbered SF series, but few are magazines in the traditional sense. Most series appear frequently, often weekly, and feature translated or original short novels, perhaps only one or two per volume, and frequently drastically abridged. They are bibliographically parallel to the old dime novel series, which were sequentially numbered but in no way constituted a continuous series publication. Most of these titles are excluded from this listing of magazines to avoid compounding the confusion as to their actual form. The titles listed here are all SF magazines, or are listed for clarification. A brief appendix identifies additional titles which are sometimes identified as magazines.

ANDROMEDA

Dates: October/November 1978–July/August 1980 (5 issues).
Editor: Hans-Jurgen Frederichs.
Publisher: SF Club Deutschland.

For over twenty years, since 1955, the Science Fiction Club of Germany had published its official fanzine, *Andromeda*, on an entirely amateur basis, issuing ninety-five issues in that period. In 1978 Hans-Jurgen Frederichs offered to establish the magazine as a professional publication, and it was converted to a slick, attractive magazine similar to *Omni*, though with fewer pages and considerably less financial backing. The first four issues were transitional, featuring mostly news and articles, with only one piece of fiction per issue, and that a short-short of German origin. The attempt to raise the magazine to professional status proved abortive, with too little income from advertisements, and a low circulation. The agreement with Frederichs was dissolved, and *Andromeda* reverted to its status as a club magazine.

COMET

Dates: May 1977–June 1978 (8 issues).
Editors: Nos. 1–3, Hans Joachim Alpers, Ronald Hahn, Werner Fuchs; Nos. 4–8, Renate Stroik.
Publisher: Tandem Verlag.

An attractive large-format magazine with profuse color illustrations, *Comet* featured a mixture of material: articles, interviews, reviews, cartoons and comic strips, plus four or five stories per issue. Most fiction was translated from American sources. The first three issues were edited by a consortium of three editors who, while still serving as a team, had individual responsibilities for the first three issues: Alpers for the first issue, and Hahn for the second and third, both working with Fuchs. After the third issue, Renate Stroik, dissatisfied with sales of 10,000 to 15,000, took over the editorship and reduced the size of the issues from 116 pages to 68 pages. The fourth issue did not appear until February 1978. Low payments for material resulted in low quality, and sales dropped below 8,000. *Comet* was suspended after its eighth issue. The same publisher tried another version, *Comet Sonderband*, as noted below.

COMET SONDERBAND

Dates: 1978 (1 issue).
Editor: Renate Stroik.
Publisher: Tandem Verlag.

Following the failure of *Comet*, Tandem tried a new direction with *Comet Sonderband*, a 116–page magazine which featured three long stories: "The Winds of Zarr" by Richard Tierney, "Der Geraubte Engle" by Mischa Morrison (H. J. Alpers) and "Time Wants a Skeleton" by Ross Rocklynne. The magazine was unattractive, and apparently sales were poor, since the magazine was discontinued.

COSMONAUT: MAGAZIN FÜR SCIENCE FICTION

Dates: December 1980–1984.
Editor: Not known.
Publisher: Michael Kunath, Würzburg.

Cosmonaut, published twice yearly, features stories by internationally known authors as well as by novices, SF classics, interviews, book reviews, movie reviews, art and letters. It is in that group of magazines which are a cross between the traditional magazine and the paperback book, yet is clearly called "magazin" in its title. The 140–page issues are attractively printed on good-quality paper and feature good stories and graphics.

DEUTSCHES SCIENCE FICTION MAGAZIN

Dates: August/September 1981–.
Editor: Wolfgang Dulm (Uwe Draber).
Publisher: Printy, Hanover.

This publication was founded by a group of SF fans in collaboration with a printer, with the intention of establishing an all-German magazine. The first issue was large-sized, printed on slick paper, with fifty-two pages, and featured articles, news, reviews, a story competition and three stories: two of German origin, and a translation of Robert Sheckley's "Love, Inc." The print run was between 3,000 and 5,000 copies, and the intention was to sell the magazine chiefly by subscription. Issues appeared irregularly.

GALAXIS

Dates: March 1958–May 1959 (15 issues).
Editor: Lothat Heinecke.
Publisher: Moewig Verlag, Munich.

This German edition of *Galaxy*, despite the high quality of the contents, met with little success, possibly because the authors were, at the time, little known to the general German readership. Uwe Luserke has stated that "*Galaxis* was an experiment that had been started too early for success."

HEYNE SCIENCE FICTION MAGAZIN

Dates: November 1981–[Summer] 1985.
Editor: Wolfgang Jeschke.
Publisher: Heyne Verlag, Munich.

Germany's latest SF magazine is a colossal venture with issues running from 300 to 400 pages each. Published quarterly with a print run of over 20,000, *Heyne Science Fiction Magazin* is aimed at reaching a wide readership. It publishes fiction by German writers along with translated fiction, and has extensive features: reviews, portfolios, interviews, bibliographies, essays, news notes, cartoons and even a radio play. It is of high quality, both in content and appearance, and ranks as one of the best SF magazines in the world.

KABINETT DER LEIDENSCHAFTEN

Dates: 1950–1951 (2 issues).
Editor: Not known.
Publisher: Mertins Verlag, Hamburg.

Kabinett der Leidenschaften was a weird-fiction magazine containing twelve stories per issue. Each issue featured a story from the then-popular Frank Kenney pulp series. One classic by Guy de Maupassant was published, with the remainder of the stories by unknown German pulp writers, possibly pseudonymous. The format was approximately six by nine inches, with eighty pages per issue.

M. Z. (MEINE ZEITUNG)

Dates: 1924–1926 (33 [?] issues).
Editor: Walter Flechsig.
Publisher: Tummler Verlag, Chemnitz (1924); Berliner Verlag für Volksliteratur (1925–1926).

M.Z. was a horror magazine patterned after the U.S. magazines of that time. Each issue contained about fifteen short stories of the horror-adventure genre, including one installment of a serial. Stories were illustrated with black and white drawings. The material was by popular German pulp writers of the period. In the third year, the title was changed to *Das Magazin für Alle*. The format was approximately six by nine inches, with ninety-six pages per issue.

DER ORCHIDEENGARTEN

Dates: April 1919–May 1921 (51 issues).
Editors: Karl Hans Strobl and Alf von Czibulka.
Publisher: Dreilander Verlag, Munich.

Featuring new German stories alongside classics from all over the world, all adorned with a beautiful array of artwork, *Der Orchideengarten* ranks as one of the world's first fantasy magazines, along with the Swedish *Hugin*. Because it featured material from a variety of writers and artists, rather than being the work of a single author, it is perhaps the most deserving claimant to the title of first fantasy magazine.

PERRY RHODAN SONDERHEFT

Dates: Spring 1978–June 1981 (28 issues).
Editors: 1978–May 1980, Hans Gamber; June 1980–January 1981, Helmut Gabriel; February 1981, Walter Fuchs; March 1981–June 1981, Hans-Jurgen Frederichs.
Publisher: Eric Pabel Verlag, Rastatt.

The original Perry Rhodan series of dime novels has appeared regularly since 1961 and is now the world's longest running SF series. It was not a magazine, but its success resulted in spinoff magazines in Germany, Italy and the United States. *Perry Rhodan Sonderheft*, which changed its name to *Perry Rhodan Magazin* after the sixth issue, was a large-format, forty-eight-page magazine that was more closely related to *Star Wars* during its early issues. It initially featured biographies of the actors from *Star Wars*, an interview with George Lucas, and the usual fan material. It reached an initial circulation of 120,000 issues and achieved monthly publication status, but as the novelty faded, so did sales. A new editor failed to revitalize the sales but did improve the quality of the fiction and increase the size of the magazine to seventy-two-page issues. The last editor, Frederichs, developed an *Omni*-like concept for the magazine, but low sales forced its suspension before the new concept was tested in sales.

SOLARIS

Dates: April 1982–.
Editor: Uwe Luserke.
Publisher: Jürgen Mercker, Gerlingen.

Solaris is one of Germany's newest magazines. Unlike *Heyne Science Fiction Magazine*, it is retaining the traditional slick format and is limiting itself to a small circulation (under 10,000 copies). The magazine is a blend of fantasy and science fiction and features both new material and translations, along with interviews, news and reviews. It includes color interior art, an unusual feature.

SPACE TRAVEL

Dates: 1981–.
Editor: K.-H. Schmitz.
Publisher: Ubergrenzen Verlag, Bonn.

Although the first issue was a fanzine with a small print run, the second issue was to have a print run of 60,000 copies, with newsstand distribution but it failed to appear. Contents include SF stories, articles and artwork.

2001

Dates: April 1978–January/February 1979 (5 issues).
Editor: Uwe Nielsen.
Publisher: Budo-Sport-Verlag, Neu-Isenberg.

Issued by the publisher of a local karate magazine, with little advance notice, *2001* was attractively done but lacked attention-getting covers. The general layout lacked direction, although it was clear that the publisher was aiming it at a young readership (which was already satiated with the many *Perry Rhodan* look alikes). The editor had many British contacts, and as a result the magazine carried a British news column and much British artwork. The fifth issue was retitled *Nova 2001*.

UTOPIA MAGAZIN

Dates: Winter 1955–August 1959 (26 issues).
Editors: Nos. 1–2, Walter Ernsting; Nos. 3–20, Walter Spiegl and Norbert Wolfl; Nos. 21–26, Norbert Wolfl (under the pseudonym Bert Koeppen).
Publisher: Erich Pabel Verlag, Rastatt.

Titled *Utopia-Sonderband* for the first two issues, this was the first genuine German SF magazine, planned as a companion to the various "Utopia" book series from the publisher. It published mostly translations of U.S. and U.K. stories from a variety of sources, plus a number of articles, many of German origin. It was digest-sized, and the page count dropped constantly, from 128 in the early issues to 96 in the final issues. Sales were in the 20,000–copy range, but as the page count and the quality of both content and appearance dropped, sales declined until the magazine was suspended.

APPENDIX: GERMANY

The following titles are included here for clarification, either because the title is similar to a magazine title or because they have been previously identified as magazines.

ANALOG

Dates: 1981–.
Editor: Hans Joachim Alpers.
Publisher: Moewig Verlag, Munich.
This pocketbook series features selections from the American *Analog*.

GALAXY

Dates: 1965–1970 (14 issues).
Editors: Nos. 1–9, Walter Ernsting; Nos. 10–14, Walter Ernsting and Thomas Schlück.
Publisher: Heyne Verlag, Munich.
This pocketbook series features selections from the American *Galaxy*.

ISAAC ASIMOV'S SCIENCE FICTION MAGAZIN

Editor: Wolfgang Jeschke.
Publisher: Heyne Verlag, Munich.
A pocketbook anthology series, selected from the American *Isaac Asimov's Science Fiction Magazine*, it is not a magazine in spite of its title.

KAPITAN MORS

Dates: ca. 1908–1913 (over 165 issues).
Editor: Not known.
Publisher: Druckund Verlag.
Not technically a magazine, the Kapitan Mors adventures were a series of German dime novels under the general title of *Der Luftpirat*. The series has often been suggested as being one of the first SF magazines and is included here for clarification. Each issue ran about thirty-two pages and told of the adventures of a Captain Nemo-like character, called by Franz Rottensteiner a "Cosmic Robin Hood" in his *The Science Fiction Book*.

KOPERNIKUS

Dates: 1980–.
Editor: Hans Joachim Alpers.
Publisher: Moewig Verlag, Munich.
 This is a paperback anthology series.

MAGAZINE OF FANTASY AND SCIENCE FICTION
(Series title)

Dates: 1963–.
Editors: Nos. 1–9, Charlotte Winheller; Nos. 10–14, Walter Ernsting; Nos. 15–42, Wulf H. Bergner; Nos. 43–, Manfred Kluge.
Publisher: Heyne Verlag, Munich.
 While not a standard SF magazine, an edition of the *Magazine of Fantasy and Science Fiction* is published. A regular selection of material from the American magazine is made and published as part of the Heyne SF Series. Some fifty-six selections have been published to date, most of which bear as their title the title of the lead story.

POLARIS

Editor: Franz Rottensteiner.
Publisher: Heyne Verlag, Munich.
 This is a paperback anthology series featuring both stories and articles.

SCIENCE FICTION STORIES

Dates: 1970–1982 (92 issues).
Editor: Walter Spiegl.
Publisher: Ullstein, Berlin.
 This paperback anthology series reprints from both magazines and other anthologies.

SOLARIS

Dates: August/September 1982–.
Editor: Uwe Luserke.
Publisher: Jurgen Mercker.

Issues typically contain two or three stories—mostly first German printings—writers' portraits, interviews, articles on SF, a series segment on the history of the SF magazines, news, reviews and interior illustrations.

ULLSTEIN 2000

Ullstein 2000 is the general title of Ullstein's paperback SF line, usually two titles per month. This series title is sometimes mistakenly cited as a magazine.

HUNGARY

Consultant: *Peter Kuczka*

GALAKTIKA

Dates: Fall 1972–.
Editor: Peter Kuczka.
Publisher: Kozmosz Konyvek, Budapest.

Galaktika features both original Hungarian fiction and translations from America, France, Spain, Germany, Italy and other countries. Each 128–page issue carries ten to fifteen articles and stories, along with reviews. *Galaktika* presents the most balanced reflection of the world SF situation currently available and is considered by Mike Ashley and Sam J. Lundwall as one of the best magazines in the world. In spite of the language barrier, this magazine should be represented in all science fiction and fantasy research collections. Hungary also has an active SF club, the Kozponti Tudomanyos club, which publishes *Pozitron* and an amateur magazine called *Andromeda*, produced by the Veszprem Chemical University group.

ISRAEL

Consultant: *Nachman Ben-Yehuda*

COSMOS

Dates: 1958 (4 issues).
Editor:
Publisher: Tash-Ted, Tel Aviv.

Cosmos was a magazine devoted entirely to translations of SF stories. Among the writers whose stories appeared are Henry Kuttner, Murray Leinster, Isaac Asimov, Parker, Robert Sheckley, Fredric Brown and others. The magazine gave credit to authors, but not to the translators.

COSMOS

Dates: 1979 (6 issues).
Editor: D. Kol.
Publisher: "Atid," Ramat HaSharon.
  Cosmos was the Hebrew version of *Isaac Asimov's Science Fiction Magazine*. The Israeli magazine was wholly translated from the U.S. original, including stories and departments. It included a local "Letters to the Editor" column and some original Israeli science fiction. Among Israel's best SF magazines *Cosmos* was second only to *Fantasia 2000*.

FANTASIA 2000

Dates: December 1978–1984 (44 issues).
Editor: Aharon Hauptman; Gabi Peleg.
Publisher: Nos. 1–15, A. Tene, Tel Aviv; Nos. 16–44, Hyperion, Tel Aviv.
  By far the most professional SF magazine to appear in Israel, *Fantasia 2000* maintained high quality in both appearance and content. Fiction included translated stories (most from *The Magazine of Fantasy and Science Fiction*), plus a few original Israeli stories. Departments included Isaac Asimov's science column from the American magazine, letters to the editor, SF news from around the world, profiles of major SF writers and a variety of articles. *Fantasia 2000* gave the Israeli reader, for the first time, an accurate idea of what good-quality SF is all about.

FLASH GORDON

Dates: 1963 (7 issues).
Editor: Not known.
Publisher: Ramdor, Tel Aviv.
  This magazine-thriller is devoted entirely to the adventures of Flash Gordon. The various issues were written by H. L. Halder (possibly a pen name) and could be described as an Israeli form of space-western.

MADA DIMIONI

Dates: 1958 (13 issues).
Editor: Not known.
Publisher: Not known.

This magazine emphasized short "action" stories translated without credit to either author or translator. Despite this oversight and the cheap appearance, the translations were of good quality.

OLAM HaMAHCAR

Dates: 1979? (1 issue).
Editors: Amir Gavrelli, Jacob Or.
Publisher: Khotam, Tel Aviv.

It included translated stories by A. E. van Vogt and others, information and articles about UFOs, the space shuttle, movies and cartoons. The magazine did not credit either authors or translators.

ITALY

Consultants: Gianni Montanari and Gianfranco de Turres

Note: A series of profiles of the Italian SF magazines appeared in the Italian magazine *Wow* in the early 1970s.

ALPHA TAU

See I NARRATORI DELL 'ALPHA TAU.

ALTAIR

Dates: October 1976–May 1977 (8 issues).
Editor: Antonio Bellomi.
Publisher: Casa Editrice "Il Picchio," Milan.

Altair was an attractive magazine that presented short novels either in translation from U.S. or U.K. sources or by Italian authors adopting non-Italian pen names. It also carried short stories, book reviews and a letter column. Publication was ceased, then restarted as *Spazio 2000*.

ASTROMAN

Dates: December 1957–January 1958 (2 issues).
Editor: Pini Segna.
Publisher: Edizioni RAID, Milan.
This magazine contained short translated stories.

AU DELÀ DU CIEL

The French-language version of *Oltre il Cielo*. See entry under France.

CORRIERE DELLO SPAZIO

Dates: April 1959–May 1963 (51 issues).
Editor: Manuel Lualdi.
Publisher: Soc. Iniziative Editorialie Aeronautiche, Milan.
A magazine of astronautics and SF, it follows much the same formula as *Oltre il Cielo*.

COSMIC

Dates: June 1957–May 1958 (3 issues).
Editor: Mario Todarello.
Publisher: Irsa Muraro Editrice, Rome.
Essentially a reprint magazine (subtitled "Selezione di Fantascienza"), *Cosmic* drew its contents primarily from its earlier companion magazine *I Narratori dell'Alpha Tau*. The stories were always Italian under bogus pen names that suggested English origins. Collectors should note that this magazine had two first issues, a preliminary Number 1 in June 1957, and an additional Number 1 in December 1957, followed by Number 2 in May 1958.

COSMO

Dates: November 1961–April 1965 (89 issues).
Editor: See *I Romanzi del Cosmo* for details on editors.
Publisher: Ponzoni Editore, Milan.
This twice-monthly reprint magazine was assembled by binding together two issues of *I Romanzi del Cosmo* from unsold returns, but featuring new covers.

COSMO

Dates: 1970–.
Editor: Gianfranco Viviani.
Publisher: Editrice Nord, Milan.
No details on this reported title have been identified.

CRONACHE DEL FUTURO

Dates: August 15, 1957–August 16/30, 1958 (24 issues).
Editor: Salvatore Cappadonia.
Publisher: Edizione Periodici Kappa, Rome.
This fortnightly magazine was published by Italian writers under anglicized pen names. It continued publication as *Le Cronache del Futuro*.

LE CRONACHE DEL FUTURO

Dates: November 30, 1958–May 30, 1959 (11 issues).
Editor: Salvatore Cappadonia.
Publisher: Editrice Maya, Rome.
This was a continuation of *Cronache del Futuro*, but from a new publisher. Work was always by Italian writers masquerading as English or American writers, and was never in translation.

GLI ESPLORATORI DELLO SPAZIO

Dates: December 1961–February 1963 (11 issues).
Editors: Nos. 1–8, Antonio Cantarella; Nos. 9–11, Aldo Crudo.
Publisher: Editrice Romana Periodici, Roma.
A monthly or bi-monthly magazine, it concentrated on longer stories and novels.

FANTASCIENZA

Dates: November 1954–May 1955 (7 issues).
Editor: Livio Garzanti.
Publisher: Garzanti gli Fratelli Treves, Milan.
These were reprint editions of *The Magazine of Fantasy and Science Fiction*.

FANTASCIENZA

Dates: May–October 1976 (3 issues).
Editors: Maurizio Nati, Sandro Permageno.
Publisher: Editrice Ciscato, Milan.
Fantascienza was planned as a monthly, but there was a long delay between the second (June) and last issues. It included translations of U.S. and U.K. stories plus articles, interviews, a letter column, book reviews, and SF fan and professional news.

FANTASIENZA SOVIETICA

Dates: September 1966–June 1967 (7 issues).
Editor: Ugo Ugolini.
Publisher: Editrice FER, Rome.
This contained translations of Soviet SF.

FANTASIA & FANTASCIENZA

Dates: December 1962–October 1963 (10 issues).
Editor: G. Jori.
Publisher: Minerva Editrice, Milan.
This was a reprint edition of *The Magazine of Fantasy and Science Fiction* but with some original material. It was published monthly except for May 1963.

FANTAVVENTURA

Dates: October–November 1961 (2 issues).
Editor: Luigi Santucci.
Publisher: Luigi Santucci, Rome.
More of a novel series than a magazine, this title featured two novels by Italian writers, under the pseudonym "Ghely Moor."

FUTURIA

Dates: September–December 1964 (4 issues).
Editor: Franco Enna.
Publisher: Zillitti Editore, Milan.
A monthly magazine featuring translations of novelettes by U.S. and U.K. writers, it was supplemented by author biographies and reviews.

FUTURO

Dates: May/June 1963–15 November 1964 (8 issues).
Editors: Nos. 1–5, Lino Aldani and Massimo Lo Jacono; Nos. 6–8, Massimo Lo Jacono.
Publisher: Editorialo Futuro, Rome.
  This bi-monthly published predominantly stories and articles by Italians, but did include one story each by Jorge Luis Borges, Stanislaw Lem and Atilla Jozsef.

GALASSIA

Dates: January–June 1953 (3 issues).
Editor: Orfeo Giovanni Landini.
Publisher: Edizioni Galassia, Milan.
  Galassia contained translations of U.S. and U.K. short novels.

GALASSIA

Dates: January–April 1957 (5 issues).
Editor: Luigi Rapuzzi Johannes, assisted by M. Maglioni, Giorgio Monicelli, P. Dalloro, C. Nadalina and E. Stern.
Publisher: Casa Editrice Galassia, Udine.
  This monthly magazine (with two issues dated April) carried short novels and stories by U.S., U.K. and Italian authors writing under pen names. Issue 2 contains a story, "Q.I. = 10.000" by Thomas H. Morehouse, which appears to be a pirating of Olaf Stapledon's *Odd John*.

GALASSIA

Dates: January 1961–February 1978 (230 issues).
Editors: Nos. 1–8, Mario Vitali; Nos. 9–59, Roberta Rambelli (assisted by Ugo Malaguti on Nos. 57–59); Nos. 60–110, Ugo Malaguti; Nos. 111–204, Vittorio Curtoni and Gianni Montanari; Nos. 205–230, Gianni Montanari.
Publisher: Casa Editrice La Tribuna, Piacenza.
  One of the major Italian SF magazines, it appeared monthly for the first 108 issues, then fortnightly until Number 188, bi-monthly for four issues, and then back to a monthly schedule from Number 194, with occasional gaps. It contained mainly U.S. and U.K. translations, but also included French, German, Russian and East European writers, along with some Italian writers. Articles, reviews, interviews and other departments appeared in issues 50–102 and 211–230.

GALAXY

Dates: June 1958–May 1964 (72 numbered issues in 70).
Editors: Nos. 1–26/27, R. Valente; Nos. 28/29–39, Mario Vitali; Nos. 40–72, Lella Pollini Rambelli.
Publishers: Nos. 1–10, Editrice Due Mondi, Milan; Nos. 11–72, Casa Editrice La Tribuna, Piacenza.

This was an Italian reprint edition of the U.S. *Galaxy*, with some original Italian material.

GAMMA

Dates: October 1965–March 1968 (27 issues).
Editors: Valention De Carlo and Ferruccio Allesandri.
Publishers: Nos. 1–5, Edizione Gamma, Milan; Nos. 6–27, Edizione dello Scorpione, Milan.

Gamma was really a semi-professional critical magazine rather than a straight fiction publication. Produced by two Milan fans, it featured articles and essays from various sources, including the British *SF Horizons*.

GEMINI

Dates: September 1977–1979 (15 issues).
Editor: Mameli Gatti.
Publisher: Edizione Diffusione Nationaleo, Milan.

ISAAC ASIMOV—REVISTA DI FANTASCIENZA

Dates: 1982–.
Editor: Vittorio Curtoni.
Publisher: Armenia SIAD Edizione, Milan.

This is a new Italian edition of *Isaac Asimov's Science Fiction Magazine* (see also *La Revista di Isaac Asimov*). Issues range to 160 pages, with new covers by Italian artists. It reprints stories, articles and features from the U.S. edition but adds Italian letters, news and occasional articles.

KADATH

Dates: October 1979–.
Editor: Francesco Cova.
Publisher: The Kadath Press, Genoa.

Kadath is a limited edition, semi-professional magazine devoted to weird fiction. Although published in Italy, the editor is aware of the non-Italian market and has increasingly enlarged an English-language section within the magazine to the extent that issue 4 was totally in English. It contains both fiction and articles, with emphasis on the *Weird Tales* school of writers. It is extremely attractive, in large size on slick paper. Pagination varies from twenty-eight to fifty-six pages per issue, and it is profusely illustrated with photographs and artwork, mostly by British and American artists.

MICROMEGA

Dates: January 1967 (1 issue).
Editor: Carlo Bordoni.
Publisher: Not known.
   This slim, twenty-eight-page semi-professional magazine contains Italian short stories and articles.

MONDI ASTRALI

Dates: January–April 1955 (4 issues).
Editor: Eggardo Beltrametti.
Publisher: Gabriele Gioggi, Rome.
   This publication consisted mostly of short stories by Italian writers with anglicized pen names, but included some articles and a letter column.

I NARRATORI DELL'ALPHA TAU

Dates: January 12–June 15, 1957 (9 issues).
Editors: Nos. 1–14, Bernardino de Rugeriis; Nos. 5–9, Mario Todarello.
Publisher: Irsa Muraro Editrice, Rome.
   This publication carried predominantly novels written by Italians under such names as Charles Beta, Peter Jota and Jim Omega (a name adopted by Peter Kolosimo). It began as a fortnightly but slipped to every three weeks, then monthly. Some of the novels were later reprinted in *Cosmic*.

NOVA

Dates: May 1967–1978 (38 issues).
Editor: Ugo Malaguti.
Publisher: Libra Editrice, Bologna.

This attractive magazine featured translations of U.S. and other SF, supplemented by Italian stories, columns and reviews.

OLTRE IL CIELO

Dates: September 16/30, 1957–January/February 1970 (154 issues).
Editors: Armando Silvestri, Cesare Falessi.
Publisher: Nos. 1–81, E. Silvestri; Nos. 82–155, Gruppo Editoriale Esse, Rome.

This magazine has been called an Italian "poor man's *Science and Invention*" since it gave emphasis to popular science articles mixed with SF from various sources. Fortnightly for the first 136 issues, it then appeared irregularly either monthly or bi-monthly. A French-language edition was published simultaneously as *Au Delà du Ciel*.

PERRY RHODAN

Dates: March 1976–1979.
Editor: Mameli Gatti (pseudonym of Antonio Bellomi).
Publisher: Solaris Editrice, Milan.

This is the Italian edition of the German magazine.

PIANETA

Dates: March 1964–July 1968 (23 issues).
Editor: Louis Pauwels.
Publisher: Not known.

An Italian edition of the French nonfiction magazine *Plantete*, it concentrated mostly on nonfiction with a heavy emphasis on UFOs and von Daniken phenomena. It printed occasional stories.

POKER D'ASSI

Dates: January–February 1959 (2 issues).
Editor: Vittorio Della Cese.
Publisher: Editrice Poker D'Assi, Rome.

This general magazine featured crime, adventure and fantastic fiction, as indicated by the subtitle, "Letteratura Gialla, Fantascienza, Enigmistica, Umorismo."

PROXIMA

Dates: April–July 1966 (4 issues).
Editors: Luigi Cozzi, Franco Filanci.
Publisher: Granillo Editore, Turin.
Proxima consisted predominantly of translations of U.S. and U.K. SF adventure novels.

I RACCONTI DEL TERRORE

Dates: June 1962–January 1963 (8 issues).
Editor: G. Sansoni.
Publisher: Not known.
Titled *Terrore* for the first two issues, this publication consisted predominantly of novels by Italians using anglicized pen names.

LA RIVISTA DI ISAAC ASIMOV

Dates: Spring 1978–November 1980 (11 issues).
Editor: Karel Thole.
Publisher: Arnoldo Mondadori, Milan.
The Italian edition of *Isaac Asimov's Science Fiction Magazine* ceased publication because the circulation of 20,000 was deemed too low by the publisher.

LA RIVISTA DI ISAAC ASIMOV—AVVENTURE SPAZIALI E FANTASY

Dates: 1981–1982 (4 issues).
Editor: Vittorio Curtoni.
Publisher: Armenia SIAD Edizioni, Milan.
This was the Italian edition of *Isaac Asimov's SF Adventure Magazine*.

ROBOT

Dates: April 1976–August 1979 (40 issues).
Editors: Michele Armenia, Laura Fasolino, Guiseppi Lippi.
Publisher: Armenia Editore, Rome.
During its existence *Robot* ranked as one of the world's top SF magazines. It featured both new and translated fiction, columns, reviews, criticism, inter-

views and news notes. In digest size, the magazine was an attractive, high-quality offering. A series of nine anthology-style special issues also appeared, identified as supplements to *Robot*.

I ROMANZI DEL COSMO

Dates: June 1957–May 1967 (202 issues).
Editors: Nos. 1–10, Giorgio Monicelli, as Tom Arno; Nos. 11–18, Luigi Johannes Rapuzzi; Nos. 19–20, F. P. Aldorin; Nos. 21–58, Marco Paini; Nos. 59–85, Gianni Tosi; Nos. 86–141, Franco Urbini; Nos. 142–169, Annico Pau; Nos. 170–202, Giancarlo Cella.
Publisher: Ponzoni Editore, Milan.

It contained predominantly novels poorly translated from U.S., U.K. and French sources, but with some Italian material under pen names. Publication was monthly or fortnightly. Unsold issues were repackaged as *Cosmos*.

I ROMANZI DEL FUTURO

Dates: March 20/25–May 20/30, 1961 (5 issues).
Editor: Salvatore Cappadonia.
Publisher: Edizione P.E.N., Rome.

A fortnightly magazine from the same editor as *Le Cronache del Futuro*, it featured some Italian novels.

I ROMANZI DI URANIA/URANIA

Dates: October 1952– (800+ issues).
Editors: Nos. 1–267, Giorgio Monicelli; Nos. 281–355, Carlo Fruttero; Nos. 355–, Carlo Fruttero and Franco Lucentini.
Publisher: Arnoldo Mondadori, Milan.

This publication contained mostly translations of U.S. and U.K. novels, but featured occasional Italian material and fillers. A magazine more in appearance than in intent, its schedule varied from weekly to fortnightly. The title changed from *Urania* with Number 153 (June 6, 1953) but has no connection with the original *Urania*.

SCIENZA FANTASTICA

Dates: April 1952–March 1953 (7 issues).
Editor: Lionello Torossi.
Publisher: Editrice Krator, Rome.

Italy's first specialized SF magazine, it was planned as a monthly but appeared irregularly. It published stories translated from *Astounding*, along with a few original Italian items. The first four issues were gathered into one volume and published as *Antologia di Scienza Fantastica*.

SF CRONACHE

Date: December 1967 (1 issue).
Editor: Gianluigi Missiaja.
Publisher: Centro Cultori Science Fiction.
    A single issue put together by the Central Italian SF Association, it contained news, articles and some Italian stories.

GLI SHOCKS

Dates: February–August 1967 (7 issues).
Editor: Teodoro Giuttari.
Publisher: Not known.
    Gli Shocks published Italian and Latin American short novels and stories.

SPAZIO 2000

Dates: June 1977–1978 (19 issues).
Editor: Antonio Bellomi.
Publisher: Editrice il Picchio.
    A continuation of *Altair*, it concentrated on translations of U.S. and U.K. novels with some Italian stories under foreign pen names, plus letters and reviews.

SUPER FANTASCIENZA ILLUSTRATA

Dates: July 1961–April 1962 (10 issues).
Editor: Gino Sansoni.
Publisher: ILE, Milan.
    This publication carried Italian novels under anglicized pen names. After the sixth issue, the title changed to *I Piu' Grandi Scrittori del Futuro*.

SUPERSPAZIO

Dates: November 1961–November 1962 (10 issues).
Editor: G. Jori.
Publisher: Minerva Editrice, Milan.
   Superspazio published Italian novels under anglicized pen names.

TERRORE

Dates: April–July 1961 (6 issues).
Editor: Salvatore Cappadonia.
Publisher: Edizione P.E.N., Rome.
   The Subtitle "I Romanzi del Terrore," helps differentiate it from another magazine of the same name. It carried Italian novels and short stories under anglicized pen names.

TERRORE (1962/1963)

   See I RACCONTI DEL TERRORE.

URANIA

Dates: November 1952–December 1953 (14 issues).
Editor: Giorgio Monicelli.
Publisher: Arnoldo Mondadori, Milan.
   Urania published good-quality translations of stories predominantly from the U.S. *Galaxy*.

URANIA

See I ROMANZI DI URANIA.

VERSO LE STELLE

Dates: 1977–1979 (8 issues).
Editor: Mameli Gatti (pseudonym of Antonio Bellomi).
Publisher: Solaris Editrice, Milan.

This is an attractive magazine concentrating on translations of lead novels by U.S. and U.K. authors, supported by short stories and filler departments by the editorial staff.

JAPAN

Consultant: *Takumi Shibano*

AMAZING STORIES

Dates: April–July 1950 (7 issues).
Editor: Not known.
Publisher: Seibundo Shinkosha, Tokyo.
Often cited as a magazine, this was an early anthology series which featured stories from both prewar and postwar issues of the U.S. *Amazing Stories* and from *Fantastic Adventures*. Stories were selected by employees of the publishing house, among them Isamu Yamashita.

HOSEKI

Editor: Not known.
Publisher: Hoseki-sha, Tokyo.
Frequently identified as a science fiction magazine, this title was actually a mystery magazine which published science fiction issues in February 1955, August 1955, September 1963 and March 1964. It is included here for clarification.

KISO-TENGAI

Dates: January–October 1974 (10 issues); April 1976–October 1981 (67 issues).
Editor: Tadao Soné.
Publisher: First series, Seiko-sha, Tokyo; second series, Kiso-Tengai-sha, Tokyo.
Loosely translated, the title means "Fantastic." The first series mixed SF and mystery stories. When the magazine failed, the editor established his own publishing company and relaunched the magazine with a pure SF lineup, featuring new and translated stories.

SEIUN

Date: January 1955 (1 issue).
Editor: Chizuo Ohta.
Publisher: Morinomichi-sha, Tokyo.
This was the first genuine Japanese attempt at a science fiction magazine. The only issue featured three American stories, one Russian story and three Japanese stories, plus some articles.

SF ADVENTURE

Dates: May 1979–.
Editor: Yoshio Sugawara.
Publisher: Tokuma-Shoten, Tokyo.
This magazine emphasizes SF adventure stories by Japanese authors, and features articles, reviews, and SF art. In addition to the stories, *SF Adventure* concentrates on art and the visual aspects of science fiction. Translated material is rare. As of August 1982, 33 issues had appeared.

SF HOSEKI

Dates: August 1979–June 1981 (12 issues).
Editor: Hisanori Taniguchi.
Publisher: Kobunsha, Tokyo.
It carried translations from *Isaac Asimov's Science Fiction Magazine*, plus original Japanese stories and articles. Issues are large, up to 300 pages.

SF MAGAZINE

Dates: February 1960–.
Editors: Nos. 1–122, Masami Fukushima; Nos. 123–185, Masara Mori; Nos. 186–198, Ryozo Nagashima; Nos. 199–225, Taku Kurahashi; Nos. 226–246, Hiroshi Hayakawa (with Kiyoshi Imaoka); Nos. 247–, Kiyoshi Imaoka.
Publisher: Hayakawa-shobo, Tokyo.
The first genuinely successful Japanese SF magazine, it started as a Japanese edition of *The Magazine of Fantasy and Science Fiction*, but gradually the ratio of original material increased until now one-half of each issue is original Japanese fiction. Recent (1982) issues show an increase in translated material. It appears monthly, with one or two extra issues per year.

STARLOG

Dates: August 1980–.
Editors: Nos. 1–7, Koh Miyamuta; Nos. 10–33, Shigahara Nakao; Nos. 34–, Ryohei Takahashi.
Publisher: Tsurumoto-Room.

Although related to the American *Starlog*, this magazine is edited independently in Japan, with more than one-half original material. Contents are more inclined toward written SF than is the case with the American title.

Note: Japan featured many "Special Science Fiction Issues" in the fifties and sixties, to satisfy the demand for quality SF in the absence of a continuing SF magazine. One of these, *Hoseki*, is cited in this listing, but the scholar should be aware that there were many more issues similar to this one. No bibliography of these special issues was discovered during the preparation of this listing.

MEXICO

Consultant: *Hector Pessina*

ANTOLOGIA DE CUENTOS FANTASTICOS, POLICIACOS Y MYSTERIO

Dates: August–November 1950 (4 issues).
Editor: Not known.
Publisher: Not known.

This is identified by Brad Day, in his *Checklist*, as an SF/mystery pulp. No further information is known.

CIENCIA-FICCIÓN ESPACIO

Dates: August 1977–.
Editor: Carlos Jaumá Guix.
Publisher: Editorial Mosaico.

A monthly, digest-sized publication, it features a glossy cover, nice layout, and fine illustrations. It contains all fiction, most being translations from the English. Issue 5 carried stories by R. Yarov and Joseph Flower, along with well-known names like Robert Sheckley, O'Donnell and Grant.

CIENCIA Y FANTASIA

Dates: September 1946–December 1957 (14 issues).
Editor: Not known.
Publisher: Novaro-Mexico, S.A.

This was a Mexican edition of *The Magazine of Fantasy and Science Fiction*, but with stories selected from various issues, rather than a direct issue-by-issue translation. Early sales were good, then declined steadily.

LOS CUENTOS FANTASTICOS

Dates: July 1948–May 1953 (44 issues).
Editor: Not known.
Publisher: Not known.

It featured material from various U.S. magazines and fanzines. The schedule was irregular, with up to three issues per month during some periods, or two to three months between issues.

ENIGMAS

Dates: August 1955–May 1958 (16 issues).
Editor: Bernandino Diaz.
Publisher: Editorial Proteo, S.A., Mexico City.

This was a monthly magazine, except for the delayed final issue. It selected material predominantly from *Startling Stories* and *Fantastic Story Magazine*, with nonfiction from other sources. Some original material was included.

ESCAPIO

See CIENCIA-FICCIÓN ESPACIO.

FANTASIAS DEL FUTURO

Date: September 1958 (1 issue).
Editor: Antonio Gascon.
Publisher: Editora Sol, S.A., Mesones.

This was a 128–page digest-sized magazine translating from *Future SF*, *Planet Stories*, *SF Quarterly* and other U.S. magazines.

NETHERLANDS

Consultants: *Eddy C. Bertin, Peter Coene, and Roelf Goudriaan*

APOLLO

Joint Dutch/Belgian publication. See under Belgium.

ESSEF

Dates: January/March 1977–1979 (9 issues).
Editor: R.A.J. Zielschot.
Publisher: R.A.J. Zielschot, Utrecht.

Two magazines appeared almost simultaneously under this title. Kees Van Toorn had planned to convert his fanzine, *Atlan*, into a professional publication printed by R.A.J. Zielschot, but at the last moment the two split, each bringing out a magazine named *Essef*. Zielschot's was a slick, thirty-two page quarterly with an emphasis on SF comic strips, but it frequently featured short fiction.

ESSEF

See ORBIT.

FANTASIE IN WETENSCHAP

Dates: December 1948–March 1949 (4 issues).
Editor: Ben Abbas.
Publisher: Ben Abbas and Lo Hartog Van Banda.

The first known Dutch SF magazine, it is now very rare. It mainly published stories by Lo Hartog Van Banda, under various pseudonyms.

GALAXIS

Dates: October 1966–February 1967 (5 issues).
Editor: Theo Kemp.
Publisher: Vector, Dordrecht.

Galaxis carried translations of stories selected from *Galaxy* from the 1953–1967 period. The stories are well selected but poorly translated.

HOLLAND-SF

Dates: 1966– (80 issues through July 1982).
Editor: Annemarie Kindt.
Publisher: NCSF, Den Haag.

Holland-SF publishes in-depth interviews and essays and medium-length critical reviews. Recent special issues featured Fred Pohl, Chris Priest, Rachel Pollack and others. It also includes news and fan notes. The primary Dutch critical journal, it is essential to all libraries with any interest in Dutch SF. For over fifteen years it has been the focal point of Dutch fandom.

HORROR

Joint Dutch/Belgian publication. See under Belgium.

MORGEN

Dates: September 1971–November 1972 (6 issues).
Editor: Manual van Loggem.
Publisher: Nos. 1–5, De Dam, Schiedam; No. 6, R.A.J. Productions, Utrecht.

The first Dutch SF magazine to offer SF of literary quality, *Morgen* contained some translated material, but mainly original Dutch and Flemish fiction. Many of the Dutch writers are still active. It included some comic and nonfiction columns and was significant as the first sign of the appearance of original Dutch SF writers. Number 6 was a small press fan edition of the contents planned for the sixth issue of *Morgen* from De Dam.

ORBIT

Dates: Autumn 1977–.
Editor: Kees Van Toorn.
Publisher: Kees Van Toorn, Rotterdam.

Orbit was Kees Van Toorn's new name for his magazine *Essef*, to avoid conflict with another magazine with the same title. It features both fiction and secondary material. Fiction is translated U.S., U.K. and Scandinavian material, with a few original Dutch stories. It also features interviews, a film column, a news column, and Dutch and Flemish fan news. It is representative of the Dutch approach to SF and is significant as the focal point of current Dutch SF.

PLANEET

Dates: January 1953 (1 issue).
Editor: N. Osterbaan.
Publisher: Durkkerijen Cevado, The Hague.

This ninety-six-page digest publication reprinted British material, mainly from *Authentic*.

SF—SCIENCE FICTION AVONTUREN IN RUIMTE EN TIJD

Dates: 1981 (10 issues).
Editors: House team.
Publisher: Meulenhoff/De Tijdruimte, Amsterdam.

Each issue had sixty-four pages, with color covers. The magazine was a promotional device for the publisher, Meulenhoff, but carried two science fiction stories per issue, plus promotional material for Meulenhoff. The stories were all by American and British writers and were all reprinted from books published by Meulenhoff.

SPACE FICTION

Date: 1951 (1 issue).
Editors: Tim Verheggen and Henk Luderichs.
Publisher: Space Fiction, Amsterdam.

It contained fiction and nonfiction, a UFO story, comics, cartoons and short reviews, and is of interest to completists only.

NORWAY

Consultant: *Johannes H. Berg*

NOVA

Dates: 1971–1979 (34 issues).
Editors: Terje Wanberg, Øyvind Myhre, Per G. Olson, Johannes H. Berg.
Publisher: Stowa Forlag.

Science Fiction-Magasinet was launched in early 1971 by Terje Wanberg, initially as a Norwegian edition of *The Magazine of Fantasy and Science Fiction.* Starting with the fourth issue, many new authors were featured, many of them Norwegian. The magazine never achieved adequate circulation to be solvent, and was supported by Stowa's SF book club. In early 1973 the name was changed to *Nova*, with "Science Fiction Magasinet" as a subtitle for a year. By 1974 the contents were a mixture of fantasy and "hard" SF translations, with fewer Norwegian writers included. From 1974 to 1979 the circulation declined, finally forcing termination of both *Nova* and Stowa Forlag.

TEMPO-MAGASINET

Dates: November 1953–March 1954 (5 issues).
Editor: Arne Ernst.
Publisher: Greens Forlag.
This magazine featured translations of U.S. fiction, predominantly from *Galaxy*.

POLAND

Consultant: *Mariusz Piotrowski*

FANTASTYKA

Dates: October 1982–.
Editor: Adam Hollanek.
Publisher: Krajowe Wydawnictwo Czasopism RSW "Prasa-Ksiazka-Ruch."
Fantastyka is the first Polish SF magazine and has a very professional appearance. It features translated stories by American, Russian and other authors, and short stories by Polish authors, supplemented by columns and critical articles.

ROMANIA

COLECTIA "POVESTIRI STIINTIFICO-FANTASTICE"

Dates: October 1, 1955–April 15, 1974 (466 issues).
Editor: Adrian Rogoz.
Publisher: Editura Scînteia, Bucharest.

This long-running supplement to *Ştiinţă şi Tehnică* most frequently consisted of one long (20–30 page) story, or part of a novel serial, with some filler material. It featured items from all over the world.

SPAIN

Consultant: *Hector R. Pessina*

ALIEN: EL MUNDO DE LA CIENCIA Y LO SOBRENATURAL

Dates: December 1981–.
Editor: Javier Viejo Comas.
Publisher: CEDISA, Barcelona.

This is undoubtedly an attempt to create a Spanish-language *Omni*. It contains articles about science and pseudo-science, UFOs, and strange phenomena, plus two or three SF stories or excerpts from books. Most of the contents are by Spanish writers, but some nonfiction is by well-known names such as Isaac Asimov. Departments include movie and book reviews. It is illustrated with many glossy photographs and features covers and portfolios of SF illustrations.

ANTICIPACION

Dates: October 1966–April 1967 (7 issues).
Editor: Domingo Santos and Luis Vigil.
Publisher: Editorial Ferma, Barcelona and Buenos Aires.

A particularly attractive magazine, it presented translations from American, French and other sources. Early issues were clearly magazine oriented, but later issues more nearly resemble short story collections.

CIENCIA-FICCION

Dates: 1982?–.
Editor: Not known.
Publisher: Ciencia-ficcion, Madrid.

This thirty-two-page pulp magazine is an attempt to publish an all-Spanish science fiction magazine with fiction and nonfiction. The quality is low, the articles weak, and the illustrations poor. It features original material from Spanish-speaking countries, but does not include the well-known Spanish writers who have been published elsewhere, such as in *Nueva Dimension*.

CONTACTO

Dates: 1981?–.
Editor: Not known.
Publisher: Not known.
A "little magazine" with stories and articles by Spanish writers, *Contacto* suffers from poor layout and unimaginative content.

ESPACIO

Dates: ca. 1950s to 1960s.
Editor: Not known.
Publisher: Not known.
Espacio was a regular space opera novel series not unlike some of the Italian "magazines" on which it may have been modeled; it may have been the Spanish edition of one of them. Further details are not available, but the publication may have run to over 200 issues.

FANTASTICA

Dates: 1948? (19 issues).
Editor: Not known.
Publisher: Not known.
This little-known magazine featured original Spanish stories.

FUTURO

Dates: 1953–1954 (34 issues).
Editor: Not known.
Publisher: Not known.
This was a regular series of short novellas translated from U.S. and U.K. sources.

ISAAC ASIMOV'S SF MAGAZINE

Editor: Not known.
Publisher: Piacazo Editores.
The Spanish edition of the U.S. magazine, it has direct translations from the U.S. issues, but the covers are by Esteban Maroto.

LUCHADORES DEL ESPACIO

Dates: 1950s?
Editor: Not known.
Publisher: Not known.
It has been reported as a companion of *Espacio*; no further details are known.

NUEVA DIMENSION

Dates: January 1968–.
Editor: Domingo Santos.
Publisher: Ediciones Nueva Dimension, Barcelona.
This is one of the world's premier SF magazines, and one of the most attractive. Each issue features stories, articles, news, notes and reviews. About two-thirds of the fiction is translated, mostly from American sources, but some original Spanish stories appear. The magazine has constantly had to battle against the authorities in Spain. The June 1970 issue, for instance, was seized by the State Police as representing a threat to security. At the 1972 Trieste SF Convention, the magazine received the award as the Best European Magazine. The title should be represented in all SF research collections. In late 1984, *Nueva Dimension* was reported to have ceased publication.

S.I.P.

Dates: ?–1962 (over 200 issues).
Editor: Not known.
Publisher: Not known.
This is a space opera novel series, probably translated from the Italian, and possibly a companion series to *Espacio*. It is included here for clarity, since it is sometimes reported as a magazine.

SWEDEN

Consultants: *John-Henri Holmberg and Sam Lundwall*

GALAXY

Dates: September 1958–June 1960 (19 issues).
Editor: Henrik Rabe.
Publisher: Not known.

The Swedish edition of the U.S. *Galaxy* featured one or two original Swedish stories per issue. It originated from the same publisher as the Swedish edition of *Mad Magazine*.

HÄPNA!

Dates: March 1954–January 1966; Winter–Autumn 1969 (137 numbers in 119 physical issues).
Editors: First series, Kjell Edstrom; second series, Sam Lundwall.
Publisher: First series, Kindberg, Jonkoping; second series, Lundwall Fakta & Fantasi.

Published as a labor of love by the brothers Kurt and Karl-Gustaf Kindberg, *Häpna!* was never a financial success. It ceased publication in 1966 due to the illness of Kurt Kindberg. Contents were predominantly U.S. stories, with some U.K. stories and a scattering of Swedish and Danish originals. Covers came from several sources, with *New Worlds* a favorite. *Häpna!* is important for having started Swedish SF fandom. The four "issues" dated 1969 were four pages (one folded A4 sheet) with reprinted items from the original *Häpna!* run. They were never widely distributed and were not available for sale. They existed solely to legally protect the title *Häpna!* for the publisher.

HUGIN

Dates: April 1916–December 1920 (82 issues).
Editor: Otto Witt.
Publisher: Hugin Forlag.

Sometimes claimed as the world's first SF magazine, this was almost totally the product of writer/editor/publisher Otto Witt. It featured articles, reviews, stories and novels on the theme of science in the future. It is historically important as an indication of the worldwide development of an interest in science and the fiction of science, but *Hugin* apparently had little influence on the development of SF as we know it. It is more accurately equated with Gernsback's "Experimenter" magazines, which also featured SF stories. The magazine was usually thirty-two pages in length and had a circulation of about 10,000 copies. It is now extremely rare, with only two sets believed to exist. One set is in the Swedish Royal Library, and the other, Witt's own file copy, is owned by Sam Lundwall.

JULES VERNE MAGASINET

Dates: October 1940–February 1947 (332 issues); May 1969–.
Editors: First series, Rolf Ahlgren; second series, Bertil Falk, 1969–1971; Sam Lundwall, 1972–.
Publishers: First series, not identified; second series, Falk, 1969–1971; Askild & Karnekul, 1972; Delta Forlag, Bromma, 1973–.

The first series was a weekly pulp magazine. It relied heavily on material from the American magazines and reprinted the entire Captain Future corpus, leading to the establishment of a solid core of Captain Future fans in Sweden. It also reprinted extensively from the Ziff-Davis magazines. Originally an attractive digest-sized ₁magazine, it changed to the pulp format. Among the SF material were occasional non-SF stories and articles. As the magazine continued, the ratio of SF to non-SF gradually decreased, until by the final year SF was a rarity on its pages. It also began featuring regular comic strips from U.S. sources, including Superman, Batman and Jungle Jim. Gradually the subtitle, "Veckans Aventyr," was superimposed over the main title. Concurrent with these changes was a gradual drop in circulation, finally resulting in the cessation of the magazine.

It was revived in 1969 by SF fan Bertil Falk as a quarterly fan magazine, but due to economics it was dropped in 1971. It was revived again in 1972 by Askild & Karnekul, who issued it as a thirty-six-page slick magazine. Sam Lundwall became editor, then purchased the magazine. In 1974 he changed the format to a large pocketbook style, with no cover artwork, and a more literary approach. Still quarterly, it relies mostly on reprints from *The Magazine of Fantasy and Science Fiction*, which are supplemented with columns, reviews and critical articles from Sweden and other sources. Circulation is approximately 2,500, and it is near its 400th issue.

NOVA SCIENCE FICTION

Dates: March 1982–.
Editors: John-Henri Holmberg and Per W. Insulander.
Publisher: Laissez faire produktion AB, Stockholm.

This magazine features translations from U.S. and U.K. sources, as well as original stories by Swedish authors. Quarterly 100–page issues appeared in 1982–1983.

TURKEY

ANTARES

Dates: March 1974–.
Editor: Sezar Erkin Ergin.
Publisher: Kultur Dergisi.

X-BILINMEYEN

Dates: April 1976–.
Editor: Selma Mine.
Publisher: Bahariye Kusukestamesi.
  Both these magazines appear to be more magazines about SF in all its forms than primarily fiction magazines. They do include some fiction from a variety of sources, and some Turkish fiction. *Antares* published only Turkish stories in its early issues. They provide the only existing focus for SF in Turkey.

U.S.S.R.

MIR PRIKLIUCHENII

Dates: 1910–1930.
  Sometimes reported as a "science fiction" magazine, *Mir Prikliuchenii* was more an adventure magazine like *Argosy* that sometimes carried SF. Willy Ley, in the February 1963 *Galaxy*, said:

The first science fiction magazine before World War I was Russian. It began in about 1903, and its title was *Mirpriklusheniya*, "The World of Adventures." The early issues, I have been told, consisted mainly of translations of Jules Verne, but with a sprinkling of Russian authors, one of whom was a lady specializing in interplanetary romances. The magazine still existed in 1923 (I have seen issues from that year) but it was apparently discontinued at a later date.

Research has now shown that the magazine did not, in fact, start until 1910. That date still places the magazine earlier than *Hugin* or *Kapitan Mors* but, as Ley himself later discovered, *Mir Prikliuchenii* was not an SF magazine. Sam Moskowitz, in correspondence, reports:

> *Mirpriklusheniya* was an adventure magazine like *The Argosy*, that also ran science fiction. There are copies in the Library of Congress. . . . In the twenties it sometimes had a cover illustrating a science fiction story, like the US but almost never more than one story or serial installment of a story in an issue.

In fact, Russia has never had a proper science fiction magazine, the nearest it has come being technical magazines like *Iskatel* and *Teknika-Molodezhi* that featured SF stories.

YUGOSLAVIA

Consultant: *Krsto Mazuranic*

Note: In addition to the magazines listed below, there is a bulky science fiction almanac called *Andromeda*, which has appeared three times since 1976. It features both SF and nonfiction, and is edited by Gavrilo Vućković for BIGZ in Beograd.

GALAKSIJA

Dates: April 1972–.
Editor: Gavrilo Vućković.
Publisher: BIGZ, Beograd.

Although this has been identified as a science fiction magazine, it is to all intents and purposes a popular science magazine, featuring astronomy, physics, ecology, history, occult and *ESP* material. It is, as its subtitle suggests, "the magazine for promoting science," and any SF it may carry is incidental. The misunderstanding is fostered by the use of colored futuristic artwork, including work by Ludek Pesek, Chesley Bonestell and some Soviet artists.

KOZMOPLOV

Dates: March 1969–June 15, 1970 (24 issues).
Editor: Gavrilo Vućković.
Publisher: Duga, Beograd.

Another borderline case, *Kozmoplov* was originally the green supplement to an entertainment magazine entitled *Duga* (''Rainbow''), so all its supplements were a different color. This supplement soon became ''The Magazine for Astronautics and Science Fiction,'' but only about 25 percent of its contents ever related to SF at best, and as time passed the SF content grew smaller. The format was similar to that of *Sirius*.

SIRIUS

Dates: July 1976–.
Editor: Borivoj Jurković.
Publisher: Vjesnik, Zagreb.

Sirius is Yugoslavia's first and only genuine SF magazine. It was the result of the efforts of SF fans there who organized an association, then collaborated with a major publisher to establish the new magazine. It sells about 30,000 copies per month and features short stories, mainly translations from the U.S., U.K., or U.S.S.R., plus occasional items from France and Germany. Contributions by Yugoslav writers have steadily increased, and the country now has a promising stable of SF writers. A special issue, *YU-Sirius*, featured only Yugoslav writers.

Index to Major Cover Artists

Most publishers know that it is the cover that sells the magazine—initially. Thereafter the quality of the magazine and its contents sustains that sale, but it is the cover that first catches the eye. The title and an author's name may have an additional effect, but they are secondary to that first impact of the artwork. The cover artist, therefore, has a significant part to play in publishing and marketing, and in the SF field this is of a singular quality. While most magazines can rely simply on the photo of a pretty girl on the cover, and while specialist magazines dealing with subjects like gardening, computers or concurrent affairs will have equally relevant covers, the SF magazine has to achieve much more. Not only must it indicate the contents of the magazine by its cover, but its cover must also present to a potential reader an image of something that does not exist in the world as we know it. The picture must be entirely conjectural and totally imaginative.

The SF artist is thus a specialist without equal. He must have a mastery of technical, astronomical and animate drawing skills, must have sufficient scientific knowledge to make the drawing reasonably accurate, and must have a vivid imagination. Such combinations are rare—even among SF artists!

Most book and magazine artists have had a raw deal. Their work is seldom acknowledged or credited. In the SF field, however, many of the artists are recognized for their abilities and are frequently credited. The following index attempts to detail all identifiable cover artists. Where an artist has not been credited, an attempt has been made to identify his work, but this has not always been possible. I have not listed artists for the non-SF associational magazines such as *Argosy* or *The Black Cat*. Neither have I detailed reprinted covers. I have also restricted the list to those artists who have painted more than one cover—there are many who appeared just once and vanished—unless the artist is well known.

The details included are the artist's name, followed by the magazine issue of his first cover. Beneath are listed all magazines for which he has painted covers and the number of covers (as of December 1984).

ACHILLEOS, CHRIS [*Galaxy* Jul/Aug 73]

ADKINS, DAN L. [*If* Oct 66]
    If 3; *Amazing* 2; *Galaxy* 1; *Fantastic* 1

ADRAGNA, ROBERT [*Fantastic* Dec 62]
   Fantastic 3; *Amazing* 2

AINSWORTH, K. P. [*Uncanny Tales* (Canadian) Mar 42]
   Uncanny Tales 6

ALEJANDRO. See CANEDO, ALEJANDRO

ALEXANDER, PAUL [*Asimov's* Jan/Feb 78]
   Asimov's SF Adventure 3; *Asimov's* 1

ANDERSON, ALLEN [*Planet Stories* Win 42]
   Planet Stories 31; *2 Complete Science Adv.* 7

ANDERSON, DARREL [*Eternity* 2, 1973]
   Eternity 4

ANGELINI, GEORGE [*Analog* Apr 27, 1981]
   Asimov's 4; *Analog* 2

ARBIB, RICHARD [*Galaxy* Oct 51]
   Galaxy 2

ARFSTROM, JON [*Weird Tales* Jan 52]
   Weird Tales 3

BARBER, THOMAS, JR. [*Amazing Stories* Mar 76]
   Galileo 5; *Amazing* 4; *Weird Tales* 4; *Unearth* 1

BARLOWE, WAYNE [*Fantastic* Jul 80]
   Analog 7; *Asimov's* 7; *Fantastic* 1

BARR, GEORGE [*Fantastic* Apr 62]
   Asimov's 4; *Fantastic* 2; *Forgotten Fantasy* 1; *Amazing* 1

BARR, KENNETH J. [*Nebula* Aug 58]
   Nebula 3

BASH, KENT [*F & SF* Oct 80]
   F & SF 2; *Amazing* 1

BAUMHOFER, WALTER [*Doc Savage* Mar 33]
   Doc Savage 43; *Dime Mystery* 27 +

BEAR, GREG D. [*F & SF* Aug 76]
   F & SF 1; *Galaxy* 1

BEEKMAN, DOUG [*Amazing* Sep 76]
   Analog 4; *Amazing* 1; *Fantastic* 1

BELARSKI, RUDOLPH [*Terence X. O'Leary's War Birds* 1935]
   Startling Stories 8; *Thrilling Wonder* 7; *Orbit* 5(?); *Captain Future* 2; *Future* 1;
   T. X. O'Leary's War Birds ?; *Thrilling Mystery* ?

BERGER, DAVID [*Horror Stories* Dec 36/Jan 37]
   Dime Mystery ?; *Horror Stories* ?

BERGEY, EARLE K. [*Strange Stories* Aug 39]
   Thrilling Wonder 59; *Startling Stories* 58; *Captain Future* 13; *Fantastic Story
   Mag.* 8; *Strange Stories* 7; *Future* 2; *Space SF* 2; *Space Stories* 1; *SF Adventures*
   1; *Avon SF Reader* 1

BERRY D. BRUCE [*Imaginative Tales* May 58]
    Imag. Tales 1; *Weirdbook* 1

BERRY, PHIL [*Fantastic* Jan 59]
    Amazing 1; *Fantastic* 1; *If* 1

BIERLEY, JOHN [*Fantastic* Feb 77]
    Fantastic 1 (but not *Amazing* Mar 77 as credited)

BINDER, JACK [*Astonishing* Feb 40]
    Astonishing 2; *Super Science Stories* 1; *SF Quarterly* 1

BIRMINGHAM, LLOYD [*Fantastic* Nov 61]
    Amazing 10; *Fantastic* 8; *Analog* 2

BLAISDELL, PAUL [*Spaceway* Jun 54]
    Spaceway 5; *Other Worlds* 3; *F & SF* 1

BLAKESLEE, FREDERICK [*G-8* 1933]
    G-8 ?; *Dusty Ayres* 12

BLAMIRE, LARRY [*Galileo* 8, May 78]
    Galileo 3; *Galaxy* 1

BLANDFORD, E. L. [*Authentic* Apr 56]
    Authentic 8 [Note: E. L. Blandford may be an alias of John Mortimer, but this has not been verified.]

BOAS, MARCUS [*Fantastic* Oct 75]

BODE, VAUGHN [*If* Nov 67]
    If 6; *Galaxy* 3; *Amazing* (with Larry Todd) 3; *F & SF* 1; *Fantastic* (with Todd) 1

BOK, HANNES [*Weird Tales* Dec 39]
    Weird Tales 8; *Future* 4; *Other Worlds* 4; *Fantasy Fiction* 4; *Fantastic Universe* 4; *SF Quarterly* 3; *Stirring* 3; *Imagination* 2; *Marvel SF* 2; *Cosmic* 1; *Planet* 1; *Space SF* 1; *Science Stories* 1; *F & SF* 1; *If* 1; *Bizarre* (1941) 1

BONESTELL, CHESLEY [*Astounding* Oct 47]
    F & SF 38; *Astounding/Analog* 12; *Galaxy* 2

BOYLE, BRIAN [*Galaxy* Sep/Oct 72]
    Galaxy 8; *If* 5

BRADSHAW, M. [*New Worlds* Apr 55]
    New Worlds 5; *SF Adventures* 2

BRAND, T. [*Thrills, Inc.* 1]
    Thrills, Inc. 12 (2 reprinted on *Amazing Science Stories*)

BRAUTIGAM, DON [*Destinies* Nov/Dec 78]
    Destinies 1; *Asimov's* 1

BROSNATCH, ANDREW [*Weird Tales* Nov 24]
    Weird Tales 15

BROWN, HOWARD V. [*Astounding* Oct 33]
    Astounding 53; *Thrilling Wonder* 28; *Startling Stories* 9

BRUNDAGE, MARGARET [*Oriental Stories* Spr 32]
    Weird Tales 66; *Oriental Stories* 6; *Golden Fleece* 2

BRUNO, FRANK [*Fantastic* Apr 63]
    Fantastic 2; *Worlds of Tomorrow* 1

BULL, REINA M. [*New Worlds* Aut 51]
    New Worlds 2; *Science Fantasy* 2

BUNCH, JOHN [*Galaxy* Jan 51]
    Galaxy 2

BURGE, JERRY [*Witchcraft & Sorcery* Jan 71]
    Witchcraft & Sorcery 3

BURLESON, JOE [*Asimov's* Feb 15, 1982]
    Asimov's 7; *Twilight Zone*, 2

BURR, LINDA [*Asimov's* Jul 83]
    Asimov's 2

CAESARI, VICTOR [*New Worlds* 2, 1946]
    New Worlds 1; *Supernatural Stories* 1

CALDWELL, CLYDE [*Space & Time* 17, Nov 72]
    Unearth 3; *Questar* 1; *Space & Time* 1

CAMPANILE, DARIO [*F & SF* May 75]
    F & SF 2

CANEDO, ALEJANDRO [*Astounding* Dec 46]
    Astounding 10

CARTER, HUBERT [*Mag. of Horror* Sum 66]
    Mag. of Horror 2; *Startling Mystery Stories* 1

CARTIER, EDD [*Unknown* Dec 39]
    Unknown 4; *Astounding* 1; *Doc Savage* 1

CASTELLON, HECTOR [*Amazing* Dec 65]
    If 2; *Amazing* 1; *F & SF* 1

CASTENIR, RALPH [*Amazing* Sep 54]
    Amazing 1; *Fantastic* 1

CAVANAGH, RALPH [*Thrills, Inc.* 14]
    Thrills, Inc. 4

CAWTHORN, JIM [*Science Fantasy* Oct 62]
    Science Fantasy 2; *New Worlds* 2

CHADWICK, PAUL [*F & SF* Mar 81]
    F & SF 5

CHAFFÉE, DOUG [*Galaxy* Apr 67]
    If 5; *Galaxy* 3; *Fantastic* 2; *Worlds of Tomorrow* 1; *Amazing* 1

CHARETTE, JOHN [*Dragonbane* Spr 78]
    Space & Time 2; *Dragonbane* 1; *Dark Fantasy* 1

CHATTO, KEITH [*Future* (Aus) No. 1]
    Future 2; *Popular SF* 2 (Both Australian)

CIVILETTI/CIVILLITTI [*Space SF* Sep 53]
    Space 1; *Rocket* 1

CLEWELL, ROBERT [*Startling Mystery* Spr 70]
Mag. of Horror 2; *Startling Mystery* 1

CLOTHIER, ROBERT [*New Worlds* 5, 1949]
New Worlds 10; *Nebula* 6

COGGINS, JACK [*Galaxy* May 52]
Galaxy 9; *Thrilling Wonder* 6; *F & SF* 4; *Fantastic Story Mag.* 2; *Startling Stories* 1; *SF Quarterly* 1

CONKLIN, BRUCE S. [*Dark Fantasy* 18, Dec 78]
Dark Fantasy 1; *Space & Time* 2

CONRAD, RUPERT [*Fantastic* Jul/Aug 53]
Beyond 2; *Fantastic* 1

CORBEN, RICHARD [*F & SF* Sep 67]
F & SF 1; *Ariel* 1

COX, AL B. [*Fantasy & Terror* 6, 1974]
Fantasy & Terror 1; *Weirdbook* 2

COYE, LEE BROWN [*Weird Tales* Jul 45]
Weird Tales 10; *Whispers* 2; *Fantastic* 1; *Toadstool Wine* 1

CRAWFORD, ROBERT [*Asimov's* Apr 13, 1981]
Asimov's 3; *Analog* 2

CROZETTI, LORA [*Fantasy Book* 2, 1947]
Fantasy Book 2

DALZELL, BONNIE [*F & SF* Apr 76, with R. Sternbach]
Galaxy 2; *F & SF* 1

DAVIDSON, KEVIN [*Vertex* Jun 73]
Vertex 2

DAVIES, GORDON C. [*Wonders of the Spaceways* 5, 1952]
Authentic 3 + ; *Tales of Tomorrow* 3; *Worlds of Fantasy* 3; *Futuristic Science Stories* 1; *Wonders of the Spaceways* 1

DAVIS, DON [*Amazing* Sep 72]
Amazing 3; *F & SF* 2; *Vertex* 1

DAVIS, JACK [*Shock* May 60]
Shock 3

DAVIS, ROGER [*Weird World* No. 1, 1955]
Weird World 2 [Note: may be the same "Davis" who illustrated *Authentic* and is suspected as being a pseudonym for John Richards.]

DAY, DAN [*Space & Time* Oct 79]
Space & Time 2; *Dark Fantasy* 1

DAY, GENE [*Dark Fantasy* Jun 73]
Dark Fantasy 10; *Space & Time* 1

DE SOTO, RAFAEL M. [*Ace Mystery*, Sep 36]
Spider 44; *Fantastic Novels* 2; *Famous Fantastic Mysteries* 1; *Ace Mystery* 1; *Operator #5* 1

DEAN, MAL [*New Worlds* Oct 68]
  New Worlds 4; *Other Times* 1

DELAY, HAROLD S. [*Golden Fleece* Oct 38]
  Golden Fleece 6; *Weird Tales* 4

DEMBER [*Galaxy* Mar 58]
  Galaxy 12; *Worlds of Tomorrow* 2; *If* 2

DICKISON, LARRY [*Copper Toadstool* Jun 79]
  Copper Toadstool 1; *Dark Fantasy* 1

DiFATE, VINCENT [*Analog* Nov 69]
  Analog 22; *Asimov's* 4; *Destinies* 2; *F & SF* 2; *Amazing* 1; *Cosmos* 1; *Galaxy* 1;
  Vertex 1; *Whispers* 1

DILLON, LEO and DIANE [*F & SF* Aug 72]
  F & SF 2

DIXON, DON [*F & SF* Jun 74]
  F & SF 2

DOLD, ELLIOTT [*Miracle Stories* Apr/May 31]
  Miracle 2; *Cosmic Stories* 1

DOLGOV, BORIS [*Weird Tales* Nov 46]
  Weird Tales 5

DOLLENS, MORRIS SCOTT [*F & SF* Nov 57]
  Spaceway 4; *Gamma* 3; *F & SF* 1; *Fantastic* 1; *Venture* 1

DOOLIN, JOSEPH [*Weird Tales* Dec 25]
  Weird Tales 2

DOORE, CLARENCE [*Fantastic Universe* Mar 54]
  Amazing Stories 2; *Fantastic Universe* 2; *SF Adventures* 1

DOWLING, LELA [*Rigel* Fall 81]
  Rigel 1; *Fantasy Book* 1

DRAKE, A. [*Planet Stories* Win 39]
  Planet Stories 5

DREW, JOHN [*Horror Stories* Feb/Mar 37]
  Horror Stories ?; *Terror Tales* ?; *Dime Mystery*?

DRIGIN, SERGE R. [*Scoops* Feb 10, 1934]
  Scoops 20; *Fantasy* 3

DUILLO, JOHN [*Fantastic* May 60]
  Fantastic 2

DURANT, CHARLES [*The Thrill Book* Jul 15, 1919]
  Thrill Book 2

DWOSKIN, STEPHEN [*New Worlds* Apr 68]
  New Worlds 2

EAGLESON, DUNCAN [*F & SF* Mar 82]
  F & SF 3

EASLEY, JEFF [*Chacal* Win 76]
  Chacal 2; *Amazing* 1

EBEL, ALEX [*Space SF* Feb 53]
  Space SF 2; *Fantastic Story Mag.* 1

EBERLE, JOSEPH [*Weird Tales* Mar 52]
  Weird Tales 2

EDWARDS, BILL [*Weird Tales* Win 73]
  Weird Tales 2

ELLIS, DEAN [*Analog* Nov 77]
  Analog 4; *Destinies* 2; *Amazing* 1; *Universe* 1

EMBLETON, RON [*Futuristic Science Stories* 13, 1953]
  Futuristic Science Stories 3

EMSHWILLER, EDWARD [*Galaxy* Jun 51]
  F & SF 71; *Galaxy* 46; *Science Fiction Stories* 25; *Infinity* 19; *Future* 18; *Amazing Stories* 10; *SF Quarterly* 10; *Fantastic* 10; *Super Science Fiction* 9; *Astounding* 8; *Startling Stories* 8; *SF Adventures* (2nd) 8; *Venture* 8; *Fantastic Universe* 6; *If* 6; *Thrilling Wonder* 3; *Space Stories* 3; *Fantastic Story Mag.* 2; *Satellite* 2; *SF Adventures* (1st) 1; *Rocket Stories* 1; *Wonder Story Annual* 1; *Vanguard* 1

ENGLE, ROBERT V. [*Infinity* Nov 55]
  Infinity 1; *SF Adventures* 1

EPPERLY, R. R. [*Weird Tales* Mar 23]
  Weird Tales 1; *Fantastic Adventures* 1

FABIAN, STEPHEN E. [*Eternity* 1, Jul 72]
  Galaxy 11; *Fantastic* 11; *Amazing* 10; *Whispers* 3; *Eternity* 2; *Asimov's* 2; *Weirdbook* 5; *Fantasy Tales* 2; *Asimov's Adventure* 1; *Witchcraft & Sorcery* 1; *Sword & Sorcery Annual* 1; *Dark Fantasy* 1; *Fantasy Book* 1

FACEY, GERALD [*Futuristic Science Stories* 1, 1950]
  Worlds of Fantasy 4; *Supernatural Stories* 4; *Futuristic Science Stories* 3; *Tales of Tomorrow* 2; *Wonders of the Spaceways* 1

FAGG, KENNETH [*If* Mar 53]
  If 12

FARLEY, G. M. [*Weirdbook* 2, 1969]
  Weirdbook 4

FINLAY, VIRGIL [*Weird Tales* Feb 37]
  Famous Fantastic Mysteries 27; *Fantastic Universe* 25; *Weird Tales* 20; *Fantastic Novels* 7; *Galaxy* 6; *If* 3; *Super Science Stories* 3; *Other Worlds* 3; *Future* 2; *Amazing* 2; *Worlds of Tomorrow* 2; *Astonishing* 1; *Astounding* 1; *Planet Stories* 1; *Science Stories* 1; *Universe* 1; *Science Fiction Stories* 1

FITZGERALD, RUSSELL [*F & SF* May 68]
  F & SF 2

FORTE, JOHN R., Jr. [*Future* Aug 41]
  Future 4

FOSS, CHRIS [*Amazing Stories* Aug 80]

FOX, H. [*Supernatural Stories* 11, 1957]
  Supernatural Stories 66

FOX, MATT [*Weird Tales* Nov 44]
> *Weird Tales* 11

FRANK[enberg], ROBERT [*Fantastic* Jan/Feb 53]
> *Fantastic* 1; *Amazing* 1

FRAZETTA, FRANK [*Ariel* 2, 1977]
> *Ariel* 1; *Questar* 1

FREAS, FRANK KELLY [*Weird Tales* Nov 50]
> *Astounding/Analog* 112; *Planet Stories* 11; *F & SF* 11; *Super Science Fiction* 9; *Science Fiction Stories* 8; *Fantastic Universe* 7; *SF Quarterly* 5; *2 Complete Science Adv.* 4; *Future* 4; *If* 4; *Weird Tales* 3; *Asimov's* 2; *Amazing* 3; *Tops in SF* 1; *Satellite* 1; *Haunt of Horror* 1; *Odyssey* 1; *Galaxy* 1; *Galileo* 1; *SF Monthly* 1

FREFF [*Galaxy* Jan 75 (with W. Pini)]
> *Galaxy* 2

FUQUA, ROBERT (real name Joseph Tillotson) [*Amazing* Oct 38]
> *Amazing* 26; *Fantastic Adventures* 8

GARLAND, MICHAEL [*F & SF* Dec 82]
> *F & SF* 2

GARRISON, JIM [*Space & Time* 23, Mar 74]
> *Space & Time* 1; *Weirdbook* 1; *Fantasy & Terror* 1

GAUGHAN, JACK [*Fantasy Book* 6, 1950]
> *Galaxy* 38; *If* 29; *F & SF* 21; *Analog* 15; *Asimov's* 7; *Worlds of Fantasy* 4; *Worlds of Tomorrow* 3; *Cosmos* 2; *International SF* 2; *Fantasy Book* 1; *Fantastic* 1; *Odyssey* 1

GELOTTE, MARK [*Space & Time* 9, Jul 1970]
> *Space & Time* 8; *Fantasy & Terror* 1

GIBBONS, GEORGE A. [*F & SF* Aug 52]
> *F & SF* 3

GILBERT, MIKE [*F & SF* Feb 70]
> *F & SF* 1; *Analog* 1; *If* 1

GILDEA, STEVE [*Unearth* Win 77]
> *Unearth* 2

GILMORE [*Astounding* Dec 39]
> *Astounding* 2

GIUNTA, JOHN [*Weird Tales* Mar 44]
> *Saturn* 5?; *Weird Tales* 3

GLADNEY, GRAVES [*Dime Mystery* Apr 38]
> *Shadow* 60; *Astounding* 4; *Unknown* 3; *Dime Mystery* 1+

GORDON, DONNA [*Dragonfields* 3, Sum 80]
> *Dragonfields,* 2

GURNEY, JAMES [*F & SF* Apr 83]
> *F & SF* 3

GUTIERREZ, ALAN [*Rigel* Win 82]
> *Rigel* 5; *Fantasy Book* 1

HAMMEL, TIM [*Dark Fantasy* May 76]
  Copper Toadstool 4; *Dark Fantasy* 3

HARDY, DAVID [*Vision of Tomorrow* Mar 70]
  F & SF 37; *Analog* 3; *If* 3; *Vision of Tomorrow* 2; *Ad Astra* 1; *Amazing* 1; *Galaxy* 1; *SF Monthly* 1

HARRIS, ROGER [*Science Fantasy* Jun/Jul 64]
  Science Fantasy 3

HARTMAN, C. L. [*Amazing* Feb 40]
  Amazing 2

HEALY, JOHN [*Gamma* Feb 65]
  Gamma 2

HICKMAN, STEVE [*Fantastic* May 76]
  Fantastic 1; *Amazing* 1 (Mar 77, not as credited); *Destinies* 1

HIGGINS, DAVID [*Ad Astra* 1, 1978]
  Ad Astra 2

HINGE, MIKE [*Amazing* Nov 70]
  Amazing 8; *Analog* 5; *Fantastic* 2

HINTON, WALTER HASKELL [*Fantastic Adventures* Aug 48]
  Fantastic Adventures 2; *Imagination* 1

HOWETT, JOHN NEWTON [*Terror Tales* Oct 34]
  Terror Tales 23 + ; *Operator 5* ?; *Horror Stories* 16 +

HUGHES, BILL [*Forgotten Fantasy* Oct 70]
  Forgotten Fantasy 3

HUNT, STEVEN [*Asimov's* mid-Dec 83]
  Asimov's 2

HUNTER, ALAN [*Nebula* Aut 52]
  Nebula 2

HUNTER, MEL [*Galaxy* Feb 53]
  F & SF 31; *If* 15; *Galaxy* 12; *Fantastic Universe* 7; *Spaceway* 3; *Satellite* 3; *Amazing* 2; *SF Adventures* 1; *Universe* 1

ISIP, M. [*Unknown* Mar 40]
  Unknown 2

JAKUBOWICZ [*New Worlds* Sep/Oct 64]
  New Worlds 2

JOINER, RALPH [*If* May 52]
  If 3

JONES, EDDIE [*Nebula* Nov 58]
  Vision of Tomorrow 4; *Nebula* 3; *Vortex* 2; *Supernatural Stories* 1; *Alien Worlds* 1; *F & SF* 1

JONES, JEFF [*Fantastic* Apr 70]
  Amazing 5; *Fantastic* 4; *Witchcraft & Sorcery* 1; *Galileo* 1

JONES, ROBERT GIBSON [*Fantastic Adventures* Aug 42]
Fantastic Adventures 46; *Amazing* 43; *Other Worlds* 6; *Universe* 4; *Science Stories* 1; *Mystic* 1

JORDAN, SYDNEY [*New Worlds* Jan 61]
New Worlds 3

KALUTA, MICHAEL W. [*Fantastic* Dec 70]
Fantastic 3

KATO, GARY [*Space & Time* 26, Sep 74]
Space & Time 5

KEITH, GABE [*Fantastic* Oct 58]
Fantastic 4; *Amazing* 1

KENNEDY CHARLES A. [*Weird Tales* Jan 51]
Weird Tales 2

KIDD, THOMAS [*Amazing* Jul 83]
Analog 3; *F & SF* 2; *Amazing* 1

KIDWELL, CARL [*Mag. of Horror* Aug 65]
Mag. of Horror 2; *Startling Mystery* 1

KIRBY, JOSH [*Authentic* Mar 57]
Authentic 6; *Vertex* 1

KIRK, TIM [*Forgotten Fantasy* Apr 71]
Whispers 2; *Forgotten Fantasy* 1

KOFOED, KARL [*Asimov's* Jun 79]
Asimov's 4

KOHN, ARNOLD [*Fantastic Adventures* Jul 45]
Amazing 13; *Fantastic Adventures* 9; *Other Worlds* 1

KOSZOWSKI, ALLEN [*Space & Time* Mar 77]
Space & Time 4

KRAMER, VERNON [*Fantastic* Nov/Dec 53]
Fantastic 8; *Amazing* 1

KRENKEL, ROY G. [*Weirdbook* 11, 1977]

KRUPA, JULIAN S. [*Amazing* Jun 40]
Amazing 6 (also in reissues of *Amazing Quarterly*)

KRUPOWICZ, R. J. [*F & SF* Sep 83]
F & SF 2

KRUSZ, ARTHUR [*Beyond* May 54]
Beyond 2

KUHLHOFF, PETE [*Weird Tales* May 45]
Weird Tales 3

KURKA, ANTON [*If* Jan 53]
If 3

LAKEY, VAL (now Val Lakey Lindahn) [*Analog* Feb 1, 1982]
Analog 5; *Asimov's* 5; *Twilight Zone* 1

MAITZ, DON [*F & SF* Jan 83]

MALLY, R. M. [*Weird Tales* Jun 23]
Weird Tales 9

MALONEY, TERRY [*New Worlds* Mar 56]
New Worlds 19; *Science Fantasy* 7; *SF Adventures* 4 [Note: Includes work under aliases "Jarr" and Jose Rubios.]

MANSO, LEO [*Avon SF & Fantasy Reader* Jan 53]
Avon SF & Fantasy Reader 2

MAROTO, ESTEBAN [*Fantastic* Apr 73]
Fantastic 2

MARTIN, BOB [*Planet Stories* Sum 46]
Planet Stories 3

MATTHEWS, RODNEY [*Vortex* Jan 77]
Vortex 3

MATTINGLY, DAVID [*Questar* Feb 80]
Amazing Stories 2; *Asimov's* 2; *Questar* 1; *F & SF* 1

MAVOR, ELINOR [*Fantastic* Apr 79]
Fantastic 4; *Amazing* 3

MAYORGA, GABRIEL [*Super Science Stories* May 40]
Astonishing 3; *Super Science Stories* 1; *Thrilling Wonder* 1

MAZEY and SCHELL [*F & SF* Nov 74]
F & SF 6

MELTZER, DAVIS [*Universe* 1, 1971]
Universe 1; *Destinies* 1

MERCER, RALPH [*Twilight Zone* Sep 81]
Twilight Zone 2

MILLER, IAN [*Amazing Stories* Sep 81]
Amazing 2; *Interzone* 2

MILLER, RON [*Amazing* Apr 74]
Amazing 1; *Analog* 1; *Galileo* 1; *Fantastic* 1

MILLER, WALT [*Astounding* Jun 50]
Astounding 6

MOLL, JOHN B. [*Mind Magic* Aug 31]
Mind Magic/Myself 3

MOORE, CHRIS [*Ad Astra* 6, 1979]
Ad Astra 2

MOREY, LEO [*Amazing Stories* Feb 30]
Amazing 77; *Amazing Quarterly* 12; *Comet* 3; *Astonishing* 2; *Super Science Stories* 2; *Future* 2; *Cosmic Stories* 1; *Fantastic Adventures* 1; *Stirring Science Stories* 1; *SF Quarterly* 1

MOROL, AGOSTA [*Science Fantasy* Mar 65]
Science Fantasy 2; *Impulse* 1

MORRILL, ROWENA [*Amazing Stories* Nov 81]

MORROW, GRAY [*Worlds of Tomorrow* Jun 64]
  Perry Rhodan 100 + ; *If* 14; *Galaxy* 9; *F & SF* 8; *Fantastic* 7; *Worlds of Tomorrow*
  5; *Amazing* 3; *Mag. of Horror* 1; *Haunt of Horror* 1

MORTIMER, JOHN E. [*Authentic* Mar 56]
  Authentic 4

MOSKOVITZ, HARRY S. [*Mind Magic* Jun 31]
  Mind Magic/Myself 3

MULFORD, STOCKTON [*Fantastic Adventures* May 40]
  Fantastic Adventures 2; *Amazing* 1

NASEMANN, GABI [*New Worlds* Nov 68]
  New Worlds 6

NAYLOR, RAMON [*Amazing Stories* Jan 48]
  Fantastic Adventures 2; *Amazing* 1

NAZZ, JAMES [*Asimov's* Sep 82; *Twilight Zone* Sep 82]

NICOLSON, JOHN [*Tales of Wonder* 1, 1937]
  Tales of Wonder 8

NOBLE, LARRY [*Asimov's* Oct 26, 1981]
  Asimov's 1; *Analog* 1

NUETZELL, ALBERT A. [*Science Stories* Feb 54]
  Amazing 7; *Fantastic* 2; *Science Stories* 1; *F & SF* 1

ORBAN, PAUL [*Astounding* Dec 48]
  Astounding 4; *Space SF* 1; *Future SF* 1; *SF Stories* 1

OUGHTON, TAYLOR [*Amazing Stories* Jun 59]
  Amazing 1; *Fantastic* 1

PALLADINI, DAVID [*F & SF* Apr 77]
  F & SF 2

PALMER, DELOS [*Ghost Stories* Feb 28]
  Ghost Stories 7

PARKE, WALTER [*Fantastic Adventures* Feb 46]
  Amazing 1; *Fantastic Adventures* 1

PARKHURST, H. [*Planet Stories* Fall 44]
  Planet 7

PASTOR, TERRY [*Ad Astra* 5, 1979]
  Ad Astra 2

PAUL, FRANK R. [*Amazing Stories* Apr 26]
  (Science) Wonder Stories 77; *Amazing Stories* 40; *(Science) Wonder Quarterly*
  14; *Science Fiction* 12; *Air Wonder* 11; *Amazing Quarterly* 7; *SF Plus* 4; *Famous*
  Fantastic Mysteries 3; *SF Quarterly* 3; *Comet* 2; *Future* 2; *Amazing Annual* 1;
  Dynamic Science Stories 1; *Scientific Detective* 1; *Marvel Science Stories* 1; *Fan-*
  tastic Adventures 1; *Planet Stories* 1; *Fantastic Novels* 1; *Satellite* 1

PAWELKA, GORDON [*Astounding* Mar 52]
  Astounding 4

PEDERSON, JOHN Jr. [*Galaxy* May 57]
  Galaxy 12; *If* 12; *Amazing* 5; *F & SF* 3; *Worlds of Tomorrow* 2; *Fantastic* 1
PENNINGTON, BRUCE [*SF Monthly* 4, 1974]
  SF Monthly 7
PERL, H. W. [*Strange Tales* Feb 46]
  Strange Adventures 2; *Futuristic Stories* 2; *Strange Tales* 1
PETILLO, ROBERT [*Fantastic* Oct 80]
  Fantastic 1; *Amazing* 1
PETRIE, C. BARKER Jr. [*Weird Tales* Feb 26]
  Weird Tales 6
PHILLIPS, BARYE W. [*Amazing Stories* Mar 52]
  Amazing 4; *Fantastic* 2
PIERARD, JOHN W. [*Ares*, Mar 81]
  Ares 3
PINI, WENDY [*Galaxy* Jul 74]
  Galaxy 8; *If* 1
PIOCH, RAY [*Satellite* Mar 59]
  Satellite 2
PITT, STANLEY [*Thrills Inc.* 21, 1952]
  Selected SF 5; *Thrills Inc.* 2; *Vision of Tomorrow* 2
PITTS, JIM [*Fantasy Tales* 1, 1977]
  Fantasy Tales 6
POPP, WALTER [*Amazing Stories* Jun 52]
  Startling Stories 6; *Amazing* 5; *Fantastic Adventures* 5; *Thrilling Wonder* 4; *Fantastic Story Mag.* 2; *Space Stories* 1
POULTON, PETER [*Future* Nov 51]
  Future 2
POWERS, RICHARD M. [*Galaxy* Feb 52]
  Galaxy 2; *Beyond* 2; *Analog* 2; *Fantastic* 1; *Star* 1
QUIGLEY, RAY [*Weird Tales* Dec 38]
  Weird Tales 3
QUINN, GERARD [*New Worlds* Jan 52]
  New Worlds 36; *Science Fantasy* 24; *Nebula* 3; *SF Adventures* 3; *Vision of Tomorrow* 2; *Extro* 2
RAE, G. M. [*Uncanny Tales* (Canadian) May 42]
  Uncanny Tales 2
RAINEY, D. [*Supernatural Stories* 37, Nov 60]
  Supernatural Stories 10
RANEY, KEN [*Space & Time* 31, Jul 75]
  Space & Time 2; *Dark Fantasy* 1
RANKIN, HUGH [*Weird Tales* Aug 27]
  Weird Tales 15

RATTIGAN, JAMES [*Nebula* Dec 54]
   Nebula 6

REISENBERG, SIDNEY [*The Thrill Book* Mar 1, 1919]
   Thrill Book 10

REMBACH, WILLIAM. See VALIGURSKY, ED

RICHARDS, JOHN [*Authentic* 30, Feb 53]
   Authentic 27; *Vargo Statten* 11 [Note: Includes work under the presumed alias "Davis."]

RITTER, BOB [*If* Jan 61]
   If 1; *Galaxy* 1

RIVOCHE, PAUL [*Stardust* 9, 1979]
   Stardust 2

ROBERTS, KEITH [*Science Fantasy* Jan 65]
   Impulse 10; *Science Fantasy* 5; *New Worlds* 6

ROBERTS, W. J. [*Tales of Wonder* Sum 38]
   Tales of Wonder 6; *Fireside Ghost Stories* 1; *Tales of Ghosts & Haunted Houses* 1

ROGERS, HUBERT [*Astounding* Feb 39]
   Astounding 58; *Super Science Stories* 1

ROGNAN, LLOYD [*Imaginative Tales* Nov 55]
   Imaginative Tales 10; *Imagination* 8

ROLAND, HARRY [*Fantastic* Jul 73]
   Fantastic 3

ROMERO, EDWARD ART [*Space & Time* 16, Aug 72]
   Eternity 4; *Space & Time* 1

ROSS, A. LESLIE [*Future* Jul 52]
   Future 3; *SF Quarterly* 2; *Dynamic* 1

ROTH, JAMES [*F & SF* Aug 64]
   F & SF 2

ROZEN, GEORGE [*Captain Future* Win 40]
   Shadow 198; *Planet Stories* 3; *Doc Savage* 3; *Captain Future* 1

RUGER, Jno [*Scientific Detective Monthly* Jan 30]
   Scientific Detective/Amazing Detective 7

RUTH, ROD [*Fantastic Adventures* Aug 41]
   Fantastic Adventures 3; *Amazing* 1

ST. JOHN, J. ALLEN [*Oriental Stories* Win 32]
   Amazing Stories 13; *Fantastic Adventures* 11; *Weird Tales* 9; *Oriental Stories/ Magic Carpet* 2; *Other Worlds* 1; *Mystic* 1

SALOMANI, TITO [*Questar* Jun 81]
   Twilight Zone 3; *Questar* 1

SALRAN, B. [*Cosmos* Sep 53]
   Cosmos 3

SALTER, GEORGE [*F & SF* Win/Spr 50]
   F & SF 9

SANCHEZ, JOHN M. [*Analog* Apr 79]
  Analog 2

SAUNDERS, NORMAN [*Ace Mystery* May/Jun 36]
  Famous Fantastic Mysteries 5; *Marvel* 5; *Mysterious Traveler* 5; *A. Merritt's Fantasy* 4; *Fantastic Novels* 3; *Eerie Mysteries* 4; *Secret Agent X* 3+; *Uncanny Tales* 3?; *Mystery Adventure* 3?; *Ace Mystery* 2; *Amazing Stories* 1; *Captain Hazzard* 1; *Dynamic Science Stories* 1; *Eerie Stories* 1; *Planet Stories* 1; *Super Science Stories* 1; *Uncanny Stories* 1 and probably many more

SAVIUK, ALEX [*Space & Time* 2, Fall 67]
  Space & Time 7

SCHELL. See MAZEY and SCHELL

SCHELLING, GEORGE L. [*Amazing Stories* May 62]
  Worlds of Tomorrow 5; *Fantastic* 3; *If* 3; *Galaxy* 3; *Amazing* 2; *Analog* 1; *Cosmos* 1

SCHMAND, RICHARD (sometimes listed as Robert Schmand) [*Startling Mystery* Sum 69]
  Startling Mystery 3; *Mag. of Horror* 2; *Weird Terror Tales* 1

SCHNEEMAN, CHARLES [*Astounding* May 38]
  Astounding 6

SCHOENHERR, JOHN [*SF Adventures* Jan 58]
  Analog 75; *SF Adventures* 1; *Galileo* 1

SCHOMBURG, ALEX [*Thrilling Wonder* Oct 51]
  Amazing Stories 19; *Fantastic Universe* 10; *Fantastic Story Mag.* 8; *Startling Stories* 8; *Fantastic* 7; *Asimov's* 7; *Satellite SF* 6; *F & SF* 6; *SF Plus* 3; *Future SF* 3; *Dynamic SF* 2; *SF Adventures* (1st) 2; *Thrilling Wonder* 1; *Wonder Story Annual* 1; *Galaxy* 1; *SF Stories* 1; *Rocket Stories* 1; *SF Quarterly* 1; *Analog* 1

SCOTT, H.J. [*Ka-Zar* Oct 36]
  Ka-Zar 3; *Marvel* 3; *Future* 3

SCOTT. H.W.
  Unknown 6; *Doc Savage* 1

SENF, C. C. [*Weird Tales* Mar 27]
  Weird Tales 45

SETTLES, JAMES B. [*Amazing Stories* Sep 42]
  Amazing 4; *Fantastic Adventures* 2; *Other Worlds* 2

SHAW, BARCLAY [*F & SF* Mar 79]
  F & SF 11

SHELTON, RICHARD T. [*F & SF* Jun 56]
  F & SF 2; *Venture* 1

SHERRY, ROBERT C. [*Super Science Stories* Sep 40]
  Astonishing 4?; *Super Science Stories* 2; *Future* 1

SIEGEL, NORMAN [*Fantastic Universe* Nov 58]
  Fantastic Universe 2

SIGMOND, A. [*Amazing Stories* Jan 33]
  Amazing 7; *Amazing Quarterly* 1

SILVEY, W. H. [*Weird Tales* Jul 53]
    Weird Tales 3

SMITH, BARRY WINDSOR [*Ariel* 3, 1978]

SMITH, MALCOLM [*Amazing Stories* Jan 42]
    Imagination 21; *Other Worlds* 19; *Amazing* 6; *Fantastic Adventures* 5; *Imaginative Tales/Space Travel* 5; *Universe* 3; *Mystic* 2

SOLOVIOFF, NICHOLAS [*F & SF* Sep 54]
    F & SF 6

STANLEY, DORIS [*Ghost Stories* Aug 28]
    Ghost Stories 5

STARK, JAMES [*Nebula* Jan 56]
    Nebula 9

STATON, JOE [*Fantastic* Sep 73]
    Fantastic 2

STEADMAN, BROECK [*Analog* Jul 80]
    Analog 2; *Asimov's* 1; *SF Digest* 1

STEIN, MODEST [*Unknown* Oct 39]
    Shadow 37; *Doc Savage* 34; *Unknown* 1; *Astounding* 1

STERANKO, JIM [*Infinity* 1, 1970]
    Infinity 3

STERNBACH, RICK [*Analog* Oct 73]
    Analog 14; *Galaxy* 9; *F & SF* 8; *If* 3

STEVENS, DALTON [*Ghost Stories* Apr 30]
    Ghost Stories 14

STEVENS, LAWRENCE STERN [*Super Science Stories* Nov 42] [Note: Some of the following may be the work of Peter Stevens.]
    Famous Fantastic Mysteries 26; *Super Science Stories* 9; *Fantastic Novels* 5; *Amazing Stories* 3; *A. Merritt's Fantasy* 1

STEVENS, PETER [*Astonishing Stories* Dec 42] [Note: The following have been positively identified by Robert Weinberg.]
    Famous Fantastic Mysteries 13; *Fantastic Novels* 7; *Astonishing* 1

STEVENSON, E. M. [*Weird Tales* Apr 26]
    Weird Tales 5

STEWART, (C) JOHN [*Authentic* Apr 55]
    Authentic 3

STINE, ROGER [*Shayol* 1, Nov 77]
    Shavol 2; *Asimov's* 1

STONE, BILL [*Mag. of Fantasy* Fall 49]
    Fantasy Fiction/Stories 2; *F & SF* 1

STONER, ELMER C. [*Witch's Tales* Nov 36]
    Witch's Tales 2

STOUT, WILLIAM [*Coven 13*, Sep 69]
    Coven 13 4

STOWE, D. A. [*Authentic* Oct 55]
  Authentic 2

STRIMBAN, BOB and JACK [*Galaxy* Dec 52]
  Galaxy 2

SUMMERS, LEO RAMON [*Fantastic Adventures* Feb 52]
  Fantastic 16; *Amazing* 8; *Analog* 5; *Fantastic Adventures* 4

SWANSON, ROBERT [*If* Oct 54]
  Analog 2; *If* 1

SWIATEK, EDMOND [*Amazing Stories* Mar 49]
  Fantastic Adventures 3; *Amazing* 2

TANNER, BERT [*F & SF* Apr 65]
  F & SF 11; *Venture* 6

TERRY, WILLIAM E. [*Imagination* Jan 52]
  Imagination 14

THEOBALD, RAY [*Worlds of Fantasy* 11, 1953]
  Supernatural Stories 19; *Wonders of the Spaceways* 3; *Worlds of Fantasy* 2;
  Futuristic Science Stories 1; *Tales of Tomorrow* 1; *Out of This World* 1

THOMAS, GENE [*Analog* Jul 61]
  Analog 2

TILBURNE, A. R. [*Weird Tales* Nov 38]
  Weird Tales 10

TILLEY, ROBERT J. [*New Worlds* Nov 64]
  New Worlds 2

TIMMINS, WILLIAM [*Astounding* Sep 42]
  Astounding 53

TODD, LARRY S. [*Fantastic* Oct 71]
  Amazing Stories 3; *Fantastic* 1 (both with Vaughn Bode)

TURNER, HARRY [*Tales of Wonder* Sum 40]
  Tales of Wonder 1; *Science Fantasy* 1

TURNER, ROLAND [*Tales of Tomorrow* 3, 1951]
  Tales of Tomorrow 3; *Futuristic Science Stories* 3; *Wonders of the Spaceways* 3;
  Worlds of Fantasy 2; *Supernatural Stories* 2; *Out of This World* 1

UTPATEL, FRANK [*Whispers* Jun 75]
  Whispers 2

VALIGURSKY, ED [*Fantastic Adventures* Nov 51] [Note: Includes work under the alias
  William Rembach.]
  Amazing Stories 49; *Fantastic* 32; *Fantastic Adventures* 3; *If* 3; *Dream World* 2;
  Amazing SF Novel 1; *Startling Stories* 1

VALLEJO, BORIS [*Questar* Feb 81]

VAN DONGEN, H. R. [*Super Science Stories* Sep 50]
  Astounding/Analog 46; *Super Science* 3; *SF Adventures* (1st) 3; *Worlds Beyond*
  2; *Space SF* 1

VESS, CHARLES [*Space & Time* 48, Jul 78]
    Space & Time 1; *Fantasy Book* 1

VIDMER, RENE [*Beyond* Nov 53]
    Beyond 3; *Galaxy* 1

VON GELB [*Oriental Stories* Oct/Nov 30]
    Oriental Stories 5

WALDMAN, BARRY [*F & SF* Aug 57]
    F & SF 2; *SF Adventures* 1

WALKER, NORM [*Vertex* Jun 74]
    Vertex 2

WALOTSKY, RON [*F & SF* May 67]
    F & SF 39; *Infinity* 2

WATKINS, BOB [*If* Nov 54]
    If 2

WAYNE, BILL [*Weird Tales* Sep 50]
    Weird Tales 2

WEIMAN, JON [*Asimov's* Nov 82]
    Asimov's 2

WELKER, GAYLORD [*Astounding* Dec 52]
    Astounding 1; *Amazing* 1

WENZEL, PAUL E. [*Space Travel* Sep 58]
    If 8; *Galaxy* 4; *Space Travel* 2; *Worlds of Tomorrow* 2; *Fantastic* 1

WESSOLOWSKI, HANS [*Amazing Stories Quarterly* Fall 29]
    Astounding 41; *Strange Tales* 7; *Amazing Stories* 5; *Amazing Quarterly* 2; *Thrilling Wonder* 2; *Astonishing* 1; *Marvel* 1

WHELAN, MICHAEL [*Asimov's* Sep/Oct 78]
    Asimov's 1; *Destinies* 1; *Quest/Star* 1; *Amazing* 1

WHITE, NAT [*Analog* Mar 63]
    Analog 2

WHITE, TIM [*SF Monthly* 2/2, 1975]
    SF Monthly 2

WILSON, GAHAN [*F & SF* Mar 68]
    F & SF 4

WISE, DENNIS [*Stardust* 3, 1976]
    Stardust 2

WITTMACK, E. FRANKLIN [*Weird Tales* Mar 43]
    Weird Tales 2

WOLFE, COREY [*Fantasy Book* May 82]
    Fantasy Book 4

WOLTERS, FRED [*Mag. of Horror* Nov. 64]
    Mag. of Horror 3 (+ 1 cover reprinted)

WOOD, WALLACE [*Galaxy* Oct 57]
    Galaxy 6

YANKUS, MARK [*Asimov's* Aug 82]
  Asimov's 3
YASUDA, HISAKI [*Asimov's* May 84]
  Asimov's 2
YOUNG, VIVIENNE [*New Worlds* Nov 67]
  New Worlds 2
ZIRN, RUDOLPH [*Terror Tales* Sep 34]
  Terror Tales ?; *Dr. Death* 3

In terms of output these are the top fifty-five cover artists together with the total number of covers produced.

1. Ed Emshwiller (276)
2. George Rozen (205)
3. Kelly Freas (190)
4. Frank R. Paul (183)
5. Earle K. Bergey (152)
6. Gray Morrow (148 +)
7. Jack Gaughan (124)
8. Virgil Finlay (106)
9. Leo Morey (102)
10. Robert Gibson Jones (101)
11. Ed Valigursky (91)
12. Howard V. Brown (90)
13. Alex Schomburg (88)
14. Brian Lewis (81)
15. John Schoenherr (77)
16. Mel Hunter (75)
17. Margaret Brundage (74)
18. Modest Stein (73)
19. Gerard Quinn (70)
20. Graves Gladney (68)
21. H. Fox (66)
22. Malcolm Smith (61)
23. Hans Wessolowski (59)
    Hubert Rogers (59)
25. Harold McCauley (57)
26. H. R. van Dongen (55)
27. William Timmins (53)

28. Chesley Bonestell (52)
29. Stephen Fabian (51)
30. John N. Howett (50 +)
31. Raphael M. DeSoto (49)
32. David Hardy (49)
33. C. C. Senf (45)
34. Lawrence Stevens (44)
35. Norman Saunders (41 +)
36. Hannes Bok (41)
    Ron Walotsky (41)
38. Allen Anderson (38)
    John Richards (38)
40. J. Allen St. John (37)
41. John Pederson, Jr. (35)
    Vincent DiFate (35)
43. Robert Fuqua (34)
    Rick Sternbach (34)
45. Leo Ramon Summers (33)
46. Terry Maloney (30)
47. Milton Luros (29)
48. Rudolph Belarski (27)
    Ray Theobald (27)
50. S. R. Drigin (23)
    Arnold Kohn (23)
    Walter Popp (23)
    Jack Coggins (23)
54. Peter Stevens (21)
    Keith Roberts (21)

Chronology

1882
The Argosy

1895
The Black Cat

1905
All-Story

1913
Science and Invention

1919
The Thrill Book

1923
Weird Tales

1926
Amazing Stories
Ghost Stories

1927
Amazing Stories Annual
Tales of Magic and Mystery

1928
Amazing Stories Quarterly

1929
Air Wonder Stories
Mind, Inc.

Wonder Stories
Wonder Stories Quarterly

1930
Astounding Stories of Super-Science (Analog Science Fiction/Science Fact)
Oriental Stories
Scientific Detective Monthly

1931
Mind Magic Magazine
Miracle Science and Fantasy Stories
The Shadow
Strange Tales of Mystery and Terror

1932
Dime Mystery Magazine

1933
Doc Savage
G-8 and His Battle Acres
The Spider

1934
Dusty Ayres and His Battle Birds
Marvel Tales
Operator #5
Scoops
Secret Agent X
Tales of Mystery and Detection
Tales of the Uncanny
Terror Tales

1935

Dr. Death
Horror Stories
The Mysterious Wu Fang
Mystery Adventures
Terence X. O'Leary's War Birds
Thrilling Mystery

1936

Ace Mystery
Dr. Yen Sin
Fanciful Tales of Time and Space
Flash Gordon Strange Adventure Magazine
Ka-Zar
The Witch's Tales

1937

Fireside Ghost Stories
Tales of Terror
Tales of Crime and Punishment
Tales of Wonder

1938

Captain Hazzard
Fantasy
Ghosts and Goblins
Golden Fleece Historical Adventure
Marvel Science Stories

1939

Dynamic Science Stories
Eerie Mysteries
Famous Fantastic Mysteries
Fantastic Adventures
Future Fiction
Jungle Stories
The Octopus
Planet Stories
Science Fiction
The Scorpion
Startling Stories
Strange Stories
Tales of Ghosts and Haunted Houses
Thrills
Uncanny Tales
Unknown/Unknown Worlds

1940

Astonishing Stories
Captain Future
Comet
Fantastic Novels
Science Fiction Quarterly
Stardust
Super Science Stories
Uncanny Tales
Weird Story Magazine

1941

Bizarre
Cosmic Stories
Eerie Tales
Science Fiction
Stirring Science Stories
Uncanny Stories

1942

Astonishing Stories
Super Science Stories
Yankee Science Fiction
Yankee Weird Shorts

1943

Weird Pocket Library (?)

1945

Occult
Weird Shorts (?)

1946

Fantasy
Futuristic Stories
New Worlds
Outlands
Strange Adventures
Strange Love Stories
Strange Tales
Thrilling Stories

1947

Avon Fantasy Reader
Fantasy Book
The Vortex

1948

The Arkham Sampler

1949

A. Merritt's Fantasy Magazine
The Book of Terror
Captain Zero
The Magazine of Fantasy and Science Fiction
Other Worlds Science Stories

1950

Cosmic Science Stories
Fantastic Story Quarterly
Fantasy Fiction
Futuristic Science Stories
Galaxy Science Fiction
Gripping Terror
Imagination
Out of This World Adventures
Science Fantasy
Tales of Tomorrow
Thrills Incorporated
Two Complete Science-Adventure Books
Wonder Story Annual
Worlds Beyond
Worlds of Fantasy

1951

Amazing Science Stories
Authentic Science Fiction
Avon Science Fiction Reader
The Mysterious Traveler Magazine
Sheena, Queen of the Jungle
Suspense
Ten Story Fantasy
Wonders of the Spaceways

1952

American Science Fiction [Magazine]
Brief Fantastic Tales (?)
Dynamic Science Fiction
Fantastic
Fantastic Science Fiction
If/Worlds of If
Nebula Science Fiction
Science Fiction Adventures

Space Science Fiction
Space Stories

1953

Avon Science Fiction and Fantasy Reader
Beyond Fantasy Fiction
Cosmos Science Fiction and Fantasy Magazine
Fantastic Universe
Fantasy Magazine
Future Science Fiction
Mystic Magazine
Orbit Science Fiction
Popular Science Fiction
Rocket Stories
Science-Fiction Plus
Science Stories
Spaceway [Science Fiction]
Tops in Science Fiction
Universe Science Fiction
Vortex Science Fiction
Worlds of the Universe

1954

Imaginative Tales
Out of This World
Science Fiction Digest
Space-Fact and Fiction
Supernatural Stories
Vargo Statten Science Fiction Magazine

1955

Infinity Science Fiction
Science-Fiction Monthly
Selected Science-Fiction Magazine
Weird World

1956

Satellite Science Fiction
Science Fiction Adventures

1957

Amazing Stories Science Fiction Novel
Dream World
Macabre
Phantom
Saturn
Screen Chills and Macabre Stories

Space Science Fiction Magazine
Tales of the Frightened
Venture Science Fiction

1958

Science Fiction Adventures
Star Science Fiction
Vanguard Science Fiction

1959

Super-Science Fiction

1960

A Book of Weird Tales
Fear!
Science Fiction Library
Shock
Weird and Occult Library

1962

Thriller

1963

Gamma
Magazine of Horror
Prize Ghost Stories
True Twilight Tales
Venture Science Fiction
Worlds of Tomorrow

1964

Tales of Terror from the Beyond
Treasury of Great Science Fiction Stories

1965

Bizarre! Mystery Magazine
Great Science Fiction

1966

Alien Worlds
Famous Science Fiction
The Girl from U.N.C.L.E. Magazine
Impulse
The Man from U.N.C.L.E. Magazine
Space and Time
Startling Mystery Stories
Thrilling Science Fiction

1967

The Arkham Collector
Beyond Infinity
International Science Fiction
Science Fiction Classics
Science Fiction Yearbook

1968

Weirdbook
Worlds of Fantasy

1969

Coven 13
Strange Fantasy
Vision of Tomorrow
Weird Terror Tales

1970

Adventures in Horror
Astounding Stories Yearbook
Bizarre Fantasy Tales
The Black Cat
Fantastic Adventures Yearbook
Forgotten Fantasy
Science Fantasy
Science Fiction Adventures Yearbook
Science Fiction Classics Annual
Space Adventures
The Strangest Stories Ever Told
Weird Mystery

1972

Eternity Science Fiction

1973

Dark Fantasy
Etchings & Odysseys
The Haunt of Horror
The Literary Magazine of Fantasy and Terror
Vertex
Whispers

1974

Kadath
Midnight Sun
Science Fiction Monthly
Sword & Sorcery Annual

1975

Stardust
Toadstool Wine
Void Science Fiction and Fantasy

1976

Ariel, The Book of Fantasy
Chacal
Galileo
Isaac Asimov's Science Fiction Magazine
Odyssey
Other Times
Phantasy Digest
S.F. Digest

1977

Argosy Special
Copper Toadstool
Cosmos Science Fiction and Fantasy
  Magazine
Erotic Science Fiction Stories
Fantasy Tales
Shayol
Sky Worlds
Unearth
Vortex

1978

Ad Astra
Asimov's SF Adventure Magazine
Dragonfields
Omni
Questar
The Sorcerer's Apprentice

1980

Something Else

1981

Chillers
Fantasy Book
Rigel
Rod Serling's The Twilight Zone Magazine
Science Fiction Digest

1982

Extro
Interzone

1983

Last Wave

Bibliography

Index Sources

Ashley, Mike. *The Complete Index to Astounding/Analog: Being An Index to the 50 Years of Astounding Stories—Astounding SF & Analog: January 1930–December 1979 together with the Analog Annual, the Analog Yearbook, & the John W. Campbell Memorial Anthology.* Oak Forest, Ill.: Robert Weinberg Publications, 1981.

——. *Fantasy Reader's Guide. Number One: The John Spenser Fantasy Publications.* U.K.: Cosmos Literary Agency, 1979.

Australian Science Fiction Association. *Index to British Science Fiction Magazines: 1934–1953.* 7 vols. Canberra City: Australian Science Fiction Association, [1968?]–1975.

Boyajian, Jerry and Kenneth R. Johnson. *Index to the Science Fiction Magazines: 1977.* Cambridge, Mass.: Twaci Press, 1982.

——. *Index to the Science Fiction Magazines: 1978.* Cambridge, Mass.: Twaci Press, 1982.

——. *Index to the Science Fiction Magazines: 1979.* Cambridge, Mass.: Twaci Press, 1981.

——. *Index to the Science Fiction Magazines: 1980.* Cambridge, Mass.: Twaci Press, 1981.

——. *Index to the Science Fiction Magazines: 1981.* Cambridge, Mass.: Twaci Press, 1982.

——. *Index to the Science Fiction Magazines: 1982.* Cambridge, Mass.: Twaci Press, 1983.

——. *Index to the Science Fiction Magazines: 1983.* Cambridge, Mass.: Twaci Press, 1984.

——. *Index to the Semi-Professional Fantasy Magazines: 1982.* Cambridge, Mass.: Twaci Press, 1983.

——. *Index to the Semi-Professional Fantasy Magazines: 1983.* Cambridge, Mass.: Twaci Press, 1984.

Cockcroft, Thomas G.L. *Index to the Weird Fiction Magazines.* Lower Hutt, New Zealand: T.G.L. Crockcroft, 1962–1964. 2 vols. Rev. ed. 1967; rpt. New York: Arno Press, 1975.

Cook, Frederick S. *Fred Cook's Index to the Wonder Group*. Grand Haven, Mich.:
    Frederick S. Cook, 1966.
Day, Bradford M. *The Complete Checklist of Science-Fiction Magazines*. Woodhaven,
    N.Y.: Science-Fiction and Fantasy Publications, 1961.
———. *An Index on the Weird & Fantastica in Magazines*. South Ozone Park, N.Y.:
    Bradford M. Day, 1953.
Day, Donald B. *Index to the Science-Fiction Magazines 1926–1950*. Portland, Ore.: Perri
    Press, 1953. Rev. ed. Boston: G. K. Hall, 1982.
Gernsback, Hugo. *Evolution of Modern Science Fiction*. New York: Hugo Gernsback,
    1952.
Hall, Hal W. *The Science Fiction Magazines: A Bibliographical Checklist of Titles and
    Issues Through 1982*. Bryan, Tex.: SFBRI, 1983.
Hemmings, John D. "Fan Publications Index." In *Fandom Directory. No. 6. 1984–1985
    Edition*. Ed. Mariane S. Hopkins. San Bernardino, Calif.: Fandom Computer
    Services, 1984.
Lewis, Anthony R. *Index to the Science Fiction Magazines 1966–1970*. Cambridge,
    Mass.: New England Science Fiction Association, 1971.
Metcalf, Norm. *The Index of Science Fiction Magazines 1951–1965*. El Cerrito, Calif.:
    J. Ben Stark, 1968.
New England Science Fiction Association. *The N.E.S.F.A. Index. Science Fiction Mag-
    azines: 1971–1972 and Original Anthologies: 1971–1972*. Cambridge, Mass.:
    NESFA Press, 1973.
———. *The N.E.S.F.A. Index. Science Fiction Magazines: [1973] and Original An-
    thologies: [1973]*. Cambridge, Mass.: NESFA Press, 1974.
———. *The N.E.S.F.A. Index to the Science Fiction Magazines and Original Anthologies
    1974*. Cambridge, Mass.: NESFA Press, 1975.
———. *The N.E.S.F.A. Index to the Science Fiction Magazines and Original Anthologies
    1975*. Cambridge, Mass.: NESFA Press, 1976.
———. *The N.E.S.F.A. Index to the Science Fiction Magazines and Original Anthologies
    1976*. Cambridge, Mass.: NESFA Press, 1977.
———. *The N.E.S.F.A. Index to the Science Fiction Magazines and Original Anthologies
    1977–1978*. Cambridge, Mass.: NESFA Press, 1983.
———. *The N.E.S.F.A. Index to the Science Fiction Magazines and Original Anthologies
    1979–1980*. Cambridge, Mass.: NESFA Press, 1982.
———. *The N.E.S.F.A. Index to the Science Fiction Magazines and Original Anthologies
    1981*. Cambridge, Mass.: NESFA Press, 1982.
———. *The N.E.S.F.A. Index to the Science Fiction Magazines and Original Anthologies
    1982*. Cambridge, Mass.: NESFA Press, 1983.
Pavlat, Robert and William Evans. *Fanzine Index . . . Listing Most Fanzines Through
    1952 Including Titles, Editors' Names and Data on Each Issue*. Flushing, N.Y.:
    Harold Palmer Piser, 1965.
Parnell, Frank H., comp. *Monthly Terrors: An Index to Weird Fantasy Magazines Pub-
    lished in the United States and Great Britain*. Westport, Conn.: Greenwood Press,
    1985.
Roberts, Peter. *British Fanzine Bibliography. Part One: 1936–1950*. U.K.: Peter Roberts,
    1978.
———. *British Fanzine Bibliography. Part Two: 1951–1960*. U.K.: Peter Roberts, 1978.
———. *Guide to Current Fanzines*. 5th ed. U.K.: Peter Roberts, 1978.

Stone, Graham. *Australian Science Fiction Index 1925–1967*. Canberra City: Australian Science Fiction Association [1968].

Strauss, Erwin S. *The MIT Science Fiction Society's Index to the S-F Magazines, 1951–1965*. Cambridge, Mass.: The MIT Science Fiction Society, 1965.

Tuck, Donald H. *The Encyclopedia of Science Fiction and Fantasy Through 1968. Volume 3: Miscellaneous*. Chicago: Advent, 1982.

Weinberg, Robert and Lohr McKinstry. *The Hero Pulp Index*. rev. ed. Evergreen, Colo.: Opar Press, 1971.

Surveys and Histories

Ashley, Michael. *The History of the Science Fiction Magazines*. 4 vols. London: New English Library, 1974–76, 1978.

Blackbeard, Bill. "The Pulps." In *Concise Histories of American Popular Culture*. Ed. M. Thomas Inge. Westport, Conn.: Greenwood Press, 1982.

Carter, Lin. "Lost Cities, Forgotten Ages: The Rise of Fantasy in the American Pulp Magazines." *Imaginary Worlds: The Art of Fantasy*. New York: Ballantine, 1973.

Carter, Paul A. *The Creation of Tomorrow: Fifty Years of Magazine Science Fiction*. New York: Columbia University Press, 1977.

Cawelti, John G. *Adventure, Mystery, and Romance: Formula Stories As Art and Popular Culture*. Chicago: University of Chicago Press, 1976.

Cioffi, Frank. *Formula Fiction? An Anatomy of American Science Fiction, 1930–1940*. Contributions to the Study of Science Fiction and Fantasy, No. 3. Westport, Conn. and London: Greenwood Press, 1982.

del Rey, Lester. *The World of Science Fiction: 1926–1976: The History of a Subculture*. New York: Garland Publishing, 1979; rpt. Ballantine, 1979.

Goulart, Ron. *Cheap Thrills: An Informal History of the Pulp Magazines*. New Rochelle, N.Y.: Arlington House, 1972; rpt. as *An Informal History of the Pulp Magazines*. New York: Ace, 1973.

Greenland, Colin. *The Entrophy Exhibition: Michael Moorcock and the British "New Wave" in Science Fiction*. London and Boston: Routledge & Kegan Paul, 1983.

Gruber, Frank. *The Pulp Jungle*. Los Angeles: Sherbourne Press, 1967.

Gunn, James. *Alternate Worlds: The Illustrated History of Science Fiction*. Englewood Cliffs, N.J.: Prentice-Hall, 1975; rpt. New York: A & W Visual Library, 1976.

Hall, H. W. "Science Fiction Magazines." In *Anatomy of Wonder: A Critical Guide to Science Fiction*. 2nd ed. Ed. Neil Barron. New York and London: R. R. Bowker, 1981.

Jones, Robert Kenneth. *The Shudder Pulps: A History of the Weird Menace Magazines of the 1930's*. West Linn, Ore.: FAX Collector's Editions, 1975.

Lundwall, Sam J. "The Magazines." *Science Fiction: What It's All About*. New York: Ace, 1971.

———. "Adventures in the Pulp Jungle." *Science Fiction: An Illustrated History*. New York: Grosset & Dunlap, 1978.

Moskowitz, Sam. "A History of Science Fiction in the Popular Magazines, 1891–1911." *Science Fiction by Gaslight: A History and Anthology of Science Fiction in the Popular Magazines, 1891–1911*. Cleveland: World, 1968; rpt. Westport, Conn.: Hyperion Press, 1974.

———. "A History of 'The Scientific Romance' in the Munsey Magazines, 1912–1920." *Under the Moons of Mars: A History and Anthology of "The Scientific Romance" in the Munsey Magazines, 1912–1920.* New York: Holt, Rinehart and Winston, 1970.

Nicholls, Peter, ed. *The Science Fiction Encyclopedia.* U.K.: Granada, 1979; and Garden City, N.Y.: Doubleday, 1979.

Reynolds, Quentin James. *The Fiction Factory, or From Pulp Row to Quality Street: The Story of 100 Years of Publishing at Street and Smith.* New York: Random House, 1955.

Rogers, Alva. *A Requiem for Astounding.* Chicago: Advent, 1964.

Sampson, Robert. *Yesterday's Faces: A Study of Series Characters in the Early Pulp Magazines. Volume I—Glory Figures.* Bowling Green, Ohio: Bowling Green University, Popular Press, 1983.

————. *Yesterday's Faces: [A Study of Series Characters in the Early Pulp Magazines]. Volume II: Strange Days.* Bowling Green, Ohio: Bowling Green University, Popular Press, 1984.

Scholes, Robert and Eric S. Rabkin. "A Pulpy America." *Science Fiction: History, Science, Vision.* New York: Oxford University Press, 1977.

Weinberg, Robert. *The Weird Tales Story.* West Linn, Ore.: FAX Collector's Editions, 1977.

————. "The Horror Pulps." In *Horror Literature: A Core Collection and Reference Guide.* Ed. Marshall B. Tymn. New York and London: R. R. Bowker, 1981.

Wertham, Fredric. *The World of Fanzines: A Special Form of Communication.* Carbondale: Southern Illinois University Press, 1973.

Marshall B. Tymn

Index

Magazines and descriptive material in Section IV relating to non-English language magazines and material detailed in the appendices are not included in the index. The fictional characters discussed in this book are likewise omitted from the index. Page numbers of magazine profiles are in *italics*. Major references in the notes following the magazine entries are indexed and indicated by ''n'' after the page number. ''SF'' is alphabetized as if spelled out.

Contributors

Brian Aldiss is a renowned science fiction author. He has written a history of science fiction, numerous short stories, and many novels. His current project is the immense Helliconia novel in three volumes, *Helliconia Spring*, *Helliconia Summer*, and *Helliconia Winter*.

Albert I. Berger is research associate at the Sleepy Hollow Restorations, Inc., and is preparing a history of the Rockefeller house at Pocantico Hills, N.Y. Formerly on the faculties of the Universities of Montana and Maryland, he is the author of the forthcoming *The Magic That Works: John W. Campbell and the American Response to Technology*. His articles on science fiction have appeared in *The Journal of Popular Culture* and *Science-Fiction Studies*, which has described his essays as "establishing [him] as one of the leading authorities on American SF."

Wendy Bousfield is bibliographer for English and American language and literature/linguistics at Bird Library, Syracuse University. She is the author of *Catalog of the Maurice M. Tinterow Collection of Works on Mesmerism, Animal Magnetism, and Hypnotism* and *Edgar Allan Poe: Paradox and Ambivalence as a Narrative Technique*, and a contributor to *Acquisition of Foreign Materials for U.S. Libraries*.

Joseph Payne Brennan is affiliated with the Yale Library and has published sixteen books, including such short story collections as *The Dark Returns*, *Stories of Darkness and Dread*, and *The Shapes of Midnight*. He has received awards from the Poetry Society of America as well as the 1982 World Fantasy Convention Award for Life Achievement. His stories have been adapted for radio and television and his *The Calamander Chest* was recorded with narration by Vincent Price.

Edwin Casebeer is chairman of the English Department at Indiana University–Purdue University at Indianapolis. He is the author of *Hermann Hesse* in the Writers for the

Seventies series, *How to Survive in College*, and three stories which appeared in *Evergreen Review*.

Thomas D. Clareson is chairman of the Department of English at the College of Wooster. He was the first president of the Science Fiction Research Association (SFRA) and received the SFRA Pilgrim Award in 1977. He is a representative of the Popular Culture Group at the Modern Language Association Delegate Assembly. He is the editor of *Extrapolation* and the author of *SF Criticism: An Annotated Bibliography, Robert Silverberg: A Critical Overview, Robert Silverberg: A Primary and Secondary Bibliography, Science Fiction in America: 1870s–1930s: An Annotated Bibliography,* and the *Some Kind of Paradise: A History of Science Fiction in America* (Greenwood Press, 1985).

John Robert Colombo is well known in his native Canada as "the Master Gatherer" for his innumerable compilations of Canadiana. The best known are *Colombo's Canadian Quotations* and *Colombo's Canadian References*. He has compiled the country's first anthology of fantastic literature, *Other Canadas*, as well as such specialized anthologies as *Friendly Aliens* and *Windigo*. He has also published *Blackwood's Books*, a bibliography devoted to Algernon Blackwood. He is a member of the Science Fiction Research Association and works as a communication consultant in Toronto.

Nicholas S. DeLarber is a member of the Science Fiction Research Association, a freelance writer, and a reviewer for the *SF & Fantasy Review*. He holds a Bachelor of Arts degree in English from the University of Missouri at Rolla and was a graduate teaching assistant at Bowling Green State University for several years. He is presently engaged in research into the works of Manly Wade Wellman and Harlan Ellison, fiction involving occult detectives, and magazine science fiction and fantasy.

Howard DeVore, a member of First Fandom, has been involved with science fiction since 1936 and owns one of the better private collections in the Midwest. A government civil servant, he is also a part-time rare book dealer and owner of Misfit Press. He issues his own magazines for Fantasy Amateur Press and Spectator Amateur Press Society and has published the reference work, *A History of the Hugo, Nebula, and IFA*, which he updates annually.

Steve Eng is on the board of Marshall Tymn's *The Year's Scholarship in SF, Fantasy and Horror*. His work has appeared in such reference books as Don Herron's *The Dark Barbarian* (Greenwood Press, 1984), Marshall Tymn's *Horror Literature*, and Frank N. Magill's *Survey of Modern Fantasy Literature*. His criticism and articles appear in such periodicals as *Books at Iowa, Gothic, Nyctalops, The Portland Review, Science Fiction & Fantasy Book Review*, and *The Romantist*. His specialty is fantasy poetry. He has edited Mary Elizabeth Counselman's verse in *The Face of Fear*, and his poetry has appeared in such magazines as *The Twilight Zone Magazine* and *Amazing SF*.

Robert Ewald is professor of English at Findlay College in Ohio and a medieval scholar. He is a regular reviewer for *SF & Fantasy Review* and the author of a forthcoming study of Clifford Simak. He has been a fan of science fiction, fantasy, and weird fiction for forty-five years.

Craig Shaw Gardner was one of a number of writers discovered by that springboard magazine for budding talent, *Unearth*. Apart from reviewing movies, he has sold stories to a number of magazines and anthologies including *Chrysalis 2*, *Dragons of Light*, *Flashing Swords 5*, and *Perpetual Light*.

Hal W. Hall is head of the Special Formats Division at Texas A & M University. He is a former member of the board of directors of the Science Fiction Research Association, former editor of the *SFRA Newsletter,* and a member of the editorial board of *Extrapo- lation*. His publications include *Science Fiction Book Review Index* (annual since 1970), *Science Fiction Book Review Index 1923–1973, Science Fiction Book Review Index 1974– 1979, Science Fiction and Fantasy Research Index* (annual), *Science/Fiction Collections: Fantasy, Supernatural & Weird Tales* (ed.), and *The Science Fiction Magazines: A Checklist of Titles and Issues Through 1982*.

Thomas W. Hamilton is the director of Wagner College Planetarium on Staten Island. He is the author of two books in the computer field, numerous articles dealing with the space program, planetariums, and astronomy education, and several unpublished SF stories.

Jon Harvey, a B.Sc. and Ph.D. in mathematics and computing, became interested in fantasy through comic books. His first publishing venture was a comic fanzine, *Seminar*. After producing a fantasy/folklore magazine, *Balthus,* he created Spectre Press in the mid–1970s. The press published a number of hardbacks and paperbacks, including Adrian Cole's first Voidal story and Brian Lumley's first poetry collection. Harvey was in charge of the British Fantasy Society in the mid- to late 1970s. He is currently lieutenant commander in the Royal Navy, instructing in computer software and hardware.

Donald M. Hassler is professor of English at Kent State University and is currently serving as treasurer of the Science Fiction Research Association. He is the author of *Hal Clement, Patterns of the Fantastic*, and a monograph on Erasmus Darwin, and is coeditor (with Carl B. Yoke) of *Death and the Serpent* (Greenwood Press, 1985).

Stephen Holland has been collecting science fiction since childhood and began researching British publishing, especially the period of the early fifties, about four years ago. He is writing a book on the small British publishers of that period and is coauthor of a book on British science fiction from 1949 to 1955.

Theodore Krulik teaches at Bushwick High School in Brooklyn, N.Y. His essay on teaching science fiction has appeared in *Extrapolation*, and he is a contributor to *The Intersection of Science Fiction and Philosophy*, edited by Robert E. Myers, and *Critical Encounters II*, edited by Tom Staicar. He is the author of a forthcoming book-length study of the major works of Roger Zelazny.

Gordon Larkin, a free-lance writer, was involved in the British fantasy scene during the last half of the 1970s, contributing poems, short stories, and reviews to many of the small press magazines on both sides of the Atlantic. He was editor of the British Fantasy Society's bimonthly bulletin and a member of the editorial board of *Fantasy Media*. Since then, he has been collaborating on a fantasy novel and also on television scripts, not necessarily of a fantastic nature.

George J. Laskowski, Jr., teaches mathematics at Kingswood School Cranbrook in Bloomfield Hills, MI. He has been a science fiction fan since childhood and has a library containing several thousand volumes of science fiction. Active in SF fandom since 1975, he attends several conventions a year, has appeared on panels and as Fan Guest of Honor, and publishes the fanzine *Lan's Lantern*.

Donald Lawler is professor of English at East Carolina University. He is the current editor of *Victorians Institute Journal*. His publications include *Approaches to Science Fiction*, *Vonnegut in America* with Jerome Klinkowitz, and *The Picture of Dorian Gray* (forthcoming). He served as consulting editor to the *Survey of Science Fiction Literature* (5 vols.) and the *Survey of Modern Fantasy Literature* (5 vols.). He has also contributed to *Twentieth Century Science Fiction Writers*, edited by Curtis C. Smith, and *Dictionary of Literary Biography, Vol. 8: Twentieth Century American Science Fiction Writers*, edited by Davis Cowart and Thomas L. Wymer.

Russell Letson teaches English at St. Cloud State University. He has published articles on Philip José Farmer, Robert Silverberg, Jack Vance, Robert Heinlein, and others, and is currently completing a book on Jack Vance. He is a contributor to *The Mechanical God*, edited by Thomas P. Dunn and Richard D. Erlich (Greenwood Press, 1982) and the forthcoming *Science Fiction Fandom*, edited by Joe Sanders.

Gordon Linzner's short stories have appeared in *Rod Serling's* The Twilight Zone *Magazine*, *The Magazine of Fantasy and Science Fiction*, *Fantasy Book*, the paperback anthology series Swords Against Darkness, and diverse small press magazines. He has edited and published the small press science fiction/fantasy magazine *Space and Time* since 1966.

Robert A.W. Lowndes is currently production associate of *Radio-Electronics*, *Special Projects*, *Hands-On Electronics*, and *Computer Digest*. He began his career as free-lance editor of *Future Fiction* and *Science Fiction Quarterly* and then became editorial director of the entire pulp chain for Columbia Publications, editing *Future, Science Fiction Quarterly*, *Science Fiction Stories*, and *Dynamic Science Fiction* as well as detective, western, and sports titles. He has also been moonlight editor of Avalon's science fiction book list, editor of *Magazine of Horror*, *Startling Mystery Stories*, *Famous Science Fiction*, *Weird Terror Tales*, *Bizarre Fantasy Fiction*, and *Exploring the Unknown*, and associate editor and later managing editor of *Sexology* and *Luz*.

Robert Madle was involved in the earliest aspects of science fiction fandom. One of the ten fans at the first science fiction convention in 1936, he attended all of the early conventions and was involved in the organization of some of them. He also organized the Philadelphia Science Fiction Society in 1936. He wrote the column "Inside Science Fiction" for *Science Fiction Quarterly*, and his articles have appeared in such magazines as *Future*, *Dynamic SF*, and *SF Adventures*. He was Fan Guest of Honor at the World SF convention in 1977.

Joseph J. Marchesani teaches English at the Hazleton Campus of the Pennsylvania State University. A member of the Science Fiction Research Association and a book reviewer for the *SF & Fantasy Review*, he has published essays on Horace Gold and on teaching science fiction. At present, he is working on a study of *Galaxy Science Fiction* and the practice of science during the cold war.

Will Murray is editorial director of Odyssey Publications, editor of *Duende*, and past editor of *Skullduggery*. He is the author of *The Duende History of the Shadow Magazine* and coauthor of *The Man Behind Doc Savage*, *Secret Agent X: A History*, and *The Assassin's Handbook*. He is a contributor to *Twentieth Century Crime and Mystery Writers*, *Twentieth Century Science Fiction Writers*, and *Mystery, Detective, and Espionage Magazines* (Greenwood Press, 1983). His articles and fiction have appeared in *Ellery Queen's Mystery Magazine*, *The Armchair Detective*, *Clues*, *Paperback Quarterly*, *Starlog*, *Crypt of Cthulhu*, *Lovecraft Studies*, *Comics Collector*, *Xenophile*, *Nemesis Inc.*, and many other magazines. He received the Lamont Award in 1979.

Frank H. Parnell is author, with the assistance of Mike Ashley, of *Monthly Terrors* (Greenwood Press, 1985) and a contributor to Donald H. Tuck's *Encyclopedia of Science Fiction and Fantasy*, Peter Nicholl's *Encyclopedia of Science Fiction*, and Mike Ashley's *Who's Who in Horror and Fantasy Fiction*. He has been collecting science fiction and fantasy magazines since World War II and has close to a full file of *Weird Tales*.

Joe Sanders is professor of English at Lakeland Community College in Mentor, Ohio. He is the author of numerous reviews and essays, as well as of *Roger Zelazny: A Primary and Secondary Bibliography* and the forthcoming *E. E. "Doc" Smith*.

Graham B. Stone has been a stalwart of Australian science fiction fandom for over forty years. He holds a B.A. in Psychology and is a member of the Library Association. He currently works at the National Library, Canberra. Actively involved in the Australian sf magazine scene during the 1950s, he has subsequently concentrated on sf bibliography and is the compiler of the *Australian Science Fiction Index* and the *Index to British Science Fiction Magazines*.

Milton Subotsky is film producer and writer for Amicus Productions Ltd. His films include *The Land That Time Forgot*, *At the Earth's Core*, *Dr. Who and the Daleks*, *Invasion Earth 2150 A.D.*, *They Came from Beyond Space*, *The Martian Chronicles*, *The Vault of Horror*, *Asylum*, and *The Birthday Party*. He lives in London.

James Grant Thiessen is proprietor of Pandora's Book Ltd. in Manitoba, Canada, and was editor and publisher of *The Science Fiction Collector/Megavore* and *The Tanelorn Archives*. He is a contributor to Robert Weinberg's *The Weird Tales Story*, L. W. Currey's *Science Fiction and Fantasy Authors*, Michael Cook's *Mystery, Detective, and Espionage Magazines*, (Greenwood Press, 1983), and other reference works. His articles have been published in various publications, including *The Science Fiction Collector/Megavore*, and *Famzine* (Italian).

Raymond H. Thompson teaches English at Acadia University in Wolfville, Nova Scotia. His main research interest is the Arthurian legend in both medieval and modern literature. He is currently serving as associate editor of the *Arthurian Encyclopedia*. His study of modern Arthurian fiction, *The Return from Avalon*, will be published in 1985. He is also the author of *Gordon R. Dickson: A Primary and Secondary Bibliography* and a contributor to Carl B. Yoke and Donald M. Hassler's *Death and the Serpent* (Greenwood Press, 1985).

Bruce Tinkel has been involved with science fiction for over twenty years and has one of the largest collections of science fiction books and magazines in the New York area. He has an MBA from Adelphi University and is an accountant with a major New York firm.

Robert Weinberg is a full-time book dealer specializing in science fiction and fantasy material. In the past ten years he has written two books and over one hundred articles, and has edited forty collections of material from and about the pulps. He was awarded a World Fantasy Award in 1978 and a Lamont Award in 1983 for his work in the fantasy and pulp fields. He is science fiction consulting editor for two major publishing houses and is currently working on the forthcoming *Biographical Dictionary of Science Fiction Artists*.

Milton T. Wolf is Collection Development Librarian for the University of Nevada–Reno. He has an A.B. from Pennsylvania State University and an A.M.L.S. from the University of Michigan. He is past editor of *Technicalities*, a member of the Science Fiction Research Association, and a contributor to *Shaping Library Collections for the 1980's*.

About the Editors

Marshall B. Tymn, Professor of English at Eastern Michigan University, is Director of the national Workshop on Teaching Science Fiction and Fantasy. The author of numerous reference books and articles on science fiction and fantasy literature, Dr. Tymn is series editor of Contributions to the Study of Science Fiction and Fantasy (Greenwood Press series) and the annual bibliography, *The Year's Scholarship in Science Fiction, Fantasy and Horror Literature*. He is currently President of the International Association for the Fantastic in the Arts.

Mike Ashley is coauthor of *Monthly Terrors: An Index to the Weird Fantasy Magazines Published in the United States and Great Britain* (Greenwood Press, 1985). He has written some twenty books, most recently *The History of the Science Fiction Magazines, Who's Who in Horror and Fantasy Fiction, The Seven Wonders of the World*, and *The Illustrated Book of Science Fiction Lists*, as well as more than one hundred articles published in scholarly and popular magazines.